FINANCIAL MANAGEMENT
Cases and Readings

FINANCIAL
MANAGEMENT
cases and readings

PEARSON HUNT, D.C.S.
Edmund Cogswell Converse Professor
of Finance and Banking

VICTOR L. ANDREWS, Ph.D.
Associate Professor of Business Administration

Both of the Graduate School of
Business Administration, Harvard University

1968
RICHARD D. IRWIN, INC.
Homewood, Illinois

First Printing, January, 1968

Case material of the Harvard Graduate School of Business Administration is made possible by the cooperation of business firms who may wish to remain anonymous by having names, quantities and other identifying details disguised while maintaining basic relationships. Cases are prepared as the basis for class discussion rather than to illustrate either effective or ineffective handling of administrative situations.

Foreword

The well-worn metaphor about building bridges may be used once again to describe the purpose of this book. The value of cases in courses aimed at the training of professional managers has been established for many years. Teachers accustomed to using cases will, we hope, find the collection in this book a valuable teaching tool. Even those who prefer to introduce the subject of corporation finance by other methods will find cases such as those presented in this book useful at the second level of study.

During the years since publication of *Cases in Financial Management,* the predecessor of this book, there have been important achievements in interrelating the various sections of financial decision making in a body of concepts. Also, methods of processing data have been developed to a level unrecognizable to a student of finance in the 1940's. Finally, descriptive studies of the institutions of the financial world have reached a higher level of detail and appositeness. We have endeavored to assemble cases and readings that comprise a nexus of these developments. We hope that those who know well the voluminous literature of the field will agree that our choice will give the student not only the values inherent in these materials themselves, but also the ability to read other parts of the literature with an enlarged "vocabulary" of concepts, techniques, and styles of presentation.

If this attempt at bridge building is successful, the thoughtful user of this book will be able to travel on either bank of the intellectual ravine that divides theory from practice, and to cross from one side to the other when the need arises.

Our obligations to those who gave their permission for the reprinting of their work are acknowledged as the source of each is cited. We are grateful to each of them, and to the tradition of the academic world which encourages this means of disseminating knowledge.

Nearly all the cases in this book are copyrighted by the President and Fellows of Harvard College, and are used with their permission. Each of them has been edited by one of the authors, so final responsibility for their quality rests on us. Several of them, however, were planned and written under the direction of others. We are grateful to Robert F. Vandell, now a Professor at the University of Virginia, for his development of The Cuno Engineering Corporation and Mid-America Pipeline Company cases. We are indebted to our colleagues, John McArthur, who prepared the General Holdings Corporation case, and Keith Butters, who is responsible for the case of the Amalgamated Manufacturing Corporation. We are indebted also to Mr. Charles Young for permission to use Marrud, Inc. Research assistants too numerous to name carried out field work in gathering cases, and suffered while their drafts were mutilated on the professorial desk.

Since the first publication of *Cases in Financial Management* in 1960, all published collections of Harvard finance cases have benefited from the editorial work of Carolyn Stubbs. She has again done the detailed work required to transfer from the manuscript to this printed book, and there are many less errors as a consequence. We are grateful to her, as our predecessors have been, and as others will be.

Boston, Mass.   P.H.
December, 1967   V.L.A.

Table of Contents

PART I. Funds Allocation

1. THE ANALYTICAL PROBLEMS OF FUTURE CASH FLOWS AND MAXIMIZATION CRITERIA IN CAPITAL BUDGETING 3

Economy Shipping Company 3
The Bowl Inns 8
Liberty Petroleum Company 21
Electricircuit, Inc. 31
How to Evaluate New Capital Investments, *John G. McLean* . . 41
Capital Budgeting and the Problem of Reinvesting Cash Proceeds, *Harold Bierman and Seymour Smidt* 57
Weaknesses of Accelerated Depreciation as an Investment Stimulus, *E. Cary Brown* 62
Three Problems in Rationing Capital, *James H. Lorie and Leonard J. Savage* 73
The Excess Present Value Index—A Theoretical Basis and Critique, *H. Martin Weingartner* 86

2. OPTIMUM ALLOCATION OF FUNDS BY LINEAR PROGRAMMING . . 98

Rectified Liquors, Inc. 98
Florida Fertilizers Co. (A) 100
Florida Fertilizers Co. (B) 107
Florida Fertilizers Co. (C) 109
Allen Brothers Charcoal Company 111
Nel-Max Cookies, Inc. 117
Rationing of Resources: Two-Product Projects, *William Beranek* . 123
Application of Linear Programming to Financial Budgeting and the Costing of Funds, *A. Charnes, W. W. Cooper, and M. H. Miller* . 146

3. ALLOCATION OF FUNDS IN DIVISIONALIZED CORPORATIONS . . . 184

General Holdings Corporation 184
Seaton Company 189
Ultramedia Inc. 206
Lilliputian Ball Bearings Company 227
Accounting Implications of a Mathematical Programming Approach to the Transfer Price Problem, *Nicholas Dopuch and David F. Drake* 234

4. ADMINISTRATION OF CASH FLOWS AND LIQUID ASSETS 248

Northeast Airlines, Inc. 248
Shoretex Corporation 268

Are Compensating Balance Requirements Irrational? *Richard G. Davis and Jack M. Guttentag* 275

The Transactions Demand for Cash: An Inventory Theoretic Approach, *William J. Baumol* 280

Managing the Corporate "Money" Position, *Federal Reserve Bank of Philadelphia* 291

5. GOVERNING AND MINIMIZING THE COST OF FUNDS COMMITTED TO RECEIVABLES 303

Taurus Industries, Inc. 303

Bell Campinas, S.A. 315

Jones & Lamson Machine Company 322

Koehring Finance Corporation 336

Sears Roebuck Acceptance Corp. 347

Using Credit for Profit Making, *Merle T. Welshans* 358

Captive Finance Companies, *Victor L. Andrews* 377

Commercial Paper, *Federal Reserve Bank of Cleveland* 398

6. VALUATION OF A FIRM 406

Wm. Filene's Sons Company 406

The Cuno Engineering Corporation 418

Burlington Mills Corporation—Pacific Mills 440

A Note on Takeover Bids and Corporate Purchases of Stock, *Manuel F. Cohen* 459

PART II. Managing the Capital Structure

7. INTERRELATED PROBLEMS OF CREATING AND SUPPORTING THE CAPITAL STRUCTURE 471

1. LIMITS ON THE USE OF DEBT

Mid-America Pipeline Company 471

Textron Inc. 485

American Machine & Foundry Company 503

Hercules Machine Tool Company, Inc. 518

Merrimack-Essex Electric Company 534

2. DIVIDEND POLICY

Marrud, Inc. 547

The Lamson & Sessions Co. 561

Continental Leasing Corporation 575

Rochester Gas and Electric Corporation 595

On the Problem of Capital Budgeting, *Diran Bodenhorn* 615

Corporate Income Taxes and the Cost of Capital, *Franco Modigliani and Merton H. Miller* 633

New Framework for Corporate Debt Policy, *Gordon Donaldson* . 643

Dividends, Earnings, Leverage, Stock Prices and the Supply of Capital to Corporations, *John Lintner* 666

3. Decapitalization

Union Pacific Railroad Company 706

Motec Industries, Inc. 721

Why Companies Are Buying Back Their Own Stock, *Leo A. Guthart* 739

A Review of Livingston's *The American Stockholder, Bayless Man-*
ning 749

8. Refining the Security Pattern 765

Oren Weaving Company, Inc. 765

Galesburg Pulp Company 774

Quality Plastics, Inc. 783

9. Acquisitions and Mergers 794

Amalgamated Manufacturing Corporation 794

Litton Industries, Inc. 806

Lestoil Products, Inc. 825

Hightower Company 840

10. Markets and Intermediaries 854

S. D. Warren Company 854

Speedata Equipment, Inc. 873

Cutter & Dunlop, Inc. 893

How the Investment Banker Functions, *Opinion of Judge Harold R.*
Medina 909

Pricing a Corporate Bond Issue: A Look behind the Scenes, *Ernest*
Bloch 916

The Private Route to New Capital, *Jean Ross-Skinner* 923

APPENDIX

Appendix 933

PART I

Funds Allocation

Chapter *1*   The Analytical Problems of Future Cash Flows and Maximization Criteria in Capital Budgeting

ECONOMY SHIPPING COMPANY

I

IN THE SPRING of 1950 the controller of the Economy Shipping Company, located near Pittsburgh, was preparing a report for the executive committee regarding the feasibility of repairing one of the company's steam riverboats or of replacing the steamboat with a new diesel-powered boat.

The Economy Shipping Company was engaged mainly in the transportation of coal from the nearby mines to the steel mills, public utilities, and other industries in the Pittsburgh area. The company's several steamboats also, on occasion, carried cargoes to places as far away as New Orleans. All the boats owned by Economy were steam powered. All were at least 10 years old, and the majority were between 15 and 30 years old.

The steamboat the controller was concerned about, the *Cynthia*, was 23 years old and required immediate rehabilitation or replacement. It was estimated that the *Cynthia* had a useful life of another 20 years provided that adequate repairs and maintenance were made. Whereas the book value of the *Cynthia* was $39,500, it was believed that she would bring somewhat less than this amount, possibly around $25,000, if she was sold in 1950. The total of immediate rehabilitation costs for the *Cynthia* was estimated to be $115,000. It was estimated that these general rehabilitation expenditures would extend the useful life of the *Cynthia* for about 20 years.

New spare parts from another boat, which had been retired in 1948, were available for use in the rehabilitation of the *Cynthia*. An estimate of their fair value, if used on the *Cynthia*, was $43,500, which was their book value. Use of these parts would, in effect, decrease the immediate rehabilitation costs from $115,000 to $71,500. It was believed that if these parts were sold on the

3

market they would bring only around $30,000. They could not be used on any of the other Economy steamboats.

Currently, the Cynthia was operated by a 20-man crew. Annual operating costs for the 20-man crew would be approximately as follows:

Wages	$110,200
Vacation and sickness benefits	1,880
Social security payments	2,400
Life insurance	1,800
Commissary supplies	15,420
Repairs and maintenance	24,400
Fuel	34,500
Lubricants	550
Miscellaneous service and supplies	12,000
Total	$203,150

It was estimated that the cost of dismantling and scrapping the *Cynthia* at the end of her useful life after the overhaul would be offset by the value of the scrap and used parts taken off the boat.

II

An alternative to rehabilitating the steamboat was the purchase of a diesel-powered boat. The Quapelle Company, a local boat manufacturer, quoted the price of $325,000 for a diesel boat. An additional $75,000 for a basic parts inventory would be necessary to service a diesel boat, and such an inventory would be sufficient to service up to three diesel boats. If four or more diesels were purchased, however, it was estimated that additional spare parts inventory would be necessary.

The useful life of a diesel-powered boat was estimated to be 25 years; at the end of that time the boat would be scrapped or completely rehabilitated at a cost approximating that of a new boat. The possibility of diesel engine replacement during the 25-year life was not contemplated by the controller, since information from other companies having limited experience with diesel-powered riverboats did not indicate that such costs needed to be anticipated; but a general overhaul of the engines, costing at current prices $60,000, would be expected every 10 years.

One of the features the Quapelle Company pointed out was the 12% increase in average speed of diesel-powered boats over the steamboats. The controller discounted this feature, however. The short runs and lock-to-lock operations involved in local river shipping would prohibit the diesel boats from taking advantage of their greater speed, since there was little opportunity for passing and they would have to wait in turn at each lock for the slower steamboats. In 1950, out of about 40 boats only two diesel boats were operating on the river. The controller felt it would be many years, if at all, before diesel boats displaced the slower steamboats.

After consulting the Quapelle Company and other companies operating

diesel-powered boats, the controller estimated that the annual operating costs
of such a boat would total $156,640, broken down as follows:

```
Wages for a 13-man crew............................$ 77,300
Vacation and sickness benefits........................  1,320
Social security payments.............................  1,680
Life insurance......................................  1,170
Commissary supplies................................ 10,020
Repairs and maintenance*........................... 21,700
Fuel.............................................. 28,800
Extra stern repairs.................................  2,000
Miscellaneous service and supplies................... 12,650
        Total.......................................$156,640
```
* Excluding possible major overhaul of diesel engines.

Although the Economy controller had not considered the matter, the user
of this case may assume that at the end of the 20th year the diesel boat would
have a realizable value of $32,500 and the inventory of parts of $37,500.

III

The controller was also concerned at this time with a city smoke ordinance,
which had been signed in 1948 to take effect in 1952. To comply with the
regulations of the ordinance, all hand-fired steamboats had to be converted to
stoker firing. Several of the Economy steamboats were already stoker fired;
the *Cynthia,* however, was hand fired. The additional cost of converting the
Cynthia to stoker firing was estimated to be $40,000, provided it was done at
the same time as the general rehabilitation. This $40,000 included the cost of
stokers and extra hull conversion and was not included in the $115,000
rehabilitation figure. The controller also knew that if $115,000 were spent
presently in rehabilitating the *Cynthia* and it was found later that no relief or
only temporary relief for one or two years was to be granted under the smoke
ordinance, the cost of converting to stoker firing would no longer be $40,000,
but around $70,000. The higher cost would be due to rebuilding, which would
not be necessary if the *Cynthia* was converted to stoker firing at the time of
her general rehabilitation.

Conversion would reduce the crew from 20 to 18, with the following
details:

```
Wages...........................................$100,650
Vacation and sickness benefits........................  1,650
Social security payments.............................  2,200
Life insurance......................................  1,620
Commissary supplies................................ 13,880
Repairs and maintenance*........................... 24,400
Fuel*............................................. 34,500
Lubricants*........................................    550
Miscellaneous service and supplies*................... 12,000
        Total.......................................$191,450
```
* These costs would remain the same, whether the crew was 20 or 18 men.

IV

All operating data the controller had collected pertaining to crew expenses were based on a 2-shift, 12-hour working day, which was standard on local riverboats. He had been informed, however, that the union representing crew members wanted a change to a 3-shift, 8-hour day. If the union insisted on an 8-hour day, accommodations on board the steamers or the diesels would have to be enlarged. The controller was perturbed by this, because he knew the diesels could readily be converted to accommodate three crews whereas steamers could not. How strongly the union would insist on the change and when it would be put into effect, if ever, were questions for which the controller could get no satisfactory answers. He believed that the union might have a difficult time in getting acceptance of its demands for three 8-hour shifts on steamers, since because of space limitations it would be very difficult, if not impossible, to convert the steamers to hold a larger crew. The controller thought that the union might succeed in getting its demands accepted, however, in the case of diesel-powered boats. One of the diesel boats currently operating in the Pittsburgh area had accommodations for three crews, although it was still operating on a 2-shift basis. The diesel boats that the Quapelle Company offered to build for Economy could be fitted to accommodate three crews at no additional cost.

V

Another factor the controller was considering at this time was alternative uses of funds. In the spring of 1950, Economy had sufficient funds to buy four diesel-powered boats; however, there were alternative uses for these funds. The other projects the management was considering at this time had an estimated return of at least 10% after taxes. The income tax rate at the time was 48%.

The company was conservatively managed, and in 1950 had no long-term debt outstanding. Its net worth exceeded $2 million. The company occasionally used unsecured bank loans to provide working capital during seasonal periods of peak need. In the spring of 1950, the company's liability for bank loans amounted to $150,000, which had been borrowed at 3% interest. The prime loan rate in New York City at the time was 2%.

VI

As a further inducement toward a contract to build a diesel boat, the Quapelle Company offered to rent a diesel boat to Economy. The rental terms offered by the Quapelle Company called for annual payments of $21,700 for 15 years, plus $5,700 per year for an interest charge. At the end of 15 years, when the Quapelle Company had, in effect, recovered the value of the boat, it would charge a nominal rental of $2,850 a year. Title to the boat would continue to remain in the hands of the Quapelle Company. Economy would incur all costs of operating and maintaining the boat, including general overhaul every 10 years, and would still need to invest $75,000 in a basic spare parts inventory.

THE BOWL INNS

In August, 1964, Justin McCarthy was trying to decide whether he should make an additional investment in his new bowling alley venture, The Bowl Inns. Mr. McCarthy was a partner in a law firm in Boston, Massachusetts. He had recently inherited some money, which he felt could earn about 5% before taxes if invested in the usual media, and he had decided to use these funds to open a business that would be more profitable, and to operate it in his spare time. After some investigation, he had decided that an amusement business, which could take advantage of the increased amount of leisure time enjoyed by the population, would find a ready market. He had finally selected tenpin bowling as a suitable amusement. Tenpin bowling was more popular in the midwestern and western parts of the United States, but Mr. McCarthy felt that it was likely to spread into New England, and that a tenpin bowling alley in the right location in the Boston area would be successful.

During 1963, Mr. McCarthy had spent a considerable amount of his leisure time searching for a suitable location for his first bowling alley. He ultimately selected and purchased a site on Route 9, west of Boston, for $30,000. The lot was in a rapidly developing commercial area and had some frontage on the busy highway.

In July, 1964, Mr. McCarthy completed a complicated financial transaction with Mr. Anderson, a real estate developer and general construction contractor. Mr. Anderson paid Mr. McCarthy $30,000 for the Route 9 location, and agreed to erect on the site a building suitable for a 16-lane bowling alley, whose operations could begin in about a year. Mr. McCarthy obtained a 15-year lease on the building at an annual rent of $16,800, to be paid monthly from the time the building was available for installation of the alleys, with an option to renew for an additional 10 years at a reduced rental. Mr. Anderson was responsible for paying all taxes and insurance, and for maintaining the building. The lease provided that the building was to be air-conditioned, and Mr. Anderson was to be responsible for the initial air-conditioning equipment and for its maintenance. Mr. McCarthy knew that bowling was a seasonal sport, more popular in the winter, but he hoped that an air-conditioned facility would reduce the seasonality of his business. Further details of the lease appear on pages 14 and 15.

In checking on the reasonableness of the proposed rental, Mr. McCarthy learned from a client who was a contractor that a building of this nature, ready for the installation of bowling equipment and with adequate parking space, would cost about $130,000. At the same time, it was estimated that taxes, insurance, and maintenance on an owned building would average $1,800 a year.

Mr. McCarthy had had no previous experience in the bowling alley business, but he attempted to estimate what his operating expenses would be. He planned to hire a full-time manager, because he would be able to devote only general supervision to the operation of the business. He estimated the manager's salary at about $6,000 a year. He also knew that he would need to hire two additional persons: a cashier-clerk at $4,000 a year, and a janitor and utility man for about $3,600 a year. He estimated his heating and electricity bill at approximately $4,000 a year, to cover the costs of lights, operation of the air-conditioning equipment, and heat for the building during the winter. Costs of supplies and maintenance were difficult to estimate, particularly maintenance because the new alleys would require a minimum amount, but as they aged, maintenance costs would no doubt rise. He estimated an average annual expenditure of $8,000 for these expenses. Payroll taxes and workmen's compensation insurance would amount to approximately 5% of his labor costs. He used an average figure of 40% for federal income taxes because of the small size of the enterprise.[1]

In late July, 1964, Mr. McCarthy contracted with a firm in Chicago, Illinois, for the installation of 16 bowling alleys. The cost of these alleys and accessory equipment was just under $4,000 each, a total of $60,000. The Chicago firm told Mr. McCarthy he could expect from the hardwood alleys a life of about 15 years. Mr. McCarthy made a down payment of $30,000, and the supplier permitted him to pay off the balance over 5 years in equal monthly payments (interest and principal) of $625, amounting to $7,500 a year. This scheme is presented in further detail on pages 14 and 15.

Mr. McCarthy planned to permit an outside operator to establish and run the concessions in his first Bowl Inn. These concessions, which would rent bowling shoes and lockers as well as offer a full line of refreshments, were expected to provide Mr. McCarthy with a net income of $10,000 a year, and he would not need to invest $22,500 in equipment or to undertake the management of the concessions. The income offered was about the same as Mr. McCarthy had hoped to obtain, before depreciation, under a manager employed by him.

Thus, by August, 1964, Mr. McCarthy's plans for the Route 9 Bowl Inn were complete except for the decision as to whether he should buy or lease the pinsetting machines needed to equip his alleys. He had definitely eliminated the alternative of using pinboys for manual pinsetting. This decision was based on a variety of strong reasons, including the desire to offer the most modern equipment and the wish to avoid behavioral and reliability problems often encountered with pinboys.

[1] See page 16 for possible depreciation schemes and tax shields from depreciation and other legislative grants.

PINSETTING MACHINES

Two makes of pinsetting machines were available: Speedy pinsetters, made by the Griswold Machine Corporation of Everett, Massachusetts, and Reliable pinsetters, made by Old Reliable Machine Tool Corporation of Akron, Ohio. Both machines could be either bought or leased.

Purchase

Both companies charged $2,900 per machine, and 16 machines would be required, representing a total outlay of $46,400. Freight and installation charges on the Reliable machines were paid by the manufacturer. On Speedy machines, the manufacturer charged the customer $125 per machine for installation and estimated that the freight cost to Mr. McCarthy would be an additional $10 per machine. The parts of Reliable machines were guaranteed for 1 year; the Speedy warranty covered only 90 days.

Financing could be arranged by both companies. Reliable agreed to finance 75% of the cost of the machines over 48 months, and Speedy would finance 80% over 36 months. Both firms charged interest of 6% per year on the total original amount of the loan. For instance, if the purchase was financed by Speedy, Mr. McCarthy would make a down payment of $9,280, plus freight and installation of $2,160, and in each of the 3 following years he would pay $12,373 on the principal (one third of $46,400 − $9,280), plus $2,227 in interest (6% of $37,120). The installment payments of $1,217 would be paid each month for 36 months. Both these plans are described in further detail on pages 14 and 15.

Lease

Speedy machines could be leased under the following conditions. The rent on each Speedy machine was $725 a year, paid monthly for 4 years, and would probably be $450 thereafter. An initial lease of 4 years would be required, followed by 4-year leases at the option of the lessee. The rental fee after the initial lease period was uncertain because very few machines had been in operation for 4 years, and fees for subsequent lease periods would be subject to renegotiation, as would any purchase options. Freight and installation costs on the Speedy machines would be paid by the customer; insurance on the machines would be paid by the manufacturer.

The rental fee on Reliable machines was 10 cents a string, with a minimum fee of $40 a month on an initial lease for 4 years. Subsequent 4-year leases could probably be negotiated at 5 cents a string and $40 a month minimum. The manufacturer of the Reliable machines paid the freight, installation, and insurance costs.

The manufacturers of both the Speedy and the Reliable pinsetters employed servicemen to do major repair work on the machines. Most alleys, however, did their own minor repair work and maintenance, and Mr. McCarthy expected that he would have to hire a maintenance man for $3,900 a year whether he bought or rented the machines. If the machines were purchased, Mr. McCarthy expected that after the initial warranty period special maintenance services purchased from the manufacturer might cost an average of $50 per year per machine. These services would be provided at no cost by the manufacturer if the machines were leased.

Lease payments were deductible for tax purposes in the year in which paid. If the machines were purchased, they could be depreciated for tax purposes over an 8-year life.

Since Mr. McCarthy had had no prior business experience and was starting his bowling venture in a relatively untried area, both manufacturers expected him to personally guarantee the fulfillment of the leasing contract, even though he planned to incorporate the Bowl Inn as a separate entity. Under either purchase arrangement, the manufacturers were willing to limit their interests to the chattel mortgage on the machines, since the down payment provided a cushion against possible default.

VOLUME OF BUSINESS

One of the important considerations, in Mr. McCarthy's opinion, was the volume of business that the new Bowl Inn might achieve. In his initial planning, he tried to estimate the volume of business, after deciding that the alleys would be open every day of the year from 2 P.M. to 11 P.M., although he knew that the evening hours were much more popular for bowling. Initially, he had thought of charging 25 cents a string before 5 P.M., and 35 cents from 5 P.M. until 11 P.M. With these prices, which were the going rates in the area for manually set pins, he expected to obtain 100% utilization of his alleys from 7 to 10 P.M.; about 60% utilization from 5 to 7 P.M. and 10 to 11 P.M.; and perhaps a 40% utilization during the afternoon hours. The capacity of the pinsetting machines was about 8 strings an hour for each of the 16 machines.

Mr. McCarthy reconsidered his pricing problem, however, since speed was one of the primary advantages of machines over pinboys, and he thought he should exploit this. He knew that most bowlers, and league bowlers in particular, liked the greater speed of bowling with machines and might be expected to pay a premium for this advantage. He was less sure that afternoon bowlers would be so inclined, as they represented few bowlers of league caliber. Since he had decided to offer machines, he felt he might be able to charge 40 cents a string from 5 P.M. to 11 P.M., while leaving the afternoon price at 25 cents a string. Mr. McCarthy's best estimate of volume and revenue with these prices is shown in Exhibit 1.

As he pondered the possible range of revenues he could expect to encounter, Mr. McCarthy thought that his best estimate of $92,350 a year was as likely to be exceeded as it was to be underachieved. Although at the proposed prices about $147,000 of revenue could be produced in a year of capacity operations, he was sure that in no circumstances could the revenues exceed $100,000 or be below $75,000 with the hours and prices he had planned. He further believed that actual revenue was just as likely to be within the range of plus or minus $5,000 of his best estimate as it was to be outside of this range. The upper range of his revenue estimates, was, of course, rather limited by capacity constraints, especially during the prime evening hours, while the downward range was much more dependent on his ability to forecast the acceptance of his venture by the seekers of leisure-time diversions. Mr. McCarthy had no doubts about the credit standing of the prospective concessionaire.

ADDITIONAL FACTORS

Although the possible down payments for purchased machines and certain other expenditures would have to be made during the period of construction, Mr. McCarthy decided to ignore such questions of timing and to assume that all preliminary costs could be treated as if they occurred on the date of opening the alleys.

There were some additional factors that Mr. McCarthy had to consider. Each machine would require electrical power extensions costing about $150. Also, his annual property insurance costs of $275 would rise by $12.75 per machine purchased, and his property taxes (in addition to the $1,800 mentioned on page 9) would rise from about $1,450 a year to $2,400 if he bought the machines. Electrical power costs at .1 cent per string were expected to amount to about $250 a year.

Mr. McCarthy examined both makes of machines in operation and came to the conclusion that there was little difference in their reliability or speed. The Speedy machine was perhaps slightly less noisy, but on the whole each did the job satisfactorily. In addition, there seemed to be no reason why one machine would last longer than another, although just how long they would last was difficult to determine. They would surely last for 5 years, and probably for 10. All machines could be easily modified as a part of normal maintenance activities, the manufacturers said, to keep abreast of design improvements. If this was done, the machines would almost certainly last for 10 years. There had been almost no major improvements over the past three years, and neither of the companies appeared to be working on any radical improvements for the near future.

Mr. McCarthy was quite optimistic about the potential success of his Route 9 Bowl Inn. He felt that his judgment in launching the venture had been substantiated, because he had recently been approached by Carl Peterson, operator of a nearby amusement park, who offered to buy him out (that is, take over the lease and make the remaining payments on the alleys, which were being installed) for $40,000. Mr. McCarthy felt that this prospective $10,000 immediate profit was partly in compensation for his efforts in locating the site and getting the business underway, but also reflected the potential high profitability of the enterprise. Mr. McCarthy declined to sell because he did not need the money and was hoping to use the Route 9 Bowl Inn as the first of a chain of such ventures.

Mr. McCarthy still had approximately $45,000 available for investment in his bowling alley venture. He thought that about $5,000 would be needed for insurance prepayments, for working capital, and for a safety margin, and the remaining $40,000 could be drawn on to make the down payment on the pinsetting machines if he decided to purchase them.

During his investigation of bowling as an investment, Mr. McCarthy had learned that forecasts of a return of 8 to 12% after taxes on total invested capital were not unusual. While he wanted to promote this enterprise as a sideline and was willing to drain his bank accounts for the purpose, he felt that ultimately he should be adequately compensated for his time, trouble, and risk. Even though this was his first venture, he was sure that he would have started another kind of enterprise had bowling not been a possibility.

Exhibit 1

THE BOWL INNS

MR. McCARTHY'S BEST ESTIMATE OF VOLUME AND REVENUE AT ROUTE 9

(1) Period	(2) Hourly Machine Capacity (Strings)	(3) Capacity Utilized	(4) Strings per Hour (2) × (3)	(5) Strings in Period (1) × (4)	(6) Revenue per String	(7) Revenue in Period (5) × (6)
2 P.M. to 5 P.M.	128	40%	51	153	25¢	$ 38.25
5 P.M. to 7 P.M.	128	50	64	128	40	51.20
7 P.M. to 10 P.M.	128	90	115	345	40	138.00
10 P.M. to 11 P.M.	128	50	64	64	40	25.60
Total estimated revenue per day ...						$253.05

365 days at $253 per day = $92,350 per year

Appendix A

The following material is designed to reduce the time a student must spend on calculations. The exact material to be used will depend partly on the assignment given by the teacher and partly on what the student selects.

PART I. Determination of rate of interest implicit in schemes where the payment covers both interest and principal amounts.

To permit reference to the tables most frequently available, annual compounding is used and rates are rounded to the nearest percent.)

Lease of land and building. Annual rental of $16,800 per year for 15 years provides $160,000.

Present value of 15-year annuity at 6% = $163,166
at 7% = $153,013

6% is the better approximation (6.302% by computer).

Purchase of 16 alleys. Payment of $7,500 per year for 5 years provides $30,000.

Present value of 5-year annuity at 7% = $30,752
at 8% = $29,945

8% is the better approximation (7.931% by computer).

Purchase of 16 Reliable machines. Payment of $10,788 per year for 4 years provides $34,800.

Present value of 4-year annuity at 9% = $34,950
at 10% = $34,197

9% is the better approximation (9.195% by computer).

Purchase of 16 Speedy machines. Payment of $14,600 per year for 3 years provides $37,120.

Present value of 3-year annuity at 8% = $37,616
at 9% = $36,857

9% is the better approximation (8.753% by computer).

PART II. Subdivision, where necessary, of annual payments between principal and interest.

Purchase of 16 alleys. 5-year annuity of $7,500 at 8%.

Year	Annual Payment	Principal	Before-Tax Interest	After-Tax Interest	Tax Shield
1	$7,500	$ 5,100	$2,400	$1,440	$960
2	↑	5,508	1,992	1,195	797
3		5,949	1,551	931	620
4	↓	6,425	1,075	645	430
5	7,500	6,939	561	337	224
Rounding error		79	(79)	(47)	(32)
		$30,000	$7,500		

14

Lease of land and building. Rental of $16,800 per year for 15 years at 6%.

Year	Annual Payment	Principal	Before-Tax Interest	After-Tax Interest	Tax Shield
1.....................	$16,800	$ 7,200	$ 9,600	$5,760	$3,840
2.....................	↑	7,632	9,168	5,501	3,667
3.....................		8,090	8,710	5,226	3,484
4.....................		8,575	8,225	4,935	3,290
5.....................		9,090	7,710	4,626	3,084
6.....................		9,635	7,165	4,299	2,866
7.....................		10,213	6,587	3,952	2,635
8.....................		10,826	5,974	3,584	2,390
9.....................		11,476	5,324	3,194	2,130
10....................		12,164	4,636	2,782	1,854
11....................		12,894	3,906	2,344	1,562
12....................		13,668	3,132	1,879	1,253
13....................		14,489	2,311	1,387	924
14....................	↓	15,357	1,443	866	577
15....................	$16,800	16,279	521	313	208
Rounding error.........		(7,588)	7,588	4,553	3,035
		$160,000	$92,000		

Purchase of 16 Reliable machines. 4-year annuity of $10,788 at 9%.

Year	Annual Payment	Principal	Before-Tax Interest	After-Tax Interest	Tax Shield
1.....................	$10,788	$ 7,656	$3,132	$1,879	$1,253
2.....................	↑	8,345	2,443	1,466	977
3.....................	↓	9,096	1,692	1,015	677
4.....................	$10,788	9,915	873	524	349
Rounding error.........		(212)	212	127	85
		$34,800	$8,352		

Purchase of 16 Speedy machines. 3-year annuity of $14,600 at 9%.

Year	Annual Payment	Principal	Before-Tax Interest	After-Tax Interest	Tax Shield
1.....................	$14,600	$11,259	$3,341	$2,005	$1,336
2.....................	↕	12,273	2,327	1,396	931
3.....................	$14,600	13,377	1,223	734	489
Rounding error.........		211	(211)	(127)	(84)
		$37,120	$6,680		

PART III. Information concerning depreciation and related charges open to The Bowl Inns.

Additional First-Year Allowance

NOTE.—Although this privilege should be noted, it is recommended to instructor and student that the allowance be ignored in working out the case.

20% of tangible personal property (new or used) may be deducted from income in the first year of use, reducing the depreciable value to 80%.

Limits

Assets must have a useful life of over 6 years.
Does not apply to real estate.
Cannot exceed $2,000 in any year.

Investment Credit

The amount of the credit depends on the depreciable life of the asset:

Life	Percentage of Depreciable Value
1–3 years	0 %
4–5	$2\frac{1}{3}$
6–7	$4\frac{2}{3}$
8 or more	7

The credit applies to almost all tangible depreciable property, but not to buildings. Its use does not reduce the depreciable value of the property. As much as $25,000 may be deducted from tax liability, plus no more than one fourth of the remaining liability in any year. But unused credit may be carried back and forward.

Alternative depreciation schedules permissible for federal income tax purposes.

GENERAL NOTE.—For depreciable assets purchased new, businesses are allowed the choice of one of four alternative patterns of depreciation charges.

1. Straight line.
2. Declining balance.
3. Declining balance shifting to straight line.
4. Sum of years' digits.

Only the second of these patterns can be applied to the original cost of the asset without deduction of estimated salvage value. In the following tables, which present the amounts of expense allowable for the depreciable assets of the Route 9 Bowl Inn, *no salvage value* has been assumed in any case, and the declining balance method has not been computed because it never accumulates to the full cost of the asset. In each case, the minimum time permitted by the Internal Revenue Service has been taken.

BUILDING AND EQUIPMENT: $130,000 COST; 40-YEAR LIFE

Year	Straight Line			Declining Balance and Straight Line			Sum of Years' Digits		
	Before-Tax Expense	Accumulation	Tax Shield	Before-Tax Expense	Accumulation	Tax Shield	Before-Tax Expense	Accumulation	Tax Shield
1	$3,250	$ 3,250	$1,300	$6,500	$ 6,500	$2,600	$6,341	$ 6,341	$2,536
2		6,500		6,175	12,675	2,470	6,183	12,524	2,473
3		9,750		5,866	18,541	2,346	6,024	18,548	2,410
4		13,000		5,573	24,114	2,229	5,866	24,414	2,346
5		16,250		5,295	29,409	2,118	5,707	30,121	2,283
6		19,500		5,030	34,438	2,012	5,548	35,669	2,219
7		22,750		4,778	39,216	1,911	5,390	41,059	2,156
8		26,000		4,540	43,756	1,816	5,231	46,290	2,092
9		29,250		4,312	48,068	1,725	5,073	51,363	2,029
10		32,500		4,096	52,164	1,638	4,914	56,277	1,966
11		35,750		3,892	56,056	1,557	4,757	61,034	1,903
12		39,000		3,697	59,753	1,479	4,598	65,632	1,839
13		42,250		3,513	63,266	1,405	4,440	70,072	1,776
14		45,500		3,337	66,603	1,335	4,281	74,353	1,712
15		48,750		3,169	69,772	1,268	4,122	78,475	1,649
16		52,000		3,011	72,783	1,204	3,964	82,439	1,586
17		55,250		2,861	75,644	1,144	3,805	86,244	1,522
18		58,500		2,718	78,363	1,087	3,647	89,891	1,459
19		61,750		2,582	80,945	1,033	3,488	93,379	1,395
20		65,000		2,453	83,398	981	3,328	96,707	1,331
21		68,250		2,330	85,728	932	3,171	99,878	1,268
22		71,500		2,330	88,058		3,012	102,890	1,205
23		74,750		2,330	90,388		2,854	105,744	1,142
24		78,000		2,330	92,718		2,695	108,439	1,078
25		81,250		2,330	95,048		2,536	110,975	1,014
26		84,500		2,330	97,378		2,378	113,353	951
27		87,750		2,330	99,708		2,219	115,572	888
28		91,000		2,330	102,038		2,060	117,632	824
29		94,250		2,330	104,368		1,902	119,534	761
30		97,500		2,330	106,698		1,743	121,277	697
31		100,750		2,330	109,028		1,586	122,863	634
32		104,000		2,331	111,359		1,427	124,290	571
33		107,250		2,330	113,689		1,269	125,559	508
34		110,500		2,330	116,019		1,110	126,669	444
35		113,750		2,330	118,349		952	127,621	381
36		117,000		2,330	120,679		793	128,414	317
37		120,250		2,331	123,010		634	129,048	254
38		123,500		2,330	125,340		476	129,524	190
39		126,750		2,330	127,670		317	129,841	127
40	3,250	130,000	1,300	2,330	130,000	932	159	130,000	64

ALLEYS: $60,000 COST; 15-YEAR LIFE

Year	Straight Line			Declining Balance and Straight Line			Sum of Years' Digits		
	Before-Tax Expense	Accumulation	Tax Shield	Before-Tax Expense	Accumulation	Tax Shield	Before-Tax Expense	Accumulation	Tax Shield
1	$4,000	$ 4,000	$1,600	$8,000	$ 8,000	$3,200	$7,500	$ 7,500	$3,000
2		8,000		6,934	14,934	2,774	7,000	14,500	2,800
3		12,000		6,009	20,943	2,404	6,500	21,000	2,600
4		16,000		5,207	26,150	2,083	6,000	27,000	2,400
5		20,000		4,513	30,663	1,805	5,500	32,500	2,200
6		24,000		3,911	34,574	1,564	5,000	37,500	2,000
7		28,000		3,390	37,964	1,356	4,500	42,000	1,800
8		32,000		2,755	40,719	1,102	4,000	46,000	1,600
9		36,000		2,755	43,474		3,500	49,500	1,400
10		40,000		2,754	46,228		3,000	52,500	1,200
11		44,000		2,754	48,982		2,500	55,000	1,000
12		48,000		2,755	51,737		2,000	57,000	800
13		52,000		2,754	54,491		1,500	58,500	600
14		56,000		2,754	57,245		1,000	59,500	400
15	4,000	60,000	1,600	2,755	60,000	1,102	500	60,000	200

	Straight Line			Declining Balance and Straight Line			Sum of Years' Digits		
Year	Before-Tax Expense	Accumulation	Tax Shield	Before-Tax Expense	Accumulation	Tax Shield	Before-Tax Expense	Accumulation	Tax Shield

16 MACHINES: $46,400 COST; 8-YEAR LIFE

Year	Before-Tax Expense	Accumulation	Tax Shield	Before-Tax Expense	Accumulation	Tax Shield	Before-Tax Expense	Accumulation	Tax Shield
1	$5,800	$ 5,800	$2,320	$11,600	$11,600	$4,640	$10,311	$10,311	$4,124
2	←	11,600	←	8,700	20,300	3,480	9,022	19,333	3,609
3		17,400		6,525	26,825	2,610	7,733	27,066	3,093
4		23,200		4,895	31,720	1,958	6,444	33,510	2,578
5		29,000		3,670	35,390	1,468	5,156	38,666	2,062
6		34,800		←	39,060	←	3,867	42,533	1,547
7	→	40,600	→		42,730		2,578	45,111	1,031
8	5,800	46,400	2,320	3,670	46,400	1,468	1,289	46,400	516

16 ELECTRICAL CONNECTIONS: $2,400 COST; 8-YEAR LIFE

Year	Before-Tax Expense	Accumulation	Tax Shield	Before-Tax Expense	Accumulation	Tax Shield	Before-Tax Expense	Accumulation	Tax Shield
1	$ 300	$ 300	$ 120	$ 600	$ 600	$ 240	$ 533	$ 533	$ 213
2	←	600	←	450	1,050	180	467	1,000	187
3		900		337	1,387	135	400	1,400	160
4		1,200		253	1,640	101	333	1,733	133
5		1,500		190	1,830	76	267	2,000	107
6		1,800		←	2,020	←	200	2,200	80
7	→	2,100	→		2,210		133	2,333	53
8	300	2,400	120	190	2,400	76	67	2,400	27

FREIGHT AND INSTALLATION: $2,160 COST; 8-YEAR LIFE

Year	Before-Tax Expense	Accumulation	Tax Shield	Before-Tax Expense	Accumulation	Tax Shield	Before-Tax Expense	Accumulation	Tax Shield
1	$ 270	$ 270	$ 108	$ 540	$ 540	$ 216	$ 480	$ 480	$ 192
2	←	540	←	405	945	162	420	900	168
3		810		304	1,249	122	360	1,260	144
4		1,080		227	1,476	91	300	1,560	120
5		1,350		171	1,647	68	240	1,800	96
6		1,620		←	1,818	←	180	1,980	72
7	→	1,890	→		1,989		120	2,100	48
8	270	2,160	108	171	2,160	68	60	2,160	24

BAR, RESTAURANT, LOCKERS, ETC.; $22,500 COST; 10-YEAR LIFE

Year	Straight Line			Declining Balance and Straight Line			Sum of Years' Digits		
	Before-Tax Expense	Accumulation	Tax Shield	Before-Tax Expense	Accumulation	Tax Shield	Before-Tax Expense	Accumulation	Tax Shield
1	$2,250	$ 2,250	$ 900	$4,500	$ 4,500	$1,800	$4,091	$ 4,091	$1,636
2	↑	4,500	↑	3,600	8,100	1,440	3,682	7,773	1,473
3		6,750		2,880	10,980	1,152	3,272	11,045	1,309
4		9,000		2,304	13,284	922	2,864	13,909	1,146
5		11,250		1,843	15,127	737	2,455	16,364	982
6		13,500		1,475	16,602	590	2,045	18,409	818
7		15,750		1,474	18,076	↑	1,637	20,046	655
8		18,000		1,475	19,551		1,227	21,273	491
9		20,250		1,474	21,025	↓	818	22,091	327
10	2,250	22,500	900	1,475	22,500	590	409	22,500	164

LIBERTY PETROLEUM COMPANY

In the fall of 1965, the officers of Liberty Petroleum Company were considering what price to bid for a large tract of timberland in southern Georgia. The proposed acquisition involved a considerable amount of cash as well as a major commitment in a field of endeavor that was relatively new to Liberty.

For years an important integrated oil company, Liberty in the late 1950's began a program of diversification into many agricultural and industrial chemical fields. The company had grown steadily throughout its history, but especially so in the early 1960's as the demand for its products increased greatly. Annual sales for the year 1965 were expected to amount to about $360 million and total assets to about $550 million. Net profits would be about $45 million, and the return on invested capital 11.5%.[1]

DIVERSIFICATION PROGRAM

In the course of its diversification program, Liberty purchased a major interest in Duride Corporation in 1963. Duride was a producer of natural glues and resins for the plywood industry, and for the particleboard and pulp and paper industry. Its plant was located in northern California, but at the time of acquisition by Liberty the Duride management was in the process of constructing an additional plant in the Southeast to supply the rapidly growing southern pine plywood industry. The Liberty executives felt that Duride was a natural extension of its petrochemical diversification activities, since Duride consumed both phenol and urea, which Liberty was already producing, as well as formaldehyde, which Liberty planned to develop.

In late 1964, under the direction of the president, a group of officers began to analyze the merits of diversification into the forest products industry, primarily the plywood manufacturing field. Such diversification would embody a wood fiber and chemicals concept, which was rapidly coming to the fore in industry literature. According to industry sources, the chemical value in forest products such as plywood, particleboard, and other types of building

---

[1] Invested capital (or capitalization) is usually the difference between total assets and current liabilities. If the amounts are large, intangible assets may be deducted, and portions of the current debt that are expected to roll over may be added.

materials would in a very short period of time be at least equal to the value of the fiber content. Liberty was already supplying certain basic raw materials for plywood and particleboard through its interest in Duride. It appeared that by this means Liberty would continue to be in a position to supply the various plastic coatings and lamination materials that in future years would occupy a prominent role in the fabrication of such building products. The acquisition of a plywood company by an oil company would not be unprecedented. One of Liberty's competitors, a large midwestern oil company, had made a similar move the previous year.

Liberty therefore entered the forest products field by the acquisition of United Plywood Company, a customer of Duride. United Plywood was one of the country's largest plywood manufacturers, with four plants in the Pacific Northwest and one in Georgia, the last a part of the rapidly growing pine plywood industry in the South. Despite limited financial resources, United Plywood had been one of the first companies to undertake an expansion program in the South. Many of its stronger competitors had subsequently followed. The Liberty executives had been impressed by the youthful and aggressive management of United Plywood, and had felt that if these people had the capital availability that Liberty could provide, and which United Plywood lacked, the company could experience considerable growth.

THE DUNCAN TIMBERLANDS

United Plywood's southern pine plywood mill was adjacent to the timber reserves owned by the Duncan family in southern Georgia. The Duncan family owned roughly 100,000 acres of prime pine timberland in the area, and in the early 1960's had begun looking for a way to realize on the value of its properties. Hence, when United Plywood had come into the South in 1963 to investigate raw material supplies for a plywood plant, the association between United Plywood and the Duncan timberlands had been a natural one. In late 1964, United Plywood was awarded a contract for the right to the sawtimber growth on the Duncan properties for a period of 15 years; the growth amounted to between 12 and 18 million board feet per year. United Plywood also made similar contracts with several smaller landowners in the area.

When discussing long-range plans with officers of United Plywood late in 1965, the president of Liberty learned that the Duncan family would soon sell its property for reasons of estate planning. Since the Liberty officers had already considered the possibility of a greater commitment in forest products, it appeared logical for them to consider the acquisition of the Duncan timber properties, adjacent to United Plywood's southern mill. In addition, it appeared that the Duncan properties might also have some interest to Liberty from a mineral standpoint, although no surveys of this possibility had been made.

The Liberty officers felt that they must reach a decision quickly because of the competition for timberlands. Further evaluation of the possible acquisition became the task of Henry Jonas, assistant treasurer of Liberty.

It was understood that the Duncan family would sell for cash. The figure of $18 million had been mentioned. During the preceding 12 to 18 months, timber properties in the South had been selling for values regarded by people in the industry as exorbitant. High prices were being paid by companies whose managements felt that they must have a position in southern pine timber if they were to remain a factor in their industry. They were paying what might be termed "insurance" values for large tracts of property. Although the Liberty officers were aware of this type of competition for large properties, certain circumstances indicated to them that Liberty might be able to purchase timberlands for what the Liberty management would consider a price more realistic than $18 million.

The dominant circumstance was that United Plywood held the right to the sawtimber growth on the Duncan property, and this right was accompanied by a very favorable stumpage or sawtimber price, since the contract had been entered into before the increase in values had been established. To a third party purchaser looking for a southern pine timber position for either plywood or pulp and paper manufacture, this circumstance meant, first, that the growth from the property would be unavailable to it during the first 15 years of its ownership, because the growth was already committed to the United Plywood mill. In other words, the property must be held for the first 15 years simply as a passive investment. Second, even if the third party purchaser was willing to hold the property during that period simply as an investment, the capitalized earnings value it could afford to pay for the property would be rather modest because of the low price at which the timber was committed to United Plywood.

Liberty's valuation of the property, of course, would also be inhibited by this circumstance. Since Liberty owned United Plywood, it actually would indirectly achieve the benefit of the advantageous price itself.

With these thoughts in mind the executives of Liberty retained the forestry consulting firm of Jackson & Jackson, Natchez, Mississippi, to prepare a valuation of the Duncan properties. It was agreed that the analysis should proceed from cash flow estimates and not accounting data. Thus it would be necessary to determine the after-tax cash flows expected in each of the years to be studied. In addition, since the cash flows would be affected by the assumptions made (because of the tax shields developed from depletion expenses, which were based on cost), it was decided to explore the results from purchase prices of $10, $15, $18, and $20 million.

METHOD OF VALUATION

The valuation might be sensitive to two factors in the environment. The first was the pattern of sawtimber and pulpwood selling prices to be assumed for the sales from the property in the future years after expiration of the 15-year contract. It was finally decided to test the valuation under three pricing patterns, the low, medium, and upper price projections. These levels were based on historical records and the judgment of the consultants.

The second environmental factor the valuation might be sensitive to was the timber-cutting pattern under which the property would be managed. One cutting pattern would involve the assumption of sustained yield management, wherein the cut from the property would be limited to the annual growth from the property. Based upon accepted rules of thumb regarding restocking and sales price, the value of the property at the end of 30 years would be $14,592,870, which was taken as the terminal value for the analysis. This figure was expected to approximate the book value of the property at that time.

A second cutting pattern was an accelerated cut, wherein the property would actually be cut at a rate exceeding the annual growth, thereby gradually depleting the property. This assumption would be studied to see whether an acceleration of timber revenues would have an effect on the present values of the property significant enough to give the technique serious consideration. The study was especially important given the severe reduction in terminal value with the use of an accelerated cut. A happy medium had to be found regarding the degree of acceleration, however, so that the property would retain some value to the plywood mills in terms of a long-term source of raw material supply. For example, it would have been possible to assume a cut that within a few years would leave the forest lands producing only pulpwood and yielding no sawtimber at all for the plywood mills. Such a result would have been somewhat in conflict with the original goal of purchasing the properties. At the end of 30 years, this cutting method would leave mostly pulpwood, with an estimated final value for the property of $7,714,634.

To summarize the first steps of the analysis, it was decided to analyze the property under three different price conditions, two different cutting pattern conditions, and four purchase price assumptions. This required working out 24 different detailed cash flow calculations. Jackson & Jackson was instructed to make the calculations of value before giving effect to any method of financing that might be chosen for the project. They thus prepared an all-equity cash flow analysis based upon the stated assumptions.

The analysis began with an estimate of potential cash receipts for each of 30 years under the 24 sets of assumptions. The estimate involved assumptions as to the amount of timber to be taken from the land and the prices to be paid for various grades of timber. That is, the expected yields of pine pulpwood, pine sawtimber, hardwood pulpwood, and hardwood sawtimber for each of the 30 years were multiplied by the prices assumed to be applicable to those items and years.

The consultants next estimated the various expenses associated with management of the timberland. These included the costs of surveying, administration, and sales, as well as the capitalized cost for planting and the equipment necessary to maintain the property as a continuing source of timber supply. Estimates were made for each of the 30 years to determine an inflow–outflow relationship between sales and expenses.

Since tax regulations made provision for depletion of natural resources, the final segment of the consultants' report concerned detailed projections of future inventory and depletion accounts. These projections too were made for a 30-year period on an annual basis so that a yearly federal tax figure could be estimated, given the applicable 25% tax rate. This permitted determination of the net annual cash throw-off on an all-equity basis.

Discounted cash flow rates of return on investment were then calculated by computer for each of the 24 combinations of purchase price, cutting pattern, and selling price. Graphic summaries of the results are presented in Exhibits 1 and 2. Exhibit 1 illustrates the rates of return associated with the various purchase prices under the assumption of a sustained cut at three different price levels. Exhibit 2 is similar except for the assumption that an accelerated rate of cut would be utilized on the property.

FINANCING

After studying the all-equity charts, the Liberty executives decided that the most reasonable set of assumptions was that of a sustained yield cut and a medium price level. Since Liberty used 7.5% as the cost of its invested capital, the purchase obviously was not feasible at the asking price of $18 million. The internal rate of return at that price was 4.8%. In fact, a price slightly under $12 million was indicated. This amount would surely be unsatisfactory to the Duncans.

On hearing of this decision, the consultants suggested that the rate of return on Liberty's investment might be increased by the use of a loan secured by the value of the timberlands. Another client of theirs had recently obtained from a large insurance company a 15-year, 5.4% direct reduction mortgage loan of 50% of the purchase price of a similar property. The consultants therefore were authorized to explore the effects of using debt to finance half of the $18 million asking price of the Duncan property.

The consultants' analysis then proceeded to adjust the all-equity flows for the effect of $9 million of debt financing, thus reducing Liberty's equity investment to $9 million. It was assumed, on the basis of the recent loan made by the insurance company, that the principal amount of the financing was to be amortized over 15 years. In essence, then, the all-equity cash flows derived were reduced by the sum of the annual principal payments on the investment and the after-tax cost of the interest payments. It was then possible to relate the after-financing cash flow to the unfinanced amount of the purchase price in terms of the discounted cash flow rate of return on equity (the amount considered to be at Liberty's risk).

Exhibit 3 indicates the effect of this analysis and the rate of return anticipated from the resulting flows. The irregularity in the cash flows, which may be observed in column 1, resulted from the care with which the estimates were made. These estimates reflected changing patterns in the kinds of wood cut and the use of accelerated depreciation following periodic replacements of plant items as needed. They were accepted by the Liberty officers as being realistic for the analysis of the property.

Analysis of the results from column 4 of Exhibit 3 showed that this method of financing did not produce a sufficient return from the proposed project because the internal rate of return was 5.4%. A member of the consulting group then commented that some of their clients felt that assigning a portion of the cash flow to the repayment of the financing did not accurately reflect the nature of the timber property involved. Implicit in retiring the loan was the assumption that the debt capacity of the project was declining. Presumably, given the initial existence of the debt capacity and the use of a sustained-yield cutting scheme, the debt capacity would not fall, and the project could be refinanced as needed.

The consultants argued that use of a conventional approach to leverage had locked the analysis into an assumption that was no more applicable to the project than any other wrong assumption, such as one concerning price level or cutting pattern. The asset was one that would not depreciate over time but, if anything, would appreciate over time. Not only were large, well-stocked tracts of timber such as this one becoming increasingly scarce, but, in fact, the trees themselves were growing at a rate that would increase the total inventory of fiber over the long term. It seemed that in these circumstances the debt capacity of the project was going to increase rather than decrease.

With these thoughts in mind, the consultants developed a second approach to leverage for presentation to the Liberty management. This approach reflected the financing of the project by what might be called "perpetually outstanding debt." The flows from the all-equity analysis were reduced only by the after-tax cost of the interest payments on the outstanding debt. The principal amount of the financing was assumed to be paid back out of the salvage value derived from the project in year 30, when the calculation was arbitrarily terminated. The net effect of this approach, of course, was to leave a much larger cash flow available for payout and a higher rate of return on the equity portion of the investment. The results are shown in column 6 of Exhibit 3, from which an internal rate of return of 6.6% was computed. While less than 7.5%, it was within the bounds of possibility, in Mr. Jonas' opinion.

Finally, the consultants pointed out that if continuous discounting was used, instead of the end-of-year discounting that had been the Liberty management's practice, the internal rate of return would rise to 6.8%. (See Exhibit 4 for a summary of the rates mentioned above.)

It was Mr. Jonas' task to appraise the work of the consultants, selecting the figures that he decided were based on appropriate assumptions, and even making alterations if they were justified. He would then prepare for the committee of senior officers his recommendations as to the price the company should consider the absolute maximum, citing the necessary evidence to justify his conclusions.

Although discounted cash flow calculations had been presented to this committee before, the ideas about the use of debt were novel to its members, so Mr. Jonas knew that his choice would have to be explained very clearly. In particular, he anticipated that there would be questioning concerning the terminal values chosen.

Exhibit 1

LIBERTY PETROLEUM COMPANY
Sustained Yield Cut
Rates of Return Associated with Various Purchase Prices
and Three Pricing Patterns

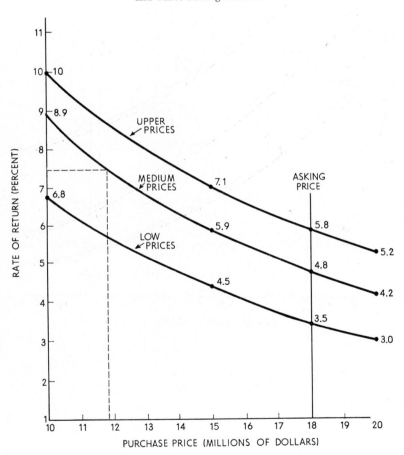

Exhibit 2

LIBERTY PETROLEUM COMPANY
ACCELERATED YIELD CUT
Rates of Return Associated with Various Purchase Prices
and Three Pricing Patterns

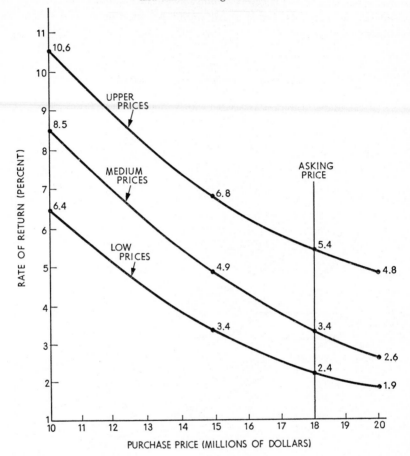

Exhibit 3

LIBERTY PETROLEUM COMPANY

ALL-EQUITY CASH FLOWS RELATED TO $18 MILLION PRICE AND ADJUSTMENTS
CAUSED BY POSSIBLE DEBT PROGRAMS
(Tabulated Figures in Thousands)

Year	All-Equity Cash Flows	$9 Million Loan, Payment of $890,000 Annually			$9 Million Loan, Constant	
		Applied to Principal	Interest after 48% Tax	Adjusted Cash Flows	Interest after 48% Tax	Adjusted Cash Flows
1......	$ 439	$(405)	$(253)	$ (218)	$(253)	$ 186
2......	657	(426)	(241)	(11)	↑	404
3......	732	(450)	(229)	53		480
4......	805	(474)	(217)	115		553
5......	855	(499)	(203)	152		602
6......	928	(526)	(189)	212		676
7......	624	(555)	(175)	(106)		371
8......	740	(585)	(159)	(4)		487
9......	804	(616)	(143)	45		551
10......	869	(650)	(125)	94		617
11......	916	(685)	(107)	125		664
12......	1,167	(722)	(88)	357		914
13......	1,285	(761)	(68)	457		1,032
14......	843	(802)	(46)	(5)		590
15......	805	(845)	(24)	(64)		552
16......	1,237	...	...	1,237		984
17......	824	...	...	824		571
18......	587	...	...	587		334
19......	754	...	...	754		502
20......	1,437	...	...	1,437		1,184
21......	1,328	...	...	1,328		1,075
22......	1,372	...	...	1,372		1,119
23......	1,366	...	...	1,366		1,114
24......	1,361	...	...	1,361		1,108
25......	1,356	...	...	1,356		1,102
26......	1,139	...	...	1,139		886
27......	1,090	...	...	1,090		837
28......	1,086	...	...	1,086		833
29......	1,083	...	...	1,083	↓	830
30......	1,035	...	...	1,035	(253)	782
Terminal value 30......	14,593	...	...	14,593	...	5,593
Rate of return..	4.8%	...	...	5.4%	...	6.6%

Exhibit 4

LIBERTY PETROLEUM COMPANY

TABULATION OF RATES OF RETURN AND PRESENT VALUES FROM
EXHIBIT 3

Financing Method	Rate of Return	Present Value at 7.5%
All equity	4.8%	$11,981,299
Amortized debt	5.4	5,523,890
Perpetual debt Annual discounting	6.6	7,968,699
Perpetual debt Continuous discounting	6.8	8,219,682

ELECTRICIRCUIT, INC.

IN LATE MAY, 1964, Vito Rappasadi, treasurer of Electricircuit, Inc., was considering the company's future investment and financing program. Anticipated normal growth, introduction of a new product line, and modification of the company's inventory control system together would require substantial external financing. However, the opportunities for such financing were severely restricted by the company's financial condition.

COMPANY BACKGROUND INFORMATION

Electricircuit, Inc., had been founded on Long Island and incorporated in New York in 1954 by four young electrical engineers. At the outset, stock in the company had been wholly owned by this group of four. Later, stock options had been granted to three particularly desirable managers as an inducement to join the company. These options had been exercised, and in 1964 the entire equity was owned by the seven men, in approximately equal blocks. The seven also held all the top management positions and composed the board of directors.

In the period from formation through 1963, Electricircuit had enjoyed considerable success. The product line had been expanded from one original product to include several lines of proprietary items sold as components for digital systems. In the form of packaged circuits (modules), these products performed decision control, storage, and ancillary functions as components of digital systems. They were primarily produced for off-the-shelf sale to customers who used them in systems of their own design and manufacture. Company profit came principally from the sale of these proprietary products.

As the company had expanded, it had also begun the manufacture-to-order of a variety of special purpose systems, which applied digital techniques to computing, information handling, control tasks, and data processing. The systems were used in space equipment, navigation and positioning systems, signal processing, data converters, and a variety of other end uses associated directly or indirectly with government expenditures for military and nonmilitary purposes. This business accounted for roughly one fourth of Electricircuit's billings. The company profited from the inclusion of its products in these systems, but little if any additional profit had been gained from the provision of engineering services.

Electricircuit's proprietary products were subject to a high rate of obsolescence in an extremely competitive market. Although protected by patents, these items were always exposed to the competition of alternatively engineered products performing the same function. Typically, the company's new products had achieved about three fourths of their highest sales level in the year they were introduced. Peak volumes had been reached and maintained in the second and third years, but these years normally had been followed by steep decay and virtual worthlessness by the sixth or seventh year. Competitive developments had cut short this 6- to 7-year cycle for about 10% of the new products that the company had introduced during the past 10 years, and on those occasions Electricircuit had been forced to absorb substantial inventory write-offs.

Thus, the danger of being technically leapfrogged was a very real one. It had been met by unstinting expenditures on research and development to improve existing product lines and add new ones. Company officials had been successful in recruiting and holding a strong research group, and this group, supported by ample budgetary allocations, had created enviable market respect for the quality of the company's products. The seven owner-managers were determined to maintain that reputation.

Over the years, continuing expansion had led to a number of changes in Electricircuit's internal organization. Sales outlets had been established in southern California, and late in 1962 a plant had been constructed there for the design and production of systems for the West Coast space industry. Earlier, production of proprietary products had been shifted from Long Island to a wholly owned subsidiary in North Carolina largely because of the availability of a low-wage labor force in that area. Production operations at the subsidiary consisted almost entirely of hand assembly and wiring of modules and allied components. Other managerial offices remained at the original site on Long Island.

In the period after 1960, rapidly widening product acceptance had almost trebled the company's sales (Exhibit 1), and its investment in current assets had expanded accordingly (Exhibit 2). Short-term loans, secured by the pledge of receivables, had been obtained from Electricircuit's Long Island bank to support this growing requirement. With isolated exceptions, the bank had been willing to lend 85% of the face amount of the receivables, and this banking arrangement had proved generally satisfactory until early 1964. At that time, an officer of the bank had made it clear that Electricircuit had reached the limit of the credit line that the bank was willing to extend in the absence of some improvement in the company's capital structure. New equity or junior debt financing would qualify Electricircuit for a larger loan, if the company so desired and the requisite security was available, but the loan limit would continue to be set in terms of the ratio of bank debt to junior claims (equity plus subordinated debt, if any) that existed at the end of 1963. This assumed no deterioration in earnings or financial condition.

As 1964 had worn on and sales had continued to increase, the company had been forced to sharply cut its cash balance to meet its growing financing needs. Positive earnings had been realized in approximately the same proportion to sales as in 1963, but the retention of these earnings had failed to alter the bank's stand on additional financing. When approached in April, the loan officer had been reluctant to extend additional credit on the basis of unaudited interim statements, but more importantly he had pointed out that the growth of equity had produced only a modest change in the company's debt–equity ratio. Moreover, about one half of the earnings had been invested in highly specialized equipment, and to that extent the bank had not benefited either from replenishment of the company's deposit balance or, as a creditor, from the increased protection that investment in more liquid assets might have provided.

GROWTH PROSPECTS

In late May, Mr. Rappasadi prepared the following forecast of Electricircuit's year-end current asset position, to help in assessing the company's immediate financing problems.

Cash		$ 135,000
Receivables		2,720,000
Inventory		
Raw materials	$436,000	
Work in process	529,000	
Finished goods	311,000	1,276,000
		$4,131,000

The forecast assumed a year-end sales rate of $13.6 million and a corresponding cost of goods sold figure of $8.1 million. Actual sales for the year were estimated at $12 million. These estimates had been employed with some confidence in projecting working capital requirements, since sales in recent months and impressions of customers' production plans for the rest of the year pointed unmistakably toward continued growth. Receivables had been estimated at 20% of sales, and raw materials and work in process at a four-week rate of usage. Finished goods, on the other hand, had been projected at little more than a two-week supply.

During preceding months, finished goods inventory had been deliberately reduced in relation to sales as other cash requirements had mounted. Mr. Rappasadi believed that continued curtailment of investment in finished goods inventory was likely to be costly, but lacking other immediate sources of funds he also felt that the stock of finished goods would have to be held to the projected level if the company was to avoid an acute cash emergency. As it was, cash had been projected at merely its current level.

Beyond 1964, the marketing manager had estimated that sales of the company's current products would reach $16 million in 1965. Without major product innovation, he thought that sales could probably be maintained at that level in 1966, but if past patterns prevailed, he expected that the following year would see a decline, which might amount to as much as $4 or $5 million. The exact forecast for 1965 was based primarily on the marketing group's knowledge of government appropriations for ongoing defense and space programs. It could be upset by project cancellations, but that was considered highly unlikely for the projects concerned. On the other hand, the plateau and descent pattern of the more distant estimates emphasized the importance of maintaining Electricircuit's technical preeminence.

INVESTMENT POSSIBILITIES

Mr. Rappasadi saw two possible opportunities for investment that might improve the projected sales pattern and its profit consequences in the future. One involved the introduction of a major new product line, and the other a revision of the company's finished goods inventory control system.

The new product line, which had been under development for the past two years, performed comfortably to military specifications and was believed to possess technical qualities that would give it significant competitive advantages. All the items making up the line were in a late stage of development, and the line was currently scheduled for introduction at the turn of the year. Market reception was difficult to estimate with any degree of precision, but the marketing manager was confident that the line would contribute sales of at least $2 million in 1965 and a further increment of at least $0.5 million in 1966. The line would be priced to give the same coverage of costs as was provided by the company's other proprietary products.

To put the line into production in the North Carolina plant would require about $100,000 for specialized equipment. That plant had been built to accommodate more growth than had yet been realized, and therefore no additional outlays were anticipated for production facilities. However, the marketing manager had estimated that a budget allocation of $35,000 would be needed to introduce and promote the line if it was to achieve its full potential.

The second investment possibility—increasing stocks of finished goods—grew out of widespread feeling that economizing in that direction had already been pushed far beyond justifiable limits. Expediting had become commonplace in juggling production schedules, with costly consequences, and orders had been lost to competitors with disturbing frequency when customers had been notified of long but necessary delivery delays. Mr. Rappasadi, therefore, had ordered a review of the company's entire inventory control system.

The area of concern, as a result of that study, had been narrowed to the finished goods segment of total inventory. Some improvements seemed possible in balancing raw material stocks, but it was not thought that this would lead to any appreciable change in the relationship of total raw material inventory to production volume. Lead time required by the purchasing department and limited interchangeability of parts among product lines combined to fix the required total at roughly a four-week supply level. Work in process inventory seemed similarly intractable. Allocation of shop labor, timing of lot starts, schedules, and so on were already being decided on grounds of optimum production arrangements, as the production manager saw them. Technical changes, necessitating work stoppages, often had to be introduced during the in-process stage; therefore, the production manager and the engineering group as well attached considerable value to the flexibility allowed by a four-week production period.

By contrast with its approval of current raw material and in-process control practices, the report recommended complete revamping of the system being used to determine finished goods inventory levels. The current system, in brief, was based on specific item-by-item sales forecasts for the coming quarter. Given those forecasts, goods were scheduled into production in quantities that would raise the level of existing stocks to the anticipated sales requirement. Recently, as noted above, financial circumstances had made it necessary to cut stocks below the target levels that would have been set in more normal circumstances, but the report's condemnation of the system was independent of that experience.

Its basic criticism centered on the system's dependence on quarterly sales forecasts and the invariable inaccuracy of such estimates. Replacement demand could be predicted with tolerable margins of error, but the same was not true of new orders. They were typically received at erratic intervals. Moreover, they constituted a large part of the total demand for most products.

To cope with the problem, the report urged adoption of a system of buffer stocks, which would be set with more careful regard to the costs, returns, and risks associated with inventory maintenance. To that end, data had been compiled on five possible inventory-sales levels representing substantially different inventory policies (Exhibit 3). In each case, the lost-sales estimate had been derived from computer simulations (using appropriate reorder points and reorder quantities) of the demand experience of major product lines.

Since Electricircuit was currently operating with lower finished goods stocks than those contemplated by any one of the five policies, Mr. Rappasadi was particularly impressed by the magnitude of the lost-sales figures. On the other hand, he was also impressed by the inventory investment required to cut those losses by appreciable amounts. Any significant change in inventory policy would therefore tend to enlarge the financing problems that already lay ahead.

FINANCING ALTERNATIVES

As noted earlier, those problems had come to a head at the beginning of 1964, when Electricircuit's bank had refused to increase its line of credit in the absence of some prior strengthening of the company's capital structure. That development had not been completely unanticipated. In 1963, Mr. Rappasadi had begun to explore the possible issuance of subordinated long-term debt with several investment bankers and representatives of lending institutions. All the discussions had been unsuccessful, however, and as a result Electricircuit had been forced to finance the acquisition of a new headquarters building and its West Coast plant with sale-and-leaseback financing. The two buildings together had been constructed at a cost of $950,000 and had been leased by Electricircuit for a 10-year period at a combined annual rental of $280,000. The leases contained 10-year renewal options at the same annual rentals, but no repurchase option. At the time, Mr. Rappasadi had estimated that the two plants probably would be worth half their original cost at the end of 10 years, and little or nothing at the end of 20 years. Both deals had been arranged with a private group of wealthy New York investors.

The same group had also indicated its willingness to lend the company an additional $500,000 to $1 million at any time at an annual interest rate of 18%. While the loan would be subordinated to bank debt and would permit an increase of the type of secured financing that the bank was currently providing, it would not be without its own restrictive covenants:

1. Cash dividend payments and company purchase of its own stock would be prohibited.
2. No additional debt would be allowed other than bank borrowing and other short-term liabilities arising in the normal course of business, or long-term debt specifically subordinated to this loan.
3. Current assets would have to exceed the sum of current liabilities and all long-term debt by at least $800,000.
4. Default on any provision would automatically accelerate the due date of principal and accrued interest to the date of default.

Interest payments would be payable semiannually, but the principal would not become due for five years. Prepayment in full would become permissible at the end of 3 years at a penalty of 10% and at the end of 4 years at 6%, but only with funds from operations.

Concern about weakening of control and earnings dilution made a public sale of common stock seem highly questionable to some of the company's owner-managers. They felt that earnings would continue to improve and cited the company's recent growth record as evidence of the possible cost of bringing in outside shareholders at an inopportune point in the company's development. On the other hand, Mr. Rappasadi had found that underwriters repeatedly expressed the opinion that Electricircuit's only hope for adequate long-term financing was additional common stock. That meant a public offering, since none of the current stockholders had additional funds to invest.

Increasingly tight financial straits during 1964 had pressed Mr. Rappasadi to pursue the subject. Expressions of interest had been obtained from several underwriters, but only one, Bayles and Bayles, had expressed willingness to underwrite a stock issue. After many conversations, company visits, and a preliminary study of Electricircuit's financial records, the senior partner of

Bayles and Bayles had indicated to Mr. Rappasadi that an issue of common stock to net the company up to $1 million would probably be feasible in early autumn. Offering price to the public would be about $10.50 per share. The brevity of Electricircuit's history of good earnings would be a drawback, but Mr. Bayles explained that he counted on the company's unusual growth record to make that price attainable. The net proceeds to Electricircuit, however, would be closer to $8. The spread between the two prices would cover the underwriter's compensation and risk and all costs of preparing the issue. In addition, the company would agree to sell warrants to Bayles and Bayles for $10,000 to purchase 10,000 shares of stock. The warrants would be exercisable after 1 year at $13.50 per share.

If the terms of a deal were finally agreed on, Bayles and Bayles would attempt to assemble a syndicate for which it would act as lead underwriter. The syndicate would be organized to provide wide geographic dispersion and insure a distribution of shares that would pose no threat to existing management. For a period of a year or so after the sale, Bayles and Bayles would make an informal market for Electricircuit's stock in limited quantities. Although the firm was not an active over-the-counter dealer, it sometimes made an aftermarket in issues it had originated, largely for the benefit of customers who might be forced to dispose of their stock in emergency circumstances.

Mr. Rappasadi found it difficult to evaluate the terms of this offer. Inquiries addressed to acquaintances in the financial community uncovered some opinion that the company should hold out for a higher price. These sources cited a number of recent growth issues that had sold in the 30 times price–earnings range. In addition, they noted that the economy showed strong signs of extending its longest postwar boom and that the stock market was currently at a record high.

Although Mr. Rappasadi realized that of all the firms approached Bayles and Bayles had been the only one to express any interest in underwriting a new issue, he decided to review the above opinions with Mr. Bayles. While Mr. Bayles agreed that both the economy and stock market were unusually strong, he interpreted these developments as cause for apprehension concerning the new-issues market. He was uncertain about how long these favorable conditions could continue, and foresaw a possible break in the market at any time. In a sharply falling market, an unseasoned over-the-counter stock such as Electricircuit's was apt to fare much worse than average. In pricing Electricircuit's proposed issue, the underwriter therefore had tried to allow both for some immediate capital appreciation and for the fact that it would be selling the issue to its customers at or near the top of a particularly strong market. Bayles and Bayles was particularly mindful of the second fact because of its agreement to maintain an informal market for Electricircuit common stock. As for the price of so-called comparable issues, the firm disagreed with the critics. The issues referred to were generally smaller, often had a small cash dividend to provide downside price support, and had been sold two or three months earlier in quite different market conditions. For all these reasons, Bayles and Bayles declined to reconsider the offering price.

An alternative to external equity financing was continued reliance on the plowback of earnings with no payment of dividends. Mr. Rappasadi thought. that the outlook for expansion and the profitability of contemplated funds commitments probably threw doubt on the wisdom of that policy, but he was uncertain about the amount and type, or types, of outside financing to recommend to his fellow shareholders.

Exhibit 1

ELECTRICIRCUIT, INC.

INCOME STATEMENTS FOR YEARS ENDED DECEMBER 31, 1961–63
(Dollar Figures in Thousands)

	1961	1962	1963
Net sales	$3,616	$5,544	$10,637
Cost of goods sold*	2,368	3,758	6,325
Gross profit	$1,248	$1,786	$ 4,312
Research and development expense	422	529	1,097
Selling, general, and administrative expense†	782	1,105	2,376
Interest expense	30	40	93
Income from operations	$ 13	$ 112	$ 746
Other income	2	7	20
Other deductions	(7)	(9)	(92)
Income before tax	$ 8	$ 110	$ 675
Federal income tax	3	45	329
Net Income	$ 5	$ 65	$ 346

* Included in cost of goods sold:

	1961	1962	1963
Depreciation, amortization, and maintenance	$31	$ 52	$117
Rental charges	40	80	210
State and local taxes (excluding payroll)	1	1	4
Total	$72	$133	$331

† Included in selling, general, and administrative expense:

	1961	1962	1963
Depreciation, amortization, and maintenance	$11	$ 18	$ 40
Rental charges	19	39	101
State and local taxes (excluding payroll)	10	17	66
Total	$40	$ 74	$207

Exhibit 2

ELECTRICIRCUIT, INC.

BALANCE SHEETS AS OF DECEMBER 31, 1961–63
(Dollar Figures in Thousands)

	1961		1962		1963
CURRENT ASSETS					
Cash.............................		$ 279		$ 303	$ 347
Accounts receivable................		693		1,260	2,255
Inventories					
Raw materials...................	$128		$337		$372
Work in process.................	187		373		537
Finished goods..................	244		311		407
Total inventory...............		$ 559		$1,022	$1,317
Prepaid expenses..................		8		13	24
Total Current Assets.........		$1,539		$2,598	$3,943
FIXED ASSETS					
Gross fixed assets..................	$212		$298		$537
Less: Accumulated depreciation....	72		120		155
Net Fixed Assets............		140		178	382
Total Assets................		$1,679		$2,776	$4,325
CURRENT LIABILITIES					
Notes payable*...................		$ 541		$1,072	$1,804
Trade accounts payable............		159		401	484
Accrued expenses.................		129		246	240
Provision for taxes...............		9		56	383
Other............................		20		102	160
Total Current Liabilities......		$ 858		$1,876	$3,072
STOCKHOLDERS' EQUITY					
Common stock, stated value 50 cents.		$ 318		$ 328	$ 360
Paid-in surplus...................		486		489	464
Retained earnings.................		17		83	429
Total Stockholders' Equity....		$ 821		$ 900	$1,253
Total Liabilities and Capital...		$1,679		$2,776	$4,325
Number of shares outstanding		636,086		655,122	719,746

* Secured by the pledge of all receivables.

Exhibit 3

ELECTRICIRCUIT, INC.

SELECTED FINANCIAL DATA ON POSSIBLE INVENTORY POLICIES
(Dollar Figures in Thousands)

Alternative	Ratio of Inventory to Cost of Goods Sold*	Total Investment in Finished Goods Inventory*	Annual Sales Loss because of Stockouts	Annual Combined Setup, Warehouse, Handling, and Insurance Costs†
A.....	4.9% (18 days' sales)	$ 381	$495	$21
B.....	6.5 (24 days' sales)	505	301	25
C.....	8.9 (32 days' sales)	692	150	30
D.....	11.8 (42 days' sales)	917	56	35
E.....	14.2 (51 days' sales)	1,103	17	37

* Based on forecast annual cost of sales rate of $8.1 million. Inventory valued at direct cost.
† Interest expense and/or other financing costs are not included.

Exhibit 4

ELECTRICIRCUIT, INC.

BALANCE SHEET, AS OF APRIL 30, 1964 UNAUDITED
(Dollar Figures in Thousands)

CURRENT ASSETS

Cash......................................		$ 135
Accounts receivable........................		2,510
Inventories		
Raw materials..........................	$410	
Work in process........................	506	
Finished goods.........................	310	1,226
Prepaid expenses..........................		30
Total Current Assets..................		$3,901

FIXED ASSETS

Gross fixed assets.........................	$612	
Less: Accumulated depreciation..........	168	
Net Fixed Assets....................		444
Total Assets.......................		$4,345

CURRENT LIABILITIES

Notes payable*...........................	$1,795
Trade accounts payable....................	530
Accrued expenses.........................	246
Provision for taxes†......................	245
Other....................................	143
Total Current Liabilities.............	$2,959

STOCKHOLDERS' EQUITY

Common stock, stated value 50 cents........	$ 360
Paid-in surplus...........................	464
Retained earnings.........................	562
Total Stockholders' Equity...........	$1,386
Total Liabilities and Capital.........	$4,345
Number of shares outstanding..............	719,746

* Secured by the pledge of receivables.
† Tax liabilities as of April 30 reflect a large, first-quarter adjusting payment. At year-end, "Provision for taxes" normally equals the federal corporate income tax for the year just ended, plus approximately $75,000 state and local tax accruals.

HOW TO EVALUATE NEW CAPITAL INVESTMENTS *

By John G. McLean†

In evaluating new investment projects, why are return-on-investment figures preferable to years-to-pay-out figures?

Of various possible methods for calculating return on investment, why is the discounted-cash-flow procedure likely to yield the best results?

What techniques and assumptions will help executives who want to make practical use of the discounted-cash-flow method?

Obviously, I cannot answer these questions satisfactorily for all companies. I shall attempt only to describe some of the answers developed by the Continental Oil Company. Faced with a need for better methods of evaluating investment proposals, management decided in 1955 to adopt the discounted-cash-flow method. The procedures adopted, the reasons for choosing them, and the results obtained during the past three years may serve as a useful "case example" for other companies to study.

Of course, the techniques that I shall describe were not invented by Continental. They have been used for centuries in the field of finance and banking and have been fully described in many textbooks and articles in the field of industrial management and business economics during the past 25 years. It is only recently, however, that they have been applied in the industrial field, and their usage is still limited to a fairly small number of companies.

MANAGEMENT CONCERN

Prior to 1955, we had relied heavily—as many oil companies do—on years-to-pay-out figures as the primary means of judging the desirability of investments and as a yardstick for measuring one investment opportunity against another. We had also made use of return-on-investment figures computed in a variety of different ways, which I shall describe later.

* Reprinted by permission from the *Harvard Business Review,* Vol. 36 (November–December 1958), p. 59–69.

† Senior Vice President, Continental Oil Company.

In the latter part of 1954 our financial group, consisting of the controller, the financial vice president, and myself, undertook a comprehensive review of the techniques we were then using in making capital investment decisions. We were concerned about this matter because of the large amounts of new money we found it necessary to channel back into the oil business each year. Characteristically, oil companies have a very high rate of capital turnover because they operate assets which deplete at high rates, and large amounts of new funds must be reinvested each year if earnings are to be maintained and increased.

The capital expenditures of Continental Oil, for example, normally run in the neighborhood of $100 million per year, or about $385,000 each working day—roughly twice our net income, which is about $50 million per year. To the best of my knowledge, there are few, if any, other major industries with such a high ratio of capital expenditures to current net income.

In the oil business, therefore, the making of capital investment decisions assumes considerably more significance as a part of top management's job than is usually the case. In our own situation it was apparent that the management judgment exercised in directing the flow of new funds into our business had a very significant bearing upon current and future earnings per share and a profound influence on the long-term growth and development of our company. We decided, therefore, that we should make a maximum effort to develop the best possible yardstick for comparing one investment opportunity against another and for evaluating the returns that particular projects would earn on the stockholder's dollar.

NEW TECHNIQUES

As a background for outlining the new techniques which our financial group recommended as a result of its study and which were later implemented throughout the company, let me first outline the steps which are normally involved in the appraisal of new capital investments:

1. Estimate the volume of sales, prices, costs of materials, operating expenses, transportation costs, capital investment requirements, strength and nature of competition, rates of obsolescence or depletion, and other economic and business factors.
2. Summarize basic estimates of annual income, life of project, and capital investment in convenient form for appraisal purposes. (Commonly used yardsticks include years to pay out and return on investment.)
3. Exercise managerial judgment in determining whether or not:
   (a) The anticipated return is large enough to warrant the business risks involved;
   (b) The investment opportunity is attractive in view of the various alternative opportunities for capital spending;
   (c) The timing of the investment is right relative to anticipated developments in the near future.

The discounted-cash-flow techniques which we introduced in 1955 had to do only with Step 2; that is, with the way we did our arithmetic in adding up the basic estimates of annual incomes, life of project, and capital investments to arrive at payout and return on investment.

It was clearly recognized that there was nothing in the discounted-cash-flow method which would make it any easier to estimate the items listed in Step 1 or which would improve the accuracy of those estimates. It was likewise recognized that there was nothing in the discounted-cash-flow techniques which would relieve management at any level of the responsibility for exercising judgment on the various matters listed under Step 3. We were concerned fundamentally, at this time, with improving the mechanics of our capital investment analyses in order that management might render better judgments on the three points under Step 3.

Payout vs. Return

Our first recommendation was that we use the return-on-investment figures as the primary yardstick for evaluating new capital investments and pay much less attention to years-to-pay-out figures than had been our custom in the past.

Our reason for de-emphasizing payout figures was simply that they do not provide an adequate means of discriminating among new investment opportunities. They merely indicate how long it will take to recover the original capital outlay and do not tell us anything about the earning power of an investment. There is, of course, no point in making investments which just give us our money back. The true worth of an investment depends on how much income it will generate *after* the original outlay has been recovered, and there is no way that can be determined from a payout figure. Generally speaking, payout figures are reliable measures of the relative worth of alternative investments only when the income-producing life of all projects under consideration is about the same—which is far from the case in our particular situation.

To illustrate how misleading payout figures can be, I have prepared an example consisting of three different projects, each involving an investment of $125,000 (see Exhibit I).

At first glance, you might be inclined to say that this is all pretty simple—all you have to do is look at both the payout period and the total estimated life to reach a correct decision. And it *is* relatively easy if the payout periods are all the same, as they are in this example, or even if the payout periods are different but the total economic lives are the same.

Unfortunately, however, we are usually looking at projects where there is a difference in both the payout period and the project life. Under such circumstances, it becomes very difficult to appraise the relative worth of two or more projects on the basis of payout periods alone. For example, consider the three projects shown in Exhibit II.

It was for these reasons that our financial group recommended that in the future we make use of return-on-investment figures as our primary guide in

Exhibit I

DIFFERENCES IN RATES OF RETURN WHEN PAYOUT PERIODS ARE EQUAL

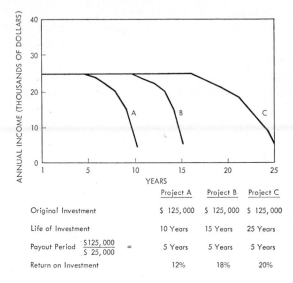

	Project A	Project B	Project C
Original Investment	$ 125,000	$ 125,000	$ 125,000
Life of Investment	10 Years	15 Years	25 Years
Payout Period $\frac{\$125,000}{\$\ 25,000}$ =	5 Years	5 Years	5 Years
Return on Investment	12%	18%	20%

The annual income generated by the investments begins at $25,000 and then declines in later years in each case as shown on the graph. Since the annual incomes are identical in the early years, each project has the same payout period; namely, five years. By this standard of measurement, therefore, the projects would be equal from an investment standpoint. But actually the returns on investment range from 12% per year for Project A, which has the shortest life, to 20% per year for Project C, which has the longest life.

evaluating new projects rather than the payout figures which had customarily been our main guide in the past.

Alternative Calculation

Our second recommendation had to do with the procedures used in calculating the return-on-investment figures. There are at least three general ways to make the calculation:

(1) In the first method, the return is calculated on the *original investment;* that is, the average annual income from a project is divided by the total original capital outlay. This is the procedure we had been using in our producing, refining, petrochemical, and pipeline departments.

(2) In the second method, the return is calculated on the *average investment.* In other words, the average annual income is divided by half the original investment or by whatever figure represents the mid-point between the original cost and the salvage or residual land value in the investment. This is the procedure which was used in our marketing department for calculating returns on new service station investments.

Exhibit II

FAILURE OF PAYOUT PERIODS TO RANK INVESTMENTS
IN ORDER OF DESIRABILITY

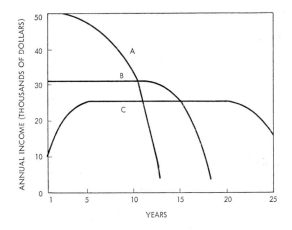

	Project A	Project B	Project C
Original Investment	$ 372,000	$ 267,000	$ 230,000
Life of Investment	13 Years	18 Years	25 Years
Average Annual Income, after Taxes before Depreciation	$ 37,200	$ 26,700	$ 23,000
Payout Based on Average Income	10 Years	10 Years	10 Years
Payout Based on Actual Income	8 Years	8.7 Years	11.5 Years
Return on Investment	5%	8%	8.5%

The payout periods here range from 8 years in the case of Project A, which has a high initial income and a short life, to 11.5 years in the case of Project C, which has a low initial income and a long life. On the basis of payout periods, therefore, Project A would appear to be the best of the three. Actually, however, the true rates of return on investment range from 5% for Project A to 8.5% for Project C. The order of desirability indicated by payout periods is thus exactly the reverse of that indicated by return-on-investment figures.

(3) The third procedure—the *discounted-cash-flow* technique—bases the calculation on the investment actually outstanding from time to time over the life of the project. This was the procedure used in our financial department in computing the cost of funds obtained from various sources or in estimating the yields we might obtain by investing reserve working capital in various types of government or commercial securities.

These three methods will produce very different results, and the figures obtained by one method may be as much as twice as great as those obtained by another—i.e., a project that showed a return of 10% under the procedures used in our refining department could show as much as 20% under the procedures used by our marketing department, and might show 15% or 18% under those used by our financial department.

It was clear, therefore, that we must settle on one of these three methods and use it uniformly throughout all departments of the company. Otherwise, we would be measuring some investments with long yardsticks, others with short yardsticks, and we would never be sure exactly what we were doing.

Relative Advantages

Our selection of discounted cash flow was based on three primary considerations:

It gives the true rate of return offered by a new project. Both of the other methods merely give an approximation of the return. The original-investment

Exhibit III

COMPARISON OF RETURN-ON-INVESTMENT
CALCULATIONS

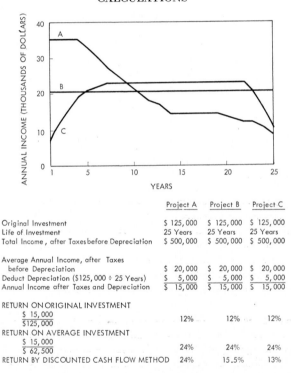

	Project A	Project B	Project C
Original Investment	$ 125,000	$ 125,000	$ 125,000
Life of Investment	25 Years	25 Years	25 Years
Total Income, after Taxes before Depreciation	$ 500,000	$ 500,000	$ 500,000
Average Annual Income, after Taxes before Depreciation	$ 20,000	$ 20,000	$ 20,000
Deduct Depreciation ($125,000 ÷ 25 Years)	$ 5,000	$ 5,000	$ 5,000
Annual Income after Taxes and Depreciation	$ 15,000	$ 15,000	$ 15,000
RETURN ON ORIGINAL INVESTMENT $\frac{\$ 15,000}{\$125,000}$	12%	12%	12%
RETURN ON AVERAGE INVESTMENT $\frac{\$ 15,000}{\$ 62,500}$	24%	24%	24%
RETURN BY DISCOUNTED CASH FLOW METHOD	24%	15.5%	13%

These three projects all require the same original outlay, have the same economic life, and generate exactly the same total income after taxes and depreciation. The return on the original investment would be 12%, and the return on average investment 24% in each case. By these standards, therefore, the projects would appear to be of equal merit. Actually, however, Project A is by far the best of the three because it generates a larger share of its total income in the early years of its life. The investor thus has his money in hand sooner and available for investment in other income-producing projects. This highly important difference is clearly reflected in the discounted-cash-flow figures, which show 24% for Project A, 15.5% for Project B, and 13% for Project C.

method usually understates the return, while the average-investment method usually overstates the return. By contrast, the discounted-cash-flow method is a compromise and usually gives figures lying in between those that would be obtained by the other two methods.

It gives figures which are meaningful in relation to those used throughout the financial world in quoting interest rates on borrowed funds, yields on bonds, and for various other purposes. It thus permits direct comparison of the projected returns on investments with the cost of borrowing money—which is not possible with the other procedures.

It makes allowance for *differences in the time* at which investments generate their income. That is, it discriminates among investments that have (a) a low initial income which gradually increases, (b) a high initial income which gradually declines, and (c) a uniform income throughout their lives.

The last point was particularly important to us, because the investment projects which we normally have before us frequently have widely divergent income patterns. Refining projects usually have a relatively uniform annual income, because they must be operated at 75% to 100% of capacity from the time they go on stream in order to keep unit costs at reasonable levels. On the other hand, producing wells yield a high initial income, which declines as the oil reservoir is depleted; while new service station investments have a still different pattern in that they frequently increase their income as they gain market acceptance and build up their volume of business.

As an illustration of the usefulness of the discounted-cash-flow method in discriminating among investments with different income patterns, consider the three examples presented in Exhibit III.

SIMPLE APPLICATION

To facilitate the adoption of the new system on a company-wide basis, we recommended a very simple application. Assumptions were made at many points in order to reduce the complexity of the calculations involved. In most instances, we found the range of possible error introduced by these simplifying assumptions to be negligible relative to that involved in the basic estimates of income, costs, and economic life of a project. As a further means of facilitating the computations, we prepared a number of special arrangements of the discount tables.

Uniform Income

The procedures that we developed for investments with a uniform annual income are illustrated in Exhibit IV.

The payout period is computed in the usual manner by dividing the cash flow after taxes into the original investment. Then, since the life of the project is estimated at 15 years, the payout period is carried into the 15-year line of a cumulative discount table, and the column in which a matching number is found indicates the discounted-cash-flow rate of return. The numbers in this table are simply sums of the discount factors for the time periods and rates

Exhibit IV

APPLICATION OF DISCOUNTED-CASH-FLOW METHOD IN A SITUATION WITH UNIFORM INCOME

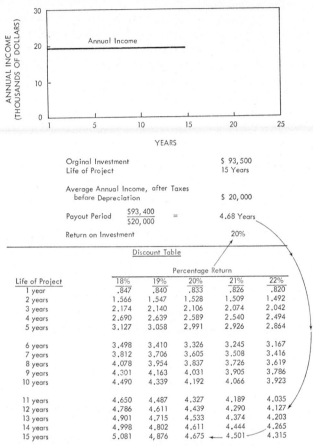

			YEARS		

| Orginal Investment | $ 93,500 |
| Life of Project | 15 Years |

| Average Annual Income, after Taxes before Depreciation | $ 20,000 |

| Payout Period | $\frac{\$93,400}{\$20,000}$ = | 4.68 Years |

| Return on Investment | 20% |

Discount Table

Life of Project	Percentage Return				
	18%	19%	20%	21%	22%
1 year	.847	.840	.833	.826	.820
2 years	1.566	1.547	1.528	1.509	1.492
3 years	2.174	2.140	2.106	2.074	2.042
4 years	2.690	2.639	2.589	2.540	2.494
5 years	3.127	3.058	2.991	2.926	2.864
6 years	3.498	3.410	3.326	3.245	3.167
7 years	3.812	3.706	3.605	3.508	3.416
8 years	4.078	3.954	3.837	3.726	3.619
9 years	4.301	4.163	4.031	3.905	3.786
10 years	4.490	4.339	4.192	4.066	3.923
11 years	4.650	4.487	4.327	4.189	4.035
12 years	4.786	4.611	4.439	4.290	4.127
13 years	4.901	4.715	4.533	4.374	4.203
14 years	4.998	4.802	4.611	4.444	4.265
15 years	5.081	4.876	4.675	4.501	4.315

indicated. Thus, $4.675 is the present worth of $1.00 received annually for 15 years, discounted at a 20% rate.

It is apparent, therefore, that the discounted-cash-flow procedure involves nothing more than finding the discount rate which will make the present worth of the anticipated stream of cash income from the project equal to the original outlay. In this case, the anticipated cash flow of $20,000 per annum for 15 years has a present worth equal to the original outlay—$93,400—when discounted at 20%. Alternatively, it can be said that the discounted-cash-flow procedure simply computes the rate of return on the balance of the investment actually outstanding from time to time over the life of the project, as illustrated in Exhibit V.

The cash flow of $20,000 per annum, continuing over 15 years, is shown in Column 1. Some part of this must be set aside to return the original outlay

Exhibit V

RETURN CALCULATED BY DISCOUNTED-CASH-FLOW METHOD

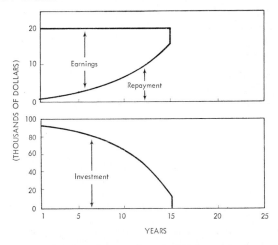

Year	Annual Income	Repayment of Investment	Available for Earnings	Investment Outstanding	Return on Investment
1	$ 20,000	$ 1,298	$ 18,702	$ 93,510	20%
2	20,000	1,558	18,442	92,212	20
3	20,000	1,869	18,131	90,654	20
4	20,000	2,243	17,757	88,785	20
5	20,000	2,692	17,308	86,542	20
6	20,000	3,230	16,770	83,850	20
7	20,000	3,876	16,124	80,620	20
8	20,000	4,651	15,349	76,744	20
9	20,000	5,581	14,419	72,093	20
10	20,000	6,698	13,302	66,512	20
11	20,000	8,037	11,963	59,814	20
12	20,000	9,645	10,355	51,777	20
13	20,000	11,574	8,426	42,132	20
14	20,000	13,888	6,112	30,558	20
15	20,000	16,670	3,330	16,670	20
	$300,000	$93,510	$206,490	0	

over the 15-year period, as shown in Column 2. The remainder, tabulated in Column 3, represents the true earnings.

On this basis, the balance of the original capital outlay outstanding (not yet returned to the investor) at the beginning of each year is shown in Column 4. The ratio of the earnings to this outstanding investment is 20% year by year throughout the life of the project, as shown in Column 5. The graph at the top of the form shows the declining balance of the investment and the division of the annual cash flow between repayment of principal and earnings.

It will immediately be recognized that the mechanism of the discounted-cash-flow procedure here is precisely the same as that involved in a household mortgage where one makes annual cash payments to the bank of a fixed amount to cover interest and payments on the principal. This is the reason for my earlier statement; i.e., that the discounted-cash-flow procedure gives rates of return directly comparable to the interest rates generally quoted for all financial purposes. It is worth noting that in this particular case the conventional procedure of computing a return on the original investment would have given a figure of 15%. Had the calculation been based on the average investment, a figure of 30% would have been obtained (assuming straight-line depreciation in both cases and zero salvage value).

Increasing Income

Our application of the discounted-cash-flow procedure in a situation with increasing income—e.g., investment in new service stations—is illustrated in Exhibit VI. In this case, we assume a build-up of income during the first 5 years, a 20-year period of relatively stable income, and a 5-year period of declining income at the end of the station's life (assumptions now undergoing modification in the light of recent statistical studies of volume performance).

To simplify the calculations and to avoid discounting the income on a

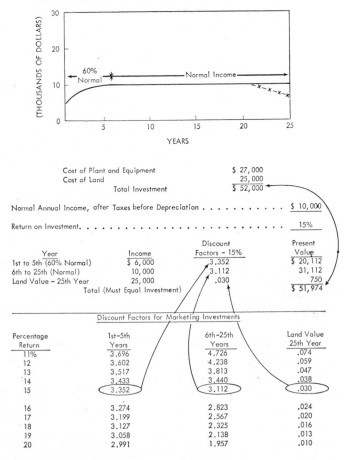

Exhibit VI

APPLICATION OF DISCOUNTED-CASH-FLOW METHOD
IN A SITUATION WITH INCREASING INCOME

Cost of Plant and Equipment	$ 27,000
Cost of Land	25,000
Total Investment	$ 52,000

Normal Annual Income, after Taxes before Depreciation . . . . $ 10,000

Return on Investment. 15%

Year	Income	Discount Factors – 15%	Present Value
1st to 5th (60% Normal)	$ 6,000	3.352	$ 20,112
6th to 25th (Normal)	10,000	3.112	31,112
Land Value – 25th Year	25,000	.030	750
Total (Must Equal Investment)			$ 51,974

Discount Factors for Marketing Investments			
Percentage Return	1st–5th Years	6th–25th Years	Land Value 25th Year
11%	3.696	4.726	.074
12	3.602	4.238	.059
13	3.517	3.813	.047
14	3.433	3.440	.038
15	3.352	3.112	.030
16	3.274	2.823	.024
17	3.199	2.567	.020
18	3.127	2.325	.016
19	3.058	2.138	.013
20	2.991	1.957	.010

year-by-year basis, however, we break the calculations into three parts. We assume that the income in the first to the fifth years is roughly comparable to a uniform series of payments of 60% of the normal level. We also ignore the decline in income at the end of the life, since it would have little effect on the results, and assume that the normal level of income will continue for the sixth to twenty-fifth years. And, finally, we assume that the land would, or could, be sold at the end of the twenty-fifth year at its original cost.

We have thus been able to make use of a special, and much simplified, discount table like the one shown at the bottom of Exhibit VI. The first column contains the sum of the discount factors for the first five years, and the second column shows the sum of the factors for the sixth to twenty-fifth years. The last column shows the present worth of $1.00 received 25 years from now. These factors may then be applied directly to the three segments of the anticipated cash flow from the project in the manner shown. The calculation proceeds by trial and error until a series of factors, and a corresponding discount rate, are found which will make the present value of the future cash flow equal to the original outlay.

Declining Income

Our application of the discounted-cash-flow procedure in a situation of declining income is shown in Exhibit VII. In this case—e.g., an investment in producing wells with a gradually depleting oil reservoir—we have found, again, that the cash flow can usually be divided into three pieces, with a uniform annual income assumed for each. The first year must be treated separately, since the cash flow is usually high as a result of the tax credits for intangible drilling costs. We then select a middle and end period of varying lengths, depending on the characteristics of the particular well, and simply assume an average annual income throughout each period.

These assumptions make it possible to use a simplified arrangement of the discount tables. The first line contains the discount factors for the first year alone, while the remainder of the table consists of cumulative factors beginning in the second year.

The factors for the first year and the middle period may then be read directly from the table, and the factor for the end period is obtained by deduction, as shown. The calculation proceeds by trial and error until discount factors are found which will make the present value of the cash flow equal to the original outlay—in this case 22%.

Irregular Cash Flow

Somewhat more complicated applications of the discounted-cash-flow procedure occur whenever the cash flow is more irregular. To illustrate, here are two special situations:

A. *Oil Payment Deals.* Exhibit VIII shows the application when the problem is to analyze the profitability of acquiring a producing property under an oil payment arrangement.

Exhibit VII

APPLICATION OF DISCOUNTED-CASH-FLOW METHOD IN A SITUATION WITH DECLINING INCOME

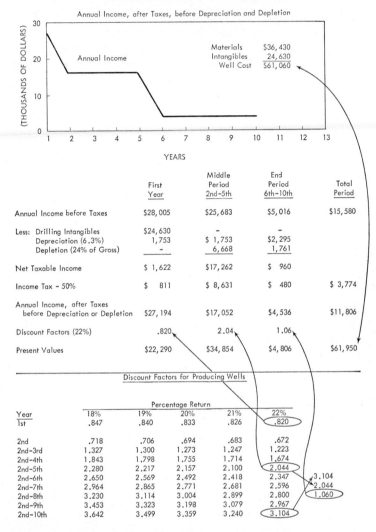

	First Year	Middle Period 2nd–5th	End Period 6th–10th	Total Period
Annual Income before Taxes	$28,005	$25,683	$5,016	$15,580
Less: Drilling Intangibles	$24,630	–	–	
Depreciation (6.3%)	1,753	$ 1,753	$2,295	
Depletion (24% of Gross)	–	6,668	1,761	
Net Taxable Income	$ 1,622	$17,262	$ 960	
Income Tax – 50%	$ 811	$ 8,631	$ 480	$ 3,774
Annual Income, after Taxes before Depreciation or Depletion	$27,194	$17,052	$4,536	$11,806
Discount Factors (22%)	.820	2.04	1.06	
Present Values	$22,290	$34,854	$4,806	$61,950

Discount Factors for Producing Wells

Year	18%	19%	Percentage Return 20%	21%	22%
1st	.847	.840	.833	.826	.820
2nd	.718	.706	.694	.683	.672
2nd–3rd	1.327	1.300	1.273	1.247	1.223
2nd–4th	1.843	1.798	1.755	1.714	1.674
2nd–5th	2.280	2.217	2.157	2.100	2.044
2nd–6th	2.650	2.569	2.492	2.418	2.347	3.104
2nd–7th	2.964	2.865	2.771	2.681	2.596	2.044
2nd–8th	3.230	3.114	3.004	2.899	2.800	1.060
2nd–9th	3.453	3.323	3.198	3.079	2.967
2nd–10th	3.642	3.499	3.359	3.240	3.104

The total cost of the property is $35 million, of which $30 million is supplied by an investor purchasing an oil payment. The terms of sale provide that he shall receive a specified percentage of the oil produced until he has recovered his principal and interest at 6%. The remaining $5 million is supplied by the new operator, who purchases the working and remaining interest and who agrees to do certain additional development drilling as shown in Column 1.

The cash flow after expenses accruing to the operator from the properties is shown in Column 2. Column 3 shows the operator's net cash flow after deduction of the development expenses in Column 1. It is negative in the first two years, and remains small until the oil payment obligation is liquidated. Thereafter, it

Exhibit VIII

APPLICATION OF DISCOUNTED-CASH-METHOD IN A SITUATION WITH IRREGULAR CASH FLOW (A)

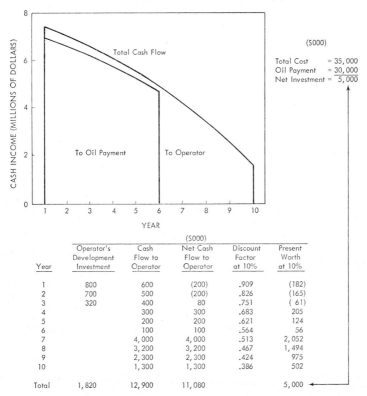

($000)

Total Cost   = 35,000
Oil Payment   = 30,000
Net Investment = 5,000

Year	Operator's Development Investment	Cash Flow to Operator	Net Cash Flow to Operator	Discount Factor at 10%	Present Worth at 10%
1	800	600	(200)	.909	(182)
2	700	500	(200)	.826	(165)
3	320	400	80	.751	(61)
4		300	300	.683	205
5		200	200	.621	124
6		100	100	.564	56
7		4,000	4,000	.513	2,052
8		3,200	3,200	.467	1,494
9		2,300	2,300	.424	975
10		1,300	1,300	.386	502
Total	1,820	12,900	11,080		5,000

increases sharply and ultimately amounts to more than twice the original investment of $5 million. The discounted-cash-flow method recognizes that most of this income does not become available until late in the life of the project, and the resulting return on investment is 10% per annum. (If the same total income had been received in equal annual installments, the return would have been 15%.)

In situations of this kind, it is difficult to see how the analysis could be handled without resorting to the discounted-cash-flow approach. The conventional methods of calculating rates of return would give wholly misleading results.

B. *Water Flood Project.* Exhibit IX contains a second application of the discounted-cash-flow approach to situations in which the income generated by an investment is irregular. Normally, the free flow of oil from a reservoir (primary recovery) diminishes with the passage of time. In some cases, however, secondary recovery measures, such as injection of water into the reservoir, may result in a substantial increase in the total amount of oil produced.

The problem is to determine the profitability of acquiring a small producing property. The primary reserves have been nearly exhausted, and an investment of $2.5 million will be needed at the appropriate time for a water flood to accomplish recovery of the secondary reserves. No immediate payment will be made to

Exhibit IX

APPLICATION OF DISCOUNTED-CASH-FLOW METHOD IN A SITUATION WITH IRREGULAR CASH FLOW (B)

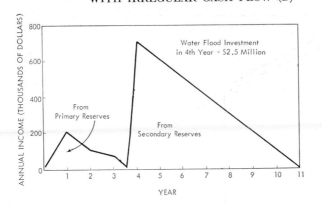

Water Flood in 4th Year   (Figures in Thousands)

Year	Cash Flow	Present Worth of Cash Flow At:						
		10%	20%	28%	30%	40%	49%	50%
1	$ 200	$ 182	$167	$156	$154	$143	$134	$133
2	100	83	69	61	59	51	45	44
3	50	38	29	24	23	18	15	15
4	-1,800	-1,229	-868	-671	-630	-469	-365	-356
5	600	373	241	175	162	112	82	79
6	500	282	167	114	104	66	46	44
7	400	205	112	71	64	38	24	23
8	300	140	70	41	37	20	12	12
9	200	85	39	21	19	10	5	5
10	100	39	16	8	7	3	2	2
Total	+650	+198	+42	0	-2	-8	0	+1

the selling party, but he will receive a $12\frac{1}{2}\%$ royalty on all oil produced from the property, whether from primary or secondary reserves.

The calculations in Exhibit IX are made under the assumption that the water flood investment will be made in the fourth year. During the first three years all the primary reserves will be recovered, and income in the fourth to the tenth years will be attributable solely to the water flood project.

As shown by the table, the discounted-cash-flow analysis gives *two solutions* to this problem. At both 28% and 49%, the net present worth of the cash flow is zero; i.e., the present worth of the cash income is equal to the present worth of the $2.5 million investment. The correct solution is 28%, because the net present worth is declining as we move from the lower to the higher discount rates. The reverse is true at the 49% level.

In general, two solutions may arise whenever the net cash flow switches from positive to negative at some stage in the life of the project, possibly as a result of additional capital outlays required at that time, as in the case of secondary recovery projects. It is important, therefore, to recognize the possibility of two solutions and not to settle for the first one found. A false solution can easily be identified by noting the direction of change in the present worths as higher discount rates are introduced in the trial-and-error calculations.

Bench Marks

As a final step in applying the discounted-cash-flow procedure to our business, it was necessary to develop some bench marks that could be used in appraising the figures resulting from the calculations.

As a starting point, we recommended that approximately 10% after taxes be regarded as the minimum amount we should seek to earn on investments involving a minimum of risk, such as those in new service stations and other marketing facilities. We further recommended that the minimum acceptable level of returns should be increased as the risks involved in the investment projects increased. Accordingly, we set substantially higher standards for investments in manufacturing, petrochemical, and exploration and production ventures.

We arrived at these bench-mark figures by considering:

Our long-term borrowing costs.

The returns which Continental and other oil companies have customarily earned on their borrowed and invested capital (substantially more than 10%).

The returns which must be earned to make our business attractive to equity investors.

The returns which must be earned to satisfy our present shareholders that the earnings retained in the business each year are put to good use.

In this latter connection, it may be noted that whenever we retain earnings instead of paying them out as dividends, we in effect force our stockholders to make a new investment in the Continental Oil Company. And clearly, we have little justification for doing that unless we can arrange to earn as much on the funds as the stockholders could earn by investing in comparable securities elsewhere.

CONCLUSION

The discounted-cash-flow method rests on the time-honored maxim that "money begets money." Funds on hand today can be invested in profitable projects and thereby yield additional funds to the investing company. Funds to be received at some future date cannot be profitably invested until that time, and so have no earning power in the interim. For this reason, a business concern must place a *time value* on its money—a dollar in hand today is much more valuable than one to be received in the distant future. The discounted-cash-flow method simply applies this general concept to the analysis of new capital investments.

The procedures which I have been describing in regard to the discounted-cash-flow method of analyzing new capital investments were adopted by Continental's top management in the fall of 1955 and were implemented throughout the company. Our subsequent experience in using the discounted-cash-flow approach may be summarized as follows:

We have found it to be a very powerful management tool. It is an extremely effective device for analyzing routine investments with fairly regular patterns of cash flow, and also for analyzing very complicated problems like those involved in mergers, acquisitions of producing properties under oil payment arrangements, and other ventures that require a series of capital outlays over a period of many years and generate highly irregular cash flows.

We have also found that the discounted-cash-flow techniques are far easier to introduce and apply than is commonly supposed. We had anticipated considerable difficulty in gaining acceptance of the new methods and in teaching people throughout the organization to use them; however, this turned out to be a very minor problem. Once the new methods were properly explained, they were quickly adopted throughout our operating and field organizations, and the mechanics of the calculations presented no problems of any importance.

There is one major theoretical and practical problem in using the discounted-cash-flow procedure for which we have not yet found a fully satisfactory solution. This problem is that of developing a return-on-investment figure for whole departments or groups of departments which may be computed year by year and compared with the returns calculated under the discounted-cash-flow procedures at the time individual investment projects were undertaken. Clearly, division of the cash income or the net income after taxes and depreciation by either the cost of the investment or the depreciated investment for the department as a whole will not produce statistics comparable to the discounted-cash-flow figures.

On the whole, our experience with the discounted-cash-flow techniques has been very satisfactory. To my mind, these techniques represent part of the oncoming improvements in the field of finance and accounting. Just as new technological discoveries continually bring us new opportunities in the fields of exploration, production, manufacturing, transportation, and marketing, so too there are occasionally new techniques in finance and accounting that offer opportunities to improve operations. The discounted-cash-flow method of investment analysis falls in that category, and I would expect that steadily increasing application will be made of it by industrial companies in the years ahead.

CAPITAL BUDGETING AND THE PROBLEM
OF REINVESTING CASH PROCEEDS *

By Harold Bierman† and Seymour Smidt‡

RECENTLY the internal rate of return has received considerable support as a criterion for determining the economic value of investments.[1] The internal rate of return of an investment is defined as the rate of discount that equates the present value of the cash expenditures required by the investment with the present value of its cash proceeds.[2] The conventional procedure recommended by rate-of-return advocates might be described as follows. Consider all possible investment proposals. For each one calculate its rate of return. Array these proposals according to their rates of return. Then decide on a rule for determining the cutoff rate. The cutoff rate is the rate of interest which determines whether an investment will be undertaken. Investments with a rate of return higher than the cutoff rate will be undertaken; other investments will not be undertaken.

There is no general agreement on the question of how the cutoff rate should be determined. It is in keeping with the spirit of the rate-of-return approach to suggest that the cutoff point be equal to the firm's "cost of capital," the definition of which will not be discussed in this paper. But it is generally recognized that many firms are reluctant to issue new securities to finance investments. For these firms the amount invested is limited to the cash proceeds (or a fraction of these proceeds) generated by current operations. The two methods of setting the cutoff rate of return correspond to Lorie and

* Reprinted by permission from the *Journal of Business*, 30 (October 1957), pp. 276–79.

† Professor of Accounting, Graduate School of Business and Public Administration, Cornell University.

‡ Assistant Professor of Managerial Economics, Graduate School of Business and Public Administration, Cornell University.

[1] See Joel Dean, *Managerial Economics* (Englewood Cliffs, N.J.: Prentice-Hall, Inc., 1951), pp. 551–610.

[2] The rate of return is termed "internal," since it refers to the rate of return computed for internal capital-budgeting purposes. Since the term rate of return will only be used in this context in this paper, the term "internal" will be understood to precede "rate of return" hereafter.

Savage's distinction between the selection of investments given a cost of capital and the selection given a fixed sum for investment.[3]

RATE-OF-RETURN APPROACH AND MUTUALLY EXCLUSIVE INVESTMENTS

It has been recognized that the rate-of-return approach may not lead to the correct decision if the array of investment proposals include two or more mutually exclusive investments and that, for mutually exclusive investments, the assumptions made as to how the cash proceeds are to be reinvested must be given special attention.[4] In particular, the amounts earned by each such investment up to a common future date must be compared. The common future date should be at least as far in the future as the terminal date of the longest-lived of the investments. "Mutually exclusive," in this context, refers to a set of investment proposals only one of which will be undertaken, since accepting one of the proposals in the set reduces the earning possibilities of the other proposals to a point where they are no longer worthy of consideration (for example, the choice of buying a ferry or building a bridge to carry cars and trucks across a river). For present purposes a pair of investment proposals can be assumed to be *either* mutually exclusive or independent, though in practice the distinctions are seldom so clear.

A brief example will illustrate the incongruities that can occur when investment proposals are ranked according to their rates of return and when the reinvestment of cash proceeds is ignored.

Assume that A and Z are investments with the following characteristics:

Investment*	Year	Earnings	Cost of Investment	Per Cent Rate of Return
A	0	. . . . . .	$100	20
	1	$ 20	. . . .	. .
	2	120	. . . .	. .
Z	0	. . . . . .	$100	25
	1	$100	. . . .	. .
	2	31.25	. . . .	. .

* Investments are made at the beginning of year 1.

The better investment seems to be investment Z, since it promises the higher rate of return. But, as Solomon points out, we cannot decide with the information at hand. We need to know at what rate cash proceeds, available at the end of year 1, can be reinvested. Suppose the marginal *reinvestment* rate at the beginning of year 2 is 5 per cent. Then investment A would result in a total cash accumulation of $141 (105 per cent of $20 + $120) by the end of

[3] See James H. Lorie and Leonard J. Savage, "Three Problems in Rationing Capital," *Journal of Business*, XXVIII, No. 4 (October, 1955), pp. 229–39.

[4] See Ezra Solomon, "The Arithmetic of Capital-budgeting Decisions," *Journal of Business*, XXIX, No. 2 (April, 1956), pp. 124–29.

the second year, while investment Z would result in a cash accumulation of only $136.25 (105 per cent of $100 + $31.25). In this instance investment A would be preferable to investment Z, although the rate of return on Z is higher than on A.

It is important to note that both investments in the above example had the *same useful life*. Obviously, the possibility that rate-of-return calculations will incorrectly rank investment proposals is *not* limited to situations in which the terminal life of the two proposals is different. It is clear from this example that a ranking of investment according to their rates of return will not always correspond to a ranking of these same investments according to their profit potential, if the reinvestment of cash proceeds is ignored.[5]

IS IT NECESSARY THAT THE INVESTMENTS BE MUTUALLY EXCLUSIVE?

Solomon's conclusion, from examples such as these, is that, in the case of *mutually exclusive* investment proposals, it is necessary to make an "explicit estimate of the yield to be derived from the cash flows generated by each of the alternatives being considered."[6] This conclusion gives the impression that we do *not* need to consider the yields generated by reinvesting cash proceeds *unless* the investment proposals are mutually exclusive.

It might be argued that, except for mutually exclusive investments, it is not necessary to rank investments in order of their profitability to make appropriate investment decisions. All that is required is that proposed independent investments be divided into two groups—those accepted and those rejected—so that each investment among those accepted is more profitable than any alternative among those investments rejected. If the use of the rate-of-return criterion accomplishes such a division, we would be justified in using it. Unfortunately, it does not always succeed.

Suppose that a firm has succeeded in dividing its available investment proposals into two groups such that each investment in the group of those accepted is more profitable than any alternative among the group not accepted but that the funds available for present capital investment are not exhausted. Enough funds are available for one more investment, and, since the choice is between investment proposals A and Z, a capital rationing decision must be made. The proposals are *not mutually exclusive*, because both could be undertaken if sufficient funds were available. The firm wishes to choose whichever of the two proposals is more profitable. Yet, if the firm uses a

---

[5] Some of the recent literature on capital budgeting has failed to recognize that the internal rate of return and the present value criterion may give contradictory rankings of two investment proposals even when the same life-span is considered for each. For example, see Romney Robinson, "The Rate of Interest, Fisher's Rate of Return over Cost and Keynes' Internal Rate of Return: Comment," *American Economic Review*, XLVI, No. 5 (December, 1956), pp. 972–73. On the other hand, this point seems implicit in Solomon's article (*op. cit.*), although he does not explicitly consider comparisons of investments with the same life-span.

[6] *Op. cit.*, p. 129.

rate-of-return criterion to choose between the two, it may make the wrong decision for the same reason that this criterion could lead to a wrong decision if the two investments were in fact mutually exclusive.[7]

WHEN DOES THE RATE-OF-RETURN CRITERION GIVE INCORRECT RESULTS FOR INDEPENDENT INVESTMENTS?

If a firm expects that in all relevant future years the added cash proceeds that can be earned by today's investments can be reinvested to earn r per cent per year, then any investment proposal available now whose expected rate of return is greater than r per cent will be more profitable than any whose rate of return is less than r per cent.[8] If the firm uses the ordinary rate-of-return criterion, accepting all independent investment proposals whose rate of return is greater than r per cent and rejecting all others, it will tend to make correct investment decisions.

On the other hand, if a firm expects that in some relevant future years the rates at which it will be able to reinvest the cash proceeds of present investments will be higher or lower than r per cent, then it is possible that some present investment proposals whose rates of return are less than r per cent will be more profitable than some others whose rates of return are greater than r per cent. Under these circumstances the use of the rate-of-return criterion to make investment decisions will not always lead to correct results.

The possibility that the rate-of-return criterion can lead to incorrect results even for independent investments can be illustrated by an example. Suppose a firm discovered that its available funds would be exhausted if all investments with rates of return greater than 15 per cent were accepted. If additional funds available in the next year could be invested at a rate of return of 20 per cent, for one more year, then investment C would be preferable to investment B, because it would lead to total earnings at the end of the second year of $135.60. Yet this investment would have been rejected if the rate-of-return criterion were followed:

Invest-ment	Year	Earnings	Cost of Invest-ment	Per Cent Rate of Return
B	0	. . . . . .	$100	. .
	1	. . . . . .	. . . .	15
	2	$131.25	. . . .	. .
C	0	. . . . . .	$100	13
	1	$113	. . . .	. .
	2	. . . . . .	. . . .	. .

[7] Throughout this article we ignore the effects of discontinuities in the investment proposals (see Lorie and Savage, *op. cit.*, p. 232).

[8] In some special cases an investment proposal may not have a unique rate of return (*ibid.*, p. 237). The correct procedure in this case is described by Solomon (*op. cit.*, pp. 127 ff.).

In cases like this a short-lived investment (or one with larger earnings in the early years) may be more profitable but have a lower rate of return than a long-lived investment (or one with larger earnings in the later years). Similarly, if the rate at which additional funds available next year could be reinvested is expected to be less than 15 per cent, then some investments with longer pay-out periods may be more profitable but have lower rates of return than others with a shorter pay-out.

CONCLUSION: USEFULNESS OF RATE-OF-RETURN APPROACH

1. We argue that a ranking of mutually exclusive investment proposals in terms of their relative profitability may not correspond to a ranking according to their rates of return. We emphasize that this does not depend on the relative lives of the proposals.

2. For mutually exclusive investments the question of how cash proceeds arising in all years are to be reinvested must be considered.

3. A firm is justified in using the rate-of-return approach for choosing between independent investments (and ignoring the rate at which the cash proceeds can be reinvested) only if it can be confident that the cutoff rate in the future will be constant and will be the same as it is currently. A constant cutoff rate is more likely to obtain where the firm's cutoff rate is equal to its cost of capital than when the amount of investments to be undertaken is determined by funds available from internal sources.[9] However, if a firm does not typically accept all the investment proposals that promise to earn a rate of return greater than its cost of capital, whether because it is subject to some form of capital rationing or for other reasons, then it is likely that its cutoff rate will vary from year to year. In this case the rate-of-return criterion will not necessarily assure an appropriate choice of capital investments.

4. Since the rate at which cash proceeds can be reinvested will vary from year to year, the amounts that can be earned by reinvesting these funds must be explicitly considered.

---

[9] The cost of capital will change but probably not so much as a cutoff rate determined by investment opportunities and the internal supply of funds.

WEAKNESSES OF ACCELERATED DEPRECIATION AS AN INVESTMENT STIMULUS *

By E. Cary Brown†

INTRODUCTION

LIKE ANY OTHER ITEM that enters into the determination of taxable income, the amount of depreciation allowed for tax purposes affects business decisions. Variations in it can change the rate at which business firms find it worthwhile to purchase depreciable assets, and thus alter productive capacity and the rate of economic growth. Cyclical fluctuations in capital formation may also be modified both in amplitude and in length through depreciation modifications. And, since tax allowances may also affect business accounting, they may enter into decisions about prices, wages, dividends, and the like.

In addition to these economic effects, depreciation allowances have equity consequences in that they alter the definition of income and the amount of taxes different business firms pay. This question—the effects of various depreciation methods on the accuracy with which income is measured—has been the primary focus of past discussions. Important as it is, I intend to give primary attention to certain of the economic consequences of accelerated depreciation methods—methods that are not designed to improve the measurement of income or achieve greater equity, but rather to stimulate certain economic effects.

The economic aspects of depreciation policy have received increasing public attention during World War II and in the immediate postwar years. Many countries adopted various kinds of accelerated programs to achieve one

---

* Reprinted from *Federal Tax Policy for Economic Growth and Stability*, Joint Committee on the Economic Report, 84th Congress, 1st session, pp. 495–504. The arguments herein are not stated at the level of the firm as are those of most of the readings in this book. Rather, the effects of alternative schemes of depreciation and other devices available to public policy on investment incentives and investing ability are viewed in a macroeconomic context. By a simple switch of view, however, the implications of the author's demonstrations and logic can be read equally well for their impact at the level of the firm.

† Professor of Economics, Massachusetts Institute of Technology.

or more economic results. England, for example, was motivated primarily by the desire to stimulate the replacement of obsolete plants and to gain a stronger position in postwar world markets. Sweden had used rather extreme forms of optional depreciation for countercyclical reasons even before World War II. Canada's depreciation program was geared to deflationary prospects in the immediate postwar period, and was intended as a shot in the arm to pick up deficient demand. None of these initial programs has stood without modification. When deficient demand turned into excess demand and inflation threatened, all of these programs were suspended or modified. Canada not only stopped but actually reversed its policy by postponing normal depreciation on assets purchased in inflationary period.

In 1954 the United States embarked on such a program for the first time in a peacetime period. An examination and appraisal of this specific program in the following section represents an introduction to an analysis in the last section of the major problems connected with any kind of accelerated-depreciation device.

APPRAISAL OF 1954 DEPRECIATION LEGISLATION

The Internal Revenue Code of 1954 permitted unrestricted use of the sum-of-year-digits depreciation for the first time,[1] the declining-balance method at double the straight-line rate,[2] and any other methods that give no more than this latter method over the first two-thirds of the useful life of an asset. In addition, existing methods of depreciation, such as the straight line, were continued. These new methods were limited to new depreciable assets with a life of 3 or more years, the costs of which were attributable to 1954 or later years.

This legislation falls into the accelerated-depreciation category. It was clearly designed to speed the rate of economic growth rather than to improve the equity of the income tax. The administration's case rested on hoped-for economic effects of the change in depreciation policy, not on whether or not the definition of taxable income would be improved, and no evidence was brought forth indicating existing depreciation methods were inadequate or inaccurate in measuring income. Moreover, the new methods were made applicable only to new assets acquired after a certain period, rather than to all assets of a particular kind. Obviously, if the primary desire were equity, limitations on the kinds of assets that could get special treatment would be inappropriate.

How well can these provisions be expected to achieve their goal of economic growth through investment stimulation? Any specific decision by business management about the purchase of new depreciable assets will be

---

[1] The sum-of-year-digits method results in a depreciation rate determined by dividing the number of years remaining in an asset's life by the sum of each of the digits in its life.

[2] The declining-balance method applies a constant depreciation rate to initial cost less total depreciation already taken.

likely to take into account the fact that taxes can be postponed under the new depreciation methods. Depreciable assets thus become more profitable to invest in than they previously were. This postponement of taxes permits a more rapid recovery of the cost of the asset, thus saving interest and reducing risk. These are factors increasing the incentive to invest. In addition, the ability to invest is increased through the reduction in taxes presently payable, and the consequent increase in working capital.

Incentives to Invest

Consider, first, the effect of the new policies on investment incentives. The value of the postponed taxes to a firm will depend on the rate of discount for risk or interest that is used in the investment decision and on the tax rate. The present value of tax postponement can then be expressed as a percentage of the cost of the depreciable asset whose purchase is contemplated. Table 1

Table 1

PRESENT WORTH OF DEPRECIATION DEDUCTIONS AS PERCENT OF COST OF ASSET SUM-OF-THE-YEARS-DIGITS AND STRAIGHT-LINE METHODS

Length of life	Sum-of-the-year-digits discount rates of—			Straight-line discount rates of—			Excess of SYD over SL discount rates of—		
	4 per-cent	12 per-cent	20 per-cent	4 per-cent	12 per-cent	20 per-cent	4 per-cent	12 per-cent	20 per-cent
10	85%	66%	50%	81%	55%	39%	4%	11%	11%
20	75	48	33	68	36	22	7	12	11
30	68	38	25	57	25	15	11	13	10
40	61	31	20	49	20	11	12	11	9
50	56	26	16	43	16	9	13	10	7
100	37	14	9	24	8	5	13	6	4

Source: E. Cary Brown, "The New Depreciation Policy Under the Income Tax: An Economic Appraisal," *National Tax Journal*, VIII (March 1955), p. 92.

shows the difference between the present worth of sum-of-year-digits depreciation and straight-line depreciation under various assumed discount rates and asset lives. The present value of the tax postponement from using sum-of-year-digits depreciation can then be found by multiplying these figures by whatever tax rate one wishes, on the assumption that future tax rates remain unchanged.

These data reveal that the stimulus to investment in depreciable assets is modest at best, and is surprisingly little affected by the expected life of the asset or by the rate of discount applied to it. Given a particular rate of discount, the present value of the tax savings from the new method rises as the expected life of the asset rises until it reaches a maximum and then begins to taper off. Given the expected life of the asset, the present value of the tax savings rises as the discount rate rises, but again it reaches a maximum and then tapers off. Over a fairly wide range of asset lives and of rates of discount, the tax savings from the new method computed at a 50-percent rate appear to be about 5 percent of the initial cost of an asset. In other words, it is as if investment yields after tax were increased roughly by about 5 percent (not 5 percentage points). For example, it would mean that 10 percent yields would now be 10½ percent, 20 percent yields 21 percent, and so on. This is nearly an across-the-board increase in yields. It does not appear to be directed toward particular types of firm, degrees of risk, or the like. It then becomes strikingly similar in its incentive effects to a cut in the income-tax rate.

Ability to Invest

The 1954 depreciation revisions will also change the ability to invest in depreciable assets. The amount of taxes postponed by a particular firm will depend on the rate of growth of its depreciable-asset purchases, on future tax rates, on the expected lives of its depreciable assets, and on the extent to which it avails itself of the new methods. Moreover, these postponed taxes can become virtually a permanent reduction. While taxes are only temporarily postponed on one particular depreciable asset since early excess depreciation is offset by later deficient depreciation, the continued purchase of depreciable

Table 2

AGGREGATE STRAIGHT-LINE AND SUM-OF-YEAR-DIGITS
DEPRECIATION GROWTH IN DEPRECIABLE-ASSET
PURCHASES 3 PERCENT PER YEAR 20-YEAR
ASSETS, 50 PERCENT TAX RATE
[In billions]

Year	Purchases of depreciable assets*	Depreciation		
		Straightline	Sum-of-year-digits	Difference (SYD–SL)
1	$27.8	$ 1.3	$ 2.6	$1.3
2	28.7	2.8	5.0	2.2
3	29.6	4.3	7.8	3.5
4	30.4	5.7	10.3	4.6
5	31.4	7.3	12.8	5.5
6	32.3	8.8	15.2	6.4
7	33.3	10.5	17.4	6.9
8	34.4	12.3	19.7	7.4
9	35.4	14.0	21.9	7.9
10	36.4	15.7	24.2	8.5
11	37.6	17.7	26.0	8.3
12	38.7	19.5	28.0	8.5
13	39.8	21.3	29.6	8.3
14	41.1	23.5	31.6	8.1
15	42.3	25.5	33.0	7.5
16	43.6	27.6	35.4	7.8
17	45.0	30.0	37.0	7.0
18	46.4	32.3	38.6	6.3
19	47.6	34.3	39.8	5.5
20	49.2	37.0	41.2	4.2

* Assumed to grow 3 percent per year from a base of $27 billion.
Source: Ibid., p. 88.

assets continues this temporary postponement. As long as the firm continues to purchase depreciable assets at the old rate, the tax postponement never has to be made good. The temporary postponement through excess depreciation on these new purchases matches deficient depreciation on old purchases. Only when the firm's purchases of depreciable assets shrink, or when it liquidates, are the postponed taxes ever recovered. When the firm increases its rate of purchase of depreciable assets the permanent tax postponement actually grows.

Estimates of the amount of revenue losses from the new methods have been made by the staff of the Joint Committee on Internal Revenue Taxation, on the assumption that purchases of depreciable assets continue at present rates. These show that the amount of tax reduction will start out modestly in the first fiscal year at less than one-half billion dollars, rise rapidly to over $1 billion in 1960, and gradually decline to zero by 1970. But if there is growth in the rate of purchases, the tax reduction will be considerably larger. Assuming a rate of growth of 3 percent as in the past, my estimates (table 2) place the figures at over $2 billion in 5 years, over $4 billion in 10 years, nearly $4 billion in 15, over $2 billion in 20 years, from which point on the revenue loss would grow at 3 percent per year.

What fraction of this large increase in net income after taxes will find its way into further purchases of depreciable assets is impossible to predict on the basis of present knowledge. But this improvement in working capital would be available for capital formation—either inventories or fixed capital, for debt repayment, for payment of dividends, or for retention as added working capital. Undoubtedly some will be used for purchases of depreciable assets.

Appraisal

The 1954 depreciation revisions then represent a costly method of getting a modest investment stimulus. There are other, cheaper alternatives. For example, a cut in the corporate income-tax rate of $2\frac{1}{2}$ percentage points would appear to achieve the same investment stimulus by increasing yields after tax by about 5 percent.[3] Moreover, the distribution of this incentive would be approximately the same as that achieved by the new depreciation methods.

Such a cut in the tax rate on present corporate income would amount to about $1 billion per year and would grow in 20 years, assuming 3-percent growth, to less than $2 billion. In comparison, the new depreciation methods will reduce corporate taxes by a larger amount in virtually every year. As a rough guess, the difference would be $30 billion over the first 20 years.[4] It

---

[3] For corporations subject to the 30-percent rate, the rate reduction would have to be $3\frac{1}{2}$ percentage points.

[4] Total business expenditures on plant and equipment in 1954 are estimated at $27 billion, of which the Council of Economic Advisers estimates $23 billion to be corporate. The estimate in the text is based on table 2, assumes a 50-percent tax rate and reduces this result by the ratio of corporate to total purchases of depreciable assets—84 percent. The total revenue loss, personal and corporate, would run to $35 billion.

seems fairly clear that direct rate reduction should be substituted for the new depreciation methods as a cheaper way of getting the same investment stimulus.

GENERAL PROBLEMS OF ACCELERATED DEPRECIATION

In view of these conclusions regarding the 1954 depreciation revisions, a number of more general questions arise. Is accelerated depreciation inherently a more costly way of creating an investment incentive than a straight rate reduction? When its incentive effects are strengthened, does it create other problems? For example, how does it affect the cyclical timing of investment? How are pricing and other decisions affected?

Relative Incentive Effects of Accelerated Depreciation

These conclusions regarding the 1954 depreciation changes cannot generally be applied to accelerated depreciation since there are many other forms it can take. Other forms permit full or fractional write-off of the cost of assets in the year acquired or over a 5-year period and have received considerable attention. One important feature of such plans as compared with the recent one enacted in the United States is that the accelerated-depreciation portion of the allowance is the same regardless of the expected economic life of the depreciable asset. The firm is thus led to decide between two assets of different ages solely on their economic merits, and not on their favorable or unfavorable treatment under the tax law.[5]

A second feature of these accelerated-depreciation methods is that they enhance the position of the risky investor as compared with the safe investor over a wider range of asset lives. And, finally, they offer a sharply higher investment incentive than present methods, and, if pushed far enough, can provide more per dollar of revenue loss than that achieved by rate reduction.

If these methods can overcome one part of the criticism of existing methods, what then are the remaining ones? The major criticisms are the effects on economic stability and on business decisions about prices, wages, and dividends.

Effects on Timing of Investment Purchases

Accelerated depreciation can affect the timing of investment either by creating cyclical changes in financial ability or in investment incentives.

1. *Ability to Invest.* A common charge against accelerated depreciation is that it will reduce the sensitivity of tax yields to economic fluctuations, since it weights current rates of investment more heavily in computing depreciation than do normal methods. It tends to increase disposable income of firms at a time of boom through decreasing their taxes. In a depression, when rates of

---

[5] It can be noted parenthetically that the present form of the allowance discriminates against longer-lived assets.

purchase of depreciable assets are subnormal, accelerated depreciation falls below normal, and the resulting increase in taxes decreases business disposable income. If this were inevitable, accelerated depreciation would reduce the countercyclical effectiveness of income taxes on business firms.

But before examining this question, a few factors should be placed in perspective. First, while it is perfectly clear that accelerated depreciation responds more quickly than normal depreciation in situations of long-run growth, it is not so clear that this is true for short-run fluctuations, whether superimposed on an underlying situation of growth or of stability.

Second, much depends on whether economic fluctuations in the future are minor, such as in 1923, 1927, 1949, and 1954, or major, such as 1921 or the great depression of the thirties. If the fluctuations are minor, virtually no countercyclical issue arises. In 1949, for example, business purchases of depreciable assets (in real terms) were about 10 percent below the rate in 1948 and in 1950; in 1954, they were 6 percent less than the 1953 rates. Different kinds of depreciation could vary by no more than these amounts, and ordinarily would by considerably less. But, a fluctuation of this magnitude is less than $1 billion in taxes, surely not a size of first-order importance. If, on the other hand, fluctuations will be major, different depreciation methods have quantitative significance. Real purchases of depreciable assets in 1933, for example, fell to less than one-third of their 1929 rate and did not really recover until after World War II.

But even though it is possible for various depreciation methods to have quantitatively significant differences when there are major economic fluctuations, there is no presumption against accelerated depreciation in favor of normal methods. Whether it will behave more or less cyclically than normal depreciation depends on the kind of cyclical pattern in the purchase of depreciable assets, the duration of the business cycle, and the durability of assets.

The following illustration will emphasize the danger of generalizing about this. Suppose cyclical fluctuations are symmetrical over a period of 8 years—the usually accepted average length of major business cycles so far observed. Suppose, further, that all depreciable assets have a life of 20 years. Five-year depreciation is then noticeably more stabilizing than normal 20-year depreciation in that it results in less depreciation in the upswing (first 4 years in table 3) and more in the downswing (last 4 years in table 3). One-year depreciation, on the other hand, increases depreciation in the upswing relative to the use of a 20-year period since it would follow the pattern of purchases.

An illustration of this kind obviously does not establish accelerated depreciation as more countercyclical than normal depreciation. The results depend on the particular assumptions underlying the illustration. While the ones chosen are not unreasonable, different results could be obtained by altering the shape or duration of the cycle, the average length of life of asset, and the methods of depreciation. One-year depreciation, for example, would

Table 3

COMPARISON OF CYCLICAL DEPRECIATION PATTERNS
8-YEAR SYMMETRICAL CYCLE, 20-YEAR ASSETS

Period	Purchases of depreciable assets*	Amount of depreciation under depreciation period of—		
		5-year	8-year	Normal 20-year
1............................129		166	200	188
2............................200		152	200	188
3............................271		166	200	195
4............................300		200	200	205
5............................271		234	200	212
6............................200		248	200	212
7............................129		234	200	205
8............................100		200	200	195

* Purchases in period $t = 100\left(1 + \sin\frac{\pi}{4}\right)$.

clearly have a cyclical pattern. But this illustration does eliminate the belief that accelerated depreciation necessarily or presumptively reduces the countercyclical effectiveness of the tax. No general answer, therefore, seems possible in the abstract. These doubts about the direction, coupled with the relative quantitative unimportance of the amounts should reduce worry about this aspect of the question.

2. *Cyclical Effect of Investment Incentives.* This, of course, is not the whole story. Accelerated depreciation has been accused of stimulating investment incentives cyclically, even under constant tax rates. The case rests on the following considerations. In the boom profits are high. Business firms are aware of their ability to write off rapidly the cost of depreciable assets purchased, and are encouraged to invest in them. In the depression, on the other hand, losses are sustained and rapid depreciation cannot provide added stimulus. Indeed, if the period of losses is expected to be followed by a period of profits, a rapid writeoff may actually be disadvantageous to the individual firm.

For this result to follow it is necessary that tax deductions be lost if they are not taken in a year of boom or high activity. That is to say, other years in the cycle are either low profit or loss years. But recent economic history has given us two recessions with high profits—1949 and 1953. In 1949 the number of profitable corporations fell by less than 2 percent and their income declined about one-sixth to slightly over $30 billion. Deficit corporations increased 14 percent and their deficits rose $0.6 billion to $2.4 billion. The 1954 recession appears to have fallen even less heavily on corporate profits. These, of course, are aggregate amounts. Separate industries or firms could have been affected in different ways. But still it seems a safe generalization that relatively few profitable firms slipped so far as to make deficits. In contrast, in 1932 the number of profitable corporations dropped nearly 200,000 from 1929; aggregate net income fell from $11.7 billion in 1929 to $2.2 billion. Deficit corporations in the same period rose from 187,000 to 369,000; net losses from $2.9 billion to $7.8 billion. If future cyclical swings are like those of recent years, depreciation could be absorbed in a recession almost as easily as in a boom. If they are like the great depression of the thirties, it will be much harder to absorb depreciation in depression years.

But even in this case expenses in loss years, even when they cannot be fully deducted from income of that year, can reduce taxes of other years. Under present law a 2-year carryback and a 5-year carryforward of losses is provided. Under these circumstances, it is unlikely that firms would fail to receive some tax benefit from accelerated depreciation in a year of loss. Only if they never really expected to make profits in the next 5 years, and did not make them in the 2 preceding years, would this be true. In such a situation, taxes would have little or no effect on their investment decisions in either a boom or recession.

Moreover, a special assumption must be made about the formation of business expectations about future income in order for the described result to take place. A firm must expect good years to be succeeded by bad, and bad years to be followed by good. The usual complaint about business behavior is that this cyclical behavior is usually not expected; that instead there is a tendency toward the belief that existing conditions will continue. There is overinvestment in good years because it is expected to be justified by the continuance of large future profits; underinvestment in depression years because weak markets are expected to last indefinitely. If business firms expect existing levels of profits to continue, accelerated depreciation, even without loss offsets, would not have much cyclical effect on investment incentives. Expected continuance of boom profits would not induce the firm to rush its investment in order to secure a full offset from accelerated depreciation. Expected continuance of depression losses would not induce the firm to postpone investment to a time in which accelerated depreciation could be taken.

Finally, accelerated depreciation, if used for tax purposes, may also be used in the firm's accounts. If it is, it could reduce book profits after taxes in a boom and decrease them in a depression. (Whether or not it actually will was analyzed in the preceding section.) While some students of business behavior place considerable emphasis on this factor as a damper on business optimism in a boom and a cushion under depression pessimism, it is probably too minor to warrant emphasis as a stabilizer.

EFFECTS ON OTHER BUSINESS DECISIONS

The possibility that accelerated depreciation may be used by business firms in their own accounts may have a significant effect on other managerial decisions, however. There is, to be sure, no inherent reason why accelerated depreciation will be used in business accounts, nor, if used, that it must enter into managerial decisions. The tax law permits separate sets of books. But what evidence is available points toward the continuation of past practices under which book depreciation tended to conform to tax depreciation.[6]

If used in the firm's accounts and in business decisions, accelerated depreciation may raise prices through artificially overstating costs, depending on the degree and kind of competition the particular firm faces. Such an eventuality could lead to a decrease in the quantity demanded of the firm's products, and some slackening of the demand for enlarged capacity. If demand did not fall off at the new prices, there would result some redistribution of income from consumers to business, with perhaps, some effect on aggregate demand. On the other hand, failure to raise prices could reduce profits and perhaps dividends.

Existing knowledge does not allow an accurate prediction of the consequences flowing from the use of accelerated depreciation in managerial decisions. It seems sufficient to point out here that it represents an artificial, distorting influence on decisions. These decisions would be improved if based on as accurate a measure of depreciation as can presently be made by accountants, engineers, managers, economists, and other interested groups. This is a major weakness in the use of accelerated depreciation as an investment stimulus. What are the alternatives? Two obvious ones present themselves: rate reductions and investment credits.

ALTERNATIVE STIMULATING DEVICES

Rate reductions cannot achieve the same effects as some of the extreme forms of accelerated depreciation do. For example, 1-year depreciation substantially eliminates the disincentive effects of the income tax, yet large yields of taxes would still be collected under it. This same effect could be achieved by rate reductions only by virtual elimination of yields. In view of the pressing financial needs of the country, elimination of tax yields does not seem a fruitful approach to tax revision at the present time.

Tax credits, over and above normal depreciation, upon the purchases of depreciable assets can, however, duplicate the incentive effects of accelerated depreciation. They can be granted in the year when the asset is purchased or spread over several years subsequent to its purchase. (A carryforward of unused tax credits would, of course, be a feature of any such plan to avoid

---

[6] "Adoption by many corporations of accelerated depreciation for corporate accounting, when they adopt it for taxes, is indicated." William J. Edmonds, "The Effect on Business Decisions of Changes in Tax Depreciation Policy," *National Tax Journal*, VIII (March 1955), p. 113. But note this qualification: "Subsequent information reaching the author indicates a trend among large companies toward the declining-balance method for tax purposes but with no changes contemplated in accounting practices at this time." P. 112 n. Preliminary results of a study by Prof. E. K. Smith confirm the view that firms using the new depreciation methods for tax purposes will also tend to use it in their own accounts.

discriminating against firms with low profits or losses in any particular year.) Tax credits also have the important advantage that they would not creep into business accounts and distort business decisions. Since normal depreciation would be deducted from the firm's taxable income, it would ordinarily be used in the firm's accounts. These tax credits could be varied from time to time as economic conditions warranted without creating a major wrench in business accounting policies. The British after a number of years of experimentation with accelerated depreciation have gone over to what they call an investment allowance system which permits a 10-percent credit for industrial buildings and a 20-percent credit for machinery and equipment. Careful study of their experience has not yet been made but is urgently needed.

The tax credit for investment can be made to stimulate economic growth still further by limiting it to expenditures on depreciable assets in excess of normal depreciation. Then, only if the firm were spending more than the amount necessary to maintain the book value of existing depreciable assets would additional tax reduction be granted. Static and declining firms would receive only normal depreciation on their replacement purchases; growing firms would receive normal depreciation on all purchases plus a tax credit for purchases in excess of normal depreciation. In order to avoid encouraging business concentration through growth by the purchase of existing firms and assets, the tax credit should be restricted to purchases of new assets. This distinction is now made under the 1954 law and seems relatively easy to handle administratively.

One further advantage of the tax credit for investment in depreciable assets is that it nicely complements the most satisfactory method of eliminating or reducing double taxation of dividends, namely, the tax credit to corporations for dividend payments. Corporations could then receive a tax credit either for purchase of depreciable assets or for dividend payments; the tax consequences of decisions about retention and use or payment as dividends could be placed roughly on a par.

CONCLUSIONS

1. The 1954 depreciation changes are a more costly way of securing an investment stimulus similar to that achieved by reducing the corporate income tax around $2\frac{1}{2}$ percentage points.

2. Accelerated depreciation provides a stimulus to investment that cannot be duplicated by rate reduction. It does not involve a reduction in the countercyclical effectiveness of the income tax of any serious magnitude. It does, however, tend to distort business decisions about prices and dividends.

3. Tax credits for investment provide the same kind of stimulus but avoid this distortion. They can still further stimulate growth by being limited to the excess of expenditures for new depreciable assets over normal depreciation.

THREE PROBLEMS IN RATIONING CAPITAL*

By James H. Lorie† and Leonard J. Savage‡§

I. INTRODUCTION

CORPORATE EXECUTIVES face three tasks in achieving good financial management. The first is largely administrative and consists in finding an efficient
procedure for preparing and reviewing capital budgets, for delegating authority and fixing responsibility for expenditures, and for finding some means for
ultimate evaluation of completed investments. The second task is to forecast
correctly the cash flows that can be expected to result from specified investment proposals, as well as the liquid resources that will be available for
investment. The third task is to ration available capital or liquid resources
among competing investment opportunities. This article is concerned with
only this last task; it discusses three problems in the rationing of capital, in
the sense of liquid resources.

1. Given a firm's cost of capital and a management policy of using this cost
to identify acceptable investment proposals, which group of "independent"
investment proposals should the firm accept? In other words, how should the
firm's cost of capital be used to distinguish between acceptable and unacceptable investments? This is a problem that is typically faced by top management
whenever it reviews and approves a capital budget.

Before presenting the second problem with which this paper deals, the use
of the word "independent" in the preceding paragraph should be explained.
Investment proposals are termed "independent"—although not completely
accurately—when the worth of the individual investment proposal is not
profoundly affected by the acceptance of others. For example, a proposal to
invest in materials-handling equipment at location A may not profoundly
affect the value of a proposal to build a new warehouse in location B. It is
clear that the independence is never complete, but the degree of independence

* Reprinted by permission of the authors from *The Journal of Business*, 28 (October
1955), pp. 229–39.

† Professor of Business Administration, University of Chicago.

‡ Professor of Statistics, University of Chicago.

§ This work was supported in part by the Office of Naval Research and in part by
Joel Dean Associates.

is markedly greater than for sets of so-called "mutually exclusive" investment proposals. Acceptance of one proposal in such a set renders all others in the same set clearly unacceptable—or even unthinkable. An example of mutually exclusive proposals would be alternative makes of automotive equipment for the same fleet or alternative warehouse designs for the same site. The choice among mutually exclusive proposals is usually faced later in the process of financial management than is the initial approval of a capital budget. That is, the decision as to which make of automotive equipment to purchase, for example, typically comes later than the decision to purchase some make of equipment.

2. Given a fixed sum of money to be used for capital investment, what group of investment proposals should be undertaken? If a firm pursues a policy of fixing the size of its capital budget in dollars, without explicit cognizance of, or reference to, its cost of capital, how can it best allocate that sum among competing investment proposals? This problem will be considered both for proposals which require net outlays in only one accounting period and for those which require outlays in more than one accounting period. In the latter case, special difficulties arise.

3. How should a firm select the best among mutually exclusive alternatives? That is, when the management of an enterprise, in attempting to make concrete and explicit proposals for expenditures of a type which is included in an approved capital budget, develops more than one plausible way of investing money in conformance with the budget, how can it select the "best" way?

After presenting our solutions to these three problems, we shall discuss the solutions implied by the rate-of-return method of capital budgeting.[1] These solutions are worthy of special attention, since they are based on a different principle from the solutions that we propose, and since the rate-of-return method is the most defensible method heretofore proposed in the business literature for maximizing corporate profits and net worth.

II. THE THREE PROBLEMS

A. Given the Cost of Capital, What Group of Investments Should Be Selected?

The question of determining the cost of capital is difficult, and we, happily, shall not discuss it. Although there may be disagreement about methods of calculating a firm's cost of capital, there is substantial agreement that the cost of capital is the rate at which a firm should discount future cash flows in order to determine their present value.[2] The first problem is to determine how

---

[1] This method was developed by Joel Dean, who has probably done more than anyone else in applying the formal apparatus of economics to the solution of capital-budgeting problems in their business context.

[2] One of the difficulties with the concept of cost of capital is that in complicated circumstances there may be no one rate that plays this role. Still worse, the very concept of present value may be obscure.

selection should be made among "independent" investment proposals, given this cost or rate.

Assume that the firm's objective is to maximize the value of its net worth—not necessarily as measured by the accountant but rather as measured by the present value of its expected cash flows. This assumption is commonly made by economists and even business practitioners who have spoken on the subject. It is equivalent to asserting that the corporate management's objective is to maximize the value of the owner's equity or, alternatively, the value of the owner's income from the business. Given this objective and agreement about the significance of the firm's cost of capital, the problem of selecting investment proposals becomes trivial in those situations where there is a well-defined cost of capital; namely, proposals should be selected that have positive present values when discounted at the firm's cost of capital. The things to discount are the net cash flows resulting from the investments, and these cash flows should take taxes into account.

There is nothing unusual or original about this proposed solution. It is identical with that proposed by Lutz and Lutz,[3] and is an economic commonplace. Joel Dean in his writings has developed and recommended a method which typically yields the same results for this problem, although the principle of solution is somewhat different, as is discussed later in this article.

The principle of accepting all proposals having positive present value at the firm's cost of capital is obvious, since the failure to do so would clearly mean forgoing an available increment in the present value of the firm's net worth. The principle is discussed here only because it seems a useful introduction to the somewhat more complicated problems that follow. An interesting property of this principle is that adherence to it will result in the present value of the firm's net worth being at a maximum at all points in time.

B. Given a Fixed Sum for Capital Investment, What Group of Investment Proposals Should Be Undertaken?

Some business firms—perhaps most—do not use the firm's cost of capital to distinguish between acceptable and unacceptable investments but, instead, determine the magnitude of their capital budget in some other way that results in fixing an absolute dollar limit on capital expenditures. Perhaps, for example, a corporate management may determine for any one year that the capital budget shall not exceed estimated income after taxes plus depreciation allowances, after specified dividend payments. It is probable that the sum fixed as the limit is not radically different from the sum that would be expended if correct and explicit use were made of the firm's cost of capital, since most business firms presumably do not long persist in policies antithetical to the objective of making money. (The profit-maximizing principle is the one that

---

[3] Friedrich Lutz and Vera Lutz, *The Theory of Investment of the Firm* (Princeton: Princeton University Press, 1951). The solution proposed here is identical with the maximization of $V - C$, where V is the present value of future inflows and C is the present value of future outflows. This is discussed in chap. ii of the Lutz book.

makes use of the firm's cost of capital, as described previously.) Nevertheless, there are probably some differences in the amount that would be invested by a firm if it made correct use of the firm's cost of capital and the amount that would be invested if it fixed its capital budget by other means, expressing the constraint on expenditures as being a maximum outlay. At the very least, the differences in the ways of thinking suggest the usefulness to some firms of a principle that indicates the "best" group of investments that can be made with a fixed sum of money.

The problem is trivial when there are net outlays in only one accounting period—typically, one year. In such cases, investment proposals should be ranked according to their present value—at the firm's cost of capital—per dollar of outlay required. Once investment proposals have been ranked according to this criterion, it is easy to select the best group by starting with the investment proposal having the highest present value per dollar of outlay and proceeding down the list until the fixed sum is exhausted.[4]

The problem can become more difficult when discontinuities are taken into account. For large firms the vast majority of investment proposals constitute such a small proportion of their total capital budget that the problems created by discontinuities can be disregarded at only insignificant cost, especially when the imprecision of the estimates of incomes is taken into account. When a project constitutes a large proportion of the capital budget, the problem of discontinuities may become serious, though not necessarily difficult to deal with. This problem can become serious because of the obvious fact that accepting the large proposal because it is "richer" than smaller proposals may preclude the possibility of accepting two or more smaller and less rich proposals which, in combination, have a greater value than the larger proposal. For example, suppose that the total amount available for investment were $1,000 and that only three investment proposals had been made: one requiring a net outlay of $600 and creating an increment in present value of $1,000; and two others, each requiring a net outlay of $500, and each creating an increment in present value of $600. Under these circumstances, the adoption of the richest alternative, the first, would mean forgoing the other two alternatives, even though in combination they would create an increment in present value of $1,200 as compared with the increment of $1,000 resulting from the adoption of the richest investment alternative. Such discontinuities deserve special attention, but the general principles dealing with them will not be worked out here, primarily because we do not know them.

We shall, however, deal with the more serious difficulties created by the necessity to choose among investment proposals, some of which require net

---

[4] We mention, for completeness, that the outlay or the present value, or both, for a proposal can be negative. Proposals for which the outlay alone is negative—something for nothing—are always desirable but almost never available. Proposals for which both the outlay and the present value are negative can sometimes be acceptable if something sufficiently profitable can be done with ready cash expressed by the negative outlay. The rules which we shall develop can be extended to cover such cases.

cash outlays in more than one accounting period. In such cases a constraint is imposed not only by the fixed sum available for capital investment in the first period but also by the fixed sums available to carry out present commitments in subsequent time periods. Each such investment requires, so to speak, the use of two or more kinds of money—money from the first period and money from each subsequent period in which net outlays are required. We shall discuss only the case of investments requiring net outlays in two periods, for simplicity of exposition and because the principle—although not the mechanics—is the same as for investments requiring net outlays in more than two periods.

Let us start with a very simple case. Suppose that all the available opportunities for investment that yield a positive income can be adopted without exceeding the maximum permitted outlay in either time period 1 or time period 2. Clearly, no better solution can be found, because all desirable opportunities have been exhausted. This simple case is mentioned not because of its practical importance, which is admittedly slight, but because it may clarify the more complicated cases that follow.

Next, consider a slightly more complicated case. Suppose that the opportunities available require more funds from either time period 1 or time period 2 than are permitted by the imposed constraints. Under these circumstances, the problem becomes somewhat more complicated, but it still may not be very complicated. It is still relatively simple if (1) the best use of money available in period 1 does not exhaust the money available in period 2 or (2) the best use of money available in period 2 does not exhaust the money available in period 1. In either case the optimum solution—that is, the solution which results in the greatest increment in the net worth of the firm, subject to the two stated constraints—is the one that makes the best possible use of the funds available for investment in one of the two time periods.

This statement is justified by the following reasoning. The imposition of additional restrictions upon the freedom of action of any agency can obviously never increase the value of the best opportunity available to that agency. In the problem at hand, this means that the imposition of an absolute dollar constraint or restriction in time period 2 can never make it possible to make better use of dollars available in time period 1 than would have been possible in the absence of that constraint. Thus, if the best possible use is made of the dollars available in time period 1, the imposition of a restriction relating to time period 2 can never mean increased possibilities of profit from the use of funds available in time period 1. Therefore the maximization of the productivity of dollars available in time period 1 will constitute a maximization of productivity subject to the two constraints as well as to the one constraint. The reasoning is equally valid if we start with the constraint referring to time period 2 and maximize productivity of money available in that time period and then think of the effect of the additional constraint imposed for time period 1.

Unfortunately, typical circumstances will probably make the relatively simple solutions unavailable. The solution to the relatively complex problem will—abstracting from discontinuities—require expending the full amount available for investment in each period. To illustrate how the solution is to be reached, consider the average actual net outlay of the two periods as being an outlay in a single "virtual" period, and consider the average net outlay that is permitted by the constraints as being the average permitted outlay for the "virtual" period. Plan a budget for this "virtual" period according to the method of the one-period problem with which this section begins. That is, ration the capital available in the "virtual" period among the available investment opportunities so as to maximize the firm's net worth according to the principles stated in the discussion of the one period problem. If, by accident, this budget happens to require precisely those outlays which are permitted for the first and second periods, it is easy to see that the problem has been solved. No other budget with a higher present value can be devised within the stated constraints for periods 1 and 2.

Typically, the happy accident referred to in the preceding paragraph will not occur. The optimum use of the average amount available for investment in the two periods will typically result in expending too much in one period and not so much as is permitted in the other. Indeed, the happy accident was mentioned only as a step in explaining one method that will work. Though a simple average will almost never work, there is always some weighted average that will, and it can be found by trial and error. We shall describe in some detail a method that is mathematically equivalent to this method of weighted averages. In this method the solution is found by choosing, for suitable positive constants p_1 and p_2, those, and only those, proposals for which the following quantity is positive: $(y - p_1c_1 - p_2c_2)$. Here, y is the present value of the proposal; c_1 and c_2 are the present values of the net outlays required in the first and second periods, respectively; and the multipliers p_1 and p_2 are auxiliary quantities for which there does not seem to be an immediate interpretation but that nonetheless help in solving the problem.[5]

Initially, the values of p_1 and p_2 will be determined by judgment. Subsequently, they will be altered by trial and error until the amounts to be expected in the first and second periods, according to the rule just enunciated, are precisely the amounts permitted by the constraints. The initial choice of values for p_1 and p_2 is not very important, since a graphical process can usually lead rapidly to the correct values.

Certain special possibilities are worth noting. Proposals of positive present value may have negative cost, that is, release cash, for either period. Some proposals of zero or negative present value may be acceptable because they release cash for one period or both. All such possibilities are automatically covered by the rule as stated and by the rules to be given for later problems.

Finding the correct values for p_1 and p_2 is sometimes not easy—especially when combined with the problem of selecting among mutually exclusive

---

[5] The multipliers, p_1 and p_2, are closely related to what are known in mathematics and in economics as "Lagrange multipliers."

alternatives—but the task is usually as nothing compared to the interests involved or compared to many everyday engineering problems.[6] The following example may clarify the process.

Nine investments have been proposed. The present value of the net outlays required in the first and second time periods and the present values of the investments are as shown in Table 1. The finance committee has stated that

Table 1

Investment	Outlay, Period 1 (c_1)	Outlay, Period 2 (c_2)	Present Value of Investment
a.	$12	$ 3	$14
b.	54	7	17
c.	6	6	17
d.	6	2	15
e.	30	35	40
f.	6	6	12
g.	48	4	14
h.	36	3	10
i.	18	3	12

$50 and $22 will be available for capital investment in the first and second periods, respectively. We shall consider these amounts to have present values of $50 and $20, respectively. According to the principle stated above, we must now find appropriate multipliers, p_1 and p_2.

Multipliers p_1 and p_2 were initially set at 1 and 3, respectively. With these values, only for investment d was the expression $(y - p_1c_1 - p_2c_2)$ positive and therefore acceptable. This would have resulted in net outlays of only $6.00 and $2.00 in periods 1 and 2, respectively. Clearly, the values initially chosen for p_1 and p_2 were too great. On the other hand, values of 0.1 and 0.5 for p_1 and p_2, respectively, are too low, resulting in a positive value of $(y - p_1c_1 - p_2c_2)$ for all investments and required outlays in periods 1 and 2 far exceeding the permitted outlays.

Values of 0.33 and 1 for p_1 and p_2 result in a near-perfect fit. The expression $(y - p_1c_1 - p_2c_2)$ is positive for investments a, c, d, f, and i. These investments require outlays of $48 and $20 in the first and second periods, as near the permitted outlays of $50 and $20 as discontinuities permit. No other group of investments that is possible within the stated constraints has a greater present value than $70, the present value of this group.[7]

C. Selecting the Best among Mutually Exclusive Alternatives

Before moneys are actually expended in fulfillment of an approved capital budget, the firm usually considers mutually exclusive alternative ways of

---

[6] It is true, however, that the numbers in engineering problems are less conjectural; hence the cost of calculation is more likely to be considered worthwhile.

[7] For the three-period problem the relevant quantity is $(y - p_1c_1 - p_2c_2 - p_3c_3)$ rather than $(y - p_1c_1 - p_2c_2)$.

making the generally described capital investment. When the firm is operating without an absolute limit on the dollars to be invested, the solution to the problem of selecting the best alternative is obvious. (Throughout this article, it is assumed that decisions regarding individual investment proposals do not significantly affect the firm's cost of capital.) The best alternative is the one with the greatest present value at the firm's cost of capital.

When the firm is operating subject to the constraint of an absolute dollar limit on capital expenditures, the problem is more difficult. Consider, first, the case in which there are net outlays in only one time period. The solution is found by the following process:

1. From each set of mutually exclusive alternatives, select that alternative for which the following quantity is a maximum: $(y - pc)$. Here, y is the present value of the alternative, c is the net outlay required, and p is a constant of a magnitude chosen initially according to the judgment of the analyst. (Remember that the alternative of making no investment—that is, accepting $y = 0$ and $c = 0$—is always available, so that the maximum in question is never negative.)

2. Compute the total outlays required to adopt all the investment proposals selected according to the principle just specified.

3. If the total outlay required exceeds the total amount available, p should be increased; if the total amount required is less than the amount available for investment, p should be reduced. By trial and error, a value for p can be found that will equate the amount required for investment with that available for investment.

It should be clear that as the value of p is increased, the importance of the product, pc, increases, with a consequent increase in the probability that in each set of mutually exclusive alternatives, an alternative will be selected that requires a smaller net outlay than is required with a smaller value for p. Thus, increasing p tends to reduce the total amount required to adopt the investment proposals selected according to the principle indicated in (1) above. Conversely, reducing p tends to increase the outlay required to adopt the investment proposals selected according to this principle.

When there are net outlays in more than one period, the principle of solution is the same. Instead of maximizing the quantity $(y - pc)$, it is necessary to maximize the quantity $(y - p_1c_1 - p_2c_2)$, where again c_1 and c_2 are the net outlays in the first and second periods and p_1 and p_2 are auxiliary multipliers.

Up to this point, we have not discussed the problem of rationing capital among both independent investment proposals and sets of mutually exclusive investment proposals. Superficially, this problem seems different from the one of rationing among mutually exclusive proposals only, but in fact the problems are the same. The identity rests upon the fact that each so-called "independent" proposal is and should be considered a member of the set of proposals consisting of the independent proposal and of the always present proposal to do nothing. When independent proposals are viewed in this way, it can be seen that the case of rationing simultaneously among independent proposals and sets of mutually exclusive proposals is really just a special case of rationing among mutually exclusive proposals according to the principles outlined in the preceding paragraph.

The mechanics of solution are easily worked out. All that is required in order to make the solution the same as the solution for what we have called "mutually exclusive" sets of alternatives is that each so-called "independent" proposal be treated as a member of a mutually exclusive set consisting of itself and of the alternative of doing nothing. Once this is done, it is possible to go into the familiar routine of selecting from each set that proposal for which the expression $(y - pc)$, or its appropriate modification to take account of constraints existing in more than one time period, is a maximum. Again, of course, that value of p will have to be found which results in matching as nearly as discontinuities permit the outlays required by the accepted proposals with the outlays permitted by the stated budgetary constraints.

III. SOME COMPARISONS WITH THE RATE-OF-RETURN METHOD OF CAPITAL RATIONING[8]

Since the rate-of-return method of capital rationing is fully described elsewhere, we shall describe it only briefly.[9] As in the methods described previously, attention is focused exclusively on net cash flows rather than on the data produced by conventional accounting practices. Investment proposals are ranked according to their "rate of return," defined as that rate of discounting which reduces a stream of cash flows to zero, and selected from this ranking, starting with the highest rate of return.

The rate-of-return solution to the three problems that are the subject of this paper is discussed below.

A. Given the Cost of Capital, What Group of Investments Should Be Selected?

The rate-of-return solution to the problem of selecting a group of independent proposals, given the firm's cost of capital, is to accept all investment proposals having a rate of return greater than the firm's cost of capital. This solution is necessarily identical with the solution proposed previously, except when the present value of some of the proposals is other than a steadily decreasing function of the cost of capital. An intuitive substantiation of this statement is achieved by an understanding of Figure 1. In Figure 1, I–I indicates the present value of an investment at different rates of interest, Oa is the firm's cost of capital, Ob is the rate of return on the investment, and aa' is the present value of the investment at the firm's cost of capital. It should be

[8] Joel Dean has pioneered in the development of methods of capital rationing that have an understandable relationship to profit maximization, in contrast to methods still quite widely used in business that rely on such criteria as payback, average return on book investment, etc. The method that he advocates is called the "rate-of-return" method.

[9] See Joel Dean, *Capital Budgeting* (New York: Columbia University Press, 1951); "Measuring the Productivity of Capital," *Harvard Business Review*, Vol. XXXII (January-February, 1954).

Figure 1

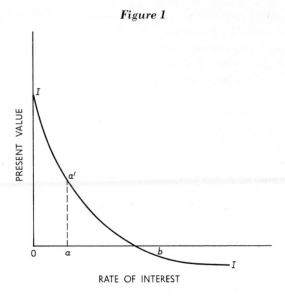

clear from the diagram that any proposal that has a positive ordinate (present value) at the firm's cost of capital will also have a rate of return (*x*- intercept) greater than the cost of capital. (However, it usually takes a little longer to find an intercept than to determine the value of an ordinate at one point.)

Under what circumstances can the present value of an investment proposal be something other than a steadily decreasing function of the cost of capital? Some investment proposals can intersect the *x* axis at more than one point. In particular, investment proposals having initial cash outlays, subsequent net cash inflows, and final net cash outlays can intersect the *x* axis more than once and have, therefore, more than one rate of return. Investments of this nature are rare, but they do occur, especially in the extractive industries. For example, an investment proposal might consist of an investment in an oil pump that gets a fixed quantity of oil out of the ground more rapidly than the pump currently in use. Making this investment would require an initial net outlay (for the new pump), subsequent net incremental cash inflow (larger oil production), and final net incremental cash outlay (the absence of oil production, because of its earlier exhaustion with the use of the higher capacity new pump).[10] The present value of an investment in such a pump could look like Figure 2. In Figure 2, *I–I* indicates the present value of the investment, *Oa* is the firm's cost of capital, *Ob* and *Oc* are the two rates of return on the investment, and *aa'* is the present value of the investment at the firm's cost of capital.

---

[10] These incremental flows are measured with reference to the flows that would have resulted from the use of the smaller pump. Thus the final net outlay is not absolute but rather by comparison with oil (money) that would have been produced had the smaller pump been in use.

Figure 2

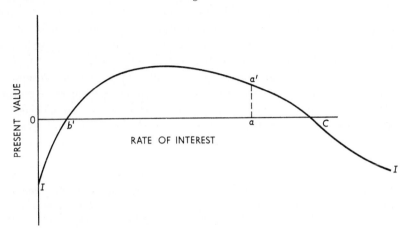

The reasoning behind this apparent paradox of the double rate of return is as follows:

1. As the cost of capital of the firm approaches zero, the present value of the investment proposal approaches the algebraic sum of net cash flows and will be negative if this sum is negative.

2. As the cost of capital increases, the present value of the final net cash outflow diminishes in importance relative to the earlier flows, and this diminution can cause the present value of the entire proposal to become positive.

3. If the cost of capital continues to increase, the significance of all future cash flows tend to diminish, causing the present value of the proposal to approach the initial outlay as a limit.

The rate-of-return criterion for judging the acceptability of investment proposals, as it has been presented in published works, is then ambiguous or anomalous. This is in contrast to the clarity and uniform accuracy of the decisions indicated by the principle proposed earlier, which relates to the present value of an investment at the cost of capital rather than to a comparison between the cost of capital and the rate of return.[11]

B. Given a Fixed Sum for Capital Investment, What Group of Investment Proposals Should Be Undertaken?

The rate-of-return solution to the problem of allocating a fixed sum of money—without reference to cost of capital—among competing proposals is to order the proposals according to their rate of return and to proceed down the ladder thus created until the available funds are exhausted. The group of investment proposals selected by the use of this principle can be different, and probably would usually be different, from the group selected when the crite-

---

[11] The rate-of-return rule could be easily modified to remove this ambiguity or anomaly by specifying that the relevant rate of return is the one at which the investment is a decreasing function of the rate of interest.

rion is present value rather than rate of return. A difference between the two groups would not exist if the available capital funds were just equal to that amount which would permit investment in all those proposals having a rate of return at least equal to the firm's cost of capital, and only those proposals, and if the anomalies mentioned under Section A were not present.

The preceding statements are equivalent to saying that the groups of investments that would be chosen by the use of the two principles or criteria would necessarily be the same only if the fixed sum to be invested happened to be the optimum sum and that investment of any other sum could result in selection of different groups of proposals by use of the two principles. This difference would result from the fact that the different principles can result in a different ranking of proposals within the group that would be accepted if the optimum amount were invested. Table 2 indicates the validity of the statement that the ordering of two investment proposals according to their rate of return

Table 2

Period	Net Cash Flows	
	Investment A	Investment B
0– year..........................	–$ 85	–$ 90
0–1 year..........................	+ 17	+ 21
1–2 years..........................	+ 35	+ 33
2–3 years..........................	+ 68	+ 57
3–4 years..........................	+ 131	+ 94
4–5 years..........................	+ 216	+ 155
5–6 years..........................	+ 357	+ 255
6–7 years..........................	+ 546	+ 420
7–8 years..........................	+ 555	+ 695
8–9 years..........................	+ 345	+ 1,150
Present value at 20%.............	+ 606	+ 853
Rate of return...................	66%	62%

can be contrary to their ordering according to their present value per dollar of outlay.

The example of Table 2 illustrates that a proposal with a higher rate of return can have a lower present value and that, therefore, the two rules can conflict. The present value rule maximizes the present value of the firm's net worth—by definition—and the rate-of-return rule therefore may not.

This discrepancy is undoubtedly of small practical significance. In the first place, firms that ration their capital rationally use the firm's cost of capital as the constraint rather than an absolute dollar sum; and under such rational behavior the two rules yield the same results, with the exception noted previously. (Undoubtedly, no firms long persist in setting absolute dollar constraints that differ significantly in their effects from the cost-of-capital constraint.) In the second place, the present values of investment proposals, expressed as functions of the cost of capital, are often thoughtful enough not to intersect above the x axis (the rate-of-interest axis), a necessary condition for a conflict between the rate-of-return and present-value principles.

C. Selecting the Best among Mutually Exclusive Alternatives

The rate-of-return solution to the problem of selecting the "best" among mutually exclusive investment alternatives, although occasionally tricky in practice, is simply explained as follows:

1. Compute the rate of return for that investment proposal, among the set of mutually exclusive proposals, requiring the least initial net outlay.

2. If the rate of return on the investment requiring the smallest outlay exceeds the firm's cost of capital (or other cutoff rate), tentatively accept that investment. Next, compute the rate of return on the incremental outlay needed for the investment requiring the second lowest outlay. If that rate exceeds the firm's cutoff rate, accept the investment requiring the greater outlay in preference to that requiring the lesser. Proceed by such paired comparisons (based on rates of return on incremental outlay) to eliminate all but one investment.

3. If the rate of return on the proposal requiring the least outlay does not exceed the firm's cutoff rate, drop it from further consideration, and compute the rate of return for the proposal requiring the next least outlay. If that rate exceeds the firm's cutoff rate, that investment proposal becomes the bench mark for the first paired comparison. If that rate does not exceed the firm's cutoff rate, drop that proposal from further consideration. The process just described is to be repeated either until a proposal is found with a rate of return exceeding the cost of capital or until all proposals have been eliminated because their rates of return do not exceed the cutoff rate.

The rate-of-return solution to the problem of selecting the best among mutually exclusive investment alternatives is especially subject to the ambiguities and anomalies mentioned under Section A, because the costs and revenues associated with incremental investments required for proposals included in mutually exclusive sets are much more likely to have unusual time shapes and reversals than are the costs and revenues associated with independent investments.

SUMMARY

We have given solutions to three problems in budgeting capital so as to maximize the net worth of the firm. The solutions that we have given differ in principle from those implied by the rate-of-return method of capital rationing. The difference in principle can lead to differences in behavior. Differences in behavior will be rare in coping with problems of the first and third sorts, and will be relatively frequent for problems of the second sort. When differences do exist, the rate-of-return solution does not result in maximizing the present value of the firm's net worth.

THE EXCESS PRESENT VALUE INDEX—A THEORETICAL BASIS AND CRITIQUE *

By H. Martin Weingartner†

INTRODUCTION

SEVERAL RECENT TEXTBOOKS in management accounting and related fields[1] have proposed use of the Excess Present Value Index (the ratio of the present value of cash inflows to the initial outflow) in making investment decisions.[2] This article provides a mathematical foundation for the Excess Present Value Index [EPVI], and examines its properties in order to state more precisely the limitations which must be imposed on its use in capital budgeting problems. No review of the criteria for investment decisions is undertaken, nor is there proposed a single "best" tool in place of the EPVI. Instead, the framework provided by a simple mathematical programming model is used to make an evaluation of investment decision methods such as the EPVI.

---

* Reprinted by permission from the *Journal of Accounting Research*, 1 (Autumn 1963), pp. 213–24. The interested reader will want to note that the pathbreaking volume from which this article was drawn in essence is noted in footnote 8.

† Professor of Business Administration, University of Rochester.

[1] Robert N. Anthony, *Managerial Accounting* (Homewood, Ill.: Richard D. Irwin, Inc., 1960), pp. 554–5; Charles T. Horngren, *Cost Accounting, A Managerial Emphasis* (Englewood Cliffs, N.J.: Prentice-Hall, Inc., 1962), pp. 409–15, 604–10; Carl L. Moore and Robert K. Jaedicke, *Managerial Accounting* (Cincinnati: South-Western Publishing Co., 1963), p. 524. See also Robert Lindsay and Arnold W. Sametz, *Financial Management: An Analytical Approach* (Homewood, Ill.: Richard D. Irwin, Inc., 1963), pp. 73–75; and Norman N. Barish, *Economic Analysis for Engineering and Managerial Decision-Making*, (New York: McGraw-Hill Book Co., Inc., 1962), pp. 142–43, 234–35.

[2] The term "Excess Present Value Index" is supplied by Horngren, while Anthony, Moore and Jaedicke, and Lindsay and Sametz call it the "Profitability Index" and Barish calls it the "Premium Worth Percentage." However, Lindsay and Sametz and Barish use the net present value in the numerator with a resulting index which differs from the above by unity. Moore and Jaedicke use the "present value of the cash flows" in the numerator which presumably is intended to be the cash *inflows* since the ratio is required to be "better than 1 to 1" for acceptance [*op. cit.*, p. 524]. Lindsay and Sametz use the present value of the cash outlays in the denominator which, if different from the denominator used by the other authors, is suggestive of some of the difficulties to be discussed below. Because the term "Profitability Index" has been used by others to represent the discounted-cash-flow-rate-of-return (or internal rate of return) we shall use the longer label "Excess Present Value Index," abbreviated to *EPVI*.

Under the assumption of complete certainty and perfect capital markets (i.e., in a world in which the outcomes of all acts are known with probability one, and entrepreneurs may borrow or lend at a single market rate of interest),[3] maximization of the economic welfare of the owners of an enterprise implies maximization of the net present value (inflows less outflows) of total investment when discounting is done at the firm's opportunity cost of capital—the market rate of interest.[4] In the presence of capital rationing, i.e., when some limitation on the amount a firm can spend for capital investment is imposed either from within or without, this implication fails to hold. It is then no longer possible to disengage the investment decision from the decision to consume—to assume that owners can adjust their income streams to their preferred consumption patterns via the market alone.[5] We shall side-step this issue, to which no definitive answer has been provided to date, by assuming, for the moment, that if capital rationing exists, it is a short-term phenomenon, limiting expenditures only in the current period of a year or two. Some justification for such a limitation may be found in the lead times and cost of large financial market transactions or in periods of managerial change in which the financial "status quo" is to be maintained. Clearly, no firm should want to limit expenditures, aside from profitability considerations, over the long run.[6] Hence we shall continue to use maximization of net present value as the criterion for investment decisions, initially computing present values at the market rate of interest.

THE BASIC MODEL

Under these assumptions we may formulate the problem of maximizing the net present value of investments subject to an expenditure ceiling by means of the following model. Let b_j = the net present value of an investment project, computed at the market rate of interest, r (assumed to remain constant over time for simplicity only); let c_j = the current outlay required for project j; let C be the expenditure ceiling; and let x_j = the fraction of project j accepted, i.e., $x_j = 1$ if the project is accepted, and $x_j = 0$ if it is not. We then wish to

$$Maximize \sum_{j=1}^{n} b_j x_j \qquad (1a)$$

[3] The assumption of certainty is almost universal in the literature on criteria for investment decisions, the most prominent exception being portfolio selection, which is not our concern here. Perfect capital markets are also generally assumed, although we shall make references to some notable exceptions below.

[4] Irving Fisher probably deserves credit for the first rigorous derivation of this proposition. See his *The Theory of Interest* (New York: The Macmillan Company, 1930). A more recent restatement is Jack Hirshleifer, "On the Theory of Optimal Investment Decision," *Journal of Political Economy*, LXVI, No. 4 (August, 1958) pp. 329–52, reprinted in Ezra Solomon, ed., *Management of Corporate Capital* (Glencoe, Ill.: The Free Press, 1959).

[5] See Hirshleifer, *op. cit.*

[6] The common use of capital budgets as administrative control devices without economic significance is irrelevant for this discussion.

subject to constraints

$$\sum_{j=1}^{n} c_j x_j \leq C \tag{1b}$$

to express the limitation on expenditures, and

$$0 \leq x_j \leq 1, \qquad j = 1, \ldots, n \tag{1c}$$

to rule out duplication of investment projects at the same values of b_j and c_j.

The requirement that a project be either accepted or rejected, that $x_j = 0$ or 1, implies that the formulation in (1) is an integer programming problem.[7] The solution to this problem leads to the selection of those investment alternatives that maximize the total present value of all investments, that is, of the entire investment program, subject to the assumptions and constraints explicitly stated. However, our use of this model here is solely for the purpose of revealing the structure of the problem that must be solved, as well as the limitations which must be placed on the solution, and not to suggest its use for numerical calculation.

A relaxation of one of the assumptions in the above model enables us to derive some important propositions for the *EPVI*. If we assume the expenditure ceiling not to be completely rigid we may drop the requirement that the x_j take on only the integral values of 0 or 1, with the consequence that the problem given in (1) becomes a *linear* programming problem, permitting use of the properties of linear programming solutions. Integer programming solves the problem of indivisibilities which arise when a few projects are of sufficient size as to potentially exhaust the budgeted funds, and when it may be advantageous to utilize small, if less attractive, projects to fully utilize the limited funds. Linear programming, in contrast, permits the inclusion of a fraction of a project—an x_j between zero and unity—in the optimal solution. Geometric considerations permit us to assert that at most a single x_j will take on a proper fractional value for the problem stated. While practical implications are not our primary concern here, it is possible to regard fractional acceptance as a signal for expansion of the ceiling by an amount sufficient to permit acceptance of the marginal project *in toto*, or to reject it, leaving some funds unemployed.[8]

---

[7] Integer programming applies to linear programming problems in which some or all variables are required to take on integer values. See Ralph E. Gomory, *An Algorithm for Integer Solutions to Linear Programs*, IBM Mathematics Research Project, Technical Report No. 1, Princeton University, November 1958, reprinted in *Recent Advances in Mathematical Programming*, ed. Robert L. Graves and Philip Wolfe (New York: McGraw Hill, 1963). See also George F. Dantzig, "On the Significance of Solving Linear Programming Problems with Some Integer Variables," *Econometrica*, XXVIII, No. 1 (January, 1960), pp. 30–44.

[8] This problem and related ones are treated more fully in H. Martin Weingartner, *Mathematical Programming and the Analysis of Capital Budgeting Problems* (Englewood Cliffs: Prentice-Hall, Inc., 1963); reissued by Markham Publishing Company, Chicago, Illinois, 1967.

DERIVATION OF THE EPVI

To derive the *EPVI* we need only to analyze the dual to the linear programming problem given in (*1*).[9] To facilitate interpretation, we associate the variable ρ with the budget constraint (*1b*) and the variables μ_j with the upper bound constraints (*1c*). The dual problem then is

$$\textit{Minimize} \quad \rho C + \sum_{j=1}^{n} \mu_j \tag{2a}$$

Subject to

$$\rho c_j + \mu_j \geq b_j, \quad j = 1, \ldots, n \tag{2b}$$

$$\rho, \mu_j \geq 0. \tag{2c}$$

If we signify the optimal values of our variables by placing an asterisk next to them, we may make several observations about the solutions to the primal and dual problems. First, from (*1a*) it is clearly the case that $x_j^* = 1$ only if $b_j > 0$. That is, no project is accepted unless its net present value is greater than zero.[10] This is the straightforward present value criterion for investment decisions. Second, if the budget constraint is inoperative, i.e., if sufficient funds are available for the acceptance of all projects having positive net present values, then the strict inequality

$$\sum_{j=1}^{n} c_j x_j^* < C$$

also implies

$$\rho^* = 0$$

as a condition of optimality.[11] Under these circumstances, if, in addition $x_j^* > 0$ then the corresponding dual constraint (*2b*) is met as an equality, which means that

---

[9] To every linear programming problem there corresponds another linear programming problem, called the dual, which makes use of the same data as the original, or primal, problem. If the primal has a finite optimum, then the dual also shares this property, and the value of the primal optimum is the value of the dual optimum. See, e.g., George Hadley, *Linear Programming* (Reading: Addison-Wesley, 1962), or any text in linear programming.

[10] This obvious result holds only in the absence of certain kinds of inter-relationships between projects which have, so far, been neglected. For simplicity in exposition we neglect occurrences of "degeneracy," which can arise here when a project is accepted although its net present value is exactly zero. These offer no difficulty in theory, and hence they will be ignored for the remainder of this article.

[11] See, for example, the notion of "complementary slackness" in A. W. Tucker, "Dual Systems of Homogenous Linear Relations," *Linear Equalities and Related Systems*, ed. H. W. Kuhn and A. W. Tucker (Princeton, N.J.: Princeton University Press, 1956), pp. 15 ff.

$$\mu_j^* = b_j > 0. \qquad (3)$$

If, in contrast, the expenditure ceiling is binding, so that at least one project with positive net present value is partially or wholly rejected, then $\rho^* > 0$. In this situation, for accepted projects (i.e., for projects with $x_j^* > 0$) the corresponding dual constraint $(2b)$ again holds as an equality, but with the consequence (after transposing and using condition $(2c)$)

$$\mu_j^* = b_j - \rho^* c_j > 0. \qquad (4)$$

Making use of the fact that $\rho^* > 0$, we may rewrite (4) to assert

$$b_j/c_j > \rho^* \qquad (5)$$

for accepted projects in this rationing situation. But since, presumably, $c_j > 0$ for all projects (all projects require net expenditures in the budget year[13]) we may also assert from (3) that

$$b_j/c_j > 0 \qquad (6)$$

in the non-rationing situation, in which either no budget ceiling exists, or if it does exist, it is inoperative.

Results (5) and (6) translate themselves directly into the *EPVI*. If we add unity to each side of the inequality, doing so by adding c_j to both numerator and denominator on the left side, we immediately obtain the *EPVI* criterion[14]

$$EPVI_j = \frac{b_j + c_j}{c_j} > 1 \qquad (7)$$

for both rationing and non-rationing situations. A stronger condition holds in the presence of effective capital rationing:

$$EPVI_j = \frac{b_j + c_j}{c_j} > \rho^* + 1 > 1. \qquad (8)$$

Since the b_j were defined as the *net* present values, the quantities

$$\frac{b_j + c_j}{c_j}$$

---

[12] Again, disregarding the possibility of the knife edge condition of degeneracy in the primal problem. See note 10.

[13] There is, of course, no logical requirement why this should be the case, and situations where it is not may easily be constructed. For our present problem such projects may be treated outside the model, although this framework, more fully developed in *Mathematical Programming and the Analysis of Capital Budgeting Problems, op. cit.*, may be made to encompass it with ease.

[14] Before adding c_j to both numerator and denominator we have the criterion as stated by Barish, and with the previous qualification, by Lindsay and Sametz. See note 2.

are the ratios of the "excess present value" to cost, or the ratios of the present value of inflows to cost.[15] We have therefore the first half of the *EPVI* criterion, although at least partly at variance with its usual form: All acceptable projects under the present assumptions must have an *EPVI* greater than unity; and greater than unity plus some positive quantity (to be discussed below) when capital rationing is effective.

Before elaborating on these results we must first establish the other half of the criterion: that all projects not satisfying (5) or (6) for their respective situations should be rejected. This follows from similar arguments on the dual constraints. If $x_j^* = 0$, then necessarily $\mu_j^* = 0$ and dual constraint (2b) is a strict inequality.[16] This implies

$$0 > b_j \tag{9}$$

for rejected projects in the non-rationing situation, and

$$\rho^* c_j > b_j \tag{10}$$

that is

$$b_j/c_j < \rho^*$$

with effective rationing. Clearly, these conditions reduce to the counterparts to conditions (7) and (8); to wit, when capital is not effectively rationed, an *EPVI* less than unity leads to rejection of the project, while in the presence of a binding expenditure ceiling, an *EPVI* less than the yet-to-be-determined quantity $1 + \rho^*$ similarly implies rejection. That is, in the latter case it may well be that even an *EPVI* greater than unity leads to rejection since here $\rho^* > 0$.

INTERPRETATION OF ρ^* AND DETERMINATION OF THE APPROPRIATE CUTOFF

When capital rationing is not a problem, the *EPVI* criterion, under the conditions used to derive it, stands as is. Also, when a single period budget-ceiling limits expenditures, recourse to linear programming for the determination of the numerical value of ρ^* is unnecessary. A procedure originally derived by Lorie and Savage[17] suffices to carry out the selection of projects; this procedure can be made to yield the quantity ρ^* as a by-product.

---

[15] The c_j are the rationed quantities in the rationing situation. If cash inflows take place in the budget year, either they are excluded from consideration for the budgetary ceiling since they do not accrue strictly to that single asset alone, or the quantities c_j are themselves net of inflows.

[16] Again except in the case of degeneracy, in which increasing this x_j^* above zero would not affect the value of the solution.

[17] J. H. Lorie and L. J. Savage, "Three Problems in Rationing Capital," *Journal of Business*, XXVIII, No. 4 (October, 1955), pp. 229–39; reprinted in Ezra Solomon, ed., *The Management of Corporate Capital* (Glencoe, Ill.: The Free Press, 1959). For an

To select the best set of investment projects one merely ranks them by the ratios of their net present value to their cost or by their $EPVI$'s and accepts all those from the top down that the expenditure ceiling allows. The first project which cannot be included *in toto* may be used to obtain the quantity ρ^*, if this is desired. If project k is the marginal one, $\rho^* = b_k/c_k$.[18]

From its derivation and from considerations of dimensionality, it should be clear that the quantity ρ^* is in the nature of an interest rate. Its origin in the dual constraints (2b) indicates that it is an evaluator of the budget ceiling, that it measures the maximum rate of return which may be obtained by loosening the ceiling by one dollar. Thus it yields the premium which acceptable projects must earn, over and above the rate of interest used to compute their net present values. When rationing is not effective or not present this premium is zero, and the criterion is equivalent to acceptance of all projects with positive net present values. In this instance ranking is not required, and it is not clear what ranking by $EPVI$ (or, for that matter, any other criterion such as discounted cash flow rate of return) really means.[19]

A PARTIAL SUMMING UP

It may be useful to summarize what we have learned about the $EPVI$. As mentioned, the $EPVI$ criterion holds as stated in the absence of effective capital rationing or any other capital market imperfection which vitiates the use of a single discount rate (or at least a single, known rate for each future period). However, under these circumstances the $EPVI$ criterion is equivalent to the present value criterion and is no more informative than this more simple tool. It allows selection of all acceptable projects and rejection of the non-acceptable ones (from an economic point of view). In this situation ranking of projects is not necessary since optimization requires selection of *all* acceptable projects, and the question of comparing projects is not strictly relevant.

When capital expenditures are limited in the current period, the $EPVI$ criterion requires qualification, and its expression must be modified. While it is possible to use the $EPVI$ for the purpose of ranking projects, the appropriate cutoff is not known except "after the fact." Thus it is, strictly speaking, not an investment criterion in the sense of a rule that applies to each alternative

---

analysis of the Lorie-Savage solution see H. M. Weingartner, *Mathematical Programming, op. cit.* The strict combinatorial problem solved by use of integer programming or enumeration methods is not encompassed in the Lorie-Savage solution, nor do they arrive at the precise value of ρ^*.

[18] We may show this as follows: Assume that (a) $0 < x_k^* < 1$ and (b) $x_j^* = 1$, $j = 1, \ldots, k-1$; $x_l^* = 0$, $l = k+1, \ldots,$ n. Then $\mu_k^* = 0$ (by complementary slackness) and also from (4) $0 = b_k - c_k\rho^*$ or $\rho^* = b_k/c_k$. If the $k-1$ projects in (b) exactly exhaust the budgeted funds C then $x_k^* = 0$. However, it is still true that $b_k - c_k\rho^* = 0$. This is an instance of degeneracy.

[19] The basis for ranking may be found in entirely different origins. Discussion of this problem is not germane here, but will appear in a forthcoming article with M. H. Miller.

separately but only a device for accomplishing the selection of projects once they are all listed. The method does not take care of the problem of indivisibilities in that some collection of smaller projects may effectively use up remaining budget dollars even though their *EPVI*'s are lower than the first rejected one.

More important, the derivation of the *EPVI* above made use of only a single budget ceiling. When outflows take place in more than the current year, *EPVI* must be rejected or modified. For example, if outflows also take place in the year following and a similar expenditure ceiling exists, then the *EPVI*, even when redefined to include the present value of the following year's flow, no longer serves as a rationing device and use of programming methods or other more sophisticated analyses is indicated.[20] When funds are limited only in the current year, but net outflows in later years are associated with at least some projects, then the EPVI must be redefined. In this situation the numerator consists of the net present value plus the current year outlays, divided by the latter. Future outlays enter into the net present value, but not otherwise. For ranking purposes, a more straightforward calculation would make use of the ratio of the net present value to current outlay. However, the point to be emphasized is that the *EPVI* criterion does not hold in its original form even for ranking purposes; that in modified form, it is adequate for ranking provided that future outlays will not also be rationed.

Finally, an assumption used in the mathematical derivation but not otherwise discussed is that of independence between the investment alternatives. This property holds whenever the value (and cost) of a project is the same regardless of which other projects are also accepted. We have used the property by simply adding present values and costs in the function to be maximized and in the budget constraint, expressions (*1a*) and (*1b*), respectively. Absence of independence, as for example when some projects are mutually exclusive, is the subject to which we turn next.

MUTUALLY EXCLUSIVE ALTERNATIVES

A general treatment of the possible interrelationships which may exist between investment proposals is beyond the scope of the present paper and is available elsewhere.[21] It is sufficient for our purposes to assert that the programming framework may be employed to advantage, and that analyses of the resulting dual problems provide further insights into the common investment criteria in the presence of such interdependencies. We shall utilize the remainder of this paper to illustrate some pitfalls which stem from the use of *EPVI* when projects are mutually exclusive.[22] By use of simple numerical ex-

---

[20] See *Mathematical Programming, op. cit.*

[21] *Ibid.*

[22] Some of these observations have been made by George Terborgh in rebuttal to Joel Dean and Winfield Smith. See his "Some Comments on the Dean-Smith Article on the MAPI Formula," *Journal of Business*, XXIX (April, 1956), pp. 138–40; reprinted in Ezra Solomon, ed., *Management of Corporate Capital, op. cit.*

amples we shall also illustrate a common error in the employment of the discounted cash flow rate of return for these problems. Since the difficulties of limited capital expenditures were discussed earlier, we shall assume no capital rationing for the examples below. Assume that, of two mutually exclusive projects, one has a higher net present value than the other when discounting is done at the opportunity cost of funds. More concretely, assume $b_1 > b_2$— project 1 is preferred to project 2. What can be said about the respective $EPVI$'s? Is it necessarily the case that $EPVI_1 > EPVI_2$? The answer to this question is negative. In fact, this ordering of projects by $EPVI$ is reversed whenever

$$\frac{b_1}{b_2} < \frac{c_1}{c_2}. \tag{11}$$

From (11) it follows that

$$\frac{b_1}{c_1} < \frac{b_2}{c_2}.$$

since both b_i and c_i are positive quantities. From this it is obvious that

$$EPVI_1 = \frac{b_1 + c_1}{c_1} < \frac{b_2 + c_2}{c_2} = EPVI_2.$$

To illustrate we suppose that the first project has a net present value of $1000 and requires an investment of $500 in the initial year. Project two is assumed to have a net present value of $800 and requires an outlay of $200 in the first year. This is an instance in which (11) holds, i.e.,

$$\frac{b_1}{b_2} = \frac{\$1000}{\$800} < \frac{\$500}{\$200} = \frac{c_1}{c_2}.$$

Thus

$$EPVI_1 = \frac{\$1000 + \$500}{\$500} = 3 < EPVI_2 = \frac{\$800 + \$200}{\$200} = 5.$$

That is, the $EPVI$ criterion would lead to selection of the project with the lower net present value which would make a lower net contribution to the wealth of the owners of the firm. What does the rate of return criterion say in this situation?

Unfortunately, the discounted cash flow rate of return is frequently misused in choosing between mutually exclusive alternatives. The *incorrect* application of the rate of return method involves a comparison (ranking) of the rates of return computed for the two projects separately and selection of the one with the higher rate.[23] As Alchian has emphasized some time ago,[24] appropriate use of Fisher's rate-of-return-criterion requires calculation of that rate of interest which leads to indifference between the two mutually exclusive alternatives.[25] In this instance, the choice between the competing projects requires knowledge of the appropriate cutoff rate or market rate of interest and no relative criterion is sufficient for selection. The preferred project is that one whose net present value at the *market rate* is higher. This may be translated into the following criterion making use of the rate of return. If the rate of return computed on the differences between the series of cash flows of the two projects is higher than the market rate, choose that project whose inflows are generally farther from the present, since that project will have the higher net present value at the market rate. If, however, the rate of return on the differences is lower than the market rate, the converse leads to the correct selection. We may use an example to illustrate this point.

We suppose, as before, that project one has a net present value of $1000 and requires an outlay of $500, while project two has a net present value of $800 and requires an outlay of $200. Further, we assume the market rate of interest to be 10%, and that cash flows occur as in Table 1.

Table 1

Year of Flow*	Cash Flow for	
	Project 1	Project 2
0	($500)	($200)
1	—	1100
2	—	—
3	—	—
4	—	—
5	2416	—

* All flows are assumed to take place at the end of the year.

Note: Parentheses signify outflows.

Since the present values and outlays are the same as before, the *EPVI*'s remain the same—in percentage terms, 300% and 500%, respectively. If one computes the rate of interest which makes the discounted value of the inflows equal to the outflow for each project separately, as is commonly done, the

---

[23] The confusion probably stems from inculcation of the idea of *ranking* independent investments in the absence of budget constraints by Joel Dean. Dean fails to emphasize that discounted-cash-flow-rate-of-return is an over-all accept-reject criterion, still based on the cost of capital, and he erroneously applies ranking to situations of capital rationing ("autonomous financing"). He also omits discussion of mutually exclusive investments. See his *Capital Budgeting* (New York: Columbia University Press, 1951), Ch. 4.

[24] A. A. Alchian, "The Rate of Interest, Fisher's Rate of Return Over Cost, and Keynes' Internal Rate of Return," *American Economic Review*, XLV (December, 1955), pp. 938–43; reprinted in Ezra Solomon, ed., *Management of Corporate Capital, op. cit.*

[25] Multiple rates which have this property can arise, although we ignore this possibility in our present discussion. See Lorie and Savage, *op cit.*

resulting rates of return are 37% and 450% for projects 1 and 2, respectively. Choosing the one whose rate of return (thus computed) is higher leads to the *same incorrect* selection as the *EPVI* criterion. That is, the rankings are identical, and both are incorrect. If, however, that rate of interest is computed which makes the net present value of project 1 equal to the net present value of project 2, then the result is a rate of approximately 14%. Given a cut off rate of 10%, project 1 is preferred to project 2, as it should be.

A slightly different example will help to bring out the nature of the rate of return and the *EPVI* criterion. We continue to compare two projects with net present values of $1000 and $800 and with outlays of $500 and $200, respectively. However, the timing of the cash flows is assumed to be as in Table 2. The only difference between the flows in Table 1 and Table 2 is that

Table 2

Year of Flow	Cash Flow for	
	Project 1	Project 2
0	($500)	($200)
1	1650	1100

project 1 here has an inflow of $1650 in year 1 instead of $2416 in year 5. Thus both projects have their outflows and inflows in the same period, and, of course, their *EPVI*'s remain as before. The separate rates of return (following improper usage) are 230% for project 1, and 450% (as before) for project 2. The naive application of the rate of return as well as the *EPVI* criterion would signal selection of the second project even though its net present value, as computed at the opportunity cost of funds, is lower. Fisher's rate of return here is 83%. At any rate of interest up to 83%, project 1 is superior to project 2. This must clearly be the case since the incremental investment of $300 required to move up from project 2 to project 1 returns more than the 10% opportunity cost of capital.[26]

In both examples, the separate rates of return and *EPVI*'s resulted in the same (incorrect) ranking of the two projects. This need not be the case as the following calculations will show. Assuming the same net present values and outflows for our two projects as before, but assuming that the timing of flows occurs as in Table 3, we arrive at some different outcomes. Project 1 is thus identical with the same project in Table 2, while project 2 has its inflow in year 5. The separate rates of return are now 230% and approximately 54%,

<hr/>

[26] Ezra Solomon attributes the difficulty in the example of Table 1 to the difference in the lives of the two projects. [See "The Arithmetic of Capital-Budgeting Decisions," *Journal of Business*, XXIX (April 1956), pp. 125–6, reprinted in *Management of Corporate Capital, op. cit.*] The present example shows that even with identical terminal dates naive use of rate of return yields incorrect results. Solomon also errs in saying "when comparing two projects requiring different outlays, it is necessary to compare 'present value per dollar of outlay' [EPVI] rather than the absolute present value of the projects." [*Op. cit.*, p. 127.]

Table 3

Year of Flow	Cash Flow for	
	Project 1	*Project 2*
0	($500)	($200)
1	1650	—
2	—	—
3	—	—
4	—	—
5	—	1756

respectively, while the *EPVI*'s are, as before, 300% and 500%. The result is a reversal in ranking. Fisher's rate of return here is just over 7%. With a market rate of interest of 10% we therefore accept project 1 since its closer inflow is worth more at the higher market rate. This is again consistent with the present value, as it necessarily must be.

CONCLUSIONS

Our earlier summary of implications of the *EPVI* criterion has adequately disposed of it for situations of capital rationing as well as those in which capital constraints are absent, when independent projects alone are considered. Our examples of mutually exclusive alternatives reinforce the conclusion that the *EPVI* does not provide aid in the choice among such alternatives. In two examples, ranking by means of the *EPVI* and by separate rates of return led to the same incorrect choice. In the third example, these rankings were different, and the *EPVI* criterion resulted in the wrong choice. In all these instances, the present value criterion and Fisher's rate of return yield similar answers which are correct in the absence of capital rationing or more complex interrelationships between investments, but they are not to be taken as universally applicable either.[27] Of importance here is the observation that it is impossible to make the choice between mutually exclusive alternatives without some knowledge of the (opportunity) cost of capital; ranking devices designed to by-pass this difficult task must necessarily fail.

---

[27] See *Mathematical Programming, op. cit.*

Chapter 2   Optimum Allocation of
Funds by Linear Programming

RECTIFIED LIQUORS, INC.

RECTIFIED LIQUORS, INC., engaged in the production and sale of two kinds of hard liquor. Unlike a fully integrated distillery, however, the company was a rectifier only. That is, it purchased intermediate-stage products in bulk, purified them by repeated distillation, mixed them, bottled the product under its own brand names, and sold to commercial channels. One product was a bourbon branded as Old Wishbone; the other was Old Backbone, a blended whiskey, sometimes known regionally as rye. Sales of each product were quite independent of the other. In the firm's experience, market limits on sales had never come into play short of the firm's producing capacity.

Labor was not a significant constraint on the firm. Machine capacity as indicated, though, was inadequate to produce all that the firm might sell. The bourbon required three machine hours per bottle, but because of additional blending requirements, Old Backbone absorbed a total of four hours of machine time per bottle. A total of 20,000 machine hours was available in the current production period.

Higher quality made the direct operating costs (principally labor and materials) of Old Wishbone $3 per bottle in contrast with the blended whiskey costs of $2 per bottle. *Excluding* collections of receivables from sales made during the current production period, funds available to finance labor and cost of materials were planned at $4,000. Collection experience on bourbon and whiskey sales varied from time to time. However, it was anticipated that 44% of bourbon sales and 31% of whiskey sales made from current production would be collected during the same production period, and the cash proceeds would be available to finance operations. All direct costs would be paid during the production period, and none accrued. The level of accruals otherwise would remain unchanged on balance.

Price margins tolerated by the market differed on the two products. Old Wishbone sold to the distributive channels at $5 per bottle and Old Backbone at $4.50 per bottle.

Planning for company activities during the approaching production period had led to some disagreement among the members of management. Disagreement centered about two issues. First, the production and marketing managers on one hand and the treasurer-controller on the other were unable to agree about the most desirable product mix and production volume to schedule. Second, the production manager and the treasurer-controller were unable to agree on a proposal to expend $500 for repair of decrepit machinery currently lying idle. It had been estimated that 3,000 machine hours could be added to capacity for the coming production period by this expenditure, although it was quite likely that the machines would again be inoperable by the end of the period. The treasurer-controller acknowledged the need for additional machine capacity, but argued that the severity of the firm's working capital straits made it inadvisable to divert any cash from financing current production.

FLORIDA FERTILIZERS CO. (A)

FLORIDA FERTILIZERS CO. was a small but well-known and growing manufacturer and distributor in the southeastern states of a specialized fertilizer and a multipurpose water-soluble insecticide. Although it had been incorporated in 1917, its common stock was still closely held by members of a few families. Company growth had taken place mostly after World War II, and particularly in the later 1950's and the 1960's. In the late 1950's, the company profitably diversified into insecticide production and distribution from its previous exclusive concentration on fertilizer. Plant facilities and offices were located in the community where the company had been founded.

In early January, 1966, John Branson, treasurer of Florida Fertilizers Co., was pondering a decision that would be reflected ultimately in the company's production rates, product mix, and profit during the coming peak production months of March, April, and May. An assistant had just submitted a pro forma balance sheet incorporating an estimate of the amount of financing to be available for raw materials at the end of February (see Exhibit 1). With this and other information, Mr. Branson would decide, after reaching agreement with some other members of management, on the composition and quantities of raw materials to be ordered for use in production in March and after. Also to be decided was an issue as to whether during this important season the company should attempt to maintain a stockpile of about 30-days usage of raw materials, including packaging materials, to insure continuity of production.

FINANCING

For many years, Florida Fertilizers had relied on the Osceola National Bank for short-term financing of seasonal needs under lines of credit negotiated annually. During Mr. Branson's tenure as treasurer, arrangements for the coming fiscal year's financing had always been made in July. An understanding regarding loan limit and repayment was reached with the bank, and until very recently had been adhered to with little difficulty each year. With the exception of 1965, Florida Fertilizers had been out of the bank for at least one month, and usually for several months, every year within Mr. Branson's recollection. However, accelerating growth of sales had strained working capital for a few years before 1965, and loan repayment had become progressively more difficult. These developments culminated when it proved impossible to liquidate bank indebtedness in the summer of 1965. When a new credit agreement was negotiated at that time, a limit of $2.5 million was established by the bank on its credit, and for the first time Mr. Branson had been asked to agree to a series of restrictions, which had the practical effect of limiting bank debt and trade credit indebtedness to $3 million at any time during fiscal 1966. This put a ceiling, in the loan officer's words, "on the creditors' partnership in company risk." The bank's objection to greater indebtedness and a larger credit of its own was that at the time immediately before peak production, short-term assets consisted preponderantly of raw materials, providing little liquid asset protection for creditors.

Although these loan and debt limits might cramp operations in 1966, Mr. Branson had been forced to consent to them because it appeared impolitic to seek a banking connection elsewhere on short notice and because Osceola National had been generous enough over many past years. Also, Mr. Branson was aware that tight money prevailed, making the availability of a new loan from another bank very uncertain at best.

The remainder of Florida Fertilizers' negotiated debt was a $2 million term loan, the last two years' worth of a larger loan which had been amortized serially. Quarterly installments of $250,000 amortized yearly obligations of $1 million. Restrictive provisions operative under this debt contract were less constraining than the bank's.

Equity constituted the remainder of the company's financing, aside from trade credit and accrued liabilities.

PRODUCTION OPERATIONS

Because of its limited financial capacities, Florida Fertilizers could not engage in vertically integrated production operations. Capital equipment requirements in production of raw materials and intermediate stage products in both fertilizers and insecticide exceeded the firm's capabilities. Moreover, in fertilizer manufacture the production of superphosphate, the basic ingredient, required level year-round operations, implying the accumulation of large off-season inventories. Instead, Florida Fertilizers operated a dry mixing plant, purchasing all the materials needed, compounding them to the desired grade, bagging, and distributing the product for final sale. By confining production operations to mixing and bagging refined materials and by seasonal ordering, the company was able to minimize financial demands.

Processed materials arrived at the plant on freighters, barges, and in railroad hopper cars. Materials were unloaded, stored in bins, charged into mixing machines when needed, and fed ultimately into automatic bagging machines.

The mixing and bagging machines had hoppers leading to outlets that emptied into bags on a rack. After filling, the rack was automatically replaced by another. This mixing and bagging machinery could be used for both products, and although the company had originally equipped for fertilizer production, it was this versatility that had made possible diversification into insecticide in recent years. A single bagging operation took about 16 seconds for 50-pound insecticide bags and 20 seconds for 80-pound bags of fertilizer. The company operated 8 such bagging machines, each capable of filling 5 bags simultaneously. An eight-hour working day was customary.

MARKETING

Both fertilizer and insecticide were sold under the brand name Flo-Gro. About one half of yearly sales of both items were concentrated in the spring months. The remainder of yearly sales was distributed about evenly through the other nine months except for June (see below for June raw material requirements in production). Orders for the peak season were booked in large volume during the winter, but shipments remained low until early March. Orders were subject to revision to the time of shipment.

The company sold in the Southeast, particularly in Florida, Georgia, Alabama, and South Carolina, both through retail outlets, such as grain, feed, and hardware stores and agricultural cooperatives, and directly to a very few extremely large farms. Insecticide was also sold to municipalities for use in insect control programs. Company salesmen solicited orders from some 13,000 accounts. Characteristically, orders from either retail outlets or customers buying in bulk involved significant quantities. Fertilizer and insecticide were offered to both types of customers at the same set of prices. Fertilizer was sold either by the ton or in 80-pound bags. Insecticide was sold by the pound or in 50-pound bags. However, bulk prices of both products were straight multiples of the smaller unit quantities. Overwhelmingly, shipments of both products were in bags because retail outlets accounted for a great preponderance of company sales, and transactions by these outlets took place in relatively small quantities.

From recent sales and new order data it seemed that in 1966 the company would enjoy sales opportunities far better than in recent years. Anticipated increases in allotted acreages under government agricultural control programs were the probable source of the improvement. In any event, from current reports Mr. Branson and Harlow Wilson, the sales manager, estimated that the only significant limit on fertilizer sales would be company processing capacity. On the other hand, Mr. Wilson argued that if the sales force devoted a maximum effort to it, sales of insecticide could reach 600,000 bags in the March–May period. Moreover, he contended that this was the most profitable policy to pursue, and that company production capacity should be given over entirely to insecticide if this proved necessary. He based his argument on the higher profit per bag of insecticide over fertilizer. (See the per bag cost estimates for insecticide and fertilizer in Exhibit 2.) Mr. Wilson had been the person chiefly responsible for the entry into insecticide production shortly after he came to the firm as a part of a youth movement in management.

Despite a potential downward revision, Mr. Branson felt that the cost estimates for each product shown in Exhibit 2 were reasonable, since very little of the labor required in company operations was specialized and more was readily available at the same wage rates. Seasonal labor had been used in the past, and there was no reason to assume that it would not be available in the amounts needed in 1966, whatever they proved to be.

In the company's experience, there had been no fixed relationship between the quantities of fertilizer and insecticide sold, and there was no apparent reason why the firm would not be free to vary its output of each as best suited its own needs. For this reason, Mr. Branson was swayed somewhat by Mr. Wilson's contentions, but the direct costs per bag of fertilizer and insecticide, and thus cash requirements in production, were quite different. Hence, it was not clear whether it would be better to devote the company's limited financing in the March–May period to producing a large number of bags of fertilizer at low profit per bag or to a small number of bags of insecticide at high profit per bag.

CONDITIONS UNDERLYING PLANNING

Purchase orders must be placed about 60 days in advance of need. Hence, Florida Fertilizers would order materials very early in January for March production. If market conditions or other reasons made it necessary, plans for April and May materials purchases could be altered as late as early February and March, respectively. This appeared unlikely, however, so for the present decision it would be assumed that production planning for the 64 working days in the period March through May could treat the period as a unit, and production would be at a level pace throughout the 13 weeks (a local holiday reduced the total of working days). Conventional cash budgeting would be used to govern intraweekly and intramonthly variations in cash flow once the production schedule for the period as a whole determined output rates and product mix. Sales for the period would be about equally distributed through the three months. Extraordinary events, such as weather phenomena and cyclical variations in consumption of certain crops, had altered this pattern at times in the past.

Several considerations other than those previously cited affected Mr. Branson's planning for cash flow during the peak months. June production requirements had been historically low relative to the other eight off-season months. The best guess available in January was that Florida Fertilizers must reach the end of May with funds of about $500,000 available for raw materials and packaging inventories to support June production requirements.

Collections of receivables on insecticide and fertilizer sales did not behave similarly. For insecticide, collections would lag sales about an average of 45 days. Collections on fertilizer sales were slightly faster. The following rule of thumb applied fairly well: 10% of a month's sales would be collected during the same month, half in the month following, and 37% in the second month following. The remaining 3% would be collected unpredictably or written off as bad debts.

Cash outflows for March through May, other than for production payments, were foreseen as follows:

	March	April	May
Fixed cash operating expenses...........	$114,000	$114,000	$114,000*
Dividend.............................	. . .	. . .	325,000
Quarterly estimated tax................	. . .	600,000	. . .
Quarterly term loan amortization.......	. . .	. . .	250,000
	$114,000	$714,000	$689,000

* Approximately one week's expenses would be accrued at month-end and paid in the following month.

The $72 thousand accrual shown on the pro forma balance sheet for February 28, 1966, related to miscellaneous items. For cash flow planning it could be assumed that this item would remain unchanged on balance throughout the planning period. Other accruals, including direct labor expense, were entirely independent of this sum.

Wages were paid every two weeks, usually at the end of the first and third weeks in each month. Trade suppliers furnished the processed materials used in production on terms of net 30 days, and because of the company's dependence on continuity of relationships with outside suppliers, Mr. Branson adhered to these terms as scrupulously as possible. For purposes of financial planning it could be assumed that the company would be continuously indebted to trade vendors for 30 days' usage of materials during the March–May season. Bank debt would be used as needed to the limit of $2.5 million.

Exhibit 1

FLORIDA FERTILIZERS CO. (A)

PRO FORMA BALANCE SHEET, AS OF FEBRUARY 28, 1966

(Dollar Figures in Thousands)

ASSETS		
Cash		$ 116
Accounts receivable, net		1,110
Finished goods inventory		
Fertilizer	$ 32	
Insecticide	18	50
Raw materials and packaging—available for commitment		2,658
Current Assets		$ 3,934
Prepaid expenses		$ 98
Plant and equipment	$17,225	
Less: Accumulated depreciation	9,144	
Plant and equipment, net		8,081
Total Assets		$12,113

LIABILITIES		
Bank notes		$ 400
Trade accounts		2,600
Wages and other payables		72
Estimated tax liability for January–February		193
Current maturity of term loan		1,000
Current Liabilities		$ 4,265
Term loan		$ 1,000
Net worth		
Capital stock	$1,000	
Earned surplus	5,848	
Total		6,848
Total Liabilities		$12,113

Exhibit 2

FLORIDA FERTILIZERS CO. (A)

ESTIMATED PRODUCTION COSTS PER BAG OF
FERTILIZER AND INSECTICIDE

Fertilizer, sale price per 80-pound bag...................... $2.45
Cost:
    Processed minerals and other raw materials.............. 1.50
    Packaging, labels, etc.................................. 0.14
    Variable direct and indirect labor...................... 0.13
    Variable machine operating expense...................... 0.01
        Total... $1.78
    Gross profit at 27.3%............................... $0.67
Insecticide, sale price per 50-pound bag.................... $9.00
Cost:
    Chemicals.. 6.23
    Packaging, labels, etc.................................. 0.14
    Variable direct and indirect labor...................... 0.13
    Variable machine operating expense...................... 0.01
        Total... $6.51
    Gross profit at 27.7%............................... $2.49

FLORIDA FERTILIZERS CO. (B)

IN EARLY JANUARY, 1966, John Branson, treasurer of Florida Fertilizers Co., studied the recommendations in a consultant's report concerning production rates and product mix during the coming peak sales months of March, April, and May. The report explained that its recommended combination of output and sales rates would give Florida Fertilizers the highest attainable profit within the limits of its production and financial capacities.

While Mr. Branson could not quarrel directly with the technical basis of the report, he was aware that the consultant had originally been instructed to base his recommendations only upon an analysis of the peak period as a single unit of time. It was apparent to Mr. Branson that his company experienced great differences in cash flow from month to month. Since the consultant maintained that cash flow was a principal limitation on the firm's output, and hence profit, Mr. Branson thought it might be possible to schedule output by month rather than for the peak season as a whole, thus stretching the productivity of the firm's financial resources. In anticipation of discussing the matter with the consultant, Mr. Branson assembled the data he thought would be required for a month-by-month analysis.

The peak production period in 1966 had 64 working days, scheduled unevenly—23 in March, 20 in April, and 21 in May. Fixed cash outflows for the period were scheduled in data previously supplied to the consultant. In addition to the sales made from production during the months in question, cash inflows would be realized from receivables and finished goods anticipated to be on hand at the end of February. An analysis of sales forecasts produced the data shown in Exhibit 1. Receivables collections were assumed to follow the pattern recently experienced. Finished goods of $32,000 worth of fertilizer and $18,000 worth of insecticide would be sold in March, and the resulting receivables collected on the same schedule.

Exhibit 1

FLORIDA FERTILIZERS CO. (B)

ESTIMATED MONTH OF ORIGIN OF RECEIVABLES
TO BE HELD AT FEBRUARY 28
(Dollar Figures in Thousands)

Product	Month of Origin			Total
	December	January	February	
Fertilizer.............	$12	$133	$164	$ 309
Insecticide.............	...	216	585	801
Total..........	$12	$349	$749	$1,110

FLORIDA FERTILIZERS CO. (C)

AFTER RECEIVING an amended report from a consultant, John Branson of the Florida Fertilizers Co. deliberated over the possibility of a reduction of the company's operating cash balance. The amended report recommended a certain mix of fertilizer and insecticide in the company's production over the months March–May, 1966. Changes from the previous report's recommendations reflected alterations in assumptions employed by the consultant after Mr. Branson submitted supplementary data.

Previously, the consultant had treated the entire three-month production planning period as a unit, but the more detailed cash flow data enabled him to find the best fertilizer–insecticide mix by choosing output over monthly intervals. Also, in the consultant's earlier calculations the contemplated policy of maintaining a 30-day stockpile of raw material had proved too restrictive in its preemption of funds. With Mr. Branson's consent the policy was abandoned. Instead, Mr. Branson intended to control raw materials and intramonthly cash flow by scheduling purchase orders and payments to vendors by the weekly cash budgeting techniques already in use in Florida Fertilizers. This control over weekly operations by traditional methods would be aimed at realizing the monthly production goals recommended by the consultant.

At the outset of their planning, Mr. Branson had instructed the consultant to treat the $116,000 cash balance shown on the February 28, 1966, balance sheet as an inviolable minimum need for operating purposes. When the amended report was submitted, the consultant observed that some of the figures emerging from his work indicated that profit would be improved if additional funds were found to finance production. He argued that operating cash of $116,000 was excessive, and that perhaps a reduction of $50,000 could be tolerated. Mr. Branson was not satisfied yet that such a sizable reduction left a safe minimum, but the prospect of raising output and profit by, in essence, simply rearranging his current asset structure at the beginning of the March–May period was appealing.

Mr. Branson was curious about the return he might expect on each dollar of working cash reduction. If it proved impossible to reduce operating cash by the full $50,000 proposed by the consultant, an intermediate figure might still be worthwhile in its effect on profit. Mr. Branson thought that a unit profitability estimate would be helpful in gauging the desirability of undertaking the progressively greater risk entailed in lower operating cash balances. Since the time for placement of orders for raw materials for March production had already passed, Mr. Branson wondered if there was an expeditious way to ascertain the effects of a reduced cash balance on the production mix that maximized profit.

ALLEN BROTHERS CHARCOAL COMPANY

ALLEN BROTHERS CHARCOAL COMPANY was a small, family-owned company located in New Hampshire. Majority ownership had recently passed to Charles Allen, the current president. In January, 1966, Mr. Allen was preparing his annual plan for the coming year's production schedule and funds requirements. With the approval of the board of directors, Mr. Allen would present a budget for funds, and possibly a request for increased credit, when he visited the Indian Bonnet Bank. For this reason, he now faced the choice of seasonal versus level production, and the problem of estimating levels of output and consequent funds needs during the next 12 months.

HISTORY

Allen Brothers Charcoal Company was formed in the early 1900's by Mr. Allen's grandfather. The company produced by the open-pit method for a number of years and because of vigorous demand realized good profits despite the crudity of its production methods. During World War I, however, a large number of major concerns began deriving the chemicals associated with wood distillation, and sold the resulting charcoal as a by-product. Simultaneously, the use of charcoal for heating and cooking purposes began to decline. This combination of developments severely depressed charcoal prices.

In response to this pressure, Allen Brothers began to produce charcoal in steel beehive kilns to take advantage of the low fixed costs and mobility of such operations. Its production methods remained essentially unchanged until World War II. During the war, synthetic chemicals undercut the market of many companies that had previously sold charcoal as a by-product only, forcing them to rely wholly on charcoal sales. Under the ensuing market pressures, the geographic advantages of Allen Brothers became important and allowed it to continue profitably.

In 1964, the company underwent a series of major changes. First, it made arrangements with a local sawmill to provide raw material on a continuing basis. The sawmill supplied scrap edgings and slabs associated with the production of lumber, all at a cost of $11 per cord of stacked lumber delivered to the Allen Brothers yard. In the same year, the company built a battery of new masonry-construction kilns to replace the worn steel beehive kilns. This

111

battery of 16 kilns, each capable of holding 3 cords of wood, cost $9,600, not including peripheral equipment. Additional kilns could be constructed at a cost of $600 each.

PRODUCTION PROCESS

In the kiln, a controlled heat converted wood to charcoal in a drying and a coaling stage. The yield obtained from the raw material input was dependent on the amount of carbon in the wood and the carbonization conditions employed in the burn. The heat needed for drying and to initiate coaling conditions was provided by burning a portion of the wood. The amount of burning was controlled by limiting and regulating the amount of air entering the kiln.

After an initial surface zone of dry wood had been established, further heating charred the wood to form charcoal progressively throughout a kiln charge. Water vapor and gases escaped through various kiln stacks. Since Allen Brothers produced charcoal primarily for domestic use, it was necessary that high coaling temperatures be maintained with hardwood raw material to obtain a reasonably clean and smokeless finished product. To achieve consistently high yields of satisfactory charcoal, each kiln was fitted with regulatory thermocouples so that coaling temperatures were maintained between 850° and 950°.

Allen Brothers allowed the sawmill wood to dry for at least six months in order to reduce the drying time in the kiln as much as possible. Therefore, the company maintained a six-month supply of wood at all times. Purchases of raw material on hand in early January, 1966, had been distributed about evenly through the preceding six months.

The yield obtained from the raw material under these conditions was about 30% in 1966, although individual burns varied. On an input of three cords of wood, a yield of charcoal weighing 2,000 pounds was expected under normal conditions. At average prices, raw material costs for a single burn were $33.

Charcoal production involved a number of separate phases, each of which had to be accomplished under rigid time requirements. Raw material was transported by a forklift truck to the door of the kiln and was stacked in the kiln by hand. The front of the kiln was shut by constructing a cinder block wall in it and sealing the joints with lime mortar. The kiln was then ignited. Control of the burning was obtained entirely by opening or closing air inlets at the sides of the kiln. A burn too hot called for partially closing these inlets; a burn too slow called for opening them wider. An operator had to be present during the first two hours of ignition and at various times during carbonization.

After the kiln was fully closed to stop carbonization, it was allowed to cool for about 120 hours, with sporadic checks made to investigate the extent of cooling taking place. On completion of cooling, the front door wall was torn down and the charcoal unloaded by hand from the kiln. The charcoal was bagged and warehoused before shipment to either jobbers or local markets. If the charcoal was to be sold to industrial users or briquetters, however, bagging was omitted and the finished product was unloaded directly into large trucks, which transported it immediately to the company's spur track for railroad shipment. Because no bagging was involved in this process, unloading took only about two man-hours.

All told, 136 hours were consumed in a single kiln cycle for production of bagged charcoal. Bulk production required 133 hours per cycle, the difference being attributable to the difference in time required for unloading. In operations of ordinary efficiency, about 5 cycles could be completed per month, or 15 1/2 cycles per 91-day calendar quarter.

Since the kilns were operated on a rotational basis and many of the tasks required three men working simultaneously, the labor force was separated into three-man crews, each responsible for 16 kilns. To operate the 16 kilns, a crew was required on each of the 3 shifts per 24 hours of operations. Thus, four full-time crews were employed in total, and part-time labor was used to fill out requirements for operations seven days per week.

The work force in 1966, other than a supervisor and a clerk, was composed entirely of local labor, which was readily available at a cost of $1.25 per hour. The supervisor, a man of long experience in the business and not easily replaced, was employed regardless of current production rates.

MARKETING SYSTEM

Charcoal was sold for the household market in 10-pound bags at an average price of $105 per ton. Sales of bagged charcoal to jobbers and local markets occurred from April through September. Off-season production of bagged charcoal was stored in a local warehouse where Allen Brothers had the option of renting space as needed. Storage cost was $5 per ton of packaged charcoal per quarter.

In the recent past, Allen Brothers had been forced by its extreme shortage of funds to adhere rigidly to credit terms of net 30 in the household segment of the market. In sales to industrial buyers, however, other charcoal manufacturers extended 60-day terms, and Allen Brothers was forced to meet these terms. Sales to commercial users or briquette manufacturers were at $81 a ton, unpackaged, F.O.B. the plant. Bad debt losses had been negligible on sales to both market segments.

FINANCIAL PROBLEMS

The most difficult problem facing Mr. Allen at this time concerned the allocation of available cash. He began his analysis with the balance sheet for 1965, the year just completed (Exhibit 1).

The local bank, the Indian Bonnet Bank, had previously extended an open line of credit of $12,000 at 8% per annum, payable quarterly, and it had also loaned on a long-term note secured by the company's peripheral equipment, principally forklift trucks. The two final payments of $2,000 each on this note were due on February 1 and June 1, 1966. It seemed safe to anticipate that without pressure the bank would again apply the same $12,000 ceiling on the line of credit. Mr. Allen was planning to argue strenuously that this ceiling would limit output and profit.

Indian Bonnet Bank had always overlooked its customary minimum balance requirements in the case of Allen Brothers, but the company had always consented to maintain an acid test ratio (cash plus receivables divided by current liabilities defined to include the remaining estimated tax for the year) of 1 to 1 throughout the duration of a loan. The bank had refused to consider use of a current ratio because the inventory was, in its view, of problematical value.

Mr. Allen had contemplated an attempt to secure loan accommodations elsewhere. Because of the company's extremely small size and limited net worth, however, long-term debt was not likely to be available from other sources. This was especially true since the collateral value of the supporting equipment had deteriorated, and it was unlikely that even the Indian Bonnet Bank could be induced to refinance a term loan on this security.

PLANNING

The planning task was essentially one of deciding output mix and volume with existing financial resources. Mr. Allen's current problem was to draw up for presentation to the board and to the bank a plan that would maximize company profits during the coming year. Relevant direct costs are given in Exhibit 2, as Mr. Allen estimated them for 1966.

The supervisor was paid $6,000 a year and one clerk was employed at $4,800 a year. Added to these costs was Mr. Allen's salary of $8,000 a year. Wages were paid every two weeks, usually at the end of the second and fourth weeks in each month. Direct labor costs per ton of charcoal are itemized in Exhibit 3.

Cord wood was paid for immediately. Although this imposed a hardship on the company, it was treated as essential because the local supply of edgings lowered the company's raw material costs to substantially below those of competitors, and prompt payment served as a decisive attraction to the supplier.

Since each kiln could be operated only as needed, it was not considered sensible to treat depreciation on an annual basis. Instead, the depreciation charge was figured on the basis of a 200-burn life per kiln, which amounted to $3 per burn. Another fixed cost was the charge for depreciation of peripheral equipment such as tractors, sheds, and loading forks.

Recent renegotiation of the warehouse contract had resulted in an agreement that storage charges for warehousing would be paid quarterly in the future. Taxes also were paid on a quarterly basis. Income tax liability for 1965 had been completely discharged. Estimated tax payments for 1966 were as follows:

March	June	September	December
$150	$150	$212	$212

Previous company procedure had been to produce at a level rate 12 months a year in order to have sufficient inventory to meet seasonal demand for bagged charcoal. Bagged charcoal was sold only during the summer, since jobbers paid only a below-cost price during off months. Any excess production beyond the amount sold in bulk was stored in bags to meet the later household demand. Bulk charcoal could not be stored for significant time periods because of its susceptibility to adverse weather.

Since the company's financial resources were extremely limited, it appeared questionable to Mr. Allen whether the off-season accumulation of inventories, which accompanied level production, was justifiable. He thought that seasonal production of bagged charcoal, closely geared to demand, would enable the company to capture the benefit of higher markup on this packaging style, while minimizing inventory accumulations and raising total output and profit above levels previously experienced. An argument had been made that added capacity would expand profits, but Mr. Allen felt sure that his cash flows were too tight to allow expenditures on fixed assets. In production planning it was customary to assume 91-day calendar quarters.

Exhibit 1
ALLEN BROTHERS CHARCOAL COMPANY
BALANCE SHEET AS OF DECEMBER 31, 1965

ASSETS

Cash		$ 3,500
Accounts receivable		4,500
Inventory		
Raw material	$16,500	
Finished goods	4,200	20,700
Total Current Assets		$28,700
Property and plant	$ 9,600	
Less: Accumulated depreciation	4,800	4,800
Equipment	$20,000	
Less: Accumulated depreciation	8,000	12,000
Total Assets		$45,500

LIABILITIES AND NET WORTH

Accrued labor expense	$ 1,680
Notes payable	4,000
Total Current Liabilities	$ 5,680
Capital stock	10,000
Earned surplus	29,820
Total Liabilities and Net Worth	$45,500

Exhibit 2

ALLEN BROTHERS CHARCOAL COMPANY

ANALYSIS OF DIRECT COSTS FOR 1966

Sacked Charcoal

Price per ton.................................$105.00
Cost
    Labor....................................... 35.00
    Raw material............................... 33.00
    Repair.....................................   3.00
    Sacks......................................   5.00
    Miscellaneous*.............................   5.00
        Total Cost............................ \$ 81.00
Contribution per ton.........................\$ 24.00
    Bulk Charcoal
Price per ton.................................\$ 81.00
Cost
    Labor....................................... 27.50
    Raw material............................... 33.00
    Repair.....................................   3.00
        Total Cost............................ \$ 63.50
Contribution per ton.........................\$ 17.50

* Includes promotion and other similar expenditures,

Exhibit 3

ALLEN BROTHERS CHARCOAL COMPANY

DIRECT LABOR COST PER TON OF CHARCOAL, ESTIMATED FOR 1966

	Sacked	*Bulk*
Load......................................	5 hours	5 hours
Wall......................................	3	3
Carbonize.................................	8	8
Cool......................................	4	4
Unload....................................	8	2
	28 hours	22 hours

Labor cost, \$1.25 per hour
Direct labor—sacked = \$35 a ton
Direct labor—bulk = \$27.50 a ton

NEL-MAX COOKIES, INC.

NEL–MAX COOKIES and crackers were sold in supermarkets, grocery stores, and specialty food shops throughout the Midwest. The company produced and distributed a wide line ranging from plain crackers to fancy cookies in gift-wrapped packages. Sales reached a peak of $12.3 million in 1965.

Recognizing that cash flow was becoming a major problem of Nel–Max, the vice president–finance and treasurer, Jeff Kabat, contemplated an approach to divisional cash flow planning based on programming estimates of profit potential and funds flow requirements of operations. Mr. Kabat decided to conduct a pilot study covering the last four months of 1966 at one of the sales divisions before completing his recommendation to the monthly officers' meeting. He selected the Illinois Sales Center for this purpose. He hoped to extend such planning to all profit centers and to the company as a whole.

COMPETITIVE SITUATION

Nel–Max faced two types of competition. Most important were the "Big Three"—National Biscuit Company, Sunshine Biscuits, Inc., and United Biscuit Company. Several medium-size companies operating in Nel–Max's territory offered additional competition. The product lines of the large companies were essentially the same as Nel–Max's although they put more emphasis on crackers and on product variety. The smaller companies generally specialized in high-priced fancy cookies.

The Nel–Max product line could be conveniently classified into crackers and plain cookies, which provided a gross margin of 40%, and fancy cookies, which yielded a 60% gross margin. The former were sold primarily to supermarkets; specialty food shops were the major market for fancy cookies.

Because there was little genuine product differentiation in Nel–Max's market, competition focused in significant measure upon service to customers and attention to detail by company representatives. In several respects this led to a requirement for a large sales force. Order-taking, stock-checking, and replenishing merchandise were all time-consuming tasks. Also, personal association of salesmen with customers often bore high returns. Although supermarkets generally allocated fixed shelf space to each of the important firms in the area, the relationship of the salesman to the store manager influenced the treatment Nel–Max products might receive, e.g., space for special promotions.

As a sales inducement, Nel–Max management also offered relatively long credit terms of net 60 for orders of crackers and plain cookies and net 75 for fancy cookies.

ORGANIZATION

The company was organized into four divisional profit centers—production and three sales divisions—each headed by a vice president. The production center, considered the home office and the central corporation, provided many of the necessary staff services for the sales divisions. Each sales division, however, was responsible for its own financial planning within policy constraints. The president, Jeffrey Allen, met monthly with the vice presidents.

The board of directors consisted of the president and four members representing some 2,000 stockholders. These board members were an officer of the company's principal bank, an investment banker, and vice presidents of a supplier and a customer. Meetings were held monthly, usually after the officers' meeting. The board maintained a close interest in operating results and major capital expenditures.

PRODUCTION

The plant, together with the home office, was located in a four-story building served by a spur track of the Rock Island Railroad. The ground floor was used for warehousing and shipping, and the second and third floors contained offices and manufacturing. The fourth floor was rented to another firm. Major items of equipment were six 200-foot continuous band ovens, a battery of dough mixers handling about 600,000 pounds of flour and shortening per week, several kneading machines, packaging lines serving the ovens, and five icing, sandwiching, and coating lines. Most of the equipment was of very advanced design at the time of installation and had been kept in good condition, according to Scott Morris, vice president of production. Several conveyor arrangements allowed continuous product flow. Two-shift operation of production facilities prevailed.

Production scheduling was complicated, owing to the large variety of products offered. The most difficult problem was dovetailing inventories and current requirements of the three sales divisions. To facilitate this scheduling, the sales divisions were required to order one month in advance of desired delivery.

SALES DIVISIONS

Mr. Allen believed that the lines of authority had become blurred under the preceding management. "Nobody knew who was to tell what to whom," he said. He stated that "decentralization was introduced to provide an organizational framework that would increase the motivation of employees." He was convinced that morale and employee turnover had benefited from the adoption of profit centers. In addition, the president believed that divisionalization had improved the company's asset allocation because each vice president was able to pay constant attention to information about his division's use of resources.

An intrinsic part of divisionalization of operations and measurement of profit-center performance was formulation of prices to be applied to financial transfers between the central corporation and the sales divisions. Assets were furnished to the sales divisions by the central corporation under certain restrictive conditions and on given cost terms. It was the responsibility of division management to forecast sales, and to budget for financial needs accordingly. The performance measure employed for profit centers operated so as to reflect favorable results with minimal funds usage.

In the measure of profit performance both the production and the sales divisions received full credit for the gross margin on sales because determination of accurate transfer prices had proved impossible.

FINANCE

Mr. Kabat had spent much of his career in consulting. During a special assignment for another biscuit company in the later 1950's, he had attracted Mr. Allen's attention. In 1963, he was asked to join the company as assistant to the newly appointed president, and was promoted to vice president soon thereafter.

In addition to instituting profit centers, Mr. Kabat established a cost surveillance program, which required compilations of average costs for each product at least three times a year. The latest figures (August 31, 1966) to emerge under this system showed that the gross margins on sales of the two major product groups, based on the expected mix within each, had not changed.

The sales divisions were held accountable by direct and indirect means for their employment of current assets. The balance sheet of the Illinois Sales Center in Exhibit 1 is an illustration of a resulting financial statement.

Operating cash of $125,000 was furnished to each of the sales divisions "free." However, it was considered by management that, by appropriate investment, divisions should earn 0.5% per month on any cash held in excess of this balance. Profit estimation reflected this anticipation. In planning, it was assumed that the earning rate would apply to the excess cash held at the end of a month; earnings and the related cash receipts would occur during the next month.

Astute inventory management was vital to good sales division performance for two reasons. First, the division's ending inventory level served as the basis for a noncash intracompany charge. Monthly carrying cost was computed as 1% of that month's ending inventory. Second, this inventory and outstanding purchase orders were required by policy to exceed one and one-half times the next month's planned sales at cost. The redundant portion was required, against the protests of sales division managers, as a safeguard against fluctuations in demand in excess of anticipated levels. This safety cushion insured the desired level of customer service.

The amount owed to the production center for inventory was analogous to trade credit from the sales center's standpoint. Terms to all sales centers were identical. Payment for deliveries of fancy cookies had to be sent immediately, while remittances for crackers and plain cookies could be postponed for one month as a sales stimulant for these lower margin products.

To preserve divisional autonomy, Mr. Kabat had established relatively few guidelines for divisional financial planning. Each sales division, in fact, was permitted to arrange its own short-term financing needs through a local bank. The anticipated monthly excess cash and loan balances for each division during the study period, except for the Illinois Sales Center which enjoyed a $200,000 line of credit for the same months, are shown in Exhibit 2.

The Illinois Sales Center borrowed from its bank at a monthly rate of 0.75% on the debt outstanding at the end of the month, making payment and recording cost in the next month. Provision of a permanent $125,000 operating balance by the central financial organization more than met compensating balance requirements of the bank. The home office reserved authority for long-term borrowing to itself.

Another financial requirement imposed on each division was a $200,000 payment to the home office in February, May, August, and November. These payments represented reimbursements for services and depreciation charges and some of the division's profits. The timing coincided with Nel–Max's dividend payments to stockholders.

ILLINOIS SALES CENTER

An analysis of the Illinois Sales Center's records made in connection with the prospective study yielded the following data.

FIXED MONTHLY OPERATING COSTS

Salesmen's salaries	$ 50,000
Warehouse and delivery	37,500
Promotion and advertising	30,000
Administrative expenses	7,500
Depreciation of automobiles, trucks, etc.,—all original cost is on home office books	10,000
Allocated service charges from home office	10,000
Total	$145,000

All cash operating expenses were incurred and paid within the same month.

ORDERS PLACED AT COST WITH THE PRODUCTION DIVISION:

	Crackers and Plain Cookies	Fancy Cookies
June	$ 50,000	$ 70,000
July	60,000	75,000
August	66,000	80,000

SALES (AT SALE PRICE) DURING:

June—actual	80,000	150,000
July—actual	80,000	150,000
August—actual	100,000	170,000
September—expected maximum	110,000	200,000
October—expected maximum	195,000	375,000
November—expected maximum	225,000	450,000
December—expected maximum	190,000	450,000

Sales in the next calendar year were less certain, but provisionally it was planned that ending inventory and goods on order from the production center in December would be the same as that shown on the August 31 balance sheet in Exhibit 1.

Collections were somewhat slower than the formal credit terms would suggest, but did not require a careful examination at this time. Collections on sales for the last few months, for practical purposes, conformed to the average collection experience shown below:

	Crackers and Plain Cookies	Fancy Cookies
Second month after month of sale	.5	.25
Third month after month of sale	.5	.75

Exhibit 1

NEL–MAX COOKIES, INC.

BALANCE SHEET OF ILLINOIS SALES CENTER AS OF AUGUST 31, 1966

Cash		$125,000
Short-term investments		. . .
Accounts receivable		652,500
Inventory		
Crackers and plain cookies	$ 90,000	
Fancy cookies	120,000	210,000
		$987,500
Trade credit (to production center)		$ 60,000
Short-term bank debt		. . .
Intracompany equity account		927,500
		$987,500

Exhibit 2

NEL-MAX COOKIES, INC.

ANTICIPATED EXCESS CASH AND LOAN BALANCES

	Home Office and Production	Indiana	Minnesota
Line of Credit...................	$300,000	$200,000	$150,000
September 30, 1966			
Excess cash....................	200,000	50,000	...
Loan balance..................	...	...	150,000
October 31, 1966			
Excess cash....................	100,000	...	...
Loan balance..................	...	...	50,000
November 30, 1966			
Excess cash....................	300,000	...	50,000
Loan balance..................	...	100,000	...
December 31, 1966			
Excess cash....................	100,000	...	150,000
Loan balance..................	...	200,000	...

RATIONING OF RESOURCES:
TWO-PRODUCT PROJECTS *

By William Beranek†

THE PREVIOUS chapter has illustrated how *single-product* projects involving certainty, linear relationships, and the absence of outlays for durables could be tested for single-period payback. This chapter extends the analysis to embrace *two-product* projects and in doing so introduces the reader to the subject of linear programing. Projects which involve the scheduling of more than two products require the simplex method for their analysis. . . .

When a given amount of resources are allocated to a departmental production manager, he determines his optimal rates of output by the process of suboptimization. But determining the amount of resources which should be made available to a department, and especially in the face of over-all firm *financial constraints*—e.g., existing cash balance, available trade credit and limited external sources of money, and balance sheet constraints like a minimum current or acid test ratio—is a financial problem, a problem which usually cannot be suboptimized with satisfactory results.

The first part of the chapter illustrates the graphical solution to a two-product scheduling problem on the assumption that liquid resources sufficient to achieve any desired schedule are on hand. Following this, we introduce the additional resource restraints of (a) a limited cash balance, (b) limited trade credit, and (c) limited capacity to borrow short-term cash. Finally, we shall illustrate the development of shadow prices and their use in evaluating financial constraints and policies.

TWO-PRODUCT PROJECTS

Consider two products which can be produced simultaneously with the same facilities. This contrasts with the type of project considered in Chapter 3

---

* It is quite unusual to reprint a chapter from a textbook in another instructional volume, and because of this novelty the authors of this book owe a particular debt of gratitude to William Beranek and to Richard D. Irwin, Inc., author and publisher, for permission to reprint this chapter from *Analysis for Financial Decisions*, 1963.

† Professor of Finance, University of Wisconsin

where the existing facilities were assumed to be capable of producing two or more products, but not simultaneously.

As before, assume that the rate of deterioration of our existing durable goods does not depend upon either the production rates or the sales rates of these products. All expenditures are for non-durables and we continue to assume certainty. No inventories of finished goods are held at the beginning of the period; no inventories are required at the end of the period. The intermediate goal is maximizing the rate of profits for the coming period. Our objective is to seek the rate of resource use, and the production schedule of both products, such that our intermediate goal is achieved. Finally, we shall assume initially that liquid resources available for expenditure are more than adequate to achieve any optimal rate of output and sales.

Demand Constraints

Let X denote the amount demanded per period for product A, Y the amount demanded per period for product B. Let p_x denote a specific price for product A, p_y a specific price for product B. At these prices, the rates of demand for products A and B are bounded by X_0 and Y_0 respectively. This means, for example, that at the price $p_{\bar{x}}$ any amount up to X_0 of product A may be sold during the period. We may express these constraints in the following form:

$$X \leq X_0$$
$$Y \leq Y_0. \tag{4.1}$$

The graph of the linear inequalities (4.1) is provided by Figure 1. Given our X and Y axis, all points on and to the left of the vertical line X_0 represent

Figure 1
GRAPH OF DEMAND RESTRICTIONS

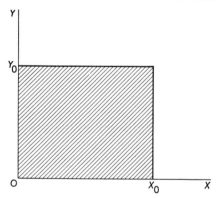

the statement $X \leqq X_0$. In the same way we plot the points corresponding to the statement $Y \leqq Y_0$. Since neither X nor Y can be negative—i.e., we must have $X \geqq 0$, $Y \geqq 0$—the set of points satisfying (4.1) must be given by the

shaded area represented by the rectangle—$X = X_0$, $Y = Y_0$, $X = 0$, $Y = 0$
—and its boundaries. Note that this set of points is a graphic method of representing all possible sales combinations of products A and B.[1]

Let $X_0 = 50$ units, $Y_0 = 40$ units. Since there is to be no inventory at the end of the period, we will never produce more than we can sell during the period. Therefore X, the rate of demand for product A, denotes as well the rate of output of product A. Similarly, we may let Y stand for the rate of output of product B.

Capacity Constraints

Products A and B require processing in two departments. In the machine shop the products go through a lathe operation requiring one hour of labor time for product A, two hours of labor time for product B. The assembly department requires two man-hours to assemble product A, 1.5 man-hours for product B.

For the coming period, 100 hours of labor time are available for the machine shop, while 120 are available for assembly.

This information may be summarized on a graph. The additional restrictions of limited labor time define the capacities of both the machine shop and the assembly department. Let us look at the machine shop. Since we require one hour of labor time to process one unit of product A, and two hours of labor time to process one unit of product B, it must be true that

$$X + 2Y \leq 100. \tag{4.2}$$

We can graph this expression in two stages. First, plot the straight line of the implied linear equation. This determines a boundary. Thus $X = 100 - 2Y$ is plotted on Figure 2 to yield the line labeled "100." Second, observe that all points satisfying (4.2) which are not on the line 100 must lie exclusively to one side of the line. To see that this statement is true, consider the following argument. Supose the capacity of the machine shop were 90 rather than 100 hours. Then the restriction would read: $X + 2Y \leq 90$. If the equation which is embedded in this restriction, $X + 2Y = 90$, is plotted on Figure 2 it would lie below but parallel to the line 100. Repeating the procedure for a capacity of 80 hours would produce another parallel line lying below the line labeled "90." If this procedure were repeated for successively smaller and smaller capacities, the corresponding lines would lie farther and farther to the southwest. There are an infinite number of such parallel capacity lines which can be plotted below the line 100. Any point on any of these capacity lines must therefore satisfy the restriction (4.2) while any point on a capacity line lying above—i.e., to the northeast—of the capacity line 100 contradicts the statement (4.2). Therefore, all points satisfying (4.2) must lie either on or to one side of the line $X + 2Y = 100$.

[1] It is also the solution to the system of inequalities (4.1). In other words, for the points contained within this set, statements (4.1) are both true.

Figure 2

ILLUSTRATION OF ADDITIONAL CAPACITY LINES

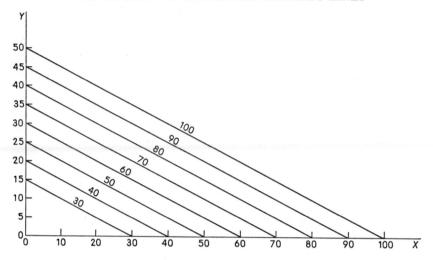

It is not necessary, of course, to plot several capacities in order to determine the complete graph of an inequality. It is sufficient to choose some point at random, say, $X = 0$, $Y = 0$, and substitute its co-ordinates into the inequality, say, (4.2). The point $X = 0$, $Y = 0$ will either satisfy the restriction (4.2) or it will not. If it does, then all points on the side of the line containing the point $X = 0$, $Y = 0$ will also satisfy (4.2). If the restriction (4.2) is violated by the point $X = 0$, $Y = 0$, then this point does not lie within the set of points satisfying (4.2). Hence, the points which satisfy (4.2) must lie on the side opposite to that which contained the tested point $X = 0$, $Y = 0$.

In our case, the point $X = 0$, $Y = 0$ satisfies the restriction (4.2). Therefore, the remaining points which satisfy (4.2) must lie below the line $X = 100 - 2Y$. These points plus those on the line represent all machine shop attainable outputs of products A and B. In Figure 3, the machine shop capacity line is labeled *MS* and the partial shading immediately below it indicates the side of *MS* which contains the remaining points satisfying (4.2).

We proceed in a similar manner with the assembly department restriction. We have

$$2X + 1.5Y \leq 120. \tag{4.3}$$

This expression implies a boundary

$$2X + 1.5Y = 120,$$

or

$$X = 60 - .75Y,$$

and its graph is the line labeled A, Figure 3. By applying the test of an arbitrary point, say, $X = 0$, $Y = 0$, we conclude that the remaining points satisfying (4.3) lie below the line $X = 60 - .75Y$. The partial shading on one side of the line A, Figure 3, indicates on which side of A these points lie.

Since we can only sell what we produce, the set of points which satisfy both demand and productive capacity restrictions must be given by the shaded area (and its boundary) of Figure 3. Certain demand combinations cannot be

Figure 3

GRAPH OF DEMAND AND CAPACITY RESTRICTIONS

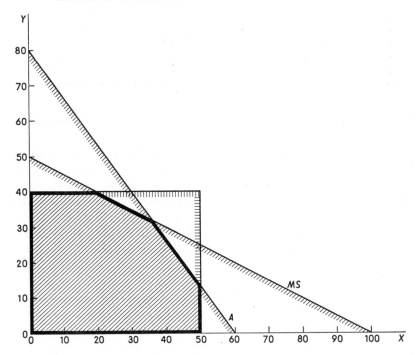

achieved because of capacity limitations of either the machine or the assembly department.

Figure 3 shows all output combinations of products A and B which satisfy all restrictions, both demand and capacity and the added fact that X and Y must be nonnegative. Observe that for any two points within this set, the locus of points on the straight line which connects these two points also lies within the set. Any set of points which has this property is said to be a *convex* set. The points represented by the shaded area in Part I, Figure 4, for example, constitute a convex set while in Part II, the shaded area is not a convex set since it is possible to find two points, p_1 and p_2, with the line segment connecting them not lying wholly within the set.

We can now set forth the following definition: if the co-ordinates of every

Figure 4

ILLUSTRATION OF A CONVEX SET, PART I, AND A
NONCONVEX SET, PART II

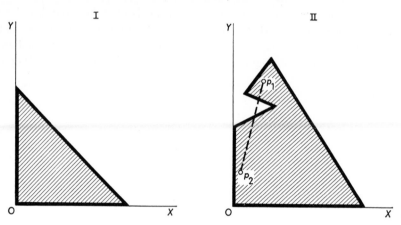

point within a convex set of points satisfy the nonnegativity requirement, then the convex set is a *feasible* set.

The absence of a convex set is apparent when the restrictions which one sets up for a problem cannot all hold—i.e., cannot all be true—at the same time. This can easily happen in the process of formulating restrictions and in such cases these conflicts must be removed before one can proceed with a linear programing solution.[2]

We have reproduced our feasible set of points in Figure 5 as the area that is represented by the polygon and the points on its boundary.

Profit Function

Before we can go further, we must develop a linear relationship which connects the rate of profits with the rate of output of our two products. Labor time in the machine shop costs $3.00 per hour and in the assembly department, $2.50 per hour. There is no penalty imposed upon the firm for failing to utilize its total labor capacity. Given the labor costs in each department and the man-hours required to produce each product we conclude that it costs $8.00 to produce a unit of X, $9.75 to produce a unit of Y. Let p_x and p_y be $10.00 and $10.75 respectively. Unit profit of X must therefore be $2.00, the unit profit of Y, $1.00. Hence P, profits before fixed costs, must be

$$P = \$2.00X + \$1.00Y. \tag{4.4}$$

The production schedule of products A and B which maximizes profits—i.e., equation (4.4)—is given by a point within our feasible set.

The linear programing problem then consists of finding that point (called

---

[2] It is still possible to solve such problems in two variables but not with the technique of linear programing.

the "optimum point") within the feasible set such that profits are maximized. Or, what is saying the same thing, we seek that point which maximizes (4.4) subject to the constraint that the point must lie within the feasible set—i.e., must satisfy linear inequalities (4.1), (4.2), and (4.3) and the nonnegativity requirements on all variables.

Equation (4.4) is often called the *objective function* which, in linear programing, is always a linear equation. There is no requirement, however,

Figure 5
ATTAINABLE OUTPUT AND SALES COMBINATIONS, PRODUCTS A AND B

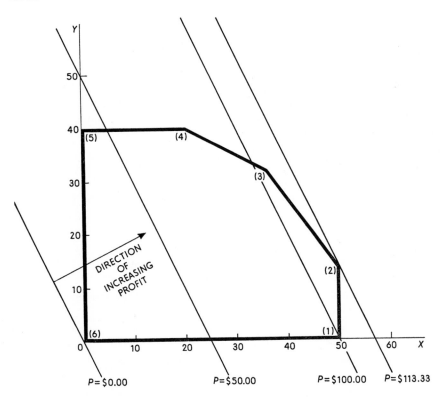

that one must always maximize the value of an objective function. Problems often arise which contain as an objective function a linear cost equation and the motive in such cases is to *minimize*, rather than to maximize, the value of the objective function.

Formally, linear programing consists of maximizing (or minimizing) a linear function (the objective function) subject to (1) a set of linear constraints (linear inequalities and/or equalities), and (2) the further restriction that each variable must be nonnegative.

Let us turn now to the problem of finding that point within our feasible set which maximizes (4.4).

Locating the Optimum Point

In Figure 5 our feasible set of points consists of the area represented by the polygon and the points on its boundary. If we set $P = \$0.00$ in expression (4.4) and plot the resulting linear equation on Figure 5, it would appear as the line denoted by $P = \$0.00$. This is an *iso-profit* line. Each point on such a line denotes a combination of X and Y which yields the same profit as any other point on that line. Hence, every output combination on the line $P = \$0.00$ would provide a profit of $\$0.00$. Other iso-profit lines in Figure 5 correspond to $P = \$50.00$, $P = \$100.00$ and $P = \$113.33$. Conceivably we could plot every possible iso-profit line which intersects our feasible set. Then, by following the iso-profit line with the highest profit we would eventually reach a point in our feasible set. This is an optimal point for it is feasible and it maximizes our objective function. But this procedure is not necessary. We can locate the optimal point without having to draw every possible iso-profit line which cuts our feasible set.

In our example, observe that iso-profit lines representing higher and higher profits lie farther and farther to the northeast. This corresponds to moving in the direction of the arrow on the graph of Figure 5. Eventually we will reach a profit line which lies entirely outside of our feasible set. We have gone too far. We step backwards until we meet the highest profit line which contains at least one point within the feasible set. This is the point we seek.

Clearly, the point of maximum profits will always lie on the boundary of the feasible set. Regardless of the slope of the iso-profit line, if we move at right angles to it in the direction of increasing profits we will eventually bump into the boundary of our feasible set. The line of maximum profits may lie on a segment of the boundary, in which case all points on the segment are optimal, or it may simply intersect a corner of the feasible set. At any rate, it is seen that a corner, or strictly speaking, a vertex, of the feasible set will be an optimum point.

This is the hint we need to provide a more efficient computational procedure. To solve the problem, it suffices to evaluate (4.4) at each vertex. The optimum production and distribution schedule is given by that corner which is associated with the maximum value of P.

The corners of the problem may be found by the following procedure. The equations we employed in establishing the boundary of the feasible set intersect at corners. Therefore, the co-ordinates of a vertex must satisfy the two intersecting equations simultaneously.

The six vertices in our problem are numbered on the graph of Figure 5. The co-ordinates of these points must be provided by the solutions to the following pairs of equations:

> **Point (1)** $X = 50, Y = 0$.
> **Point (2)** $X = 50$
> $\qquad\qquad 2X + 1.5Y = 120$,
> $\qquad\qquad$ hence $Y = 40/3$.

Point (3) $X + 2Y = 100$
$2X + 1.5Y = 120,$
hence $X = 36,\ Y = 32.$
Point (4) $Y = 40$
$X + 2Y = 100,$
hence $X = 20.$
Point (5) $X = 0,\ Y = 40.$
Point (6) $X = 0,\ Y = 0.$

The value of P corresponding to each of these points is:

Point	Profit
(1)....................	$100.00
(2)....................	$113.33
(3)....................	$104.00
(4)....................	$ 80.00
(5)....................	$ 40.00
(6)....................	$ 0.00

Point (2), with co-ordinates $X = 50,\ Y = 40/3$, is the optimal point. However, $Y = 40/3$ implies a fractional rate of output for product B which, in our problem, is meaningless. While we may produce partially completed units, we can sell only completed units. Hence our solution must be expressed in terms of integers.

We must examine all points in the neighborhood of the point $X = 50$, $Y = 40/3$ which contain as co-ordinates numbers that are exclusively integers. We could round $Y = 40/3$ to its nearest feasible integer, 13, and leave X equal to 50. The point $X = 50,\ Y = 13$ is certainly feasible. Or we could consider the point $X = 49,\ Y = 13$ which, while being feasible, is inferior to the feasible point $X = 50,\ Y = 13$. Finally we could consider the point $X = 49,\ Y = 14$ which is feasible since it satisfies (4.3), the only limiting equation since $X = 49$ clearly satisfies the demand barrier, $X = 50$. Since the marginal profit of X is greater than the marginal profit of Y, this point is also inferior to the point $X = 50,\ Y = 13$. All other admissible neighborhood points are either not feasible or clearly inferior to the point $X = 50$, $Y = 13$.

The optimal production schedule consists of producing 50 units of A and 13 units of B. The maximum profit is thus $113.00.

The profit of $113.00 may be compared to the fixed costs which must be incurred. If fixed costs are less than $113.00, then the pay-back period is one; if greater, then the project should not be adopted unless it promised payoffs in the future. This would place it in the multiperiod analysis classification, a topic for later discussion.

Other Linear Costs

We have assumed the production of items which require only labor as the variable factor input. Suppose there are other variable unit costs, such as raw material, for example, which must be incurred in the production of products

A and B. As long as the unit costs of raw materials remain constant with changes in the rate of output, the cost and profit functions will remain linear. This problem can then be solved by linear programing. For example, if raw material for product A costs $.75 per unit of output, while the material for B costs $.50 per unit of output, then the unit cost of X increases to $8.75 = $8.00 + $.75$, the unit cost of Y to $10.25 = $9.75 + $.50$. The profit function then becomes

$$P = \$1.25X + \$.50Y. \tag{4.4a}$$

An alteration in the profit function does not change the feasible set of output possibilities. The reader should verify the fact that with this profit function the optimal production schedule is still given by the point $X = 50$, $Y = 13$, with a profit before fixed costs in this case of $69.00.

The Value of Added Capacity

In planning the acquisition of additional capacity it is useful to determine the *value* of such added capacity. That is, what is a unit of additional capacity worth to the firm? In Chapter 3 we learned to compute such values by finding the *maximum* amounts we would pay for variable factors per unit of output and for fixed factors. We shall extend this principle to the two-product case.

Suppose we contemplate expanding the capacity of the assembly department with the addition of 10 hours of labor time. The total capacity would then be 130 hours and the new restriction becomes

$$2X + 1.5Y \leq 130.$$

Our new feasible set is depicted in Figure 6 by the shaded area and its boundary. Assume that the cost of each additional hour of labor time remains at $2.50 and that the profit function is still equation (4.4). Then each vertex and its associated profit is

	Vertex	*Profit*
(1)	$X = 50$, $Y = 0$	$100.00
(2)	$X = 50$, $Y = 20$	$120.00
(3)	$X = 44$, $Y = 28$	$116.00
(4)	$X = 20$, $Y = 40$	$ 80.00
(5)	$X = 0$, $Y = 40$	$ 40.00
(6)	$X = 0$, $Y = 0$	$ 0.00

With this added capacity the optimal schedule of $X = 50$, $Y = 20$ will yield $120.00 of profit, or $7.00 more than the $113.00 of profit which is forthcoming from an assembly capacity of 120 hours. When this profit increment of $7.00 is divided by the increment of 10 hours of assembly capacity we obtain $.70, the incremental profit per unit of additional labor time. Since assembly labor costs $2.50 per hour, we would be willing to pay as much as $3.20 per hour for such additional labor time. In other words, if we were forced to pay $3.20 per hour for such additional labor (perhaps because of overtime requirements) we would break even on the added capacity.

The value, or worth, of $.70 per hour of added capacity represents the value of an hour of existing assembly capacity, too. While it has been given various appellations, the most frequent ones include "shadow" price, "accounting" price, "implicit" price, and "evaluator."

Since each point in the feasible set has an associated profit we can compute

Figure 6
FEASIBLE SET WITH ADDED ASSEMBLY CAPACITY

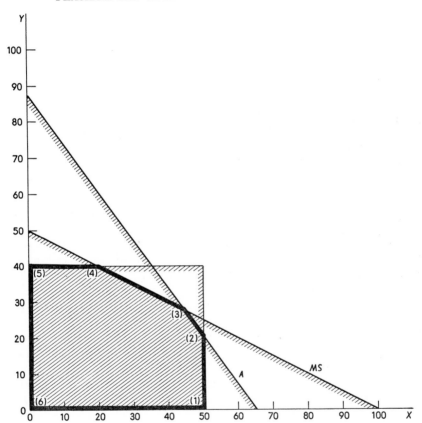

conceivably a shadow price for a given capacity for each of these points. For this reason, we must distinguish between the shadow price for a given capacity computed at the optimal point, called the "optimal shadow price," and the shadow price determined at a nonoptimal point. In the example above, then the shadow price of $.70 per hour of labor time in the assembly department is optimal.

An optimal shadow price may be computed for each department, each restriction. Of course, unless the department's capacity is providing the barrier to greater profits—i.e., is limiting—its shadow price will be zero. This reflects the fact that resources in short supply—i.e., those being used to capacity—are more valuable than the additional capacity which can be added to already existing abundant capacities. In the example at hand, the limiting capacities are the rate of demand for product A and the assembly department. Since a shadow price is the value of a unit of existing capacity, the sum of the shadow price of each restriction multiplied by its associated capacity must equal the total value of all capacities. While we will not prove the statement here, it happens that when this total value is computed with *optimal* shadow prices, it is always equal to the total profit of the optimum point—i.e., to the optimal profit. In other words, the total value of the capacities, when utilized optimally, is equal to the total optimal profit.

In the computation of a shadow price by the above method, the arbitrary change in capacity should never be so large as to render the capacity nonlimiting. In other words, the resulting capacity must be a barrier to greater profits. Observe that this condition was satisfied in the example above.

Expenditure Constraints

To return again to our original problem we note that its solution explicitly assumed that our limited resources were adequate to achieve any optimal production schedule. Suppose this is not the case. To be exact, suppose we have an amount of cash, say, C_u, available for both fixed and total variable costs and that expenditures for these costs must be paid in cash during the period from the available balance, C_u. Cash from sales to be made during the period will not be received until subsequent periods and hence, is not available for expenditure during the coming period. Therefore, our expenditures on variable factor inputs, V, cannot exceed $C_u - F$, or

$$V \leq C_u - F, \tag{4.5}$$

where F denotes fixed cash costs. Expression (4.5) becomes an operative restriction, a barrier which may narrow even more the attainable output combinations.

To illustrate, suppose $C_u = \$600.00$, $F = \$200.00$. Then $C_u - F = \$400.00$. Given our labor and raw material costs it must follow that V for our problem is given by

$$V = \$8.75X + \$10.25Y.$$

Therefore restriction (4.5) for our problem must be

$$\$8.75X + \$10.25Y \leq \$400.00. \tag{4.6}$$

Our new feasible set appears in Figure 7. It consists of the shaded area plus the points which lie on the boundary of this area. The expenditure limitation line is denoted by *EL*. Observe that now both the machine shop and the assembly department restrictions are no longer limiting—they have been pushed into the background by the new expenditure restriction.

With the profit function (4.4a)—i.e., $P = \$1.25X + \$.50Y$—we can proceed as before and find the corner of this new feasible set which yields maximum profits. Point (1) of Figure 7 is optimal but the best neighborhood point with integer co-ordinates is the point $X = 45$, $Y = 0$. This schedule

Figure 7
FEASIBLE OUTPUT AND SALES COMBINATIONS WITH EXPENDITURE LIMITATION

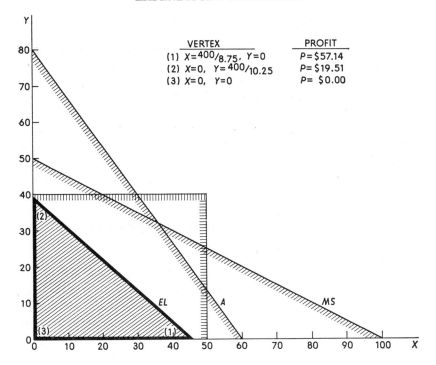

	VERTEX	PROFIT
(1)	$X = 400/8.75$, $Y = 0$	$P = \$57.14$
(2)	$X = 0$, $Y = 400/10.25$	$P = \$19.51$
(3)	$X = 0$, $Y = 0$	$P = \$0.00$

will consume $393.75 of the available cash and leave $6.25 in the cash balance.

The Shadow Price of the Cash Balance

Suppose, instead of contemplating the borrowing of cash we were to compute the optimal shadow price of the limiting cash balance. This value is equal to the *maximum* rate of interest we would pay per period for each additional dollar of borrowed funds. Since each dollar in the existing cash balance has an interest cost of zero, each dollar of incremental profit on the added funds could be expended for interest without impairing total profits.

This optimal shadow price expresses the optimal rate of earnings per period per dollar of cash. In this sense, any optimal shadow price represents an opportunity rate, the amount of profit foregone if one unit of a given capacity is withdrawn or switched to another project.

The optimal shadow price of the cash balance may be viewed not only as the maximum rate of interest to pay on borrowed funds but also as the worth of other liquid resources. For example, it may be viewed as the worth of an optimally employed dollar of trade credit. In such cases, failure to take the customary cash discount for prompt payment—i.e., taking advantage of the full period of credit but at the cost of foregoing the cash discount—may be regarded as a full-period credit cost as against the alternative of settling promptly with no penalty. In other words, if the trade credit liability is to be discharged during the discount period, the cost of the credit is zero and the shadow price of the cash balance reflects the full worth of a dollar of such an opportunity. However, if the obligation cannot be discharged within the discount period, then the foregone discount per dollar of credit is to be compared to the optimal shadow price of the cash balance. Such trade credit would not be acquired unless its cost per dollar were equal to or less than the optimal shadow price of the cash balance.

Similarly, the profitability of financing a larger output by obtaining cash from the sale of existing marketable securities may be compared to the optimal shadow price of the cash balance. A necessary condition for the switching of resources from securities to cash is that the return per dollar invested in securities be equal to or less than the optimal shadow price of the cash balance.

ADDITIONAL FINANCIAL CONSTRAINTS

Trade Credit and Accrued Labor

If we can obtain resources on a line of credit from suppliers, or labor time from our employees on an accrued basis, then, in the manner of the single-product case, we can extend the analysis to include such interest-free debt. As in the single-product case, we must find the optimal rates of output corresponding to a new expenditure limitation.

To illustrate, suppose we modify the previous problem to include the possibilities of using both trade credit and accrued labor as sources of financing. Suppose that trade credit for acquiring raw material only is available in any amount up to $25.00. Also assume that wages of up to $200.00 may also be obtained. From this point, the analysis may take one of several different directions depending upon the precise nature of the constraints, if any, to be imposed upon the cash balance. Assume, for sake of illustration, that available cash is to be used for outlays before any trade credit or accrued wage expense is to be incurred. Then, this problem can be solved in two stages. In stage one we find the optimal schedule on the assumption that available resources are restricted to the cash on hand. In stage two, we find the optimal expansion in output which is financed by trade credit and accrued labor.

The previous analysis provides the optimal schedule if available resources consist solely of the existing cash balance. This solution constitutes the completion of stage one. It consists of $X = 45$, $Y = 0$ and a residual cash balance of $6.25. However, note that it is profitable to expand output further since capacity and sales limitations have not been met and incremental profits are positive (see Figure 7).

In the analysis of stage two, we must determine the available labor capacities in both the machine shop and the assembly department and the available demand for both products. Since the cost of the stage-one schedule of 45 units of X and 0 units of Y will be paid from the $400.00 in cash which is available for variable costs, the available labor time in the machine shop for stage two is 55 hours (100 hours of capacity less 45 hours used to produce 45 units of X). Similarly, the assembly department has 30 hours of labor time available for stage two after deducting 90 hours required to produce 45 units of X from the capacity of 120 hours. Excess demand for X is 5, for Y, 40 units. If we let X' and Y' denote output of X beyond 45 units and output of Y beyond 0 units, respectively, these new limitations become

$$X' + 2Y' \leq 55 \text{ Machine shop.}$$
$$2X' + 1.5Y' \leq 30 \text{ Assembly.}$$
$$X' \leq 5 \text{ Unsatisfied demand for } X.$$
$$Y' \leq 40 \text{ Unsatisfied demand for } Y.$$

Expenditure restrictions consist now of the two statements:

$$\$ .75X' + \$ .50Y' \leq \$ 25.00 \text{ Trade credit.}$$
$$\$8.00X' + \$9.75Y' \leq \$200.00 \text{ Accrued labor.}$$

The graph of these restrictions is given by Figure 8. The constraints provided by the machine shop, assembly department, and available trade credit and accrued labor are denoted by MS, A, TC and AL respectively. The feasible set is represented by the shaded area and its boundary.

There are four points to be evaluated. Since each form of credit is assumed to be costless, the stage-one profit function applies to stage two, namely, equation (4.4a). The optimal point is $X' = 5$, $Y' = 20/1.5$, where we use $(5)\$.75 + (20/1.5)\$.50 = \$10.42$ of trade credit and $(5)\$8.00 + (20/1.5)\$9.75 = \$170.00$ of accrued labor expense.

The optimal output consists of 50 units of product A and $20/1.5$ units of product B, a fact which the student should verify. The excess cash of $6.25 carried over from stage one may be applied to reduce trade credit, accrued labor expense, or both.

Current Ratio Constraint

We may introduce other financial constraints, like a minimum current or acid test ratio. In Chapter 3 the problem involving a current ratio constraint assumed that trade credit was perfectly substitutable for *any* cash expenditure on variable costs. In the initial stages of the analysis to follow we shall assume that the only unit variable cost is labor expense, and this item may be paid in cash or accrued. This means that we can pool our liquid resources of cash with the available accrued labor. The analysis preceding this section explicitly assumed that pooling was prohibited, that credit was to be employed only if the cash balance was exhausted. We also had two distinct sources of credit—trade and accrued labor—and the use of each was restricted as to purpose:

Figure 8
FEASIBLE SET CORRESPONDING TO STAGE TWO

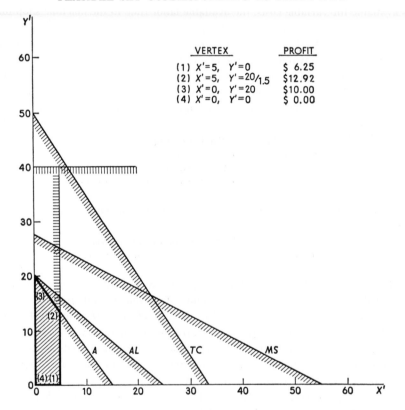

VERTEX			PROFIT
(1)	$X'=5,$	$Y'=0$	$ 6.25
(2)	$X'=5,$	$Y'=20/1.5$	$12.92
(3)	$X'=0,$	$Y'=20$	$10.00
(4)	$X'=0,$	$Y'=0$	$ 0.00

trade credit for acquiring raw material, accrued labor for the services of labor. For these reasons, we were led to the two-stage type of analysis.

Let us illustrate a problem in which we can pool liquid resources with accrued labor. Following this the problem will be modified to reflect the impact of a current ratio constraint. Let C_u, our beginning cash balance, be $400.00, $F = 100.00, and the maximum amount of AL be $300.00. Fixed costs must be met with cash payments during the current period. Unit variable costs of $8.00 for X and $9.75 for Y consist solely of labor expense. Any portion of the liability associated with variable costs may be paid in cash when the liability is incurred, or the payment may be delayed until the end of the next period in which case the amount owing at the end of the current period is reflected in the accrued labor account, a current liability. At any rate, total liquid resources available for labor expense must be $400.00 − $100.00 + $300.00 = $600.00. Since total variable costs are given by $8.00X + $9.75Y the liquid resource restriction becomes

$$\$8.00X + \$9.75Y \leq \$600.00. \tag{4.7}$$

Assume that the original demand and capacity restraints apply in this case—i.e., $X \leq 50$, $Y \leq 40$, as well as the capacity restrictions (4.2) and (4.3). The resulting feasible set appears in Figure 9 with the resource barrier (4.7) represented by the line EL.

With unit selling prices of X and Y remaining at $10.00 and $10.75 respectively, the profit function is still given by (4.4), namely, $P = \$2.00X + \$1.00Y$.

The student should verify the fact that the optimal rate of profits is provided by the point $(X = 50, Y = 13)$, our original solution. Total variable costs, which in this case equal total labor cost, amount to $526.75.

The extent to which we accrue labor expense, or pay for the liability as it is incurred will depend upon other policies. Suppose, for example, that one of

Figure 9

FEASIBLE SET WITH RESOURCES EXPANDED BY AVAILABLE CREDIT

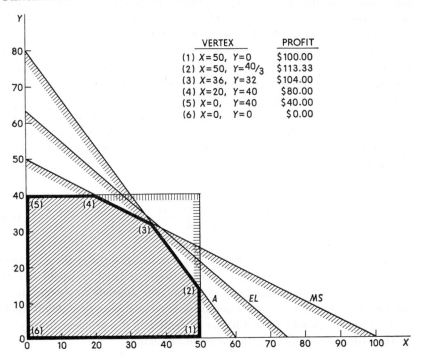

VERTEX	PROFIT
(1) X=50, Y=0	$100.00
(2) X=50, Y=40/3	$113.33
(3) X=36, Y=32	$104.00
(4) X=20, Y=40	$80.00
(5) X=0, Y=40	$40.00
(6) X=0, Y=0	$0.00

our policies provides that we exhaust the accrued labor potential before dipping into the cash balance which remains after paying fixed costs. Observe that utilizing cash for labor expense is not prohibited; rather, that the policy consists of a scheme of priorities in which available accrued labor expense is to be used first, and only when this source is used to the limit do we then resort to the cash balance. It is in this sense that we speak of the policy: preservation of the cash balance. If our policy provides for the preservation of the cash balance, then the optimal production schedule provides that we employ credit to the limit of $AL = \$300.00$, which implies that the beginning cash balance is reduced by a total of \$326.75—\$226.75 to meet variable costs and \$100.00 for fixed costs.

Now following the Chapter 3 procedure, let us assume that β—the proportion of the total dollar value of our sales on account—is equal to $\frac{3}{4}$ and that payment for such credit sales will not be received until sometime during the following period. One fourth of the sales volume is therefore for cash and, let us assume, such cash may be used for expenditures during the current period.

Since the maximum amount of accrued labor is used by the previous solution, these additional conditions do not alter the solution values of $X = 50$, $Y = 13$, and $AL = \$300.00$. However, cash from current sales in the amount of \$159.94—i.e., $\frac{1}{4}[\$10.00(50) + \$10.75(13)]$—is available for expenditure during the current period. Therefore, the cash balance need not be reduced by \$326.75 but only by $\$326.75 - \$159.94 = \$166.81$. At the end of the period the cash balance will be \$233.19, receivables will equal \$479.81, and current liabilities will amount to \$300.00. If we assume that these are the only current assets and current liabilities, the current ratio would then be $(\$479.81 + \$233.19)/\$300.00 = \$713.00/\$300.00$.

Let us modify the problem further by introducing an additional constraint. Suppose we seek to preserve the cash balance subject to the constraint that the current ratio must equal three. Since our current ratio for the above solution, \$713/\$300, is greater than one and less than three, and since our end-of-period cash balance is greater than zero, it is possible to increase our current ratio by the substitution of cash for current liabilities. To solve for the optimal amount of accrued labor and the optimal cash drain, d, we define, as in Chapter 3, the current ratio restriction as

$$\frac{\$479.81 + \$233.19 - d}{\$300.00 - d} = 3, \qquad (4.8)$$

where $d \leq \$233.19$. Thus $d = \$93.50$, a value which satisfies the constraint $d \leq \$233.19$. However, if this constraint were violated it would not be possible to achieve the planned rate of output. The schedule would have to be modified to reflect this constraint and there is no assurance that output would not have to be reduced to zero. Chapter 13 deals with this problem directly.

The cash budget which emerges is given as follows:

Cash Budget for Period 1

Cash receipts: Cash expenditures............$420.25

    From cash sales of X........$125.00

    From cash sales of Y......... 34.94

        Total................$159.94

Deficit...................... 260.31

        Total............$420.25   Total.............$420.25

BORROWING SHORT-TERM FUNDS

The preceding discussion has dealt with noncost short-term credit. We now introduce the possibility of borrowing money at a given rate of interest for the purpose of financing output. These funds may be employed to hire the services of labor, to acquire raw materials, or both. In this sense, the analysis is simplified, but in another sense we have an added complication: since the amount of interest constitutes a cost, the profit function must be altered to reflect this fact.

We shall assume that our given resources—i.e., those that we have at hand—are to be exhausted first before recourse is had to borrow money at interest. Let r denote the rate of interest per period for which funds are available. The analysis is then made in two stages. First, find the point of optimum profits corresponding to our given resources. If such limited resources are a barrier to greater profits, then stage-two analysis proceeds exactly as it did in our earlier example of trade credit financing. The unit costs of both X' and Y' are increased by the financing charges r ($8.75) and $r(\$10.25)$, respectively, and hence our profit function becomes

$$P = [\$10.00 - (1 + r)\$8.75]X' + [\$10.75 - (1 + r)\$10.25]Y'. \qquad (4.9)$$

It may happen that r is sufficiently large to produce, for some product, a negative incremental profit. If so, then the rate of output for such a product is *frozen* at its stage-one solution.

Recall that in stage-two analysis each capacity limitation, each restriction, must be adjusted to reflect the impact of the solution at stage one. An expenditure limitation equation is then defined which brings into the problem the maximum amount of funds that are available at the rate of interest r. For example, suppose we may borrow up to $500.00 at 2 per cent interest per period. Then the stage-two expenditure limitation statement becomes

$$(1 + .02)\$8.75X' + (1 + .02)\$10.25Y' \leq \$500.00. \qquad (4.10)$$

Expressions (4.9) and (4.10), in combination with the adjusted capacity restrictions, constitute the frame for solving the borrowed funds problem.

Of course, as funds are borrowed to expand output, the current section of our balance sheet will reflect this short-term indebtedness. It may be that the output which maximizes profits also entails a level of bank borrowing which violates a current position constraint. . . .

LINEAR PROGRAMING—A FINAL EXAMPLE

Assume that we are producing two products, 1 and 2, with rates of output X_1 and X_2 respectively, that we have one productive capacity, an assembly operation with a capacity of 100 hours per period, and that we have an opening cash balance of $1,000.00 Cash from current sales will not be received until the next period while all variable costs must be paid in cash when incurred. Our problem is to maximize the value of the profit function

$$P = 20X_1 + 20X_2,$$

subject to the restrictions

$$2X_1 + X_2 \leq 100.00 \text{ Assembly capacity,}$$
$$10X_1 + 20X_2 \leq \$1,000.00 \text{ Cash balance,}$$

and to the nonnegativity restriction

$$X_1, X_2 \geq 0.$$

Observe that all necessary incremental profits, coefficients of production, and coefficients of cash utilization are given in the above expressions.

On the assumption that fractional products may be produced and sold, the student should verify the following results. The optimal value for both X_1 and X_2 is 100/3, the optimal profit is $4,000/3, and both capacities are limiting. The optimal shadow price per unit of assembly capacity is $20.00/3, per unit of opening cash balance, 2/3. The total value of existing capacities must be ($20.00/3) 100 + (2/3) $1,000.00 or $4,000/3, which is equal, of course, to the optimal profit.

Observe the difference in procedure which is required to compute shadow prices when an outlay must be made for utilizing a unit of existing capacity versus the case where no outlay is required for the same purpose. The latter case corresponds to the above example where it is assumed that no costs are incurred to use either a unit of the 100 units of assembly capacity or $1.00 of the opening cash balance. The shadow price of a unit of a given capacity is then the change in profits if one unit of that capacity, obtained without charge, is added to the existing capacity and optimally employed. If, however, an outlay is required to use a unit of the existing capacity, e.g., labor time, then the shadow price of that capacity is the change in profits if one unit of labor time, at existing unit wage costs, is added to the existing supply of labor and optimally employed.

The first example in this chapter contained the important assumption that the available cash was more than adequate to achieve any optimal rate of output with existing production and demand capacities. Since the capacity of the cash balance was not limiting, the shadow price per unit of opening cash was zero. And since we had excess cash we could speak of the shadow price of, say, a unit of machine shop labor time, as the maximum amount we would spend for an additional unit of that capacity. In the example at hand, however, the opening cash balance is *limiting* and if we were to acquire one additional unit of assembly capacity from funds in our opening cash balance we would be foregoing the value—i.e., the profit—which those funds would generate if they were used for operations rather than for the expansion of assembly capacity. In this case, therefore, we must evaluate a joint cost, which can be done as follows. Assuming that the unit of added assembly capacity will not endure beyond the current period (that it is, for example, a unit of labor time) then the maximum amount we would pay for an added unit of assembly capacity, optimally employed, from our *opening* cash balance must be the optimal shadow price per unit of assembly capacity divided by the optimal shadow price per unit of opening cash balance, or ($20.00/3)/(2/3) = $10.00. In other words, an expenditure of $10.00 from our opening cash balance (which will leave only $990.00 for expenditure on variable costs) will entail sacrificing (2/3) $10.00 or $20.00/3 in profits, the value of the unit of added assembly capacity.

To see that optimal profits remain unchanged after this adjustment consider the following argument. Since assembly capacity is now 101 units we could give up a unit of X_2 and add a unit of X_1. In the cash equation $20.00 is freed by reducing X_2 by one unit. $10.00 of this amount is used to pay for the additional unit of assembly capacity and the remaining $10.00 to finance the additional unit of output in X_1. Since marginal profit of X_1 is equal to the marginal profit of X_2 total profits remain unaltered.

If we were required to incur a cash cost for each dollar of trade credit, then the maximum amount we would pay for such credit is ⅔ of a dollar. As was pointed out before, such a cost would arise if one were to forego a cash discount. In such cases the appropriate cost per dollar of credit for comparison to the shadow price of the cash balance is the ratio of the size of the discount to the amount of the *net* rather than the gross billing.

We have noted earlier that suppliers of resources often either explicitly or implicitly require that we maintain a level of liquid assets in some ratio to our total current liabilities. Suppose a trade creditor specifies that we maintain at least one dollar in the cash balance for every three dollars of credit he extends. Trade credit is assumed to be perfectly substitutable for any cash outlay. Is such an offer acceptable?

Each dollar which is preserved in the cash balance is foregoing ⅔ of a dollar of profit, but this enables us to obtain three dollars of trade credit which will yield $3.00(⅔) or $2.00 of profit. The net difference is $2.00 − (⅔)$1.00, a positive value and therefore a necessary condition for accepting the offer is satisfied.

It is essential to remind the student that a given shadow price remains valid only so long as the associated capacity is still limiting. For example, if the $3.00 increase in trade credit above had rendered the liquid resource constraint nonlimiting, the shadow price of each dollar of trade credit would not have been ⅔ of one dollar.

SUMMARY

This chapter was concerned with determining the optimal allocation of resources in two-product projects when we are faced with (1) certainty and (2) payoff functions and constraints which are linear expressions. In such cases linear programing may be applied to solve the problem. This tool consists of maximizing (or minimizing) a linear function subject to a set of linear constraints. The optimal allocation of resources determines the production schedule—i.e., the "product mix"—and the extent to which alternative sources of funds are used.

To solve a problem with the use of linear programing observe the following steps:

1. Frame the problem by translating into analytic expressions the objective and the restrictions. If linear programing is to be used these expressions, of course, must either be linear or safely approximated by linear forms.

2. Graph the restrictions and the nonnegativity constraints. Problems which cannot be graphed can be solved by the methods of Chapter 13.

3. If a feasible set does not exist then it is impossible to go further. If it exists then locate the co-ordinates of its corners by solving the pairs of equations which intersect on the boundary of the set.

4. Find the value of the objective function corresponding to each corner.

5. The vertex associated with the maximum (or the minimum, as the case may be) value of the objective function is the optimal point.

A shadow price indicates the value of a unit of capacity and hence, the maximum additional amount we would pay per unit of additional capacity under the specified conditions of the problem.

If different sources of funds, such as the cash balance and trade credit, are perfectly substitutable, then their available supplies may be pooled and expressed in one restriction. If, however, one source is to be exhausted before another is tapped, then the problem may be solved in two stages. If substitution is not possible, then separate expressions must be developed, one for each restriction.

If the borrowing of cash at a given rate of interest is an available alternative, then this problem, too, may be solved in two stages. Here the objective function for stage two must reflect the interest cost. This will solve the problem, however, on condition that there are no current position restrictions.

The optimal shadow price of the cash balance indicates the optimal return per dollar of opening cash, the maximum rate of interest, per period which the firm can afford to pay for borrowed money and still break even, and the lowest rate of return which must be forthcoming from marketable securities in order to hold, for the coming period, one dollar of securities rather than cash. It also enables one to compute the cost of other financial constraints, such as minimum current, quick, or acid test ratios.

APPLICATION OF LINEAR PROGRAMMING
TO FINANCIAL BUDGETING
AND THE COSTING OF FUNDS*

By A. Charnes,† W. W. Cooper,‡ and M. H. Miller§

I. INTRODUCTION

THE PURPOSE of this paper is to explore ways in which the theorems and computational apparatus of linear programming might be brought to bear on the allocation of funds within an enterprise. The rational deployment of a firm's resources requires (simultaneous) consideration of at least the following closely related questions.

1. Given the structure of the firm's assets, what operating program—in the sense of plans for production, purchases, and sales over the relevant planning interval—will yield the firm the greatest prospective net returns in the light of its profit and other objectives? That linear programming can contribute to a solution here has been amply demonstrated by its many successful applications to such planning problems (some quite large) in a variety of contexts.[1] For a number of reasons reported applications have so far been concentrated heavily in the production area; but, as we shall try to show, there is no reason

---

* Reprinted by permission from *The Journal of Business*, 32, (January 1959), pp. 20–46. This paper is a revised version of an ONR research report which was first presented at the Symposium on Operational Models, jointly sponsored by the Chemical Corps Engineering Command and New York University held at Army Chemical Center, Maryland, January 17, 1957. Part of the research underlying this paper was undertaken for the project "Planning and Control of Industrial Operations" at Carnegie Institute of Technology and part for the project Methodological Aspects of Management Research" at Purdue University. Both projects are under contract with the United States Office of Naval Research. Reproduction of this paper in whole or in part is permitted for any purpose of the United States government, Contract Nonr-760-(01), Project NRO47-011, and Contract Nonr-1100-(05), Project NRO47-016.

† Research Professor of Applied Mathematics and Economics, Northwestern University.

‡ Ford Distinguished Research Professor, Graduate School of Industrial Administration, Carnegie Institute of Technology.

§ Edward Eagle Brown Professor of Finance and Economics, University of Chicago.

[1] See, e.g., [6] (in the Bibliography) and the references therein.

why the same techniques cannot be used for financial planning or, more to the point, joint operating and financial planning.

2. What is the "yield" to the firm of each of the various possible changes in its asset structure, assuming that these assets are employed to maximum advantage? Here linear programming offers a way of bypassing some of the technical difficulties which have been encountered in connection with attempts to evaluate projects (as proposed, e.g., in [16] or [21]) on the basis of their "rates of return."[2] In addition, with a programming formulation, some of the harder parts of the task of tracing through the interactions of proposed investments with each other and with existing facilities can be left to the mathematics.

3. What is the opportunity cost of funds in the firm, in the sense of the prospective rate of yield on an increment of funds committed to the enterprise and optimally employed during the planning interval? Knowledge of this opportunity cost is required for determining, among other things, whether the "yield" of a proposed investment is sufficient to justify its undertaking. Under some conditions this opportunity cost of funds can be determined in advance and independently of the actual operating and investment decisions. Such is the case when the firm has the power to borrow or lend unlimited quantities of funds in the capital markets at a constant rate. When, on the other hand, the firm is subject to "capital rationing"[3] or when its planning must be undertaken subject to liquidity constraints, the use of some predetermined external yield rate for purposes of internal allocations is not, in general, appropriate or feasible.[4] Here, again, however, a linear programming approach may represent one way to by-pass some of the difficulties. It is possible, as we shall show, to modify standard linear programming formulations by incorporating the funds components of the profit objective directly among the constraining relations on programs. This procedure provides a measure of the marginal internal yield of funds and one which takes account of the feedback between operations and finance when funds are limited. It can also be made to yield evaluations of some of the "qualitative" restrictions which are features of many actual financing arrangements.

Since linear programming is still a relatively new tool of management, it may perhaps be well to begin with some preliminary remarks about its nature.

---

[2] Rate of return is defined for this purpose as that rate of interest which makes the present value of the project equal to its cost. For discussions of the technical deficiencies of this method of ranking projects (which include possible non-uniqueness and possible inability to rank mutually exclusive projects) see [26], [29], and [22].

[3] For the analysis presented here "capital rationing" will be taken in its familiar sense of implying a situation in which a firm has access to only a maximal amount of funds. Higher offer prices either will not call forth additional funds or will call them only on terms which are unacceptable—as when creditors or new investors stipulate significant changes in the control of the firm (see [14], [15], and [20]).

[4] In particular, it is not feasible to use an external rate for, say, computing "present values" of proposed projects or to serve as a "cut-off" rate for screening projects. For a demonstration of the inadequacy of these standard approaches when capital markets are imperfect see [22].

II. LINEAR PROGRAMMING: DIRECT AND DUAL RELATIONS

Consider, for example, the following ingredients of a very simple buying, selling, and storage problem for a warehouse manager contemplating possible purchase, sale, and storage patterns over the $j = 1, 2, \ldots, n$ periods which constitute his "planning horizon." Let

B = the fixed warehouse capacity;
A = the initial stock of inventory in the warehouse;
x_j = the amount to be purchased in period j;   (1)
y_j = the amount to be sold in period j;
p_j = sales price per unit prevailing in period j; and
c_j = purchase price per unit prevailing in period j.

Given the p_j and c_j, how should this firm program its activities—that is, determine values x_j and y_j—in order to maximize its profits?

All programs must honor the constraints. As an example, let it be assumed that the firm sells under conditions of "perfect competition" so that potential sales at a given price p_j may be of any size. Sales must, however, be executed from inventory on hand at the start of any period so that at, say, period i the cumulative sales of the firm must conform to

$$\sum_{j=1}^{i} y_j \leq A + \sum_{j=1}^{i-1} x_j.$$

Also, while the firm can buy any quantity of goods, it cannot store more than its net available capacity allows; that is,

$$\sum_{j=1}^{i} x_j \leq B - A + \sum_{j=1}^{i} y_j.$$

The problem as described can be represented by the following mathematical model.[5]

$$\text{maximize } \pi = \sum_{j=1}^{n} p_j y_j - \sum_{j=1}^{n} c_j x_j \qquad (2a)$$

subject to the $i = 1, 2, \ldots, n$ buying constraints,

---

[5] Notice that what is being maximized is *undiscounted* cumulative profits. This assumption can be interpreted as implying that an "adequate" allotment of funds has been granted to the manager and that no further decisions about withdrawals of funds or new commitment of funds are to be made until the horizon period is reached. Later examples will cover cases in which the funds allotted may not be "adequate" to permit the manager to undertake every profitable transaction as well as cases in which external market opportunities for borrowing and lending are considered explicitly. The relation of these and other cases to the standard discounting approach in dynamic models will be discussed further below.

$$\sum_{j=1}^{i} x_j - \sum_{j=1}^{i} y_j \leq B - A, \tag{2b}$$

and to the n selling constraints,

$$-\sum_{j=1}^{i-1} x_j + \sum_{j=1}^{i} y_j \leq A. \tag{2c}$$

Also the variables

$$x_j, y_j \geq 0, j = 1, 2, \ldots, n \tag{2d}$$

for all purchases and sales are constrained to assume non-negative values.

If each of the mathematical expressions (2b)–(2c) are written explicitly for $i = 1, 2, \ldots, n$, the kinds of expressions obtained are shown in (3a) and (3b).

$$
\begin{aligned}
x_1 && -y_1 && \leq B - A \\
x_1 + x_2 && -y_1 - y_2 && \leq B - A \\
\cdots\cdots && \cdots\cdots && \cdots\cdots \\
x_1 + x_2 + \cdots + x_n && -y_1 - y_2 - \cdots - y_n && \leq B - A
\end{aligned}
\tag{3a}
$$

and

$$
\begin{aligned}
&& y_1 && \leq A \\
-x_1 && +y_1 + y_2 && \leq A \\
-x_1 - x_2 && +y_1 + y_2 + y_3 && \leq A \\
\cdots\cdots && \cdots\cdots && \cdots\cdots \\
-x_1 - x_2 - \cdots - x_{n-1} && +y_1 + y_2 + y_3 + \cdots + y_n && \leq A.
\end{aligned}
\tag{3b}
$$

When the coefficients which appear alongside the variables in these expressions are detached and arrayed, as in Figure 1, a rather striking pattern, called the "structure" of the model, emerges. The non-zero coefficients[6] are either $+1$ or -1. They can be arrayed as a series of triangles (with one smaller than the others) positioned as shown. To check that this is so, simply drop the variables shown at the top of the table (corresponding to the stub labeled "λ") alongside the 1's, 0's, and -1's as schematically indicated by the triangles in the body of the table. Form the resulting expressions, one for each row of the diagram. The triangles opposite the t's (in the stub) will then give the expressions (3a). Those alongside the u's will give the expressions (3b). Finally, if the process is continued into the last row (labeled "p"), the functional (2a), for which a maximum is sought, can be secured.

---

[6] I.e., the first expression in (3a) may be considered to be the same as $+ 1x_1 + 0x_2 + \cdots + 0x_n - 1y_1 - 0y_2 - \cdots - 0y_n \leq B - A$, and the same kinds of expressions may be written for the other constraints. All coefficients are then seen to be $+1$, -1, or 0.

Figure 1
SCHEMA FOR A SIMPLE WAREHOUSING MODEL

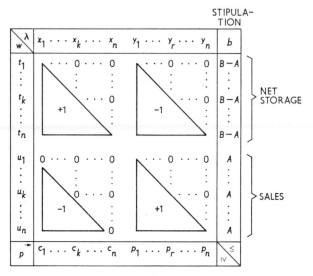

The algebraic expressions thus secured may be called the "direct" problem. To each such direct linear programming problem there is always another (linear programming) problem which can be formed from exactly the same data. It is called the "dual" problem.

The dual to (2) is

$$\text{minimize } E = \sum_{k=1}^{n} (B - A)t_k + \sum_{k=1}^{n} Au_k \tag{4b}$$

subject to

$$\sum_{i=k}^{n} t_i - \sum_{i=k+1}^{n} u_i \geq -c_k, \quad k = 1, 2, \ldots, n \tag{4c}$$

and to

$$-\sum_{i=r}^{n} t_i + \sum_{i=r}^{n} u_i \geq p_r, \quad r = 1, 2, \ldots, n. \tag{4c}$$

That is, values are sought for the variables u and t which make E a minimum while honoring the $2n$ expressions, (4b) and (4c), along with the non-negativity requirements

$$t_i, u_i \geq 0, \quad i = 1, 2, \ldots, n. \tag{4d}$$

The schema of Figure 1 assists in forming the dual as well as the direct problem. Whereas the direct problem was formed from the *rows*, its dual is formed from the *columns* of this same table. Thus, at $k = 1$, the first dual inequality is secured by positioning the variables t and u alongside the $+1$'s, the -1's (and the single zero) on the left margins of the two left-hand triangles to give $t_1 + t_2 + \cdots + t_k + \cdots + t_n - u_2 - u_3 - \cdots - u_r - \cdots - u_n \geqq - c_1$. Continuing in this same manner until the right-hand vertices of these two triangles on the left are reached, the final dual constraint for (4b) is found to give $t_n \geqq - c_n$, since u_n has a zero coefficient in this column. Continuing to the margin of the next two triangles, the first of the n expressions in (4c) is found to be $- t_1 - t_2 - \cdots \rightarrow t_k - \cdots - t_n + u_1 + u_2 + \cdots + u_r + \cdots + u_n \geqq p_1$. Each of the remaining constraints is found in like manner until the final one is secured as $t_n + u_n \geqq p_n$. The functional which gives the value E for (4a) for any given t's and u's is obtained from the right-hand or "stipulations" *column* as

$$(B - A)t_1 + (B - A)t_2 + \cdots + (B - A)t_{n} + Au_1 + Au_2 \cdots + Au_n.$$

There is a theorem, known as the "dual theorem of linear programming,"[7] which asserts that the optimum values, min. $E = E^*$ and max. $\pi = \pi^*$,[8] are equal, so that $E^* = \pi^*$.[9] In the present case this gives

$$\sum_{j=1}^{n} p_j y_j^* - \sum_{j=1}^{n} c_j x_j^* = \sum_{k=1}^{n} (B - A)t_k^* + \sum_{k=1}^{n} Au_k^*. \qquad (5a)$$

To make sense as an equation, both sides of these expressions must give the same units of measure. The p_j's and c_j's are in terms of dollars per unit and the y_j's and x_j's are in terms of the units—say, tons—in which purchases and sales can be effected in period j. Thus, π^* represents the total dollars (of profit) which can be (optimally) obtained over the entire horizon $j = 1, 2, \ldots, n$. The right-hand side, which gives E^*, must therefore equal the same number of dollars. Now $(B - A)$ is, say, tons of net warehouse capacity available, while A represents tons of starting inventory. Therefore, t_k^* must be stated in terms of dollars per ton of net warehouse capacity available in period k, and u_k^* must, similarly, be in dollars per unit of initial (opening) inventory considered at period k.

The t^*'s and u^*'s can therefore be used to "evaluate" these assets. To see what is involved, suppose the firm acquires (or wishes to consider acquiring)

---

[7] See [24(2)], where it was first given.

[8] Certain additional refinements which are primarily directed to questions of mathematical consistency and the existence of solutions are also contained in this theorem but will not be dealt with here (see [24(2)]). For a more elementary exposition (and related management interpretations) see [10]. The relation of this theorem to general economic questions is studied in [17].

[9] Starred values will be used to indicate optimum values.

in, say, period 1 an extra ton of warehouse capacity. Then these same dual evaluators may apply[10] to give[11]

$$\sum_{k=1}^{n} (B+1)t_k^* - \sum_{k=1}^{n} A(t_k^* - u_k^*)$$

$$= (B+1) \sum_{k=1}^{n} t_k^* - A \sum_{k=1}^{n} (t_k^* - u_k^*), \quad (5b)$$

with a new total dollar value E^{**} which is larger than E^* by

$$\sum_{k=1}^{n} t_k^*.$$

Since the dual theorem also applies to this new problem, it asserts (without requiring advance knowledge of the actual direct program composition) that optimal use of this new resource makes possible new program values which will give a new total profit

$$\pi^{**} = \pi^* + \sum_{k=1}^{n} t_k^* \geq \pi^*.[12]$$

In this sense the values of the dual variables serve as "evaluators." They provide, beforehand, a means of determining the consequent increments (or decrements) in profits, costs—and like values—which can be secured if optimal use is made of proposed asset changes.[13]

The enhanced power that linear programming receives from the relations

---

[10] These remarks will be qualified later to indicate how ranges within which the t^*'s and u^*'s remain unchanged can be ascertained.

[11] Note that $\Sigma(t_k^* - u_k^*)$ gives the net inventory value, the terms t_k^* representing costs (i.e., opportunity costs) resulting from the utilization of otherwise available warehouse space and the u_k^* representing gains resulting from either (or both) purchase economies or selling possibilities. Cf. [5] for further discussion.

[12] The inequality allows the case $\pi^{**} = \pi^*$ but never $\pi^{**} < \pi^*$, because, by virtue of the non-negativity constraints, every $t_k^* \geq 0$, so that

$$\sum_{k=1}^{n} t_k^* \geq 0.$$

[13] More generally, these are called changes in the "stipulations" to allow for the fact that they are not confined to physical assets but may also apply to constraints arising from prescribed policies of the business, legal requirements, etc. For example, a policy which requires "relatively stable" employment may become a constraining relation with a stipulation. A constraining relation is to be distinguished from the "objective" (e.g., profit maximization), which is incorporated in the functional. See [10] for further discussion.

of duality that have been established will be illustrated in the sections to follow. This will be done by tracing through, *mutatis mutandis*, the simultaneous interactions of asset changes and optimal program compositions which can be generated from one type of demonstration model. It will then be apparent how the dual theorem makes it possible to consider one linear problem in place of what might otherwise appear as a series of complicated non-linear problems.

This last statement is predicated on the choice of a suitable rule of computation. That is, the rule must be selected so that, in solving one problem (direct or dual), a solution to the other one is also secured without extra calculations. Since such rules of computation are available (e.g., the simplex method of Dantzig [24(1)]), this choice can always be made, and there need be no trouble on this point.

III. FINANCIAL CONSTRAINTS AND THEIR EVALUATION

To see how the methods of linear programming (including duality) can help to disentangle some of the interactions between financial and operating policies, consider what happens when the dual theorem is applied to financial (liquidity) constraints such as

$$\sum_{j=1}^{i} c_{j-\epsilon} x_{j-\epsilon} - \sum_{j=1}^{i} p_{j-\tau} y_{j-\tau} \leq M_0 = \underline{M} \equiv \overline{M}, \ i = 1, \ldots, n. \qquad (6)$$

In these expressions the subscripts indicate lags,[14] $j - \epsilon$ and $j - \tau$, in, respectively, payments and receipts; M_0 represents initial cash[15] available; and $\underline{M}$, a balance which it is (for whatever reasons)[16] desired to maintain at all times.

Each of these financial stipulations in equation (6)—whose force is to limit purchases by the manager to the original allotment of funds plus the cash in excess of required minimal holdings generated by operations—can be associated with a dual variable. Let these variables be called v_k. The dimensional analysis given in connection with equations (5a) and (5b) can be immediately extended to these new constraining relations. It is then seen that the v's must be stated in terms of dollars per dollar invested—assuming optimal use of the additional investment—or, more precisely, dollars per unit time per

---

[14] Leads may also be inserted, and even more complicated expressions may be used. For this exposition, however, only the simplest cases (which retain some degree of interest) will be examined.

[15] Other measures of liquidity may, of course, be used if desired, and constraints may be entered for each relevant component of liquidity at any or all time periods for which they may be pertinent.

[16] E.g., because of an allotment schedule, transaction or precautionary motivation, etc. If desired, the stipulations may be altered to M_i, different for each time period.

dollar invested (or withdrawn). These are the dimensions of compound interest.

IV. LINEAR PROGRAMMING AND MODEL TYPES

At this point it may be helpful to outline the strategy which will be followed in the remaining sections of this paper. Attention will be centered on questions of interpretation rather than on issues, such as computational efficiency or mathematical theory. Numerical examples and schematic illustrations (such as Fig. 1) will therefore be used to carry the burden of the analysis. These examples (and resulting interpretations) will be oriented mainly toward standard constructs in economics and finance, and only the simplest kinds of cases will be used. For example, even though it may seem to lend an air of artificiality to the "financial constraints," risk and related considerations will be left aside in order to avoid introducing still further complications into this exposition.[17]

The prototype from which these examples will be synthesized has already been given in the expressions (2). In that form it is known as the "warehousing model" of linear programming. Originally formulated by Cahn [2],[18] this model has been generalized from its original formulation as a single-commodity, one-warehouse, fixed-price example to include multiple warehouses and products, prices which vary with quantities bought and sold, etc.[19]

The warehousing model to be used here will cover only the single-product, one-warehouse case. Suitably adjusted, it contains all essentials which are required for the proposed yield analyses in extremely simple form. These include fixed facilities, inventory carrying charges (to be imputed), and transactions across time which involve payables and receivables (and, therefore, a distinction between cash flows and accruals).

Attention should be drawn toward one other aspect of these models. Most linear programming applications to management planning have revealed families of rather striking structural similarities in a wide variety of situations. These structural elements have made it possible to devise analytical and computational techniques which, when compared with more general techniques, are highly efficient for models with these structural properties. This has made it possible to deal with problems whose size would otherwise be forbidding.

The transportation model of linear programming is an example which can be used to illustrate one such "model type." Originally formulated for optimal

---

[17] Cf. [11] for further discussion. Later papers will include such probabilistic (risk) considerations.

[18] The formulation given here, however, rests on the one first used in [3] and [5].

[19] See [5] for further discussion and suggested methods of computation for these models. See also [1] for a formulation of one case into functional equations—a formulation which is equivalent in that it yields the same (optimum) solutions as its algebraic counterpart.

movement of goods from origins to destinations,[20] it has since been general-ized[21] in ways which also make it applicable to such seemingly alien problems as the assignment of personnel to jobs, the analysis of electrical networks,[22] etc. Moreover, when "model approximations"[23] are allowed, still wider classes of problems are encompassed within this one type. Thus, as exhibited in [6],[24] machine- and shop-loading models of certain kinds can also be included in this category.

As a different example, consider the problem of blending gasolines in a refinery.[25] If the elements for a "blending model" are diagrammed, a rather striking pattern of rectangles and echelons is obtained for the non-zero coefficients. These same elements are found in many processes of chemical manufacture, in mixing formula feeds for animals, and even in models that have been used for studying the traffic flows in a network of city streets.[26]

Still other examples could be cited. The potential importance of these model types as a guide for applications is probably sufficiently clear. In any event, these ideas have been discussed elsewhere and therefore need not be repeated here in full detail.[27] The essential notion is that many (if not most) problems of management planning can be synthesized from various combina-tions of a few model types (or approximations) which serve as basic ingre-dients.

Operations research, or related activities, will provide the tests required to establish the exact scope of potential applications of the model-type con-structs. In the meantime there is a sufficient accumulation of evidence to make a study of any member of one of these classes a worthwhile scientific pursuit.[28]

There is little question that the warehouse model, suitably generalized, is an important member of one such class: "The warehousing problem is of interest in its own right. It is also worthy of study for other reasons. On the one hand it represents a generalization of simpler transportation models;[29] on the other hand it is the simplest example of a large and important class of

---

[20] See, e.g., [24(3)].

[21] These generalizations have become known as "distribution models," which are intended to be comprehended here as models of "transportation type."

[22] Including non-linear networks of both electrical and hydraulic varieties. See, e.g., [7].

[23] I.e., models which have (or can be made to have) approximately the structure of a known (exact) model type.

[24] See this reference for further discussion, including a discussion of methods for securing and controlling the approximations.

[25] Cf. [9]; see also [19] for a report of further extensions and applications.

[26] See [4].

[27] See [5] and [6].

[28] E.g., for purposes of devising special methods of analysis, study of its properties in relation to other members of the class, etc.

[29] Cf. [28] for an explicit formulation given after these remarks were published.

dynamic models."[30] Indeed, in the latter connection, it may serve as a model approximation for much more complicated problems.[31]

V. WAREHOUSE MODEL WITH A FINANCIAL CONSTRAINT

Instead, therefore, of considering a large and complicated example of the kind that might occur in practice, a smaller one can be used to study essential properties of the larger ones in ways which can be usefully applied to them as well. For this purpose a small "warehouse model" involving only ten variables and fifteen constraints[32] can be used to initiate the desired explorations. Further possible extensions (e.g., from a one-commodity to multiple-commodity cases) will become evident as the discussion proceeds.

To simplify the presentation (and analysis), it is desirable to transform the problem, commencing with Figure 1, into a simpler equivalent. Therefore, by reference to equation (4), define the new cumulative variables

$$T_k = \sum_{i=k}^{n} t_i$$

$$U_k = \sum_{i=k}^{n} u_i \tag{7}$$

so that $T_n \equiv t_n$ and $U_n \equiv u_n$. Then the entire problem in (4) may be stated in the following simpler form:

$$\text{min. } E = (B - A)T_1 + AU_1$$

subject to

$$T_k \geq U_{k+1} - c_k, \; T_{k-1} \geq T_k, \; T_n \geq - c_n,$$
$$U_r \geq T_r + p_r, \; U_{r-1} \geq U_r, \tag{8}$$
$$T_r, \; U_r \geq 0,$$

where $U_0 \equiv U_1$, $T_0 \equiv T_1$, by reference to these cumulative variables.[33]

---

[30] Quoted from [5]. See also [12] for a formulation with financial constraints in the context of "dyadic" linear programming models.

[31] See the model discussed in [6] for scheduling (over time) the flows of oil from a series of wells, while allowing for non-linearities arising from pressure drops due to the oil flows.

[32] There are actually twenty-five constraints when non-negativity (of each variable) is also counted. (Undue worry about questions of consistency or uniqueness may be avoided by noting that the basic orientation is toward *inequalities* rather than *equations*.)

[33] Henceforth all values c_j, p_j will be assumed to be non-negative so that constraints such as $T_n \geq -c_n$ may be regarded as redundant and eliminated from further consideration.

The relevance of the dual relation between (2) and (4) has already been noted. This same relation evidently holds between (2) and (8), since the latter, in essence, simply cumulates the variables (and hence their values) in (4). In other words, the proper cumulants for any solution of (4) give the results required in (8); conversely, by a suitable arrangement for decumulation, any results secured for (8) can be used to give the corresponding values of (4).

An optimal solution of a direct problem such as (2) automatically provides the values w_i^* for the corresponding dual variables. They may be read immediately from the optimum "tableau"[34] of the direct problem. The possibility of altering any stipulation in the direct problem without necessarily altering the (optimal) values for any dual variable has already been noted. Indeed, it is possible (in general) to vary more than one stipulation at a time without altering any of the dual evaluators, but such variations cannot be arbitrarily undertaken. Because of existing methods of computation, however, no great trouble need arise in practical applications. It is possible quickly to ascertain whether any proposed set of variations will affect the values w_i^*.[35] If such alterations are encountered, it is then possible to ascertain new optimal values w_i^* (and the new direct programs) without having to initiate calculations from scratch.[36]

Although the required adjustments to the program and dual variables can readily be generated in actual computation, for simplicity of presentation, it will be assumed, unless otherwise noted, that only variations in stipulations which permit maintenance of the "previous pattern" of direct activities are of interest.[37]

---

[34] A tableau refers to the tabular arrangement used to effect the calculations. See [10] for further details on this or other technical terms used in this paper.

[35] A sufficient condition for the values of the dual variables w_i^* to remain unchanged when stipulations change is that no change in the optimum set of "basis vectors" occurs. Call this collection of basis vectors G and its inverse G^{-1}. Let $G^{-1}b = Y_0 \geq 0$ represent the optimum program achieved from the set b of initial stipulations. If b is replaced by a new set $\hat{b}$, the new program $G^{-1}\hat{b} = \hat{Y}_0$ may be readily generated. If $\hat{Y}_0 \geq 0$, then the new program is also optimal, and a fortiori the values w_i^*, achieved with b, will remain unaffected by the change from b to $\hat{b}$. See [10].

[36] E.g., by the modified simplex method of Charnes and Lemke [13] and the dual method of Lemke [25]. The dual method starts with a solution $\hat{Y}$, not necessarily nonnegative but does arrange to have $w^* \geq 0$. With this start, the dual method continues to an optimum at

$$\hat{\hat{Y}}^* \geq 0, \quad \hat{\hat{w}}^* \geq 0.$$

This is precisely what is required when alterations in the initial $w_i^* \geq 0$ are to be considered. Machine codes (due to R. Graves, of Standard Oil Co., Indiana) are available, it may be noted, which combine the dual and modified simplex methods for use on electronic calculators.

[37] In the specific context of the warehousing problem under discussion, a pattern may be described as follows. Under the initial set of stipulations, purchases and sales will be undertaken at positive levels in some periods and at zero levels in others. This will form a "pattern" of non-zero values—these values occurring in the periods when transactions

To the basic warehousing model, (2), a financial constraint of the following simple form of (6) is now added:

$$\sum_{j=1}^{i} c_j x_j - \sum_{j=1}^{i-1} p_i y_i \leq \overline{M}, i = 1, 2, \ldots, n. \tag{6a}$$

In this case all purchases are made in cash, and sales are made on an accrual basis with realization in cash one period later.

Figure 2 extends the schema of Figure 1 to incorporate these n additional "financial constraints." The two new triangles at the bottom contain the c_k and $-p_k$, respectively, drawn from (6a). Also new dual variables, v_k, $k = 1, 2, \ldots, n$ are inserted in the w column to facilitate formation of the dual constraints.

Defining new cumulative variables

$$V_k = \sum_{i=k}^{n} v_i$$

$$W_k = 1 + V_k \tag{9}$$

in a fashion analogous to equation (7), the dual of this problem may be stated as

$$\text{min. } E = (B - A)T_1 + AU_1 + \overline{M}V_1$$

subject to

$$T_k \geq U_{k+1} - c_k W_k; T_{k-1} \geq T_k \geq 0, \quad U_r \geq T_r + p_r W_{r+1}; U_{r-1} \geq U_r \geq 0,$$
$$W_{r-1} \geq W_r \geq 1. \tag{10}$$

The values T_1^*, U_1^*, and W_1^* which these variables assume at an optimum then provide the desired (incremental) evaluators: T_1^* applies to $(B - A)$; U_1^*, to A; and V_1^*, to $\overline{M}$. In particular, V_1^* is the incremental (opportunity cost) cumulative, or compound, internal yield rate. It shows the net amount to which an additional dollar invested in the firm will accumulate if left to mature to the end of the planning horizon.

This relation of duality may be stated in economic as well as mathematical terms. Management can proceed by either of the following routes: either it can proceed directly to maximize profits subject to its capital (and physical) limitations or, alternatively, it can proceed to allocate its resources, including

---

actually occur. This pattern will be regarded as constant under any variation in the stipulations only so long as none of the previously zero levels becomes positive. This characterization is, rigorously speaking, too strong (see n. 35). All that is really required (as a sufficient condition) is that no change in "basis" shall occur. This constant-pattern assumption may be regarded as an extension or adaptation of the usual type of *ceteris paribus* assumptions.

Figure 2

WAREHOUSING MODEL WITH FINANCIAL CONSTRAINT.

w \ λ	$x_1 \cdots x_k \cdots x_n$	$y_1 \cdots y_r \cdots y_n$	b
t_1			$B - A$
t_k	$+1$	-1	$B - A$
t_n			$B - A$
u_1	$0 \cdots 0 \cdots 0$		A
u_k	$0 \cdots 0$; -1	-1	A
u_n	0		A
v_1		$0 \cdots 0 \cdots 0$	$\bar{M}$
v_k	c_k	$0 \cdots 0$; $-P_r$	$\bar{M}$
v_n		0	$\bar{M}$
p	$-c_1 \cdots -c_r \cdots -c_n$	$P_1 \cdots P_r \cdots P_n$	$\leq$ IV

liquid resources, by a minimizing principle. These resources should then be allocated among competing uses until they are driven to the lowest incremental (value) level admitted either by outside conditions (e.g., the market) or by non-negativity—whichever holds first.

VI. A NUMERICAL ILLUSTRATION

The data of Table 1 can be used for a readily calculated example. The results are shown in Figure 3. Here the direct program variables are written in the body and their (numerical) optimizing values at the top. The purchase prices, c, and the selling prices, p, are shown at the bottom. By inserting the numbers at the top for each x and y and the numbers at the bottom for each c and p, it is found that all constraints are satisfied either as equations or as the inequalities shown in the column which is second from the right-hand end. Also, the program profits, $6,825, may be calculated as the difference between cash receipts and expenditures where the former are extended to include the collections at the end of period 5.[38] This "profit" includes the sale of the initial inventory but not the "cost" thereof, since this cost was presum-

---

[38] Or beginning of period 6. The awkwardness arising from a fixed finite horizon will be dealt with in subsequent papers which are being prepared in collaboration with J. Dreze.

Table 1

DATA FOR WAREHOUSING MODEL WITH SIMPLE FINANCIAL CONSTRAINT: ONE-PERIOD LAG

A = 100 = opening inventory ⎫ "Tons" or
B = 125 = warehouse capacity ⎬ equivalent
                                      ⎭ units

M_0 = 1,000 = initial cash balance
$\underline{M}$ = 500 = minimum cash balance
n = 5 = number of "periods"

Period (j)	Unit Cost (c_j)	Unit Sales Price (p_j)
1	25	20
2	25	35
3	25	30
4	35	25
5	45	50

ably incurred prior to the planning interval and hence does not enter into optimizing decisions during the interval.[39]

It will be observed that the solution of the direct problem involves the purchase of 20 units in the first period—the maximum quantity permitted by the available funds $(M_0 - \underline{M})$ of $500—and the sale in period 2 of these units plus the initial 100 units of opening inventory. The proceeds of this sale are realized in cash by period 3, and the funds generated are reinvested in 125 units of inventory in the period—the maximum permitted by the warehouse capacity. The inventory acquired in period 3 is then liquidated in period 5.

The values for the dual variables appear in the stub of Figure 3. The profit figure (and also optimality) may therefore be readily checked by reference to the dual theorem. Substitution in equation (10) yields

$$\text{min. } E = E^* = (B - A)T_1^* + AU_1^* + \overline{M}V_1^* = 25 \times 25 + 100 \times 60 + 500 \times 2/5 = \$6{,}825, \quad (11)$$

the same as $\pi^* = $ max. π as required by the dual theorem.

The values $T_1^* = \$25$ and $U_1^* = \$60$ used above are, of course, simply the cumulants of the t^*'s and u^*'s shown in the stub of Figure 3. The value $T_1^* = \$25$ asserts that a one-unit increment in net warehouse capacity $(B - A)$ will, if used optimally (i.e., by permitting the purchase of an additional unit of inventory in period 3), increase the total profit by $25. An additional unit of initial inventory will provide an increment of $U_1^* - T_1^* = \$35$. That is, if a new direct problem is constructed with $\hat{A} = 101$ in place of $A = 100$, the profit level will increase by $35 to a new level of $6,860, as may be readily verified.

These valuations hold, of course, only within prescribed limits. Thus, if the firm acquires more than 168 "tons" of warehouse capacity, a new value $T_1^* = 0$ will obtain. At this capacity level—or greater—the warehouse restric-

---

[39] Except when taxes (and like matters) are considered. It is then necessary to include specific rules—LIFO, FIFO, etc.—on inventory valuation.

Figure 3
VARIABLES AND VALUES FOR THE ILLUSTRATION OF TABLE 1

Dual	Direct	x (20)	x (0)	x (125)	x (0)	x (0)	y (0)	y (120)	y (0)	y (0)	y (125)	Inequality	Stipulation
0 = t_1		x_1					$-y_1$					<25	
0 = t_2		x_1	$+x_2$				$-y_1$	$-y_2$				<25	$B - A$
10 = t_3		x_1	$+x_2$	$+x_3$			$-y_1$	$-y_2$	$-y_3$			=25	
15 = t_4		x_1	$+x_2$	$+x_3$	$+x_4$		$-y_1$	$-y_2$	$-y_3$	$-y_4$		=25	
0 = t_5		x_1	$+x_2$	$+x_3$	$+x_4$	$+x_5$	$-y_1$	$-y_2$	$-y_3$	$-y_4$	$-y_5$	<25	
0 = u_1							y_1					<100	
0 = u_2		$-x_1$					y_1	$+y_2$				=100	
10 = u_3		$-x_1$	$-x_2$				y_1	$+y_2$	$+y_3$			=100	A
0 = u_4		$-x_1$	$-x_2$	$-x_3$			y_1	$+y_2$	$+y_3$	$+y_4$		<100	
50 = u_5		$-x_1$	$-x_2$	$-x_3$	$-x_4$		y_1	$+y_2$	$+y_3$	$+y_4$	$+y_5$	=100	
0 = v_1		c_1x_1					$-p_1y_1$					=500	
2/5 = v_2		c_1x_1	$+c_2x_2$				$-p_1y_1$	$-p_2y_2$				=500	
0 = v_3		c_1x_1	$+c_2x_2$	$+c_3x_3$			$-p_1y_1$	$-p_2y_2$	$-p_3y_3$			<500	$\overline{M}$
0 = v_4		c_1x_1	$+c_2x_2$	$+c_3x_3$	$+c_4x_4$		$-p_1y_1$	$-p_2y_2$	$-p_3y_3$	$-p_4y_4$		<500	
0 = v_5		c_1x_1	$+c_2x_2$	$+c_3x_3$	$+c_4x_4$	$+c_5x_5$						<500	
Dual Values / Direct Prices	-25 ($-c$)	-25	-25	-25	-35	-45	20	35	30	25	50 (p)		

tion would never be binding.[40] Moreover, a minimum capacity of 120 "tons" is necessary to validate the result $T_1^* = \$25$, since reductions below this level would render the net storage capacity rather than the cash constraint binding in period 1.[41] In short, the evaluations $T_1^* = \$25$ and $U_1^* - T_1^* = \$35$ are valid only so long as the status of a previously critical constraint is not altered.[42]

For the financial constraint, Figure 3 shows values of $V_1^* = 2/5$ or $W_1^* = 1 + V_1^* = 7/5$. The financial constraint is binding only in period 1. An extra dollar committed in period 1 would permit additional purchases in period 1 and hence additional sales in period 2. Thus each extra dollar would accrue to $\$35/\$25 = 7/5 = W_1^* = 1 + V_1^*$ by period 2.[43] Thereafter no further accumulation takes place, since physical capacity rather than cash is the effective constraint on purchases. If the financial constraint were binding in other periods as well as the first, then, by equation (9), new values v_j^* and $j \geq 3$ would be added to V_1^* which would reflect the possibility of further accruals realized not only from the initial cash but also from the profits realized from their (optimal) employment. In the present example, since all values subsequent to v_2^* are zero, $W_3^* = W_4^* = W_5^* = 1$, and no further accretion occurs.

VII. JOINT ANALYSIS OF FINANCIAL AND OTHER CONSTRAINTS

The internal yield rates V_j^* acquire added interest insofar as they can be used to assess alternative applications of funds—for example, as they can be used to evaluate alterations of other stipulations such as warehouse capacity. Consider, therefore, the desirability of altering $B = 125$ to $\hat{B} = 126$, with $\bar{M} = \$500$. As previously noted, this would yield an increment to total profit of $T_1^* = \$25$ by permitting a one-unit increase in the following transaction: Buy in period 3 at \$25 and sell in period 5 at \$50.

Of course, the cost of securing this additional unit of capacity must also be considered. Suppose this cost to be \$20 and suppose, furthermore, that the additional facility will be worth nothing at the end of the fifth period. The net return on the investment, $5/20 = 25$ per cent, is clearly not sufficient to justify a diversion of funds from the original allotment, since the cost of the cash diversion as measured by V_1^* is 2/5, or 40 percent. Moreover, the investment in this added facility would not be warranted even if an extra \$20 could be secured at zero cost from external sources. Any increment $\Delta M_0 < \$125$, in

---

[40] Excess capacity has, of course, a zero opportunity cost over the alternatives considered. If leasing out, or leasing in, were also included in the model, however, this value would change.

[41] Information of this character, rendered in schedular form, would present a "demand curve" for warehouse capacity, given the level of the other constraints (see [10]).

[42] See n. 35 above for a more exact statement.

[43] Just as the value $T_1^* = 25$ remained valid for variations $120 \leq B \leq 168$ so the value $V_1^* = 2/5$ remains valid for variations $\underline{M} \leq M_0 \leq \$1,125$, or $0 \leq \bar{M} \leq \$625$.

liquid funds, can be more profitably employed in effecting purchases at period 1 prices and selling them in period 2.

On the other hand, under the liquidity constraints assumed for the firm, the extra warehouse space might be worth acquiring provided "suitable" financing terms were offered by the builder. If, for example, the builder were willing to give terms of 50 per cent down and 50 per cent in period 3, then the cost of the diversion of funds would be only $10 V_1^* + \$10 V_3^* = \$4$, which is less than the $5 net increment to profit which can be generated from the extra space. Thus, even at the same "interest rate" (here zero), the form of the financing arrangement enters significantly into the resource-allocating decisions when liquidity is to be considered as an appropriate part of the profit-maximizing machinery.

Other such "financial effects" (which can enter to modify standard propositions about rational patterns of profit maximization behavior) might be considered at this point. Suppose, for example, that a tax payment of $1,100 is due in period 2 and that, in anticipation of this payment, the firm eliminates all other considerations of liquidity in this period. In particular, the requirement $\bar{M} = \$500$ is replaced by $\bar{M} = -\$100$, the entire available cash resources being held in readiness for the payment. Under these conditions the constant pattern assumption cannot be maintained.[44] In particular, the firm is required to undertake "distress sales." At an optimum it must discontinue its "profitable" period 1 purchases and replace $x_1^* = 20$ by $\hat{x}_1^* = 0$. Also it will replace $y_1 = 0$ by $\hat{y}_1^* = 5$ and reduce $y_2 = 120$ to $\hat{y}_2^* = 95$, and leave the remaining transactions at their previous levels.[45]

The pattern variation encountered in this (tax) example also alters the dual evaluators. In particular, the value $v_2^* = 2/5$ is changed to $\hat{v}_2^* = 3/4$. This alteration provides a measure of what may be called the "money cost" (incremental and compounded) of this tax. The same tax collected in other periods would have no such money cost. Thus the period 2 collection of $1,100 reduces the level of total profit from $6,825 to $5,550, so that the profit reduction exceeds the $1,100 tax by $175. Alternatively, a later collection period would allow this firm to reap an extra $175 of profit.[46]

---

[44] If this same tax were imposed and collected in period 1, a contradiction would appear. Under the stated conditions there is no way to generate the funds required. This can be interpreted as causing the firm "to go out of business." (The dual would then show either an infinite value or no solution. Because this aspect of the dual theorem is not really being examined in this paper, no further attention will be paid to it here.) Note, however, that, if the model were altered so that the firm might allow discounts for immediate (cash) payment by customers, it would then be able to continue operations. The way to incorporate such features in the model will be evident from subsequent discussion.

[45] That these alterations must occur is apparent from an examination of the second-period financial constraint: $c_1 x_1 + c_2 x_2 - p_1 y_1 \leq -100$ or $y_1 = (100 + c_1 x_1 + c_2 x_2)/p_1$, which shows that any values $x_1, x_2 \geq 0$ force larger period 1 sales under any regime of positive prices. The minimum of such "loss sales" (in this example all reproduction costs are higher) occurs with $\hat{x}_1^* = \hat{x}_2^* = 0$ and $\hat{y}_1^* = 5$.

[46] See n. 45, where a still earlier collection period would cause a contradiction in the problem as stated. Notice, also, that this raises a question of optimum collection periods, as well as amounts, as part of the problem of the tax-revenue policy. Questions can also evidently be raised about standard versions of shifting and incidence theory.

Not only can the dual variables be used in this way to evaluate investment and financing opportunities but they can be made to yield most of the standard constructs of the theory of investment. Consider, for example, the question: "What is the maximum cost at which another unit of warehouse capacity would be just worth acquiring out of opening funds?" This may be rephrased analytically as find the value β which satisfies

$$(1 + V_1^*)\beta \equiv W_1^*\beta = T_1^*. \tag{12}$$

With $T_1^* = \$25$ and $W_1^* = 7/5$, the solution is $\beta = \$17\frac{6}{7}$ per unit. An analogous procedure may be used, of course, to find the maximum amount to pay for an additional unit of opening inventory. This value, $\hat{\beta}$, can readily be shown to be \$25, since the values of W_1^*, U_1^*, and T_1^* in the expression $W_1^*\,\hat{\beta} = U_1^* - T_1^*$ are 7/5, \$60, and \$25, respectively. The values obtained for β and $\hat{\beta}$ can be interpreted as the "present value" of each kind of additions to the firm's physical assets, assuming their optimal employment over the planning interval. Alternatively, W_1^* can be interpreted as an (internal) "discount factor"—one which allows for the repercussions of investment on liquidity as well as profitability.

Further insight into the nature of the evaluators may be gained by recalling that traditional theory represents the productive opportunities for funds by a function such as the one shown in Figure 4A. Here F_0 represents initial

Figure 4A

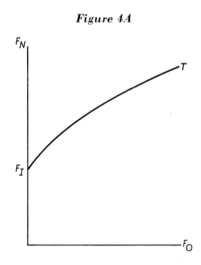

funds and F_n final funds, when opportunities are utilized to maximum advantage over the horizon.[47] For ease of comparison with the present case, this diagram has been modified to allow for the presence of initial inventory. This has a conversion value such that, even when $F_0 = \$0$ is invested, an accumula-

---

[47] For simplicity of exposition investment is here shown as increasing from left to right. This reverses the usual portrayal of the opportunity function. See, e.g., [22].

tion of $F_n = F_I$ will nevertheless occur via sale of inventory[48] on the most advantageous terms. Such a sale, of course, converts inventory first to receivables and then to cash which is thereafter available for reinvestment.

The range $0 - F_I$ in Figure $4A$ is perhaps best regarded as a discontinuity, or "jump," at $F_0 = \$0$, and the slope of T thereafter can be interpreted (in the usual fashion) as 1 plus the marginal rate of return on invested funds for $F_0 > \$0$. More precisely, it should be called the "marginal productive rate of return" (see [22]) in order to avoid possible confusion with what has come to be known as the "internal rate of return" in the literature of capital budgeting.[49]

The productive opportunity locus does not appear explicitly in the programming formulation. It is, however, implicit in the formulation and can be derived by parametric variations of the cash stipulation. Such a locus for the example of Figure 3 is given in Figure $4B$. For this example, $F_0 = M_0 - \underline{M}$

Figure 4B

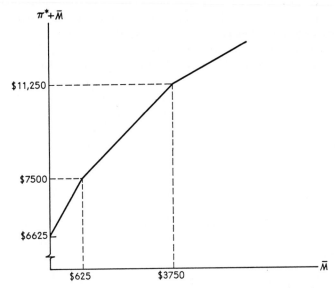

---

[48] Other assets may also be liquidated and the diagram adjusted further for these possibilities if desired.

[49] See, e.g., Dean [16] or Hill [21]. As noted earlier (n. 5 above), this concept has serious deficiencies as a means for making capital budgeting decisions. In particular, these internal rates do not always give correct rankings of investment opportunities even when liquidity considerations can be ignored. When liquidity considerations are present, even more severe difficulties are encountered. The use of "present values" as a basis for ranking projects has been suggested as an alternative to "internal rates of return," at least when liquidity considerations are absent. But, as noted in [22], ambiguous results are possible even in this case—e.g., when borrowing and lending rates differ. Then the proper discount rate is not a given (independent of decisions) but, as in the case for W^*_I, is a variable whose value is to be ascertained as part of the problem. These remarks apply a fortiori when rationing or liquidity considerations are present.

and $F_N = \pi^* + \bar{M}$. The function consists of three linear segments. The first segment reflects the return when $F_0 = \$0$, so that the inventory conversion ultimately gives $\pi^* = \$6,625$. As positive allotments of liquid funds are made, the profits of the firm rise at a constant rate to the point B, where $M_0 - \underline{M} = \$625$. The slope of the curve in this section—i.e., one plus the marginal productive rate of return—is, of course, $W_1^* = 1 + V_1^* = 7/5$, which maintains over the range $0 < M_0 - \underline{M} < \$625$. From $\$625$ to $\$3750$, W_1^* has a value of $6/5$. Beyond this range, liquid funds cease to be a binding constraint on production, and the marginal productive rate of return becomes zero.

VIII. EVALUATION OF THE INDIVIDUAL PERIOD CONSTRAINTS

There are additional analogues between the standard constructs of marginal productivity analysis and the lower-case variables t_k^*, u_k^*, and v_k^*. They are, however, of a rather looser sort—in part because of the lack of a standard dynamic version of the firm in economic theory and in part because of semantic problems. Logically, there is no trouble with the status of the dual variables in this or any other programming problem. The trouble, if any, arises only when an attempt is made to make these symbols correspond with real-world counterparts in existing economic institutions.

Consider, for example, the value $u_3^* = \$10$ in Figure 3. This is associated with variations of A, the "initial" inventory, in period 3. It is desired to study the consequences of varying only the value $A = 100$ in period 3 and only in the selling constraint. In particular, no comparable variation in the stipulation $(B - A)$ which applies to the third-period buying constraint will be admitted.

To interpret such a variation, it is necessary once more to consider the nature of this selling constraint. It states, essentially, that all sales must be made from inventory. Thus, if $A = 100$ is replaced by $\hat{A} = 99$ in the third period, the following adjustments occur to achieve a new optimum: $y_2^* = 120$ is replaced by $\hat{y}_2^* = 119$, and $x_3^* = 125$ is replaced by $\hat{x}_3^* = 124$. All other program values are unaffected. Tracing through the effect of the indicated adjustment, it is found that total profit is reduced by the indicated amount, $u_3^* = \$10$.

It might seem that the reduced purchases in period 3 would cause a reduction in the highly profitable period 5 sales. It must be remembered, however, that only a period 3 variation in "initial" inventory is being considered. All other values of A are held constant. In fact, the one-unit reduction in period 2 sales is effected precisely to avoid this contingency and to allow the more profitable period 5 sales to be executed at their previous (maximal) level.

The effect of varying A in a selling and not in the corresponding buying constraint is to "free" the associated purchases from the necessity of clearing through the warehouse. In subsequent periods, however, adjustments must be made, since the values of A in the selling constraint have their counterparts in the buying constraints as well. A study of the structure of Figure 3 will reveal that in certain circumstances this can cause the firm to sell "forward" by increasing some preceding value of y in order to "make room" for the subsequent purchases. That is, the sale is made, even though goods are not on hand, on condition that a subsequent purchase will also be made "to cover" the transaction.

The present example does not permit an easy illustration when A is varied upward; that is, any upward variation of A in the inventory constraint requires the computation of a new optimum program and thereby violates the constant-pattern assumption. For example, if $A = 100$ is replaced by $\hat{A} = 101$, the value $y_3^* = 0$ is replaced by $\hat{y}_3^* = 1$, and $x_3^* = 125$ is replaced by $\hat{x}_3^* = 126$.[50] Essentially, then, the firm is selling a unit purchased in the same period under these circumstances.

As an alternative method of illustrating the nature of the selling constraint and its evaluators, consider the possibility of altering A in two periods. Let $A = 100$ be changed to $\hat{A} = 101$ in periods 2 and 3. The firm will then utilize this across-period possibility by selling an additional unit at \$35 in period 2 and buying an additional unit in period 3 at \$25, for a total incremental gain of $u_3^* = \$10$.

A similar across-period approach helps to clarify the interpretation of the variables t^* as they apply to net warehouse capacity. Here the variation is on B while A is held constant. An additional unit of warehouse space in period 4, which is available until sales are effected in period 5, is worth $t_4^* = \$15$, since it would make possible a purchase in period 4 at \$35 for sale in period 5 at \$50. If available one period earlier, the space gains an additional value $t_3 = \$10$, since the extra purchase can be made at period 3 prices, which are \$10 less than those of period 4.[51]

In this interpretation the values t_j^* measure the added profit which can be secured by having extra capacity available one period earlier than $j + 1$. These values are, so to speak, the "time derivatives" of the profit stream relative to the available capacity. They can be thought of (in value terms) as the marginal product of "not waiting"—along lines made familiar by the Austrian concepts of "waiting" and "periods of production." The parallel can perhaps be drawn a bit stronger by thinking in terms of a construction program. With $n = 5$, the enlargement is worthless if it first materializes in this period. Accelerating the program by one period—say, at premium or bonus rates—would be worth up to $t_4^* = \$15$. If the date when additional space is available can be moved up to period 3, it is worth $T_3^* = t_3^* + t_4^* + t_5^* = \$25$. Availability in still earlier periods adds nothing further, since cash rather than capacity is the effective constraint for this business in periods 1 and 2. The

[50] Also $u_3^* = 10$ and $u_2^* = 0$ are replaced, respectively, by $\hat{u}_3^* = 5$ and $\hat{u}_2^* = 5$, while $v_2^* = 2/5$ and all other $v^* = 0$ is replaced by $\hat{v}_2^* = 1/5$ and $\hat{v}_1^* = 1/5$. The cumulants $U_1^* = \$60$ and $V_1^* = 2/5$ are not affected, but their constituent elements (the items now being examined) are. This variation also illustrates why the constant-pattern assumption is too strong with respect to the upper-case dual evaluators.

[51] It is possible also to think of the firm's capacity as deteriorating over time and, by cumulating in reverse, to interpret the t^*'s as maintenance evaluators. This topic will be dealt with in later papers.

marginal cost of "not waiting" would therefore be the extra construction cost incurred adjusted for the marginal cost of funds, as measured by the relevant W^*'s or V^*'s.

Tracing through the v_j^*'s is somewhat more involved, so that their further analysis is best reserved for later sections. The following general characterization will, for the moment, suffice. From the earlier discussion of W_1^* as a "discount factor" it is clear that W_1^* can be expressed as

$$W_k^* = (1 + r_k)(1 + r_{k+1}) \ldots \times (1 + r_{n-1})(1 + r_n), \tag{13}$$

where r_k is the marginal productive rate of return (optimum incremental yield rate) for period k. From equation (13) and the definition of W^* it also follows that

$$\frac{W_k^*}{W_{k+1}^*} = 1 + r_k. \tag{13a}$$

But $v_k^* = r_k W_{k+1}^*$ and $V_k^* \equiv W_k^* - 1$,
so that

$$v_k^* = r_k W_{k+1}^* = r_k(1 + V_{k+1}^*). \tag{14}$$

The lower-case evaluator, v_k^*, is therefore the product of two terms: (i) the marginal productive rate of return on funds for that period and (ii) the further accumulation made possible by their continued reinvestment in subsequent periods. With the precaution that W_{k+1}^* and V_{k+1}^*, like v_k^* itself, are constant only for a certain range of funds, it may be said that v_k^* represents the compound rate of accumulation of an additional dollar invested in that period and maintained in the business up to the horizon.

IX. EVALUATING TRADE CREDIT AS A SOURCE OF FUNDS

A simple extension of the previous model makes it possible to examine the effects of trade credit. Figure 5 presents the essential features when suppliers are willing to extend credit to the firm with a one-period lag. The schema simply extends that of Figure 2, with a new column of triangles (on the left) and new variables $x_1', x_2', \ldots, x_n'$ and costs $- c_1', - c_2', \ldots, - c_n'$ associated with these opportunities.

Such credit opportunities may involve penalties (such as loss of discounts) as compared with prompt payment, so that, in general, $c_j' \geqq c_j$. The purpose of the present discussion is, however, to illustrate how the dual evaluators may be brought into play even when such premiums are absent. By assuming, therefore, that $c_j' = c_j$, for $j = 1, 2, \ldots, n$, it will be possible (i) to simplify the discussion and (ii) continue with the data of Table 1 for the remainder of this section.

Figure 5
SCHEMA FOR TRADE CREDIT

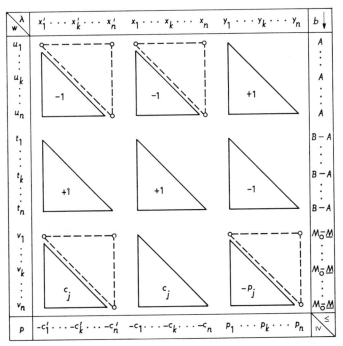

Table 2 shows an optimum program returning (accrued) profits of $7,450 = $14,200 − $6,750, as may be calculated from the details shown under the heading "Income and Expense." In addition to physical details shown to the left of the "Income and Expense" columns, certain elements of "Financial Position" are shown on its right in order to facilitate tracing the cash and credit positions. Finally, the values for the dual evaluators are shown in the last three columns.

New values are now secured for T_1^* and U_1^*, but V_1^* remains at the same level as in Figure 2. Cash position remains binding in period 1. Extension of trade credit provides no assistance in this period, since sales are not effected until period 2 and cash is not realized until period 3. Starting in period 2, however, the opportunities provided by trade credit become apparent, and new purchases and sales are executed which could not previously be utilized.

The difference in program profits between Figure 2 and Table 2 indicates that it would have been worth the firm's while to have paid up to $625 for these credit facilities. This is justified, however, only if such payment can be withheld until the close of business. Suppose, however, that it cannot. The cumulative marginal yield on funds, $V_1^* = 2/5$, must then be considered. An easy application of preceding concepts then gives

$$CW_1^* = \Delta\pi = \$625, \tag{15}$$

Table 2
DIRECT AND DUAL OPTIMUM FOR TRADE CREDIT MODEL
(Data from Table 1 and Details from Fig. 4)

Period	Price ($/Ton)		Purchases (Tons)		Sales (Tons)	Income and Expense ($)		Financial Position (Close of [$] Period)			Dual Variables ($/Unit)		
								Cash on Hand	Credit Position				
			Credit	Cash		Expendi-			Accounts Receiv-	Accounts			
	p_j	c_j	x'_j	x_j	y_j	tures	Receipts		able	Payable*	t_k	u_k	v_k
1	20	25	...	20	...	500	....	500	....	....	...	...	...
2	35	25	125	...	120	3,125	4,200	500	4,200	3,125	5	10	2/5
3	30	25	82	43	125	3,125	3,750	500	3,750	2,050	10	5	...
4	25	35	...	...	...	....	....	2,200	....	....	15	...	...
5	50	45	...	...	125	....	6,250	2,200	6,250	....	0	50	...
Total..	...	...	207	63	370	6,750	14,200	8,450	....	....	$T_1 = 30$ $U_1 = 65$ $V_1 = 2/5$		

* Exclusive of any accounts outstanding for the initial inventory.

or $C = \$446.43$ as the present cash equivalent of such a final period payment.

Of course, it is not customary to pay for this kind of credit directly. The funds may, if desired, be thought of rather as a "deposit" left with suppliers or (following the more usual custom) as an additional working-capital requirement imposed on the firm as a condition precedent to receiving such credit extensions. In either case, the issue is one of accounting for the "cost"— $\$178.57 = \$625 - \$446.43$—of this further restriction.

Suppose, therefore, that an additional $\$446.43$ of the firm's funds is impounded by one device or the other and consider once more the program of Table 2. This new stipulation requires the firm to contract its period 1 purchases by 17.857 units, thus reducing its period 2 profit accrual (and total net realization) by the indicated $\$178.57$. This, therefore, is the cost of such a reservation of funds. The "capital equivalent" of trade credit extended at the beginning of business is therefore $\$446.43$, which accumulates to $\$625$ by the end.

X. BORROWING AND LENDING MODELS

It is possible to extend these imputation procedures in a variety of ways. Distributed lags on payments to vendors can be introduced to evaluate these opportunities, and distributed lags on receivables, if inserted, can be used to impute their carrying cost. Evaluation of "stretching" and like phenomena can thereby be encompassed in the analysis.

By means of the devices indicated in [5], it is possible to encompass multiple commodity considerations and varying prices as well. Some interest attaches, of course, to such extensions from the point of view both of realism and of theoretical clarification. In the interests of brevity, however, these extensions will be avoided. Attention will be directed, instead to opportunities associated with borrowing and lending so as to place the examples of this paper in better perspective against standard applications of capital and interest theory.

Suppose the firm has unlimited power to borrow and lend at constant (and equal) rates of interest. This approximates the assumption of perfect capital markets and makes it possible to restrict attention to a single type of security.[52] Specifically, it will be assumed that the firm can make contracts to borrow or lend at given interest rates for a term equal to the time remaining up to the horizon. With principal and interest thus assumed repayable only at the end of the planning period, it is possible to simplify matters. Interest and income (on lending) can then be handled in the functional without introducing additional constraints.[53]

---

[52] See [27].

[53] Under the assumption of unlimited borrowing and lending nothing important appears to be lost by this approach. The interest drain (per period) would then simply lead the firm to borrow compensating amounts without affecting the dual evaluators. Of course, when capital is rationed, this proposition is no longer valid.

For this purpose let the new variables

m_j = amount to be borrowed in period j = 1, 2, ..., n,
n_j = amount to be lent in period j = 1, 2, ..., n,   (16)

be introduced into the problem in order that the amounts to be borrowed and loaned can be simultaneously ascertained with the program of purchases and sales. Then the terms

$$- \sum_{j=1}^{n} m_j[(1 + d_j)^{n+1-j} - 1] + \sum_{j=1}^{n} n_j[(1 + d_j)^{n+1-j} - 1],   (17)$$

where d_j = the given rate of interest prevailing in period j, can be adjoined to the functional of the direct problem—see equation $(2a)$—in order to allow for the interest cost and income associated with borrowing the amounts m_j and lending the amounts n_j.[54] Since financial position is also affected, it is necessary to replace equation (8) by the following expressions:

$$\sum_{j=1}^{i} c_j x_j - \sum_{j=1}^{i-1} p_j y_j - \sum_{j=1}^{i} m_j + \sum_{j=1}^{i} n_j \leq \bar{M}.   (18)$$

The assumption that all loans and borrowings are repaid only at the end of period n makes it unnecessary to insert the accumulation factors used in (17). It is unnecessary, also, to introduce new constraints.

Figure 6 presents the schema. The data of Table 1 will continue to serve for illustration, when supplemented by the data of Table 3. These numbers

Table 3

$(1 + e_1)^5 - 1 = 1/3$
$(1 + e_2)^4 - 1 = 1/4$
$(1 + e_3)^3 - 1 = 1/5$
$(1 + e_4)^2 - 1 = 1/8$
$(1 + e_5) - 1 = 1/16$

have been chosen with $e_j \cong 1/16$ to approximate a constant interest rate of $6\frac{2}{3}$ per cent.

Inserting these values and the information contained in Table 1, the optimum program is derived in Table 4. Net operating income[55] has now risen to $7,500 compared with the $6,825 total profit under the conditions of Figure

---

[54] Under these assumptions an equivalent functional could, of course, be defined in terms of "discounted" profits. It is simpler, however, to state the analysis in the same form as in preceding cases. It will then be seen that the V^*'s are directly related to the external (borrowing and lending) rates under the indicated assumptions.

[55] See n. 39 above.

Figure 6
SCHEMA FOR BORROWING AND LENDING

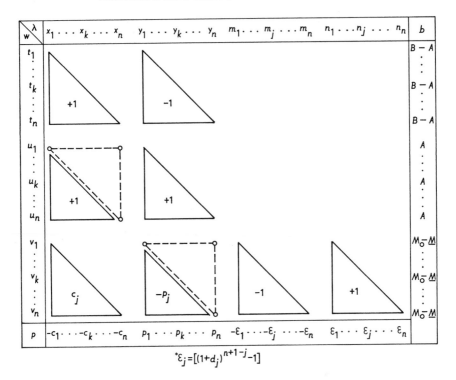

$$^*\varepsilon_j = [(1+d_j)^{n+1-j}-1]$$

3. However, the borrowing necessary to finance this higher level of operations entails an interest expense of, approximately, $822.92, which is, in part, recouped by lending to return $718.75. When the net interest charges of $104.17 are deducted, the level of total profits becomes $7,395.83 for an increment of $570.83 compared to the case (Fig. 3) when these opportunities were absent.

From a theoretical standpoint the important fact about the assumption of unlimited borrowing and lending power is that it effectively eliminates the cash constraint and therefore transfers the entire effect of financial considerations to the functional. On this assumption the purchases and sales are determined entirely by the pattern of prices, the interest rate, and the technological constraints.[56]

The matter may also be stated in another way which leads directly to an interpretation of the dual evaluators v_k^*. Having another dollar available in any period would simply lead the firm either to reduce its scheduled borrowing

---

[56] It is perhaps worthwhile to stress again that this disappearance of financial considerations is a consequence of the assumption of perfect capital markets. Whenever capital rationing is effectively present, the cash-flow consequences of financing arrangements will have an influence on production (and investment) decisions.

Table 4
OPTIMUM PROGRAM: BORROWING AND LENDING

Period		Price		Direct Problem					Dual Problem		
				Purchases (Tons)	Sales (Tons)	Borrowing ($)	Lending ($)	Cumulative Net Borrowing ($)			
	c_j		p_j	x_j	y_j	m_j	n_j		t_k	u_k	v_k
1......	.25		20	25	0	125	0	125	26/3	0	1/12
2......	.25		35	125	125	3,125	0	3,250	5/2	43/4	1/20
3......	.25		30	125	125	0	1,250	2,000	75/8	15/4	3/40
4......	.35		25	0	0	0	3,750	−1,750	85/8	0	1/16
5......	.45		50	0	125	0	0	−1,750	0	50	1/16
Total	.		.	....	...	.....	.....	......	31 1/6	64 1/2	1/3

or to increase its scheduled lending.[57] This may be validated by scrutinizing the values V_k^* as $k = 1, 2, \ldots, 5$ in succession. Reading from Table 4, it is found that $V_1^* = 1/3$ the same as $(1 + e_1)^5 - 1$ in Table 3. Also $V_2^* = 1/4$, the same as $(1 + e_2)^4 - 1$, and so on. In short, the V_k^*'s now correspond to the market earning and borrowing rates in successive periods. Hence any such value, V_k^*, corresponds to the compound accumulated earnings (or savings) possible from having an extra dollar available in period k and continuing this investment, plus the earnings thereon in the business of buying, selling, lending, and borrowing.

By equations (11) and (14) it follows that

$$v^* = V^* - V_{k+1}^* = r_k W_{k+1}^*, \tag{19}$$

where (in this case) r_k is the market rate of interest. Translating the present example into analytic terms,

$$v_j^* = [(1 + r)^{n+1-j} - 1] - [(1 + r)^{n-i} - 1] = r(1 + r)^{n-i}. \tag{20}$$

Thus $v_1^* = V_1^* - V_2^* = 1/3 - 1/4 = 1/12$ represents, in this case, the *earnings on the earnings* at the constant market rate, r, after the loan is liquidated at the end of the period.

These borrowing and lending contracts at constant market rates of interest can be used for still further clarification. Consider, for example, the evaluators T_k^* and t_k^*. The value of T_1^* has risen from $25 per unit (Fig. 3) to $31\frac{1}{8}$ per unit (Table 4).[58] Also, $t_k^* > 0$ in all periods save the last, where the selling constraint effectively eliminates the value of this facility. Hence the introduction of these borrowing and lending opportunities not only increases the value of this facility but also tends to even out the value fluctuations across the periods.

It may be noted that, although the value of T_1^* in Table 4 exceeds its correspondent in Figure 3, this is not true for all T_k^*. Thus $T_4^* = \$85/8$ is less than its corresponding level, $15, in Figure 3. This reduction occurs because using this facility in period 4 for a period 5 sale now adjusts for a non-zero accumulated interest cost. That is, the correct cost calculation is

$$p_5 - c_4(1 + r)^2 = \$50 - \frac{\$35 \times 9}{8} = \frac{\$400 - \$315}{8} = \frac{\$85}{8}.$$

Although an extra unit of warehouse capacity which is available for the last two periods still permits a $15 increment to profit, it is necessary also to consider the accumulated interest cost associated with this transaction. The cor-

---

[57] It follows from this that parametric programming over values of $(M_0 - \underline{M})$ will not lead to a tracing-out of the productive opportunity locus such as that of Figure 4B. Instead, given any vector of interest rates, we obtain only one "point" on that function, namely, the point at which the marginal productive rates of return of each period are equal to the interest rates of the periods. The entire function, if there were any use for it, could be generated by dropping the borrowing and lending vectors and repeating the procedure used to obtain Figure 4B.

[58] In order to ascertain the corresponding present value see equation (12).

rect evaluation is therefore automatically supplied by T_4^* in Table 4, and like remarks apply to the remaining values T_k^*. It should occasion no surprise, therefore, that all values save T_1^* are reduced in passing from Figure 3 to Table 4.[59]

It is interesting also to trace through the effects on the values t_k^* and to do so in a manner which is different from the one used in Section VI. Consider, therefore, the formula

$$t_1^* = p_2(1 + z)^3 - c_1(1 + z)^5 . \qquad (21)$$

It is desired now to find that rate of interest, z, which would lead the firm to abandon the period 1 purchase and the period 2 sale. When this occurs, the "slack" associated with the first buying constraint will be in the "basis," and the value $t_1^* = 26/3$ will be replaced by $\hat{t}_1^* = 0$. It therefore follows that

$$z = 2 \sqrt{\frac{p_2}{c_1}} - 1, \qquad (22)$$

or $z = 28$ per cent[60] is this rate. Corresponding critical levels may be established for the other values t_k^*.

XI. SOME POSSIBLE FURTHER EXTENSIONS

The preceding examples are only selected (simple) illustrations of ways in which the incremental (opportunity cost)[61] yield factors made available from the dual can be used. The model can be extended to embrace multiple commodities and facilities, inside and outside investment opportunities at various rates (along with conditional lending),[62] and other standard features of financial analysis.[63] Moreover, as already noted, there is no reason why

---

[59] The matter may be summarized by saying that loosening the financial constraints sets up two opposing forces relative to this capacity. Easing of the restrictions on borrowing makes the facility more productive. Easing of the restrictions on lending raises the opportunity cost of the co-operating resources and thus tends to lower its net marginal productivity.

[60] More exactly, $(28 + \eta)$ per cent, $\eta > 0$.

[61] Any use of interest for judging investment opportunities is, of course, an opportunity cost valuation. Usually, but not necessarily (cf. [23], chap. xvii), it is a "money cost." That is, it is a measure of the income which must be foregone by absorbing otherwise available funds in the proposed alternative. The principle of opportunity cost (strictly interpreted) therefore requires that these yields be calculated incrementally and at the highest rates which can be secured from possible alternatives. This is true whether formulas based on the simpler $(1 + r)^n$ or the more general

$$\prod_{j=1}^{n} (1 + r_j) = (1 + r_1) \times (1 + r_2) \times \ldots (1 + r_n)$$

are used.

[62] E.g., working capital, dividends, and reduced opportunities for further borrowing (or credit).

[63] Including tax considerations, obsolescence phenomena, etc.

such financial constraints cannot be incorporated in any linear programming problem. Finally, the activity analysis constructs of Koopmans [24] have been shown to be capable of reformulation (and complete solution) by means of linear programming,[64] so that, at least in principle, these constructs can be extended to economy-wide models for exploring, say, funds and income flows between various economic sectors, networks of transactions between banks and business firms (along with "terms of trade"), etc.

Exactly how (or whether) these possibilities can be used depends, of course, on the nature of the problem confronted. But it should be noted that most problems may be formulated in a variety of ways. In this paper the strategy has centered largely on evaluations within limited realms of variations,[65] but this is not the only possible approach. It is possible, for example, to commence instead with a given asset mixture simply as a preliminary to studying other possibilities. The additional data generated by the calculations can then be used to examine proposed changes in asset mix and volume without requiring that the calculations be initiated anew for each such proposed mixture. Indeed, if desired, the problem may be parameterized, and a sequence of tableaus can then be generated by allowing the parameters—A, B, etc.—to vary according to prescribed rules.[66] This will provide the corresponding optimal program for each range of parameter variations. It will also supply the dual evaluators. Thus, by relatively simple comparisons for the cost of each such asset mix, it should be possible to secure a basis for choice.

The use of a limited and fixed horizon (apparent throughout the models studied) appears to be a defect which these programming approaches share with alternatives that have been suggested. But, on further analysis,[67] it turns out that mathematical methods may also be brought to bear on this problem in ways which provide optimal rules for fixing horizon and subhorizon dates by reference to the available parameters.

The size of the problems that may be encountered in actual applications also needs to be considered. The possible use of model types (and approximations thereto) has already been suggested as one possible way of pushing back these boundaries. Supplemented by electronic computer aids (now available), these boundaries may be pushed back even further, especially as special codes (now in process of preparation by commercial computer firms) become available.

It must be remembered, too, that computer designs are in rapid evolution. Moreover, properly oriented business research can (at least conceivably) help to accelerate this evolution in particular directions. For example, it may be

[64] See [6].

[65] E.g., on the "constant pattern" assumption.

[66] Cf. [18] for a method which covers all possible mixes. Usually, however, only "efficient-point programs" will be of interest. The parameterization methods described in [6] may then be used to restrict examinations to this subset of possibilities.

[67] These results are being readied for release in a research report being prepared in collaboration with J. Dreze.

possible to design a "financial module" (analogue or digital) as part of a sequence of "modules"[68] in a larger machine. A summary presentation is given in the Appendix to illustrate how such research might proceed by reference (only) to the relatively simple cases covered in this paper.

APPENDIX

One approach would be to separate the business into two interrelated parts, according to whether funds flows or physical flows are being viewed for transaction analysis purposes. To commence the desired analytical decomposition, let

$$
\begin{aligned}
\mathcal{C}_j &= c_j x_j \\
\mathcal{P}_j &= p_j y_j.
\end{aligned} \tag{23}
$$

Then the model of, say, Figure 2 becomes

$$
\text{max.} \ -\sum_{j=1}^{n} \mathcal{C}_j + \sum_{j=1}^{n} \mathcal{P}_j
$$

subject to

$$
\sum_{j=1}^{i} x_j - \sum_{j=1}^{i} y_i \leq B - A
$$

$$
\sum_{j=1}^{i} \mathcal{C}_j - \sum_{j=1}^{i-1} \mathcal{P}_j \leq \bar{M}
$$

$$
-\sum_{j=1}^{i-1} x_j + \sum_{j=1}^{i} y_j \leq A
$$

$$
\begin{aligned}
- c_j x_j + \mathcal{C}_j &= 0 \\
- p_j y_j - \mathcal{P}_j &= 0
\end{aligned} \tag{24}
$$

with $i, j = 1, 2, \ldots, n$.

The diagram of Figure 7 may be compared with Figure 2 to see what resulted from this transformation. The first pair of triangles in Figure 7 represent physical transactions into and out of the warehouse. The next pair represent transactions into and out of the firm's net cash balance. The third pair of triangles are also physical and appear directly under the first pair because of inventory interrelations.

The diagonals directly below the triangles now provide the rest of this "double-entry" system. $\mathcal{C}_j$, for any j, brings the firm closer to its cash limit, but, at an exchange of $-c_j$ per unit, it creates x_j which (i) relaxes the sales

---

[68] This term is borrowed from the field of electronic computer design. A modular design may be thought of as a sequence of submachines (modular units) co-ordinated into one larger unit where each of the modules is designed to handle particular problems with specialized efficiency.

constraint (third pair of triangles) and (ii) tightens storage (first pair of triangles). Conversely, any y_j relaxes the constraints (starting on the diagonal) for the first pair of triangles, tightens those for the third pair, and, at the rate p_r, relaxes the cash condition one period later. In short, $-c_j$ and p_r are the rates at which cash is converted to goods, while $-1/c_j$ and $1/p_r$ are the rates at which goods are converted to cash in any transactions between the business, which is thus sectorized. Thus the echelons, at the bottom of Figure 7, serve to relate the two parts of the business (physical and funds) at the indicated exchange rates.

It is now desired to carry these transformations one stage further in order to secure a network analogue. Consider, therefore, the period 1 transactions. All sales must be made from inventory and all purchases from initial cash. Therefore, let

$$\begin{aligned} g_1 &= A - y_1 = \textbf{goods on hand after sale,} \\ \mathcal{R}_1 &= \bar{M} - c_1 x_1 = \textbf{cash available after purchase.} \end{aligned} \quad \text{(25a)}$$

Next define

$$\begin{aligned} h_1 &= g_1 + x_1 = \textbf{goods available for second-period sales,} \\ \mathcal{F}_2 &= \mathcal{R}_1 + p_1 y_1 = \textbf{funds available for second-period purchases,} \end{aligned} \quad \text{(25b)}$$

so that

$$g_2 = h_1 - y_2. \quad \text{(25c)}$$

As is also readily seen, non-negativity is retained along with $h_1 \leq B$.

Continuing in this manner, the following equations emerge:

$$\begin{aligned} h_j &= x_j + g_j \\ \mathcal{F}_j &= c_j x_j + \mathcal{R}_j \end{aligned} \quad \text{(26a)}$$

and, also,

$$\begin{aligned} \mathcal{F}_{j+1} &= p_j y_j + \mathcal{R}_j \\ h_{j-1} &= y_j + g_j, \end{aligned} \quad \text{(26b)}$$

with all variables constrained to be non-negative and $h_j \leq B$, $j = 1, 2, \ldots, n$.

With these transformations the functional becomes

$$\sum_{j=1}^{n} (\mathcal{F}_{j+1} - \mathcal{R}_j) - \bar{M} + \mathcal{R}_1 - \sum_{j=2}^{n} (\mathcal{F}_j - \mathcal{R}_j) = \mathcal{F}_{n+1} - \bar{M}. \quad \text{(27a)}$$

The storage constraints are reduced to

$$\sum_{j=1}^{i} (h_j - g_j) - A + g_1 - \sum_{j=2}^{i} (h_{j-1} - g_j) \leq B - A, \quad \text{(27b)}$$

or

$$h_i \leq B$$

Figure 7

MODEL OF FIGURE 2 SEPARATED INTO PHYSICAL AND FUND FLOWS

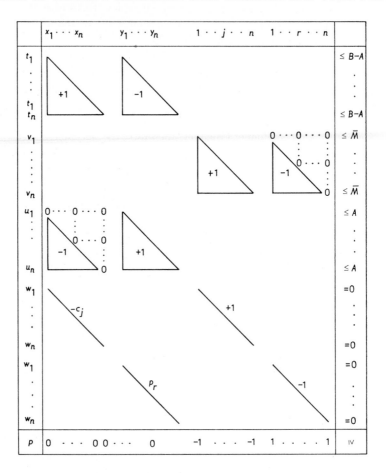

for $i = 1, 2, \ldots, n$. The sales constraints, in turn, become

$$-\sum_{j=1}^{i-1} (h_j - g_j) + A - g_1 + \sum_{j=2}^{i} (h_{j-1} - g_j) \le A, \qquad \text{(27c)}$$

or, simply, $g_i \ge 0$. The financial constraints are similarly reduced to

$$\bar{M} - \mathcal{R}_1 + \sum_{j=2}^{i} (\mathcal{F}_j - \mathcal{R}_j) - \sum_{j=1}^{i-1} (\mathcal{F}_{j+1} - \mathcal{R}_j) \le \bar{M}, \qquad \text{(27d)}$$

or $\mathcal{R}_i \ge 0$.

Hence the originally stated problem is replaced by

$$\text{max. } \mathcal{F}_{n+1}$$

Figure 8

WAREHOUSE—FUNDS-FLOW NETWORK

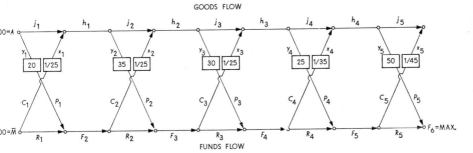

Note: All values $h \leq B$, the gross warehouse capacity.
Source: A. Charnes and W. W. Cooper, "The Use of Model Types in Some OR Applications to Business Planning" (two lectures in a series sponsored and published by the University of Michigan Seminar on Operations Research, October, 1957).

subject to

$$h_i \leq B,$$

with

$$x_i + g_i - h_i = 0$$
$$c_i x_i + \mathcal{R}_i - \mathcal{F}_i = 0$$
$$p_i y_i + \mathcal{R}_i - \mathcal{F}_{i+1} = 0$$
$$y_i + g_i - h_{i-1} = 0 \tag{28}$$

and

$$y_1 + g_1 = A$$
$$c_1 x_1 + \mathcal{R}_1 = M,$$

where $h_i, g_i, x_i, y_i, \mathcal{F}_i, \mathcal{R}_i \geq 0$, $i = 1, 2, \ldots, n$.

These transformations convert Figure 7 into Figure 8, which may be viewed as a directed graph, as shown by the arrows. There is a goods-flow and a funds-flow axis, each oriented in the same direction and connected as shown.

Alternatively, this figure may be viewed as a capacitated[69] network. The sources (e.g., of electrical current) are the initial inventory and (net) cash balance. The currents along these two similarly oriented branches are connected by the arrows moving across the diagram with the boxes containing current amplifiers and deamplifiers. The value at the final sink, distinguished as $\mathcal{F}_6$, is to be made a maximum. That is, values y and x, from and to the goods flow, or values $\mathcal{C}$ and $\mathcal{P}$, from and to the funds flow, are to be determined so that the current flowing into $\mathcal{F}_6$ will be as great as possible.

It is interesting to observe the central role played by the funds-flow axis. As the one commodity case is extended, it will be found that (under suitable conditions) direct hookups with the goods-flow axes for commodities already present may be avoided. But all commodities will be hooked directly into the

---

[69] Because of the condition $h \leq B$ noted at the bottom of Fig. 8.

funds-flow axis, which thereby establishes their interrelations (along with the corresponding yield rates) at every node on this axis. The central importance of this axis both for co-ordination and for alternative (opportunity) cost evaluations is thus brought out in a clear and striking manner. It is conjectured that these (funds-flow) connections will be found in any model type for which incremental yield evaluations are required for financial planning purposes.

BIBLIOGRAPHY

[1] BELLMAN, R. "On the Theory of Dynamic Programming—a Warehousing Problem," *Management Science*, II, No. 3 (April, 1956), 272–75.

[2] CAHN, A. S. "The Warehouse Problem," *Bulletin of the American Mathematical Society*, LIV (October, 1948), 1073–80.

[3] CHARNES, A., and COOPER, W. W. "Duality, Regrouping and Warehousing." (ONR Research Memorandum No. 19.) Pittsburgh: Graduate School of Industrial Administration, Carnegie Institute of Technology, June, 1954.

[4] ———. "Extremal Principles for Simulation Traffic Flows in a Network," *Proceedings of the National Academy of Sciences*, January, 1958.

[5] ———. "Generalizations of the Warehousing Model," *Operational Research Quarterly*, IV (December, 1955), 131–72.

[6] ———. "Management Models and Industrial Applications of Linear Programming," *Management Science*, IV, No. 2 (October, 1957), 38–91.

[7] ———. "Non-linear Network Flows and Convex Programming over Incidence Matrices," *Logistics Research Quarterly*, V, No. 2 (June, 1958).

[8] ———. "Nonlinear Power of Adjacent Extreme Point Methods in Linear Programming," *Econometrica*, XXV, No. 1 (January, 1957), 132–53.

[9] CHARNES, A., COOPER, W. W., and MELLON, B. "Blending Aviation Gasolines: A Study in Programming Interdependent Activities in an Integrated Oil Co.," *Econometrica*, XX, No. 2 (April, 1952), 135–59.

[10] CHARNES, A., COOPER, W. W., and HENDERSON, A. *An Introduction to Linear Programming.* New York: John Wiley & Sons, 1953.

[11] CHARNES, A., COOPER, W. W., and SYMONDS, G. H. "Cost Horizons and Certainty Equivalents: An Approach to Stochastic Programming of Heating Oil," *Management Science*, IV, No. 3 (April, 1958), 235–63.

[12] CHARNES, A., COOPER, W. W., and MILLER, M. "Dyadic Programs and Subdual Methods." Lafayette: Purdue University Research Project for Methodological Aspects of Management Science, 1957.

[13] CHARNES, A., and LEMKE, C. E. "A Modified Simplex Method for Control of Round-Off Error in Linear Programming," *Proceedings, Association for Computing Machinery, Pittsburgh Meeting, May 1952.*

[14] COOPER, W. W. "Research on the Business Firm—Discussion," *American Economic Review, Papers and Proceedings of the 67th Annual Meeting,* XLV, No. 2 (May, 1955), 559–64.

[15] ———. "Revisions to the Theory of the Firm," *American Economic Review,* XXXIX, No. 6 (December, 1949), 1204–22.

[16] DEAN, JOEL. *Capital Budgeting.* New York: Columbia University Press, 1951.

[17] DORFMAN, R., SAMUELSON, PAUL A., and SOLOW, R. M. *Linear Programming and Economic Analysis.* New York: McGraw-Hill Book Co., 1958.

[18] GASS, S. I., and SAATY, T. L. "The Computational Algorithm for the Parametric Objective Function," *Logistics Research Quarterly*, II, Nos. 1 and 2 (March and June, 1955), 39–45.

[19] GARVIN, W. W., CRANDELL, H. W., JOHN, J. B., and SKELLMAN, R. A. "Applications of Linear Programming in the Oil Industry," *Management Science*, III, No. 4 (July, 1957), 407–30.

[20] HART, A. G. *Anticipations, Uncertainty, and Dynamic Planning.* ("Studies in Business Administration," Vol. XI, No. 1.) Chicago: University of Chicago Press, 1940.

[21] HILL, HORACE, G., JR. *A New Method for Computing the Rate of Return on Capital Expenditure.* Berwyn, Pa.: Horace G. Hill, 1953.

[22] HIRSHLEIFER, JACK. "On the Theory of Optimal Investment Decision," *Journal of Political Economy*, LXVI, No. 4 (June, 1958), 329–52.

[23] KEYNES, J. M. *The General Theory of Employment, Interest and Money.* New York: Harcourt, Brace & Co., 1939.

[24] KOOPMANS, T. C. (ed.). *Activity Analysis of Production and Allocation.* (Cowles Commission for Research in Economics, Monograph No. 13). New York: John Wiley & Sons, 1951.

    (1) DANTZIG, G. B. "Maximization of a Linear Function of Variables Subject to Linear Inequalities"

    (2) GALE, D., KUHN, H. W., and TUCKER, A. W. "Linear Programming and the Theory of Games"

    (3) KOOPMANS, T. C., and REITER, S. "A Model of Transportation"

[25] LEMKE, C. E. "The Dual Method of Solving the Linear Programming Problem," *Naval Research Logistics Quarterly*, I, No. 1 (March, 1954), 36–47.

[26] LORIE, J. H., and SAVAGE, L. J. "Three Problems in Capital Rationing," *Journal of Business*, XXVIII, No. 4 (October, 1955), 229–39.

[27] MODIGLIANI, FRANCO, and MILLER, MERTON H. "The Cost of Capital, Corporation Finance and the Theory of Investment," *American Economic Review*, XLVIII, No. 3 (June, 1958), 261–97.

[28] PRAGER, W. "On Warehousing Problems," *Operations Research*, V, No. 4 (August, 1957), 504–12.

[29] SOLOMON, E. "The Arithmetic of Capital-budgeting Decisions," *Journal of Business*, XXIX, No. 2 (April, 1956), 124–29.

Chapter 3   Allocation of Funds in Divisionalized Corporations

GENERAL HOLDINGS CORPORATION

ONE OF THE critical problems confronting management and the board of General Holdings Corporation in the early 1960's was the determination of a minimum acceptable rate of return on new capital investments. While this question had been under discussion within the company for several years, so far the people involved had been unable to agree even on what general concept of a minimum acceptable rate they should adopt. They were about evenly divided between using a single cutoff rate based on the company's overall weighted average cost of capital and a system of multiple cutoff rates said to reflect the risk–profit characteristics of the several businesses or economic sectors in which the company's subsidiaries operated. In late 1963, management was asked by the board to restudy the issue of single versus multiple cutoff rates and to recommend which approach the company should follow in the future.

General Holdings Corporation was formed in 1923 with the merger of several formerly independent firms operating in the oil refining, pipeline transportation, and industrial chemical fields. Over the following 40 years, the company integrated vertically into exploration and production of crude oil and marketing refined petroleum products, and horizontally into plastics, agricultural chemicals, and real estate development. The company was organized as a holding company with semiautonomous operating subsidiaries working in each of the above areas of activity. Its total assets exceeded $2 billion in 1963, and its capital expenditures averaged about $150 million a year in recent years.

Although management was unable to decide whether the company should use single or multiple cutoff rates, it had worked tentatively with a single corporatewide rate for about five years. The company's basic capital budgeting approach during this period had been to accept all proposed investments with a positive net present value when discounted at the company's estimated weighted average cost of capital. As cost of capital was defined and used in this process, the company, in effect, accepted projects down to the point where there would be no dilution in expected earnings per share of common stock.

The cost of capital discount rate used in the net present value discounting procedure was 10%, estimated as follows: First, an estimate was made of the expected proportions of future funds sources. Second, costs were assigned to each of these sources. Third, a weighted average cost of capital was calculated on the basis of these proportions and costs. Finally, this weighted average was adjusted upward to reflect the fact that no return at all was earned on a substantial proportion of the company's investments.

On the basis of the company's financing experience during the 1950's, company officials estimated that future capital investments would be financed about one third from debt and two thirds from depreciation and retained earnings combined. The company had not sold common stock for many years and had no plans to do so in the foreseeable future.

The primary consideration behind the costs assigned to the above funds sources was to avoid accepting projects with expected returns so low that the stockholders' expected earnings per share would be diluted. If the stockholders could reinvest their funds at a higher rate of return outside the company than management could inside, so the argument ran, the funds involved should be distributed to the stockholders rather than invested or reinvested internally. With this objective in mind, the company's future cost of debt was estimated at 2.5% after taxes, assuming a one third proportion of debt to total fund sources. Depreciation and retained earnings were thought to be exactly the same as common stock from the stockholders' point of view. In costing depreciation and retained earnings, therefore, the management started with the reciprocal of the company's probable long-term price–earnings ratio. This ratio was thought to be about 15 times. In addition, however, because this 15-times ratio was thought to reflect an assumed continuation of past growth in earnings per share, an adjustment was made, reducing the assumed price–earnings ratio to 10 times. The lower ratio was thought to reflect more accurately the long-term relationship between current market prices and expected earnings per share.

Combining these proportions and costs, the company's weighted average cost of capital came out at 7.5%.

Source	Estimated Proportions of Future Funds Sources	Estimated Future Cost, After Taxes
Debt.................................	33%	2.5%
Depreciation and retained earnings..........	67%	10.0%
Weighted Average Cost..............		7.5%

This 7.5% assumed that at least 7.5% would be earned on the total capital employed by the company. In fact, however, total capital employed included

not only successful projects but also unsuccessful projects and certain necessary investments that resulted in little, if any, return. About 25% of the company's investments typically fell into the second and third categories. Thus, to earn 7.5% on an overall basis it was necessary to earn at least 10% after taxes on the 75% of the company's projects where an actual return was expected. This is the 10% discount rate that was used by the company in determining the net present value of proposed capital expenditures.

The idea of using the single 10% discount rate on a corporatewide basis had been strongly opposed from the beginning by several of the operating subsidiaries of General Holdings. These subsidiaries argued that the internal allocation of funds by the parent company among its principal operating subsidiaries should be based upon a system of multiple target rates of return reflecting the unique risk–profit characteristics of the industry or economic sector in which each subsidiary operated.

Those arguing in favor of multiple target rates of return usually began by pointing out that General Holdings Corporation was really just a holding company with a number of operating subsidiaries in several related and unrelated industries. Each of these operating affiliates faced numerous competitors and a unique risk–profit environment. Some of these competitors operated in only one industry or economic sector; others were parts of more complex groupings, such as General Holdings. However this might be, those arguing in favor of multiple cutoff rates did so on the grounds that given the underlying strategic decision to be in, say, pipelines or refining or plastics, the parent company had then to adopt minimum acceptable rates of return related to the competitive risk–profit characteristics inherent in each area.

To do otherwise was alleged to have two important undesirable outcomes. The first of these was that a high companywide rate, such as the company's present 10% discount rate, resulted in the company or its affiliates not going into some highly profitable ventures. Gas transmission pipelines were an often-cited example of this. Gas pipelines had been ruled out by General Holdings in the past because the regulated 6% return on invested capital was well below the company's 10% minimum. In spite of this low regulated return, however, gas transmission companies were typically highly leveraged because of the limited economic risk involved in their operation, and their common stocks often sold in the 30 times price–earnings range. Since this was double General Holdings' normal price–earnings ratio, it was argued that the company's stockholders would have benefited had the parent company allowed its pipeline affiliate to expand along with the gas transmission industry.

The second undesirable outcome of using a high single cutoff rate was that it was said to favor investment projects or alternatives with low initial funds commitments almost without regard to the subsequent operating cost streams that could be expected to follow. In part, this was simply reiterating the point that the company had been underinvesting in the low risk parts of its business or businesses. But more was involved. Where operating economies of scale were concerned, particularly in capital intensive areas, a higher than justified rate penalized high initial investment–low operating cost alternatives in favor of low initial investment–high operating cost alternatives or projects. In short, the company tended to underinvest initially at the expense of higher future operating costs, and deferred related investments whose importance was underrated as a result of using an inappropriately high discount rate in low risk situations.

The specific alternative proposed by the supporters of multiple cutoff rates in lieu of a single companywide rate involved determining several rates, based on the estimated cost of capital inherent in each of the economic sectors or industries in which the company's principal operating subsidiaries worked. Weighted average cost of capital cutoff rates reflecting their specific risk–profit environments would be determined for the company's production-exploration, pipeline transportation, refining, and marketing affiliates in the oil industry, as well as for its plastics, industrial chemicals, agricultural chemicals, and real estate subsidiaries operating outside the oil industry. For example, cutoff rates of 16%, 11%, 8%, and 6%, respectively, were proposed for the production-exploration, chemicals, real estate, and pipeline parts of the business. All the other rates proposed fell within this range. The suggestion was that these multiple cutoff rates determine the minimum acceptable rate of return on proposed capital investments in each of the main operating areas of the company.

It was proposed that the weighted average cost of capital in each operating sector be developed as follows. First, an estimate would be made of the usual debt and equity proportions of independently financed firms operating in each sector. Several such independents competed against each of the company's affiliates. Second, the costs of debt and equity given these proportions and sectors would be estimated in accordance with the concepts followed by the company in estimating its own costs of capital in the past. Third, these costs and proportions would be combined to determine the weighted average cost of capital, or minimum acceptable rate of return, for discounting purposes in each sector.

These multiple hurdle or discount rates had been calculated for several periods in the past, and invariably their weighted average, when weighted according to the company's relative investment in each sector, exceeded the company's actual overall average cost of capital. This differential was attributed to the fact that the sector hurdle rates calculated as described above tended to overlook the risk diversification benefits of many investments undertaken by General Holdings. As compared with a nonintegrated enterprise operating in any given branch, a vertically and horizontally integrated firm such as General Holdings enjoyed some built-in asset diversification as well as important captive markets between certain of its vertically integrated parts. For example, the risks associated with a refinery investment by an integrated company like General Holdings were said to be much less than for an identical investment made by an independent. It was proposed that this diversification premium be allocated back and deducted from the multiple subsidiary discount rates in proportion to the relationship of the investment in each subsidiary to the company's total assets.

While it had been impossible to accurately appraise the overall impact of changing from a single rate to multiple target rates, it could be foreseen that both the company's asset structure and the probable size of its future capital expenditures would be affected. It was anticipated, for example, that up to one third of future capital expenditures might be shifted from one to another operating sector or affiliate with the adoption of multiple hurdle rates. In addition, the company's expected average annual capital budget could easily increase from $150 million to $175 million or more. An annual budget of this magnitude would force reconsideration of the company's traditional debt, common stock, and dividend policies.

As management and the board of General Holdings began their latest review of the controversy between using single or multiple minimum acceptable cutoff rates, the officers of the operating subsidiaries were asked to restate their positions. Those behind the present single target rate contended that the stockholders of General Holdings would expect the company to invest their funds in the highest return projects available. They suggested that without exception the affiliates backing multiple rates were those that were unable to compete effectively for new funds when measured against the corporate group's actual cost of capital. Against this, the multiple hurdle rate proponents pointed out again that if the parent company was serious about competing over the long run in industries with such disparate risk–profit characteristics as they faced, it was absolutely essential to relate internal target rates of return to these circumstances. They felt that division of the overall corporate investment pot should be based primarily on the company's long-term strategic plans. It was against this background that the final choice between single versus multiple cutoff rates had to be decided.

SEATON COMPANY

In early 1965, the Seaton Company was one of the largest fully integrated producers of aluminum and aluminum products in the United States. Aluminum accounted for slightly more than 75% of the company's gross revenues. The remaining 25% of revenues resulted from the company's interests in chemicals (10%), electrical equipment (7%), beryllium (5%), and real estate (3%). In almost every year since the end of World War II, the company's gross revenues had increased substantially over those for the preceding year. By 1964, they were slightly more than $700 million. The company experienced its highest growth rate during the period from 1950 through 1964, when revenues increased by a factor of six. Unfortunately, profit increases did not match the increases in revenues. After-tax return on investment fell from 15% in 1950 to just over 5% in 1964. Earnings per share fell from $3.80 in 1950 to $1.80 in 1964.

In the postwar period, sales of aluminum and aluminum products had been the largest growth area for the company, and had increased as a percentage of total sales during almost every year. As aluminum had been in large part responsible for the sales increases, it had also been the major cause of the drastic drop in after-tax return on investment. After-tax return in the aluminum division had fallen from 17% in 1950 to just under 3% in 1964.

The central analysis department made financial analyses for all capital expenditure proposals involving investments of $25,000 or more. It was the responsibility of analysts in this department to review the sales, pricing, and expense forecasts relating to each proposal and to prepare rate-of-return analyses and recommendations for the senior corporate officers. The recommendations reviewed possible risks in each project and suggested a course of action (approval or rejection) to be followed. The central analysis department was also charged with establishing the methods of analysis used and with recommending improvements. Changes had frequently been made to reflect changing conditions in the industries in which the company participated. The director of the department since mid-1962 had been George Romain. He reported to Joseph DeMato, manager–corporate planning. Mr. DeMato, in turn, reported to Robert Sherman, vice president–finance, and controller.

During the summer of 1964, Mr. Romain undertook an analysis of Seaton's capital budgeting policies and procedures. In recent years, he had become increasingly concerned with the apparent inconsistencies between assumptions made in the capital budgeting system and the changing aspects of the aluminum industry. A major industry expansion in the early and middle 1950's had led to overcapacity, which was still evident in 1965. During this period, corporate strategy had called for entering any product line that would provide a contribution to fixed charges and would have a payback period short enough to insure corporate liquidity. Consequently, during this period the central analysis department had analyzed projects in terms of after-tax rate of return on the incremental cash flows involved and also in terms of payback. During the first few years, payback had been considered the most important, but as capacity operations appeared possible in the next few years, payback had diminished in importance and central analysis had required a higher incremental ROI for a project to be acceptable. Mr. Romain immediately asked Mr. Sherman for permission to develop a new capital budgeting system for aluminum fabricating facilities. In May, 1965, Mr. Romain presented to Mr. Sherman a proposal outlining the system he and his staff envisioned. At the same time, he requested authorization to work out in detail and to install the new system.

Mr. Romain proposed that three major changes be made in the present system.

1. The transfer price used to transfer aluminum to fabricating facilities would be changed. The existing system used a full-cost transfer price, which merely allowed for the return of capital invested in prior processing facilities. The proposed system would use a higher transfer price, calculated to provide at least a minimum acceptable after-tax return (8%) on investments in prior processing facilities. This transfer price would be used only in capital budgeting analyses.

2. The approval of new fabricating facilities would be made in two categories. The first category would include all projects that promised the minimum acceptable return on prior processing facilities as well as an adequate return on the fabricating investment (no less than 15%). These projects would be permanent in that they would be expected to remain in Seaton's product line as long as they were profitable. The second category would include those short projects that did not meet the above criteria but would provide a satisfactory after-tax return (15%) on the incremental cash flows involved. Because basic aluminum capacity could be expanded only in large increments, it was expected that all expansion programs would be followed by a period of overcapacity.[1] Temporary products were to be produced when capacity was too great to be used by permanent products alone. Temporary products were to be discontinued when the aluminum used in their production was needed in permanent products.

3. Expansion of prior processing facilities, including bauxite mining, alumina production, and reduction facilities, would be undertaken only if the expansion was needed to fill the demand for permanent products.

Mr. Sherman was not sure what action to take on either Mr. Romain's proposed system or his request for permission to undertake further study. Mr. Sherman was convinced that the system, if it could be made to work and if the line managers would obey the signals given, could result in a significant

---

[1] Basic means either large fabricating and/or reduction.

increase in return on investment. In the past, Seaton managers had emphasized growth in sales and in market share, both measured in pounds of
aluminum shipped. Return on investment was secondary. The proposed system would elevate ROI to far and away the most important goal for the
company.

Mr. Sherman realized that approval of the work done so far would mean,
in effect, approval of the detailed system Mr. Romain would then develop. He
therefore believed that before taking any action he should analyze the system
in great detail in order to determine what it would do in a wide range of
possible situations.

PROBLEMS ENCOUNTERED IN EXPANSIONS

The economics of aluminum production processes made the analysis required for investigation of investment proposals quite different from the
analysis needed in most other manufacturing industries. The peculiar features
of the industry had caused severe problems, especially during periods of
general expansion.

The first area of difference arose because the minimum investment by
which primary production (the series of processes producing aluminum ingot
or hot metal from bauxite) could be expanded was very large and would
significantly increase capacity. As an example, the smallest economic investment for building a new reduction facility would increase Seaton's capacity
by 150,000 tons of hot metal, a 20% increase. Besides requiring large
increases in capacity, expansion in primary production required a large
investment per unit of output. Whereas the investment required to produce 1
ton of steel varied between $100 and $150, the investment to produce a
similar weight of aluminum varied between 10 and 25 times as much. Lead
times to reach production in the various processes varied between three and
five years. Because of these facts, very few firms were fully integrated back to
bauxite.

A second problem of the industry resulted from the economic increments of
expansion for each process, which were quite different in size. In most cases,
both the investment required and the increase in capacity involved were
greater as the process was farther away from the final product. For example,
Seaton planned to build a facility to produce siding panels for mobile homes.
This plant would annually process 1,000 tons of aluminum and would cost
$90,000 to equip. At the other end of the process, the next planned increment
to expand bauxite mining would cost $50 million and would have a capacity
of 1.5 million tons of bauxite—roughly 300,000 tons of aluminum ingot.

A third problem area was caused by the almost complete absence of
dependable markets outside a firm for the output of processes prior to the
production of aluminum ingot. Therefore, a firm could not rely on balancing
production by either purchasing or selling partially processed aluminum. This
situation was not expected to change significantly.

During 1964, almost 10% of Seaton's ingot production was sold without further processing to independent fabricators, and another 12% was sold in a semifinished state to fabricators. The remainder was fabricated and marketed by Seaton. In contrast, Seaton sold no bauxite and only a negligible amount of alumina to outsiders.

These factors had caused serious difficulties for the industry in the late 1950's and early 1960's. During that period, primary producers, including Seaton, had expanded vigorously. As an example, industry smelter capacity increased from 1.4 million tons in 1954 to 2.5 million in 1960. Capacity in 1960 would have been even higher if many planned projects had not been halted in various stages of construction. Price wars and the financial drains of maintaining idle capacity reduced industry profits by almost 50% between 1954 and 1960. To utilize expanded capacity and to provide at least some contribution toward fixed charges, the industry introduced many otherwise unacceptable product lines, and return on investment dropped for most companies. Failure to discontinue these products as demand for more profitable products increased had resulted in a 1965 situation that required expansion of primary capacity to supply the ingot demand if all product lines were to be maintained.

The overexpansion of the late 1950's, while creating havoc in the industry in the early 1960's, had decreased the importance of expansion problems in the late 1960's. First, many of the expansion projects started in the 1950's were still only partially completed in 1965 and would require relatively small investments to expand capacity at many levels of production in order to meet forecasted demand through 1970-73. Also, new processes being developed would decrease the size and investment needed in the minimum economic-sized plant. Mr. Sherman expected that these developments would decrease the deviation and magnitude of the industry's cyclic swings between overcapacity and undercapacity.

THE CAPITAL BUDGETING SYSTEM IN USE IN 1965

The capital budgeting system used by the Seaton Company in 1965 required an IPR (investment proposal request) for every investment proposed, regardless of size. This report summarized the financial aspects of the proposed investment as well as the competitive and strategic reasoning behind the proposal. Exhibit 1 charts the routing of IPR's for projects of $25,000 or more from the originating plant through the various stages of approval and review back to the originating plant. The routing for IPR's originating in plants is described below. Only slight modifications in this procedure were required for IPR's originating at other locations. Mr. Romain did not propose that this routing be changed. His recommendations concerned only the financial analysis of projects to be made by the central analysis department.

The plant engineer at the originating plant assembled all data to be included in the IPR. His work was reviewed and approved by the plant controller and the plant manager. In most cases, investments involving amounts less than $10,000 could be approved by the plant manager. In a few instances, these IPR's required approval by the division manager. When this was the case, the IPR's were routed in the same way as those for projects involving $10,000 or more but less than $25,000 (discussed below). Each month a summary report of all investments approved at the plant level was forwarded to the head office for review by the responsible division manager.

All projects involving investments of $10,000 or more required the approval of one or more executives at the head office. IPR's for less than $25,000 were forwarded directly to the responsible division manager for final approval. IPR's for $25,000 or more received more detailed examination.

IPR's for $25,000 or more were forwarded first to the manager–engineering planning at the head office. He recorded each IPR in a control log and forwarded copies to the appropriate division engineer and to the central analysis department. When each approving authority completed his work on a particular IPR, he returned it to the manager–engineering planning for recording and forwarding to the next person in line. In this way, records of each IPR's progress were maintained.

The IPR went from the division engineer to the manager–engineering at the head office, and then in sequence to the division controller, the operations manager, and the division manager. When the division manager had approved, the IPR was sent to the vice president–manufacturing for review by the top executives.

Each approving authority reviewed and commented on only those attributes of the proposed investment that involved his particular area of competence. The division engineer and the manager–engineering at the head office checked the technical aspects of the project to insure that all alternatives had been analyzed and that the project took advantage of experience and ideas developed in other plants. The division controller made sure that the needed management reports could and would be collected and distributed if and when the project was approved. All the other levels of approval (except the central analysis department) reviewed proposals to be certain that they were in line with division objectives.

If minor changes were necessary for approval at any step in the process, the manager–engineering planning arranged for them to be made in the head office and for the originating plant to be advised of the changes. If large or basic changes were required, he returned the IPR to the plant engineer with a memorandum outlining the reasons for return. Copies of the memorandum were sent to all persons who had had an interest in the prior progress of the IPR. The plant engineer could resubmit the IPR either after the changes had been made or accompanied by an explanation of why the changes could not be made.

The central analysis department was charged with analyzing the financial aspects of a project after its feasibility had been thoroughly established. The objective was to determine whether the project would yield a rate of return commensurate with the risks involved. To accompany the IPR, the analyst assigned to a project wrote a memorandum summarizing his findings, the risks involved in the project, and his recommendation for further action. The analyst's report was reviewed by Mr. Romain and routed directly to the vice president–finance, and controller.

The central analysis department could not approve or reject projects, but could only recommend a course of action to persons reviewing the proposals at a later date. Mr. Romain had made it a policy, however, to suggest to the managers of the originating plants any changes that he believed were desirable to insure higher level approval. Most of his suggestions had been incorporated into the proposals.

After a project had been approved by the final authority, the IPR went back to the central analysis department and to the manager–engineering planning and the purchasing department. Purchasing returned the IPR to the manager of the originating plant and also notified the property accounting department at the head office so that it could prepare the necessary ownership contracts and papers.

Mr. Romain estimated that approval of an IPR took from two weeks to two months. Approval times varied with the number of requests being reviewed at a given time, the number of changes to be made, the complexity of the particular project, and the availability of funds.

THE APPROVAL WORK OF THE CENTRAL ANALYSIS DEPARTMENT

The central analysis department separated all projects for financial analysis into four categories:

1. Cost reduction and replacement projects (except fabricating projects).
2. Additions to primary capacity.
3. Additions to and replacements of fabricating facilities.
4. Projects that were not to be or could not be analyzed on a rate-of-return basis.

1. Projects involving *cost reduction and replacement* of mining and reduction facilities were analyzed by using present value techniques to determine the after-tax internal rate of return associated with the incremental cash flows forecasted for the project. Company policy did not dictate a minimum return criterion, but most projects accepted had shown an expected after-tax internal rate of return of at least 20%. It was company policy to attempt to evaluate the rate of return afforded by each project in light of the risks associated with that project.

2. Decisions to *expand primary aluminum capacity* were based almost exclusively on forecasts of the amount of primary aluminum needed to meet the expected demand for both existing and planned end products. Annually, five-year sales forecasts by product line were developed by division marketing

managers as part of the company's long-range planning efforts. The manufacturing division then transformed these forecasts into metal supply and demand forecasts.

When it became evident to the manufacturing divisional managers that expansion of a process or facility was required, they had compiled reports comparing the forecasts of demand for the next five years with the estimates of existing and planned aluminum availability. The report was submitted to top management along with recommendations as to the most advantageous methods and plant additions to implement the expansion.

The central analysis department was required to review these recommendations but was not authorized to make changes in the forecasts. If an analyst believed a forecast was unreasonable, he could suggest to the division that the estimate be revised. Alternatively, he could use the forecasts submitted and include his opinion in his recommendations.

At all times the engineering department of each division in the production process prior to fabrication had designs and locations established for the next several increments of expansion. These plans were reviewed and revised every two years or whenever significant technological innovations occurred. Mr. Romain was certain that the planned plants were as low in cost and as well designed as any in the industry.

Mr. Romain summarized the problem he saw as follows: "Our present system tells us when to expand primary capacity to allow us to keep up with the demand for our products. But it does not tell us which of the products we have now are worth expanding primary supply in order to keep. We could drop or reduce participation in many of our products and use the freed-up aluminum elsewhere."

3. The analysis of *additions to fabrication facilities* involved the calculation of an internal rate of return for the project. The investment figure used included estimates of working capital, preoperating expenses, and initial promotion, in addition to plant and equipment. Cash inflows reflected estimates of incremental sales as well as an allowance for scrap.

Both direct and allocated costs were included in cash outflow amounts. Rules of thumb, believed to reasonably approximate the effect of the project on factory, division, and corporate overhead, were used to allocate these costs. All manufacturing costs, except those for aluminum raw material, were developed from the industrial engineering forecasts.

For capital budgeting decisions, aluminum was transferred to proposed fabricating facilities on a full-cost basis. The transfer cost was calculated to include all the manufacturing costs, overhead, and depreciation connected with prior facilities. Therefore, the transfer costs were calculated to ensure at least the return of the capital invested in prior facilities, but did not provide for any profit on these investments.

The company had no policies setting minimum return criteria for fabricating facilities. Mr. Romain thought that few projects had been accepted with after-tax expected returns below 15%. Although Mr. Romain recommended approval of proposed expansions to existing product lines expecting a return of as low as 25%, he did not like to recommend for approval investments in new products promising less than 30%. He said, "We try to weigh the expected rate of return against the risks involved in each individual situation."

4. To analyze *projects that were not to be or could not be analyzed on a rate-of-return basis,* the central analysis department first reviewed all investment and expense figures and then calculated the net present value cost of the project. The discount rate used in all calculations was the minimum acceptable rate of return, 8% after taxes. The analyst prepared a memorandum on his findings and forwarded it along with the IPR to the manager–engineering planning. No recommendations for further action were included.

THE PROPOSED SYSTEM

Mr. Romain proposed three changes in the capital budgeting system. First, he proposed the development of new transfer prices. These processing prices would be calculated as the prices at which the aluminum stock used as a raw material in the fabrication process would have to be sold in order to provide a minimum acceptable return (8% after taxes) on all prior facilities required in the production of that stock. Furthermore, they were to be calculated assuming the aluminum stock used would be produced in the next planned expansion of basic capacity in prior operations. This method of analysis would take into account the effect of the proposed investment on the constant need to expand prior processing facilities. The transfer prices would have no relation to actual market prices for the stock. The transfer prices would not be used in the company's management control systems, but only for investment proposal analysis.

Second, he proposed that suggested fabricating investments be analyzed so as to fall into one of two categories. The first category—permanent—would include all projects that would yield an after-tax return on investment of at least 15%. This would ensure at least an 8% after-tax return on prior processing facilities and a 15% return on the more risky fabricating facilities. If a project did not meet this criterion, it would be considered as a potential temporary project—the second category. Projects were to be approved as temporary only when there was excess primary and prior fabricating capacity that could not be used in category 1 products. Temporary projects were to be abandoned as soon as the aluminum employed could be used in permanent projects. The product life to be used in the analysis of a potential temporary project would be determined through a comparison of the forecasted supply and demand for the type of stock needed. Mr. Romain expected product life for most projects to vary from three to five years. To be approved as a temporary project, an investment proposal would be expected to yield at least a 20% after-tax internal rate of return on the incremental cash flows involved.

If unused aluminum capacity was not available, the analysis for a temporary project could assume that the aluminum supply would be shifted from a less profitable existing product line using the same aluminum stock as a raw material. Approval of the transfer assumed in the analysis would be required before final approval could be given to the potential temporary project. This process would result in an upgrading of the profitability of the less profitable products.

Third, Mr. Romain proposed that all existing product lines be analyzed in the same manner as new products in order to classify them as either permanent or temporary products. Products that fell in the temporary category and were not judged desirable for strategic reasons would be proposed for abandonment when the aluminum used in them could be fabricated into more profitable products. New investment proposals possibly falling into category 2 would be compared with the group of existing products classified as temporary. Some of these new proposals were expected to replace the existing products. Mr. Romain estimated that one half of the aluminum poundage used in 1964 was in existing products that did not meet MRP (minimum return prices) criteria. This would mean that sales of category 1 products could increase by 100% before new primary capacity would be needed. In addition, after-tax return on existing investment could increase from 3 to 10% or more.

Mr. Romain believed the proposed capital budgeting system would allow Seaton to increase profits and return on investment with minimal new investment through selective selling and reduced participation in less profitable product lines. He had made a sample study of several existing products and had found products with after-tax internal rates of return on the total investment required (based on the next expected increments of expansion) ranging from 0 to 25%.

Mr. Romain was convinced that either reducing participation or eliminating many product lines could be done without serious marketing implications. First, most of the products that might be dropped appeared to be sold on a price basis and seemed to have little, if any, market differentiation and demand cross elasticity with other more desirable product lines. Many were sold as the result of bids presented by Seaton. In reducing participation in these lines, Mr. Romain believed Seaton could choose to either not bid or bid high enough to ensure losing the contract. If cross elasticity of one of these products was believed to exist with more profitable product lines, this fact could be considered in the analysis. Products found to have such relationships would be retained.

Mr. Romain had worried about the possible problems involved in reentering fabrication of a product on a temporary basis after it had been dropped. He concluded that those products requiring heavy marketing outlays and a long time (more than one year) for reentry on a profitable basis would not be reconsidered. He believed that many products could be very easily reincorporated in the product line. He also believed that this step would not often be necessary; possibly one in four products might be reentered. He planned to recommend that Seaton should not completely withdraw from producing a product if it seemed likely that the product would be reincorporated in the line within three years. Instead, the company should scale down operations to a level that would maintain a foothold in the market. In addition, he believed that there were, and would continue to be, enough new product proposals generated to supply much of the expected need for temporary products.

THE CALCULATION OF TRANSFER PRICES

Mr. Romain expected that the first step his department would take to install the proposed system would be a calculation of new aluminum transfer prices for all processes, to be called minimum return prices (MRP). Such a price was to be the minimum selling price for the output of a process or series of processes necessary to earn a minimum acceptable return on the investment needed to build a new economic-sized plant to produce that output. The investment and cost figures to be used would be those estimated by the industrial engineering department of the division for the next planned increments of expansion. MRP's would be calculated for each process. The transfer price to each process would be the MRP selling price for the prior production step. Therefore, the MRP for any process would provide a minimum return for all prior processes.

The level of operations to be assumed would not be full capacity but would reflect expected minimum operating conditions. Expected minimum operating conditions were defined as the minimum risk level of operations—one in which mining, reduction, and hot metal facilities were operating at an average rate of 90% and casting facilities at an average 75% of capacity. These rates were lower than experienced by the company in any of the previous 10 years.

Mr. Romain believed that if facilities could be operated at these average rates of capacity or better, Seaton could expect to earn an amount equivalent to its cost of capital, which was estimated to be 8%. He reasoned that with the expected growth in demand for Seaton's products, the wide diversity of end uses for each of its semifinished products, and its strong position in the market, operation at this average level would provide a reasonable return for the common stockholders on a more or less risk-free basis.

Exhibit 2 presents a production flow chart showing where MRP's were to be calculated. MRP costs were to be revised every two years, and sooner if significant technological developments occurred.

Exhibits 3 and 4 give sample figures for the calculation of the MRP for hot metal. The present value, at 8%, of the investment and its depreciation tax shield was to be computed from a schedule showing the amounts and times of all quantities needed to establish the facility. As shown in Exhibit 3, the net figure was $405,506. From this number would be obtained the annual receipt necessary to earn 8% on the investment and to gain the return of the capital used. In this case, the amount of the annuity was $39,733. Assuming a 48% tax rate, the before-tax number was $76,409.

Since the capacity of this investment was 1 million pounds a year, the "capital adder" was 7.64 cents per pound. As shown in Exhibit 4, this capital adder would be included in the MRP charged to the next layer in the production process for the hot metal used by it, just as the hot metal level was charged an MRP for alumina.

The suggested method of calculating the internal rate of return for a proposed fabricating investment would differ from the existing method only in that the MRP would be used instead of the full-cost transfer price. If the project showed an adequate after-tax return (usually 15%), it would be recommended for approval. If not, it would be further analyzed as a potential temporary project.

THE DEMAND–AVAILABILITY GRAPH

Mr. Romain believed a significant number of existing product lines should be dropped because they did not meet the minimum return criteria and, therefore, would not justify expanding prior processing facilities in order to continue them. He proposed that a demand–availability graph (DAG) be constructed for each group of fabricated products using the same aluminum raw material. This graph would suggest an order in which these products should be dropped, as well as an estimate of the time at which they should be dropped. The DAG could also be used to project the need for new primary capacity. Exhibit 5 shows a sample graph for all products fabricated from thin sheet. Other DAG's were to be constructed for other groups of products fabricated from other types of aluminum stock.

The first step in preparing a DAG would be calculations of MRP's for all end products. The MRP's would be those prices at which the fabricated products would have to be sold to provide at least the minimum acceptable return on all assets involved (8%). The MRP's for aluminum raw material inputs would be the same as those used in the analysis of new products. Because demand for all product groups was expected to increase, Mr. Romain believed each existing product should provide a return on total investment high enough to warrant expanding prior processing facilities in order to keep that product in the Seaton line.

The next step would be a comparison of each product's MRP with its actual sales price. If the sales price was the same as or higher than the MRP, the product would be yielding an adequate return on investment. If the product was selling for less than the MRP, it would be a candidate for discontinuance. The difference between the MRP and the sales price for a product would be a measure of that product's desirability to Seaton. The greater the excess of sales price over MRP, the more profitable the product would be. Conversely, those products whose MRP showed the greatest premium over the sales price should be discontinued first.

The annual demand (as measured in pounds of aluminum raw material expected to be used) for each product was then forecasted. The aluminum availability, both existing and planned, was also determined.

The sample DAG for products fabricated from thin sheet was constructed from this information as follows (see Exhibit 5). The horizontal axis was in years; the vertical axis was in millions of pounds of aluminum. The dotted line recorded the expected supply of aluminum that would be available to the class of products being analyzed. The solid lines recorded the amount of aluminum forecasted to be needed by each product line in the group; that is, the vertical distance between each set of solid lines reflected the volume in pounds of aluminum raw material forecasted to be demanded by that product. The product lines were ordered on the graph according to their desirability to Seaton; those near the bottom of the graph were the most profitable and therefore the most desirable. The figures in parentheses recorded the excess of selling price over MRP. Therefore, the solid line between products E and F marked the cutoff point between permanent and temporary products.

Products A through E were expected to meet minimum return criteria. Products F through K were not. Product K, however, although not profitable in early 1965, was expected to meet MRP standards by late 1966 and therefore would be continued. Products F through J were to be considered for discontinuance.

When a new product proposal using thin sheet as an input was being analyzed for acceptance as a temporary investment, it would be analyzed as if aluminum were to be shifted from Product J into the new product. If approved, the new product would be inserted into the graph in the appropriate spot.

The use of DAG would have a profound effect on the expansion of prior processing facilities. Exhibit 5 indicated that the need to expand facilities to produce thin sheet would be postponed from 1966 until after 1969. The intersection of a product's demand line and the aluminum availability line (dotted) forecasted the year during which that product would presumably be phased out. As an example, product H would most likely be phased out in 1968, assuming product K developed as expected and was retained.

Exhibit 1

SEATON COMPANY

ROUTING OF INVESTMENT PROPOSAL REQUESTS OF $25,000 OR MORE FROM
PLANTS IN ALUMINUM DIVISION
(Routing of Original Copy Only)

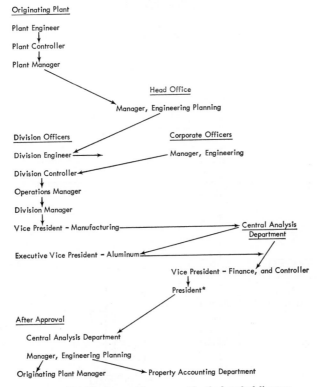

* IPR's for over $100,000 also must be approved by the board of directors.

Exhibit 2

SEATON COMPANY

FLOW CHART FOR PRODUCTION PROCESSES SHOWING WHERE
MRP ARE TO BE CALCULATED

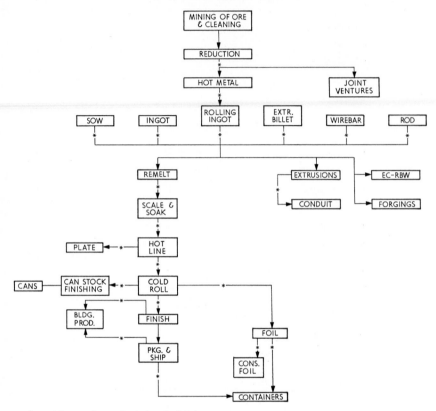

* = minimum return price to be calculated.

Exhibit 3

SEATON COMPANY

ESTIMATED CASH FLOW AND MINIMUM RETURN ON INVESTMENT CALCULATION
FOR HOT METAL FACILITIES
PER MILLION POUNDS OF ALUMINUM*

	Fixed Asset Capital Outlay			Working Capital	Pre-operating Expense	Total Investment	Depreciation†
	Land	Buildings	Equipment				
......	$12,100	$118,020	$450,000	$ 6,000	$4,100	$590,220	...
....	...	...	...	5,500	...	5,500	$ 80,468
2......	...	...	...	...	...	...	74,137
3......	...	...	...	...	...	...	67,806
4......	...	...	...	...	...	...	61,475
5......	...	5,000	25,000	...	...	30,000	59,466
6......	...	...	...	...	...	...	52,791
7......	...	...	...	...	...	...	45,915
8......	...	...	...	...	...	...	39,440
9......	...	...	...	...	...	...	32,765
0......	...	5,000	25,000	...	...	30,000	30,412
1......	...	...	...	...	...	...	23,392
2......	...	...	...	...	...	...	16,371
3......	...	...	...	...	...	...	9,353
4......	...	...	...	...	...	...	8,103
5......	...	5,000	25,000	...	...	30,000	11,174
6......	...	...	...	...	...	...	9,578
7......	...	...	...	...	...	...	7,982
8......	...	...	...	...	...	...	6,710
9......	...	...	...	...	...	...	5,436
0......	...	...	...	...	...	...	4,161
ation...	(12,100)	(60,000)	(57,000)	(11,500)	...	(140,600)	...
Total	...	$ 73,020	$468,000	...	$4,100	$545,120	$646,936

...t value at 8%...............................	608,917	(423,772)
...hield (after tax)‡............................	(203,411)	(203,411)
...t value of investment........................	405,506	...

...tment of PV of investment to before-tax ...ount....................................

$$\frac{405,506}{0.52} = 779,819$$

...nt required per period (received continu-...ly) to recover investment at 8%................

$$779,819 \times .097983 = 76,409$$

...amount expressed in cents per pound............

$$\frac{76,409}{1,000,000} = 7.64¢ \text{ per pound}$$

*ssumed rate of production is 90% of rated capacity.
uildings and repairs: sum of years' digits for 20 years. Equipment: sum of years' digits for 12 years.
ax rate assumed at 48%.

Exhibit 4

SEATON COMPANY

CALCULATION OF MINIMUM RETURN PRICE FOR
HOT METAL

	Cents per Pound
1. Manufacturing costs	
Alumina MRP	5.25
Carbon	1.62
Other materials	.52
Total Materials	7.39
Labor	2.61
Power	.95
Other potroom costs	.60
Hot metal service	.17
Total Labor and Burden	4.33
Total Manufacturing	11.72
2. General and administrative costs	
Plant	.50
Division	.23
Corporate	.55
Total General and Administrative	1.28
3. Capital adder (from Exhibit 3*)	7.64
MRP Price for Hot Metal	20.64

* This capital adder reflects only investment in the reduction of alumina. The capital adders for prior steps in production of alumina are reflected in the alumina MRP transfer price.

Exhibit 5

SEATON COMPANY

DAG CHART FOR END PRODUCTS USING THIN SHEET

NOTE.—The numbers in parentheses represent the cents per pound by
which the selling prices in 1965 exceeded (+) or were lower than (−) minimum
return prices.

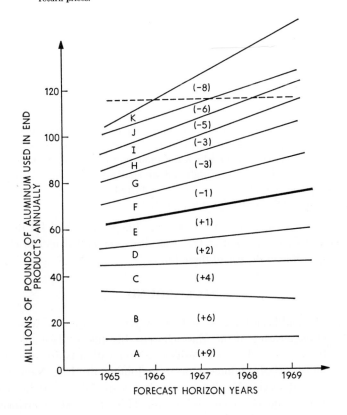

ULTRAMEDIA INC.

DURING THE LATTER half of 1965 the capital budget situation in Ultramedia underwent a dramatic change. The following passage is taken from a letter sent to all divisional general managers by Mr. Peter Clark, vice president for operations:

We have reviewed in some detail the capital equipment budget requests for the first half of 1966. These requests amount to a record total of almost $3 million. While most of the programs for which the funds are requested are necessary and important, the total figure is too high and we shall have to squeeze it a bit. . . . We are asking you again to review your requests and to cut out or delay any items that are not absolutely needed for this period.

Divisions were asked, also, to review any funds authorized for the current budget period which had not at that time been committed and to effect any economies possible in the use of these funds.

BACKGROUND

Ultramedia had been founded in 1946 by Jeremy Wise. Mr. Wise majored in electrical engineering at the Massachusetts Institute of Technology, graduating in 1938, and worked as a design engineer with a major manufacturer of industrial electrical equipment prior to joining the U.S. Navy in 1942. During his naval service Mr. Wise trained as a specialist in radio detection and ultra-high frequency communications. This experience convinced him that high-frequency engineering would play an increasingly important part in the postwar electrical industry. (The concept of a distinct electronics industry had not appeared at this time.) Mr. Wise became convinced, also, that existing testing and calibration equipment was inadequate to the needs of this developing technology, and he set about thinking of ways in which the equipment might be improved.

By 1946 Mr. Wise had developed a number of instruments that seemed to him to have characteristics superior to any then available, and on his release from the Navy in that year he decided to produce these instruments for sale instead of returning to his former employer. The initial batch was produced by Mr. Wise working alone in a rented barn close to his house. The entire batch was purchased by a nearby producer of radio equipment, and repeat orders quickly followed. A period of rapid expansion now began, characterized by an abundance of orders but continual financial difficulties, as Mr.

Wise's personal resources were quickly exhausted and he was forced to rely heavily upon personal loans at this time.

The venture prospered, and within five years all loans had been retired and the organization began to generate adequate funds to finance its further expansion. New products were regularly developed and the company, which became a corporation in 1954 under the name Ultramedia Inc., was recognized as an established factor in the new electronics industry.

This case is concerned primarily with the capital budgeting process in Ultramedia during the period 1963–67. By this time the company had become an acknowledged leader in the field of electronic measuring, testing, and recording instruments. Sales in 1967 were approaching $70 million per annum, having increased rapidly throughout the previous decade. (A six-year summary of sales and income is provided as Exhibit 1.) Ultramedia consisted at this date of five operating divisions, two of them previously independent companies that had been acquired by Ultramedia. There was also a European subsidiary company located in Italy, which undertook sales, servicing, and some limited assembly of instruments for the European market. The bulk of Ultramedia production, however, took place in four plants in the eastern United States.

Throughout this period Mr. Wise continued to guide the destinies of the company, serving both as chairman of the board and as chief executive. Ultramedia had made a first public stock offering in 1957, but had offered for sale only 20% of the outstanding equity at that time. Although employee stock option and stock purchase plans existed, in early 1967 Mr. Wise still owned more than 50% of the company's common stock.

The financing of the company's expansion out of retained earnings and depreciation had become a key concept in Mr. Wise's philosophy. The use of debt was not completely precluded, and short-term bank borrowing was used from time to time. The retirement of any such debt was treated as a matter of high priority, however, and debt funds remained a relatively small part of the company's long-term capitalization, as evidenced by the balance sheets in Exhibit 2. The funds generated by operations were expected to be adequate to maintain and replace existing fixed assets and to provide sufficient new capital equipment and working capital to sustain the company's growth from year to year, and until 1965 adequate funds were in fact so generated. An analysis of sources and uses of funds in the period 1964–66 is provided as Exhibit 3.

THE CAPITAL BUDGET REVIEW PROCEDURE IN ULTRAMEDIA

Capital budget proposals were submitted twice yearly, each proposal covering one six-month budget period. The proposals were prepared by divisional manufacturing–engineering staffs with the assistance of divisional accounting staffs, and were then reviewed by the divisional general manager. Proposals were then forwarded to the corporate central headquarters, where they were reviewed by the appropriate staffs: by Building Services in the case of requests for new structures and improvements to buildings and by Central Manufacturing–Engineering for all manufacturing and test equipment. The review performed by these staffs concentrated upon the standardization of processes and equipment and sought to ensure that all items proposed were the best value obtainable. The basic economic justification for the proposals was rarely, if ever, questioned. The requests were then submitted to the Executive Council, a group of senior corporate executives under the chairmanship of Mr. Wise.

In practice, the only review of the economic basis of proposals was that performed by the divisional general managers. Approval by the Executive Council was virtually automatic. In these circumstances the divisions frequently requested, and were granted, larger capital budgets than they required. Statistics reported at the end of each budget period indicated that in many cases only some 80% of the funds authorized for a period were in fact expended or committed during that period. This era, prior to mid-1965, may best be summarized as operating under conditions of capital abundance. Capital budget expenditures by divisions for the period 1963–67 are shown in Exhibit 4.

THE BUDGET CRISIS OF 1965

The implications of the budget cutback of 1965, to which reference was made in the opening paragraphs of this case, were very significant. It was no longer possible to provide funds for every project for which a division could advance a plausible case. Unless there should be a basic change in the company's attitude to the use of debt, it would obviously now be necessary to allocate funds among competing projects. Some basis would be required upon which this allocation could be made. Of prime urgency and importance was the problem of the distribution of funds among the divisions, in the light of their widely differing product characteristics and maturities, capital intensities, and rates of growth.

In early 1967 no solution to the problem had yet been found. This case seeks to present the context within which a solution was being sought and to portray the development of thinking about capital budgeting in Ultramedia and the opinions of some of the executives most directly concerned with the problem in 1967.

LARRY MALDEN JOINS ULTRAMEDIA

In July 1965 Larry Malden joined Ultramedia as a process engineer in Central Manufacturing–Engineering. Mr. Malden had attended the Harvard Business School after qualifying as an electrical engineer, and had completed his studies for the MBA degree in May 1965. His first assignment was to examine Central Manufacturing–Engineering's role in the company's capital budget system. The review of capital budget proposals by the central staffs, hitherto largely a formality, had become in the new conditions of capital scarcity rather than capital abundance a very real review and screening process as the company tried to reduce the capital equipment requests to a level consistent with the funds available.

The company treasurer's office played little part in the review and selection procedure. Almost all the projects reviewed were for electronic equipment or automatic machine tools of a highly technical nature and it was considered that only in the appropriate corporate staff was there the necessary technical knowledge to make a competent evaluation of the projects.

Mr. Michael Slavin, manager of Central Manufacturing–Engineering, was well aware of the lack of any real decision rule upon which the review procedure could be based. He realized, also, that divisional general managers were likely to have strong views about the rejection of projects proposed by their divisions, and that if no sound basis for allocation could be found the problem was likely to become a highly political one as each general manager attempted to obtain the best possible share of whatever funds were available. He decided to give to Mr. Malden, therefore, the task of reviewing the position and of making recommendations. He asked Mr. Malden to examine the basis upon which Mr. Wise and the Executive Council should make capital equipment budget allocations and review capital equipment projects, and how the supporting information to be presented to them should be organized.

Larry Malden later said:

I think I realized from the beginning that we were going to need a whole new budgeting system, not just a rehash of the existing Executive Council submissions procedure. Somehow we had to have a way of tying it into strategy, cash flow—to look at the basic question of why we had a capital budget.

The problem was where to begin. I decided to extract from the files all the letters and memoranda on the subject of capital budgets during the last few years, and to use these to fill in the background before I spent much time talking to the executives concerned.

One memorandum, from Mr. Clark, the vice president for operations, to all divisional general managers in October 1964, summarized the basic review procedure at the time:

"For a number of years now we have been using a simple procedure in the parent group for reviewing capital equipment budgets in the divisions. The procedure is employed at the beginning and the midpoint of each financial year and involves submitting a list of the capital equipment items expected to be purchased for the ensuing six-month period. These lists are forwarded to Central Finance where they are summarized and passed to the Central Manufacturing–Engineering office for review and coordination. The final budgets from Central Manufacturing–Engineering are then submitted to the Executive Council for approval.

"This procedure . . . has enabled us to materially maximize the use of our capital dollars, avoid unnecessary duplication of equipment and facilities, etc. Moreover, it is a very good monitor of where our capital dollars are going.

"Large items of machinery and equipment usually require some justification and very large items may require a fairly comprehensive analysis including return on investment figures."

Mr. Malden continued:

One question which came to mind was: On the basis of what evidence do the Executive Committee decide how large the sum available for capital expenditures is? In other words, who estimates future sources and uses of funds, and how is the estimate made? I talked to Douglas Owen, assistant treasurer, about this, and discovered that the forecast is Doug's responsibility. The divisional staffs make sales and cost estimates for their respective products and these estimates are reviewed by the vice president for operations and then sent to Doug. His staff already has lists of all currently authorized capital projects and the expected pattern of payments in connection with these projects. Doug uses this information to produce a one-year cash flow forecast. The forecast is in fact made twice a year, always for a period of 12 months ahead. This cash flow forecast is always available to the council when they consider the budget requests, and it is on this basis that they decide how much can be spent.

Douglas also confirmed something that I already suspected—that the review by the Council was something of a formality and that the real decisions were taken by Mr. Wise and Peter Clark.

I discovered that Doug also produced a five-year Long-Range Cash Flow Projection Worksheet, usually referred to as the "five-year plan." The figures used for years two to five were recognized to be rather unreliable, however. [An example of this worksheet is appended as Exhibit 5.]

I asked Doug about the trade-off between the different uses of funds. His figure for the total available for new capital expenditure was based upon certain assumptions about inventories, for instance, and a revised inventory policy resulting in a smaller expansion in inventories in the coming period would make more funds available for capital purchases. He told me:

"I use a rule-of-thumb guide to inventory levels, that the inventory turnover should be about 4½ times a year. If I am wrong about this, then obviously I am making a mistake about the funds available for capital budget purchases, but I think it works out pretty well. Obviously there are exceptions. One division is now building a computer, and its inventory has had to rise considerably. Another thing that happened last year is that some people got wind of the idea that we were going to tighten up on things and told their purchasing agents to stock up! Our inventories rose by $2 million because of that!

"I don't think that our policies on receivables or accounts payable affect our capital budget in any way—obviously they do if you have reached the limit of your debt capacity and have to start stretching your payables, but we are not in that position. Admittedly we don't make much use of debt but we will use it if we have good reason to—we used quite a lot of short-term bank debt last year. Sure, we had cutbacks, but we didn't go without anything we really needed. I think we had been getting a bit too lavish in our budget, especially with buildings. We were putting up more capacity than we really needed. But, of course, it was rather hard on those divisions which were already occupying their space 110%."

Mr. Malden went on:

You will notice the reference in Mr. Clark's letter to return on investment figures. The position on this was that earlier in 1964 John Brown, corporate accounting manager, had sent to all operations and finance managers a memorandum explaining the Internal Rate of Return method of project evaluation. The memorandum said that the Executive Council would in future require IRR figures for all capital expenditure proposals considered by them. I have the impression, though, that a lot of executives didn't understand the method too well, and in that context this next letter is interesting.

This is a letter sent by Michael Tetley, the company treasurer, to all operation and finance managers in March 1965:

"The desirability of simplifying and making more meaningful the calculation of return on investment performance measurement has become very apparent. Effective with your next financial report, please convert your return on investment calculation to the following concept, which can best be described as a modification of the 'assets employed' theory.

$$\frac{\text{Current 3-month net profit}}{\text{Current 3-month net shipments}} = \text{Net Profit Rate}$$

$$\frac{\text{Current 3-month net shipments} \times 4}{\substack{\text{Inventory, Property, Plant and}\\ \text{Equipment at cost at beginning}\\ \text{of period}}} = \text{Turnover}$$

$$\text{Net Profit Rate} \times \text{Turnover} = \text{Return on Assets Employed.}$$

Cash and accounts receivable are excluded. Fixed assets are recorded at their original cost so that one division does not have the advantage of a heavily depreciated facility over a division operating a new plant. Leased and rented facilities will be assigned a value for incorporation in these calculations."

The next really interesting memorandum is one produced by my immediate superior, Stuart Archbold, in August 1965—and it is interesting because it is the first mention anywhere in the files of the special budgeting problems that exist in a multidivisional company such as this. Stuart is outlining in this memorandum his views about Central Manufacturing–Engineering's role in the review procedure, and after saying that the division should be fully responsible for minor and routine expenditures, goes on to state:

"The areas requiring detailed attention from Manufacturing–Engineering would probably be large individual items, new processes and the problem of general divisional funds allocations. We should also be responsible for post audits on expenditures made. I feel that these responsibilities cannot really be carried out objectively by divisional manufacturing–engineering personnel, and that they cannot be accomplished by accounting because of a lack of technical process understanding.

"I would suggest that the divisions be free to undertake projects below a certain sum, say $10,000, up to a definite annual total—say $100,000. All items over these limits should be reviewed by Central Manufacturing–Engineering

1. For process implications
2. To be balanced among the divisions in proportion to their relative needs and to the potential total savings available."

Finally, there are two letters here which are important because they illustrate the first attempt to develop a decision rule upon which the allocation of funds to divisions could be based. The following memorandum was issued by the Treasurer's Office in November 1965, shortly after the budget review at which the capital shortage had become apparent for the first time.

"The Executive Council has requested that we lay down some better guide rules for capital budgeting amounts. Mr. Wise came up with the following suggestion: the total corporate budget should be roughly equal to the depreciation allowance plus the total value of all existing assets multiplied by the percentage growth expected during the coming period."

And in January 1966, Stuart Archbold wrote to the vice president for operations, Mr. Clark:

"At the November meeting on capital equipment budgets it was suggested that general guidelines for capital budgeting, at least for manufacturing capital expenditures, be laid down.

"I am making a recommendation for the next budget compilation and review. This recommendation is acceptable to Peter Renfrew (corporate accounting manager).

1. Generate an over-all company budget target in accordance with the formula developed by Mr. Wise.
2. Break the over-all budget down by divisions on the same basis.
3. Have Manufacturing–Engineering review all projects over $10,000 for process implications.
4. Review the sum total of individual projects to insure that they do not exceed the limits established in 1.) and 2.) above."

This was pretty much the position when I started looking at this problem in mid-1966. We were aware that the increasing complexity of most of our activities would probably mean that we could not in the future hope to finance all new buildings and equipment out of earnings, that we would therefore have to make some kind of allocation, and that the question of how much to authorize for each division was going to be an important one. And we had a decision rule, the "Budget Formula" devised by Mr. Wise, which had been used as the basis of the allocations for the second half of financial 1966.

I had considerable doubts about the usefulness of the "Budget Formula"; it seemed to be a clumsy device and I did not believe that allocation made on this basis would be in the company's best interests. Now, talking to Mike Slavin, I found that he had similar reservations. Mike told me:

"The formula is now pretty well discredited, and we shall probably not use it for the 1967 budgets. As I see it, there are three things wrong with the formula:

1. The accounting rate of depreciation we use is unrealistic—it bears no relation to the real working life of the machinery.
2. The 'projected growth rate' is pretty hard to determine, especially for individual divisions.
3. The 'asset base' is also pretty arbitrary. We have been more or less slack in our accounting, especially in some of the companies we have acquired, and the current book values, even before depreciation, don't really represent the relative asset structures of the divisions at all well."

I considered that these three criticisms were valid ones. Moreover, there seemed to me to be a further and even more serious flaw in the formula. The formula assumes that there is a continuous relationship between sales volume and assets required. Now, in practice the asset base will tend to be a step function. A department which has just had a major new project probably now has some spare capacity, because in requesting the new facilities the department will have had in mind not just the production needs in the coming year but probably the needs for three or four years from now. A department in this position should not need another major capital investment for some time, but the formula gives the department a larger claim on next year's capital budget, because of both the increased asset base and the resultant greater depreciation allowance. This is illogical. Moreover, it's just a perfect basis for empire building.

Before I was able to take this any further, something happened that brought the whole thing very much to a head. The divisions submitted their capital budget requests for the first half of financial 1967 and the figure was pretty staggering—over $4 million, representing an increase of 50% over the total authorized for financial 1966. It was obvious that we would not be able to finance this out of earnings, and that cuts would have to be made.

In 1965 Mr. Wise had told Peter Clark to get the divisions to revise their own budgets and see what could be cut out or postponed. This time he simply told them to cut $1 million out of the budget. Much of the responsibility for this fell on Central Manufacturing–Engineering and Mike Slavin was working on it for weeks, going around with Mr. Clark to talk to divisional general managers and reviewing all the additional justification they kept sending in. Mike told me afterwards:

"This was a job I did not enjoy at all. We still don't have any real decision rules in this area. We took out the $1 million, mostly from projects for new buildings, but it was pretty arbitrary. Some divisions got hit harder than others—particularly the Massachusetts divisions because we could get at them more easily.

"We divided all equipment up into three categories:
1. Equipment required for new products;
2. Equipment needed to increase the volume of existing products;
3. Cost-reduction programs.
Equipment required for new products was given top priority, though even some of this was back-scheduled. Cost reduction programs were hardest hit—they virtually vanished.

"In deciding on what to cut we did not pay much attention to rates of return—rather, we tried to decide which projects could wait, which could be done differently, etc. But there is no getting away from the fact that a lot of perfectly good projects were turned down." [Examples of two of the projects rejected at this time are appended as Exhibits 6 and 7.]

Mr. Malden concluded:

I have been talking to a number of company executives about our capital budgeting during the last few weeks and there is certainly a fairly general acceptance of the need to find a better basis than we have at the moment.

EXTRACTS FROM INTERVIEWS WITH OTHER EXECUTIVES OF ULTRAMEDIA INC.

Mr. Peter Clark, Vice President for Operations

This has become a real problem recently. The divisions used only to make use of about 80% of the capital equipment budgets authorized. Now they use 100% and the size of the budget is increasing all the time. All our buildings and equipment keep getting more complex and expensive. The divisions have been rather more interested in maximizing shipments than in return on investment, I think.

Some aspects of our current system make me very unhappy. In the past we have used the idea that routine projects like replacements should come out of depreciation and that special projects such as equipment needed for new products must have some provision over and above depreciation. One problem, of course, is deciding what allocation to make to a new division, or a company we have just acquired. Another problem is, how do you support a weak division? The divisions in most need of funds might be just those with the poorest present performance. We have to look at future prospects as well. Then there is the problem of growth products versus mature ones—very important, but it is not easy to say when a product is mature in this industry. And it is very difficult to relate any piece of equipment to a particular product anyway. [Notes on the products and performance of the divisions are given in Exhibit 8.]

Mr. Michael Tetley, Vice President and Treasurer

There is no science in the allocation of capital budget funds or of research budget funds, and we certainly have no predetermined formula for making these allocations to divisions. If any division has shown that its sales estimates are fairly accurate, this makes a good impression and that division stands a better chance of having its projects approved. We do take rate of return into consideration—calculated on the basis of accounting profit for the period divided by the book cost of all assets employed, including fully depreciated ones.

The way we work is to determine first of all just how much we are going to have to spend, on the basis of our volume projections and of sources and uses of funds forecasts based upon those projections. One of the difficulties is that if top management does not have quite such an optimistic view of prospects in the coming period as some of the divisional people, then we have to keep pushing everything back.

In the past we have generated enough profit to meet all our needs, but last year this was not so. We are not working under capital rationing; we will use bank borrowing if there is a good case for doing so. Many of the projects we postponed could in fact be put back without any real hardship, and the really urgent ones did go through.

Mr. Nigel Waddington, Director of Corporate Management Services

For years capital budgets have been approved automatically, and then been underspent. In fact, divisions would submit a project and if they did not hear anything back from top management about it, they assumed that it was O.K. to go ahead and spend the money.

It is not possible for the divisional people to see the overall corporate picture. We must have some form of allocation to the divisions in accordance with our overall operating situation and our plans for the future.

Mr. Martin Saliss, General Manager of the Communication Equipment Division

In putting in my six-month capital budget requests, I don't really have any clear idea as to how much I should be shooting for. I know that the divisions are now competing for capital funds. There are some discretionary funds after the items needed for testing new products, etc., have been provided for, and these are the funds we compete for. I guess you just get in there and try to rustle up whatever funds you can.

I'm not sure that we always get as large a share as we are entitled to—top management sometimes seem to lose sight of the fact that this division produces 30% of the company's total profits.

Sometimes I see that the company's accounts receivable have gone up by x million dollars and I can't help saying, "Boy, what I could do with a lousy 5% of that!"

Mr. Michael Slavin, Manager of Central Manufacturing– Engineering

I have been giving some thought to this question of capital budgeting. My current thinking is that we should have a "base line" of necessary expenditure for each division, and a surplus over and above the sum of all these base lines, which will be available for discretionary spending and for which the divisions will compete. I would like to see them all making competitive submissions for these funds. But the allocation of the discretionary funds would not be made purely on rate of return grounds. Top management should be involved in that it would have to decide which division should get what. We need to know a lot more about all this.

A FINAL INTERVIEW WITH LARRY MALDEN

Finally, Mr. Malden was asked to summarize his current position on the capital budgeting problem, and to try to indicate in what direction his thinking was developing. After some thought he replied:

For some time my main concern was to find some basis upon which we could make the allocation to divisions a fairly automatic process. The "Budget Formula" is not adequate, for reasons we have already been over, and is now pretty well discredited, but I have been thinking in terms of some other rule-of-thumb, perhaps something based largely upon divisional payroll. Now I am moving away from that approach.

Mike's ideas about a base line and discretionary funds above that base are interesting, but there are some problems there—not the least of which is that the divisions are going to keep back their best projects to use in the fighting!

I think we have been getting too much bogged down in detail on our capital budgeting—and that we have been looking at too short a time scale. How can we make meaningful projections of needs for land and buildings on a six-month basis? The five-year projection is certainly a step in the right direction, but even that is only just beginning to be taken seriously.

Somehow we have to look further ahead and try to get some idea as to what the divisions are going to need as much as five years from now. But how do you do this with 5 different divisions and an overseas subsidiary, all making a wide range of products of a great diversity of types and with some divisions introducing as many as 20 new products a year? Do you realize that more than 40% of our current products have been in production less than three years? That only 15% of them have been in existence for six years or more? And yet somehow we have to come to some kind of conclusion about how important the different fields are going to be to us in x years time and plan our capital expenditures accordingly.

Think about just two of the divisions for a moment, Communication Equipment and Medical Electronics. Communication is working hard on integrated circuitry: we have a prototype integrated circuit facility already and some of our new instruments embody this technology. The exciting thing about this field is that the very smallness of integrated circuit equipment is going to make it possible to work at far higher frequencies than we have ever before achieved, but we have no idea at this time what new products may come out of this. Then look at our medical equipment division. Last year their growth rate was 5%, the lowest in the company. This year they introduced a new patient-monitoring device and their sales to date are 41% up on last year! A whole new field of medical applications is opening up there.

When I was doing capital budgeting at HBS it seemed to be pretty straightforward but somehow none of it fits the situation we have here.

Brief descriptions of the product ranges produced by the 5 divisions and the factors expected to influence their performances during the next five years are appended as Exhibit 8.

Exhibit 1
ULTRAMEDIA INC.

SUMMARY OF SALES AND EARNINGS, 1961–66
(In Thousands of Dollars)

	1961	1962	1963	1964	1965	1966
Net receipts from sales	$31,472	$39,369	$41,042	$45,030	$55,051	$68,329
Deductions:						
Cost of goods sold	18,602	23,068	24,579	26,576	31,608	39,346
Selling and general expenses	8,411	10,844	11,214	12,098	14,247	17,833
Interest	85	59	57	32	77	255
Total	$27,098	$33,971	$35,850	$38,706	$45,932	$57,434
Income before taxes on income	$ 4,374	$ 5,398	$ 5,192	$ 6,324	$ 9,119	$10,895
Federal and foreign income tax	2,238	2,805	2,663	2,952	4,430	5,062
Income after tax	$ 2,136	$ 2,593	$ 2,529	$ 3,372	$ 4,689	$ 5,833
Minority interests	. . .	11	20	26	54	17
Net income	$ 2,136	$ 2,582	$ 2,509	$ 3,346	$ 4,635	$ 5,816
Preferred dividends	123	135	135	135	135	. . .
Balance available to common shareholders	$ 2,013	$ 2,447	$ 2,374	$ 3,211	$ 4,500	$ 5,816

Exhibit 2

ULTRAMEDIA INC.

BALANCE SHEETS AS OF OCTOBER 31, 1964–66
(In Thousands of Dollars)

Assets	1964	1965	1966
Current assets	$19,577	$24,187	$32,871
Property, plant, and equipment, at cost	12,588	15,580	21,204
Less: Depreciation	4,553	5,401	6,614
Net property, etc.	$ 8,035	$10,179	$14,590
Other assets	888	1,036	1,431
Total assets	$28,500	$35,402	$48,892
Less: Current, accrued, and deferred liabilities	5,903	9,824	16,997
Net assets	$22,597	$25,578	$31,895

Capitalization			
Long-term debt	$ ...	$ 156	$ 264
Minority interests	144	60	77
Preferred stock	149	...	...
Common stock	7,715	8,850	10,044
Retained earnings	14,589	16,512	21,510
Total capitalization	$22,597	$25,578	$31,895

Exhibit 3

ULTRAMEDIA INC.

SOURCES AND USES OF FUNDS, YEARS ENDED OCTOBER 31, 1964–66
(In Thousands of Dollars)

	1964	1965	1966
Net income	3,346	4,635	5,816
Increases in working capital	(2,441)	(689)	(1,511)
Capital accounts:			
Increases in property, plant and equipment	(1,498)	(3,141)	(5,624)
Less: Depreciation	371	848	1,213
Net	(1,127)	(2,293)	(4,411)
(Increases) or decreases in other assets	62	(148)	(395)
Support of Capitalization:			
Increases in long-term debt	(97)	156	108
Preferred dividends	(135)	(135)	—
Common dividends	(418)	(792)	(818)
Retirement of preferred stock	..	(1,785)	..
Increases in minority interests	80	(84)	17
New stock issues	730	1,135	1,194
Net for support of existing capitalization	160	(1,505)	501

Exhibit 4

ULTRAMEDIA INC.

CAPITAL BUDGET EXPENDITURE BY DIVISIONS, 1963–67
(In Thousands of Dollars)

Year	Communi- cation Equipment Division	Labora- tory Equipment Division	Digital Recording Division	Medical Electronics Division	Dataplot Division	Ultra- media (Italy)	Total
Land, Buildings, and Construction							
1963	140	120	60	10	59	5	394
1964	305	220	160	15	114	10	824
1965	624	420	400	37	285	28	1,794
1966	820	540	726	323	470	251	3,130
1967*	1,100	890	729	403	743	105	3,970
1967†	705	645	570	330	585	40	2,875
Plant, Equipment, and Vehicles							
1963	220	174	97	15	77	10	593
1964	230	140	144	26	120	14	674
1965	437	230	150	225	275	30	1,347
1966	720	415	464	320	525	50	2,494
1967*	1,065	1,110	1,090	482	782	51	4,580
1967†	905	795	698	424	760	30	3,612
Total Capital Expenditures							
1963	360	294	157	25	136	15	987
1964	535	360	304	41	234	24	1,498
1965	1,061	650	550	262	560	58	3,141
1966	1,540	955	1,190	643	995	301	5,624
1967*	2,165	2,000	1,819	885	1,525	156	8,550
1967†	1,610	1,440	1,268	754	1,345	70	6,487

* Requested.
† Authorized.

Exhibit 5

ULTRAMEDIA INC.

EXAMPLE OF LONG-RANGE CASH FLOW PROJECTION WORKSHEET—
COMMUNICATION EQUIPMENT DIVISION
(In Thousands of Dollars)

	Actual 1966	Target 1967	Long-Range Plans			
			1968	1969	1970	1971
Shipments.....................	16,000	17,250	18,500	21,000	25,000	29,000
Cash sources:						
Pretax profit.................	2,750	3,000	3,500	4,250	5,000	5,750
Depreciation.................	350	390	400	475	550	700
Increases in borrowing........	...	...	...	...	...	...
Increases in A/cs payable......	300	450	600	690	750	850
Other......................	(200)	70	50	70	...	...
Total Cash Sources..............	3,200	3,910	4,550	5,485	6,300	7,300
Cash Uses:						
Taxes......................	1,200	1,350	1,550	2,000	2,300	2,800
Land and buildings...........	820	705	750	1,500	800	650
Equipment and autos.........	720	905	1,100	1,200	1,400	1,500
Increases in receivables........	150	180	200	210	230	250
Increases in inventories........	550	570	650	790	1,020	1,250
Other......................	...	...	...	...	...	...
Total Cash Uses...............	3,440	3,710	4,250	5,700	5,750	6,450
Cash Excess or (Shortage)...........	(240)	200	300	(215)	550	850

Exhibit 6

ULTRAMEDIA INC.

COMMUNICATION EQUIPMENT DIVISION'S REQUEST FOR
PERMISSION TO PURCHASE A BROWN & SHARPE AUTOMATIC SCREW-CUTTING MACHINE

In September 1966, the Communication Division submitted to the Manufacturing–Engineering staff a request for a half-inch capacity automatic screw-cutting machine to be included in the division's 1967 capital budget. This submission had been proposed by divisional manufacturing–engineering and approved by the divisional accounting staff and by the divisional general manager, Mr. Martin Saliss. The submission consisted of the Capital Equipment Justification, the Capital Equipment Expenditure Guide, and the Rate of Return and Payback Calculation Sheet, all reproduced in full in this exhibit, plus a list of the parts to be made on the machine and their annual usages.

Exhibit 6 *(Continued)*

CAPITAL EQUIPMENT JUSTIFICATION

Name of Project:	Brown & Sharpe Automatic Screw Machine
Project Cost:	$20,285
Project Rate of Return:	61.4%
Purpose of Project:	The purpose of this project is to reduce the cost of some of the parts that are now being sub-contracted by this division. It will enable us to cut down on our inventory due to a shorter lead time and will give us a better opportunity to control the quality of the parts.

Proposed Equipment:

Machine Cost	$12,830
Accessory Cost	5,007
Controls Cost	
Tooling	1,257
Freight	468
Installation	150
Sales Tax	573
Total Cost	$20,285

CAPITAL EQUIPMENT EXPENDITURE GUIDE

	Hours				Present (Subcontracting)		Proposed	
	Present		Proposed		Cost	Advantage	Cost	Advantage
	M/C	Labor	M/C	Labor	Cost	tage	Cost	tage
Set-up		289		289	$	$	$	$
Run		2,350		700				
Total		2,639		989		10,900	10,900	
Overhead:								
Indirect Labor						...	...	
Fringe Benefits						1,187	1,187	
Maintenance						112	112	
Tooling						2,500	2,500	
Repair						175	175	
Lubrication & Supplies						1,609	1,609	
Power						264	264	
Taxes & Insurance						10	10	
Other Relevant Costs:								
Floor Space						1,820	1,820	
Subcontracting					49,146			49,146
Material						9,295	9,295	
Other								
Total						27,872		49,146

Operating Advantage (or Disadvantage) $21,274

Exhibit 6 (Continued)

RATE OF RETURN AND PAYBACK CALCULATION

Investment:

Capitalized Cost	20,285
Expense	...
Total Cost	20,285
Less Value of	
Present Equipment	...
Net Capital	20,285

Depreciation:

Method	Sum-of-years'-digits
Depreciable Life	5 years

Year	Advantage Cash Flow	Deprecia- tion	Taxable Income	Tax @48%	Cash Flow After Taxes	P.V. @60%	P.V. @65%
0	−20,285				−20,285		
1	+21,274	7,091	14,183	6,808	14,466	9,041	8,767
2	+21,274	5,672	15,602	7,489	13,785	5,384	5,063
3	+21,274	4,255	17,019	8,169	13,105	3,198	2,917
4	+21,274	2,836	18,438	8,850	12,424	1,895	1,675
5	+21,274	1,417	19,857	9,531	11,743	1,120	948
6							
7							
8							
9							
10							
Total						20,638	19,370

Interpolation

$$60\% + \frac{353 \times 5}{1268} = 61.4\%$$

Discounted Rate of Return: 61.4%

Payback: 1.42 years

The Communication Equipment Division's request for permission to purchase an automatic screw-cutting machine was reviewed by Michael Slavin, corporate manufacturing–engineering manager. After thorough examination of the submission Mr. Slavin wrote to the Communication Equipment divisional manufacturing manager as follows:

"Per your request, a rather thorough review has been made. The following comments are listed in order of importance:

1. Based on the submitted data, your division is paying $15.00 per hour for subcontracted screw machine work. Divisions at this location have this work done (including variance) for less than $10.00 per hour. At a $10.00 rate the R.O.I. would drop from 61% to 15%.

2. Your estimate of tooling costs appears to be low. Tooling costs both for any items previously made on conventional machines or pulled-in from subcontractors will average about $100 per part. An additional $4,000 during the first year would not be unrealistic.

3. A 10-year depreciated life would be more realistic than a 5-year life.

4. You appear to have depreciated the operating advantage instead of the purchase price!

Exhibit 6 (Continued)

5. One of the parts on your list, 1440–ZZ105, has an annual usage of 500,000. It's hard to believe that we could compete with a Chicago 'sweat shop' on this one.
6. An 80% efficiency factor on cycle time should be used. With this efficiency, which is realistic, the utilization would climb to two shifts and with this load it certainly makes sense to think in terms of automatic machinery. But we should consider other alternatives—conventional turrets, turrets with Sandex attachments and auto lathes.

"I should be glad if you would think about the above comments and, if they are justified, recalculate the R.O.I. to determine if the proposed investment makes sense at this time."

On October 13 Mr. Slavin received the following reply from divisional manufacturing–engineering:

"In answer to your letter of September 30, reviewing our justification for the Brown & Sharpe screw machine.

1. I think you are assuming that all the work we have listed is being done on an automatic screw machine by our subcontractor. This is not the case. Some of these parts are currently made in our shop, and we believe that some of the parts sent out are made on turret lathes.
2. In regard to the tooling costs, I have consulted with our cost engineer and he is confident that he can get by with $2500, due to the similar nature of many of these parts.
3. The depreciation has been recalculated on a 10-year basis. We are now depreciating the purchase price, not the annual saving.
4. The 80% efficiency factor is now being used."

Enclosed with this letter were new Capital Equipment Expenditure Guide and Rate of Return Calculation sheets. These indicated that the expected annual saving was now $17,889 and that, using the 10-year depreciation and working life basis, the rate of return would be 52.4%.

The revised submission was discussed by Mr. Slavin, Mr. Clark, vice president for operations, and Mr. Wise. It was postponed indefinitely.

Exhibit 7

ULTRAMEDIA INC.

Laboratory Equipment Division's Request for Authorization to Purchase New Type KB24 Oscilloscopes and Related Equipment

In December 1966, the Manufacturing–Engineering staff received from the Laboratory Equipment Division a request for permission to purchase two new oscilloscopes. These instruments were manufactured by another division of Ultramedia, Communication Equipment Division, and had been introduced into the division's product line six weeks previously to replace an older model of oscilloscope, the KA22. The new oscilloscope was designed to be a part of a compatible range of plug-in units such as time bases and dual trace plug-ins. The pricing procedure used in such cases of intracompany purchases was for the purchasing division to be charged 55% of the normal list price of the instruments. The price of the equipment here being considered was:

Exhibit 7 (Continued)

2 type KB24 Oscilloscopes @ $1,100 list	=	$2,200
2 type KB241 Dual Trace Units @ $750 list	=	1,500
2 type KB244 Time Bases @ $530	=	1,060
		$4,760
@ 55% list price	=	$2,618

This equipment was required for purposes of final testing and quality control of various signal generators and microwave test equipment manufactured by the Laboratory Equipment Division. The equipment currently in use for this purpose consisted of three type HA17 oscilloscopes, all approximately 10 years old. The type HA17 had been out of production for more than three years, although the Communication Equipment Division continued to offer replacement parts and servicing facilities for this model.

The design features of the type KB24 series equipment and the plug-in units available considerably reduced the changeover or set-up time required for changing from the testing of one type of instrument to another; divisional production was on a batch basis and three or four types of instrument might be expected to pass through each testing station in the course of one day. The new instruments were also considerably more compact than the other oscilloscopes, an important point in the Laboratory Equipment Division, which was producing approximately 2½ times as much output as that for which its buildings and facilities had been designed.

The most important reasons for the requested oscilloscopes, however, were those the divisional management believed it could not quantify. The KB24 was an attractive product: the questions of styling, convenience, and labelling of controls, etc., had been given careful consideration in its design stages. The older type HA17 looked like a piece of military surplus equipment of the vintage of World War II. The type KB24, although smaller in over-all dimensions, had 60% more viewing screen area, making it much less tiring to use. The divisional production manager, Peter Spooner, expressed his feelings about the oscilloscopes thus:

We pride ourselves on being right at the frontiers of the technology in which we operate. Many of our products are "state-of-the-art" equipment. This is the kind of thing we keep stressing to our staff—the need to keep right up to date, to look for a new approach. Some of this stuff we are doing here is practically basic research, especially in the microwave field. And we expect people to use equipment that should be in a museum. I can't express the importance of having the latest equipment in dollars and cents, but I am damn sure that it is important all the same.

No formal economic justification was made for this equipment. The submission was made verbally to Mr. Clark and Mr. Slavin, and was turned down. By early 1967 Mr. Spooner had made three attempts to obtain this equipment, all without success.

Exhibit 8

ULTRAMEDIA INC.

NOTES ON DIVISIONAL PRODUCTS, PERFORMANCE, AND FUTURE PROSPECTS

Communication Equipment Division

The products of this division included signal generators, microwave test equipment, and general-purpose audio, visual, and communications instrumentation. Sales revenues in recent years had increased at the rate of 29% per annum, slightly higher than the company average. The microwave field was becoming increasingly important, and more than 50% of divisional sales in 1966 were of high-price low-volume microwave test and calibration equipment. Integrated circuit technology was expected to assume prime importance in this field and the division had developed a pilot integrated circuit facility. The division was also moving towards a systems approach, producing instrumentation to be used in conjunction with the computer being developed by the Dataplot Division. The new products were expected to sell to a market quite distinct from that in which most sales had been made in the past. Semiconductor manufacturers were expected to be major purchasers.

The Communication Equipment Division produced 24% of total corporate revenues in 1966. It was estimated that sales would increase by 25% yearly over the 5-year long-range planning period 1967–1971. This division's profitability, in terms of both return upon sales and return upon assets (fixed assets plus inventories), was higher than that of any other Ultramedia division in 1965–1966. (See table at end of this exhibit.) The rate of return on sales of individual products varied very widely between 0% and 40%.

Laboratory Equipment Division

This division produced measuring and analyzing equipment for the chemical industry. Products included viscometers, gas chromatographs, CHN analyzers, etc. Any attempt to forecast growth prospects in this field was complicated by the extreme segmentation of the chemical industry and the fact that growth rates in various segments varied between 8% and 30% per annum. Divisional sales in recent years had increased by an average of 28% yearly. The basic area of chromatography, in which the division was particularly well established, was expected to grow a little more than 15%, but the chemical field as a whole was thought to be a promising one and future sales were expected to increase by at least 25% yearly. The sales of this division amounted to 22% of company revenues in 1966. The Laboratory Equipment Division's profitability in terms of return on sales and return on assets approximated the company average during the period 1964–1966.

Digital Recording Division

This division had traditionally concentrated upon a range of low-price high-volume digital counters, of which it had become a major producer. Competition had become increasingly severe in recent years, however, and the growth rate of 21% per annum was below the corporate mean of 26%. In an attempt to counter this trend the division had been diversifying into nuclear instrumentation and

Exhibit 8 (Continued)

frequency standards, the latter being considered particularly promising. In this division, too, integrated circuits were expected to be increasingly important, and development work in this field was underway.

Digital Recording products amounted to 20% of total company sales in 1966, a smaller proportion than in previous years. Future sales growth was estimated at 18% per annum. The division's rates of return on sales and on assets employed decreased relative to those of other divisions but were still approximately equal to the company averages during the period 1965–1966. Certain individual products were unprofitable in 1966.

Medical Electronics Division

The "traditional" products of this division were analog-recording devices for medical use, predominantly electro-cardiograph recorders. Sales in 1966 made up 15% of the company total, and the rate of growth had been the lowest in the company at 8% per annum.

In mid-1966 a range of patient-monitoring and diagnostic equipment was introduced and immediately generated considerable interest and demand. Sales in the latter half of 1966 were more than 40% greater than in the corresponding period of 1965, and orders on hand at the end of 1966 amounted to 5 months' production at the rate planned for 1967. It was estimated that demand for this equipment would increase by 35% yearly throughout the planning period, and that the advent of Medicare would result in demand for the division's traditional products increasing at 14% per year. Rates of return on sales and on assets employed were lower than those of any other division but increased sharply during 1966.

Dataplot Division

This division specialized in the development of data handling systems, and prior to 1965 had concentrated upon high-quality tape decks and input-output devices for use with computers produced by other manufacturers. Sales had increased at the rate of 25% yearly, and in 1966 amounted to 19% of company revenues.

In the fall of 1966 the division introduced a small computer of its own design and manufacture. The market for such a computer was estimated to be $100 million in 1967, increasing to $350 million by 1971. Dataplot hoped to avoid head-on competition with the established computer producers by selling this machine as part of a total instrumentation system in conjunction with the products of other divisions, particularly the Communication Equipment Division. Divisional sales were expected to increase very rapidly in 1968–1969 and at a lower rate thereafter, giving an over-all rate of increase of 35% through the planning period. The division's return on sales and on assets remained close to the company average during 1964–1966.

Exhibit 8 (Continued)

Division	Sales (In Thousands of Dollars)			Percent Rate of Sales Growth		Net Profit before Tax as Percent of Sales Revenues			Percent Net Profit as Return on Assets†		
	1964	1965	1966	1964–66	1967–71*	1964	1965	1966	1964	1965	1966
Communication Equipment	9,500	12,450	16,017	29	25	16	23	19	30	38	36
Laboratory Equipment	8,880	12,200	15,025	28	25	20	22	18	26	34	28
Digital Recording	9,300	11,160	13,670	21	18	21	22	18	28	32	30
Medical Electronics	8,900	9,100	10,250	8	30	4	3	10	12	14	22
Dataplot	8,450	10,141	13,367	25	35	14	16	16	26	30	32
Total Ultramedia	45,030	55,051	68,329	26	27	14	17	16	26	35	30

* Estimated.
† The asset base used by the company in calculating these returns consisted of undepreciated fixed assets plus inventories.

LILLIPUTIAN BALL BEARINGS COMPANY

IN MARCH 1967, Steven Miller, president of Lilliputian Ball Bearings Company, announced at a meeting of the executives that he was studying a change in the firm's intracompany pricing. Current corporate practice forced interdivisional integration of operations by policy. Mr. Miller was convinced that there was a better solution through transfer prices to the problems posed to corporate control by autonomous divisional management.

Lilliputian, a manufacturer of both commercial and precision grades of ball bearings, became one of the industry's few integrated producers through its acquisition of a steel ball supplier in 1963. The company then had facilities for fabricating all ball bearing components and assembling them into the finished product. This vertical integration assured supply and improved quality control of the steel balls used in bearings. A managerial complexity created by the merger was controlling operations in northern and southern California, where the Bearing and Ball Divisions, respectively, were located. Mr. Miller hired a consultant to devise a set of transfer prices that would force the two division managers to production decisions serving both their own and the company's best interests. The consultant's efforts were unsuccessful. As a result, the product mix for each division was dictated by the corporate staff. This procedure made the evaluation of divisional performance somewhat arbitrary, according to the parties concerned.

Bearing engineers operating from six sales offices sold the Lilliputian products throughout the United States. These salesmen worked closely with customers in adapting and designing bearings for specific purposes. The company served approximately 2,200 customers, excluding the military services, which accounted for 42% of sales. Although only a small number of firms specialized in bearings, the industry was keenly competitive because divisions of larger companies and foreign enterprises sold similar products.

PRODUCTS

A ball bearing consisted of an inner ring to fit on a rotating shaft and an outer ring to be held in a support housing, which was usually stationary. The two rings were separated by the rolling elements—the steel balls, some of which in the Lilliputian product lines had outside diameters as small as $\frac{1}{40}''$. Usually a retainer was assembled between the rings to separate the balls for minimum contact, thereby providing optimum performance. To further ensure such performance, tolerance requirements for some products were as minute as one millionth of an inch (.000001″). The smallest bearing Lilliputian manufactured had an outside diameter of $\frac{1}{12}$″.

The purpose of a ball bearing was to replace the sliding friction of a rotating shaft by the rolling friction between the bearing balls and rings. Mr. Miller vividly portrayed this benefit by saying that "anyone who had accidentally stepped on a cluster of marbles resting on a hard floor could appreciate the relatively friction-free properties of a ball bearing." With less drag in rolling friction, the performance of machinery and equipment was improved and prolonged.

On the basis of the criterion of dimensional tolerance requirements, two major product lines could be distinguished for the Bearing Division. The first was the commercial grade (lower quality), which was priced at $22 per dozen bearings on the average and was sold to manufacturers of potentiometers, small motors, miniature clutches and brakes, computers, calculators, and typewriters. The second was the precision or instrument grade, which had an average price of $32 per dozen bearings, and was used by manufacturers of gyroscopes, autopilots, synchros, tape recorders, fuel control systems, aircraft cameras, and high-speed dental handpieces. Although hundreds of different bearings were produced in each grade, with prices depending upon order quantity, Mr. Miller believed that these two groups and average selling prices were adequate for a study of intracompany prices. A previous engineering and financial analysis showed that the profit contribution per dollar of cash usage and the profit contribution per machine hour were approximately the same for all the products within each classification.

The Ball Division also had two major product lines, which were differentiable by quality. Both of these product lines could be sold to a variety of industrial users, including nonintegrated members of the bearing industry and manufacturers of ball-point pens, in addition to the Bearing Division of Lilliputian. The average market prices for the quantity of steel balls contained *in a dozen bearings* were $5 for commercial steel balls and $10 for precision steel balls.

OPERATIONS

The basic manufacturing operation in the Bearing Division was the removal of metal from the heat-hardened rings by abrasive grinding. Grinding, although relatively slow, permitted close control of the rate at which metal was taken off. Surfaces were then finished to extreme fineness. In total, about 40 steps were required to produce individual rings from the raw material, which cost about $2 per dozen sets of inner and outer rings, regardless of quality. Mr. Miller felt that it was only necessary to divide these steps into two segments—grinding and finishing—because ordinary production planning could be used to balance individual machine load within each phase. The heat-treatment, cleaning, assembly, and inspection operations were not considered to be relevant to this study, except for their variable costs, for two reasons. First, heating capacity was excessive and, second, the existing number of handworkers and inspectors would not restrict increases in sales, since it was company policy to hire and retain these highly skilled employees regardless of the level of output. The Grinding and Finishing Departments had monthly machine capacities of 25,500 hours and 36,000 hours, respectively.

The Ball Division could also be conveniently separated into two sections whose functions were similar to those in the Bearing Division. The Machining Department had a monthly machine capacity of 42,000 hours, and the Finishing Department had 12,000 machine hours available.

RELATIONSHIPS BETWEEN DIVISIONS

Although the Ball Division had a ready market for its products, in 1963 the corporate staff imposed a requirement, with management's consent, that internally produced steel balls be used by the Bearing Division. Both division managers were dissatisfied with the resulting production schedules. Moreover, they believed the evaluation of their performance based on return on investment was defective because the divisions could not select the most profitable course of action given the prevailing set of transfer prices and outside market prices. The managers did not dispute their respective investment bases. They agreed, however, that the efficiencies resulting from integration must be allocated in a meaningful manner if a fair evaluation was to be achieved. The anticipated efficiencies included the following:

1. Lower total cost for the completed ball bearing because outside suppliers of steel balls would not receive their markups.
2. Possible reductions in time demands on Bearing Division machinery as a result of better quality control in the Ball Division.
3. Cash savings, if any, from the lower product costs.

The goal of Mr. Miller's pricing study, therefore, was to devise transfer prices which, by embodying cost savings available from integration of operations, would prevent suboptimal autonomous production scheduling. The correct setting of transfer prices, coupled with free choice between internal and external markets by division managers, would maximize company profits while preserving divisional autonomy and profit responsibility.

The Bearing Division paid $3 to external suppliers for the commercial-grade steel balls needed in one dozen bearings. Manufacturing cost for these steel balls in the Ball Division was $3.60. This price-cost disparity was justified by better quality. Although Lilliputian's commercial-grade bearings were salable containing balls of either quality, the internally produced steel ball created some efficiencies in the manufacturing operations of the Bearing Division.

Precision-grade steel balls per one dozen bearings cost the Bearing Division $8 from external sources, while the Ball Division's manufacturing cost was $6. As a result, a direct cash saving to the corporation resulted if the Bearing Division used the Ball Division's output. The $10 outside selling price for Lilliputian's precision steel balls was indicative of their high quality. This quality produced time savings in the Grinding Department of the Bearing Division, although the savings were partially offset by additional operations in the Finishing Department.

Exhibit 1 summarizes the manufacturing cost and machine times compiled during the engineering and financial study for each possible combination of purchase and sale of steel balls. The question marks (?) represent the items remaining to be determined in finding the transfer prices.

FINANCIAL INFORMATION

A limit on cash available for operations was the only corporate resource that caused further divisional interactions; that is, excessive use of cash by one division would necessitate curtailment of operations in the other.

Because of the lead time in planning operations, Mr. Miller believed that the study, which was conducted in March, should be used to plan June production rates, product mix, and profit for each division and the company as a whole. He estimated that $75,000 would be available for operations after payment of all known obligations, including the fixed expenses for June, which are listed in Exhibit 2.

Both divisions placed purchase orders for external materials one month before the desired delivery and, with the exception noted below, used the material in the month in which it was received. Terms were net 30 days. However, in order to ensure continuity of integrated operations, the company maintained a two-month lead in ordering the basic materials to be used by the Ball Division in the steel balls sold to the Bearing Division. These materials were delivered during the month preceding the month of use and were paid for in the month of use. If the optimal production schedule indicated purchase of steel balls externally, elimination of the safety stock maintained under the policy of integrated operations would result as shown in Exhibit 2. Internal transfer of steel balls, however, would require maintenance of the appropriate safety stock.

All labor and variable overhead costs were paid for in the month in which they were incurred.

A review of collection experience disclosed that the Bearing Division could anticipate an average receipt in the month of sale of $12 per dozen precision bearings sold and $8 per dozen commercial bearings sold. The Ball Division usually carried in accounts receivable 27 days of external sales of precision steel balls and 15 days of external sales of commercial steel balls.

See Exhibits 3 and 4 for the company's recent financial statements.

Exhibit 1

LILLIPUTIAN BALL BEARINGS COMPANY

UNIT VARIABLE COSTS AND MACHINE HOURS—BEARING AND BALL DIVISIONS

	Bearing Division (steel balls per dozen bearings)				Ball Division (steel balls per dozen bearings)			
	Precision Grade		Commercial Grade		Precision Grade		Commercial Grade	
	(externally supplied steel balls)	(steel balls from Ball Division)	(externally supplied steel balls)	(steel balls from Ball Division)	(sold externally)	(sold to Bearing Division)	(sold externally)	(sold to Bearing Division)
Selling price	$32.00	$32.00	$22.00	$22.00	$10.00	$?	$5.00	$?
Cost:								
Raw material	$ 2.00	$ 2.00	$ 2.00	$ 2.00	$ 2.90	$2.90	$0.40	$0.40
Steel balls	8.00	?	3.00	?	...	...	...	...
Labor and overhead	15.00	12.00	10.50	9.00	3.10	3.10	3.20	3.20
Total cost	$25.00	$?	$15.50	$?	$ 6.00	$6.00	$3.60	$3.60
Beginning contribution	$ 7.00	$	$ 6.50	$	$ 4.00	$	$1.40	$
Machine hours:								
Ball Division								
Machining Dept					1.5 hrs.	1.5 hrs.	2.4 hrs.	2.4 hrs.
Finishing Dept					.3 hrs.	.3 hrs.	.2 hrs.	.2 hrs.
Bearing Division								
Grinding Dept	3 hrs.	1.5 hrs.	1 hr.	1.5 hrs.				
Finishing Dept	2 hrs.	2.5 hrs.	2.5 hrs.	2 hrs.				

Exhibit 2

LILLIPUTIAN BALL BEARINGS COMPANY

FORECASTED CASH AVAILABLE FOR JUNE OPERATIONS

Estimated cash balance, June 1, 1967
(under present purchases-sales procedure)............$ 90,000
Collections of prior months' accounts receivable........... 250,000
$340,000

Fixed cash expenses..................................$100,000
Payments of prior month's accounts payable............. 60,000
Estimated tax payment.............................. 30,000
Loan repayment..................................... 25,000
Semiannual cash dividend............................ 60,000
Minimum cash balance............................... 25,000
$300,000

Estimated cash available for June operations
(under present purchases-sales procedure)............$ 40,000
Add: Eliminate policy requirement of inventory
safety stock..................................... 35,000
Cash available for June operations without
integrated production policy.......................$ 75,000

Exhibit 3

LILLIPUTIAN BALL BEARINGS COMPANY

CONSOLIDATED BALANCE SHEET AS OF DECEMBER 31, 1966
(Dollar Figures in Thousands)

Assets

Cash...		$ 138
Accounts receivable (net).............................		306
Inventory: Raw materials and finished goods..............		117
Plant, property, and equipment........................	$3,573	
Less: Reserves for depreciation........................	1,715	
Net balance.....................................		1,858
Total assets...................................		$2,419

Liabilities and Equity Capital

Notes payable.......................................		$ 93
Accounts payable....................................		75
Accrued taxes......................................		77
Current portion of long-term debt......................		100
Long-term debt.....................................		675
Deferred federal taxes................................		87
Common stock......................................	$ 100	
Capital in excess of par value.........................	73	
Retained earnings...................................	1,139	
Total stockholders' equity........................		1,312
Total liabilities and equity capital................		$2,419

Exhibit 4

LILLIPUTIAN BALL BEARINGS COMPANY

CONSOLIDATED INCOME STATEMENT
FOR THE YEAR ENDED DECEMBER 31, 1966
(Dollar Figures in Thousands)

Net sales..$4,378

Costs and expenses, including materials, labor, and
  depreciation.......................................$3,481
Selling and administrative expenses, including
  interest...   602
                                                      $4,083

Income before taxes..................................$ 295
Provision for income taxes*..........................   119
Net income...$ 176

* The investment credit used by the company to reduce current federal income taxes amounted to $25,000 in 1966 as compared with $18,000 in 1965.

ACCOUNTING IMPLICATIONS OF A MATHEMATICAL PROGRAMMING APPROACH TO THE TRANSFER PRICE PROBLEM *

By Nicholas Dopuch† and David F. Drake‡

THIS PAPER examines several cross-disciplinary efforts to solve problems of intra-firm resource allocation in an attempt to determine their possible significance to managerial accounting. For this inquiry, a system of transfer prices is defined as a set of internally derived prices for guiding the intra-company transfer of productive resources. We assume that this system is restricted to optimal allocation of a fixed set of productive goods and services; that is, the supply of these goods is given, and the transfer price problem is the short-run efficiency problem—how can a firm "best" utilize a fixed quantity of tangible and intangible resources.

DECENTRALIZATION, INFORMATION-PROCESSING AND TRANSFER-PRICES

The need for a transfer pricing system develops from a delegation of that authority for which central management is ultimately responsible. This "decentralization" ranges in degree from the control of a single variable to that of complete freedom in determining levels, types, combinations, customers, and sources of inputs or outputs for an entire division.

Presumably, decentralization is chosen in the expectation that the resulting organizational structure will better serve the firm's objectives or goals. Two general arguments which favor decentralization are: (1) the employees will be better motivated and this increased motivation will lead to an increase in productivity; and (2) decentralized managers are in better position to process

* Reprinted by permission from the *Journal of Accounting Research*, (Spring 1964), pp. 10–24.

† Assistant Professor of Accounting, University of Chicago.

‡ Assistant Professor of Accounting, University of Chicago.

information concerning resource allocation.[1] Although these are interrelated, our interest is in the assumed economies of information processing.

Part of the accounting function is to determine the type of information to be collected and the method of its classification for the purposes of both decision-making and evaluation throughout all management levels. Traditionally, accounting employs a single information system to aid both in decision-making and in interpreting the results of the decision-making process. For example, the use of standard costs is predicated upon an information system resulting from managerial goals (decisions made) and the measurement of events in reference to these goals (evaluation-control).

Consequently, the accountant will wish to judge the impact of various proposals for transfer pricing on the system's ability to perform simultaneously both objectives—the providing of information leading to the optimal allocation of a specific quantity of resources and the generation of the complementary information which can be used to control and evaluate the allocation decision.[2]

A related interest in this allocation problem may be derived as a corollary to this basic methodology. If the accounting method is successfully implemented, only those individuals actually making the allocation decisions can be evaluated by the system. Thus, we must examine proposed pricing systems in terms of the system's ability to guide that group in management most likely to make the allocation decisions.

In the pages following the notion of information processing is developed as a basis for examining the potential applications of recent developments in programming to the accounting problem of transfer pricing. We first consider the situations where "real" prices are available for both decision-making and evaluation. This facilitates analysis of those situations requiring artificial prices. It is in the derivation of artificial prices that the benefits from programming methods are to be reaped.

"Real" Prices and Intra-Firm Resource Allocation

If resources are bought and sold in a competitive market, real prices exist for use in the firm's internal transactions. Such prices assume that the outputs of supplying divisions can be sold at the given market price which permits the assumption of constant acquisition price to the purchasing divisions. Given these conditions, the resulting market prices satisfy the decision-making needs of divisional managers; also, they enable top management to evaluate the general degree of effectiveness of divisional managers.

---

[1] For a detailed account of the behavioral aspects, see George Benston, "The Role of the Firm's Accounting System for Motivation," *Accounting Review*, Vol. XXXVIII (April, 1963), pp. 347–354. The economics of information processing are implicit in competitive economic models. For example, see F. Hayek, *Individualism and Economic Order* (Chicago: University of Chicago Press, 1948), especially Ch. 4.

[2] See Joel Dean, "Decentralization and Intracompany Pricing," *Harvard Business Review*, v. 33 (July–August, 1955), p. 67.

Fundamentally, "real" prices are effective under these overall conditions because they reflect the opportunity costs of the intra-firm transactions.[3] That is, if the manager of one division is willing to supply a unit of output to another division, his price should reflect, as a minimum, the amount he could have received from his next best alternative. The opportunity cost is constant over all ranges of output. Similarly, the purchasing manager should not be made to pay a price greater than that of his next best alternative which is also constant over his range of demand. These conditions prevent or discourage attempts to misquote or rig the prices to be employed. Also, these are the ideal conditions for the use of an income figure as a control and evaluative device for central management in their comparisons of performances which indicate the relative degree to which opportunities are seized by divisional managers.

If the divisions do not operate under these conditions of competition, central management must recognize that the resulting market prices may not represent the opportunity costs of divisional transactions. Under these conditions the demand curves of the selling divisions will be downward sloping for increasing levels of sales to outside firms and/or the supply curves will be upward (or downward) sloping for greater levels of purchases made from outside firms. In order to achieve an optimal allocation of the firm's resources, it is necessary to work with the revenue and cost functions of both the supplying and the purchasing divisions since the relative slopes of the functions will vary between divisions.[4] Thus, it is necessary to relieve one of the divisions of profit responsibility. However, it might be more practical to accept market price as an approximation of the opportunity cost of intra-firm transactions since the data needed to centralize the decision-making process may be available only after considerable delay.

A compromise solution seems reasonable especially if cross-elasticity of demand exists between the outputs of related divisions. Under such circumstances an optimal solution to the firm's allocation problem would require a system of "taxes" and "bounties" to supplement market prices (depending on whether the sales of one division had a favorable or unfavorable effect on another division's sales).[5] Such a system might require more administrative effort than appears reasonable. Moreover, the ability to design the system of

---

[3] A qualification is necessary to the extent the price obtained by the supplying division in the open market is less than the price which must be paid on the open market by the purchasing division. This situation exists because of the economics of integration. The equilibrium conditions for such situations have been worked out by J. Gould, London School of Economics, in a paper forthcoming in the *Journal of Business.* Its main point of relevance to this paper is its concern over the weakness in the procedures of obtaining equilibrium which generally involve divisional negotiation. We believe, however, that the conditions for evaluation reduce the dangers which could develop.

[4] Jack Hirshleifer, "On the Economics of Transfer Pricing," *The Journal of Business,* v. 29 (July, 1956), pp. 172–184.

[5] Jack Hirshleifer, "Economics of the Divisionalized Firm," *The Journal of Business,* v. 30 (April, 1957), pp. 96–108.

taxes and bounties presupposes (perfect) knowledge of the cost and revenue functions in which case decentralization would serve no useful purpose.

We may conclude that in general the existence of market prices for divisional outputs will provide a basis for transfer prices which either allows complete decentralization—perfect competition—or which allows degrees of decentralization based upon the considerations above. An outside set of prices not only provides a reasonable measure of the opportunity costs of diverting units to related divisions, but it suggests that other firms are operating under conditions similar to the decentralized divisions. References are thereby established for the evaluation of the decentralized managers.

In the event still more complete programs of decentralization are desired under conditions of imperfect competition, these may be achieved through processes of negotiation where the transfer prices are determined in reference to cost and revenue functions of respective divisions. In evaluating the resulting performances of the divisional managers, however, the central management may be evaluating their ability to negotiate rather than their ability to control economic variables. Accordingly, the information economies of decentralization may be more apparent than real.

Intra-Firm Transfers—"Real" Prices Not Available

The more complex problems of intra-firm pricing develop, however, when the firm produces its own specialized resources but desires a program of decentralization.[6] The assumption of specialized resources implies that either no market exists for these resources (other than internally) or that market prices for related items are irrelevant for the short-run. In other words, the market place offers no alternative to either the purchasing or the supplying divisions so that other methods must be developed to determine the opportunity costs of divisional transactions. One general approach in determining transfer prices for these situations involves the use of various measures of standard or actual costs. These include full-cost, full-cost plus, and marginal or variable costs.[7]

If no market exists for the specialized resource, the opportunity costs of supplying units of output are limited to the marginal costs of producing additional units.[8] A purchasing division would continue to make additional purchases until the cost of obtaining the inputs (the transfer-price) is equal to the additional revenue obtained from selling the final output. A measure of decentralization is possible since the manager of the purchasing department has control over the level of inputs he will purchase.

---

[6] In fact, Dearden uses the extent of availability of market prices as a basis for classifying approaches to the transfer-price problem. See John Dearden, "Interdivisional Pricing," *Harvard Business Review*, v. 38 (January–February, 1960), pp. 117–125.

[7] Howard Greer, "Divisional Profit Calculation—Notes on the 'Transfer Price' Problem," *N.A.A. Bulletin*, Vol. XLIII (July, 1962), p. 6.

[8] It will be recalled that we are limiting our discussion to time-horizons which are not sufficient to permit investment decisions.

Since the manager of the supplying division is not given the authority to determine his level of output, his performance can not be evaluated by a traditional measure of profit or loss. Any attempts to develop reports of profitability must lack the substance to motivate the manager of the supplying divisions, given the conditions just considered. It is more rational, therefore, and at least as useful, to apply more traditional measures of cost control to evaluate the results of the manager of the supplying division.

It is evident that transfer prices based upon full-cost or full-cost plus do not provide a basis for determining the optimal output levels of the divisions; these prices do not reflect the opportunity costs of the divisional transactions. Further, it is doubtful that these prices will motivate divisional managers in an appropriate manner. While it is obvious that all divisions affect the final profit of the firm, it does not seem useful to develop some form of profit and loss statement based upon full cost or full-cost adjusted by mark-ups. Because the amount of profit is so far-removed from the control of the managers of supplying divisions, it is not likely that these measures will lead to the appropriate actions on their parts. Indeed, systems of standard costs and flexible budgets are intended to overcome this deficiency which extends the evaluation of performance beyond the effective span of control.

From this, it is concluded that marginal cost of production or distribution can be used as a basis for transfer prices when market prices are not relevant to the output of the supplying divisions. Marginal costs can reflect the opportunity costs of divisional transactions.

Market Prices Not Available—Alternative Uses of Fixed Facilities

These marginal costs remain sufficient, however, only in the event the demand for the outputs of the supplying divisions is limited to one purchasing division. Assuming several divisions desire the output of the supplying division, and the facilities are limited, the opportunity cost of supplying any one division as opposed to another is the greater of the marginal costs of producing the output or the revenue lost by diverting the resource from alternative uses.

Conceivably the manager of the supplying division could allocate his scarce facility to the most profitable output, e.g., on the basis of the highest net contribution per unit of scarce facility. In this event the managers of the purchasing divisions will no longer control their input levels. In this respect, the manager of the supplying division tends to occupy a position similar to one central management might occupy with as much efficiency. It is doubtful that an elaborate program of decentralization would be developed in these situations.

A more serious limitation to this procedure arises when the operations of the organization involve the use of substantial fixed facilities common to a large range of possible outputs. The conditions of interdependence then require a formal programming solution since no single supplying manager is in a position to determine an optimal allocation without affecting the activity levels of other supplying divisions of the organization. That is, a formal solution must be obtained by a more centralized management using the techniques of linear and non-linear programming. We wish now to consider whether these formal solutions are consistent with programs of decentralization.

The Application of Programming to Transfer Pricing: Linear Restraints and Linear Objective Functions

It is generally accepted that, to the extent the problem can be formulated properly, linear programming offers a technique for allocating scarce resources among different choices of output. The problem here is to determine whether the allocation ought to be carried out by divisional managers, and assuming this procedure is considered feasible, what amount of information will be required by the divisional managers in order to accomplish these allocations.

The application of linear programming to the transfer pricing problem is based upon the relationship between the primal and dual solutions in the linear programming problem. That is, "To every linear programming problem there is an associated, sometimes somewhat artificial, minimization problem and vice versa."[9] The symmetry of these problems is such that, ignoring theoretical complications, the optimal solution of the primal is equal to the optimal solution of the dual. In simple notation, max $z = $ min Z (see the Appendix).

The optimal values of the dual variables have often been called "shadow prices," since they are considered to reflect the imputed values of the scarce resources implied in the primal problem. These prices are believed to offer the basis for a system of transfer prices. Specifically:

Decentralized administration . . . has many advantages, but it is important to note that its success depends upon the establishment of proper accounting prices . . . we have now seen that linear programming can be used for this purpose and is thus a significant aid as well as an alternative cost-accounting guidance.[10]

It is necessary to consider this proposal in more detail.

If we suppose that top management has solved the optimization problem, it possesses the information needed to determine both the types and the amounts of the outputs which should be produced. Presumably, top management could send the complete solution to the divisional managers or, rather, direct them

---

[9] William J. Baumol, *Economic Theory and Operations Analysis* (Englewood Cliffs, N.J.: Prentice-Hall, Inc., 1961), p. 91. The notations used here and in the Appendix correspond to those used by G. Hadley, *Linear Programming* (Reading, Mass.: Addison-Wesley Publishing Co., 1962), Chapter 8. We are ignoring theoretical complications in these statements.

[10] R. Dorfman, P. A. Samuelson, and R. M. Solow, *Linear Programming and Economic Analysis* (New York: McGraw-Hill Book Co., 1958), p. 184. See also G. Hadley, *op. cit.*, p. 485, and W. Baumol, *op. cit.*, p. 327.

to produce given levels of various products. With this knowledge we must wonder why a program of decentralization is desired.

Before considering this question, however, we should point out that the existence of "shadow prices" is not a sufficient condition to lead to an implementation of the optimal solution by divisional managers.[11] That is, shadow prices will only permit these managers to select the types of outputs which should be produced, but the exact levels of outputs must be determined by alternative means. Conceptually, the calculation of these output levels would presuppose the ability to solve large systems of simultaneous equations. While this may be possible, it does not seem a feasible manner of implementation. We might by-pass this problem by assuming some practical method has been determined which will reduce the likelihood that divisional managers will authorize production of nonoptimal levels of output.[12] Our main concern is the degree to which programming permits decentralized operations. We can approach this problem by considering the alternative forms of information economies which may exist.

EVALUATION OF DIVISIONAL MANAGERS

It seems evident that the allocation problem is best solved by centralized management when conditions permit a practical linear programming solution. However, the calculation of a linear programming solution is only part of the overall allocation problem.

For example, organizations may be designed in such a manner that divisional managers would still be in the best position to collect current information concerning input prices, output demands, and so on. Thus, while central management coordinates the activities of the firm, the input data used to solve the allocation problem are supplied by divisional managers. This would permit these managers to choose the most economic combinations of input factors for the types of possible outputs, the sources of supply, the outlets for the outputs, etc. Thus a considerable, and significantly important, degree of decentralization would be possible under these circumstances. The imputed prices sent by central management would simply be a means of implementing the solution to the firm's allocation problem, but the accuracy of the data used to derive the solution would actually be a responsibility of the decentralized divisions.

The evaluation of the performances of these decentralized managers, given these conditions however, would be a somewhat more difficult problem. The central management could use the programming solution as a means of estimating the profit of the firm. Later the actual performances of the divisions could be compared to the anticipated profits to determine how well they anticipated technical coefficients and input and output prices, including the degree to which they followed or were able to follow the optimal solution. If

[11] See G. Hadley, *op. cit.*, Ch. 11.
[12] *Ibid.*

the profit performances of the firm could be compared to the performances of other firms, central management would also have a method of indirectly evaluating the ability of the divisional managers to determine the most economical means for producing the possible outputs.

An alternative approach might involve the establishment by central management of the input standards for the various outputs within a formal system of standard costs. Although this reduces the attainable degrees of decentralization, a knowledge of the imputed values of the resources would still prove useful. For example, the lower level managers could be encouraged to review input and output variables continually in order to determine if the original solution remains optimal. More specifically, solutions to linear programming problems permit a storing of information needed to determine the degree to which changes in certain of the variables are critical to the original solution. The ranges of those changes in the values of the optimal set of variables which would alter the solution could be transmitted by central management for comparison by divisional managers to actual events. Essentially, a program of decentralization would be developed on the basis of the techniques of parametric programming since the positive activities will form the matrix of the coefficients of the optimal solution.

In conclusion, these and other possibilities of information economies may exist which offset the apparent need for highly centralized operations when using linear programming to solve the allocation problem. Indeed, some of the techniques of non-linear programming, which we shall mention shortly, implicitly assume that such information economies are real. In all instances, however, the evaluation of performances must be developed in terms of the limits of decentralization which exist. In the applications of programming we have seen that these limits are somewhat peculiar, and the evaluative framework may develop to be similarly so.[13]

NON-LINEAR PROGRAMMING

In recent years developments in non-linear programming have taken place which may offer advantages to the transfer price problem when the problem-situations involve non-linear functions.[14] Unfortunately, non-linear solution techniques are rather complex so a discussion of the implication of these techniques must be in general terms only.

One of these developments, the decomposition principle,[15] offers a possible

---

[13] Some of the characteristics of the situations of equilibrium and information processing just described are not completely unlike the conditions for equilibrium in a socialist economy. For example, see O. Lange, F. M. Taylor and B. E. Lippincott (ed.), *On the Economic Theory of Socialism* (Minneapolis: The University of Minnesota Press, 1938, second printing, 1948), pp. 72–82.

[14] Philip Wolfe, "Recent Developments in Non-Linear Programming," *The Rand Corporation—R-401-Pr.*, May, 1962.

[15] For example, see G. B. Dantzig and P. Wolfe, "Decomposition Principle for Linear Programs," *Operations Research*, v. 8 (January–February, 1960), pp. 101–11; a related article appears in *Econometrica*, v. 29 (October, 1961), pp. 767–78.

basis for negotiation between top management and the divisional managers. The techniques for the decomposition principle, while resembling the techniques of linear programming, are beyond description here, but very briefly the approach takes advantage of the fact that not all the constraints in the linear programming problem are common to all the activities.

More specifically, the original matrix is structured so that sets of equations form smaller linear programming problems which are linked together by a common set of constraints. The system may be solved in the usual manner, but it may be more feasible to solve the individual problems and then attempt to find a convex combination of the individual solutions which will satisfy optimally the common constraints as well. In the process of determining the optimal solution to the overall problem, new "prices" are generated which are then used in re-solving the smaller problems. It can be envisioned that individual managers, who would be in charge of the activities represented in the smaller problems, and who could not optimize their activities independently of each other, would send their individual programming solutions to a central management where the new prices would be generated and then sent back to the divisional managers. The process is repeated until the optimal solution is obtained. The relevant point is that, if this method can be applied in practice, it will provide a basis for negotiation between the departmental and central management levels. In this respect it would not be necessary for the divisional managers to negotiate with each other. This in itself may be an advantage since situations of negotiation between divisional managers may degenerate into personal conflicts.[16]

The overall process may be difficult to apply in practice, however, because of the possible extent of negotiations which might be necessary before the convergence to an optimum takes place. If the needed negotiations are extensive, the departmental managers will spend considerable time calculating solutions. On the other hand, the organizational structure may be so complex that the individual divisional managers can better process information concerning their activities than can a central management which must coordinate the activities of several divisions. Additionally, this type of structure may even permit central management more opportunity to compare the performance of divisonal managers to each other or to other "outside" firms. In any respect, the system of prices which is developed using these techniques should be less arbitrary than the prices which are developed utilizing the accounting methods of costs or by referring to non-relevant market prices.

Methods of determining prices have been suggested for use where non-linear functions of several variables are to be maximized subject to constraints.[17] In the process of maximizing these functions under constraints, the

---

[16] Joel Dean, *op. cit.*, p. 67.

[17] A simple illustration is contained in Baumol, *op. cit.*, pp. 56–58; for additional applications see also Paul H. Daus, W. M. Whyburn, *Introduction to Mathematical Analysis* (Reading, Mass.: Addison-Wesley Publishing Co., 1962), pp. 166–168; and

marginal value of the resources constraining the problem may also be computed. These prices would be applicable, for example, where the managers of two or more divisions demand the services of a single resource (the constraint). In that case the activities of each manager are no longer independent.

The practical use of non-linear programming as a basis for transfer prices is not immediately at hand since efficient methods for solving large systems of non-linear programming problems are still being developed.[18] Consequently, an evaluation of the uses of these methods for accounting purposes would be premature, although some of the remarks made earlier regarding the possibilities of information economies will apply under these programming conditions also.

Other implications. The shadow prices relative to scarce resources provide the accountant with a method for developing an analysis of whether to increase or abandon the organization's specialized resources.[19] These prices indicate the "worth" of these resources to the final profit of the firm. The complexities of multi-product firms may be such that an informal method of analysis is no longer feasible. The use of these prices in evaluating the possibilities of increasing or decreasing facilities is not as straight forward as it might seem unless it is assumed that all resources are increased or decreased as a complete unit. The methods of parametric programming are really needed to determine the effect of changing the available capacity of a single facility.

This suggests an implication of programming for systems of standard costs. Most systems of standard costs are based on engineering estimates of transferring the incomplete units from division to division. If the only choice which exists at all stages of completion is either to complete or not to complete the unit, then the standard variable costs may be considered as appropriate measures of the opportunity costs of producing the unit up to various stages of completion. If the facilities are being strained, the standards must be adjusted to include the opportunity costs of using the facility to produce the product or unit. This situation may occur when the firm's fixed facilities are capable of producing more than one type of output. Thus, programming may have relevance to standard cost systems to the extent that the imputed values of the scarce facilities may be incorporated within the system as a means of measuring the opportunity costs of processing the units of output.[20] In this

H. W. Kuhn and A. W. Tucker, "NonLinear Programming," in J. Neyman (ed.), *Proceedings of the Second Berkeley Symposium on Mathematical Statistics and Probability* (Berkeley: University of California Press, 1951), pp. 481–92.

[18] A late summary of these techniques by W. S. Dorn is contained in "Non-Linear Programming—A Survey," *Management Science*, v. 9 (January, 1963), pp. 171–208.

[19] Dorfman, Samuelson, and Solow, *op. cit.*, p. 184.

[20] This view is not inconsistent with the recommendations made by Moonitz and Sprouse concerning the valuation of inventories. See R. T. Sprouse and Maurice Moonitz, *A Tentative Set of Broad Accounting Principles for Business Enterprises, Accounting Research Study, No. 3* (New York: American Institute of Certified Public Accountants, 1962).

manner the engineering standards may be adjusted to reflect the economic conditions. The standards, therefore, will be useful for decision-making and control purposes. The more common standard cost systems seem to be designed to accomplish the single purpose of controlling divisional transactions to insure that they remain consistent with some centralized plan. If no alternative exists but to carry out the plan, the standards are sufficient. If other alternatives exist, these must be reflected within the system of standard costs. Programming may offer a means of accomplishing this need.

CONCLUSION

No attempt has been made in this paper to develop the mathematical techniques which are necessary to implement a system of transfer prices, although an appendix has been included to illustrate more fully some of the remarks. Rather, our purpose was to consolidate the material on transfer prices in order to evaluate the basis for applying programming. Further interest in the mathematical techniques can best be served by referring to the sources suggested.

One thing has become apparent in this discussion. The faith in a simple measure of performance such as a profit and loss index is not completely warranted in the area of transfer pricing. If real prices exist for units of outputs at the stages where decision-making concerning resource allocation is appropriate, then these prices will serve both the function of decision-making and the function of evaluation. A profit and loss index is as appropriate here as it is for external reporting on a firm's economic results.

If it is necessary to develop fictitious prices, however, the concurrent accomplishment of these two objectives seems difficult. While it may be possible to develop a system of prices which will guide the divisional managers in a manner consistent with an overall plan of resource allocations, the same system of prices cannot be relied on to motivate divisional managers toward some higher level of profits since they will have only a token amount of control over these profits. On the other hand, we may develop a system of prices which will permit the calculation of divisional profits or losses, but the system may not permit the determination of the optimal allocation of the firm's resources.[21]

As a general conclusion we suggest that the relationships between the decision-making and the control and evaluation phases of managerial functions be kept in the forefront in considering the design of accounting systems for programs of decentralization regardless of the degree to which decentralization will be carried out. In this respect the increasing applications of

---

[21] We do not deny the need to establish a conceptual system of measurement, given the objectives of the accounting system. For an attempt in this direction, see G. Shillinglaw, "Toward a Theory of Divisional Income Measurement," *Accounting Review*, v. 37 (April, 1962), pp. 208–216.

programming to solve the allocation problems of complex firms can no longer be ignored by accountants.

APPENDIX

Consider the following linear programming problem:

$$8x_1 + 3x_2 + 4x_3 + x_4 \leq 7$$
$$2x_1 + 6x_2 + x_3 + 5x_4 \leq 3$$
$$x_1 + 4x_2 + 5x_3 + 2x_4 \leq 8$$
$$\text{Max } z = 3x_1 + 4x_2 + x_3 + 7x_4$$

The problem may also be represented with the use of the vectors a_1, a_2, a_3, and a_4 as:

$$x_1a_1 + x_2a_2 + x_3a_3 + x_4a_4 \leq b \text{ where } a_1 \text{ is the vector } \begin{bmatrix} 8 \\ 2 \\ 1 \end{bmatrix},$$

$$a_2 \text{ is the vector } \begin{bmatrix} 3 \\ 6 \\ 4 \end{bmatrix}, \text{ etc.}$$

The dual to this problem may be formulated as:

$$8w_1 + 2w_2 + w_3 \geq 3$$
$$3w_1 + 6w_2 + 4w_3 \geq 4$$
$$4w_1 + w_2 + 5w_3 \geq 1$$
$$w_1 + 5w_2 + 2w_3 \geq 7$$
$$\text{Min } Z = 7w_1 + 3w_2 + 8w_3$$

If A is the matrix of the vectors, a_1, a_2, a_3, a_4, and c is the vector of prices of the x_5, the symmetry of the maximization and the minimization problem may be indicated in the following manner:

Primal	Dual
$Ax \leq b$	$A'w \geq c'$
$\text{Max } z = cx$	$\text{Min } Z = b'w$

where the primes in the dual indicate the transpose of the matrix A and the vectors c and b. This symmetry is further indicated by the fact that if an optimal basic feasible solution is obtained for the primal, and is represented as max $z = c_B x_B$; the scalar product z will equal the minimum value Z of the dual. That is:

$$\text{Min } Z = b'w = \text{Max } z = c_B x_B \quad \text{so} \quad b'w(= w'b) = c_B x_B$$

Fortunately, the general procedures of the simplex method can be used to derive sufficient information to compute the value of the optimal solution to the dual problem, assuming the primal is being solved directly. To illustrate how the value of the dual variables may be determined and *also* how this knowledge may be utilized for transfer prices, the initial and final tableaux of the maximization problem are given below. The variables x_5, x_6, and x_7 are the slack variables necessary to convert the inequalities of the problem into equalities.

Initial Tableau

C_B	Vectors in basis	b	a_1	a_2	a_3	a_4	a_5	a_6	a_7
0	a_5	7	8	3	4	1	1	0	0
0	a_6	3	2	6	1	5	0	1	0
0	a_7	8	1	4	5	2	0	0	1
	$z,\ z_j - c_j$	0	−3	−4	−1	−7	0	0	0

$$x_1 = x_2 = x_3 = x_4 = 0$$
$$x_5 = 7; \quad x_6 = 3; \quad x_7 = 8$$

Final Tableau

C_B	Vectors in basis	b	a_1	a_2	a_3	a_4	a_5	a_6	a_7
3	a_1	32/38	1	9/38	19/38	0	5/38	− 1/38	0
7	a_4	10/38	0	42/38	0	1	−2/38	8/38	0
0	a_7	252/38	0	59/38	171/38	0	−1/38	−15/38	1
	$z,\ z_j - c_j$	166/38	0	169/38	19/38	0	1/38	53/38	0

$$x_1 = 32/38; \quad x_4 = 10/38; \quad x_7 = 252/38; \quad x_2 = x_3 = x_5 = x_6 = 0$$

Recalling that max $z = c_B\, x_B$, we have $c_1\, x_1 + c_4\, x_4 + c_7\, x_7 = z$, or

$$[3 \quad 7 \quad 0] \begin{bmatrix} 32/38 \\ 10/38 \\ 252/38 \end{bmatrix} = 166/38$$

since min $Z = $ max z or $c_B\, x_B = w'b$, then $w'b = 166/38$.

It will be noted that the vectors a_5, a_6 and a_7 represent the vectors of the coefficients of the slack variables which correspond to the resources b_1, b_2, b_3. Since the $z_j - c_j$ row indicates the net marginal change in z caused by increasing the values of the variables $x_1, x_2, \ldots, x_7$ by an additional unit, the values $1/38$, $53/38$, and 0 under the columns a_5, a_6, and a_7 represent the change in profit of having either an additional unit of b_1, b_2, b_3 available or have a unit stand idle. We can assume then that these values are the imputed values of the resources b_1, b_2 and b_3 respectively, and in terms of the previous equations, $c_B\, x_B = b'w (= w'\, b) = $ max $z = $ min Z, we have

$$[3 \quad 7 \quad 0] \begin{bmatrix} 32/38 \\ 10/38 \\ 252/38 \end{bmatrix} = [7 \quad 3 \quad 8] \begin{bmatrix} 1/38 \\ 53/38 \\ 0 \end{bmatrix} = 166/38$$

The same information is obtainable through another and more general method. That is, if we assume that a_1, a_4, and a_7 are the vectors in the basic solution, and that they are represented as the matrix B, we have $Bx = b$. Premultiplying both sides by the inverse of B, $B^{-1} Bx = B^{-1} b = Ix = B^{-1} b$, or $x = B^{-1} b$. Using the previous notation, $x_B = B^{-1} b$. Thus $z = c_B\, x_B = C_B(B^{-1} b)$.

Similarly, since $b'w = w'b = c_B x_B$, $w'b = (c_B B^{-1})b$. The values of the dual variables w_j can therefore be determined by pre-multiplying the inverse of the matrix of the vectors in the basis by the prices of the variables in the solution. For example, if B is the matrix

$$\begin{bmatrix} a_1 & a_4 & a_7 \\ 8 & 1 & 0 \\ 2 & 5 & 0 \\ 1 & 2 & 1 \end{bmatrix}; \quad B^{-1} = \begin{bmatrix} 5/38 & - & 1/38 & 0 \\ -2/38 & - & 8/38 & 0 \\ -1/38 & - & 15/38 & 1 \end{bmatrix}$$

$$w' = c_B B^{-1} = [3 \quad 7 \quad 0] \begin{bmatrix} 5/38 & - & 1/38 & 0 \\ -2/38 & - & 8/38 & 0 \\ -1/38 & - & 15/38 & 1 \end{bmatrix} = \begin{bmatrix} 1/38 \\ 53/38 \\ 0 \end{bmatrix}$$

It should be noted that the inverse, B^{-1}, is also contained in the columns a_5, a_6, a_7, of the final tableau and they are also the columns which contained the original identity matrix in the initial tableau.

Similarly the vectors of coefficients for any solution, call them y_j, can be obtained by the equation $B^{-1} a_j$. For example, a_2 in the final solution which is represented as y_2 can also be determined by the equation:

$$y_2 = \begin{bmatrix} 5/38 & - & 1/38 & 0 \\ -2/38 & - & 8/38 & 0 \\ -1/38 & - & 15/38 & 1 \end{bmatrix} \begin{bmatrix} 3 \\ 6 \\ 4 \end{bmatrix} = \begin{bmatrix} 19/38 \\ 42/38 \\ 59/38 \end{bmatrix}$$

Suppose then the manager is given the shadow prices of the resources, 1/38, 53/38, 0. He determines that to produce x_1 he needs to "purchase" 8 units of b_1, 2 units of b_2, and 1 unit of b_3. His cost will be $8(1/38) + 2(53/38) + 1(0) = 114/38 = \$3$. For each unit of x_1 he produces he receives \$3, so that he breaks even on producing x_1. Similarly, he determines that he will lose 169/38 on each unit of producing x_2 and 19/38 on each unit of x_3; but he will break-even on each product of x_4. It will be noted that these values correspond to those in the $z_j - c_j$ row under the columns a_1, a_2, a_3, and a_4. This is not entirely coincidental, for $z_j = c_B y_j = c_B (B^{-1} a_j) = w' a_j$. Applying the process further to a_5, a_6, a_7, it can be determined that only the expressions $c_1 - w'a_1$, $c_4 - w'a_4$, and $c_7 - w'a_7 = 0$. From this the manager can conclude, unless there are alternative optima or unless the solution is degenerate, that these vectors form the matrix of basis vectors, the matrix B. If he can determine B^{-1}, he will be able to determine the levels of x_1 and x_4 and x_7 (slack) since $x_B = B^{-1} b$.

Chapter 4 Administration of Cash Flows and Liquid Assets

NORTHEAST AIRLINES, INC.

On January 15, 1960, Harry Zimmerman, assistant treasurer of Northeast Airlines, Inc., received the financial reports of the company's operations for the year ended December 31, 1959. He noted that on sales of $31,458,472 the company had suffered a reported loss of $7,061,983 for the year, including $3,044,896 in cash outflow. Operating losses throughout the year had resulted in substantial and continuous pressure on the company's cash position. As of December 31, 1959, Northeast Airlines had a negative working capital position of approximately $4.7 million.

In considering what he, as a financial officer, might do to relieve the pressure on working capital, Mr. Zimmerman recognized that he had little influence over the level and timing of operational receipts and disbursements. However, he felt that he was responsible for the efficient use of the company's working capital assets. He knew that pressures on working capital were ultimately reflected in the cash account. Therefore, he thought that his initial step in analyzing the use of working capital assets should focus on the management of cash. Anything that he could do to increase the effective use of Northeast Airlines' cash resources would directly reduce the financial pressures on the company.

Since joining the company as assistant treasurer in July, 1958, Mr. Zimmerman had concentrated mainly on improving internal accounting procedures and the control of financial operations. Disbursements to vendors, payroll, and ticket refunding procedures, for example, had been redesigned and integrated into a punched card accounting system. Cash receipts, billings, and accounts receivable records were also carried on punched cards. As of January, 1960, the company's internal accounting system was functioning smoothly, with accountability and control over assets firmly established.

Mr. Zimmerman recognized that establishing internal efficiency of procedural operations was only the first step toward efficient resource management. Although the company's balance sheet on December 31, 1959, showed approximately $2.1 million in cash, $1.3 million of this sum was required to be held in an inactive collateral deposit account against equipment trust obligations. Thus, only $800,000 was available for operations. On that date, a substantial part of the available funds was tied up in check clearance through the banking system, in internal check processing, and in deposits in the company's receiving banks. The internal daily cash report for December 31 showed only $116,000 in the company's checking accounts available for general disbursement. Mr. Zimmerman thought that changing the company's banking procedures offered the possibility of releasing a substantial amount of funds for operational use. He was not sure, however, what lines these modifications should take.

Northeast Airlines, Inc., with main offices in Boston, Massachusetts, served the New England area locally and also longer haul routes extending down the East Coast to Miami, Florida. The company had received approval from the Civil Aeronautics Board in September, 1956, to fly the Florida route, and thus was transformed from a regional airline to a competitor of two major airlines on an important domestic route.

Between December 31, 1955, and December 31, 1959, the company made substantial purchases of flight equipment to service its expanded route system. During this period, the company's total assets increased from $6.9 million to $35.6 million; gross investment in flight equipment increased from $5.3 million to $31.3 million.

After opening of the Florida service in the spring of 1957, Northeast Airlines began to incur increasing losses in spite of substantial increases in revenues. The introduction of new and expensive flight equipment raised the company's overall break-even load factor to 59% at the end of 1959. This development, combined with actual load factors in the 45–55% range, resulted in substantial operating losses and severe pressure on working capital. The company was able to continue in business and obtain required bank credit only because of the willingness of an investment company, the Atlas Corporation, to advance funds through notes subordinated to the company's bank credit. These subordinated notes carried an interest charge of 5.5%, and as of December 31, 1959, totaled $12.3 million. Also, at the end of 1959 the Atlas Corporation was the company's principal stockholder, with approximately 56% of the outstanding common stock. The investment company was represented on Northeast Airlines' board of directors.

CASH MANAGEMENT AT NORTHEAST AIRLINES

Northeast Airlines' revenues came from passenger service, air freight, mail, and miscellaneous services. Approximately 95% of total revenues in 1959 came from passenger service. Cash receipts from other than passenger service are excluded from discussion in this case study.

General Nature of Operational Cash Flow

Cash receipts and expenditures at Northeast Airlines were subject to particular seasonal, monthly, and weekly patterns. The company had two peak yearly seasons—one in the summer, when it served the New England resort business, and the other in the winter, during the Florida tourist season. Since aircraft maintenance, flight crew payroll, and flight support services all tended to fluctuate with passenger revenues or flying time, inflows and outflows of cash tended to peak at reasonably predictable times during the year. Exhibit 1 shows the monthly record for 1959 cash operating revenues and expenditures as reflected in the accounting records. This exhibit shows only operational cash flows and cumulative cash losses; cash flow for the company as a whole for the year 1959 is shown in Exhibit 2. Intramonthly and intraweekly patterns of cash flow are discussed below.

System of Cash Disbursement

The major cash payments required of Northeast Airlines consisted of accounts payable to vendors, payroll, credit obligations, taxes, and ticket refunding. The internal system of cash disbursement functioned along the following line, using vendor disbursement as an example.

All vendor bills were paid through the company's central accounting office in Boston. On receipt of a vendor's invoice for payment, an accounting distribution card was key punched to reflect the charge to the appropriate account or accounts. The aggregate of all accounting distribution cards reflected, for a specific period, all the vendors' bills presented for payment. At the time the accounting distribution card was originally punched, a cash payment card was also summary-punched and filed by payment date. All the cash cards coming due on each payment date were automatically sorted by vendor number. A punched card payment check was then written automatically, signed by the appropriate officer, and mailed. A summary check disbursement card for each vendor payment was held on file and eventually collated against the canceled check as a control over error or fraud in the check cashing process. On the day the check was mailed to the vendor, the accounting distribution cards covered by the check were posted into the accounting system to reflect payment of the bill in the appropriate accounts.

Other cash disbursements, including payroll, were handled similarly; payment was always made by checks issued through the company's Boston office. The company prepared all its own checks. All disbursement checks were written against accounts in two Boston banks—the First National Bank of Boston and the National Shawmut Bank of Boston. Although Northeast Airlines' internal accounting system reflected an immediate decrease in cash on the preparation and mailing of checks, the cash balances in the company's checking accounts were not drawn down until the checks were presented to the banks for payment. Although at times this disbursement float was large, the company's policy was to attempt to maintain in the disbursing accounts current cash balances sufficient to meet all checks outstanding. No attempt was made to continuously play the float and decrease working capital requirements in this manner. However, occasionally in short-run periods of cash stringency checks had been written against deposits that had been received at out-of-town banks and were to be transferred to Boston in a day or so.

System for Cash Receipts

Passenger revenues were derived 45% from sales at airport and central ticket offices operated by the company, 40% from sales through independent travel agencies, and 15% from sales under credit card plans.

Travel Agency Receipts

Approximately 1,450 travel agencies across the country issued tickets for Northeast Airlines. Payment on agency sales was due from each agency twice a month, on the 15th and at month-end. These payment dates had been arbitrarily set by Northeast when it had been decided to collect agency receipts twice a month. On these dates, each agency with payment due forwarded to Northeast Airlines' central accounting office in Boston a ticket accounting report, individual ticket coupons, and a check covering all sales to the payment date. Individual tickets were issued to and sold by each agency in numerical sequence. Each payment check, therefore, covered a sequential block of tickets sold. Payment to Northeast Airlines was computed by the agencies on the basis of ticket price less a commission of 10% on first class, 7% on tourist, or 5% on family plan sales. Ticket agencies had no recourse to Northeast Airlines on losses that resulted from extending credit or accepting bad checks. In order to audit the agencies, individual ticket coupons from agency sales were matched at later times against coupons collected from passengers at the actual time of travel. Ticket agency checks were recorded and posted into the company's accounting system, and then deposited in one of the two Boston disbursing banks, normally within 24 hours of receipt. Exhibit 3 shows the geographical distribution of ticket agency sales for December, 1959.

Credit Card Receipts

Credit cards were of two major types—the Air Travel Plan (A.T.P.) system, sponsored by the airlines, and independent credit plans, such as Diners' Club, Carte Blanche, and American Express. Each A.T.P. credit card was issued by one airline but usable on all. The card-issuing airline was responsible for all collections from the customer. When an A.T.P. card was used on another airline, that airline billed the issuing airline for the sale and turned the receivable over for collection.

An airlines' clearinghouse at a New York bank had been organized to expedite this process. Weekly, Northeast Airlines sent A.T.P. credit sales lists and verifying ticket coupons directly to card-issuing airlines. However, card-issuing airlines were billed by Northeast through the clearinghouse bank. On the 15th of each month, the clearinghouse bank balanced the accounts among the airlines and made settlement by intercompany deposit transfer. Each airline member of the clearinghouse carried a special account in the bank. Thus, the only actual transfers among the airlines consisted of funds to clear net balances. Since Northeast Airlines was almost always a net receiver of funds from this clearance activity, no minimum balance was carried in the clearinghouse bank account. All funds received from A.T.P. clearance were transferred by wire to a Boston bank on the day of clearance.

Under the A.T.P. credit plan, each customer's account was invoiced by Northeast Airlines on the 20th of each month for the charges of the preceding month, and the credit card holder was then given 10-day terms of payment. Offsetting this extension of credit was a required deposit of $425 for each account. The 20th was chosen as the invoicing date because at that time of month company personnel were under least pressure from other accounting and reporting work. On January 1, 1960, Northeast Airlines had 181 A.T.P. credit card accounts, predominantly with business firms.

Independent credit card plans were currently being introduced for use on Northeast flights. Diners' Club credit cards had been accepted beginning on January 1, 1960, the Carte Blanche plan was to be introduced on February 4, and use of American Express credit cards was currently under negotiation with the credit card company. The Northeast management considered the introduction of these credit plans primarily a service to its customers. It did not expect these plans to have significant impact on the revenues of the company.

Terms of reimbursement on independent credit card sales varied with the plan. The Diners' Club followed a monthly billing cycle. Payment in full was made to Northeast Airlines on the 15th of each month for all sales through the 27th of the prior month. Ticket coupons, showing the credit that had been extended against Diners' Club cards, were forwarded daily from individual ticket offices to the central accounting office. If at any time Diners' Club's current month's billings totaled more than $100,000, Northeast was reimbursed for 40% of the total within 5 days after the 27th of the month; the remaining balance was due in full, as indicated above, on the 15th of the following month.

Payment under the Carte Blanche credit card plan was to be distinctly different. When a Northeast ticket office sold a ticket against a Carte Blanche card, it would fill out a previously provided sight draft on the Hilton Credit Corporation for the appropriate amount. The sight draft would be printed on an envelope into which the validating ticket sale coupon was to be sealed. The sight draft would be treated by the ticket office as a check, deposited into its receiving bank, and cleared through the banking system as a check drawn on the Hilton Credit Corporation. Thus, for sales under the Carte Blanche plan, Northeast Airlines was to receive funds as soon as it normally did when a personal check was used for payment.

As of January 15, the final terms of billing and the selling commission under the American Express credit card plan were under negotiation. Mr. Zimmerman expected that the billing terms finally agreed to would resemble those of the Diners' Club plan.

Under the Diners' Club and Carte Blanche credit card plans, Northeast Airlines was reimbursed on the basis of ticket price less a 4% commission charge. All the credit card companies had full responsibility for collections from their credit card users. They had no recourse to Northeast Airlines either on sales that resulted in bad debt losses or on sales arising from fraudulent use of their credit cards.

Ticket Office Receipts—the Receiving Bank System

All other passenger ticket sales were made through 45 airline ticket offices located at airports along Northeast Airlines' route, or through 25 central ticket offices located in the downtown areas of cities the airline served. These ticket offices were staffed and managed by Northeast's personnel. Approximately 30% of the ticket office sales were made on a cash basis, with the remaining sales being paid for by personal check or credit card. Every ticket office filled out a daily ticket report listing individual sales and total daily receipts. These ticket reports were mailed each day to the company's central accounting office in Boston. On receipt of a ticket report from a ticket office, the listed sales were immediately reflected in the company's accounting system by a debit to cash and a credit to unearned revenue. As the passengers were actually flown, credit was given to earned revenue.

Although the daily sales by a ticket office were thus accounted for and reflected in the cash account of the company as a whole, the funds were not available for use until they reached the company's disbursing banks in Boston. To service the 70 ticket offices, a system of 52 receiving banks had been established. Each ticket office daily deposited its total cash and check receipts in a local receiving bank. Typically, these deposits were made each afternoon, although some of the larger ticket offices made deposits two or three times a day. After the daily receipts of a ticket office had been deposited, the receiving bank mailed a deposit notice to Northeast Airlines' central accounting office in Boston. The deposit notices were checked by the accounting office against the daily ticket reports received from the ticket offices. This control procedure ensured that all cash and check receipts from ticket sales had been deposited and correctly credited to Northeast Airlines' accounts at the various receiving banks.

Transfer of Funds from the Receiving Banks to the Disbursing Banks

In accordance with standing instructions from the company, every Tuesday each receiving bank transferred to one of the two Boston disbursing banks all funds deposited during the previous seven days. That is, all deposits through Monday night were transferred on Tuesday. Certain receiving banks always transferred funds to the First National Bank of Boston, while the rest transferred funds to the National Shawmut Bank of Boston.

The only exception to this transfer procedure was the receiving bank in Montreal. In addition to receiving ticket office deposits of approximately $2,000 to $3,000 a day, this bank also disbursed Canadian funds as required by the company's Canadian operations. Northeast Airlines maintained in the

Montreal bank a balance of between $35,000 and $55,000 (Canadian funds). Deposits of Canadian funds into this bank on balance exceeded disbursements. At intervals the company sold Canadian exchange through the First National Bank of Boston and thus effected a transfer of Canadian funds out of the Montreal bank, receiving an equivalent dollar credit to its account at the First National Bank. For the Montreal bank, then, there was no fixed schedule for transfer of funds.

Each receiving bank was allowed to retain a minimum compensating balance, previously agreed on by the receiving bank and Northeast Airlines. The minimum balance was based on the number and size of deposits, and typically was $1,000, $2,000, $3,000, or $5,000. The total of all minimum balances retained in the receiving bank system was approximately $125,000. This sum represented a permanent investment of cash in the receiving bank system. With the exception of the Montreal bank, none of the receiving banks provided services other than receiving and transferring funds.

The receiving banks transferred all of the week's ticket office deposits regardless of whether deposited checks had been cleared through the local Federal Reserve bank check clearance system. The minimum balances retained in the receiving banks thus not only compensated the banks for their services but also acted as a buffer against uncollected funds and as a reserve should any deposited check bounce after the funds had been transferred to Boston. When a bad check was returned to a receiving bank, the check was forwarded to the company's accounting office, along with a notice that the account was being charged for the amount involved. The minimum balance was then reestablished in the receiving bank from the following week's deposit. Northeast Airlines pursued collection on all bad checks from its Boston office.

Methods of Fund Transfer

Also as part of their permanent instructions, the receiving banks were asked to transfer funds to the Boston banks by wire wherever possible, and otherwise by bank sight drafts mailed directly to the Boston banks. Approximately 25 of the 52 receiving banks had access to the bank wire transfer service. These banks either subscribed to the wire service at a flat monthly rate or paid a $1.25 fee for each wire transfer transaction. Except for a very few banks there was no direct charge to Northeast Airlines, the cost being covered by the receiving bank's compensating balance. Wire funds were immediately available for disbursement on receipt at the Boston banks. Bank sight drafts similarly were recognized by the Boston banks as a deposit of immediately usable funds. Those banks without access to wire transfer typically served ticket offices in smaller New England towns. Such towns were rarely more than two days away from Boston by mail.

From a receiving bank's point of view, there was an important difference between transfer of funds by wire and by sight draft. Wire funds were immediately lost from the receiving bank's cash balances, but sight draft funds were not lost until the draft cleared through the banking system and was presented for payment at the issuing bank. If a sight draft was mailed from a receiving bank late on Tuesday, was received at a Boston bank on Thursday, and then required two days for clearance back to the issuing bank, the receiving bank would not lose the funds involved until the following Monday. Thus, the receiving bank would retain the use of the funds for six extra days. If a receiving bank was a correspondent of the Boston disbursing bank and maintained correspondent balances in Boston, the receiving bank would lose funds immediately on receipt of the sight draft in Boston through a transfer from its account balance. Nevertheless, even in this case the receiving bank retained the funds for two days longer than if wire transfer were used.

Northeast Airlines had noted a reluctance on the part of some of its receiving banks to wire funds to the Boston banks. In times of money market tightness, such as December, 1959, some of the receiving banks seemed to have ignored the standing instructions to transfer by wire, and had "inadvertently" sent bank sight drafts by mail to cover the required Tuesday transfer even where wire transfer was available.

Exhibits 4, 5, and 6, on a daily basis for the month of December, 1959, show examples of funds flow through several of the receiving banks, the transfer of funds from these receiving banks to Boston, the deposit of these funds into Northeast Airlines' disbursing account, and the notification to the company of the funds' availability for disbursement.

Receipt of the Funds in the Disbursing Banks

On receipt of funds transferred from the receiving banks, the First National Bank and the National Shawmut Bank credited them to a general disbursing account. Both banks had instructions to mail to Northeast Airlines each day a form showing the funds received from each receiving bank. On receipt of this deposit advice, the company's central accounting office then compared the funds received with the funds which should have been transferred, based on the deposit notices forwarded from the receiving banks during the previous week. The transferred funds were available for immediate use by Northeast Airlines.

Aside from the general disbursing account in each bank, the company maintained three special accounts at the First National Bank and one special account at the National Shawmut Bank. The two special disbursing accounts at the First National Bank were a payroll account and a passenger ticket refund account. Periodically, funds were transferred from the general disbursing account to the special disbursing accounts and then paid out as checks were presented. Funds were transferred in an amount sufficient to cover specific blocks of checks issued. The third special account at the First National Bank was a deposit account for the Parker House ticket office in Boston. The First National Bank acted as a receiving bank for this ticket office and its normal practice was to transfer to the company's general disbursing account each Tuesday all deposits above a $5,000 minimum balance. From the bank's point of view this was simply an accounting transfer from one account balance to another.

In addition to a general disbursing account, the National Shawmut Bank carried one special account for Northeast Airlines. This special account was a deposit account for the company's ticket office located at Logan International Airport in Boston. The National Shawmut Bank acted as a receiving bank for this ticket office by accumulating funds in the deposit account during the week and transferring to the general account each Tuesday funds in excess of a $5,000 minimum balance.

In the two disbursing banks, Northeast Airlines thus maintained two accounts for general disbursement, two accounts for special disbursement, and two accounts for receiving local ticket office deposits. The activity in each of these accounts for the month of December, 1959, as reflected in the actual bank statements is shown in Exhibits 7 and 8, as is the aggregate daily balance for the combined accounts. Minimum compensating balances were not required in any of the disbursing accounts. Northeast did not receive from the Boston banks any special services other than those discussed above. However, the First National Bank of Boston had participated in the equipment trust financing of the company's most recent acquisition of flight equipment.

Management of Disbursing Account Balances—the Daily Cash Report

Internal control of disbursing account balances was exercised on the basis of information compiled into a daily cash report. Exhibit 9 shows Northeast's daily cash report for December 1, 1959. The daily cash report was made up each morning, beginning balances being carried over from the previous day's close. Daily receipts listed for the two general disbursing accounts consisted of funds deposited directly by the company plus the sum of the deposit advice notices received that day from the Boston banks. Thus, receiving bank funds were not brought into the general disbursing account cash balance and considered available for disbursement until the company was notified of their arrival in Boston. Disbursements on the daily cash report were totaled from the checks written during the day. The closing balance was based on beginning balance, plus receipts, less disbursements.

According to the internal cash report of December 1, 1959, both general disbursing accounts had shown negative closing balances for that day. To offset these cash deficiencies, the company had held back certain checks from mailing. However, no check that involved a cash discount for payment within a specified time period was ever held back. Mr. Zimmerman recognized that the National Shawmut Bank's general disbursing account had shown, on December 1, a negative cash balance of $32,000, even after the checks held back had been considered. He knew, however, that in this account there generally were receiving bank funds that had been transferred to and deposited in Boston, but on which notification had not as yet been received. He therefore did not feel that the company was writing checks against disbursement float, which would be contrary to its policy. Mr. Zimmerman had frequently been in contact with the two Boston banks in recent months, attempting to reconcile the actual funds received with those anticipated.

Closing balances in the passenger refund and payroll accounts were not considered by Mr. Zimmerman to be available for use elsewhere, since they were scheduled for specific disbursement. The balance in the passenger refund account was particularly vulnerable, since the field ticket offices wrote the refund checks. Thus, these checks often were presented for payment before the central office knew they had been written. Funds were periodically transferred into this account in blocks of $50,000 as the central accounting office received ticket refund reports from the various ticket offices and estimated total passenger refund commitments.

The cash flow and cash balances in the receiving bank system were included on the daily cash report. Receipts were based on the daily accumulation of ticket sales reports received from the ticket offices. Disbursements consisted of transfers shown on the Boston banks' deposit advice notices for the day. The receiving banks' cash balances, of course, were not available for disbursement, but they did give Mr. Zimmerman some indication of the funds that would be transferred to Boston during the week. Thus, he could plan his tentative major disbursements several days in advance, knowing the funds that would be flowing in. Also included on the daily cash report were remarks about the major disbursements made and any other relevant information.

Exhibit 10 summarizes the daily cash reports for the month of December, 1959. Exhibit 11 compares, for each day of December, the available cash balances as shown on the internal daily cash reports with the cash balances actually carried in the disbursing banks.

Mr. Zimmerman forecasted the first six months of 1960 as a period of continued cash loss. He wondered what action would be most appropriate in meeting this cash deficiency and what change in the company's cash management system, if any, would most effectively contribute to easing the chronic pressure on the disbursing account cash balances. He was reluctant to borrow from the Atlas Corporation more funds than were absolutely necessary. Finally, he wondered whether the company's cash accounting and reporting system provided him with the type of information he needed for effective cash management and, if not, what revision was needed.

Exhibit 1

NORTHEAST AIRLINES, INC.

CASH OPERATING REVENUES AND EXPENSES BY MONTH, AND TOTAL CASH LOSSES
FOR THE YEAR 1959
(Dollar Figures in Thousands)

	Cash Operating Revenues	Cash Operating Expenses*	Cash Inflow (Outflow) from Operations	Cumulative Cash Inflow (Outflow) from Operations
January	$2,747	$2,559	$ 188	$ 188
February	2,519	2,467	52	240
March	3,063	2,696	367	607
April	2,788	2,608	180	787
May	2,497	2,654	(157)	630
June	2,589	2,658	(69)	561
July	2,855	2,849	6	567
August	2,981	2,828	153	720
September	2,460	2,755	(295)	425
October	2,185	2,792	(607)	(182)
November	2,189	2,689	(500)	(682)
December	2,683	3,021	(338)	(1,020)

Total operating cash loss	$1,020
Total interest and special charges	1,354
Total miscellaneous cash charges	671
Total Cash Loss in 1959	$3,045

* Total operating expenses less depreciation.

Exhibit 2

NORTHEAST AIRLINES, INC.

STATEMENT OF CASH FLOW YEAR ENDED DECEMBER 31, 1959
(Dollar Figures in Thousands)

INCREASES

Equipment purchase notes	$ 2,502
Long-term loan subordinated, Atlas Corporation	6,468
Disposition of flight equipment	427
Disposition of ground property	24
Disposition of land	3
Depreciation and amortization	4,017
Decrease in accounts receivable	1,092
Decrease in prepayments	(112)
Increase in accounts payable	2,108
	$16,530

DECREASES

Net loss from operations	$ 7,062
Fixed asset expenditures	3,515
Payment of bank term loan	3,769
Decrease in unearned transportation revenue	254
Increase in expendable parts and supplies	467
Increase in investments	32
Deferred charges	1,106
	$16,205
Net Cash Increase	$ 325
Cash balance beginning of period	1,761
Cash Balance, 12/31/59	$ 2,086

Exhibit 3

NORTHEAST AIRLINES, INC.

TOTAL TRAVEL AGENCY SALES BY STATE, DECEMBER 1959
(Dollar Figures in Thousands)

Location of Ticket Agency	December Sales	Approximate Mailing Time to Boston in Days
Connecticut	$ 23	1
Delaware	5	2
Florida	156	3
Maine	69	1
Maryland	11	2
Massachusetts	407	1
New Hampshire	29	1
New Jersey	41	1
New York	433	1
Pennsylvania	93	2
Rhode Island	6	1
Vermont	11	1
Virginia and District of Columbia	20	2
Quebec	15	2
Total Travel Agency Sales	$1,319	

Exhibit 4

NORTHEAST AIRLINES, INC.

AN EXAMPLE OF FUNDS FLOW THROUGH THE RECEIVING BANK SYSTEM, DECEMBER, 1959
MERCHANTS NATIONAL BANK, NEW BEDFORD, MASSACHUSETTS
(Dollar Figures in Thousands)

December, 1959	Receiving Bank's Books			Credited to Northeast's Account in Boston	Deposit Advice Received by Northeast from Boston Bank
	Deposit by Ticket Office	End of Day Balance	Transfer to Boston		
Opening balance.........		$6	...	...	...
Tue 1...............	$1	3	$4	...	...
W 2...............	1	4	...	...	...
T 3...............	1	5	...	$4	...
F 4...............	1	6	...	...	$4
S 5...............	1	7	...	...	...
S 6...............		...	...	...	...
M 7...............	1	8	...	...	...
T 8...............	0	2	6	...	...
W 9...............	1	3	...	6	...
T 10...............	1	4	...	...	6
F 11...............	1	5	...	...	...
S 12...............	1	6	...	...	...
S 13...............		...	...	...	...
M 14...............	1	7	...	...	...
T 15...............	1	3	5	...	...
W 16...............	1	4	...	5	...
T 17...............	1	5	...	...	5
F 18...............	1	6	...	...	...
S 19...............	0	6	...	...	...
S 20...............		...	...	...	...
M 21...............	1	7	...	...	...
T 22...............	1	3	5	...	...
W 23...............	0	3	...	5	...
T 24...............	0	3	...	...	...
F 25 holiday..........		...	...	...	...
S 26...............	0	3	...	...	...
S 27...............		...	...	...	...
M 28...............	2	5	...	...	5
T 29...............	0	2	3	...	...
W 30...............	0	2	...	3	...
T 31...............	1	3	...	...	3

NOTE.—All funds transferred from the Merchants National Bank by mailed draft in Boston funds. The minimum balance allowed the Merchants National Bank was $2,000.

Exhibit 5

NORTHEAST AIRLINES, INC.

An Example of Funds Flow through the Receiving Bank System, December, 1959
The Chase Manhattan Bank, New York
(Dollar Figures in Thousands)

December, 1959	Receiving Bank's Books			Credited to Northeast's Account in Boston	Deposit Advice Received by Northeast from Boston Bank
	Deposit by Ticket Office	End of Day Balance	Transfer to Boston		
Opening balance........ ...	...	$37	...	...	...
Tue 1...............	$12	13	$36	$36	...
W 2...............	8	21	...	...	...
T 3...............	4	25	...	...	...
F 4...............	8	33	...	...	$36
S 5...............	...	...	...	...	...
S 6...............	...	...	...	...	...
M 7...............	5	38	...	...	...
T 8...............	10	11	37	37	...
W 9...............	7	18	...	...	...
T 10...............	9	27	...	...	37
F 11...............	7	34	...	...	...
S 12...............	...	...	...	...	...
S 13...............	...	...	...	...	...
M 14...............	11	45	...	...	...
T 15...............	12	13	44	...	...
W 16...............	9	22	...	44	...
T 17...............	9	31	...	...	...
F 18...............	10	41	...	...	...
S 19...............	...	...	...	...	...
S 20...............	...	...	...	...	...
M 21...............	9	50	...	...	...
T 22...............	11	12	49	49	...
W 23...............	10	22	...	...	...
T 24...............	4	26	...	...	...
F 25 holiday........	...	...	...	...	...
S 26...............	...	...	...	...	...
S 27...............	...	...	...	...	...
M 28...............	7	33	...	...	93
T 29...............	14	15	32	32	...
W 30...............	7	22	...	...	...
T 31...............	7	29	...	...	32

Note.—All funds transferred from The Chase Manhattan Bank by wire. The minimum balance allowed The Chase Manhattan Bank was $1,000. This bank held a special and inactive deposit of $1,260,000, which more than justified the small balance in the receiving account.

Exhibit 6

NORTHEAST AIRLINES, INC.

An Example of Funds Flow through the Receiving Bank System, December, 1959
Industrial National Bank, Miami, Florida
(Dollar Figures in Thousands)

December, 1959	Receiving Bank's Books			Credited to Northeast's Account in Boston	Deposit Advice Received by Northeast from Boston Bank
	Deposit by Ticket Office	End of Day Balance	Transfer to Boston		
Opening balance........	...	$16	...	...	...
Tue 1..............	$4	9	$11	...	...
W 2..............	2	11	...	$11	...
T 3..............	1	12	...	...	...
F 4..............	1	13	...	...	$11
S 5..............	...	...	...	...	...
S 6..............	...	...	...	...	...
M 7..............	5	18	...	...	...
T 8..............	3	8	13	13	...
W 9..............	2	10	...	...	...
T 10..............	2	12	...	...	13
F 11..............	3	15	...	...	...
S 12..............	...	...	...	...	...
S 13..............	...	...	...	...	...
M 14..............	5	20	...	...	...
T 15..............	1	6	15	15	...
W 16..............	3	9	...	...	...
T 17..............	2	11	...	...	...
F 18..............	3	14	...	...	15
S 19..............	...	...	...	...	...
S 20..............	...	...	...	...	...
M 21..............	6	20	...	...	...
T 22..............	3	8	15	15	...
W 23..............	4	12	...	...	...
T 24..............	2	14	...	...	...
F 25 holiday........	...	...	...	...	...
S 26..............	...	...	...	...	...
S 27..............	...	...	...	...	...
M 28..............	5	19	...	...	15
T 29..............	7	12	14	14	...
W 30..............	1	13	...	...	...
T 31..............	3	16	...	...	14

Note.—All funds transferred from the Industrial National Bank by wire. The minimum balance allowed the Industrial National Bank was $5,000.

Exhibit 7

NORTHEAST AIRLINES, INC.
BOSTON BANKS' STATEMENTS, DISBURSING ACCOUNTS ACTIVITY DECEMBER, 1959
(Dollar Figures in Thousands)

December, 1959	National Shawmut Bank of Boston General Account					The First National Bank of Boston General Account					First National Bank Passenger Refund Account			First National Bank Payroll Account			Total Disbursement Accounts			
	Deposits from Northeast	Deposits from Receiving Bank Transfers	Total Deposits	Checks Paid	Day End Balance	Deposits from Northeast	Deposits from Receiving Bank Transfers	Total Deposits	Checks Paid	Day End Balance	Transfers into Account	Checks Paid	Day End Balance	Transfers into Account	Checks Paid	Day End Balance	Total‡ Deposits	Total‡ Checks Paid	Day End Balance	
Opening balance					$719					$179			($8)†			$127			$1,017	
Tue 1		$86	$86	$393	413	$39		$39	$166*	51		$4	(12)	$107	$70	$127	$125	$526	616	1
W 2		103	103	36	480		$21	21	62*	10	$50	6	32		46	164	124	100	640	2
T 3	$1	14	15	29	465	44	17	61	12	58		4	28		26	118	75	71	643	3
F 4				116	349	103		103	18	143		3	25		23	92	103	160	586	4
S 5																				5
S 6																				6
M 7				34	315	111	1	112	182*	73		5	20	170	70	169	112	121	577	7
T 8		143	143	18	440	108	4	112	1	184		2	18		70	99	255	91	741	8
W 9		72	72	57	455	94	40	134	5	314		5	13		30	69	206	97	851	9
T 10		32	32	31	457	58	14	72		385		4	9		17	52	104	53	903	10
F 11				10	447		13	13	11	387		4	5		8	44	13	33	883	11
S 12																				12
S 13																				13
M 14		113	113	41	406	27	1	28	189*	226		3	2	185	87	142	28	135	776	14
T 15		128	129	6	513	201	5	206	3	430		5	(3)		40	102	319	54	1,042	15
W 16	1			22	619		31	31	10	452		3	(6)		35	67	160	71	1,132	16
T 17				29	590	12	13	25	197	279		5	(11)	190	52	205	25	93	1,063	17
F 18		15	15	24	581				8	271		4	(15)		57	148	15	93	985	18
S 19																				19
S 20																				20
M 21		1	1	60	522	169		169	221*	219	50	9	26	170	140	178	170	210	945	21
T 22		159	159	57	625	249	7	256	193	281		2	24		48	130	415	300	1,060	22
W 23	282	52	334	88	870	193	33	226	3	504		5	19		32	98	560	128	1,491	23
T 24		18	18	66	822		18	18	54*	468	50	6	63		43	55	36	119	1,408	24
F 25 holiday																				25
S 26																				26
S 27																				27
M 28		28	28	62	789		15	15	199*	284		10	53	185	51	189	43	137	1,315	28
T 29	76	122	198	57	930		3	3	20	267		7	46		76	113	201	160	1,356	29
W 30	12	44	56	302	683	112	35	147	3	411		10	36		32	81	203	347	1,211	30
T 31	168		168		851	73	3	76	6	482		9	27		41	40	244	56	1,400	31

* Indicates overdraft on the account.
† Includes funds transferred into passenger refund and payroll accounts.
‡ Excludes interaccount transfers.

SOURCES: Bank statements and transfer records.

Exhibit 8

NORTHEAST AIRLINES, INC.

Boston Banks' Statements

DEPOSIT ACCOUNTS ACTIVITY AND TOTAL CASH BALANCE, DECEMBER, 1959

(Dollar Figures in Thousands)

December, 1959	National Shawmut Bank of Boston Airport Deposit Account			The First National Bank of Boston Parker House Deposit Account			Total Cash Balance, Boston Deposit Accounts	Total Cash Balance, Boston Disbursing Plus Deposit Accounts
	Deposits	Transfers	Day End Balance	Deposits	Transfers	Day End Balance		
Opening balance		$35	$40	$3		$ 8	$48	$1,065
Tue 1	$ 8		13	1		11	24	640
W 2	5		18	2		12	30	670
T 3	7		25			14	39	682
F 4	4		29			14	42	628
S 5	..		..	..		..	..	..
S 6	..		..	..		..	..	..
M 7	21		50	1		15	65	642
T 8	5	45	10	2		17	27	768
W 9	6		16	1		18	34	885
T 10	6		22			18	40	943
F 11	8		30	3	$11	10	39	922
S 12	..		..	..		..	..	..
S 13	..		..	..		..	..	..
M 14	16		46	1		11	56	832
T 15	7	41	12	2		13	24	1,066
W 16	7		19			13	32	1,164
T 17	6		25	1		14	39	1,102
F 18	6		31	1		15	46	1,031
S 19	..		..	..		..	..	..
S 20	..		..	..		..	..	..
M 21	19		51	1		16	66	1,011
T 22		40	11	2		18	29	1,089
W 23	11		22	1		19	41	1,532
T 24	5		27		11	8	35	1,443
F 25 holiday	..		..	..		..	..	..
S 26	..		..	..		..	..	..
S 27	..		..	..		..	..	..
M 28	16		43	2		10	53	1,368
T 29	6	38	11	1		11	22	1,378
W 30	5		16	1		12	28	1,239
T 31	8		24			12	36	1,436
	$5,000 minimum balance			$5,000 minimum balance				

Exhibit 9

NORTHEAST AIRLINES, INC.

EXAMPLE OF COMPANY'S DAILY CASH REPORT DECEMBER 1, 1959
(Dollar Figures in Thousands)

Bank Account	Beginning Balance	Receipts	Disburse-ments	Closing Balance	Checks Held Back
First National Bank, general disbursing account............	$ 41	$10	$141*	($89)	$ 91
National Shawmut Bank, general disbursing account........	(251)	67	1	(185)	153
Passenger refund account........	66	50	...	116	...
Payroll account................	125	...	...	125	...
Ticket office receiving banks......	641	...	77†	564	...
Chase Manhattan Bank, equipment collateral account (inactive)....................	...	...	...	1,260	...

REMARKS: Passenger refund transfer.......$50
            IBM run of checks............$91

---

* Includes transfer to passenger refund account.
† Indicates transfers to Boston disbursing accounts.

Exhibit 10

NORTHEAST AIRLINES, INC.

SUMMARY OF COMPANY'S DAILY CASH REPORTS DECEMBER, 1959
(Dollar Figures in Thousands)

	National Shawmut Bank of Boston General Disbursing Account			The First National Bank of Boston General Disbursing Account			First National Bank Passenger Refund Account			First National Bank Payroll Account			Total General Disbursing Accounts			Total Receiving Bank Accounts			Total Cash Balance, General, Disbursing Accounts Plus Receiving Bank Accounts
December, 1959	Receipts	Disbursements	Cash Balance	Receipts	Disbursements	Cash Balance	Receipts	Disbursements	Cash Balance	Receipts	Disbursements	Cash Balance	Receipts	Disbursements	Cash Balance	Total Receipts	Total Transfers	Day End Balance	
Opening balance			($251)			$41			$66			$125			($210)			$641	$431
Tue 1	$67	$1	(185)	$10	$141*	(89)	$50						$77	$142	(274)		$77	564	290
W 2		17	(202)	44		(46)							44	17	(247)			564	317
T 3	20	3	(185)	123		78					178	(53)	143	3	(107)	$141	43	662	555
F 4	143	279	(321)	112	170*	20				170		117	255	449	(301)		143	519	218
S 5																			
S 6																			
M 7	14	1	(308)	125		145							139	1	(163)	35	31	523	360
T 8		29	(337)	95		240							95	29	(97)			523	426
W 9	1	18	(354)	61		301							62	18	(53)		5	518	465
T 10	142	10	(222)	41		342							183	10	120		183	335	455
F 11		18	(240)	27	185*	184				185	175	127	27	203	(56)	113		448	392
S 12																			
S 13																			
M 14	32	9	(217)	64	192*	56				190		317	96	201	(161)	175	45	578	417
T 15		322	(539)	151	192*	15							151	514	(524)		1	577	53
W 16		13	(552)	16		31							16	13	(521)		4	573	52
T 17	113	50	(489)	77		108	50			170	371	116	190	50	(381)	116	126	563	182
F 18		64	(553)	104	220*	(8)							104	284	(561)	124		687	126
S 19																			
S 20																			
M 21		5	(558)	248		240	50						248	5	(318)	94		781	463
T 22	15	25	(568)	193	3	430				185		301	208	28	(138)	119	16	834	746
W 23	461	258	(365)		235*	195							461	493	(170)		179	705	535
T 24																			
F 25 holiday																			
S 26																			
S 27																			
M 28	371	22	(16)	40	4	232					178	123	411	26	215	58	337	426	641
T 29	18	16	(14)	144		376							162	16	362	149	50	525	887
W 30	40	240	(213)	74	26	424				280			114	266	210	54	28	551	761
T 31	341	23	105	39	451*	12		$151†	65		279	124	380	474	116	94	279	366	482

* Includes funds transferred to passenger refund and payroll accounts.
† Cumulative total for month.
NOTE.—At all times during the month, Northeast carried $1.26 million in cash in an equipment collateral deposit account in The Chase Manhattan Bank.

Exhibit 11

NORTHEAST AIRLINES, INC.

COMPARISON OF RECORDED AVAILABLE CASH BALANCES IN DISBURSING
ACCOUNTS, COMPANY REPORTS VERSUS BOSTON BANKS' STATEMENTS
(Dollar Figures in Thousands)

December, 1959	Available Cash Balance According to Company Reports*	Available Cash Balance According to Bank Statements†	Difference
Opening balance..................	($210)	$1,017	$1,227
Tue 1.........................	(274)	616	890
W 2.........................	(247)	640	887
T 3.........................	(107)	643	750
F 4.........................	(301)	586	887
S 5.........................	. . .	. . .	. . .
S 6.........................	. . .	. . .	. . .
M 7.........................	(163)	577	740
T 8.........................	(97)	741	838
W 9.........................	(53)	851	904
T 10.........................	120	903	783
F 11.........................	(56)	883	939
S 12.........................	. . .	. . .	. . .
S 13.........................	. . .	. . .	. . .
M 14.........................	(161)	776	937
T 15.........................	(524)	1,042	1,566
W 16.........................	(521)	1,132	1,653
T 17.........................	(381)	1,063	1,444
F 18.........................	(561)	985	1,546
S 19.........................	. . .	. . .	. . .
S 20.........................	. . .	. . .	. . .
M 21.........................	(318)	945	1,263
T 22.........................	(138)	1,060	1,198
W 23.........................	(170)	1,491	1,661
T 24.........................	. . .	1,408	. . .
F 25 holiday.................	. . .	. . .	. . .
S 26.........................	. . .	. . .	. . .
S 27.........................	. . .	. . .	. . .
M 28.........................	215	1,315	1,100
T 29.........................	362	1,356	994
W 30.........................	210	1,211	1,001
T 31 closing balance...........	116	1,400	1,284

* Includes funds in two general disbursing accounts only. Company considered passenger
refund and payroll account balances committed.
† Includes funds in all disbursing accounts.

SHORETEX CORPORATION

LATE IN OCTOBER, 1957, Montgomery Brewster, a member of the board of directors of the Shoretex Corporation, wrote to Mark T. Henry, the treasurer, as follows:

Chicago
October 22, 1957

DEAR MARK:

I received the September figures at a time when things were not too busy at the office, so I have had time to compare them with the condition of the company at the beginning of the year. It seems to me that we are falling into the happy position of having too much money on hand.

As you know, I am going to be in Houston just before Thanksgiving, and I would like to sit down with you for two or three hours to go over all the aspects of our company's operations that affect the size of the cash account. I think we should work out a figure that represents the amount necessary to comfortably take care of our needs, and then decide on a policy for any excess.

.   .   .   .

With best wishes.

Sincerely,
(*Signed*) BREW

The Shoretex Corporation was a chemical manufacturing company. Its general offices were located in Houston, Texas, and its plant was on the Gulf Coast nearby. It also had a research laboratory and pilot plant in the outskirts of Houston for the development of new products. A small manufacturing subsidiary was nearing completion in Europe. The company had been formed in 1950 by a group of wealthy people to exploit certain technical developments that had been worked out by a small research laboratory owned by the group.

Patent protection on one group of related chemicals among the company's products gave it a strong competitive position in this type of product, and thus a high margin of profit on its own sales as well as large royalties from licensees overseas.

The principal raw materials of the Shoretex Corporation were by-products from refinery and chemical operations. These materials were processed in a continuous stream installation, which put the products through the complicated series of separations and reactions that produced the various final products.

The company had built a tank farm to permit the quantity storage of a certain intermediate product that could be directed into several final products, depending on demand. It also used some of this storage capacity to hold quantities of raw materials in order to adjust the flow of receipts and plant input.

Raw materials were obtained on long-term contracts, which required the company to estimate its needs 60 days in advance and to take within 10% of the quantities scheduled throughout the life of the contract. Fixed-price arrangements for these materials had been obtained on favorable terms.

In addition to the highly profitable line of patented chemicals, which were used principally as raw materials in the pharmaceutical industries, the company sold a wide variety of specialty chemical products. It also delivered large quantities of hydrogen by pipeline to nearby chemical plants, and accounted for the proceeds of these sales by reducing the cost of manufacture of certain of its products. As a result of this variety of products, the company had many customers, all industrial concerns, who used Shoretex products as raw or intermediate materials in their own production.

Many of the Shoretex products were highly competitive and very sensitive to price competition, since several other chemical companies were able to supply materials of the same specification. The sales department, however, had shown itself able to keep up with the competitive situation, and no difficulty had been experienced in moving the products of the company. On occasion, substantial concessions had been made both in price and credit terms in order to keep the plant at near-capacity levels. These special concessions, together with certain other unforeseeable events, often resulted in wide fluctuations in budgeted monthly sales and accounts receivable. Other important elements affecting budget estimates were: wide fluctuations in foreign sales; adverse weather, which influenced sale of agricultural chemicals; changes in product mix because of competition; and new product developments.

The research laboratories were constantly at work to improve the production processes and the quality of the final product, and especially to discover new products that could be made of the raw materials received by the Shoretex Corporation.

Each member of the board of directors received monthly financial statements, from which the data in Exhibits 1 and 2 have been taken. Mr. Brewster, who was particularly interested in financial matters, also had received a copy of the cash budget of the company, which was kept up to date monthly by the entry of actual figures. Figures from this comparison for the first nine months of 1957 appear in Exhibit 3; the budgeted figures for the last three months of 1957 are in Exhibit 4. Exhibit 5 shows monthly sales from September, 1956, through September, 1957.

Exhibit 1

SHORETEX CORPORATION

BALANCE SHEETS, DECEMBER 31, 1956, AND SEPTEMBER 30, 1957
(In Thousands)

ASSETS	December 31, 1956		September 30, 1957	
Current assets:				
Petty cash...............................		$ 3		$ 3
Cash in bank:				
Payroll.................................	10		10	
General.................................	168		282	
Total Cash............................		$ 181		$ 295
U.S. Treasury 90-day bills....................	...		$ 27	
State and municipal obligations................	...		40	
Total Short-Term Reserve...............		...		67
Accounts receivable, net.....................		331		376
Inventories and supplies.....................		742		823
Total Current Assets....................		$1,254		$1,561
Advances to subsidiary.......................		64		117
Plant:				
Land, buildings, machinery, fixtures (cost)......$1,663			$1,829	
Less: Allowance for depreciation............. 680			819	
Net Plant..............................		983		1,010
Construction in process.......................		147		24
Deferred charges.............................		51		51
Total Assets........................		$2,499		$2,763
LIABILITIES				
Current liabilities:				
Trade creditors............................		$ 260		$ 134
Quantity discounts offered....................		...		59
Other accruals.............................		45		58
Dividend payable...........................		27		...
Federal income tax accrued...................$ 83			$ 397	
Profit-sharing bonus accrued..................	...		43	
Current maturity debentures.................	70		70	
	$ 153		$ 510	
Less: U.S. Treasury 90-day bills.............	134		510	
Total Current Liabilities.................		$ 351		$ 251
Other debentures.............................		587		517
Capital:				
Reserve, contingencies.......................$ 210			$ 210	
Common stock.............................	336		336	
Capital surplus.............................	131		137	
Earned surplus, 12/31/56.....................	884		884	
Net royalties, year to date....................	...		151	
Net profits, year to date.....................	...		324	
Less: Dividends paid, year to date...........	...		(47)	
Net Capital............................		1,561		1,995
Total Liabilities......................		$2,499		$2,763

Exhibit 2

SHORETEX CORPORATION

INCOME, EXPENSE, AND SURPLUS ITEMS, NINE MONTHS ENDING
SEPTEMBER 30, 1957
(In Thousands)

Net sales......................................			$3,286
Manufacturing costs*.........................	$2,160		
Less: By-product sales.......................	17		
Net manufacturing costs......................		$2,143	
Sales expense................................	$ 148		
Quantity discounts offered....................	59		
Administration...............................	98		
Research.....................................	93		
Overhead costs*.............................		398	2,541
Operating profit.............................			$ 745
Discounts earned.............................	$ 3		
Other income................................	18	$ 21	
Interest expense.............................	$ 22		
Profit sharing...............................	43		
Other expenses..............................	1	66	45
Net before income tax........................			$ 700
Estimated income tax.........................			376
Net Profit...................................			$ 324
Surplus items:			
Royalty payments............................		$ 202	
Estimated income tax........................		50	$ 152
Assets sold over book value...................			6
Dividends declared...........................			47

* Including depreciation $155

Exhibit 3

SHORETEX CORPORATION

BUDGET AND ACTUAL CHANGES IN CASH AND SECURITIES, MONTHLY, JANUARY–SEPTEMBER, 1957

(In Thousands)

	January Budget	January Actual	February Budget	February Actual	March Budget	March Actual	April Budget	April Actual	May Budget	May Actual	June Budget	June Actual	July Budget	July Actual	August Budget	August Actual	September Budget	September Actual	Total Budget	Total Actual
Operations:																				
Gross profit	$97	$95	$140	$101	$192	$142	$188	$159	$168	$151	$156	$147	$101	$152	$131	$108	$67	$88	$1,240	$1,143
Adjustments:																				
Depreciation	17	15	19	17	19	17	17	17	18	18	18	17	18	18	19	18	19	18	164	155
Inventories	(16)	(9)	33	(27)	55	9	20	20	29	3	(3)	(9)	(13)	36	(21)	(53)	(50)	(52)	37	(82)
Accruals	1	(5)	(4)	16	6	22	6	29	(6)	(9)		42	0	24	(3)	7	1	10	(2)	116
Accounts receivable	(21)	(25)	(177)	(50)	1	(54)	(91)	(86)	48	59	62	(54)	82	47	(17)	47	76	68	(37)	(46)
Accounts payable	(30)	(33)	15	(55)	8	(40)	(4)	18	10	16	10	(31)	(20)	0	(2)	4	9	(8)	(4)	(129)
Selling administration, research	(44)	(41)	(47)	(47)	(22)	(50)	(49)	(51)	(43)	(55)	(21)	(25)	(31)	(44)	(40)	(44)	(36)	(34)	(333)	(391)
Royalties					34	49				33	51	23				29	58	67	143	201
Net effect on cash	$4	$(3)	$(21)	$(45)	$293	$95	$87	$106	$224	$216	$273	$110	$137	$235	$67	$116	$144	$137	$1,208	$967
Capital:																				
Advances to foreign subsidiaries	$(47)	$(34)	$(9)	$(9)	$(30)	$(1)	$(9)	$(10)	$(2)	$(2)	$(6)	$(12)	$(12)	$(12)	$(10)	$(9)	$(7)	$(18)	$(17)	$(54)
Construction			(36)	(12)	35	(7)			(20)	(10)	(16)	12		(6)				(15)	(187)	(115)
Insurance recovery										31									35	43
Net effect on cash	$(47)	$(34)	$(45)	$(21)	$5	$(8)	$(9)	$(10)	$(22)	$19	$(22)	$(12)	$(12)	$(18)	$(10)	$(9)	$(7)	$(33)	$(169)	$(126)
Financial:																				
Income tax			$(13)	$(13)	$(33)	$(38)					$(34)	$(34)					$(42)	$(42)	$(109)	$(114)
Interest															$(13)	$(13)			(26)	(26)
Debt reduction											(27)	(27)			(127)	(70)			(127)	(70)
Dividends	$(27)	$(27)															(13)	(20)	(67)	(74)
Net effect on cash	$(27)	$(27)	$(13)	$(13)	$(33)	$(38)					$(61)	$(61)			$(140)	$(83)	$(55)	$(62)	$(329)	$(284)
Combined effect on cash	$(70)	$(64)	$(79)	$(79)	$265	$49	$78	$96	$202	$235	$190	$37	$125	$217	$(83)	$24	$82	$42	$710	$557
Cash and securities beginning	315	315	245	251	166	172	431	221	509	317	711	552	901	589	1,026	806	943	830	315	315
Cash and Securities Ending	$245	$251	$166	$172	$431	$221	$509	$317	$711	$552	$901	$589	$1,026	$806	$943	$830	$1,025	$872	$1,025	$872

Exhibit 4

SHORETEX CORPORATION

BUDGETED CHANGES IN CASH AND SECURITIES, MONTHLY, OCTOBER–DECEMBER, 1957
(In Thousands)

	October Budget	November Budget	December Budget	3 Months Total Budget
Operations:				
Gross profit	$ 55	$ 57	$ 62	$ 174
Adjustments:				
Depreciation	19	19	19	57
Inventories	(63)	(60)	(57)	(180)
Accruals	(4)	7	5	8
Accounts receivable	18	(12)	12	18
Accounts payable	(2)	7	50	55
Selling, administration, research	(39)	(39)	(37)	(115)
Royalties	...	...	56	56
Profit sharing	...	(45)	...	(45)
Net effect on cash	$ (16)	$ (66)	$110	$ 28
Capital:				
Advances to foreign subsidiaries	...	...	...	...
Construction	$ (7)	$ (7)	$ (6)	$ (20)
Insurance recovery	...	...	...	...
Net effect on cash	$ (7)	$ (7)	$ (6)	$ (20)
Financial:				
Income tax	...	...	$(42)	$ (42)
Interest	$ (1)	$ (1)	(1)	(3)
Debt reduction	...	...	...	...
Dividends	...	...	(13)	(13)
Net effect on cash	$ (1)	$ (1)	$(56)	$ (58)
Combined effect on cash	$ (24)	$ (74)	$ 48	$ (50)
Cash and securities beginning	1,025	1,001	927	1,025
Cash and Securities Ending	$1,001	$ 927	$975	$ 975

Exhibit 5

SHORETEX CORPORATION

GROSS MONTHLY SALES, SEPTEMBER–DECEMBER, 1956,
JANUARY–SEPTEMBER, 1957
(In Thousands)

	Pharmaceutical	General	Total
1956:			
September	$ 85	$204	$289
October	54	184	238
November	60	187	247
December	68	179	247
1957:			
January	120	173	293
February	147	174	321
March	214	192	406
April	250	193	443
May	242	189	431
June	217	187	404
July	213	205	418
August	134	206	340
September	102	201	303

ARE COMPENSATING BALANCE REQUIREMENTS IRRATIONAL? *

By Richard G. Davis and Jack M. Guttentag†

IN A RECENT ARTICLE in this *Journal*, Douglas Hellweg argues that "by eliminating compensatory balance requirements, a bank can enlarge its own earnings while at the same time reducing the effective rate of interest paid by the borrower."[1] These requirements are therefore, or so Hellweg argues, irrational, and it is a puzzle that they ever became so firmly imbedded in banking practice.[2]

Hellweg illustrates his case somewhat as follows: Consider a thousand dollar loan with a contract interest rate of 4 per cent and a 20 per cent compensatory balance requirement. Since the borrower has the use of only $800, he pays an effective rate of 5 per cent. If, instead, the bank advanced $800 at a 5 per cent contract rate but with no required balance, the borrower would be just as well off. The bank, however, would be *better* off because it would not have to hold required reserves against deposits represented by the compensating balance. Thus, in the first case above, where a compensatory balance is required, the lender's income is $40 (0.04 × $1,000), but $40 of reserves is tied up (assuming a reserve ratio of 20 per cent). If the bank advances $800 at 5 per cent with no balance required, its income is $40 (0.05 × $800) *plus* the return it can obtain on the $40 of required reserves released through the reduction of deposits by $200. The additional income can be shared with the borrower in the form of a lower contract rate, so that both parties can be better off without the compensating balance requirement.

---

* Reprinted by permission from *The Journal of Finance*, 17 (March 1962), pp. 121–26.

† Economist and Chief, respectively, for the Domestic Research Division, Federal Reserve Bank of New York. The authors are indebted to Frederick W. Deming for helpful suggestions and comments.

[1] Douglas Hellweg, "A Note on Compensating Balance Requirements," *Journal of Finance*, XVI (March, 1961), p. 80.

[2] Like Hellweg, we are defining compensating balances as balances required of a borrower by a bank as a condition for granting a loan. Such balances, however, can serve other purposes as well, such as compensating a bank for services rendered.

The burden of this note is that Hellweg's argument applies to a special case; this case exists and requires explanation, but it does not describe compensating balance relationships generally.

Hellweg has forgotten that most businesses require substantial average balances to bridge day-to-day gaps between payments and receipts and sometimes for other purposes as well. Since compensating balance requirements are most often stated in terms of average deposits over a period, balances held to meet normal cash needs may also serve to satisfy such requirements.[3] As long as the required balance does not exceed the average balance a borrower would normally maintain in the absence of the requirement (call this the "voluntary balance"), it represents no burden to the borrower.[4] In such cases the balance requirement does not reduce the effective supply of funds made available from a loan of given nominal size and therefore does not increase the effective cost of such a loan.

Let us return to Hellweg's example and assume that the borrower voluntarily seeks to hold balances of $200. Under these conditions the borrower is not indifferent as between a $1,000 loan at a contract rate of 4 per cent with a $200 compensatory balance and an $800 loan at 5 per cent with no balance. While the interest cost is $40 in both cases, the required-balance-cum-4 per cent case gives the borrower $200 more in usable funds.

Where voluntary balances equal or exceed required balances, the requirement, far from being a burden, can in fact be advantageous to both lender and borrower. Thus a bank could solicit the business of a borrower with larger working balances by offering him a contract rate of interest lower than that charged to non-depositors on condition that the borrower accept a balance requirement. The requirement represents no burden to such a borrower but merely guarantees that his deposits will be held at the lending bank rather than elsewhere.[5] It thus appears that there is a significant borrower interest in compensating balance requirements, and its origins probably are traceable to this fact. Whenever borrowers have large working balance needs, competition for deposits will tend to bring about a compensating balance arrangement. (Once instituted, of course, these arrangements restrict further competition.) It is thus no accident that these arrangements have arisen on loans to that type of borrower ordinarily holding large working balances

[3] See George Garvy, *Deposit Velocity and Its Significance* (New York: Federal Reserve Bank of New York, November, 1959), p. 32.

[4] The largest part of voluntary balances would ordinarily be held for transactions purposes, but precautionary and speculative motives also play a role. Indeed, the latter motives probably account for the largest part of the differences in voluntary balances of firms of the same general size and type. Such differences, as we shall see, may figure importantly in situations where required balances exceed voluntary balances—the special case that Hellweg describes.

[5] A similar point has been made by Donald Hodgman (see "The Deposit Relationship and Commercial Bank Investment Behavior," *Review of Economics and Statistics*, XLIII [August, 1961], pp. 257–68). Much of his treatment of the compensating balance problem, however, while highly suggestive, suffers from a failure to make use of the distinction between voluntary and required balances.

(business firms) and are virtually non-existent on other types of loans, such as mortgage loans, consumer loans, or farm loans.[6]

In general, for any given effective yield to a bank—and there are a theoretically infinite number of combinations of contract rate and compensatory balance requirement that will give it the same yield—the lowest effective rate to the borrower is realized when the compensatory balance requirement is exactly equal to the voluntary balance. A proof of this is given in an appendix note.

On the whole, compensatory balances are an eminently rational practice both from the standpoint of the individual borrower and from the standpoint of the individual bank in a unit banking system. (Whether it is advantageous to the banking system as a whole is another matter.) It is true that compensatory balances in excess of voluntary balances are irrational, for the very reason Hellweg presents—required reserves are increased by the compensating balance, and no offsetting benefit is derived by either party. But this is a far cry from saying that compensatory balance requirements are per se irrational.

Two questions remain. The first is why compensating balances need be required where they equal or fall short of voluntary balances. The answer, as already intimated, is simply that the compensating balance requirement in this case serves to guarantee the lending bank that the borrower will hold his working balance with it rather than elsewhere. Such assurance is particularly important where the lender has made a concession in contract rate on the understanding that he will obtain a balance. If the borrower were not required to keep his working balance at the lending bank, he might find it advantageous to transfer all or part of the balance to another bank because of its more convenient location, as compensation for services, or to obtain additional loans at a favorable rate.[7]

The second question is why compensating balance requirements, in some cases, do come to exceed voluntary balances. Among the most striking indications that the Hellweg case does exist is the recent development of a new financing device known as "link-financing." Under a link-financing arrangement a borrower who wishes to withdraw the entire amount of his bank loan but is nevertheless obliged to hold a compensating balance arranges to pay a third party to deposit funds with the bank for the purpose of meeting the bank's balance requirement. Because of the costs involved, this device would be attractive only to firms for whom required balances exceed voluntary balances.[8]

---

[6] The same point is made *ibid.*, p. 261.

[7] This does not imply, it may be noted, that compensating balance requirements necessarily reflect hard and fast agreements that spell out the obligations of borrowers in precise detail. On the contrary, usually the requirements take the form of informal understandings. Indeed, where a customer voluntarily holds balances in excess of those the bank would ordinarily require, the latter may studiously avoid broaching the subject.

[8] See J. Guttentag and R. Davis, "Compensating Balances," *Monthly Review*, Federal Reserve Bank of New York (December, 1961), pp. 205–210.

In such cases, why is there not a mutually advantageous reduction in the requirement and simultaneous increase in contract rate? For a number of reasons, one or both of these adjustments may not be considered feasible or desirable. Thus a bank may wish to maintain uniform balance requirements among borrowers of the same general class, and this would restrict its ability to reduce requirements to particular borrowers whose voluntary balances are unusually small. Similarly, upward adjustments in contract rates may be restrained by the bank's desire to maintain uniform rates for similar types of borrowers; by legal rate ceilings; and by borrower resistance toward paying a higher contract rate (offset by a lower balance requirement) in cases where they consider the rate a "status symbol" of a firm's credit standing. Equal treatment may be an administrative convenience as well as a requirement of good bank-customer relations. Compensating balances may be the most convenient way of charging for bank services, despite the added cost to the bank of holding reserves against idle deposits.

In addition, some banks may seek to maximize deposits rather than earnings.[9] This may be due less to deliberate choice (wherein one goal is given precedence over another) than to the implicit assumption by bankers that larger deposits necessarily result in larger profits. It is easy to see how banks might be unaware of the profit potential in lower balance requirements for selected borrowers. Indeed, even if the banker understands the general principle perfectly, it may be too costly in terms of both administrative time and potential disruption of bank-customer relations to ferret out cases of this sort.

Appendix Note

For any given profit to a bank, the lowest effective cost to the borrower of a given quantity of effective funds (i.e., the loan amount less the excess of required balances over desired balances) is achieved where the required dollar balance is equal to the desired balance. Let

> x = required balance (in dollars),
> y = contract rate of interest,
> u = desired effective loan size (in dollars),
> s = desired balance (in dollars),
> r = required reserve ratio,
> b = opportunity cost to the bank per dollar of reserves,
> L = loan size,
> p = net profit on loans,
> e = effective interest rate to borrower.

The loan volume giving the borrower effective funds of u is

$$L = u - s + x \quad \text{when} \quad x \geq s,$$
$$L = u \qquad\qquad \text{when} \quad x \leq s.$$

---

[9] Such behavior would be analogous to the behavior of the sales-maximizing firm recently examined by W. J. Baumol in *Business Behavior, Value, and Growth* (New York: Macmillan Co., 1959).

The net profit to the bank on a loan is defined as the gross interest proceeds minus the opportunity cost of reserves used up (whether through withdrawals or as required reserves held against compensating balances). The net profit on a loan L thus is

$$p = yL - b(L - x) - brx \quad \text{when} \quad x \geq s, \tag{1}$$
$$p = yL - b(L - s) - brs \quad \text{when} \quad x \leq s. \tag{1a}$$

When L is sufficient to give the desired effective quantity of funds,

$$p = y(u - s) + yx - brx + b(s - u) \quad \text{when} \quad x \geq s, \tag{2}$$
$$p = yu - b(u - s) - brs \quad \text{when} \quad x \leq s. \tag{2a}$$

The lender's isoprofit functions showing various combinations of contract rate and required balance which result in a given net profit (and the desired amount of effective funds) are given by

$$y = \frac{p + brx - b(s - u)}{u - s + x} \quad \text{when } x \geq s, \tag{3}$$

$$y = \frac{p + bs(r - 1)}{u} + b \quad \text{when } x \leq s. \tag{3a}$$

The effective rate to the borrower for the given desired effective loan volume is

$$e = \frac{y(u - s + x)}{u} \quad \text{when } x \geq s, \tag{4}$$

$$e = y \quad \text{when } x \leq s. \tag{4a}$$

Substituting equation (3) in equation (4), we get

$$e = \frac{p + brx - b(s - u)}{u} \quad \text{when } x \geq s. \tag{5}$$

Since

$$\frac{de}{dx} = \frac{br}{u} > 0,$$

any value of x greater than s is clearly more costly to the borrower than is a value of x equal to s. For values of x less than s, the lender's net profit and the effective cost to the borrower, even with y constant, are the same as at s. Thus the given net profit could be maintained at the minimum effective cost to the borrower for any x such that

$$o \leq x \leq s.$$

The bank, however, would not set x below s, lest the borrower transfer part or all of his desired balance to some other bank.

THE TRANSACTIONS DEMAND FOR CASH:
AN INVENTORY THEORETIC APPROACH *

By William J. Baumol†

A STOCK of cash is its holder's inventory of the medium of exchange, and like an inventory of a commodity, cash is held because it can be given up at the appropriate moment, serving then as its possessor's part of the bargain in an exchange. We might consequently expect that inventory theory and monetary theory can learn from one another. This note attempts to apply one well-known result in inventory control analysis to the theory of money.[1]

I. A SIMPLE MODEL

We are now interested in analyzing the transactions demand for cash dictated by rational behavior, which for our purposes means the holding of those cash balances that can do the job at minimum cost. To abstract from precautionary and speculative demands let us consider a state in which transactions are perfectly foreseen and occur *in a steady stream.*

Suppose that in the course of a given period an individual will pay out T dollars in a steady stream. He obtains cash either by borrowing it, or by withdrawing it from an investment, and in either case his interest cost (or

---

* Reprinted by permission from the *Quarterly Journal of Economics*, 66 (November, 1952), pp. 545–56.

† Professor of Economics, Princeton University.

[1] T. M. Whitin informs me that the result in question goes back to the middle of the 1920's when it seems to have been arrived at independently by some half dozen writers. See, e.g., George F. Mellen, "Practical Lot Quantity Formula," *Management and Administration*, Vol. 10 (September 1925). Its significant implications for the economic theory of inventory, particularly for business cycle theory, seem to have gone unrecognized until recently when Dr. Whitin analyzed them in his forthcoming *Inventory Control and Economic Theory* (Princeton University Press) which, incidentally, first suggested the subject of this note to me. See also, Dr. Whitin's "Inventory Control in Theory and Practice" (elsewhere in this issue, *supra*, p. 502), and Kenneth J. Arrow, Theodore Harris, and Jacob Marschak, "Optimal Inventory Policy," *Econometrica*, Vol. 19 (July 1951), especially pp. 252–55. In addition to Dr. Whitin, I am heavily indebted to Professors Chandler, Coale, Gurley, Lutz, Mr. Turvey, and Professor Viner, and to the members of the graduate seminar at Harvard University, where much of this paper was first presented.

interest opportunity cost) is i dollars per dollar per period. Suppose finally that he withdraws cash in lots of C dollars spaced evenly throughout the year, and that each time he makes such a withdrawal he must pay a fixed "broker's fee" of b dollars.[2] Here T, the value of transactions, is predetermined, and i and b are assumed to be constant.

In this situation any value of C less than or equal to T will enable him to meet his payments equally well provided he withdraws the money often enough. For example, if T is \$100, he can meet his payments by withdrawing \$50 every six months or \$25 quarterly, etc.[3] Thus he will make $\dfrac{T}{C}$ withdrawals over the course of the year, at a total cost in "brokers' fees" given by $\dfrac{bT}{C}$.

In this case, since each time he withdraws C dollars he spends it in a steady stream and draws out a similar amount the moment it is gone, his average cash holding will be $\dfrac{C}{2}$ dollars. His annual interest cost of holding cash will then be $\dfrac{iC}{2}$.

The total amount the individual in question must pay for the use of the cash needed to meet his transaction when he borrows C dollars at intervals evenly spaced throughout the year will then be the sum of interest cost and "brokers' fees" and so will be given by

$$\frac{bT}{C} + \frac{iC}{2} \tag{1}$$

---

[2] The term "broker's fee" is not meant to be taken literally. It covers all non-interest costs of borrowing or making a cash withdrawal. These include opportunity losses which result from having to dispose of assets just at the moment the cash is needed, losses involved in the poor resale price which results from an asset becoming "secondhand" when purchased by a nonprofessional dealer, administrative costs, and psychic costs (the trouble involved in making a withdrawal) as well as payment to a middleman. So conceived it seems likely that the "broker's fee" will, in fact, vary considerably with the magnitude of the funds involved, contrary to assumption. However, *some* parts of this cost will not vary with the amount involved—e.g., postage cost, bookkeeping expense, and, possibly, the withdrawer's effort. It seems plausible that the "broker's fee" will be better approximated by a function like $b + kC$ (where b and k are constants), which indicates that there is a part of the "broker's fee" increasing in proportion with the amount withdrawn. As shown in a subsequent footnote, however, our formal result is completely unaffected by this amendment.

We must also extend the meaning of the interest rate to include the value of protection against loss by fire, theft, etc., which we obtain when someone borrows our cash. On the other hand, a premium for the risk of default on repayment must be deducted. This protection obtained by lending seems to be mentioned less frequently by theorists than the risk, yet how can we explain the existence of interest free demand deposits without the former?

[3] In particular, if cash were perfectly divisible and no elapse of time were required from withdrawal through payment he could make his withdrawals in a steady stream. In this case he would never require any cash balances to meet his payments and C would be zero. However, as may be surmised, this would be prohibitive with any b greater than zero.

Since the manner in which he meets his payments is indifferent to him, his purpose only being to pay for his transactions, rationality requires that he do so at minimum cost, i.e., that he choose the most economical value of C. Setting the derivative of (1) with respect to C equal to zero we obtain[4]

$$-\frac{bT}{C^2} + \frac{i}{2} = 0 \,,$$

i.e.,

$$C = \sqrt{\frac{2bT}{i}}. \tag{2}$$

Thus, in the simple situation here considered, the rational individual will, given the price level,[5] demand cash in proportion to the square root of the value of his transactions.

Before examining the implications of this crude model we may note that, as it stands, it applies to two sorts of cases: that of the individual (or firm) obtaining cash from his invested capital and that of the individual (or firm) spending out of borrowing in anticipation of future receipts. Since our problem depends on non-coincidence of cash receipts and disbursements, and we have assumed that cash disbursements occur in a steady stream, one other case seems possible, that where receipts precede expenditures. This differs from the first case just mentioned (living off one's capital) in that the individual now has the option of withholding some or all of his receipts from investment and simply keeping the cash until it is needed. Once this withheld cash is used up the third case merges into the first: the individual must obtain cash from his invested capital until his next cash receipt occurs.

We can deal with this third case as follows. First, note that any receipts exceeding anticipated disbursements will be invested, since, eventually, interest earnings must exceed ("brokerage") cost of investment. Hence we need only deal with that part of the cash influx which is to be used in making payments during the period between receipts. Let this amount, as before, be T dollars. Of this let I dollars be invested, and the remainder, R dollars, be withheld, where either of these sums may be zero. Again let i be the interest rate, and let the "broker's fee" for withdrawing cash be given by the linear expression $b_w + k_w C$, where C is the amount withdrawn. Finally, let there be

---

[4] This result is unchanged if there is a part of the "broker's fee" which varies in proportion with the quantity of cash handled. For in this case the "broker's fee" for each loan is given by $b + kC$. Total cost in "broker's fees" will then be

$$\frac{T}{C}(b + kC) = \frac{T}{C}b + kT.$$

Thus (1) will have the constant term, kT, added to it, which drops out in differentiation.

[5] A doubling of *all* prices (including the "broker's fee") is like a change in the monetary unit, and may be expected to double the demand for cash balances.

a "broker's fee" for investing (depositing) cash given by $b_d + k_d I$ where the b's and the k's are constants.

Since the disbursements are continuous, the $R = T - I$ dollars withheld from investment will serve to meet payments for a fraction of the period between consecutive receipts given by $\dfrac{T - I}{T}$. Moreover, since the average cash holding for that time will be $\dfrac{T - I}{2}$ the interest cost of withholding that money will be $\dfrac{T - I}{T} i \dfrac{T - I}{2}$. Thus the total cost of withholding the R dollars and investing the I dollars will be

$$\frac{T - I}{2} i \frac{T - I}{T} + b_d + k_d I .$$

Analogously, the total cost of obtaining cash for the remainder of the period will be

$$\frac{C}{2} i \frac{I}{T} + (b_w + k_w C) \frac{I}{C}.$$

Thus the total cost of cash operations for the period will be given by the sum of the last two expressions, which when differentiated partially with respect to C and set equal to zero once again yields our square root formula, (2), with $b = b_w$.

Thus, in this case, the optimum cash balance after the initial cash holding is used up will again vary with the square root of the volume of transactions, as is to be expected by analogy with the "living off one's capital" case.

There remains the task of investigating $R/2$, the (optimum) average cash balance before drawing on invested receipts begins. We again differentiate our total cost of holding cash, this time partially with respect to I, and set it equal to zero, obtaining

$$-\frac{T - I}{T} i + k_d + \frac{Ci}{2T} + \frac{b_w}{C} + k_w = 0 ,$$

i.e.,

$$R = T - I = \frac{C}{2} + \frac{b_w T}{Ci} + \frac{T(k_d + k_w)}{i} ,$$

or since from the preceding result, $C^2 = 2T b_w / i$, so that the second term on the right hand side equals $C^2/2C$,

$$R = C + T \left(\frac{k_w + k_d}{i} \right).$$

The first term in this result is to be expected, since if *everything* were deposited at once, C dollars would have to be withdrawn at that same moment to meet current expenses. On this amount two sets of "broker's fees" would have to be paid and no interest would be earned—a most unprofitable operation.[6]

Since C varies as the square root of T and the other term varies in proportion with T, R will increase less than in proportion with T, though more nearly in proportion than does C. The general nature of our results is thus unaffected.[7]

Note finally that the entire analysis applies at once to the case of continuous receipts and discontinuous payments, taking the period to be that between two payments, where the relevant decision is the frequency of investment rather than the frequency of withdrawal. Similarly, it applies to continuous receipts and payments where the two are not equal.

II. SOME CONSEQUENCES OF THE ANALYSIS

I shall not labor the obvious implications for financial budgeting by the firm. Rather I shall discuss several arguments which have been presented by monetary theorists, to which our result is relevant.

The first is the view put forth by several economists,[8] that in a stationary state there will be no demand for cash balances since it will then be profitable to invest all earnings in assets with a positive yield in such a way that the required amount will be realized at the moment any payment is to be made. According to this view no one will want any cash in such a stationary world, and the value of money must fall to zero so that there can really be no such thing as a truly static monetary economy. Clearly this argument neglects the transactions costs involved in making and collecting such loans (the "broker's fee").[9] Our model is clearly compatible with a static world and (2) shows that

---

[6] Here the assumption of constant "brokerage fees" with $k_d = k_w = 0$ gets us into trouble. The amount withheld from investment then is never greater than C dollars only because a strictly constant "broker's fee" with no provision for a discontinuity at zero implies the payment of the fee even if nothing is withdrawn or deposited. In this case it becomes an overhead and it pays to invest for any interest earning greater than zero.

For a firm, *part* of the "broker's fee" may, in fact, be an overhead in this way. For example, failure to make an anticipated deposit will sometimes involve little or no reduction in the bookkeeping costs incurred in keeping track of such operations.

[7] If we replace the linear functions representing the "broker's fees" with more general functions $f_w(C)$ and $f_d(I)$ which are only required to be differentiable, the expression obtained for R is changed merely by replacement of k_w, and k_d by the corresponding derivatives $f_w'(C)$ and $f_d'(I)$.

[8] See, e.g., Frank H. Knight, *Risk, Uncertainty and Profit* (Preface to the Re-issue), No. 16 in the series of Reprints of Scarce Tracts in Economic and Political Science (London: The London School of Economics and Political Science, 1933), p. xxii; F. Divisia, *Économique Rationelle* (Paris: G. Doin, 1927), chap. XIX and the Appendix; and Don Patinkin, "Relative Prices, Say's Law and the Demand for Money," *Econometrica*, Vol. 16, April 1948, pp. 140–45. See also, P. N. Rosenstein-Rodan, "The Coordination of the General Theories of Money and Price," *Economica*, N. S., Vol. III, August 1936, Part II.

[9] It also neglects the fact that the transfer of cash takes time so that in reality we would have to hold cash at least for the short period between receiving it and passing it on again.

It is conceivable, it is true, that with perfect foresight the difference between money

it will generally pay to keep some cash. The analysis of a stationary monetary economy in which there is a meaningful (finite) price level does make sense.

Another view which can be reexamined in light of our analysis is that the transactions demand for cash will vary approximately in proportion with the money value of transactions.[10] This may perhaps even be considered the tenor of quantity theory though there is no necessary connection, as Fisher's position indicates. If such a demand for cash balances is considered to result from rational behavior, then (2) suggests that the conclusion cannot have general validity. On the contrary, the square root formula implies that demand for cash rises less than in proportion with the volume of transactions, so that there are, in effect, economies of large scale in the use of cash.

The magnitude of this difference should not be exaggerated, however. The phrase "varying as the square" may suggest larger effects than are actually involved. Equation (2) requires that the average transactions velocity of circulation vary exactly in proportion with the quantity of cash, so that, for example, a doubling of the stock of cash will *ceteris paribus*, just double velocity.[11]

A third consequence of the square root formula is closely connected with the second. The effect on real income of an injection of cash into the system may have been underestimated. For suppose that (2) is a valid expression for the general demand for cash, that there is widespread unemployment, and that for this or other reasons prices do not rise with an injection of cash. Suppose,

---

and securities might disappear since a perfectly safe loan could become universally acceptable. There would, however, remain the distinction between "real assets" and the "money-securities." Moreover, there would be a finite price for, and non-zero yield on the former, the yield arising because they (as opposed to certificates of their ownership) are not generally acceptable, and hence not perfectly liquid, since there is trouble and expense involved in carrying them.

[10] Marshall's rather vague statements may perhaps be interpreted to support this view. See, e.g., Book I, chap. IV in *Money, Credit and Commerce* (London, 1923). Keynes clearly accepts this position. See *The General Theory of Employment, Interest and Money* (New York, 1936), p. 201. It is also accepted by Pigou: "As real income becomes larger, there is, prima facie, reason for thinking that, just as, up to a point, people like to invest a larger proportion of their real income, so also they like to hold real balances in the form of money equivalent to a larger proportion of it. On the other hand, as Professor Robertson has pointed out to me, the richer people are, the cleverer they are likely to become in finding a way to *economize* in real balances. On the whole then we may, I think, safely disregard this consideration . . . for a close approximation. . . ." *Employment and Equilibrium*, 1st ed. (London, 1941), pp. 59–60. Fisher, however, argues: "It seems to be a fact that, at a given price level, the greater a man's expenditures the more rapid his turnover; that is, the rich have a higher rate of turnover than the poor. They spend money faster, not only absolutely but relatively to the money they keep on hand. . . . We may therefore infer that, if a nation grows richer per capita, the velocity of circulation of money will increase. This proposition, of course, has no reference to *nominal* increase of expenditure." *The Purchasing Power of Money* (New York, 1922), p. 167.

[11] Since velocity equals $\dfrac{T}{C} = \dfrac{i}{2b} C$ by (2).

moreover, that the rate of interest is unaffected, i.e., that none of the new cash is used to buy securities. Then so long as transactions do not rise so as to maintain the same proportion with the square of the quantity of money, people will want to get rid of cash. They will use it to demand more goods and services, thereby forcing the volume of transactions to rise still further. For let ΔC be the quantity of cash injected. If a proportionality (constant velocity) assumption involves transactions rising by $k \Delta C$, it is easily shown that (2) involves transactions rising by more than twice as much, the magnitude of the excess increasing with the ratio of the injection to the initial stock of cash. More precisely, the rise in transactions would then be given by[12]

$$2k \, \Delta C + \frac{k}{C} \, \Delta C^2 \, .$$

Of course, the rate of interest would really tend to fall in such circumstances, and this would to some extent offset the effect of the influx of cash, as is readily seen when we rewrite (2) as

$$T = C^2 i / 2b. \tag{3}$$

Moreover, prices will rise to some extent,[13] and, of course, (3) at best is only an approximation. Nevertheless, it remains true that the effect of an injection of cash on, say, the level of employment, may often have been underestimated.[14] For whatever may be working to counteract it, the force making for increased employment is greater than if transactions tend, *ceteris paribus*, toward their original proportion to the quantity of cash.

Finally the square root formula lends support to the argument that wage cuts can help increase employment, since it follows that the Pigou effect and the related effects are stronger than they would be with a constant transactions velocity. Briefly the phenomenon which has come to be called the Pigou effect[15] may be summarized thus: General unemployment will result in reduction in the price level which must increase the purchasing power of the stock of cash provided the latter does not itself fall more than in proportion with prices.[16] This increased purchasing power will augment demand for commodi-

---

[12] This is obtained by setting $k = C i / 2b$ in (3), below, and computing ΔT by substituting $C + \Delta C$ for C.

[13] Even if (2) holds, the demand for cash may rise only in proportion with the money value of transactions when all prices rise exactly in proportion, the rate of interest and transactions remaining unchanged. For then a doubling of all prices and cash balances leaves the situation unchanged, and the received argument holds. The point is that b is then one of the prices which has risen.

[14] But see the discussions of Potter and Law as summarized by Jacob Viner, *Studies in the Theory of International Trade* (New York, 1937), pp. 37–39.

[15] See A. C. Pigou, "The Classical Stationary State," *Economic Journal*, Vol. LIII, December 1943.

[16] Presumably the "broker's fee" will be one of the prices which falls, driven down by the existence of unemployed brokers. There is no analogous reason for the rate of interest to fall, though it will tend to respond thus to the increase in the "real stock of cash."

ties[17] or investment goods (either directly, or because it is used to buy securities and so forces down the rate of interest). In any case, this works for a reduction in unemployment.

Now the increase in the purchasing power of the stock of cash which results from fallen prices is equivalent to an injection of cash with constant prices. There is therefore exactly the same reason for suspecting the magnitude of the effect of the former on the volume of transactions has been underestimated, as in the case of the latter. Perhaps this can be of some little help in explaining why there has not been more chronic unemployment or runaway inflation in our economy.

III. THE SIMPLE MODEL AND REALITY

It is appropriate to comment on the validity of the jump from equation (2) to conclusions about the operation of the economy. At best, (2) is only a suggestive oversimplification, if for no other reason, because of the rationality assumption employed in its derivation. In addition the model is static. It takes the distribution of the firm's disbursements over time to be fixed, though it is to a large extent in the hands of the entrepreneur how he will time his expenditures. It assumes that there is one constant relevant rate of interest and that the "broker's fee" is constant or varies linearly with the magnitude of the sum involved. It posits a steady stream of payments and the absence of cash receipts during the relevant period. It deals only with the cash demand of a single economic unit and neglects interactions of the various demands for cash in the economy.[18] It neglects the precautionary and speculative demands for cash.

These are serious lacunae, and without a thorough investigation we have no assurance that our results amount to much more than an analytical curiosum. Nevertheless I offer only a few comments in lieu of analysis, and hope that others will find the subject worth further examination.

1. It is no doubt true that a majority of the public will find it impractical and perhaps pointless to effect every possible economy in the use of cash. Indeed the possibility may never occur to most people. Nevertheless, we may employ the standard argument that the largest cash users may more plausibly be expected to learn when it is profitable to reduce cash balances relative to transactions. The demand for cash by the community as a whole may then be

---

[17] The term "Pigou effect" is usually confined to the effects on consumption demand while the effect on investment demand, and (in particular) on the rate of interest is ordinarily ascribed to Keynes. However, the entire argument appears to antedate Pigou's discussion (which, after all, was meant to be a reformulation of the classical position) and is closely related to what Mr. Becker and I have called the Say's Equation form of the Say's Law argument. See our article "The Classical Monetary Theory; the Outcome of the Discussion," *Economica*, November 1952.

[18] I refer here particularly to considerations analogous to those emphasized by Duesenberry in his discussion of the relation between the consumption functions of the individual and the economy as a whole in his *Income, Saving and the Theory of Consumer Behavior* (Cambridge, Mass., 1950).

affected similarly and by a significant amount. Moreover, it is possible that even small cash holders will sometimes institute some cash economies instinctively or by a process of trial and error not explicitly planned or analyzed.

2. With variable b and i the validity of our two basic results—the non-zero rational transactions demand for cash, and the less than proportionate rise in the rational demand for cash with the real volume of transactions—clearly depends on the nature of the responsiveness of the "brokerage fee" and the interest rate to the quantity of cash involved. The first conclusion will hold generally provided the "broker's fee" never falls below some preassigned level, e.g., it never falls below one mill per transaction, and provided the interest rate, its rate of change with C and the rate of change of the "broker's fee" all (similarly) have some upper bound, however large, at least when C is small.

The second conclusion will not be violated persistently unless the "brokerage fee" tends to vary almost exactly in proportion with C (and it pays to hold zero cash balances) except for what may roughly be described as a limited range of values of C. Of course, it is always possible that this "exceptional range" will be the one relevant in practice. Variations in the interest rate will tend to strengthen our conclusion provided the interest rate never decreases with the quantity of cash borrowed or invested.[19]

---

[19] For people to want to hold a positive amount of cash, the cost of each holding must be decreasing after $C = 0$. Let b in (1) be a differentiable function of C for $C > 0$ (it will generally be discontinuous and equal to zero at $C = 0$). Then we require that the limit of the derivative of (1) be negative as C approaches zero from above, where this derivative is given by

$$\text{(i)} \quad -b\frac{T}{C^2} + \frac{T}{C}b' + \frac{i + i'C}{2}.$$

Clearly this will become negative as C approaches zero provided b is bounded from below and b', i, and i' are all bounded from above.

The second conclusion, the less than proportionate rise in minimum cost cash holdings with the volume of transactions, can be shown, with only b not constant, to hold if and only if $b - b'C + b''C^2$ is positive. This result is obtained by solving the first order minimum condition (obtained by setting (i), with the i' term omitted, equal to zero) for $\dfrac{T}{C}$

and noting that our conclusion is equivalent to the derivative of this ratio with respect to C being positive.

Now successive differentiation of (i) with the i' term omitted yields as our second minimum condition $2(b - b'C) + b''C^2 > 0$ (note the resemblance to the preceding condition). Thus if our result is to be violated we need

$$\text{(ii)} \quad b - Cb' \leq -b''C^2 < 2(b - Cb'),$$

which at once yields $b'' \leq 0$. Thus if b' is not to become negative (a decreasing *total* payment as the size of the withdrawal increases!) b'' must usually lie within a small neighborhood of zero, i.e., b must be approximately linear. However we know that in this case the square root formula will be (approximately) valid except in the case $b = kC$ when it will always (by (i)) pay to hold zero cash balances. Note incidentally that (ii) also yields $b - Cb' \geq 0$ which means that our result must hold if ever the "brokerage fee" increases more than in proportion with C.

Note, finally, that if i varies with C the first order condition becomes a cubic and, provided $\infty > i' > 0$, our conclusion is strengthened, since T now tends to increase as C^3.

It would perhaps not be surprising if these sufficient conditions for the more general validity of our results were usually satisfied in practice.

3. If payments are lumpy but foreseen, cash may perhaps be employed even more economically. For then it may well pay to obtain cash just before large payments fall due with little or no added cost in "brokers' fees" and considerable savings in interest payments. The extreme case would be that of a single payment during the year which would call for a zero cash balance provided the cash could be loaned out profitably at all. Cash receipts during the relevant period may have similar effects, since they can be used to make payments which happen to be due at the moment the receipts arrive. Here the extreme case involves receipts and payments always coinciding in time and amounts in which case, again, zero cash balances would be called for. Thus lumpy payments and receipts of cash, with sufficient foresight, can make for economies in the use of cash, i.e., higher velocity. This may not affect the rate of increase in transactions velocity with the level of transactions, but may nevertheless serve further to increase the effect of an injection of cash and of a cut in wages and prices. With imperfect foresight, however, the expectation that payments may be lumpy may increase the precautionary demand for cash. Moreover, the existence of a "broker's fee" which must be paid on lending or investing cash received during the period is an added inducement to keep receipts until payments fall due rather than investing, and so may further increase the demand for cash.

4. The economy in a single person's use of cash resulting from an increase in the volume of his transactions may or may not have its analogue for the economy as a whole. "External economies" may well be present if one businessman learns cash-economizing techniques from the experiences of another when both increase their transactions. On the diseconomies side it is barely conceivable that an infectious liquidity fetishism will permit a few individuals reluctant to take advantage of cash saving opportunities to block these savings for the bulk of the community. Nevertheless, at least two such possible offsets come to mind: (a) The rise in the demand for brokerage services resulting from a general increase in transactions may bring about a rise in the "brokerage fee" and thus work for an increase in average cash balances (a decreased number of visits to brokers). If cash supplies are sticky this will tend to be offset by rises in the rate of interest resulting from a rising total demand for cash, which serve to make cash more expensive to hold. (b) Widespread cash economizing might require an increase in precautionary cash holdings because in an emergency one could rely less on the ability of friends to help or creditors to be patient. This could weaken but not offset the relative reduction in cash holdings entirely, since the increase in precautionary demand is contingent on there being some relative decrease in cash holdings.

5. A priori analysis of the precautionary and the speculative demands for cash is more difficult. In particular, there seems to be little we can say about the latter, important though it may be, except that it seems unlikely that it

will work consistently in any special direction. In dealing with the precautionary demand, assumptions about probability distributions and expectations must be made.[20] It seems plausible offhand, that an increase in the volume of transactions will make for economies in the use of cash for precautionary as well as transactions purposes by permitting increased recourse to insurance principles.

Indeed, here we have a rather old argument in banking theory which does not seem to be widely known. Edgeworth,[21] and Wicksell[22] following him, suggested that a bank's precautionary cash requirements might also grow as the square root of the volume of its transactions (!). They maintained that cash demands on a bank tend to be normally distributed.[23] In this event, if it is desired to maintain a fixed probability of not running out of funds, precautionary cash requirements will be met by keeping on hand a constant multiple of the standard deviation (above the mean). But then the precautionary cash requirement of ten identical banks (with independent demands) together will be the same as that for any one of them multiplied by the square root of ten. For it is a well-known result that the standard deviation of a random sample from an infinite population increases as the square root of the size of the sample.

---

[20] See Arrow, Harris and Marschak, *op. cit.* for a good example of what has been done along these lines in inventory control analysis.

[21] F. Y. Edgeworth, "The Mathematical Theory of Banking," *Journal of the Royal Statistical Society*, Vol. LI (1888), especially pp. 123–27. Fisher (*loc. cit.*) points out the relevance of this result for the analysis of the cash needs of the public as a whole. The result was independently rediscovered by Dr. Whitin (*op. cit.*) who seems to have been the first to combine it and (2) in inventory analysis.

[22] K. Wicksell, *Interest and Prices* (London, 1936), p. 67.

[23] The distribution would generally be approximately normal if its depositors were large in number, their cash demands independent and not very dissimilarly distributed. The independence assumption, of course, rules out runs on banks.

MANAGING THE CORPORATE "MONEY" POSITION*

"Our job is production. We are not in the investment business." So stated an official of a large business corporation in explaining the principles followed in managing the company's cash and short-term investment positions. This statement probably reflects the attitude of management of many nonfinancial corporations.[1] Production is the primary source of income.

Nevertheless, many companies have found that they can derive considerable income by investing cash not currently needed in operations. This policy of investing excess corporate cash has attracted considerable attention in recent years. It has also raised a number of questions. What is the basic philosophy underlying these investment programs? Do rising short-term rates activate idle corporate cash balances? What is the effect of corporate policies on velocity of circulation of money? Has the policy of investing excess cash reduced corporate deposits in the banks? What kinds of securities are popular with corporate investors?

This article attempts to throw some light on these questions. It deals primarily with how business corporations manage their "money" position—cash and short-term investments. It is based largely on information obtained from interviews with officials of corporations of varying size and types of business activity. The article also shows postwar trends in corporate cash and Government securities.

NATURE OF THE PROBLEM

Corporations handle a huge amount of cash. Last year, sales of manufacturing corporations alone—a rough indication of cash inflow—exceeded $350 billion. Cash receipts are never in just the right amount and at just the right time to meet expenditures. Sometimes the cash inflow is larger, at other times smaller than current expenses. The problem is to keep enough cash on hand to meet expenses, but not to have idle cash that earns no income.

Several postwar developments have encouraged corporations to pay closer attention to cash. A substantial rise in tax liabilities requires the accumulation of funds (or borrowing) to meet large quarterly tax payments. Rising costs

---

* Federal Reserve Bank of Philadelphia, *Business Review*, March, 1961.
[1] Unless otherwise noted, corporation as used in this article refers to nonfinancial corporations.

and increases in plant and equipment mean that larger sums must be charged to depreciation reserves. Higher interest rates make it more expensive to hold idle cash. The favorable results achieved by some large corporations from investing excess cash have been an inducement for other corporations to adopt similar policies.

A prerequisite for effective portfolio management is determination of the minimum cash balance consistent with the company's operating needs. A helpful device used by a number of corporations is cash budgeting—projecting the company's cash inflow and outflow. Cash-flow analysis usually consists of more detailed estimates for the near-term and rougher estimates for the longer-term future. Some companies make rough projections for several years in advance—five or even ten years. Ability to project the cash flow accurately is influenced by the regularity and stability of the company's income and disbursements.

Cash projections serve two main purposes. The estimates, together with experience, enable officials to have a much better idea of the minimum amount of cash required for operations. Projections are also useful in managing the short-term investment portfolio.

The size of the cash balance maintained by a corporation is influenced by factors other than direct operating needs. Management may prefer to "play it safe"—to have a cushion for unforeseen developments. Some companies maintain "good" balances with their major banks to promote good will and to improve access to bank credit when money is tight. Other companies pare bank balances more closely, endeavoring only to compensate the banks for account activity and other services rendered.

PRINCIPLES OF PORTFOLIO MANAGEMENT

The primary objectives in managing the corporate investment portfolio are to derive income from cash not currently needed in operations and to have cash "on the barrel head" whenever needed. Thus safety and liquidity as well as yield are important considerations in investing temporary excess receipts. Emphasis on these factors varies among corporations, depending on such things as the volatility of the cash flow, accuracy of cash projections, and the attitude of management. Even though there are no hard and fast lines dividing them, corporations can be classified into three general groups with respect to their short-term investment policies.

One group consists of companies that follow a quite conservative approach. Some buy only short-term Treasury bills; others limit their portfolios to short-term Government securities. Little if any attempt is made to space maturities to meet a series of anticipated cash needs.

This conservative approach in managing short-term investments may reflect several factors. For one thing, it is likely to be employed by companies with relatively little cash to invest. Corporations with only small amounts of excess cash to invest would derive little additional income for the extra time required in the management of a more diversified portfolio. In the words of one official, "the additional income would not be worth the effort and risk." A volatile cash flow and hence inability to estimate cash needs accurately often cause management to put great stress on liquidity. The view that the job of a business corporation is to produce goods and services may well result in little emphasis being placed on the management of cash and short-term investments.

The investment policy of a second group of corporations is characterized by a more diversified investment portfolio but with a relatively slow rate of turnover. These companies invest in a greater variety of short-term securities in order to obtain a better yield without unduly sacrificing liquidity. Liquidity is achieved, in part, by spacing maturities so that run-offs will provide cash just prior to lump-sum disbursements such as tax, dividend, and interest payments. When funds are to be invested, the tendency is to select securities (acceptable under the company's investment policy) of the desired maturity currently affording the higher return. Once acquired, securities are held until maturity; they are rarely sold in an effort to get a better return.

The most distinguishing characteristic of companies in the third group is active management of the portfolio to get the maximum return consistent with safety and the individual company's liquidity needs. Portfolios are more diversified both as to type of security and maturity. More attention is devoted to cash-flow projections in order that maturities can be better adapted to anticipated needs. As a result, a portion of the portfolio may be in very short maturities, another in securities maturing within a year, and if there is a significant yield advantage a part may be in maturities up to two or three years or even longer.

Corporations in the third category do not hesitate to sell and re-invest to take advantage of yield differentials among maturities as well as among different types of securities. The price of a security usually rises and the yield falls as it approaches maturity. The average return on a portfolio of Treasury bills, some officials pointed out, may often be improved by investing in the 91-day bill, selling as it approaches maturity, and reinvesting in another 91-day bill. Another device sometimes used is adjusting maturities in anticipation of changes in rates—shortening maturities in anticipation of rising rates and lengthening them when rates are expected to fall. A few companies avoid maturities that are exceptionally popular because of uniform tax and dividend payment dates. Experience indicates a better yield can usually be obtained by buying somewhat shorter maturities and employing the funds, perhaps in a repurchase agreement, in the interval between maturity and the actual cash need; or the net yield may be improved by buying a slightly longer maturity and selling it just prior to the date the funds are needed. Active management of the investment portfolio results in a considerably higher rate of turnover than is characteristic of companies in the first and second groups.

COMPOSITION OF THE PORTFOLIO

Government securities are by far the most popular form of investment for nonfinancial corporations, both in terms of total amount and number of companies. The safety, broad market, and wide range of maturities available in Governments are strong appeals to most corporate investors.

There is a tendency, however, for more corporations to branch out into other types of investments such as Government agency issues, short-term state and municipal securities, commercial paper, and finance company paper. Only a small number enter into repurchase agreements, and apparently few companies buy foreign securities to take advantage of yield differentials, although some acquire such securities in connection with their foreign operations. Thus far, time deposits have not been a substantial outlet for corporate funds.

Finance company paper and repurchase agreements, in addition to affording somewhat higher yields than a Government security of comparable maturity, are attractive to some companies because the maturity can usually be tailored to individual corporate needs. Some companies shy away from repurchase agreements because they are not in a position to appraise the credit

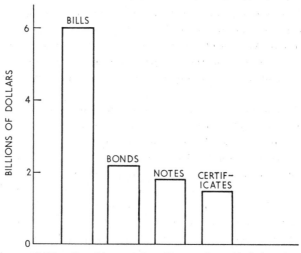

CORPORATE HOLDINGS OF MARKETABLE
GOVERNMENT SECURITIES*
(NOVEMBER 30, 1960)

* 497 nonfinancial corporations: Treasury Ownership Series.

risk involved; others, regarding r.p.'s as a form of loan, do not want to get into the "lending business." Time deposits are not considered a suitable outlet, especially by large corporations. One disadvantage is that the rate is usually attractive only in a period of recession when market rates are low and there is little demand for funds. Banks are less willing to accept time deposits in such periods because of the difficulty of investing them profitably, and corporate officials are reluctant to press them to do so. For large corporations, the limited amount that can be put on time deposit and the fact that deposits must be scattered among a large number of banks are other disadvantages. The issue of negotiable time certificates of deposit, recently announced by some large banks, may prove more attractive for corporate funds.

Corporate portfolios are heavily concentrated in short maturities. Holdings of Government securities as of the end of last November were mainly in short-term issues—52 per cent in Treasury bills, 13 per cent in certificates, 16 per cent in Treasury notes, and 19 per cent in bonds, mostly of short maturity.

CORPORATE HOLDINGS OF GOVERNMENTS
BY MATURITY CLASS*
(NOVEMBER 30, 1960)

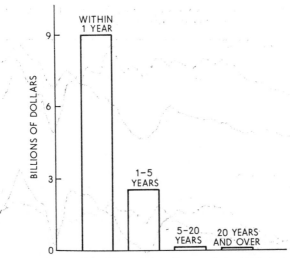

* 497 nonfinancial corporations: Treasury Ownership Series.

The distribution of Governments by maturity shows that the bulk of corporate holdings matured within one year and practically all of the remainder, within one to five years. Data are not available on investments other than Governments, but the interviews indicated these investments are also of short maturity.

INFLUENCE OF MARKET RATES

Two possible effects of interest rates on corporate management of short-term investments need to be distinguished—the effect of the level of rates on the volume of corporate funds put into short-term assets, and the effect on the allocation of funds among different types of investments.

There is little evidence that cyclical changes in the level of interest rates have any significant direct effect on the volume of funds a corporation puts into short-term investments. One of the guiding principles in portfolio manage-ment is to put all cash in excess of a minimum working balance into some liquid earning asset. Once a company has initiated such a program, it is not feasible to discontinue investing excess cash just because market rates decline. Out-of-pocket expense incurred in handling the investment portfolio is quite small. There is no express policy of intensifying efforts to economize cash as interest rates rise, according to all of the officials interviewed. In fact, some stated that when profits from operations are small—usually a period of recession when interest rates are also low—they intensify their efforts to get the best possible return from the investment portfolio.

High market rates may attract some additional funds by inducing corporations to initiate a program of investing excess cash. It may well be that if data were available they would show that most corporations started their programs of short-term investments in periods of relatively high interest

CORPORATE GOVERNMENTS AND INTEREST RATE ON
TREASURY BILLS,* 1947–60

* 91-day bill, quarterly average.
† New series.

rates. Even so, the volume attracted by rising rates in recent years has probably been relatively small. Large corporations have been investing excess funds for many years—some used the call loan market for this purpose in the twenties—and they hold a substantial part of all corporate cash.

There has been a tendency in recent years for corporate holdings of Governments and short-term rates to move upward and downward together. But the movement of both seems to result primarily from a common cause, cyclical fluctuations, rather than rate changes inducing corresponding changes in corporate holdings of Governments. Business recovery is usually accompanied by an increase in market rates; it is also accompanied by an accumulation of corporate cash available for investment as receipts rise more rapidly than disbursements.

Interest rates are influential in allocating corporate funds among alternative types of investments. Funds are attracted to those types of securities offering the higher yields, and anticipation of changes in rates may lead to some shortening or lengthening of maturities.

IMPACT ON VELOCITY

The effect of corporate investment policies on the velocity of money appears to be mainly secular rather than cyclical. Corporate cash balances have moved generally upward during the postwar period. There is no observable tendency for cash holdings to decline as market rates rise, and increase as rates fall.

The development of cash saving techniques enables corporations to handle a larger volume of business with the same amount of cash. A substantial rise in sales relative to cash balances of manufacturing corporations since 1954 is evidence of a more efficient use of cash. Cash saving techniques and the spread of such techniques to other corporations occur gradually and tend to produce a secular rise in velocity. Moreover, for reasons already

MANUFACTURING CORPORATIONS—
CASH AND SALES, 1947–60

* New series.
† Total for quarter.

given, it seems likely that the major part of the secular impact on velocity has already occurred.

EFFECT ON BANK DEPOSITS

Corporations have increased their bank deposits substantially in the postwar period despite the trend toward investing excess cash in short-term securities. Their cash balances totaled $35 billion at the end of last September, an increase of 58 per cent since the first quarter of 1947.

Corporate purchases of securities typically transfer deposits from buyer to seller—and frequently from one bank to another—but they do not usually decrease total deposits of the banking system. Such purchases result in a loss of deposits for the banking system only when commercial banks are sellers of the securities the corporations are buying. This may well happen in periods of business recovery and strong credit demands when banks sell short-term Governments to get funds for loans; however, when the loans are made, deposits are increased. The net effect, therefore, is a shift in assets with no change in total deposits.

GROWING MARKET FOR GOVERNMENTS

Corporations have become an important market for Government securities. Their holdings of Treasury obligations exceeded $20 billion at the end of last September, an increase of nearly 40 per cent since early 1947.

CORPORATE CASH BALANCES AND
GOVERNMENTS, 1947–60

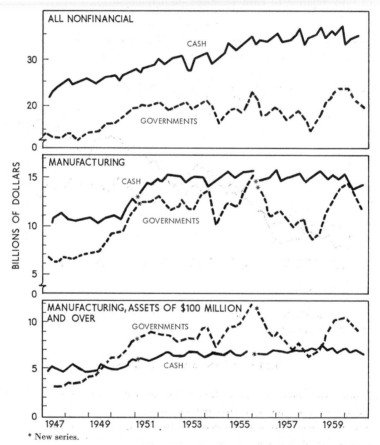

* New series.

The nature of the corporate market is revealed more clearly by the distribution of corporate holdings. Manufacturing corporations owned well over one-half of the total. A breakdown for manufacturing companies available by size groups shows that Government securities are concentrated in the large companies with assets of $100 million and over. The large companies are also a growing market. They have more than doubled their holdings of Gov-

CORPORATE GOVERNMENTS AND TAX LIABILITIES, 1947–60

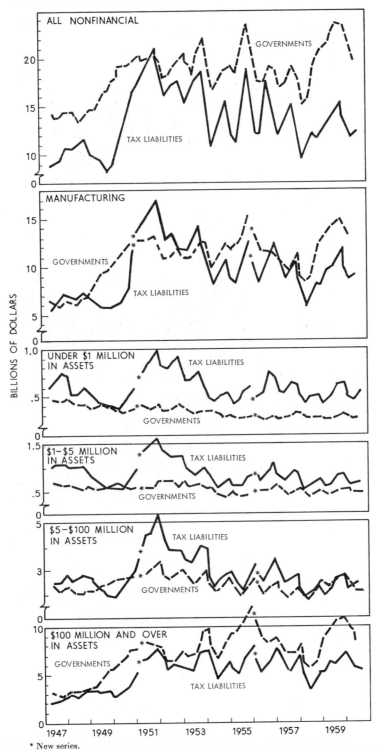

* New series.

MANUFACTURING CORPORATIONS—
GOVERNMENTS AND TAX LIABILITIES,
1947–60 (BY INDUSTRY)

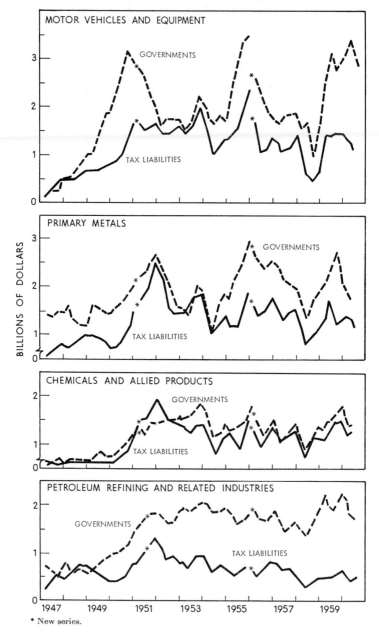

* New series.

ernments since early 1947. Small companies, on the other hand, are not as yet a significant factor in the market. Their investment in Governments is small compared with their cash balances, and they have gradually reduced their holdings of Governments in the postwar period.

Four industries—motor vehicles and equipment, primary metals, petroleum, and chemicals—hold about three-fifths of the Governments owned by manufacturing corporations. Government portfolios of the first two industries show marked cyclical fluctuations. Companies in these industries typically build up their holdings of Governments in the recovery phase of the cycle and then draw them down as taxes and other expenditures rise relative to receipts.

Tax liabilities have become quite large; they are a significant influence in the behavior of the Government portfolios of corporations. There is a tendency for holdings of Governments and tax liabilities to move upward and downward together, even though corporations follow the policy of investing all cash not needed in operations and as a working balance. The net effect of corporate investment policies is a tendency to accumulate Governments in the intervals between tax dates, and for the portfolio to decline as securities are liquidated to raise cash for the tax payments.

The characteristics of the corporate market explain the emphasis on short-term investments. The bulk of the net cash inflow is invested in anticipation of large short-term liabilities such as taxes, interest, and dividends; and, as already explained, most companies space maturities to provide the cash for these needs. Furthermore, the cash flow of some of the large corporate holders is subject to marked cyclical fluctuations, making it difficult to estimate cash needs accurately. The resulting uncertainty increases the need for liquidity.

The size and characteristics of the corporate market are of considerable significance in formulating debt management policies. The recent trend toward more diversified portfolios indicates that Government securities are likely to encounter stronger competition from other high-quality, short-term investments. The implications of corporate investment policies for debt management, however, are beyond the scope of this article.

CONCLUSIONS

Corporations apparently in increasing numbers are using the money market to bridge temporary gaps between cash receipts and expenditures. Cash in excess of operating and working balance requirements is invested in high-quality, short-term marketable assets; these assets are converted into cash as needed to meet temporary excess expenditures. Use of the money market to adjust its cash position benefits the corporation. The resulting increase in the number of participants and volume of operations, in turn, enables the money market to perform its functions more efficiently.

Policies pursued in managing cash and short-term investments vary among corporations, reflecting such things as the attitude of management and size of the company. Companies with a large volume of funds to invest and with a more specialized staff can benefit from refined techniques that would not be feasible for the small corporation.

There is no evidence that corporate investment policies impair significantly the effectiveness of monetary restraint; their impact on velocity is mainly secular, not cyclical. The velocity effect occurs as more corporations adopt short-term investment programs and as those already pursuing them develop more effective cash-conserving techniques. The fact that corporations try to keep excess cash fully invested regardless of the level of market rates indicates that their investment policies are not a significant influence on cyclical fluctuations in velocity.

Chapter 5 Governing and Minimizing the Cost of Funds Committed to Receivables

TAURUS INDUSTRIES, INC.

NEAR THE END of 1966 Steven Winslow, General Credit Manager of Taurus Industries, Inc., was preparing a report for the treasurer in which he would recommend that a system of credit management, which had been developed and pilot-tested over a period of nearly four years, be adapted to computer administration. Credit managers would function in capacities of surveillance and research aimed at continuous improvement of the data and methods upon which the computer relied.

He noted that at this time more than 500,000 trade customers had credit accounts with Taurus Industries, and that by 1971, extrapolating current rates, the company would be extending credit to about 818,000 trade customers. Currently, about 200 new accounts were being added daily.

One aspect of the current pilot system particularly merited scrutiny, namely, the way in which credit limits were assigned to individual accounts. In addition, Mr. Winslow was concerned with the relationship between the mechanism for setting credit limits and the company's total of funds committed to accounts receivable. Other questions related to whether or not, in setting customer credit limits, distinctions should be made with respect to the different profit margins prevailing on product lines; whether opportunity losses on the funds tied up in overdue accounts should be recognized in some way; and what use, if any, should be made of scoring systems in customer selection.

THE CONTINUING GROWTH IN RECEIVABLES

Taurus's principal customers were, typically, general contractors and building materials retailers, wholesalers, and manufacturers. Between 1956 and

1965, receivables nearly doubled (from \$65 million to \$125 million) while sales rose by half (from about \$600 million to about \$900 million). A recent balance sheet is presented in Exhibit 1. The relationships between sales and receivables growth for both this company and all manufacturing corporations can be studied in Exhibit 2. Exhibit 3 summarizes the company's sources and applications of funds for 1956–1965.

THE CREDIT OPERATION IN THE 1950's

Through the middle 1950's, the company experienced no particular difficulties with growth in receivables. Bad debt losses generally ran low, not exceeding \$500,000 yearly. During this period the company was divisionalized, each division being a manufacturing entity with the exception of the Sales Division. There were about 3,500 large, direct "factory customers" who purchased from manufacturing divisions. The balance of sales was made through the Sales Division.

In the 1957–58 recession the company encountered collection problems, not only among "factory" accounts but also among accounts serviced by the Sales Division. Bad debt expense in 1957 was \$1,062,000; in 1958 it was \$766,000. At that time, the company sold to roughly 80,000 customers. Credit was administered by every selling unit. For example, the Sales Division had about 75 "mother" warehouses, each of which had its own credit department. As this particular distribution and warehousing system developed, the "mother" warehouses sponsored some satellite units and each of these also maintained its own credit department. These highly decentralized arrangements made it possible for a customer to maintain separate credit accommodations at each one.

Because of the difficulties experienced by the company, particularly with respect to bad debt losses, Taurus Industries, Inc. established a corporate Credit Department in 1958. At its inception, the department consisted of only a few persons. Mr. Winslow entered the department in July 1959 as General Credit Manager. His initial efforts were directed at developing efficient supervision of accounts and credit extension procedures, as well as achieving better bad debt experience. In addition, there was some thought about the possibility of centralizing credit functions through the use of a computer. The company had been using a computer in various inventory applications for several years, and it had been a desire of the management to put the computer to greater use.

THE ZONE ACCOUNTING CENTER

As a pilot study in 1962, Mr. Winslow instituted a Zone Accounting Center (ZAC), which was the initial attempt to supervise accounts receivable with a computer. The first ZAC had a total of 40,000 accounts. Its underlying idea was dependence on a credit limit, assigned to each account, as the major element of credit control. All customer transactions, such as purchases and payments, were provided as input data to the computer. Using this information and the assigned credit limits, the computer would identify and print out daily the name of each ZAC account owing a balance in excess of its credit limit. The number of dollars an account was over its limit was printed alongside the name. Appearance of an account on the report was intended to caution sales personnel at the warehouses that further credit should not be extended. Continued appearance on the report would lead to a succession of collection measures.

Various methods were used initially to assign credit limits to the ZAC accounts. Credit managers considered whatever data were available, including the maximum historical amount outstanding on an account. In some cases, credit limits were merely based on subjective appraisals, and, in a few cases, the assignment was somewhat arbitrary. Mr. Winslow felt that, however imperfect the method might be, there ought to be a limit on each account as a means of restricting the company's exposure to possible bad debt losses.

THE CREDIT LIMIT FORMULA

In late 1962 Mr. Winslow developed a method by which credit limits could be assigned, more or less routinely, to customer accounts. There were about 250,000 customer accounts at this time. His idea was to arrive at a credit limit that would take into account a number of factors, including the ability of the customer to pay, his pay habits, and various operating and performance ratios as obtained from its financial statements. The procedure is described in Exhibit 4, using hypothetical "Company A" as an example. At first, Mr. Winslow felt that the credit limit alone, if set through the use of his proposed scheme, would be a sufficient tool for credit administration. Since the customer's pay habits (prompt, slow, etc.) would be a factor in the computation of the credit limit, he felt at that time that there would probably be no need for a traditional "receivables aging schedule."

As the use of this limit-setting method became widely applied, a policy was adopted whereby the dollar amount of a credit limit determined who would be responsible for final approval, according to the following table.

Amount of Credit Limit	Person Responsible for Setting Limit
$ 0 –$ 5,000	Field credit representative at the field offices or credit analysts at the regional offices.
$ 5,000–$ 25,000	District Credit Manager at the Regional Office.
$25,000–$ 75,000	Regional Credit Manager at the Regional Offices.
$75,000–$125,000	Product Credit Manager at the head office.
Over $125,000	General Credit Manager.

In addition, every salesman was given the authority to set a starting limit of 10% of the customer's net worth on an account (not to exceed $500), to obtain the opening order.

Realizing that the use of the credit limit formula was a time-consuming process and that about 200 new accounts had to be assigned limits daily,

Mr. Winslow abbreviated the process somewhat by the use of Dun & Bradstreet ratings to set limits on the smaller accounts. However, he decided that any credit limit of $25,000 or more must be justified by the use of the formula described in Exhibit 4.

Under this system, credit limits were periodically reviewed and a review was automatically made when an account appeared on the "over credit limit" report. Additionally, a salesman could request that a particular limit be reviewed if he felt an increase or decrease was justified.

To this point credit limits were calculated manually and assigned by personnel of the Credit Department with the computer functioning only in a data-keeping role.

THE EXPERIENCE WITH ZAC AND THE CURRENT CREDIT OPERATION

For a number of years, two monthly measures had been computed in the Credit Department, namely, "days' sales outstanding" and "percentage of receivables over 3 months in age." These measures were charted month-by-month, as in Exhibit 5, and it was expected that through their use evaluation of certain aspects of the credit limit system would eventually be possible. Mr. Winslow felt that neither of these measures was meaningful when applied to total receivables; he thought they ought to be adjusted for such factors as seasonality and difference in product lines. After a period of time, though, it was noted that the collection experience with ZAC accounts was slightly better than with non-ZAC accounts, and, in fact, the "days' sales outstanding" figure was reduced by a few days. Therefore a systematic program was followed under which nearly all accounts were added to the credit limit system. The accounts were grouped into several Zone Accounting Centers, each group containing the accounts in a particular geographic area. Near the end of 1966, 460,000 accounts had been "on the computer" for six months or more. At this time, only 60,000 existing accounts were not administered in this way, and it was expected that most of them would be gradually added to the system.

Near the end of 1966 the credit system was administered through the Credit Department at company headquarters in Cincinnati, at five regional credit offices, and at about 16 one-man or two-man field offices throughout the country. By this time there were no longer separate credit departments in the various warehouses and distribution centers.

One of Mr. Winslow's goals was to absorb all new accounts through 1970 with virtually no increase in his department's personnel, then numbering 105. The cost of the credit function was regularly calculated, and efforts were made to steadily reduce the administrative cost per account.

RECEIVABLES AGING AS AN ALTERNATIVE

In reflecting upon the results achieved by late 1966, Mr. Winslow concluded that the next logical step was the automatic setting of credit limits by the computer. This could be accomplished with appropriate financial data as inputs, such as customer balance sheets and records of customer payments. Before any definite steps were to be taken in this direction, however, and before refinements in the limit-setting procedure were made, both he and the company treasurer thought that a decision should be made about whether or not the limit mechanism should become the single element of control in the company's supervision of trade credit. There were responsible arguments for using other means of regulating the company's exposure to credit risk. One of these was the traditional application of receivables aging, which did not require the use of a credit limit. Under such a system a computer could be programmed to identify all accounts with outstanding amounts of a specified age. The actual format would provide a breakdown of the amounts owed on a particular account in terms of how long they had been outstanding, as for example:

Name of Account	
Account Number	
under 30 days	$www
30–60 days	$xxx
60–90 days	$yyy
over 90 days	$zzz
Total Amount Due	$Total

Using this method, a complete, up-to-date aging schedule for every account could be prepared whenever desired. Some of Taurus's credit managers still preferred to have this kind of information. One regional credit manager argued for a presentation of this sort on the basis that a customer could be automatically and quickly notified when his account became overdue. However, it was recognized that a system of this sort, while it eliminated the need to set a credit limit on each account, would produce a much greater volume of information. Mr. Winslow regarded this as a disadvantage. He also felt that if an aging schedule, rather than a credit limit, was used, the company might be unable to effectively limit its exposure to bad debt losses.

A number of individuals in the company remained unconvinced of the appropriateness of the credit limit concept. In fact, Mr. Winslow was not wholly convinced that the daily "over-credit limit" report was an effective indicator of the accounts that eventually turned into bad debt write-offs. Moreover, without information on age of accounts it was unclear how use could be made of the data on opportunity losses on funds tied up in delinquent accounts.

PROFIT CENTER CONSIDERATIONS

The use of profit centers superimposed certain considerations on the company's credit management. The performance of product managers was judged largely on the basis of profits earned by their respective product lines. Also, the structure of costs and margins was quite different among the different product lines. Thus, ostensibly there appeared to be no reason why product managers should not determine how much of their gross margins they would permit to be absorbed in bad debt losses.

Whether or not bad debt losses were minimized was therefore not particularly relevant, Mr. Winslow thought. He viewed his functions in this respect as one of maintaining loss rates, i.e., ratios of bad debts to sales, which were to be developed by product managers for their specific products. These loss rates were not yet established as Mr. Winslow prepared his report. To an interviewer he said, "I would criticize a credit manager if he went over *or* under the bad debt provision. What we're trying to do is to have established loss rates on each product line. We're saying to our sales people that this is the rate we, the Credit Department, will maintain for them." If differentiations were drawn in credit limits along product lines, the decisions of the individual product managers would determine, in effect, the terms of credit, including credit limit, which the Credit Department would extend. One unresolved matter was the precise fashion in which expected bad debt losses would be incorporated in a system that tied credit limits to margin differences on product lines.

FINANCIAL IMPLICATION OF THE CREDIT LIMIT CONCEPT

In the massive effort required to computerize nearly a half million accounts and to train a staff of credit managers and personnel, very little had been done within the Credit Department relating to the total dollar commitment placed in accounts receivable. Toward the end of 1966, receivables amounted to 15% of the company's total assets.

It was clear that the existing method of setting credit limits on accounts determined, in effect, the total amount of funds represented by receivables in the asset structure. Since an individual credit limit was based primarily on the net worth of a customer, Mr. Winslow realized that it might be useful to know the extent to which the total dollar commitment in receivables was influenced by changes resulting from the formula. The Credit Department had not progressed far in collecting data of this type, however. Trade associations were potential sources of information. The Paint and Wallpaper Association of America, for example, reported in its magazine, *Decorating Retailer*,[1] that a representative sample of its 11,500 retail dealer-members increased their net worths by an average of 25.2% in 1964. The 1965 comparable figure was 10.0%. The National Industrial Conference Board periodically released information about home builders and general contractors which indicated that yearly increases of 5%–10% in average net worth were usual.

The corporate capital budgeting process did not include any economic analysis with respect to expanding accounts receivable, except when new accounts receivable were associated with capital expansion plans, as, for example, with a new plant. In such a case, new accounts receivable were es-

---

[1] *Decorating Retailer*, published by Paint and Wallpaper Association of America, Inc., August, 1965, p. 28; and August, 1966, p. 8.

timated and included as a part of required working capital, and the project was evaluated by means of a discounting technique. Otherwise, no attempt was made to evaluate incremental receivables as a separate investment. Some members of the Credit Department argued that in the absence of explicit profitability tests for committing funds to receivables, means should be sought for limiting this investment. Various suggestions other than those mentioned heretofore were made inconclusively toward this end, but no action was taken.

One idea suggested repeatedly along another line was that the increasingly widespread methods of "discriminant analysis" used by trade corporations selling to consumers be adapted to trade credit administration for Taurus Industries, Inc. Although this idea was incompletely articulated, if it followed current practice in consumer credit analysis, records of payment experience with its customers would be examined by statistical means. A scoring system would be devised weighting various characteristics such as liquidity, debt levels, profit margins, and length of time in business, and prospective customers would be evaluated accordingly. Accumulation of a certain "cut off" score either would or would not qualify the prospect for receipt of credit from Taurus Industries.

Exhibit 1

TAURUS INDUSTRIES, INC. CONSOLIDATED BALANCE SHEET
(Dollar Figures in Thousands)

	December 31 1965	1964
ASSETS		
Current Assets:		
Cash	$ 35,391	$ 42,305
United States Government and other marketable securities—at lower of cost or market (Quoted market value: 1965, $24,662,000; 1964, $13,435,000)	24,662	13,413
Notes and accounts receivable (less estimated losses: 1965, $5,184,000; 1964, $4,995,000)	125,321	112,092
Inventories	163,394	155,826
Prepayments and other current assets	11,842	13,038
Total current assets	360,610	336,674
Investments	52,283	42,603
Property—at cost:		
Land	13,371	12,873
Buildings, machinery, and equipment, mineral deposits, etc.	907,897	842,865
Total	921,268	855,738
Less: accumulated depreciation and depletion	519,475	479,547
Property, Net	401,793	376,191
Other assets	25,954	28,024
TOTAL	$840,640	$783,492

Exhibit 1—Continued

TAURUS INDUSTRIES, INC. CONSOLIDATED BALANCE SHEET
(Dollar Figures in Thousands)

	December 31	
LIABILITIES	*1965*	*1964*
Current Liabilities		
Notes payable—bank	$ 26,242	$ 29,231
Current maturities of long-term debt	3,707	1,000
Accounts payable and sundry accruals	82,705	74,020
Domestic and foreign taxes on income	39,872	36,050
Total current liabilities	152,526	140,301
Long-term debt	16,209	15,606
Deferred credits	35,913	34,103
Accumulated provisions for maintenance, insurance, pensions, etc.	13,061	10,826
Minority interest in consolidated subsidiaries	23,073	21,735
Capital and retained earnings:		
Common stock—authorized, 12,500,000 shares, par value $10 each; issued 1965, 10,770,760 shares; 1964, 10,750,725 shares	207,374	206,288
Earnings retained for use in the business (after transfers to capital)	402,396	362,469
Less common stock in treasury (1965, 156,535 shares; 1964, 127,710 shares) at cost	(9,912)	(7,836)
Capital and retained earnings	599,858	560,921
TOTAL	$840,640	$783,492

Exhibit 2

TAURUS INDUSTRIES, INC.

PERCENTAGE INCREASE IN SALES AND RECEIVABLES—BASE YEAR 1954
CONSOLIDATED (ADJUSTED FOR 1963 INCREASE IN NUMBER OF SUBSIDIARIES
CONSOLIDATED) COMPARED WITH ALL MANUFACTURING CORPORATIONS

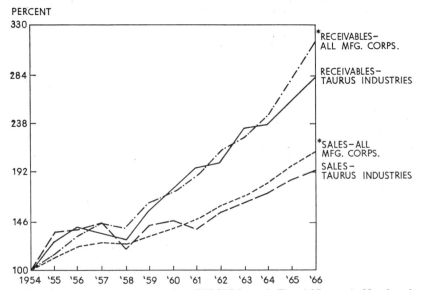

PERCENT

RECEIVABLES— ALL MFG. CORPS.

RECEIVABLES— TAURUS INDUSTRIES

SALES—ALL MFG. CORPS.

SALES— TAURUS INDUSTRIES

* Data for 1954 to 1964, inclusive, are from FTC-SEC Quarterly Financial Reports for Manufacturing Corporations. Data for 1965 and 1966 are from reports issued by the Credit Research Foundation, Inc.

Exhibit 3

TAURUS INDUSTRIES, INC.

STATEMENT OF SOURCES AND APPLICATIONS OF FUNDS, 1956–65

(Dollar Figures in Millions)

	1965	1964	1963	1962	1961	1960	1959	1958	1957	1956
Sources of Funds										
From operations	$ 58.1	$ 49.0	$ 45.6	$43.0	$34.6	$47.6	$ 44.1	$32.1	$ 58.0	$ 55.4
Depreciation and other non-cash charges	54.0	48.4	48.5	35.2	35.2	35.8	34.0	32.3	27.0	19.1
Total from operations	112.1	97.4	94.2	78.2	69.8	83.4	78.1	64.4	85.0	74.5
Increase in long-term debt	0.6	—	23.7	0.1	—	—	11.1	—	—	0.1
Loans from banks	—	5.2	—	—	—	—	—	—	—	—
Sale of marketable securities	—	3.4	30.2	—	9.9	—	—	6.1	33.1	40.3
Increase in current liabilities, excluding those noted separately	15.2	—	35.4	6.6	—	1.0	20.7	11.1	—	—
Miscellaneous sources*	7.3	5.3	13.0	4.4	4.4	—	8.1	—	4.0	(0.5)
	$135.2	$111.3	$196.5	$89.3	$84.1	$84.4	$118.0	$81.6	$122.1	$114.4
Applications of Funds										
Expenditures for property and investment	$ 79.7	$ 57.3	$130.7	$37.9	$30.3	$25.1	$ 42.5	$42.4	$ 69.1	$ 66.4
Cash dividends paid	26.6	25.5	23.9	23.0	22.7	22.3	21.8	21.8	27.2	27.1
Retirement of long-term debt	—	3.4	0.3	5.3	5.4	6.3	4.7	5.0	5.0	4.3
Retirement of bank loans	3.0	—	—	—	4.0	6.9	—	0.2	—	—
Increase in receivables	13.2	3.2	22.3	2.5	8.7	(5.4)	20.2	(5.0)	(1.7)	3.0
Increase in inventories	7.6	7.2	14.8	0.7	(2.7)	1.3	23.3	(7.1)	0.4	23.7
Increase in other current assets, mainly cash and prepayments	3.1	3.1	4.5	12.5	6.0	22.9	5.5	—	12.8	(13.5)
Decrease in current liabilities, excluding those noted separately	—	11.6	—	—	9.8	5.1	—	24.3	9.3	3.4
Purchase of Treasury shares	2.1	—	—	7.3	—	—	—	—	—	—
	$135.3	$111.3	$196.5	$89.2	$84.2	$84.5	$118.0	$81.6	$122.1	$114.4

* Principally deferrals and exercise of stock options.

Exhibit 4

TAURUS INDUSTRIES, INC.

ANALYTICAL PROCEDURE FOR ESTABLISHING A CREDIT LIMIT*, WORK FORM

Customer _____ *"A" Company Inc.*
Statement Dated _____ *12/31 --*
Net Worth _____ *93,000*

Basic Information	Rating Used	Contribution to Credit Limit
1. Basic Allowance – 10% of Net Worth		$ *9,300*
2. Requirements (What % of customer's total labor and material supplied?)	*30* %	*4,650*
3. Pay Habits (Rating – Circle Appropriate Symbol)	H Ⓖ N F P	*4,650*
4. Years in Business	*7* Yrs.	*2,325*
(a) Sub Total (1 thru 4)		$*20,925*

Financial Statement Analysis

	Rating Used	Contribution to Credit Limit
5. Profit Margin – (Before Income Taxes)	*2* %	*372*
6. Current Ratio – (Current Assets ÷ Current Liabilities)	*1.74* to 1	*4,650*
7. Quick Ratio – (Cash & Receivables ÷ " ")	*.96* to 1	*4,650*
8. Current Debt/Inventory Ratio – (Current Liab. ÷ Inv.)	*1.28* to 1	*(4,650)*
9. Inventory/Working Capital Ratio – (Inventory ÷ Net Working Capital)	*1.06* to 1	*(4,650)*
10. Net Worth/Debt Ratio – (Net Worth ÷ Total Debt)	*.96* to 1	*(4,650)*
11. Quality of Receivables (Days Sales Outstanding)	*52* Days	*930*
12. Inventory Turnover (Cost of Sales ÷ Inventory)	*6.6* Times	*4,650*
(b) Sub Total (a. plus 5 thru 12)		$*22,227*

13. Judgment Factors – Where factors other than those presented in Items 1 through 12 above should be considered in establishing Limit, explain fully and add or deduct Assigned Dollar Value.
Explanation:

Trend of comparative statements shows slight decline in all major ratios   *(2,000)*

Maximum Credit Limit $*20,227*

Actual Credit Limit Assigned $*20,000*

* See explanation on following page.

Exhibit 4—Continued

EXPLANATION OF SPECIFIC ALLOWANCE FOR WORK FORM—
"ANALYTICAL PROCEDURE FOR ESTABLISHING CREDIT LIMITS"

	Rating	Contribution to Credit Limit (Percent of net worth)
1. Where "Intangibles" (Goodwill, Research & Development Expenses, Etc.) are substantial in amount, deduct from Net Worth before applying formula.		
2. *Requirements*—What portion of customer's requirements is to be supplied? (Actual or estimated Sales to customer–Cost of Sales.)	Under 25%	–0–
	25 to 50%	+ 5
	Over 50%	+10
3. *Will he pay?* What is the customer's payment record? Based on Trade Clearances *and* past record of payments, rate the customer's payment habits:		
Discounts, or pays promptly where Net terms only available—	High	+10
Pays promptly where Discount terms available—	Good	+ 5
Pays per agreed, special terms or no experience—	Neutral	–0–
Occasionally late in meeting obligations—	Fair	– 2½
Considerably late in meeting obligations—	Poor	– 5
4. *Years in Business*	Under 3 years	–0–
	3 to 10 years	+ 2½
	Over 10 years	+ 5
5. *Profit Margin*—For each 1% of Profit (Loss) Margin, add (deduct) 2/10th of 1% of Net Worth as "Contribution to Credit Limit." Profit Margin defined as Net Income before Income Taxes divided by Net Sales.		
6. *Current Ratio*—Indicates Margin of Protection to Current Creditors	2 to 1–Higher	+10
	1.25 to 1–2 to 1	+ 5
	.75 to 1–1.25 to 1	–0–
	Under .75 to 1	– 5
7. *Quick Ratio*—Measure extent to which current debt can be liquidated without relying on inventory.	2 to 1–Higher	+15
	1 to 1–2 to 1	+10
	.80 to 1–1 to 1	+ 5
	.50 to 1–.80 to 1	–0–
	Under .50 to 1	– 5
8. *Current Debt to Inventory Ratio*—Indication of reliance on unsold inventory to meet current obligations.	.65 to 1–Lower	+10
	.65 to 1–1 to 1	–0–
	1 to 1–Higher	– 5
9. *Inventory to Working Capital Ratio*—Consideration as to Over or Under stocked condition.	.50 to 1–1 to 1	+ 5
	.25 to 1–.50 to 1	–0–
	Under .25 to 1 *and* Over 1 to 1	– 5

Exhibit 4—Continued

EXPLANATION OF SPECIFIC ALLOWANCE FOR WORK FORM—
"ANALYTICAL PROCEDURE FOR ESTABLISHING CREDIT LIMITS"

	Rating	Contribution to Credit Limit (Percent of net worth)
10. *Net Worth to Debt Ratio*—Measures soundness of over-all capital structure and margin of protection to all creditors.	Over 2 to 1 1 to 1–2 to 1 Under 1 to 1	+10 + 5 − 5
11. *Quality of Receivables*—(Gross Trade Receivables divided by Average Daily Sales) Test of Credit and Collection Policies and Liquidity of Receivables. Minimum standard for additional credit consideration would be "Net Selling Terms Plus Thirty Days." For each 10 days under this minimum standard add 1% of Net Worth to potential Credit Limit.		
12. *Inventory Turnover*—Measures control and quality of inventory and, to an extent, sales capacity.	10 to 30 times 5 to 10 times Under 5 and Over 30 times	+10 + 5 –0–
13. *Judgment Factors*—Include in the category marketing, security, growth potential and other factors not specifically covered previously.		

Exhibit 5

TAURUS INDUSTRIES, INC.

CHART OF PERCENTAGE OF RECEIVABLES OVER THREE MONTHS IN AGE AND OF DAYS'
SALES OUTSTANDING, 1964–66

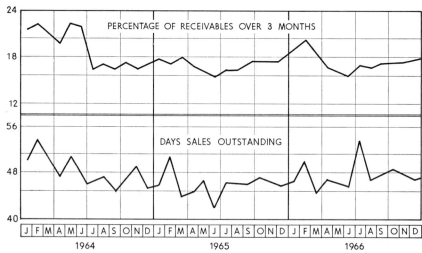

BELL CAMPINAS, S.A.

AT ITS MEETING in August, 1962, the board of directors of Bell Manufacturing Company, a consumer hard goods producer, voted to increase the company's investment in its Brazilian subsidiary, Bell Campinas. Bell had been active in foreign markets for many years. In fact, some Bell products in lines where the company was a latecomer were better accepted abroad than domestically. In 1961, 72% of total sales were in foreign markets.

Bell Campinas was organized in 1959 to assemble and distribute refrigerators in Brazil. Although sales in Brazil had increased substantially each year (see Exhibit 1), the market had grown only in conjunction with the availability of consumer credit. Bell had experienced a similar association of the growth of consumer credit and advancing consumer hard goods sales in other countries, including the United States. Liberal credit terms were extraordinarily important to inflation-conscious Brazilian consumers, who insisted on incurring indebtedness to turn the galloping price rise to advantage. In July, management had decided to extend installment purchase terms from 12 to 24 months to assure sales. To finance the refrigerator sales forecast for the first six months of Bell's fiscal year on the extended credit terms, Bell Campinas would need 1,875 million cruzeiros (Cr$) or $5.137 million at the then existing pegged free rate of 365 cruzeiros to the U.S. dollar[1] (Exhibit 1). Other funds needs would be met from Campinas' internal sources.

The parent company was willing to commit equity capital to Campinas only to the extent of 80% of plant and equipment book value, 20% of cash and receivable contracts, and 90 days of inventory requirements. These equity participation limits, set in the summer of 1961 for all Bell subsidiaries operating in inflationary economies with weak currencies, reflected top management's desire to limit Bell's exposure to exchange losses. These limits applied to investments made subsequent to the decision. The cost of excessive

---

[1] Throughout the postwar period, Brazil had had one of the world's most complex multiple exchange systems. Former President Quadros moved to establish a single free exchange rate. Aside from special arrangements concerning coffee and cacao exports, this had been achieved. Yet the pegged free rate had not kept pace with basic economic forces tending to accelerate the rate of cruzeiro deterioration. This had given rise to an active parallel market. The so-called free rate was pegged by the Bank of Brazil, the only institution permitted to deal in foreign exchange at this time. If Bell were to provide dollars (or other foreign exchange) for its subsidiary, these funds could move legally only through the Bank of Brazil at the pegged rate. In the parallel market during August, the exchange rate was approximately Cr$555 per U.S. dollar. Transactions in this market were not sanctioned by the Brazilian Government.

exposure is reflected in Campinas' profitability in fiscal 1960 and 1961, when equity was the only significant source of the subsidiary's funds (Exhibits 1 and 2). In compliance with this standard, it would be necessary to obtain Cr$1.5 billion, from outside sources in this instance. At the conclusion of the August meeting, the board had asked the vice president of finance, Mr. Senturia, to prepare a financing plan.

Mr. Senturia realized that his recommendation must take into account Brazil's inflation, the weakening exchange rate, and the impact of taxation. The financing plan must enable Campinas to survive government and monetary regulations. At the same time, it must accommodate Campinas' return visits to the Brazilian money markets. In sum, his recommendation must reflect the company's intention to remain in Brazilian markets for many years.

Brazil had enjoyed a recent period of considerable growth, a development made all the more remarkable in view of the imbalance prevailing in the economy. Inflationary conditions had caused the cost of living to increase 15-fold since 1948. The inflation encouraged imports and discouraged exports by making domestic prices higher than international prices. Consequent painful balance of payments corrections had entailed severe import restrictions. Despite this turbulence in the economy, the country's industrial output increased 100% in real terms between 1946 and 1962.

In 1960 and 1961, the pace of inflation had accelerated. The following governmental expenditures, among others, contributed to a large deficit in each of these years: substantial financial resources had been required to support the increasing coffee inventory; the construction of the new capital, Brasilia, had cost the government 73 billion cruzeiros; former President Kubitschek had undertaken large-scale industrial projects. Finally, government administration had been inefficient. These deficits were financed substantially by monetization of the public debt—i.e., by the creation of bank deposits and the issuance of paper money (see Exhibit 3)—and it was this that fueled the inflation. By the same token, this period was one of considerable expansion of the banking system's claims on the government. The prospects for further inflation in 1962 were aggravated by a 40% wage increase approved for federal employees.

In 1961, the already high level of annual government deficits was stepped up in the budgets for 1962 and 1963. In addition, Premier Neves publicly noted in 1962 that the proposed budgets failed to take into account the cost of projected 40% wage increases as well as the rapidly increasing deficits of the railway system. The rate of the free cruzeiro had weakened from 40 to the dollar in 1953 to an average of 74 in 1955, to 90 in 1957, to 205 in 1960, and to 315 in 1961.

Chronic inflation had colored the evolution of Brazilian financial institutions and imposed limitations on the availability of funds for industrial concerns. Although the stock of money had increased markedly in recent years (Exhibit 3), the growth of commercial bank deposits was inhibited by the imposition of an interest rate ceiling on commercial bank loans, which handcuffed the banks in competition for deposits. Unaffected by rate restrictions, private finance companies were better able to obtain cruzeiro deposits. Other financial institutions, such as savings banks, insurance companies, and pension funds, had preferred investments in real estate to commercial loans, since real estate provided an effective hedge against inflation. As a result, only an infant capital market existed for would-be industrial borrowers to utilize as a means of effecting the financing required for large-scale and rapid transfers of real resources to growth industries. Also, government spending to finance enlarged coffee inventories, massive real estate projects, and the burgeoning administrative apparatus of government tended to deprive industry of the economy's real resources.

In July, 1962, the Brazilian Superintendency of Money and Credit (SUMOC) issued a directive that, in effect, gave the Bank of Brazil a monopoly on legal foreign exchange transactions. This measure, coupled with existing import and export remittance regulations, provided the government with substantial control of foreign exchange in its attempt to preserve hard currency reserves. Bell could readily provide Campinas with foreign capital in the form of currency or banking transfers because the Bank of Brazil needed hard currencies. Mr. Senturia was not at all certain, however, that future remittances from the subsidiary to the parent company could move through this market. The Bank of Brazil was unwilling to cover foreign exchange transactions at the present time—i.e., the bank would exchange cruzeiros for dollars but would not, in return, exchange dollars for cruzeiros.

The latest SUMOC directive was merely one of many restrictive measures likely to be introduced during this troubled time. The exchange market was knotted by currency regulations that imposed an artificial rate of exchange and inhibited currency movements. Bell's foreign exchange during August would, of necessity, move through the official market at Cr$365 per U.S. dollar without cover, or illegally through the parallel market at approximately Cr$555 per U.S. dollar without cover. Since the Brazilian government officials reviewed corporate financial statements frequently and in detail, it was both difficult and risky to circumvent the required procedure of requesting authorization for dollar investments from the Bank of Brazil.

A number of alternative paths to accomplish the projected currency transfer had emerged from discussions with Bell's bankers and several similarly situated corporate treasurers. The alternatives proved numerous enough to necessitate grouping them for analytical convenience into those with and those without exchange rate risk. Two possibilities—(1) a direct loan from the parent company to Bell Campinas and (2) establishment of a financing subsidiary—fell into the risk category. Several possibilities, enumerated below, involved little or no exposure to deteriorating exchange rates.

The first alternative bearing currency risk would have the parent company make available to the Brazilian subsidiary a bank draft for the amount required in U.S. dollars. This amount would then be sold for free cruzeiros to the Bank of Brazil. The Brazilian company would need to repay these funds in subsequent months by repurchasing U.S. dollars in the free market when cover later became available at the then prevailing exchange rate. On one prior occasion, Bell had made a loan of $100,000 to its Brazilian subsidiary in November, 1960, to be repaid in July, 1961. This amount was sold in the free exchange market at the rate of 205 cruzeiros to the dollar, and this gave the Brazilian subsidiary 20.5 million cruzeiros. In order to repay in July, 1961, the subsidiary had to pay 30 million cruzeiros to buy the $100,000 at the then existing exchange rate of 300 cruzeiros to the dollar.

It was the Bell policy to charge 10% per annum payable in dollars on all loans made to its subsidiaries. Interest on Campinas borrowing, however, was deductible in computing profits subject to the Brazilian corporate profits tax, which for Campinas would be approximately 30%.

A second alternative, involving minimal exchange risk, was the swap transaction. A swap loan was an arrangement between the Bank of Brazil and the United States parent of the Brazilian subsidiary. The U.S. parent would lend a given amount in dollars to the Bank of Brazil, depositing the dollars in its New York account. The Bank of Brazil, in return, would make a loan of an equivalent number of cruzeiros to Campinas. The exchange rate the Bank of Brazil would apply would be less favorable to Bell than the prevailing free exchange rate. (On a previous occasion, when the rate was Cr$265 per U.S. dollar and commercial banks were permitted to engage in swap transactions, a Brazilian bank, Banco do Campinas, applied a rate of Cr$210 per dollar; thus Bell had to deposit $100,000 in order to provide Campinas with Cr$21 million, while at the free rate it would have had to exchange only $79,245.)

The Bank of Brazil rates for swap transactions varied between Cr$180 and Cr$200 per dollar during August. Longer contracts and larger amounts commanded more favorable rates. If the transaction could be arranged, Mr. Senturia was confident that Bell could obtain a 6-month swap loan sufficient to cover Campinas' additional receivables need of Cr$1.5 billion (excluding the parent's equity contribution) at a rate of Cr$180 per U.S. dollar. There would be no interest charged on either the dollar or the cruzeiro balance. Since the swap loan would tie up Bell dollar funds, however, a 10% interest charge per year payable in dollars would be required of Campinas on the dollars deposited in New York. This interest payment would not be tax deductible in Brazil because this dollar deposit was not loaned to Campinas. The interest payment would, perforce, be exposed to the vagaries of the free exchange rate of cruzeiros for dollars.

All the possible methods of meeting Campinas' funds needs without exposure to the risk of currency deterioration relied on financing within the financial structure of Brazil, thereby avoiding the need to trade currencies and undergo currency risk.

As one alternative without currency risk, the Brazilian subsidiary might be able to borrow its cruzeiro requirement from local banks. Under the influence of a ceiling rate imposed by SUMOC, the interest rate currently charged by

Brazilian commercial banks was 14% after additional charges were included. The advantage of this method was that the subsidiary could repay the loan in cruzeiros, benefiting from any inflation and avoiding the risk of exchange losses.

The major drawback with this method, however, was that local banks did not have an abundant supply of cruzeiros.[2] In general, they were willing to make loans for only relatively small amounts up to Cr$5 million, and for periods not to exceed 120 days. The local bank in some instances expected the parent company to maintain compensating balances and to allow the bank to handle the borrower's commercial transactions. If this expedient were adopted, Mr. Senturia felt that the local subsidiary should not enter into loan agreements with more than 20 local banks because of these unwanted complications.

It was also possible either to discount Campinas' receivables with recourse at Brazilian commercial banks or to borrow cruzeiros from local private finance companies. In both cases, Campinas could readily obtain the required cruzeiros. Mr. Senturia's assistant had computed the cost of discounting the receivables to be 30% after including income lost on internally financed receivables. Of the 30% cost, 18% would be deductible in computing profits subject to Brazilian corporate taxes. It would cost approximately 36% per annum to borrow cruzeiros from private finance companies, all of which would be deductible.

The final alternative consisted of establishing a finance company in Brazil to facilitate Campinas' borrowing outside the existing financial institutions. Under this arrangement, Campinas would issue bills of exchange cosigned by the finance company and denominated in cruzeiros.[3] These bills could be sold to investors on the Brazilian stock market, where such bills were actively traded. With an investment of $1 million in the proposed finance company, which would guarantee the bills of exchange, it was felt that Campinas would be able to issue bills in excess of its immediate working capital requirements.

Campinas would be charged 10% per annum for the investment in the finance company, which would tie up Bell funds. In addition, Campinas would incur the cost of discounting the bills of exchange. (In August, 1962, 6-month bills of exchange denominated in cruzeiros were being discounted at 18% per annum in Rio.) The vice president believed these cost components would be tax deductible, since all funds would be advanced to Brazilian corporations.

With the background information collected and alternative financing methods identified, Mr. Senturia had now to make his recommendation. He recognized that in large measure the appropriate financing method would

---

[2] Cruzeiros in large measure were deposited in private finance companies, which were not subject to the SUMOC directive and therefore were able to exact a 30–40% lending rate per annum.

[3] A bill of exchange is a common form of commercial draft drawn between parties to foreign trade. The draft signifies the indebtedness of one of the parties to the other. Bills of exchange are marketed in most financial centers throughout the world. They usually are sold at a discount.

depend on future economic and political development in Brazil. More particularly, since the alternatives available varied in the amount of funds exposed to currency exchange rate risk, anticipations about the pace of inflation and the resultant deterioration of exchange rates must play a major role in the policy choice. With the number of possibilities posing a bewildering problem, Mr. Senturia decided to first choose the best of the alternatives not involving exchange risk, and then to compare it with each of the two possibilities entailing risk. A possible means of choosing the best in this last comparison would necessitate an estimate of losses or gains anticipated during the six months on the alternative with currency risk.

Exhibit 1

BELL CAMPINAS, S.A.

SELECTED FINANCIAL DATA
(In Millions of Cruzeiros)

	Fiscal (August 31)			Forecast for First Six Months of Fiscal 1963
	1960	1961	1962	
Time sales	Cr$1,253	Cr$2,043	Cr$4,218	Cr$2,816
Total sales	1,794	2,524	5,943	3,118
Year-end time sales receivable*	787	1,541	2,704	4,579
Net earnings subject to exchange fluctuation	517	884	2,185	1,206
Return on net worth subject to exchange adjustment	24%	30%	71%	...
Return on investment after adjustment for foreign exchange loss	2%	7%	42%	...

* Ending balance.

Exhibit 2

BELL CAMPINAS, S.A.

BALANCE SHEETS AS OF AUGUST 31, 1960–62
(In Millions of Cruzeiros)

ASSETS	1960	1961	1962
Cash...................................	Cr$ 168	Cr$ 198	Cr$ 203
Time sales receivable.....................	787	1,541	2,704
Accounts receivable......................	414	517	648
Foreign receivables......................	...	4	3
Deposits for exchange....................	8	17	21
Compulsory deposits.....................	...	36	49
Advances, merchandise—long term........	...	...	27
Inventory...............................	79	96	118
Finished	...	...	...
In process	268	312	411
Fixed assets............................	943	1,821	2,059
Total...........................	Cr$2,667	Cr$4,542	Cr$6,243

LIABILITIES			
Notes payable—bank overdrafts..........	...	...	Cr$ 3
Bills discounted..........................	...	...	3
Accounts payable (short term).............	Cr$ 483	Cr$ 812	1,749
Accounts payable (long term).............	...	600	1,245
Reserve for federal taxes.................	30	81	165
Other liabilities.........................	...	103	61
Legal reserves...........................	102	147	141
Other reserves...........................	268	373	409
Common stock..........................	1,531	1,531	1,531
Earned surplus..........................	253	895	936
Total...........................	Cr$2,667	Cr$4,542	Cr$6,243

Exhibit 3

BELL CAMPINAS, S.A.

THE RATE OF INFLATION IN BRAZIL

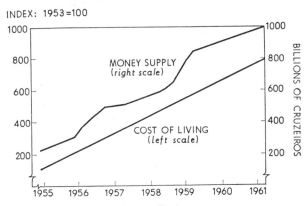

SOURCE: International Monetary Fund.

JONES & LAMSON MACHINE COMPANY

In June, 1960, Norman T. Harrison, treasurer of Jones & Lamson Machine Company, was considering whether the lease plan currently offered as a means of financing the sale of company products should be revised to include a terminal value allowance. This allowance was an amount to be deducted from the original sales value of the equipment in arriving at the principal amount (net of interest and other charges) to be paid by the customer during the lease period for use of the equipment. It represented an estimate of the market value the equipment would have at the termination of the lease.

Three alternatives were already open to customers for purchasing Jones & Lamson products:

1. Outright purchase on open account.
2. Conditional sales contract.
3. Profitivity lease plan.

Evaluation of the implications, advantages, and disadvantages of the proposed lease plan with terminal value allowance was somewhat complicated because the company had acquired only a few months of experience under the profitivity lease plan, which provided for no terminal value allowance. Mr. Harrison's task, nonetheless, was to decide whether the plan should be revised and, if so, whether the change should be effective at once or at some later date.

HISTORY OF THE COMPANY

Jones & Lamson Machine Company of Springfield, Vermont, had been incorporated in 1876. Since then, it had continuously enjoyed a reputation as a manufacturer of high quality products in the machine tool industry. In recent years, it had kept abreast of competition through the development of new electronically controlled turning and grinding machine tools. The product line in 1960 consisted of turret lathes, Fay automatic lathes, thread grinders, positioning tables, boring machines, and optical comparators. The price ranges of the principal products in 1960 are given in Exhibit 1.

Wide cyclical swings in sales were typical in the industry. During the last 10 years, Jones & Lamson's sales volume had ranged from $7.891 million in 1950 to a high of $29.684 million in 1953, and down to $10.911 million in 1959. The company had suffered losses from operations in years 1958 and

1959, the first such losses in the 10-year period. Selected financial statements appear in Exhibits 2 and 3.

In addition to the outright sale of its products, the company had made several lease plans and conditional sales contract plans available to customers in past years. The first conditional sales contract arrangement offered by the company had been financed through a large national finance company, the Commercial Finance Corporation, at a cost to the customer of 6% on the unpaid balance. Management had objected to this plan for three reasons.

1. The customer was required to make a 25% down payment.
2. The Commercial Finance Corporation held back from Jones & Lamson nearly 20% of the purchase price until such time as the customer had fulfilled his obligations under the contract.
3. Jones & Lamson was not completely isolated from the transaction after the sale was completed, but remained responsible for any default or claim arising under the contract.

Beginning in 1958, the company had switched its financing of sales under conditional sales contracts from the Commercial Finance Corporation to a large commercial bank, which had long been its principal banking connection. The interest cost to the customer was the same and the company still remained liable for default or claims under the contract, but this arrangement provided an advantage to Jones & Lamson in that the bank did not hold back any part of the purchase price from the company. Thus, the company did not have any of its funds tied up in financing sales under this plan.

The conditional sales contract was advantageous to certain customers in that it enabled them to purchase new equipment without paying the full price at the time of sale. The bank was willing to spread payments for periods up to five years. It did not solve the financing problem for all customers, however, since it also required a 25% down payment.

Also available to Jones & Lamson's customers in years past had been two types of lease arrangements, one with an option to purchase the equipment during or at the expiration of the lease term, and the other without this option. The company had financed these lease plans through the Commercial Finance Corporation, which had managed the leases and set the terms. Both of these plans had required from the customer a 10% security deposit, which was not returned until termination of the lease, and three monthly rental payments in advance of the date of shipment. The next monthly rental payment was due on the first day of the fourth month following shipment. The effective interest cost to the customer under these plans was approximately the same as the 6% interest cost under the conditional sales contracts.

When a sale had been made, the Commercial Finance Corporation advanced the company 55% of the cash value of the equipment and amortized the balance on an annual basis over the life of the lease. Thus, under this arrangement Jones & Lamson financed 45% of the original selling price, which was gradually amortized over the period of lease. Although the cash outlay required of customers was less than under the conditional sales contract, management had objected to financing the declining balances with company funds. For this reason, in 1959 the company discontinued making sales under these lease arrangements.

REASONS FOR INTRODUCTION OF THE PROFITIVITY LEASE PLAN

Prompted by management's concern regarding the low level of sales and the resulting losses from operations in 1958 and 1959, Mr. Harrison undertook a study of the machine tool market. As a result of talking with a number of machine tool and equipment users, he concluded that the replacement market had not developed as anticipated because many users were delaying replacement of old machine tools in order to conserve funds for other business purposes. It was apparent to him that a large majority of these companies were overlooking the inflation factor in the replacement analysis, and that the real saving to be made by purchasing now rather than later was therefore being underestimated. Elaborating on this point, Mr. Harrison thought that historical trends seemed to indicate a continually rising price and wage index in the future. He believed, therefore, that a replacement decision should take into account the estimated savings offered by replacing now, owing to the probability of still higher equipment prices at a future date and rising wage rates applicable to the labor savings available through immediate replacement.

Mr. Harrison also discovered in his survey that several potential customers were suffering from a deficiency in available after-tax funds with which to replace old machines with new, higher-priced ones, even though their computations often indicated that replacement would be profitable.

Confronted with this evidence, Mr. Harrison first devised a replacement formula that brought into consideration the inflation factor. Company salesmen circulated this formula among prospective customers in the hope that its use would result in better and more favorable estimates of the savings available and would aid in selling the company's products.

Second, to overcome the problems of customers' shortage of funds and reluctance to invest available funds in new machine tools, Mr. Harrison decided that the company should offer a plan under which the customers would not be required to make an initial outlay of funds and could reasonably expect to offset the annual cost of replacement with savings on new equipment.

On the basis of his survey and his general knowledge of the machine tool market, Mr. Harrison then speculated about the potential value of such a plan. He believed that by the end of 1 year it would not be unreasonable to expect that 10–12.5% of the company's total sales volume would be made under this plan. He foresaw a reasonable possibility that a plan of this nature would account for approximately 25% of sales at the end of 18 months, and perhaps as much as 50% in the long run.

Other members of management were enthusiastic about the possibilities of this lease plan. They agreed that it provided an opportunity to make sales that might otherwise be lost because of the limited funds situation of many potential customers.

LIMITING CONDITIONS ON ESTABLISHMENT OF THE PROFITIVITY LEASE PLAN

Drawing on views expressed by management regarding the company's experience under the previous lease plans, Mr. Harrison determined the limiting conditions to guide him in making financial arrangements for the new plan. He knew that management did not intend to tie up company funds in providing working capital for customers. In addition, the company did not have sufficient personnel with the necessary skills and knowledge of the finance and credit business to handle any significant sales volume under a company-financed plan. If possible, management also wanted to isolate the company from the transaction in such a way that the customer and the financial intermediary would be dealing directly with each other after the sale was made.

THE PROFITIVITY LEASE PLAN

In the fall of 1959, with the criteria and limiting conditions for a time payment sales plan clearly in mind, Mr. Harrison began his search for suitable financial arrangements. Bank officials of the company's then existing banking connections and several other large banks expressed the opinion that this kind of investment of bank assets without a required deposit or down payment was both questionable in its appropriateness and undesirable from their point of view.

During this period, the Third National Bank of a city several hundred miles away had approached Jones & Lamson on the general possibility of participating in financing of machine tool sales. Impressed with this inquiry and having heard that the bank was extremely progressive, Mr. Harrison called on the Third National Bank and presented his proposal. Subsequent discussions and negotiations led to establishment of the profitivity lease plan, which went into effect January 1, 1960.

This plan involved a five-year lease period. It contained neither a terminal value allowance nor an option to purchase the equipment under lease. Monthly lease payments to be made by the customer amounted to $20.50 per thousand dollars of sales value of the equipment when new.[1] At the end of the five-year lease period, the customer had the following alternatives:

---

[1] The monthly rental payment rate was arrived at as follows:

Selling price of equipment	$1,000
Bank add-on charges, 4.6% per annum	230
	$1,230
	÷ 60 months
	$20.50 per month

1. Continue to lease on a year-to-year basis at one tenth of the original lease rental rate.
2. Return the equipment to the company with no further obligation (freight paid by Jones & Lamson).
3. Lease (or buy) new replacement equipment.

When returned by the customer, used equipment under this plan was to be sold to secondhand dealers at a negotiated price.

Mr. Harrison thought that the main advantages accruing to customers under the profitivity lease plan were (1) the opportunity to acquire new equipment without an initial cash outlay and (2) the right to continue leasing beyond the five-year lease period at a very nominal rental rate.

Provisions of the agreement with the Third National Bank permitted Jones & Lamson to assign to the bank, on the date equipment was shipped to the customer, both the financial interest in the lease and the title in the equipment. Jones & Lamson, however, was to remain responsible for a normal one-year guarantee. The bank agreed to pay Jones & Lamson the selling price of the shipped equipment within 30 days after receiving notice of shipment. Under this arrangement, the company avoided tying up its own funds to finance sales and escaped any financial risk involved in carrying customer credit.

The profitivity lease plan was set up on a five-year basis for two reasons. First, the bank did not want to carry a lease for a longer period, although it had indicated a willingness to inquire whether longer terms would be possible through an arrangement with an insurance company for periods exceeding five years. Second, the company officers believed that real savings on new equipment would be greatly reduced by the end of this period. Because of these factors, the agreement with the Third National Bank specified that all right, title, and interest in a lease and the equipment covered would revert to Jones & Lamson after the five-year term had expired. If the customer elected to continue leasing at the reduced rental rate, all payments subsequently made would be the property of the company.

In the negotiations, the Third National Bank had insisted on the right to reject lease assignments of any customers who did not appear to be reasonable credit risks. At the same time, it was agreed that the company was not under obligation to assign lease contracts that it chose to finance with company funds. However, it was not the management's intention to finance sales to customers who were rejected by the bank as poor credit risks.

An informal part of the financial arrangement was that the company would maintain a balance of at least $50,000 with the Third National Bank. In June, 1960, Mr. Harrison did not know of any unfavorable reactions to this new banking relationship on the part of existing banking connections.

EXPERIENCE UNDER THE PROFITIVITY LEASE PLAN

As of June, 1960, the Third National Bank had not refused to finance a sale to any customer who purchased under the plan. Management was also encouraged by the number of new customers apparently attracted by the plan, as evidenced by the customer analysis in Exhibit 4. Mr. Harrison expressed confidence that sales volume under this plan would gain momentum as knowledge of its availability spread. His confidence was increased because the plan had accounted for approximately 5.5% of net orders received in the first 7 months of 1960. (See Exhibit 5 for a summary of new orders received in the years 1955–60).

In the market surveys conducted by the company, it had been discovered that the biggest deterrent to leasing equipment from the lessee's point of view was fear or uncertainty about the position of the Internal Revenue Service on allowing rental payments as an income tax deduction. Mr. Harrison thought that the current IRS regulations (excerpts in Exhibit 6) were somewhat arbitrary and capricious on this matter. As a result of this evidence, he concluded that a lease plan that offered assurance of full rental payments as allowable tax deductions in the year paid would have a definite appeal to some potential customers. Under the profitivity lease plan, wherein the customer obtained an option to continue leasing beyond the original lease term at a greatly reduced rate, this certainly did not exist.

TERMINAL VALUE LEASE PLAN

To overcome the tax problem, Mr. Harrison and other executives undertook, in the spring of 1960, the design of a new lease plan, to be called the terminal value lease plan. Not all the details had been worked out by June, 1960, but certain features had been established.

1. The lessee would be committed to turn back the equipment at the end of the original lease period.

2. The lessee would not have the privilege of renewing the lease or purchasing the equipment.

3. The lessee would pay during the lease term an amount totaling less than 100% of the original value of the equipment, plus bank add-on charges estimated at 4.6% per annum on the original equipment value. The amount of equal monthly rental payments would depend on the equipment value, the lease period, and the corresponding terminal value. The following schedule of lease periods and terminal values would be used:

Lease Period	Terminal Value (Percentage of Original Value of Equipment)
3 years	25%
5	20
7½	15
10	10

It was intended that all other terms of the terminal value lease plan would be the same as those under the profitivity lease plan.

Mr. Harrison had not yet approached the Third National Bank regarding arrangements for financing the terminal value lease plan. He hoped that terms and conditions similar to those under the profitivity lease plan would be available. For example: At the time of a sale under the terminal value lease plan, the bank would advance 100% of the purchase price to Jones & Lamson and title to the equipment would be transferred to the bank for the lease period. At the end of the lease term, title would revert to Jones & Lamson, and the company would pay the bank the terminal value of the equipment. Exhibits 7 and 8 compare the effects on the company and on a customer of sales under the profitivity lease plan and under the terminal value lease plan.

If the bank did accept this arrangement for financing sales under the plan, Jones & Lamson would be financially isolated from the transaction until the expiration of the lease period. In this way, the company would be in a position to treat the transaction as an outright sale, and the customer would *lease* from the bank. At the end of the lease period, however, the company would receive the used equipment from the customer, and the terminal value amount would be carried in the inventory account until the used equipment could be sold.

The other possibility, of course, was that the bank would be willing to advance only the purchase price less the terminal value allowance. In this event, Jones & Lamson would be required at the outset to finance the terminal value allowance with its own funds. These funds would be tied up until the used equipment could be sold at some date following the term of the lease.

To aid in weighing the financial implications of the problem before him, Mr. Harrison prepared funds flow estimates for 1960 and 1961, given in Exhibit 9.

THE SECONDHAND MARKET FOR MACHINE TOOLS

The company had always followed a policy of selling only new equipment of its own manufacture. It rarely accepted a trade-in from a customer. Most manufacturers in this field, however, maintained a close working relationship with several dealers in the used machine tool and equipment business for the purpose of helping customers to dispose of used equipment. Jones & Lamson worked closely with several such dealers.

Mr. Harrison knew that these secondhand dealers were generally in a position to carry large inventories of used equipment. He also knew that experience indicated that Jones & Lamson's standard machine tools and equipment had commanded a relatively high value in the used equipment market over many years. For these reasons, he was confident that a suitable arrangement could be worked out with several secondhand dealers in order to minimize the amount of used inventory to be carried by Jones & Lamson. In this way, the risks involved in the secondhand market would be largely eliminated.

The arrangement that Mr. Harrison had in mind would be set up so that at the end of the lease term a used equipment dealer would establish the trade-in value of the used equipment. The equipment would then be sold to the dealer at this price, and Jones & Lamson would absorb the difference (gain or loss) between trade-in value and the contracted terminal allowance value. In turn, the customer would have these options available: (1) lease (or buy) new replacement equipment; (2) purchase the old equipment from the secondhand dealer at a competitive price as is, reconditioned, or rebuilt.

Owing to their competitive needs, buyers of used machine tools were usually concerned with the speeds and tolerances of such equipment. For this reason, they generally purchased rebuilt equipment on which speeds and tolerances were guaranteed. The cost of rebuilding general-purpose machine tools and equipment frequently amounted to as much as 50% of the cost of manufacturing new equipment. The price range of rebuilt and guaranteed equipment typically ran from 70–85% of new price, depending on its age and its speeds and tolerances as compared with new equipment, and on business conditions in the industry. To properly evaluate the risks involved in the used equipment market, Mr. Harrison had determined that the influence of the inflationary price curve over recent years was the same on prices of both new and used equipment. The cyclical swings in demand for new and used equipment also generally followed a similar pattern.

Exhibit 1

JONES & LAMSON MACHINE COMPANY

TYPICAL PRICE RANGE OF PRODUCTS MOST
COMMONLY IN DEMAND IN 1960

Turret lathes	$15,000–$50,000
Single spindle automatic lathes	20,000– 45,000
Tracer lathes	40,000– 50,000
Thread and form grinders	30,000– 55,000
Optical comparators	1,500– 20,000
Small precision machine tools	5,000– 12,000

SOURCE: Records of company.

Exhibit 2

JONES & LAMSON MACHINE COMPANY

STATEMENT OF FINANCIAL CONDITION AS OF DECEMBER 31, 1959
(In Thousands)

ASSETS

Cash	$ 1,116
Receivables	1,672
Life insurance, cash value	134
Tax claim	701
Inventories (cost or standard cost)	4,598
Total Current Assets	$ 8,221
Property, plant, and equipment (net)	4,180
Other assets	561
Total	$12,962

LIABILITIES

Current	$ 1,248
Deferred income taxes	472
Capital stock, $20 par value	5,146
Surplus	6,096
Total	$12,962

SOURCE: Annual report of the company for 1959.

Exhibit 3

JONES & LAMSON MACHINE COMPANY

STATEMENT OF INCOME AND EXPENSE
(In Thousands)

	1955	1956	1957	1958	1959
Net sales........................	$16,813	$25,401	$22,013	$ 9,540	$10,911
Cost and expenses...............	15,061	20,770	18,851	10,368	11,770
Depreciation and amortization....	629	372	445	470	483
Operating profit (loss)...........	$ 1,123	$ 4,259	$ 2,717	($ 1,298)	($ 1,342)
Other income, net...............	199	(225)*	236	188	105
Income taxes (credit)............	684	2,463	1,635	(612)	(701)
Net profit (loss)................	$ 638	$ 1,571	$ 1,318	($ 498)	($ 536)
Dividends......................	418	354	515	322	257

* Includes net loss of $431,469 on liquidation of subsidiary.
SOURCE: *Moody's Industrials.*

Exhibit 4

JONES & LAMSON MACHINE COMPANY

ANALYSIS OF CUSTOMERS FOR FIRST SIX MONTHS OF 1960

Product Line	Total Number of Customers	Total Number of New Customers	Lease Plan Customers	New Lease Plan Customers	Conditional Sales Customers	New Conditional Sales Customers
Turret........................	41	25	9	8	2	1
Fay automatic lathe............	9	1	...	...	...	...
Thread grinder.................	12	2	...	...	...	...
Positioning table...............	4	...	1	...	...	...
Boring machine................	15	11	2	2	...	...
Comparator....................	192	100	14	12	16	12
Totals.................	273	139	26	22	18	13

Of total customers, 51% were new customers.
Of lease plan customers, 85% were new customers.
Of conditional sales customers, 72% were new customers.
SOURCE: Records of company.

Exhibit 5

JONES & LAMSON MACHINE COMPANY

NET ORDERS RECEIVED, 1955–60

Year	Total Net Orders	Outright Sales	Lease	Conditional Sales Contract	Total Domestic Orders	Foreign Orders*
1955............	$24,483,632	$22,954,231	$224,860	$ 730,390	$23,909,481	$ 574,151
1956............	24,450,813	21,996,761	45,200	1,087,019	23,128,980	1,321,833
1957............	15,783,664	14,187,757	3,245	737,057	14,928,059	855,605
1958............	8,815,740	7,583,395	48,038	317,822	7,949,255	866,485
1959............	13,057,200	11,861,943	. . .	539,654	12,401,597	655,603
1960 (first 7 months only)..	7,564,186	5,467,041	413,457	141,128	6,021,626	1,542,560

* Foreign orders are not included in figures for outright sales, lease sales, or conditional sales contract sales.

SOURCE: Records of company.

Exhibit 6

JONES & LAMSON MACHINE COMPANY

IRS REGULATIONS GIVING GUIDES FOR TAX TREATMENT
OF LEASES OF EQUIPMENT

The following excerpts from the tax regulations of the Internal Revenue Service in 1960 are taken from the Prentice-Hall *Federal Tax Report Bulletin.*

Guides to be used in determining the treatment, for Federal income tax purposes, of leases of equipment used in the trade or business of the lessee.

. . . .

Sec. 3.02. In deciding whether a taxpayer is entitled to a deduction for any payments claimed to represent rentals . . . it is necessary to determine whether by virtue of the agreement the lessee has acquired, or will acquire, title to or an equity in the property.

. . . .

Sec. 4.01. Whether an agreement, which in form is a lease, is in substance a conditional sales contract depends upon the intent of the parties. . . . In ascertaining such intent no single test, or any special combination of tests is absolutely determinative. . . . However, . . . in the absence of compelling persuasive factors of contrary implication an intent warranting treatment of a transaction for tax purposes as a purchase and sale rather than as a lease or rental agreement may . . . be said to exist if, for example, one or more of the following conditions are present:

. . . .

(c) The total amount which the lessee is required to pay for a relatively short period of use constitutes an inordinately large proportion of the total sum required to be paid to secure transfer of the title. . . .

(d) The agreed rental payments materially exceed the current fair rental

Exhibit 6—Continued

value. This may be indicative that the payments include an element other than compensation for the use of property. . . .

(*e*) The property may be acquired under a purchase option at a price which is nominal in relation to the value of the property at the time when the option may be exercised, as determined at the time of entering into the original agreement, or which is a relatively small amount when compared with the total payments which are required to be made. . . .

. . . .

Sec. 2.02.

(*d*) Agreements which provide for the payment of "rental" for a short original term in relation to the expected life of the equipment, with provision for continued use over substantially all of the remaining useful life of the equipment. During the initial term of the agreement, the "rental" approximates the normal purchase price of the equipment, plus interest, while the rentals during the remaining term or renewal period or periods are insignificant when compared to the initial rental. These agreements may or may not provide for an option to acquire legal title to the equipment upon the termination of the initial period or at any stated time thereafter.

(*e*) Agreements similar to the arrangement in (*d*) above, but with the added factor that the manufacturer of the equipment purports to sell it to a credit or finance company, which either takes an assignment of such an existing agreement with the user or itself later enters into such an agreement with the user. In some instances, the lessor may be a trustee acting for or on behalf of the original vendor.

. . . .

Sec. 4.02.   The fact that the agreement makes no provision for the transfer of title or specifically precludes the transfer of title does not, of itself, prevent the contract from being held to be a sale of an equitable interest in the property.

. . . .

Sec. 4.05.   In the absence of compelling factors indicating a different intent, it will be presumed that a conditional sales contract was intended if the total of the rental payments and any option price payable in addition thereto approximates the price at which the equipment could have been acquired by purchase at the time of entering into the agreement, plus interest and/or carrying charges. . . .

Sec. 4.06.   If the sum of the specified rentals over a relatively short part of the expected useful life of the equipment approximates the price at which the equipment could have been acquired by purchase at the time of entering into the agreement, plus interest and/or carrying charges on such amount, and the lessee may continue to use the equipment for an additional period or periods approximating its remaining estimated useful life for relatively nominal or token payments, it may be assumed that the parties have entered into a sale contract, even though a passage of title is not expressly provided in the agreement. Agreements of the type described in section 2.02(*d*), and (*e*), above, in general, will be held to be sales contracts.

Source: Prentice-Hall, Inc., *Federal Tax Report Bulletin*, September 1, 1955, Par. 77, 416 (Rev. Rul. 55–540. IRB 1955–1935). Reprinted by permission of Prentice-Hall, Inc.

Exhibit 7
JONES & LAMSON MACHINE COMPANY
COMPARISON OF CASH FLOWS (NET AFTER TAXES AT 50%) OF CUSTOMER UNDER
PROFITIVITY LEASE PLAN AND TERMINAL VALUE LEASE PLAN
Example: Customer Purchases $12,000 of Equipment at Beginning of Each Lease Period

Year	Profitivity Lease Plan*		Terminal Value Lease Plan†			
	Treated as Lease by IRS	Treated as Purchase by IRS‡	3-Year Lease§ (25% Terminal Value)	5-Year Lease‖ (20% Terminal Value)	7½-Year Lease¶ (15% Terminal Value)	10-Year Lease** (10% Terminal Value)
1	$1,476	$1,139	$ 1,776	$ 1,236	$ 956	$ 816
2	1,476	1,479	1,776	1,236	956	816
3	1,476	1,782	1,776	1,236	956	816
4	1,476	2,062	1,776	1,236	956	816
5	1,476	2,324	1,776	1,236	956	816
6	148	(157)	1,776	1,236	956	816
7	148	(145)	1,776	1,236	956	816
8	148	(134)	1,776	1,236	956	816
9	148	(122)	1,776	1,236	956	816
10	148	(108)	1,776	1,236	956	816
	$8,120	$8,120	$17,760	$12,360	$9,560	$8,160

* Customer is committed only for the first five years. For purposes of comparison, assumption is made that rental of equipment for an additional five years at the reduced rental rate is economically feasible for the customer.

† The bank's add-on charges under the terminal value lease plans were computed on the entire purchase price of the equipment ($12,000).

‡ Depreciation computed on double declining balance for the first five years and straight line basis for the second five years. Assumption is made that bank add-on charges are allowable as a tax deduction at a constant rate (approximately 9% on a present value basis) applied to a declining average annual principal balance over estimated 10-year life.

§ Customer has use of new equipment every three years, but is committed only for 3-year rental payment periods.

‖ Customer has use of new equipment every five years, but is committed for 5-year rental payment periods.

¶ Customer is committed for 7½-year rental payment periods.

** Customer is committed for 10-year rental payment period.

Exhibit 8

JONES & LAMSON MACHINE COMPANY

Comparison of New Equipment Sales to Customer and Used Equipment Purchases from Bank*
Under Profitivity Lease Plan and Terminal Value Allowance Plan

Example: Assuming Jones & Lamson Sells $12,000 of New Equipment to the Customer at Beginning of Each Lease Period

End of Year	Profitivity Lease Plan† Sales	Terminal Value Lease Plan							
		3-Year Lease Plan (25% Terminal Value)		5-Year Lease Plan (20% Terminal Value)		7½-Year Lease Plan (15% Terminal Value)		10-Year Lease Plan (10% Terminal Value)	
		Purchases	Sales	Purchases	Sales	Purchases	Sales	Purchases	Sales
0	$12,000	...	$12,000	...	$12,000	...	$12,000	...	$12,000
1	...	...	...	...	...	...	...	...	...
2	...	...	...	...	...	...	...	...	...
3	...	$3,000	12,000	...	...	...	...	...	...
4	...	...	...	...	...	...	...	...	...
5	...	...	...	$2,400	12,000	...	...	...	...
6	...	3,000	12,000	...	...	...	...	...	...
7	...	...	...	...	...	$1,800	12,000	...	...
8	...	...	...	...	...	...	...	...	...
9	12,000	3,000	12,000	...	...	...	...	...	...
10		...	...	2,400	12,000	...	...	$1,200	12,000
	$24,000	$9,000	$48,000	$4,800	$36,000	$1,800	$24,000	$1,200	$24,000

* Purchase of used equipment from bank is made at terminal value amount as originally set up under corresponding lease plan. These amounts will be carried in inventory until the equipment is sold to a secondhand dealer or otherwise disposed of. Sale of used equipment is not considered in these figures.
† Assuming that customer elects to lease for 10-year period.

Exhibit 9

JONES & LAMSON MACHINE COMPANY

FUNDS FLOW ESTIMATES FOR 1960 AND 1961
(In Thousands)

FUNDS PROVIDED	1960	1961
From operations............................	($300)	$ 750
Depreciation and amortization..............	460	480
Total...............................	$160	$1,230
Dividends declared........................	257	257
Net Funds Provided..................	($ 97)	$ 973
Increase or (decrease) in working capital.......	($200)	500
Total Funds Provided.................	$103	$ 473

FUNDS APPLIED		
Purchase of new plant and equipment.........	$103	$ 423
Increase in noncurrent assets.................	. . .	50
Total Funds Applied..................	$103	$ 473

(   ) Indicates deficit.
SOURCE: Forecast by company.

KOEHRING FINANCE CORPORATION

In June, 1958, Orville Mertz, vice president of the Koehring Company in Milwaukee, was considering formation of a wholly owned subsidiary as a means of financing installment sales receivables and inventory-secured distributors' notes. Koehring was a widely diversified multidivision manufacturer of heavy machinery, primarily construction equipment. It competed against a few much larger manufacturers across several product lines, as well as against a larger number of intermediate and smaller sized companies in a single line or a few product lines each. Koehring stock was widely held and traded actively over the counter.

In the preceding 5 fiscal years, Koehring's receivables had risen from 8% to more than 14% of sales. In addition, sales growth and mergers had contributed to greatly enlarging receivables in absolute terms from $2.1 million at the end of 1953 to approximately $8 million at the end of 1957. In early 1958, the company adopted a program of financing customer and distributor notes with its own funds under several different arrangements. Another part of the same program—a system of loan guarantees offered by the company—had been a vain attempt to induce banks to absorb the receivables, but the greater burden had fallen directly on Koehring. In the first half of 1958, requests for longer terms had become more rather than less common. Exhibit 1 shows that despite a sales decline, receivables had continued to rise after the previous fiscal year-end in November, 1957. This pattern of receivables growth had been quite common in Koehring's industry through the late 1950's, and a number of Koehring's competitors had formed subsidiaries as a device for financing their ballooning deferred payment receivables. Several economic indicators pointed to an early end of the recession that had started late in 1957,[1] and a rising sales rate thereafter would renew the pressure on Koehring's funds. Inventory reduction had supplied ample liquidity thus far in 1958, but Mr. Mertz knew that it was only a question of time until inventory rebuilding and receivables growth made his working capital financing an acute problem.

Whatever solution was finally devised, however, Mr. Mertz believed that it would involve either recourse to debt or the disposal of receivables. Mid-1958 projections placed internally generated funds at about $2.9 million for the

---

[1] Company shipments in the quarter ending in February, 1958, had been only 65% of the corresponding quarter's shipments 1 year earlier; but for the quarter ending in May, the figure was 76%, and the trend had accelerated in June with seasonal pickup and what seemed to be cyclically reviving construction expenditures.

year—about $1.7 million of depreciation and something over $1.2 million of profit—against planned expenditures for plant and equipment of slightly over $1 million and debt service requirements of slightly under $.5 million for sinking funds and $.6 to $.7 million of interest. In addition, preferred stock dividends of over $.2 million and common stock dividends of more than $.8 million were anticipated. Since the sale of equity was inadvisable in a recession year and viewed askance by the board of directors in any event, the alternatives were reduced to adding debt or disposing of receivables by sale or discounting. Substantial amounts of long-term and short-term debt were already outstanding (see the balance sheets in Exhibit 1). It was particularly distressing that Koehring had been unable to meet the annual clean-up requirements on its bank borrowings in the last two years. (See footnote to Exhibit 2.) If Koehring issued more debt, it would be at the price of using up a part of the company's debt capacity, which was already somewhat pressed.

FINANCING THROUGH BANKS OR INDEPENDENT FINANCE COMPANIES

One alternative was the factoring or discounting of Koehring's deferred payment receivables with banks or independent finance companies. Although he had not fully investigated this possibility, Mr. Mertz doubted its viability. If limited loan capacity and unwillingness to buy construction machinery paper were partly responsible for secondary demand on manufacturers for financing, there was little reason to think that the banks would be receptive to the purchase of receivables from Koehring itself. Mr. Mertz thought the same observations probably applied to independent commercial finance companies. Even assuming the availability of financing to Koehring itself from either or both of these two possible sources, however, significant loss of control from exclusive reliance on external sources with indeterminate commitments might be entailed. Nevertheless, placement of the retail receivables with banks or independent finance companies could substantially lessen the burden on Koehring's resources, and so remained an alternative with some attraction.

Since commercial finance companies often limited the amount of financing extended on receivables to an approximation of the sales price less markup as a means of reducing risk of loss on repossession, it would be fortunate if commercial finance companies financed as much as 75% of the sale price of equipment less the buyer's down payment, and it would not be surprising if the percentage was less. Effective interest rates could run from 12 to 15%, if not higher, and loan service charges, including the cost of audits, would be borne by the finance companies' customers.

Another impairment of control would be Koehring's inability to regulate the risk assumed on retail paper. Outside lenders would undoubtedly require some assurance of the quality of the receivables. This requirement might prove cumbersome if Koehring decided to alter the risk it wished to assume from time to time, depending on the sales rate.

A related point was the problem of financing wholesale paper. For many years, Koehring had financed distributors' inventories, and was continuing to do so. Banks and independent finance companies were always reluctant, at best, to lend on inventory other than automobiles because of the notoriously high risk and limited return. Only when a tie-in of lucrative retail paper was offered would these lenders assent to wholesale financing. A sales finance company president's testimony before a congressional subcommittee, which Mr. Mertz had recently read, had explained that president's attitude toward wholesale financing of dealer automobile inventories.

There prevails a tendency to believe wholesale financing is a plain, simple, safe, bank-lending type of operation. It is not this at all. The risks in wholesale automobile financing are considerable; the amounts involved very large. It is the finance company, however, that is left holding the bag when economic dislocations take place, dealers go out of business, dealers sell cars for which they are unable to pay, find themselves in a frozen position, or have many other reasons for not being able to pay their debts.

Although Mr. Mertz had no doubt that wholesale financing involved substantial risk, he knew that it would be literally impossible for Koehring to omit providing for distributor inventory financing. If an arrangement was concluded with an outside lender, enforceable provision for inventory financing would be imperative.

An additional disadvantage of using independent finance companies was the possibility of jeopardizing Koehring's relations with its distributors and customers. Often, Koehring overlooked slow payment of individual accounts when a long history of association warranted it, but an independent finance company certainly would relentlessly dun slow accounts.

FINANCING THROUGH THE PARENT OR A CREDIT CAPTIVE

The alternative, as Mr. Mertz saw it, was to finance both retail and wholesale paper within Koehring, as in the past, or through a captive finance company. The internal course would mean further borrowing, probably bank loans.

Formation of a credit captive was seemingly an eligible device. It intrigued Mr. Mertz particularly because of the manifest success that Koehring's rivals enjoyed with theirs. Koehring's large competitors—Caterpillar, International Harvester, Clark Equipment, and, most recently, Allis–Chalmers—all had formed captives in the preceding decade. For many years, the Euclid Division of General Motors, which manufactured earthmoving machinery, had used the credit facilities of Yellow Manufacturing Acceptance Corporation, a GM captive.

Operation of the captives seemed to have several financial advantages. Existence of the captives made it possible for the parents to divest themselves of growing receivables and free funds for other parent uses. What appeared especially interesting to Mr. Mertz was the reported ability of the captives to pyramid debt in multiples of several times their equity bases in capital structures much more similar to those of independent finance companies than to industrial corporation norms. In circumstances that made Koehring's use of increased debt almost certain, this feature was particularly attractive. In answer to Mr. Mertz's request for capital structure data on Koehring's competitors and their captives, a staff assistant had supplied the information contained in Exhibits 5 and 6.

Since it was evident that a captive must rely on bank financing, at least in the early years of its life, Mr. Mertz canvassed the loan officers in Koehring's regular group of six banks. Stenographic transcriptions of some recollections of four of these conferences and a verbatim reproduction of an arithmetic illustration used by one banker appear below.

Bank A

Favors formation of a captive company. Says it would be a good means to beat the problem of the annual clean-up requirement, which is now becoming a near necessity. Selling receivables to a captive would enable the parent to liquidate its bank indebtedness. Argued that this would improve the parent's balance sheet. Used an example to show the process.

Company A		Company B	
CA..............	$100	CA..............	$250
Deferred rec.......$50		Deferred rec......$150	
CL..............	50	CL..............	200
NWC............	$ 50	NWC............	$ 50
FA.............	50	FA.............	50
NW.............	$100	NW.............	$100

Balance sheet of company B is much worse than that of company A, even though both have the same net working capital and fixed asset and equity structures. But if company B forms a captive, and parent sells $150 of deferred payment receivables to it:

Company B		Captive	
CA..................$ 70		Deferred rec............$150	
CL.................. 50		CL.................... 120	
NWC................$ 20		Equity.................$ 30	
Investment in captive...... 30			
FA.................... 50			
NW..................$100			

Says he feels more secure lending to a finance company than to a parent company anyway, because the receivables are good security. Claims that bank examiners treat loans to finance companies much more leniently than corresponding loans to nonfinancial corporations.

Bank B

Emphasized that separation of deferred payment receivables in a captive finance company would make it easier to apply standards of evaluation and debt limits traditionally applied by banks to finance companies. Debt limits placed on independent finance companies and tests of their balance sheets cannot be applied to a manufacturing company, but if a subsidiary is formed these tests and financing limits apply with minor modification.

Prefers to have a Koehring captive hold receivables rather than buy them directly from us, because our captive can make sure legal requirements for adequate security are met where paper is recorded in the individual states. Also, says we can hold safety of collateral under surveillance, but banks cannot. Confirmed that it was easier to deal with bank examiners if receivables-secured loans are made to finance companies.

Bank C

Thinks captive finance companies are simply another device for stretching equity even thinner than it is now in corporate finance generally, which is plenty thin, according to him.

Contends that in the case of captives the security is inferior to that offered creditors by an independent finance company because receivables of captives are less diversified. Also, wholesale paper held by captives is weaker security than the retail receivables held by independent finance companies.

Insists that there is little or no preference on his part between lending on receivables held in escrow or in a collateral trust and lending on those held by a captive finance company.

Expressed confidence in our management, however, and said that our long borrowing history with the [name of bank withheld] was sufficient to enable us to procure a line of credit for a captive.

Bank D

Pointed out that in many instances they evaluate parent and captive finance companies as a unit, and limit the combination's borrowing to a ceiling. Either the parent or the captive can use as much of the line as it wants, but the two together cannot borrow more than the limit. However, he also said his bank extended credit lines to parent and captives separately in other cases, and made no direct statement that it was their intention to make the line an "either or" proposition in our case. Our deposit balances have always been ample at this bank. I believe we will have no difficulty on this score.

As a basis for further discussion with his bankers, Mr. Mertz prepared a booklet describing his plan for a proposed subsidiary, which he had decided to call Koehring Finance Corporation. Excerpts appear in Exhibit 2; also from the booklet are pro forma balance sheets for Koehring Finance, reflecting the plan for its financing at different operating levels (Exhibit 3), and a pro forma balance sheet for the parent company, reflecting the formation of the subsidiary (Exhibit 4). Mr. Mertz was virtually certain that arrangements for financing the subsidiary could be consummated substantially as planned. However, he was bothered by two misgivings. First, although it was popularly supposed that formation of a subsidiary raises the debt-bearing capacity of parent and captive combined, and though relatively little difficulty had been experienced in making preliminary arrangements for Koehring Finance, Mr. Mertz was curious about the ultimate effect that the removal of receivables

from the asset structure of the parent would have on its ability to raise
additional outside financing in the future. Second, Mr. Mertz felt strongly
that any decision about receivables financing must be made in full recognition
of its probable consequences for equity prices and, in turn, the company's
cost of capital.

Exhibit 1

KOEHRING FINANCE CORPORATION

CONDENSED BALANCE SHEETS AND SELECTED FINANCIAL DATA FOR KOEHRING COMPANY

(Dollar Figures in Thousands)

	November 30, 1957	February 28, 1958	May 31, 1958
ASSETS			
Current assets:			
Cash	$ 2,288	$ 1,278	$ 2,614
Notes and accounts receivable:			
Installment and deferred notes	3,921	2,634	2,823
Distributors' notes—floor planning		1,172	1,348
Trade accounts	4,075	4,455	5,091
Miscellaneous	152	56	222
Less: Loss reserve	(178)	(179)	(183)
Net receivables	$ 7,970	$ 8,138	$ 9,301
Inventories	26,259	24,983	22,031
Other	572	586	578
Total Current Assets	$37,089	$34,985	$34,524
Investments	187	180	180
Net fixed assets	11,184	10,979	10,977
Other assets	13	13	13
Total Assets	$48,473	$46,157	$45,694
LIABILITIES			
Current liabilities:			
Notes payable	$ 6,990	$ 5,816	$ 5,406
Trade accounts payable	1,289	1,115	1,236
Long-term debt due within 1 year	488	488	488
Accruals	3,990	3,049	2,834
Total Current Liabilities	$12,757	$10,468	$ 9,964
Long-term debt:			
4¼% notes	$ 3,078	$ 7,932	$ 7,870
5¼% notes	4,500		
4¾% first mortgage bonds	436	436	410
Total Long-Term Debt	$ 8,014	$ 8,368	$ 8,280
Stockholders' investment:			
5%, cumulative convertible preferred	$ 4,317	$ 4,317	$ 4,311
Common stock and paid-in capital	12,124	12,167	12,150
Retained earnings	11,261	10,837	10,989
Total Net Worth	$27,702	$27,321	$27,450
Total Liabilities and Capital	$48,473	$46,157	$45,694
Market value of long-term securities:			
Long-term debt, yield adjusted	$ 7,819	$ 8,477	$ 8,367
Preferred stock, yield adjusted	4,212	4,311	4,297
Common stock, at bid price	20,567	24,543	20,226
Earnings after tax, year ended November 30, 1957	$ 1,937		
Interest paid, year ended November 30, 1957	660		

Exhibit 2

KOEHRING FINANCE CORPORATION

EXCERPTS FROM "FORMATION OF KOEHRING FINANCE SUBSIDIARY"

The cash and working capital management for a manufacturing activity differ considerably from that of a financing activity. The more liquid character of deferred payment notes receivable is distinct from plant and equipment or basic inventory requirements, and lends itself to financing through a finance company subsidiary rather than attempting to blend these requirements with those of the manufacturing parent.

We discussed with Caterpillar Tractor Company and Allis-Chalmers Manufacturing Company the formation and operation of their successful finance company subsidiaries. As a result of these talks, and analysis of our circumstances, we plan to establish a finance company similar to theirs in many respects, but with adaptations to meet Koehring requirements.

It is the purpose of this presentation to outline to you our proposed method of operation and related bank loan requirements.

It is intended that the finance company be organized as a wholly owned subsidiary. Of the authorized capital stock, Koehring would initially buy $250,000 at par. In addition, the finance company would issue and the parent company would buy, at par, the 6% subordinated debentures of the finance company in the amount of $1 million. These would be repayable in equal installments, annually over a 20-year period, commencing 5 years after sale.

Additional sales of both common stock and debentures might be made from time to time to support the operations of the finance company at a higher level of activity, if that were justified by experience and the success of the operation.

The remaining cash requirements of the finance company would be met by use of its short-term lines of credit with its principal banks, which will be the banks that Koehring Company uses presently.

It is our intent to have a maximum period on any transaction [i.e., receivable] of five years, but to keep very limited the number of deals written for such a period. We presently have only a very few outstanding for as long as 3 years; 86% of the total amount outstanding is due within 1 year.

Paper to be purchased by the finance company would be purchased from the parent company on a without-recourse basis. The parent company would warrant that the paper was valid and properly recorded. It is planned that the paper be purchased on a basis that would create a 10% reserve fund against which credit losses could be charged unless the parent company exercised an option to buy back defaulted notes.

Our lenders have agreed to the amendments to our long-term loan agreements[1] that are necessary to enable us to form such a subsidiary finance company.

---

[1] A footnote to the balance sheet published in the *Annual Report* for 1957 read in part: ". . . short-term borrowings are limited [under the long-term loan agreements] to $12,000,000 with the further requirement that the Company be free of such borrowings for a period of 90 days annually."

Agreement had been obtained in principle from the insurance companies holding the long-term debt to change this provision to read ". . . short-term borrowings are limited to $12,000,000 (not including debt of the unconsolidated Koehring Finance Corporation) with a further requirement that the consolidated companies be free of such borrowings for 90 days annually."

Exhibit 2—Continued

Our present planning is that we will set up an initial bank line of about $5 million. The beginning balance sheet will be as shown in [Exhibit 3]. You will notice that our pro forma statements contemplate a 90-day clean-up period each year. By staggering this period evenly over each year, a maximum of 75% of the line will be outstanding at any one time. This method of operating would result in a program whereby we would not exceed a short-term debt to equity ratio of about 3 to 1.

Exhibit 3

KOEHRING FINANCE CORPORATION

Pro Forma Balance Sheets
(Dollar Figures in Thousands)

Assumptions

1. 4 to 1 subordinated debenture to capital stock ratio.
2. 4 to 1 bank line to capital ratio.
3. 75% of total bank line outstanding as an average maximum assuming 90-day clean-up required each year at each bank.
4. 20% compensating balance required for total line.
5. 10% of average receivables withheld as reserve.
6. Koehring Inter-American (a Western Hemisphere Trade Corporation) will retain their financed receivables at the outset.

	Pro Forma Beginning Basis	Maximum Customer Paper to Be Financed and Corresponding Bank Line and Capital Requirements		
Bank line	$5,000	$5,000	$6,000	$7,000
Assets				
Cash	$1,000	$1,000	$1,200	$1,400
Receivables	$3,500	$4,444	$5,333	$6,222
Less: Reserve	350	444	533	622
Net	$3,150	$4,000	$4,800	$5,600
Total Assets	$4,150	$5,000	$6,000	$7,000
Liabilities				
Bank loans	$2,900	$3,750	$4,500	$5,250
Capital				
Subordinated debentures	$1,000	$1,000	$1,200	$1,400
Capital stock	250	250	300	350
	$1,250	$1,250	$1,500	$1,750
Total Liabilities	$4,150	$5,000	$6,000	$7,000

Exhibit 4

KOEHRING FINANCE CORPORATION

PRO FORMA BALANCE SHEETS FOR KOEHRING COMPANY REFLECTING FORMATION OF KOEHRING FINANCE CORPORATION

(Dollar Figures in Thousands)

	5/31/58 Statement	Adjust- ments	Pro Forma Beginning Balances	Pro Forma Forecasted Balance at 8/31/58
ASSETS				
Cash	$ 2,610	$(1,250)* 3,150† (2,900)‡	$ 1,610	$ 1,250
Receivables				
Notes	$ 4,000	(3,150)†	$ 850	$ 900
Other	5,300		5,300	5,300
	$ 9,300		$ 6,150	$ 6,200
Inventories and miscellaneous				
assets	22,600		22,600	21,000
Total Current Assets	$34,510		$30,360	$28,450
Investments	180	1,250*	1,430	1,400
Fixed assets	11,000		11,000	10,600
Total Assets	$45,690		$42,790	$40,450
LIABILITIES				
Short-term loans				
U.S.	$ 4,000	(2,900)‡	$ 1,100	. . .
Canada	1,400		1,400	. . .
Total	$ 5,400		$ 2,500	. . .
Other payables	4,560		4,560	$ 4,700
Total Current Liabilities	$ 9,960		$ 7,060	$ 4,700
Long-term loans	8,280		8,280	8,100
Net capital and surplus	27,450		27,450	27,650
Total Liabilities	$45,690		$42,790	$40,450
Current ratio	3.46		4.30	6.05

* Investment in Finance Corporation: $250,000 capital stock and $1 million debentures.

† Sale of notes receivable to finance corporation at 90% of face value (except Koehring Inter-American notes).

‡ Payoff of short-term debt.

Exhibit 5

KOEHRING FINANCE CORPORATION

SELECTED OPERATING AND BALANCE SHEET FIGURES IN 1957*
FOR EIGHT MACHINERY MANUFACTURERS
(Dollar Figures in Millions)

COMPANIES WITH CAPTIVES

	Allis-Chalmers	Cater-pillar	Clark Equipment	International Harvester
Parent Company				
Book value				
Current liabilities	$ 84.0	$100.9	$ 15.4	$ 147.7
Accruals	61.7	100.9	15.4	147.7
Negotiated short-term debt due in 1 year	22.3	.0	.0	.0
Long-term debt	92.1	100.0	31.0	100.0
Equity	297.5	293.3	57.9	773.4
Total Liabilities and Capital	$473.6	$494.2	$104.3	$1,021.1
Earnings after tax	$ 17.80	$ 39.80	$ 8.23	$ 45.60
Interest paid	5.78	2.13	1.95	3.52
Market value†				
Negotiated debt due in 1 year	$ 22.3	$ 0.0	$ 0.0	$ 0.0
Long-term debt	79.4	96.5	31.0	83.4
Equity	183.2	542.0	79.1	498.8
Total Market Value	$284.9	$638.5	$110.1	$ 582.2
Captive Finance Subsidiary				
Negotiated debt due in 1 year‡	$ 21.4	$ 12.2	$ 30.7	$ 275.0
Long-term debt	...	...	...	35.0
Equity of parent	6.1	7.4	6.2	49.1
Total Liabilities and Capital	$ 27.5	$ 19.6	$ 36.9	$ 359.1
Earnings after tax	na	$ .23	$ .36	$ 1.70
Interest paid	$ .35e	.21e	1.05e	10.24e
Consolidated§				
Book Value				
Current liabilities	$105.4	$113.1	$ 46.1	$ 422.7
Long-term debt	92.1	100.0	31.0	130.0
Equity	297.6	294.3	58.8	787.5
Total Liabilities and Capital	$495.1	$507.4	$135.9	$1,340.2
Earnings after tax	$ 17.80+	$ 40.00	$ 8.59	$ 47.30
Interest paid	6.13e	2.34e	3.00e	13.76e
Market Value‖				
Negotiated debt due in 1 year	$ 43.7	$ 12.2	$ 30.7	$ 275.0
Long-term debt	79.4	96.5	31.0	110.8
Equity	183.2	542.0	79.1	498.8
Total Market Value	$306.3	$650.7	$140.8	$ 884.6

* For International Harvester, figures are for fiscal year ending October 31, 1957. All others are for December 31, 1957.

† Market value of long-term debt was estimated by adjusting yield to reflect market rate movements. The new price was estimated for each year-end. Market value of the equity was based on the year-end price and number of shares outstanding. Negotiated debt due in one year carried at book value.

‡ Negotiated short-term debt for the subsidiary includes a minor amount of accruals in each case.

§ None of the captive companies were consolidated with their parents in published financial statements, and none of the parents guaranteed the debt of their subsidiaries.

‖ Market value of long-term debt was estimated by adjusting yield to reflect market rate movements. The new price was estimated for each year-end. Market value of the equity was based on the year-end price and number of shares outstanding. Negotiated debt due in one year carried at book value.

e = estimated.

na = not available.

Exhibit 5—Continued

COMPANIES WITHOUT CAPTIVES

	Baldwin-Lima-Hamilton	Blaw-Knox	Link Belt	Worthington
Book Value				
Current liabilities	$ 29.4	$ 32.0	$ 22.5	$ 42.2
Accruals	27.4	26.5	22.5	30.7
Negotiated short-term debt due in 1 year	2.0	5.5	0	11.5
Long-term debt	0	19.7	0	25.0
Equity	112.4	54.4	85.2	86.3
Total Liabilities and Capital	$141.8	$106.1	$107.7	$153.5
Earnings after tax	$ 6.48	$ 7.01	$ 10.11	$ 9.92
Interest paid	0.57	1.06	0	1.64
Market Value‖				
Negotiated debt due in 1 year	$ 2.0	$ 5.5	$ 0.0	$ 11.5
Long-term debt	0	17.2	0	22.3
Equity	40.8	41.9	87.8	78.0
Total Market Value	$ 42.8	$ 64.6	$ 87.8	$111.8

Exhibit 6

KOEHRING FINANCE CORPORATION

SELECTED FINANCIAL DATA FOR EIGHT MACHINERY MANUFACTURERS
FISCAL YEAR-END 1957

Company	Debt to Total Book Value*	Debt to Total Market Value†	Return on Total Book Value‡	Return on Total Market Value§	Return on Market Value of Equity‖
Allis-Chalmers—consolidated	31.3%	40.2%	5.5%	7.8%	9.7%
Caterpillar—consolidated	27.6	16.7	10.4	6.5	7.4
Clark Equipment—consolidated	51.2	43.8	9.6	8.2	10.9
International Harvester—consolidated	34.0	43.6	5.1	6.9	9.5
Baldwin-Lima-Hamilton	1.7	4.7	6.2	16.5	15.9
Blaw-Knox	31.7	35.1	10.1	12.5	16.7
Link Belt	0.0	0.0	11.9	11.5	11.5
Worthington	29.7	30.2	9.4	10.3	12.7

* % Debt to total book value equals: [negotiated short-term debt due in 1 year + book value of long term debt] divided by [total book value of liabilities and capital, not including accruals].

† % Debt to total market value equals: [negotiated short-term debt due in 1 year + market value of long-term debt] divided by [total market value of liabilities and capital, not including accruals].

‡ % Return on total book value equals: [earnings after tax + interest paid] divided by [total book value of liabilities and capital, not including accruals].

§ % Return on total market value equals: [earnings after tax + interest paid] divided by [total market value of liabilities and capital, not including accruals].

‖ % Return on equity equals: earnings after tax divided by market value of equity.

SEARS ROEBUCK ACCEPTANCE CORP.

SEARS ROEBUCK ACCEPTANCE CORP. (SRAC) was a wholly owned subsidiary of Sears Roebuck and Co. It was organized November 16, 1956, to purchase installment receivables arising from domestic retail and mail-order sales of the parent. Sears' initial investment in the stock of the acceptance corporation was $35 million. Arrangements were made with a group of New York banks and one Philadelphia bank to set up lines of credit totaling $60 million. With this $95 million, the finance subsidiary began operations.

About a month after its inception, the acceptance corporation's short-term notes, or commercial paper,[1] were offered to investors through a brokerage firm. Additional lines of credit were offered by banks and were accepted.

During January, 1957, the acceptance corporation sold its first long-term debenture issue of $50 million through a syndicate of underwriters.

By March 1, SRAC was approaching a borrowing ratio of 4 to 1, i.e., borrowing $4 for every $1 of capital stock plus subordinated debt (called the capital base). (See Exhibit 1.) Although not a restriction of the indenture agreement, nor a limitation set by the commercial bankers, SRAC's board of directors regarded a debt ratio of 4 to 1 as an appropriate ceiling at this early point in the company's existence. Therefore, the acceptance corporation's capital base was broadened by a $15 million contribution from the parent. At the same time, SRAC's underwriters sold to the public $25 million of subordinated debentures. These two additions increased the acceptance corporation's capital base to $75 million and expanded its senior debt limit to $300 million. It remained for SRAC's management to recommend an appropriate instrument (or instruments) to increase borrowing, and to suggest a timetable for running off the unused short-term borrowing capacity.

To that point, the acceptance corporation had depended on bank borrowing and the sale of commercial paper for its short-term financing requirements. SRAC's commercial paper dealer had placed a volume of roughly $16 million on its behalf after early December. The volume of paper placed and

---

[1] Commercial paper refers to single-name, unsecured notes of both financial and non-financial corporations. These notes are sold at a discount. Yields vary with maturities and with the flux of demand and the supply of loanable funds. Borrowers use commercial paper as a substitute for, or as a supplement to, short-term bank loans. Lenders hold these notes as a part of their liquid reserves, or as a short-term earning outlet for temporarily idled funds. In the case of small or medium-sized banks, the notes also serve as an investment supplemental to loans where loan demand is below the desired level at acceptable rates and risks.

outstanding during the acceptance corporation's history is summarized in Exhibit 2.

On the morning of March 15, 1957, Donald MacArthur, the first president of SRAC and treasurer of the parent company, was in the process of deciding whether or not to recommend to the parent finance committee that SRAC place its commercial paper directly rather than through a dealer. Working with Mr. MacArthur on this problem was Donald W. Hansen, assistant treasurer, who had been brought to Sears from Commercial Credit Company at the time the acceptance corporation was formed. As manager of Commercial Credit's midwestern bank relations department, Mr. Hansen had nine years of experience in the direct placement of paper. After weighing all the factors, he was to present to Mr. MacArthur a clear picture of the benefits against the possible consequences of direct placement of notes; then Mr. MacArthur would ultimately transmit the recommendation to Sears' finance committee.

Although earlier calculations that he and his associates had prepared favored direct placement of the commercial paper, Mr. Hansen questioned some of the assumptions they rested on. Even if the projected cost savings were eventually to materialize, Mr. Hansen was not at all certain that SRAC should begin placing its own paper in a tight money market when even the U.S. Treasury was having difficulty in refunding maturing obligations. Furthermore, it was felt that a recommendation to cease placement through the company's dealer and to commence placing directly would encounter among committee members resistance stemming from nonfinancial considerations. The firm's dealer had been a friend and principal underwriter for the parent company for many years, and it was likely that the committee would be reluctant to chance a breach of relations.

SEARS ROEBUCK INSTALLMENT SALES

Sears was the world's largest general retail merchandising organization, with net sales of over $3.5 billion during the fiscal year ended January 31, 1957. Installment sales accounted for approximately 44% of the total. Sears' installment receivables outstanding on January 31, 1957, amounted to $1,039,128,814 in 8,587,764 accounts—an average of $121 per account. SRAC's purpose at inception was to absorb increases in installment accounts, plus approximately $200 million of installment contracts held by Sears. Although Sears announced that initially it would continue to sell accounts to banks, the acceptance corporation might be asked in the future to purchase receivables now held by banks, which amounted to roughly $450 million. Lengthening credit terms and a growing proportion of installment sales in Sears' total sales promised to expand the demand on SRAC's capacities even beyond this level in the very long term.

Installment contracts that the acceptance corporation purchased were paid out, on the average, in nine and one half months. Also, Sears' cash flow was subject to substantial variation with the seasons, the weather, and other influences. Both of these factors pointed to a preponderance of short-term borrowing for SRAC.

Commercial Paper

Financial qualifications for sellers of commercial paper are exacting. When underlying demand and supply conditions permit the market to flourish, the commercial paper rate reflects the superior quality of the paper's issuers. Because of the importance of financing cost to SRAC, as outlined below, management was determined to take advantage of its ability to tap this market and its rate.

Cost of debt was especially important to the acceptance corporation because, except for relatively low operating expenses, the company's profit was the difference between the rate received on receivables contracts purchased from Sears and the cost of money. The rate received from Sears early in 1957 was 5.25%. The company's cost of money had been computed as of February 28, 1957, and was as shown in Exhibit 3. It was apparent that commercial paper was SRAC's cheapest source, even including the dealer's commission.

The advantage of placing notes through a dealer lay, first, in the dealer's maintenance of a staff of sales specialists who were experienced in day-to-day transactions in the money markets and who knew which investors would be interested in purchasing the acceptance corporation's notes. Second, the dealer distributed the notes and arranged for transferring funds. Since the cost of the dealer's services was .25% per annum of the outstanding balance, the fee was wholly variable. Mr. Hansen knew that a flourishing commercial paper market, including ample fund supplies, depended on a differential between the bank borrowing rate and the rates for short-term government securities. The rates for these securities during recent periods are plotted and shown in Exhibit 4. It was comforting to management to know that the status of the commercial paper market at the present time was largely the dealer's worry.

Nevertheless, the disadvantages of placing through dealers were numerous. The most obvious was the .25% commission, which would be saved if SRAC were to sell directly. Perhaps even more important, however, was the limitation imposed by reliance on the dealer for development of potential markets. In placement through dealers there was no personal contact between borrower and ultimate lender. The acceptance corporation did not know who was investing in its paper, and therefore could not follow up at maturity with a reminder to try to gain a replacement. Also, the dealer firms placed with banks a substantial portion of the paper they handled. Since banks are limited by law on the amount of paper they can buy in any one name, Mr. Hansen doubted the feasibility of using them as principal purchasers of SRAC's notes. SRAC had in mind an immediate goal of maintaining $85 million outstanding, in contrast with the dealer's $20 million (estimated). To accomplish this objective, efforts would necessarily be concentrated on large nonfinancial corporations. If the absorptive capacity of this portion of the commercial paper market significantly eclipsed that of the dealer market, this would be an important pillar in SRAC's long-range plans to meet the increasing demands of its parent company.

If the company decided to place paper directly, the name Sears Roebuck Acceptance Corp. not only would come before financial officers of corporations and executive officers of banks but would be discussed by finance committees, executive committees, and boards of directors. This exposure would be beneficial during subsequent public flotations of debt.

Lines of credit maintained with certain banks would play a role in SRAC's financial planning, irrespective of whether commercial paper was sold to dealers or placed directly. If dealer placement was relied on, bank borrowing would make up the difference between the projected $20 million commercial paper to be maintained outstanding and total short-term financing needs. On the other hand, if direct sales became SRAC's policy election, not only would bank borrowing be needed to fill any gap in fund supplies but also open lines of bank credit would be maintained as a guarantee against the risk of being unable to refinance commercial paper at some time. It was customary to keep deposits in the lending banks to maintain lines of credit. The proportion of deposits maintained to the amount of the line of credit varied with the borrower and with activity of the account. Usual terms required stronger borrowers to maintain deposits equal to 10% of inactive lines of credit and 15% against active lines, but the same figures for intermediate-sized and small borrowers were 10% and 20%. There was some possibility for SRAC that banks could be induced to treat its deposits and those of its parent company as indistinguishable for this purpose.

The Cost of Direct Placement

In order to estimate the cost of direct placement to the acceptance corporation, several factors were considered. First, the company would need to hire men to place its notes with investors. GMAC, largest in the field, had eight such men; C.I.T., second in size, had three; Commercial Credit Company had six. Although such specialized individuals were not easily obtained, Mr. Hansen was prepared to recommend that if the company decided to place its own paper SRAC should initially place full-time contact men in New York and Chicago. Two men would be sufficient until these markets were more fully developed. To attract qualified men, the acceptance corporation would have to offer approximately $10,000 salary.

Advertising for an activity of this type would be limited to rate sheets and annual reports, because direct promotion in newspapers or magazines was prohibited by state blue-sky laws. Mr. Hansen estimated that the incremental cost of these activities and clerical assistance would amount to $15,000 per annum.

The mechanics of note issuance and transferring funds would be performed by corporate trust departments of large banks in selected cities for $2.50 per transaction.

Additional costs would be initially incurred in terms of a rate premium to be paid by the acceptance corporation on large transactions. Management had agreed that in order to encourage the acceptance of directly placed paper and to maintain outstandings at a suitable level it would be desirable to offer a premium of .125% on purchases of SRAC paper in amounts exceeding $1 million. As a matter of policy, the brokerage firm handling the placement of SRAC notes would not permit any direct placement by the company it was representing. If direct placement began, the broker's efforts on SRAC's behalf would terminate. Furthermore, the brokerage firm would not divulge the names of SRAC note purchasers. (As this was bearer paper, and usually held in custody by a bank, endorsements seldom appeared when the notes were presented for payment.) It was for these reasons that an initial premium as a sales weapon was considered essential. It was difficult to predict how long the premium would be required, but Mr. Hansen thought that under favorable money market conditions the rate incentive might be lifted after the first six months of operations.

Competition and the Market

Despite what he thought was a cost advantage of direct placement, Mr. Hansen was quite concerned with the competition SRAC would face in the direct placement field. A new name would encounter difficulty in entering an oligopsony composed of five companies who were the entirety of direct sellers. These companies—General Motors Acceptance Corporation, Commercial Credit Company, C.I.T., Associates Investment Company, and General Electric Credit Corporation—at mid-1955 accounted for 70% of total commercial paper placements. In Exhibit 5, the amount of paper placed through brokers and in direct sales is illustrated by year for the period after the 1920's. Almost entirely, the paper issued by nonfinancial corporations is included in the total sold through brokers.

The commercial paper rate was ordinarily .25 to .5% higher than U.S. Government securities of comparable maturity. When government rates changed significantly, one of the companies would take the lead and raise or lower rates. The others followed almost immediately. It was for this reason that Mr. Hansen was hesitant about the acceptance corporation's proposed rate incentive plan to force entry into the direct placement market. Although rate concessions appeared to be the best device for getting on the approved lending list of corporate treasurers, reaction of other commercial paper sellers was not predictable.

In addition to reviewing the competitive structure within the commercial paper industry, Mr. Hansen also studied other investment media competing with commercial paper for short-term investors' funds. The principal competitive instruments for short-term funds were obligations of the federal government, whose advantages were their unmatched liquidity and marketability. Holdings of such securities and other short-term investments by nonfinancial corporations during recent years are listed in Exhibit 6. The holdings of commercial paper classified according to functional class of investor at a recent date are shown in Exhibit 7.

Exhibit 1

SEARS ROEBUCK ACCEPTANCE CORP.

BALANCE SHEET AS OF FEBRUARY 28, 1957

ASSETS

Current assets:

Customer installment contracts (including installments
maturing after one year) purchased from Sears Roebuck and Co. without recourse.................... $156,771,076
Less portion of purchase price withheld pending collection (including allowance for uncollectible accounts of $1,567,710)........................... 15,789,391

		$140,981,685
Cash...		742,292
Accounts receivable from Sears Roebuck and Co........		3,397,897
Prepaid interest on:		
Notes payable to banks.........................$	483,333	
Commercial paper outstanding....................	173,492	656,825
Total Current Assets...........................		$145,778,699
Organization expense.................................		38,302
Unamortized debenture discount and expense...........		998,157
		$146,815,158

LIABILITIES AND STOCKHOLDERS' EQUITY

Current liabilities:		
Notes payable to banks............................		$ 50,000,000
Commercial paper outstanding......................		10,753,000
Accrued interest on debentures.....................		373,802
Federal income taxes..............................		326,163
Other accrued taxes...............................		248
Unearned discount.................................		18,899
Other accrued expenses............................		7,813
Total Current Liabilities.......................		$ 61,479,925
4⅝% debentures, due 1972..........................		50,000,000
Stockholders' equity:		
Capital stock, par value $100 per share; authorized, 500,000 shares; issued and outstanding, 350,000 shares...$35,000,000		
Earned surplus, January 31, 1957.....................	235,035	
Net income for February, 1957.......................	100,198	35,335,233
		$146,815,158

Exhibit 2

SEARS ROEBUCK ACCEPTANCE CORP.

COMMERCIAL PAPER PLACEMENT AND VOLUME OUTSTANDING,
DECEMBER 12, 1956–MARCH 15, 1957

First Transaction, December 12, 1956

	Outstanding*	Cumulative Volume Placed†
December 31, 1956	$ 8,620,000	$ 8,620,000
January 15, 1957	11,185,000	12,233,000
January 31, 1957	11,188,000	13,248,000
February 15, 1957	11,878,000	14,818,000
February 28, 1957	10,753,000	15,758,000
March 15, 1957	11,070,000	16,878,000

* Outstanding refers to the balances of short-term notes outstanding as of the recorded dates.

† Volume Placed refers to the aggregate volume of notes placed by SRAC's broker in the company's behalf after the first transaction.

Exhibit 3

SEARS ROEBUCK ACCEPTANCE CORP.

PERTINENT DATA ON RELATIVE COST OF MONEY, FEBRUARY, 1957

Bank Loans

Total credit lines	$136,650,000
Average unused credit lines	86,171,429
Average, gross credit lines in use	50,478,571
Less: Prepaid discount on borrowing date	506,663
Average balance required to support lines	9,000,000
Average net credit lines in use	40,971,908
Discount charged out during month	157,044
True per-annum cost, based on net credit lines*	4.93%

Short-Term Notes

Average daily outstanding, gross	11,722,464
Average daily outstanding, after discount	11,488,434
Discount charged out	34,754
True per-annum cost, based on net available	3.89%
Gross outstandings as of February 28, 1957	10,753,000
Volume, fiscal year to date (January 31 to February 28)	2,510,000

Long-Term Debt

Average outstanding, gross	50,000,000
Average net available after discount and expenses	48,898,362
Interest, discount, and expense charged out	180,803
True per-annum cost, based on average net available	4.82%

Total Debt

Average outstanding, gross	112,201,035
Average net funds available after interest, discount, and expenses	101,358,704
Total interest, discount, and expenses charged out	372,601
True per-annum cost, based on average net available	4.76%

* The following procedure is used to compute true per-annum cost: (a) discount charged out during month is converted to an average daily discount and then to an annual discount, multiplying the daily figure by 360; (b) the resulting annual discount figure is divided by average credit lines in use to ascertain true per-annum cost, based on net credit lines. The true per-annum cost for the other financial instruments is similarly computed.

Exhibit 4

SEARS ROEBUCK ACCEPTANCE CORP.

MONTHLY AVERAGES OF WEEKLY YIELDS FOR THREE-MONTH TREASURY BILLS,
PRIME COMMERCIAL PAPER, AND PRIME BANK LOAN RATE

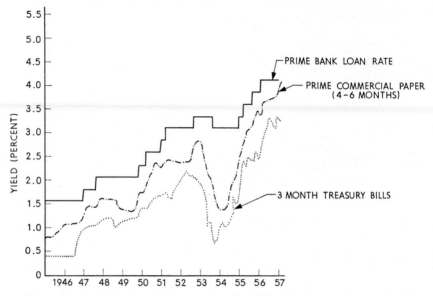

SOURCE: Standard & Poor's monthly average of weekly yields.

Exhibit 5

SEARS ROEBUCK ACCEPTANCE CORP.

VOLUME OF COMMERCIAL PAPER OUTSTANDING BY CHANNEL OF
DISTRIBUTION AND NUMBER OF ISSUERS

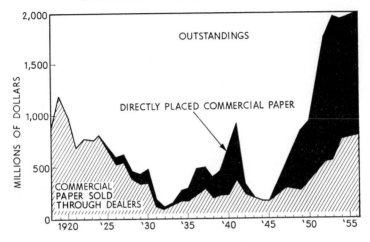

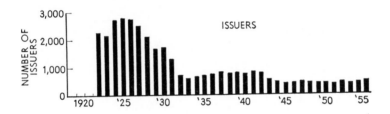

Exhibit 6

SEARS ROEBUCK ACCEPTANCE CORP.

Short-Term Investments Portfolio of 276 Large Corporations
(000,000's omitted)

	1952 Amount	%	1953 Amount	%	1954 Amount	%	1955 Amount	%
Treasury securities								
91-day bills	$ 2,919.3	33.3	$ 2,804.7	29.7	$ 2,534.2	28.3	$ 3,177.0	26.9
180 days or less	1,459.7	16.6	2,025.1	21.4	2,713.5	30.3	2,809.3	23.8
181 days–1 year	1,364.5	15.6	1,211.7	12.8	1,703.0	19.0	2,461.9	20.9
Over 1 year	2,189.4	25.0	2,431.8	25.7	1,197.8	13.4	1,767.4	15.0
Total Treasuries	$ 7,932.9	90.5	$ 8,473.3	89.6	$ 8,148.5	91.0	$10,215.6	86.6
Securities held under repurchase agreements (mostly Treasuries)	$ 351.0	4.0	$ 423.0	4.5	$ 192.2	2.2	$ 643.8	5.5
Government agency securities	38.9	.4	41.4	.4	38.7	.4	118.6	1.0
Tax-exempt securities	12.6	.1	47.2	.5	155.0	1.7	240.4	2.0
Foreign government securities	105.1	1.2	48.4	.5	48.6	.5	81.3	.7
Directly placed commercial paper	166.4	1.9	222.3	2.4	215.3	2.4	280.9	2.4
Dealer placed commercial paper	117.6	1.4	155.1	1.6	115.8	1.3	163.3	1.4
All other securities	39.0	.5	45.8	.5	48.5	.5	45.9	.4
Total All Securities	$ 8,763.5	100.0	$ 9,456.5	100.0	$ 8,962.6	100.0	$11,789.8	100.0
Cash	$ 6,065.8		$ 5,966.0		$ 6,222.8		$ 6,418.6	
Other current assets	25,260.6		26,586.6		26,432.6		27,814.8	
Total current assets	40,089.9		42,009.1		41,618.0		46,023.2	

SOURCE: *Fortune*, August, 1956, composite of survey made of 276 nonfinancial corporations. Quoted from *Fortune* by permission.

Exhibit 7

SEARS ROEBUCK ACCEPTANCE CORP.

ESTIMATE OF HOLDINGS OF DIRECTLY PLACED COMMERCIAL PAPER BY
FUNCTIONAL CLASS
September 30, 1955

Holder	Percent of Total
Domestic nonfinancial corporations	54.90
Foreign corporations and banks	7.73
Insurance companies, life and casualty	7.40
Domestic commercial banks	6.80
Pension and trust funds	5.55
Colleges	2.50
Brokers on account of customers	8.94
Individuals and miscellaneous	6.18
Total directly placed commercial paper	100.00

SOURCE: Board of Governors of the Federal Reserve System, *Consumer Instalment Credit* (Washington, D.C.: U.S. Government Printing Office, 1957), Part II, p. 363.

USING CREDIT FOR PROFIT MAKING *

By Merle T. Welshans†

MORE AND MORE U.S. corporations are treating their credit departments as profit centers. Discarding the traditional approach of "What can credit do for sales?" credit managers more frequently are asking the broader question, "What can credit do for profits?"

Liberalizing credit practices, many financial executives report, has boosted corporate profits.

These are among the findings of a survey of experiences and attitudes of credit managers and other executives having major trade credit responsibility. The survey was sponsored by the National Association of Credit Management and the *Harvard Business Review*.

Other pertinent results of the survey include these highlights:

Although credit managers welcome the attention that top management usually devotes to credit policy, some managers complain that they are not permitted enough initiative to change credit practice and that they are excluded from deliberation on sales, pricing, and product strategy.

Assisted by electronic data processing, companies increasingly are making more profound analyses of their own credit operations, surveying competitors' practices, and conducting simulated sales and profitability studies, to permit more meaningful decisions on policy.

Receivables as percentages of assets and sales have grown during the present prolonged business expansion, a majority of respondents said. Government statistics covering all manufacturers reflect similar growth.

Throughout the history of the nation, credit granted by manufacturers, wholesalers, jobbers, and other business units as sellers of goods has served as one of the most important forms of current financing. The evolution of specialized and highly efficient financial institutions and intermediaries has not diminished the importance of trade credit; indeed, it continues to show striking growth both in absolute amounts and in relation to other sources of financing.

This article explores the experience of the surveyed companies in growth of

---

* Reprinted by permission from the *Harvard Business Review*, Vol. 45 (January-February 1967), pp. 141–56

† Professor of Finance, Washington University.

receivables, and discusses their credit practices, their motives for changing credit policy and strategy in doing it, the relationship to sales and profits, measurement of the effectiveness of credit practices, and the involvement of top management and other executives in decisions on these matters.

SCOPE OF SURVEY

A total of 825 usable responses were received from companies completing detailed questionnaires. All size and major product area classifications were represented in the sample drawn from the membership of the National Association of Credit Management. Respondents were instructed to frame their replies from the viewpoint of their own particular zone of responsibility—whether for the company as a whole, for a division, or for a subsidiary. More than two thirds of the individuals completing the questionnaire indicated that they had eight years or more of experience in corporate trade credit management. The range of sales volume and the general industrial classification of responding firms are shown in Exhibit I.

Exhibit I

PROFILE OF SURVEYED COMPANIES

	Percent of respondents
A. *Sales volume*	
Less than $1 million	7.3%
$1 million to $4.9 million	22.7
$5 million to $9.9 million	12.9
$10 million to $49 million	27.1
$50 million to $99 million	10.7
$100 million to $499 million	13.6
$500 million to $999 million	3.3
$1 billion or more	2.4
B. *General industrial classification*	
Consumer durable goods	23.7%
Consumer nondurable goods	24.8
Producers' goods	25.1
Construction, mining, oil	12.3
Other	14.1

In addition to the questionnaires, personal interviews were conducted with the financial executives of 20 corporations, which were selected on the basis of diversity of size and of product lines. Before the mailing of the questionnaire, 5 company interviews were conducted; and the remaining 15 companies were interviewed following receipt of the questionnaires.

INCREASING MAGNITUDE

The survey confirms published statistics on the growth of trade credit (summarized in the appendix to this reading).

Contributing to Growth

More than one half of all the companies surveyed reported increases in receivables as a proportion of both sales and total assets (see Exhibit II).

Exhibit II

CHANGES IN RECEIVABLES AND PROFITS,
1966 AS COMPARED WITH 1963

	Much higher	Moderately higher	About the same	Moderately lower	Much lower
Receivables in relation to sales are	13%	40%	27%	16%	4%
Receivables as a percent of total assets are	12	43	29	13	2
Profits as a percent of sales are	20	42	23	11	4
Profits as a percent of total assets are	16	43	25	12	4

Among the types of industries reporting relatively large increases in receivables are construction, oil, and mining.

Considering the national growth in receivables in terms of aggregates, some writers have described the situation as "out of hand." But, except for rare instances, the financial executives surveyed seem to be fully aware of the magnitude of their problems and responsibilities and of the increasing challenge of their credit decisions.

Far from looking upon receivables increases as unfortunate, they feel that liberalized credit practices have increased the profitability of corporate sales efforts. About 60% of the responding companies show higher profits in relation to both sales and assets compared with 1963.

While it is true that the increased profits derived from a wide variety of influences, financial executives offered many examples of the contribution of trade credit to such results. This one was frequently cited:

A customer is able to maintain a more complete line of inventory because of liberalized credit. Not only does the customer benefit, but the supplying firm enjoys expanded sales and higher profits.

Some respondents noted that often they can provide financing in the form of credit to customers who fail to qualify for institutional financing. Thus the selling firm assumes additional risk in pursuit of higher profits.

The relatively small firms covered in the survey indicated particular concern over their own liquidity or general financial positions in pursuing aggressive trade credit practices. Interviews with the bankers who serve them revealed a similar concern. I have discussed this problem separately (see the box on pages 369–70).

According to some credit executives, the current high interest in inventory control has caused undue increases in receivables; that is, to keep their own inventory levels low, some companies ship goods on especially attractive terms. The customers then, in effect, hold the supplier's inventory, and the supplier holds the receivables. Inventory positions look better and receivables look worse—but nobody is looking at receivables, anyway. Some consider this a meaningless, if not dangerous, accommodation to a current managerial fad.

Special Facets

To discern some special facets of trade credit practice, these questions were asked:

1. *Does your firm extend especially liberal trade credit in connection with the introduction of new products?*

One out of five firms answered *yes* to this question. Manufacturers of consumer durable goods indicated a somewhat greater liberality of credit than did other firms. Respondents from the central administration of multidivision companies also indicated greater liberality, which may be explained by the fact that very large companies do develop and introduce more new products.

2. *Is granting of trade credit to high-risk or marginal customers influenced by the extent of excess productive capacity?*

One third answered *yes;* two thirds answered *no.* The construction industry and manufacturers of producers' goods showed a higher proportion of *yes* answers, reflecting the importance of high levels of activity in industries with heavy fixed costs. Large firms in general also gave a greater-than-average response of *yes*—reflecting, perhaps, a greater awareness of the smaller incremental risk exposure on marginal accounts during periods of excess productive capacity.

3. *Is granting of trade credit to high-risk or marginal customers influenced by the profit margin on the particular items sold?*

One half of the respondents answered *yes;* one half answered *no.*

CHANGES IN PRACTICE

Use of trade credit as a competitive sales tool requires flexibility to be able to modify credit conditions swiftly and frequent review of credit terms in the company's markets.

Judging by the experience of the respondents to this survey, changes in trade credit practice usually apply to all product lines, although in a significant number of cases selected product lines receive special treatment (see Exhibit III).

Planned or Unplanned

By far the most important reason given for changes in trade credit practice is the necessity of meeting fast-changing competitive conditions (see Exhibit

Exhibit III

HOW CREDIT CHANGES WERE APPLIED IN 1964 AND 1965,
BY COMPANY SALES VOLUME

	Less than $1 million	$1 million to $4.9 million	$5 million to $9.9 million	$10 million to $49 million	$50 million to $99 million	$100 million to $499 million	$500 million to $999 million	$1 billion or more
All product lines	62%	67%	62%	54%	53%	33%	35%	35%
All established product lines	11	7	3	8	5	7	2	—
Selected established lines	8	4	19	16	15	28	30	24
New product lines exclusively	3	5	6	3	5	4	—	—
Both selected established and new products	3	6	5	9	14	17	13	28
Selected geographic areas	8	1	3	2	—	1	7	3

IV). This frank admission of expediency as a motivating factor seems to reflect the importance of flexibility in trade credit activities rather than inadequate planning.

If respondents can be believed, in fewer than 10% of all cases an "unplanned drift in credit practices" has been responsible for increasing receivables levels. In another equally small percentage of cases, credit practices have been changed as a result of deliberate credit experimentation (referred to again later)—which is the opposite of "unplanned."

The executives were also asked whether certain other circumstances obliged the company to alter its trade credit practices. These circumstances

Exhibit IV

REASONS FOR CHANGE IN CREDIT PRACTICES IN 1964 AND 1965,
BY COMPANY SALES VOLUME

	Less than $1 million	$1 million to $4.9 million	$5 million to $9.9 million	$10 million to $49 million	$50 million to $99 million	$100 million to $499 million	$500 million to $999 million	$1 billion or more
Credit experimentation	23%	9%	7%	5%	3%	8%	3%	—
Unplanned drift from established practice	3	14	15	7	3	6	3	—
Expediency to meet competitive conditions	34	33	50	49	33	43	37	38%
Experimentation and unplanned drift	7	4	—	1	2	1	—	—
Experimentation and expediency	20	26	14	24	32	27	47	33
Unplanned drift and expediency	13	14	14	14	27	15	10	29

Exhibit V

CIRCUMSTANCES INFLUENCING COMPANY'S CREDIT PRACTICES

Changes in company's liquidity or financial position	31%
Changes in company's inventory position	24
Changes in company's cost of acquiring capital	21
Changes in company's unused productive capacity	24
Changes in the financial condition of customers	86

are listed in Exhibit V, with the percentage of respondents who feel they are influential.

There were 96 firms that answered questions on the impact of corporate acquisition on credit practice. Of these, 54 said that acquisition of companies having credit practices different from theirs resulted in changes in their own practices. Managers of 42 subsidiaries said that acquisition by other companies had pronounced influence on their own credit practices as well as on their general credit policies.

Terms and Limits

Reported changes in the discount or net period divide roughly between companies that have lengthened and those that have shortened their terms

Exhibit VI

NATURE OF CHANGES IN CREDIT PRACTICES BY PRIMARY INDUSTRY

	Consumer durable goods	Consumer non-durable goods	Producers' goods	Construction, mining, oil	Other
Lengthened discount and/or net terms period	30%	24%	29%	24%	15%
Reduced discount and/or net terms period	27	24	22	29	26
No change or not applicable	43	52	49	47	59
Relative increases in credit limits	33%	40%	30%	41%	27%
Relative decreases in credit limits	24	17	33	22	29
No changes or not applicable	43	43	37	37	44
Increase in service charges on past-due accounts	23%	11%	23%	28%	26%
Decrease in service charges on past-due accounts	1	—	1	—	—
No changes or not applicable	76	89	76	72	74

(see Exhibit VI). Companies in the former category tend to be large and engaged in manufacture of producers' goods and consumer durable goods.

About one third of the respondents said that their credit limits had been increased, while about one fourth indicated decreases. A high frequency of increases in credit limits characterizes the construction industry and producers of consumer nondurable goods.

Service Charges

Only about one firm in every five indicated that it had imposed or increased service charges on past-due accounts. Several credit managers stated flatly that they not only refused to consider service charges, but that they would not continue approving credit for customers who did not take their discounts. Without exception, their companies sell products to firms in highly competitive and low profit-margin fields. They explained that, under these competitive conditions, a customer could not survive without taking all available discounts, and to deal with customers who did not take the discount meant time-consuming effort, if not ultimate loss.

The fact remains that most of the credit managers interviewed have a strong preference for service charges—especially during the present period of high money costs—as opposed to the few who consider them only an excuse for poor departmental collection performance.

Among those companies that impose service charges, there is little agreement on the appropriate amount. Several credit managers prefer a flat $\frac{1}{2}$ of 1% per month; others, perhaps more conscious of the cost of money to their firms, favor $1\frac{1}{2}\%$ per month. Most, however, indicated they charge 1% per month.

Some respondents expressed concern about possible violation of usury laws when service charges exceed the legal maximum interest rate. In some states, proof of violation can result in the creditor's loss of the entire service or interest charge. One credit manager expressed much impatience with such considerations, however, claiming that the average weighted cost of capital for his firm after taxes was 12%; to be held accountable for usury because of imposing service charges of less than that amount, in his view, is the height of legal folly.

Frequency of Review

More than one third of the companies surveyed make annual reassessments of credit practice; 10%, semiannual reassessments. (These ratios are broken down in Exhibit VII.) A far larger number of companies claimed continuing attention to the appropriateness of trade credit practices. With near-unanimous emphasis on the necessity of adjusting to fast-moving developments, the firms that undertake seminannual and annual reassessments also reported giving continuous, informal attention to credit, rather than relying solely on periodic reviews. Most of the producers' goods companies, for instance, were in this category.

SALES AND PROFITS

Exhibit VIII reveals a conviction on the part of most respondents that changes in credit practices have increased profits. Interestingly enough, a

Exhibit VII

CHANGE IN CREDIT PRACTICES, BY VARIOUS LEVELS OF OPERATIONS

	Central adminis- tration, multi- division company	Single division, multi- division company	Sub- sidiary	Single location company	Other
Percent of responses represented by each level of operations	36%	23%	6%	32%	3%
Credit practices have changed within the last two years*	55%	58%	57%	47%	62%
Frequency of reappraisal of credit practices*					
Semiannually	8%	4%	7%	17%	19%
Annually	35	38	41	42	35
Continuously	57	58	52	41	46

* Percent of respondents at each level of operations.

Exhibit VIII

IMPACT OF CREDIT PRACTICE CHANGES ON SALES AND PROFITS, BY PRIMARY INDUSTRY

	Con- sumer durable goods	Con- sumer non- durable goods	Pro- ducers' goods	Construc- tion, mining, oil	Other
Led to an increase in sales volume	47%	34%	30%	33%	29%
Led to a decrease in sales volume	3	1	1	4	4
Had relatively little effect on sales volume	50	65	69	63	67
Increased the profitability of total sales	58%	53%	53%	49%	59%
Decreased the profitability of total sales	6	7	4	9	2
Had relatively little effect on sales profitability	36	40	43	42	39

smaller percentage of them feel that changes in practices have also increased sales volume.

The companies responding fall into three distinct groups: (1) those for whom more generous trade credit practices have increased both sales and profits; (2) those for whom more restrictive credit practices have had little or no effect on sales, but have increased profitability on sales; and (3) those for whom liberalized trade credit practices have maintained existing sales volume, but have reduced profitability.

The first group is represented primarily by producers of consumer durable goods. Among the comments reflecting this attitude:

"[More liberal credit] made possible a floor plan for dealer sales—a high profit-margin category of our product line."

"Fixed overhead per unit of output decreased as a result of expanded sales to marginal accounts, increasing overall profits."

"Moved products otherwise unsalable."

"Permitted establishment of a sales office in a new geographic area as a result of increased volume of sales."

Comments offered by respondents in the second group:

"More restrictive credit practices have resulted in a faster turnover of receivables, reducing risk and losses on bad debts."

"Restriction on sales to marginal risks has permitted greater concentration on better accounts."

"Enforcement of cash discount policies has resulted in reduced number of days credit sales outstanding."

"More vigorous collection practices, along with service charges on past-due accounts, has reduced average investment in receivables, increasing return on overall company investment."

Comments from the third group:

"We have provided longer terms in order to maintain our present sales position. Result was more money invested in receivables and accompanying pressure on profits."

"Competition has forced us to lengthen credit terms, and our bad debt losses seem to increase as the number of days of credit sales outstanding increases."

Study and Experimentation

Executives of approximately 40% of the companies interviewed claimed that before changes in credit practices were made, they had studies conducted to determine the potential effect on sales volume and profitability. Of the companies making credit-sales studies, about 60% base them on a "survey of competitive practices."

Some of the firms that engage in sales and profitability studies employ the experimental technique of varying credit practices on a product basis and on a geographic basis; others utilize computers to simulate sales-credit relationships; and still others simply observe reaction to overall change in practices.

Large firms, as might be expected, show a higher incidence of sales and profitability studies and experimental techniques; and respondents representing the central administration of multidivision companies, probably reflecting their size, also make substantial use of such studies. (Here is evidence of credit practice leadership.) At the other extreme, respondents from construction companies place a heavy reliance on surveys of competitive practices, with little attention to sales-profit studies.

In virtually all the companies responding to these questions, trade credit practice studies are carried out by company personnel. Consulting firms apparently direct very little attention to this aspect of corporate management.

MEASURING EFFECTIVENESS

Appraising results of credit administration is a difficult task. Most companies continue to rely on time-tested yardsticks, but some are venturing into consideration of their credit operations as profit centers.

Traditional Techniques

Of the responding firms, 65% use historical ratios and standards in determining the effectiveness of their credit offices (see Exhibit IX). While

Exhibit IX

WAYS OF MEASURING PERFORMANCE OF THE CREDIT DEPARTMENT

Historical ratios and standards	65%
Its contribution to company sales	21
Its contribution to company profits	34
Budgeted goals and standards	23
Other	12

many companies employ more than one measurement, the preference is for contribution to profits (34%) rather than contribution to sales (21%) as a guide.

A number of credit managers feel that, with rapidly changing markets and product lines, applying historical ratios and standards to measure departmental performance has become useless in some instances and misleading in others. Allocation of departmental operating funds also fails, in some cases, to reflect the changing responsibilities of credit management.

A very few companies reported the use of "indexes of quality" as a measuring stick. These have been described in recent journal articles,[1] and it is highly probable that some companies have attempted to apply them to their own receivables. Basically, such indexes provide a composite picture of the condition of receivables at a particular moment.

In answer to the question of how the credit department's contribution to company profitability is appraised, respondents frequently made reference to analysis of marginal accounts. On the other hand, there are a few firms that make estimates of company profits on the basis of sales only to their well-rated customers, in contrast to actual profits. Other firms undertake detailed studies to determine the causes of changing levels of receivables. (The credit managers of a few family-owned businesses said they are unable effectively to determine their contribution to profitability, since they do not have access to their company's financial statements.)

---

[1] For example, "A New Gauge for Receivables," *Credit and Financial Management,* September 1966, p. 20.

Profit Centers

Perhaps more significant than the specific techniques used to measure the credit department's contribution to company profits is the frequent reference to the concept of the credit department as a profit center. Many credit managers frankly stated that only through such an approach to their duties could they ever hope to play the strategic role in company affairs that they feel is warranted by their work.

One response developed somewhat as follows:

When we extend trade credit, we commit some of the resources of our firm to support receivables. We are investing the funds of our firm to earn a profit, just as is the production manager who purchases additional equipment, the purchasing agent who stocks raw materials or merchandise inventories, or the advertising executive who undertakes a promotional campaign. Extending credit has its initial impact on company sales, but our ultimate goal is to increase profits.

We should expand our investment in receivables to the point where the added demand for the firm's product ceases to provide as much revenue as the costs incurred. We can also increase our net revenues by reducing costs through credit operations. For example, in some cases we can use seasonal dating, reduce our warehousing costs, and, at the same time, make possible regular production levels throughout the year. Such economies arise by stimulating the incentive for early customer inventory purchases.

Credit executives inclined toward this departmental profit orientation admit that it is a far easier thing to say than do; that the real trick is to determine how the effectiveness of their efforts can be measured. Yet they suggest that the problem of identifying all relevant costs with relevant revenues in any phase of business is extremely challenging and that, given the same attention, trade credit may prove to be one of the most amenable facets of business operations for the application of this approach. One credit executive provided this example:

His company was considering accepting a contract on a construction project that would require two years to complete. On the basis of the proposed contract price, the credit manager voiced strong opposition to the project. Considering the cost of capital involved in supporting the 10% of the contract amount to be retained by the disbursing agent (until completion of the project), the contract would not yield the rate of return sought by the company, he told his superiors. Needless to say, the credit manager's recommendation and the logic with which he backed it caused much consternation, but it also resulted in a reappraisal of procedures. He commented to me, "Difficult as it is to make a science of our activities, the act of trying results in uncovering many facts that would otherwise be glossed over."

Computer Utilization

As it has for all aspects of business operation, the computer has begun to play a role in the credit departments of many businesses. Thus, 20% of responding firms are making substantial use of computers in their credit

What Smaller Companies Can Do

The predicament of the medium sized or small company faced with increasingly liberal trade credit practices on the part of large competitors is a most difficult one. Dun & Bradstreet has found that receivables difficulties rank first as a fundamental cause of business failure. As a setting for discussing it, consider a typical situation:

The firms in a particular industry have expanded their productive capacity and in the process have increased their break-even points. Furthermore, the fixed-cost component of total costs has risen more rapidly than has the variable-cost component, as a result of investment in labor-saving production equipment. The greater proportion of fixed costs to variable costs causes profits to fall rapidly when sales fail to reach the break-even point. (Conversely, once volume exceeds that point, profits rise rapidly.) So the smaller firms in the industry must do everything in their power to maintain high sales levels.

As a further complication, these companies have drawn down their cash resources while expanding, to a far greater extent than have their large competitors. The latter are in a position to expand sales at their expense by offering more liberal credit terms—an offer most welcome to customers at a time of high money costs and pressure on their own liquid resources.

The predicament of the small firms is obvious. On the one hand, accommodation of credit demands by additional investment in receivables will put extreme pressure on their dwindling cash resources (external sources are no longer readily available). On the other hand, if they fail to meet their large competitors' liberalized trade credit terms, they may expect sales to shrink drastically.

This bleak description of an all too common situation these days offers ample force to the argument for long-range planning *before* such conditions are created. A carefully paced rate of expansion (compatible with a well-balanced capital structure) may require much managerial discipline during periods of strong economic expansion, but the alternative is often financial disaster.

While there often may be no solution for small firms that find themselves in the plight described above, they may have feasible courses of action to take. Some of these are:

Offering special services to customers. (Their nature cannot here be specified, but smaller companies, by virtue of their size and flexibility, have typically claimed their niche in the nation's industrial complex by competing on the basis of factors other than price or credit terms.)

Guaranteeing supplementary lines of credit between the customer and the customer's bank through "buy-back" agreements or other arrangements.

Selling or otherwise disposing of certain product lines to concentrate financial resources on those that are more productive of profits. (A strategic contraction of activities may free funds to accommodate increasing trade credit demands.)

What Smaller Companies Can Do—*Continued*

Entering into "sale and lease-back" agreements, thereby preserving control of company assets and generating substantial increases in working capital to support further investment in receivables.

Accounts receivable financing. (Finance companies that provide funds on the basis of accounts receivable as collateral can play a strategic role in assisting firms under liquidity pressures. The typical 1% per month interest charge for this service should be regarded as an excessive cost of money only if it worsens the small firm's profit position. But failure to accommodate trade credit demands because of this presumed high cost of receivables financing could result in a serious sacrifice of profits.)

---

activities, and 23% moderate use. There still are many firms, however, which have not yet made use of company computers in the credit department (28%) or have not used computers in any capacity (29%).

Simplifying and speeding up work procedures are among the reasons cited by credit executives for the use of computers by their departments. More important, however, is the frequently expressed hope that more meaningful information can be accumulated and organized for analysis and interpretation. According to several credit managers, the information now available to the credit department through electronic data processing makes possible more prompt and meaningful reports to top management, while top management itself is developing a greater awareness of credit activities because of this improved communication.

MANAGING CREDIT

The respondents were asked to indicate those positions in their companies which had primary influence on setting credit policy and supervising practice. The results are outlined in Exhibit X. Examination of the returns reveals that the credit manager's importance in these activities grows as the size of the company increases.

Exhibit X

EXECUTIVES PRINCIPALLY INFLUENCING
CREDIT OPERATIONS

	Credit policy	Credit practice
President	18%	8%
Financial vice president	10	4
Treasurer	18	13
Credit manager	24	42
Controller	7	9
Marketing vice president or sales manager	7	9
A well-balanced team effort	16	15

Far from resenting their lack of dominant influence in setting policy, most credit managers, judging by their reactions when interviewed, in fact welcome participation by representatives of the functional areas of their business, and especially desire participation by the president or other chief executive officer. Once policy is set, however, the typical credit manager displays a strong preference for primary control over credit practices.

Top Management's Role

Some respondents accused top-level executives of failure to stimulate lower-level initiative and reluctance to adopt methods of making credit a better tool—methods frequently urged by subordinates. The most obvious and generally cited example of shortsightedness was top management's attitude toward bad debts.

To minimize losses on bad debts is simple—just reject all but the most strongly rated customers. What has escaped top management teams, many credit managers believe, is the realization that deliberate assumption of trade credit risk can contribute to profits. A number of them complained of a lack of freedom to use initiative in handling marginal accounts.

Belying the usual impression of basic incompatibility between credit and sales, the vast majority of respondents indicated that they enjoy the best of relationships with their marketing divisions. Less than 10% reported any serious controversy over trade credit activities.

Many credit managers are concerned, however, over a notable lack of participation on their part in sales, price, and product strategy sessions. Almost without exception, credit managers feel that their firms are forgoing important matters of strategy by slighting the credit function in their deliberations. Apparently the value of their counsel to customers goes without challenge; yet often they cannot effectively provide equally significant counsel to their own companies. In their judgment, the importance of investment in receivables and the impact of credit strategy on business operations are two good reasons why they *should* be included.

According to their reports, 41% of the respondents *seldom* are given the opportunity to participate in general planning sessions, and 30% have it *occasionally*; while only 15% have the opportunity *often*, and only 14% *most of the time*. One credit executive observed that it had taken him 10 years to gain recognition for the strategic contribution of credit management—but he said it was worth it; he is now included in all important market planning sessions.

Intercompany Activity

Credit managers made frequent mention of the necessity for intercompany cooperation in the control of poor credit risks. Cooperation to date has primarily taken the form of an improved flow of information to central credit interchange offices.

Credit managers consider fraud-prevention activities to depend heavily on intercompany cooperation. Another form of intercompany relationship which was reported in the interviews as extensive is customer counseling. Despite the possible pitfalls of advising customer companies, which were stressed by those interviewed, the general feeling is that customer counseling is unavoidable. Apparently, some credit executives actually devote a major proportion of their time to this counseling, and in fact they expect these responsibilities to expand even more.

CONCLUSION

The survey reveals that top management exerts a strong influence on the formulation of credit policy, but relies heavily on credit managers and other financial executives to implement and administer practices. The vast majority of respondents make continuous evaluation of competitive practices and pressures, rather than depending on regular credit practice reassessment. Somewhat surprisingly, a consensus indicated general harmony with sales and marketing departments, contradicting the familiar notion of constant friction.

Perhaps the most significant finding is the overwhelming number of credit and financial executives who claim a profit contribution from their activities. And the reports show the greatest growth of receivables for those companies with the best profit records. Descriptions of credit practices designed to turn a profit, such as a present-value approach to investment in receivables and experimentation with various credit practices—and rejection of historical "what can we do for sales" attitudes—give tangible evidence of profit consciousness and more dynamic thinking in the credit field.

Credit executives noted frequently that introduction of electronic data processing to their departments not only freed them from time-consuming detail, but enabled them to conduct more meaningful research, such as simulation exercises and studies to determine the desirability of marginal accounts. Even so, several feel concern that their departmental resources are inadequate to permit them to explore fully the many profit-related opportunities available to them.

Many respondents expressed the hope that the speed and completeness of reports processed by computers would promote recognition by top management of the importance of the credit management function. They also demonstrated a commendable desire to be included in their company's general planning sessions, in light of the vast potential for strategic competitive practices and the expanding role of credit management in business.

APPENDIX

THE GROWTH OF TRADE CREDIT

The balance sheet item of "receivables" for manufacturing corporations, as reported by the Federal Trade Commission and the Securities and Exchange Commission, has grown by almost $40 billion in the last 10 years. More important, this increase is proportionately greater than that of any other single asset category of business—rising from an average of 15.5% of total assets in 1956 to 18.1% through the second quarter of 1966.

With the increasing cost of acquiring corporate capital, it is natural that attention would be drawn to this application of funds. The surge in receivables buildup during the present business expansion reveals that the largest businesses have experienced a greater growth of receivables as a percentage of total assets than firms of lesser size (see Figure 1). And, although the buildup of receivables for the category of smallest firms—those with assets of less than $1 million—has been more modest, this class of assets now on the average is roughly equal to the net investment in plant, property, and equipment combined.

Nor can this growth of receivables be accounted for simply on the basis of increased sales volume, receivables having increased as a percentage of sales as well as of assets in the last decade. This statistical fact is confirmed by the National Association of Credit Management figures on growth of the average number of days' credit sales outstanding.

(There has been no general increase, however, in past-due accounts. This may be explained in part by the more frequent practice of customer firms of withholding payment until the very end of their terms periods, thus conserving corporate funds. This practice is, of course, only one of the many responses to increasing costs of corporate capital. A more important explanation, however, seems to be the lengthening of terms by some creditors.)

While the ratio of receivables to sales for companies exceeding $1 billion in assets has increased since the beginning of the present economic expansion in early 1961, receivables compared with sales for firms of lesser size actually have declined slightly (see Figure II). The largest companies, which account for 27% of sales of all manufacturers, have been able to afford strategic incremental investment in receivables. Figure II gives a breakdown of receivables/sales experience during the five-year period by asset size.

373

Figure I

TRADE RECEIVABLES AS A PERCENT OF TOTAL ASSETS, BY SIZE OF
COMPANY, FOR THE CURRENT ECONOMIC EXPANSION

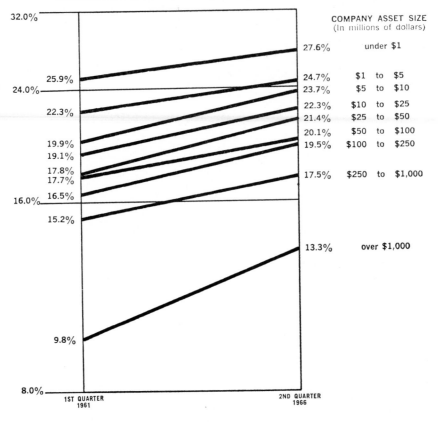

Figure II

TOTAL RECEIVABLES AS A PERCENT OF NET SALES, U.S. MANU-
FACTURING CORPORATIONS BY ASSET SIZE

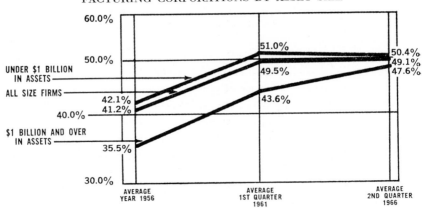

How much added financial vulnerability has resulted from this growth of receivables? One significant measure of financial strength is the liquidity position of the firm. This measure is calculated by dividing the total of corporate cash plus U.S. government securities by total current liabilities. The higher the percentage, the more liquid the firm. While the liquidity position of corporations exclusive of the largest size category has fallen from 69% in 1956 to 28% through the second quarter of 1966, the largest corporations have experienced a decline from 86% to 43% (see Figure III). Here is more

Figure III

CASH & U.S. GOVERNMENT SECURITIES AS A PERCENT OF CURRENT LIABILITIES (LIQUIDITY POSITION), U.S. MANUFAC- TURING CORPORATIONS BY ASSET SIZE

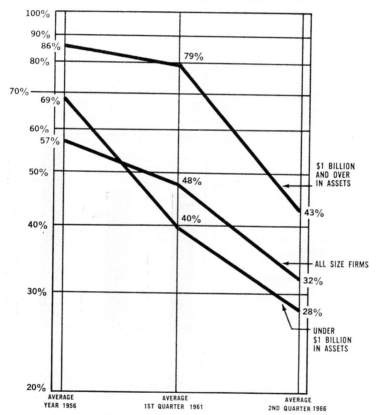

evidence that the strong financial positions of the largest corporations have made possible their heavy increase in receivables investment.

With the liquidity positions of the largest corporations now reduced se- verely and with the cost of corporate capital at a high level, it would not be surprising to see an abrupt reduction in the rate of growth of receivables on the part of the largest corporations. As Figure II indicates, the smaller companies controlled their receivables rigorously during the present economic expansion, reflecting the fact that they had strained their liquidity positions to danger points during the preceding five years. Their present vulnerable liquidity positions must be a result of the business boom rather than liberalized trade credit practices.

Forecasts of the economic growth of the United States in the next decade indicate that it will exceed that of the last 10 years. Among the reasons given is the expectation that expansion phases of cyclical activity will be longer, while periods of contraction will be shorter and less severe than before. To the extent that this is true, business will rely increasingly on external financing to support expansion. Figure IV shows the extraordinary rate of growth of external financing during the present expansion period compared to two previous periods of expansion. Greater external financing will place continuing pressure on the cost of capital. As one of the most significant forms of external financing, trade credit demands attention not only as a strategic marketing device but as a source of funds.

Figure IV

COMPOUND ANNUAL RATE OF INCREASE IN EXTERNAL
AND INTERNAL FINANCING, NONFARM NONFINANCIAL
CORPORATE BUSINESS, IN THREE EXPANSIONS

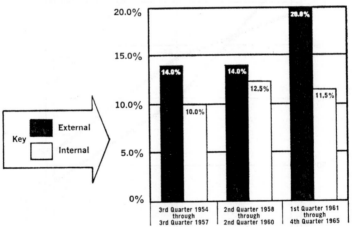

Sources: Data for Figures I, II, and III obtained from Federal Trade Commission and Securities and Exchange Commission; data for Figure IV obtained from Office of Business Economics, U.S. Department of Commerce.

CAPTIVE FINANCE COMPANIES *

By Victor L. Andrews†

DURING THE 1950's and early 1960's, the managements of a sizable number of the nation's largest nonfinancial corporations elected the captive finance company—that is, a subsidiary company holding notes receivable produced in connection with the parent corporation's sales—as a device for raising needed debt capital. The basic attraction of the captives has been their alleged ability to pyramid debt upon equity in multiples of several times—in conspicuous contrast with their parent companies' more modest ratios.

The captive companies' debt outstanding has mounted to astonishing aggregates. In 1961, the year of latest available data, for example:

The commercial banking system had better than $1 billion at stake in the captives through direct loans.

The great number of nonfinancial corporations and banks which lend to captives through the commercial paper market had more than $1 billion committed.

Long-term lenders—the insurance companies, pension funds, and personal trusts which feed money into the corporate bond market—had more than $1.2 billion on loan to the captives.

The foregoing organizations are not the only ones interested in credit captives. Others with a vested interest are:

Executives of the parent corporations, who may be restive about the risks involved.

Shareholders in the parent companies.

Managements of rival corporations, who may feel envious and/or puzzled about what the corporations with captive finance companies have achieved.

Financial analysts in pension funds, mutual funds, insurance companies, and bank trust departments, who are interested in assessing the future of corporations with captive finance companies.

Independent finance companies, which consider captives to be arch rivals.

Despite the great growth of the subsidiaries and the breadth of interest vested in them, however, there has been no decisive, clear statement by

* Reprinted by permission from the *Harvard Business Review*, Vol. 42 (July–August 1964), pp. 80–92.
† Associate Professor of Business Administration, Harvard University.

management or by the lending community of why the captive is an advance in financing technique. Indeed, this statement may be overly generous: within my experience, at least, there is a pronounced tendency to answer a question on this score with folklore, to confuse financial matters with operating considerations, to attribute the captives' existence to someone else's ignorance, or to beg the question altogether.

The principal financial issue is whether the administration of cash flows, dismemberment of assets and liabilities, and consequent reapportionment (perhaps gerrymandering) of risk in parent-plus-captive is a departure in financing technique that is somehow superior to the financing of a parent as a single unit. Can the sum of the parts be more than the whole? As a first step toward resolving this issue, I propose to address two interrelated questions:

(1) Is there a ground in logic for presuming that the operation of a financing subsidiary enables a parent corporation to shoulder debt indirectly without its celebrated Jekyll-and-Hyde impact on internal company cash and earnings flows? As a part of this question it is necessary to consider the captive finance company as a collateral device and to reason out the implications for the risks assumed by various classes of creditors.

(2) Is there ground for thinking that the equity market should incorporate an allowance in its pricing of the stock of a parent company to recognize the risk imposed by debt issued by a finance subsidiary?

In part, this article is a challenge to the managements of nonfinancial corporations and to the lending fraternity to desist from a conspiracy of silence and to help hammer out the answers to these questions. To preview my attitude, I retain fundamental reservations about the reality of the "debt capacity" which the operation of a captive bestows on its user. Furthermore, I think that the stock of a parent company is subject to market reaction to the leverage risk of operating a financing subsidiary.

TRENDS OF DEVELOPMENT

The corporate universe is always a net lender to other segments of the economy—to consumers, government, unincorporated businesses. Loans outstanding from the aggregate of corporations in the form of accounts receivable always exceed indebtedness on their own payables. On balance, then, corporations are one of our economy's principal lenders. The net flow of credit from corporations to others has been variable in absolute volume per unit of time and relative to other uses of corporate funds in different periods of economic history. In the 1950's corporate receivables expanded with intermittent spells of quiescence. Manufacturing corporations, which hold the preponderance of corporate receivables, underwent an almost continual rise of their net credit outstanding.[1]

---

[1] Martin H. Seiden, *Trade Credit: A Quantitative and Qualitative Analysis*, unpublished dissertation quoted by Robert Lindsay and Arnold W. Sametz in *Financial Management: An Analytical Approach* (Homewood, Illinois: Richard D. Irwin, Inc., 1963), pp. 291–297.

The growth of captive finance companies is but one of this panorama's facets, albeit a quantitatively imposing part of the whole. In the 1950's and 1960's, lengthening credit terms caused the receivables of many companies to gobble up funds so rapidly that, coupled with other uses of funds, demands ran well ahead of cash generated internally. Barring the marketing of new stock issues, which have been as scarce for manufacturers and trade corporations as the proverbial hen's teeth, the only means of finance left open was new debt, and many managements elected to segregate burgeoning receivables and their debt financing into a wholly owned financing subsidiary. The result, as the box (on page 384) states, was a multibillion dollar business.

A pervasive force in casting some of the outlines of a captive are its connections with the types of financing blandished by the parent company in its sales rivalries. From the mid-1950's on, thinly financed small trade corporations and unincorporated trade businesses pressed demands for financing their inventory and their deferred-payment sales contracts up the line to manufacturers. Rationing of small businesses at the hands of the banks during a period of general monetary policy restraint may have forced the distributive channels to this expedient. Also, crude data suggest that declining rates of output relative to capacity may have made manufacturers willing lenders for the lift this would give to sales.

In any event, the credit captives of manufacturers have had asset structures composed of inventory loans to dealers and distributors and deferred-payment sales contracts. Net growth of the credit outstanding from manufacturers' captives to dealers and distributors—wholesale financing—absorbed some $700 million of the net growth of the captives' loans after 1946. About $3.7 billion flowed into the financing of deferred-payment sales. The evidence of this latter kind of transaction shows on a captive's balance sheet as retail notes receivable—"retail paper"—whether the parent company is a manufacturer financing time sales to other businesses or a trade corporation financing consumers.

The nature of credit demands on the parent companies in the various industries is reflected in the asset distribution of their captives. The details of the assets by industry of the 62 captives sampled in 1961 appear in Exhibit I. The reader will note, incidentally, that the industry concentration of assets follows the concentration of the number of financing subsidiaries in the four S.I.C. industry groups mentioned in the boxed insert on page 384.

ALLEGED ADVANTAGES

In my opinion, practitioners often and writers sometimes mistake some of the operating characteristics of the financing affiliates as their distinctive features. For instance, it is often argued that the *purpose* of captive finance companies is to support parent company sales by absorbing notes receivable. Or some will say that a valuable check is created by insulating the captive's credit-granting and credit-supervising function from the influence of an exuberant credit-brandishing sales staff.

Exhibit I

INDUSTRY DISTRIBUTION OF THE ASSETS OF A SAMPLE
OF 62 CAPTIVE FINANCE COMPANIES, 1961
(Dollars in Millions)

Assets	Nonelectrical machinery		Electrical machinery		Transportation equipment	
Cash and securities..$	61.7	5.9%	$ 107.1	7.4%	$ 86.7	9.4%
Notes receivable						
Wholesale........	396.1	38.0	202.0	14.0	124.0	3.5
Retail...........	574.5	55.0	1,111.5	77.0	686.8	4.7
Total........	970.6	93.0	1,313.5	91.0	810.8	8.2
Other assets........	11.4	1.1	23.3	1.6	22.1	2.4
Total.............$1,043.7		100.0%	$1,443.9	100.0%	$919.6	100.0%

But such reasoning is wide of the mark. The functions of receivables absorption and credit surveillance of the captives are not distinctive. It seems clear that both these functions could be and usually are executed perfectly well within a nonfinancial corporation without a subsidiary. So must it be with any of the fund-allocating and/or administrative functions of the captives. The real question, and here the only question, is what can be had with captive finance companies that cannot be had without them?

Debt-Raising Capacities

The answer lies, seemingly, in their debt-raising capacities. Part A of Exhibit II shows for 1962 the liability structures and their equivalents in percentages for five large financing affiliates with parent companies in various product markets. First, let us consider only their broad outlines:

All the captives shown have some short-term notes payable outstanding. With the exception of Clark Equipment Credit Corporation, the proportion of notes payable plus routine accruals and payables to total financing ranges upwards of two-thirds for all companies. The maximum is Allis-Chalmers Credit's four-fifths (which has been reduced subsequently with a long-term debt privately placed). Three of the five captives—Borg-Warner Acceptance, Clark Equipment Credit, and Sears, Roebuck Acceptance—have long-term debt outstanding to external creditors. Only one captive leans on its parent for a substantial percentage of its total financing.

It is common practice in analysis of the capital structures of finance companies to consider the proportion between senior debt and the risk-bearing base, i.e., the sum of equity and subordinated debt. (In this case, subordinated debt is both external and parent-supplied.) This ratio is in the neighborhood of 4 to 1 for all captives shown except Sears, Roebuck Acceptance, for which it is considerably higher at this date.

Thus, these captives have succeeded in pyramiding $4 or better of senior debt on each $1 of equity or subordinated debt. This is the "secret" of their appeal. In interview after interview that I have held with parent-company and bank-loan officers, the debt/risk capital ratios boasted by the subsidiaries have been singled out as the touchstone for their formation and operation.

Exhibit I—Continued

INDUSTRY DISTRIBUTION OF THE ASSETS OF A SAMPLE
OF 62 CAPTIVE FINANCE COMPANIES, 1961
(Dollars in Millions)

Miscellaneous manufacturing		Retail trade		All others		Total	
$ 1.7	0.7%	$ 10.2	1.2%	$ 33.6	15.3%	$ 301.0	6.4%
—	—	—	—	33.4	15.2	755.5	16.0
250.0	98.3	811.5	98.0	142.5	64.8	3,576.8	76.0
250.0	98.3	811.5	98.0	175.9	80.0	4,332.3	92.0
2.5	1.0	6.4	0.8	10.4	4.7	76.1	1.6
$254.2	100.0%	$823.1	100.0%	$219.9	100.0%	$4,709.4	100.0%

The effects of having the captives are readily apparent. As Part B of Exhibit II shows:

Only two of the parent companies have short-term notes outstanding, and for one of these two the notes are proportionately insignificant in total financing. Thus, of the five parent companies' balance sheets, only Massey-Ferguson's shows a significant amount of negotiated short-term debt outstanding. For the rest, routine accruals and payables comprise all or virtually all of current indebtedness. All the parents have some long-term debt outstanding, ranging from about 3% of total financing in the case of Borg-Warner to nearly 24% in the case of Clark Equipment.

The debt/equity ratios appearing at the foot of the parent-company balance sheets exhibit a wide range. The highest ratio, nevertheless, is 1.23 in the case of Massey-Ferguson, and there seems to be little question for each parent of a clear contrast with its subsidiary on this score.

The instances shown of captive company financing are not isolated. A tabulation of the claims structures in 1961 of a sample of 62 captives, excluding General Motors Acceptance Corporation, is contained in Exhibit III along with a breakdown of the total by size class and with percentage equivalents of the absolute dollar sums. The summation column indicates a total financing of $4.7 billion. Parent equity comprises 15% of the total, and parent-supplied debt slightly over another 8%. The ratio of senior debt to equity and subordinated indebtedness for this group of companies in its entirety is almost exactly 3 to 1.

Examination of the detail in the table will reveal departures from this generality within size classes. But differences of detail are rather beside the point here. What is clear is that throughout the size structure of captives, one dollar of parent company funds is parlayed into several other dollars of externally supplied debt.

Role of Collateral Value

The foundation of the captives' capacities in this regard is the high collateral value of their receivables, which are also virtually their only asset.

Exhibit II

LIABILITY STRUCTURES OF FIVE CAPTIVE FINANCE COMPANIES
AND PARENT CORPORATIONS, RESPECTIVE
FISCAL YEAR-ENDS FOR 1962
(Dollars in Thousands)

	Borg-Warner		Allis-Chalmers	
A. CAPTIVE COMPANIES				
Notes payable	$ 72,833	59.4%	$ 68,145	78.5%
Accrued liabilities and accounts payable	8,776	7.1	1,125	1.3
Total	81,609	66.5	69,270	79.8
Parent company loans				
Short-term	...	...	...	...
Long-term subordinated	4,500	3.7	10,000	11.5
Total	4,500	3.7	10,000	11.5
External long-term debt				
Senior	15,000	12.2	...	...
Subordinated	10,000	8.2	...	...
Total	25,000	20.4	...	...
Equity	11,538	9.4	7,566	8.7
Total liabilities and equity	$122,647	100.0%	$ 86,836	100.0%
Senior debt/equity and subordinated debt	4.27		3.94	
B. PARENT COMPANIES				
Notes payable	...	...	$ 23,670	4.7%
Accrued liabilities and accounts payable	$ 89,309	19.1%	61,890	12.3
Current installments on long-term debt	...	...	...	...
Total current liabilities	89,309	19.1	85,560	17.0
Long-term debt	13,070	2.8	86,135	17.0
Reserves*	3,959	0.8	20,355	4.0
Equity	362,673	77.3	312,900	62.0
Total	$469,011	100.0%	$504,950	100.0%
Debt/equity ratio	.28		.52	

* Includes deferred income taxes, provision for warranties, and other co itingencies.

In essence, receivables are debt contracts with a defined schedule of cash inflow to the lender. Thus, the assets have a schedule of liquidation with a high degree of assurance because default and loss rates are low (barring outright mismanagement) and because there is safety for the lender in the credit of large numbers of unconnected, unrelated debtors on the receivables. In short, the captives' main asset has the same high collateral value that has made the receivable common in secured financing.

Once a sale of receivables from parent to captive is consummated, the deal is usually final. Exceptions to this do exist (e.g., the right of partial recourse of some captives to their parents, some few instances of full recourse, and occasional extensions of parent guarantees), but they are few. The captive's independence implies that the security of its receivables is unencumbered. Thus, because a captive has clear title to liquid assets and lacks the risks associated with nonfinancial businesses, it is a prime credit shell.

Although the captive is merely a departure in collateral form, another device for establishing clear claim of a creditor on realizable value, it is particularly adapted to the needs of a nonfinancial corporation. A manufac-

Exhibit II—Continued

LIABILITY STRUCTURES OF FIVE CAPTIVE FINANCE COMPANIES
AND PARENT CORPORATIONS, RESPECTIVE
FISCAL YEAR-ENDS FOR 1962
(Dollars in Thousands)

Massey-Ferguson		Clark Equipment		Sears Roebuck	
A. CAPTIVE COMPANIES					
59,000	72.4%	$ 44,520	47.5%	$ 468,937	70.4%
1,543	1.9	1,571	1.7	4,920	0.7
60,543	74.3	46,091	49.2	473,857	71.1
4,983	6.1	...	...	...	...
4,000	4.9	...	...	...	...
8,983	11.0	...	...	...	...
...	...	28,966	30.9	100,000	15.0
...	...	8,500	9.1	25,000	3.8
...	...	37,466	40.0	125,000	18.8
11,924	14.7	10,077	10.8	67,603	10.1
$ 81,450	100.0%	$ 93,634	100.0%	$ 666,460	100.0%
4.11		4.04		6.20	
B. PARENT COMPANIES					
$ 80,024	15.0%	...	...	...	...
119,526	22.4	$ 31,762	21.5%	$ 403,428	14.7%
4,339	0.8	...	...	...	...
203,889	38.2	31,762	21.5	403,428	14.7
90,113	16.9	35,000	23.6	350,000	12.8
16,704	3.1	955	0.6	288,807	10.5
222,822	41.8	80,319	54.3	1,699,904	62.0
$533,528	100.0%	$148,036	100.0%	$2,742,139	100.0%
1.23		.82		.38	

turer's distributive channels and point-of-sale contacts enable it to acquire notes receivable from widely dispersed and sometimes remote geographic regions which conventional lenders, especially commercial banks, simply cannot reach. Moreover, in many product lines the manufacturer's marketing personnel, through their ordinary contacts with dealers and distributors, can maintain surveillance of the notoriously risky inventory-secured wholesale paper. Repossession by a captive does not entail losses to the extent ordinarily sustained by a financial institution in such proceedings because the parent company can ordinarily remarket the merchandise with little difficulty. Thus, wholesale paper, usually shunned by independent finance companies and never liked, becomes palatable enough to serve as a form of collateral value for loan security.

LINKS WITH PARENT

The character and viability of a captive company as a financial vehicle depend on its link to the parent company's sales and cash flow.

Role of Operating Agreement

Because a captive is in business only with its parent, its functions and financial character are molded exclusively by the operating agreement be-

---

MULTIBILLION DOLLAR BUSINESS

What is a captive finance company? How many are there? What companies have them? How much business do they do? Here are the highlights of a study that I made of these questions:

The definition of "captive finance companies," employed in data gathering, had two parts. First, with the exception of a few captives in retail trade, only subsidiaries of nonfinancial parent corporations engaged in national or regional marketing (usually national) were included. Secondly, for inclusion in the sample, the assets of the financial subsidiaries in question must have been composed predominantly of notes receivable.

Within the definition cited, an extensive search identified 14 financing affiliates as operating before 1946, and births subsequent to that date raised the total of those operating actively for some period after World War II to 125 through the end of 1961. Births were concentrated heavily during the 1954–1957 period.

Overwhelmingly, the captives operating actively were and are concentrated in four of the Standard Industrial Classification (S.I.C.) industry groups—electrical machinery, nonelectrical machinery, transportation equipment and, to a lesser degree, retail trade. The roster of companies involved reads like a social register of corporations—General Electric, Borg-Warner, Philco, Motorola, Westinghouse, and others in appliances; Caterpillar, International Harvester, Koehring, and Allis-Chalmers in earth moving and other heavy machinery; John Deere and Massey-Ferguson in farm equipment; Clark Equipment, Pullman, and Fruehauf in truck trailers; International Telephone & Telegraph, Stromberg-Carlson, and General Telephone in telephone equipment; Cessna and Beech in small aircraft; Sears Roebuck, Montgomery Ward, Gamble-Skogmo, Macy, and Spiegel in retail trade; White Motor and Mack in trucks; and so on.

For each year of operation after World War II, balance sheets for a continually enlarging sample of financing subsidiaries were assembled. Through 1961 the sample had reached 62 companies in size. Yearly balance sheets were put on punched cards, and tabulations with various breakdowns were run off.*

Excluding GMAC, the net expansion of credit outstanding from this group of credit captives approximated $4.4 billion for the years 1946–1961. To finance this massive flow of credit, the financing affiliates tabulated drew a net $3.4 billion from the funds markets over the 1946–1961 span.

We are hardly talking a game of penny-ante!

* For more details of the methodology employed, see Victor L. Andrews, "Captive Finance Companies: Their Growth and Some Speculations on Their Significance," *Industrial Management Review*, Fall 1961, p. 27.

Exhibit III

LIABILITIES OF A SAMPLE OF CAPTIVE FINANCE COMPANIES, 1961
(Dollars in Millions)

Liabilities	Size class of assets											
	Under $10		$10–$25		$25–$100		$100–$250		$250 and over		All classes	
Short-term debt												
Negotiated												
Bank loans	$41.3	54%	$106.7	47%	$317.8	35%	$358.6	20%	$ 331.9	19%	$1,156.3	24.6%
Commercial paper	—		24.0	11	66.4	7	345.3	20	577.0	34	1,012.7	21.5
Total	41.3	54	130.7	58	384.2	42	703.9	40	908.9	53	2,169.0	46.1
Accruals and payables	1.6	2	3.1	1	20.5	2	38.4	2	80.0	5	143.6	3.0
Parent company loans												
Short-term	4.4	6	9.7	4	123.6	14	55.0	3	22.3	1	215.0	4.6
Long-term subordinated	6.6	9	14.3	7	47.5	5	72.5	4	39.0	2	179.9	3.8
Total	11.0	15	24.0	11	171.1	19	127.5	7	61.3	3	394.9	8.4
External long-term debt												
Senior	6.0	8	26.5	12	160.3	18	468.7	26	364.8	21	1,026.3	21.8
Subordinated	1.0	1	—	—	28.1	3	95.5	6	62.5	4	187.1	4.0
Total	7.0	9	26.5	12	188.4	21	564.2	32	427.3	25	1,213.4	25.8
Loss reserves	0.5	1	2.2	1	16.0	2	21.5	1	31.6	2	71.8	1.5
Equity	15.3	20	37.8	17	128.5	14	328.9	18	206.2	12	716.7	15.2
Total	$76.7	100%	$224.3	100%	$908.7	100%	$1,784.4	100%	$1,715.3	100%	$4,709.4	100.0%
Number of companies tabulated	15		15		19		9		4		62	

tween the two. (A handful of the subsidiaries have evolved into aggressive buyers of outside receivables and are income-oriented, but will be ignored in this discussion. Undeniably, though, they are a very different critter.) Formal operating arrangements between parent and captive typically consist principally of an agreement that the latter will purchase receivables generated in the course of the former's business. For our purposes, the most important feature of such an operating agreement is its implicit definition of the affiliate's scale of operations and of the means by which it is to generate an earnings stream.

By way of illustration, the agreement between one manufacturer and its subsidiary says:

> [The parent] agrees to offer the Company [i.e., the captive] all wholesale and retail obligations acquired or created by the parent in the regular course of its business.

A similar agreement between a trade corporation and its credit subsidiary must also be cited in contrast:

> The Company has entered into an agreement with [the parent] . . . under which [the parent] sells and assigns to the Company all conditional sales contracts, exclusive of Contracts under the . . . Revolving Charge Plan, arising out of merchandise sales made by [the parent] in those retail and mail order outlets mutually agreed upon from time to time. . . . Either party has the right on 60 days' notice to terminate this Agreement except as to Contracts previously purchased.

The size of a subsidiary's assets and (the other side of the coin) its need for funds are determined entirely by the volume of receivables "offered" by its parent. Agreement to transfer receivables will channel to the captive prospective cash inflows locked up in receivables. Hence, a statement such as that in the first quotation, which specifies that *all* retail and wholesale paper acquired by the parent will be funneled into the captive, rather clearly associates its size potential, and ultimately its cash inflow, with the sales fortunes of the parent company. Furthermore, the meaning of the word "all" is subject only to a very limited amount of gratuitous interpretation and reinterpretation. By contrast, scale of operations and permanency of existence are considerably more vague in the case of the captive mentioned in the second quotation. In either instance, however, realization of parent-company sales is the indispensable ingredient of the captive's life.

Controlled Earnings

The operating agreement also defines a captive finance company's visible means of support. Some parent companies reimburse captives with fees, but usually the interest burden of the captive company's debt financing must be met from its earnings on receivables held. Consequently, the terms on which they are purchased determine the captive's ability to cover interest charges and installments of long-term debt retirement. To quote again for illustration:

The General Operating Agreement provides that it is the intent of the parties that the relationships between [the parent] and the Company covered by this Agreement shall generally be on terms which in the regular course of business will afford reasonable compensation for the financing services rendered by the Company to [the parent] in respect of [the parent's] products.

Other agreements could be cited which specify that purchase prices and/or other forms of compensation are variable and negotiable, occasionally indicating that they are designed to produce a certain earnings coverage of fixed charges on debt of the corporation. In short, the captives are kept by their parents, not as courtesans usually, but simply as cash and earnings flow dependents. Retention by the parent of the right and ability, direct or indirect, to control volume and terms of acquisition of receivables makes the captive's cash flow a managed variable—managed by a party which is neither creditor nor debtor.

It might be added that, because of the arbitrariness of "earnings" of the type of captive under consideration here, attempts by officers of independent finance companies to compare their earnings with those of captives are an exercise in utter futility.

The dependency of a captive is underscored by the neither-fish-nor-fowl nature of its operating agreement with its parent. Usually, the basic document is a letter of agreement stating the parties' intentions. So far as I can discern, it is not a contract. Indeed, the meaning such a "contract" would have is open to question, since there seems little doubt that a wholly owned subsidiary would do its parent's bidding in any event.

Interestingly enough, statements have appeared in the prospectuses of bond issues publicly floated by some captives which constitute an admission of the power of the parent company over the captive's cash flows. For instance:

New York State laws effectively limit the investments of the insurance industry, one of the dominant fund suppliers to the long-term corporate debt market, to bonds of issuers which have covered their interest obligations one and one-half times in either of the preceding two fiscal years and on an average over the last five. A quotation from a comparatively recent public issue by a captive will illustrate implicit recognition of the parent's ability to *define* what the captive's cash flow will be to meet the intent of the New York legal constraint:

"The purchase price at which the Corporation [the captive] may acquire accounts . . . is designed to produce an earnings coverage of at least one and one-half times the fixed charges on debt of the corporation."

CASE EXAMPLE

Having examined the captive-parent company relationship in a general way, let us take a simplified but realistic example of a hypothetical company. Three separate stages will be considered:

1. Situation of the parent before creating the captive.
2. Formation of the captive.
3. Situation after both parent and captive have financed expanding assets by added debt.

Stage 1: Financial Pressure

Let us call the company Heavy Equipment Maker, Inc. (HEM). When management first begins to think of creating a captive, its financial position is as follows:

The balance sheet of HEM is shown in Exhibit IV; see the figures in columns I and III. Following several years of intermittently expanding sales and rather stead-

Exhibit IV

BALANCE SHEETS OF HEAVY EQUIPMENT MAKER, INC. AND CAPTIVE COMPANY

(In Thousands of Dollars)

Assets			Liabilities		
	I. Before Captive	II. After Captive		III. Before Captive	IV. After Captive
A. PARENT COMPANY					
Current assets			Current liabilities		
Cash	$ 1,500	$ 1,500	Short-term bank loans	$11,200	—
Government securities	—	—	Accruals and payables	9,000	$ 9,000
Receivables			Current maturity of		
Notes			long-term debt	1,000	1,000
Wholesale	2,000	—	Total current		
Retail	12,000	—	liabilities	$21,200	$10,000
Open book	6,600	6,600			
Inventory	30,000	30,000	Long-term debt	17,000	17,000
Total current assets	$52,100	$38,100			
Equity in captive	—	2,800			
Fixed assets	25,000	25,000	Net worth	38,900	38,900
Total assets	$77,100	$65,900	Total liabilities	$77,100	$65,900
B. CAPTIVE COMPANY					
Notes receivable					
Wholesale		$ 2,000	Short-term bank loans		$11,200
Retail		12,000	Parent equity		2,800
Total assets		$14,000	Total liabilities		$14,000

NOTES: Earnings before interest and taxes at 12% per annum of assets: $9.252 million
Interest at average interest rate of 5% per annum on debt outstanding: $1.460 million
Pretax profit — $7.792 million
Assume tax rate of 50%
Pretax equivalent of current maturity of long-term debt: $2 million
Earnings coverage of interest burden: 6.3 times
Earnings coverage of interest plus pretax equivalent of current maturity of long-term debt: 2.67 times

ily lengthening credit terms, HEM possesses a $20.6 million portfolio of receivables. A minor fraction of the total consists of ordinary open-book trade credit. The remaining $14 million, however, is composed of $12 million of deferred payment "retail" receivables contracts with final purchasers and $2 million of "wholesale" paper secured by HEM products in the inventories of the distributors in

HEM's marketing chain. The gradual expansion of these receivables has dried up what was once a liquidity reserve of Treasury bills.

Because receivables growth has outpaced the internal generation of cash, it has forced increasing reliance on continuous rollover of unsecured short-term bank debt, which amounts to $11.2 million at the time of our reading. The outlook for receivables growth is one of intensification rather than respite. Since the "short-term" debt has grown whiskers with successive renewals, there is some pressure on the vice president for finance to find a permanent way out. The debt and equity composition is virtually 50–50 (1 to 1, in ratio terms)—not exaggerated but high enough to hint that continued debt financing of receivables growth may hit a bottle-neck. Liquidity coverage in the form of cash held plus prospective cash inflows in the form of receivables relative to current liabilities is a trifle better than 1 to 1.

The memoranda at the foot of the balance sheet indicate the risk and income positions of creditors and equity holders:

During the year preceding the balance-sheet date, HEM earned a return of 12% on its assets after all operating costs, or in other words, a little over $9 million (before interest and taxes) returned to security holders. The debt outstanding bears an average interest rate of 5%, and this earns the creditors $1.46 million per year. The remainder of pretax earnings, of course, returns to shareholders and the government. The interest burden of $1.46 million is covered 6.3 times by earnings before interest and taxes.

In the coming year, $1 million of the long-term debt is due to mature. These are after-tax dollars: to meet the payment HEM must earn $2 million before taxes. The total pretax long-term debt drain, then, will consist of interest of $1.46 million plus the $2 million, or $3.46 million. Earnings before interest and taxes of $9.252 million will cover this two and two-thirds times.

Stage 2: Captive Formed

Not surprisingly, the enticements of owning and operating a captive finance company—whether real or imagined—catch the eye of the financial vice president, and he succumbs. Accordingly, the Heavy Equipment Finance Company (HEFCO) is sired. This leads to a two-piece corporation and the two-piece balance sheet shown in columns II and IV.

On the face of it, HEM's situation is transmuted. Pestiferous short-term debt has been wiped off the slate, and HEM's debt/equity ratio is now a revivified .695 in contrast to the previous borderline 1 to 1. Seemingly, the result is an unqualified success for the parent company. (This clean-as-a-hound's-tooth effect has been of some importance to financial management. Most parent companies deconsolidate their financing subsidiaries in annual reporting, and the prospect of a spick-and-span parent company balance sheet understandably exercises some magnetism.)

It is now HEFCO's job to raise and administer the funds committed to its parent-generated receivables. HEFCO operates, let us say, under an agreement with its parent to buy without recourse receivables the latter may offer which have originated in connection with dealer and distributor or customer financing, but the agreement is terminable with notice.

Wholesale and retail notes receivable of $2 million and $12 million, respectively, have become the asset structure of HEFCO. Simultaneously, HEFCO has assumed, in effect, liability for the old $11.2 million short-term debt.

The intrinsic security of the cash flow of HEFCO's assets earns it a convenient debt/equity ratio characteristic of many captives. HEFCO is able to boast of debt to its bank of $11.2 million on an equity base of $2.8 million. This is a ratio of 4 to 1. The contrast with the parent company's previous headscratching over its manufacturer's norm of 1 to 1 is a thing of beauty. Moreover, the problem of added financing for receivables expanding in the future is broken wide open; every added $1 of the parent's equity in HEFCO will support $4 of loans from the banks.

Illusions. Closer scrutiny, however, is justified. A notation of $2.8 million invested in HEFCO appears on the asset side of the parent company's balance sheet—the same $2.8 million, of course, which appears as equity on the claims side of HEFCO's balance sheet. Readers who return to HEM's pre-captive balance sheet and mentally pair the unsecured $11.2 million bank debt then outstanding with the $14 million of notes receivable simultaneously held (wholesale and retail), will see that the $2.8 million difference between the two figures is nothing more or less than HEM's equity in the same notes receivable then outstanding. Since HEFCO's sole asset is the same $14 million notes receivable, the parent's equity of $2.8 million in its subsidiary is the same equity held in notes receivable before they were splintered away. The transmutation of the balance sheets is, perhaps, mere alchemy.

Some may argue that the pre-captive debt/equity ratio supposed here is not realistic. But consider secured financing of manufacturer's receivables which provides a loan value of 75%. Equity of 25% is retained by the borrower. This is a debt/equity ratio of nothing other than 3 to 1; and an 80% to 20% split is a ratio of 4 to 1, the value assumed in the foregoing example. Consumer receivables have often commanded loan values of 90%; this gives the borrower the benefit of a 9 to 1 debt/equity split. In brief, the same collateral value operates in the achievement of a high debt/equity ratio in other contexts as it does in the example assumed.

Risk, Income, and Cash Flow. No change has ensued in the aggregate returns to creditors and equity holders. The amount of debt outstanding is precisely equal to its total before severance of the receivables limb from the parent body. Assuming that the average interest rate remains constant, the interest burden remains constant. Since no change in the schedule of debt retirement is implied, debt service—interest plus the pretax equivalent of annual debt retirement—remains constant too. Thus, for the corporate entity as a whole *total* coverage of debt service by earnings before interest and taxes remains *completely unchanged* by formation of the captive.

Note, too, that formation and separate financing of the subsidiary in no way shields the cash and earnings flows of the parent company from the interest burden of the subsidiary's debt. That is, expenses of the parent company realized in the sale of receivables to its subsidiary are the latter's income. The excess of this income to the subsidiary over its expenses is net earnings; when consolidated, that is, changed back to the original pocket in the same pair of pants, these earnings contribute to the parent's net income. Thus, interest expenses paid by the subsidiary affect parent-company net income as much as if the parent had paid them directly. Even if captive company income is not consolidated for accounting presentation, the parent's underlying equity in assets of the subsidiary grows by the amount of the latter's net income.

The same reasoning applies to the cash drain of debt repayments made by the subsidiary: inevitably they are drawn from cash flow of the parent company. If an excess of cash flow piles up in the captive for some reason, it takes but a stroke of a pen to loan it back to the parent or pay a dividend. Both expedients can effect a transfer of money as needed. Similarly, the parent can loan to the captive as needed. Again it is clear that parent and captive are a single liquidity unit.

Stage 3: Subsequent Growth

Is this the end of the argument? If dismemberment of the asset and liability structures of a nonfinancial corporation creates additional "borrowing capacity" and if a captive company is bound by creditor-imposed limits to a certain debt/equity ratio, as is the case in reality, the only place where added debt can be evidenced is on the balance sheet of the parent company. Those who maintain that operation of a captive enhances or manufactures debt capacity must be prepared to argue that it somehow avoids or softens the usual effects of debt on the corporation. To test this view, let us take our example a stage further:

Time has passed in the lives of parent and financing affiliate. Both have experienced asset growth, as can be seen in their balance sheets, but a period of stability is now at hand. Expanding sales have boosted all assets proportionately, including notes receivable. HEFCO has husbanded a modest increment of $700 thousand in its parent-company equity into a total expansion in its resources of $3.5 million— the $700 thousand and an increase of debt of four times this amount (see Exhibit V).

To reduce the pressure of short-term liabilities (however remote the possibility that they would ever be withdrawn by the lenders), a long-term debt issue of $8 million with equal annual repayments is placed privately by HEFCO with some insurance companies. Fully used bank lines of $6 million are maintained with a group of banks, the remnant of the previously larger short-term debt. HEFCO observes its banks' modest requirement of compensating balances of 10% of the $6 million in active use, which gives it the cash balance shown of $600 thousand.

These credit lines are independent of those of the parent company except that they are maintained at the parent's banks of deposit.

Asset growth has forced HEM to draw on the postulated additional borrowing capacity. Hence, borrowing from banks reappears on HEM's balance sheet; since

Exhibit V

BALANCE SHEETS AFTER GROWTH

(In Thousands of Dollars)

Assets		*Liabilities*	
A. PARENT COMPANY			
Current assets		Current liabilities	
Cash	$ 1,875	Accruals and payables	$ 9,900
Government securities	—	Bank loans	12,276
Receivables		Current maturity of long-	
Notes	—	term debt	1,000
Open-book	8,250	Total current	
		liabilities	$23,176
Inventory	37,500	Long-term debt	16,000
Total current assets	$47,625		
Equity in captive company	3,500		
Fixed assets	31,250	Net worth	43,199
Total assets	$82,375	Total liabilities	$82,375
B. CAPTIVE COMPANY			
Cash	$ 600	Short-term bank loans	$ 6,000
Notes receivable		Current maturity of long-term	
		debt	500
Wholesale	2,417	Long-term debt	7,500
Retail	14,483	Parent equity	3,500
Total assets	$17,500	Total liabilities	$17,500

NOTES: Earnings before interest and taxes at 12% per annum of consolidated assets: $11,565
Interest at an average interest rate of 5% per annum on outstanding interest-bearing debt: $2,163
Pretax profit: $9,402
Assume a tax rate of 50%
Pretax equivalent of current maturity of long-term debt: $3,000
Earnings coverage of interest burden: 5.3
Earnings coverage of interest plus pretax equivalent of current maturity of long-term debt: 2.2

Stage 2, bank debt has reappeared for the purpose of financing $12.276 million of HEM's $16.475 million asset expansion.

How does HEM's additional debt affect the position of the company's claimants—creditors and equity holders?

REALISTIC PERSPECTIVE

Counting all debt, accruals and interest-bearing alike, debt/equity ratios are as follows:

Parent company	.907
Captive company	4.000
Consolidated	1.231

The earnings-flow protection of debt service is reduced. Under our assumptions, parent and captive have been fortunate enough to continue borrowing at an unchanged average interest rate of 5% despite alteration of the capital structure. On the new amount of interest-bearing debt outstanding, the interest burden has mounted to $2.163 million. Earnings coverage has dropped from 6.3 to 5.3 times. In turn, coverage of interest plus the pretax equivalent of the current installments of long-term debt retirement has slipped from the previous 2.67 times to 2.2 times. Thus, risk of default in the aggregate has *increased*.

It is evident now that the popularly employed ordinary balance-sheet tests of debt proportions applied to parent and/or captive separately would understate aggregate debt pressure. More important, there is an essential unity of parent and captive as cash-flow and earnings entities; balance-sheet tests of separate pieces omit completely the more significant question of aggregate coverage of debt service.

Short-Term Creditors

The basic security of short-term lenders must rest on the security of receivables in existence at one moment in time. For a captive's creditors this protection is usually good. On the receivables outstanding at a given time, prospective interest income is well defined because the receivables have changed hands between parent and captive on known terms. Cash provided by receivables run-off would liquidate short-term indebtedness in the event of their shrinkage. Thus, for the captive's short-term creditors, liquidity protection is clear.

However, we made the assumption earlier that parent and subsidiary maintain lines of credit separately but with the same banks. In real life this is the usual case. Under such an arrangement, increases in the total of loans made by an institution to parent and captive can only lower the degree of liquidity protection it enjoys. For example:

The loans of HEFCO's banks are adequately secured, as we have noted, but the same banks also now have painted themselves into a corner where they lend to a parent corporation denuded of its folio of notes receivable. In short, HEM's banks are lenders to a company which has a current asset structure composed of minor amounts of operating cash and open-book receivables but mostly inventory which can be reduced to liquidity only by normal turnover or by forced sale.

What the captive has, the parent does not. If the notes receivable of a captive finance company are prime liquid assets and premium collateral, it follows that the attractiveness of its parent to a creditor is diminished. Thus, the position of a parent company's creditors, both short- and long-term, seems materially *weaker* than before formation of the captive.

The preceding point makes clear the oversight in the oft-repeated catechism that the parent company will "stand behind" the obligations of its financing affiliate. I wonder whether, barring outright mismanagement or fraud, the well-defined cash flow of the subsidiary's extant receivables does not make it a far better bet to survive adversity than its parent, which would labor under pressure with an illiquid asset structure. In any case, though, if we picture a situation in which for some reason the subsidiary cannot meet its debt obligations, it is clear that the parent could be helpful only if (1) it has maintained excess liquidity reserves (while the subsidiary has been borrowing!) or (2) it has kept its hands free by not employing its own debt capacity. In the last case there would seem to be little point in having employed the subsidiary as a debt vehicle; for the parent might as well have done the same job alone.

Long-Term Creditors

Consider the position of HEFCO's long-term creditors. HEFCO floated a 16-year amortizing bond issue of $8 million. This means that, with equal annual repayment installments, $500 thousand after taxes ($1 million before taxes) must be repaid annually, and under the assumption of a corporate-wide interest rate of 5%, an interest bill in the first year of $400 thousand (on the long-term debt alone) is incurred. This cash drain of $1.4 million in pretax terms must be met out of the spread between the price paid for receivables and cash inflow from receivables collection.

Given the usual operating agreement, the sole earning assets of HEFCO will be parent-generated receivables. Thus, flagging sales of the parent would rob HEFCO of the ability to earn. Aside from this customary business risk, the basic security characteristic of creditor-borrower relationships is missing. The ability of the parent company to terminate its relationship with the captive is a vague and nebulous but nonetheless real weakness of a loan to a captive. Any reply that this escape valve is a mere legality is not sufficient: if legalities do not matter, why are note agreements still written?

To look at the matter in still another way, if a long-term lender were to say that the ambiguities of the captive company's earnings and cash flow do not disturb him because of his confidence in the parent company's good business prospects and intention to maintain the subsidiary, this would be equivalent to purchasing captive debt on the faith and credit of the parent. This would, in turn, be equivalent to buying a debenture (i.e., unsecured bond) of the parent. If this is in fact the lender's attitude, what point is there in a parent company's having a credit subsidiary for its supposedly superior segregated collateral value and fund-raising capacities?

Effects of Leverage

The debt borne by a credit subsidiary exerts leverage on the return on its parent company's net worth. This leverage effect is indirect but nevertheless real. As was brought out earlier, fixed-interest charges borne by the subsidiary affect the parent company's net income, albeit by a roundabout route. This establishes a link between market treatment of parent company common stock and subsidiary interest charges.

The effects of fixed-interest charges and fluctuating revenue on HEM's return on equity are shown in Part A of Exhibit VI. The same assumption with respect to interest burden is used as in Exhibit V. In Part B of Exhibit VI we see the return on book value of equity for a company identical with

Exhibit VI

EFFECTS OF LEVERAGE ON RETURN ON EQUITY

(Dollars in Thousands)

	Earnings before interest and taxes on total corporate assets						
	9%	*10%*	*11%*	*12%*	*13%*	*14%*	*15%*
A. HEAVY EQUIPMENT MAKER, INC.							
Earnings before interest and taxes	$8,674	$9,638	$10,601	$11,565	$12,529	$13,492	$14,456
Interest	2,164	2,164	2,164	2,164	2,164	2,164	2,164
Profit before tax	6,510	7,474	8,437	9,401	10,365	11,328	12,292
Income tax @ 50%	3,255	3,737	4,218	4,700	5,182	5,664	6,146
Profit after tax	3,255	3,737	4,219	4,700	5,183	5,664	6,146
Return on book value of net worth	7.5%	8.7%	9.8%	10.9%	12.0%	13.1%	14.2%
B. IDENTICAL UNLEVERED COMPANY							
Earning before interest and taxes (profit before tax)	$8,674	$9,638	$10,601	$11,565	$12,529	$13,492	$14,456
Income tax @ 50%	4,337	4,819	5,300	5,782	6,265	6,746	7,228
Profit after tax	4,337	4,819	5,301	5,783	6,264	6,746	7,228
Return on book value of net worth	5.0%	5.6%	6.1%	6.7%	7.2%	7.8%	8.3%

HEM in every respect except that it does not have debt; all its financing is equity save for accruals and payables. In contrast with the unlevered company, the mean value of return on net worth is raised for HEM by leverage, but the range of possible income results is widened appreciably and the actual result made more problematical over exactly the same range of earnings on assets.

During the 1950's and early 1960's these classic effects of leverage were at work on many parent companies, but short recessions and recurrent booms ironed out variability in profit rates. Obviously, this happenstance should not lead us to overlook the impact of subsidiary-borne interest charges on parent companies' return on equity in the future.

Risk and Income Analysis

The investment in a captive's receivables is an earning asset which, aside from its effects (ignored here) on realization of additional sales by the parent, has an impact on revenue. Also, it is literally impossible to say what is the return on captive-company assets; their revenue is subject to negotiation with the parent, and except for the very large ones, their cost figures are arbitrary allocations between parent and captive. Thus, we have no way of knowing a plausible assumption with respect to the return on their assets. Moreover, holdings of expanded liquid receivables may cushion the risks of debt. So long as these pieces in the jigsaw puzzle are missing, a complete analysis of the risk assumed by creditors and equity holders is checkmated.

CONCLUSION

Hopefully, the foregoing has made clear that the typical operating arrangement between a parent and its captive makes the latter a creature of the former's will to divert a portion of its prospective cash inflows. A nonfinancial parent company has but one stream of cash inflow to be split up, and no matter how many pieces are carved out, it is the sum of those pieces. Similarly, profits for the shareholders of the parent cannot be manufactured by trading assets and services at a price within the same over-all corporate entity. Thus, parent and captive are essentially one unit for analysis of liquidity, cash inflow, and profit.

I think that, wittingly or unwittingly, the banking system has absorbed considerably increased risk exposure in lending to parent-captive combines; that long-term lenders have loaned to many captives which have little control over their ability to earn debt service; that the creditors of parents with captives lend, in essence, to organizations with reduced liquidity protection and hence greater risk; and that managements of nonfinancial parent corporations have taken no account of the effects on their stock prices of leverage introduced to their profit flows by subsidiary-borne debt. In short, the rush of lenders and borrowers to debt finance mushrooming receivables has preceded a rounded consideration of risk. In addition, the usual analytical practices as they are almost invariably applied to financial data have been altogether inadequate for revealing the full meaning of the growth of the captives.

It is a good bet that a keystone of the rapid spread of financing subsidiaries in the 1950's and 1960's was a shift of institutional lender preferences toward increased risk for the sake of increased income. The desire for a rising loan-to-deposit ratio made the commercial banking system, particularly the large city banks, fertile ground for loan applications to finance receivables. Also, after excess capacity developed widely in corporate manufacturing in the mid-1950's, demands for long-term debt to finance plant and equipment expenditures shrank, thus heightening the receptivity of the corporate capital market to long-term debt issues of the captives.

If nonfinancial corporations found the ready financing a congenial answer to their need for lengthened credit terms, it is no surprise and no sin that a marriage of the minds was consummated. What is argued here is that rather than marry in haste and repent at leisure, both borrowers and lenders can well afford some dispassionate reflection. In particular, the former should pay more attention to the question of whether the equity values under their stewardship have been enhanced or diminished by the use of captives.

A full-scale analytical attack on the problems in financial analysis posed by the operation or desire to operate financing subsidiaries will be difficult. A captive grafted on its parent creates a hybrid financial entity—half financial, half nonfinancial. The capital structure appropriate to such a creature is surely unlike the more familiar contours of nonfinancial parent alone. Some may be inclined to defend the separate financing of parent and captive as the appropriate form. However, since parent and captive are essentially a single liquidity-cash-flow unit, this view seems speciously simple. The conclusion is unavoidable that business needs much more concrete information on the behavior of cash flows in hybrid financial-nonfinancial corporations.

COMMERCIAL PAPER *

THE TERM commercial paper has been used traditionally to describe the various types of short-term credit instruments issued by business and banking firms to raise funds. In recent years, however, the term has been employed more and more to mean specifically the short-term promissory notes issued by a relatively small group of business firms that borrow funds in the money market.

As the meaning of the term has narrowed, the use of commercial paper to raise funds has increased markedly. Over the entire postwar period, following the wartime episode when the use of commercial paper had been reduced substantially, the amount of commercial paper outstanding climbed to a level nearly five and a half times as great as the prewar record level reached in 1920. At the end of 1963 the amount of commercial paper reached a total of $6.7 billion outstanding.

The commercial paper market, as defined above, is the oldest of the various segments of the short-term money market. Although the market can be traced in financial history as far back as the early 1800's, the present form was developed early in the twentieth century. Then, as now, business firms rated highly by the market obtained short-term funds by issuing unsecured notes on a discount basis through a small number of commercial paper dealers. The maturities of the unsecured notes have usually ranged from four to six months, although, currently, some are as short as five days while others run over nine months. The denominations of the notes vary, but they are for the most part in multiples of $5,000.

One of the most significant developments in the postwar commercial paper market, as compared with the market during the early part of the century, has been the marked growth in the amount of commercial paper placed directly with investors by a number of the largest sales finance companies. During the 1920's and early 1930's all borrowing and lending by major industrial concerns carried on in the commercial paper market was done through commercial paper dealers. The introduction of directly placed paper took place in the mid-1930's. After making fairly sizable inroads, the amount of directly placed commercial paper was reduced to virtually nothing during the abnormal credit situation of the war period. Since 1945, however, finance paper placed directly with investors has moved into prominence in the com-

---

* Reprinted by permission from *Money Market Instruments*, Federal Reserve Bank of Cleveland, 2d ed., (January 1967), pp. 41–47.

mercial paper market, usually amounting to more than three times the amount of paper placed through dealers.

The rapid postwar growth in the commercial paper market, and especially the more recent expansion, has paralleled the growth in the demand for working capital on the part of business firms. Since the market is not generally considered a source of permanent working capital, borrowers use it mainly to supplement short-term bank loans in meeting peak seasonal and cyclical needs. On the other hand, the sales finance companies that are active

Figure 1
COMMERCIAL PAPER OUTSTANDING
Directly Placed Finance Paper and Paper Placed through Dealers

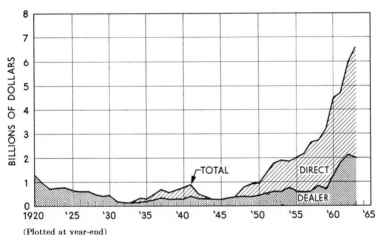

(Plotted at year-end)
Source of data: Board of Governors of the Federal Reserve System.

in the directly placed market, in order to satisfy a growing yet highly flexible demand for their services, have tapped the market continuously.

The extent to which firms have been able to satisfy their working capital demands by selling commercial paper has, of course, depended upon the supply of funds available in the market at any one time. During the 1920's, commercial banks were the major suppliers of funds in this market, holding about 90 percent of the amount outstanding. Country banks and small city banks, in particular, held a large volume of commercial paper as secondary reserves.

In the past several years, although banks have continued to acquire commercial paper, there has been a large-scale entry of new types of purchasers. Recent purchasers include diverse groups such as nonfinancial corporations, pension and trust funds, insurance companies, and college endowment funds. Of these, non-financial corporations are estimated to hold over 50 percent of outstanding paper.

The continuous growth in the liquid funds of these groups, which have provided a major portion of the supply of funds to the market, has been an important factor in the postwar growth as well as in the recent expansion of the use of commercial paper.

As a result of the influx of new buyers, one of the striking features of the present commercial paper market is that it is increasingly becoming a market in which various institutions in competition with the banking system are meeting part of the short-term credit demands of business firms.

FEWER BORROWERS IN DEALER MARKET

From a relatively low level at the end of the war, the amount of paper placed through dealers, which accounts now for a minority share of the commercial paper market, has recovered to the extent that the dollar volume

Table I

NET WORTH OF COMMERCIAL PAPER BORROWERS
(5 selected years)

Firms with net worth of:	Percentage distribution of borrowers				
	1945	1950	1955	1960	1963
Over $25 million..................	4.5	10.3	19.4	32.7	41.6
$5 to $25 million..................	14.7	24.7	34.8	37.0	39.9
$1 to $5 million...................	57.3	56.9	42.9	28.5	18.0
Less than $1 million...............	23.5	8.1	2.9	1.8	0.5
	100.0	100.0	100.0	100.0	100.0

Source: National Credit Office, New York, New York

is about 150 percent as large as the 1920 level when all commercial paper was placed through dealers. In striking contrast to the postwar expansion in dealer paper, however, has been the sharp drop in the number of borrowers in the market. In 1963 only 416 qualified firms offered paper through dealers, as compared with nearly 4,400 during the 1920's. Since borrowers have not numbered more than 450 in any year in the postwar period, the greatest portion of the decline in the number of borrowers obviously occurred prior to World War II. Thus, the entire expansion since 1945 in outstanding dealer paper has originated from less than one-tenth of the number of firms selling paper during the 1920's.

During the postwar period, there has been a marked trend toward relatively larger firms using the market as a source of short-term funds. As shown in Table I, 80.8 percent of the borrowers had a net worth of under $5 million in 1945, whereas only 18.5 percent had a net worth of under $5 million in 1963. The trend cannot be attributed to short-term cyclical influences because the movement toward the $5–25 million and the over $25 million classes has taken place steadily throughout the postwar period.

The nature of the dealer commercial paper market is such that only large firms with impeccable credit ratings and well-known to investors can sell commercial paper. At present, ten dealers purchase the unsecured promissory notes of business firms. Since dealers do not endorse the notes when purchased and since holders may wish to dispose of the notes before maturity, the name of the company largely must sell itself. Furthermore, notes are sold with the provision that investors can return them if they are not satisfied with the firm's record. As may be expected, however, losses have been practically negligible.

Although investors in the commercial paper market are located throughout the United States as well as in some foreign countries, particularly Canada, borrowers in the market have been concentrated near the money market centers of New York and Chicago. Historically, about 80 percent of the borrowers have been located in the eastern half of the United States.

Table II
PERCENTAGE DISTRIBUTION OF COMMERCIAL
PAPER BORROWERS ACCORDING
TO INDUSTRIES

	1951	1961	1963
Manufacturers			
Food Processing	15.1	10.0	8.7
Textiles	17.1	6.9	8.4
Metal Products	4.5	5.7	5.8
Other	12.3	15.5	18.0
Total	49.0	38.1	40.9
Finance			
Automobile	11.1	24.1	17.8
Small Loans	5.3	8.3	10.3
Other	3.5	5.1	4.8
Total	19.9	37.5	32.9
Wholesalers	19.0	8.6	7.9
Retailers			
Department Stores	6.8	6.6	5.5
Other	3.5	3.4	2.9
Total	10.3	10.0	8.4
Miscellaneous	1.8	5.7	9.9
	100.0	100.0	100.0

Source: National Credit Office, New York, New York

Despite the decline in the number of borrowers in the commercial paper market, a considerable variety of borrowers continues to be represented. As shown in Table II the principal classifications of borrowers include manufacturers, finance companies, wholesalers, and retailers. During 1963, manufacturers and finance companies taken together, comprised about three-fourths of the total number of borrowers. The manufacturers' group included food and related products, textiles, and metal products; automobile finance companies accounted for the major part of the financial classification.

Although requirements for issuing commercial paper are relatively rigid, the market does provide an important alternative source of funds for seasonal and cyclical needs for qualified firms. In addition, there is a prestige factor that tends to enhance the firm's ability to borrow in the long-term end of the market.

Another factor in the use of commercial paper as an alternative source of credit has been the statutory ceiling on bank loans to a single large borrower. Because of the rapid growth in financing needs, many major industrial concerns have found themselves at the legal maximum of commercial banks. Further expansion of loans from commercial banks is thus realizable only through resort to additional banks.

ROLE OF FINANCE COMPANIES IN THE DIRECTLY PLACED PAPER MARKET

During the postwar period, the directly placed commercial paper market has expanded steadily to become an important source of short-term funds for the large sales finance companies. An exceptionally rapid expansion in directly placed paper began early in 1959.

With the entrance of additional companies in 1960 and 1961, there are at least twelve sales finance companies, including the four largest that place commercial paper directly with investors. The finance companies borrowing short-term funds in this way have developed the staffs and facilities necessary for selling their paper to investors continuously throughout the year.

Since the end of World War II, sales finance companies have been under constant pressure to meet the very large increase in the demand for their services. To meet such demand, which consists primarily of automobile dealer financing, the finance companies have relied heavily upon borrowed funds. The expansion in automobile credit has fluctuated widely from year to year. As a result, sales finance companies, in order to maintain flexibility, have borrowed largely by means of short-term obligations.

The sources of funds available to the sales finance companies, of course, include both short- and long-term borrowing, as well as capital accounts. However, the use of short-term credit has been the most flexible of the various sources of funds.

RATES ON COMMERCIAL PAPER

The open market rates on commercial paper are relatively sensitive indicators of changes in the supply and demand for short-term funds. The open market rate is announced by major dealers on the paper of their prime borrowers. The rate has usually been from one-fourth to one-half percent above the Treasury bill yield, resulting in yield differentials that make commercial paper attractive to investors.

The prime commercial rate usually has been at least one percent below the prime rate charged by major commercial banks to their top-quality borrowers. The differential in this case offers interest cost savings to borrowers in the commercial paper market. However, the spread between the commercial paper rate and prime bank rate tends to understate somewhat the actual difference in cost of borrowing. Since commercial banks have set minimum balance provisions that require some proportion of the borrowed funds to be kept on deposit with the bank, the actual cost of bank funds available for use may be greater than the stated rate.

At the same time, however, the spread between the bank rate and the rate on commercial paper placed through dealers overstates the differential between the two rates in that dealers charge a commission usually amounting, on an annual basis, to about one-fourth percent of the amount of the unsecured notes.

The rate on directly placed commercial paper of the sales finance companies generally has been slightly below the rate of borrowers in the dealer market. Although sales finance companies in the directly placed market publish their rates separately, changes in the rates of one company are usually followed closely by changes in the rates of other companies. Offered rates are listed according to the maturity of the notes and usually have a differential of 1.25 percent between the notes of five to twenty-nine days and those over nine months.

The amount of commercial paper outstanding began to grow rapidly during 1959, especially during the first half of 1960. The increase in outstanding paper during 1959, however, was due wholly to the activity in the directly placed market of the sales finance companies. It was not until the beginning of 1960, when the demand for this type of credit became more widespread, that the amount of outstanding paper placed through dealers expanded rapidly.

An impetus to the expansion in dealer commercial paper in 1960 was a widening in the differential between the rate on commercial paper placed through dealers and the bank rate for prime borrowers. As shown in the accompanying chart, the average differential between the bank rate and the commercial paper rate moved from .69 percent in the first quarter of 1959 down to .23 percent in the fourth quarter, before lengthening to an average differential of .62 percent in the first half of 1960. Since the spread has customarily been about one percent, the cost of commercial paper relative to bank credit was rather large throughout most of the period from early 1959 through mid-1960. During the last half of 1960 and throughout 1961, however, the spread between the bank rate and the commercial paper rate widened to 1.35 percent and 1.54 percent, respectively. Thus, the cost of commercial paper relative to bank credit throughout the latter period became more attractive to commercial paper borrowers.

The average differential between the rate on commercial paper placed through dealers and the bank rate for prime borrowers again narrowed during 1962 and 1963. In the fourth quarter of 1963, for example, the average differential was .59 percent. In contrast, although the volume of commercial paper placed through dealers continued to expand rapidly during 1962, dealer paper declined by 7.6 percent in 1963.

One factor in the ability of major corporations to obtain funds in the commercial paper market, particularly during the sharp increase in the use of commercial paper during 1960, was the level of the rate on commercial paper

Figure 2

SELECTED SHORT-TERM MONEY RATES

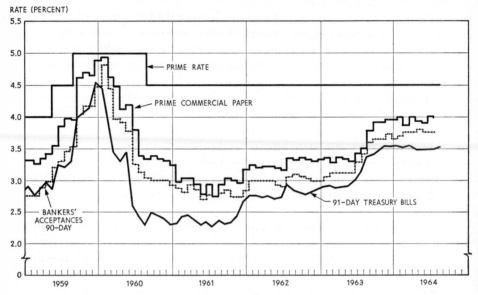

Source of data: Board of Governors of the Federal Reserve System.

relative to Treasury issues with comparable maturity. The average spread between the dealer paper rate and the Treasury bill rate during 1959 was .57 percent, but it averaged 1.09 percent during 1960. Because of a faster increase in the rate on Treasury bills during the succeeding three years, the average differential narrowed to the more customary percentage of about one-half.

SEASONAL PATTERNS IN DATA

One feature common to the firms that place their paper through dealers is the seasonal nature of their operations. For these firms, commercial paper serves as a source of funds to finance seasonally large inventories or a particularly large volume of accounts receivable. For example, large retailers, such as department stores, sell commercial paper to finance heavy inventories during the fall and Christmas seasons. Also, textile mills and food processing firms, such as flour mills, tap the market during harvest seasons to accommodate the large purchases of cotton and grain.

As evidenced by the monthly data on commercial paper placed through dealers, the amount outstanding increases at the end of the summer, rising to a seasonal maximum during November. Outstandings increase again during February, reaching a peak in March, before declining through the summer months.

Since the large sales finance companies in the directly placed market sell paper continuously throughout the year, a relatively small amount of monthly fluctuation of paper outstanding might be expected. In fact, during the early part of the past decade, this was largely the case, as the amount outstanding rose consistently throughout the year and contracted sharply only during the month of December.

In the past few years, however, swings in the monthly magnitudes have become sharper. Downswings have occurred not only in December, but also during the months of April, June, and September. The timing of such seasonal downswings corresponds to the tax payment months of corporations. During these months, when corporations are less liquid, the finance companies increase their use of lines of bank credit so as to satisfy continuing needs for relatively large amounts of short-term credit.

Chapter 6   Valuation of a Firm

WM. FILENE'S SONS COMPANY[1]

IN 1949, the management of Federated Department Stores, Inc., took steps to combine into the parent corporation four subsidiaries the parent company had controlled for many years through ownership of a large majority of the shares. In the case of Wm. Filene's Sons Company, Federated owned 99.21% of the 500,000 shares of common stock, which was the only class of stock outstanding. The minority interest in Filene's consisted of 3,958 shares, held by several owners. Federated offered to exchange 1.25 shares of its common stock for each share of Filene's, and questions arose as to the fairness of the value placed on Filene's stock, as expressed by this exchange ratio.

In describing its own operations and those of Filene's, the Federated Stores corporation stated:

Federated Department Stores, Inc., is a Delaware corporation, incorporated in 1929, with its principal office at Federated Building, Cincinnati 2, Ohio. Its business, conducted directly and through five principal subsidiaries, is the operation of eight major department and specialty stores, together with fourteen branch stores. Each of the major stores is the dominant or a leading institution of its kind in its community.

. . . .

. . . Wm. Filene's Sons Company (Filene's), established in 1851 and incorporated as a Massachusetts corporation in 1912, operates the leading specialty store in Boston, Massachusetts, and branch stores in nine other New England communities, including the B. Peck Company department store in Lewiston, Maine. . . .

Each of the eight major stores [in the Federated Stores group], Abraham & Straus, Bloomingdale, Filene's, Lazarus, Shillito, Foley, Halliburton's and Boston Store, is operated as an independent unit, whether it be a subsidiary corporation or a division of Federated. Each store is an integral part of the community in which it is located. Each store has its own management, and dictates its own policies with respect to operations, personnel, merchandising, [buying], and other matters.

---

[1] Based on the record of the arbitration proceeding. Material has been condensed and paraphrased, and some detail is omitted. No facts or arguments have been added.

HOW THE EXCHANGE RATIO WAS REACHED

In developing the proposed ratio of exchange, the Federated Stores employed a firm of financial consultants, which considered many factors.

The consultants first noted that while Federated Stores stock was frequently traded on the New York Stock Exchange, Filene's stock, although sometimes quoted on the over-the-counter market, was traded very infrequently. It was concluded that the value of Filene's stock could not be measured by such nominal quotations, but that the market prices of Federated Stores stock reflected "the opinions of informed buyers and sellers [about this stock] and thus furnish the best evidence of value."

One element in the proposed value for the Filene's stock was developed by using a price–earnings ratio for Federated and multiplying this by the earnings per share. The result was called the "adjusted fair market value." Throughout their work, the consultants used the earnings as they had been reported from time to time, since later corrections could not have influenced prices before they were made.

It was decided to give no attention to the dividend policies of the two companies, since "earnings afforded a common basis of measurement." However, it was noted that Filene's had paid 44.8% of earnings during 10 years, while Federated Stores had paid 36.7%.

The adjusted fair market value of Filene's was computed to be $35.41 on July 30, 1949. In the final result, this figure had a weight of 75%.

The other 25% of the fair exchange value was assigned to the book value of the common stock of Filene's, which was $33.05 on July 30, 1949. Thus, the resulting figure was $34.82.

In connection with the use of book value as a part of the final figure, the consultants said: "Although we felt that . . . book value . . . had to be taken into consideration . . . experience shows that market appraisals generally give more weight to earning power."

When the consultant's figure of $34.82 was divided by $28.50, the July price of the stock of Federated Stores, an exchange ratio of 1.222 for 1 was indicated. The directors of Federated Stores voted to offer the ratio of 1.25, thus offering market value in Federated stock of $35.63 per share of Filene's.

Following a special stockholders' meeting, holders of 1,681 shares of Filene's stock on November 26, 1949, voted against the plan and demanded that their shares be evaluated as of that date by arbitrators, and that they be paid in cash.[2] On that date, the stock of Federated sold at $32.75 per share.

A board of arbitrators was duly appointed. Over a period of weeks, this board received briefs, and heard arguments by attorneys and evidence from expert witnesses.[3]

---

[2] Massachusetts General Laws, chap. 146, sec. 46.

[3] The arguments of the two sides are presented without any indication of which witness brought the material into the proceeding.

ARGUMENTS BY FILENE'S REPRESENTATIVES

The position of Filene's representatives was that the stock should be evaluated at $35 per share. They felt that it was first necessary to define value, since the statute does no more than require that a value be determined. Filene's argued that value in this case must mean the proportionate interest in the going concern that a stockholder offered for sale, for no liquidation was anticipated in 1949.

It was then argued for Filene's that the value of any stock investment reflected the future earning power and dividends of the corporation, appraised in the market where the securities of comparable companies were being traded, for a buyer could not be expected to pay more for Filene's stock than for a similar stock, if available. On this point, it was said: "It must be realized that there is not likely to be any other identical property, but by examining a sufficiently wide group of companies . . . a range of generally accepted . . . value for similar property will be ascertainable."

With reference to intangible values, it was said: "To the extent that a business has goodwill, such goodwill must be reflected in its earnings. The process of capitalizing earnings at the rate at which earnings are capitalized by buyers and sellers of comparable businesses, or the shares thereof, therefore includes in the value so determined whatever 'goodwill value' the business may have."

In support of the $35 valuation, a considerable amount of information was submitted concerning the earning power of Filene's. With reference to the past, the figures as reported were adjusted in various ways. One set of adjusted figures changed the earnings by showing what they would have been if the federal income tax rate had uniformly been 38%, the rate in 1949. Another set adjusted the reported figures by omitting the earnings of R. H. White's, a subsidiary sold in 1944, and including in all years the earnings of Peck's, a store purchased in 1948. These figures were presented on both a FIFO and a LIFO basis, since Filene's went to LIFO accounting in 1941. Exhibit 1 presents Filene's earnings as reported and adjusted. The fiscal years used varied with different persons who presented evidence, and so the comparable figures for all the periods are not available.

If the reader wishes to reduce these figures to a per share basis, the figure of 500,000 outstanding shares applies throughout.

Evidence was submitted to show that the growth trend of department store sales in the New England area, and especially downtown Boston, was not so strong as in other areas of the country. On the other hand, Filene's was shown to be maintaining its share of the market, and its basement store showed a stronger growth trend than the Boston average. It was generally admitted that Filene's was a leader in the establishment of branch stores, and that the management was competent.

Information was also submitted concerning Filene's dividend policy. The record of dividends is shown in Exhibit 2. With reference to the future of dividends, the age of the buildings of Filene's main store was compared unfavorably with the new Jordan Marsh building across the street, and it was argued that the need to make capital investments both in the main store and in any new branches would affect cash dividend policy in the future. The same need was advanced as the justification of the strongly liquid position of the company.

The major argument in support of Filene's was that comparisons with the market prices of common stocks of other stores would show that a price of $35 to $40 per share was not unreasonable.

One series of tables, using earnings and other data as reported, was based on an extensive list of 21 stores, which were said to be: "(a) department store and specialty store companies whose businesses are reasonably comparable to Filene's; (b) common stocks which are relatively well regarded investment-wise; and (c) common stocks having active markets [but] not, as of November 26, 1949, subject to abnormal circumstances." Several of the stocks chosen were not listed, but traded over the counter in local markets.

A condensation of the tables for the 21 stores appears as Exhibits 3 and 4. The argument of the Filene's representatives, which was based on the tables, appears below Exhibit 3. The common unit of measurement used was the ratio of the price of each stock at November 26, 1949, to an average of the earnings for that stock. Since Filene's earnings were known, the argument was that a suitable ratio could be selected from the tabulation, to be used with the Filene's earnings to give a suitable market price.

From the price–dividend ratios, it was argued in a similar way that a price of $35 for Filene's was generous, especially since the need for large investments in new buildings and equipment, referred to above, was expected to keep dividends from increasing sharply.

Noting that there was considerable variation among the stores used as to method of evaluating inventory, sale or holding of receivables, ownership or rental of property, and reliance on debt or preferred stock, the representatives of Filene's selected four stores for a more careful comparison. The purpose was to find a figure for the total capitalization of Filene's. A figure for the total capitalization of each store was built up from the market values (as of November 26, 1949) of the outstanding securities, plus an imputed principal value of annual rental expenses for leased property. The total capitalization so reached was compared with earnings before the charges on the items included in the capitalization, and the resulting ratio was applied to Filene's earnings, also taken before rents, interest, or taxes.

The witness who prepared the figures from which Exhibit 5 has been prepared testified that he placed the greatest reliance on the comparison with Best's. In his opinion, taking into account the unfavorable location of the main store, Filene's stock was not worth more than $40 per share. The reader will note that the ratio of 7.4 in Exhibit 5, applied to the Filene's earnings of $4.2 million, gives a figure of $31.1 million for total capitalization. After deducting $12.1 million for the principal value represented by rents, $19 million, or $38 per share, remains as the value of Filene's common stock.

A comparison of market prices and book values for the original list of 21 stores was also made. It was summarized by the Filene's representatives as follows:

1. A very small number of specialty or department store common stocks have, on an historical basis, consistently shown annual mean prices higher than year-end book values.

2. The bull market years of 1937, 1945 and 1946 were the only periods during which such common stocks showed relatively high frequency of mean prices in excess of book values.

A price of $35 for Filene's would result in premiums over book value at 1/29/49 of 8.5%. Such a relationship indicates a full value for Filene's in relation to book values particularly when it is remembered that Filene's owns little real estate whereas many of the other companies own real estate that may have a market value in excess of book value.

As a final point regarding the determination of fair market value, the Filene's representatives mentioned that there might be a discount due to the limited marketability of Filene's stock, but offered no measure for this discount.

ARGUMENTS OF THE DISSENTING STOCKHOLDERS

The representatives of the dissenting stockholders attacked the position of Filene's by arguing that the attempts to measure the value of Filene's stock from the market values of other stocks were not pertinent. Dissenting stockholders were asking for an equitable liquidation of their portion of the business, and the "intrinsic value" was what was to be determined.

Value must be ascertained exclusively by searching for all of the assets, tangible and intangible, and [subtracting the] liabilities of this company to arrive at the arithmetic conclusion for which these proceedings have been brought. . . . That all these vital elements, having tremendous value, should be completely discounted by Federated, and heavy weight put upon market quotations of [other] stocks dealt in on the open market . . . challenges both logic and simple good faith.

The dissenters developed a value for the Filene's stock of between $97 and $100 per share, chiefly by restating the values of the assets shown in the balance sheet of January 29, 1949 (the latest publicly available on November 26), shown in Exhibit 6.

The dissenters' viewpoint toward the figures on the balance sheet will be stated in the order in which they appear in Exhibit 6, except for the remarks on goodwill, which will be summarized last.

Cash and U.S. securities were accepted as stated, although it was noted that Filene's had a more liquid position than many other stores. No comparative figures were given with reference to this statement.

The amounts of reserves against possible losses on receivables were challenged, as the percentages seemed unreasonably high to the dissenters. Later in the proceeding, testimony brought out that actual losses had been $267,800 in the year ending January 31, 1950, against reserves of $306,000 at the beginning of the year.

As to inventory, after some argument with Filene's representatives, it was agreed that the LIFO value was under current market by about $1.8 million. This amount would be taxable as ordinary income if Filene's were to shift from LIFO to FIFO. This would be true of other capital gains, if they were recognized.

As to the land, buildings, fixtures, and equipment, it was pointed out that these assets, being booked at cost less depreciation, were greatly understated with reference to the inflated prices of November, 1949. An increase of $3 to $4 million was suggested.

The value of Filene's leasehold arrangements, it was argued, should be added to the balance sheet, but not simply as an asset offsetting a capitalized rental for a liability. The argument was that Filene's lessors would be glad to construct new buildings for a tenant so clearly able to pay an appropriate rent. It was argued that this opportunity for large-scale financing represented a hidden net value of $5 million.

In discussing the liabilities, the dissenters argued that $177,000 of the reserve for possible assessments of taxes should be added to surplus, since only $221,000 had been required to be paid by November, 1949.

It was also argued that the increase in surplus due to earnings, amounting to $1.155 million from January 29 to November 30, should be considered, since the above adjustments were proposed from a January 29 balance sheet.

The sum of the maximum increases in net worth proposed by the dissenters and listed above amounted to about $12.4 million. In addition, it was argued that Filene's had a substantial value in its goodwill. The evidence of the existence of this goodwill was found in the nationally known reputation of Filene's, in its basement, in its location, its buying power as the country's largest specialty store, its good labor relations, and in its "hidden assets."

The dissenters evaluated goodwill by a procedure that is sometimes used by courts and the Board of Tax Appeals, as follows.

The net tangible assets were given current values by the adjustments as proposed above. The value so invested was taken as capable of producing the going rate of return. The dissenters' representatives differed on the appropriate going rate. The range was from a low of 4.5%, a figure selected because diversified investments were currently producing this rate, to a high of 6%. The high figure was about two thirds of recent results as reported for specialty stores. The one-third reduction was made because the dissenters thought it was to be presumed that typical stores also enjoyed hidden values in their balance sheets.

As an example of the application of this argument, if one were to multiply the rate of 4.5% by Filene's suggested net tangible assets of about $29 million, an earnings figure of $1.305 million would result. In fact, in the 12 months ending July 31, 1949, Filene's earned $3.104 million after taxes. Therefore, goodwill could be said to have caused earnings of $1.799 million. This figure, capitalized at 10%, adds about $18 million to the value of Filene's, justifying a total value of $29 million plus $18 million, or $47 million, which is $94 per share.

The dissenters furnished several calculations on this method, using different rates, asset values, and earnings averaged over various periods, but they all tended to the conclusion that the shares should be valued at $100 or slightly less.

The dissenters also introduced facts regarding the May Company purchase of Kaufmann's Department Store in 1946. This was the same kind of transaction as the Federated-Filene's merger. The price paid, measured by the market value of the May stock given to the Kaufmann stockholders, was 244% of the stated values on the Kaufmann balance sheet. The same ratio applied to Filene's would make the stock worth $39.4 million or $78 per share. This evidence was used to weaken the Filene's tabulation of market prices related to book value, and the conclusions drawn therefrom.

In reply, the Filene's representatives stated that 1946 was a year in which stock values were high, so that the stock of May's also was selling well above book values. The implication they saw was that a 1949 sale of Kaufmann's would have seen a different price, although perhaps the same ratio of exchange of shares. It appeared that the Kaufmann-May exchange was based on the market value of the two stocks.

The dissenters suggested that an allowance should be added for the dividends that would have been paid to their shares in the year that had elapsed since November 26, 1949, if Filene's had remained independent.

As a final argument, the dissenters claimed that a value should be assigned to the $80,000 per year savings that the Federated Stores had announced it expected to gain from the merger of the four stores, with an appropriate portion added to the Filene's value.

Exhibit 1

WM. FILENE'S SONS COMPANY

FILENE'S NET EARNINGS FOR COMMON STOCK
(In Thousands)

Year Ending	As Reported	Adjusted to a Uniform 38% Income Tax Rate	Adjusted to Remove White and Add Peck in All Years	
			LIFO	FIFO
1/31/40	$ 877	$ 673	na*	$ 908
1/31/41	586	508	na	673
1/31/42	912	911	$ 858	888
7/31/42	1,196	1,346	na	na
1/31/43	na	na	931	947
7/31/43	1,142	2,085	na	na
1/31/44	na	na	1,105	1,123
7/31/44	1,351	2,468	na	na
2/3/45	na	na	2,384	2,391
8/4/45	1,408	3,303	na	na
2/2/46	na	na	1,192	1,191
8/3/46	2,175	3,189	na	na
2/1/47	3,013	3,074	3,136	3,487
1/31/48	2,553	2,668	2,657	3,012
1/29/49	3,242	3,253	3,242	3,192
7/31/49	3,104	na	3,104	na
Six months to 7/31/49	1,089	1,104	1,089	979

* na = not available in the record.

Exhibit 2

WM. FILENE'S SONS COMPANY

FILENE'S DIVIDENDS

Year Ended	Dividends as Percent of Reported Earnings Paid Out	Annual Dividends per Share
1/31/40	57.0%	$1.00
1/31/41	85.3	1.00
1/31/42	54.8	1.00
7/31/42	41.8	1.00
7/31/43	43.8	1.00
7/31/44	37.0	1.00
8/4/45	35.5	1.00
8/3/46	28.7	1.25
2/1/47	29.0	1.75
1/31/48	47.0	2.40
1/29/49	43.2	2.80

Exhibit 3

WM. FILENE'S SONS COMPANY

SELECTED PRICE–EARNINGS RATIOS FROM TABLE SHOWING 21 STORES

Prices of November 26, 1949, Divided by Earnings for Various Periods as Shown

	Earnings, Year 1948	*Earnings, Year Ending 7/30/49*	*Estimated Earnings, 1949*	*3-Year Average Earnings, 1946–48*	*5-Year Average Earnings, 1944–48*	*10-Year Weighted* Average Earnings, 1939–48*	*Average Earnings, Selected Years, 1939, 1940, 1947, 1948*
High.......	13.7	9.0	9.4	10.2	12.6	13.7	13.6
Median.....	5.2	6.1	6.7	5.3	6.6	7.2	8.4
Low........	3.7	3.4	5.0	3.2	4.2	4.9	5.7
Filene's Earnings, per Share, Averaged for Periods Above							
	$ 6.48	$6.21	$5.15	$ 5.87	$ 4.39	$ 3.84	$ 3.41
Ratios for Filene's at Price of $35							
	5.4	5.6	6.8	6.0	8.0	9.1	10.3

* Weights most recent year 10, and drops weight by 1 as years become more remote.

ARGUMENTS FROM DATA SUMMARIZED IN ABOVE TABLE

1. Price of $35 for Filene's is reasonable in relation to 1948 earnings. Note that Filene's ratio of 5.4 is only a shade lower than Federated (5.6) and Best (5.6). Also that it is higher than Hecht (5.0), Rich's (4.5), Schuster (5.1), Arnold Constable (5.2), Marshall Field (4.0), and Joseph Horne (4.9), all of which are very highly regarded businesswise and investmentwise.

2. At $35, Filene's ratio of 5.6 appears reasonable in relation to earnings for the 12 months ended 7/30/49, although it is higher than many well-regarded investments.

3. In relation to estimated 1949 earnings, a price of $35 for Filene's would produce a price–earnings ratio of 6.8, which is not out of line. It should be noted that the number of 1949 earnings estimates was limited.

4. At $35, Filene's would be rather fully priced in relation to three-year average earnings (1946–48). The resulting ratio of 6.0 is higher than all the remaining companies except Meier & Frank (10.2) and Woodward & Lothrop (9.1), both of which are abnormally high, and May (7.2), Macy (7.0), and Federated (6.6).

5. A price of $35 for Filene's is high in relation to average earnings for the other periods covered in Table II. This may be demonstrated by the following comparison of Filene's with Best, which, incidentally, enjoys a high and seasoned investment rating among specialty and department store common stocks.

Exhibit—Continued

Earnings Basis	Price–Earnings Ratios	
	Filene's at $35	Best at 11/26/49
5-year average (1944–48)............................	8.0	7.6
10-year average (1939–48)...........................	11.9	10.1
10-year weighted average............................	9.1	8.3
4-year average (1939, 1940, 1947, 1948)...............	10.3	8.4

Note that the above ratios of Filene's are higher than those of Best, whereas Best enjoys one of the highest investment ratings in the country for specialty stores.

6. Filene's records of growth and growth prospects were not outstanding at 11/26/49.

7. The vitality and growth prospects of the Boston area as of 11/26/49 were not impressive. In addition, Filene's did not enjoy the advantages of broad geographical diversification.

8. While Filene's occupies a leading position as a specialty store, it is not a department store and ranks second in sales to Jordan Marsh (Allied unit).

9. As of 11/26/49, there appeared to be no particular factors to suggest that the future earnings trends at Filene's would be more favorable than those of leading companies in the specialty and department store industry. On the other hand, Filene's future earnings may suffer because its plant is not in as good physical condition as most stores with whom the foregoing comparisons have been made.

Exhibit 4

WM. FILENE'S SONS COMPANY

SELECTED PRICE–DIVIDEND RATIOS FROM TABLE SHOWING 21 STORES
Prices of November 26, 1949, Divided by Dividends for
Various Periods as Shown

	Dividends 1948	5-Year Average Dividends 1944–48	10-Year Average Dividends 1939–48
High.......................	55.0	30.6	44.1
Median.....................	13.6	16.2	22.0
Low.......................	9.0	11.0	15.5
Filene's Dividend, per Share, Averaged for Periods Above	$ 2.40	$ 1.64	$ 1.32
Ratios for Filene's at Price of $35	14.6	21.3	26.5

Exhibit 5

WM. FILENE'S SONS COMPANY

DETAILED COMPARISON WITH SELECTED STORES BASED ON BALANCE SHEETS
AS OF JANUARY 1, 1949
Prices of November 26, 1949, and Earnings of Year Ending January 1, 1949
(In Millions)

	Filene's	Best & Co.	Ed Schuster	Rich's	May Department Stores
Capitalization:					
Market in which traded... ...		N.Y.S.E.	O.T.C.	O.T.C.	N.Y.S.E.
Market values of outstanding securities......	?	$20.9	$12.6	$14.1	$188.1
1948 rents, capitalized at 8%..............	$12.1	3.1	0.4	8.0	26.6
Total..............	?	$24.0	$13.0	$22.1	$214.7
Earnings before capitalization charges:					
	LIFO	FIFO	LIFO	FIFO	LIFO
1948...................	$ 4.2	$ 3.3	$ 1.4	$ 2.6	$ 22.4
Capitalization ÷ earnings...	?	7.4	9.4	8.5	9.6

Exhibit 6

WM. FILENE'S SONS COMPANY

BALANCE SHEET
(In Thousands)

ASSETS		January 29, 1949	November 26, 1949*
Current assets:			
Cash..		$ 2,780⎱	$ 4,602
U.S. government securities................		1,894⎰	
Due from customers:			
30-day charge accounts..................	$3,809	⎱	3,728
Less: Reserve........................	150	3,659⎰	
Revolving budget accounts..............	$2,781	⎱	2,366
Less: Reserve........................	139	2,642⎰	
Other installment accounts..............	$ 223	⎱	355
Less: Reserve........................	17	206⎰	
Other accounts receivable................		198	...
Merchandise inventories, chiefly LIFO.......		4,776	6,515
Refundable federal taxes on income........		679	553
Supplies and prepaid expenses..............		446	458
Total Current Assets...............		$17,280	$18,577
Investment in Associated Merchandising			
Corp....................................		125⎱	
Cash-surrender value of executives' life in-			264
surance.................................		21⎰	
Miscellaneous.............................		21	
Land, at cost.............................		250⎱	
Buildings on own land, at cost..............	$1,407		
Less: Depreciation......................	640	767⎰	1,967
Buildings on leased land at cost.............	$1,147		
Less: Amortization.....................	108	1,039⎰	
Store fixtures and equipment..............	$3,740		
Less: Depreciation.....................	1,119	2,621	2,713
Goodwill.................................		...	...
Total Assets......................		$22,124	$23,521
LIABILITIES			
Current debt..............................		$ 5,415	$ 5,892
Long-term debt...........................		67	50
Reserve for possible assessments of taxes for			
prior years...........................		398	287
For executives' deferred compensation con-			
tracts.................................		107	...
Common stock............................		5,000	5,000
Earned surplus...........................		11,137	12,292
Total Liabilities....................		$22,124	$23,521

* Unaudited statement as of date of vote by Filene's stockholders on the merger proposal.

THE CUNO ENGINEERING CORPORATION

To PROVIDE for more orderly growth and improved evaluation of acquisition opportunities, Mr. Patterson, chairman and chief executive of the American Machine & Foundry Company, established a planning staff in 1958. By the spring of 1960, this group had produced several major special reports in addition to its more routine task of analysis of possible acquisitions. One of the areas to which the planning staff had directed its attention was water treatment. Early in 1960, Peter J. West of the AMF planning staff was again considering the desirability of acquiring The Cuno Engineering Corporation through an exchange of shares.

For some time, AMF's research and development laboratories had been exploring the area of dialytic treatment of salt and brackish water. In the process of dialytic treatment, the liquid to be conditioned was separated into compartments by ion-exchange membranes of alternate types, which would permit either negative or positive particles to pass. When current was applied to the solution, the particles in the solution flowed toward the proper electrodes and grouped themselves in alternate compartments as they were stopped by the ion-exchange membranes. As a result, the solution in half of the compartments was less saline than the original substance, and the solution in the other compartments was more saline. AMF's research group was experimenting not only in water treatment but also in the use of the dialytic method in broader fields, such as the treatment of pickling liquors in the steel industry.

Members of the planning division recognized the long-range possibilities created by the increasing water shortage in many parts of the world. Many areas were served only by naturally brackish water, which required some treatment before it would be potable. Treatment of brackish water was one step, AMF executives believed, toward the treatment of sea water. Moreover, the possibility of using developments in the water desalinization area for still other purposes indicated to the planning staff that they should approach the problem in the general terms of liquid conditioning.

A liquid-conditioning system required a pump, a treatment section, and a polishing filter. The pump was a standard product, manufactured by many firms, and could easily be procured when AMF had developed a treatment system. The polishing filter would have to be improved beyond its current refinement, but these advances were probably well within the capabilities of engineers in the field. Successful entrance into the liquid-conditioning market also would require suitable marketing channels. AMF executives thought that they could acquire such a distribution system by purchase of a company already in the area, preferably closely related to the areas AMF had been exploring. However, the key problem in an entrance into the liquid-conditioning field was the necessity of overcoming the various technical difficulties, not the acquisition of the ancillary equipment lines or marketing channels. AMF executives were not concerned about competition because they felt that the company's research group could be expected to produce results at least as fast as the research laboratories of other major companies in the water treatment area. Partly as a by-product of recent findings developed from experiments involving more economical production of atomic energy, the AMF executives believed that AMF had gained a technological advantage, and they were anxious to push developments ahead rapidly.

Although in 1959 AMF had no immediate plans for acquiring any firms in the liquid-conditioning business, the planning staff had considered several companies as possible candidates for acquisition, and had made brief studies of their operations. Several firms had been informally approached, but no commitment had been made by the beginning of 1960.

One of the firms the planning group had investigated in the summer and fall of 1959 was The Cuno Engineering Corporation of Meriden, Connecticut. The reports prepared at that time pointed out the limited position that Cuno would offer in AMF's expansion into the water and liquid treatment field. As a result, Cuno was not formally approached by the AMF executives in 1959. Selected portions of the report concerning Cuno appear in Exhibit 1.

In February, 1960, Murray McConnel, president of Cuno, notified Morehead Patterson, chairman of AMF, that he and his associates were interested in selling their interest in Cuno and that a merger offer had been made to Cuno by another firm in the filter business. Mr. McConnel was interested in learning whether the AMF executives might want to merge AMF with Cuno and, if so, what terms would be satisfactory. Because Mr. Patterson and Walter Bedell Smith (AMF's vice chairman) had been members of Cuno's board of directors for some years and Mr. McConnel had been on AMF's board, the corporate officials were well aware of the potential conflicts of interest in the situation and agreed to conduct their negotiations on an arm's-length basis. Mr. Patterson requested the planning division to make a review of Cuno and prepare a recommendation for action, along with suggested purchase terms. Peter J. West, a recent graduate of the Harvard Business School and a member of AMF's planning staff, was assigned this task.

THE CUNO ENGINEERING CORPORATION

The Cuno Engineering Corporation had been founded in 1912. It was not the largest company in the filter industry, but it had a reputation for engineering excellence and market service in its segment of the market. By specializing in industrial filters rather than in the automotive filter market, the company had avoided the price competition involved in supplying original equipment to automobile manufacturers.

Cuno's products could be divided into three main classifications. The first included a broad line of industrial filters, which accounted for about 70% of net sales; the second, a line of home water filters, which accounted for about 10% of net sales; the third, a line of automobile cigarette lighters, which accounted for about 20% of net sales.

Industrial Filters

The types of industrial filters manufactured by Cuno enabled it to produce and market equipment designed to filter any fluid—liquid or gas—that could be pumped. Such filtering was usually employed to remove foreign particles from a fluid used in a piece of equipment and so prevent damage to the working parts of the equipment, or to remove foreign particles from a consumer product such as paint, soap, or chocolate. In nearly all cases, Cuno's filters were precision products engineered to do specific filtering tasks. They were produced in small quantities rather than in mass. The most important types of Cuno industrial filters were the following.

Auto-Klean. This precision filter contained equally spaced discs of metal and was capable of providing positive removal of all particles larger than .0035 inch. The filter was a permanent, all-metal type that could be cleaned at any time, manually or automatically, without interrupting the flow of the fluid being filtered. The Auto-Klean filter was used in cleaning fluids, greases, lubricants, and coolants in machine tools, engines, compressors, and pumps.

Flo-Klean. This motor-driven filter was intended for use in filtering large volumes of liquids. The permanent, all-metal filtering element consisted of a stationary cylindrical cage; around the outer surface was wound a wire with the spacing between rows as close as .0025 inch. The filter had a continuous and automatic backwash cleaning mechanism. The Flo-Klean filter was used primarily for removing particles from water, coolants, cutting oil, and other like fluids, particularly in connection with large machines or groups of machines such as steel mills, grinding machines, and paper machines.

Micro-Klean. This filter of the replaceable cartridge type was capable of filtering micronic-size particles out of liquid or gas. The degree of filtration attainable ranged from 5 microns (.0002 inch) to 75 microns (.003 inch). Important users of the filter included paint, varnish, and enamel manufacturers; jet engine producers, diesel engine manufacturers; and industries using air-operated instruments and tools.

Micro-Screen. This line of filters had elements of woven wire mesh, sometimes sintered. They were used for hydraulic and fuel systems on aircraft, missiles, and missile launching facilities, and in cleaning various process fluids.

Poro-Klean. This line had a filtering element of porous sintered metals produced from various powdered metals, notably stainless steel. The filters were particularly suited for handling fluids where extreme conditions of corrosion, temperature, and differential pressure could be encountered. Their unusual properties led to successful use in the rapidly expanding fields of atomic energy, aircraft and guided missiles, and the chemical process industries. These uses included fuel filtering on jet engines, filtering in hydraulic systems on aircraft and guided missiles, and filtering of various process fluids, including such chemicals as polymers for use in production of film and synthetic fibers.

Home Water Filters

The newest of Cuno's main product groups included a line of filters for the filtration of water in the home as it came from city and municipal water supplies, from wells, or from other private sources. The most important product in this group was the Aqua-Pure, which utilized a white cellulose replaceable cartridge contained in a durable plastic housing with a transparent sump. It removed particles of iron, rust, dirt, grit, sand, and algae from household water systems.

Automobile Cigarette Lighters

Cuno was one of the three largest manufacturers of automobile cigarette lighters in the United States. Its main customers for cigarette lighters were automobile manufacturers, which normally accounted for about 90% of Cuno's sales of lighters.

FINANCIAL BACKGROUND ON CUNO

The filter business was a highly competitive one. In 1958 and 1959, a number of the larger companies in the industry had shown negligible profits or actual losses. Cuno, however, had an excellent financial record. Exhibit 2 gives 1957 and 1958 balance sheets, and Exhibit 3 gives income statements for 1955–58. Cuno's earnings had shown excellent growth except in 1958, when profits fell off because of the decline in the industrial segment of the economy and also because of unusual expenses incurred in the development of the Cuno line of home water filters. The company's sales in 1957 were 130% of 1955 sales, and 1957 net profits were 167% of 1955 profits. Final figures for 1959 sales and profits were expected to show gains over 1957.

In 1955, Cuno had reorganized its financial structure. To replace a two-class common stock capitalization, one class of common stock was created and a new preferred stock was issued.[1] The new preferred stock was offered to the public along with some of the new common stock. A total of 100,000 units was

---

[1] The new common stock had a par value of $1. The new preferred stock, which was entitled to annual cumulative dividends of $1, had a stated value of $14 a share and was callable in whole or in part at $17. Beginning on April 1, 1957, an annual sinking fund of 20% of net earnings, not exceeding $60,000 in any year, was to be used to retire preferred stock by purchase at not more than $17 or by call at $17. The consent of 50% of the preferred stock was required for the issue of debt of a maturity over 1 year for purposes other than to refund indebtedness or to retire all the preferred stock.

issued at $16.50 per unit of one preferred share and one common share. The net proceeds, $1.5 million, were used to help retire bank loans of about $2.2 million and to acquire the stock of the Connecticut Filter Corporation for $250,000.

Cuno had about 1,200 common stockholders in 1959, down from 1,367 at the end of 1956. Of the 287,260 shares of common stock outstanding at the end of 1959, Mr. McConnel, Cuno president, and Mrs. McConnel held 36.1%, and the other directors and officers as a group held 29%. Directors and officers could also influence another 4%, held in trust or by their wives and children. The directors and officers as a group held about 6% of the preferred stock, either directly or as trustees. The Cuno stock was traded over the counter, but the market was thin.

Cuno had been aggressively managed. Its product distribution was well organized, production costs were falling as a percentage of sales, and about 1.5% of net sales was spent on its development department. The company's products were considered to be the most sophisticated in the industry, and its engineering capability was, according to customers, second to none. Mr. McConnel, who had been president since 1949, was becoming concerned about the company's continued existence after his retirement. In addition, Mr. and Mrs. McConnel had a substantial portion of their personal savings invested in Cuno stock and were interested in planning the disposition of their estate. Therefore, in late 1959 Cuno's board of directors began to look for a prospective buyer.

CUNO–AMF RELATIONS

For several years, Morehead Patterson, board chairman of AMF, and Walter Bedell Smith, vice chairman, had served on the board of directors of Cuno, and Mr. McConnel had served as a director of AMF. The two groups of executives held each other in high regard, and it was natural that the interest of AMF's executives should be attracted to Cuno when they decided to enter the liquid-conditioning field. However, AMF had not made a formal offer to Cuno's management—in fact, had not yet made a decision regarding the desirability of acquiring Cuno—when word of the pending offer to Cuno was received. According to Mr. Patterson's information, the proposed acquisition was to be on the basis of a market-for-market exchange of stock, which at current prices (Exhibit 4 lists Cuno's stock prices) represented about $6 million for the common stock and about $1.4 million for the preferred. Because Cuno's management had a knowledge of AMF's manner of operation and knew AMF's management, it was anxious to know whether AMF would meet the alternative offer or on what terms AMF would be interested.

Mr. Patterson's Position

Despite the relatively negative conclusions of AMF's 1959 reports on Cuno, Mr. Patterson argued that if AMF was going to enter the liquid-conditioning field and would eventually be interested in Cuno or a similar company, then AMF should buy Cuno at once. He believed that Cuno offered AMF several advantages that AMF would not have when going cold turkey into a firm. AMF's management knew and respected the Cuno management. AMF's executives were reasonably familiar with Cuno's problems. Mr. McConnel was likewise familiar with AMF's practices and outlook. Moreover, if AMF delayed and Cuno was purchased by some other firm in the liquid-conditioning business, AMF might find it necessary at a later date to buy a much larger firm, some of whose divisions might not fit well into AMF's growth plans.

Mr. Patterson was also aware that AMF's stock was trading at a favorable price–earnings multiple in February, 1960. (Exhibit 5 gives prices of AMF common stock monthly from January, 1959, through February, 1960.) He did not know how long this condition would continue and believed that AMF should take immediate advantage of its favorable market evaluation to follow out its growth plan.

Mr. West's Analysis

In approaching his analysis, Mr. West had the benefit of a substantial file on Cuno, which had been built up during the prior six months. One of the earliest memoranda, dated July 20, 1959, was written for a member of Mr. Patterson's staff.

If AMF plans to enter the chemical processing, water treating, and fluid handling equipment field with a broad spectrum of products, then Cuno may be a desirable acquisition. If, on the other hand, AMF decides to operate primarily in the domestic water field, then we should not consider acquisition, but perhaps we should consider only licensing Cuno's Aqua-Pure line. In any event, we would specify or use some Cuno filters in our industrial and domestic desalter applications.

After the decision had been made to take a broader view of the liquid treatment field, a more detailed analysis of Cuno was prepared. This document (Exhibit 1), written early in August, 1959, was far from enthusiastic, although it pointed out certain advantages that would result to AMF from the acquisition. After this report had been discussed for several weeks, the AMF executive office asked for a possible purchase price estimate. This estimate, prepared in October, 1959, before the 2 for 1 split of AMF stock in November, 1959, appears as Exhibit 6.

The October, 1959, estimates had suggested a price substantially less than the price represented by the market-to-market offer of February, 1960. Mr. West therefore requested additional data on Cuno's 1959 sales and profits. The memorandum he was provided is reproduced as Exhibit 7.

Before he could make a meaningful recommendation, Mr. West decided, he must make a four-phase analysis. First, he would study and perhaps revise the documents and reports he had been given, in order to be sure that they provided the best calculations and projections of earnings. At the least they ought to be revised in light of Cuno's 1959 profits. Second, Mr. West was interested in the alternatives to Cuno that might be offered by other sources. He therefore prepared information regarding some of the more profitable companies in the industry. Exhibit 8 presents sales, profit, and return figures for four firms in addition to Cuno. Third, he would consider how to acquire the preferred stock.[2] Since AMF had not previously been faced with the problem of buying preferred stock, no policies had been set regarding a desirable way of paying for it. Mr. West wondered whether any special treatment of the preferred stockholder was called for. Fourth, Mr. West thought that perhaps he ought to consider the advantages to AMF of acquiring a less successful, more stagnant company. Although he did not propose to do much detailed investigating, he thought he ought to answer to his own satisfaction the question of whether AMF might not profit most by buying a company in difficulty for a relatively depressed price and then rehabilitating it, rather than buying a firm like Cuno, which was doing well.

Exhibit 1

THE CUNO ENGINEERING CORPORATION

PRELIMINARY ANALYSIS OF THE CUNO ENGINEERING CORPORATION
AS A PROPOSED ACQUISITION

Excerpts from Report Prepared by AMF Planning Staff

Source: AMF Executive Office
Date Suggested: July, 1959   *Date of Analysis:* August 3, 1959
Location:

.   .   .   .

Business:

.   .   .   .

Price Asked:

It is understood that the principal Cuno stockholders desire a tax-free market-for-market exchange of common stock. Based on the study to date, from AMF's point of view the most desirable way of obtaining a tax-free reorganization would require retirement by Cuno of its 88,515 outstanding preferred shares. A total of $1,504,755 would be necessary for this purpose. The number of AMF common shares to obtain the Cuno common is 62,334.

Performance and Growth Aspects:

.   .   .   .

Cuno's wide range of industrial filters indicates that they should be able to maintain a growth rate at least equal to the level of general industry. The recent emphasis on replacement type filters should give them an increasing volume of recurring business at probably attractive profit ratios. Continuation of their past aggressive product development program should encourage growth at a rate in excess of that for general industry. . . .

---

[2] In January, 1960, the Cuno directors had voted to redeem 20,000 of the 87,605 preferred shares outstanding at the end of 1959. The sinking fund would retire a further 3,500 shares in April, 1960.

Exhibit 1—Continued

Discussion:

. . . .

A positive factor is that Cuno is in an industry with a volume in excess of $100 million per year and growing. There is every indication, moreover, that special engineered filter applications of particular interest to Cuno will continue to grow.

Cuno's reputation is highly respected in the segments of the filter industry where it operates. . . . Moreover, in analyzing Cuno's acquisition value, another positive factor is the very broad range of industries served. Therefore, it is not dependent on the vicissitudes of any one or even a few industries. This broad customer base will be even further expanded as Cuno establishes its line of Aqua-Pure home water filters.

The Cuno reputation has, in large part, been derived from its aggressive product development program. The exercise of sound applications engineering, research and development, and contract research with Johns Hopkins University have led to new product developments, such as the Micro-Klean cartridge, the Aqua-Pure domestic water filter, and the Poro-Klean porous stainless steel filter, as well as to unique and valuable applications of the above products. In 1958, Cuno spent $300,000 on engineering and R.&D., and $30,000 for R.&D. consulting. These expenses amounted to 5.5% of 1958 sales. It should be noted that Cuno's development work is directed toward improved methods of dealing with undissolved solids as opposed to chemical processes leading to the removal of dissolved impurities.

Cuno's pretax returns on total assets exceed the AMF criterion by a comfortable margin (Schedule III). . . .

A further positive factor is that Cuno's acquisition would give AMF Atomics another entry into the auxiliary equipment side of the nuclear power, propulsion, and research reactor fields. This fits in with AMF Atomics' objectives. In another area, it should be noted that our recently developed thin film, AMFab, has considerable potential as a filter material as do several of the other AMF films; therefore, the Cuno filter line might be married to our AMFab film with possible mutual benefit. Significantly, Cuno's lines of filter equipment have general application to the broad field of liquid conditioning, which is expected to experience above average growth in the future.

In the event that a "pooling of interests" type of merger may not be feasible, the consequences of a conventional acquisition approach must be considered. With a market-for-market common stock exchange and calling of the preferred stock, a total of $4,561,000 of goodwill would be created. By amortizing the goodwill created over 10 years, the yearly charge against future earnings would be $7.32 per AMF share exchanged (Schedule III). In all probability, this charge would result in a dilution of AMF's future stated earnings.

It should also be noted that Cuno's sales volume represents only a 3% to 6% share of the overall filter business and thus would not make AMF a dominant company in the industry. This factor, however, is modified by the fact that Cuno maintains a strong position in certain specialized segments of that industry.

Finally, Cuno *would not* provide AMF with important technological know-how necessary to the solution of key problems relating to AMF's liquid-conditioning interest. The problems presented by dissolved minerals such as iron, calcium,

Exhibit 1—Continued

magnesium, sulphur, and salt are considered to be the critical factors in liquid processing both domestically and industrially.

Furthermore, the presence of dissolved compounds is not only the immediate problem but also is expected to be the increasingly critical factor in the future. Cuno would bring to AMF an excellent pool of knowledge pertaining to the filtering of undissolved solids but relatively little know-how with respect to the removal of dissolved impurities. It should be mentioned, however, that in certain areas and applications there is a definite need for a liquid-conditioning filter, and in these applications Cuno might well provide the technology required. But in this case Cuno would provide the auxiliary or accessory equipment related to the field of liquid processing and not the technology critical to the solution of key liquid conditioning problems.

In summary, Cuno would offer the following opportunities and disadvantages.

POSITIVE

1. It is available.
2. Cuno is in a large, growing industry.
3. Cuno has an excellent reputation due to, among other things, its aggressive product development program.
4. Cuno serves a broad range of industries.
5. Cuno's profit performance exceeds AMF criteria.
6. Cuno could contribute to programs for AMF Atomics and GOVPG.

NEGATIVE

1. Cuno might be too small to qualify for a "pooling of interests" approach.[1] However, the size factor is only one of several considerations to be weighed before a definite conclusion can be made in this regard. The alternative is a high goodwill factor.
2. Cuno would not make AMF the dominant factor in filtering.
3. Cuno would not bring to AMF the key technology necessary to the solution of the critical liquid-conditioning problems expected in the future.

Recommendation:

AMF acquisition of Cuno Engineering Corporation is attractive only as a later adjunct to the prior establishment of a primary AMF proprietary position in: first, the water conditioning field; second, the water systems field.

[Schedules II, III, and IV below]

Prepared by: Planning Division, American Machine & Foundry Company

---

[1] In an acquisition with pooling of interests, the balance sheet accounts of the two businesses are simply added for consolidated presentation. (Footnote supplied.)

Exhibit 1—Continued

Schedule II—The Cuno Engineering Corporation, Analysis of Balance Sheet Changes
(000's Omitted)

	At 6/30/59 Unaudited	Loan to Retire Preferred at $17 Call Price	At 6/30/59 as Adjusted	Elimination of Preferred	Balance Sheet Assumed
ASSETS					
Cash and governments.	$ 916	$1,505	$2,421	$(1,505)	$ 916
Receivables.	615		615		615
Inventories.	1,316		1,316		1,316
Other.	58		58		58
Total Current Assets.	$2,905		$4,410		$2,905
Plant, property, and equipment (net).	$ 801		$ 801		$ 801
Patents.	32		32		32
Other (investment, Cuno Oil Filter Company).	110		110		110
Total Assets.	$3,848		$5,353		$3,848
LIABILITIES					
Notes payable.	$ 125		$ 125		$ 125
Accruals.	390		390		390
Income taxes.	295		295		295
Total Current Liabilities.	$ 810		$ 810		$ 810
Long-term debt (due 1960).	$ 63		$ 63		$ 63
Long-term debt due AMF.		$1,505	1,505		1,505
Preferred stock ($14 stated value), 88,515 shares.	1,239		1,239	$(1,239)	...
Common stock ($ par), 280,502 shares.	281		281		281
Capital surplus.	702		702	(266)	436
Earned surplus.	753		753		753
Common stock net worth.	$1,736		$1,736		$1,470
Total Liabilities and Equity.	$3,848		$5,353		$3,848

Exhibit 1—Continued

SCHEDULE III—THE CUNO ENGINEERING CORPORATION, PRO FORMA HISTORICAL SALES, EARNINGS, RETURN RATIOS, ETC., BASED ON SUBSTITUTION OF LOAN AT 5% FOR PREFERRED STOCK ISSUE
($000's Omitted Except per Share)

Period	Net Sales	Pre-tax Profits	% of Sales	Taxes	Net Profits	Total Assets Employed	% Pre-tax to T.A.E.	Net per Cuno‡ Share	Net per AMF Share Exchanged‖			
									Earned	Stated¶		AMF's Own Net/Share**
										10-Year	30-Year	
6 months to:												
6/30/59	$ 3,430	$ 628*	18.3%	$ 327*	$ 301*	$ 3,848	32.6%†	$1.07	$ 4.82	$ 1.16	$3.60	$2.27
6/30/58	2,918	395*	13.5	205*	190*	3,870	20.4†	0.68	3.05	(0.61)	1.83	1.25
Year:												
1958	6,009	897*	14.9	466*	431*	3,769	23.8	1.54	6.91	(0.41)	4.47	2.96
1957	7,139	1,355*	19.0	705*	650*	3,971	34.1	2.32	10.43	3.11	7.99	3.17
1956	6,298	1,016*	16.1	528*	488*	3,560	28.5	1.74	7.83	0.51	5.39	2.39
1955	5,494	751	13.7	390	361	3,240	23.2	1.29	5.79	(1.53)	3.35	1.22
1954	4,123	462	11.2	168	185§	2,746	16.8	0.66	2.97	(4.35)	0.53	1.02
Average, 1956–58	6,482	1,089	16.8	566	523	3,767	28.9	1.86	8.39	1.07	5.95	2.84
Data on AMF, 1958	230,877	22,997	10.0	11,989	11,008	231,404	9.9	...	...	...	...	2.96

* Actual historical earnings, plus preferred dividends, less $75,238 annual interest at 5% on [proposed] $1,504,755 loan to retire preferred stock, 88,515 shares at $17 call rate. [Preferred dividends: 1956, $98,350; 1957, $96,302; 1958, $93,563; 6 months to 6/30/59, $47,000.]
† Annualized.
‡ Based on 280,502 Cuno common shares outstanding, 6/30/59.
§ After deduction of investment loss of $109,000.
‖ Based on 62,334 AMF shares at $96.75 close, 8/3/59, to meet $21.50 market for Cuno common shares, or a total price of $6,030,793.
¶ After deductions for goodwill amortization. Total goodwill would be $4,561,000. This amounts to $7.32 per AMF share on a 10-year, and $2.44 on a 30-year, amortization basis.
** Based on 6 months to June 30 and 3,602,875 AMF shares outstanding.

Exhibit 1—Continued

SCHEDULE IV—THE CUNO ENGINEERING CORPORATION, OUTLOOK FOR SALES, EARNINGS, RETURN RATIOS FOR THE YEARS 1959 THROUGH 1964, BASED ON ACQUISITION BY AMF AND SUBSTITUTION OF LOAN ADVANCE AT 5% FOR PREFERRED STOCK ISSUE

($000's Omitted Except per Share)

(Revised August 10, 1959)

Period	Net Sales*	Pre-tax Profits	Taxes†	Net Profits	Total Assets Employed‡	% Pre-tax to T.A.E.	Net Worth§	Net Earnings per AMF Share Exchanged‖			AMF's Own Outlook** Per Share
								Earned	Stated¶		
									10-Year	30-Year	
At acquisition...	...	...	...	...	$3,848	...	$1,470	...	...	...	...
1959...	$ 7,745	$1,554	$ 808	$ 746	4,136	37.6%	1,758	$11.97	$ 4.65	$ 9.53	$4.68
1960...	8,708	1,723	896	827	4,882	35.3	2,504	13.27	5.95	10.83	5.88
1961...	9,580	1,913	995	918	5,709	33.5	3,331	14.73	7.41	12.29	6.72
1962...	10,610	2,135	1,110	1,025	6,627	32.2	4,249	16.44	9.12	14.00	7.25
1963...	11,675	2,367	1,231	1,136	7,652	30.9	5,274	18.22	10.90	15.78	8.11
1964...	12,810	2,590	1,347	1,243††	8,788	29.5	6,410	19.94	12.62	17.50	9.08

* Sales are based on Cuno's forecast without alteration. 1959 forecast appears slightly optimistic based on 6 months performance.

† Taxes at 52%.

‡ Increased by amount of net profits.

§ At start of period.

‖ Based on 62,334 AMF shares at $96.75 close, 8/3/59, to meet $21.50 market for Cuno common shares, or a total price of $6,030,793. This amounts to $7.32 per AMF share on a 10-year amortization basis, and $2.44 on a 30-year amortization. Total goodwill would be $4,561,000. This amounts to $7.32 per AMF share on a 10-year amortization basis, and $2.44 on a 30-year amortization basis.

¶ After deductions for goodwill amortization. Total goodwill would be $4,561,000.

** Per long-range forecast, 1959 through 1962, and on a straight-line percentage increase in 1963, 1964.

†† 1964 net profit calculated on the basis of 9.7% of net sales, percentage obtained from Cuno's profit forecasts for 1960–63.

Exhibit 2

THE CUNO ENGINEERING CORPORATION

BALANCE SHEETS OF THE CUNO ENGINEERING CORPORATION AND
CONSOLIDATED SUBSIDIARIES AS OF DECEMBER 31, 1957 AND 1958*
(Dollar Figures in Thousands)

ASSETS	1957	1958
Cash..	$ 816	$ 712
Accounts receivable, net............................	585	605
Inventories...	1,603	1,432
Prepaid expenses and deposits..........................	65	59
Total Current Assets..........................	$3,069	$2,808
Investment in subsidiary, at cost.......................	...	109
Plant, property, and equipment........................	2,060	2,118
Less: Depreciation and amortization..................	1,194	1,299
Net property.....................................	$ 866	$ 820
Patents and trademarks, less amortization...............	34	32
Deferred charges..	3	...
Total Assets................................	$3,971	$3,769

LIABILITIES AND STOCKHOLDERS' INVESTMENT		
Loans payable..	$ 100	$ 125
Accounts payable...	146	144
Accruals..	260	222
Federal and state taxes......................................	500	332
Total Current Liabilities........................	$1,006	$ 823
Loans payable..	250	125
Preferred stock†...	1,332	1,278
Common stock, $1 par‡.....................................	270	277
Capital surplus..	569	662
Retained earnings..	544	604
Total Liabilities and Stockholders' Investment......	$3,971	$3,769

* An unaudited balance sheet as of June 30, 1959, is contained in Schedule II of Exhibit 1.
    † $1 cumulative; no par; stated value $14; 95,121 shares outstanding in 1957, and 91,301 shares in 1958.
    ‡ 270,375 shares outstanding in 1957; 276,752 shares in 1958.
    NOTE.—Most of the figures in these exhibits have been rounded to the nearest whole number. Hence, totals do not always agree.
    SOURCE: Annual Reports of The Cuno Engineering Corporation. Exhibit prepared at the Harvard Business School.

Exhibit 3

THE CUNO ENGINEERING CORPORATION

CONSOLIDATED INCOME STATEMENT FOR YEARS ENDED DECEMBER 31, 1955–58
(Dollar Figures in Thousands Except for per Share Data)

	1955	1956	1957	1958
Net sales.......................$	5,494	$ 6,298	$ 7,139	$ 6,009
Cost of sales...................	3,445	3,876	4,018	3,656
Selling, administration, general expenses......................	1,242	1,460	1,842	1,546
Operating profit.................$	806	$ 962	$ 1,279	$ 807
Other income (deductions):				
Purchase discounts.............$	11	$ 13	$ 15	$ 10
Discounts allowed..............	(35)	(43)	(45)	(44)
Royalties.....................	2	4	1	2
Interest paid..................	(21)	(21)	(18)	(14)
Miscellaneous.................	(14)	(27)	1	17
Income before federal income taxes..$	750	$ 887	$ 1,233	$ 777
Provision for federal income taxes...	390	442	630	389
Net income.....................$	361	$ 445	$ 602	$ 387
Dividends on preferred stock......	...	98	96	94
Earnings applicable to common stock........................$	361	$ 347	$ 506	$ 294
Shares of common stock outstanding at end of period.............	250,000	262,500	270,375	276,752
Per share of common stock:				
Earnings....................$	1.44	$ 1.32	$ 1.87	$ 1.06
Cash dividends...............	...	...	0.12½	0.50
Stock dividends...............	...	5%	3%	2%

SOURCE: Annual Reports of The Cuno Engineering Corporation. Exhibit prepared at the Harvard Business School.

Exhibit 4

THE CUNO ENGINEERING CORPORATION

BID AND ASKED PRICES OF COMMON AND PREFERRED STOCK* OF
THE CUNO ENGINEERING CORPORATION
January, 1958–February, 1960

	Common Stock		Preferred Stock	
	Bid	Ask	Bid	Ask
1958				
January	17	18⅝	15	16
February	15	16	14½	15½
March	16½	17¼	14¾	...
April	15¾	16½	15	16
May	14½	15½	15	16½
June	14	15	15	16½
July	13¾	14¼	15¾	16½
August	14	14¾	16	16¾
September	12½	13¼	15½	17
October	13¼	14⅞	16	17
November	14¾	15½	15¾	16¾
December	15½	16¼	15¾	16¾
1959				
January	16¼	17¼	16	16½
February	17	18	15¾	16¾
March	16½	17½	16	17
April	21¾	22½	16	16¾
May	20½	21¼	16	16¾
June	20¾	21½	16	16¾
July	20½	21¼	16	...
August	20¾	21¼	16	17
September	19½	20½	16	16¾
October	21	22	16¼	17¼
November	23	...	16¼	...
December	21	23	16¼	16¾
1960				
January	19½	21	16¼	17¼
February	20½	21½	16¼	...

* Prices as near as possible to closing day of month.
SOURCE: *Bank and Quotation Record.* Exhibit prepared at the Harvard Business School.

Exhibit 5

THE CUNO ENGINEERING CORPORATION

COMMON STOCK PRICES OF AMERICAN MACHINE & FOUNDRY COMPANY
JANUARY, 1959–FEBRUARY, 1960
(Adjusted for 2 for 1 Stock Split in November, 1959)

	Low	High
1959		
January	$26\frac{3}{4}$	$29\frac{7}{16}$
February	$27\frac{5}{8}$	$31\frac{3}{4}$
March	$30\frac{5}{8}$	$36\frac{3}{8}$
April	$34\frac{1}{2}$	$44\frac{3}{4}$
May	$38\frac{3}{4}$	$44\frac{3}{4}$
June	$37\frac{5}{16}$	$47\frac{1}{2}$
July	$45\frac{1}{4}$	50
August	$43\frac{1}{4}$	$49\frac{11}{16}$
September	$41\frac{5}{8}$	$45\frac{5}{8}$
October	$43\frac{3}{8}$	$50\frac{15}{16}$
November	$46\frac{1}{8}$	50
December	$48\frac{1}{8}$	$52\frac{3}{8}$
1960		
January	$49\frac{1}{2}$	$59\frac{7}{8}$
February	50	57

SOURCE: *The Commercial and Financial Chronicle.* Exhibit prepared at the Harvard Business School.

Exhibit 6

THE CUNO ENGINEERING CORPORATION

ESTIMATE OF PURCHASE PRICE OF THE CUNO ENGINEERING CORPORATION

The Cuno Engineering Corporation—Acquisition Price Considerations

This study considers various approaches to the determination of a reasonable price for Cuno Engineering. The matter of a reasonable price cannot be divorced from a consideration of the peculiar advantages Cuno might contribute to attaining AMF's liquid conditioning objectives. In my opinion, Cuno should not be considered as the keystone acquisition with which to launch AMF into this new field, since it will not bring with it any unique strengths in technology or market directly and significantly related to our objectives. Because of this view, I have arrived at a determination of price based on Cuno's inherent value as an investment independent of potential contributions it might make to our efforts in the field of liquid conditioning.

Because of the very small percentage of Cuno's common stock in the hands of the public and because there is very limited trading in this stock (over the counter), the prices quoted are not considered to represent a true market evaluation of the company. In fact, it is doubtful that the major stockholders have an actual market for their stock. If Mr. McConnel, for example, were to put 10 to 20% of his common stock on the open market, it is probable that the price would be driven far below current quotations of 19½ bid, 21½ asked.

Cuno's projections of sales and earnings, as shown in Schedule IV of the Preliminary Analysis [Exhibit 1] dated August 3, 1959, and plotted in Schedule I attached, should not be used as a basis for an acquisition price because:

Exhibit 6—Continued

1. Actual sales and earnings for the first 6 months of 1959 [projected on an annual basis] are only 88.6% and 69.5% of Cuno's forecast.
2. A trend line projection of 6-year historical earnings, as shown on Schedule I of this memorandum, indicates a much slower profit growth than estimated by Cuno.

It is further clear that AMF will sooner or later be forced to tie up, for an indeterminate period, at least $1 million to offset the cash drain that would be created by their retirement of $1,504,755 worth of preferred stock. This factor should be weighed heavily in the determination of a purchase price.

The following represent several approaches to establishment of a price:

1. Book value.
2. Capitalization of historical earnings.
3. Market price of Cuno common stock.
4. Present value of future earnings.
5. A 25% upgrading of expected AMF earnings on shares exchanged.

Book Value

As of June 30, 1959, the common stock book value was $1.736 million; however, the premium of $266,000 for retirement of preferred reduces this to $1.47 million. The cash advance of $1 million would increase this to an effective price of $2.47 million.

The projected earnings for Cuno indicate that it would be unrealistic to assume that we could purchase Cuno for such a low price.

Capitalization of Historical Earnings

Current market prices of Fram and Purolator, both considerably larger and more actively traded, are at an average of 10 times annualized 1959 earnings. On this basis, the earnings [as adjusted for an AMF purchase in Schedule III, Exhibit 1] of Cuno for 1956, 1957, 1958, and 6 months of 1959, which averaged $534,000, would establish a price of $5.34 million. The addition of 1954 and 1955 gives a 5½-year average of $446,000, or a price of $4.46 million.

If proper allowance is made for the expected cash advance of $1 million, the resultant price range of $3.46 to $4.34 million is a more realistic evaluation than the book value.

Market Price of Cuno Common Stock

On the basis of the asked quotation of 21½ at September 25, 1959, the market price for the 280,504 common shares outstanding at June 30, 1959, would be $6.031 million.

As noted earlier, the artificial nature of the market for this common stock obviates this approach as a realistic price consideration.

Present Value of Future Earnings

Our projection of future net income and the present values of these earnings at 10, 15, and 20% discount rates are shown on Schedule II, attached. Further adjustment is made for an assumed residual value of the business after 10 years and subtraction of the AMF cash advance, which is expected to be at least $1 million. On this basis, the present value of future earnings, as adjusted, is:

At 10% discount......................$5.462 million
At 15% discount...................... 3.927
At 20% discount...................... 2.885

Exhibit 6—Continued

This approach appears to contain more logic than any of the others mentioned, because it makes due allowance for the element of risk inherent in entry into a new industry. It also evaluates Cuno as an investment for AMF and allows calculation of the purchase price at varying rates of return.

A 25% Upgrading of Expected AMF Earnings on Shares Exchanged

Schedule III, attached, shows the calculation of the number of AMF shares at the current price of $89 that would be exchanged for projected Cuno earnings to allow a 25% upgrade in expected AMF earnings per share. On this basis, it would appear that the maximum number of shares would be the 73,128 shown for 1964 earnings. At $89, this would amount to a price of $6.508 million. However, it is also clearly shown that the projected growth in AMF earnings far exceeds that for Cuno; therefore, at a constant $89 per share, the number of shares and the resultant price would continue to reduce each year.

In view of the disparity in growth rates of earnings projected for the two companies, this approach to pricing provides a very unsatisfactory yardstick.

Recommendation

Any price up to approximately $4 million appears justified, provided a "pooling of interests" approach is assured.

SOURCE: Prepared by the planning division, October, 1959.

SCHEDULE I—PROJECTED SALES AND PROFITS OF THE CUNO ENGINEERING CORPORATION

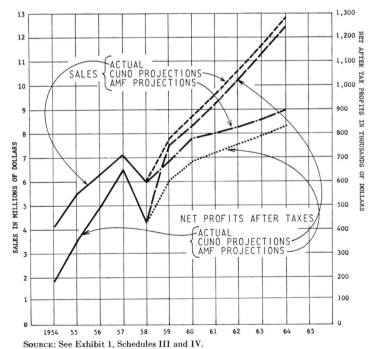

SOURCE: See Exhibit 1, Schedules III and IV.

Exhibit 6—Continued

SCHEDULE II—PRESENT VALUE OF PROJECTED CUNO AFTER-TAX EARNINGS
(In Thousands)

Year	Estimated Earnings (After Tax)	Present Value at Discount		
		10%	*15%*	*20%*
1960........................	$ 680	$ 618	$ 592	$ 566
1961........................	720	595	544	500
1962........................	750	563	494	434
1963........................	790	540	452	381
1964........................	830	515	413	334
1965........................	870*	491	376	291
1966........................	910*	467	342	254
1967........................	950*	444	311	221
1968........................	1,000*	424	284	194
1969........................	1,050*	405	259	170
Subtotal.................	$ 8,550	$5,062	$4,067	$3,345
Plus assumed residual value.....................	$ 4,000	$1,400	$ 860	$ 540
Subtotal.................	$12,550	$6,462	$4,927	$3,885
Less AMF cash advance.......	$ 1,000	$1,000	$1,000	$1,000
Total.................	$11,550	$5,462	$3,927	$2,885

* Based on a conservative projection of the trend shown in Schedule I.

SCHEDULE III—CALCULATION OF AMF SHARES EXCHANGED ON BASIS
OF 25% UPGRADE OF AMF PROJECTED EARNINGS PER SHARE

Year	Cuno Estimated Earnings after Tax		25% Upgrade on AMF Earnings per Share*		AMF Shares		Value at $89 per AMF Share
1959........600		÷	5.85	=	102,564	=	$9,128,200
1960........680		÷	7.35	=	92,517	=	8,234,000
1961........720		÷	8.40	=	85,714	=	7,628,546
1962........750		÷	9.06	=	82,781	=	7,367,509
1963........790		÷	10.14	=	77,909	=	6,933,901
1964........830		÷	11.35	=	73,128	=	6,508,392

* See Schedule IV, Exhibit 1, for base figures.

Exhibit 7

THE CUNO ENGINEERING CORPORATION
REPORT ON 1959 EARNINGS OF THE CUNO ENGINEERING CORPORATION

February 15, 1960

In 1959, this company had net sales of $7.3 million and net income of $635,000. These results were slightly under the company's forecast, as shown following.

	Actual	*Forecast*	*% under Forecast*
Sales......................	7,260	7,745	6.3%
Net income...............	635	746	14.9%

Despite failure to meet its forecast, Cuno's sales reached a new high, and the $1.1 million sales decline in 1958 was fully recovered. Similarly, the previous high in net income of $602,000 during 1957 was exceeded in 1959. It is interesting to note that Cuno's rather sharp dips in sales—16%—and in profits—36%—during 1958 were fully recovered in 1959. Cuno's vulnerability in previous recessions, such as 1949–50 and 1953–54, has not been studied.

Cuno's net worth at December 31, 1959, was $3.2 million, and its market value is approximately double this, including preferred stock.

Because of the potential value of Cuno to AMF in the areas of (*a*) liquids filtering, i.e., home water use, (*b*) filtering materials, i.e., films, (*c*) atomic energy filtering applications, this company should be kept firmly in mind as a possible follow-up to our more current acquisition plans in water conditioning.

Exhibit 8

THE CUNO ENGINEERING CORPORATION

FIVE-YEAR COMPARISON OF THE CUNO ENGINEERING CORPORATION WITH FOUR OTHER COMPANIES IN THE INDUSTRY

	The Cuno Engineering Corporation	American Machine & Metals, Inc.	Duriron Company, Inc.	Fram Corporation	Purolator Products, Inc.
Net sales, index (1954 = 100)					
1954	100	100	100	100	100
1955	133	139	119	112	117
1956	153	161	155	108	143
1957	173	183	172	114	161
1958	146	177	140	129	150
Average, 1956–58	157	174	156	117	152
Pre-tax profits, index (1954 = 100)					
1954	100	100	100	100	100
1955	184	115	101	141	154
1956	217	157	172	93	82
1957	302	169	191	93	101
1958	190	132	101	165	100
Average, 1956–58	237	153	155	117	94

Pre-tax profits, return ratios on:

	The Cuno Engineering Corporation			American Machine & Metals, Inc.			Duriron Company, Inc.			Fram Corporation			Purolator Products, Inc.		
	Sales	Total Assets	Net Worth*	Sales	Total Assets	Net Worth	Sales	Total Assets	Net Worth*	Sales	Total Assets	Net Worth	Sales	Total Assets	Net Worth
1954	9.9%	14.9%	23.5%	14.7%	24.6%	38.8%	13.3%	17.2%	26.7%	8.5%	17.4%	31.5%	12.8%	24.6%	43.5%
1955	13.7	23.1	37.4	12.3	20.5	35.3	11.2	14.2	28.5	10.6	21.8	38.1	16.8	31.5	52.5
1956	14.1	24.7	38.0	14.3	25.2	42.7	14.7	21.2	40.5	7.3	13.5	21.7	7.4	13.3	22.8
1957	17.3	31.2	45.4	13.6	24.3	39.1	14.8	22.4	34.4	6.9	13.5	21.2	8.0	15.8	26.7
1958	12.9	20.6	27.4	10.9	16.9	28.6	9.6	11.8	17.6	10.8	17.6	33.4	8.6	15.4	25.6
Average, 1956–1958	14.9	25.8	36.8	12.9	21.8	36.3	13.2	18.4	29.8	8.5	15.4	25.8	8.0	14.9	25.3

Ratio of market price to:†

	The Cuno Engineering Corporation				American Machine & Metals, Inc.				Duriron Company, Inc.				Fram Corporation				Purolator Products, Inc.			
	Book Value		Earnings‡		Book Value		Earnings		Book Value		Earnings‡		Book Value		Earnings		Book Value		Earnings	
	High	Low	High	Low	High	Low	High	Low	High	Low	High	Low	High	Low	High	Low	High	Low	High	Low
1954	na	na	na	na	1.1X	0.7X	7.1X	4.2X	1.0X	0.7X	6.7X	4.4X	na	na	na	na	1.9X	1.0X	9.4X	5.1X
1955	na	na	na	na	1.5	1.0	8.3	5.5	1.1	0.9	8.1	6.6	na	na	na	na	3.0	1.6	10.9	5.9
1956	3.3X	1.4X	9.1X	3.8X	1.5	1.1	7.8	6.0	1.4	0.9	7.2	4.6	1.3X	1.1X	12.2X	9.5X	2.3	1.7	25.4	19.0
1957	4.0	2.3	11.0	6.4	1.7	1.2	9.2	6.4	1.5	1.0	8.8	6.2	1.3	0.8	13.1	7.7	1.6	1.0	13.0	7.7
1958	3.0	2.2	16.0	11.8	1.9	1.3	14.0	9.5	1.2	0.9	13.6	10.7	1.7	0.8	9.7	4.9	2.1	1.1	15.2	8.1
1958 net sales (in thousands of dollars)	$6,009				$43,613				$12,307				$30,285				$35,366			

* Includes preferred stock: Cuno, all years; Duriron, 1954.
† On shares outstanding each year-end.
‡ Common stock only.
na = not available.

Exhibit 8—Continued

Principal Products

The Cuno Engineering Corporation:

Industrial filters; automobile cigarette lighters.

American Machine & Metals, Inc.:

Instruments to indicate, record, and control pressure, temperature, flow, level, or position for industrial processes and for other applications; pressure transducers for aircraft and missile systems; special-application fractional horsepower motors for industrial and commercial machinery, aircraft and automotive devices, and domestic appliances; filters and centrifugals for liquid–solid separation in process industries; materials testing equipment and related instrumentation; fans and blowers for industrial applications; commercial laundry machinery; springs, mechanical and electrical assemblies, fatigue testers, spring testers, and force indicators; manganese dioxide for dry cell batteries; manganese carbonate ores; zinc, lead, and silver concentrates.

Duriron Company, Inc.:

Corrosion- resistant equipment and castings, such as pumps, valves, pipe, and fittings; fans, ejectors, steam jets, etc.

Fram Corporation:

Lubricating oil filters, fluid separator filters, gasoline filters; crankcase ventilators and carburetor air filters; replacement cartridges.

Purolator Products, Inc.:

Filters (and replaceable elements and cartridges) for filtration of such substances as oil, gasoline, air, water, paints, sugar, food products, toothpastes, drugs, beverages, chemicals, etc.

SOURCE: *Moody's Industrial Manuals*. Prepared at the Harvard Business School.

BURLINGTON MILLS CORPORATION—

PACIFIC MILLS

IN 1954, the management of Burlington Mills Corporation decided that there would be substantial advantages in bringing Pacific Mills under Burlington Mills' control. The financial method chosen to achieve control was a direct offer of $50 a share in cash, first for a large block of Pacific Mills shares held by Ely & Walker Dry Goods Company, and next for 285,000 shares on a first-come, first-served basis from the other Pacific Mills' stockholders. Later, an exchange offer was made to stockholders who had not taken advantage of the cash offer.

SOME BACKGROUND ON BURLINGTON MILLS CORPORATION

In 1923, J. Spencer Love and associates started Burlington Mills, Inc., to operate a small 200-loom plant engaged in the manufacture and sale of woven cotton fabrics. Subsequently, the plant facilities were converted to the weaving of rayon fabrics, and numerous additional plants were acquired. In 1934, Burlington Mills Company, Inc., succeeded to the business of Burlington Mills, Inc., Burlington Mills Company (a copartnership), and five other corporations engaged in the same general business.

On February 15, 1937, a new company was incorporated in Delaware under the name Burlington Mills Corporation to merge Burlington Mills Company, Inc., Rayon Fabrics Corporation, and Duchess Fabrics Corporation. The new company operated 22 plants; 14 were in North Carolina, 3 in Tennessee, and 1 in Virginia. It concentrated on the manufacture of rayon fabrics, although it also produced cotton goods. The total number of employees on March 1, 1937, was 6,750. Mr. Love was president and a director of the new company, and its largest stockholder. In 1954, he was president and chairman of both the board and executive committee.

In the period from 1937 to 1953, the company expanded greatly. Through the sale of common stock, preferred stock, and notes, and through exchange of securities, it acquired the properties of 31 other companies. At the end of 1953, Burlington Mills Corporation directly or through subsidiaries operated 76 plants in 46 communities in 10 states and Canada, Colombia, and Mexico. Production machinery included 14,000 looms, 875,000 spindles, and 2,250 knitting machines, and employees numbered over 30,000.

The company manufactured woven and knitted fabrics of rayon, acetate, nylon, and other synthetic yarns and combinations, as well as fabrics of cotton, wool, and combinations of natural and synthetic fibers. In addition, it operated throwing and spinning units to produce yarn for its own use and, to some extent, cotton yarn for sale. It merchandised all its own products. Principal products were fabrics for women's and men's wear, automotive and industrial fabrics, upholstery and drapery materials, fabrics and finished products (such as bedspreads) for the home, men's and women's hosiery, and ribbons. The company was integrated from the purchase or spinning and throwing of yarns to the finishing and sale of products in the greige or finished state. Financial data on Burlington Mills Corporation are given in Exhibits 1, 2, and 3. In Exhibit 4 are selected common stock prices, 1937–53.

SOME BACKGROUND ON PACIFIC MILLS

Pacific Mills was incorporated in Massachusetts in 1850 by members of the Lawrence and Lowell families. The initial capital of $1 million was represented by 1,000 shares of $1,000 par value. Through the sale of additional stock and mainly through stock dividends, the capital stock was increased to $40 million by 1922, represented by 400,000 shares of $100 par, and surplus at this time exceeded $7.6 million. During the depression, the stock was changed to no-par value in 1934 to correct an impairment of capital, and it was split two for one in 1946.

On January 2, 1954, Pacific Mills had an authorized common stock issue of 1.5 million shares. Of this total, 966,805 shares were issued, with 7,753 in the company's treasury and 959,052 outstanding in the hands of stockholders. Ely & Walker Dry Goods Company owned 170,131 shares, but apart from this block of shares no one else was known to own directly or beneficially so much as 10% of the stock.

During the early 1900's, Pacific Mills acquired several plants, and in 1916 it bought its first southern mills in South Carolina. From its inception, its principal business was the production of printed, dyed, and bleached cotton goods, cotton warp, and wool dress goods. In 1954, it produced diversified lines of fabrics and finished products woven of wool, worsted, cotton, rayon, and blends of natural and synthetic fibers. The products included fabrics for men's, women's, and children's apparel, automobile fabrics, specially treated cloths for varied industrial uses, and such home furnishings as sheets and towels, sold in finished form. Pacific Contour Sheets, introduced in 1949, had proved successful in increasing both the sales and the prestige of the company. Pacific Mills had its own sales organization, with sales offices in nine cities throughout the country, and had developed several strong brand names.

At the end of 1953, the company owned 14 plants, 6 for woolen and worsted production and 8 for cotton and rayon. Beginning in the early 1940's, the management had engaged in an extensive rehabilitation program. The large plants operated for many years in Dover, New Hampshire, were sold in

1940, and cotton manufacturing operations were consolidated in North and South Carolina. New equipment and modern improvements were installed in the southern plants. The latest equipment for the manufacture of rayon fabrics was added in a southern plant purchased in 1945. The worsted division in Lawrence was modernized and reduced in size; and the company built five small plants in the South, with up-to-date equipment for manufacturing and finishing woolen and worsted fabrics. On December 31, 1953, the company had 9,500 employees, a decline from 11,450 in 1947.

Exhibits 5, 6, and 7 contain financial data on Pacific Mills, and Exhibit 8 gives prices and sales volume of the common stock for selected periods from 1949 to July, 1954.

LOWENSTEIN OFFER FOR PACIFIC MILLS STOCK

On July 2, 1954, Leon Lowenstein, chairman of the board of M. Lowenstein & Sons, Inc., issued a statement to the effect that on July 1 he had told the executive committee of Pacific Mills that he was prepared to offer Pacific Mills stockholders $45 cash per share for their stock.[1] Lowenstein & Sons, a textile company, had a net income of $7,165,257 on sales of $180 million in 1953. On the day of this announcement, Pacific Mills common stock reached a high of 37 and closed at 35¾, up 2⅞ for the day.

At first, officials of both Pacific Mills and Ely & Walker refused to comment, but a few days later a spokesman for Pacific Mills said that his company would be opposed to the $45 offer. He said that the $45 figure assigned practically no value to the "thoroughly modern, up-to-date plant, machines and equipment" of Pacific Mills, on which the company had spent over $35 million since 1940.[2] The Lowenstein offer was never made directly to the Pacific Mills stockholders.

PURCHASE OF PACIFIC MILLS STOCK BY BURLINGTON MILLS

As early as 1951, Mr. Love of Burlington Mills had approached Henry Bliss, president of Pacific Mills, with regard to a possible merger. The management of Pacific Mills could see no reason for recommending such action to the stockholders, and the matter was dropped. When Mr. Love heard about the Lowenstein offer on Friday, July 2, 1954, he reasoned that the management of Ely & Walker might prefer to sell its holdings of Pacific stock to a company other than Lowenstein & Sons. Lowenstein & Sons was already a strong competitor of Ely & Walker in the cotton printing field, and its position would be strengthened by the acquisition of Pacific Mills. Burlington Mills, on the other hand, was not in the cotton printing field. Mr. Love therefore sent word to Ely & Walker that Burlington Mills was interested in

---

[1] *Daily News Record*, July 6, 1954.

[2] *The Wall Street Journal*, July 6, 1954.

buying the Pacific Mills stock. He also talked with Mr. Bliss during the weekend, hoping to enlist his cooperation. However, Mr. Bliss still wanted Pacific Mills to remain independent. It was his opinion that Ely & Walker would reject offers for its Pacific Mills stock and, further, that other stockholders would do likewise on the recommendation of the Pacific Mills management.

On Tuesday, July 6 (Monday was a holiday), the president of Ely & Walker telephoned Mr. Love. It appeared to him that Lowenstein & Sons might get control of Pacific Mills by its public offer of $45 a share for stock that had sold as low as $23 earlier in the year. Mr. Love and the treasurer of Burlington Mills went to St. Louis to meet the Ely & Walker executives on Thursday, July 8, to negotiate the purchase of approximately 200,000 shares of Pacific Mills common stock. At 5:30 P.M. on July 8, they agreed on a price of $50 a share.[3] Of these shares, 170,131 were purchased from the Ely & Walker Company and the rest from officers and stockholders of the company.

Burlington Mills' announcement of the purchase and an offer to buy from other stockholders an additional 285,000 shares of Pacific Mills common stock at $50 cash per share appeared on the Dow-Jones news ticker at 10:19 A.M. on Friday, July 9.[4] At first, the offer was made only to stockholders proving ownership at the close of business on Thursday, July 8. Nevertheless, on Friday, 15,200 shares of Pacific Mills stock changed hands, and trading had to be suspended for 22 minutes during the flood of orders that came after the announcement. The stock closed up 6⅛ at 42⅛. On the same day Burlington Mills common stock went up ½ to 12¾, and 17,500 shares were traded. Late Friday, a further announcement by Burlington Mills removed the ownership deadline.

Letters setting forth details of Burlington Mills' offer were mailed to all Pacific Mills stockholders on Saturday, July 10. The stock was widely distributed,[5] and letters directed west of the Rocky Mountains were airmailed. In this letter, which stockholders began to receive on Monday, the deadline for acceptance of the offer was set at 3:30 P.M., Wednesday, July 21. The stock was to be received by the New England Trust Company in Boston by that

---

[3] Press release from the New York Stock Exchange, August 27, 1954.

[4] *Ibid.*

[5] The distribution of Pacific Mills common stock in March, 1951, was:

Holdings	No. of Stockholders	Total Shares
1 to 99 shares	4,263	110,607
100 to 999 shares	1,644	359,225
1,000 shares and over	115	489,220*

* Includes Ely & Walker company's 170,031 shares.

In June, 1954, the pattern of ownership was much the same; the total number of stockholders dropped slightly to around 5,400, approximately 70% of whom held less than 100 shares.

time, and would be purchased on a first-come, first-served basis. The offer was contingent on Burlington Mills' acquiring no less than 285,000 shares.

The chairman of the board of Ely & Walker company confirmed that Burlington Mills had purchased not less than 170,000 and not more than 200,000 shares of Pacific Mills common stock from his company and its officers. Ely & Walker made a profit of over $5.5 million on the sale, since the shares had been carried on its books at cost at an average price of $17.31 a share since the 1940's. The chairman said that his firm had sold its Pacific Mills holdings because "we couldn't turn it down; the offer was too good to let go by."[6]

A director of Pacific Mills said that the Pacific Mills management had not been consulted as to the terms of the offer, and that the offer had been made entirely independently of the board of directors of Pacific Mills. After the first announcement by Burlington Mills, he said, the Pacific Mills management had urged that the offer be made on a pro rata basis instead of a first-come, first-served basis; but the Burlington Mills officers had replied that the offer was made as it was because of what seemed to them extremely sound business reasons.[7]

On Monday, July 12, Pacific Mills common stock closed at $44\frac{3}{8}$, up $2\frac{1}{4}$; 21,000 shares were traded that day. Burlington Mills common stock closed at $14\frac{1}{4}$, up $\frac{1}{2}$; 29,400 shares changed hands.

Late on Tuesday, July 13, 8 days before the deadline, Burlington Mills announced that 292,500 shares had been received and accepted and that no further shares should be tendered. On Thursday, July 15, approximately 250,000 shares not purchased were returned to their owners.[8] Altogether, Burlington Mills acquired 493,145 shares, or about 52% of the outstanding shares, at a cost of $24,564,672, according to its report to the Securities and Exchange Commission.[9]

REASONS FOR THE ACQUISITION OF CONTROL OF PACIFIC MILLS

Late in July, Mr. Love, chairman of the board of Burlington Mills, gave a press conference on the reasons for acquiring control of Pacific Mills. He was quoted by *America's Textile Reporter* as follows.

. . . acquisition of controlling interests in Pacific Mills Corp. and Goodall-Sanford, Inc.,[10] primarily represents a continuation of long-term plans on the part

---

[6] *Daily News Record*, July 12, 1954.

[7] *The Wall Street Journal*, July 14, 1954.

[8] Press release from the New York Stock Exchange, August 27, 1954.

[9] *Daily News Record*, September 9, 1954.

[10] Goodall-Sanford, Inc., was a Maine corporation engaged in preparing, spinning, weaving, dyeing, and finishing blends of mohair, wool, and synthetic fibers to produce fabrics sold under the Palm Beach and other trademarks, and in producing plastics and other coated fabrics. Burlington Mills acquired a controlling interest in July, 1954. Footnote added.

of Burlington to strengthen its future position in the textile industry through diversification of operation into major fields.

. . . the recent acquisitions permit Burlington to expand its distribution and selling contacts and operations into end products heretofore not part of the Burlington line.[11] Such rounding out of lines, he said, is almost essential to the well-being of a large company in a highly competitive period.

Mr. Love also pointed out that reasonably full use of existing cash and credit facilities to increase broad earning bases is warranted today as a result of an easing in the credit and money situation.

He also cited the following points as reasons prompting the recent acquisitions by Burlington Mills.

1. The growing importance of blends of all fibers, including the new fibers, emphasizes the need of diversification.

2. Strong brand names and experienced executive and sales personnel, assets not reflected directly in the balance sheets, are very valuable portions of acquisitions in today's highly competitive markets.

3. Many economies and improvements should be possible over a period of time through joint effort in effective utilization of facilities. . . .

"The strong and respected position within the industry long held by Pacific Mills under Henry M. Bliss' leadership, its fine personnel, its wealth of experience, its modern manufacturing facilities and its highly respected consumer products, make it an important acquisition to the Burlington organization," Mr. Love said.

"The Pacific Mills operation has long been an efficient one and as such Burlington will not recommend any consequential changes in its manufacturing or merchandising operations or policies beyond such improvements as might normally be made in any operation, particularly with the combination of experience and executive man power that will be available."[12]

Some banking circles were of the opinion that Burlington Mills acquired control of Pacific Mills to obtain greater diversification and thus assume a stronger financial standing in the long run. It was pointed out that the textile industry was at the bottom of a recession, which was an excellent time for a big organization like Burlington Mills to expand. The bankers regarded the Pacific Mills plants as fairly modern and "an excellent buy." One leading banking official said, "We would be happy to lend them all the money they desire."[13] Burlington Mills had negligible bank loans; its long-term debt consisted of $80.63 million of notes issued to life insurance companies.

The Wall Street Journal commented as follows.

But Pacific also is one of the two largest producers of finished cotton prints. Its woolen and worsted production is considerably greater than Burlington's Peerless division's. So there is relatively little overlap of one company's products with the

---

[11] For instance, Pacific Mills produced sheets and terry towels, products in which Burlington Mills had no operation at all. Footnote added.

[12] *America's Textile Reporter*, Vol. LXVIII, No. 30 (July 29, 1954).

[13] *Daily News Record*, July 20, 1954.

others. Acquisition of control of Pacific, consequently, will give Burlington an important position in the converted (that is, finished) cotton goods industry, together with another line of consumer products, and greatly increase its earnings opportunities in the woolen, worsted and blended fabric line.

In addition, Pacific's management has a high reputation. The company has eight cotton and rayon plants and six woolen and worsted plants, all but one—the worsted unit—in the South. The Southern plants are all new within the past 10 years. Pacific has been a good money-maker since Mr. Bliss took over the helm, earning an average of $4.7 million or about $5 a share over this past decade.[14]

FURTHER DEVELOPMENTS

The *Daily News Record* reported that at a meeting on July 27, 1954, the directors of Pacific Mills were informed that both sales and profit for the first half of 1954 had declined in relation to the similar period in 1953. For the 6 months ended July 3, 1954, the newspaper said, the company had net sales of $53,499,000 and net profit of $694,157. The profit, equal to 72 cents a share, included 43 cents a share from the sale of nonmanufacturing property. In the first half of 1953, sales had been $62,027,000 and net income $1,231,412, equal to $1.28 a share. The president said, however, that sales and earnings for the first six months of 1954 "do not reflect the more optimistic tone that seems to prevail in the market for textiles." At the same directors' meeting two officers of Burlington Mills were elected to the directorate of Pacific Mills.[15]

Early in August, 1954, Burlington Mills announced that its sales and profits had declined. Consolidated net sales for the 9 months ended July 3 were $243,532,000, and profits were $5,594,000, compared with sales of $276,071,000 and net earnings of $6,611,000 for the similar period in 1953.[16]

INVESTIGATION BY THE NEW YORK STOCK EXCHANGE

On first learning of the offer, in accordance with its usual practice the New York Stock Exchange suggested that shares be accepted on a pro rata basis over at least a 10-day period, so that the greatest possible number of Pacific Mills stockholders could take advantage of the offer. However, Burlington Mills officers, concerned lest a competitive bid be made, decided to act as swiftly as possible. During the latter half of July, stockholders of Pacific Mills, especially those living at a distance from Boston and New York, complained to Burlington Mills that they had not had a chance to sell their shares to Burlington. On the first-come, first-served basis, many tenders had been turned down. The complaints of the disappointed stockholders led the Stock Exchange to investigate the transaction.

---

[14] *The Wall Street Journal*, July 12, 1954.

[15] *Daily News Record*, July 28, 1954.

[16] *America's Textile Reporter*, Vol. LXVIII, No. 32 (August 12, 1954).

Asked at a press conference if he thought the little shareholders got a raw deal, Mr. Love replied, "Certainly not. Look at what the shares are now. I think the shareholder is doing all right. The stock is considerably above what it was."[17] Shortly afterward, two representatives of Burlington Mills, a director and the secretary, met with the officials of the Stock Exchange to explain their company's action.

The New York Stock Exchange announced the conclusions of its investigation in a press release on August 27, 1954.

The New York Stock Exchange announced today that it had found no evidence of intent by Burlington Mills Corporation to discriminate against stockholders of Pacific Mills and Goodall-Sanford, Inc., in connection with its offers last month to purchase limited amounts of the common stocks of those companies from their stockholders. The Exchange's statement was based on information supplied by officials of Burlington Mills and information it had obtained independently. Burlington's management, the Exchange added, appears to have acted in good faith and in the best interests of its own stockholders in both transactions.

The meeting of Burlington officials with the Exchange followed complaints that the interests of stockholders of Pacific Mills and Goodall-Sanford, particularly those living at a distance from New York City and Boston, had been affected adversely by terms of the offers.

Declination by Burlington of numerous tenders of Pacific Mills stock by owners in many parts of the country was necessitated by an unanticipated heavy and immediate response to Burlington's first-come, first-served offer.

. . . .

A SUBSEQUENT OFFER TO REMAINING PACIFIC MILLS STOCKHOLDERS

On September 21, 1954, it was reported that Burlington Mills was seeking to acquire the remaining outstanding common shares of Pacific Mills through an exchange offer. The company would offer to exchange $\frac{1}{3}$ share of a new Burlington Mills $4\frac{1}{2}\%$ second preference stock and $1\frac{1}{5}$ shares of common stock for each share of Pacific Mills common stock. The second preference stock had been authorized previously but never issued.

The exchange offer was made officially to Pacific Mills stockholders in a letter dated October 15, 1954, and a prospectus. The letter read as follows.

Burlington Mills Corporation hereby offers to you the privilege of exchanging each share of capital stock of Pacific Mills held by you for $\frac{1}{3}$ of a share of new $4\frac{1}{2}\%$ Second Preference stock and $1\frac{1}{5}$ shares of Common Stock of the Corporation. This offer will expire on November 5, 1954, unless extended by us and is subject to the terms and conditions described in the accompanying Prospectus.

Since the acquisition by us in July, 1954, of approximately 52% of the outstanding stock of Pacific Mills, many of you have expressed the desire that we make a further offer to acquire your stock. Accordingly, this exchange offer is now

---

[17] *Daily News Record,* July 26, 1954.

made and will remain open, as mentioned above, for a period sufficiently long to give stockholders of Pacific Mills ample opportunity to act upon its acceptance.

Various features of the offer will be of particular interest to you. Perhaps the most noteworthy of these, from your standpoint, is that exchanges under the offer will be tax free to you if sufficient stock is exchanged by all of the Pacific Mills stockholders.[18] Also, such exchanges will enable you to continue your investment through ownership of stocks of Burlington Mills, a corporation which has an established record of leadership, progressive management, earnings and growth and which, through its highly diversified lines of business, products and distribution, its research facilities, and strong financial condition, is in a sound position to meet the intense competitive conditions of today.

Further, your income position upon the exchange will be enhanced, on the basis of the dividend rate of our new Second Preference Stock and the current annual dividend rates of the common stocks of Burlington Mills and Pacific Mills. On such basis, the total annual dividends on our stocks issued in the exchange will aggregate $2.22 per share of Pacific Mills stock, as compared with $1.40 per share, the current annual rate on the Pacific Mills stock.

In addition, the new Second Preference Stock, which has a redemption price and preference value over Common Stock of $100 per share, has been approved for listing on the New York Stock Exchange in the interest of its marketability and will be entitled to the benefits of a Purchase Fund, to be set aside annually out of earnings as described in the Prospectus, in an amount equal to 4% of the total shares issued, to be used for the purchase and retirement of such Stock.

We consider this offer to be eminently fair to the stockholders of Pacific Mills, and believe you will conclude, upon your review of the terms and benefits of the offer, the relative earnings, business and financial positions of the two corporations, the price range of the stock of Pacific Mills over the past several years and other factors mentioned in the Prospectus, that it is in your interest to make the exchange.

. . . .

The accompanying prospectus included pertinent information about Burlington Mills and Pacific Mills, and the provisions of the stock issues offered in the exchange. It added figures for 1949–53 to compare the dividends per share actually paid by Pacific Mills with those represented by the exchange; these are given in Exhibit 9. The chart in Exhibit 10 (figures also taken from the prospectus) shows for the period 1952 through October 12, 1954, the range of sales prices of Pacific Mills common stock and Burlington Mills common stock as well as 4% preferred stock, an issue prior to the new 4½% second preference stock.

---

[18] The prospectus added the statement that tax counsel was of the opinion that the exchanges would qualify as tax free to Pacific Mills stockholders if Burlington Mills owned at least 80% of the outstanding Pacific Mills stock immediately after the exchanges. Footnote added.

Exhibit 1

BURLINGTON MILLS CORPORATION

CONDENSED CONSOLIDATED BALANCE SHEETS AS OF OCTOBER 3, 1953,
AND JULY 3, 1954
(In Thousands)

ASSETS	October 3, 1953	July 3, 1954 (Unaudited)
Current assets:		
Cash	$ 25,480	$ 18,573
U.S. government securities at cost	12,101	30,113
Accounts receivable, net	42,688	37,227
Notes and accounts receivable	392	409
Inventories (lower of cost or market):		
Greige and finished goods	$ 47,022	$ 40,391
Work in process	11,103	11,157
Raw materials	29,012	25,362
Total Inventories	$ 87,137	$ 76,910
Supplies and other prepaid expenses	2,251	3,042
Total Current Assets	$170,050	$166,274
Fixed assets, at cost:		
Land and improvements	$ 2,665	$ 2,669
Buildings	64,128	65,235
Machinery, fixtures, and equipment	102,806	106,195
Total Fixed Assets	$169,599	$174,099
Less: Accumulated depreciation and amortization	47,417	52,809
Net Fixed Assets	$122,182	$121,290
Investments and other assets	8,503	8,526
Total Assets	$300,734	$296,090

LIABILITIES		
Current liabilities:		
Accounts payable	$ 12,665	$ 15,447
Accrued liabilities	7,941	7,568
Bank loans of foreign subsidiaries	283	376
Taxes based on income, estimated	14,331	8,648
Total Current Liabilities	$ 35,221	$ 32,039
Long-term debt (to insurance companies)	80,630	80,543
Stockholders' equity:		
Cumulative preferred stock*	$ 17,024	$ 16,455
Preferred stock†	14,550	13,850
Preference stock‡	...	...
Common stock	7,079	6,931
Capital surplus	59,852	58,387
Retained earnings	86,378	87,886
Total Stockholders' Equity	$184,883	$183,509
Total Liabilities	$300,734	$296,090

* Issuable in series; authorized 226,000 shares of $100 par value; outstanding at July 3, 1954, 4% series, 124,495 shares, and 3½% series, 40,055 shares.

† Issuable in series; cumulative; authorized 245,500 shares of $100 par value; outstanding 4.20% series; 70.9% of shares outstanding in July, 1954, owned by 2 insurance companies.

‡ Issuable in series; cumulative; authorized 400,000 shares of $100 par value; issued, none.

SOURCE: Burlington Mills Corporation, *Prospectus* for 4½% second preference stock and common stock, October 14, 1954.

Exhibit 2

BURLINGTON MILLS CORPORATION

CONSOLIDATED STATEMENT OF EARNINGS, YEAR ENDED OCTOBER 3, 1953,
AND NINE MONTHS ENDED JULY 3, 1954
(In Thousands)

	October 3, 1953	July 3, 1954 (Unaudited)
Net sales......................................	$360,839	$243,532
Cost of sales, exclusive of depreciation and amortization.............................	303,366	206,081
	$ 57,473	$ 37,451
Selling, administrative, and general expenses.................................	$ 23,527	$ 16,476
Depreciation and amortization................	8,588	7,016
	$ 32,115	$ 23,491
	$ 25,358	$ 13,960
Other income:		
Interest and dividends received..............	$ 377	$ 445
Miscellaneous income (deduction)............	836	(85)
	$ 1,212	$ 360
	$ 26,570	$ 14,320
Other deductions:		
Charitable donations.......................	$ 482	$ 362
Interest charges...........................	2,580	1,992
Miscellaneous.............................	644	84
	$ 3,707	$ 2,439
Profit, before taxes based on income............	$ 22,864	$ 11,882
Provision for taxes based on income:		
Federal income and excess profits taxes.......	$ 10,480	$ 5,521
Foreign taxes.............................	615	309
State taxes...............................	892	458
	$ 11,987	$ 6,288
Net Earnings for the Period..................	$ 10,877	$ 5,594

SOURCE: Burlington Mills Corporation, *Prospectus* for 4½% second preference stock and common stock, October 14, 1954.

Exhibit 3

BURLINGTON MILLS CORPORATION

FINANCIAL SUMMARY, 1944–53*

(In Millions)

	1944	1945	1946	1947	1948	1949	1950	1951	1952	1953
Net sales	$92.8	$108.2	$141.5	$217.0	$288.2	$263.5	$287.0	$310.1	$320.3	$360.8
Earnings before taxes on income	12.3	14.5	24.5	41.8	65.4	33.1	48.7	27.1	16.4	22.9
Taxes on income	8.3	9.5	11.6	16.9	29.2	14.9	21.6	13.4	7.8	12.0
Net earnings	4.0	5.0	12.9	24.9	36.2	18.2	27.1	13.7	8.6	10.9
Working capital	25.5	28.4	37.1	57.4	91.8	104.3	106.6	133.3	129.9	134.8
Long-term debt	4.9	….	15.6	15.6	25.6	35.5	35.7	66.1	65.7	80.6
Stockholders' equity	34.8	45.5	67.9	86.5	122.5	133.0	151.7	171.0	174.6	184.9
Fixed assets, at cost	21.3	24.7	40.9	53.7	72.5	84.5	108.5	134.7	147.2	169.6
Fixed assets, less depreciation and amortization	12.0	13.2	27.5	38.3	52.6	61.2	77.6	99.5	106.4	122.2
Number of common shares, outstanding, in millions†	5.2	5.2	5.2	5.3	6.0	6.0	5.9	6.5	6.7	7.1
Figures per Share of Common Stock, in Dollars:†										
Earnings before taxes on income	$ 2.38	$ 2.80	$ 4.73	$ 7.94	$ 10.90	$ 5.54	$ 8.20	$ 4.19	$ 2.47	$ 3.23
Taxes on income	1.61	1.83	2.24	3.22	4.86	2.49	3.64	2.07	1.18	1.70
Preferred dividends	0.06	0.09	0.18	0.21	0.19	0.18	0.13	0.19	0.20	0.18
Earnings after preferred dividends	0.71	0.88	2.31	4.51	5.85	2.87	4.43	1.93	1.09	1.35
Common dividends	0.35	0.41	.78	1.00	1.33	1.00	1.41	1.35	1.00	0.60
Book value	5.75	5.65	7.07	10.31	14.33	17.45	21.06	21.37	21.35	21.66

Number of stockholders: 1953, 19,817
1952, 19,209
1951, 15,726

* For fiscal years ended in September or early October except for figures for common dividends, which are on a calendar year basis.
† Adjusted for stock splits (see Exhibit 4 for splits).
SOURCE: Burlington Mills Corporation, annual reports.

Exhibit 4

BURLINGTON MILLS CORPORATION

PRICE RANGES OF COMMON STOCK, 1937 TO 1953

Period	Range	Stock Splits
1937	$18 at issue	. . .
1937–45	47¾– 5¾	. . .
1945	—	2 shares for 1
1945–46	59¾–20⅜	. . .
1946	—	2 shares for 1
1946–51	38⅜–13¾	. . .
1951	—	3 shares for 2
1951–53	23¼–10¼	. . .
1953	17 –10¼	. . .

SOURCE: *Moody's Industrials.*

Exhibit 5

PACIFIC MILLS

BALANCE SHEETS AS OF JANUARY 3, 1953, JANUARY 2, 1954, AND JULY 3, 1954

(In Thousands)

ASSETS	January 3, 1953	January 2, 1954	July 3, 1954
Current assets:			
Cash	$ 4,525	$ 4,643	$ 3,552
Accounts and notes receivable, net	15,749	17,366	13,667
Inventories:			
Raw materials	$ 4,489	$ 3,043	$ 4,614
Work in process, including grey cloth	13,858	13,825	17,768
Finished goods	7,639	9,002	9,678
Supplies	1,313	797	770
Total Inventories	$27,298	$26,668	$32,830
Total Current Assets	$47,572	$48,676	$50,048
Premium deposits with mutual insurance companies	$ 428	$ 419	$ 419
Property, plant, and equipment	$54,975	$55,158	$55,549
Less: Reserves	24,783	25,576	25,931
Net Property, Plant, and Equipment	$30,192	$29,582	$29,617
Prepaid expenses and deferred charges	488	448	438
Other assets	9	9	9
Total Assets	$78,690	$79,134	$80,532

LIABILITIES AND CAPITAL	January 3, 1953	January 2, 1954	July 3, 1954
Current liabilities:			
Notes payable, banks	$ 5,103	$ 4,000	$ 8,000
Accounts payable	2,588	2,122	1,868
Accrued liabilities, wages, salaries, etc.	1,565	1,632	767
Employees' deposits for income and social security taxes and purchase of savings bonds	364	329	416
Provision for taxes:			
Federal income taxes	$ 2,279	$ 2,553	$ 928
Less: U.S. Treasury savings notes	1,005	304	308
	$ 1,274	$ 2,249	$ 620
Other federal and state taxes	561	538	577
Total Current Liabilities	$11,455	$10,861	$12,248
Deferred credits	63	...	...
Reserve for self-insurance, workmen's compensation	98	109	97
Reserve for tax contingencies	2,000	...	...
Capital stock (Authorized 1 million shares, issued 966,805 shares, no-par value, $24,170,125; less 7,753 shares in treasury, $193,825)	23,976	23,976	23,976
Capital surplus	9,685	9,685	9,685
Retained earnings	31,412	34,503	34,526
Total Liabilities and Capital	$78,690	$79,134	$80,532

SOURCE: Pacific Mills, Annual Report for 1953; and Burlington Mills Corporation, *Prospectus* for 4½% second preference stock and common stock, October 14, 1954.

Exhibit 6

PACIFIC MILLS

STATEMENTS OF EARNINGS, YEARS ENDED JANUARY 3, 1953, AND JANUARY 2, 1954,
AND SIX MONTHS ENDED JULY 3, 1954
(In Thousands)

	Year Ended January 3, 1953	Year Ended January 2, 1954	6 Months Ended July 3, 1954 (Not Audited)
Net sales	$111,070	$121,235	$53,499
Cost of goods sold*	99,480	108,554	49,101
Gross profit on sales	$ 11,591	$ 12,681	$ 4,398
Less: Selling, general, and administrative expenses	6,834	7,089	3,578
Income from operations	$ 4,756	$ 5,592	$ 820
Other income:			
Interest and discounts	$ 189	$ 220	$ 127
Profit on disposal of fixed assets	109	109	542
Miscellaneous	103	106	26
Total Other Income	$ 400	$ 436	$ 695
Total before Income Deductions	$ 5,157	$ 6,028	$ 1,515
Income deductions:			
Interest	$ 628	$ 642	$ 274
Provision for doubtful accounts	134	99	. . .
Miscellaneous	2	204	2
Total Income Deductions	$ 763	$ 945	$ 276
Total before Provision for Income Taxes	$ 4,394	$ 5,084	$ 1,239
Provision for estimated income taxes:			
Federal taxes	$ 2,175	$ 2,410	$ 480
State taxes	195	240	65
	$ 2,370	$ 2,650	$ 545
Net Income to Earned Surplus	$ 2,024	$ 2,434	$ 694

* Including plant depreciation of $876,586 for six months ended July 3, 1954; $1,751,034 for 1953; and $1,730,631 for 1952.

SOURCE: Burlington Mills Corporation, *Prospectus* for 4½% second preference stock and common stock, October 14, 1954.

Exhibit 7

PACIFIC MILLS

FINANCIAL SUMMARY, 1944–53

(In Millions)

	1944	1945	1946	1947	1948	1949	1950	1951	1952	1953
Net sales	$74.3	$64.0	$78.3	$90.6	$112.8	$98.8	$128.6	$122.0	$111.1	$121.2
Earnings before income taxes and contingencies	12.2	10.1	19.2	19.1	21.9	6.9	10.9	1.7	4.4	5.1
Federal and state income taxes	8.8	7.4	7.7	7.8	8.5	2.8	4.8	0.8	2.4	2.7
Provision for contingencies	1.5	0.8	2.0	3.0	3.0	...	...	...	...	...
Balance of net earnings to surplus	1.9	2.0	9.5	8.4	10.4	4.1	6.1	0.9	2.0	2.4
Notes and acceptances payable	...	...	...	...	3.7	3.3	8.3	13.8	5.1	4.0
Working capital	23.3	22.5	27.3	31.4	35.0	34.0	37.0	34.8	36.1	37.8
Net worth:										
Capital stock	$19.8	$19.8	$19.8	$21.8	$ 22.9	$22.9	$ 24.0	$ 24.0	$ 24.0	$ 24.0
Capital surplus	7.6	7.6	7.6	8.6	9.1	9.1	9.7	9.7	9.7	9.7
Earned surplus	1.5	2.5	8.8	13.1	18.8	29.7	31.8	30.8	31.4	34.5
Reserve for contingencies	5.4	5.6	7.1	9.0	12.0	2.0	2.0	2.0	2.0	...
Total Net Worth	$34.3	$35.6	$43.4	$52.6	$ 62.8	$63.7	$ 67.5	$ 66.5	$ 67.1	$ 68.2
Taxes per share (959,052 shares)	$ 9.20	$ 7.71	$ 7.98	$ 8.08	$ 8.88	$ 2.89	$ 5.01	$ 0.88	$ 2.47	$ 2.76
Net per share (959,052 shares)	1.95	2.01	9.91	8.73	10.87	4.29	6.39	0.94	2.11	2.54
Cash dividends per share (not adjusted for stock dividends)	1.00	1.25	2.37½*	3.00*	3.50*	3.50	2.50*	2.00	1.50	1.40
Number of stockholders	3,300†	3,300†	3,800†	3,800†	3,800†	na	6,000†	6,022	5,895	5,561
Number of shares outstanding (in thousands)‡	792	792	792	873	915	915	959	959	959	959

* Plus a 5% stock dividend.
† Approximate number.
‡ Adjusted for 1946 two-for-one stock split.
SOURCE: Pacific Mills, Annual Report for 1953.

Exhibit 8

PACIFIC MILLS

COMMON STOCK PRICES AND SALES VOLUME, JUNE 30, 1954–JULY 26, 1954

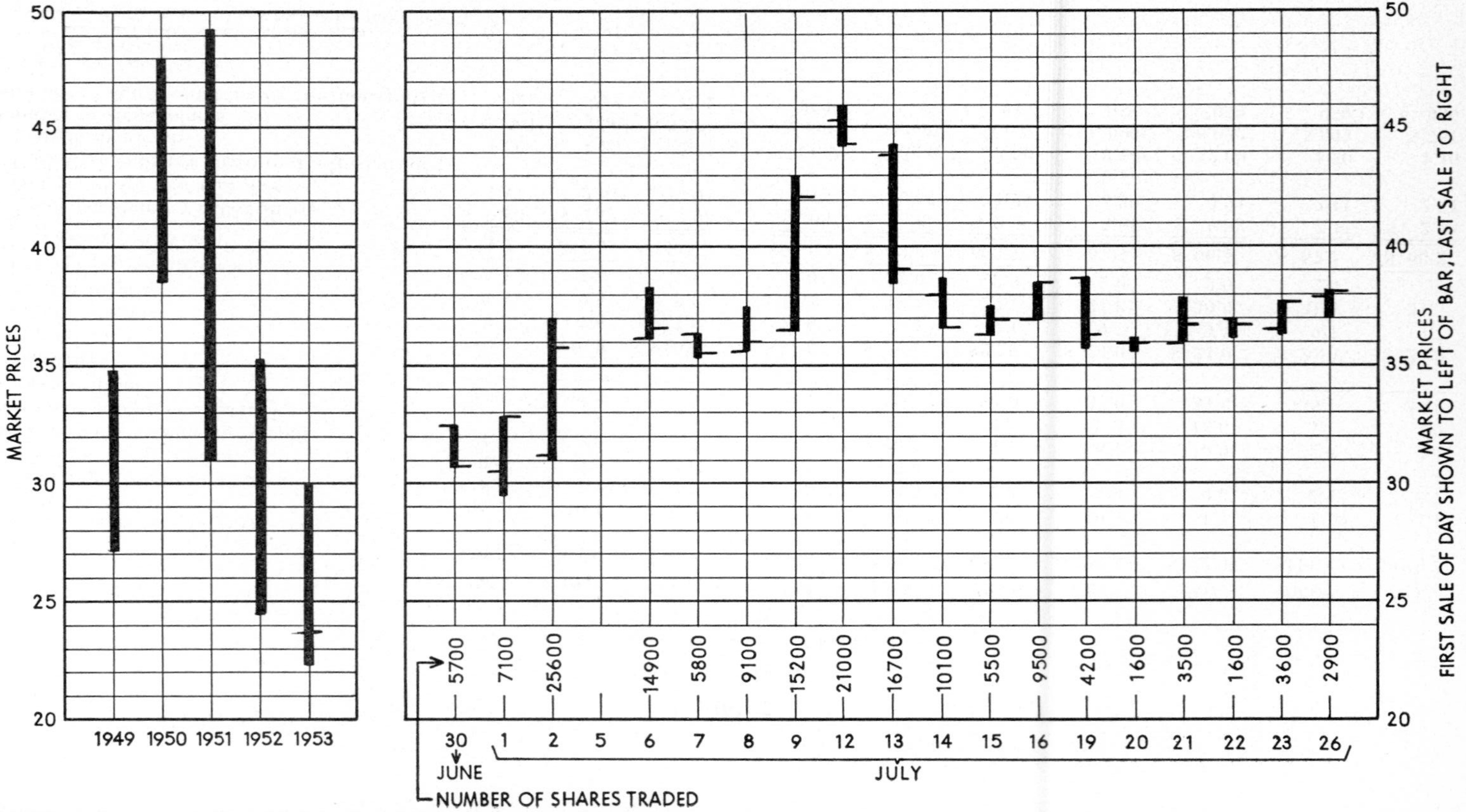

Exhibit 9

PACIFIC MILLS

COMPARISON OF DIVIDENDS ACTUALLY RECEIVED WITH THOSE
REPRESENTED BY THE EXCHANGE OFFER PROPOSED BY
BURLINGTON MILLS, 1949–53

Year	Pacific Mills Dividend per Share	Burlington Mills Exchange Offer
1949	$3.34*	$2.70†
1950	2.39*	3.19†
1951	2.00	3.12†
1952	1.50	2.70
1953	1.40	2.22

* Adjusted for 5% stock dividend paid in 1950.
† Adjusted for three-for-two splitup of common stock in March, 1951.
SOURCE: Burlington Mills Corporation, *Prospectus* for 4½% second preference stock and common stock, October 14, 1954.

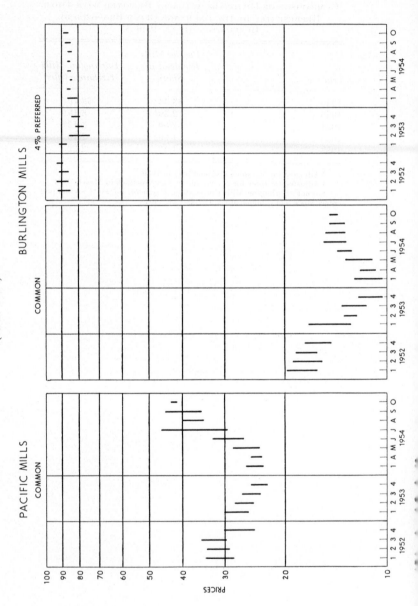

Exhibit 10

RANGE OF SALES PRICES OF PACIFIC MILLS COMMON STOCK AND BURLINGTON 4% PREFERRED AND
COMMON STOCKS, NEW YORK STOCK EXCHANGE,* 1952–OCTOBER, 1954
(Ratio Scale)

A NOTE ON TAKEOVER BIDS
AND CORPORATE PURCHASES OF STOCK*

By Manuel F. Cohen†

THE subject of this note is a new and developing concern in securities regulation: The protection of public investors in connection with the acquisition of control by cash tender offers—so-called takeover bids—and the acquisition by a company of its own stock.

TAKEOVER BIDS

As I am sure you know, the acquisition of control by cash tender offers has become much more common in the past few years than ever before. This is probably due in part to the greater availability of cash for this purpose, and the relative ease this method offers for acquiring other companies. It is certainly simpler, and perhaps less costly, than a proxy fight for control. To illustrate the increased use of the device, during the last year there have been 29 cash takeover bids involving companies listed on the New York Stock Exchange and 15 involving companies listed on the American Stock Exchange. This compares with only 8 cash takeover bids in 1960 involving stocks listed on both exchanges.

It is interesting to contrast the regulatory requirements applicable to cash tender offers with those which apply when an offer is made by one company to exchange its shares for shares of another. The exchange offer, as you know, requires registration under the Securities Act of 1933. The law recognizes that the shareholder whose stock is sought by means of the exchange offer is in the position both of a seller and a buyer: that is, he is selling the security he presently owns, and buying the security offered to him. The shareholder

---

* Reprinted by permission from *The Business Lawyer*, 22 (November 1966), pp. 149–57.

† Chairman of Securities and Exchange Commission; member of the New York and District of Columbia Bars. Adapted from an address on June 28, 1966 before the American Society of Corporate Secretaries, Inc. at Colorado Springs, Colorado. The Securities and Exchange Commission, as a matter of policy, disclaims responsibility for any private publication by any of its members. The views expressed herein are those of the author and do not necessarily reflect the views of the Commission or its staff.

therefore gets a prospectus, explaining all material facts about the offer. He knows who the purchaser is, what plans have been made for the company, and is in a position to make an informed decision either to hold his original security or exchange it for the other. The disclosures, as in the case of a proxy contest, are filed with the Commission and are subject to statutory requirements and sanctions, which operate for the protection of the opposing parties as well as the shareholder. Now look at the situation when the tender offer is solely for cash. The investment decision is similar—the choice whether to retain the original security or sell it is, in substance, little different from the decision made on an original purchase of a security, or on an offer to exchange one security for another. In many cases of cash tender offers, however, the public investor does not even know the identity of the purchaser, much less what the purchaser plans to do with the company if the takeover bid is successful.

Two substantially identical bills now pending before the Congress would correct this failure to require adequate disclosures. The bills, S. 2731 introduced by Senator Harrison Williams of New Jersey, Chairman of the Subcommittee on Securities of the Banking and Currency Committee, and H.R. 14417, introduced by Harley O. Staggers, Chairman of the House Interstate and Foreign Commerce Committee, would amend the Securities Exchange Act of 1934. They are designed primarily to require disclosure of material information *before* a person acquires control whether by a cash tender offer or by open market purchases. The bills would require this disclosure by any person holding, or intending to acquire, beneficial ownership of more than 5% of a class of equity security registered under Section 12 of the Exchange Act. It would apply with respect to listed companies and those larger over-the-counter companies registered as a result of the Securities Acts Amendments of 1964.

Specifically, the bills would require official disclosure concerning:

(1) the name, background, and security holdings in the issuer, of the person making the takeover bid and of his associates;

(2) the source of funds to be used in the acquisition; and if borrowed, the name of the lender;

(3) any special arrangements that might exist with respect to the securities, such as option contracts, guarantees against loss, or the giving or withholding of proxies, and the name of the other party to the arrangement;

(4) the person's market activity in the company's securities; and

(5) any additional matters which the Commission finds are necessary for the protection of investors.

If the purchases are to be made to acquire control, or representation on the issuer's board of directors, the purchaser would also be required to disclose his plans for the future conduct and continuation of the issuer. Any material changes in the information field would be required to be reported.

The basic principle of investor protection underlying the two bills is simple: Investors should be informed of the identity, background, future plans and other material information about anyone seeking to acquire control of their company before they sell securities to that person. This is necessary if public investors are to stand on an equal footing with the acquiring person in assessing the future of the company and the value of its shares. Further, the bills recognize that the need of investors for full and complete information in arriving at a decision to *sell* securities is just as great as when they are arriving at a decision to *buy* securities—a concept which is inherent in the Exchange Act.

The proposed legislation would, of course, subject a new class of persons to the reporting requirements of the Exchange Act; that is, persons not yet in control. But it would not represent a change in the fundamental policy underlying the federal securities laws that investors should be fully informed of all material facts before reaching an investment decision. I believe you will agree that information about control, or a potential change in control, which is so clearly essential to an informed decision to *buy* securities, is equally important in reaching an informed decision to *sell* securities—whether for cash, or in exchange for other securities.

Information about a potential change in control can be particularly essential to an informed decision. A change in control brings with it the possibility of different operating results and different investment results, or perhaps the possibility of realizing on a company's liquidation value. This may be either good, or bad, depending on the facts and circumstances involved. But no investor can reach a conclusion on the possible effects of a change in control until the facts are available to him.

It is argued by some that the basic factor which influences shareholders to accept a tender offer is the adequacy of the price. But, I might ask, how can an investor evaluate the adequacy of the price if he cannot assess the possible impact of a change in control? Certainly without such information he cannot judge its adequacy by the current market price. That price presumably reflects the assumption that the company's present business, control and management will continue. If that assumption is changed, is it not likely that the market price might change? An example will show why. Assume that a company's stock sells for $5 per share—its going concern value as assessed by investors. Its earnings are poor; its prospects dim; its management uninspired. Is a cash tender offer of $6 per share adequate? Or do we need more information? Suppose a person believes that with control he can liquidate the company and realize $15 per share, or maybe more. Certainly the company's shareholders would want to know about liquidation plans. Indeed, it is the plan to liquidate which makes the bidder willing to pay more than $5 per share. Whether or not the company's liquidation value is generally known is not important, for without someone to carry out the liquidation, this value is unobtainable. If the company's shareholders, at the time of the tender offer, know of the plan to liquidate, would they consider $6 per share adequate? I think a reasonable question arises.

I do not need to make the example so dramatic. Assume simply that the offeror has a proven record of accomplishment in the company's field, as opposed to a present management which has not done well. This factor alone would undoubtedly affect investors' assessments of the future worth of the company's securities. While the disclosure required by the bills might discourage some tender offers, it is perhaps a small price to pay for an informed choice by shareholders.

The importance of a potential change of control illustrates why the shareholder to whom even a cash offer is made is, in a sense, a purchaser as well as a seller of a security. A change in control can result in what amounts to a new, or at least vastly changed, company. A decision not to accept the offer amounts to a decision to buy into that new company. It is anomalous, therefore, to treat the cash tender offer differently from the exchange offer, and require—as we do now—full disclosure for one, but not the other. Another relevant factor which should be considered is that when management is opposed to the takeover bid, in fairness to the shareholders it should have a real opportunity to make its case, either in opposition to the proposed change in control or with respect to any aspect of the bid, whether it is the price or any other pertinent consideration.

That takeover bids should be regulated and shareholders provided with basic information has been recognized for many years in a number of foreign countries. To name some, Australia, Canada, France, Germany, Italy, the Netherlands and England have all adopted rules regulating takeover bids in one way or another. While we looked at all these laws before making our comments on the proposed bills, we looked particularly at the proposed legislation for regulating takeover bids which is now pending before the legislature in Ontario, Canada. Theirs was the most recent consideration of this problem. The guiding principle of the drafters of this legislation was set out in the Report of the Attorney General's Committee on Securities Legislation in Ontario, known (after its Chairman) as the Kimber Report. It states: "Shareholders should have made available to them, as a matter of law, sufficient up-to-date relevant information to permit them to come to a reasoned decision as to the desirability of accepting a bid for their shares." This, however, must be balanced against the need to insure that new regulations do "not unduly impede potential bidders or put them in a commercially disadvantageous position vis-a-vis an entrenched and possibly hostile board of directors of an offeree company."

In considering the provisions of the pending bills to regulate tender offers, we agreed with the Kimber Report that this balancing of interests is appropriate. While we favored the legislation in general, we thought that certain changes might improve its overall operation.

We suggested to the Senate and House Committees considering the bills that a person should not be required to disclose open market purchases until five days after they were made. We did not think a person could effectively come close to acquiring control in the market within that short period.

As introduced, the bill required that a tender offer be made known to the offeree company 20 days prior to making the offer to shareholders. We suggested instead that the offering material be filed with the Commission on a confidential basis five days in advance, and additional offering material at least two days before its use. This would allow us an opportunity to examine material to assure compliance with the law, but would not give an opposed management a period in which to mobilize its resources and take action against the offer, at a time when the offeror could not solicit tenders or otherwise make his case.

We also suggested that any recommendation to shareholders to accept or reject the tender offer, whether by management or others, be subject to regulation. In this way the opponents in an opposed takeover bid would be placed on an equal footing. Each would be subject to equivalent disclosure and anti-fraud regulations. In a general sense, our approach would apply the same principles and examination procedures to opposed takeover bids that we have developed in proxy contests. In these contests each side has an opportunity fairly to present his story in accordance with the same disclosure requirements and standards.

Indeed, in developing our approach to these bills we relied heavily on our experience with the proxy rules, and particularly proxy contests. The disclosures would be similar to many we now require, and the technique of pre-filing on a confidential basis has worked extremely well. We believe that we can keep up with the hectic pace of contested takeover bids just as we have been able to keep up with proxy battles.

I might note that the rules of the Board of Trade in England regulating takeover bids require the offer to be filed with the offeree company three days before it is made to shareholders. Although this requirement was not criticized in the Jenkins Report which reconsidered England's securities regulation in 1962, we differed with this approach. Legally, the offer is being made to shareholders, not to the company. In some instances the interest of all persons would probably be best served by an initial approach to the offeree company's board of directors. There are cases, however, where the offeror may justifiably believe that this approach would hinder the success of the bid. In some it might even insure its failure.

The Commission recommended several other changes in the bills as introduced in Congress. It was originally proposed that a statement describing the offer be filed with the Commission and mailed to the offeree company at least 20 days before the solicitation commenced. This would have given shareholders 20 days to evaluate a tender offer. As indicated above, we believed this might give management an unwarranted advantage when the offer is opposed. However, since time for careful consideration of the offer by shareholders is desirable and management should have a reasonable opportunity to present its case, we suggested that shareholders be allowed seven days after the offer is made to withdraw any shares they may have tendered.

For similar and additional reasons we also wanted to avoid having shareholders rush to accept an offer. To accomplish this, we suggested that where the person making the offer takes less than all the shares tendered, he should be required to take them on a pro rata basis. Further, we recommended that where a tender offer price is increased, that all persons having tendered shares, whether or not already taken up, be given the increased offering price. In this way we intended to remove a purely fortuitous factor from the calculation of the amount shareholders should receive for their shares, and to avoid the discriminatory effect of paying some holders more than others.

We also wanted to improve the way in which shareholders could learn the facts about a takeover bid. The bills would require a person making a takeover bid to file a statement with the Commission and the company, but nothing in the bill required delivery of information to shareholders. Information filed with the Commission is, of course, available to the public. But we wanted to assure that the information reaches shareholders and their advisers promptly and in full. We recommended, therefore, that all written tender offers and advertisements concerning them contain such information as the Commission may determine is necessary for the protection of investors. This would assure that shareholders would have at their fingertips all the information necessary to evaluate the offer.

We made numerous other suggestions concerning the bills, but they were largely technical and I will not go into them now. However, before I leave the subject of takeover bids, I would like to point out that we did differ substantially from the drafters of the Ontario proposed legislation on one matter: Whether a cash takeover bid could be made by an undisclosed principal. The Ontario legislation would allow it. The bills before Congress would not. And we think properly so. From the Kimber Report we learned that the drafters of the proposed Ontario legislation thought that to require this disclosure would be to discourage some takeover bids. We believe, however, that this possibility was simply a price which had to be paid so that investors could make an informed investment decision. As I explained before, the managerial ability of the person making a takeover bid, as reflected by his past performance, may be overwhelmingly different from that of present management. The materiality to shareholders of the identity of the potential control person, we believe, is simply too great not to require that it be disclosed.

COMPANY PURCHASES OF ITS OWN SECURITIES

The two bills also contain provisions relating to cash purchases by a company of its own registered equity securities. They would specifically authorize the Commission to adopt rules requiring a company which purchases its own shares, to disclose:

(1) the reason for the purchase of its stock;
(2) the source of funds;
(3) the number of shares to be purchased;
(4) the price to be paid, and
(5) the method of purchase.

The bills would also authorize the Commission to require the issuer to file additional financial or other information necessary for the protection of shareholders.

The practice of companies acquiring their own securities, like takeover bids, has been a growing phenomenon, particularly as companies have generated cash balances greater than needed to finance their projected growth. In an article published in the April 1965 issue of the *Harvard Business Review,* it was noted that the total number of shares reacquired by companies has been rising steadily over the past years. The author found that between 1954 and 1963 the average percentage increase year to year was close to 20% for companies listed on the New York Stock Exchange.

The purchase by a company of its own securities can be the subject of a number of abuses and special circumstances requiring disclosure to the seller, whether the purchases are by a tender offer or made in the open market. One of these potential abuses was the subject of the Commission's recent action to enjoin the Georgia-Pacific Corporation from engaging in fraud and manipulation in connection with purchases of Georgia-Pacific stock by an employee stock bonus trust managed by officers of the company. In essence, the complaint[1] alleged that purchases of Georgia-Pacific stock by the trust had been used to raise the market price of the stock while Georgia-Pacific was engaged in corporate acquisitions. This, the Commission alleged, reduced the number of shares Georgia-Pacific was required to issue in certain of these acquisitions. Georgia-Pacific had not disclosed this activity to the shareholders of the companies it acquired. Without admitting or denying the allegations, Georgia-Pacific consented last May to an injunction against violation of certain provisions of the Federal securities acts.[2] The company agreed to have an independent trustee administer the trust. To help eliminate the market effect of future stock purchases, Georgia-Pacific also agreed to a number of restrictions which would govern the independent trustee's actions. Among these is an agreement that purchases will be made through only one broker at a time; this prevents one broker from competing with another to fill an order for the same customer. The trust will not make any bid or purchase at the opening of the New York Stock Exchange nor execute orders within one hour before the close. Purchases in any one day are not to exceed 10% of the average daily trading volume for the preceding four weeks, and purchases on any one day are to be kept within 10% of that day's volume, except that purchases of 300 shares may be made despite these restrictions. To eliminate further the market effect of the trust's purchases, Georgia-Pacific agreed that no bid would be placed, and no purchase made, at a price in excess of the last sale price. In this way the trust's purchases will not lead the market up. Finally, Georgia-Pacific agreed to make appropriate disclosure to the companies it seeks to acquire about the daily volume and prices of purchases by the trust, Georgia-

---

[1] For a copy of the complaint see *SEC* v. *Georgia-Pacific Corporation,* CCH Fed. Sec. L. Rep. ¶91,680 (April 27, 1966).

[2] *SEC* v. *Georgia-Pacific Corporation,* CCH Fed. Sec. Rep. ¶96,690 (May 24, 1966).

Pacific, and its officers, directors, and more-than-10% stockholders. This disclosure is to be made at the time serious negotiations commence. The information is to be given for the previous 30 days, and each week thereafter, until negotiations are broken off or the amount of securities to be issued by Georgia-Pacific, or the formula for determining this amount, is agreed upon and, if necessary, approved by shareholders.

A few days before the settlement of this case Genesco, Inc. had disclosed in its prospectus that it had adopted a somewhat similar procedure for controlling purchases of Genesco stock by its employee benefit plans to avoid possible violation of the anti-fraud and anti-manipulative provisions of the Federal securities acts. As these actions illustrate, we have several rules which already apply in this area, and I believe that we have additional rule-making power, which has not yet been exercised, under the existing statutes. We welcome, however, the specific statutory authority which the pending bills would give us.

CONCLUSION

In conclusion, I would like to point out that the bills now pending before Congress would fill a hiatus which presently exists in the protection offered under the federal securities laws to investors selling their securities for cash. The Securities Act of 1933 was designed to protect investors against fraud and to give them adequate information when they *purchase* securities. The Securities Exchange Act was designed to protect investors through a combination of disclosure, anti-fraud, anti-manipulative and regulatory requirements in both the purchase and sale of securities. But I think it is safe to say that our primary emphasis and thought over the years has been on protecting investors in the purchase of securities. This, of course, has been the area of greatest abuse in the past. And certainly the loss which an investor suffers when a stock he purchases declines in price seems at first blush more tangible than the loss an investor suffers when he sells securities that later rise in price. But is it any less a loss to that seller who would not have sold had he been in possession of all the facts? I think not.

We have taken action before to protect investors in the sale of their securities. We have adopted rules to protect investors when they sell their securities and we have supported them in private law suits. Nevertheless, the development of the law has left a gap in securities regulation protecting investors selling their securities pursuant to a cash takeover bid. While it is probable that we can adopt rules regulating takeover bids without legislation, it may be desirable to make this power entirely clear. Certainly the bills now pending before Congress, with the changes we have recommended, would provide more complete protection to shareholders than we can provide without their passage.

If we are to retain and build investors' confidence in the integrity of our securities markets, so vital to the free flow and development of capital in our country, we must place all participants in the securities markets in a position to compete on an equal footing with respect to the availability of significant facts about a company, its management and its securities. This is the premise on which our securities markets are supposed to work, and all Americans, whether shareholders or not, have a vital stake in making sure that it is a correct one.

PART II

Managing the Capital Structure

Chapter 7　Interrelated Problems of Creating and Supporting the Capital Structure

1. *Limits on the Use of Debt*

MID-AMERICA PIPELINE COMPANY

On February 20, 1960, Robert E. Thomas, president of Mid-America Pipeline Company (MAPCO) and chairman of the executive committee of Missouri-Kansas-Texas Railroad Company (KATY), was considering methods of completing a financing program involving the promotion of a new $70 million pipeline venture. In January, The Prudential Insurance Company of America had agreed to purchase at a discount approximately $45 million face value in first mortgage bonds and a convertible promissory note, provided MAPCO's management could raise an additional $28.5 million in subordinated securities by April 10, 1960.

Two prominent investment houses had indicated their willingness to organize the underwriting of a package of the junior securities, which would consist of subordinated debentures and common stock. The first set of terms considered was the sale at $73.50 per unit of 410,000 units, consisting of 2 shares of common stock and a 6½%, $50 subordinated debenture, but it did not appear to offer sufficient growth prospects to attract enough investors for a successful underwriting. Mr. Thomas was reviewing two alternative packages, which might prove to be marketable while still serving the interest of the promoters.

The promoters of MAPCO proposed to construct and operate a common carrier pipeline for the transportation of liquefied petroleum gases (LPG), such as propane and butane, from producing plants in West Texas, New Mexico, and the Texas and Oklahoma Panhandle areas to delivery points in the upper Middle West. The products would be marketed by either the original shippers or their customers. The proposed route is shown in Exhibit 1. In these market areas, LPG is used extensively as fuel for home heating, cooking, and refrigeration. Commercially, it is used as fuel for tractors, trucks, forklifts, and other vehicles, and in various farm equipment, such as weed burners, where close control of temperature is necessary.

In 1959, railroads accounted for substantially all of the LPG traffic volume into the proposed marketing area. Considering all sources, 60–70% of the LPG consumed in the market area came from the gasoline plants in the producing area to be served by MAPCO.

HISTORICAL PERSPECTIVE

Under the necessity of increasing earnings over the long run, KATY had turned to diversification as a means of achieving this end. Only limited funds were available for such ventures, however, since most of the cash flows were needed to modernize the railroad property and to meet the burden requirements of the capital structure.[1] Better utilization of valuable railroad property was next considered as a more promising approach to diversification. It was in this context that the pipeline venture had first been proposed.

In the fall of 1957, Mr. Thomas, then chairman of the executive committee of KATY, had organized a plan to build a pipeline, using the rights-of-way of the KATY and an eastern railroad. This idea proved unworkable and the initial proposal was set aside, but the idea of a pipeline to the upper Middle West still proved intriguing. Because of low rates, KATY derived no income from revenues associated with the shipment of LPG. Thus, a pipeline involving this area would not cause losses for the railroad. Eventually, a new pipeline proposal was developed with no use of the railroad's right-of-way.

The proposal was regarded as quite attractive by the railroad's management, especially since it would involve diversification into an industry without material prospect of labor difficulties. Nevertheless, KATY's management sought profit prospects sufficient to compensate for its risks, although no specific minimum rate of return had been mentioned.

In late 1959, two large investment houses each advanced $40,000 in return for 26,333 shares apiece of the newly formed Mid-America Pipeline Company. At about the same time, KATY, through an affiliated company, advanced $255,000 in cash and $265,000 in the imputed value of rights and titles to

---

[1] By the end of 1952, KATY had restored its interest payments to a completely current basis for the first time since 1934. The accumulation of preferred dividends was so large, however, that the management decided to file a plan for voluntary stock modification under the Mahaffie Act, which in 1948 had added Section 20b to the Interstate Commerce Act. The KATY's final plan, approved by the Interstate Commerce Commission in 1958 as amended, eliminated the preferred arrearages but set up sizable current charges on income, resulting both from the new securities issued and from required payments into a capital improvement fund. In addition, important debt issues were nearing maturity.

preliminary studies, reports, options, shippers' letters of intent, etc., pertaining to MAPCO. In return, the affiliated company, Southern Management Company, received 26,334 shares of the new firm's common stock and a $480,000 promissory note, which was to be automatically converted into 316,000 common shares when the sale of securities to the public was completed. The value per common share used in these exchanges was approximately $1.52. In the event that the promotion was unsuccessful, or its proposed terms unsatisfactory, KATY retained claim to the unconsumed portion of the assets it had advanced.

ENGINEERING STUDIES

To prepare estimates of investment requirements, revenues, and costs, KATY employed the Stone & Webster Service Corporation, a consulting firm with extensive management and engineering experience in the design and evaluation of chemical and utility facilities, including pipelines. Extracts of these estimates are shown in Exhibit 2. In this exhibit, the first year of operation may be taken as 1961.

The estimated construction cost for the pipeline was $69 million, including financing costs during the construction period, line fill, and a $3 million allowance for contingencies. These estimates, given the safety factor included in the contingency allowance, were regarded as a maximum. At the volume forecast, working capital would require an additional $700,000, about half of which would vary with changes in billing.

Annual operating costs could be forecast with a fair amount of accuracy and were likely to remain comparatively fixed regardless of the pipeline throughput. These costs were subject to modest inflationary pressures, although perhaps less than costs of competitive forms of transportation would be. The pipeline itself was not expected to require major outlays for maintenance (e.g., pipe replacement) for more than 40 years.

It was not anticipated that MAPCO would pay a dividend on the common stock for several years. Funds generated from operations and available after debt servicing would be required to finance ancillary pipelines or for other growth purposes. Although the timing of these pipeline additions could be paced somewhat, opportunities for highly profitable investments were expected to range between $5 and $7 million annually, offering the equity holders returns after taxes of 10% or more, depending on leverage. Opportunities of this magnitude would require use of external funds as well as all available funds generated from operations. Therefore, the proposed initial capitalization of the venture was considered particularly important, since it could influence the future availability of external sources of funds.

Revenues Forecast

Studies by MAPCO indicated that the area in which it would have economic access to sources of supply included 116 plants with an aggregate production of about 270,000 barrels of LPG per day. Not all of these plants were to be connected to the pipeline's gathering system, and not all the production of the plants connected was likely to be shipped in the pipeline. For example, one company operating in the area and producing approximately 30% of the daily production of natural gas liquids used its own pipeline to capacity and shipped the rest of its production in other ways.

An independent expert had confirmed that the sources of propane, butane, and natural gasoline in the area of the plants to be serviced by MAPCO had adequate reserves to provide the pipeline with natural gas liquids at or near its proposed initial capacity for the next 20 to 25 years. Exploration was still being carried on in the area, and it was likely that additional reserves would be found in the foreseeable future.

MAPCO had already begun negotiations to provide pipeline connections to approximately 30 of the larger plants in the gathering area. These negotiations were in various stages of completion. MAPCO had received letters of intent from 13 companies, but they were not identical, or in some instances even similar, in form and were not considered to be firm commitments for shipment of definite volumes of products. Therefore, MAPCO could not make any precise estimates of the potential supply from such shippers.

The letters offered data on the volume of LPG shipped to or sold in the pipeline market area by each shipper over the past five-year period. The letters in general stated, first, that the shipper thought a pipeline system of the size and location proposed would be beneficial to it. Second, they noted that any use of the pipeline system would be subject, among other conditions, to: (1) a connecting line to certain specified producing plants; (2) MAPCO's filing of certain tariff rates and regulations; (3) delivery in the market area of LPG that conformed in quality to specifications outlined; (4) satisfactory transportation service beginning by specified dates; and, most important, (5) shipping costs to point of use that were competitive with alternative methods of shipping. If these conditions were met, the shippers expressed an intention to use the line in various degrees for varying lengths of time, usually five years or more.

Volume estimates had come from the 13 intended users of the pipeline in two forms: (1) firm commitments for volume throughputs from one area to another and (2) rough estimates of possible usage in each state. The usage estimates were analyzed to determine what volume would be likely to go into the pipeline on a competitive basis and to forecast actual usage derived therefrom. At the moment, approximately 6,500 barrels per day represented firm commitments from these producers, whereas 25,640 barrels per day approximated the probable usage of the pipeline by shippers that had provided only estimates of possible demand. As economic conditions were envisioned, however, it seemed unlikely that volume would average less than 25,000 barrels per day once the transition period was completed.

Information in these letters of intent was used by Stone & Webster for its forecast of product load and revenue. The conclusion was that by the fourth year of operation MAPCO was assured of utilization amounting to 100% during the prime shipping season and to 50% of a year's total line capacity.

The potential volumes from these commitments and estimates, differentiated by market area and modified for future growth in size of market, constituted the entire inflow of revenues projected for MAPCO in Exhibit 2. Stone & Webster's forecast did not estimate any revenue from any shipper who did not provide a letter of intent, even though several additional users seemed likely.

COMPETITION

The proposed 2,184 mile pipeline system would have a number of significant advantages over truck or rail movements. For example, the current rail rate from producing plants in Eunice, New Mexico, to St. Paul, Minnesota, was $1.73 per barrel. MAPCO proposed to charge 95 cents for the same service. In addition, the pipeline could operate under all weather conditions, a factor that would favorably affect the storage and servicing costs of various LPG wholesalers and retailers in the market area, since LPG use was highly seasonal.

MAPCO had planned its pipeline to meet anticipated demands from continued growth in LPG use in the marketing area. (Exhibit 3, showing sales of propane over the six years 1954–59, provides some basis for estimating growth beyond 1960.) The efficiencies of pipeline operations were such that installation and operation of large-diameter pipelines, like the one MAPCO proposed, were not materially more costly than that of smaller lines. Costs per unit of throughput fell with volume. It was therefore unlikely that a competitor could develop a more efficient competing facility once the MAPCO installation was in place.

There was always the possibility that LPG production might be initiated in producing areas closer to the proposed service areas of MAPCO, thus providing a more economical source of supply for the proposed marketing area. There had been some recent speculation that LPG deposits in Canada might eventually be piped into the American market. Known fields in Canada were more distant from the terminal marketing areas than were the proposed sources of MAPCO. Nonetheless, there was some danger the region might eventually be serviced competitively by pipelines fed from a trans-Canada system.

Other transportation systems were not likely to compete effectively on a price basis with a long-haul pipeline throughout this region. The southwestern railroads had already proposed an overall reduction of 21 cents per barrel (43 gallons), long haul, to discourage construction of the proposed MAPCO line. The southwestern railroads would be the principal sufferers, since they would lose all the long-haul traffic. The straight-haul loss by the western trunk lines would be replaced in part by short-haul traffic away from the pipeline terminals. In order to effect the interjurisdictional rate reduction, a majority of the western and southwestern railroads had to vote in favor of it. Each railroad carried one vote, and in this combined meeting 20 western and 7 southwestern railroads would be voting.

Several of the intended users of MAPCO's facilities owned their own tank-car rail fleets. Initially, these shippers would not enjoy the full benefits of the envisioned transportation savings, because their out-of-pocket costs in the rail transport were lower than those described earlier. However, these shippers were expected to gradually transfer their fleets to service other transportation needs. Stone & Webster estimated that only 40% of potential volume from these sources could be gained initially but that 100% of available volume would be shipped by pipeline by the fourth year (see Exhibit 2). It was conceivable, however, that the process might take five years.

REGULATION

The MAPCO pipeline would be a common carrier of petroleum products in interstate commerce, and as such its business would be subject to the jurisdiction of the Interstate Commerce Commission. The accounts of the company had to be kept in a manner prescribed by the Commission. It would be required to file its tariff rates with the Commission and to make periodically a complete report on its operation.

The Commission's attitude toward earnings was expected to be as follows:

The Commission recognized that the hazards of the uncertain future of pipeline common carrier business justified a somewhat larger rate of return (8%) than would be reasonable to expect in a more stable industry. Product lines were considered even more hazardous a venture thus warranting a 10% return. [This rate setting reflected] the traditional fair rate on fair value concept enunciated in *Smyth* v. *Ames*. Return is allowed on property after allowing for the effects of replacement cost [e.g., caused by inflation] changes.[1]

FINANCING

Senior Financing

The Prudential Insurance Company of America had agreed to supply the senior funds, provided MAPCO could raise an additional $28.5 million from subordinated securities. Prudential agreed to pay $42 million ($200,000 to go to the banking firms as intermediaries) in return for (1) $42 million in face value of 15-year first mortgage bonds carrying a 6% interest rate, and (2) a $3 million face convertible promissory note bearing a 6% interest rate and due on November 1, 1975. In effect, these issues were to be purchased at the discount price of $93⅓ per $100, to yield about 6.7%.

Most new pipelines were secured by throughput agreements guaranteed by major oil companies. Thus, the credit of the guaranteeing oil company protected the debentures. For MAPCO, a first mortgage was necessary because the letters of intent were not adequate security, although they were pledged to Prudential as a part of the loan agreement.

---

[1] SOURCE: Legal briefs prepared on behalf of MAPCO.

The first mortgage was to be an open-end lien against all of MAPCO's physical property to be constructed at any time during the life of the bonds. The open-end contract allowed MAPCO to increase the first mortgage debt up to $500 million. Any new funds secured, however, would have to be matched with equity funds on the basis of 60% in mortgage funds and 40% in equity funds. MAPCO could look to any source for these funds, and the new supplier of capital would participate in a first lien against *all* the physical assets of the pipeline and be on an equal footing with Prudential.

The proposed mortgage, however, was not to cover the following types of property: (1) working capital, that is, cash, receivables, and inventory (line fill) ; (2) any investments in securities; (3) any natural gas or oil producing properties acquired by the company.

Initial estimates indicated an aggregate of $69 million of mortgageable property. These bonds would be callable at $102 but could not be refunded from the proceeds of a new bond issue. Sinking fund requirements are shown in Exhibit 4. Dividends could be paid, or stock acquired, only to the extent of 80% of accumulated net earnings as yet undistributed. Finally, the loan would become due and payable in the event of a default on any security outstanding.

The convertible promissory note, which matured November 1, 1975, did not carry a sinking fund requirement but could be prepaid in whole or in part, after May 1, 1965, at 200% of the principal amount. Any $1,000 portion of the note could be converted into common shares after May 1, 1961, at the rate of 100 shares per $1,000 of note. This privilege was protected against dilution if shares should be sold at any time at a price less than $10 a share.

These loans were to be taken down over the period of construction in accordance with a specified formula.

The Subordinated Capital

In planning the rest of the capitalization, Mr. Thomas and representatives of the underwriting firms were aware that pipeline companies often had debt-to-capitalization ratios of 90%. However, the absence of throughput agreements made MAPCO a more risky venture initially and would influence the amount of senior securities permissible. Once the venture was successful and shippers were more or less committed by tie-in facilities to use the proposed pipeline, larger sums of debt than those outstanding to Prudential might be considered more reasonable.

These considerations led the underwriters to the concept of a package of subordinated debt and common shares to raise the remaining $28.5 million. During the period of uncertainty existing before the pipeline was fully operating, many equity investors would keep the subordinated debt in their own hands. When the situation stabilized, these securities presumably could be marketed at prices more favorable than those feasible initially.

As the underwriters saw it, the interest rate on the subordinated debt securities had to be set above the 6% rate on the Prudential loans. On the other hand, various additional considerations led the underwriters to want to avoid a rate of 7% or higher. A coupon rate of 6½% was therefore set, although Stone & Webster had used 6% in its tabulations.

For exploratory purposes, the promoters hypothesized a unit of a 6½%, $50-par, 20-year subordinated debenture and 2 shares of common stock. They planned to sell 410,000 units at $73.50 each to raise $30.135 million before underwriting fees and issue costs of about $1.5 million and $250,000, respectively. In Exhibit 5, this is Proposal A.

From June 1, 1970, through June 1, 1975, the required annual sinking fund payment on the debentures would be the least of (1) $500,000 or (2) 40% of net earnings for the preceding calendar year, or (3) 80% of net earnings after January 1, 1961, after deduction of all earnings expended for acquisition of stock or debentures. From 1976 on, the sinking fund payment would be $2.5 million annually. Purchase on the open market was permissible to satisfy sinking fund requirements. The debentures were callable at par value but, except for a refunding, the provisions of the first mortgage bonds prevented all redemptions before 1970 and permitted redemption only in limited amounts thereafter. Initially, the amount of these debentures would be $20.5 million, but the indenture would permit adding $1 million to the outstanding issue.

This package was designed to appeal to the private investor in the high income tax bracket, who would be willing to take somewhat higher risks for substantially higher income if it could be realized on favorable tax terms. For the original buyer, the initial return of 4.4% on the unit before consideration of dividends and capital gains would tend to put a floor under the market price of the securities to somewhat limit downside market risks, but this was regarded as much less material. The shares were expected to carry the bonds until the major uncertainties were clarified.

Since buyers of the type envisioned would be largely depending on the investment banker's recommendation, the reputations of the underwriting firms were deeply involved. The two underwriters would be obliged to rely on a syndicate to market the new issue. Many of the participants would accept the principal underwriters' pricing, but those who might not would be more influential on the terms of the final scheme. These firms could be expected to carefully review available analyses and perhaps initiate further tests before settling on the suggested pricing. Since the most recent pipeline underwriting six months before had sagged below its issue price shortly after issue, analysis of the MAPCO proposal would be scrutinized with particular care.

Some investors would want to sell the subordinated debenture almost immediately. The underwriters considered it probable that certain institutional investors and trusts would be willing to buy such a security at $38. For investors in high tax brackets, the after-tax yield at this price was significantly higher than the yield on prime-grade securities because of the capital gain implicit in the heavy discount.[1] Once projected MAPCO revenues were real-

---

[1] The tax laws have now (1966) been changed. If bonds that were issued after 1954 at a discount are sold before maturity but held for at least six months, a pro rata portion

ized, the subordinated debentures would probably sell at par or slightly better, depending on interest rate conditions.

Once the units were sold, they would begin trading on an as-split basis. Assuming the market was free, the opening prices would determine the tax basis of the securities in calculations of taxable capital gains and losses. Thus, if the subordinated debentures initially sold at $40, the capital gains tax would be measured on the basis of this price as the purchase cost. The purchase cost for the common shares would then be determined by proration. In this example, each of the two shares would have a value of $16.75. The par values of the securities had no significance for tax purposes.

This proposal had been reviewed from many angles. For example, the units were being packaged in a way that seemed most likely to appeal to investors in high income tax brackets. The plan also left the promoters with working control and promised them substantial profits if the venture succeeded.

Two points about the proposal gave the promoters the greatest concern. The underwriters feared that the appreciation potential implicit in the proposal would not afford adequate incentive to the investor, principally because the investor could not see his common stock holdings doubling in value within five years with a fair amount of certainty. It was also important that the price of the unit should rise 5–10% after issue and hold at that level for several months or even longer. The proposed underwriting seemed to be priced too high to achieve these objectives.

At the same time, the group recognized that MAPCO would be assuming obligations of $65.5 million senior to the equity, all with maturities within 20 years. In contrast, the total net cash proceeds to the company would be as follows:

Underwriting firms................................	$ 80,000
KATY Railroad, through affiliate....................	255,000
Prudential loans (net).............................	41,800,000
Equity package (net)...............................	28,385,000
Total.......................................	$70,520,000

Equity was obviously thin, and risks could be too high.

ALTERNATIVES

At the conclusion of these preliminary sessions, the MAPCO management and the underwriters decided to further explore two alternatives. These were: alternative B1—410,000 units, consisting of $3\frac{1}{2}$ shares of common stock and a $6\frac{1}{2}\%$, $50-par subordinated debenture, at a price of $73.50 a unit; alternative B2—3 million shares of common stock at $10 a share.

Mr. Thomas was about to review the implications of these alternatives preparatory to the final series of negotiations with the underwriters. To help with this objective, he had drawn up Exhibit 5, evaluating the alternatives in

---

of the discount is treated as ordinary income. All gain above this proportion is taxed as long-term capital gain. Thus, if a 10-year bond purchased at 90% of par is sold after 2 years at 93, it is taxed as follows: 2 points are regular income; 1 point is capital gain.

terms of net profit, cash flow, and earnings per share for the fifth year at
selected sales volumes. These included one of $18 million, which went beyond
the letters of intent relied on by Stone & Webster but was within the capacity
of the line with capital expenditures not exceeding the annual $5 to $7
million referred to above. Mr. Thomas had also collected certain data,
shown in Exhibit 6, for evaluating the market price behavior of somewhat
comparable companies. Unhappily, all these companies had throughput guarantees and established records, attributes notably missing in MAPCO's case.

Exhibit 1

MID-AMERICA PIPELINE COMPANY
PROPOSED PIPELINE ROUTE AND TERMINAL LOCATIONS

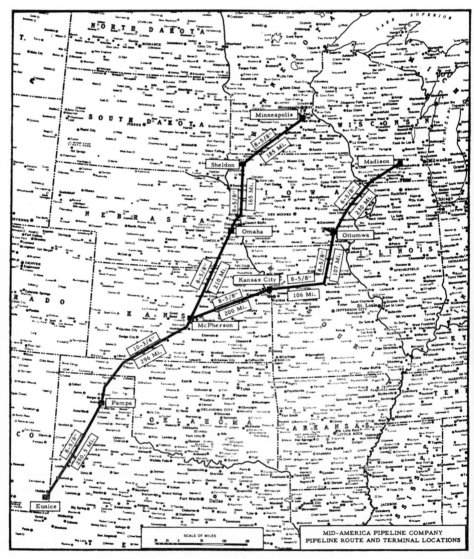

MID-AMERICA PIPELINE COMPANY
PIPELINE ROUTE AND TERMINAL LOCATIONS

Exhibit 2

MID-AMERICA PIPELINE COMPANY

Pro Forma Income and Expense Statement, Based on Operating Estimates by Stone & Webster Service Corporation and on the Original Financing Proposal Made by the Underwriters*

(Dollar Figures in Thousands)

	Construction Period	Year 1	Year 2	Year 3	Year 4	Year 5 No Federal Income Taxes	Year 5 Full Taxes
Operating revenues	…	$ 6,151	$9,279	$11,286	$12,527	$12,909	$12,909
Operating revenue deductions:							
Operation and maintenance							
Payroll	…	$ 1,607	$1,655	$ 1,704	$ 1,756	$ 1,808	$ 1,808
Pumping station power	…	203	306	372	413	426	426
Other	…	601	613	625	637	650	650
Depreciation	…	2,300	2,312	2,312	2,312	2,312	2,312
Taxes:							
General	…	760	775	791	807	823	823
Federal income	…						889
Total Operating Revenue Deductions	…	$ 5,471	$5,661	$ 5,804	$ 5,925	$ 6,019	$ 6,908
Utility operating income	…	$ 680	$3,618	$ 5,482	$ 6,602	$ 6,890	$ 6,001
Interest:							
Bonds	$ 842	$ 2,520	$2,520	$ 2,465	$ 2,329	$ 2,185	$ 2,185
Subordinated debentures	808	1,333	1,333	1,333	1,333	1,333	1,333
Convertible debentures	90	180	180	180	180	180	180
Amortization of debt discount and expense	174	315	315	442	425	410	410
Interest, other	85	…	…	…	…	…	…
Interest, charged to construction (credit)	(1,999)						
Total Income Deductions	…	$ 4,348	$4,348	$ 4,420	$ 4,267	$ 4,108	$ 4,108
Net income (loss)	…	$(3,668)	$ (730)	$ 1,062	$ 2,335	$ 2,782	$ 1,893
Times earned, after federal income tax:							
Interest on bonds	…	0.3	1.4	2.2	2.8	3.2	2.7
Interest on long-term debt	…	0.2	0.9	1.4	1.7	1.9	1.6
Total income deductions	…	0.2	0.8	1.2	1.5	1.7	1.5
Shares of common stock outstanding, end of period	1,215,000	1,215,000	1,215,000	1,215,000	1,215,000	1,215,000	1,215,000
Earned per common share, end of period	…	…	…	$ 0.87	$ 1.92	$ 2.29	$ 1.56

* $42 million 6% first mortgage bonds; $3 million convertible promissory note; $20.5 million 6½% subordinated debentures; 1.215 million common shares, of which 820,000 shares were to be sold to the public in the proposed units.

Exhibit 3

MID-AMERICA PIPELINE COMPANY

SALES OF PROPANE—ANNUAL AVERAGE BARRELS PER DAY

States	1954	1955	1956	1957	1958	1959
Iowa.................	5,600	6,400	6,900	7,000	6,600	8,900
Kansas...............	6,500	7,300	8,400	8,900	8,500	11,200
Minnesota............	6,100	6,600	7,200	7,600	9,300	11,400
Missouri..............	7,000	7,700	9,300	9,800	12,000	14,100
Nebraska.............	4,100	4,400	4,900	5,200	5,000	6,200
North Dakota..........	2,300	2,600	2,800	2,900	1,900	2,700
South Dakota..........	2,900	3,400	3,800	3,700	2,800	3,500
Wisconsin.............	4,900	5,900	6,200	6,300	6,800	9,500
Total...........	39,400	44,300	49,500	51,400	52,900	67,500

Exhibit 4

MID-AMERICA PIPELINE COMPANY

SCHEDULE OF SINKING FUND PAYMENTS ON THE FIRST MORTGAGE
BONDS, 6% SERIES DUE 1975

Year*	Amount (in Thousands)
1963...	$2,213*
1964...	2,347
1965...	2,491
1966...	2,643
1967...	2,803
1968...	2,974
1969...	3,155
1970...	3,347
1971...	3,551
1972...	3,767
1973...	3,997
1974...	4,240
1975, May 1......................................	2,216
November 1, maturity........................	2,256

* In semiannual installments, May 1 and November 1.

Exhibit 5

MID-AMERICA PIPELINE COMPANY

FORECASTS OF CASH FLOW AND NET PROFITS IN FIFTH YEAR FOR SELECTED SALES
VOLUMES, INCLUDING SERVICING OF MORTGAGE BONDS AND NOTE HELD BY
THE PRUDENTIAL INSURANCE COMPANY OF AMERICA
(Dollar Figures in Thousands)

Revenue.....................	$ 7,000	$ 9,000	$11,000	$13,000	$18,000
Deductions:					
Operation and maintenance....	2,440	2,550	2,700	2,875	3,275
Depreciation and amortization.	2,722	2,722	2,722	2,722	2,722
Taxes, general...............	823	823	823	823	823
Interest, Prudential mortgage and note..................	2,365	2,365	2,365	2,365	2,365
Total Deductions.........	$ 8,350	$ 8,460	$ 8,610	$ 8,785	$ 9,185

Exhibit 5—Continued

Operating income (loss) before income taxes and subordinate financing	($1,350)	$ 540	$ 2,390	$ 4,215	$ 8,815

A. The Underwriters' Original Proposal

Sale of 410,000 units, made up of one 6½%, $50 subordinated debenture and 2 common shares. Promoters to hold 395,000 shares. Total shares outstanding: 1,215,000.

Income statement

Interest	$ 1,333	$ 1,333	$ 1,333	$ 1,333	$ 1,333
Net income (loss) before taxes	($2,683)	($ 793)	$ 1,057	$ 2,882	$ 7,482
Federal income tax at 50%	...	...	529	1,441	3,741
Net profit (loss)	($2,683)	($ 793)	$ 528	$ 1,441	$ 3,741

Cash flow

Profit (loss)	($2,683)	($ 793)	$ 528	$ 1,441	$ 3,741
Depreciation and amortization	2,722	2,722	2,722	2,722	2,722
Mortgage payment	(2,491)	(2,491)	(2,491)	(2,491)	(2,491)
Capital expenditures	(200)	(200)	(200)	(200)	(200)
Net cash flow	($2,652)	($ 762)	$ 559	$ 1,472	$ 3,772
Earned per share	($ 2.21)	($ 0.65)	$ 0.43	$ 1.19	$ 3.08
Cash flow per share	($ 2.18)	($ 0.63)	$ 0.46	$ 1.21	$ 3.10

B. Alternative Proposals

1. Sale of 410,000 units, made up of one 6½%, $50 subordinated debenture and 3½ common shares. Total shares outstanding 1,830,000.

Income statement

Interest	$ 1,333	$ 1,333	$ 1,333	$ 1,333	$ 1,333
Net income (loss) before taxes	($2,683)	($ 793)	$ 1,057	$ 2,882	$ 7,482
Federal income tax at 50%	...	...	529	1,441	3,741
Net income (loss)	($2,683)	($ 793)	$ 528	$ 1,441	$ 3,741

Cash flow

Profit (loss)	($2,683)	($ 793)	$ 528	$ 1,441	$ 3,741
Depreciation and amortization	2,722	2,722	2,722	2,722	2,722
Mortgage payment	(2,491)	(2,491)	(2,491)	(2,491)	(2,491)
Capital expenditures	(200)	(200)	(200)	(200)	(200)
Net cash flow	($2,652)	($ 762)	$ 559	$ 1,472	$ 3,772
Earned per share	($ 1.47)	($ 0.43)	$ 0.29	$ 0.79	$ 2.04
Cash flow per share	($ 1.45)	($ 0.42)	$ 0.31	$ 0.80	$ 2.06

2. Sale of 3,000,000 common shares. Total shares outstanding, 3,395,000.

Income statement

Net income (loss) before taxes	($1,350)	$ 540	$ 2,390	$ 4,215	$ 8,815
Federal income tax at 50%	...	270	1,195	2,108	4,408
Net income (loss)	($1,350)	$ 270	$ 1,195	$ 2,107	$ 4,407

Cash flow

Profit (loss)	($1,350)	$ 270	$ 1,195	$ 2,107	$ 4,407
Depreciation and amortization	2,722	2,722	2,722	2,722	2,722
Mortgage payment	($2,491)	($ 2,491)	(2,491)	(2,491)	(2,491)
Capital expenditures	(200)	(200)	(200)	(200)	(200)
Net cash flow	($1,319)	$ 301	$ 1,226	$ 2,138	$ 4,438
Earned per share	($ 0.40)	$ 0.08	$ 0.35	$ 0.62	$ 1.30
Cash flow per share	($ 0.39)	$ 0.09	$ 0.36	$ 0.63	$ 1.31

Exhibit 6

MID-AMERICA PIPELINE COMPANY

COMPARATIVE STATISTICS FOR FIVE PIPELINE COMPANIES, 1956-60

	Sales (Millions)	Working Capital (Millions)	Net Plant (Millions)	Earnings per Share	Dividend per Share	Price/Earnings Ratio	Dividend Yield	Dividend Payout Ratio	Average Market Price	Ratio of Senior Debt to Capitalization	Ratio of All Debt to Capitalization
Buckeye Pipe Line Company											
1956	$21.8	$ 4.5	$ 47.6	$1.13	$0.60	10.8	4.9%	53%	$12.20		
1957	21.8	2.6	49.6	1.01	0.70	12.1	5.7	70	12.20		
1958	21.2	4.8	49.9	1.13	0.70	11.5	5.4	61	12.90		
1959	22.6	0.8	54.2	1.31	0.73	11.9	4.6	56	13.50		
1960	23.1	2.2	64.7	1.33	0.80	12.5	4.8	60	16.60	53%	53%
Interprovincial Pipe Line Company											
1956	$41.8	$15.8	$207.7	$1.92	$1.10	20.7	2.8%	57%	$39.75		
1957	41.1	1.3	222.6	1.89	1.40	26.1	2.8	72	49.50		
1958	49.2	0.3	224.7	2.51	1.80	18.2	3.9	72	45.75		
1959	54.2	8.0	218.7	3.08	2.25	17.3	4.2	73	53.30		
1960	53.4	6.9	215.3	3.05	2.80	18.9	4.9	91	57.75	58%	58%
National Transit Company											
1956	$ 1.9	$ 0.06	$ na	$0.13	$0.10	38.0	2.0%	77%	$ 5.0		
1957	2.1	0.2	na	0.19	0.20	25.2	4.1	105	4.8		
1958	2.0	0.09	na	0.17	0.15	25.3	3.5	90	4.3		
1959	2.1	0.1	$ 1.5	0.20	0.15	20.0	3.8	75	4.0		
1960	2.0	0.1	1.5	0.21	0.15	14.3	5.0	71	3.0	11%	11%
Oklahoma Mississippi River Products Line, Inc.											
1956	$ 4.9	$ na	$ na	$0.42	$0.25	14.7	4.0%	60%	$ 6.2		
1957	6.4	na	na	0.65	0.25	9.5	4.0	38	6.2		
1958	5.0	na	na	0.41	0.25	15.0	4.0	61	6.2		
1959	5.2	8.0	17.9	0.48	0.20	10.4	4.0	42	5.0		
1960	4.9	6.9	17.2	0.48	0.20	9.4	4.5	42	4.5	49%	63%
Trans Mountain Oil Pipe Line Company											
1956	$23.0	$ na	$ na	$0.93	$0.20	18.3	1.1%	21%	$17.0		
1957	27.7	na	na	1.10	0.40	18.2	2.0	36	20.0		
1958	13.0	na	na	(0.02)	...	...	...	...	11.5		
1959	15.5	5.3	118.9	0.22	0.15	58.1	1.1	68	13.0		
1960	17.9	5.6	114.1	0.46	0.40	21.8	4.0	87	10.0	69%	69%

na = not available.

TEXTRON INC.

In May, 1961, the management of Textron Inc. was contemplating which of two financial plans should be recommended to the board of directors as the method for bringing about the merger of Spencer Kellogg & Sons, Inc., into the Textron family.

TEXTRON INC.

Textron, incorporated in Rhode Island in 1928, had long been important in the domestic textile industry. In 1953, the company began diversification into consumer and industrial areas in an attempt to enlarge and stabilize its earnings base. This goal was sought largely through acquisitions of existing businesses. Operations were conducted through divisions and subsidiaries, which operated with a considerable degree of autonomy, subject to centralized administrative supervision.

In 1960, Textron operated 25 divisions in various industries, with product sales as follows: automotive, 17%; consumer, 24%; defense, 22%; industrial, 20%; and textiles, 17%. The company's largest divisions included: Amerotron Company, textiles; Burkart, industrial batting and polyurethane foam; Campbell, Wyant and Cannon Foundry Company, castings; Dalmo Victor Company, airborne radar antennae; Federal Industries, plastic-coated fabrics; Hall-Mack Company, bathroom accessories; Homelite, power chain saws, generators, and marine engines; Shuron Optical Company, eyeglass frames, lenses, and ophthalmic machinery; Nuclear Metals, Inc., research; Townsend Company, fasteners and metal parts; The Waterbury Farrel Foundry & Machine Co., heading machines and presses; Pittsburgh Steel Foundry Corporation, steel castings; Weinbrenner, shoes; and Bell Aerospace Corporation, rocket engines, helicopters, landing gear, and electronics. Subsidiaries included Textron Pharmaceuticals, Inc., ethical drugs; Photek, Inc., photocopy and thermocopy papers and machines; and Textron Electronics, Inc.

Textron had financed its expansion by means of a wide variety of securities, including subordinated debentures, convertible subordinated debentures, a term loan from The Prudential Insurance Company of America, conditional sales contracts, several issues of preferred stock (only one of which was outstanding in 1961), and common stock. The long-term debt and capital stock outstanding as of April, 1961, are listed in Exhibit 1, and the 1957–60 annual price ranges of the three debenture issues and the outstanding pre-

ferred stock are given in Exhibit 2. The three issues of subordinated debentures totaled $45 million. All were rated Ba by Moody's bond service.[1]

From 1957 to 1960, Textron's consolidated sales increased by 50%, and net
income advanced 63%. However, as a result of a growing number of shares
outstanding, per share earnings rose only 28%. (Exhibits 3 and 4 present
selected financial data.) The company was quickly exhausting a tax loss carry-
forward, and management estimated that in 1962 the company would be
paying full taxes. The effective tax rates applicable to Textron's earnings for
the years 1957 through 1960 were as follows:

$$
\begin{array}{ll}
1957 & 0\% \\
1958 & 0 \\
1959 & 4 \\
1960 & 16
\end{array}
$$

Before considering the effects of the Kellogg acquisition, Textron had approximately $8 million in tax carry-forward losses applicable to future years. In
the past, tax losses applicable to any given year had been frequently increased
by the process of acquisition.

Several security analysts had remarked that Textron's capital structure, the
debt–equity ratio, and the two overhanging convertible security issues tended
to keep the price of the company's common stock at relatively low levels.
Management thought that the prospects of increased taxes tended to keep the
price below its true investment value. It regarded the price–earnings ratio of
the shares as unrealistically low in comparison with the ratios of other
industrial companies. In Exhibits 5 and 6, changes in market prices of
Textron stock from 1957 to 1960, its price-earnings ratios, and its dividend
yields are compared with those of Moody's 125 industrial stocks. Actual
market prices are given in Exhibit 7.

Textron had increased the cash dividend on its common stock 25% since
1957. The dividend yield was consistently higher than the average for
Moody's 125 industrial stocks, as is shown in Exhibit 6. Although the debt
issues imposed restrictions on dividend payments, the limitations were not
considered serious. The most restrictive provisions were those attached to the
term loan from Prudential. These provided that the company could not pay
cash dividends or make net purchases of its own common stock in excess of
75% of consolidated income after January 2, 1960, nor let consolidated
working capital drop below $70 million. Net working capital on April 1, 1961,
was $92 million.

In the past, Textron's ability to quickly raise large sums of money and to
offer a wide range of types of securities had been considered important factors
in the company's successful acquisitions program. Experience indicated that

---

[1] Moody's Manuals describe the Ba rating as follows: "Bonds which are rated Ba by
Moody's are judged to have speculative elements; their future cannot be considered as
well assured. Often the protection of interest and principal payments may be very moderate
and thereby not well safeguarded during both good and bad times over the future. Uncertainty of position characterizes bonds in this class."

several small but growing organizations had joined the Textron family partly because the parent company was in a strong financial position and would act as a source of funds for their future expansion.

Textron's long-range plans included further acquisitions to assure its reaching its corporate objective of $600 million sales, $25 million after-tax earnings, and a return on equity of 20%. In order to accomplish these ends, the company needed a large debt capacity. The management was unable to translate future debt needs into numerical terms, however, since there was no way of telling what merger opportunities were likely to arise. Nonetheless, fearing dilution of earnings per share, management had strong doubts about the desirability of using equity financing to acquire and merge companies in the future.

SPENCER KELLOGG & SONS, INC.

Spencer Kellogg & Sons, Inc., founded in 1894, had become a leading producer and refiner of vegetable fats and oils extracted principally from soybeans, cottonseed, linseed, coconuts, and castorbeans. These products, which accounted for the bulk of the company's sales, were purchased by makers of edible or industrial products. The company also manufactured a number of related items, such as cottonseed and linseed meals. In addition, it produced oil-modified synthetic resins used in the composition of special paints and varnishes. Through two important feed divisions, Kellogg marketed a considerable amount of dairy and poultry feeds.

Over the decade 1950–60, the soybean crushing industry had not kept pace with the growth of the American economy. Kellogg's sales in 1960 were 14% below 1957 levels, and net income had fallen over 20% for the same period. Earnings per share in 1960 dropped to 83 cents, just covering the company's traditional 80 cents dividend. Exhibits 5, 6, 7, 8, and 9 present financial data for Kellogg.

Despite the recent declines, the management of Textron felt that the stable nature of Kellogg's business, plus its strong debt-free capitalization, made the company an attractive prospect for merger. In fact, for over five years, on and off, Textron had negotiated with Kellogg over the possibilities of a merger. In January, 1961, it was rumored that Kellogg had received from an unnamed source a cash offer for its assets and business. Shortly after, Textron management renewed talks with Kellogg officers.

It appeared that the Kellogg management was hesitant about selling the entire company for cash, because it strongly believed that it had a responsibility to both stockholders and employees to keep a going concern. Management felt stockholders deserved a better fate than total sale of assets followed by a liquidating dividend, which would force them to reinvest their funds in another business. Nevertheless, continually unprofitable performance of the company's soybean division suggested that withdrawal from this operation would be a strategic move. The Kellogg officers indicated that as an alternative to sale of the entire company they were considering selling only the soybean plants and machinery. Although these assets had a book value in excess of $15 million, it was expected that there would be a loss on the sale. The proceeds from the sale would be used in research and development of new products, and possibly to launch an acquisition program in other industries.

The Textron management pointed out that Kellogg's acquisition program would be aided by a merger with Textron, since Textron had gained professional experience in the area of acquisitions, and possessed the contacts and resources necessary to succeed in the highly competitive search for attractive companies. They also said that a merger with Textron by an exchange of shares, unlike a cash sale, would be tax-free for Kellogg shareholders. In addition, instead of nonincome-producing cash, Kellogg stockholders would then be holding shares in a multiindustry company that offered an unusual opportunity for diversification and a larger dividend yield than Kellogg's, based on a current market prices.

MERGER NEGOTIATIONS

In several subsequent meetings, held in May, 1961, the top managements and boards of directors of both Kellogg and Textron reached agreement on valuation. On May 24, they decided that the assets and business of Kellogg would be transferred to Textron on an exchange of six sevenths (86%) of a share of Textron common stock for each share of Kellogg. Based on the 1.25 million outstanding common shares of Kellogg and outstanding Kellogg options, the transaction would involve 1,081, 560 shares of Textron stock.

On the preceding day, May 23, the price of Textron common on the New York Stock Exchange had fluctuated between $27\frac{1}{8}$ and $26\frac{1}{8}$, and the market price of Kellogg, also listed on that Exchange, had varied between $20\frac{1}{8}$ and $19\frac{3}{4}$. Exhibit 7 presents market prices for the two companies from 1958 to May 23, 1961, and trading volume for the most recent weeks in April and May. Textron management believed that the heavy trading volume and recent strength in the market price of Kellogg securities were directly attributable to rumors of the pending merger. On the basis of the exchange agreement, Textron was giving approximately $22 worth of market value for each Kellogg share. Despite their recent market rise, the Kellogg shares were still selling at a $2 discount from the value of the Textron shares receivable in exchange. In all likelihood, however, this margin would shrink as Wall Street arbitragers began to trade in both securities.

Since 1959, Textron had acquired 337,500 shares of its own stock in the open market at an average cost of $22.75 a share. The Textron management planned to exchange this treasury stock for Kellogg shares. Beyond these, approximately 744,060 additional shares of Textron common stock were needed to complete the merger.

There were several alternatives for raising such a large block of stock. The chosen financial plan, management felt, must coincide with Textron's objectives of making the merger a completely tax-free exchange for Kellogg share-holders, minimizing the earnings dilution of Textron shares, and permitting Textron to remain financially flexible for future acquisitions and mergers. Management also wanted to make Textron common stock a more attractive investment so that the market price of the shares would improve. And last, Textron was interested in formulating a financial plan that the general investment community would sanction as the soundest method of merging Kellogg into Textron.

After approval by Textron's board of directors, the merger plan would require sanction by a majority of Textron's stockholders. The Kellogg share-holders also were required to vote on the merger at a special stockholders' meeting. Management believed that the manner of securing the necessary shares to complete the transaction would affect the attractiveness of the merger. Within this framework of potentially conflicting interests, management outlined two plans of action.

Plan 1

Plan 1 included the use of an invitation to tender.[2] Although the Securities and Exchange Commission generally prohibited companies from purchasing their own shares in the open market for subsequent distribution in mergers or acquisitions, Textron's two-year precedent of buying shares in the open market was sufficient ground for the SEC's approval of a tender offer. Under this plan, Textron would publicly announce that for a limited time it was offering to purchase up to 744,060 shares of its outstanding stock for a specified price, which would probably be set at $28 a share, representing an expenditure of $20,833,680.

Textron had already made arrangements whereby it could borrow up to $22 million to cover all the costs of purchasing the tendered shares and completing the acquisition; and Prudential had agreed to the necessary modifications of the term loan restrictions. The money was committed by a group of New York and Boston banks and would be repayable by Textron over a three-year period: $10 million (45%) during the first year, $7 million (32%) during the second year, and the remainder, $5 million (23%), during the third year. The loan would carry an interest charge of 5%, which was .5% above the prime commercial rate in May, 1961. Thus, interest costs would be approximately $642,000 for the rest of 1961, $600,000 in 1962, and $250,000 in 1963.

A three-year bank loan would impose a heavy cash burden on Textron in the next few years. Payment of current maturities on the long-term debt already outstanding would amount to about $4 million annually for the years 1961–65. Textron planned to dispose of Kellogg's soybean facilities, which had a book value of $15 million. The proceeds from such a sale were

---

[2] An *invitation to tender* is a method of purchasing securities. The prospective buyer announces its intention of making purchases under specified terms, and invites owners to indicate their acceptance, that is, to *tender* their securities.

estimated at $8 million. There would also result a $7 million tax loss to be carried forward against Textron's future earnings. In the first quarter of 1961, Textron's net income was only $275,000, as against $3.361 million reported for the same quarter a year earlier. A general upturn in the economy, however, suggested that Textron's profit performance for the next three quarters would show a marked improvement. A leading investment service estimated that Textron's earnings before interest and taxes for 1961 would be approximately $20 million and that Kellogg would add approximately $2.5 million to pre-tax earnings. Management believed this forecast to be realistic.

In 1962, the company's profits would be aided by elimination of the major plant start-up expenses experienced in 1961 and by anticipated improvement in the general economy. Although it was too early to make projections for 1962, the same advisory service forecast that Textron might earn close to $30 million before interest and taxes.

Management estimated that capital expenditures for 1961 and 1962 would approximate $10 to $11 million each year. Depreciation and other noncash charges for the same period were expected to equal these costs. If necessary, most of the planned capital expenditures could be postponed for several years, since Textron's plants and equipment were in excellent condition. (Exhibit 10 presents a statement of sources and uses of funds.)

In management's opinion, the success of Plan 1 would depend greatly on stockholders' reaction to the merger. In light of the attractive proposed merger with Kellogg, in which Textron's earnings per share were subject to little dilution, Textron management was apprehensive that an insufficient number of stockholders would be willing to sell their shares a few dollars above the current market price.

Plan 2

Under Plan 2, Textron would issue new shares in the amount needed (744,060 shares) to complete the transaction. Although this method of financing permitted greater flexibility and involved fewer risks than Plan 1, the per share earnings of Textron would suffer dilution. Exhibit 11 compares earnings per share and dividends under the two plans. Pro forma balance sheets reflecting the two plans appear as Exhibit 12.

Since Textron had outstanding convertible subordinated debentures and convertible preferred stock, with protection against dilution written into their covenants, approximately 86,000 additional shares would be added to their conversion privileges on acceptance of Plan 2. Thus, these securities, which currently were convertible into approximately 574,000 shares of common stock, would become exchangeable for nearly 660,000 shares of common stock.

As in Plan 1, Textron would dispose of Kellogg's soybean facilities. The proceeds from the sale would be free for any corporate use deemed desirable.

No matter which plan was decided on, in the final analysis the success of the merger was dependent on approval by the stockholders of both Textron and Kellogg. The Textron management believed that speculators and short-term capital gain holders might own as much as a quarter of the Textron common stock outstanding. This group were not considered strong or desirable shareholders.

The Textron management believed that Kellogg shareholders were conservative investors who would be strong holders. It was assumed that the majority of Kellogg shareholders had purchased their stock a good many years earlier at prices well below those of 1961, and had subsequently realized a paper profit. Trading activity in the stock was extremely light—an indication that there was very little in the way of demand or supply for the shares. For example, the number of Kellogg shares traded in 1959 was 250,000, as compared with 3 million for Textron. In 1960, only 130,000 Kellogg shares changed hands, while Textron traded in excess of 1 million shares.

Kellogg had consistently avoided long-term debt, and had paid a dividend on its capital stock every year since incorporation in 1912. In fact, in the past safety of principal and generous dividends had been considered the two guideposts of Kellogg's financial policy.

Exhibit 1

TEXTRON INC.

LONG-TERM DEBT AND CAPITAL STOCK OUTSTANDING, APRIL, 1961

Long-term debt (inclusive of current maturities)
Note payable, The Prudential Insurance Company of America, $5\frac{7}{8}\%$, due serially from
1966 to 1975 . . . . $25,000,000
Unsecured notes, mortgages, and conditional
sales contracts   15,241,678
5% subordinated debentures, due May 1,
1984   30,000,000
15-year, 5% subordinated sinking fund debentures, due February 1, 1970   9,411,750
5% convertible subordinated debentures, due
January 1, 1971. Convertible into common
stock at $31.77 per common share to December 31, 1963 (177,114 shares); $38.58 to December 31, 1967; and $45.39 to December 31,
1970.* Conversion privilege protected
against dilution   5,626,900
$85,280,328

Capital stock
$1.25 cumulative, convertible preferred stock,
no par value (stated value $25). Convertible
into 1.0785 common shares per preferred
share (396,672 common shares).* Conversion
privilege protected against dilution . . . .   367,800 shares
Common stock, 50 cents par value, issued† . . . . . 4,976,530 shares
Less: Common stock in treasury† . . . . 337,500 shares
Common Stock Outstanding . . . .   4,639,030 shares

* See Exhibit 7 for recent market prices of Textron common stock.
† These figures do not include 10,000 shares held in the treasury and restricted for options.

Exhibit 2

TEXTRON INC.

ANNUAL PRICE RANGES OF DEBENTURES AND CONVERTIBLE PREFERRED STOCK
1957–60

Year	Debenture 5's, 1970	Debenture 5's, 1984	Convertible Debenture 5's, 1971	$1.25 Cumulative Convertible Preferred Stock
1957	82–73	. . .	81½–60	21 –15⅛
1958	92–73½	. . .	96½–61½	24 –15⅜
1959	95–90	93–85	116½–87	31⅞–23
1960	96–90	100–85	94 –85	26½–22¾

Exhibit 3

TEXTRON INC.

CONSOLIDATED SALES, INCOME, DIVIDENDS, AND BURDEN

(Dollar Figures in Thousands)

	Year Ended December 31				Quarter Ended	
	1957	1958	1959	1960	April 3, 1960	April 3, 1961
Sales..........	$254,575	$244,227	$308,202	$383,188	$82,513	$90,034
Earnings before interest and taxes..........	13,016	14,746	21,829	21,969	5,525	1,956
Interest expense..........	$ 4,320	$ 3,990	$ 4,531	$ 5,113	$ 1,045	$ 1,529
Preferred dividends, including tax related*..........	826	764	567	549	137	177
Current maturities paid on long-term debt, including tax related*..........	2,283	4,769	4,000	3,210	790	1,020
Total Burden..........	$ 7,429	$ 9,523	$ 9,098	$ 8,872	$ 1,972	$ 2,726
Burden coverage (based on earnings before interest and taxes) exclusive of common stock dividends (times)..........	1.8	1.5	2.4	2.5	2.8	0.7
Federal taxes..........	$		$ 655	$ 2,688	$ 1,119	$ 152
Net income..........	8,696	10,756	16,643	14,168	3,361	275
Cash dividends paid						
Preferred stock..........	826	764	544	461	115	115
Common stock..........	3,501	4,349	5,691	5,922	1,449	1,440
Burden coverage (based on earnings before interest and taxes) inclusive of common stock dividends and their tax related* (times)..........	1.2	1.1	1.5	1.4	1.5	0.4

* Tax related: 1957, 0%; 1958, 0%; 1959, 4%; 1960, 16%; 1961, 35%.

Exhibit 4

TEXTRON INC.

CONSOLIDATED ASSETS, FINANCIAL POSITION, AND PER SHARE PERFORMANCE
(Dollar Figures in Thousands)

Year Ended December 31

	1957	1958	1959	1960
Total assets, less reserves....$	178,282	$ 187,638	$ 218,713	$ 271,829
Capital expenditures........	6,600	4,320	23,210	14,100
Long-term debt, less current maturities..........	56,517	53,763	62,238	83,520
Debt–equity ratio..........	0.7 to 1	0.6 to 1	0.5 to 1	0.7 to 1
Depreciation and other noncash charges..........$	8,457	$ 8,581	$ 9,080	$ 9,691

PER SHARE DATA

	1957	1958	1959	1960
Earnings per common share*..................$	2.25	$ 2.51	$ 3.61	$ 2.89
Dividends per common share..................	1.00	1.00	1.19	1.25
Payout ratio..............	44%	40%	33%	43%
Book value per share*.......$	17.99	$ 18.22	$ 22.49	$ 23.53
Common shares outstanding at end of year........	3,550,593	4,349,366	4,783,009	4,672,429

* Based on average number of shares outstanding during period.

Exhibit 5

TEXTRON INC.

SELECTED COMPARISONS OF TEXTRON, SPENCER KELLOGG, AND
MOODY'S 125 INDUSTRIAL COMMON STOCKS

MARKET PRICES (1957=100)*
(RATIO SCALE)

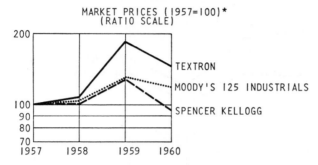

PRICE/EARNINGS RATIOS

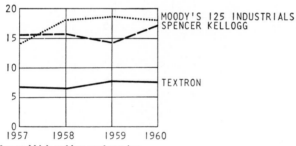

* Average of annual high and low market prices.

Exhibit 6

TEXTRON INC.

COMPARISON OF DIVIDEND YIELDS OF TEXTRON AND SPENCER
KELLOGG WITH MOODY'S 125 INDUSTRIAL STOCKS

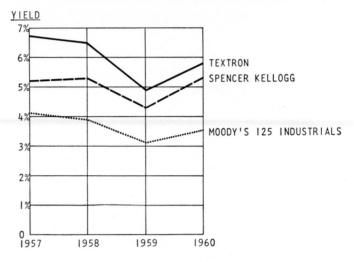

Exhibit 7

TEXTRON INC.

PRICE RANGES OF TEXTRON COMMON STOCK AND KELLOGG CAPITAL STOCK SINCE 1958
(New York Stock Exchange Quotations)

	Textron Common Stock		Kellogg Capital Stock	
	High	Low	High	Low
1958:				
First quarter	$13\frac{1}{4}$	$10\frac{7}{8}$	15	$12\frac{1}{8}$
Second quarter	$12\frac{1}{2}$	$9\frac{7}{8}$	$16\frac{3}{8}$	$12\frac{3}{4}$
Third quarter	$16\frac{1}{2}$	11	$17\frac{1}{2}$	$15\frac{1}{8}$
Fourth quarter	$21\frac{7}{8}$	$15\frac{3}{8}$	$18\frac{5}{8}$	$16\frac{1}{2}$
1959:				
First quarter	$24\frac{7}{8}$	$19\frac{3}{4}$	$21\frac{1}{4}$	$17\frac{7}{8}$
Second quarter	$26\frac{3}{8}$	$21\frac{7}{8}$	$20\frac{7}{8}$	17
Third quarter	$29\frac{5}{8}$	$21\frac{5}{8}$	$18\frac{1}{4}$	$16\frac{1}{8}$
Fourth quarter	$25\frac{7}{8}$	$22\frac{1}{2}$	$17\frac{1}{2}$	16
1960:				
First quarter	$24\frac{3}{4}$	$19\frac{7}{8}$	$16\frac{5}{8}$	$13\frac{3}{4}$
Second quarter	$23\frac{3}{8}$	$19\frac{1}{2}$	$15\frac{1}{4}$	$13\frac{1}{2}$
Third quarter	$21\frac{3}{4}$	$18\frac{3}{4}$	$16\frac{3}{4}$	$13\frac{5}{8}$
Fourth quarter	$22\frac{3}{8}$	19	$15\frac{7}{8}$	$13\frac{5}{8}$
1961:				
First quarter	$29\frac{3}{8}$	$21\frac{5}{8}$	$19\frac{7}{8}$	$14\frac{1}{8}$

	Textron			Kellogg		
Week Ending	High	Low	Trading Volume (in hundreds)	High	Low	Trading Volume (in hundreds)
April 14, 1961	$28\frac{1}{2}$	27	370	$18\frac{1}{2}$	18	66
April 21, 1961	$27\frac{7}{8}$	$26\frac{1}{4}$	310	$21\frac{1}{4}$	$18\frac{1}{4}$	470
April 28, 1961	$27\frac{1}{2}$	$25\frac{5}{8}$	358	20	$18\frac{1}{2}$	88
May 5, 1961	$26\frac{1}{4}$	$24\frac{3}{4}$	711	20	$18\frac{5}{8}$	30
May 12, 1961	$25\frac{7}{8}$	25	315	20	$18\frac{3}{4}$	139
May 19, 1961	$27\frac{3}{8}$	$25\frac{3}{8}$	501	21	$19\frac{3}{8}$	185
Day Ending						
May 22, 1961	$27\frac{1}{4}$	$25\frac{7}{8}$	157	$19\frac{7}{8}$	$19\frac{3}{4}$	6
May 23, 1961	$27\frac{1}{8}$	$26\frac{1}{8}$	56	$20\frac{1}{8}$	$19\frac{3}{4}$	31

Exhibit 8

TEXTRON INC.

CONDENSED BALANCE SHEET OF SPENCER KELLOGG & SONS, INC.,
AND SUBSIDIARY AS OF MARCH 25, 1961 (UNAUDITED)
(Dollar Figures in Thousands)

ASSETS

Current assets:

Cash...	$ 2,976
U.S. government securities at cost.....................	50
Receivables..	12,075
Inventories at lower of cost or market.................	32,729
Prepaid expenses...................................	685
Total Current Assets..........................	$48,515
Property, plant, and equipment, net......................	$23,556
Investments and other assets..........................	4,038
	$76,109

LIABILITIES AND NET WORTH

Current liabilities:

Notes payable.....................................	$24,288
Accounts payable and accrued expenses................	2,486
State, local, and other taxes.........................	541
Federal taxes, estimated.............................	646
Total Current Liabilities......................	$27,961
Reserve for self-insurance.............................	$ 1,000

Net worth:

Capital stock, par value $1, 1,250,000 shares outstanding, at stated value...............................	$18,586
Retained earnings...................................	28,562
	$76,109

Exhibit 9

TEXTRON INC.

CONSOLIDATED SALES, INCOME, DIVIDENDS, FINANCIAL POSITION, AND NUMBER OF COMMON SHARES OF SPENCER KELLOGG & SONS, INC.

(Dollar Figures in Thousands)

	Fiscal Years Ended August 31				Seven-Month Periods Ended	
	1957	1958	1959	1960	3/26/60	3/25/61
Sales	$ 134,778	$ 128,370	$ 130,517	$ 115,995	$ 64,522	$ 69,597
Other income	469	482	655	669	587	441
Total income	$ 135,247	$ 128,852	$ 131,172	$ 116,664	$ 65,109	$ 70,038
Earnings before taxes	$ 2,762	$ 2,687	$ 3,432	$ 2,069	$ 1,105	$ 1,333
Federal taxes	1,453	1,437	1,802	1,036	585	738
Net income	$ 1,309	$ 1,250	$ 1,630	$ 1,033	$ 520	$ 595
Number of shares outstanding, end of year	1,312,095	1,251,700	1,251,700	1,250,000	1,251,700	1,250,000
Earnings per share*	$ 1.00	$ 1.00	$ 1.30	$ 0.83	$ 0.42	$ 0.48
Dividends per share	0.80	0.80	0.80	0.80	0.40	0.40
Total assets, less reserves	54,244	52,347	55,467	52,459	na	na
Provision for depreciation	1,892	1,801	2,022	2,105	1,216	1,252
Book value per share*	36.57	37.39	37.90	37.64	na	na

* Based on number of shares at end of year.

na = not available

Exhibit 10

TEXTRON INC.

STATEMENT OF SOURCES AND USES OF FUNDS, 1957–60, AND ESTIMATES FOR 1961 AND 1962 UNDER MERGER PLANS 1 AND 2

(Dollar Figures in Thousands)

	Year Ended December 31				1961		1962	
	1957	1958	1959	1960	Plan 1 Treasury Shares and Tender	Plan 2 Treasury Shares and New Stock	Plan 1 Treasury Shares and Tender	Plan 2 Treasury Shares and New Stock
Sources:								
Net income after taxes and interest	$ 8,696	$10,756	$16,643	$14,168	$12,500	$12,800	$15,700	$16,000
Depreciation and other noncash charges	8,457	8,581	9,080	9,691	10,800	10,800	11,000	11,000
Increases in long-term debt	…	…	8,475	21,282	22,000	…	…	…
Sale of Kellogg soybean facilities	…	…	…	…	8,000	8,000	…	…
Other sources	192	…	5,408	…	…	…	…	…
Total	$17,345	$19,337	$39,606	$45,141	$53,300	$31,600	$26,700	$27,000
Uses:								
Current maturities paid on long-term debt	$ 2,283	$ 4,769	$ 3,840	$ 2,696	$13,934	$ 3,934	$11,039	$ 4,039
Capital expenditures	6,600	4,320	23,210	14,100	10,000	10,000	10,000	10,000
Retirement of preferred stock	1,774	2,056	6,321	…	…	…	…	…
Reductions in long-term debt	2,361	2,754	544	461	440	440	440	440
Preferred dividends	826	764	…	…	…	…	…	…
Common dividends	3,501	4,349	5,691	5,922	6,221	7,151	6,221	7,151
Tender of 744,060 shares	…	…	…	…	20,834	…	…	…
Expenses related to merger	…	…	…	…	1,166	1,166	…	…
Other uses	…	325	…	21,962	…	…	…	…
Total	$17,345	$19,337	$39,606	$45,141	$52,595	$22,691	$27,700	$21,630
Surplus or (deficit)					$ 705	$ 8,909	$(1,000)	$ 5,370

Exhibit 11

TEXTRON INC.

COMPARISON OF HISTORICAL AND PRO FORMA DIVIDENDS AND EARNINGS PER SHARE,
FOR TEXTRON AND KELLOGG, 1957–60

The following tabulations of earnings per share for the years 1957 through 1960 present historical and pro forma figures for Textron and Kellogg based on alternative assumptions as to the source of shares of Textron common stock to be used to consummate the acquisition of Kellogg.

	Textron		Kellogg	
	Historical*	Pro Forma†	Historical‡	Pro Forma
EARNINGS PER SHARE				
a) Assuming issuance of treasury shares and use of an invitation to tender:				(6/7 Textron Share)
1957	$2.25	$2.27	$1.00	$1.95
1958	2.51	2.50	1.00	2.14
1959	3.61	3.61	1.30	3.09
1960	2.89	2.82	0.83	2.42
b) Assuming issuance of treasury shares and authorized but unissued stock:				(6/7 Textron Share)
1957	$2.25	$2.00	$1.00	$1.71
1958	2.51	2.22	1.00	1.90
1959	3.61	3.20	1.30	2.74
1960	2.89	2.53	0.83	2.17
CASH DIVIDENDS PER SHARE				
				(6/7 Textron Share)
1957	$1.00	...	$0.80	$0.86
1958	1.00	...	0.80	0.86
1959	1.19	...	0.80	1.02
1960	1.25	...	0.80	1.07

* From Exhibit 4.

† Pro forma earnings per share for alternative (a) were calculated as follows: Income figures were based on the arithmetical combination of the consolidated net incomes of the two companies for their respective fiscal years, after reflecting for Textron a charge for interest (net of federal income taxes) applicable to funds to be provided for the invitation of tenders through bank loans. Numbers of shares were the average numbers outstanding each year plus the treasury shares as of December 31, 1960 (313,200 shares).

Pro forma earnings for alternative (b) were based on the combination of the two companies' consolidated net incomes and on the average numbers of shares outstanding plus 1,081,560 shares.

‡ From Exhibit 9.

Exhibit 12

TEXTRON INC.

PRO FORMA CONDENSED BALANCE SHEETS REFLECTING THE ACQUISITION OF KELLOGG
UNDER TWO ALTERNATIVES*
(Dollar Figures in Thousands)

	Plan 1 *Assuming Issuance of 337,500 Treasury Shares and a Success- ful Tender of 744,060 Shares*	Plan 2 *Assuming Issuance of 337,500 Treasury Shares and 744,060 Shares of Authorized but Unissued Stock*
ASSETS		
Cash and U.S. government securities	$ 15,865	$ 15,865
Accounts receivable, net	61,206	61,206
Inventories	120,425	120,425
Other current assets	5,575	5,575
Total Current Assets	$203,071	$203,071
Total fixed and other assets	138,556	138,556
Total Assets	$341,627	$341,627
LIABILITIES AND CAPITAL		
Notes payable	$ 40,636	$ 40,636
Accounts payable and accruals	42,790	42,790
Federal income taxes	3,880	3,880
Current maturities of long-term debt	13,934	3,934
Total Current Liabilities	$101,240	$ 91,240
Long-term debt	$ 93,430	$ 81,430
Other liabilities	4,426	4,426
Excess of book value over purchase price of net assets of Kellogg	18,641	18,641
CAPITAL STOCK AND SURPLUS		
$1.25 convertible preferred stock (367,800 shares)	$ 9,195	$ 9,195
Common stock, 50 cents par value 4,976,530 outstanding†	2,489	. . .
5,720,590 outstanding†	. . .	2,876
Capital surplus	72,324	93,937
Earned surplus	39,882	39,882
Total Capital Stock and Surplus	$123,890	$145,890
Total Liabilities and Capital	$341,627	$341,627
Book value per share	$ 26.79	$ 27.15

* Figures based on unaudited balance sheets: Textron, April 1, 1961; Kellogg, March 25, 1961.
† These figures do not include 10,000 shares held in the treasury and restricted for options.

AMERICAN MACHINE & FOUNDRY COMPANY

In December, 1958, David S. Meiklejohn, vice president and treasurer of American Machine & Foundry Company (AMF), was reviewing the company's financial condition and its cash and earnings forecasts for the year 1959. He was preparing a recommendation, to be submitted at the AMF board of directors meeting, January 6, 1959, regarding the company's two convertible debenture issues—one in the amount of $4.388 million outstanding at 4¼%, the other in the amount of $12.286 million outstanding at 5%. The question to come before the board was whether the company should plan to force conversion of the debentures in early 1959 by calling either or both of them for redemption. As of December, 1958, conversion of the 4¼'s outstanding would result in 140,400 additional common shares, and conversion of the 5's would add 321,200 shares. Approximately 3.347 million common shares were already outstanding.

COMPANY BACKGROUND

AMF was a large, diversified company engaged in manufacturing, selling, and leasing special automatic and semiautomatic machinery and equipment. It was composed of over 20 wholly owned domestic and international subsidiaries, with manufacturing plants and sales offices located throughout the United States and in many foreign countries. Its varied products included: cigarette making and packing machines for the tobacco industry; stitching machines for the apparel and shoe industries; ovens, wrapping machines, and slicing machines for the baking industry; pinspotters, alleys, and pins for the bowling industry; bicycles and power shop equipment for the consumer; reactors, control systems, and remote handling equipment for the atomic energy field; radar, electronic, and missile control equipment for the defense industry; motors, engines, and special equipment for general industries. Consolidated gross sales and rentals of the company and its subsidiaries had grown from $27.517 million in 1950 to a high of $261.754 million in 1957. Management expected 1958 gross sales and rentals to total approximately $230 million.

A growing recreation field in recent years had enabled AMF to take good advantage of its bowling line, particularly the automatic pinspotter. Although the 1958 recession had decreased the company's overall earnings and profits, leases of bowling equipment were running nearly two thirds greater in 1958 than in 1957. As AMF had continued to improve its position of leadership in this field, the need for funds to finance investment in leased bowling equipment had been a problem of increasing proportions. In fact, investment in bowling machines and equipment leased to customers had grown from $1,424,476 in 1950 to approximately $112 million in 1958; the 1958 figure was an increase over 1957 of $21 million. In an effort to free cash to help support the tremendous growth in sales and in investment in bowling equipment leased to customers, the company for several years had followed the practice of leasing rather than buying most of its own manufacturing plants.

Exhibits 1–4 present selected data on AMF's financial condition and operations.

CONVERTIBLE DEBENTURES ISSUED, 1956

In December, 1955, Mr. Meiklejohn received from the accounting department a cash forecast for 1956, showing that the company would need at least $10 million by year-end to meet the cash requirements for the year's operations. This amount was over and above funds that would be provided by borrowing[1] against new investment in bowling equipment to be leased to customers. The possibility of raising $10 million through short-term borrowing was not considered as an alternative because the funds would be needed on a long-term basis. The company followed a policy of using short-term borrowing capacity only for seasonal requirements and bridging financing, and therefore tried to be out of debt on a short-term basis at the end of each year.

In the spring of 1956, Mr. Meiklejohn consulted with an investment banking firm for recommendations on the matter. After discussions with several institutional lenders and others, the investment banking firm came to the conclusion that AMF could not raise $10 million through a straight debt issue on satisfactory terms. AMF's relatively disappointing earnings during 1955 and its debt position were given as the primary reasons for this conclusion. AMF was also advised that a common stock issue to raise the funds would be inadvisable at that time, because a common stock offering had been made in 1955 and another issue coming so soon thereafter would probably have a depressing effect on market price.

It was recommended that AMF raise the funds through an issue of subordinated convertible debentures. Mr. Meiklejohn favored this method for several reasons: (1) it presented an opportunity to raise funds through a device that substantially amounted to selling common stock at a premium above market price; (2) AMF's long-term debt holders would view such an issue as equivalent to equity; (3) if AMF's sales and rentals should take an unexpected slump, the debentures could still be sold by the company on a bond-yield basis; (4) if the unexpected slump should happen to continue, AMF would be in a position to retire the debentures with cash released by resulting decreases in receivables, inventories, and investment in leased equipment.

---

[1] See pages 506 and 507 for description of borrowing method.

Therefore, convertible debentures seemed to provide AMF with the greatest flexibility in light of the company's circumstances.

At a special stockholders' meeting on June 26, 1956, the stockholders authorized the issuance of subordinated convertible debentures by an affirmative vote of 85%. The following day, June 27, a $10.897 million offering of 25-year debentures was made to stockholders, with subscription rights expiring on July 11. The interest rate was set at $4\frac{1}{4}\%$, and the conversion price, protected against future dilution, was set at $32.50 for 10 years, based on a closing price of 30 for AMF common on that day. (In December, 1958, the adjusted conversion price on this issue was $31.25.) Of the total offering, 95.67% was subscribed by exercise of warrants, and a tabulation of market prices during the period showed little effect on the price of AMF common stock.

Soon after the sale of the $4\frac{1}{4}\%$ convertible debentures, it became obvious to Mr. Meiklejohn that AMF's cash needs would exceed forecasts. Revised forecasts for the remainder of 1956 and for the year 1957 indicated a need of at least $10 million additional long-term money by December 31, 1957. This sum was in addition to another $20 million, which Mr. Meiklejohn thought could be raised during the period by borrowing against expected new investment in leased equipment.

Again the investment banking firm was consulted for recommendations. A straight debt issue was ruled out on substantially the same grounds as before. Since AMF was planning to issue common stock in 1957 for the purpose of acquiring two companies, it was thought that the sale of an additional block of stock at this time might have a depressing effect on the market price.

After discussing the problem with the investment bankers, Mr. Meiklejohn decided that AMF should sell another issue of subordinated convertible debentures. The investment banking firm at first recommended that the $4\frac{1}{4}\%$ outstanding debentures, which were then selling at $125–29, should be called and conversion forced prior to sale of the new issue. However, in November, 1956, shortly after this recommendation, it became evident that a tremendous amount of new money would be raised by U.S. corporations in early 1957 to finance general business expansion. The investment banking firm became concerned about the delay involved in first calling the outstanding issue to force conversion and then making an offer to stockholders of a second debenture issue. In view of this, Mr. Meiklejohn decided that it would be best to sell the new issue without calling the first.

On January 24, 1957, without the earlier conducted formality of a special stockholders' meeting, a $12,725,800 offering of 20-year subordinated convertible debentures was made to AMF stockholders, with subscription rights expiring on February 7. The interest rate was set at 5%, and the conversion price, protected against future dilution, was set at $38.25 for 20 years (based on a January 22 closing market price of $35.50 for AMF common).[2] Of the

---

[2] Excerpts from the conversion provisions of this issue as contained in the indenture, which were almost identical with those of the $4\frac{1}{4}\%$ issue, are given in Appendix A.

total offering, 96.3% was subscribed by exercise of warrants. The closing market prices of AMF common during the period from announcement date (December 21, 1956) to expiration date (February 7, 1957) fell from $37.25 to $33.50.

CALL DEBENTURES AND FORCE CONVERSION IN 1959— FACTORS CONSIDERED

Management of AMF was confidently expecting that 1959 would be a record year in terms of sales, rentals, and profits. However, several members of management believed the company's rental business had reached a point where, instead of creating a demand for cash, it would provide a positive cash flow for expansion of the company's other business and for debt reduction. Partly in this light, the directors had recently voted to increase quarterly cash dividends on AMF common stock from 40 to 50 cents a share. Exhibit 5 presents the company's forecast of cash requirements and sources for the year 1959. Sales and rentals for 1959 were estimated at $275 million, and earnings before interest, lease obligations, and taxes were estimated at $40 million.

As Mr. Meiklejohn reviewed the forecasts, however, he recalled that in recent years investment in leased bowling equipment had continually exceeded management's expectations. In late 1957, for example, it had been forecast that 7,000 new automatic pinspotters would be leased during 1958. It was now apparent that new pinspotters leased in 1958 would total at least 10,000. While the cash reduction as now forecast would not particularly strain AMF's cash position, he thought that it would be undesirable to risk reducing it any further. In this light, Mr. Meiklejohn was somewhat reluctant to place a high degree of confidence in the 1959 forecast of investment in pinspotters included in the forecast of companywide cash requirements and sources (Exhibit 5).

Mr. Meiklejohn also recalled that in late 1956 the company had obtained an increase in its line of credit for financing pinspotter leases, but only after overcoming a very noticeable reluctance on the part of some of the financing institutions. As of December 31, 1957, the full line of credit (a 15-year loan of $60 million) had been taken down by the company except for an unused $6 million special cushion, which had been provided for in the agreement to finance unanticipated pinspotter leases at 100% of equipment cost. Of the loan, $20 million had been placed with a group of banks and included maturities for the first 5 years, payable at the rate of $5 million a year for 4 years beginning in 1959; $40 million had been placed with 2 insurance companies and included maturities for the remaining 10 years of the 15-year period. The $60 million loan was based principally on the credit of AMF Pinspotters, Inc., a wholly owned subsidiary which had practically no other liabilities; however, it was guaranteed by AMF, the parent company. The principal basis for credit to the subsidiary was the minimum rental of $800 a year guaranteed in the pinspotter leases (10-year), which involved an AMF investment of approximately $2,000 for each pinspotter covered. The loan agreement required that the minimum rental ($800) times the unexpired terms of all pinspotters on lease must not be less than at least three times the outstanding amount of the loan. This requirement was covered by a significant margin of safety, but Mr. Meiklejohn questioned whether the banks and insurance companies would yet be willing to consider another increase in AMF's line of credit.

It seemed to Mr. Meiklejohn that if past experience of underestimating the next year's sales and investments in leased equipment should repeat itself, then some external financing late in 1959 would be difficult to avoid. In December, 1958, the market price of AMF common stock was at a level that would almost assure 100% conversion of both debenture issues if called for redemption. Mr. Meiklejohn knew that forcing conversion would greatly increase the company's financing flexibility. He knew that a delay in such action was always subject to the risk of the market. If general business or political conditions that depressed the market were to develop, the opportunity for forcing conversion might be lost for some time. On the other hand, AMF common stock would have to fall substantially from its price level to prevent forcing conversion of the debentures, probably over 21% for the convertible 5's and 35% for the convertible 4¼'s. Exhibit 6 presents recent market performance of AMF common stock and convertible debentures. Exhibit 7 presents a comparison of AMF common stock with Moody's 125 Industrial Stocks.

A provision in the company's agreement with certain long-term lenders required that an underwriting be secured for call of convertible debentures unless market price of AMF common stock on the call date was at least 150% of the conversion price. This was to protect the asset security position of debt holders in the company by providing assurance that AMF would not be required to pay out cash for redemption of any debentures not converted by the holders. An underwritten call arrangement would involve an agreement with an investment banking firm wherein debentures turned back for cash redemption would be taken up by the underwriter, converted to common stock, and held for investment or for sale to the public. In any event, those holders redeeming for cash instead of converting would create no cash drain on the company if the call was underwritten. As long as the market price of AMF common stock remained above 46⅞, the necessity and expense of an underwritten call on the 4¼% debentures could be avoided. A price of 57⅜ or above was necessary, however, to avoid an underwriting of the 5% debentures. Mr. Meiklejohn had obtained an estimate of $100,000 as the underwriting fee on the call of the 5's at this time. This expense probably could have been avoided in very recent weeks when the common reached its all-time high of 59¾.

Mr. Meiklejohn thought that a gradual voluntary conversion of the 4¼% debentures would continue, owing to the cash dividend yield on the common stock. Holders of these debentures were in a position to receive a 6.4% yield on their investment by converting, as compared with 4.25% if they did not convert. He also thought that voluntary conversion of the 5% debentures would not be significant until the common dividend was again increased. Cash dividend yield on investment after conversion of a 5% debenture would be only 5.23%.

Exhibit 1

AMERICAN MACHINE & FOUNDRY COMPANY

PRELIMINARY CONSOLIDATED STATEMENT OF FINANCIAL CONDITION FOR
COMPANY AND SUBSIDIARIES, AS OF DECEMBER 31, 1958
(Dollar Figures in Thousands)

ASSETS

Current assets:		
Cash...		$ 21,000
Receivables......................................		56,000
Inventories (at cost or market, whichever is lower)....		41,000
Other..		2,500
Total Current Assets.........................		$120,500
Property, plant, and equipment, net (at cost)*.........		23,000
Bowling machines and equipment leased to customers...	$112,000	
Less: Reserve for depreciation.....................	30,700	
		81,300
Patents, licenses, developments, investments, and other		
(net)..		6,700
		$231,500

LIABILITIES, CAPITAL STOCK, AND SURPLUS

Current liabilities:		
Current maturities on long-term debt..............		$ 6,900
Accounts payable and accrued liabilities............		20,300
Federal, state, and other taxes (after deducting U.S.		
government securities, at cost, $4,000)............		7,800
Total Current Liabilities.....................		$ 35,000
Long-term debt, less maturities included in current		
liabilities......................................		93,600
Deferred federal income taxes......................		6,850
Minority interest in subsidiary.....................		150
Preferred stock..................................	$ 8,150	
Common stock and surplus (issued and outstanding,		
3,347,000 shares, $7 par)........................	88,250	
	$ 96,400	
Less: treasury stock, preferred and common (at cost)..	500	95,900
		$231,500

* Aggregate annual rental payments for property, plant, and facilities on long-term leases at December 31, 1958, including rentals on properties sold and leased back, approximated $1.985 million.

Exhibit 2

AMERICAN MACHINE & FOUNDRY COMPANY

Selected Data on Consolidated Sales, Income, Dividends, Financial Position, Burden Coverage, and Common Stock for Company and Subsidiaries
(Dollar Figures in Thousands)

			Year		(Preliminary)
	1954	1955	1956	1957	1958
Sales	$ 117,143	$ 130,936	$ 175,225	$ 227,504	$ 184,140
Rental income from leased equipment	9,364	14,065	22,833	34,250	46,735
Total sales and rentals	$ 126,507	$ 145,001	$ 198,058	$ 261,754	$ 230,875
Earnings before interest, lease obligations, and taxes	$ 9,215	$ 11,516	$ 21,646	$ 28,775	$ 28,300
Interest expense	$ 1,347	$ 1,727	$ 2,670	$ 4,639	$ 5,298
Annual rental payments for property and facilities under long-term lease	na	na	1,266	1,968	1,985
Preferred dividends*	757	763	741	721	682
Retirement of preferred stock*	479	340	557	482	750
Current maturities paid on long-term debt*	4,130	7,810	10,300	16,800	3,660
Total burden	$ 6,713	$ 10,640	$ 15,534	$ 24,610	$ 12,375
Burden coverage, exclusive of common dividends (times)	1.4	1.1	1.4	1.2	2.3
Net income	$ 4,023	$ 4,774	$ 8,976	$ 11,782	$ 11,000
Cash dividends paid:					
Preferred stock	$ 363	$ 366	$ 355	$ 346	$ 327
Common stock	2,149	2,479	2,863	4,192	5,600
Shares of common stock outstanding at December 31†	2,238,372	2,660,204	2,847,923	3,258,739	3,347,000
Earnings per share at December 31 (after preferred dividend)	$ 1.64	$ 1.66	$ 3.03	$ 3.51	$ 3.19
Total assets, less reserves	105,662	132,625	182,385	225,619	231,500
Long-term debt, less current maturities	30,150	38,467	67,480	102,868	93,600

* Including tax related (52%).
† Listed on the New York Stock Exchange.
na = not available.

Exhibit 3

AMERICAN MACHINE & FOUNDRY COMPANY

CONSOLIDATED STATEMENTS OF SOURCE AND DISPOSITION OF FUNDS FOR
COMPANY AND SUBSIDIARIES
(Dollar Figures in Thousands)

					Year
	1954	*1955*	*1956*	*1957*	*(Preliminary)* *1958*
Source of Funds:					
Net earnings..............	$ 4,023	$ 4,774	$ 8,976	$ 11,782	$11,000
Depreciation and other noncash charges..........	4,611	6,080	8,351	11,857	15,700
Federal income taxes deferred................	...	...	555	3,408	1,850
Sale of 5% cumulative preferred stock...........	556	...	...	...	...
Sale of common stock.......	104	6,322	172	91	540
Long-term borrowing.......	21,415	8,318	38,242	92,926	...
Decrease in working capital other than cash.........	...	...	...	...	7,270
Held by subsidiaries when acquired................	522	245	320	595	...
Total...............	$31,231	$25,739	$56,616	$120,659	$36,360
Disposition of Funds:					
Investment in leased machines...............	$10,584	$10,869	$22,669	$ 25,260	$21,700
Property, plant, and equipment..............	3,437	3,988	5,820	4,808	2,600
Retirement of preferred stock...................	230	163	267	231	360
Long-term debt paid or transferred to current liabilities...............	*	*	8,783	54,544	6,900
Dividends paid............	2,512	2,845	3,218	4,538	5,930
Increase in working capital other than cash..........	12,020	6,778	6,276	22,358	...
Other items, net...........	498	1,088	2,266	3,930	870
Total...............	$29,281	$25,731	$49,299	$115,669	$38,360
Increase (decrease) in cash..	$ 1,950	$ 8	$ 7,317	$ 4,990	$(2,000)

* Netted against long-term borrowing in years 1954 and 1955.

Exhibit 4

AMERICAN MACHINE & FOUNDRY COMPANY

CONSOLIDATED SCHEDULE OF LONG-TERM DEBT, INTEREST RATES, AND FUTURE MATURITIES
FOR COMPANY AND SUBSIDIARIES
(Dollar Figures in Thousands)

	Total 12/31/58 (Preliminary)	Interest Rate	Maturities in year indicated				
			1959	1960	1961	1962	1963
Notes payable to insurance companies	$ 1,050	3¾%	$ 150	$ 150	$ 150	$ 150	$ 150
	1,000	4¾	100	100	100	100	100
	5,000	4¾	...	425	425	425	425
	40,000*	5¾	...	...	...	...	2,000
Note payable to banks	20,000*	5	5,000	5,000	5,000	5,000	...
Sinking fund debentures	14,000	4	500	500	1,500	1,500	1,500
First mortgage note	1,750	3	1,000	750	...	...	...
Convertible subordinated debentures	1,040	4¾	105	105	105	105	105
	12,236†	5	...	...	...	...	...
	4,388‡	4¼	...	...	...	...	...
Totals	$100,514		$6,855	$7,030	$7,280	$7,280	$4,280
Estimated annual rental payments for property and facilities under long-term lease			$2,200	$2,400	$2,500	$2,700	$3,000

* Loaned against bowling equipment as described on pages 506 and 507.
† Call prices started at 105, and beginning January 31, 1961, declined to par at maturity.
‡ Call prices started at 104¼, and beginning June 30, 1963, declined to par at maturity.

Exhibit 5

AMERICAN MACHINE & FOUNDRY COMPANY

FORECAST OF CONSOLIDATED CASH REQUIREMENTS AND SOURCES FOR
COMPANY AND SUBSIDIARIES, YEAR 1959
(Dollar Figures in Millions)

Requirements:

Investment in leased machines	$22.0
Additions to property, plant, and equipment	4.5
Other investments	3.0
Redemption of preferred stock	0.3
Cash dividends on preferred stock	0.3
Cash dividends on common stock	6.8
Increase in receivables and inventories	3.0
Current maturities on long-term debt	6.9
	$46.8

Sources:

Net earnings*	$16.0
Depreciation and other noncash charges	16.0
Increase in tax liabilities (including increase in deferred federal income taxes, $1.8)	7.5
U.S. government securities (offset against tax liabilities on 1958 balance sheet)	4.0
	$43.5
Decrease in cash	$ 3.3

* Deductions included for annual rental payments on property and facilities under long-term lease were $2.2 million.

Exhibit 6

AMERICAN MACHINE & FOUNDRY COMPANY

RECENT MARKET PERFORMANCE OF AMF COMMON STOCK AND CONVERTIBLE DEBENTURES

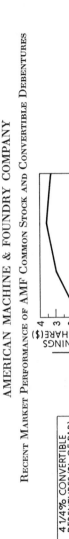

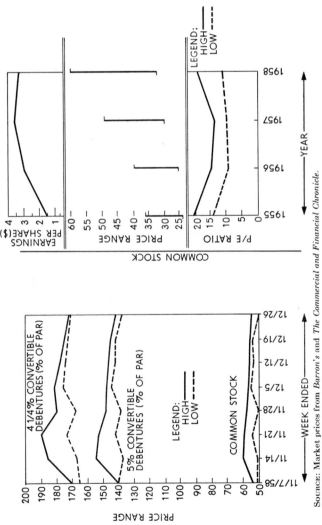

SOURCE: Market prices from *Barron's* and *The Commercial and Financial Chronicle*.

Exhibit 7

AMERICAN MACHINE & FOUNDRY COMPANY

SELECTED COMPARISONS OF AMF COMMON STOCK DATA WITH
MOODY'S 125 INDUSTRIAL STOCKS

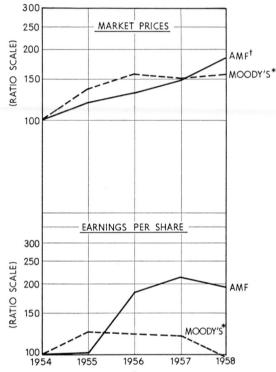

* Averages from Moody's 125 industrial stocks.
† Average of annual high and low market prices.

Appendix A

General Provisions for Conversion of the 5% Debenture Issue, Taken from the Indenture

. . . .

ARTICLE FOUR
Conversion of Debentures

Section 4.01. *Conversion Privilege.* Subject to and upon compliance with the provisions of this Article Four, at the option of the holder, any Debenture, or any portion of the principal amount thereof which is $100 or a multiple thereof, may, at any time on or before February 1, 1977, or in case such Debenture or some portion thereof shall be called for redemption prior to such date, then with respect to such portion thereof as is so called, until and including, but (if no default is made in making due provision for the payment of the redemption price) not after, the date fixed for such redemption, be converted at 100% of so much of the principal amount of such Debenture as is so converted, into Common stock at the conversion price in effect at the date of conversion.

Section 4.02. *Manner of Exercise of Conversion Privilege.* In order to exercise the conversion privilege, the holder of any Debenture or Debentures to be converted shall surrender such Debenture or Debentures, together with all unmatured coupons thereto appertaining, if any, to the company at any time during usual business hours at its office or agency in the Borough of Manhattan, City and State of New York, and shall give written notice to the company at such office or agency that the holder elects to convert such Debenture or Debentures, or a specified portion thereof. Such notice shall also state the name or names (with address) in which the certificate or certificates for shares of Common Stock which shall be issuable on such conversion shall be issued. . . . Such conversion shall be deemed to have been effected immediately prior to the close of business on the date (hereinafter called the date of conversion) on which such notice shall have been received by the company and such Debenture or Debentures shall have been surrendered as aforesaid, . . . but such conversion shall be at the conversion price in effect at the close of business on the date of such surrender. No adjustment shall be made for interest accrued on any Debenture that shall be converted or for dividends on any Common Stock that shall be issued upon the conversion of such Debenture as provided in this Article Four.

. . . .

Section 4.03. *Fractions of Shares.* The company shall not be required to issue fractions of shares of Common Stock upon conversions of Debentures. If more than one Debenture shall be surrendered for conversion at one time by the same holder, the number of full shares which shall be issuable upon conversion thereof shall be computed on the basis of the aggregate principal amount of the Debentures (or specified portions thereof) so surrendered. If any fraction of a share of Common Stock would, except for the provisions of this Section 4.03, be issuable on the conversion of any Debenture or Debentures (or specified portions thereof), the company shall, at its option, either (a) purchase such fraction for an amount in cash equal to the current value of such fraction (i) computed, if the Common Stock shall be listed or admitted to unlisted trading privileges on the New York Stock Exchange, on the basis of the last reported sale price of the Common Stock on such Exchange on the last business day prior to the date of conversion upon which such a sale shall have been effected, or (ii) computed, if the Common Stock shall not be so listed or admitted to unlisted trading privileges, on the basis of the average mean of the bid and asked prices for the Common Stock in the over-the-counter market in New York, New York, on the last business day prior to the date of conversion as reported by the National Quotation Bureau, Inc., or (b) issue scrip of the company in lieu thereof. . . .

Section 4.04. *Conversion Price.* The basic conversion prices at which Common Stock shall be issuable upon conversion of Debentures shall be the following principal amounts of Debentures for each share of Common Stock: $38.25 if converted on or before February 1, 1967, and $43.25 if converted thereafter and on or before February 1, 1977.

The conversion price shall be the applicable basic conversion price or, after adjustment as provided in this Article Four, the conversion price as so adjusted.

Section 4.05. *Adjustment of Conversion Price.* The conversion price shall be subject to adjustment from time to time as follows:

(a) Except as hereinafter provided, in case the company shall at any time after the date of this Indenture issue or sell any shares of Common Stock (including shares held in the company's treasury) for a consideration per share less than the conversion price in effect immediately prior to the issuance or sale of such shares, or without consideration, then, and thereafter successively upon each such issuance or sale, the conversion price in effect immediately prior to each such issuance or sale shall forthwith be reduced to a price determined by dividing

(i) an amount equal to (A) the total number of shares of Common Stock outstanding immediately prior to such issuance or sale multiplied by the conversion price in effect immediately prior to such issuance or sale, plus (B) the consideration, if any, received by the company upon such issuance or sale, by

      (ii) the total number of shares of Common Stock outstanding immediately after such issuance or sale.

. . . .

(b) In case the company shall at any time after the date of this Indenture, issue options or rights to subscribe for shares of Common Stock (including shares held in the company's treasury), or issue any securities (other than the Debentures, and scrip certificates issued pursuant to Section 4.03) convertible into or exchangeable for shares of Common Stock, for a consideration per share less than the conversion price in effect immediately prior to the issuance of such options or rights or convertible or exchangeable securities, or without consideration, the conversion price in effect immediately prior to the issuance of such options or rights or securities shall be reduced to a price determined by making a computation in accordance with the provisions of subsection (a) of this Section 4.05, . . .

(c) In case the company shall at any time subdivide or combine the outstanding shares of Common Stock, the conversion price shall forthwith be proportionately decreased in the case of subdivision or increased in the case of combination.

(d) On the date when the new basic conversion price becomes effective (as provided in Section 4.04), the conversion price shall be the last preceding conversion price increased to an amount which shall bear the same proportion to such new basic conversion price as the last preceding conversion price bore to the preceding basic conversion price.

. . . .

HERCULES MACHINE TOOL COMPANY, INC.

In July, 1957, Timothy O'Brien, treasurer of Hercules Machine Tool Company, Inc., received a letter from the executive vice president of Universal Life Insurance Company, discussing the Hercules company's recent request for an increase of $1.02 million in its outstanding term loan. The vice president, Harry Nielson, noted in the letter that the finance committee had tentatively approved the increase, which would raise the term loan to a total of $4.380 million at $5\frac{1}{2}\%$, payable over $14\frac{1}{2}$ years. The offer depended, however, on the Hercules company's acceptance of certain conditions proposed by the finance committee. A copy of the suggested loan agreement was enclosed in the letter. Mr. O'Brien immediately began a study of the proposed loan restrictions in an effort to estimate their acceptability from his company's point of view.

Hercules Machine Tool Company, Inc., with headquarters in Springfield, Massachusetts, produced a variety of specialized machine tools primarily for use in the manufacture of furniture. The line included such items as planers, glue jointers, automatic lathes, saws, sanders, and drill presses.

The firm had been founded in 1919 by Horace Stockton. He managed the company until his retirement in 1954, when Horace Stockton, Jr., became president. The Stockton family owned approximately 25% of the outstanding common stock. The family had always maintained effective working control, however, because the remaining shares were widely distributed. The company's stock was traded in the over-the-counter market. (See Exhibit 1 for details on the common stock.)

As the result of an $8.2 million research and development program, which had been under way since World War II, the Hercules company had steadily expanded its product line. Although most of the new machine tools were designed primarily for use by furniture manufacturers, the company was also trying to diversify into other types of products in order to offset the somewhat cyclical nature of the furniture industry. For example, it had developed new wire-winding equipment, which had extensive applications in the steel industry. In addition, the research organization was engaged in a variety of special projects for United States government agencies. In the fiscal year ended June 30, 1956, these activities had accounted for 4.7% of sales.

Most of the company's products were sold by its own sales force operating from regional offices in principal cities of the New England, midwestern, and southern states, as well as in Ottawa, London, and Paris. The company sold a large quantity of its equipment to foreign industry. Export sales usually accounted for approximately 20% of annual volume; Canada, Great Britain, and continental Europe provided the largest foreign markets.

In addition to sales of new machine tools, the Hercules company also sold replacement parts for its equipment. In recent years, these sales had ranged from 5 to 10% of total annual volume. The company also leased some of its equipment to a growing number of customers who preferred this arrangement to outright purchase. In 1957, approximately 10% of the company's annual net profit resulted from leasing.

Immediately after World War II, the company's sales had expanded suddenly as furniture manufacturers throughout the country placed large orders for new production equipment of virtually every type. The management expected at that time to maintain a substantially higher sales volume for some years because of the expanded level of postwar industrial and consumer demand. To help finance this growth, in March, 1947, the company sold to the public $1.95 million of 5.50 cumulative convertible preferred stock. In 1947, the treasurer, Mr. O'Brien, also negotiated a $2.4 million, $14\frac{1}{2}$-year, $3\frac{1}{2}$% direct placement loan with Universal Life Insurance Company. Previously, the company had financed its operations primarily through retained earnings. It had never used any medium- or long-term debt.

The proceeds of the loan were used to finance higher production and sales and necessary additions to fixed assets. The very profitable results of the immediate postwar years permitted Mr. O'Brien, in the summer of 1950, to prepay the remaining portion of this term loan, together with the required premium of $1\frac{3}{8}$%.

In May, 1952, the company again negotiated a direct placement loan—$3.6 million, 15-year, $4\frac{1}{4}$%—with Universal Life. The company used $1.2 million of the proceeds to pay expenses incurred for new tooling and $2.4 million to increase working capital and to acquire certain new capital assets. The terms and conditions of this loan agreement are shown in Exhibit 2.

In the following years, the company encountered increasingly severe competition and sharply fluctuating industrial demand for machine tools. Although sales increased moderately in 1954 and 1955, and gave evidence of increasing further in 1956, the company's profitability remained substantially below the levels of previous years, primarily because of much keener price competition throughout the machine tool industry. In order to strengthen the company's competitive position, the management decided in 1956 to undertake a factory modernization program designed to lower manufacturing costs.

To finance this activity, Mr. O'Brien renegotiated with Universal Life the 1952 loan, which had been reduced to $2.88 million by February, 1956. Universal Life agreed to the request that the loan be increased to the original $3.6 million, thus providing the Hercules company with an additional $720,000 for factory modernization. The revised loan agreement, covering $3.6 million of $4\frac{1}{2}$% notes payable over 15 years, was signed in March, 1956. Exhibit 2 shows certain provisions required by the finance committee of Universal Life in connection with the new loan.

On completion of the agreement, the company proceeded with its modernization program. Mr. O'Brien estimated that the company would realize annual pre-tax savings of approximately $240,000 because of the new production arrangements. These estimates subsequently proved correct. The new manufacturing economies and generally improved business conditions in the furniture industry resulted in a considerable improvement in the company's operations during 1956 and 1957. Exhibit 3 includes summary financial data from 1947 to 1957. Exhibits 4 and 5 show balance sheets and statements of income for the years ended June 30, 1954–57.

Early in 1957, two major developments occurred that promised to improve the company's prospects for higher sales and earnings. The first was the research department's successful completion of a lengthy series of tests that it had been conducting with several new multipurpose power attachments for furniture-making machinery of standard design. The tests had proved highly satisfactory, and trial users of the equipment were enthusiastic. These power attachments permitted substantial increases in the flexibility and productivity of regular production machinery, either by increasing the output of a general-purpose machine, such as a standard drill press, or by extending the operations and applications of more specialized furniture-making equipment, such as sanders and glue jointers. The new attachments, patented and named the Multi-Flex line, included such items as a drill press adapter, which allowed multiple drillings, and a new lathe attachment, which permitted automatic duplication of certain standard parts. There were 6 new multipurpose machine tool attachments in the line, ranging in price from $300 to $1,200 a unit, and the director of research and development expected at least 4 more attachments to enter production within the next 2 years.

One particularly favorable aspect of the Multi-Flex attachments was the broader diversification that the company could achieve through the sale of these products to other light manufacturing industries, in addition to the furniture industry. Since the potential applications for this equipment extended beyond the rather cyclical furniture industry, the management believed that the Multi-Flex line would lend greater stability to future sales and earnings. Judging by enthusiastic consumer reaction during the two-year test period, the director of marketing believed the line could easily raise the company's sales annually by an average of about 15% (see Exhibit 6).

The director of marketing had supervised an extensive market research program during 1956 to learn more about the potential applications for Multi-Flex attachments. His estimates showed that there were approximately 600,000 standard machine tools in American industry capable of using the new line. The director believed that Multi-Flex tools could be sold effectively with the existing sales force. He realized that the company would have to hire new salesmen to provide broad geographical sales coverage. Nevertheless, he did not foresee greatly increased marketing expenses in connection with the new products.

Company officers hoped to begin manufacturing Multi-Flex attachments by

November, 1957. Production of the new line would require some relocation and additions to the existing plant and equipment. The production manager estimated that expenditures for new machines and tooling for Multi-Flex manufacture would total about $600,000 (see Exhibit 7).

The second major development in 1957 was the award, after lengthy negotiations, of a large subcontract to the Hercules company by Imperial Electric Company, an important national manufacturer of electrical equipment. The subcontract called for specialized, high-precision machining on parts of a new antiaircraft weapon recently developed by the U.S Navy. The Hercules management forecast that the subcontract would result in additional sales of $2 million annually, with an average gross margin of 20% over an expected 5-year period.

In order to meet the requirements under the subcontract, the production manager estimated that new equipment would be required totaling $390,000, in addition to expenses of $60,000 for relocation and rearrangement of certain plant facilities (see Exhibit 7). Approximately half of this machinery later would be converted to the manufacture of other products if the company did not receive any additional defense business. During the subcontract negotiations, the Imperial Electric management had indicated that if the Hercules company's work proved satisfactory, additional contracts could be expected in the future for the same or similar work.

The treasurer, Mr. O'Brien, realized that although these new developments promised higher levels of future sales and earnings, the company would require some assistance in financing the new Multi-Flex tooling and the machine tools for the defense subcontract. Low rates of profit in recent years had reduced working capital to such an extent that expansion could not be financed entirely from internal sources.

In order to anticipate the probable financing requirements, a member of Mr. O'Brien's staff prepared a five-year financial forecast of the balance sheets and income statements, taking into consideration the anticipated effects of the Multi-Flex line and the defense subcontract. The purpose of this preliminary forecast, which made no provision for any additional outside financing, was to permit Mr. O'Brien to decide when the company should seek financial assistance and what amounts might be required. After analyzing the forecast and discussing the future outlook with the president and the sales and production managers, Mr. O'Brien decided to request an immediate increase of about $1 million in the term loan with Universal Life. In May, 1957, the Hercules company owed Universal Life $3.36 million at $4\frac{1}{2}\%$, under the loan originally established in 1952 at $3.6 million and renegotiated in 1956 on a 15-year basis.

After completing his study of fund requirements, Mr. O'Brien called on Harry Nielson, executive vice president of Universal Life, to discuss the recent new developments and to explain the proposal to increase the term loan. Mr. Nielson's participation in negotiations on the previous loans had made him familiar with the company's products and its financial history. In addition, before this first meeting, late in May, Mr. O'Brien sent copies of his financial forecasts to Mr. Nielson as a basis for preliminary discussion.

Early in June, Mr. O'Brien supplied a new set of forecasts, given in Exhibits 6–9, to include both the proposed financing and a schedule of repayments suggested by Mr. Nielson. During the month Mr. Nielson also visited the company's plant in Springfield, Massachusetts, in order to see production models of the Multi-Flex line and to talk with the management about the company's future prospects.

After a final meeting in New York late in June, Mr. Nielson promised to submit the Hercules company's loan request to the finance committee of Universal Life for preliminary consideration. Mr. Nielson pointed out, however, that because of the Hercules company's disappointing profits in recent years and its relatively high debt burden the finance committee would probably insist on stringent protective provisions in the event an increase in the loan was granted. Mr. Nielson particularly stressed the desirability of an increase in equity investment as a means of financing the expansion.

Although Mr. O'Brien agreed that the company's present financial condition indicated a need for more equity capital, he said that he was reluctant to recommend the sale of more common stock at a time when earnings were depressed. He pointed out that because of the Multi-Flex line and the Imperial Electric subcontract, earnings would improve substantially in the near future. He also emphasized that the Stockton family preferred to avoid issuing a large block of common stock at this time. The family believed that a sale of stock as a means of raising long-term funds would be too expensive, particularly in view of expected levels of sales and profits in the years ahead.

Since the Stockton family wanted to maintain effective working control of the company, it would be necessary for them to purchase their pro rata share in a new issue. Mr. O'Brien said that a large sale of common stock at this time might cause difficulties for certain members of the family. However, he told Mr. Nielson that a common stock offering two or three years hence would probably prove more satisfactory to the company and to the Stockton family.

Several days after their third meeting, Mr. O'Brien received the following letter from Mr. Nielson.

UNIVERSAL LIFE INSURANCE COMPANY

NEW YORK CITY, N.Y.

July 8, 1957

Mr. Timothy O'Brien, Treasurer
Hercules Machine Tool Company, Inc.
Springfield, Massachusetts

DEAR MR. O'BRIEN:

Our Finance Committee has approved in principle the $1,020,000 increase in your term loan, which would bring the amount outstanding to $4,380,000 on terms of 5½% interest under 14½-year notes. I am attaching to this letter a detailed copy of the proposed loan provisions suggested by the committee. [See proposed provisions in Exhibit 2.]

As I indicated to you during our preliminary discussions, we are asking for more extensive restrictive provisions in connection with this loan agreement. In particular, the committee has requested that your firm issue 12,000 common stock warrants providing us with an option to buy your stock at 20. Although we do not normally ask for options of this kind, we feel the extra degree of risk in this case justifies our request. The highly cyclical problems faced by your industry during the past few years, combined with your greatly reduced profitability during this time, increase the risk materially from our point of view.

I should also emphasize that the Finance Committee agrees with me about the desirability of raising some additional outside capital—preferably equity or debt subordinated to our loan agreement. Specifically, we propose that you arrange for the prior or concurrent sale of at least $360,000, and preferably $600,000, of subordinated notes. We should also prefer that these notes be convertible into common stock in order to provide for the future reduction of your debt burden. We feel that this supplementary financing would be an essential condition to any increase in our term loan.

This loan proposal is subject to acceptance within two weeks, upon receipt of which we will request the firm of Cheatham and Hyde of New York to act as our special counsel for the preparation of the required loan documents and opinions. As is customary in transactions of this nature, legal fees and expense will be paid by the borrower.

In the event you have any questions about this loan proposal, or if you would like to raise any questions about the common stock warrants or other restrictive provisions we have proposed, please contact me at once and I shall be glad to discuss these matters with you.

> Very sincerely,
> (*signed*) HARRY NIELSON
> *Harry Nielson*

Exhibit 1

HERCULES MACHINE TOOL COMPANY, INC.

COMMON STOCK DATA FOR YEARS ENDED JUNE 30, 1947–57

Number of shareholders, June 30, 1957:
  Preferred, 385
  Common, 660
Where traded:
  Preferred, over the counter
  Common, over the counter
Dividends: No common dividends paid since 1952; preferred dividends paid regularly.

Year Ended June 30	Net Profit (Thousands)	Common Shares (Thousands)	Earnings per Share*	Range of Bid Prices†	Price–Earnings Ratios
1947	$ 890	346	$ 2.48	$13¼–8½	5.3–3.4
1948	1,456	346	3.90	12½–9½	3.2–2.4
1949	2,191	347	6.05	11–7	1.8–1.2
1950	872	347	2.31	13¼–8¼	5.7–3.6
1951	554	347	1.41	13⅛–8¼	9.3–5.9
1952	53	347	(0.02)ᵈ	9⅛–6	. . .
1953	(1,030)ᵈ	347	(3.13)ᵈ	6¼–4¼	. . .
1954	152	347	0.28	10–4¾	35.7–17.0
1955	(236)ᵈ	362	(0.80)ᵈ	26¾–11½	. . .
1956	785	367	2.02	24½–13½	12.1–6.7
1957	557	371	1.40	19–13	13.6–9.3

* After preferred dividends.
† May 27, 1957, market price: bid, 18; ask, 19.
ᵈ Deficit.

Exhibit 2

HERCULES MACHINE TOOL COMPANY, INC.

RESTRICTIVE PROVISIONS OF TERM LOANS

	Term Loan of May 1952	Term Loan of March 1956	Provisions Proposed on July 8, 1957 for New Term Loan
1. Amount, Term, and Rate:	$3,600,000, 15-year, 4¼% notes.	$3,600,000, 15-year, 4½% notes due 1971.	$4,330,000, 14½-year, 5½% notes. A $1,020,000 increase in the currently outstanding balance.
2. Warrants:	None.	None.	Detachable warrants to purchase 12,000 shares of common stock at 20 for ten years will be attached to the notes.
3. Date of Issue:	May, 1952	March, 1956	The notes will be dated as of the date of the closing, which shall be on October 15, 1957, or such other date as shall be agreed upon.
4. Interest:	Payable quarterly.	Payable quarterly.	Payable quarterly on the outstanding balance on February 1, May 1, August 1, and November 1 of each year, beginning November 1, 1957.
5. Fixed Sinking Fund:	$240,000 per annum.	$240,000 per annum.	$300,000 annually, beginning one year from the loan agreement.
6. Contingent Sinking Fund:	Commencing June 30, 1953, 20% of net income in excess of $350,000, such payments not to exceed $250,000 in any one year.	Commencing June 30, 1957, 20% of net income in excess of $350,000, such payments not to exceed $250,000 in any given year.	Beginning with the fiscal year ended June 30, 1958, the company will make an annual additional payment of principal equal to 20% of net income earned in excess of $350,000, with the contingent payment in any one year not to exceed $350,000.
7. Optional Prepayments:	Company may pay without premium up to the maximum of $250,000 per annum (not cumulative) whether or not required by contingent provision. Company may pay in full or multiples of $75,000 on any	Company shall have the noncumulative option to prepay up to $250,000 a year at par. All other optional prepayments shall be subject to a premium of 4½% the first year and reducing to par the last year. Con-	a) Noncallable for a refunding at a lower rate of interest prior to November 1, 1967. b) The proceeds of the exercise of the warrants may be used to prepay the notes at par.

	c) interest date by giving 30 days' prior written notice with premium of 104 the first year and reducing ¼ of 1% each year thereafter with the last two years at par. Contingent and optional prepayments will be applied to notes with the latest maturity.	c) Otherwise permitted upon the payment of a premium of 5½% the first year ending June 30, 1958, reducing 0.43% each year thereafter. Contingent and optional prepayments will be applied to the notes with the latest maturity.
8. *Indebtedness:*	No additional funded debt permitted except purchase-money mortgages up to 60% of cost or fair value of after acquired property and shall not exceed $250,000 in the aggregate.	None except purchase-money mortgages not to exceed 60% of the cost or fair value of after acquired real property, and not to exceed $250,000 in the aggregate.
		None permitted except: a) The notes as indicated above. b) Subordinated debt (as defined below). c) Purchase-money mortgages not to exceed 60% of the cost or fair value of after acquired real property with a maximum of $250,000 in the aggregate at any time outstanding. d) Unsecured current borrowings. e) Indebtedness incurred for financing customers' obligations under conditional sales contracts and leases of machinery.
9. *Working Capital:*	Cash and receivables plus 60% of inventory must at all times equal the total of total current liabilities plus funded debt.	Cash and receivables plus 60% of inventories must equal the total of current liabilities and funded debt.
		Cash and receivables plus 60% of inventories must always be at least equal the total of current liabilities and unsubordinated funded debt.
10. *Dividends:*	Payable only out of earnings subsequent to 6/30/51.	Dividends (other than stock dividends), stock retirements, and purchases of all classes of stock other than the outstanding $5.50 convertible preferred stock shall not exceed net income earned subsequent to December 31, 1955, after deducting all payments made on the notes.
		Dividends (other than stock dividends and dividends paid on the presently outstanding $5.50 convertible preferred stock), stock purchases and retirements, and subordinated debt purchases and retirements shall not exceed net income earned subsequent to June 30, 1957, after deducting all payments on the above notes. Dividends on the presently outstanding

Exhibit 2—Continued

	Term Loan of May 1952	Term Loan of March 1956	Provisions Proposed on July 8, 1957 for New Term Loan
		Dividends and sinking-fund requirements at the present rates on the presently outstanding $5.50 convertible preferred stock are excepted from this provision.	$5.50 convertible preferred stock shall not be paid if such dividends would cause the sum of dividends (other than stock dividends) on all classes of stock, stock purchases and retirements, and subordinated debt purchases and retirements to exceed $180,000 plus net income earned subsequent to June 30, 1957, after deducting all payments made on the notes.
11. *Leases:*	Not mentioned.	Sale and leaseback only with consent.	Leases with an unexpired term of more than three years shall not exceed an amount to be agreed upon.
12. *Subordinated Debt (Definition):*	Not mentioned.	Not mentioned.	(Minimum, $360,000.) Subordinated debt shall be funded debt (*a*) which is only repayable as to principal from monies available under Paragraph 10, and (*b*) as to which payments of interest and principal are prohibited in the event of insolvency or an event of default under the Note Agreement. This subordinated debt should be convertible into common stock.
13. *Other Provisions:*	Bonus payments to officers and key personnel shall not exceed the scale paid for the fiscal year ending 6/30/51.	Investments, loans, and advances limited to investments in direct obligations of the U.S. government and up to $250,000 in wholly owned subsidiaries. Merger and consolidation only with consent. Other provisions as in the presently outstanding loan agreement.	To be substantially similar to those in the presently outstanding loan agreement.

Exhibit 3

HERCULES MACHINE TOOL COMPANY, INC.

SUMMARY FINANCIAL DATA FOR YEARS ENDED JUNE 30, 1947–57

(Dollar Figures in Thousands)

Year, June 30	Working Capital	Net Worth	Net Sales	Depre- ciation	Pre-tax Income	Net Income	Preferred Dividends Paid
1947.....	$6,215	$6,894	$11,836	$216	$1,596	$ 890	$ 23
1948.....	6,545	7,939	18,937	242	2,232	1,456	107
1949.....	7,253	9,106	25,260	276	3,709	2,191	94
1950.....	6,076	9,326	16,135	264	1,680	872	72
1951.....	5,867	9,794	15,468	281	997	554	65
1952.....	8,627	9,534	18,185	323	152	53	60
1953.....	7,740	8,645	13,060	362	(1,014)[d]	(1,030)[d]	56
1954.....	7,518	8,742	14,316	371	164	152	56
1955.....	7,037	8,452	16,088	436	(234)[d]	(236)[d]	53
1956.....	7,254	9,217	20,785	510	796	785	41
1957.....	7,765	9,301	18,054	648	732	557	39

Year, June 30	Debt Requirements* Times Earned		% Earned on Sales (before Tax)	% Earned on Invested Capital (before Interest and Tax)
	Interest Only	Interest, Sinking Fund, Tax Related		
1947.............	6.6	1.8	13.5%	17.0%
1948.............	9.3	2.6	11.8	20.6
1949.............	15.4	4.3	14.7	34.8
1950.............	7.0	1.9	10.4	18.2
1951.............	4.1	1.2	6.4	10.5
1952.............	0.6	0.2	0.8	2.0
1953.............	. . .	. . .	. . .	. . .
1954.............	0.7	0.2	1.1	2.6
1955.............	. . .	. . .	. . .	. . .
1956.............	3.3	0.9	3.8	7.9
1957.............	3.0	0.8	4.1	7.5

* Maximum debt requirement:

Interest on $4,380,000 at 5½%	=	$240,900
Sinking fund, annual requirement	=	300,000
Tax related to the sinking fund	=	325,000
		$865,900

[d] Deficit.

HERCULES MACHINE TOOL COMPANY, INC.

BALANCE SHEETS AS OF JUNE 30, 1954–57

(In Thousands)

ASSETS	1954		1955		1956		1957	
Current assets:								
Cash	$ 1,054		$ 821		$ 910		$ 788	
U.S. Treasury obligations	1,207						. . . . .	
Accounts and notes receivable, net	1,504		3,146		3,359		2,984	
Inventories	5,339		6,530		7,277		8,066	
Prepaid expenses	128		349		132		116	
Total Current Assets	$ 9,232		$10,846		$11,678		$11,954	
Other assets	128		374		1,216		788	
Land, building, machinery, equipment	$7,716		$8,070		$9,251		$9,254	
Less: Reserve for depreciation	3,595		4,028		4,396		4,704	
Land, etc., net	4,121		4,042		4,855		4,550	
Patents	1		1		1		1	
Total Assets	$13,482		$15,263		$17,750		$17,293	

LIABILITIES AND CAPITAL

	1954		1955		1956		1957	
Current liabilities:								
Accounts payable	$ 470		$ 1,003		$ 1,421		$ 1,367	
Notes payable, banks*	. . . .		1,200		360		263	
Customer advances on contracts	28		166		868		686	
Accruals	739		902		1,237		1,079	
Debt installment, current maturity	240		240		240		280	
Local, state, miscellaneous taxes	197		258		276		317	
Federal and foreign income taxes	40		40		22		197	
Total Current Liabilities	$ 1,714		$ 3,809		$ 4,424		$ 4,189	
Deferred income	146		362		749		723	
Long-term debt	2,880		2,640		3,360		3,080	
$5.50 preferred stock†	1,014		778		751		718	
Common stock	2,256		2,491		2,539‡		2,575‡	
Earned surplus	5,472		5,183		5,927		6,008§	
Total Liabilities and Capital	$13,482		$15,263		$17,750		$17,293	

* Bank loans in 1956 and 1957 represented borrowing on 90-day renewable notes.
† Decrease in preferred stock account between 1954 and 1955 resulted primarily from conversion into common stock; decreases in other years reflect the operation of a small sinking fund.
‡ Changes in the outstanding common shares in 1956 and 1957 resulted from exercise of stock options by officers. As of June 30, 1957, options at prices ranging from $7.25 to $9.60 a share were outstanding on a total of 15,000 shares.
§ There was a special charge against earned surplus in 1957.

Exhibit 5

HERCULES MACHINE TOOL COMPANY, INC.

STATEMENT OF INCOME, YEARS ENDED JUNE 30, 1954–57
(In Thousands)

	1954	1955	1956	1957
Net sales and other operating revenues	$14,316	$16,088	$20,785	$18,054
Other income	71	56	152	127
	$14,387	$16,144	$20,937	$18,181
Costs and expenses:				
Cost of goods sold	$ 9,459	$11,437	$14,345	$11,261
Selling and administrative expense	4,176	4,283	4,948	5,221
Depreciation	371	436	510	648
Interest expense	138	143	222	221
Other	79	79	116	98
Total Costs and Expenses	$14,223	$16,378	$20,141	$17,449
Income (loss) before taxes	$ 164	$ (234)	$ 796	$ 732
U.S. and foreign taxes (estimate)	12	2	11	175
Net Income (Loss)	$ 152	$ (236)	$ 785	$ 557
Preferred dividends	$ 56	$ 53	$ 41	$ 39

Exhibit 6

HERCULES MACHINE TOOL COMPANY, INC.

FORECAST OF NET INCOME AFTER PROPOSED EXPENDITURES AND FINANCING,
JULY 1, 1957, THROUGH JUNE 30, 1962
(In Thousands)

	1958	1959	1960	1961	1962
Net sales	$20,316	$26,136	$30,348	$34,128	$38,406
Cost of sales, standard	12,078	15,204	17,526	19,746	22,454
Gross margin, standard	$ 8,238	$10,932	$12,822	$14,382	$15,952
Manufacturing variances	$ 1,380	$ 1,920	$ 2,396	$ 2,610	$ 2,940
Selling expense*	2,760	2,880	3,070	3,324	3,480
Administrative expense*	1,560	1,662	1,800	2,040	2,280
Development expense	516	750	900	1,020	1,020
Depreciation	720	738	756	780	804
	$ 6,936	$ 7,950	$ 8,922	$ 9,774	$10,524
Net income from operations	$ 1,302	$ 2,982	$ 3,900	$ 4,608	$ 5,428
Royalties received	235	144	144	144	144
Net income before taxes	$ 1,537	$ 3,126	$ 4,044	$ 4,752	$ 5,572
Provision for taxes	804	1,620	2,052	2,460	2,880
Net Income after Taxes	$ 733	$ 1,506	$ 1,992	$ 2,292	$ 2,692
Earnings per common share	$ 1.88	$ 3.96	$ 5.27	$ 6.08	$ 7.16

(Based on the 371,000 shares outstanding June 30, 1957; after preferred dividends, making no allowance for the small annual preferred sinking fund; and assuming no further conversion of preferred shares.)
   * Including prorated interest expense.

Exhibit 7

HERCULES MACHINE TOOL COMPANY, INC.

FORECAST OF FIXED ASSETS AS OF JUNE 30, 1958–62,
INCLUDING PROPOSED EXPENDITURES

	1958	1959	1960	1961	1962
Land, building, machinery, equipment (gross), beginning of year	$ 9,098	$10,508	$11,108	$11,588	$12,188
Additions*	1,410	600	480	600	600
Total	$10,508	$11,108	$11,588	$12,188	$12,788
Allowance for depreciation	5,310	5,892	6,504	7,140	7,812
Net, End of Year	$ 5,198	$ 5,216	$ 5,084	$ 5,048	$ 4,976

Special additions to property, 1958:

Machine tools, regular production	$ 360
Machine tools, Imperial Electric	210
Tooling, Imperial Electric	180
Plant rearrangement	60
Tooling, Multi-Flex line	600
	$ 1,410

* The year 1958 includes additions required for the Multi-Flex line and the Imperial Electric subcontract. The years 1959–62 include normal additions only.

Exhibit 8

HERCULES MACHINE TOOL COMPANY, INC.

FORECAST OF BALANCE SHEET AS OF JUNE 30, 1958–62,
AFTER PROPOSED EXPENDITURES AND FINANCING
(In Thousands)

	1958	1959	1960	1961	1962
ASSETS					
Current assets:					
Cash......................	$ 811	$ 805	$ 682	$ 1,074	$ 1,483
Accounts and notes receivable, net...........	3,029	3,640	4,020	4,200	4,740
Inventories................	8,197	9,600	11,280	12,960	14,640
Prepaid expenses..........	449	240	240	240	240
Total Current Assets...	$12,486	$14,285	$16,222	$18,474	$21,103
Other assets, including lease machine inventory.........	1,274	1,266	1,264	1,422	1,455
Land, building, machinery, equipment, net.............	5,198	5,216	5,084	5,048	4,976
Total Assets..........	$18,958	$20,767	$22,570	$24,944	$27,534
LIABILITIES AND CAPITAL					
Current liabilities:					
Accounts payable..........	$ 970	$ 1,032	$ 1,080	$ 1,175	$ 1,238
Notes payable, banks.......	394	430	490	562	610
Customer advances on contracts................	180	180	180	180	180
Reserve for income taxes....	804	1,620	2,052	2,460	2,880
Accrued taxes.............	403	408	414	420	426
Accrued expenses.........	990	856	769	829	889
Debt installment, current maturity*...............	377	531	628	650	650
Employees' deposits........	108	110	113	115	118
Total Current Liabilities...........	$ 4,226	$ 5,167	$ 5,726	$ 6,391	$ 6,991
Deferred income.............	733	664	583	688	675
Long-term debt.............	4,003	3,472	2,844	2,194	1,544
Net worth..................	9,996	11,464	13,417	15,671	18,324
Total Liabilities and Capital............	$18,958	$20,767	$22,570	$24,944	$27,534

* Based on assumption that the new term loan would require fixed payments of $300,000 annually and contingent payments not to exceed $350,000 annually.

Exhibit 9

HERCULES MACHINE TOOL COMPANY, INC.

DETAILS ON EXPECTED RESTRICTIONS OF TERM LOAN, JUNE, 1957
(In Thousands)

	1958	1959	1960	1961	1962
1. Working capital restrictions:					
Cash..........................	$ 811	$ 805	$ 682	$ 1,074	$ 1,483
Accounts, notes receivable.........	3,029	3,640	4,020	4,200	4,740
Inventory (60% of book value).....	4,918	5,760	6,768	7,776	8,784
	$8,758	$10,205	$11,470	$13,050	$15,007
Less: Current liabilities and					
funded debt...............	8,229	8,639	8,570	8,585	8,535
Excess....................	$ 529	$ 1,566	$ 2,900	$ 4,465	$ 6,472
2. Computation of contingent prepayment:*					
Net income....................	$ 733	$ 1,506	$ 1,992	$ 2,292	$ 2,692
Less: Exemption...............	350	350	350	350	350
	$ 383	$ 1,156	$ 1,642	$ 1,942	$ 2,342
20% of remainder†	77	231	328	350	350
Plus: Required payment.........	300	300	300	300	300
Total Annual Payment........	$ 377	$ 531	$ 628	$ 650	$ 650

* Assuming annual required payment of $300,000.
† Assuming such payments will not exceed $350,000 in any one year.

MERRIMACK-ESSEX ELECTRIC COMPANY

EARLY IN 1958, the treasurer of the Merrimack-Essex Electric Company was considering the possibility of refunding the company's outstanding $20 million, 5⅝%, Series B first-mortgage bond issue due in 1987. These bonds had been sold under competitive bidding to a syndicate of underwriters on November 6, 1957, to yield proceeds to the company of 100.699, resulting in an interest cost of 5.6%. The underwriting syndicate, headed by Kidder, Peabody & Co. Incorporated and White, Weld & Co., resold the bonds to the public at 101.826 and accrued interest, providing a yield to investors of 5.5%.

The Merrimack-Essex Electric Company, formerly named Essex County Electric Company, was incorporated under the laws of Massachusetts as a public service corporation on January 28, 1953. Effective October 1, 1953, the company acquired, through consolidation, the electric properties and businesses of three former subsidiaries of New England Electric System, and in July, 1957, four other subsidiaries of New England Electric System were merged into it. All the properties and businesses of the consolidated and merged companies were located in northeastern Massachusetts. Merrimack-Essex, as the continuing company, was engaged in the generation, purchase, and sale of electricity in a 460-square-mile area with a population in 1957 of approximately 465,000. Principal cities served were Haverhill, Lawrence, Lowell, Newburyport, and Salem. New England Electric System, a holding company, controlled Merrimack-Essex through ownership of 80.6% of the common stock after the merger. In announcing its intention to merge the several operating utilities, the holding company commented:

> Merger of the five subsidiaries was proposed in pursuance of our policy to permit larger and more efficient units . . . the resultant company, to be called Merrimack-Essex Electric Company, will provide a more suitable and economic vehicle for future financing and will be able to effect operating economies and render improved service to customers.

Prior to the merger, Merrimack-Essex had outstanding $5 million principal amount of 3¼%, Series A first-mortgage bonds, and $3.45 million principal amount of short-term notes payable to New England Electric System and to banks with varying interest rates of 4% or 4½%. As a result of the 1957 merger, Merrimack-Essex acquired a number of new financial responsibilities. Pursuant to the merger agreement, it assumed: (1) a $2.75 million 2⅝% first-mortgage bond issue, due in 1979, of Lawrence Electric Company; (2) a $6 million 3¾% debenture, due in 1959, of The Lowell Electric Light

534

Corporation; and (3) a responsibility for $11.15 million principal amount of 4% or 4½% short-term notes payable to New England Electric System and to banks, making a total of $19.7 million of debt assumed in connection with the merger. The proceeds of the short-term debt of the consolidated company, $14.6 million, had been used to finance an extensive construction and modernization program.

In addition to these new financial responsibilities, certain legal problems arose regarding specific indenture provisions of the assumed Lawrence bond issue, which limited Merrimack-Essex's freedom to operate its combined electric properties. The management had planned to issue bonds soon after the merger in order to refund the outstanding short-term notes payable; therefore, because of these legal and operating difficulties, it was decided to increase the refunding in order to permit calling the two assumed bond issues. Elimination of these obligations would simplify the company's capital structure and would eliminate the legal and operating problems referred to above.

The treasurer therefore began to make preliminary arrangements early in September, 1957, for an offering of approximately $20 million of bonds later in the year. He realized that because of current money market conditions the interest costs of such an issue would probably be quite high. Interest rates for all types of debt obligations had been rising steadily since 1955, and by mid-1957 yields on top-rated corporate bonds, such as Moody's Aaa group, had reached the highest levels since the late 1930's. In spite of this long and steady rise, the opinions of leading economists and financial analysts were divided concerning the outlook for interest rates in the immediate future. Many predicted that current borrowing costs would level off and remain on a relatively high plateau pending resumption of more vigorous economic expansion. A few experts predicted still higher rates in the next few months, while still others forecast a decline, particularly if business activity should show signs of decreasing.

The treasurer knew that Merrimack-Essex could wait a few months in the hope that interest rates might decline, but could not afford an indefinite delay since the construction notes and the assumed bond and debenture issues represented either temporary or somewhat inconvenient forms of financing. He had to decide whether Merrimack-Essex should proceed at once to issue new bonds in spite of currently unfavorable interest costs, or whether the company should defer action pending improved money market conditions.

The following quotation from the First National City Bank of New York's *Monthly Letter* in August, 1957, reflects general economic sentiment at that time.

Looking toward the Fourth Quarter

Expecting no marked change in business before fall, if then, businessmen are now trying to appraise the outlook for the late months of the year. Latest available figures indicate that, while new orders are in good volume, they are not equal to shipments. Backlogs therefore are declining. This may be only a lull; in any case it is not decisive, for unfilled orders are large even in industries where the trend has been downward for some time. By early fall, however, a pickup will be needed in many lines if output is to be sustained. Meanwhile industrial capacity is increasing. The prospect for more than seasonal improvement in operations is weakened by the change from inventory liquidation to accumulation already noted. If the fall upturn is disappointing, doubts may arise as to the size of plant and equipment expenditures in 1958.

On the other hand, the business changes are moderate, activity in the aggregate holds at or close to record levels, and there is little evidence of any shift in current thinking sufficient to cause modification of long-range investment programs. The backlog of corporate financing which will come either to the public market or to the banks in the fall is enormous. This persistent demand for business capital, despite higher interest rates, is one of the best indications that plans for expansion and modernization are being carried through. Adding the continuous strength in the service industries and the requirements for highways, schools, and other local government projects, it seems plain that business will have strong support. Moreover, a fourth-quarter stimulus from the automobile industry is probable. Competition is acute, new-model changes will be substantial and selling efforts vigorous, and more of the people who bought new cars during the 1955 boom should be in the market again.[1]

The author of the letter concluded that several months might be required before a definite pattern emerged concerning national economic activity and conditions in the money market.

During September, the treasurer of Merrimack-Essex held several discussions with commercial and investment bankers about the immediate outlook for interest rates. On the basis of these discussions and his own opinion about probable trends, he concluded that borrowing costs might remain for some time at the currently high plateau. In that event the company could not afford to wait for a favorable change. Further, there was no assurance that interest rates might not rise even higher as a result of the growing demand for funds from public and private investors for a wide variety of capital expenditure programs. The treasurer therefore proposed, and the board of directors accepted, that the company proceed at once with its plans to issue $20 million in first-mortgage bonds.

On October 2, 1957, the company filed a registration statement for the proposed bonds with the Securities and Exchange Commission. This statement contained all necessary information about the bonds except the coupon, selling price, and call prices, which would be determined later under competitive bidding. The management stated that proceeds from the $20 million issue would be used as follows:

A. $2,750,000—to finance the redemption of 2⅝% first-mortgage bonds of the Lawrence Electric Company assumed by Merrimack-Essex in merger.
B. $6,000,000—to retire a three-year, 3¾% debenture bond of The Lowell Electric Light Corporation, also assumed in merger.

---

[1] First National City Bank of New York, *Monthly Letter on Business and Economic Conditions*, August, 1957, pp. 87–88.

C. $11,250,000—to be used to repay, in part, short-term note indebtedness bearing interest at 4% and 4½% payable to banks and to New England Electric System. The total of such indebtedness was $14,600,000.

The SEC issued an order on October 22, authorizing the company to proceed with the sale, and Merrimack-Essex announced it would receive competitive bids for the bonds. The winning bid was submitted on November 6 by Kidder, Peabody & Co. and White, Weld & Co. and associates. This group proposed a 5⅝%, Series B first-mortgage bond with net proceeds to the company of 100.699, resulting in an interest cost of 5.6%. The syndicate offered the bonds to the public, beginning November 7, 1957, at 101.826 and accrued interest, providing a yield to investors of 5.5%. The issue was successful.

A number of important changes occurred in the money markets beginning later in November. Probably the most important was a cut in the Federal Reserve's discount rate, which, in turn, triggered declines in virtually all other interest rates. The following market comments, furnished by the Irving Trust Company to *Electric Light and Power*, indicate some of the financial effects of the sudden change in Federal Reserve policy.

November 1957

The volume of electric and gas utility financing dropped to $240,838,000 in November, well below the levels of September and October. Most issues were well received and only two small gas company offerings were reported to have sold somewhat slowly.

In the early part of the month, sticky sale of the major, $250,000,000 American Telephone & Telegraph debenture offering accounted for somewhat higher rates for two electric issues: 5% on the "Aa" Dayton Power & Light bonds and 5⅝% for the "A" Merrimack-Essex issue. The Dayton issue was well received and the Merrimack-Essex offering went fairly well.

Mid-month announcement by the Federal Reserve of the reduction in the discount rate from 3½% to 3% seemed to signal change in credit policy and has been followed by higher prices generally for new issues. The "A" Houston Lighting Power 1st 4¾s, 1983 offered on a 4.65% basis were selling on a 4.57% basis on 11/29.

Prices on outstanding electric company bonds, preferred, and common stocks rose during the month.

December 1957

The month of December 1957 saw considerable improvement in the cost of senior money over the appreciably higher interest rates that prevailed through much of the year. The well received Wisconsin Public Service "Aa" 4⅜s on December 6 came on new ground, offered on a 4.30% basis to the public. This was only a few days after the successful "Aa" 4½s of Virginia Electric & Power, on a 4.47% basis. Both issues compared favorably with the lowest yield basis for a new "Aa" offering in November 1957, of 4.65%.

Further improvement was noted in December, with the "A" 4½s of Suburban Electric on December 12 on a 4.40% basis. All debt offerings with the exception of a small electric issue were quite well received. In addition, a preferred stock issue, for which there were no bids in November, was sold quickly early this month.

The volume of electric and gas utility new money financing rose almost 60% in 1957 to a total of $3,900,548,000, from $2,435,000,000 in 1956. Electric company offerings of $2,559,234,000 compared with $1,479,987,000, the year before; gas company issues totaled $1,341,314,000, up from $995,191,000 in 1956. Notwithstanding higher money cost, utilities placed substantially heavier emphasis on bond financing in 1957; similarly, common stock financing showed large gains, whereas preferred stock financing was notably lower.

January 1958

Through the first several weeks of the month most issues were well received in a continuing strong market. The "A" Columbus & Southern Ohio 1st 4⅛s, 1988, came out on January 8, as the first deal of the year, on a 4.07% basis and were "out the window." Similarly, the "Aaa" Connecticut Light & Power 1st 3⅞s, 1988, sold quickly on a 3.89% basis. However, later in the month, the "A" West Texas Utilities 1st 3⅞s, 1988, on a 3.80% basis, the "Aa" Cambridge Electric Light 3⅞% Notes, 1988, on a 3.80% basis, and the "Aa" Pacific Gas & Electric 1st 3¾s, 1978, on a 3.65% basis were considerably less well received. The Pacific Gas & Electric syndicate broke on 1/31/58 and the issue dropped in price to sell on a 3.84% basis. Indeed, the rapidly rising bond market seemed at this later date to be seeking some firmer ground, having already given recognition to the recent reductions in the discount and prime rates, and with the new Treasury 3½% issue, due in 1990, in the market.

February 1958

The month saw the largest volume of electric company preferreds in over 14 months; the total of $71,789,000 compared with the peak in October 1957, of $39,690,000. The average yield basis of the four "electric" offerings was 4.84%. Three of the issues were accorded good reception, although one sold somewhat slowly.

Reception of new issues generally was spotty during February. The bond market declined in the past several weeks almost as quickly as it had gone up in January. The month end found a substantial inventory of senior utility issues on dealers' shelves.

The first deal of the month, the "A" Central Power & Light 1st 4's, 1988, came out on the 5th on a 3.90% basis and was badly received. The Indiana & Michigan Electric "Aa" 1st 3⅞s, 1988, on the 14th, on a 3.80% basis, similarly were slow merchandise. However, the "Aa" New York State Electric & Gas 1st 3⅞s, 1988, on the 20th, were taken up quickly on a 3.80% basis. An "A" issue and two "Aa" issues followed on 3.92%, 3.95% and 4.00% basis, respectively, and were all slow sellers. Similarly, the top quality, "Aaa" Cleveland Electric 1st 3⅞s, 1988, on a 3.77% basis on the 26th moved slowly.

The final offering of the month, however, perhaps suggested a leveling off in the market; on the 28th California Electric Power brought out its "A" 1st 4½s, 1988 on a 4.40% basis and the issue was well received.

As a result of the large declines in interest rates, the treasurer of Merrimack-Essex began considering early in 1958 the possibility of refunding the $20 million, 5⅝% issue. A refunding at rates prevailing in January would result in a very sizable saving to the company. After some discussion with investment bankers and his own analysis of recent bond issues, the treasurer felt that Merrimack-Essex could probably raise $20 million at an interest cost of about 4.25 to 4.5%. In order to estimate more precisely the potential savings from the sale of new bonds, he prepared a cost comparison between the outstanding 5⅝%, Series B bonds and such a new issue at an assumed interest rate of 4¼%. After reviewing the projected savings estimates, the treasurer decided to discuss the question of a possible refunding at the next meeting of the board of directors and in the meantime to proceed with the paper work to effect a refunding.

Even though the 5⅝'s issue had been sold only 3 months ago, the treasurer believed that Merrimack-Essex should consider refunding because of the current favorable trends in interest costs. He reasoned that the company was probably paying something higher than going market rates because the 5⅝'s bonds were callable for the purpose of refunding. Since Merrimack-Essex had paid a premium for this privilege, it should be exercised at a time most favorable to the company. The treasurer was uncertain, however, about the timing of a new bond issue. He wondered whether he should wait in anticipation of even lower rates, since interest costs still remained comparatively high. The treasurer decided to present the facts to the board of directors at a special meeting and to recommend proceeding with a refunding without delay.

At a meeting held January 21, 1958, the directors of Merrimack-Essex voted, subject to approval of the stockholders, to refund the 5⅝%, Series B bonds through the issuance of Series C bonds in like principal amount. The Series C bond issue was approved by vote of the stockholders at a meeting held on January 30, 1958.

A registration statement was filed with the Securities and Exchange Commission on February 11, 1958. This registration statement contained pertinent information with respect to the Series C bonds, except the coupon, selling price, and call prices, which would be determined later by competitive bidding. The proceeds of the issue would be used, together with additional funds to be supplied by the company, to call for redemption the 5⅝%, Series B bonds. The registration statement became effective February 28, 1958, and on March 3, 1958, a public invitation was sent out for bids to be made on March 10, 1958. Beginning in mid-February, however, the bond market began to decline again under the pressure of exceptionally heavy security offerings, principally by electric utilities. Because of the extent and suddenness of the decline in bond prices, the board of directors decided to defer further action on the projected refunding. Accordingly, just prior to the bidding date, representatives of qualified bidders were notified by telephone, and by confirming telegram on March 10, 1958, that the bidding would be postponed to an indefinite date. The following quotations from *Electric Light and Power* summarize trends in the bond market during March and April.

March 1958

Most of the bond issues in March were well received. However, the "A" Georgia Power 1st 4⅛s, 1988, on a 4.07% basis to the public on March 21, found some hesitation. This compared with the more successful "A" Iowa Public Service 1st 4¼s, 1988, on a 4.25 basis early in the month.

Two public preferred stock offerings were well received, the Cincinnati Gas & Electric 4.75% preferred at par and the Public Service Electric & Gas 5.05% preferred on a 4.95% basis. The Tennessee Gas Transmission 5.16% convertible preferred at par was a slow seller.

April 1958

Most of the April bond offerings were well received. Toward the middle of the month new issues were off to slow starts, but announcement by the Federal Reserve of a cut in the discount rate from 2¼% to 1¾% on April 18, led to a quick clean-up of inventories. Many recent investment quality offerings moved quickly at premiums. Late in the month, however, a somewhat less rapid but still fairly good demand for new issues seemed to signal caution among investors.

The First National City Bank of New York's *Monthly Letter* of May, 1958, appraised business and economic conditions as follows:

The business decline has continued during April, although there are signs that the rate of fall is moderating. Apparently the industrial production index, which by March had declined 12 per cent in seven months, has dropped further; most weekly production figures, including those for steel, automobiles, paperboard, petroleum, and coal, have been down more than seasonally. In retail trade the pinch of rising consumer prices on reduced incomes is being felt. Seasonal revival in outdoor work has brought greater employment in agriculture and construction. However, total unemployment declined only about one sixth the usual seasonal amount, and the number of people receiving unemployment compensation has risen slightly. Business sentiment continues cautious, with emphasis on inventory reduction and no general move toward forward buying.

On the other hand, some business reports have a little more favorable tone. Chiefly they take the form of a leveling out in the drop of new orders, or even modest improvement, in individual companies or industries. The significance of such reports is the indication that curtailment of output and inventory reduction are beginning at last to exert their corrective influence. Hope that the recession is entering or is about to enter the "bottoming out" stage seems to be spreading. Good support for this hope can be adduced, but thus far there is little statistical proof. The only certainty is that final demand and consumption are in general running above production, and that sizable inroads on inventories are being made. At some point such drafts will no longer be possible and production and consumption will come closer together.

The great question is how much the gap will be closed by increasing output, and how much by a further decline in consumption. . . .

. . . .

While debate over anti-recession fiscal policy continued, the Federal Reserve authorities in April took two more steps to ease the cost and availability of credit. Effective April 18, Federal Reserve discount rates were reduced from 2¼ to 1¾ per cent at five Reserve Banks, including New York. By the end of the month only the Dallas Reserve Bank still was at 2¼ per cent. The discount rate has now been cut to half the level prevailing last November before the dramatic reversal of Federal Reserve credit policy, and is at the lowest level since August 1955.

Simultaneously, the Federal Reserve Board announced the third reduction this year in member bank reserve requirements. . . .

. . . .

Money rates and bond yields responded to the Federal Reserve's actions with further declines. Yields on new issues of 91-day Treasury bills, which had gone as high as 3.66 per cent last October, averaged 1.13 per cent in April. Dealers cut commercial paper rates by $\frac{1}{8}$ per cent more to $1\frac{3}{4}$ per cent on prime 4–6 months notes. Rates paid on bankers acceptances and finance company paper were also reduced. All these rates made new lows since 1955.

In the bond market, U.S. Governments responded strongly to the dual stimulus of the Federal Reserve moves and the Treasury's decision to refrain from a long-term offering on its $3.9 billion April 15 cash borrowing. The new five-year $2\frac{5}{8}$ per cent notes offered were heavily oversubscribed and at the close of the month were selling at 101 to yield 2.39 per cent. The Treasury $3\frac{1}{2}$s of 1990, issued at par only two and one half months ago, which had risen from a March low of 102 to 105 following the Treasury's financing announcement, advanced another 2 points to 107 on the strength of the Federal Reserve actions. Profit-taking cut these gains toward the close of the month.

In the corporate bond sector, yields on new issues of highest quality, which had been successively raised in February and March under the pressure of offerings, fell back in April, approaching their January low. Highest grade new corporate bonds were sold in April at an average yield around $3\frac{3}{4}$ per cent compared with $4\frac{3}{4}$ per cent or more in June 1957. State and local government borrowers also found a growing demand for their obligations, reflecting increased bank buying. Yields on representative high grade tax exempts, which had gone as high as 3.57 per cent last August, dropped to 2.89 per cent late in April.

Beginning April 22, principal commercial banks throughout the nation lowered their prime rates—the minimum charged business borrowers of the highest credit standing—from 4 to $3\frac{1}{2}$ per cent. Maintenance of the prime rate at levels substantially above those for short-term open market borrowing reflects the continued relatively strong demand for credit from banks. . . .[2]

In view of more favorable trends in the bond market in late March and April, the treasurer decided to discuss again with the board of directors the advisability of proceeding at once with the refunding of the $5\frac{5}{8}$'s Series B bonds. In order to estimate more precisely the potential savings from the sale of a new issue, he prepared a cost comparison between the outstanding $5\frac{5}{8}\%$ bonds and a new series (see Exhibit 1). In this estimate, the treasurer assumed new bonds could be sold at $4\frac{1}{2}\%$. Exhibits 2 to 4 give additional data used by the treasurer.

The treasurer planned to present his conclusions and recommendations for action on the proposed refunding at the May meeting of the board of directors.

---

[2] *Ibid.*, May, 1958, pp. 49–53.

Exhibit 1

MERRIMACK-ESSEX ELECTRIC COMPANY

REFINANCING STUDY RE: $20 MILLION FIRST-MORTGAGE BONDS, SERIES B
5⅝% DUE NOVEMBER 1, 1987

	Period May 1, 1958 to December 31, 1958	Period January 1, 1959 to November 1, 1987	Total	Average per Year 29½ Years
Old basis:				
Interest on $20 million Series B bonds at 5⅝% per annum	$750,000	$32,437,500	$33,187,500	$1,125,000
Expense of issue of Series B bonds ($75,000) prorated over 30 years	1,667	72,083	73,750	2,500
Premium on Series B bonds ($139,800) prorated over 30 years	(3,107)	(134,363)	(137,470)	(4,660)
Total Charges on Old Basis	$748,560	$32,375,220	$33,123,780	$1,122,840
New basis:				
Interest on $20 million new bonds at 4½% per annum	$600,000	$25,950,000	$26,550,000	$ 900,000
Expenses of issue of new bonds (estimated) prorated over 30 years	1,667	72,083	73,750	2,500
Estimated premium on new bonds ($300,000) prorated over 30 years	(6,667)	(293,333)	(300,000)	(10,345)
Call premium (7.46%) on Series B bonds prorated over period to November 1, 1987	33,717	1,458,283	1,492,000	50,576
Unamortized expense of issue of Series B bonds prorated over period to November 1, 1987	1,667	72,083	73,750	2,500
Unamortized premium on Series B bonds prorated over period to November 1, 1987	(3,107)	(134,363)	(137,470)	(4,660)
Expense of call of Series B bonds (trustee's fees, etc.)	10,000	. . .	10,000	339
Tax savings ($669,100) on call premium and unamortized expense less premium on Series B bonds to be deducted from amount thereof to be amortized	(15,121)	(653,979)	(669,100)	(22,681)
Duplicate interest on $20 million at 5⅝% per annum for 1 month*	93,750	. . .	93,750	3,178
Interest on borrowings required to refinance*	35,794	350,839	386,633	13,282
Total Charges on New Basis	$751,700	$26,821,613	$27,573,313	$ 934,689
Net effect before federal income taxes	$ (3,140)	$ 5,553,607	$ 5,550,467	$ 188,151
Federal income tax effect (52%)*	(7,300)	(3,272,700)	(3,280,000)	(111,186)
Net Effect	$(10,440)	$ 2,280,907	$ 2,270,467	$ 76,965

* See technical footnotes on page 543.

Exhibit 1—Continued

TECHNICAL FOOTNOTES

1. *Duplicate interest.*

Duplicate interest arises in a refunding because a 30-day call notice must be given to the bondholders of the old issue. Many managements feel that they cannot safely issue a call notice until the proceeds from the sale of new bonds have actually been received. Interest accrues on these new bonds from date of issue; hence, for a period of one month both the old and the new bonds remain outstanding.

2. *Interest on borrowings required to refinance.*

This charge represents the interest cost on the money needed to pay the 7.46% call premium, which totaled $1.492 million. Since the call premium provided a tax-deductible expense resulting in cash savings, the interest on borrowings required to refinance was based on fund needs of approximately $700,000 at 4% for 29½ years. This amount was borrowed from a group of banks on six-month, renewable notes. The Merrimack-Essex management expected to repay these notes within a five-year period.

3. *Federal income tax regulations in refunding.**

   a) The unamortized expenses of the former bond issue and the call premium are fully deductible in the year the old bonds are unconditionally called and paid.

   b) In the event the old bonds were issued at a premium, that portion of the premium not reported as income at the date of retirement must be used as an offset against retirement costs.

   c) If new bonds are issued at a premium, the premium represents income that should be amortized over the life of the bonds. Expenses incurred from a new issue must also be amortized over the life of the bonds.

4. *Income tax computations.*

The income tax effect appears higher than 52% because of several adjustments related to nonrecurring charges and credits in the year of refunding. These adjustments are shown below:

Net Adjustments

$1,492,000	Call premium at 7.46, old issue
73,750	Unamortized bond expense, old issue
$1,565,750	
(137,470)	Bond premium, old issue
$1,428,280	
669,100	Tax savings related to the above items
$ 759,180	Net special charges and credits written off in year of refunding

Total charges with new bonds.....................................$27,573,313
Less: *Net adjustments*... 759,180
Adjusted new total charges after deduction of special, nonrecurring
    refunding charges and credits.................................$26,814,133
Total charges, old bonds... 33,123,780
Total savings on refunding *before taxes*............................$ 6,309,647
Less: *Total tax* on adjusted savings (52%)......................... 3,281,016†

* Adapted from: *Federal Tax Course* (Englewood Cliffs, N.J.: Prentice-Hall, Inc., 1958), paras. 948.7,-3114.
   † See Exhibit 1—difference of $1,016 due to rounding.

Exhibit 2

NEW BOND ISSUES AND PROPOSED OFFERINGS, FEBRUARY 25 TO APRIL 15, 1958

Date	Company and Type of Issue	Year Due	Amount in Millions	Public Offering Price	Yield	Cost to Company
	Moody's Aaa					
2/26	Cleveland El. Ill., first 3⅞'s	1993	$ 30.0	$102.000	3.77%	3.80%
3/3	Baltimore Gas & El., first 4's	1993	30.0	101.134	3.94	3.98
3/25	New Jersey Bell Tel., debs.	1993	30.0	Postponed indefinitely (1)		
4/9	Duquesne Light, first	1988	15.0			
4/15	Commonwealth Edison, first	1988	50.0			
	Moody's Aa					
2/25	Penn. El., first 4's	1988	29.0	100.874	3.95	3.99
2/26	Cent. Ill. P. & L., first 4⅛'s G	1988	15.0	102.172	4.00	4.04
2/27	So. New Eng. Tel., debs. 4⅛'s	1991	30.0	102.279	4.00	4.04
3/4	Ohio Edison, first 4¼'s	1988	40.0	101.706	4.15	4.20
3/5	Union Electric, first 4⅜'s	1988	35.0	102.623	4.22	4.27
3/11	Indianapolis P. & L., first 4⅛'s	1988	8.0	102.172	4.00	4.04
3/18	Carolina P. & L., first 4⅛'s	1988	20.0	102.172	4.00	4.04
3/24	Florida Power & Light, first	1988	20.0	101.295	4.05	4.09
3/31	Wisconsin Electric Power, first 4⅛'s	1988	30.0	102.526	3.98	4.03
4/1	Idaho Power, first	1988	10.0			
4/1	Idaho Power, debs.	1983	10.0			
4/9	American Can, debs.	1988	80.0			
4/11	Aluminum Co. of America, debs.	1983	125.0			
4/14	N.E.T.&T., debs.	1993	35.0			(2)
	Moody's A					
2/27	United Gas, first & col. 4¼'s	1978	30.0	101.349	4.15	4.21
2/28	Calif. Elec. P., first 4½'s	1988	12.0	101.656	4.40	4.46
3/3	Iowa Pub. Ser., first 4¼'s	1988	10.0	100.000	4.25	4.31
3/5	Iowa-Ill. Gas & El., conv. debs. 3¼'s	1968	9.0	100.500	3.19	3.30
3/6	Columbia Gas Sys., debs. 4⅜'s, J	1983	30.0	99.623	4.40	4.45
3/20	Georgia Power, first 4⅛'s	1988	24.0	100.947	4.07	4.12
3/26	Gen. Tel. Co. of Cal., first 4⅛'s, L	1988	20.0	100.429	4.10	4.15
	Moody's Baa					
3/12	Mississippi R. Fuel, debs. 4¾'s	1978	30.0	100.500	4.71	4.79
3/18	Tenn. Gas Trans., debs.	1978	30.0	Postponed indefinitely		
3/19	Texas East Trans., first 4⅞'s	1978	25.0	99.500	4.92	5.00
4/10	Douglas Aircraft, debs.	1978	60.0			

(1) Refunding $30M, 4⅞% debentures due 1993.
(2) Refunding $35M, 4¾% debentures due 1986.
Issued: March 31, 1958.

Source: Pearson Hunt, Charles M. Williams, and Gordon Donaldson, *Basic Business Finance: Text and Cases* (Homewood, Ill.: Richard D. Irwin, Inc., 1958), p. 845.

MONEY RATES

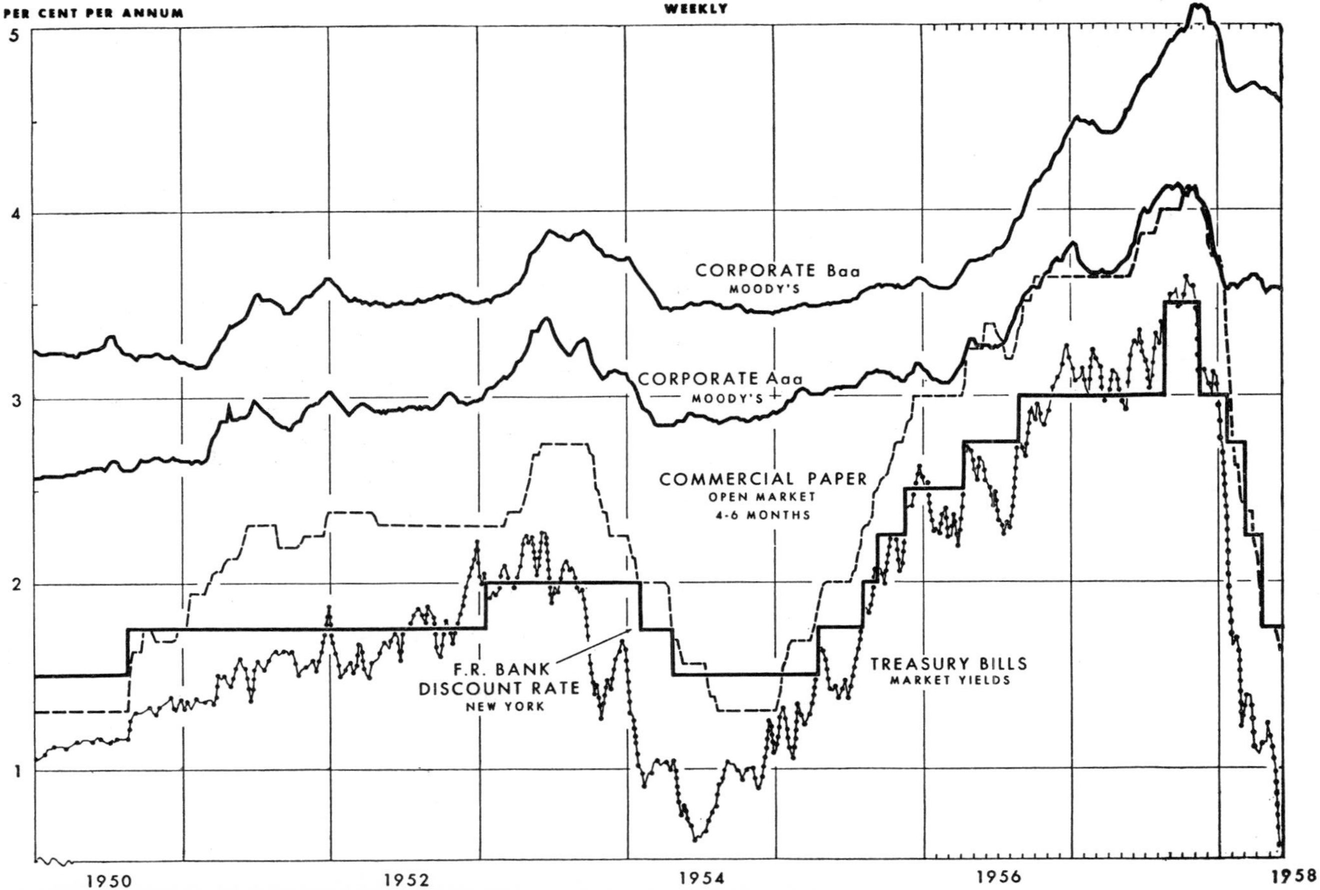

WEEKLY

PER CENT PER ANNUM

CORPORATE Baa
MOODY'S

CORPORATE Aaa
MOODY'S

COMMERCIAL PAPER
OPEN MARKET
4-6 MONTHS

TREASURY BILLS
MARKET YIELDS

F.R. BANK
DISCOUNT RATE
NEW YORK

1950   1952   1954   1956   1958

Source: Board of Governors of the Federal Reserve System.

Latest Figures Plotted: AUGUST 8

Exhibit 4

MERRIMACK-ESSEX ELECTRIC COMPANY

ADDITIONAL DATA ON THE $20 MILLION FIRST-MORTGAGE BONDS, SERIES B
5⅝%, DUE NOVEMBER 1, 1987*

Sinking Fund†

There is a sinking fund for the Series B bonds amounting to 1% of the largest principal amount of Series B bonds at any time outstanding, payable annually commencing June 1, 1959. The annual sinking-fund requirement of $200,000 (based on the initial issue of Series B bonds) may be satisfied in cash, Series B bonds, or the allocation of additional property (credited at 60% thereof), provided that the amount of additional property so allocated shall not exceed the amount of available net additional property. On any sinking-fund payment date the company may anticipate future sinking-fund obligations up to 2% of the largest principal amount of Series B bonds at any time outstanding.

Replacement Fund†

There is a replacement fund with an annual requirement, payable June 1, equal to 2¼% of the average investment in depreciable electric utility property during the preceding calendar year. Beginning June 1, 1959, and so long as any of the Series B bonds are outstanding, said percentage of 2¼% shall be changed to 2½%, or such other percentage as may be authorized in accordance with the Indenture. The annual replacement fund requirement may be satisfied in cash, bonds of any series, or by the allocation of available additional property. Additional property used to satisfy the replacement fund may be used as a credit to offset retirements.

Redemption Provisions†

The Series B bonds will be redeemable as a whole or in part at any time prior to maturity on at least 30 days' notice given as provided in the Indenture, if at the option of the company or through the application of moneys deposited with the trustee as the basis for the issuance of bonds, at the following general redemption prices, expressed as percentages of the principal amount, and if through the application of sinking fund, replacement fund, release, insurance, eminent domain, or other moneys held by the trustee, at the following special redemption prices, similarly expressed, together in each case with accrued and unpaid interest to the redemption date.

If redeemed at any time in the respective 12 months' period beginning November 1 in each of the following years:

	General Redemption Price	Special Redemption Price
1957	107.46%	101.83%
1958	107.21	101.81
1959	106.95	101.78
1960	106.69	101.75
1965	105.41	101.59
1970	104.12	101.37
1975	102.83	101.09
1980	101.55	100.72
1985	100.26	100.24

---

* The 5⅝'s Series B bonds were not traded publicly, and the company had no information on any market prices for the bonds subsequent to the issue date. Registration records for the bonds indicated that over 75% of the issue was closely held by large private and institutional investors.

† Prospectus for this issue, dated November 6, 1957.

2. Dividend Policy

MARRUD, INC.

In late October, 1964, Saul Margolis, financial vice president of Marrud, Inc., was preparing for the November meeting of the board of directors. Mr. Margolis planned to propose that regular semiannual cash dividends be adopted as a policy and that the initial dividend be 20 cents per share, to be paid in January, 1965.

During the last several years, Marrud had experienced extremely rapid growth of both sales and earnings. Although the company had never paid a cash dividend, Mr. Margolis had felt for some time that a policy of regular dividend payments would benefit both the company and its shareholders. Recent financial statements presented in Exhibits 1 and 2 indicate the magnitude of Marrud's growth.

Even though the board of directors was responsible for dividend policy, it relied to a large extent on Mr. Margolis's recommendations concerning financial matters.

COMPANY BACKGROUND

Marrud, Inc., organized in 1953, had its executive offices and central warehouse in Norwood, Massachusetts, a suburb of Boston. The company's principal business was the retail sale, in a highly competitive market, of a wide variety of drug sundries, health and beauty aids, costume jewelry, and other relatively low-priced items. This business was conducted through 362 leased departments operated in discount department stores. The company believed that it operated more leased departments in the health and beauty aids field than any other similar firm.

Marrud had achieved its rapid growth by leasing departments in new stores and purchasing departments in established stores. The table on the next page indicates how the number of retail units had expanded in recent years.

The company had also followed a policy of expansion and diversification

July 31	Number of Units in Operation
1960	49
1961	79
1962	148
1963	196
1964	345

through acquisition. Acquisition of 80% of D. W. Jewelry, Inc., in December, 1963, extended Marrud into the costume jewelry field and added approximately 97 leased jewelry departments. Control of D. W. Jewelry was acquired by the exchange of 106,852 shares of Marrud common stock for 80% of the D. W. Jewelry stock and an option to purchase the remaining 20% from the former owners at any time during 1969. The option price was indeterminate because it was based on a growth and profitability arrangement designed to motivate the management and former owners. However, the agreed price would be no less than $300,000 and probably no more that $2 million payable in cash.

To reduce its dependence on the operation of leased departments, Marrud had initiated a diversification policy when in February, 1964, it acquired a modern plant fully equipped for the manufacture and packaging of cosmetics and drugs. This acquisition was made for approximately $1.6 million in cash and notes, and was operated as Clifton Private Brands, Inc., an 80%-owned subsidiary. Clifton manufactured a number of cosmetic and drug products sold by the company in its retail departments. In addition, Clifton packaged cosmetics, drugs, and other products sold by the company under its private labels. Management estimated that 25% of Clifton's sales volume was taken by Marrud and the remainder by outside customers. Clifton had sales revenue of $400,000 for the quarter ended October 26, 1964. However, it was operating on a break-even basis and was not expected to reach a profitable volume until early 1965. Sales for fiscal year 1965 were estimated by management to be approximately $2 million.

FUTURE EXPANSION

In carrying its program of rapid expansion into 1965, Marrud had firm plans to open 53 new leased departments between November 1, 1964, and May 1, 1965. The capital required to establish a new unit varied widely, but experience indicated that $30,000 was the average amount needed for retail inventory, and $4,500 was required for fixtures. The average department employed four people. Although there were no firm plans for opening additional units after May, 1965, it was the company's policy to accept every attractive opportunity to open a new department, and it was expected that new units would continue to be opened at the rate of 50 to 75 per year.

To further reduce its dependence on leased departments, the company was planning to open a number of small retail stores located in central or downtown shopping areas. These stores would sell basically the same products

as those sold through the leased health and beauty aid and jewelry departments. Initial stocking of each of these stores was estimated to require
approximately $75,000, and $10,000 would be needed for fixtures. Plans
called for opening nine stores of this type by the end of fiscal year 1965. Each
store was expected to generate sales revenue of $350,000 to $400,000 per year
after one year of operation. In addition the company hoped to open about 25
of these stores each year, starting with fiscal year 1966.

Management was also negotiating for the purchase of a chain of 42
drugstores and franchise contracts relating to an additional 39 drugstores
affiliated with the same chain. If this acquisition was successful, it would add
$20 million of profitable sales volume during the first year of operations and
another $5 million by the end of the second year. Mr. Margolis estimated that
this acquisition would require an initial cash payment of $1 million during
fiscal year 1965 and payment of an additional $3 million in 60 monthly
installments. An additional $1.5 million would be needed during 1965 to
provide working capital for the new operation.

FINANCING OPERATIONS

Marrud common stock was closely held until 1961. At that time, the
company sold 100,000 shares to the public at $20.50 per share. In April, 1962,
the company declared a 100% stock dividend to increase the number of
outstanding shares from 500,000 to 1 million and to effectively split the stock
2 to 1. In October, 1964, 1,136,517 shares were issued, of which 6,818 shares
were held in the treasury. The stock was widely held by approximately 2,600
investors. The 450,000 shares owned by Marrud's president, J. E. Margolis,
were the only block of any size held by one individual.

Although Marrud had never paid a cash dividend and all earnings had
been retained, the company's rapid growth and its constant need for additional working capital had required it to rely heavily on debt financing. In
December, 1962, the company borrowed $3 million from The Prudential
Insurance Company of America. The loan agreement called for interest of
$5\frac{7}{8}\%$ and for warrants to purchase 25,000 shares of common stock at $10.50
per share until December 1, 1972. This loan was repaid in April, 1964, with
part of the proceeds of a new borrowing of $5.5 million from the same lender.
The new loan was due May 1, 1979, and required interest payments of $5\frac{3}{4}\%$
on the unpaid balance. Warrants to purchase an additional 5,000 shares of
common stock at $14 until May, 1979, were also issued. Annual sinking fund
payments of $300,000 were required on May 1, 1965 through 1969, and
$400,000 from 1970 through 1978. The net proceeds of $5.483 million from
this borrowing were used: (1) to retire the principal and accrued interest on
the old note; (2) to discharge the unpaid balance and accrued interest on a
first mortgage note in the amount of $541,000, which was assumed as part of
the purchase price of the recently acquired packaging plant; (3) to replenish
funds in the amount of $580,000, which were previously utilized to discharge

a second mortgage note on the same property; and (4) to provide additional working capital.

On February 1, 1963, Marrud had issued an aggregate of $750,000 principal amount of 6% convertible subordinated notes, due February 1, 1976, to two insurance companies and an employees' retirement fund. Sinking fund payments were deferred until February, 1967, when they would require an annual payment equal to 10% of the principal amount of the notes outstanding on January 31, 1967. The notes were convertible into common shares at $11.85 per share until February 1, 1965, at $12.37 until February 1, 1967, and at $13.40 until maturity. In April, 1964, one lender had converted $50,000 of these notes into 4,219 shares of common stock.

RESTRICTIONS ON DIVIDENDS

The April, 1964, loan agreement between Marrud and Prudential restricted the payment of dividends (other than stock dividends) on the common stock to 70% of consolidated net earnings after July 28, 1963, less the sum of all dividends paid, the net amount of funds committed to repurchase of stock, and all payments of principal on outstanding term debt. In addition, the agreement relating to the 6% convertible notes prevented the payment of dividends if, after giving effect to the dividend payment, consolidated tangible net worth would be less than the principal amount of all the then outstanding debt. Both loan agreements also prohibited the company from permitting consolidated working capital to be less than $6.75 million. The effect of all the above restrictions was to limit retained earnings available for dividends on July 26, 1964, to approximately $1.1 million.

LEASE COMMITMENTS

The majority of the company's departments were operated under lease agreements with store owners. The typical lease provided for a percentage rental of approximately 10% of net sales revenue of the applicable unit, and specified a minimum annual rental. In October, 1964, Marrud had leases with original terms of more than one year with an aggregate minimum annual rental of approximately $2.5 million. The company would normally be held liable for the minimum rental during the unexpired term of the lease in the event the company vacated the lease prior to its expiration.

DIVIDEND POLICY AND MARKET VALUATION

Since 1961, Marrud's stock had been traded over the counter, and its price had fluctuated considerably. Monthly high and low bid prices from June, 1961, to October, 1964, are presented in Exhibit 3. Exhibit 4 compares the price of Marrud common stock with Moody's 200 common stock average, Barron's retail merchandise group stock average, and the National Quotation

Bureau's over-the-counter index for the same period. Financial data and stock prices for a few roughly comparable companies are presented in Exhibit 5. In an effort to enhance the investment quality of the stock by increasing its marketability and reducing its susceptibility to speculative influences, Marrud had submitted an application for listing to the American Stock Exchange. This application was pending, but Mr. Margolis anticipated that it would be approved and that the stock would be listed by early December, 1964.

Mr. Margolis also thought that a regular cash dividend would enhance the investment quality of the stock. He was certain that if institutional investors became interested in the stock their buying would stabilize the price and reduce its volatility. Although Mr. Margolis did not feel that the 40-cent-per-year dividend he was considering would have any immediate effect on the stock's price, he did feel that it would support the price over the longer term. In addition, Mr. Margolis felt that it was appropriate to distribute some part of the company's rapidly growing earnings to its stockholders. Approximately 60% of the individuals who purchased shares in 1961 still held at least the number of shares they had bought initially.

To sustain the rate of growth envisaged by the company would require large amounts of new capital during the next few years. Debt financing would supply most, but Mr. Margolis anticipated that the company would also sell equity securities. If the dividend stabilized and raised the market price of the common stock, future equity issues would be less costly and less subject to speculative pressures.

Marrud's relations with its primary lender were very good, and as long as earnings and cash flow provided adequate coverage of debt service, additional debt would be available. However, Prudential followed the practice of capitalizing annual lease obligations at 10% when evaluating the company's debt position, and it was not certain what effect further increases in lease obligations would have on Prudential's willingness to provide additional amounts of funded debt.

Marrud had very little excess liquidity, and if earnings should drop sharply, particularly without a commensurate reduction in sales and working capital, it would be impossible to maintain the dividend. The discount store business was steadily becoming more competitive, and, in addition, the company's diversification plans would require larger investments per retail outlet and would also change the nature of the risks to which the company was exposed.

As part of his presentation for the board of directors, Mr. Margolis had prepared the cash forecasts for the next five years that are shown in Exhibit 6.

Exhibit 1—MARRUD, INC. AND SUBSIDIARIES

CONSOLIDATED BALANCE SHEET (000 Omitted)

	July 31 1961	July 29 1962	July 28 1963	July 26 1964	October 25 1964
ASSETS					*(Unaudited)*
Cash	$ 1,121	$ 629	$ 1,024	$ 1,230	$ 501
Accounts receivable	458	1,459	1,555	2,028	2,670
Inventory:					
Retail units	$ 1,325	$ 3,784	$ 5,803	$ 8,548	$ 10,435
Warehouse	1,119	2,695	2,793	3,168	4,256
	$ 2,444	$ 6,479	$ 8,596	$ 11,716	$ 14,691
Prepaid expenses	25	106	205	253	251
Total Current Assets	$ 4,048	$ 8,673	$ 11,380	$ 15,227	$ 18,113
Other assets	75	89	282	364	361
Property and equipment:					
Land	0	0	0	155	155
Building	0	0	0	1,058	1,058
Fixtures and equipment	210	634	1,182	2,404	2,490
Leasehold improvements	14	29	50	68	81
	$ 224	$ 663	$ 1,232	$ 3,685	$ 3,784
Less: Accumulated depreciation	78	195	320	513	590
	$ 146	$ 468	$ 912	$ 3,172	$ 3,194
Intangibles	0	292	187	408	407
Total Assets	$ 4,269	$ 9,522	$ 12,761	$ 19,171	$ 22,075
LIABILITIES AND CAPITAL					
Notes payable	$ 0	$ 2,022	$ 837	$ 1,197	$ 1,000
Current portion, long-term debt	0	0	0	300	300
Accounts payable	804	3,037	2,932	4,085	6,792
Accruals	175	218	325	517	493
Income tax payable	405	363	411	790	801
Total Current Liabilities	$ 1,384	$ 5,640	$ 4,505	$ 6,889	$ 9,386
Long-term debt:					
5¾% notes, due 1979	0	0	0	5,200	5,200
5⅛% notes, due 1974	0	0	3,000	0	0
6% conv. sub. debentures, due 1976	0	0	750	700	700
Minority interests	0	0	0	83	89
Capital:					
Common stock, $2 par	1,000	2,051	2,051	2,273	2,273
Paid-in capital	1,673	905	905	731	731
Retained earnings	212	926	1,765	3,394	3,795
	$ 2,885	$ 3,882	$ 4,721	$ 6,398	$ 6,799
Less: Treasury stock	0	0	215	99	99
Total Capital	$ 2,885	$ 3,882	$ 4,506	$ 6,299	$ 6,700
Total Liabilities and Capital	$ 4,269	$ 9,522	$ 12,761	$ 19,171	$ 22,075
Number of shares issued	500,000	1,025,446	1,025,446	1,136,517	1,136,517
No. of shares in treasury	0	0	20,081	6,818	6,818
Number of leases with terms in excess of one year	48	144	116	250	270
Annual lease obligation, in thousands	$ 515	$ 1,200	$ 1,560	$ 2,300	$ 2,500

Exhibit 2

MARRUD, INC. AND SUBSIDIARIES

Consolidated Statement of Earnings
(000 Omitted)

	52 Weeks Ended					13 Weeks Ended (Unaudited)	
	July 31 1960	July 31 1961	July 29 1962	July 28 1963	July 26* 1964	October 25* 1964	October 27* 1963
Sales	$6,608	$10,618	$20,676	$32,773	$45,832	$12,573	$10,078
Cost of goods sold	4,364	6,941	13,891	22,349	31,023	8,373	6,703
Gross margin	$2,244	$3,677	$6,785	$10,424	$14,809	$4,200	$3,375
Selling, general, and administrative expenses	1,729	2,821	5,643	8,550	12,180	3,444	2,791
Interest and amortization of debt expense	27	40	38	190	317	104	71
Net income applicable to minority interests	0	0	0	0	47	11	6
Other (income) deductions	2	(4)	(9)	(15)	(37)	(10)	(8)
Earnings before taxes	$486	$820	$1,113	$1,699	$2,302	$651	$515
Provision for federal taxes on income†	210	400	400	646	766	250	225
Write-off of nonrecurring loss, net of taxes	....	....	....	214	....	....	....
Net earnings	$276	$420	$713	$839	$1,536	$401	$290
Depreciation	na	na	$144	$157	$206	$77	na
Net earnings per share‡ (as reported)	$.69	$.84	$.71	$.83	$1.37	$.36	$.26
Net earnings per share§ (adjusted)	$.34	$.42	$.71	$.83	$1.37	$.36	$.26

* Includes D. W. Jewelry, Inc., for entire period as a pooling of interest.
† The company and its subsidiaries file individual tax returns, and the provision for federal income taxes has been computed at the separate rates applicable to each of the companies.
‡ Based on the number of shares outstanding on the last day of the period.
§ Adjusted to reflect the 100% stock dividend declared in April, 1962.
na = not available.

Exhibit 3

MARRUD, INC.

COMMON STOCK PRICES, 1961–64*

Marrud, Inc. common stock was traded over the counter. Prices shown are the monthly high and low bid prices as reported by the National Quotation Bureau. The monthly closing price is the bid price reported for the last trading day of the month.

	High	Low	Close
June, 1961	12⅞	10⅞	12¼
July	13⅝	13	13½
August	15⅜	13⅞	15¼
September	16⅝	14¼	16⅜
October	20⅝	17¾	19⅞
November	21½	18⅞	21½
December	21⅜	16½	17¾
January, 1962	19	16½	18¼
February	19¾	18⅜	18¾
March	21⅜	18¾	21⅜
April	20	19½	19½
May	18¼	11¼	11¼
June	13¼	10¼	10½
July	13½	10¾	13½
August	13¼	11¼	11¼
September	12⅝	10	10
October	9¾	8	8
November	9⅞	7⅝	9⅞
December	9⅝	8	8
January, 1963	11¼	8¼	10½
February	10¼	9⅛	9⅜
March	9¼	8⅜	8½
April	10⅜	9¼	9¼
May	9⅜	7½	7⅝
June	9⅜	7	7⅝
July	10½	7⅝	10⅜
August	10	9¼	9¼
September	9	7⅞	7⅞
October	9½	8¾	8⅞
November	9	8⅝	9
December	10⅜	8⅞	10⅜
January, 1964	13	9⅞	11¼
February	12¾	10	12½
March	15¼	12⅜	14⅝
April	14⅝	12½	12¾
May	13⅜	12	12
June	14⅜	12¾	14⅜
July	14⅛	13¼	13½
August	13½	12¾	12⅞
September	14¾	12⅞	14⅛
October	16¼	12	16

* Prices have been adjusted to reflect the 2 for 1 stock split in April, 1962. The offering price of the public offering in June, 1961, was $20.50.

Exhibit 3—Continued

MARRUD, INC.

QUARTERLY HIGH AND LOW BID PRICES FOR
MARRUD, INC., COMMON STOCK AND FOUR
QUARTER CUMULATIVE EARNINGS PER SHARE
FOR FISCAL YEARS 1961–64
Quarters Correspond to the Company's Reporting Practice, i.e., August–October, November–January, February–April, and May–July

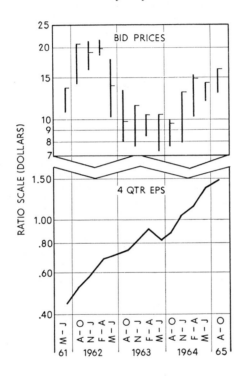

Exhibit 4

MARRUD, INC.

RANGE OF MARKET PRICES OF MARRUD, INC., COMMON STOCK, BARRON'S RETAIL MERCHANDISE GROUP STOCK AVERAGE, MOODY'S PRICE INDEX OF 200 COMMON STOCKS, AND NATIONAL QUOTATION BUREAU'S OVER-THE-COUNTER STOCK INDEX, JUNE, 1961 THROUGH OCTOBER, 1964

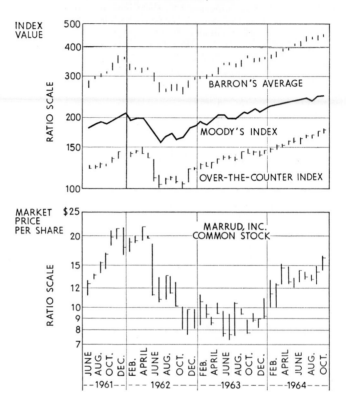

Exhibit 5
MARRUD, INC.
FINANCIAL DATA FOR SELECTED COMPANIES

Cunningham Drug Stores, Inc.

Operates directly or through wholly owned subsidiaries conventional and discount drug and variety stores, including leased drug departments in discount department stores. The common stock is listed on the New York Stock Exchange.

12 Months Ended September 30

	1960	1961	1962	1963	1964
Sales (000 omitted)	$ 54,700	$ 52,488	$ 53,189	$ 53,920	$ 57,616
Earnings after taxes (000 omitted)	1,122	755	193	407	925
Net earnings per share	$ 2.91	$ 1.96	$ .50	$ 1.06	$ 2.40
Dividends per share	1.50	1.90	1.90	.80	.80
Number of shares	385,119	385,119	385,119	385,119	385,119
Number of operating units	211	206	216	211	227
(000 omitted)					
Total assets	$ 26,096	$ 26,025	$ 25,649	$ 25,457	$ 26,889
Net working capital	11,418	12,224	11,442	11,239	12,032
Long-term debt	0	0	0	0	0
Net worth	20,102	20,306	19,767	18,975	19,592
Annual lease obligations	2,100	2,050	1,800	1,875	1,875

Gateway Sporting Goods Company, Inc.

Sells at retail and wholesale, sporting goods, photographic equipment, toys, luggage, etc., through 10 conventional sporting goods stores and licensed departments in discount department stores and mail order, school, and wholesale divisions. An initial offering of the common stock was made to the public in August, 1960, at $10 per share. The stock was split 2 for 1 in February, 1962, and listed on the American Stock Exchange in June, 1963.

12 Months Ended December 31

	1960	1961	1962	1963
Sales (000 omitted)	$ 7,709	$ 10,785	$ 15,307	$ 23,115
Earnings after taxes (000 omitted)	201	340	496	615
Net earnings per share*	$ .53	$ .71	$ 1.03	$ 1.16
Dividends per share*	.15†	.30	.32	.32
Number of shares*	379,150	479,406	479,986	528,786
Number of leased units	na	na	103	145
(000 omitted)				
Total assets	na	$ 6,076	$ 9,819	$ 11,838
Net working capital	na	3,326	5,563	6,124
Long-term debt	na	700	3,000	3,052
Net worth	na	3,128	3,544	4,352
Annual lease obligations	na	na	na	671

* Adjusted to reflect 2 for 1 stock split in February, 1962.
† Six months only.
na = not available.

Exhibit 5—Continued

Peoples Drug Stores, Inc.

Operates directly or through wholly owned subsidiaries conventional and self-service discount drugstores. The common stock is listed on the New York Stock Exchange.

	12 Months Ended December 31				9 months to
	1960	1961	1962	1963	9/30/1964*
Sales (000 omitted)........	$ 93,185	$ 98,667	$108,439	$117,654	$ 92,728
Earnings after taxes (000 omitted)...............	1,312	1,986	1,517	2,032	1,179
Net earnings per share......$	2.39	$ 3.61	$ 2.63	$ 3.51	$ 1.96†
Dividends per share........	2.00	2.00	2.00‡	2.00	2.00§
Number of shares..........	550,000	550,000	577,709	578,495	601,723
Number of operating units..	196	205	221	225	na
(000 omitted)					
Total assets...............$	32,022	$ 35,103	$ 39,913	$ 42,825	$ 45,700
Net working capital........	12,438	12,359	16,459	17,074	17,861
Long-term debt............	0	0	5,700	5,400	5,250
Net worth.................	23,815	24,701	25,054	25,960	27,199
Annual lease obligations....	3,065	3,575	3,986	4,020	na

* Unaudited.
† $1.19 for 9 months to 9/30/1963.
‡ Plus 5% stock dividend.
§ Annual rate.

Unishops, Inc.

Sells men's and boys' clothing at retail through leased departments in discount department stores. An initial offering of common stock was made on April 17, 1962, at $14 per share. The common stock was listed on the American Stock Exchange in October, 1963.

	12 Months Ended December 31				9 months to
	1960	1961	1962	1963	9/30/1964*
Sales (000 omitted).............	$8,419	$15,627	$23,630	$27,384	$22,080
Earnings after taxes (000 omitted)....................	424	702	891	1,198	517
Net earnings per share..........$	.42	$ .70	$ .85	$ 1.14	$ .49†
Dividends per share............	0	0	0	0	0
Number of shares (000 omitted)..	1,000	1,000	1,050	1,050	1,060
Number of operating units......	33	69	91	104	137
(000 omitted)					
Total assets..................	na	$ 6,302	$ 7,374	$ 9,388	na
Net working capital...........	na	811	1,915	4,623	na
Long-term debt...............	na	0	0	1,500	na
Net worth....................	na	1,655	3,103	4,301	na

* Unaudited.
† $.24 for 9 months to September 30, 1963.

Exhibit 5—Continued

MARRUD, INC.

QUARTERLY HIGH AND LOW COMMON STOCK PRICES AND FOUR QUARTER CUMULATIVE
EARNINGS PER SHARE FOR CUNNINGHAM DRUG STORES, INC., GATEWAY SPORTING
GOODS COMPANY, INC., PEOPLES DRUG STORES, INC., AND UNISHOPS, INC.
Ranges of Market Prices Shown for Second Quarter 1961 Are for the Month
of June Only
(Vertical Axes in Ratio Scale)

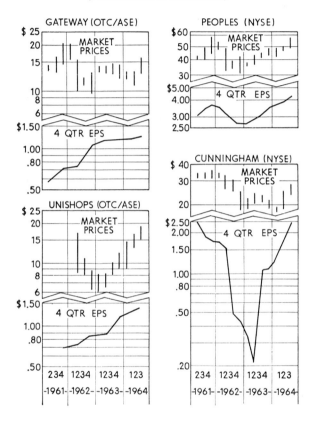

Exhibit 6

MARRUD, INC.

CASH BUDGET, FISCAL YEARS 1965–69*
(000 Omitted)

	1965	1966	1967	1968	1969
Estimated expenditures:					
Capital expenditures.................	$ 400	$ 400	$ 400	$ 400	$ 400
Net addition to working capital.......	1,750	2,500	1,740	2,290	2,960
Sinking fund payments..............	300	300	370	370	370
Dividend requirements..............	450	450	450	450	450
Total........................	$2,900	$3,650	$2,960	$3,510	$4,180
Estimated receipts:					
Net earnings......................	$1,760	$2,000	$2,400	$2,840	$3,400
Depreciation......................	340	450	560	670	780
Total........................	$2,100	$2,450	$2,960	$3,510	$4,180
Net need..........................	$ 800	$1,200	$ 0	$ 0	$ 0

* Does not include the proposed acquisition of the drugstore chain.

THE LAMSON & SESSIONS CO.

In January, 1953, Mr. Smith, chairman of the board of directors of The Lamson & Sessions Co. of Cleveland, was considering a memorandum from Mr. King, a large stockholder[1] and a director of the company. In this memorandum, Mr. King repeated two recommendations he had formerly discussed with the company's management: (1) the amount of cash dividends on the common stock should be substantially increased, perhaps to a level that would average 60% of earnings over a normal business cycle; (2) the company should negotiate a term loan larger than the one currently outstanding in order to secure adequate funds for the company's capital expansion program.

FINANCIAL HISTORY

The Lamson & Sessions Co. had been founded as a partnership in 1866 for the purpose of manufacturing nuts and bolts. With an initial capitalization of $16,000, the firm had prospered and had been incorporated in 1883 with a capitalization of $300,000, all of which had been earned since the inception of the partnership. Dividends had been paid on the common stock from 1889 to 1917 and, since the issue of preferred stock in 1918, on both classes of stock until 1932.

After World War I, the company expanded rapidly, until in 1930 the total output from its 8 plants accounted for over 10% of the total industry sales. The depression of the thirties had a severe impact on both the company and the industry. Lamson & Sessions disposed of three marginal plants and, through the closest cost control, kept losses down to a point where continued operations were possible. As the company's financial position became increasingly critical, it was necessary to take advantage of unusually liberal credit terms offered by a steel supplier in order to maintain adequate raw material inventories. The industry was characterized by a high level of competition, and in depression periods there was a tendency to sell below cost, with resultant losses and working capital shortages. In 1932, one of the company's five remaining plants alone could have produced all the nuts and bolts sold in

---

[1] Mr. King held approximately 5% of the company's common stock, part of which was managed for a family trust.

the entire country during the year. During the period from 1932 to 1941, the company's working capital situation remained critical; no common stock dividends were paid, and preferred dividends were allowed to fall into arrearage.

During World War II, the capital expansion process came to a virtual standstill, though defense orders pushed the volume of sales to an all-time high. In 1944, management was able to turn attention to the problems of postwar operations, and to the prospects of plant modernization and improvement. During the period from 1944 to 1948, capital improvements totaled $1.8 million, which was derived principally from retained earnings and depreciation charges. Though common stock dividends were resumed during the war and the preferred issue was readjusted to remove the arrearages,[2] dividends were maintained at a low level. (See Exhibit 2 for application of earnings during this period.) In 1947, the company's working capital shortage again became acute, and a three-year term loan was arranged with a group of banks. The management considered this loan a temporary expedient to enable completion of the final phases of the postwar expansion and modernization program, and to relieve the cash shortage brought about by increased tax payments. It was thought that this loan would be repaid exclusively out of retained earnings, unassisted by any new capital.

In 1949, it became apparent that the working capital crisis was not past, and that retained earnings were not sufficient for both expansion of facilities and a greater volume of sales. Accordingly, a new, longer term loan was arranged with an insurance company. The loan was for $1.5 million, 15 years at $3\frac{5}{8}\%$; $333,000 was used to retire the balance of the current loan, and the rest was added to working capital. Prepayments were made in both 1949 and 1950, leaving a balance of $1.0 million at the end of 1950. The next mandatory payment of $100,000 was thus moved ahead to 1957, though the management wanted to continue prepayments and "get the note off the books" as soon as possible.[3]

Each time before a loan was negotiated, the management had carefully investigated the feasibility of issuing additional common stock and had reluctantly concluded that the low market price of the stock in relation to its book value and prices of comparable equities precluded such a move (see Exhibits 3 and 8).

During 1950, and particularly in 1951, the impact of the Korean conflict necessitated accelerating the expansion program originally contemplated for the next four or five years. The funds required to finance the increased level of activity were again generated internally in accordance with the company's policies, resulting in a serious cash shortage. No loan payment was made in 1951. In order to reflect the increased level of profits during these years without disbursing more cash, the company paid stock dividends of 20% in

---

[2] See second footnote (†) to balance sheets, Exhibit 5.

[3] For the provisions of the term loan indenture, see first footnote (*) to balance sheet, Exhibit 5.

1950 and 10% in 1951, in addition to the cash dividend, which remained roughly the same on a per shareholders basis. On the other hand, the company reacquired 11,553 common shares for the treasury in 1951.

Although the company's cash position had not improved much during 1952, no further stock dividends were paid, since in management's opinion the continued payment of stock dividends would dilute the earnings and the book value per share. The management had long followed a policy of trying to maintain the book value per share at a level between $30 and $35, and believed that stock dividends were justified only when book value exceeded $35 per share. This level was admittedly arbitrary but was defended on the grounds that any stock with a book value under $30 tended to become a dog as far as the market was concerned, while $35 was a good value for a stock of this sort. Therefore, no further stock dividends were contemplated in the near future.

MR. KING'S MEMORANDUM

Mr. King's memorandum to Mr. Smith pointed out, in regard to dividend rates, that over the past 6 years The Lamson & Sessions Co. had paid out only 29% of its earnings in the form of common dividends. The average for all corporations in 1951 was 61%, according to an article in a financial journal.[4] Mr. King believed that dividends could be substantially increased without compromising the company's traditionally conservative financial policies, and also that such a move might favorably affect the market price of the common stock, thus facilitating future equity financing.

Mr. King further noted, in urging consideration of a larger term loan, that the company had financed its capital expansion and improvement activities, as well as its greater volume of receivables and inventories, almost exclusively out of retained earnings. Retained earnings were also currently used to retire the company's preferred stock issue on the basis of an annual program that was included in the preferred stock indenture but was not compulsory. The resultant continued cash drain brought about by these policies was reflected in the cash dividend policy, which, in Mr. King's opinion, did not properly represent the stockholders' interest.

An amount equal to 25% of the common stock dividend was set aside annually to repurchase the outstanding balance of the preferred issue, approximately $300,000 at the end of 1952. Mr. King suggested that this stock should be retired with the proceeds of a larger term loan. Such a move, using 4% money, would produce an appreciable saving over the 5% preferred dividend rate as well as over the use of earnings. The loan would free retained earnings, which approximated a 10% imputed cost, for dividends.

Mr. Smith knew that the adoption of Mr. King's proposals would constitute a substantial shift in the company's long-established policies of growing from within through the use of retained earnings, and of avoiding, where possible,

---

[4] Source of data was the Bureau of Internal Revenue.

fixed charges against income. From time to time, the company had reluctantly borrowed for short periods, and in each case had repaid loans at the earliest opportunity, usually well in advance of maturity. Mr. Smith suspected that the policies advocated by Mr. King took inadequate account of the instability of earnings characteristic of the steel products industry. (Earnings and dividend records are reproduced in Exhibit 1.) Nevertheless, he gave the proposals serious consideration, since the company's management had become increasingly concerned over the inability of retained earnings alone to furnish adequate working capital for the company's expanding level of operations.

THE OUTLOOK

The company's treasurer had recently stated in a memorandum that cash requirements for federal income tax payments would continue to be heavy in 1953, despite the accelerated tax amortization of plant expansion allowed by National Production Authority certificates of necessity. In the current excess profits tax schedule, earnings of $2.85 per share of common stock were allowed before the tax became effective. The treasurer estimated that, as in 1952, earnings during 1953 would substantially exceed this figure. Though the management felt quite sure that the excess profits tax would be allowed to expire in June, 1953, it did not feel justified in basing cash requirements on expiration of the tax. At the beginning of 1953, the earnings outlook for the coming year was very favorable, and backlogs of unfilled orders were at a high level.

Though the management did not contemplate the issue of additional common stock, such a course might become necessary in order to avoid further borrowing should future retained earnings fail to furnish adequate funds. Further, in recent months the management had given increasing attention to the problem of the common stock's marketability. A considerable amount of this stock was held in trusts and estates (see Exhibit 4); the liquidation of these holdings, if and when desired, might be somewhat unattractive because of the probable decrease in price when large quantities were put on the market. Although the stock was listed on the Midwest Stock Exchange and was also traded over the counter, it had a relatively thin market. The management believed that to a degree increased marketability could be attained by a better flow of information about the company to investors and particularly to security analysts. Accordingly, it had retained a firm of financial consultants to monitor such a program. The president of the company, Mr. Case, had talked to several gatherings of analysts and brokers in 1952 to publicize the company's operations and prospects, and he felt that his efforts had produced some results. The company was also considering registration of its stock on the American Stock Exchange. It was thought that such a move would considerably expand trading activity in the stock and aid in stabilizing its price.

During his conversations with brokers, Mr. Case had become increasingly impressed with the importance of dividend rates in determining market price and general investor interest. In order to assess the impact of dividends on market price, Mr. Case had asked the Value Line investment service to study the stock. It reported that the dividend rate was extremely important in this case. Market price data on certain other somewhat comparable companies are shown in Exhibit 8.

Both Mr. Case and Mr. Smith were much interested in the results of this study and its implications, but they believed that higher dividends would increase the market price of the stock only by the extent necessary to maintain the current yield of almost 9%. The common stocks of other firms in this industry were currently yielding from 8 to 11%; Mr. Case thought that steel products stocks were regarded as dogs and cats by the market, and were chronically undervalued. He felt that the basic strength of Lamson & Sessions stock would not be revealed except through a severe market shake-out, which would indicate those stocks that could maintain a dividend rate in the face of general business adversity. However, he was convinced of the value of public relations and a wider listing in stabilizing the price and increasing trading activity.

In regard to dividends, Mr. Case and Mr. Smith were agreed that it was better policy to maintain a regular dividend rate in cash, which could be paid in all but unusually poor earnings years, than to pay a dividend that reflected the earnings of that particular period. The second policy would produce a fluctuating dividend rate, which would inevitably result in decreased investor confidence and interest.

With regard to the long-run cash problem, Mr. Smith thought that by the end of 1953 the company's expansion program would have leveled off to a point where retained earnings might be more nearly sufficient both to provide working capital and to liquidate the outstanding debt. Estimates of future funds requirements are shown in Exhibit 7.

Mr. Smith found preparation of a forecast for the future particularly difficult. Although sales for 1953 could be predicted with reasonable accuracy, the effects of taxation on profits were not easy to estimate. Mr. Smith decided to assume that excess profits taxes would be continued through 1953. Since payment of tax liabilities promised to constitute a future problem if sales and profits fell off drastically, he chose to fund the remaining tax liability during 1953. He thought that after 1953 sales would continue a general upward trend but would be subject to cyclical reversals. Therefore, he forecasted a decline in 1954, followed by a recovery. Other items included in the forecast were less uncertain, provided that sales estimates materialized.

FORTHCOMING DIRECTORS MEETING

Despite the current cash shortage faced by the company, Mr. Smith was sure that Mr. King's proposals would find some support among the company's directors, but that they would probably stir up a sharp controversy when they came up for discussion. He wondered, therefore, what position he should take in making a recommendation to the directors when they met the following week.

As for Mr. King's proposal to negotiate a larger term loan and use such funds to retire the preferred stock, Mr. Smith suspected that replacing one prior charge with the charge of an even more senior security could work directly against the long-run goals of the company. The dollar savings of such an arrangement, he thought, were outweighed by the desirability of maintaining the maximum proportion of equity in the capitalization. Nevertheless, he planned to modify his forecasts to trace the impact of the proposal.

Mr. Smith considered the question of dividend payout to be more controversial. Although he was doubtful about how it should be analyzed, he thought that it should be appraised independent of the refinancing proposal. Mr. King's proposal would approximately double the level of the current $586,000 dividend.

Exhibit 1

THE LAMSON & SESSIONS CO.

Earnings and Dividends Records
1937–1952

Year	Depreciation and Amortization	Earned before Interest and Income Taxes	Net Income	Cost of Preferred Shares Retired	Cash Dividend Preferred	Paid‡ Common	Earnings per Common Share§	Dividends per Common Share‖	Dividend/Earnings per Common Share
1937	$333,882	$ 833,115	$ 638,402	…	…	…	$2.08	…	…
1938	218,751	(336,334)*	(377,674)*	…	…	…	(1.62)*	…	…
1939	292,384	51,900	5,353	…	…	…	(0.22)	…	…
1940	312,303	524,259	365,475	…	…	…	1.09	…	…
1941	404,334	2,218,118	734,085	…	$89,050†	…	2.28	…	…
1942	441,711	2,910,360	560,433	$122,390	64,493	$113,270	1.75	$0.40	23%
1943	531,237	3,797,318	866,866	103,512	58,002	169,904	2.86	0.60	21
1944	540,054	3,830,389	807,516	99,189	51,844	198,222	2.67	0.70	26
1945	556,102	1,185,420	476,073	141,690	45,010	283,174	1.52	1.00	66
1946	341,928	81,798	90,318	56,649	40,142	155,746	0.18	0.55	306
1947	459,958	2,502,486	1,490,852	107,288	38,651	240,698	5.13	0.85	17
1948	514,226	3,116,214	1,855,777	162,354	31,814	399,238	5.86	1.35	23
1949	351,482	1,699,374	1,026,511	93,487	25,831	373,745	3.22	1.20	37
1950	449,744	3,741,593	1,970,799	19,635	22,123	529,472	5.21	1.70	33
1951	539,950	5,530,804	1,725,058	41,475	20,293	548,548	4.26	1.50	35
1952	700,656	3,486,854	1,293,266	60,270	16,685	586,282	3.09	1.40	45

* Figures in parentheses are losses.
† Payment in cash to preferred shareholders in connection with the plan of reorganization, December 29, 1941.
‡ Stock dividends of 10% in 1948, 20% in 1950, and 10% in 1951 were also paid.
§ Computed on number of shares outstanding at the end of each year.
‖ Stated for shares outstanding the entire year.

Exhibit 2

THE LAMSON & SESSIONS CO.

EARNINGS AND THEIR APPLICATION
DECEMBER 31, 1941–SEPTEMBER 30, 1952

Changes in Surplus

Earnings 12/31/41 to 9/30/52 as reported...............	$11,873,427	
Remainder of contingency reserve restored to earned surplus..	337,228	
		$12,210,655
Preferred dividend paid............................$	407,933	
Common dividend paid.............................	3,372,021	
Preferred stock purchases...........................	959,401	
Common stock purchases in 1951...................	158,561	
		4,897,916
Remainder reinvested.............................		$ 7,312,739

Changes in Other Accounts

Cash and U.S. bonds..................................		$ 3,053,155	
Accounts receivable..................	$1,031,628		
Inventory...........................	2,476,133		
		$ 3,507,761	
Less accounts payable increase............	778,674		
Less federal tax increase................	1,565,514	2,344,188	
		$ 1,163,573	
Total working capital increase.......................		4,216,728	
Less increase in long-term debt......................		508,500	
Working capital increase after long-term debt..........			$ 3,708,228
Investment in plant and equipment, net...............			3,368,313
Other assets and deferred charges....................			236,198
			$ 7,312,739

Exhibit 3

THE LAMSON & SESSIONS CO.

BOOK VALUE PER COMMON SHARE AND MARKET RANGE
1947–1952

Year	Book Value* (on 12/31)	Market Range (Midwest Exchange)	
		High	Low
1947.........................	$33.20	14½	9
1948.........................	32.81	15¼	10
1949.........................	31.95	11⅝	8⅝
1950.........................	30.42	20	10¾
1951.........................	30.92	22¼	14¾
1952.........................	32.63	18	14

* Adjusted to reflect increasing number of shares outstanding through stock dividends (10% in 1948, 20% in 1950, 10% in 1951) and shares distributed through employee stock purchase program.

Exhibit 4

THE LAMSON & SESSIONS CO.

Distribution of Common Stock Ownership by Major Classifications and Size of Holdings

	1952	
	Number of Holders	*Shares*
BY MAJOR CLASSIFICATIONS		
Men..	656	188,668
Women..	604	142,896
Joint accounts................................	98	9,783
Fiduciaries...................................	44	52,381*
Institutions and foundations....................	2	510
Stock brokers and securities dealers..............	36	15,074
Nominees.....................................	4	9,460
Others.......................................	1	1
Total................................	1,445	418,773
BY SIZE OF HOLDINGS		
Owners of 1 to 100 shares......................	812	30,090
Owners of 101 to 999 shares....................	552	144,540
Owners of over 999 shares.....................	81	244,143
Total................................	1,445	418,773

* Includes 17,091 treasury shares.

Exhibit 5

THE LAMSON & SESSIONS CO.

COMPARATIVE CONDENSED BALANCE SHEETS, 1947–52, INCLUSIVE

(Dollar Figures in Thousands)

	December 31			October 31		
	1947	1948	1949	1950	1951	1952
ASSETS						
Cash	$ 708	$ 802	$ 1,401	$ 1,397	$ 1,409	$ 835
U.S. government securities	391	406	881	430	444	444
Accounts and notes receivable, net	1,716	1,965	1,380	2,487	2,613	2,935
Inventories	3,263	3,887	3,004	4,448	5,227	5,013
Total Current Assets	$ 6,078	$ 7,060	$ 6,666	$ 8,763	$ 9,694	$ 9,227
Property, net	5,314	5,918	6,069	6,697	7,404	7,619
Preferred stock sinking fund	71	67	42	104	260	249
Other assets	26		51	30		62
Deferred charges	17	17			28	
Total Assets	$11,506	$13,062	$12,828	$15,594	$17,386	$17,157
LIABILITIES						
Notes payable, banks	$ 333	$ 333	$ 1,104	$ 1,487	$ 2,045	$ 2,015
Accounts payable	926	1,237				
Dividends payable	79	7	6			35
Accrued	43	52	55			629
Federal and state income taxes, net	927	1,233	12	1,306	1,580	
Other						
Total Current Liabilities	$ 2,308	$ 2,862	$ 1,177	$ 2,793	$ 3,625	$ 2,679
Notes payable, banks	567	333				
Long-term loan			1,250*	1,000	1,000	1,000
Reserves—contingencies, etc.	235	235				
Preferred stock	694†	539	449	431	391	331
Common stock	2,873	3,161	3,161	3,793	4,172	4,171
Less: Treasury shares	(81)	(81)	(81)	(81)	(236)	(236)
Capital surplus	1,675	1,842	1,842	2,211	2,431	2,431
Earned surplus	3,135	4,171	5,030	5,448	6,003	6,781
Net worth	$ 8,296	$ 9,632	$10,401	$11,801	$12,761	$13,478
Total Liabilities	$11,506	$13,062	$12,828	$15,594	$17,386	$17,157
Working capital	$ 3,770	$ 4,198	$ 5,489	$ 5,970	$ 6,069	$ 6,548
Current ratio	2.63	2.47	5.66	3.14	2.67	3.44

* A 15-year term loan of $1.5 million was negotiated early in 1949; a prepayment of $250,000 was made during the year, leaving a 12/31 balance of $1.25 million, as indicated. Among the provisions of the term loan indenture were the following: (1) cash dividends, retirement of stock, and other disbursements shall not reduce working capital below $4.6 million; (2) cash dividends, retirement of stock, and other disbursements shall not exceed 70% of earnings accumulated subsequent to 12/31/48. Stock dividend distribution was not restricted by this provision.

† To eliminate preferred stock arrearages on the $100 par pre'erred stock amounting to $62 per share on 12/31/41, an adjustment was made in 1942 as follows: For each share of $100 par preferred + $62 arrearage, 3 no par new preferred shares were issued, with $10 cash and 1 share of common stock. The preferred stock was callable at $52.50 plus accrued dividends at any time after 30 days' notice, and had a liquidation value of $52.50 plus accrued dividends if action was voluntary, and $50 if involuntary. To maintain a market for the new shares, the company promised to set aside annually an amount equal to 50% of the common stock dividend, to retire preferred shares through voluntary tender. This proportion was changed to 25% of the common dividend in 1948, and retirement was made voluntary, not compulsory, on the part of the company.

‡ Parentheses denote negative figures.

Exhibit 6

THE LAMSON & SESSIONS CO.

PROFIT AND LOSS STATEMENTS, 1947–52, INCLUSIVE
(Dollar Figures in Thousands)

	1947	1948	1949	1950	1951	1952 (10 months)
Net sales..................	$19,924	$23,309	$19,607	$25,559	$32,429	$25,785
Cost of goods sold...........	14,915	17,546	15,401	19,201	23,646	19,590
Gross profit..............	$ 5,009	$ 5,763	$ 4,206	$ 6,358	$ 8,783	$ 6,195
Selling, administrative, and general expense.........	2,268	2,462	2,376	2,623	3,117	2,695
Operating profit..........	$ 2,741	$ 3,301	$ 1,830	$ 3,735	$ 5,666	$ 3,500
Other deductions:						
Employees' pension trust..	248	240	180	180	185	150
Interest charges..........	26	55	53	51	37	32
Miscellaneous............	11	7	13	3	2	5
Discount allowed........	. . .	. . .	. . .	. . .	. . .	241
Total..............	$ 285	$ 302	$ 246	$ 234	$ 224	$ 428
Other income:						
Adjustment of property account...............	. . .	$ 39	$ 24	$ 164	$ 5	$ . . .
Miscellaneous............	$ 20	7	21	6	9	4
Discount earned.........	. . .	. . .	. . .	. . .	. . .	67
Interest earned..........	. . .	16	18	20	38	20
Total..............	$ 20	$ 62	$ 63	$ 190	$ 52	$ 90
Net profit (before taxes)...	$ 2,476	$ 3,061	$ 1,647	$ 3,691	$ 5,494	$ 3,162
Federal income tax..........	970	1,190	608	1,500	2,810	{2,011
Federal excess profits tax.....	. . .	. . .	. . .	200	955	
Refund of federal tax previous years............	. . .	. . .	. . .	. . .	(11)*	. . .
State income tax..............	15	15	12	20	15	. . .
Net profit (after taxes).....	$ 1,491	$ 1,856	$ 1,027	$ 1,971	$ 1,725	$ 1,151

* Parentheses denote negative figures.

Exhibit 7

THE LAMSON & SESSIONS CO.

FORECAST OF FUTURE FUNDS REQUIREMENTS ASSUMING
CONTINUANCE OF EXISTING POLICIES
(Dollar Figures in Thousands)

	1953	1954	1955	1956
Net sales	$33,500	$29,000	$34,000	$36,000
Profit before taxes	4,075	2,725	4,200	4,550
Federal income taxes	2,150	1,450	2,200	2,400
Federal excess profits tax	425	0	0	0
Profit after taxes	$ 1,500	$ 1,275	$ 2,000	$ 2,150
Less: Preferred dividends	12	9	6	3
Earnings to common stock	$ 1,488	$ 1,266	$ 1,994	$ 2,147
Common dividends	586	586	586	586
Retained earnings	$ 902	$ 680	$ 1,408	$ 1,561
Depreciation	900	850	850	850
Cash Generated	$ 1,802	$ 1,530	$ 2,258	$ 2,411
NEEDS				
Retirement of preferred stock	$ 80	$ 80	$ 80	$ 80
Optional preretirement of long-term loan	100	100	100	100
Capital expenditures	1,000	1,000	1,750	1,750
Tax reserve	630	0	0	0
Working capital increase (decrease)	1,000	(500)	600	200
Total cash needed	$ 2,810	$ 680	$ 2,530	$ 2,130
Surplus (shortage) cash	(1,008)	850	(272)	281
Accumulated Cash Shortage	1,008	158	430	149

Exhibit 8

THE LAMSON & SESSIONS CO.

SUMMARY OF FINANCIAL AND STOCK MARKET DATA FOR COMPARABLE COMPANIES

	Moody's 125 Industrials	Lamson & Sessions Co.	Elastic Stop Nut Corp. of America	The American Screw Co.	National Lock Co.
Where traded	New York Stock Exchange (predominantly)	Midwest Stock Exchange	New York Stock Exchange	Over the counter	Over the counter
1952 Net sales ($1,000)	na	25,785*	22,670	11,048	28,718
1952 Net PAT ($1,000)	na	1,151*	1,551	591	1,916
1952 Long-term debt/capitalization (%)	na	7.4*	6.6	0	0
1952 Tangible book value per share ($)	na	32.63*	16.71	87.52	16.37
Earnings per share ($):					
1947	5.32	5.13	d0.40	9.92	2.64
1948	7.03	5.86	0.57	7.90	3.23
1949	6.60	3.22	0.79	d4.45	2.65
1950	8.45	5.21	1.33	9.59	2.79
1951	7.37	4.26	1.99	9.43	3.24
1952	7.18	3.09	3.07	5.49	3.16
6-year average	6.99	4.46	1.22	6.31	2.95
Dividends per share ($):					
1947	2.33	0.85	0	1.50	1.10
1948	2.78	1.35a	0.55	1.50	1.40
1949	3.19	1.20	0	1.00	1.50
1950	3.77	1.70b	0.70	1.50	1.00
1951	4.44	1.50a	1.15	3.40	1.00
1952	4.20	1.40	1.00	3.00	1.00
6-year average	3.45	1.333c	0.57	1.98	1.17
Dividend payout (%):					
1947	43.8	16.6	...	15.0	41.7
1948	39.6	22.2	96.5	19.0	43.3
1949	48.4	37.3	0	...	56.6

Exhibit 8 (Continued)

	Moody's 125 Industrials	Lamson & Sessions Co.	Elastic Stop Nut Corp. of America	The American Screw Co.	National Lock Co.
1950	44.6	32.6	52.7	15.7	35.8
1951	60.2	35.2	47.8	36.1	30.9
1952	58.4	45.3	32.6	54.6	31.7
6-year average	49.4	29.9	46.2	31.4	39.5

Market price range ($):

	Moody's 125 Industrials	Lamson & Sessions Co.		Elastic Stop Nut Corp. of America		The American Screw Co.		National Lock Co.	
	Average†	High	Low	High	Low	High‡	Low‡	High‡	Low‡
1947	46.1	14.5	9.0	8.9	4.8	28.0	23.0	14.5	13.0
1948	47.5	15.2	10.0	8.6	5.1	31.5	25.0	17.0	13.0
1949	46.9	11.6	8.6	8.8	6.0	26.5	20.8	17.0	14.0
1950	57.8	20.0	10.8	13.4	8.0	27.0	19.0	20.0	15.0
1951	70.7	22.2	14.8	15.0	11.0	44.5	27.0	20.5	19.0
1952	75.6	18.0	14.0	17.0	12.8	43.5	33.5	21.0	16.0

Dividend yield range (%):

	Moody's 125 Industrials	Lamson & Sessions Co.		Elastic Stop Nut Corp. of America		The American Screw Co.		National Lock Co.	
	Average	Low	High	Low	High	Low	High	Low	High
1947	5.1	5.9	9.4		0	5.4	6.5	7.6	8.5
1948	5.9	8.8	13.5	6.4	0	4.8	6.0	8.2	9.3
1949	6.8	10.3	13.9			3.8	5.8	8.8	10.7
1950	6.5	8.5	15.8	5.2	8.8	5.6	7.8	5.0	6.7
1951	6.3	6.7	10.2	7.7	10.4	7.6	12.6	4.9	5.3
1952	5.6	7.8	10.0	5.9	7.8	6.9	9.0	4.8	6.3

Average† price–earnings ratio:

	Moody's 125 Industrials	Lamson & Sessions Co.	Elastic Stop Nut Corp. of America	The American Screw Co.	National Lock Co.
1947	8.7	2.3	…	2.6	5.2
1948	6.8	2.2	12.1	3.6	4.6
1949	7.1	3.1	10.7	…	5.8
1950	6.8	3.0	8.4	2.4	6.3
1951	9.6	4.3	6.4	3.8	6.1
1952	10.5	5.2	4.8	7.0	5.9

* 10 months through 10/31/52.
† Midpoint of annual high and low.
‡ Based on quoted bid prices.
d = deficit per share.
a) Plus 10% stock.
b) Plus 20% stock.
c) Plus 6.7% stock.

CONTINENTAL LEASING CORPORATION

In early December, 1965, while Nathan Preston, financial vice president and member of the board of directors of Continental Leasing Corporation, was away on a business trip, the board held its usual year-end dividend meeting. A dividend of 40 cents per share had been established as the regular rate for the preceding three quarters. The past pattern had been to increase the regular rate at the end of the year, taking into consideration the expected earnings for the coming year (estimated at $3.68 for 1966). Nevertheless, on his return Mr. Preston learned that the board had made a compromise decision between raising the dividend as in the past and holding to the existing payment. The compromise was to declare a 5% stock dividend in addition to the 40-cent quarterly cash dividend to be paid at the end of January. This particular action came as a surprise to Mr. Preston, who had been expecting that the board would increase the cash dividend, following past policy. The event suggested that this was the appropriate occasion to make a thorough review of CLC's long-range financial forecasts and their policy implications.

Mr. Preston was particularly concerned with Continental Leasing Corporation's (CLC) dividend policy in relation to the need to retain earnings in order to provide funds for sufficient new investment to maintain the target rate of growth of 15% annually in net earnings on the common stock. This rate had been set as a minimum target by H. Edward Thain, CLC's president.

Although the stock dividend resulted in a more moderate increase in actual cash requirements for total dividend payments than would have been required if the cash dividend had been increased as he had expected, Mr. Preston had reservations about the device, which he thought would have an adverse effect on the market price of a share of the common stock.

HISTORY

CLC had been founded at the turn of the century to engage in leasing railway cars to individual shippers. Initially, the acquisition of equipment to be leased was financed on the basis of 50% debt and 50% equity. Financing of operations on this basis continued until the depression of the 1930's, when CLC's business declined almost to the point of forcing CLC into bankruptcy. A loan from the Reconstruction Finance Corporation, a federal agency, kept the firm solvent until the increase in business activity during World War II generated sufficient funds to overcome the company's financial deficiencies.

This course of events made a marked impression on the then existing management, which feared that the firm and the car leasing business might have no more than a marginal future, if that. However, profits continued to rise after the war, and the company's financial position gradually improved. Nevertheless, in 1952 the firm's financial position was still generally considered to be submarginal. Still, the management found it quite easy to issue equipment trust certificates[1] to finance some new cars, which were the first acquired in over 20 years. These equipment trust certificates were issued up to 80% of the cost of new cars with 15-year serial maturities.

Modest acquisitions of new cars continued on this basis until 1955, when CLC effected a major expansion through a merger with Packers Transportation Company. The magnitude of this acquisition in terms of common shares may be seen in Exhibit 1. The merger substantially increased the CLC fleet of cars. Though old and in poor physical condition, the Packers fleet was under lease on very favorable terms. The leases were written to yield the lessor a break-even if the cars traveled an average of 50 miles a day, and the fleet was averaging 200 miles a day.

The financial consequences of the acquisition were fourfold. First, as Packers was acquired for stock, the equity base of CLC was substantially increased. Second, Packers had an issue of preferred stock outstanding, which was replaced with a CLC issue, adding to the complexity of CLC's capital structure. Third, Packers had a large unsecured debt outstanding with the Cosmopolitan Mutual Life Assurance Company (COSMO). CLC assumed this debt and then retired all of its own debt, except the equipment trust obligations, into a larger loan with COSMO. An important provision of this loan enabled COSMO to collateralize any or all of CLC's free cars (that is, those not covered by equipment trust certificates) at any time. The effect of this provision was that it precluded any other lender from regarding the free cars as sources of security, owing to the threat posed by COSMO's right to collateralize.

Fourth, the physical condition of the Packers fleet presented a financial

---

[1] Equipment trusts are a device frequently employed by railroads and other transportation companies to finance the acquisition of new rolling stock. The equipment is held in the name of a trustee, frequently a bank, which issues equipment trust certificates to investors and leases the equipment to the railroad. The certificates have serial maturities, are usually issued for terms of 10 to a maximum of 15 years, and typically have been limited to 80% of the cost of the new equipment. As the equipment is generally believed to be (1) essential to the lessee's operations, (2) readily salable, and (3) highly mobile, the good title inherent in the trust device is considered sufficient security to insure a high-quality rating for the equipment trust certificate and to afford a low interest rate to even the most marginal borrower.

The accounting rules of the Interstate Commerce Commission, followed by CLC, specified that assets under the equipment trust arrangement should be accounted for as if there had been a conditional sale.

problem. If the abnormally high usage of the cars was to continue, a substantial investment would be required to rebuild the entire fleet. This investment was made, nevertheless, and it was decided that the cost of rebuilding would be capitalized and then written off on a 10-year basis rather than expensing the cost in a single year. The decision to spread the cost of rebuilding over 10 years resulted in a marked benefit for the 1956 reported earnings and a decline for the subsequent 9 years.

In 1957, a significant change took place in CLC's management. H. Edward Thain, who had devoted his earlier life to public service, was named president of the company. Mr. Thain was vigorous and optimistic. The board had selected him to revitalize the company and to lead it into a new period of growth. Yet, despite the optimism expressed in the naming of an aggressive and respected president, the board as a group still was uncertain about the future of the leasing business. As a consequence, the board favored "paying out earnings while they exist" over retention, as one member expressed it.

In 1958, the small outstanding preferred issue was refunded with an issue of subordinated debt. While this step produced tax savings, it created a new debt issue to add to the other two on the balance sheet and therefore made no contribution toward simplifying the capital structure. At this time, someone in management set a debt policy of 60% debt (including all forms) and 40% common stock equity.

Three years later, in 1961, the car leasing business was booming. The Packers fleet continued to make a major contribution to earnings and CLC's equity base had increased despite dividend payouts running at a rate over 50% of earnings for 1961 and the two prior years. At this time, the average age of the CLC fleet was in excess of 20 years. After reviewing this fact, the board members agreed that unless the fleet was rejuvenated the company would have to go out of business. Consequently, in 1961 the firm spent $60 million on additions to the car fleet.[2] The leases on the new cars were written to yield 7% on investment after tax but before interest. However, the existing 60–40 debt limitation forced the company to go to the market with a stock offering in order to finance the purchase. The dilution resulting from this sale was 10%.[3]

In 1962, a substantial addition to the fleet again appeared to be desirable. The market was anticipating another sale of stock, and CLC common was trading at 32, down from an earlier price of 56, although at this time sales and earnings were increasing. (Prices shown in Exhibit 6 show the price range only for the year, not what the price was at a given point in time.) No member of management wanted the company to sell common stock in the face of a 43% decline in market price, so other means of raising funds were sought. This time, a group of investment bankers supplied the funds, and CLC

---

[2] This represented an addition of approximately 3,500 new cars.

[3] Based on computing the coefficient of dilution from the formula $\Delta N/N + \Delta N$.

set up a dummy financing corporation to hold the cars in its name. CLC got the fleet additions, but the bankers got the profits.

A NEW FINANCIAL VICE PRESIDENT

In 1963, Mr. Preston joined the firm as financial vice president. Immediately he set about analyzing the firm's capital structure. Exhibit 1 shows the percentage composition of the capital structure from 1954 through the expected position at the end of 1965. Mr. Preston concluded that CLC was trying to work with a capital structure more suited to a manufacturing concern than a financial leasing company. Realizing that 80% equipment trust financing was still open to CLC, he explored the existing debt limit. He could not find out who had set the 60–40 debt limit nor what the reason for the limitation was, though the policy had been announced in the annual reports. The market was aware of the debt policy and, in Mr. Preston's opinion, recognized CLC's continued need for funds. This need was therefore discounted in the market, and the stock was barely 10% above its 1962 low. The low price for the common provided additional impetus to the review of the debt policy.

First, Mr. Preston looked at the capitalized values of the outstanding leases. For this purpose, he simply multiplied the monthly rental charge by the number of months to the expiration of the lease. For example, a 10-year lease on a given car at $200 a month would have a capitalized value of $24,000 ($200 × 120 months). The values on this basis were 1.5 times the book value of the equipment. This suggested that a higher debt ratio, as calculated on the existing book basis, might be warranted.

Second, he saw that CLC was generating substantial funds in deferred taxes as the result of accelerated amortization. The reserves, which were set up on the balance sheet but were not counted as part of the capital structure when debt ratios were computed, provided an extra margin of safety.

Finally, he concluded that as CLC's nature was that of a leasing or finance company (95% of the revenues arose from leasing), CLC could and should appropriately be compared with General Motors Acceptance Corporation or a similar firm whose debt ratios are often 85% of the capital structure, excluding current debt maturities. These three factors seemed sufficient to justify a higher debt ratio.

RECASTING THE CAPITAL STRUCTURE

Before beginning a new financing program to recast the capital structure, Mr. Preston felt that steps should be taken to rearrange the existing structure in order to simplify it and to strengthen the position of the existing and yet to be issued equipment trust certificates. He proposed setting up a new subordinated debt, which not only would consolidate all existing issues into a single issue excluding the equipment trusts but, more important, would also elimi-nate the covenant of the existing long-term debt that permitted the lender to seize CLC's free car fleet as collateral. Using the fact that the old cars would now be free of any lien, Mr. Preston approached a large investment trust management company, which had a major position in CLC common stock, to see how the idea for such an issue with full subordination might be received. Not only was the idea readily accepted but the firm also offered to buy the entire issue at 5½%, or to buy 60% of the issue for 5⅜%, or 30% of the issue at 5¼%.

After determining that it was possible to sell the subordinated debt, Mr. Preston explored the idea of adding this subordinated debt to the common stock equity to form a base for expanding CLC's borrowing on equipment trusts. He then approached some of the major holders of the outstanding equipment trust certificates to get their views on a borrowing base computed as he suggested. He found that his plan was acceptable and that he could borrow up to twice his borrowing base, subject to the limit of 80% of the cost of new equipment. For example, in 1965 after the new subordinated debt of $54.25 million was placed and the net worth was standing at $127.719 million, CLC could borrow 2($54,250,000 + $127,719,000), or $363.938 million in equipment trusts versus the $247 million of equipment trust certificates expected to be outstanding at year-end, 1965. (Note that for the purpose of computing the borrowing base Mr. Preston omitted the deferred tax reserves, because their inclusion proved too controversial for the equipment trust holders to accept.)

Mr. Preston's next step was to get the board's approval of his proposed new debt policy, which (if debt were issued to the extent shown in the above example) would result in capitalization ratios of 67% equipment trusts, 10% subordinated debentures, and 23% common equity. The board accepted Mr. Preston's proposal, and the new subordinated debt issue was placed by an investment banker who had proposed a rate lower than any suggested by the investment trust management company.[4] All outstanding debt other than the equipment trusts was then retired. (The effects of this financing may be seen in Exhibits 11 and 12.)

FINANCING BY EQUIPMENT TRUST CERTIFICATES

Equipment trust certificates seemed to be the ideal medium for CLC's senior financing. They offered good rates, a 15-year term, required no com-pensating balances, and were available at 80% of the equipment's original cost. Since the company never acquired a piece of equipment before it had a firm lease, risk appeared minimal. Further, the capitalized values of these leases were always greater than 80% of the equipment's cost, and sometimes a 5-year lease value was as great as the total cost of the new equipment. In any

---

[4] Mr. Preston expected to issue no more subordinated debt until after 1969.

event, full value of the collateral was covered within 7 or 8 years on equipment that had a book life of 25 years and a real life in excess of 35 years.

Terms of a typical CLC equipment trust certificate are given in Exhibit 2.

DIVIDEND POLICY

Exhibits 3 through 8 are presented as background for a study of dividend policy. Exhibits 3 through 7 show data for the period 1954 through 1965, and are expressed in terms of an index number with $1954 = 100$ (note that these exhibits are plotted on semi-log grids).

Exhibit 3 plots CLC's earnings, dividends, annual average stock prices, earnings yields, and dividend yields. Exhibits 4 through 7 develop company and industry comparisons of dividends, earnings per share, stock prices, and price–earnings ratios. Exhibit 8 compares the actual price–earnings ratios of CLC and the industry on arithmetic graph paper; and Exhibit 9 similarly compares ratios of earnings and of dividends to prices.

Dividend policy was one of Mr. Preston's major concerns from the time he joined CLC. He knew that the board of directors as a group was in favor of some form of increase in the dividend each and every year. The board was proud of the company's dividend record of 8 increases in the 10 years to 1965. Very few firms listed on the New York Stock Exchange could boast of a record as good. Although the published policy of the board was to pay out 50% of earnings in dividends, there was active debate over whether this should be 50% of recent earnings or 50% of the currently forecasted earnings. For the past five years, dividend payout had averaged 54% of the earnings reported for the current year. Adjustments in the quarterly rate were usually made at the December meeting of the board.

While Mr. Preston recognized the potential value of an uninterrupted series of annual cash dividend increases, his concern centered on the need to retain sufficient earnings for reinvestment in order to achieve the investment necessary to support the target of a 15% compound rate of growth in earnings without resulting in dilution. Every $2 retained served as a base for $8 of equipment trust certificates. The $10 thus provided would purchase new equipment, which would be leased out to return 14% on the investment before interest and taxes. Mr. Preston believed that achievement of this goal would serve stockholders much better than high dividend payouts.

Like many corporate officers, Mr. Preston believed that once a cash dividend rate had been established it became irrevocably fixed and was impossible to reduce, except in the most dire circumstances. This belief furnished additional motivation to his desire to limit the number and size of dividend increases and to work toward a more moderate payout ratio over the next few years. Furthermore, retaining a greater portion of earnings would give the company some control over the timing of new equity issues, so that a favorable time to issue new stock could be chosen to avoid forced sales that would dilute the existing shareholders' position. He felt that the threat of potential dilution had been a cause when CLC stock fell in 1962 and remained at a relatively low level for several months into 1963.

Mr. Preston defined dilution as arising in either of two situations: (1) selling new stock at a price substantially below a recent market high—he had in mind the 1961 high of 56—or (2) selling stock at a time when incremental earnings from the incremental equity funds raised would be less than 12% after tax.

In order to prevent a similar situation from arising in the near future, to provide flexibility in timing for any future equity additions, and to limit the number of trips that CLC would have to make to the equity market in the immediate future, Mr. Preston wanted the firm to retain sufficient earnings to permit a capital investment program that would maintain the desired growth rate in earnings. He wanted to limit the number of trips to the equity markets because he felt that if a firm developed an image of being constantly in the market for new equity funds the stock price would suffer just as much as from selling new stock at a poor time.

Clearly, small stock dividends would represent a more moderate actual increase in cash payments than the past dividend action had. But, as mentioned earlier, Mr. Preston had reservations about this action as well. He felt that over a period of time the stock market tends to forget the stock dividends and to regard the record of each share of stock without allowing for dilution.

Mr. Preston held the opinion that steady growth in earnings per share was the most important factor to the stockholders, but this opinion was held by only one other board member. The other members generalized from their own positions. Those who were of the old management group—a majority of the board—had acquired their stock at very low prices, with resulting low tax bases. They relied on CLC dividends for much of their income and did not consider sale of their shares. Furthermore, the members representing the new management had acquired their stock through stock options with the aid of bank financing. Dividends from the stock helped meet the financing costs. Finally, two directors were officers of banks with large trust departments. These gentlemen believed that dividends are the trustees' best friends. Exhibit 10 lists the directors and their shareholdings, and also shows the total distribution of shareholdings.

FINANCIAL SITUATION IN DECEMBER, 1965

In early December, 1965, the Dow-Jones Industrial Average was within 10 points of its historic high of 961 in November, 1965. One brokerage firm whose clients were known to hold important amounts of CLC common stock was recommending a shift out of speculative issues into investment-grade common stocks[5] or into high-grade bonds, which were at their most attractive yields in five years. Early in the month, the Federal Reserve Board raised the

---

[5] The brokerage firm rated CLC common as investment grade. Standard & Poor's rating for CLC common was A+.

discount rate from 4 to 4½%. There were indications that CLC might have to pay over 5% for its equipment trust certificates in 1966.

From 1955 through 1964, the price of CLC common stock had ranged from 9½ to 56. In 1965, the range was 41–53⅝, and the stock was selling around 50 in early December. The 1965 dividend rate, $1.60 annually, resulted in a yield of 3.2% on the $50 price. At estimated earnings of $3.28 a share for 1965, the price–earnings ratio would be 15.2 to 1.

The five-year financial forecasts in Exhibits 11, 12, and 13 are those that were before the board of directors at their December meeting, except that Mr. Preston had reworked them to take into account the decision to issue a 5% stock dividend in January, 1966. In making the tables, Mr. Preston had given first priority to a cash dividend, which would be the nearest 10 cents per share below the exact figure that would be 50% of anticipated earnings of the year in question. Even with this slight reduction from the 54% average of recent years, funds would not be available from internal sources to achieve in the whole period the growth goal of 15% in net profits that Mr. Thain wanted. Mr. Preston felt that these figures strongly indicated the need to adopt more consistent policies.

Exhibit 1

CONTINENTAL LEASING CORPORATION

Capital Structure Ratios, as of December 31, 1954–65

	1954	1955	1956	1957	1958	1959	1960	1961	1962	1963	1964	Pro Forma (Forecast) 1965
Index numbers of total capital structure (1954 = 100)	100	153	165	178	182	208	266	373	398	486	602	746
Index numbers of shares of common stock outstanding, adjusted for stock dividends and splits	100	177	177	177	180	193	197	219	219	220	220	221
Composition of capital structure excluding reserve for deferred taxes:												
Equipment trust certificates	4.6%	2.8%	9.2%	14.9%	18.1%	24.0%	40.6%	47.5%	50.9%	54.5%	56.4%	57.6%
Other senior long-term debt	57.4%*	34.5	29.3	24.9	21.1	15.8	10.1	5.9	3.9	6.7*	6.2*	12.6
Subordinated long-term debt	...	...	18.5	16.4	14.7	12.0	8.6	5.6	4.8	3.6	2.8	...
Preferred stock	3.6	21.2	...	...	...	...	...	...	...	...	...	...
Common stock and surplus	34.4	41.5	43.0	43.8	46.1	48.2	40.7	41.0	40.4	35.2	34.6	29.8
Total	100.0%	100.0%	100.0%	100.0%	100.0%	100.0%	100.0%	100.0%	100.0%	100.0%	100.0%	100.0%

* This represents two separate issues.

Exhibit 2

CONTINENTAL LEASING CORPORATION

Terms of a Typical Equipment Trust Certificate

General Provisions and Guarantees

The equipment trust certificates in the case of CLC had serial maturities over 15 years with $\frac{1}{15}$ maturing each year. An issue in 1965 provided dividends at the rate of 4.80% for certificates maturing in the first 5 years and 4.95% for those maturing in the final 10 years.

CLC paid the manufacturer 20% of the cost of the equipment covered in the certificate. CLC was responsible for all maintenance and repair, and for replacement of damaged and destroyed equipment. Substitution of other equipment, sales of equipment, and sublease of equipment were permitted under specified conditions.

CLC guaranteed payment of principal, dividends, and interest at 5% on any dividend arrearage that might arise. At the final maturity of the certificate, title passed from the trustee, a bank, to CLC.

The prime source of payment on the equipment trust certificates arose from the rental fee that CLC paid to the trustee for the equipment. This rental also included the trustee's fee, taxes, licenses, and any assessments imposed against the trust equipment.

The trustee was held harmless against any and all claims in any way arising out of the operation of the trust equipment. CLC further agreed to insure all equipment to at least the replacement value as determined by the American Association of Railroads.

Default

On any default, if he had written requests from the holders of 25% of the principal amount of the outstanding trust certificates the trustee was to declare the principal of all certificates then outstanding to be due and payable, but not including payment of dividends accruing after such date of declaration. The trustee could take possession of the equipment and was entitled to receive any unpaid moneys earned by the equipment.

Events of Default

1. Default in payment of any part of the rentals payable for more than 30 days.
2. Unauthorized assignment or transfer of trust equipment.
3. Failure to comply with any covenant for more than 90 days after the trustee, in writing, demanded performance.
4. Court adjudication of bankruptcy.
5. Company filing of petition in voluntary bankruptcy.

Exhibit 3

CONTINENTAL LEASING CORPORATION

INDEX NUMBERS OF EARNINGS, DIVIDENDS, STOCK PRICES,
EARNINGS YIELDS, AND DIVIDEND YIELDS, 1954–65
1954 = 100
(Vertical axis in ratio scale)

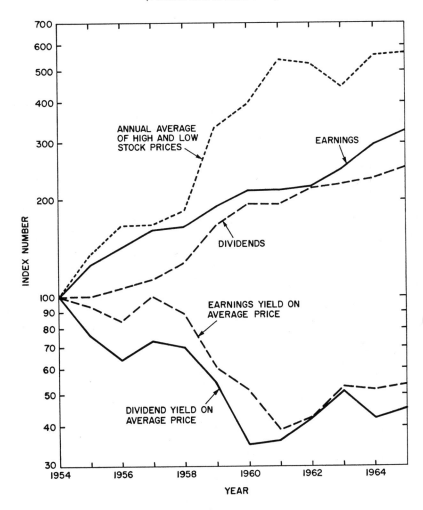

Exhibit 4

CONTINENTAL LEASING CORPORATION

INDEX NUMBERS OF DIVIDENDS PER SHARE, COMPARISON
OF COMPANY WITH INDUSTRY, 1954–65
1954 = 100
(Vertical axis in ratio scale)

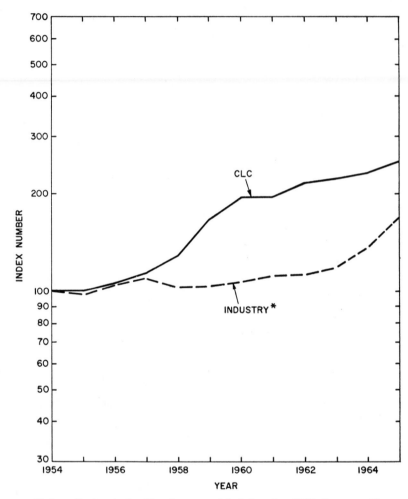

* Industry line is a simple arithmetic average of the indexes from CLC's three competitors.

Exhibit 5

CONTINENTAL LEASING CORPORATION

INDEX NUMBERS OF EARNINGS PER SHARE, COMPARISON
OF COMPANY WITH INDUSTRY, 1954–65
1954 = 100
(Vertical axis in ratio scale)

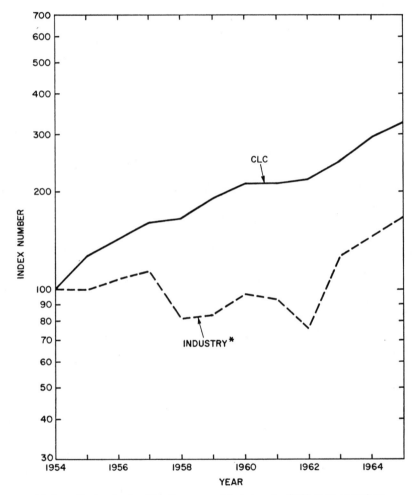

* Industry line is a simple arithmetic average of the indexes for CLC's three competitors.

Exhibit 6

CONTINENTAL LEASING CORPORATION

INDEX NUMBERS OF ANNUAL HIGH AND LOW PRICES OF COMMON STOCK,
COMPARISON OF COMPANY WITH INDUSTRY, 1954–65
1954 = 100
(Vertical axis in ratio scale)

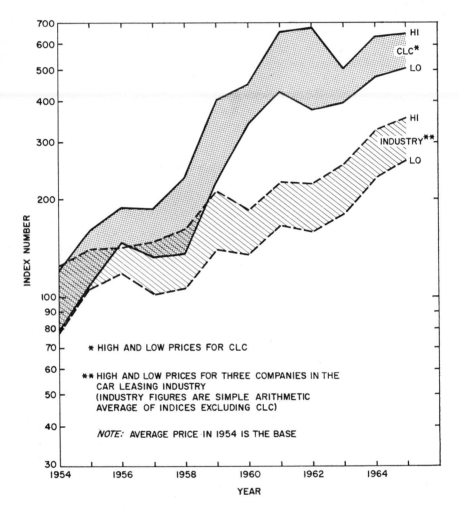

Exhibit 7

CONTINENTAL LEASING CORPORATION

INDEX NUMBERS OF PRICE–EARNINGS RATIOS, COMPARISON
OF COMPANY WITH INDUSTRY, 1954–65
1954 = 100
(Vertical axis in ratio scale)

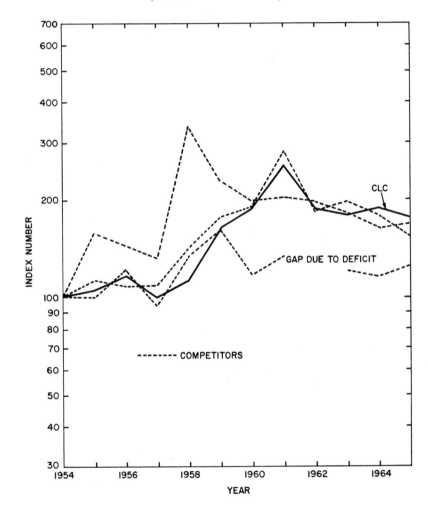

Exhibit 8

CONTINENTAL LEASING CORPORATION

AVERAGE PRICE–EARNINGS RATIOS, COMPARISON OF COMPANY
WITH INDUSTRY,* 1954–65
(Actual Figures)

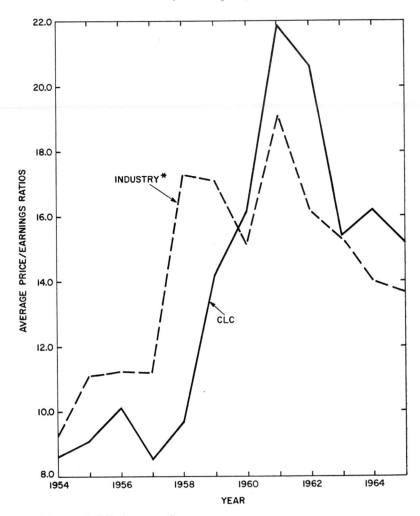

* Average of CLC's three competitors.

Exhibit 9

CONTINENTAL LEASING CORPORATION

Ratios of Earnings and Dividends to Average Market
Prices, Comparison of Company with Industry,*
1954–65
(Actual Figures)

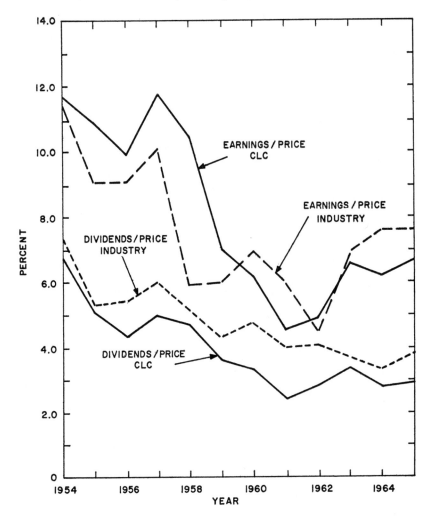

* Average of CLC's three competitors.

Exhibit 10

CONTINENTAL LEASING CORPORATION

DATA ON DISTRIBUTION OF SHAREHOLDINGS, DECEMBER, 1965

BOARD OF DIRECTORS AND SHARES HELD

Director	Number of Shares Owned
Odin W. Anderson, vice president and general manager	19,300
R. H. Davison, retired	22,756
Robert Greer, Jr., executive vice president	12,300
John E. Horngren, retired	45,371
Marshall H. Lorie, director of the Continental Trust Co.	1,000
Alex Miller, director of First National Bank	720
Charles T. Nash, retired	13,040
Nathan Preston, vice president, finance	1,500
George A. Stigler, president of Western Milling Company	400
H. Edward Thain, president	25,000
	141,387

DISTRIBUTION OF SHAREHOLDINGS

	Number of Shares	Percentage
Various investment trusts* (half was in funds managed by two management concerns)	1,978,768	39.2%
One broker's street name†	255,725	5.1
Directors as a group	141,387	2.8
Charitable foundation	48,000	1.0
Others, no one of whom held over 3%	2,619,320	51.9
	5,043,200	100.0%

Recast on the basis of influence, holdings of stock were as follows:

	Percentage	Cumulative Percentage
Investment trusts	39.2%	39.2%
Subject to one broker's influence	10.2	49.4
Subject to directors' direct influence	2.8	52.2
Holders of less than 3% interest‡	47.8	100.0

* Investment trusts, from natural inclination and also because of SEC influence, are very careful to avoid directing corporate managements. They usually vote their shares on management's proxy. In the instance of CLC, 10% of the firm's stock was all that the management of one fund felt it could hold without arousing SEC concern. This fund also held part of the subordinated debt.

† For each share in a broker's street name, the usual rule of thumb is that there is at least another share in the name of a customer of the street-name firm. In this instance, the rule would appear to give a minimum estimate, since this broker rated CLC common stock as an investment-grade growth issue attractive for longer term holding.

‡ Application of the rule of thumb as to street names would mean that a second brokerage firm influenced more than 5% of the outstanding stock, but these shares are included here in the category "less than 3% interest."

Exhibit 11

CONTINENTAL LEASING CORPORATION

PROJECTED PROFIT AND LOSS STATEMENTS FOR FIVE YEARS
ENDED DECEMBER 31, 1965–1969
(Dollar Figures in Thousands)

	1965	1966	1967	1968	1969
Gross revenues	$127,708	$148,580	$166,154	$183,647	$201,373
Operating costs	47,036	53,869	58,165	63,327	68,913
Depreciation	25,153	28,632	31,164	33,964	37,287
Gross Revenue	$ 55,519	$ 66,079	$ 76,825	$ 86,356	$ 95,173
Selling, general, and administrative expenses	9,492	10,317	11,154	12,056	13,029
Interest	13,494	17,131	20,119	22,605	24,862
Net Profit before Income Tax	$ 32,533	$ 38,631	$ 45,552	$ 51,695	$ 57,282
Provision for income taxes	15,990	19,146	22,785	25,997	28,920
Net Profit	$ 16,543	$ 19,485	$ 22,767	$ 25,698	$ 28,362
Net profit per share*	$ 3.28	$ 3.68	$ 4.30	$ 4.85	$ 5.36
Dividends per share*	1.60	1.80	2.10	2.40	2.70
Percentage growth over prior year:					
Net profit	15.1%	17.8%	16.8%	12.9%	10.4%
Net profit per share	15.1	12.2	16.8	12.9	10.4
Cash dividends per share	10.0	12.5	16.7	14.3	12.5

* 5,043,200 shares in 1965; 5,295,360 thereafter.

Exhibit 12

CONTINENTAL LEASING CORPORATION

PROJECTED STATEMENTS OF SOURCES AND APPLICATIONS OF FUNDS
FOR FIVE YEARS ENDED DECEMBER 31, 1965–69
(Dollar Figures in Thousands)

	1965	1966	1967	1968	1969
SOURCES OF FUNDS					
Net profit	$ 16,543	$ 19,485	$ 22,767	$ 25,698	$ 28,362
Depreciation	25,153	28,632	31,164	33,964	37,287
Provision for deferred taxes	11,706	14,892	17,592	19,480	18,944
Subtotal	$ 53,402	$ 63,009	$ 71,523	$ 79,142	$ 84,593
Proceeds of subordinated debt financing	54,250	. . .	. . .	. . .	. . .
Proceeds, equipment trust financing	93,000	95,480*	85,250	85,250	85,250
Total Sources	$200,652	$158,489	$156,773	$164,392	$169,843
APPLICATION OF FUNDS					
Capital expenditures	$117,890	$113,650	$109,320	$109,320	$109,320
Current maturities:					
Equipment trust	24,533	29,016	33,443	38,477	44,004
Subordinated debentures	. . .	1,550	1,550	1,550	1,550
Dividends	8,069	9,530	11,120	12,700	14,300
Debt retired from refinancing	41,912	. . .	. . .	. . .	. . .
Total Applications	$192,404	$153,746	$155,433	$162,047	$169,174
Net working capital increase	$ 8,248	$ 4,743	$ 1,340	$ 2,345	$ 669

* Includes some arrangements completed early in 1966 to finance acquisitions late in 1965.

Exhibit 13

CONTINENTAL LEASING CORPORATION

PROJECTED BALANCE SHEETS, AS OF DECEMBER 31, 1965–69
(Dollar Figures in Thousands)

	1965	1966	1967	1968	1969
ASSETS					
Net working capital	$ 22,732	$ 27,475	$ 28,815	$ 31,160	$ 31,829
Fixed assets, cost	607,395	721,045	830,365	939,685	1,049,005
Less: Accumulated deprecia- tion	(163,162)	(191,794)	(222,958)	(256,922)	(294,209)
Net Fixed Assets	$444,233	$529,251	$607,407	$682,763	$ 754,796
Prepaid and other assets	1,860	1,860	1,860	1,860	1,860
Total Assets	$468,825	$558,586	$638,082	$715,783	$ 788,485
DEBT AND NET WORTH					
Equipment trust obligations	$246,940	$313,404	$365,211	$411,984	$ 453,230
Reserve for deferred income taxes	$ 39,916	54,808	72,400	91,880	110,824
Subordinated debt	54,250	52,700	51,150	49,600	48,050
Net worth	127,719	137,674	149,321	162,319	176,381
Total Debt and Net Worth	$468,825	$558,586	$638,082	$715,783	$ 788,485
Borrowing base	$181,969	$190,374	$200,471	$211,919	$ 224,431
Excess borrowing capacity (twice borrowing base, less outstanding equipment amounts)	$116,998	$ 67,344	$ 35,731	$ 11,854	$ (4,368)
Return on net worth (using ending balance)	12.9%	14.1%	15.2%	15.8%	16.1%

ROCHESTER GAS AND ELECTRIC CORPORATION

DURING JUNE, 1960, Ernest J. Howe, president of the Rochester Gas and Electric Corporation, was reviewing the company's experience under a stock dividend policy that had been adopted in the preceding fall. In so doing, he was preparing for the coming fall, when he would be called on by the board of directors to recommend whether, in light of operations for the year 1960, a stock dividend should be declared and paid early in 1961. Mr. Howe was also particularly concerned about the fraction of 1960 earnings he should recommend to be paid out in the form of cash dividends if the board did decide to pay a stock dividend.

NEW POLICY ANNOUNCED

Late in 1959, the company had announced its new stock dividend policy in a letter to the common shareholders. This letter appeared in *The Wall Street Journal* as follows.

RELEASE . . . Nov. 25, 1959,

to holders of common stock of
Rochester Gas and Electric Corporation

On behalf of the Directors we are pleased to announce a new common stock dividend policy. The Company intends to continue to pay a regular quarterly cash dividend as it has in the past. For the present this will be the quarterly 45¢ per share which is currently being paid.

The Company also plans to consider the payment of a stock dividend once each year. Each stock dividend will require approval of the New York State Public Service Commission. The Board of Directors has today authorized the Officers to apply to the New York State Public Service Commission for permission to issue the first stock dividend of 3%. This would require the issuance of approximately 76,000 common shares. Upon receipt of necessary authorization from the New York State Public Service Commission, the Directors expect to proceed with the declaration of the stock dividend. It is planned to declare this stock dividend so that it may be distributed with the regular quarterly cash dividend of 45¢ per share on the regular dividend date in January, that is, January twenty-fifth.

. . . .

It is the objective of the company, within the limits established by regulation and sound public policy, to maximize the return on its owners' investment. The new stock dividend policy is a step in this direction. It is evident that in general those who require maximum cash income can obtain more net after taxes by selling the dividend stock than they could obtain from a cash dividend of the same amount. On the other hand, persons who wish to increase their holdings will benefit more through the receipt of a stock dividend than they would if a corresponding number of shares were purchased by using funds received from dividends paid in cash.

The growth of the Company has required large and frequent issues of rights in recent years in connection with the sale of additional common stock to stockholders to help in the financing of its increasing construction. It is believed that the new stock dividend policy should reduce the amount and frequency of rights offerings in the future. It is our belief that about the same number of shares will be issued under the plan as would be required under the former practice, as the gross construction requirements will be the same in either case. The basic difference is that if stock dividends are distributed a substantial amount of the stock will be received by stockholders as a tax free distribution, whereas if handled as an additional cash distribution followed by an issue through rights, the stockholders would be taxed at their full rate upon the added cash dividend income. Thus, it is believed that the plan should provide substantial benefit to stockholders as well as being very helpful in financing the growth of the Company.

If the plan appears to be accomplishing its objectives, it is expected to be continued. If not it will be modified or discontinued.

ROBERT E. GINNA   ERNEST J. HOWE
Chairman of the Board   *President*

BACKGROUND

The Rochester Gas and Electric Corporation of Rochester, New York, was engaged in generating, producing, and distributing electricity, gas, and steam in the city of Rochester and certain neighboring communities in the western section of New York State. In 1960, the company franchise area covered about 2,310 square miles and consisted of 4 operating districts. In total, the company served 2 cities, 69 towns, 8 counties, and 176 villages and hamlets, with a population of almost 700,000 people. (Financial background is presented in Exhibits 1–3. Exhibit 4 shows earnings, dividends, and market prices on common stock.)

A CHANGE IN THE NEW YORK LAW

In the spring of 1959, the previously existing prohibition against the issuance of stock as a dividend by utility companies in the state of New York had been removed by an amendment to the New York statutes. Just preceding this enactment, in a memorandum written by counsel for the New York State Public Service Commission and addressed to a member of the state legislature, the commission had outlined its position on the proposed amendment.

. . . in 1907 . . . the Public Service Commissions Law . . . specified the purposes for which . . . utility corporations could issue securities with Commission approval. They were: (1) acquisition of property; (2) construction, completion, extension or improvement of plant; (3) improvement or maintenance of service; (4) discharge or refunding of obligations—and the Commission had to find, preliminary thereto, that the *proceeds* of the issue were reasonably required for the purpose. Stock Dividends not being productive of proceeds, no such finding could be made. Hence—and the Commission so held—no stock dividends could be declared by utilities subject to its jurisdiction.

In 1930, upon recommendation of the Commission on the Revision of the Public Service Commissions Law—with little or no analysis of the matter, but in an aura of the disintegration of the Hopson and Insull empires which were in large measure erected upon watered securities—the prohibition was expressly spelled out in the statutes.

The purposes for which stock may be issued are still expressly enumerated and are still exclusive. Accordingly, in order to remove the prohibition against issuance of stock as a dividend, an express statutory authorization therefor is required. This the bill spells out carefully and in terms of Public Service Commission authorization to approve upon finding that the necessary protective prerequisites exist, i.e., (1) there is in fact an actual surplus which can be transferred to the capital account in an amount representative of the par or stated value of the shares to be issued as a dividend; (2) P.S.C. authorization for the transfer of such surplus to capital is forthcoming, and (3) an equivalent sum has been previously expended by the issuing corporation for property, plant, or service improvement or the refunding of its obligations—the only "purposes enumerated in this section" which are applicable. Obviously, reimbursement—another of the specified "purposes"—would not be involved in a stock dividend issuance.

It is believed that these protective prerequisites together with the improvement in utility accounting which has occurred since 1930 (enabling the Commission today to ascertain fairly readily the existence or absence of a true surplus), permit of the elimination of the present absolute prohibition against New York State utilities having resort to the stock dividend method of enhancing the attractiveness of their securities in the money market while plowing earnings back into the business. Under the review that must be made by this Commission pursuant to the form of the authorization contained in this bill, the likelihood of any repetition of utility stock dividend abuses of the past is extremely remote, if not impossible.

For these reasons the Commission is not opposed to approval of this measure.

FACTORS THAT INFLUENCED INTRODUCTION OF THE NEW POLICY

Mr. Howe had long wanted to introduce a stock dividend. It was his opinion that the removal of the statutory prohibition presented Rochester Gas and Electric with the opportunity to overcome what he regarded as "a vicious whirlpool" and the greatest frailty of utility companies from the stockholders' point of view. This difficulty was that utilities typically paid out a large fraction of earnings in the form of cash dividends and then, within a short period of time, were forced by the large funds requirements of the business to ask stockholders to reinvest their money in new common stock issues through rights offerings.

For instance, in the period from September 1, 1949, to December 31, 1959, Rochester Gas and Electric paid out $33,237,549 in cash dividends and raised $34,350,250 through rights offerings of common stock. "In the meantime," said Mr. Howe, "the United States Treasury had taken its tax bite and the stockholders ended up with less." On the other hand, as far as Mr. Howe was concerned, if it were not for the tax savings available the use of stock dividends would make "very little sense at all."

Rochester Gas and Electric's corporate charter afforded the management its choice between offering common stock to the public and offering it to existing shareholders through rights. In the past, management had always elected to issue common stock through rights because, in Mr. Howe's words, "we believed that this was what the stockholders wanted, and rights offerings were fashionable." This feeling on the part of management had been confirmed by the success that the company's rights offerings had enjoyed and by the evidence that large numbers of stockholders had subscribed to every rights offering made by the company.

In illustration of this point, Mr. Howe had received the following statistics on the company's two most recent rights offerings:

	November 25, 1955		February 5, 1959	
Shares offered for subscription upon exercise of warrants issued to stockholders	194,721	100.0%	260,774	100.0%
Shares subscribed by holders of record using all or part of rights issued to them	111,203	57.1%	165,569	63.5%
Shares subscribed by holders of record using rights issued originally to other stockholders	46,084	23.7%	55,899	21.4%
Shares subscribed by persons not holders of record	31,270	16.1%	31,213	12.0%
Total Subscription	188,557	96.9%	252,681	96.9%

However, raising funds through rights offerings was not free of costs. Carefully kept records of the company revealed that expenses incurred in connection with the 1955 offering totaled $190,110, including an underwriting commission of $70,000. In connection with the 1959 offering, the underwriting commission ($73,500) and other expenses totaled $198,903. Although of the amounts raised these costs represented only 2.35% and 1.89%, respectively, Mr. Howe realized that considerable expense would be incurred regardless of the size of the issue. In fact, company staff members had estimated that $101,500 was the cost involved in connection with a rights offering of 75,000 shares—the approximate size of the stock dividend paid for 1959.

In order to provide sufficient inducement for use of the rights to assure success of the 1955 and 1959 offerings, management had set the respective subscription prices at approximately 7% and 10% below market prices. The risks involved for the underwriter, of course, were not so great with the larger rights offering discount. The smaller discount on the 1955 offering undoubt-edly accounted in part for the greater underwriting commission per share of that issue.

Elaborating on a statement made in the 1959 letter to shareholders, Mr. Howe pointed out that the company's new policy of stock dividends would help to alleviate the burden caused by the continuing need for funds to finance new property and equipment expenditures. He thought that in the foreseeable future Rochester Gas and Electric could not hope to generate enough cash earnings to take care of its capital requirements. Exhibit 5 presents anticipated expenditures for the five years 1960–64, together with a schedule of capital expenditures for the past five years.

An alternative method of reducing the amount and frequency of outside financing would be to maintain the current cash dividend rate, thereby retaining a larger fraction of increased earnings in future years without evidencing such increases in the form of either stock dividends or higher cash dividend payout. In Mr. Howe's opinion, use of this method probably would meet considerable disfavor of stockholders and an unfavorable market reac-tion. For this reason, it had not appealed to management as a very realistic alternative. Management based its judgment in this matter on a general awareness of the preferences and prejudices of investors in common stocks, and on its prediction of the market reaction.

Another factor that in some degree influenced management's decision to introduce the new stock dividend policy was that this policy presented an opportunity, through a relatively uncomplicated accounting procedure, to capitalize a portion of the Surplus account.[1] The motivating factor here was the desire to nail down the tax savings from accelerated depreciation in the company's earnings rate base.[2] Management was hoping to accomplish this nailing down by paying an annual stock dividend in an amount sufficient to effect a transfer from Surplus to Capital Stock of approximately 90–100% of retained annual net income, including the tax savings therein. Even though the Surplus account was as much a part of the earnings rate base as the Capital Stock account, management had taken the view that it would be desirable to transfer amounts representing these tax savings from the Surplus to the permanent capitalization.

---

[1] "An ordinary stock dividend (a dividend payable in shares of common stock to holders of common stock) implies a transfer of earned surplus to capital account. Al-though the amount to be transferred is legally within the discretion of the directors, the interrelated problem of determining how many shares shall be issued as a stock dividend brings in questions of good corporate and accounting practice as well. . . .

". . . These legal requirements may be set by statute, charter, or bylaws. . . ." Lillian Doris (ed.), *Corporate Treasurer's and Controller's Handbook* (New York: Prentice-Hall, Inc., 1950), pp. 903–4.

[2] While continuing the use of straight-line depreciation in its financial statements, the company had elected to use accelerated depreciation in its federal income tax returns, with resulting reductions in taxes for the years applicable. Annual net income, therefore, was greater than it otherwise would have been by the tax savings from accelerated depreciation included therein.

FUNDS REQUIREMENTS AND RELATED ASPECTS

With regard to the new policy, Mr. Howe thought that the split between cash and stock in future dividend payments could be determined only after consideration of the cash requirements of the business. To aid him in this consideration, Mr. Howe had before him the data, shown in Exhibit 6, on the estimated sources and uses of funds for the years 1960 and 1961.

As a rule of thumb in setting the new policy, management anticipated that the cash portion of future dividends would amount to about 65% of operating earnings applicable to common stock.[3] Mr. Howe suspected that any attempt to carry further the substitution of stock dividends for cash would expose the company and its stock to unfavorable reactions from both the stockholders and the market. Exhibit 7 shows the short-run market reaction of the prices of Rochester common stock to the stock dividend policy adopted in 1959, and compares it with the market performance of stocks of two comparable utilities. Exhibits 8–10 present selected comparisons with Moody's Average of 24 Utilities.

Mr. Howe thought that the proportions of debt, preferred stock, and common stock in the company's capital structure as of December 31, 1959, were very nearly in line with those management considered desirable for the long run.

MANAGEMENT CONSIDERS THE STOCKHOLDERS

The new stock dividend policy had grown entirely out of management's philosophy and beliefs regarding what was beneficial for the stockholders and what were the preferences of stockholders. While management had recognized the desirability and probable usefulness of making a stockholder survey prior to introduction of this type of policy, it had been very reluctant to attempt such a survey because it might start rumors and create speculation and unrest in stockholder ranks and in the market. On a confidential basis, management discussed the new policy with a number of investment bankers and analysts, and the consensus was that stock dividends would be a good thing.

The stock dividend policy had been designed primarily for the benefit of the large number of individual stockholders. Management had mentally classified the company's stockholders into two groups: (1) stockholders interested in increasing their investment in the company; (2) stockholders trying to maximize their income. Under the assumption that many stockholders would reinvest their dividends anyway (through rights offerings), management viewed the new policy as beneficial to all stockholders with one major

---

[3] The 65% rule of thumb was applicable to net income from operations, less the preferred dividend. Net income from operations *did not include* tax savings from accelerated depreciation.

exception. Stockholders that had a small number of shares and wanted cash would be faced with the expense of the commission on the sale of a few stock dividend shares. The policy would work a monetary penalty against this class of holders in comparison with issuance to them of an equivalent amount in the form of an all-cash dividend.

In an effort to minimize the monetary penalty for this group of stockholders, Mr. Howe had investigated the possibility of setting up a special agency to buy and sell stock dividend shares. This agency would have facilitated the disposition of stock dividend shares with a minimum of delay and expense for those holders who preferred cash. The Securities and Exchange Commission, however, had taken the position that a registration statement would be required if such an agency were established to handle anything other than fractional shares. After talking extensively with the management of the Commonwealth Edison Company in Chicago, which had established such an agency for the convenience of its stockholders, the management of Rochester Gas and Electric decided, on the basis of Commonwealth Edison's experience, that the expense of registration was not justified. A letter from a brokerage firm regarding this question appears as Exhibit 11, and Mr. Howe's answer as Exhibit 12.

THE STOCK DIVIDEND

In November, 1959, the company petitioned the New York Public Service Commission for permission to issue 76,665 shares of common stock as a dividend, and to effect a transfer from Earned Surplus to Common Capital Stock of an amount representing the stock dividend's stated value. At a session of the Public Service Commission, held in the city of New York on January 5, 1960, the petition was approved and the issue authorized, subject to the following conditions.

1. Stated value of the stock for transfer from Earned Surplus to Common Capital Stock was to be determined by multiplying the number of shares by a figure not less than 90% of the price of the closing sale of said common stock on the New York Stock Exchange on the nearest date prior to the declaration of said dividend.
2. The cost and expense of issuing the stock dividend could not exceed $50,000.

On January 25, 1960, to stockholders of record on January 15, 1960, a 3% stock dividend amounting to 76,581 shares was paid and distributed with the regular quarterly cash dividend of 45 cents a share. Accompanying the dividend was a letter to the stockholders (see Exhibit 13), which, among other things, informed them about the tax status of the stock dividend and set forth instructions for handling of fractional interests. Management also announced in this letter that the total amount transferred to the Common Stock account from the Surplus account was $3,446,145 (76,581 shares at $45 a share.)[4]

STOCKHOLDER REACTIONS AND POLICY CONSIDERATIONS

Mr. Howe had anticipated some negative reaction from certain types and groups of stockholders. He had expected that some holders (certain types of institutions and others), not subject to federal income taxes and realizing no tax benefit from the new policy, would object on the grounds that it was costly to convert the stock dividend into the cash they preferred. He had also expected complaints from trusts and trust departments of banks, because the receipt of stock dividends by these holders often further complicated the already complex problem of allocating between trust principal and trust income.[5] Much to Mr. Howe's surprise, in the seven months that had elapsed since the new policy was announced the anticipated negative reactions had not materialized. During this period, the company had received only 14 letters from stockholders referring to this policy, and all were favorable to it.

Mr. Howe sincerely wanted to take into account the interests of stockholders in deciding whether the new policy should be continued, discontinued, or modified. Therefore, he had welcomed a suggestion, made by a professor at the Harvard Business School, that the company keep its stock transfer records in such a way as to give some insight into stockholders' desires and interests. In direct response to this suggestion, a department in the company had been instructed to determine, if possible, the number and kinds of shareholders who took advantage of the stock dividend to raise cash. Mr. Howe had been reviewing the resulting data (see Exhibit 14). He hoped to draw some useful information as a guide for his recommendations, and some useful generalizations as a guide for future policies. He was also considering what additional classifications of data could be made in the future, drawing on company stock transfer records as the primary source of meaningful information for this purpose.

---

[4] On January 5, 1960, the date prior to declaration of the stock dividend, the market price of Rochester common stock ranged from 49⅞ to 48⅞, and closed at 49. In order to comply with one condition laid down by the New York Public Service Commission, the transfer price was set at a figure *not less* than 90% of the closing sale price and was rounded to an even $45 a share.

[5] For simple illustration, legal instruments relating to trusts and estates are often drawn up in a manner that designates a party (or parties) as life tenant and another party (or parties) as remainderman. Typically, the life tenant is entitled to receive during his lifetime all income that flows from the assets represented by the trust (estate) principal, after deducting expenses incurred in acquiring the income. The remainderman, in turn, is entitled to the principal assets remaining on demise of the life tenant. All costs incurred in keeping the principal intact are typically deducted from the principal account rather than the income account. The problem of determining which costs are properly chargeable to principal as opposed to income and of determining which receipts and credits are truly for the account of one rather than the other is a very difficult one, even when the language in the legal documents is extremely clear on the matter, which often is not the case.

Exhibit 1

ROCHESTER GAS AND ELECTRIC CORPORATION

STATEMENT OF FINANCIAL CONDITION AT DECEMBER 31, 1959
(In Thousands)

ASSETS

Utility plant and property, at original cost	$258,776
Current assets	16,754
Deferred debits	4,245
	$279,775

LIABILITIES

Current liabilities	$ 14,631
Deferred credits	499
Reserves (including depreciation reserve of $46,885)	47,179
	$ 62,309

Capitalization:

Long-term debt	$101,000
Preferred stock, cumulative, par value $100 a share; 510,000 shares authorized; 370,000 shares issued and outstanding	37,000
Common stock, no par value; 3,250,000 shares authorized; 2,551,076 shares issued and outstanding*	54,266
Premium on preferred stock	83
Earned surplus	25,117
	$217,466
	$279,775

* Listed and traded on New York Stock Exchange; unlisted trading on Boston Stock Exchange.
SOURCE: Annual reports of the company.

Exhibit 2

ROCHESTER GAS AND ELECTRIC CORPORATION

STATEMENT OF INCOME AND EARNINGS RETAINED
(In Thousands)

	1955	1956	1957	1958	1959
Net income (reflects reduction in federal income taxes from accelerated depreciation)*	$6,020	$6,850	$7,336	$8,271	$10,060
Dividends on preferred stock	1,298	1,387	1,595	1,595	1,595
Earnings applicable to common stock	$4,722	$5,463	$5,741	$6,676	$ 8,465
Cash dividends on common stock	2,950	3,517	3,641	3,641	4,464
Earnings reinvested	$1,772	$1,946	$2,100	$3,035	$ 4,001

* Amounts included in net income that represent the tax savings arising from the use of accelerated depreciation on the company's federal income tax return ... $ 209 $ 377 $ 596 $ 800 $ 1,025
SOURCE: Annual reports of the company.

Exhibit 3

ROCHESTER GAS AND ELECTRIC CORPORATION

SOURCE AND DISPOSITION OF FUNDS, 1955–59

(In Thousands)

	1955	1956	1957	1958	1959	Total
Source of funds:						
Net income..............	$ 6,020	$ 6,850	$ 7,336	$ 8,271	$10,061	$ 38,538
Depreciation and net						
salvage................	4,766	5,171	5,134	5,438	5,634	26,143
Sale of bonds............	10,000	...	15,000	...	12,000	37,000
Sale of preferred stock....	...	6,000	...	...	...	6,000
Sale of common stock.....	8,015	91	...	...	10,356	18,462
Proceeds of short-term						
loans.................	7,000	14,000	5,500	10,000	14,500	51,000
Increase in other liabilities						
and credits.............	1,459	1,161	(153)	274	346	3,087
Total Funds........	$37,260	$33,273	$32,817	$23,983	$52,897	$180,230
Disposition of funds:						
Property additions........	$15,552	$22,367	$15,675	$18,809	$23,997	$ 96,400
Preferred stock dividends..	1,298	1,387	1,595	1,595	1,595	7,470
Common stock dividends..	2,950	3,517	3,641	3,641	4,464	18,213
Costs of securities retired..	...	...	...	...	...	...
Payment of short-term						
loans.................	15,200	5,800	12,700	...	22,000	55,700
Increase in other assets						
and debits.............	455	1,395	(690)	57	763	1,980
Total Disposition of						
Funds.............	$35,455	$34,466	$32,921	$24,102	$52,819	$179,763
Increase or (decrease) in						
cash..................	$ 1,805	($ 1,193)	($ 104)	($ 119)	$ 78	$ 467

SOURCE: Annual reports of the company.

Exhibit 4

ROCHESTER GAS AND ELECTRIC CORPORATION

EARNINGS, CASH DIVIDENDS, AND MARKET PRICES PER SHARE OF COMMON STOCK, 1950–59,
ADJUSTED FOR 2,551,076 SHARES OUTSTANDING AT DECEMBER 31, 1959

	1950	1951	1952	1953	1954	1955	1956	1957	1958	1959
Earnings applicable to common stock:										
From operations	$1.08	$1.01	$1.39	$1.70	$1.65	$1.77	$1.99	$2.02	$2.30	$2.91
From tax savings on accelerated depreciation	....	....	....	....	0.02	0.08	0.15	0.23	0.31	0.40
Total	$1.08	$1.01	$1.39	$1.70	$1.67	$1.85	$2.14	$2.25	$2.61	$3.31
Cash dividends*	$0.85	$0.89	$1.00	$1.08	$1.15½	$1.15½	$1.38	$1.42½	$1.42½	$1.75
Percentage of cash payout	78.7%	88.1%	71.9%	63.5%	69.2%	62.4%	64.5%	63.3%	54.6%	52.9%
Market prices†	11⅜	14⅝	16½	20¼	22⅜	26¾	25⅞	25	31	45⅛

* These figures represent total cash dividends divided by 2,551,076 shares.

† Average of the annual high and low market prices.

NOTE.—In the first 6 months of 1960, cash dividends were paid at the annual rate of $1.80 a share. Adjusted to 2,551,076 shares, cash dividends were $1.85½ a share. The average of the high and low market prices for the first 6 months of 1960 was 48 (adjusted to 2,551,076 shares).

SOURCE: Annual reports of the company; Moody's Public Utilities.

Exhibit 5

ROCHESTER GAS AND ELECTRIC CORPORATION

SCHEDULE OF CAPITAL EXPENDITURES, 1955–59, AND
PROJECTED CAPITAL EXPENDITURES, 1960–64
(In Thousands)

Year	Amount
1955	$ 15,552
1956	22,367
1957	15,675
1958	18,809
1959	23,997
Subtotal	$ 96,400
1960	$ 22,700
1961	21,600
1962	18,500
1963	17,800
1964	20,200
Subtotal	$100,800
Grand Total	$197,200

SOURCE: Annual reports and forecasts of the company.

Exhibit 6

ROCHESTER GAS AND ELECTRIC CORPORATION

ESTIMATED SOURCE AND DISPOSITION OF FUNDS, 1960–61
(In Thousands)

	1960	1961
Source of funds:		
Net income:		
From operations	$ 8,519	$ 8,274
From tax savings on accelerated depreciation	1,275	1,431
Depreciation and net salvage	6,600	7,100
Sale of bonds	27	15,000*
Sale of preferred stock	10,000†	...
Sale of common stock	67	...
Proceeds of short-term loans	10,000	4,000
Total Funds	$36,488	$35,805
Disposition of funds:		
Property additions	$22,700	$21,600
Preferred stock dividends	1,956	2,145
Common stock dividends	4,701	4,880‡
Payment of short-term loans	7,000	7,000
Increase in other balance sheet items, net	31	80
Total Disposition of Funds	$36,388	$35,705
Increase in cash	$ 100	$ 100

* This bond issue was tentatively scheduled for the first six months of 1961.
† Private preferred placement was arranged through the First Boston Corporation in New York in May, 1960.
‡ Assuming a stock dividend for year 1960 and the annual cash dividend rate maintained at $1.80 a share.
SOURCE: Forecasts of the company.

Exhibit 7

ROCHESTER GAS AND ELECTRIC CORPORATION

MARKET PERFORMANCE OF COMMON STOCK,
NOVEMBER 16, 1959–JANUARY 14, 1960
(Closing Market Prices)

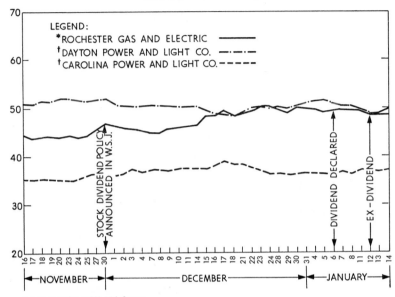

* Adjusted for 2,551,076 shares.
† Regular dividend payments made in cash only.
SOURCE: Daily quotations in *The Wall Street Journal*.

Exhibit 8

ROCHESTER GAS AND ELECTRIC CORPORATION

SELECTED COMPARISONS WITH MOODY'S AVERAGE OF 24 UTILITIES

STOCK PRICE INDEX −1950 EQUAL 100
(AVERAGE OF ANNUAL HIGH AND LOW MARKET PRICES USED FOR ROCHESTER)

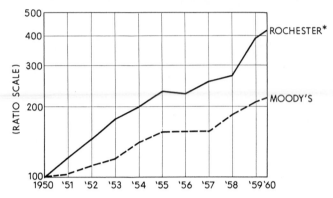

STOCK PRICE INDEX − JULY 2, 1959 EQUALS 100
(CLOSING PRICES USED FOR ROCHESTER COMMON)

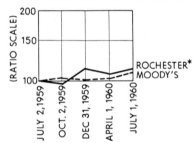

* Adjusted for 2,551,076 shares.
SOURCE: *Moody's Public Utilities;* quotations in *The Wall Street Journal.*

Exhibit 9

ROCHESTER GAS AND ELECTRIC CORPORATION

SELECTED COMPARISONS WITH MOODY'S AVERAGE OF 24 UTILITIES

EARNING PER SHARE INDEX-1951 EQUALS 100

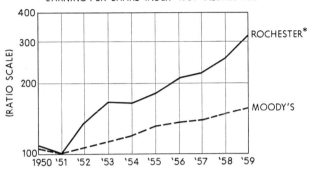

CASH DIVIDENDS PER SHARE INDEX-1950 EQUALS 100

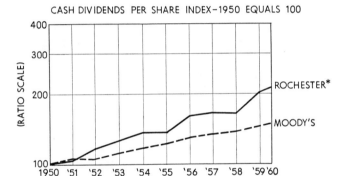

* Adjusted for 2,551,076 shares.
SOURCE: *Moody's Public Utilities.*

Exhibit 10

ROCHESTER GAS AND ELECTRIC CORPORATION

Selected Comparisons with Moody's Average of 24 Utilities

MARKET PRICE* TO EARNINGS RATIO

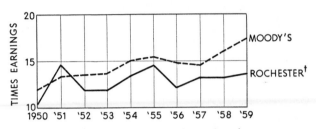

* Average of annual high and low market prices.
† Adjusted for 2,551,076 shares.

CASH DIVIDEND YIELD*

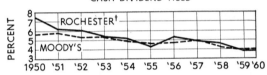

* Based on average of annual high and low market prices.
† Adjusted for 2,551,076 shares.

CASH DIVIDEND TO EARNINGS RATIO

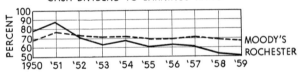

Exhibit 11

ROCHESTER GAS AND ELECTRIC CORPORATION

LETTER RECEIVED FROM BROKERAGE FIRM

COFFIN & BURR, INCORPORATED

INVESTMENT SECURITIES

70 PINE STREET

NEW YORK 5

January 12, 1960

Mr. Ernest Howe, President
Rochester Gas & Electric Co.
89 East Avenue
Rochester 4, New York

DEAR MR. HOWE:

Arthur Retallick tells me that you have not adopted the Commonwealth Edison Stock dividend plan fully, in that you do not give your stockholders the option of selling their stock dividend.

Utility analysts generally have been critical of stock dividends because they merely represented giving the stockholder something he already had. They really amounted only to giving him a small increase in his future cash dividend.

The real virtue of the Commonwealth Edison plan lies in making it *convenient* for the stockholder to sell his stock dividend and so augment his cash income. Of course, even without the stock dividend, he could have put himself in the same position by selling, say, 2% of his stock. Paying a low cash dividend, augmenting this with a stock dividend representing most of the rest of the earnings, and through stock sale arrangements, making it *convenient* for the stockholder to realize much or little of his return in cash, as he desired, constitutes the real advantage of the plan.

Mathematical analysis will show that, with most growing companies, the present value of future dividends varies little with the payout. A high payout gives immediate payments with high present value; a low payout gives higher payments ultimately, but they are in the future, so that present value works out about the same in either case. Whether a stockholder wants high present income and little growth, or low present income and a maximum of growth depends on his particular circumstances. The Chicago plan, with the stock sale arrangement, allows him to do this conveniently, and this, to my mind, is the real argument in its favor.

I will appreciate your comments.

Sincerely,

(*signed*) HUGH PASTORIZA

Exhibit 12

ROCHESTER GAS AND ELECTRIC CORPORATION

RESPONSE TO LETTER FROM BROKERAGE FIRM (EXHIBIT 11)

January 18, 1960

Mr. Hugh Pastoriza
Coffin & Burr, Incorporated
70 Pine Street
New York 5, New York

DEAR MR. PASTORIZA:

. . . .

You are quite right. The Rochester Gas and Electric's cash and stock dividend plan does not provide any special machinery by means of which stockholders may sell whole shares which they have received as the result of the stock dividend. You understand, of course, that this arrangement is made with respect to fractions. We gave very careful consideration to the idea of making special arrangements with the Transfer Agent so that stockholders could return their stock dividend to the Agent, who would arrange for its sale. This is substantially what the Commonwealth Edison Company did.

No doubt you are familiar with the experience of Commonwealth Edison. They have declared two dividends of this type: one in 1958 and another in 1959. In 1958 the number of shares declared as a dividend by Commonwealth Edison is understood to have been 360,505 shares. As it turned out, the number of shares which the stockholders wished to sell was 3,668. This had a market value of about $190,000 at the then current price of $52 per share. I do not have the details as to what happened in 1959, but I am informed that the experience followed the pattern of the preceding year.

In our case, the maximum number of shares which could be involved in the stock dividend is 76,665. If our experience with stockholders wishing to sell was similar to Commonwealth Edison's, the amount of stock which would be handled in this way would be about 770 shares. The total value of these shares would be about $38,000. We could not do a registration for this amount. In other words, it seemed to us that the service was far too expensive for the convenience the plan involves.

If you tell me that a registration should not be involved for such a small amount of stock, I must say that I agree with you fully. However, under the present wording of the statute and the attitude of the Commission and its Staff, it seems clear that this procedure is required.

. . . .

Sincerely yours,

(signed) ERNEST J. HOWE

Exhibit 13

ROCHESTER GAS AND ELECTRIC CORPORATION

LETTER TO STOCKHOLDERS TO ACCOMPANY DIVIDEND PAYMENT

January 23, 1960

To SHAREHOLDERS OF ROCHESTER GAS AND ELECTRIC CORPORATION:

. . . .

FRACTIONAL INTEREST Please read the following information and follow the instructions carefully if an Order Form for Fractional Interest has been enclosed with this letter. It is part of your stock dividend and has value.

The Order Form for Fractional Interest in terms of 100ths of a share has been issued in those cases where computation of the dividend payable results in a fraction.

Your Order Form for Fractional Interest entitles you on or before the close of business *February 26, 1960* to instruct Lincoln Rochester Trust Company, Agent, P.O. Box 1250, Rochester 3, New York, either

(a) to purchase for your account the additional fractional interest required to make up one full share and deliver to you a certificate for that full share upon payment therefor, or

(b) to sell the fractional interest and remit the proceeds to you.

The Agent will execute orders either to buy the required fraction or sell the fraction at prices determined by the Agent in its discretion, based on the then current prevailing market price for the Company's common stock on the New York Stock Exchange. No charge will be made to shareholders for any brokerage commissions, transfer taxes or fees and expenses of Lincoln Rochester Trust Company for any of the services outlined above, all of which the Company has agreed to pay.

A shareholder whose instructions are not received by the Agent prior to the close of business February 26, 1960 shall be deemed to have elected to sell his Fractional Interest, and the Agent will sell such Interest and remit the proceeds to the shareholder. Settlement of all accounts and delivery of stock certificates will be effected by the Agent as promptly as practicable. An envelope for your convenience in mailing your Order Form to the Agent (Lincoln Rochester Trust Company, P.O. Box 1250, Rochester 3, New York) is enclosed.

. . . .

TAX STATUS OF THE STOCK DIVIDEND The Company is advised by its counsel that the receipt of the stock dividend will not result in taxable income to the recipient under the present provisions of the United States Internal Revenue Code. However, if you should sell any of the shares represented by the enclosed stock certificate or any fractional interest in a share to which you are entitled as a result of the stock dividend, such sale may result in capital gain or loss for the year in which the sale is made. If more specific information is desired, it is suggested that your tax advisor be consulted.

. . . .

Sincerely yours,

(signed)   ROBERT E. GINNA   ERNEST J. HOWE
           Chairman of the Board   *President*

Exhibit 14

ROCHESTER GAS AND ELECTRIC CORPORATION

SUMMARY OF SALES OF STOCK DIVIDEND SHARES IN THE FOUR-
MONTH PERIOD, JANUARY 25–MAY 25, 1960

Stock dividend paid 1/25/60: *76,581* shares to *17,035* holders.

Sales:

1. *224* individual stockholders sold *1,325* stock dividend shares. These transactions represented sales of about *1.7%* of the total stock dividend shares issued, and about *4%* of the stock dividend shares issued to individuals.

The sales were made by about *1.3%* of the total number of stockholders, or by about *1.7%* of the individual stockholders.

2. *79* stockholders sold *768* shares, representing sales of both stock dividend shares and part of the stockholders' previous holdings.

3. *240* stockholders sold *2,350* shares, representing sales of both stock dividend shares and all of the stockholders' previous holdings.

4. *190* investment dealers and brokers sold *4,809* stock dividend shares.

5. Less than *9%* of the total stock dividend shares issued were sold for cash by the original holders during the four-month period.

SOURCE: Compiled from stockholder transfer records of the company.

ON THE PROBLEM OF CAPITAL BUDGETING*

By Diran Bodenhorn†

THE PROBLEM OF CAPITAL budgeting is to decide which of the available investment opportunities a firm should accept and which it should reject. To make this decision rationally, the firm must have an objective. The objective which economists usually assume for a firm is profit maximization. In the traditional short-run theory of the firm, capital is fixed, and the firm seeks to maximize its dollar profits. In the long run the firm can either increase or reduce its investment. It will increase investment if investment brings more than the normal rate of return on invested capital; it will reduce investment if it brings less than the normal return on invested capital; and it will maintain investment if it earns the normal return. This is the same as profit maximization if we recognize that the normal rate of return on invested capital represents a cost rather than a profit. The simple rule of profit maximization can then be applied to any investment project: a project should be accepted only if it adds to the profits of the firm after all costs, including the cost of capital, have been met.

In spite of this orientation of traditional theory, recent discussions of the capital-budgeting problem usually assume that the objective is to maximize either (a) the wealth of the owners of the firm or (b) the rate of return that the owners obtain on invested funds. Thus they suggest accepting investment projects which (a) increase the wealth of the owners of the firm or (b) yield a rate of return larger than the normal rate, since the owners would earn the normal rate if they invested elsewhere.

The three criteria—profit maximization, wealth maximization, and rate of return maximization—yield identical results as long as the earnings from the proposed investment projects are the same from year to year and extend forever. Most investment projects, however, are finite and have variable earning streams. It has been demonstrated that, for such projects, the rate of

---

* Reprinted by permission from *The Journal of Finance*, 14 (December 1959), pp. 473–92.

† Professor of Economics, Ohio State University. The author is indebted to many people for helpful comments, criticisms, and suggestions. Special mention must go to Professors Fisher, Segall, Solomon, and Wellisz, although they should not be held in any way responsible for the egregious errors which may remain.

return criterion is unsatisfactory,[1] and we shall not discuss it in this paper. Furthermore, the simple profit maximization criterion becomes ambiguous if profits vary from year to year, since the firm cannot maximize profits in each year. The solution is to use the normal rate of return to determine the present value of the variable future profits and to conclude that a project is profitable if the present value of the profits is greater than zero.

Wealth maximization requires maximizing the difference between the owners' equity in the firm and their investment in the firm. This subtraction is required because an increase in equity which is balanced by owners' investment does not increase owners' wealth, since the investment is part of the owners' wealth whether it is put into the firm or not.[2] Thus the objective is to maximize the capital gain obtained from the owners' investment.

The owners' equity is the present (discounted) value of the future earnings of the firm, whether there is a well-established market for this equity, as for companies whose stocks are traded on the security exchanges, or whether there is no market for the equity, as for most small firms. The owners' wealth will increase only if the present value of the earnings stream is larger than the owners' required investment. If the discount rate used in determining the present value of the earnings stream is the normal rate of return used in determining economic profit, then an investment project will increase the owners' wealth if and only if it yields a profit over and above the normal rate of return. Thus profit maximization and wealth maximization are equivalent.[3]

---

[1] See J. Hirshleifer, "On the Theory of Optimal Investment Decision," *Journal of Political Economy* (August, 1958), pp. 329–52; A. A. Alchian, "The Rate of Interest, Fisher's Rate of Return over Cost, and Keynes' Internal Rate of Return," *American Economic Review* (December, 1955), pp. 938–43; and Ezra Solomon, "The Arithmetic of Capital Budgeting Decisions," *Journal of Business* (April, 1956), pp. 124–29.

The major criticism of the (internal) rate of return is that it assumes that funds which are made available early in the life of the investment can be reinvested to earn the (internal) rate of return for the project as a whole. It may easily be that no such profitable investment opportunity can be found and that, if one can be found, it should be seized whether or not current investment projects make the necessary funds available. Future investment projects are relevant only if they depend upon the current investment project.

[2] Unless, of course, the owners borrow the necessary funds. But even in this case the increment in owners' wealth is the difference between the increased equity and the borrowings.

[3] Assume an investment project which requires an investment of I_0 on the part of the owners of the firm and yields an income stream $x_1, x_2, x_3, \ldots, x_n$. If the normal rate of return is r, then the "profit-maximizing" criterion says to accept the project if

$$\frac{x_1 - rI_0}{1 + r} + \frac{x_2 - rI_0}{(1 + r)^2} + \cdots + \frac{x_n - rI_0 - I_0}{(1 + r)^n} > 0.$$

The present value or present wealth criterion says to accept the project if

$$\frac{x_1}{1 + r} + \frac{x_2}{(1 + r)^2} + \cdots + \frac{x_n}{(1 + r)^n} > I_0.$$

But

$$\frac{rI_0}{1 + r} + \frac{rI_0}{(1 + r)^2} + \frac{rI_0}{(1 + r)^3} + \cdots + \frac{rI_0}{(1 + r)^n} + \frac{I_0}{(1 + r)^n} = I_0,$$

so that the two criteria are the same.

I shall therefore adopt the criterion of wealth maximization as the objective of the firm in its investment decisions.

The capital-budgeting problem is not solved, however, simply by recognizing that the firm should seek to maximize the owners' wealth. The effect of any particular investment project upon the earnings stream of the firm and the (interest) rate at which to discount this stream must both be determined before one can determine the effect on owners' equity. There are differences of opinion among economists about both the specific earnings stream and the specific discount rate to use. There are four earnings streams which have received major attention in the literature: net cash flow, net income, net income plus interest payments, and dividends. Each of these earnings streams has a companion discount rate, but there are unfortunately no standard terms to identify these rates. The purpose of this paper is to examine these four earnings streams, with their discount rates, to determine which is appropriate to the capital-budgeting problem.

I. NET CASH FLOW

The net cash flow[4] associated with an investment project in any year is defined as the difference between the (expected) cash earnings of the enterprise during that year if the project is accepted and the (expected) cash earnings during that year if the project is rejected. Cash earnings are defined as the difference between cash income and cash costs, excluding dividends. The term clearly excludes depreciation and other costs which do not require cash outlays. In assessing an investment project, the net cash flow from the project should be determined for each future year, and the present value of this income stream calculated. The discount rate to be used is the rate of interest at which the firm can either borrow or lend money. An investment project should be accepted if and only if its present value is greater than zero.[5]

This procedure is justified by the assumption that the present value of the firm is the present value of the net cash flows for the firm as a whole, i.e., for all the investment projects of the firm. Any investment project with a positive present value, therefore, adds to the present value of the firm and to the

---

[4] The use of net cash flow is advocated by such authorities as Hirshleifer, *op. cit.*; Joel Dean, "Measuring the Cost of Capital," *Harvard Business Review* (January–February, 1954), pp. 120–30; Ray I. Ruel, "Profitability Index for Investments," *Harvard Business Review* (July–August, 1957), pp. 116–32; George Terborgh, *Business Investment Policy* (Washington, D.C.: Machinery and Allied Products Institute, 1958); and James H. Lorie and Leonard J. Savage, "Three Problems in Capital Rationing," *Journal of Business* (October, 1955), pp. 229–39. Some of these authors, however, advocate the use of the rate of return rather than the present value.

[5] The initial investment in the project involves a cash outlay, and is included in the net cash flows (as a negative flow) according to this definition. Other writers sometimes suggest that the present value of the net cash flow be greater than the initial investment in the project but then exclude the initial investment outlays from the cash flows. These two versions are logically identical.

wealth of the owners. This assumption abstracts from imperfections in the capital market and accompanies the assumption that there is a single "market" rate of interest which can be used to discount any future cash payment. The method of financing the investment is immaterial, because the same interest rate is used whether equity funds or borrowed funds are involved. There is no distinction in this approach between investments financed by stocks, bonds, retained earnings, or funds supplied by a single private owner.

The objective of wealth maximization is easily justified if there is a single market rate of interest; increased wealth permits an owner to increase his consumption in any or all time periods without reducing his consumption in any time period. Increased wealth, therefore, necessarily increases the utility of the individual. Complications arise, however, if there is not a single interest rate but two rates, one which the owner pays if he borrows money and a lower rate which he receives if he lends money. Hirshleifer observes that a single entrepreneur may be better off, when borrowing and lending rates differ, if he chooses investment projects with a view to his own preferred consumption through time and does not base his decisions solely on calculations associated with the market interest rates.[6]

Hirshleifer distinguishes two cases in which this problem may arise. In one he assumes that the entrepreneur can borrow money in unlimited quantities at the borrowing rate and lend in unlimited quantities at the lending rate. The calculation of the present value of investment projects using the borrowing rate might lead the entrepreneur to make investments which would yield an income such that he would want to increase his income (consumption) in later years at the expense of income (consumption) in earlier years, by lending some of his earlier earnings. But the return that he can obtain by lending is lower than the return he can obtain by investing the money in his own firm in projects which earn a rate lower than the borrowing rate but higher than the lending rate. The extent to which he should take advantage of such projects depends on his preferred consumption pattern as well as on the rate of earnings which these projects yield.

In Hirshleifer's second case the difference between the borrowing and the lending rates arises because the borrowing rate increases as more funds are borrowed, while the lending rate remains the same. The marginal cost of capital is therefore higher than the average cost of capital, and a discrepancy between the rate of return which the entrepreneur can earn if he puts money into his own investment projects, instead of lending the money, gives rise to the same type of problem as the one which we have just discussed.

The points which Hirshleifer makes are not unique to capital budgeting. The same situation arises whenever there is a difference between the buying

---

[6] Hirshleifer, *op. cit.*, especially pp. 333–37; see also Friedrich and Vera Lutz, *The Theory of Investment of the Firm* (Princeton, N.J.: Princeton University Press, 1951), and Harry V. Roberts, "Current Problems in the Economics of Capital Budgeting," *Journal of Business* (January, 1957), pp. 12–16, for a discussion of the problems associated with different borrowing and lending rates.

price and the selling price or in any monopoly situation. Consider a farmer who has fixed resources to devote to the production of either wheat or corn. The traditional solution suggests that there are market prices for wheat and for corn, and the farmer should make his production decision so as to maximize his income. Suppose, however, that the price the farmer gets for wheat is one dollar, and he therefore decides to produce only corn. Subsequently, his wife may find that she must pay two dollars to buy wheat. It may then be that the farmer should produce wheat for his domestic consumption, and the amount of wheat which he should produce for this purpose depends on the tastes and preferences of his family, i.e., the amount of wheat which the family desires to consume at various prices. If the farmer is a net seller of wheat, he should use the selling price of one dollar in his production decision, and if he is a net buyer, he should use the buying price of two dollars in his production decision. If he neither buys nor sells, i.e., he produces only for his domestic consumption, then some intermediate price is appropriate for the production decision, and the specification of the price depends upon his utility function.[7] This refinement is not stressed in traditional analysis, presumably because it is not important and not likely to influence the outcome of an analysis.

II. NET INCOME

The problems which arise when there is more than one *borrowing* rate have also received considerable attention. Our discussion will focus on the distinction between stocks (equity capital) and bonds (debt capital), although there are clearly other methods of borrowing money, and each has its own interest rate. This and the next two sections will therefore be concerned with the capital-budgeting problem of a corporation which has two sources of capital, debt and equity.

The criterion of wealth maximization is applied to the stockholders of the corporation and implies maximizing the price of the stock the day before it goes *ex dividend*.[8] For the corporation, then, the investment criterion is to accept projects which increase the value of the stock, and much of the discussion is therefore concerned with the problem of stock valuation. The theories of stock valuation which we shall discuss assume that the price of

---

[7] In the monopoly case, traditional analysis assumes that the entrepreneur is interested in maximizing the profits of the firm. The entrepreneur, in his role as consumer, is then implicitly assumed to buy the product of his firm at market prices. This, however, does not maximize the utility of the monopolist, since the marginal cost to the monopolist of producing this commodity is lower than the price he pays when he makes his consumption decision. He could increase his utility by permitting himself to buy at marginal costs. This would increase his consumption and therefore the level of output, which would then depend upon the amount which he desires to consume, i.e., upon his utility function.

[8] The presumption is that the price of the stock drops by the amount of the dividend when it goes *ex dividend*, but the wealth of the stockholders on this date consists of the value of the stock plus the dividend. We shall have a few comments to make about the effects of dividend policy below but wish to avoid that problem at this time.

stock depends primarily upon (1) net income, (2) net income plus interest, and (3) dividend payments. These theories naturally suggest evaluating investment projects according to their effects upon that particular earnings stream which determines stock price. This is really no different from the net cash flow approach which we have just discussed, since that approach assumes that the present value of the firm—which, for a corporation, is the value of the stock—depends upon the net cash flow to the firm.

We shall discuss three approaches which use net income. The first two, put forth by Ezra Solomon in the *Journal of Business*[9] and by Modigliani and Zeman in the *Conference on Research in Business Finance*,[10] do not contain complete theories of stock prices but assume that stockholders gain if their stock increases its earnings per share. The last approach, that of David Durand,[11] does contain an explicit and complete theory of stock evaluation.

Solomon assumes that there exists at any time a net price[12] which a company can get for issuing stock and an interest rate which it must pay if it issues bonds. An investment project should be undertaken if and only if it increases the net earnings per share of stock outstanding, over what the earnings per share would be if the project were rejected. He then defines the cost of equity capital for a firm as the per share earnings if the investment project is rejected, divided by the net price of stock. If a project which is to be financed with equity capital earns more than this, it raises the per share earnings and should be accepted. He emphasizes that the cost of capital increases as investment opportunities are accepted, since each accepted project must have higher earnings per share than the average for the company as a whole and so raises the average earnings per share and therefore the cost of equity capital. Thus a project which would be acceptable if it were the first to be considered may become unacceptable if other projects are accepted first and raise the cost of equity capital.

It should be noted that Solomon is assuming that the price of new shares is independent of the investment decisions that the firm is making. If accepting the investment projects does increase the per share earnings of the firm, then this should increase the price of the shares, thereby reducing the cost of equity capital. A project may be unacceptable at one time because the cost of equity capital has been raised severely by superior projects which the management has under consideration. However, this same project may subsequently become acceptable if these superior investment projects raise the price of shares and lower the cost of equity capital. In order to predict the future cost

---

[9] "Measuring a Company's Cost of Capital," *Journal of Business*, Vol. XXVIII (October, 1955).

[10] (New York: National Bureau of Economic Research, 1952). Their paper is entitled "The Effect of the Availability of Funds, and the Terms Thereof, on Business Investment."

[11] "Costs of Debt and Equity Funds for Business: Trends and Problems of Measurement," in *Conference on Research in Business Finance* (New York: National Bureau of Economic Research, 1952).

[12] Net of flotation costs.

of equity capital, we would need a complete theory of stock prices, which Solomon does not provide.

Some projects, however, can be financed in part by the issue of bonds, and the bond rate of interest is usually lower than the cost of equity capital. Therefore, debt-financed projects can have lower earnings than equity-financed projects and still increase average earnings per share. The problem, therefore, is to decide how to finance each project. Solomon suggests that bonds can be issued by the firm only if the firm does not exceed a critical debt-to-equity ratio deemed safe by the bondholders. He implies that debt funds cannot be obtained by the firm at any price if this debt-to-equity ratio is exceeded. Thus there is a maximum debt-to-equity ratio which the firm could achieve if it were to reject all investment opportunities. There is also a maximum amount of additional debt that bondholders would accept on the basis of any new investment project, and the rest of the funds must be obtained by equity financing. The combined cost of capital using both sources of funds therefore varies from project to project and is the rate of earnings which the project must obtain in order to pay the interest on the new bonds and to maintain the earnings per share of the stock. The cost of capital for any project is a weighted average of the interest rate on bonds and the cost of equity capital, with the weights depending on the proportion of bonds that the firm can issue in support of the project.

The investment criterion suggested by Solomon's analysis is that the net income from proposed projects be discounted at the cost of capital for that project and be accepted if the present value of this income exceeds the investment cost of the project.[13] We are, however, avoiding a crucial part of the problem until we explain how the bondholders determine the maximum debt-equity ratio, since Solomon suggests that this ratio determines the cost of capital. A general theory which relates the debt-equity ratio to the interest rate for debt capital and to the price of equity issues is really required. We shall see, however, in our subsequent discussion of theories of stock price that the common solution to the problem is to assume that unlimited quantities of debt can be issued at the going market rate of interest.

Modigliani and Zeman handle the problem somewhat differently. They assume that the rate at which stockholders discount future earnings depends on the risk which the stockholders bear and that this risk depends on the amount of debt outstanding. The cost of capital (the rate at which future earnings should be discounted) is again a weighted average of the cost of equity capital and the bond rate of interest, but the proportion of bonds which can be issued in support of any project depends upon the risk to the stockholders rather than the risk to the bondholders. In fact, bonds are assumed to be entirely riskless, no matter how many are issued, and the firm can issue bonds in unlimited quantities at the going rate of interest. Management refrains from financing all projects exclusively with bonds only because

---

[13] The investment cost is not deducted from net income, as it is in the case of the cash flow, so that the present value must be greater than this cost instead of greater than zero.

this would increase the risk to stockholders. Since Modigliani and Zeman do not present a theory of the relationship between risk and stock price, they conclude that the management of the firm makes its financing decision on the basis of its attitudes toward risk rather than with a view to maximizing the price of the stock.

David Durand presents a simple theory of stock price: the value of the stock is the discounted value of the net income of the firm, and the discount rate is independent of the amount of debt outstanding.[14] A firm can determine the appropriate discount rate by dividing the earnings per share by the price per share[15] and should accept any project for which the present value of the net income exceeds the initial investment outlay. The effect of the investment project on net income depends upon the source of financing because of tax considerations and because interest is a cost, while dividends are not a cost. This theory implies, therefore, that the present value of an investment project is always higher if it is debt-financed than if it is equity-financed and that the stockholder will benefit if all projects are financed exclusively by debt.

III. NET OPERATING INCOME

Since it is obvious that some projects are financed with equity funds, Durand suggests an alternative theory of stock evaluation which we shall call the "net operating income theory."

Net operating income is defined as income after tax plus interest payments on debt. The theory states that net operating income is capitalized at a rate which depends on the asset structure and riskiness of the business, to determine the total investment value of the firm. Total investment value is defined as the value of the stocks plus the value of the bonds. The theory says that the capitalization rate is independent of the investment and the financing decisions of the firm, so that the same capitalization rate is used in determining total investment value both before and after these decisions have been made. Therefore, a firm can determine the capitalization rate, which we have been calling the "discount rate" or the "cost of capital," by dividing its net operating income by its total investment value, as determined in the market. An investment opportunity should be accepted if the expected increase in net operating income will cause an increase in total investment value large enough to cover the required financing, i.e., if the present value of the net operating income associated with the project exceeds the investment cost of the project.

The presumption is that only those investment projects which increase stock price should be undertaken, whether the net income theory or the net operating income theory is used. These two theories differ in their predictions of the effects of investment and financing decisions on the price of stock. For

---

[14] It should be emphasized that Durand only *presents* this theory; he does not *advocate* it.

[15] Corrected for flotation costs.

stock-financed investments the resulting increases in the net income and in the net operating income of the firm are the same. However, the net operating income theory discounts the increased earnings at a lower rate than does the net income theory[16] and therefore predicts a larger increase in stock price. It is possible, therefore, for the net operating income theory to predict that the stock price will increase, while the net income theory predicts that the stock price will fall. In such a case the net operating income theory would tell us to make the investment, while the net income theory would tell us that the investment was unprofitable.

The big difference between the theories, however, arises when we consider debt financing. The net operating theory implies that there is a slight advantage to the corporation for debt financing rather than equity financing.[17] Since net operating income includes interest on debt, the net operating income of the company would not be influenced by the financing decision, if it were not for the impact of the corporate income tax. The effect of this tax, however, is to increase net operating income somewhat if debt financing is used, over what it would be if stock financing were used, because interest payments are deductible for tax purposes. This leads to the rather disturbing conclusion that an increase in the bond rate reduces the cost of debt capital (i.e., the rate of return which an investment project must earn in order to be profitable), since debt financing then has a larger tax effect and a larger effect on net operating income. This is true if we stick by the basic assumption that the rate at which net operating income is discounted is not affected by investment or financing decisions. Clearly, this is incorrect, and a theory ought to be developed which ties together the bond rate of interest and the rate at which net operating income is discounted, perhaps by having these two rates depend upon the same set of market forces.

The net income theory, however, suggests a strong preference for debt financing, since the net income and therefore the value of the stock will rise if a debt-financed investment contributes anything at all to earnings above the interest charges on the debt. Thus the net income theory says that debt financing is cheaper than the net operating income theory says it is, and so it would suggest accepting investment projects for debt financing which the net operating theory would reject.

This means that the net operating income theory implies that the total investment value of a company rises very slowly if the company uses debt financing rather than equity financing.[18] The net income theory, however,

---

[16] The ratio of net operating income to total investment value will be smaller than the ratio of net income to total stock value for any firm for which the bond rate of interest is smaller than the earnings rate on stock. The ratio of net operating income to total investment value is a weighted average of the earnings rate on stock and the rate of interest on bonds, with the weights suggested by the debt-to-equity ratio.

[17] The firm would be indifferent as to financing methods if there were no corporate income tax.

[18] The net operating income theory would suggest that the total investment value is independent of the method of financing if it were not for the corporate income tax.

suggests that the total investment value of the company increases rapidly if debt financing is used rather than equity financing.

Modigliani and Miller[19] present an interesting theoretical justification for the net operating income theory. They state that this theory must be correct because otherwise investors would be paying two different prices for identical income streams. It is easiest to illustrate this idea in terms of a numerical example. Assume that there are two companies with identical net operating incomes and with the same risk attached to their incomes. One of these companies has no debt, while the other is financed 50 per cent by debt and 50 per cent by equity. Modigliani and Miller argue that these two companies will have identical total investment value because of arbitrage operations which are possible if the two are unequal.

Assume that both companies have net operating incomes of $2,000 per year and that the total investment value of the equity company, i.e., the value of its stock, is $20,000. Arbitrage will be possible if the total investment value of the debt company is different from $20,000—say, $22,000—with $11,000 of debt paying $550 interest each year and $11,000 of stock. Consider an individual who owns 10 per cent of the stock of the debt company. He has an investment of $1,100 which entitles him to an income stream of one-tenth of the net operating income, less one-tenth of the interest payment, i.e., $200 less $55, or $145 per year. Suppose that he sold his stock and borrowed enough money to buy 10 per cent of the equity company. He would need a total of $2,000, so that he must borrow $900. We introduce the assumption that all borrowers pay the same rate (5 per cent) of interest on bonds, so that the investor can borrow $900 at an interest cost of $45 per year. By investing his $2,000 in the equity company, he obtains an income stream of $200 per year less $45 per year interest, or $155 per year. He will prefer this income to the alternative of $145, no matter what his attitude toward risk, because the risk associated with the $200 of net operating income is the same for both companies, by assumption. The interest payments of $55 by the firm or $45 by the individual investor must be made (i.e., no risk), no matter who issues the debt. Therefore, the same risk is associated with the $155 income as with the $145 income and the investor will prefer the higher income stream.

The investor, therefore, will sell his stock in the debt company and buy stock in the equity company, just as long as the total investment value of the equity company is smaller than that of the debt company.[20] This sale and purchase will lower the price of the debt company's stock and also the total investment value of that company, while it raises the stock price and the total investment value of the equity company. This arbitrage continues until the total investment values of the two companies are equal.

---

[19] "The Cost of Capital, Corporation Finance, and the Theory of Investment," *American Economic Review*, Vol. LXVIII (June, 1958).

[20] This example assumes no corporate income tax. Tax considerations make the argument slightly more complicated but do not change its basic structure.

There are four points at which this analysis can be questioned:

1. The corporation may be able to borrow at a lower interest rate than the investor, or vice versa.

2. The individual investor may not consider that the risk he runs when a corporation issues bonds is as great as the risk he runs when he issues bonds himself. One of the basic attributes of corporate stock is limited liability, which provides that the stockholder is not liable for bonds issued by the corporation. The same situation would not ordinarily obtain if he were to issue the debt in his own name, and that is one reason why the bond rate of interest might differ for corporations and private individuals. This problem could be avoided if the bondholder accepted the total amount of stock which the individual investor owns in the equity company as collateral for the loan and agreed to limit the liability of the investor to the value of this collateral. It is unlikely, however, that a bondholder would be willing to do this, since he would be in a stronger position if he loaned the money directly to the company. Even if he could get these terms, an investor might easily prefer an income stream of $200 of net operating income from a company less $50 interest for which the company is liable, to an income stream of $200 net operating income less $50 interest for which he is personally liable, particularly since the corporation might not pay enough dividends in a poor year for the investor to meet the interest payment. The exactness of the substitutability of the two income streams is of vital importance, since it is the core of the arbitrage argument. If the two income streams are not identical, then one may be preferred to the other,[21] and a price differential cannot be ruled out by arbitrage.

3. It may not make sense to assume that two firms with different financial structures have the same risk. This objection is not too serious as long as there is no corporate income tax, but, if we consider this tax, the theory suggests that the total investment value should depend upon the net (of tax) operating income. Consider, then, two firms with the same net operating income but with different debt. The firm with the larger debt would have larger interest payments, lower income taxes, and therefore a lower operating income gross of tax. It is reasonable to assume, however, that the gross operating income of a firm varies directly with the total assets of the firm, so that the firm with the larger gross operating income should also have larger total assets. Therefore, the corporation with the larger debt and the smaller gross operating income should have smaller total assets than the other firm. The lower level of assets, however, would suggest a somewhat greater degree of risk associated with the income stream, and this is contrary to the original assumption.[22]

---

[21] My argument suggests that the investor would prefer to have the corporation issue the debt.

[22] If the firm with the smaller gross operating income does not have a smaller level of total assets, then it is using its assets less efficiently than the other firm, and this also suggests a somewhat greater risk in investing in the firm.

4. Modigliani and Miller assume that the total amount of risk associated with the net operating income is independent of the financing, since risk is a function only of the variability of the earnings stream and this variability is unaffected by the financial structure. Financial writers, however, frequently use the ratio of debt charges to net operating income as a measure of risk, because they are interested in the probability that the net income will be negative and that the firm cannot meet its fixed charges. The probability of a loss is clearly increased by debt issues, so that this measure of the risk is increased when debt is issued. Since debt financing also increases the risk to the bondholders, issuing debt should increase both the bond rate and the discount rate on equity earnings. Equity financing, on the other hand, should reduce the risk to both debt and equity holders and therefore reduce both discount rates. Such a relationship, of course, would raise the cost of debt financing as compared to equity financing and would explain why equity financing is sometimes used.

IV. DIVIDENDS

The dividend payout is not relevant for any of the theories so far mentioned. These theories maintain that the dividend payout does not influence the wealth of the stockholder, since a rationally managed corporation will not retain earnings unless this will result in an equivalent increase in the value of its stock. If we ignore tax considerations, the stockholder's wealth is the same whether he gets a dividend or a capital gain on his stock, and he can sell the appropriate proportion of his stock if he wishes to convert the capital gain to present income. The income stream from his remaining stock will be equivalent to the stream that he would have received had the dividend been paid out. However, the capital gains tax is generally lower than the personal income tax on dividends, and so a conflict of interest between stockholders in different tax brackets and between stockholders and management can arise with respect to the dividend payout.

M. J. Gordon and E. Shapiro[23] develop a theory of stock price based on dividend payments. They assume that the value of a stock is equal to the present (discounted) value of the dividends which will subsequently be declared on the stock. By implication, they assume that the discount rate is the same no matter how much debt the firm has incurred and so employ a net income type of theory. They could adopt a net operating income type of theory by assuming that the rate at which dividends are discounted depends on the debt-equity ratio. The authors, however, do not discuss the debt-equity problem.

They assume further (1) that the firm will always retain the same proportion, b, of its net income and (2) that the firm will always earn the same average net income, r, on each dollar of retained earnings. Dividends there-

---

[23] "Capital Equipment Analysis: The Required Rate of Profit," *Management Science* (October, 1956).

fore grow at the annual rate br. The price of the stock is equal to the discounted value of these growing dividends, using the discount rate, k. This is mathematically equivalent to assuming that the current dividend will not grow and discounting it at a rate k—br.[24] Thus we must assume that the rate of growth of the dividend (br) is smaller than the discount rate (k), or the price of the stock would be infinite.

This analysis is unsatisfactory because it assumes that the discount rate, k, the rate of return on retained earnings, r, and the proportion of earnings retained, b, are independent of one another. If the earnings rate is larger than the discount rate, then the firm could make the price of stock infinite by an appropriate choice of the proportion of income retained. Thus the earnings rate must be less than, or equal to, the discount rate. But if the earnings rate is smaller than the discount rate, the capital gain to the stockholders from retained earnings would be smaller than the amount of earnings retained, and retaining earnings would reduce their wealth, were it not for the tax considerations just discussed.

Gordon and Shapiro recognize, however, that the earnings rate depends upon the proportion of earnings retained and that this proportion is controlled by the firm. They turn to the question of how the management should determine the proportion of earnings to retain, which is the capital-budgeting problem. The crucial assumptions are that the proportion of earnings retained will be the same each year and that the rate of earnings on these retained earnings will also be the same each year and depends only on the proportion of earnings retained. They conclude that earnings should be retained until the marginal rate of return on earnings is equal to k, the rate at which future dividends are discounted.[25]

Since Gordon and Shapiro assume that dividends are a fixed proportion of net income, it makes no difference whether they discount the net income

---

[24] If Y_0 is the current net income, then the current dividend, D_0, is $(1\text{-}b)Y_0$. The current price, P_0, is

$$P_0 = Y_0\left(\frac{1-b}{k-rb}\right) = \frac{D_0}{k-rb}.$$

[25] This conclusion is incorrect. Maximizing the price of the stock on these assumptions requires additional investment, with the marginal rate of return somewhat lower than k. If r is a function of b and we choose b to maximize P_0, then we get

$$r + b\frac{dr}{db} = \frac{k-rb}{1-b}.$$

The left-hand side of this equation is the marginal rate of return on retained earnings, and the right-hand side is less than k.

This is because the assumption that r is a function of b implies that, in the neighborhood of equilibrium, additional investment this year increases the average rate of return on any given dollar investment next year. Thus it pays to make "unprofitable" investments, i.e., investments which yield less than k, this year because of the additional return which can thereby be obtained on future investments. Their conclusion would be correct if they had assumed that the rate of return on retained earnings in any year is independent of the volume of retained earnings in any other year, i.e., depends only on the volume of retained earnings in the year when the earnings are retained.

stream or the dividend stream, provided that they make the appropriate adjustment in the discount rate. Their theory can be interpreted as saying that the net income stream from a proposed investment project should be discounted to determine the effect of the proposed investment on the wealth of the stockholders and would be identical with the net income theory of Durand, except that Gordon and Shapiro suggest the use of a higher discount rate.

This higher rate does not arise because Gordon and Shapiro discount dividends rather than net income but because they make a different assumption about the level of future net income. The net income theory implicitly assumes that retained earnings will earn a rate of return equal to the discount rate, so that the resulting increase in stock value (capital gain) will be equal to the retained earnings.[26] They recognize, however, that the average rate of earnings on retained earnings is larger than the discount rate,[27] and therefore they project larger future net incomes. Since they think that the market sets the current price by discounting a larger future income stream than is suggested by the net income theory, they must also think that the market is using a higher discount rate.[28]

V. CONCLUSIONS

We have theories which suggest that (1) the net operating income, (2) the net income, and (3) the dividend streams should be discounted in determining the value of stock and (4) the net cash flows should be discounted in determining the present value of a firm. In capital budgeting we are interested in determining the effect of a particular investment decision on the value of the stock or of the firm, since this determines the effect of the decision upon the owners' wealth. Therefore, management must use the same income stream and the same discount rate in calculating the value of an investment project

---

[26] In the notation which we have been using, the net income theory says

$$P_0 = \frac{Y_0}{k}.$$

This is consistent with the Gordon-Shapiro theory if we assume $r = k$. Their analysis then says

$$P_0 = \frac{Y_0(1-b)}{k-br} = \frac{Y_0(1-b)}{k-kb} = \frac{Y_0(1-b)}{k(1-b)} = \frac{Y_0}{k}.$$

[27] If investment projects are selected so that the marginal rate of return on retained earnings is equal to the discount rate, then the average rate of return on retained earnings must be higher than this.

[28] If current net income is Y_0 and the price is P_0, the net income theory says that the discount rate is Y_0/P_0. Gordon and Shapiro say that the discount rate, k, can be obtained from the equation

$$P_0 = Y_0 \left(\frac{1-b}{k-rb} \right),$$

so that $k = Y_0/P_0 + b(r - Y_0/P_0)$. If $r > Y_0/P_0$, then $k > Y_0/P_0$.

that the market uses in determining the value of stock. Otherwise, management may accept an investment project on the assumption that it has a
positive present value and will increase the value of the stock when the market
will decide that this same investment project has a negative present value, so
that the stock price will fall.

These four income streams, however, can be reconciled. Consider, first, net
income and net operating income, which differ by the interest payments to
debt holders. For any level of net income, the stockholders do not care how
large the interest payments are, except insofar as these payments influence the
riskiness of the net income stream. Thus the conflict is not really between two
income streams but between two discount rates. The net income theory
suggests that the discount rate which stockholders apply to their earnings is
independent of the amount of debt outstanding, while the net operating
income theory suggests that this discount rate is a linear function of the
debt-to-equity ratio.[29] We conclude that stockholders are interested in net
income and leave open the question of the rate at which this income should be
discounted.

The dispute between net income and dividends should be settled in favor of
dividends. Consider a firm with a net income of $100 the first year, of which
it retains $50 and pays $50 in dividends, so that net income in subsequent
years is $105. The net income theory says that the value of this stock is the
present value of $100 this year plus $105 next year and in perpetuity. This,
however, constitutes double counting of the $50 of retained earnings and the
resulting $5 a year addition to the income stream. The correct present value of
the firm is the value of $100 this year less the $50 which is retained, so that
there is only $50 this year, and plus the $105 which will be earned in each
subsequent year. Thus the value of the stock is the present value of the net
income stream minus the present value of retained earnings. But net income
less retained earnings is dividends, so that we are really discounting the
dividend stream.

This still leaves us with a conflict between dividends and net cash flows,
and again we find that these ideas are essentially the same. The one approach
discounts the cash flows to the stockholders, while the other discounts the cash
flows to the firm. While it is customary to think of the firm as deciding how
much of the net income should be distributed and how much should be
reinvested in the firm, this assumes that the firm will reinvest all the funds
made available through depreciation and other non-cash costs. This, however,
is not necessary. The firm could pay dividends equal to the net cash flows
generated in any year. Such a policy would eventually result in the dissolution
of the firm and is not likely to be followed. In principle, however, the decision
to reinvest or to distribute to stockholders applies to the total net cash flow to
the firm in any year, and this is the flow which should be discounted in
determining the present value of an investment project, and the net cash flow

---

[29] See Modigliani and Miller, *op. cit.*, p. 271.

less any reinvested funds should be discounted to obtain the value of the stock.

We can illustrate these ideas more clearly if we assume a firm which always pays out all its net income in dividends and raises funds for new investments by issuing stock.[30] It has current net income of Y_0 and would earn this same net income each year in perpetuity if it did not make additional investments. It is going to raise the sum I_0 today for investment purposes and earn a net income of r_0I_0 on this investment each year in perpetuity. Its net income for the coming year will therefore be $Y_0 + r_0I_0$. At the end of the year it is going to pay a dividend of $Y_0 + r_0I_0$ and is going to raise the sum I_1 for investment purposes. The earnings on this investment will be an annual net income of r_1I_1 in perpetuity. At the end of the second year, the firm will raise I_2 and thereafter increase its annual net income by r_2I_2, and so on. If the market exercises perfect foresight for n years and discounts future dividends at the rate k, then the current total value of the stock, S_0, then will be

$$S_0 = \frac{Y_0}{k} + \frac{I_0(r_0 - k)}{k} + \frac{I_1(r_1 - k)}{k(1 + k)} + \frac{I_2(r_2 - k)}{k(1 + k)^2} + \ldots + \frac{I_n(r_n - k)}{k(1 + k)^n}.$$

This is the present value of the current net income plus the present value of the *net* capital gains[31] which will be obtained from future investment projects. Maximizing S_0 requires that the firm choose each successive increment of investment, I_n, so that the marginal rate of return on (dollar) investment equals the discount rate, k, provided that the average earnings rate on each year's investment depends only on that year's investment (and not on previous or subsequent years' investments).[32]

In the real world, of course, the market would not exercise perfect foresight. It would have to make guesses about future net capital gains based upon past performance and estimates of future developments. This, however,

---

[30] It would make no difference whether the firm raised new money by retaining earnings or issuing stock if it were not for tax considerations and flotation costs. It is convenient to ignore these problems for the present and introduce them later.

[31] If we invest the amount I_n, the total value of the stock should rise by at least I_n. If it rises by more than I_n, this is a *net* capital gain. If we obtain a net income of r_nI_n in each year, then the investment projects have a value of r_nI_n/k, and the capital gain is

$$\frac{r_nI_n}{k} - I_n. \qquad \text{or} \qquad \frac{I_n(r_n - k)}{k}.$$

Since this capital gain will not be obtained until we make the investment in the year n, it has a present value of

$$\frac{I_n(r_n - k)}{k(1 + k)_n}.$$

[32] The Gordon-Shapiro assumption that the rate of earnings depends on the proportion of earnings retained violates this assumption. It implies that current investments make future investments more profitable and so suggests more current investment. If we assume that current investment makes future investments less profitable, we would want to invest less and make the marginal rate of return on (dollar) investment greater than k.

is immaterial for the capital-budgeting decision: the best the firm can do is to accept projects which have a present value greater than zero when the net cash flows are discounted at the rate of k. If the market has predicted that the firm will be able to find more profitable investments than it can find, the price of the stock will fall, but there is nothing the firm can do about this. It will minimize the drop in price by continuing to use the same criterion for investment decisions.

The financing decision complicates the picture in two ways. First, it influences the average rate of return, r_i, that the firm can earn on its investments in year i. Second, it influences the discount rate, k, so that this rate must be considered as a variable, and maximizing S_0 becomes a more formidable task.

We can see the effect of the variable discount rate if we rewrite our equation as follows:[33]

$$S_0 = -I_0 + \frac{Y_1 - I_1}{1 + k_1} + \frac{Y_2 - I_2}{(1 + k_2)^2} + \frac{Y_3 - I_3}{(1 + k_3)^3} + \cdots$$

This equation says that the current value of the stock is the present value of the net cash flows to stockholders, discounted at the rate appropriate to that year. In any year, n, the firm pays in dividends Y_n and raises I_n (a negative cash flow from the point of view of stockholders), so that the net cash flow is $Y_n - I_n$. It makes no difference, except for taxes and flotation costs, whether the firm actually pays Y_n and then borrows I_n, or whether it pays only $Y_n - I_n$ and borrows nothing.

We can also look upon Y_n as the net cash flow, including depreciation and other non-cash costs, instead of as net income. Then I_n is the total amount reinvested by the firm during the year, including depreciation, i.e., it is gross rather than net investment. As long as the firm never pays out in dividends more than its current net income, this makes no difference arithmetically, but it is important conceptually to get away from the idea that an investment project earns the same net income in perpetuity. Projects have limited life-spans, and the funds made available through depreciation[34] are not necessarily put back into the same project or into other projects with the same earning power. It is therefore important for us to estimate the net cash flows created by projects financed by depreciation funds, as well as the flows created by projects financed by new funds.

This formulation also permits us to handle the personal income tax and flotation costs quite easily. We add any flotation costs to I_n[35] and subtract personal income taxes from Y_n. The capital gains tax is more complicated because it depends upon when the capital gain is realized, and whether or not

---

[33] The first term is $-I_0$ because we are calculating the value after the dividend, Y_0, is paid and before the sum I_0 is raised. If we calculated the value before the dividend was paid, then the first term would be $Y_0 - I_0$, and the equation would be more symmetrical.

[34] Another advantage of this formulation is that it is not necessary to estimate depreciation year by year, which must be done if net income is to be estimated.

[35] We use the investment net of tax, however, in estimating future cash flows.

the firm can find sufficient investment opportunities so that it is profitable to raise funds in the open market.[36]

Our conclusion is, therefore, that the net cash flow is the relevant earnings stream to use in capital budgeting because this is the earnings stream which influences stockholders' wealth. The rate at which this stream should be discounted and the effect of the financing decisions on this discount rate are the most important problems that need to be solved.

---

[36] Once we introduce personal taxes and flotation costs, all internal funds should be exhausted before any borrowing is done.

CORPORATE INCOME TAXES AND THE COST OF CAPITAL*

By Franco Modigliani† and Merton H. Miller‡

THE PURPOSE of this communication is to correct an error in our paper "The Cost of Capital, Corporation Finance and the Theory of Investment" (this *Review*, June 1958). In our discussion of the effects of the present method of taxing corporations on the valuation of firms, we said (p. 272):

The deduction of interest in computing taxable corporate profits will prevent the arbitrage process from making the value of all firms in a given class proportional to the expected returns generated by their physical assets. Instead, it can be shown (by the same type of proof used for the original version of Proposition I) that *the market values of firms in each class must be proportional in equilibrium to their expected returns net of taxes (that is, to the sum of the interest paid and expected net stockholder income)*. (Italics added.)

The statement in italics, unfortunately, is wrong. For even though one firm may have an *expected* return after taxes (our $\bar{X}^\tau$) twice that of another firm in the same risk-equivalent class, it will not be the case that the *actual* return after taxes (our X^τ) of the first firm will always be twice that of the second, if the two firms have different degrees of leverage.[1] And since the distribution of returns after taxes of the two firms will not be proportional, there can be no "arbitrage" process which forces their values to be proportional to their expected after-tax returns.[2] In fact, it can be shown—and this time it really will be shown—that "arbitrage" will make values within any class a function not only of expected after-tax returns, but of the tax rate and the degree of lever-

---

* Reprinted by permission from *The American Economic Review*, 53 (June 1963), pp. 433–43.

† Professor of Industrial Management, Massachusetts Institute of Technology.

‡ Edward Eagle Brown Professor of Finance and Economics, University of Chicago.

[1] With some exceptions, which will be noted when they occur, we shall preserve here both the notation and the terminology of the original paper. A working knowledge of both on the part of the reader will be presumed.

[2] Barring, of course, the trivial case of universal linear utility functions. Note that in deference to Professor Durand (see his Comment on our paper and our reply, this *Review*, Sept. 1959, *49*, pp. 639–69) we here and throughout use quotation marks when referring to arbitrage.

age. This means, among other things, that the tax advantages of debt financing are somewhat greater than we originally suggested and, to this extent, the quantitative difference between the valuations implied by our position and by the traditional view is narrowed. It still remains true, however, that under our analysis the tax advantages of debt are the *only* permanent advantages so that the gulf between the two views in matters of interpretation and policy is as wide as ever.

I. TAXES, LEVERAGE, AND THE PROBABILITY DISTRIBUTION OF AFTER-TAX RETURNS

To see how the distribution of after-tax earnings is affected by leverage, let us again denote by the random variable X the (long-run average) earnings before interest and taxes generated by the currently owned assets of a given firm in some stated risk class, k.[3] From our definition of a risk class it follows that X can be expressed in the form $\bar{X}Z$, where $\bar{X}$ is the expected value of X, and the random variable $Z = X/\bar{X}$, having the same value for all firms in class k, is a drawing from a distribution, say $f_k(Z)$. Hence the random variable X^τ, measuring the after-tax return, can be expressed as:

$$X^\tau = (1 - \tau)(X - R) + R = (1 - \tau)X + \tau R = (1 - \tau)\bar{X}Z + \tau R \qquad (1)$$

where τ is the marginal corporate income tax rate (assumed equal to the average), and R is the interest bill. Since $E(X^\tau) \equiv \bar{X}^\tau = (1 - \tau)\bar{X} + \tau R$ we can substitute $\bar{X}^\tau - \tau R$ for $(1 - \tau)\bar{X}$ in (1) to obtain:

$$X^\tau = (\bar{X}^\tau - \tau R)Z + \tau R = \bar{X}^\tau \left(1 - \frac{\tau R}{\bar{X}^\tau}\right)Z + \tau R . \qquad (2)$$

Thus, if the tax rate is other than zero, the shape of the distribution of X^τ will depend not only on the "scale" of the stream $\bar{X}^\tau$ and on the distribution of Z, but also on the tax rate and the degree of leverage (one measure of which is $R/\bar{X}^\tau$). For example, if Var $(Z) = \sigma^2$, we have:

$$\mathbf{Var}\ (X^\tau) = \sigma^2(\bar{X}^\tau)^2 \left(1 - \tau \frac{R}{\bar{X}^\tau}\right)^2$$

---

[3] Thus our X corresponds essentially to the familiar EBIT concept of the finance literature. The use of EBIT and related "income" concepts as the basis of valuation is strictly valid only when the underlying real assets are assumed to have perpetual lives. In such a case, of course, EBIT and "cash flow" are one and the same. This was, in effect, the interpretation of X we used in the original paper and we shall retain it here both to preserve continuity and for the considerable simplification it permits in the exposition. We should point out, however, that the perpetuity interpretation is much less restrictive than might appear at first glance. Before-tax cash flow and EBIT can also safely be equated even where assets have finite lives as soon as these assets attain a steady state age distribution in which annual replacements equal annual depreciation. The subject of finite lives of assets will be further discussed in connection with the problem of the cut-off rate for investment decisions.

implying that for given $\bar{X}^\tau$ the variance of after-tax returns is smaller, the higher τ and the degree of leverage.[4]

II. THE VALUATION OF AFTER-TAX RETURNS

Note from equation (1) that, from the investor's point of view, the long-run average stream of after-tax returns appears as a sum of two components: (1) an uncertain stream $(1 - \tau)\bar{X}Z$; and (2) a sure stream τR.[5] This suggests that the equilibrium market value of the combined stream can be found by capitalizing each component separately. More precisely, let ρ^τ be the rate at which the market capitalizes the expected returns net of tax of an unlevered company of size $\bar{X}$ in class k, i.e.,

$$\rho^\tau = \frac{(1 - \tau)\bar{X}}{V_U} \quad \text{or} \quad V_U = \frac{(1 - \tau)\bar{X}}{\rho^\tau} \, ;^{\,6}$$

and let r be the rate at which the market capitalizes the sure streams generated by debts. For simplicity, assume this rate of interest is a constant independent of the size of the debt so that

$$r = \frac{R}{D} \quad \text{or} \quad D = \frac{R}{r} \, .^{7}$$

Then we would expect the value of a levered firm of size $\bar{X}$, with a permanent level of debt D_L in its capital structure, to be given by:

---

[4] It may seem paradoxical at first to say that leverage *reduces* the variability of outcomes, but remember we are here discussing the variability of total returns, interest plus net profits. The variability of stockholder net profits will, of course, be greater in the presence than in the absence of leverage, though relatively less so than in an otherwise comparable world of no taxes. The reasons for this will become clearer after the discussion in the next section.

[5] The statement that τR—the tax saving per period on the interest payments—is a sure stream is subject to two qualifications. First, it must be the case that firms can always obtain the tax benefit of their interest deductions either by offsetting them directly against other taxable income in the year incurred; or, in the event no such income is available in any given year, by carrying them backward or forward against past or future taxable earnings; or, in the extreme case, by merger of the firm with (or its sale to) another firm that can utilize the deduction. Second, it must be assumed that the tax rate will remain the same. To the extent that neither of these conditions holds exactly then some uncertainty attaches even to the tax savings, though, of course, it is of a different kind and order from that attaching to the stream generated by the assets. For simplicity, however, we shall here ignore these possible elements of delay or of uncertainty in the tax saving; but it should be kept in mind that this neglect means that the subsequent valuation formulas overstate, if anything, the value of the tax saving for any given permanent level of debt.

[6] Note that here, as in our original paper, we neglect dividend policy and "growth" in the sense of opportunities to invest at a rate of return greater than the market rate of return. These subjects are treated extensively in our paper, "Dividend Policy, Growth and the Valuation of Shares," *Jour. Bus.*, Univ. Chicago, Oct. 1961, 411–33.

[7] Here and throughout, the corresponding formulas when the rate of interest rises with leverage can be obtained merely by substituting $r(L)$ for r, where L is some suitable measure of leverage.

$$V_L = \frac{(1-\tau)\bar{X}}{\rho^\tau} + \frac{\tau R}{r} = V_U + \tau D_L \,.^{8} \tag{3}$$

In our original paper we asserted instead that, within a risk class, market value would be proportional to expected after-tax return $\bar{X}^\tau$ (cf. our original equation [11]), which would imply:

$$V_L = \frac{\bar{X}^\tau}{\rho^\tau} = \frac{(1-\tau)\bar{X}}{\rho^\tau} + \frac{\tau R}{\rho^\tau} = V_U + \frac{r}{\rho^\tau}\tau D_L. \tag{4}$$

We will now show that if (3) does not hold, investors can secure a more efficient portfolio by switching from relatively overvalued to relatively undervalued firms. Suppose first that unlevered firms are overvalued or that

$$V_L - \tau D_L < V_U.$$

An investor holding m dollars of stock in the unlevered company has a right to the fraction m/V_U of the eventual outcome, i.e., has the uncertain income

$$Y_U = \left(\frac{m}{V_U}\right)(1-\tau)\bar{X}Z.$$

Consider now an alternative portfolio obtained by investing m dollars as follows: (1) the portion,

$$m\left(\frac{S_L}{S_L + (1-\tau)D_L}\right),$$

is invested in the stock of the levered firm, S_L; and (2) the remaining portion,

$$m\left(\frac{(1-\tau)D_L}{S_L + (1-\tau)D_L}\right),$$

is invested in its bonds. The stock component entitles the holder to a fraction,

$$\frac{m}{S_L + (1-\tau)D_L},$$

of the net profits of the levered company or

$$\left(\frac{m}{S_L + (1-\tau)D_L}\right)[(1-\tau)(\bar{X}Z - R_L)].$$

The holding of bonds yields

$$\left(\frac{m}{S_L + (1-\tau)D_L}\right)[(1-\tau)R_L].$$

Hence the total outcome is

$$Y_L = \left(\frac{m}{(S_L + (1-\tau)D_L)}\right)[(1-\tau)\bar{X}Z]$$

---

[8] The assumption that the debt is permanent is not necessary for the analysis. It is employed here both to maintain continuity with the original model and because it gives an upper bound on the value of the tax saving. See in this connection footnote 5 and footnote 9.

and this will dominate the uncertain income Y_U if (and only if)

$$S_L + (1 - \tau)D_L \equiv S_L + D_L - \tau D_L \equiv V_L - \tau D_L < V_U.$$

Thus, in equilibrium, V_U cannot exceed $V_L - \tau D_L$, for if it did investors would have an incentive to sell shares in the unlevered company and purchase the shares (and bonds) of the levered company.

Suppose now that $V_L - \tau D_L > V_U$. An investment of m dollars in the stock of the levered firm entitles the holder to the outcome

$$Y_L = (m/S_L)[(1 - \tau)(\bar{X}Z - R_L)]$$
$$= (m/S_L)(1 - \tau)\bar{X}Z - (m/S_L)(1 - \tau)R_L.$$

Consider the following alternative portfolio: (1) borrow an amount $(m/S_L)(1 - \tau)D_L$ for which the interest cost will be $(m/S_L)(1 - \tau)R_L$ (assuming, of course, that individuals and corporations can borrow at the same rate, r); and (2) invest m plus the amount borrowed, i.e.,

$$m + \frac{m(1 - \tau)D_L}{S_L} = m \frac{S_L + (1 - \tau)D_L}{S_L} = (m/S_L)[V_L - \tau D_L]$$

in the stock of the unlevered firm. The outcome so secured will be

$$(m/S_L)\left(\frac{V_L - \tau D_L}{V_U}\right)(1 - \tau)\bar{X}Z.$$

Subtracting the interest charges on the borrowed funds leaves an income of

$$Y_U = (m/S_L)\left(\frac{V_L - \tau D_L}{V_U}\right)(1 - \tau)\bar{X}Z - (m/S_L)(1 - \tau)R_L$$

which will dominate Y_L if (and only if) $V_L - \tau D_L > V_U$. Thus, in equilibrium, both $V_L - \tau D_L > V_U$ and $V_L - \tau D_L < V_U$ are ruled out and (3) must hold.

III. SOME IMPLICATIONS OF FORMULA (3)

To see what is involved in replacing (4) with (3) as the rule of valuation, note first that both expressions make the value of the firm a function of leverage and the tax rate. The difference between them is a matter of the size and source of the tax advantages of debt financing. Under our original formulation, values within a class were strictly proportional to expected earnings after taxes. Hence the tax advantage of debt was due solely to the fact that the deductibility of interest payments implied a higher level of after-tax income for any given level of before-tax earnings (i.e., higher by the amount τR since $\bar{X}^{\tau} = (1 - \tau)\bar{X} + \tau R$). Under the corrected rule (3), however, there is an additional gain due to the fact that the extra after-tax earnings, τR, represent a sure income in contrast to the uncertain outcome $(1 - \tau)\bar{X}$. Hence τR is capitalized at the more favorable certainty rate, $1/r$, rather than at the rate for uncertain streams, $1/\rho^\tau$.[9]

Since the difference between (3) and (4) is solely a matter of the rate at which the tax savings on interest payments are capitalized, the required changes in all formulas and expressions derived from (4) are reasonably straightforward. Consider, first, the before-tax earnings yield, i.e., the ratio of expected earnings before interest and taxes to the value of the firm.[10] Dividing both sides of (3) by V and by $(1 - \tau)$ and simplifying we obtain:

$$\frac{\bar{X}}{V} = \frac{\rho^\tau}{1 - \tau}\left[1 - \tau\frac{D}{V}\right] \tag{31.c}$$

which replaces our original equation (31) (p. 294). The new relation differs from the old in that the coefficient of D/V in the original (31) was smaller by a factor of r/ρ^τ.

Consider next the after-tax earnings yield, i.e., the ratio of interest payments plus profits after taxes to total market value.[11] This concept was discussed extensively in our paper because it helps to bring out more clearly the differences between our position and the traditional view, and because it facilitates the construction of empirical tests of the two hypotheses about the valuation process. To see what the new equation (3) implies for this yield we need merely substitute $\bar{X}^\tau - \tau R$ for $(1 - \tau)\,\bar{X}$ in (3) obtaining:

$$V = \frac{\bar{X}^\tau - \tau R}{\rho^\tau} + \tau D = \frac{\bar{X}^\tau}{\rho^\tau} + \tau\frac{\rho^\tau - r}{\rho^\tau}\,D, \tag{5}$$

from which it follows that the after-tax earnings yield must be:

$$\frac{\bar{X}^\tau}{V} = \rho^\tau - \tau(\rho^\tau - r)D/V. \tag{11.c}$$

This replaces our original equation (11) (p. 272) in which we had simply $\bar{X}^\tau/V = \rho^\tau$. Thus, in contrast to our earlier result, the corrected version (11.c) implies that even the after-tax yield is affected by leverage. The predicted rate of decrease of $\bar{X}^\tau/V$ with D/V, however, is still considerably smaller than un-

---

[9] Remember, however, that in one sense formula (3) gives only an upper bound on the value of the firm since $\tau R/r = \tau D$ is an exact measure of the value of the tax saving only where both the tax rate and the level of debt are assumed to be fixed forever (and where the firm is certain to be able to use its interest deduction to reduce taxable income either directly or via transfer of the loss to another firm). Alternative versions of (3) can readily be developed for cases in which the debt is not assumed to be permanent, but rather to be outstanding only for some specified finite length of time. For reasons of space, we shall not pursue this line of inquiry here beyond observing that the shorter the debt period considered, the closer does the valuation formula approach our original (4). Hence, the latter is perhaps still of some interest if only as a lower bound.

[10] Following usage common in the field of finance we referred to this yield as the "average cost of capital." We feel now, however, that the term "before-tax earnings yield" would be preferable both because it is more immediately descriptive and because it releases the term "cost of capital" for use in discussions of optimal investment policy (in accord with standard usage in the capital budgeting literature).

[11] We referred to this yield as the "after-tax cost of capital." Cf. the previous footnote.

der the naive traditional view, which, as we showed, implied essentially $\bar{X}^\tau/V = \rho^\tau - (\rho^\tau - r)D/V$. See our equation (17) and the discussion immediately preceding it (p. 277).[12] And, of course, (11.c) implies that the effect of leverage on X^τ/V is *solely* a matter of the deductibility of interest payments whereas, under the traditional view, going into debt would lower the cost of capital regardless of the method of taxing corporate earnings.

Finally, we have the matter of the after-tax yield on *equity* capital, i.e., the ratio of net profits after taxes to the value of the shares.[13] By subtracting D from both sides of (5) and breaking $\bar{X}^\tau$ into its two components—expected net profits after taxes, $\bar{\pi}^\tau$, and interest payments, $R = rD$—we obtain after simplifying:

$$S = V - D = \frac{\bar{\pi}^\tau}{\rho^\tau} - (1 - \tau)\left(\frac{\rho^\tau - r}{\rho^\tau}\right)D. \qquad (6)$$

From (6) it follows that the after-tax yield on equity capital must be:

$$\frac{\bar{\pi}^\tau}{S} = \rho^\tau + (1 - \tau)[\rho^\tau - r]D/S \qquad (12.c)$$

which replaces our original equation (12), $\bar{\pi}^\tau/S = \rho^\tau + (\rho^\tau - r)D/S$ (p. 272). The new (12.c) implies an increase in the after-tax yield on equity capital as leverage increases which is smaller than that of our original (12) by a factor of $(1 - \tau)$. But again, the linear increasing relation of the corrected (12.c) is still fundamentally different from the naive traditional view which asserts the cost of equity capital to be completely independent of leverage (at least as long as leverage remains within "conventional" industry limits).

IV. TAXES AND THE COST OF CAPITAL

From these corrected valuation formulas we can readily derive corrected measures of the cost of capital in the capital budgeting sense of the minimum prospective yield an investment project must offer to be just worth undertaking from the standpoint of the present stockholders. If we interpret earnings streams as perpetuities, as we did in the original paper, then we actually have two equally good ways of defining this minimum yield: either by the required increase in before-tax earnings, $d\bar{X}$, or by the required increase in earnings net of taxes, $d\bar{X}(1 - \tau)$.[14] To conserve space, however, as well as to

[12] The i_k^* of (17) is the same as ρ^τ in the present context, each measuring the ratio of net profits to the value of the shares (and hence of the whole firm) in an unlevered company of the class.

[13] We referred to this yield as the "after-tax cost of equity capital." Cf. footnote 9.

[14] Note that we use the term "earnings net of taxes" rather than "earnings after taxes." We feel that to avoid confusion the latter term should be reserved to describe what will actually appear in the firm's accounting statements, namely the net cash flow including the tax savings on the interest (our $\bar{X}^\tau$). Since financing sources cannot in general be allocated to particular investments (see below), the after-tax or accounting concept is not useful for capital budgeting purposes, although it can be extremely useful for valuation equations as we saw in the previous section.

maintain continuity with the original paper, we shall concentrate here on the before-tax case with only brief footnote references to the net-of-tax concept.

Analytically, the derivation of the cost of capital in the above sense amounts to finding the minimum value of $d\bar{X}/dI$ for which $dV = dI$, where I denotes the level of new investment.[15] By differentiating (3) we see that:

$$\frac{dV}{dI} = \frac{1 - \tau}{\rho^\tau}\frac{d\bar{X}}{dI} + \tau\frac{dD}{dI} \geq 1 \qquad \text{if } \frac{d\bar{X}}{dI} \geq \frac{1 - \tau\dfrac{dD}{DI}}{1 - \tau}\rho^\tau. \qquad (7)$$

Hence the before tax required rate of return cannot be defined without reference to financial policy. In particular, for an investment considered as being financed entirely by new equity capital $dD/dI = 0$ and the required rate of return or marginal cost of equity financing (neglecting flotation costs) would be:

$$\rho^S = \frac{\rho^\tau}{1 - \tau}.$$

This result is the same as that in the original paper (see equation [32], p. 294) and is applicable to any other sources of financing where the remuneration to the suppliers of capital is not deductible for tax purposes. It applies, therefore, to preferred stock (except for certain partially deductible issues of public utilities) and would apply also to retained earnings were it not for the favorable tax treatment of capital gains under the personal income tax.

For investments considered as being financed entirely by new debt capital $dI = dD$ and we find from (7) that:

$$\rho^D = \rho^\tau \qquad (33.c)$$

which replaces our original equation (33) in which we had:

$$\rho^D = \rho^S - \frac{\tau}{1 - \tau}R. \qquad (33)$$

Thus for borrowed funds (or any other tax-deductible source of capital) the marginal cost or before-tax required rate of return is simply the market rate of capitalization for net of tax unlevered streams and is thus independent of both the tax rate and the interest rate. This required rate is lower than that implied by our original (33), but still considerably higher than that implied by the traditional view (see esp. pp. 276–77 of our paper) under which the before-tax cost of borrowed funds is simply the interest rate, r.

Having derived the above expressions for the marginal costs of debt and equity financing it may be well to warn readers at this point that these expressions represent at best only the hypothetical extremes insofar as costs are

---

[15] Remember that when we speak of the minimum required yield on an investment we are referring in principle only to investments which increase the *scale* of the firm. That is, the new assets must be in the same "class" as the old. See in this connection, J. Hirshleifer, "Risk, the Discount Rate and Investment Decisions," *Am. Econ. Rev.*, May 1961, *51*, 112–20 (especially pp. 119–20). See also footnote 16.

concerned and that neither is directly usable as a cut-off criterion for invest-ment planning. In particular, care must be taken to avoid falling into the fa-mous "Liquigas" fallacy of concluding that if a firm intends to float a bond issue in some given year then its cut-off rate should be set that year at ρ^D; while, if the next issue is to be an equity one, the cut-off is ρ^S. The point is, of course, that no investment can meaningfully be regarded as 100 per cent equity financed if the firm makes any use of debt capital—and most firms do, not only for the tax savings, but for many other reasons having nothing to do with "cost" in the present static sense (cf. our original paper pp. 292–93). And no investment can meaningfully be regarded as 100 per cent debt fi-nanced when lenders impose strict limitations on the maximum amount a firm can borrow relative to its equity (and when most firms actually plan on nor-mally borrowing less than this external maximum so as to leave themselves with an emergency reserve of unused borrowing power). Since the firm's long-run capital structure will thus contain both debt and equity capital, in-vestment planning must recognize that, over the long pull, *all* of the firm's assets are really financed by a mixture of debt and equity capital even though only one kind of capital may be raised in any particular year. More precisely, if L^* denotes the firm's long-run "target" debt ratio (around which its actual debt ratio will fluctuate as it "alternately" floats debt issues and retires them with internal or external equity) then the firm can assume, to a first approxi-mation at least, that for any particular investment $dD/dI = L^*$. Hence, the relevant marginal cost of capital for investment planning, which we shall here denote by ρ^*, is:

$$\rho^* = \frac{1 - \tau L^*}{1 - \tau} \rho^\tau = \rho^S - \frac{\tau}{1 - \tau} \rho^D L^* = \rho^S(1 - L^*) + \rho^D L^*.$$

That is, the appropriate cost of capital for (repetitive) investment decisions over time is, to a first approximation, a weighted average of the costs of debt and equity financing, the weights being the proportions of each in the "target" capital structure.[16]

---

[16] From the formulas in the text one can readily derive corresponding expressions for the required net-of-tax yield, or net-of-tax cost of capital for any given financing policy. Specifically, let $\tilde{\rho}(L)$ denote the required net-of-tax yield for investment financed with a proportion of debt $L = dD/dI$. (More generally L denotes the proportion financed with tax deductible sources of capital.) Then from (7) we find:

$$\tilde{\rho}(L) = (1 - \tau)\frac{d\bar{X}}{dI} = (1 - L\tau)\rho^\tau \tag{8}$$

and the various costs can be found by substituting the appropriate value for L. In partic-ular, if we substitute in this formula the "target" leverage ratio, L^*, we obtain:

$$\tilde{\rho}^* \equiv \tilde{\rho}(L^*) = (1 - \tau L^*)\rho^\tau$$

and $\tilde{\rho}^*$ measures the average net-of-tax cost of capital in the sense described above.

Although the before-tax and the net-of-tax approaches to the cost of capital provide equally good criteria for investment decisions when assets are assumed to generate perpetual (i.e., non-depreciating) streams, such is not the case when assets are assumed to have finite lives (even when it is also assumed that the firm's assets are in a steady

V. SOME CONCLUDING OBSERVATIONS

Such, then, are the major corrections that must be made to the various formulas and valuation expressions in our earlier paper. In general, we can say that the force of these corrections has been to increase somewhat the estimate of the tax advantages of debt financing under our model and consequently to reduce somewhat the quantitative difference between the estimates of the effects of leverage under our model and under the naive traditional view. It may be useful to remind readers once again that the existence of a tax advantage for debt financing—even the larger advantage of the corrected version—does not necessarily mean that corporations should at all times seek to use the maximum possible amount of debt in their capital structures. For one thing, other forms of financing, notably retained earnings, may in some circumstances be cheaper still when the tax status of investors under the personal income tax is taken into account. More important, there are, as we pointed out, limitations imposed by lenders (see pp. 292–93), as well as many other dimensions (and kinds of costs) in real-world problems of financial strategy which are not fully comprehended within the framework of static equilibrium models, either our own or those of the traditional variety. These additional considerations, which are typically grouped under the rubric of "the need for preserving flexibility," will normally imply the maintenance by the corporation of a substantial reserve of untapped borrowing power. The tax advantage of debt may well tend to lower the optimal size of that reserve, but it is hard to believe that advantages of the size contemplated under our model could justify any substantial reduction, let alone their complete elimination. Nor do the data indicate that there has in fact been a substantial increase in the use of debt (except relative to preferred stock) by the corporate sector during the recent high tax years.

As to the differences between our modified model and the traditional one, we feel that they are still large in quantitative terms and still very much worth trying to detect. It is not only a matter of the two views having different implications for corporate financial policy (or even for national tax policy). But since the two positions rest on fundamentally different views about investor behavior and the functioning of the capital markets, the results of tests between them may have an important bearing on issues ranging far beyond the immediate one of the effects of leverage on the cost of capital.

---

state age distribution so that our X or EBIT is approximately the same as the net cash flow before taxes). See footnote 3 above. In the latter event, the correct method for determining the desirability of an investment would be, in principle, to discount the net-of-tax stream at the net-of-tax cost of capital. Only under this net-of-tax approach would it be possible to take into account the deductibility of depreciation (and also to choose the most advantageous depreciation policy for tax purposes). Note that we say that the net-of-tax approach is correct "in principle" because, strictly speaking, nothing in our analysis (or anyone else's, for that matter) has yet established that it is indeed legitimate to "discount" an uncertain stream. One can hope that subsequent research will show the analogy to discounting under the certainty case is a valid one; but, at the moment, this is still only a hope.

NEW FRAMEWORK FOR
CORPORATE DEBT POLICY*

By Gordon Donaldson†

Why are many common rules of thumb for evaluating a company's debt capacity misleading and even dangerous?

Why is outside experience and advice of limited value as a guide to top management's thinking about debt capacity?

What approach will enable management to make an independent and realistic appraisal of risk on the basis of data with which it is already familiar and in terms of judgments to which it has long been accustomed?

The problem of deciding whether it is wise and proper for a business corporation to finance long-term capital needs through debt, and, if so, how far it is safe to go, is one which most boards of directors have wrestled with at one time or another. For many companies the debt-capacity decision is of critical importance because of its potential impact on margins of profitability and on solvency. For *all* companies, however large and financially sound they may be, the decision is one to be approached with great care. Yet, in spite of its importance, the subject of corporate debt policy has received surprisingly little attention in the literature of business management in recent years. One might infer from this either that business has already developed a reliable means of resolving the question or that progress toward a more adequate solution has been slow.

In my opinion, the latter inference is closer to the truth. The debt-equity choice is still a relatively crude art as practiced by a great many corporate borrowers. It follows that there is a real opportunity for useful refinement in the decision-making process. However, there is little evidence, at present, of serious dissatisfaction with conventional decision rules on the part of those responsible for making this decision. Over the past three years I have been engaged in sampling executive opinions on debt policy, and I have found little indication of the same kind of ferment as is going on with regard to capital budgeting decisions.

---

* Reprinted by permission from the *Harvard Business Review*, Vol. 40 (March–April 1962), pp. 117–31.

† Professor of Business Administration, Harvard University.

The primary purpose of this article, therefore, is to stimulate dissatisfaction with present-day conventions regarding debt capacity and to suggest the direction in which the opportunity for improvement lies. I intend to show that the widely used rules of thumb which evaluate debt capacity in terms of some percentage of balance sheet values or in terms of income statement ratios can be seriously misleading and even dangerous to corporate solvency. I also intend to develop the argument that debt policy in general and debt capacity in particular cannot be prescribed for the individual company by outsiders or by generalized standards; rather, they can and should be determined by management in terms of individual corporate circumstances and objectives and on the basis of the observed behavior of patterns of cash flows.

The question of corporate debt capacity may be looked at from several points of view—e.g., the management of the business concerned, its shareholders or potential shareholders, and, of course, the lender of the debt capital. Because each of these groups may, quite properly, have a different concept of the wise and proper limit on debt, let me clarify the point of view taken in this article. I intend to discuss the subject from the standpoint of the management of the borrowing corporation, assuming that the board of directors which will make the final decision has the customary mandate from the stockholders to act on all matters concerning the safety and profitability of their investment. For the reader who ordinarily looks at this problem as a lender, potential stockholder, or investment adviser, the analysis described in this article may appear at first sight to have limited application. Hopefully, however, the underlying concepts will be recognized as valid regardless of how one looks at the problem, and they may suggest directions for improvement in the external as well as the internal analysis of the risk of debt.

NATURE OF THE RISKS

In order to set a background for discussing possible improvements, I will first describe briefly certain aspects of conventional practice concerning present-day decision rules on long-term debt. These observations were recorded as a part of a research study which sampled practice and opinion in a group of relatively large and mature manufacturing corporations.[1] The nature of this sample must be kept in mind when interpreting the practices described.

Hazards of Too Much Debt

The nature of the incentive to borrow as an alternative to financing through a new issue of stock is common knowledge. Debt capital in the amounts normally approved by established financial institutions is a comparatively cheap source of funds. Whether it is considered the cheapest source depends on whether retained earnings are regarded as "cost free" or not. In any case, for most companies it is easy to demonstrate that, assuming normal profitability, the combination of moderate interest rates and high levels of

---

[1] The complete findings have been published in book form; see Gordon Donaldson, *Corporate Debt Capacity* (Boston, Division of Research, Harvard Business School, 1961).

corporate income tax enable debt capital to produce significantly better earnings per share than would a comparable amount of capital provided by an issue of either common or preferred stock. In fact, the advantage is so obvious that few companies bother to make the calculation when considering these alternatives.

Under these circumstances it is apparent that there must be a powerful deterrent which keeps businesses from utilizing this source to the limits of availability. The primary deterrent is, of course, the risks which are inevitably associated with long-term debt servicing. While it is something of an oversimplification to say that the debt decision is a balancing of higher prospective income to the shareholders against greater chance of loss, it is certainly true that this is the heart of the problem.

When the word "risk" is applied to debt, it may refer to a variety of potential penalties; the precise meaning is not always clear when this subject is discussed. To most people, however, risk—so far as debt is concerned—is the chance of running out of cash. This risk is inevitably increased by a legal contract requiring the business to pay fixed sums of cash at predetermined dates in the future regardless of the financial condition at that time. There are, of course, a great many needs for cash—dividends, capital expenditures, research projects, and so on—with respect to which cash balances may prove inadequate at some future point.

Too Little Cash

The ultimate hazard of running out of cash, however, and the one which lurks in the background of every debt decision, is the situation where cash is so reduced that legal contracts are defaulted, bankruptcy occurs, and normal operations cease. Since no private enterprise has a guaranteed cash inflow, there must always be *some* risk, however remote, that this event could occur. Consequently, any addition to mandatory cash outflows resulting from new debt or any other act or event must increase that risk. I have chosen to use the term "cash inadequacy" to refer to a whole family of problems involving the inability to make cash payments for any purpose important to the long-term financial health of the business; "cash insolvency" is the extreme case of cash inadequacy. It should be emphasized that although debt necessarily increases the chances of cash inadequacy, this risk exists whether the company has any debt or not, so that the debt-equity choice is not between some risk and no risk, but between more and less.

CONVENTIONAL APPROACHES

Observation of present-day business practice suggests that businessmen commonly draw their concepts of debt capacity from one or more of several sources. Thus, they sometimes

(1) *Seek the counsel of institutional lenders or financial intermediaries (such as investment bankers)*—Most corporate borrowers negotiate long-term debt contracts at infrequent intervals, while the lender and the investment banker are con-

stantly involved in loan decisions and so, presumably, have a great deal more experience and better judgment. Further, it is apparent that unless the lender is satisfied on the question of risk, there will be no loan. Finally, banks and insurance companies have a well-established reputation for being conservative, and conservative borrowers will take comfort from the fact that if the lender errs, it will likely be on the safe side.

(2) *See what comparable companies are doing in this area of financial management*—Every business has an idea of those other companies in or out of the industry which are most like themselves so far as factors affecting risk are concerned. Since this is an aspect of corporate policy which is public information, it is natural that the debt-equity ratios of competitors will be carefully considered, and, lacking more objective guides, there will be a tendency to follow the mode and reject the extremes. This approach has an added practical appeal; group norms are important in the capital market's appraisal of a company's financial strength. If a company is out of line, it may be penalized—even though the deviation from the average may be perfectly appropriate for this company.

(3) *Follow the practices of the past*—There is a very natural tendency to respect the corporation's financial traditions, and this is often apparent with regard to debt policy. Many businesses take considerable pride in "a clean balance sheet," an *Aa* rating, or a history of borrowing at the prime rate. It would border on sacrilege to propose a departure which would jeopardize these cherished symbols of financial achievement and respectability! The fact that these standards have apparently preserved corporate solvency in the past is a powerful argument for continuing them, particularly if the implications of a change cannot be precisely defined.

(4) *Refer to that very elusive authority called "general practice," "industry practice," "common knowledge," or, less respectfully, "financial folklore"*—Remarkable as it seems in view of the great diversity among companies classified as industrials, there is widespread acceptance of the belief that an appropriate limit to the long-term borrowing of industrial companies is 30% of capitalization (or, alternatively, one third). The origin of, or rationale for, this particular decision rule has been obscured by the passage of time, but there is no doubt that it has become a widely honored rule of thumb in the decisions of both borrowers and lenders.

Fallacy of Double Standard

Without denying the practical significance of some of the considerations which have led businessmen to follow these guides in formulating debt policy, it must be recognized that there are serious limitations inherent in using them (separately or as a group) as the *only* guides to appropriate debt capacity.

First, consider the practice of accepting advice from the lender. As the lender views the individual loan contract, it is one of a large number of investments which make up a constantly changing portfolio. When negotiated it is only one of a stream of loan proposals which must be acted on promptly and appraised in terms of the limited information to which generalized standards are applied. The nature of the risk to the lender is necessarily influenced by the fact that this loan is only a small fraction of the total sum invested and that intelligent diversification goes a long way to softening the impact of individual default. Further, even when default occurs, all may not be lost; in time the loan may be "worked out" through reorganization or liquidation.

All this is small comfort to the borrower. The individual loan which goes sour—if it happens to be *his* loan—is a catastrophe. There are few business-men who can take a lighthearted attitude toward the prospect of default on a legal contract with the associated threat of bankruptcy. To most, this is viewed as the end of the road. Also, it is important to recognize that while the lender need only be concerned about servicing his own (high priority) claims, the borrower must also consider the needs which go unsatisfied during the period prior to the time of actual default when debt servicing drains off precious cash reserves.

This is not to imply that the lender is insensitive to individual losses and their effect on the business concerned; but it does mean that risk to the lender is not the same thing as risk to the borrower, and, consequently, the standards of one are not necessarily appropriate for the other. The lender's standards can at times be too liberal—as well as too conservative—from the borrower's point of view. Some will argue that, as a practical matter, the borrower must accept the debt-capacity standards of the lender, else there will be no contract. However, this implies that there is no bargaining over the upper limit of the amount that will be supplied, no differences among lenders, and/or no shopping around by borrowers. While all institutional lenders do have abso-lute limits on the risks they will take (even at a premium interest rate), there is often some room for negotiation if the borrower is so disposed. Under some circumstances there may be valid reasons for probing the upper limits of the lender's willingness to lend.

Lessons of Experience

The second source of guidance mentioned is the observed practices of comparable businesses. This, too, has its obvious limitations. Even assuming strict comparability—which is hard to establish—there is no proof that the companies concerned have arrived at their current debt proportions in a deliberate and rational manner. In view of the wide variations in debt policy within any industry group, there can be little real meaning in an industry average. And what happens if every member of the group looks to the other for guidance? The most that can be said for this approach to debt policy is that the company concerned can avoid the appearance of being atypical in the investment market so far as its capital structure is concerned. But, as in most areas of business, there is a *range* of acceptable behavior, and the skill of management comes in identifying and taking advantage of the limits to which it can go without raising too many eyebrows.

Even a company's own direct experience with debt financing has its limitations as a guide to debt capacity. At best, the evidence that a particular debt policy has not been a cause of financial embarrassment in the past may only prove that the policy was on the conservative side. However, if assurance of adequate conservatism is the primary goal, the only really satisfactory policy is a no-debt policy.

For companies with some debt the experience of past periods of business recession is only partial evidence of the protection a particular policy affords. In most industries, the period of the past 20 years has produced a maximum of four or five periods of decline in sales and earnings. This limited recession experience with the behavior of cash flows—the critical consideration where debt servicing is involved—can be misleading since cash flows are affected by a variety of factors and the actual experience in any single recession is a somewhat unique combination of events which may not recur in the future. Thus, the so-called test of experience cannot be taken at face value.

Inescapable Responsibility

In summing up a criticism of the sources from which management commonly derives its debt-capacity standard, there are two aspects which must be emphasized. Both of these relate to the practice of relying on the judgment of others in a situation where management alone is best able to appraise the full implications of the problem. The points I have in mind are as follows:

(1) In assessing the risks of running out of cash because of excessive fixed cash obligations, the special circumstances of the individual firm are the primary data that the analyst has to work with. Management has obvious advantages over outsiders in using this data because it has free and full access to it, the time and incentive to examine it thoroughly, and a personal stake in making sensible judgments about what it observes. Even the judgments of predecessors in office are judgments made on information which is inadequate when compared to what management now has in its possession—if only because the predecessor's information is now 10 or 20 years old. (Subsequently, we will consider how management may approach an independent appraisal of risk for the individual business.)

(2) The measurement of risk is only one dimension of the debt-capacity decision. In a free enterprise society, the assumption of risk is a voluntary activity, and no one can properly define the level of risk which another should be willing to bear. The decision to limit debt to 10%, 30%, or any other percentage of the capital structure reflects (or should reflect) both the magnitude of the risk involved in servicing that amount of debt *and* the willingness of those who bear this risk—the owners or their duly authorized representatives—to accept the hazards involved.

In the last analysis, this is a subjective decision which management alone can make. Indeed, it may be said that a corporation has defined its debt policy long before a particular financing decision comes to a vote; it has done this in its choice of the men who are to make the decision. The ensuing decisions involving financial risk will reflect their basic attitudes—whether they see a situation as an opportunity to be exploited or a threat to be minimized.

A most interesting and fundamental question comes up here—one that underlies the whole relationship between management and the shareholder; namely, does management determine the attitude toward risk bearing which the stockholders must then adopt, or vice versa? This is part of the broader question of whether management should choose those financial policies which it prefers and attract a like-minded stockholder group (taking the "if they don't like it, they can sell out" approach) or by some means or other determine the attitudes and objectives of its present stockholder group and attempt to translate these into the appropriate action.

I do not propose to pass judgment on this difficult problem in the context of this article. The fact is, by taking one approach or the other—or some blend—management *does* make these decisions. With respect to risk bearing, however, one point is clear: responsible management should not be dealing with the problem in terms of purely personal risk preferences. I suspect that many top executives have not given this aspect the attention it deserves.

Reasons for Current Practice

Having considered the case for a debt policy which is internally rather than externally generated, we may well ask why so many companies, in deciding how far to go in using O.P.M. (other people's money), lean so heavily on O.P.A. (other people's advice). The answer appears to be three-fold:

1. A misunderstanding of the nature of the problem and, in particular, a failure to separate the subjective from the objective elements.
2. The inherent complexity of the objective side—the measurement of risk.
3. The serious inadequacy of conventional debt-capacity decision rules as a framework for independent appraisal.

It is obvious that if a business does not have a useful way of assessing the general magnitude of the risks of too much debt in terms of its individual company and industry circumstances, then it will do one of two things. Either it will fall back on generalized (external) concepts of risk for "comparable" companies, or it will make the decision on purely subjective grounds—on how the management "feels" about debt. Thus, in practice, an internally generated debt-capacity decision is often based almost entirely on the management's general attitude toward this kind of problem without regard for how much risk is actually involved and what the potential rewards and penalties from risk bearing happen to be in the specific situation. The most obvious examples are to be found in companies at the extremes of debt policy that follow such rules as "no debt under any circumstances" or "borrow the maximum available." (We must be careful, however, not to assume that if a company has one or another of these policies, it is acting irrationally or emotionally.)

One of the subjects about which we know very little at present is how individual and group attitudes toward risk bearing are formed in practice. It is apparent, however, that there are important differences in this respect among members of any given management team and even for an individual executive with regard to different dimensions of risk within the business. The risk of excessive debt often appears to have a special significance; a man who is a "plunger" on sales policy or research might also be an arch-conservative with regard to debt. The risk of default on debt is more directly associated with financial ruin, regardless of the fundamental cause of failure, simply because it is generally the last act in a chain of events which follows from a deteriorating cash position.

There are other bits of evidence which are possible explanations for a Jekyll-and-Hyde behavior on risk bearing in business:

Debt policy is always decided at the very top of the executive structure whereas other policies on sales or production involving other dimensions of risk are shaped to some degree at all executive levels. The seniority of the typical board of directors doubtless has some bearing on the comparative conservatism of financial policy, including debt policy.

There is also some truth in the generalization that financial officers tend to be more conservative than other executives at the same level in other phases of the business, and to the extent that they influence debt policy they may tend to prefer to minimize risk per se, regardless of the potential rewards from risk bearing.

What Is a Sensible Approach?

The foregoing is, however, only speculation in an area where real research is necessary. The point of importance here is that, whatever the reason may be, it is illogical to base an internal decision on debt policy on attitudes toward risk *alone,* just as it is illogical to believe that corporate debt policy can be properly formulated without taking these individual attitudes into account.

For the purposes of a sensible approach to corporate debt policy we need not expect management to have a logical explanation for its feelings toward debt, even though this might be theoretically desirable. It is sufficient that managers know how they feel and are able to react to specific risk alternatives. The problem has been that in many cases they have not known in any objective sense what it was that they were reacting to; they have not had a meaningful measure of the specific risk of running out of cash (with or without any given amount of long-term debt).

It is therefore in the formulation of an approach to the measurement of risk in the individual corporation that the hope for an independent appraisal of debt capacity lies.

INADEQUACY OF CURRENT RULES

Unfortunately, the conventional form for expressing debt-capacity rules is of little or no help in providing the kind of formulation I am urging. Debt capacity is most commonly expressed in terms of the balance sheet relationship between long-term debt and the total of all long-term sources, viz., as some per cent of capitalization. A variation of this ratio is often found in debt contracts which limit new long-term borrowing to some percentage of net tangible assets.

The alternative form in which to express the limits of long-term borrowing is in terms of income statement data. This is the *earnings coverage* ratio—the ratio of net income available for debt servicing to the total amount of annual interest plus sinking fund charges. Under such a rule, no new long-term debt would be contemplated unless the net income available for debt servicing is equal to or in excess of some multiple of the debt servicing charges—say, three to one—so that the company can survive a period of decline in sales and earnings and still have enough earnings to cover the fixed charges of debt. As we will see shortly, this ratio is more meaningful for internal formation of policy but also has its limitations.

Now, let us go on to examine each type of expression more closely.

Capitalization Standard

Consider a company which wishes to formulate its own debt standard as a per cent of capitalization. It is apparent that in order to do so the standard must be expressed in terms of data which can be related to the magnitude of the risk in such a way that changes in the ratio can be translated into changes in the risk of cash inadequacy, and vice versa. But how many executives concerned with this problem today have any real idea of how much the risk of cash inadequacy is increased when the long-term debt of their company is increased from 10% to 20% or from 20% to 30% of capitalization? Not very many, if my sample of management information in this area has any validity. This is not surprising, however, since the balance sheet data on which the standard is based provide little direct evidence on the question of cash adequacy and may, in fact, be highly unreliable and misleading.

While we do not need to go into a full discussion here of the inadequacies of relating the principal amount of long-term debt to historical asset values as a way of looking at the chances of running out of cash, we should keep in mind the more obvious weaknesses:

1. There is a wide variation in the relation between the principal of the debt and the annual obligation for cash payments under the debt contract. In industrial companies the principal of the debt may be repaid serially over the life of the debt contract, which may vary from 10 years or less to 30 years or more. Thus, the annual cash outflow associated with $10 million on the balance sheet may, for example, vary from $500,000 (interest only at 5%) to $833,000 (interest plus principal repayable over 30 years) to $1,500,000 (interest plus principal repayable over 10 years).

2. As loans are repaid by partial annual payments, as is customary under industrial term loans, the principal amount declines and the per-cent-of-capitalization ratio improves, but the annual cash drain for repayment *remains the same* until maturity is reached.

3. There may be substantial changes in asset values, particularly in connection with inventory valuation and depreciation policies, and as a consequence, changes in the per-cent-of-capitalization ratio which have no bearing on the capacity to meet fixed cash drains.

(4) Certain off-the-balance-sheet factors have an important bearing on cash flows which the conventional ratio takes no cognizance of. One factor of this sort

which has been receiving publicity in recent years is the payments under leasing arrangements. (While various authorities have been urging that lease payments be given formal recognition as a liability on balance sheets and in debt-capacity calculations, there is no general agreement as to how this should be done. For one thing, there is no obvious answer as to what the capitalization rate should be in order to translate lease payments into balance sheet values. In my opinion this debate is bound to be an artificial and frustrating experience—and unnecessary for the internal analyst—since, as will be discussed later, it is much more meaningful to deal with leases, as with debt, in terms of the dollars of annual cash outflow rather than in terms of principal amounts. Thus, a footnoting of the annual payments under the lease is entirely adequate.)

Earnings-Coverage Standard

The earnings-coverage standard affords, on the surface at least, a better prospect of measuring risk in the individual company in terms of the factors which bear directly on cash adequacy. By relating the total annual cash outflow under all long-term debt contracts to the net earnings available for servicing the debt, it is intended to assure that earnings will be adequate to meet charges at all times. This approach implies that the greater the prospective fluctuation in earnings, the higher is the required ratio (or the larger the "cushion" between normal earnings and debt-servicing charges).

This standard also has limitations as a basis for internal determination of debt capacity:

1. The net earnings figure found in the income statement and derived under normal accounting procedures is *not* the same thing as net cash inflow—an assumption which is implicit in the earnings-coverage standard. Even when adjustments are made for the noncash items on the income statement (depreciation charges), as is commonly done in the more sophisticated applications, this equivalence cannot safely be assumed. The time when it may be roughly true is the time when we are least concerned about the hazards of debt, i.e., when sales are approximately the same from period to period. It is in times of rapid change (including recessions) that we are most concerned about debt burden, and then there *are* likely to be sharp differences between net income and net cash flow.

2. The question of what the *proper* ratio is between earnings and debt servicing is problematical. In a given case should the ratio be two to one or twenty to one? If we exclude externally derived standards or rules of thumb and insist that a company generate its own ratio in terms of its own circumstances, how does it go about doing it? Perhaps the best that could be done would be to work backward from the data of past recessions, which would indicate the low points of net earnings, toward a ratio between this experience and some measure of "normal" earnings with the intention of assuring a one-to-one relationship between net earnings and debt servicing at all times. However, if this is the way it is to be done, the estimate of minimum net earnings would itself provide the measure of debt capacity, and it would be unnecessary to translate it into a ratio. Further, as already noted, there are hazards in a literal translation of past history as a guide for the future. And what of the case where the company has experienced net losses in the past?

Does this mean that it has no long-term debt capacity? If a net loss is possible, *no* ratio between normal net earnings and debt servicing, however large, will assure the desired equality in future recessions.

The earnings-coverage standard does not appear to be widely used by industrial corporate borrowers as a basis for formulating debt policy. Where it is used, it appears either to derive from the advice of institutional lenders or investment bankers or merely to reflect the borrower's attitude toward risk bearing. Its use does not seem to indicate an attempt to measure individual risk by some objective means.

A MORE USEFUL APPROACH

Granted the apparent inadequacies of conventional debt-capacity decision rules for purposes of internal debt policy, is there a practical alternative? I believe there is, but it must be recognized immediately that it rests on data which are substantially more complex than what the conventional rules require, and involve a considerably larger expenditure of time and effort to obtain and interpret. However, in view of the unquestioned importance of the debt-equity decision to the future of individual businesses, and in view of the fact that, as will be shown later, the data have a usefulness which goes well beyond the debt-capacity decision, there is reason to give this alternative serious consideration.

The basic questions in the appraisal of the magnitude of risk associated with long-term debt can be stated with deceptive simplicity: What are the chances of the business running out of cash in the foreseeable future? How are these chances changed by the addition of X thousands of dollars of annual interest and sinking fund payments? First, it is necessary to specify whether our concern is with "running out of cash" in an absolute sense (cash insolvency) or merely with the risk of cash inadequacy, i.e., running out of cash for certain purposes considered essential to management (for example, a minimum dividend on common stock). We can consider both of these possibilities, but let us focus for the moment on the ultimate hazard, the one commonly associated with excessive debt—the chance of complete depletion of cash reserves resulting in default on the bond contract and bankruptcy.

There are, of course, a variety of possible circumstances under which a company might have its cash reserves drained off. However, considering the problem from the point of view of mature, normally profitable, and reasonably well-managed companies, it is fair to say that the primary concern with debt is with what might happen during a general or industry recession when sales and profits are depressed by factors beyond the immediate control of management. Thus, when the experienced business executive wishes to instill the proper respect for the hazards of too much debt in the minds of aggressive young men eager for leverage, he will recount harrowing tales of disaster and near-disaster in the early 1930's.

Refocusing on Problem

The data we seek are information on the behavior of cash flows during the recession periods. An internal analysis of risk must therefore concern itself not with balance sheet or income statement ratios but directly with the factors which make for changes in cash inflow and outflow. Further, since we are dealing with the common denominator of all transactions, analysis must inevitably take into account *all* major influences on cash flow behavior. In short, the problem is a company-wide problem. All decisions involving cash should be included, and where cash solvency is at stake, there can be no meaningful boundaries on risk except those imposed by the corporate entity itself.

Therefore, it is somewhat artificial to think in terms of "the cash available for debt servicing," as the earnings-coverage standard does, as if it were an identifiable hoard when a number of needs equally as urgent are competing for a limited cash reserve. Consequently, the problem to which this article was originally addressed—determining the capacity to bear the incremental fixed charges of long-term debt—is in reality a much more general one: viz., the problem of *determining the capacity to bear incremental fixed cash outflows for any purpose whatever.*

Assessing Key Factors

The analysis which is proposed in this article as a way of resolving this problem can only be briefly summarized here.[2] It includes:

1. *Identification*—At the outset, it is important to identify the primary factors which produce major changes in cash flow with particular reference to contractions in cash flow. The most significant factor will be sales volume; many of the other factors will be related in greater or lesser degree to sales. However, to cite the example of another major factor, cash expenditures for raw materials, the relationship to sales volume in a downswing is not at all an automatic one since it also depends on:

   a. The volume of finished-goods inventory on hand at the onset of the recession.
   b. The working relationship between finished goods on hand, work scheduled into production, and raw-materials ordering.
   c. The level of raw-materials inventory.
   d. The responses of management at all levels to the observed change in sales.

   For most factors affecting cash flow there will be a degree of interdependence and also a range of independent variation, both of which must be identified for the purpose of the analysis.

   2. *Extent of refinement desired*—Obviously the list of factors affecting cash flow which are to be given separate consideration could be lengthy depending on the degree of refinement desired; and the longer the list, the greater the complexity of the analysis. It is therefore essential to form a judgment in advance as to how far refinement in the analysis can or should be carried in view of the objectives of the analysis. It is possible for this cash flow analysis to range all the way from

---

[2] For a full statement, see Chapters 7–9 of *Corporate Debt Capacity*, op. cit.

simple and relatively crude approximations to the other extreme of involved mathematical and statistical formulas and even to the programing of recession cash flows
on a computer.

In their simplest form, cash flows can be considered in terms of accounting approximations derived from balance sheet and income statement data. Thus, for
example, sales revenues might be adjusted for changes in accounts receivable to
derive current cash inflow, and cost of goods sold could be converted into expenditures for goods actually produced by adjusting for changes in inventory levels.
However, the hazard of simplification is that important changes may be obscured
by combining factors that at one time may "net each other out" and at some other
time may reinforce each other. For instance, changes in dollar sales are produced
by changes in product mix, physical volume, and price.

Here is where the internal analyst has a major advantage. Experience tells him
what factors should be given separate treatment, and he has access to the data
behind the financial statements so he can carry refinement as far as he wishes.
Ideally, the analysis should be in terms of cash and not accrual accounting information; that is, it should be in terms of cash receipts (not dollar sales) and cash
expenditures for raw materials received (not an accounting allocation for raw materials according to the number of units sold).

3. *Analysis of behavior*—Given a list of all major factors affecting cash flow, the
next step is to observe their *individual* behavior over time and in particular during
recessions. The objection raised earlier to using historical evidence as a guide to
debt capacity was that, as usually employed, it is an observation of the *net* effect of
change in all these factors on particular occasions—an effect which can be seriously misleading. But if management takes the individual behavior of these factors
into account, the problem is minimized to a point where it can be disregarded.

Past experience in a company with an established position in its industry commonly leads its management to the sensible conclusion that, while it is theoretically
possible for the physical volume of sales, for example, to contract to zero in a recession period, in practice there are reasons why this is highly unlikely to occur. These
reasons relate to fundamental and enduring forces in the economy, the industry,
the competitive position of the firm, consumer buying habits, and so on. Thus,
past experience will suggest a range of recession behavior which describes the
outside limits of what recession can be expected to do in the future. These limits
I wish to refer to as the *maximum favorable limit* and the *maximum adverse limit*
(referring to the effect on cash flows and the cash position). By combining the
evidence contained in historical records and the judgment of management directly involved in the making of this history, we can describe these limits of expected behavior for all factors affecting cash flow. It will be part of our analysis
to do so, taking careful account of interdependent variation for reasons given
earlier.

4. *Expected range of recession behavior*—On the basis of such informed observation it may be concluded, for example, that the recession contraction in physical volume of sales is not expected to be less than 5% nor more than 25% of the
sales of the period immediately preceding the recession. These are the maximum
favorable and maximum adverse limits of sales for the company in question. It
may also be concluded that the recession is not expected to last less than one year
nor more than three years and that no more than 40% of the contraction will be
concentrated in the first year of the recession. Naturally, our interest focuses on

the maximum *adverse* limit, since we are attempting to assess the chances of running out of cash. By setting such boundaries on the adverse recession behavior of a major factor influencing cash flows we are beginning to set similar boundaries on the recession behavior of the cash flows themselves.

At this point a question presents itself which has major implications for the subsequent character of the analysis: Is it possible to say anything meaningful about the behavior of sales volume or any other factor *within* the limits that have just been described?

PROBABILITY ANALYSIS

It is possible that there may be some historical evidence in the company on the comparative chances or probabilities of occurrence of sales contractions of, say, 5%–11%, 12%–18%, 19%–25% (or any other breakdown of the range), but the statistical data are likely to be sketchy. It is perhaps more likely that management might, on the basis of experience, make some judgments such as, for example, that the contraction is most likely—say, five chances out of ten—to fall in the 12%–18% range; that the chances of its falling in the 5%–11% range are three chances out of ten; and that the chances of falling in the 19%–25% range are two chances out of ten.

If this kind of information can be generated for all factors affecting cash flow, then it is possible to come up with a range of estimates of the cash flow in future recession periods based on all possible combinations of the several factors, and for each estimate a numerical measure of its probability of occurrence. The whole set collectively will describe all anticipated possibilities. By totaling the separate probabilities of those combinations of events exhausting the initial cash balance, we can describe in quantitative terms the over-all chances of cash insolvency. Ideally we want to know that the chances of cash insolvency, as described by this process of analysis of cash flows are, say, one in twenty or one in fifty.

Problems to Surmount

However, in order to get such a precise measure of the risk of cash insolvency, we need estimates of probability that are within the expected range of behavior and not just the limits of behavior. There are important practical problems that stand in the way of obtaining this type of information and conducting this type of analysis:

Although the analysis suggested above appears relatively simple, in practice it could be quite complex, requiring the guidance of someone experienced in probability theory as well as in financial analysis to steer the study of cash flows around potential pitfalls. The problems center mainly on (1) accurately describing patterns of adjustment over time, and (2) assessing the varying degrees of interdependence among the variables. These difficulties are not insurmountable, however, since statisticians have resolved similar ones in the case of other types of business problems.

Past recession periods may not have provided enough experience with respect to the behavior of sales, collections, inventory levels, and so forth, on which to base firm estimates of probabilities over the entire range of possible behavior. Some companies have had only two or three recessions in the past 20 years, and even then sometimes statistics are lacking (although presumably management will have some impressions about the events). But *some* experience with varying recession circumstances is essential even to make a guess. Speaking generally, this limitation on a comprehensive appraisal of the risk magnitude is far more serious than the one of technical competence mentioned first.

Top management will not base critical decisions, such as debt policy, on data which it does not understand and/or in which it does not have confidence. This, I believe, is the primary obstacle which stands in the way of widespread use of a comprehensive cash flow analysis as a basis for risk measurement and the determination of debt capacity at the present time. Because the method is complex (particularly in contrast to the customary rules of thumb) and because the judgments on probabilities and other aspects of the analysis may appear—and may in fact be—tenuous, management may well be unwilling to use the results, particularly when corporate solvency is at stake.

However, when all this is said, the fact remains that much of present-day practice is seriously inadequate, and there is an urgent need for a more meaningful approach to the problem, particularly so far as the borrower is concerned. Thus, there is a strong incentive to explore the opportunities for partial or approximate measures of the risk of cash insolvency within the general framework suggested by the comprehensive analysis. One such approach is that to be described. Its aim is to produce an indicator of risk magnitude which can be derived from more conventional and less complex data in which management has confidence.

Analysis of Adverse Limits

The new approach focuses on the expected *limits* of recession behavior and in particular on the maximum adverse limit. It is based on the assumption that while management may be unable to assess with confidence the probabilities within the range, it usually has strong opinions as to the expected limits and would be prepared to base decisions upon such expectations. Thus, to return to the example of the sales contraction, management may be unwilling to assign the "betting odds" to the three intervals between a 5% and a 25% contraction, but it probably does have strong feelings that 25% is the "absolute" limit of adversity within the foreseeable future. This feeling is based not merely on past statistics but on an expert appraisal of all the facts surrounding the customer's buying habits and circumstances, the competitive situation, and so on.

Following this procedure leads to a set of estimates of the maximum adverse limit of recession behavior covering each factor affecting cash flow, and it is a comparatively simple matter then to come up with an estimate of the maximum adverse behavior in any future recession of net cash flow itself—in terms of the minimum dollars of net inflow (or maximum dollars of net outflow), period by period. Making similar judgments as to the maximum adverse conditions immediately preceding the recession—including prerecession cash balances—it is next possible to determine whether, under such maximum assumptions, the company would become insolvent and, if so, how soon and by how much.

This calculation in itself will give management some "feel" for the nearness or remoteness of the event of cash insolvency. It may demonstrate, as I have done in the case of certain companies, that even under these maximum adverse assumptions the company still has a positive cash balance. If this is so, the amount of this minimum balance is an objective judgment of the total amount of incremental fixed cash charges which the company could assume without *any* threat of insolvency. Making some assumptions about the nature and the terms of the debt contract, this figure could be converted into the principal amount of additional debt which could be assumed with the expectation of complete safety.

Suppose, on the other hand, that the maximum adverse assumptions produce a negative cash balance, indicating the possibility of insolvency under certain adverse conditions. This does not mean that the long-term debt is excluded (except for those managements for whom any action which creates or increases the risk of insolvency, no matter how small it may be, is intolerable). The more likely response will be that, provided the chances are "sufficiently remote," the company is fully prepared to run the risk.

Thus, we are back to the problem of assessing the magnitude of the risk and the extent to which it would be increased by any given amount of debt. As a means of gaining a more precise impression of the chances of insolvency at the adverse end of the range of recession behavior, without going through the formal process of assigning probability values, I suggest that a second adverse limit be defined for each of the factors affecting cash flow. This will be called the *most probable adverse limit*. It reflects management's judgment as to the limit of *normal* recession behavior, as opposed to the maximum adverse limit, which includes all possibilities, however remote.

Modes & Ranges

A visual representation of these two adverse limits of behavior is shown in Exhibit I. Assuming experience and expected behavior are somewhat normally distributed about a mode (i.e., the value of most frequent occurrence), there will be:

1. A range of values clustered around this point, where most of past experience has been concentrated and where "bets" as to what the future is likely to bring will also be concentrated.

2. Extremes at either end of the range representing events that have a relatively small chance of happening.

It will be seen that the most probable limit cuts off the extreme "tail" of the frequency distribution in a somewhat imprecise and yet meaningful way. In setting the limits of expected sales contractions, for example, management

Exhibit I

EXAMPLE OF MAXIMUM AND MOST PROBABLE
LIMITS OF RECESSION BEHAVIOR

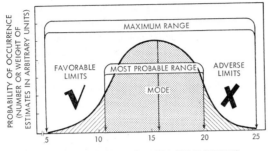

CONTRACTION OF SALES VOLUME (PERCENT)

would be saying that while sales *could,* in its judgment, contract as much as 25%, a contraction is *not likely* to exceed, say, 20%. This 20% is then the most probable adverse limit. While my terms may be new to businessmen, the distinction described is one which is commonly made and one on which judgments as to risk are often based.

From the data on the most probable adverse limits of the various factors affecting cash flow, the most probable adverse limit of recession *net* cash flows would be calculated and, from this, the most probable minimum recession cash *balance.* This last figure reflects management's best judgment as to the adverse limit of what is "likely to happen" as opposed to what "could happen" to net cash flows.

Guidelines for Policy

At this point it should be noted that, when considering cash flows from the point of view of solvency, the list of possible expenditures would be stripped down to those which are absolutely essential for continuity of corporate existence and for the generation of current income. (We will presently bring into consideration other less mandatory expenditures such as dividends and capital expenditures.) Thinking in these terms, suppose the recession cash flow analysis indicates that under the maximum adverse assumptions the minimum cash balance would be negative, say, a deficit of $1,500,000. Suppose further that under the most probable adverse assumptions the minimum recession cash balance is a surplus of $3,000,000. How are these estimates to be interpreted as a guide to corporate debt capacity?

First, it is obvious in this example that management's expectations about the factors governing cash flow include the possibility that the company could become insolvent without any additional debt. However, this possibility is considered to have a relatively remote chance of occurrence since when the analysis is restricted to the most probable limit of recession behavior, the company is left with a positive minimum cash balance. The amount of this balance is a rough measure of the *total amount of additional fixed cash outflows (e.g., debt charges) which could be incurred without creating the threat of insolvency* in the event of normal recession conditions. Thus:

If the likely limit of the recession is expected to be two years, the company could stand additional debt servicing of $1,500,000 per year of recession. This sum can be readily converted into an equivalent principal amount. Assuming a 20-year term loan repayable in equal annual installments and bearing 5% interest, an additional debt of approximately $15,000,000 could be considered safe under ordinary recession conditions.

Let me emphasize that the cash balance would not be taken as a guide to debt capacity unless management were prepared to live with some chance of insolvency—a chance which would obviously be increased by the new debt. If management were not so inclined, it would reject debt or alternatively adopt a debt limit somewhere between zero and $15,000,000. In any case, management would not increase debt *beyond* $15,000,000 unless it were prepared to accept the chance of insolvency within the most probable range of recession experience. Because of the way the most probable limit has been defined, the chances of insolvency would be expected to increase rapidly and substantially if debt were to exceed $15,000,000 by any significant amount.

There is, of course, nothing sacred about the $15,000,000 limit set by management's judgment on the limits of normal recession experience. There is no reason why some managements would not increase debt capital substantially above this figure, assuming the funds were available. Such a step depends entirely on the willingness to bear the financial risks and on the potential rewards for such risk bearing. The foregoing type of analysis does, however, perform the essential function of alerting management to the range of debt beyond which risks may be expected to increase substantially.

Practical Advantages

It is now apparent that the analytical approach proposed here produces a criterion stated in terms of *the number of dollars of debt servicing* that are acceptable within management's concepts of risk bearing at a given point in time. The criterion is derived entirely from within and is completely independent of external judgments or rules of thumb. While it is admittedly crude and approximate when compared with the theoretical ideal of risk management, I believe it to be meaningful and useful in practice and, in this as in other respects, superior to the conventional forms for expressing debt limits.

It must be added, however, that because the recommended analysis is partial and approximate, those who adopt it must use it as they use current decision rules. That is, they must use it as a general guide and not as a precision instrument. For most managements this will be entirely adequate.

BETTER DECISION MAKING

One of the real advantages of this approach to debt capacity is that it raises—and answers—a much broader question. As previously indicated, the analysis is actually concerned with the capacity to assume additional fixed cash outflows of any kind, and whatever capacity is demonstrated is not confined to debt servicing. Thus, if it is concluded from the example just given that the company in question can stand an additional outflow in recessions totaling $3,000,000, the first decision to be made by management is *how to use this capacity.*

There are a variety of ways in which the capacity may be used: to cover payments under a lease contract, to maintain a continuous research program, to stabilize employment, to pay a regular dividend in good times and bad, and so on. These are all competing uses for whatever capacity exists. With the information that the cash flow analysis provides, management now can begin to assign priorities and have some idea of how far it can hope to go in realizing its objectives. If debt servicing is given top priority, then the data have been a means of defining debt capacity.

It is because the proposed analysis has much broader significance than the question of debt (important as that question may be) that I believe the expenditure of time, effort, and money required to generate the data needed is well justified for the individual corporation. The analysis provides information which lies at the base of a whole range of financial and other decisions and has continuing significance. Moreover, most corporate treasurers have the staff and the basic data to undertake a careful and detailed study of the behavior of factors affecting cash flow.

Testing for Cash Adequacy

Up to this point the analysis of cash flows has been discussed in terms of cash solvency. As indicated earlier, this means that attention is confined to outflows which are vital to survival. It was also indicated, however, that the risk of insolvency was part of a broader family of risks, described as the risk of cash inadequacy. In discussing the question of solvency with management we often find that while there are certain expenditures which *could* be slashed to zero in an emergency, there is a reluctance to take action which would put management in a position of having to do so. These are expenditures which must be treated as mandatory for policy reasons, because management believes that to interrupt them would be detrimental to the long-term interest of the corporation. Among the best examples of such expenditures are certain minimum payments for research, for capital assets, and for preferred and common dividends.

This situation can readily be incorporated into the type of analysis outlined earlier. I refer to the method for doing this as the *test for cash adequacy* as opposed to the test for cash solvency. As soon as management has defined the "irreducible minimum" for these expenditures under recession conditions, they are merely added to the outflows of the previous analysis; then the figure generated for the maximum adverse or most probable adverse recession cash balance is the balance which remains over and above such payments. To return to the example previously used:

The effect would be to wipe out all or some portion of the most probable minimum balance ($3,000,000) or to add to the maximum adverse deficit ($1,500,000). Thus, if the irreducible minimum is considered to be two years of common dividends at $500,000 a year plus $1,000,000 of minimum capital expenditures, the result would be to cut the most probable balance back to $1,000,000. The capacity to assume additional fixed cash outflows is thereby substantially reduced. Obviously management in this case is giving priority to the dividend and capital expenditures over debt leverage—or over any other use for the funds on hand.

One of the benefits of such an analysis is to make management's priorities explicit, to recognize their competing character, and to make possible a re-evaluation of their relative importance to the company.

Making separate tests for cash solvency and cash adequacy serves another important purpose. Most discussions of the hazards of debt imply that the danger is the risk of insolvency, and this danger is usually treated with proper respect. However, our analysis may demonstrate that within the range of management's expectations there is little or no risk of insolvency but a substantial risk of cash inadequacy, particularly if large amounts of long-term debt are added. If, in the past, management has been setting limits on debt in terms of an assumed risk of insolvency and now finds that the only significant risk is that of inability to meet certain minimum dividend payments and the like, it may well be disposed to assume a greater magnitude of risk and take on more debt. A management which would reject the risk of insolvency if it exceeded a chance of one in fifty might be prepared to accept a risk of abandoning cash dividends for a year or two if the chance did not exceed, say, one in twenty.

In short, once management knows the *kind* of risk it is taking, it may begin to draw distinctions between one form of contingency and another and not operate on the general assumption that the only concern is that of possible insolvency. Better information is thus a prerequisite for better decisions.

Reappraising Present Rules

Assuming management can, by the means described, come up with an independent appraisal of its long-term debt capacity, what does this imply for existing decision rules obtained from external sources or inherited from the past? Does it mean that they will be ignored completely? The answer is likely to be no. Debt policy cannot be made in a vacuum. It must take account of the lenders' willingness to lend and also of the reactions of equity investors who make judgments on the risks inherent in the corporation.

One of the first results of the analysis, therefore, is to reappraise existing debt-capacity decision rules. To illustrate:

Suppose a company has been assuming, as many do, that it can safely incur long-term debt up to a maximum of 30% of capitalization. This rule can be translated into its equivalent of dollars of annual debt-servicing charges and directly compared with the results of the recession cash flow analysis. In view of the fact that the rule probably has been derived from external sources, it is likely that the annual debt servicing which it permits either exceeds or falls short of the amount of cash flow indicated by the internal analysis.

In view of the approximate nature of the analysis, however, this is not likely to cause a change in debt policy unless the amount of the variation is substantial. It is also possible, of course, that the existing decision rule and the cash flow analysis will produce the same result—in which case the existing rule will appear verified. But this cannot be known in advance of the analysis, and in any case the data have been converted into a form which is much more meaningful for the purposes involved.

Such a comparison gives a measure of management's attitude toward the risk that is implicit in the existing decision rule (although management probably had no clear idea of what the risk magnitude was at the time the rule was established).

The results of the cash flow analysis can also be compared with the lender's concept of debt capacity—if different from that of the corporation. While lenders are often reluctant to make statements on the outside limits of what they will lend, they will, from time to time, give indications of what they consider an appropriate capital structure for a given industry and company. If the borrower's appraisal of his capacity exceeds that of the lender, he may well decide to push the latter to the limit of his willingness to lend. Without good cash flow data, many borrowers appear reluctant to argue their case aggressively, probably because of uncertainty as to where the safe limit lies.

The results can also be related to other aspects of the debt-capacity question, such as the requirements for an A bond rating or the risk expectations of equity investors which appear to be implicit in some price-earnings ratio (assuming this can be determined). Once again, the comparison is between whatever unused debt capacity is indicated by the internal analysis and the standards imposed by external considerations with the aim of probing the acceptable and useful upper limits of long-term debt.

I have carried out this type of analysis for a sample of companies in different industries and made comparisons with existing debt-capacity standards of both the corporations themselves and their lending institutions. The data strongly indicate that there are, in fact, major inconsistencies between managements' explicit expectations regarding recession cash flows and the expectations which are implicit in accepted ratios of debt capacity. The evidence is by no means adequate to make any safe or meaningful generalization about the over-all character of industrial debt policy. Nevertheless, among the large and mature corporations which are the basis of the study the evidence seems to suggest:

Either the risks of debt have been significantly overrated by a substantial number of firms.

Or some managements tend to be unusually conservative toward this aspect of corporate risk.

FUTURE TRENDS

The trend of economic events in the past 20 years suggests that there is both a need and an opportunity for a more refined approach to the debt-equity choice in corporate structures. As the specter of the depression of the 1930's has faded into the past and confidence in our capacity to avoid a repetition of extreme economic stagnation has grown, a new generation of corporate executives has shown increasing willingness to use long-term debt financing as a source of funds for consolidation and expansion.

So long as long-term debt is avoided or kept to minor proportions, crude decision rules providing wide margins of safety are quite adequate. As the proportions of debt increase, however, the need for a sharper pencil and a more careful analysis grows. This need is further reinforced by the increase in other kinds of fixed cash commitments such as lease payments and the noncontractual but none-the-less-vital steady flows required for research, dividends, and the like. Greater stability in the economy over an extended period is likely to encourage a variety of rigidities in cash outflows, and simple rules of thumb are inadequate to cope with the problems these present.

Along with the increasing need for improved analysis has come a greater capacity to carry out this analysis. This improvement derives both from better data and from improved techniques of processing and analyzing data. Financial executives today have access to far more data on cash flows and the factors behind cash flows than they did 20 years ago—far more, in fact, than many are actually putting to use. They also have access to more sophisticated approaches to the analysis of complex data and to machines which can reduce it to manageable proportions. As time goes on and financial management becomes increasingly familiar with these tools of analysis and more aware of the opportunities they afford, the current reluctance to adopt a more complex analytical framework is bound to diminish.

But there is one hitch. However sophisticated the financial officer may be in the newer techniques, there is little merit in serving up a diet of financial data to the board of directors, as a basis for the financial decision, which is too rich for their current digestive capacity. It is for this reason that I have not attempted in this article to convert the reader to a full-scale internal analysis of risk and its components. Rather, I have taken on the more modest objective of alerting top management to four key points bearing on the debt-capacity decision:

1. While external sources of advice can and should be consulted as an aid to decision making, the question of debt capacity is essentially an internal one to be settled by management with reference to its individual circumstances and individual preferences.

2. Current rules of thumb regarding debt capacity are seriously inadequate as a framework for this decision.

3. The answer lies in a knowledge of the behavior of cash flows and in having a useful measure of the capacity to assume incremental fixed cash outflows.

4. Management needs approaches that will enable it to approximate its debt capacity within the context of data with which it is already familiar and in terms of judgments to which it has long been accustomed. The approach described in this article meets these criteria.

By accepting and acting on these points, management would take an important step forward toward debt-equity decisions in which borrowers and lenders alike could have greater confidence.

DIVIDENDS, EARNINGS, LEVERAGE, STOCK PRICES AND THE SUPPLY OF CAPITAL TO CORPORATIONS *

By John Lintner †

THE THEORY of the valuation of income streams has a central and honored place in economic doctrine.[1] Due largely to the work of Irving Fisher [10], Samuelson [29], and Hicks [15], certain important essentials are well established. Special problems arise, however, in the valuation by investors of the income stream of corporations which require careful analysis. That these special problems require further attention by the profession is clearly indicated by the fact that there are fundamental differences in the theories offered in the existing literature by eminent and highly reputable authors regarding the relationships between dividends, earnings, leverage and stock prices.

The resolution of these differences is important for our understanding of the stock market and capital markets generally. It is also essential to the resolution of the marked differences in the decision rules which have been proposed for determining the optimal capital budgets of a corporation and its optimal capital structure and reliance on different sources of financing. For these mutually inconsistent and contradictory rules[2] have all been advanced as specifications of corporate decisions to maximize the current market value of its equity capital. Given agreement on this decision-goal or "criterion of

* Reprinted by permission from *The Review of Economics and Statistics*, 44 (August 1962), pp. 243–69.

† George Gund Professor of Economics and Business Administration, Harvard University.

[1] This article is largely drawn from the longer paper presented at the meetings of the Econometric Society in St. Louis on December 29, 1960 [18]. The present paper is one part of a series of interrelated theoretical and statistical studies of corporate and financial policies which we have been conducting at the Harvard Business School under a grant of the Rockefeller Foundation for work in the general area of profits in the functioning of the economy. The Foundation's generous support for this work is most gratefully acknowledged.

[2] For a summary of these rules—and the fact that they are mutually inconsistent in the sense that they would lead to (often substantially) different decisions under given sets of circumstances—see Lintner [19].

goodness," major differences in decision rules follow directly from the differences in the assumptions the various authors have made, and more generally in the models they have used, to explain (a) the determination of stock market prices when there is no debt outstanding, and (b) the effects of leverage on those prices. In this context, the most significant differences involve the respective authors' choice of one of two basic assumptions within each of the two categories just noted.

The Valuation of Unlevered Equity. The first essential issue regarding equity values in the absence of debt is whether stock values, *ceteris paribus*, are a function of corporate earnings *independent* of dividends. One group of authors, whom we will call the "pure earnings" theorists, assert or assume the validity of this proposition as the starting point of their analysis. This group includes Durand in his famous National Bureau paper [7], the Lutzes [20], Solomon [30], Roberts [28], Kuh [16], Dean [4] and Weston [34], and perhaps most notably Modigliani-Miller who go so far as to state that "as long as management is presumed to be acting in the best interests of the stockholders, retained earnings can be regarded as equivalent to a fully subscribed, pre-emptive issue of common stock. Hence, for present purposes, the division of the (earnings) stream between cash dividends and retained earnings is a mere detail." [23, p. 226]

Other important authors, notably Walter [32], Gordon [11–13], and Gordon-Shapiro [14], and Bierman-Fouraker-Jaedicke [1] have based their whole analysis of stock prices (and of the preferences of stockholders regarding corporate capital budgets, dividends and other financing, as reflected in changes in stock prices) on the assumption or judgment of fact that valuations do and should equal the present value of expected dividend streams. Durand has also later taken this position. [8, 9] We should also note that other eminent economists writing earlier on the valuation of equities (though they did not follow through to present theories of normative corporate budgeting and financing), based their analysis squarely on dividends. This latter group includes Preinreich [27], Tinbergen [31], and J. B. Williams [35]. For all these authors, to paraphrase the Modigliani-Miller statement, "given the dividend stream, the earnings stream that happens to be associated with it is a mere detail." But this does *not* mean that stock prices are independent of (currently expected or observed) earnings and capital budgets, since current dividends are related to current earnings by way of the payout ratio and (retained) earnings and company investments are taken into account as a major determinant of the prospective growth of the dividend stream.

The real distinction between the two groups of authors is thus just what was stated above: those in the "pure earnings" group assert that unlevered stock values depend on earnings independent of dividends; those in the "dividend" group assert that they are *ceteris paribus* a function of dividends—that, in particular, the significance of the time vector of earnings (and of investments within the firm) lies in its implications *for* the prospective stream of dividends (rather than vice versa as suggested in [24, 25]; and that dividends and "payout ratios" *do* make a difference that matters in equity values, and hence in the cost of capital, even when earnings (and internal corporate investment) streams are prespecified and fixed in advance.

So much for this first essential issue. As might be expected, there are also some major differences among the "earnings" theorists as to *what* earnings are being capitalized in the market. Specifically, Dean, Roberts, Kuh, and Weston use current corporate earnings; Solomon uses "average future" earnings as did Modigliani-Zeman in [26] and Modigliani-Miller in [23] (although each of the latter averages is much different from Solomon's); and finally, Modigliani-Miller in a new paper [25] advance still a different "earnings" as their candidate for what should be capitalized. Since all these authors assume investor rationality, this issue comes down to what earnings *should* be capitalized by rational investors *if* values are to be determined as a function of earnings (and perhaps corporate investments); we show below that in these terms the discrimination is clear—and, incidentally, depends upon the resolution of the more fundamental issues emphasized before.

The Effect of Leverage on Equity Values.   On this problem, there are again two clearly defined schools of thought, both being represented and developed in Durand's National Bureau paper [7]. The first argues that the investment market in effect capitalizes the *net operating* income of the *corporation as a whole* and that this market value of the entire corporate entity is reduced by the market value of outstanding debt to determine the market value of the corporate equity. Since the central proposition of this school is that the *entity value* (the sum of debt and equity values) is independent of the proportion of debt, we will refer to this hypothesis or proposition as the "entity value" theory. This "net operating income" or "entity value" position is firmly taken by Modigliani-Miller and is implicit in Dean's earlier writing.

In sharp contrast to this model of investment market behavior is the alternative model in which the valuation of the corporate equity is determined by the capitalization of *net earnings* (after depreciation, taxes, *and* interest); the aggregate value of the corporate entity is then equal to the sum of the value of the equity so determined and the market value of the outstanding debt. This position that equity values represent the direct capitalization of the *"net earnings on equity"* is taken by Solomon, Kuh, Roberts, Weston, and presumably the Lutzes. Gordon has taken a corresponding position when equity values are assumed to depend on dividend flows.

The essential difference between the two schools may be most clearly brought out by noting the different predictions each would make regarding the effects of a substitution between debt and equity financing with fixed operating earnings and given capital budgets. Proponents of the "net operating income" position hold that the reduced net earnings due to interest *and* the increased discount rate due to added risk on equity as debt is increased, will together reduce equity values in an amount *equal to* the market value of the new debt issued—that is, the sum of the equity and debt at market values is a constant. For these authors, consequently, the optimal mix of debt and equity financing is indeterminate apart from (allegedly relatively small) tax effects.[3] In the same circumstances, the "net earnings" group hold that, in general, the reduced net earnings and increased risk together lower market values by an amount (which can be substantially) *different from* the dollar amount of the debt issue, the amount of the difference depending on the circumstances including the debt-equity ratio. For this larger group of writers, consequently, the debt-equity ratio does make a conceptually very significant difference (even in the absence of taxes), and there *is* for them a real normative problem of determining the most appropriate reliance on debt financing for any given size of capital budget.[4]

It is clear from the above discussion that—although two positions on unlevered equity valuation and two on leverage effects produce four basic models of market valuations—the essential issues involved in choosing among the four types depend upon acceptance or rejection of the necessary sets of conditions required to validate only two propositions. In their purest and most sophisticated form as advanced by Modigliani and Miller, these two propositions read: (1) *Ceteris paribus,* the valuation of unlevered equities is determined by (expectational) current earnings independent of dividends; and (2) The market valuation of the corporate entity is independent of its capitalization, apart from corporate tax differentials due to the deductibility of debt interest. If the conditions necessary or sufficient for the validity of the former proposition are not satisfied, then "dividend theories"—or, more properly perhaps, "dividend-and-earnings-and-investment" theories—must be used, since dividends *will* make a difference. Similarly, if conditions necessary or sufficient for the validity of the "entity value" theory are not satisfied, equity values will not be determined by a simple subtraction of outstanding debt from entity values, and explicit theories will be required to explain the resulting direct, variable and non-linear impact of debt-equity ratios upon equity values. The present paper consequently undertakes to determine rigor-

---

[3] See Modigliani-Miller [23], pp. 272, 294 ff. Incidentally, the relevant tax differentials for these authors are simply those following from the fact that interest is (while both retained earnings and dividends are not) a deductible expense in computing corporate income tax liabilities. These authors have not considered the implications of personal tax differentials between dividends (ordinary income) and capital gains for the optimal *mix* of debt and equity. (Cf. 48–49 below.)

[4] It should be pointed out that the validity of the entity value theory is basic not merely to the question of the proper determination of equity values, but to the further issue of whether "the cost of capital" for capital budgeting decisions is properly taken to be the weighted average cost of all equity *and* (at least long-term) debt, or whether it is simply the cost measured in terms of the owner's equity, as has also been strongly proposed—the cash flows from borrowing and debt service being deducted from those of the internal investment plan to determine *net* flows after borrowing and interest charges whose present value or rate of return is comparable with the cost of equity capital. Since these further issues involve the decision rule inferences regarding the proper size of capital budget to be drawn *from* different premises regarding the effect of leverage on equity values, which are the subject of the present paper, we must defer our examination of them to a separate manuscript [19].

ously the necessary and sufficient underlying conditions for the validity of these two central propositions.

This objective can best be accomplished by examining whether each proposition is valid under fully idealized neo-classical conditions and then, if so, whether it remains valid as we successively remove the special assumptions involved in this idealization and proceed by explicit steps to progressively more general and seemingly more realistic market conditions. Whenever either proposition is invalid, we examine the nature of the discrepancies and their implication for "dividend theories" of market values. Since the first (and in a sense, more fundamental) issue is simply whether, with earnings streams given, equity valuations are independent of dividends—and since the size of the earnings is a direct function of the size of the capital budget—*we will assume throughout* that the time-vectors of both corporate *earnings* (before interest) and *capital budgets* are *given* and invariant to the form of financing,[5] and that all substitutions in the finance-mix occur *instantaneously* and *simultaneously*. This framework is, of course, equally useful for the analysis of the second major issue raised. It must be emphasized that these assumptions establish a theoretical laboratory model in which any impact of substitutions in the finance-mix on share values (and shareholder preferences) will be strictly *independent* of changes in the size of capital budgets (and, hence, of the impact of increased investments on prices by way of their effect upon earnings and growth), and *also independent* of the shape of the time vector of discount rates k_τ—and, in particular, of whether the discount rates used at any instant in making valuations of prospective income streams are *or* are not an increasing function of futurity to allow for differences in uncertainty over the future.[6]

The entire analysis of this paper, therefore, is focused upon the single, broader issue—given the earnings and investment vectors for the present period and all future time, how does the value of the equity and the value of the corporate entity (equity value plus long-term debt) depend upon the finance-mix—which underlies the major disagreements in the current literature of corporate finance and capital budgeting. The unavoidable detail and

---

[5] In those sections in which uncertainty is introduced, it is, of course, the probability distributions of the time vectors of earnings and capital budgets which are predetermined and invariant to the form of financing. We make one exception to the statement in the text near the end of the paper when we show that this condition, even though otherwise met, *cannot* remain valid under uncertainty when there is heavy reliance on debt.

[6] Our analysis thus differs fundamentally from that of Gordon [11–13] who justifies his use of a "dividend" instead of "earnings" theory on the grounds that (a) average profitability of investments in the corporation may be greater than the average discount rate, and (b) that changes in dividends change investments which change future dividends thereby increasing the average discount rate applicable to the expected dividend stream when the vector k_τ rises with futurity due to uncertainty. Our analysis in this paper (1) permits no change in investments (and implies no change in future dividends), and (2) makes *no* restrictive assumptions regarding either the profitability of investments *or* the time shape of the discount vector k_τ. We also find dividend theories valid (when earnings theories are not) in important classes of markets under certainty.

complexity of the required analysis of these fundamentals makes it necessary to defer to another article [19] the specific implications of our results for the "cost of capital," the functional relation between equity values and size of capital budgets (assuming an optimal finance mix for each possible size of budget) and the determination of the optimal capital budgets and corporate growth under various given "profit possibility" functions.

Specifications of Market Conditions. We assume throughout—in keeping with all the authors previously cited—that:

(a) All securities (equities and debts) are traded in *purely competitive markets*. Every investor is sufficiently small relative to the market that none needs to consider the potential impact of his own actions on the then market price.[7]

(b) All purchases and sales of securities by investors are motivated solely by considerations of personal gain. *Each* investor will continue to buy and sell, until he has obtained that combination of assets he prefers to *any* other available to him, and this preferred combination will be the one which maximizes his current wealth. *Maximizing behavior is assumed to be universal.*

(c) Stock prices, like all other capital values, are equal to the *present worth* of anticipated future returns as judged by those trading in the market place. This return to the shareholder is equal to the sum of the cash dividends received while the stock is held, increased or decreased by the difference between the present price P_o and the future price at time of sale P_t.

These three conditions are of course attributes of neo-classical capital markets. We shall speak of the set of these three conditions as defining *generalized neo-classical conditions* in the capital markets.

Most authors have, in addition, implicitly or explicitly assumed the following three additional conditions:

(d) There is *no uncertainty.* Otherwise stated, *all* participants in the market are endowed with perfect prescience, and all information is *costless, certain,* and *complete* in all relevant aspects throughout the market. An important *corollary* for the present applications is: there is *precise uniformity and agreement* in the knowledge held by all actual and potential investors.

(e) There are *no transfer or transaction costs,* including new issue costs.

(f) There are either *no taxes* or at least no relevant tax differentials which have any effect on preferences or on purchases or sales.

We shall speak of capital markets satisfying the entire set of six conditions (a)–(f) inclusive as being *fully idealized neo-classical markets.* We shall correspondingly speak of markets satisfying conditions (a)–(d) inclusive as *generalized neo-classical markets with certainty.*

---

[7] We must, of course, recognize that each corporation is the sole issuer of its own securities.

Outline of Paper. Section II examines the validity of the dividend and pure earnings theories under conditions of certainty, starting with *fully idealized* neo-classical conditions, and then introducing costs and taxes. Section III introduces uncertainty—first in a specially restricted and then in more general forms (the differences depending upon whether or not there is uniformity among investors in information and subjective probability distributions). Again, the analysis is first made assuming no costs and taxes. The analysis in Sections II and III turns on investor indifference to substitutions between retained earnings (reduced dividends) and new equity issues, when there is no borrowing. Section IV then examines investor indifference to (or preferences regarding) substitutions between retained earnings and debt—and the validity of the "entity value" theory—under the same sequence of market types. At intermediate points in the paper conclusions important in the context of the literature are stated, and general conclusions are summarized at the end.

Before proceeding with this analysis, however, we should explicitly note that our results as a by-product necessarily involve a further issue in the literature not yet specifically mentioned—namely, whether the supply of capital function to the corporation is a smooth function (whether or not linear as for Modigliani and Miller and associated authors, or curvilinear as for others) *or* whether it is an essentially *discontinuous* function with a sharply rising segment or discontinuity at the point where retained funds are exhausted and *outside* capital (whether new equity or long-term debt) is first availed of. Such a discontinuity is ruled out in the writings of Modigliani-Miller, Kuh and Weston while it has been explicitly asserted[8] by Meyer-Kuh [22], Duesenberry [6] and earlier writings of the present author [17]. In the present paper we, of course, do not get into the empirical question of whether management, in fact, acts in terms of such discontinuity but are concerned solely with whether rational managements *should* act in terms of a supply-of-capital function exhibiting such a discontinuity under different specified sets of underlying assumptions.

II. DIVIDEND AND "PURE EARNINGS" THEORIES UNDER CERTAINTY

1. The Criterion

The basic theorem regarding relative prices in idealized neo-classical theory insures that security purchases and sales transactions will continue under these omniscient, frictionless, purely competitive conditions until market prices at the beginning of *each* period for *all* securities, presently and over *all* future time, have been established which will simultaneously satisfy the following *critical condition:*

---

[8] Solomon [30] also introduces a discontinuity for outside equity, though not for debt, and only to recognize issue costs and not taxes or uncertainty.

For all time periods $t\,(o \leqslant t \leqslant \infty)$: the *sum* of own-cash-returns as a ratio to own-market-price at the beginning of the period *plus* the percentage change of this price within the period must (a) be equal for all securities and (b) be equal to the market rate of interest $k(t)$.[9]

Taking current cash dividends properly as the own-cash-return, this requires

$$\frac{D_{it}}{P_{it}} + \frac{P_{i(t+1)} - P_{it}}{P_{it}} = k_t$$
$$= \frac{D_{jt}}{P_{jt}} + \frac{P_{j(t+1)} - P_{jt}}{P_{jt}} \tag{1}$$

for all possible pairs of firms, i, j and for all t, where D_t is cash dividend payments per share outstanding at the beginning of period t, P_t the price of a share at the beginning of period t (excluding any dividend in $t-1$), and k_t the market interest rate in period t, which for generality may be different for all t.

2. Analysis under Idealized Neo-Classical Conditions

2a. *The Dividend Theory.* The dividend theory asserts that the value of any share of stock at the beginning of any period is equal under neo-classical conditions to the present value of the dividend stream looking forward from the beginning of the period, just after the receipt of the last dividend. The proof that this value formula satisfies our criterion is straightforward, since this formula gives for any firm at any time t

$$P_{it} = \sum_{m=0}^{\infty} \frac{D_{i(t+m)}}{\prod_{\tau=0}^{m} (1 + k_{t+\tau})}$$
$$= \frac{1}{1 + k_t} \left[D_{it} + \sum_{m=1}^{\infty} \frac{D_{i(t+m)}}{\prod_{\tau=1}^{m} (1 + k_{t+\tau})} \right] \tag{2}$$

and since the summation in the latter bracket is $P_{i(t+1)}$, we have

$$P_{it} = \frac{D_{it} + P_{i(t+1)}}{1 + k_t}. \tag{3}$$

Substitution in the left equation of (1) reduces to the identity $k_t \equiv k_t$. The same formula for the jth firm reduces to the same identity, and things identically equal to the same thing are identically equal to each other. The dividend theory thus satisfies the required criterion for all firms and for all periods of time. Since, moreover, the length of the time unit considered is arbitrary, in the limit it will do so continuously. (See also Lintner [19].)

Because the dividend theory satisfies the criterion identically and continuously over time, we have an apparent *corollary:*

Any alternative valuation formula is valid if and only if it is identically

---

[9] Cf. Samuelson [29], Fisher [10], Hicks [15] and Dorfman, Samuelson, Solow [5].

equivalent to the dividend valuation formula. In particular, any earnings theory is valid *only if* it is identical with the dividend theory.

2b. *One Particular Set of "Earnings Theories" Is Also Valid under Idealized Neo-classical Conditions.* One obvious way to derive a valid valuation formula based on earnings is to make use of the accounting identity which says that, in any time period, funds invested F_t, must be equal to the sum of earnings before interest Y'_t and the *net* proceeds of new stock issues S_t and of new borrowing $\dot{B}_t$, *less* dividends paid D_t and interest i_tB_t on outstanding debt B_t:

$$F_t = Y'_t + S_t + \dot{B}_t - D_t - i_tB_t. \tag{4}$$

Letting Y_t be earnings at time t after deducting interest on outstanding debt [that is, $Y_t = Y'_t - i_tB_t$] equation (4) may be written

$$D_t = Y_t + S_t + \dot{B}_t - F_t. \tag{5}$$

Equations (4) and (5) are clearly valid when the variables denote company aggregates or amounts per share of currently outstanding stock at any time. Using the latter measurement and substituting in (2), we have for the price per share at time t:

$$P_{it} = \sum_{m=0}^{\infty} \frac{Y'_{t+m} + S_{t+m} + \dot{B}_{t+m} - F_{t+m} - i_{t+m}B_{t+m}}{\prod_{\tau=0}^{m} (1 + k_{t+\tau})}$$

$$= \sum_{m=0}^{\infty} \frac{Y_{t+m} - [F_{t+m} - (S_{t+m} + \dot{B}_{t+m})]}{\prod_{\tau=0}^{m} (1 + k_{t+\tau})} \tag{6}$$

which clearly satisfy the neo-classical criterion (1) because (2) does. q.e.d.

2c. *Implications Regarding Differences over What Earnings are Capitalized.* Equation (6) specifies a large number of distinct and individually valid "earnings and investment theories" because both Y_t and F_t enter with opposite sign. Both terms may be measured gross before deducting any depreciation charges, thereby preserving the "cash flow" approach *within* the corporation; but the market valuation formula is equally valid when Y_t and F_t are defined as net earnings and investment respectively after deducting depreciation on the basis of *any* formula or specification—indeed after deducting any fraction (or multiple!) of depreciation under any such formula. But while there are numerous specifications of net earnings Y_t (and investment) consistent with (6), it is nevertheless immediately apparent that price models assuming a capitalization of *current earnings* are either *not generally valid* or leave the entire weight of the determination of the capitalization multiple on implicit unspecified factors.[10] Similarly, the apparently more

---

[10] This model is valid only if the factor used to capitalize current earnings is implicitly equated to the ratio of the current period's earnings to the present value of the entire net stream shown by the right-hand side of (6); even then the model is only valid for a comparative static analysis which relies on changes in price-earnings ratios without

sophisticated proposals that the market capitalizes *average future earnings*[11] are valid under non-stationary conditions *only if* "average future earnings" are taken to be the particular weighted average of future earnings obtained by using the discount factors $[\prod_{r=0}^{m} (1 + k\tau)^{-1}]$ as weights;[12] but *even if this* average of earnings is taken to be "average earnings," then the market does *not* capitalize "average earnings"—since the same weighted average of the *investments not externally financed* (the bracketed term in the numerator of (6)) *must be deducted.* A valid model nominally capitalizing "average earnings" thus turns out to be a model capitalizing average-earnings minus average-internally-financed-investments, which in all common usage would be understood to be something very different. Moreover, the computation of such complex weighted averages is actually redundant,[13] and models capitalizing such averages are doubly subject to the same problem of implicit theorizing as was noted above for capitalizations of the current period's earnings.[14]

2d. *Further Implications.*[15]   Altogether it seems much more straightfor-

---

exploring the determinants of these changes beyond the level of proximate assumption. Specifically, when the elements on the right side of (6) are not included, the interactions between changes in these elements (or alternatively in the dividend stream) cannot be analyzed even though they together determine the change in proximate price-earnings ratios (or in price itself) which would be implied by alternative financial and investment policies.

[11] Such models have been advanced in three classic papers. Solomon [30], p. 243 simply refers to "average future earnings" and Modigliani-Zeman [26], pp. 265, 297 to "expected, net, long-run average annual earnings" without specifying weights, which must be those indicated in the text in any but strictly static contexts. Modigliani-Miller in a later paper did specify what average, identifying the earnings being capitalized at any time as a stochastic variable defined as the limit (with increasing time) of the *undiscounted* average over time of earnings per present share [23], p. 265. But definitions valid under uncertainty should be valid in the limit under certainty as all variances approach zero, and it is clear that this formulation is logically untenable in any but static conditions even in the absence of uncertainty. Indeed, it is apparent that the present value in equation (6) will *not* be proportional to the time-average (with unit weights—that is, undiscounted) of annual earnings Y_t through the future as was proposed, *except* (a) in stationary states in which the values (or more generally the expected values) of each period's own earnings per present share are strictly constant over time, *and* (b) the investment budget F_t is financed exclusively with outside funds in every period. This is true even if the discount rates k_t are constant over all future time.

[12] It will be noted that the weights are "long-term" interest rates of varying length m, not the current period's rate.

[13] The numerator of the weighted average of each stream is its present value, which is divided by the sum of the weights in order to produce an "average" which may then be capitalized in turn by the sum of the weights!

[14] The problem is made worse by the reliance on averages since any shift in financial or investment policy will, in general, modify both the discount factor appropriate to capitalize the averages and the averages which are to be capitalized—vital considerations which in turn can at best (barring use of the complete model) be covered by proximate assumption.

[15] Given the focus of this paper we do not need to develop price models comparable to equation (6) for more generalized conditions. It should be noted, however, that as it stands (6) allows for costs of issue and underpricing (since S_t and $\dot{B}_t$ are included *net*), and is valid under uncertainty if either (a) certainty-equivalents are used

ward if one wants to relate market prices to present values of earnings to use (6) directly and speak of prices as being equal to the *difference* between the present values of the earnings stream and stream of investments not externally financed, when the elements of both streams are measured per share of currently outstanding stock. But the investments not externally financed require retained earnings so we can say that an earnings theory is valid under classic competitive conditions of certainty *only* when it is *identically* reducible to the form: the value of a share is equal to the present value of the prospective *earnings* stream *less* the present value of the stream of retained earnings (both per share of presently outstanding stock). But the difference in these two present values is *identical* with the present value of the prospective stream of cash dividend payments on the presently outstanding shares.[16]

Finally, since it is this identity which validates any "earnings theory" in the acceptable set, the theory of parsimony in theory building strongly suggests primary reliance on "dividend models" rather than "earnings models" *even when* the latter are valid. And when this is done, the models have the further advantage of directly embodying a theory which asserts that the value *to investors* is the discounted worth of the prospective cash flows *to investors*. Since these flows are the dividends paid, not the earnings of the corporation without adjustment—except under particular definitions and then only in special cases which equate earnings *to* dividends (for example, 100 per cent payouts each period)—the dividend models fit directly with the vast body of economics, which has always gone directly to the cash flows of the relevant decision-maker in any capital value problem, and do so in a direct and obvious way.[17] The alternative of saying that markets capitalize earnings and

in the numerator or (b) uncertainties are properly allowed for in the k_r vector. Tax elements require separate terms.

Particular emphasis should be given to the fact that the numerator in (6) is earnings *less* investments *not* externally financed, since Modigliani-Miller shift from "average earnings" in [23] to the entire earnings stream in [25], but subtract *all* investments (that is, omit our terms S_t and $\dot{B}_t$ in the numerator—see their eq. 9, p. 415). It can be shown (using results derived later in this paper) that their equations are equivalent to (6) above (and hence are valid) *if and only if* there are no costs of issuing debt or equity *and* there is no generalized uncertainty.

[16] Bodenhorn [2], esp. p. 489 reaches the same conclusions.

[17] It was precisely for this reason that, for instance, from my earliest theoretical work in this area (reflected, for instance, in my paper "Normative Criteria for Dividend Payouts in Large Corporations," *Abstract Econometrica* [October 1958], p. 603), I have *defined* corporate net earnings for any period in terms of the maximum cash dividend which (expectationally) *could* be paid in that period consistent with (pro-forma) no outside financing *and* with the *expectation* that a similarly large dividend *could* then be paid in future periods subject to the same constraint (this pro-forma constraint tying the earnings back to earnings on present assets). This definition has the important virtues of (a) making a 100 per cent dividend payout imply a constant (expected) earnings stream if there is no outside financing, (b) tying the concept of corporate earnings relevant to investors (and thereby market values) directly to the cash flow functionals of the investors themselves, while at the same time (c) avoiding the circularity of making *corporate* earnings a function of market price change (as do the standard Hicks-Alexander variants) —when market price is the thing to be explained, and finally (d) legitimately simplifying dynamic growth models through the use of concepts of *net* earnings and investment.

internal investments which are not cash flows to the investor himself sets up a theory outside the established body of theory, and one involving apparent discrepancies requiring rationalization to show that the alternative is "really all right after all."

All this being the case, the question is naturally raised why anyone should have advanced models based on earnings rather than dividends. The reason may perhaps be that if attention is confined to *strictly idealized* neo-classical markets, then with earnings and investment streams fixed, the price of the common stock is independent of the mix of retained earnings outside equity issues and borrowing used in financing. In short, *with these restrictions,* what we have termed the "pure earnings" or "pure earnings and investment" theory is valid—the market price is independent of the dividend policy as such, and of decisions regarding the timing of dividend payments. This theorem is proved in the next subsections using the dividend model of equation (6) to establish the indifference between retained earnings (reduction in cash dividends) and outside equity financing.[18] In the following sections, the necessity of each of the indicated restrictions (or idealizations of neo-classical conditions) for the validity of the proposition is examined.

2e. *If the Earnings and Internal Investment Streams Are Fixed and Invariant, Prices Are Independent of Particular Dividends under Strictly Idealized Neo-classical Conditions with No Borrowing.* All variables used so far refer to each share of stock outstanding at the beginning of period t. Since we are going to examine trade-offs between added retained earnings and new stock issues, we need two additional variables N_t, the number of shares outstanding at the beginning of period t, and $\Delta N_t = N_{t-1} - N_t$, the number issued within period t. For brevity, we will also let asterisks denote company aggregate values. Letting $P_t^* = N_t P_t$ be the aggregate value of the company, we have from (3),

$$P_t^* = N_t P_t = \frac{1}{1 + k_t} [N_t D_t + N_t P_{t+1}]$$
$$= \frac{1}{1 + k_t} [D_t^* + N_t P_{t+1}] \tag{3a}$$

and letting $B = \dot{B} = 0$ to exclude borrowing and bond financing, we have from (5)

$$D_t^* = Y_t^* + S_t^* - F_t^*. \tag{5a}$$

The value attached to the entire enterprise at the end of the period P_{t+1}^* under present assumptions is independent of the manner in which the current period's capital budget F_t^* is financed, since this ending value depends solely upon the earnings, investments, and dividends of periods beyond the present. Specifically,

---

[18] In Section IV. 1, p. 693, we establish the validity of the corresponding theorem that under these same fully idealized conditions market price is invariant *ceteris paribus* when substitutions are made between retained earnings and debt.

$$P^*_{t+1} = (N_t + \Delta N_t)P_{t+1} = \textbf{constant} \qquad (7)$$

for all ΔN_t, where ΔN_t is the number of new shares issued in period t.[19] Further, under the current assumption of no issue costs, the ending value attributable to presently outstanding stock is equal to this end-of-period value of the entity P^*_{t+1} less the dollar amount of outside financing S^*_t:

$$N_t P_{t+1} = P^*_{t+1} - S^*_t. \qquad (8)$$

With P^*_{t+1}, Y^*_t and F^*_t fixed, $\Delta D^*_t = \Delta S^*_t = -\Delta(N^*_t P_{t+1})$ so that from (3a)

$$\Delta P^*_t \bigg|_{\Delta D^* = \Delta S^*} = 0.^{20} \qquad (9)$$

Under these conditions the valuation of securities is independent both of current dividends and outside equity financing;—and since the same substitutions can be made for *any* period, the dividend policy under these conditions must be irrelevant to market values for all dates from here to eternity.

2f. *General Observations.* First, this sweeping theorem does *not* mean that market prices are not equal to the present value of cash dividend payments—witness that the theorem has been derived from the model in which they are equal to *this* present value. The essence of the theorem is simply that, *given* the time vectors of Y_t, F_t and k_t *and fully idealized* neo-classical market conditions, *all* investors will be indifferent to *all* substitutions between the elements in the efficient set of attainable time vectors of dividend payments. We have simply shown that, given the time vector of interest rates, earnings and investments are sufficient to determine prices without reference to dividends under fully idealized neo-classical conditions because *under these conditions they are sufficient to determine the dividend vector up to a specified indifference set,* all of whose elements (dividend vectors) have the same value.

Second, we observe that these results consequently do *not* mean that the influence of earnings and investments on price is direct rather than by way of their effect upon dividends *even under fully idealized* neo-classical conditions.

Third, any inference that under more general conditions market prices are determined by the vectors of earnings and internal investments independently of the particular time path of current and future distributions of cash dividends payments would clearly be premature unless and until any such greater generality has been rigorously established. The next section examines whether such extensions can validly be made.

---

[19] Note that the present assumptions, therefore, imply that the market price per share for a company's stock has unit elasticity, when investment budgets and aggregate company earnings are predetermined and known. This property was used by Kuh [16]. Alternatively, it should be noted the present assumptions imply that the aggregate value P^*_{t+1} is "infinitely elastic" with respect to the number of shares outstanding.

[20] A similar proof of this theorem has been independently developed by Modigliani and Miller in [25].

3. Analysis under Generalized Neo-Classical Conditions of Certainty

The fully idealized neo-classical world so far examined corresponds in pure static price theory to the models in which all aspects of Spatial Economics and Public Finance are ruled out by assumption. We now move step by step to what corresponds in financial theory to the neo-classical world generalized sufficiently to admit these important parts of neo-classical analysis. Specifically, we will allow for charges analogous to transport costs by introducing costs of issuing new equity shares, and we will introduce taxes at the shareholder level. The resulting models will correspond to neo-classical Spatial Economics and Public Finance because we will retain the assumptions of certainty or prescience, universal purely competitive markets, and maximizing behavior. As we relax the other "idealizing" assumptions so far used in order, we shall retain for simplicity at each step all assumptions except the one being relaxed. We first examine whether prices are independent of dividend payouts when fixed investment budgets are financed by retained earnings and/or new share issues with no borrowing, but with positive new issue costs. This leads to the following theorem:

3a. *Under Idealized Neo-classical Conditions, Except That New Issues Involve Either Fixed or Variable Cash Expense, Market Prices Are Not Independent of Cash Dividends in Any Period When There Is No Borrowing, Even If Earnings and Internal Investment Streams Are Fixed Forevermore.* The proof of this invariance when there are no issue costs was given above in section 2e. The proof of dependence on actual dividend payments in the face of issue costs follows directly when issue costs are introduced into the equations. Let C_t be the fixed costs of undertaking a new issue of securities and c_t be the variable costs so that the total costs of a new issue will be $C_t + c_t \Delta N_t$. Since S_t^* has been defined as the *net* proceeds or cash gain of new issues, equation (5a) is unaffected as an accounting identity. Moreover, in purely competitive markets with prescience, the end-of-period value of the company P_{t+1}^* will still be a constant determined by the (unchanged) relevant vectors from that point forward in time. But the aggregate market value of the newly-issued shares is now equal to the net cash gain of the company S_t^* *plus* issue costs. Equation (8) must consequently be rewritten as

$$N_t P_{t+1} = P_{t+1}^* - (S_t^* + C_t + c_t \Delta N).\tag{8a}$$

Substituting (8a) and (5a) in (3a) then gives

$$P_t^* = N_t P_t = \frac{1}{1+k_t}[Y_t^* - F_t^* + P_{t+1}^* - (C_t + c_t \Delta N_t)],\tag{10}$$

which is clearly *not independent* of the amount of new stock issued (or even of the fact that any new stock is issued). And since the change in dividend is (inversely) related to the new stock issues, the current price P_t is *not independent* of the dividend. q.e.d. It will be noted that this conclusion was reached even though, given the prescience assumed in the model, the end-of-period price was taken as a datum. But it is apparent by iteration, that since the proof applied to any period t, the same conclusion applies to *all* periods—and therefore that P_{t+1} and P_t will depend *essentially* upon the *entire time stream of dividends.*

Moreover, even in this still prescient and purely competitive world, investors will not be indifferent to any substitutions made in financing investment budgets between retained earnings and new stock issues precisely because reliance on new issues incurs *avoidable* cash costs. Under these conditions *investors will always prefer that investment budgets be financed with retained earnings instead of new stock issues so long as retained earnings are available*—that is, so long as $D_t \leqslant Y_t$. As a further corollary, *in this prescient world, companies seeking to serve shareholder interests would never issue common stock unless retained earnings have been exhausted and investment opportunities still remain which have sufficiently high marginal returns as to justify the issue after allowing for the issuance costs involved.* Finally, since the shift from retained earnings to outside equity does involve issuance costs, there is a *vertical shift*—or a discontinuity—in the "supply of capital" function even under these prescient, purely competitive conditions. Under these conditions consequently a significant range of positions of the marginal efficiency of capital function exists for which rational optimizing company policy calls for determining the size of the capital budget by the amount of currently retainable earnings (or funds-from-operations, if gross concepts are used).

3b. *Differentials in the Personal Income Tax Structure Also Make Market Prices a Function of the Finance Mix under Otherwise Idealized Neo-classical Conditions.* Reverting to a world without costs of issuing new securities, we next examine the effect of tax differentials on market values. The essential institutional elements we want to reflect in our analysis are the facts that cash dividend receipts[21] are taxed at rates running from 20 per cent to 91 per cent while capital gains are taxed at *half* this rate or 25 per cent, whichever is *lower* (and only when "realized," which may be *never*). The effective tax differentials run from 10 per cent (20 per cent versus 10 per cent) to over 90 per cent. For present purposes the major effects of such differentials can be determined by considering a pair of taxes constant over time at a flat rate of $100\ h_p$ per cent on dividend income, and at $100\ h_g$ per cent on capital gains,[22] and letting k_τ be an after-tax rate of return or discount.[23] If we let R_{jt} be a

---

[21] Only a small group of investors (other than certain financial intermediaries) have incomes below exemptions and deductions, so that these are effective marginal rates.

[22] For simplicity, we assume that the tax is paid as accrued even if not "realized;" any benefit from deferment of tax liability on capital gains may for present purposes be translated into a lower rate h_g.

[23] The substantial complications introduced by progressive rates, non-zero capital gains rates and variation in rates over time prevent their consideration here. These elements, which are examined elsewhere, merely complicate the dividend model and reinforce the two conclusions of major concern in the present context: they make values still more

tax free return on alternative investments (say a tax exempt bond), the criterion for neo-classical equilibrium pricing given in section II.1. becomes

$$(1 - h_p)\frac{D_{it}}{P_{it}} + \frac{(1 - h_g)[P_{i(t+1)} - P_{it}]}{P_{it}} = k_t$$

$$= \frac{R_{jt}}{P_{jt}} + \frac{[P_{j(t+1)} - P_{jt}](1 - h_g)}{P_{jt}}. \tag{1a}$$

In the presence of such taxes, the basic "dividend model" of equity prices corresponding to (2) above can be specified by iteration of the left-hand equation in (1a).[24] The resulting "present value of dividends" model with taxes considered will necessarily satisfy the relevant neo-classical criterion in equation (1a)—both cross-sectionally and continuously over time—because it is derived from that criterion.[25] But the existence of the personal and capital gains tax differentials invalidates the conclusions of section 2.e above that the price P_{it} is invariant with respect to current dividend payments, and more generally to the financing mix between retained earnings and new equity issues. Consider the retention- ("costless") new equity trade-off with no borrowing. With personal and capital gains taxes, equation (3) becomes

$$P_t^* = N_t P_t = \frac{1}{1 + k_t - h_g} \times [(1 - h_p)D_t^* + (1 - h_g)N_t P_{t+1}] \tag{3a}$$

which implies using (5) and (8),

$$P_t^* = \frac{1}{1 + k_t - h_g}[(1 - h_p)(Y_t^* - F_t^*) + (1 - h_g)P_{t+1}^* - (h_p - h_g)S_t^*]. \tag{9a}$$

Since under present assumptions we have $\Delta D_t^* = \Delta S_t^*$ it follows immediately that

$$\Delta P_t^*\Big|_{\Delta D_t^* = \Delta S_t^* > 0} = -(h_p - h_g)\Delta D_t^* = -(h_p - h_g)\Delta S_t^* < 0$$

$$\text{for all } h_p > h_g. \tag{10a}$$

We have just proved that any tax differential between dividends and capital gains by itself will insure that current market prices are affected by the

---

heavily dependent upon the dividend stream per se *ceteris paribus*, and they generally serve to increase the costs of non-optimal decisions regarding the dividend streams per se.

[24] Converting the left side of (1a) to the form of (2) above and iterating, we get

$$P_{it} = \frac{(1 - h_p)\sum_{m=0}^{\infty}(1 - h_g)^m D_{i(t+m)}}{\prod_{\tau=0}^{m}(1 + k_{t+\tau} - h_g)}. \tag{2a}$$

[25] It should perhaps be noted that the vector of k_τ in the present context is not the same vector as that in (II2.) *ceteris paribus*; but this is, of course, irrelevant for present purposes. Introducing taxes into a taxless world changes the private opportunity set and hence the whole structure of equilibrium values throughout the market. The important point here is that the new set of equilibrium values satisfies the criterion.

size of the current cash distribution.[26] Moreover, if the tax on dividends is greater than on capital gains, *any substitution* of stock issues for retained earnings in the financing of a fixed investment budget in any time period will *reduce* the price of the stock, and *this is true even if there are no issuance costs involved* in the outside financing. This tax differential by itself insures that optimizing managements under conditions of certainty will finance exclusively by retained funds until this internal source is exhausted.

In all these respects, the effects of personal tax differentials are entirely similar to those of issuance costs on outside equity financing. Combining these results, we conclude that *under generalized neo-classical conditions of certainty*—that is, if *either* issuance costs on new equity *or* tax differentials between dividends and capital gains are positive: (a) the market price of the stock of unlevered firms will depend directly upon the dividend decision in *each* period (*including* the current one) even when all earnings and internal investments are predetermined forever; and (b) maximizing behavior for such firms requires that outside equity never be issued when dividends are positive.

III. DIVIDEND AND "PURE EARNINGS" THEORIES UNDER UNCERTAINTY

To this point our analysis has assumed complete certainty in keeping with neo-classical traditions. In this section we abandon this restrictive assumption and examine the effects of uncertainty upon our previous results. To simplify the analysis we will once again assume (until near the end of the section) that both issue costs and taxes are zero.

1. Classes of Uncertainty

The absence of neo-classical certainty—which implies complete prescience and agreement upon data by all decision makers—really encompasses several distinguishable sets of market conditions. First and least general is the condition of "risk" defined as conditions under which probability distributions of events are assumed *known* (in the sense of "objective" certainty) even though the particular outcomes are not specifiable beforehand. The next most general case is the one in which participants have no more than subjective probability distributions over possible events—the "real" distributions are not known—but (a) information relevant to forming these probability judgments is uniformly distributed among all decision-makers (actual and potential owners of the stocks in question in our case), *and* (b) all relevant subjective probability distributions are identical. Since no name seems to have been given to this case before, I shall call it "uncertainty with uniform information and subjective judgment," or *fully idealized uncertainty* for

---

[26] Proof of the same proposition regarding debt financing is given below in section IV3.

short, and examine its effects on share value theory in the next subsection.[27] But uniform information does not require identity in subjective probability distributions. Indeed, in the absence of special restrictive assumptions, the subjective probability distributions formed by different decision makers on the basis of identical information will normally be expected to differ among themselves,[28] and often very substantially. I shall call this case *uncertainty with uniform information and diverse judgmental distributions*. Finally, of course, there is the case in which both the "quality" and the "quantity" of information relevant to decision makers' judgments is *not* uniformly distributed. I shall refer to this situation as *generalized uncertainty*.

2. Analysis under Fully Idealized Uncertainty

The independence of current market price to current dividends, under fully idealized neo-classical conditions with investment budgets and hence earnings predetermined through time, involved proof that the *sum* of current dividend plus change in market price was some constant independent of the dividend. The corresponding proposition under uncertainty is that the *expectation* of the same sum is some constant independent of the dividend payment when the vectors of internal investment and expected earnings are predetermined, that is

$$E[(\tilde{D}_t + \Delta\tilde{P}_t) \,|\, \Psi_{1(t+\tau)}\,(\tilde{F}_\tau);\, \Psi_{2(t+\tau)}\,(\tilde{Y}_\tau) \,|\, F_1 \ldots F_\tau] = \text{constant}, \begin{cases} 0 \leq t \leq \infty \\ 0 \leq \tau \leq \infty \end{cases}, \quad (11)$$

when $\Delta P_t = P_{t+1} - P_t$; E is the expectation operator, tildes signify random variables and the $\Psi_{t+\tau}$ are the probability distributions over $\tilde{F}$ and $\tilde{Y}$ respectively in all time periods. Satisfaction of equation (11) is clearly a *necessary* condition for the validity of the corresponding conclusion under uncertainty. But it is not sufficient, for we have by simple rearrangement using (3)

$$E \frac{[\tilde{D}_t + \tilde{P}_{t+1}]}{1 + k_t} = P_t, \quad (12)$$

and

$$E \frac{[N_t\tilde{D}_t + N_t\tilde{P}_{t+1}]}{1 + k_t} = N_t P_t = P_t^*, \quad (12a)$$

---

[27] We need not consider risk per se separately since the results are identical.

[28] If it is not clear that uncertainty with uniform information is consistent with (and indeed will almost certainly result in) differing subjective probability distributions, consider the following experiment: announce to any group of "subjects" that you are about to roll a die which has had a lead slug implanted more or less in the center but that the work has been done by hand with imperfect tools by an inexperienced workman; roll the die, say 100 times, in front of the subjects, slowly, allowing each to record the results of each throw; ask each to write down his subjective probability distribution over the result of the *next* throw. With even a dozen subjects, the likelihood of all writing down the same probability distribution will (my subjective probability distribution!) be 10^{-n} with n large.

where the tilde under the discount rate indicates that it is the rate found under uncertainty. Consequently

$$\Delta P_t^* = \frac{\Delta E[\tilde{D}_t^* + N_t\tilde{P}_{t+1}]}{1 + \underline{k}_t} - \frac{\Delta \underline{k}_t \cdot E[\tilde{D}_t^* + N_t\tilde{P}_{t+1}]}{(1 + \underline{k}_t)^2} \tag{12b}$$

$$= \frac{\Delta E[\tilde{D}_t^* + N_t\tilde{P}_{t+1}] - \Delta \underline{k}_t \cdot P_t}{1 + \underline{k}_t} \tag{12c}$$

Assuming the two terms in the numerator are not by coincidence equal in size and opposite in sign, the *necessary* and *sufficient* conditions for current price to be invariant to the current dividend are therefore

$$\Delta E[\tilde{D}_t + N_t\tilde{P}_{t+1}] / \Delta D_t^* = 0 \tag{13a}$$

and

$$\Delta \underline{k}_t/\Delta D_t^* = 0; \tag{13b}$$

both being satisfied *subject to* $F_t^* = $ constant in equation (4). Since it is common observation that most investors diversify their portfolios, which implies risk aversion and concave utility functions, we will assume that k_t varies directly (and P_t and P_t^* inversely) with the variances

$$V[\tilde{D}_t + \tilde{P}_{t+1}] \text{ and } V[\tilde{D}_t^* + N_t\tilde{P}_{t+1}].$$

Under present assumptions, all actual *and* potential shareholders have a common fund of information which they interpret into *identical subjective probability distributions* regarding all relevant financial data (including market prices) for all time periods for any given common stock, *and* for all other equities and potential investments. Since all investors hold identical subjective probability distributions over all elements which affect the valuation of the stock at time $t + 1$, the distribution of $\tilde{P}_{t+1}^*$ (the *aggregate* value of the firm at that time) will be independent of which subset of investors in the market happen to hold the security, and, in particular, this distribution will be independent of the number of shares outstanding at $t + 1$. We consequently have,

$$\tilde{P}_{t+1}^* = \tilde{P}_{t+1}[N_t + \Delta N_t] = N_t\tilde{P}_{t+1}(1 + n_t), \tag{7a}$$

and

$$\tilde{P}_{t+1} = \tilde{P}_{t+1}^*/N_t(1 + n_t), \tag{7b}$$

independent of ΔN_t and of $n_t = \Delta N_t/N_t$.

Consider now a company, having probability distributions of its investment budget $\tilde{F}_t^*$, earnings $\tilde{Y}_t^*$ and dividend payout $\tilde{D}_t^*$ without issuing stock, and suppose it is considering increasing its total dividend payment by any specific amount ΔD_t^*, securing the funds to do so by issuing new stock with a corresponding value S_t^*, that is, $\Delta D_t^* = S_t^*$,[29] where using (7b), we have

$$S_t^* = \Delta N_t\tilde{P}_{t+1} = \frac{n_t\tilde{P}_{t+1}^*}{1 + n_t}. \tag{14}$$

[29] Taking the simple case starting from a base situation without new stock issues simplifies the exposition without any loss of generality.

Since there are no costs of issue, this substitution does not affect the expected value of the numerator of (12a) and condition (13a) is satisfied.

It is common knowledge, however, that the variance of market prices is very much greater than the variance of dividends. It would consequently appear that the variance of the sum $V(\tilde{D}_t + \tilde{P}_{t+1})$ could be reduced—and therefore the utility value of the return on the stock increased—by increasing dividends at the expense of the capital gains component by issuing new shares. Any such substitution consistent with the maintenance of expected values in (12a) would then clearly raise the price of the stock P_t, and price would not only not be invariant to the current dividend but would vary directly with it, *ceteris paribus*. This logic is made more persuasive by observing that substituting (14) in (12a) yields

$$\frac{E[\tilde{D}_t^* + \Delta D_t^* + \tilde{P}_{t+1}^*/(1 + n_t)]}{1 + k_t} = P_t^*. \tag{12d}$$

Adding any ΔD_t^* clearly does not affect the variance of the first two terms in the bracket, but it increases $n_t = \Delta N_t/N_t$ in the denominator of the remaining term; since the variance of $\tilde{P}_{t+1}^*$ is unchanged, the variance of the ratio would appear to be reduced in inverse proportion to the square of the (larger) denominator—which would reduce the variance of the entire bracket in the numerator, and consequently increase the value P_t^* of the shares outstanding at time t, thereby violating condition (13b) above.

Nevertheless, persuasive as such reasoning may appear, this conclusion would be in error,[30] for *under present assumptions* not only the variance but all moments of the term $\tilde{P}_{t+1}^*/(1 + n_t)$ beyond the first are invariant for any given S_t^*. This is true because $P_{t+1}^*/(1 + n_t) = P_{t+1}^* - n_t P_{t+1}^*/(1 + n_t) = P_{t+1}^* - S_t^*$, so that for any given distribution $\psi(P_{t+1}^*)$ we have $\rho[P_{t+1}^*/(1 + n_t)] = \rho[P_{t+1}^* - S_t^*] = \psi(P_{t+1}^*)$ minus some constant S_t^*. Condition (13b) above, therefore, *is* satisfied along with (13a). Moreover, since the invariance holds for *any* size of S_t^*, it continues to hold in the face of ex-ante uncertainty regarding what size will be given to $\Delta D_t = S_t^*$. It consequently follows that *fully idealized* uncertainty *per se* does not alter the conclusion reached under idealized neo-classical conditions in section (2e) above: with fixed time vectors of investments and expectations earnings $(0 \leq t \leq \infty)$, investors will be indifferent to substitutions between retained earnings and new equity issues in any time period, and the price of the stock

---

[30] I have included this misleading argument because I was blinded by its persuasiveness myself for some time, indeed until shortly after preparing [18]. Its inclusion is further indicated by the likelihood that others may be misled by these or related arguments, as shown by the fact that none of the numerous readers of [18] either spotted (or informed me) of the error in the argument. In addition, an equation corresponding to (12d) plays an important role in our later, more general, analysis. Miller and Modigliani have independently derived an alternative proof in [25] of the conclusion given in the last sentence of this paragraph. Their conclusion that this result applies to uncertainty in general, even given otherwise neo-classical conditions, is, however, quite improper, as shown below.

will be independent of the particular amount of dividends paid within any period.

It is obvious, however, that the observations made in (2f) above on the earlier similar conclusion are still relevant in an essential way. We have merely shown that *fully idealized* uncertainty in an otherwise *fully idealized* neo-classical world leaves this indifference to current dividends intact.

3. The Effect of Diverse Judgmental Distributions

We now proceed to relax these extreme idealizing assumptions. Motivation for doing so (if any is needed) is provided by the observation that under *these* conditions it will be possible for management to pay out *any* amount of dividends in any period—not merely any fraction of "current earnings" but *any multiple* thereof, however large—without any benefit or injury to any shareholder and without having any effect on the price of the stock! This corollary strongly suggests that some rather important aspects of reality have been eliminated in the idealization (or should I say sterilization?) of real world conditions of uncertainty used so far. There must be some limitations under conditions of uncertainty to shareholders' indifference to substitutions between dividends and new issues, even in the absence of issue costs and taxes. And indeed there are—as soon as the character of the uncertainty permitted is generalized, as we now show.

We have already observed that uniform information will usually be associated with differing subjective probability distributions. These differences can involve any or all of the moments of the distributions of any or all of the elements in the vectors of future events (earnings, investments, market reactions and prices, and so on) which determine current values and preferences. To simplify the analysis, consider first the situation in which the distributions of all these elements held in the minds of all current and potential shareholders is such that the variance (and all higher moments) of their resulting derived distributions of both $\tilde{P}^*_{t+1}$ and of $\tilde{P}^*_{t+1}/(1 + n_t)$ are independent of n_t. Condition (13b) for indifference to dividends is then satisfied. But there will be differences in the *expectations* (first moments) of $\tilde{P}^*_{t+1}$ whether or not new shares are issued—and this will prevent condition (13a) from being satisfied and will establish firm preferences over any potential substitution between cash dividends and new equity issues involving *any real change in the financing-mix* for given capital budgets. (For simplicity we will assume investors hold identical distributions, *including* first moments, regarding the *current period's* dividend, earnings and capital budget.)

It is clear that those who hold a stock at any given time will be those for whom its value, subjectively to them, is at least equal to its market price at that time: and, *mutatis mutandis,* for those who do not hold the stock. Given diversity in subjective estimates, we have a demand curve for the company's stock (assuming a fixed number of shares) declining to the right in the sense about to be specified, and the aggregate value will have the same shape, the vertical scale being blown up by the (fixed) number of shares. Let there be m investors in the market who might hold the given stock, and let $\xi_{ijt}(P_{jt}^*)$ be the fraction of the aggregate value of the jth company (in the absence of debt) which the ith (potential) shareholder will be willing to hold at time t if the aggregate value of the company is P_{jt}^*, given all investor's expectations regarding *all* available investment opportunities, and the amounts in the market for all securities. Consider now the valuation of the jth company, *ceteris paribus*. If P_{jt}^* is sufficiently high, no investor would be willing to hold any of its stocks and $\xi_{ijt}(P_t^*)$ would be zero. At lower potential values P_{jt}^*, some investors will be bullish enough on the jth company to hold some of its outstanding shares, and at still lower potential P_{jt}^* two things happen: (a) those $\xi_{ijt}(P_{jt}^*)$ which are already positive become larger—that is, $\delta\xi_{ijt}/\delta P_{jt}^* \leqslant 0$ with the inequality holding for some i whose $\xi_{ijt} > 0$—and (b) some investors not willing to hold any of the stock at the higher P_{jt}^*, now are willing to hold some—that is, some $\xi_{ijt}(P_{jt}^*)$ previously zero are now > 0. For both reasons we have a negatively sloped function or "aggregate demand curve" relating P_{jt}^* and $\overset{m}{\underset{i=1}{\Sigma}}\xi_{ijt}(P_{jt}^*)$. The actual market price $\tilde{P}_{jt}^*$ at any moment is a random variable with a distribution whose expected value $E_m[\tilde{P}_{jt}]$ will be established by the condition $\overset{m}{\underset{i=1}{\Sigma}}\xi_{ijt}(P_{jt}^*) = 1.0$, since all the stock must be held by someone.[31]

Now it is clear that for any given identical beliefs regarding $\tilde{D}_{jt}$, (including its mean value), there will be a similarly negatively sloped demand curve with respect to $\tilde{P}_{j(t+1)}^*$, where the actual end-of-period price $\tilde{P}_{j(t+1)}^* = E_m[\tilde{P}_{j(t+1)}^*] + \epsilon_{j(t+1)}$ in which the random variable ϵ has zero mean. Without loss of generality we can say that current shareholders are those investors for whom $E_{ii}(\tilde{P}_{j(t+1)}^*) \geqslant {}_0P_{j(t+1)}^*$ while those not now holding the stock are those investors for whom $E_{ii}(\tilde{P}_{j(t+1)}^*) \leqslant {}_0P_{j(t+1)}^*$, where ${}_0P_{j(t+1)}^*$ is the solution value of $\overset{m}{\underset{i=0(t+1)}{\Sigma}}\xi_{ij}(P_{j(t+1)}^*) = 1.0$.[32] For definiteness we may write[33] the conditional expectation of the aggregate value of the corporate equity as

---

[31] We use the expectation operator with subscript m to refer to the mean of the distribution of market price. It will be noted that our "aggregate demand curve" is simply the Wicksteed function applied to the total valuation of the corporate equity. One minor change has been made in that both the "active" and the reservation demand have been divided through by "quantity" so that the equilibrium condition is the summation of fractions held to unity instead of summation of amounts held to equal amounts which must be held.

[32] As usual in period analysis, we will assume that trading occurs only at the discrete points in time at the beginning and end of each period. Those who hold the stock at the end of trading at time t are therefore the holders of the stock at the beginning of trading at point $t + 1$.

[33] The linear form is used for simplicity; the same conclusions will follow for any exponential, hyperbolic or other form having a negative slope.

$$E_m[\tilde{P}^*_{j(t+1)} \mid Z] = {}_0P^*_{j(t+1)} [1 - b_{t+1}(Z - 1)], \; b_{t+1} > 0,$$

$$\text{where } Z = \sum_{i=1}^{m} \xi_{ij} (P_{j(t+1)})_{t+1}. \qquad (15)$$

It is understood that the relation (15) is defined relative to a given set of subjective probability distributions held by the set of m potential investors, with respect to the jth security and all other possible investments. The price of the individual shares $\tilde{P}_{j(t+1)}$ is related to $\tilde{P}^*_{j(t+1)}$ by way of

$$\tilde{P}^*_{j(t+1)} = (N_{jt} + \Delta N_{jt})\tilde{P}_{j(t+1)}. \qquad (7a)$$

Since $\Delta D^*_{jt} = S^*_{jt} = \Delta N_{jt} \tilde{P}_{j(t+1)}$, we also have

$$N_{jt}\tilde{P}_{j(t+1)} = \tilde{P}^*_{j(t+1)} - S^*_{jt} = \tilde{P}^*_{j(t+1)} - \Delta D^*_{jt}. \qquad (16)$$

We are now in a position to prove that the diversity of expected values reflected in the negative slope of the Wicksteed aggregate value function insures that shareholders will *not* be indifferent to whether cash dividends are increased (or reduced) by substituting new equity issues for retained earnings to finance given capital budgets;[34] that the "expectation" of the current price $E_m[\tilde{P}_{jt}]$ will *not* be independent of such substitutions; and that $E_m[\tilde{P}_{jt}]$ will be a function of cash dividends payments in this context. This is true because any $\Delta D_{jt} > 0$ means that current shareholders (all of whose $E_{ij}(P^*_{j(t+1)}) \underset{(t+1)}{\geq}$ ${}_0P^*_{j(t+1)}$ are *withdrawing* an amount of funds ΔD^*_t from the company, this withdrawal being financed (with investment budgets fixed and no borrowing) by issuing shares to those who have not been holding the stock (all of whose $E_{ij}(P^*_{j(t+1)}) \underset{(t+1)}{<} {}_0P^*_{j(t+1)})$. To simplify the mathematical notation, we will use $\Delta D^*_t = S^*_t > 0$ to identify the dollar amount of incremental dividend payment *not* immediately used to purchase new shares, and the *net* amount of new shares not so purchased by present shareholders.[35]

---

[34] To forestall confusion, we should emphasize that this substitution (which does involve the negative slope of the valuation function in an essential way) is quite distinct from a *stock* dividend which would merely change the number of sheets of paper representing current *unchanged* fractional holding ξ_{ij} of each shareholder in an unchanged aggregate corporate equity. Since all ξ_{ij} are unchanged by such pure stock dividends, the solution value ${}_0P^*_j$ is unchanged and the negative slope of our Wicksteed aggregate value function is irrelevant for this essentially different problem.

[35] In addition to sales to those not otherwise holding the stock, it is of course probable that some of the previous holders will (especially in this taxless, costless world) use part of the ΔD_{ijt} accruing to them to buy newly issued shares. This fact complicates the analysis but does not change the conclusions reached in the text. For suppose in the limit that all recipients of the incremental ΔD^*_{jt} immediately used all these funds to buy the new shares issued to finance the added dividend. It is then true the end result would be equivalent to a pure stock dividend and ${}_0P^*_{j(t+1)}$ would be unchanged—but it would be unchanged *only because* the present shareholders refused to accept *and retain* the added cash distribution from the company. The present shareholders would be financing precisely the same amount of the company's capital budget as if the nominal cash dividends had not been changed. *The only reason* they would continue to do so after the company had increased its cash dividend payment is that they would be worse off if they did not do so—*which means they do have a definite preference* (and are *not indifferent*) *regard-*

Using (16) along with (12a),[36] we have for any $\Delta D_t^* = S_t^* > 0$,

$$\Delta E_m[\tilde{D}_{jt}^* + N_{jt}\tilde{P}_{j(t+1)}] = \Delta D_t^* + \Delta E_m[\tilde{P}_{j(t+1)}^*] - S_t^* = \Delta E_m[\tilde{P}_{j(t+1)}^*] \qquad (17)$$

but since $S_t^*/{}_oP_{j(t+1)}^* = Z - 1$, this means by (15) that

$$\Delta E_m[\tilde{D}_{jt}^* + N_{jt}\tilde{P}_{j(t+1)}] = -b\,S_t^* = -b\,\Delta D_t^* < 0 \text{ for all } \Delta D_t^* = S_t^* > 0. \qquad (18)$$

In this costless and taxless world, the increase in dividend payment still completely offsets the S_t^* subtracted from the (conditional) expected end-of-period value of the aggregate corporate equity; but the payment of an added cash dividend *which involves a net withdrawal of cash by present shareholders from the company*[37] requires that ownership of $\Delta D_t^*/{}_o\tilde{P}_{j(t+1)}$ of this aggregate equity be transferred to others whose expectations justify *their* holding (buying) the stock only at a lower price, so that *this* shift in finance-mix and current dividend *reduces* the (conditional) expected *aggregate* market value of the company's equity *ceteris paribus*. Since the left side of (18) is negative, *shareholders will prefer that this net change in the finance mix not be made.* Moreover, by exactly similar logic with fixed investment budgets, a net *increase* in retained earnings (*reduction* in cash dividends) used to *repurchase* outstanding shares (a negative new issue) will *increase* the (conditional) expected aggregate market value $E_m[\tilde{P}_{j(t+1)}]$. Since the left side of (18) would then be positive, shareholders will have a preference *for* this kind of change in the finance mix. *In sum, diversity in investors' subjective probability distributions is sufficient to destroy investors' indifference to the effective mix of retained earnings and new equity issues used to finance given capital budgets even under otherwise fully idealized neo-classical conditions.*

So far we have used the simplifying assumption that all actual and potential shareholders' subjective distributions differ only in their first moments (expected values) and are identical for all higher moments for the jth security, and are identical among investors regarding *all* moments for all other possible investments. The results, however, are completely general. For suppose that there are differences in both the first two moments of the jth security, all others being the same. The conditional values $P_{j(t+1)}^*$, then, are functions of the doublets μ_{ij} and σ_{ij}^2 instead of the single numbers μ_{ij} and all the preceding analysis follows as before. In complete generality, if every shareholder's estimate of all moments of the jth security differ, the ξ_{ij} in our preceding derivation merely become a function of the ith shareholder's entire vector of subjectively estimated moments; assuming every investor has a consistent and

---

ing the finance-mix for given capital budgets. In all cases in which there is at least some net shift in financing—that is, in which at least some shareholders fail to buy new shares instantly in the precise amount of the incremental dividend received—new buyers must be found for some stock and the conclusion in the text follows immediately: given diverse judgmental probability distributions, the finance mix *does* make a difference both in terms of shareholder preferences and market prices.

[36] Recall that Δk_t is zero by the assumption made above that all moments of $\tilde{P}_{j(t+1)}^*$ beyond the first are invariant.

[37] The reason for this condition is given in fn. 35.

transitive ordering over these vectors, the properties of the resulting ξ_{ij} as a function of different conditional values $P^*_{j(t+1)}$ will be the same as those used above, and the rest of the analysis is unaffected.

Similarly, it is clearly immaterial whether the differences in the moments of the various shareholders' subjective distributions differ in spite of uniform information or because of differences in the quality and quantity of information available. In the latter more realistic case, one would simply expect greater diversity which should increase the negative slope of the Wicksteedian aggregate value function—the parameter "b" above.

Finally, we have implicitly assumed that all actual and potential holders of the jth security held identical subjective distributions among themselves regarding each alternative investment available in the market. Even if the relevant probability distributions are identical for the jth stock, differences among shareholders regarding various k^{th} securities $(k \neq j)$ will introduce considerations of portfolio composition which will ensure that the $\xi_{ij}(P^*_{j(t+1)})$ will have the properties attributed to them above on grounds of diversity in judgments regarding the jth security itself. When holdings of cash and borrowing are admitted, differences in investors' subjective probability distributions over general price levels, with identical distributions over everything else, will also insure this result.

4. General Conclusions Regarding Uncertainty

Under otherwise ideal neo-classical conditions (that is, no costs or taxes), we have established that *uncertainty* by itself invalidates the conclusion reached under fully idealized neo-classical conditions of certainty that current price is invariant to the equity finance mix—in particular to the size of the current (and future) cash dividend *per se*—*unless* the uncertainty is *fully idealized* in the sense that (a) *all* actual and potential shareholders in the market must have *identical subjective distributions* regarding (b) *all* relevant aspects of the future, *both* with respect to (c) the given stock and with respect to (d) *all other* investments available in the market. *Relaxation of any one or any combination of these four idealizing but unrealistic assumptions makes market price a direct function of which particular time-vector of dividend payments is chosen* (or expected to be chosen) by management, because removal of any one of these restrictions establishes a clear preference among shareholders over the particular mix of retained earnings and new equity issues used to finance a predetermined time vector of corporate capital budgets.[38] Moreover, investors in a world of generalized uncertainty will always prefer that stock issues *not* be substituted for retained earnings in

---

[38] It should perhaps be reemphasized (as in Section II.2f. above) that *even if* all these four necessary and sufficient restrictions which fully idealize the uncertainty introduced are maintained and satisfied, stock prices still depend upon the dividend vectors—and earnings, internal investments and related attributes still have their impact on stock prices by way of their implications *for* cash distributions to shareholders—the effect of the combined set of restrictions merely being to make any agreed set of vectors of earnings and internal investments sufficient to determine the dividend vectors up to a specified indifference set, all of whose elements (dividend vectors) have the same market value.

financing given capital budgets: even though any such substitution will increase current cash dividends dollar for dollar, such a substitution will *reduce* the current price of the stock. Moreover, companies seeking to serve stockholder interests should never issue common stock unless retained earnings have been exhausted and investment opportunities still remain which have sufficiently high expectations of returns as to justify the issue after allowing for the necessary "underpricing" and overt issuance costs involved.[39] As a further corollary, there is under these conditions always a vertical shift in the "supply of capital" function at the point where internal funds are exhausted and the outside equity market is tapped.

5. The Effects of General Uncertainty with Issue Costs and Taxes

So far we have considered the effects of uncertainty, issue costs, and taxes separately under otherwise fully idealized neo-classical conditions. We should now emphasize that nonuniform uncertainty is also probably the principal reason for the heavy burden of overt costs involved in making new issues— which have been officially estimated to vary from 3 per cent to 37 per cent of the net proceeds of new equity issues in non-rights offerings, and from 1.7 per cent to 8.2 per cent for rights offerings depending on industry, size of company, and size of issue.[40] These costs are largely attributable to the facts of generalized uncertainty and lack of uniform information because under these conditions information regarding the company must be gotten into the hands of those not well informed concerning it, risks must be borne by those underwriting the success of the issue, salesmanship and persuasion must be used to induce purchases by those who had not realized that the new issue would be a good one for them (even if it would, given the relevant information), and so on. Information is a free good in fully idealized neo-classical models, and *may* be assumed to be so under stringently idealized conditions of uncertainty, but in real life information is a truly economic good of central importance, having both value to the possessor and costs of production, acquisition, and dissemination. Models assuming neo-classical certainty *may* be internally consistent without introducing positive costs of issue: but if uncertainty is admitted without explicit and unrealistic assumptions of uniform information, issue costs must be admitted. Models admitting generalized uncertainty must consequently allow not only for the negative slope of the Wicksteedian conditional expected aggregate value function (the b coefficient above), but *also* for both the fixed and variable costs of flotation.

Now the right hand side of equation (18) above makes it clear that the

---

[39] This conclusion holds rigorously in the context of the models used in this paper in which expectations for future periods are independent of actual results in the current period. In more complicated (and realistic) models, in which future expectations are functions of current earnings *and* dividends, the adverse effect of reducing dividends may lead to rational decisions to issue more common stock while positive dividends are still being paid.

[40] See U. S. Securities and Exchange Commission, *Cost of Flotation of Corporate Securities, 1951–1955*, pp. 60–61. It should be noted that these figures do not include the added costs within the company from undertaking a new issue.

negative slope of the conditional expected aggregate value function created by diverse expectations means that new issues to finance increased dividends reduces the expected value of the current price P_t by a fraction b of the new issue. This is *equivalent* to a proportionate cost of new issues in a world otherwise satisfying fully idealized conditions. The introduction of anything less stringent than a fully idealized uncertainty consequently produces effects very similar to the introduction of issue costs in a world of neo-classical certainty. But *this* cost from uncertainty is most closely identified with the "underpricing" required to sell new issues, and is *an addition to* the make-ready and underwriting costs of issuing new securities. The effects of issuing costs and the "uncertainty costs" of possible trade-offs between outside equity and retained earnings are *essentially the same, and additive*.

Similarly, a comparison of the effects of general uncertainty without taxes shown above, with those of taxes shown in section II under certainty, shows that the effects of each are qualitatively the same. Allowance for real world personal income vs. capital gains differentials in a world of generalized uncertainty consequently would merely (but strongly) support the conclusions just stated regarding such uncertainty above—and would increase the size of the differentials involved in (and consequently investor preferences concerning) any possible substitutions of outside equity for retained earnings.

All our results in this section thus reinforce each other to strengthen our primary conclusions that the market price of unlevered equity will depend directly upon *what particular* time vector of *dividend* payments is made (or expected), and that it is *not* a matter of indifference to the shareholder *how* the corporation finances its internal investments.

IV. INVESTOR PREFERENCES OVER DIVIDENDS, RETAINED EARNINGS AND DEBT

In this section we examine the question of whether investors will or will not be indifferent to changes in the mix of retained earnings and debt used to finance given capital budgets. Since changes in dividends are equal (and opposite in sign) to changes in retained earnings, the same question can be put in the form of whether investors are indifferent to, or have a preference regarding, additional corporate borrowing whose net proceeds are used to increase current dividends. As will be clear, the necessary and sufficient conditions for this indifference to hold are the same as those required to validate the "entity value" theory—the proposition that the *sum* of the market values of the equity and (long-term) debt of a corporation is independent of its finance-mix, given the time vectors of its earnings-before-interest and investment budgets. Because of the general dominance of retained earnings over stock issues shown in the previous sections, we shall assume no stock issues are made. As in the preceding sections, we shall proceed systematically from fully idealized neo-classical conditions under certainty to more general and realistic assumptions. It should be emphasized that throughout the analysis we shall assume maximizing behavior and that *both* stock and bond markets are purely competitive markets for all investors.

1. With the Earnings and Investment Streams Fixed under Fully Idealized Neo-Classical Conditions of Certainty, Market Prices Are Independent of the Mix of Retained Earnings and Borrowing

It is sometimes suggested (most recently in [25] esp. 412) that under the conditions assumed (no issue costs or taxes, and especially the assumption of prescience or no uncertainty), any distinction between bonds and stocks is irrelevant so that what holds for stocks (cf. section II.2e above) will necessarily hold for bonds without separate proof. But there is one difference between bonds and stocks of some potential importance: even in these idealized markets, borrowing money generally involves interest costs, while there is no direct cost to the act of not paying a dividend. For this reason alone, separate consideration is justified. This can also provide a firm and convenient base from which to examine the differences in results required by more general and realistic assumptions.

To isolate the effects of the retained-earnings-debt trade-off without loss of generality, we set the volume of new stock issues at zero, making $\Delta N, S_t = 0$, and carry the whole analysis through on the simpler per share of stock basis. But $B_t, \dot{B}_t \neq 0$, and from (5) we have $D_t = Y'_t - i_t B_t - (F_t - \dot{B}_t)$. Since dividends are paid at the end of the period, any *incremental* borrowing $\Delta \dot{B}_t$ to permit added dividend distributions ΔD_t will also occur at the end of the period, and the other terms Y_t, $i_t B_t$ and F_t will not be affected. Also, under the assumed conditions, the act of borrowing involves no costs other than interest, so that

$$\Delta D_t = \Delta \dot{B}_t. \tag{19}$$

Using these relations in (3) we can derive

$$\Delta P_{it} \bigg|_{\Delta D_t = \Delta \dot{B}_t} = \frac{1}{1 + k_t} [\Delta \dot{B}_t + \Delta P_{i(t+1)}], \tag{20}$$

where $\Delta P_{i(t+1)}$ is the present value of the sum of interest payments on the incremental debts up to the time of its repayment and that of the repayment:

$$\Delta P_{i(t+1)} = \sum_{m=1}^{j} \frac{-i_{t+m} \cdot \Delta \dot{B}_t}{\prod_{\tau=1}^{m} (1 + k_{t+\tau})} + \frac{-\Delta \dot{B}_t}{\prod_{\tau=1}^{j} (1 + k_{t+\tau})} \tag{21}$$

when repayment is made in the jth future period.

Now, the idealized neo-classical conditions being assumed rule out costs of the act of lending as well as those of borrowings. Moreover, maximizing behavior on the part of investors under these prescient conditions means that they will invest in bonds *or* stocks with indifference if the returns are the same, and move funds from one to the other so long as there is any difference either way in the returns offered.[41] Since all potential discrepancies in return will thereby be immediately eliminated by portfolio shifts, we have the critical relation

$$i_{t+m} = k_{t+\tau} \text{ for all } \tau = m. \tag{22}$$

The change induced in ending share price is consequently equal and opposite in sign to the current borrowing, since substituting (22) in (21) yields[42]

$$\Delta P_{i(t+1)} = -\Delta \dot{B}_t, \tag{21a}$$

and further substitution in (11) gives

$$\Delta P_{it} \bigg|_{\Delta D_t = \Delta \dot{B}_t} = 0, \tag{20a}$$

which was to be proved. Finally, since the theorem holds for any t, it must hold for all time. Under the stated conditions, therefore, the fact that interest must be paid on debt while the act of making incremental retentions involves no cash outlay does not destroy the conclusion that current market price of the equity is independent of the financing mix between retentions and debt and in particular of the dividend payment. Moreover, the reader should note that the dollar equality in equation (21a) immediately validates the basic proposition of the "entity value" theory that the sum of the market value of equity and debt is invariant to the amount of debt financing undertaken. Under the fully idealized conditions assumed, the validity of the "entity value" theory is thereby established by using a model in which the value of a share is directly determined by the present value of the stream of the share's own cash flows, and without recourse to any special arguments which involve shareholders' "undoing leverage" by selling some levered stock to buy bonds of the same company. (See fn. 41 above.)

The conclusion that current share prices are invariant to trade-offs between retained earnings and borrowing to finance fixed investment budgets—or, equivalently, to the payment of dividends financed by borrowing—is, of course, subject to the same general observations made above regarding the similar conclusions with respect to stock issues under the same restricted conditions. Not only are current equity prices still determined by the set of efficient time-vectors of dividends (there simply being indifference among the elements in the set under these conditions), but more general assumptions immediately destroy investors' indifference among different dividend vectors

[41] The same propositions, of course, hold with respect to shifts between bonds and between stocks of different companies under these conditions, thereby ensuring the attainment of equilibrium positions involving precise uniformity in current returns on *all* securities throughout the market. This fact justifies our continuing to consider only a single company in the text. It should be noted, however, that attainment of this equilibrium does *not* require *any* investor to hold the bonds *and* stocks of *any* company simultaneously.

[42] Readers to whom this is not apparent will find the detail of the algebra in Conard [3], pp. 304–307.

in this efficient set and establish a unique preference ordering over the set so that there is a uniquely defined optimum choice of a *particular* dividend stream (and the associated time-vector of borrowing), given the investment and earning vectors. In particular, we note first that

2. With Costs (Other Than Interest) of Borrowing under Otherwise Idealized Neo-Classical Conditions, Market Prices Are Not Independent of Cash Dividends in Any Period When There Is No Stock Issue, Even if Earnings and Internal Investment Streams Are Predetermined

Pure competition in all markets under neo-classical conditions is clearly consistent with the existence of costs (other than interest) involved in the act of borrowing—comparable to transport costs in neo-classical spatial economics. The existence of such costs in reality is hardly open to question—and they are sufficient to make the current price of a company's equity depend directly on its dividend payment and finance mix. The proof of the invariance of price to the mix of retentions and borrowing given just above, in the absence of costs of borrowing, is clearly invalidated *unless* equations (19) *and* (21a) are simultaneously satisfied. The former is still true because we define $\Delta \dot{B}_t$ to be the *net* proceeds of borrowing, but $\Delta P_{i(t+1)}$ equals the principal of the new debt which is greater than the net proceeds by costs of acquisition or underwriting. The amount of added dividend ΔD_t made possible by any amount of borrowing will consequently be *less than* the reduction in ending price $\Delta P_{i(t+1)}$ by the amount of the fixed and variable cost of the act of borrowing. Since the act of borrowing involves avoidable costs, P_{it} is lowered by the act of substituting debt for retained earnings in *any* period, and (as in the corresponding case of stock issues) we can conclude *from these costs alone* that prices are *not independent* of cash dividends paid in any period, and also that (a) debt will not be substituted for retained earnings in otherwise idealized neo-classical markets[43] and (b) there is again a vertical displacement in the supply of capital function. Moreover, such costs, by destroying the equality in the earlier equation (21a) by themselves render the "entity value" theory invalid under otherwise fully idealized neo-classical conditions.

3. Differentials in the Personal Income Tax Structure Make Market Prices a Function of Dividends, and the Mix of Retained Earnings and Debt, under Otherwise Neo-Classical Conditions

With borrowing (assuming no costs other than interest and no equity issues), allowance for personal income taxes does not affect equations (19), (21), or (22), but (11) becomes (cf. section II3b. above)

$$\Delta P_{it}\Big|_{\Delta D_t = \Delta \dot{B}_t > 0} = \frac{1}{1 + k_t - h_g} \times [(1 - h_p)\,\Delta D_t + (1 - h_g)\,\Delta P_{i(t+1)}], \quad (11a)$$

---

[43] This conclusion is also found in Bodenhorn [2], p. 492.

which, together with the other equations listed, implies

$$\Delta P_{it}\Big|_{\Delta D_t = \Delta \dot{B}_t > 0} = -(h_p - h_g)\,\Delta D_t = -(h_p - h_g)\,\Delta \dot{B}_t < 0$$

for all $h_p > h_g$.   (11b)

Any personal tax differential thus ensures that current market prices are affected by variations in dividends financed by debt, that investors will have definite preferences regarding substitutions between retained earnings and debt in financing fixed capital budgets, and that the entity value theory will not be valid.

4. Differentials in the Corporate Income Tax Also Make Market Prices a Unique Function of Dividends and Destroy Any Investor Indifference to the Mix of Retained Earnings and Debt Otherwise Present

We now examine the effect of tax differentials within the corporate tax structure, letting corporate net income $Y_t = Y'_t - i_t B_t$—that is, income after the deduction of interest charges as well as other expenses—be taxed at a flat rate h_c. To isolate the effect of this differential treatment of interest charges compared with other earnings, we will rule out personal taxes by setting h_p and $h_g = 0$ and retain our current assumptions of no issuance costs on outside financing.[44] First of all we note that (4) and (5) become

$$F_t = (1 - h_c)(Y_t - i_t B_t) + i_t B_t + S_t + \Delta \dot{B}_t - D_t.   \qquad (4a)$$

$$D_t = (1 - h_c)Y_t + h_c i_t B_t - (F_t - S_t - \Delta \dot{B}_t).   \qquad (5a)$$

Again, we let S_t be zero to concentrate on borrowing and retentions. Equations (3), (19), (20), and (22) are still valid without change, but the change in ending price is affected. Introducing $(1 - h_c)$ into the numerator of the first term of (21), and for simplicity assuming perpetual refinancing of the current increment in debt, we have

$$\Delta P_{i(t+1)} = -(1 - h_c)(\Delta \dot{B}_t)   \qquad (21b)$$

instead of (21a), so that finally

$$\Delta P_{it}\Big|_{\Delta D_t = (\Delta \dot{B}_t) > 0} = \frac{1}{1 + k_t} \times [(\Delta \dot{B}_t) + \Delta P_{i(t+1)}]$$

$$= h_c(\Delta \dot{B}_t) = h_c\,\Delta D_t > 0.   \qquad (11b)$$

The interest-deductible corporate income tax without more, not only makes the price of the shares directly dependent on the current dividend pay-

---

[44] It is immediately clear that the corporate tax per se does not modify the conclusion of Section II3b. above—with no personal taxes and issuance costs, market price is independent of substitutions between retentions and new stock issues in financing any fixed investment budget regardless of the existence or level of the corporate tax. The corporate tax does, of course, affect the optimal size of the budget—the minimum acceptable return on the marginal internal investment—relative to any k_t ceteris paribus.

ment—but destroys the indifference of market price to current dividend found under fully idealized neo-classical conditions—it makes the price a direct and *increasing* function of the dividend. Moreover, this corporate tax has the effect of making new borrowing used to finance added current dividend payments increase *both* the debt outstanding *and* the market value of the equity so that the sum of the two—the entity value—far from being indifferent to the finance mix—is doubly increased.[45] Indeed, with certainty and no issuance costs or personal taxes, the usual assumption of unlimited possibilities of borrowing at the current market rate of interest opens the possibility of unlimitedly high current stock prices produced by unlimitedly high current dividends financed by unlimited borrowing resulting in unlimitedly high entity values for the corporation! Apart from ad hoc boundary conditions, the possibility of limits even under certainty assumptions is provided by issuance costs on debt and by personal taxes. Some of the more significant limits to the borrowing-to-pay-dividends game (and the associated increases in stock prices) are, of course, provided by the several effects of uncertainty to which we now turn. (See also fn. 39.)

5. Allowances for Uncertainty, Even When Restricted to Identical Probability Distributions and with No Costs or Taxes, Will in General Prevent Market Price from Being Independent of the Mix between Retained Earnings and Debt

As in our treatment of retained earnings and outside equity with uncertainty present, we will first consider the trade-off between retained earnings and debt under fully idealized conditions with no costs or taxes present, and with all investors (and lenders) acting in terms of subjective probability distributions which are *identical* in every relevant respect for each actual and potential security (and loan) available in the market, although the distributions, of course, differ between companies and securities. But while these assumptions were both necessary *and* sufficient to validate an indifference theorem relative to new issues, we shall show that they are *not* sufficient to do so with respect to borrowing. The reason is that (a) under these conditions, investors will be indifferent to trade-offs between retained earnings and new borrowing *if and only if the entity value theory is valid,* and (b) under these conditions the latter theory is *not* valid in general.

Consider the behavior of equation (3) for a company for which all investors hold identical probability distributions over its investment budget $\tilde{F}_t$, its earnings-before-interest $\tilde{Y}'$ and dividend $\tilde{D}_t$ respectively, *if there is no borrowing.* Suppose now the company does or does not pay an added dividend ΔD_t of some arbitrary size financed by the (equal) proceeds of new borrowing $\Delta \dot{B}_t$; both transactions to occur at the end of the tth period. Since timing is the same, neither the numerator nor the denominator will be affected by the

---

[45] Modigliani and Miller recognize that the corporate tax invalidates the entity value theory but they do not examine limits to the financing preference tax considerations introduced.

transaction *if* the expected value and variance of the sum $(\tilde{D}_t + \tilde{P}_{t+1})$ is invariant to any $\Delta D_t = \Delta \dot{B}_t$. Now we know that the expected value will be the same *if and only if* $\Delta \tilde{P}_{t+1} = -\Delta \dot{B}_t$—that is, if and only if the entity value theory is true as of time $t + 1$. The variance of the sum of (more cash ΔD_t plus lower ending price $\tilde{P}_{t+1}$) will also be the same *if* the entity value theory is valid since the (absolute) standard deviation of $\tilde{P}_{t+1}$ is then independent of the size of the then total debt $B_{t+1} = \Delta \dot{B}_t + B_t$.[46] We can consequently concentrate upon whether the expectation of the entity theory that $E(\tilde{P}_{t+1} + B_{t+1})$ is invariant to debt is generally valid even under our idealizing assumptions.

The classic arguments supporting the validity of the entity value theory in uncertain but otherwise perfect markets are those advanced by Modigliani and Miller [23]. Both their proposition that the sum of market values of equity and debt cannot be increased by corporate debt, and their proposition that this sum cannot be reduced by debt, require special and unrealistic *assumptions in addition to* (a) identical subjective probability distributions, (b) purely competitive markets, (c) maximizing behavior, and (d) no issue costs or taxes—all of which we are assuming. The proposition that the prospect of corporate leverage (with investment budgets fixed) cannot raise the sum of the market price of the stock and the debt rests on the premise that, by "rolling his own" leverage through personal borrowing against the collateral of the stock, the investor can wind up in the same funds, income, *and* risk position as if the company borrows. While the pro forma funds position and the expected value and variance of the income after interest are indeed the same, the *risk position of the investor* carrying his own debt is, in general, *inherently less favorable* than if the company does the borrowing, since the variance of price fluctuations involves him in the risk of losing both his original equity investment and the amount borrowed on its collateral. Even if the probability of the occurrence of loss is the same,[47] the conditional loss is greater because of limited liability.[48]

Similarly, even though the investor *could* use the added dividend to buy the bonds at the end of the period—and thereby prevent the entity value from being reduced by the corporate borrowing—he need not do so, and in many if not most cases *would not*—even if the risk on the bonds themselves were independent of corporate leverage. The Modigliani-Miller argument that all rational investors would do so is an inference from the linearity they assume

---

[46] Different alternative, but by hypothesis fixed, amounts of debt are subtracted from the random variable $\tilde{P}_{t+1}$ defined in the absence of leverage. The variances of two random variables differing by a constant are equal.

[47] If the entity value theory were valid this probability would be the same. We saw above that under this theory σP in dollar units is independent of debt. With $\tilde{P}_u = \tilde{P}_b + B$ as the theory asserts, it follows that $Pr(\tilde{P}_u < B) = Pr(\tilde{P}_b < 0)$, where $\tilde{P}_u$ is stock price in the absence of debt, and $\tilde{P}_b$ is stock price in the presence of debt.

[48] Cf. Bodenhorn [2] and especially Durand [9]. Limited liability, it should be emphasized, is an attribute of what is traded in the market, not a market imperfection.

in the "market line" or "investor's objective market opportunity set" [23], p. 279 and passim]—and this linearity, in turn, depends entirely on their more basic assumption (p. 268) that bonds are considered by investors to be riskless securities. But when corporate *bonds* are recognized to be *risk assets also*—as they must be for any generality even under *our* restrictive assumption of identical subjective probability distributions—the relevant market opportunity locus is *hyperbolic* or *parabolic* and *not linear*.[49] With non-linear opportunity sets, differences in investors' utility functions become relevant, optimal portfolios will differ among investors, and all efficient portfolios are *not* equally desirable to all investors at the margin even in full equilibrium. Moreover, the different portfolios along the efficiency frontier with levered *j* stock and *j* bonds in the available set of potential investments *instead of* unlevered *j* stock will, in general, differ from those when unlevered *j* is available while levered *j* and *j* bonds are not.[50] There is consequently *no* a priori *assurance* of (indeed, strong presumption against) the validity of any assertion that, when levered j^{th} company stock plus *j* bonds is offered to the market in place of unlevered *j* stock, *all* investors previously having given amounts of *j* stock in their portfolio will immediately find it optimal to have equal aggregate sums of levered *j* stock plus *j* bonds in their respective portfolios instead of the unlevered *j* stock which is no longer available.

So far our conclusion that investors generally would not buy *j* bonds in amounts and prices (or automatically increase personal leverage in amounts) that would prevent the entity value from going either to a premium or discount has been reached within the confines of an assumption that investors believe the risk on *j* bonds is independent of *j* corporation's leverage. At least beyond some moderate degree of leverage, our rational investors will neither hold nor act on such a belief. They clearly will *not* buy *j* bonds in amounts and at prices which will maintain entity values (even under present assumptions) if the resulting position indicated significant chance of *j's* bankruptcy —and this reduction in its entity value invalidates the entity value theorem.[51] It needs to be added that, with the possible exception of triangular or

---

[49] See Tobin [32], p. 85 and Markowitz [21], esp. p. 153. The locus is hyperbolic between expected return and standard deviation, parabolic on return and variance. The locus in question can be interpreted *either* as the opportunity locus for the investment of a given sum in non-cash assets, *or* as the all-inclusive opportunity locus where cash itself is subject to the "real" risk of purchasing power changes (witness the impact of inflationary or deflationary commodity-price expectations on stock prices!).

[50] This is true because "unlevered *j* stock," "levered *j* stock" and "*j* bonds" are three different investments with different *covariances* with other securities available for inclusion in portfolios. Even if the *interest payment* on *j* bonds were certain, holding the *j* bonds would involve market risks attributable to possible changes in "pure" interest rates and a random term which is unlikely to be independent of other securities.

[51] Modigliani and Miller [23] fn. 18 recognize "the danger of something comparable to 'gambler's ruin,' and they consequently "might perhaps expect heavily levered companies to sell at a slight discount." Only management prudence (and favorable market conditions) would keep the discount small—and *neither* would be required *if* the entity value theory were valid.

rectangular distributions, the probability of default and bankruptcy rises *non-linearly* with the reliance on debt even if interest rates are constant, since it will vary in the manner of the left tail of a *cumulative* probability distribution over earnings before interest. This is true even if the probability distributions over the time-vector of earnings-before-interest were independent of the size of the debt. This latter assumption has apparently been rather uniformly accepted in the theoretical literature,[52] but it is clearly unwarranted: new sales contracts may not be obtained (and existing contracts may be cancelled) if financial position is weakened by greater debts and fixed charges,[53] and real world debt instruments contain "acceleration clauses" by which any breach of the covenants make the entire remaining balance immediately due and payable. For these and many similar reasons, stochastic income streams which entail low risk in the absence of debt become subject to accelerating risk of abrupt reduction and even termination at some point in the future as debt is progressively increased.

Such prospects affect both the expected values and the variances of the *corporate* earnings-before-interest. The entity value will no longer be as large as the capital value of the original unlevered stream, so that *the price of the stock falls by more than the increment in debt* for this reason alone. In addition, the added risk *to the company* will make the interest rate on debt an increasing function of leverage, thus reducing the funds available for dividends (and net earnings after interest) more than in proportion to the added debt. Moreover, the increased risk to the company, *and* the bunching of those risks to the equity as debt increases relative to total capital, *increase* the capitalization rate on the levered equity still further.[54] It is apparent that, while the recipients of the added dividend financed by borrowing *could* use the proceeds to buy the bonds in sufficient volume and at sufficiently high (bond) prices to maintain the entity value in such circumstances, they would be foolish to do so—and they would be equally foolish to act in a way which would be rational for them *only if* others (holding the same expectations!) were in fact to do so.

We therefore conclude that purely competitive markets, maximizing behavior, absence of issue costs and taxes, and identical interest rates to personal and corporate debtors, are *not sufficient* to make investors indifferent to substitutions between retained earnings and debt in financing fixed budgets, or to validate the entity value theory, when uncertainty is admitted even

---

[52] It was advanced by Durand [7], pp. 101–102, who speaks favorably of "the rigorous analysis offered by advocates of the NOI [entity value] theory," and refers to a critic who suggests that the totality of risk is increased when a business borrows. But see also Bodenhorn [2], p. 485.

[53] Financial soundness is a condition for assurance of supply, on which procurement officers place a premium.

[54] Modigliani and Miller [23], pp. 273–6 deduce the contrary inference (capitalization factors for levered equity *declining* with increased leverage beyond some middling point) from the Procrustean Bed of their "Proposition I"—the entity value theory. Since the expected earnings stream is not independent of the leverage, the premise falls and the "paradox," as they refer to it, is resolved.

under the constraints of identical subjective probability distributions and information. *Even in this homogenized and pasteurized world, investors will still have a unique preference over particular time-vectors of dividends* unless very special *additional* assumptions are made neutralizing the asymmetrical risk position of investors providing their own leverage and the ever increasing risk to the corporate entity as its leverage increases. Moreover, all possible sets of such straight-jacketing assumptions (granting that some such sets may exist) would necessarily at best be valid only for limited ranges of corporate leverage because of the clear dominance of the impact of large leverage on the expected values of the corporate earnings before interest and the totality of its risks.

6. More General Conditions of Uncertainty Reinforce These Conclusions

Our conclusions regarding the existence of well defined investor preferences regarding particular time vectors of dividends (implemented, with investment budgets given, by associated degrees of leverage) are substantially strengthened when we relax our restrictive assumptions that information is uniformly spread among all investors and that their subjective probability distributions regarding the company are identical. If diversity in these latter respects is introduced, it becomes not only possible but probable that interest rates to many corporate debtors (with no more than moderate leverage) will be lower than those to individuals,[55] and the differences between individual investors' information and preference functions now strengthen the considerations leading to the "super-premiums" on (high-grade) corporate debt which Durand has always emphasized [7, 9]. Differences in information, interest rates, and preference functions thus reinforce the likelihood created by asymmetrical risk positions *per se* that, over the lower end of the leverage range, the *sum* of investor valuations of corporate equity and debt will be an increasing function of corporate leverage—that is, that leverage introduces "premiums" into entity values over such a range—and that investors will prefer higher dividends *cum* higher corporate debt to greater retentions and lower dividends.

Correspondingly, an argument parallel to that in section III3. above rigorously implies that as more and more debt is substituted for retained earnings in circumstances where the subjective probability distributions of potential investors vary from each other, the company's additional securities must be placed with new buyers whose subjective valuation is progressively lower (or to previous buyers at progressively lower prices). This effect compounds the forces creating the conclusions reached above that entity values will be forced to a discount—and to an increasing one—by additions to corporate leverage (at least beyond some moderate amount). *Since investors will thus have well*

---

[55] This will be true, if, for no other reason, because the costs of investigation and processing a large loan (in absolute terms) to a well known corporate name will be less per dollar of loan than those for small borrowers.

defined preferences over the dividends-retained-earnings-debt mix in both the "premium" and the "discount" range, and since the most reasonable inference from our analysis is that one range shades gradually into the other, we conclude that investors have well defined preferences over the whole range under generalized uncertainty.

So far we have ruled out issue costs, and both personal and corporate taxes, in our examination of the effects of uncertainty. But it is clear from the earlier analysis that the interest deduction under the corporate income tax increases the amount of corporate borrowing that would otherwise be optimal, the size of the current dividend investors would otherwise prefer, and the size of any premium in entity values otherwise present. Correspondingly, differentials in the personal income tax reduce the otherwise optimal amount of corporate debt in the financing of given sized capital budgets—and for high bracket investors may make the optimum corporate debt zero! For more moderate ranges of personal income tax rates, however, corner solutions will not be optimal, and the normative ideal will reflect the combined thrust of both the corporate and the personal tax along with the interacting effects of the several elements identified earlier in this section on uncertainty. Finally, costs of the act of borrowing (other than interest) are doubtless relatively small for bank loans, but beyond some point the corporate risk of such *short*-term debt will have risen to a point where a shift to longer-term private placements (which involve higher interest costs) and/or public debt issues (involving sizeable new issue costs) are justified. Again, if not a literal vertical displacement in the supply-of-capital function, there is at the least a region of steep rise beyond which the curve is relatively flatter for some range before its slope rises more rapidly again.

V. GENERAL CONCLUSIONS

1. Unlevered equity values are independent of the particular dividend vector *if, but only if*, (1) any uncertainty is fully idealized or absent, (2) there are no issue costs and (3) there are no personal tax differentials. Under these restrictions the result holds only because these conditions, together with invariant vectors of capital budgets and earnings, reduce all efficient dividend vectors to a set, all of whose (vector) elements have the same present value. *Any more general and realistic assumptions result in a well defined optimum dividend vector.* The "dividend theory" that prices are equal to the present values of the cash flow *to the investor* (that is, *cash dividends*) *remains valid even under fully generalized conditions* and should be the basis for further theoretical work. The so-called earnings theory is valid *if and only if* it is stated in forms *identically* reducible to the valuation of the cash dividend flow to the investor. In particular, the significance of the time vectors of earnings (and of company investments) lies in its implications *for* the prospective stream of *dividends*, rather than vice versa.

2. Under *fully idealized* conditions *of certainty*, alternative efficient combi-

nations of cash-dividends, retentions, and new debt for the corporation are similarly reduced to a single indifference set. Once allowance is made for (even fully idealized) uncertainty, *or* debt issuance costs, *or* personal taxes, *or* corporate taxes, *or* any combination of them, investors once again have a well defined preference ordering over the vectors in the efficient set of dividend vectors. When debt financing is available, even under the most general conditions, the optimum is still defined by the maximum present value of cash flows to the investor—in which *cash dividends are an essential element* (along with, of course, interest charges on "personal leverage" if any)—the moments of the dividend vector being, in part, a function of the amounts and conditions of corporate borrowing. This statement describes a dividend model adjusted to allow for debt financing. Once again, "earnings models" will be valid *only if* reducible to this "dividend" specification *identically.*

3. The sum of the market values of the corporate equity and debt will *not* be invariant to changes in the finance-mix (as asserted in the "entity value" theory)—in particular, stock values will not be equal to "entity value" less corporate debt—*except under fully idealized conditions of certainty.* Moreover, with uncertainty admitted, the earnings-yield is a *continuously rising* (and non-linear) function of corporate leverage—at least beyond some initial range—and not a declining function of leverage beyond some point as inferred from the entity value theory.

4. Except under fully idealized conditions of certainty, there is a vertical displacement, or at least a small region of very steep rise, in the supply-of-capital function to the corporation.

5. All the above conclusions follow from an analysis in which all substitutions in the finance-mix are instantaneous and identical in timing; they are consequently *independent* of the shape of the time-vector of discount rates k_τ—and, in particular, of whether the discount rates used at any instant in making valuations of prospective income streams are or are not an increasing function of futurity to allow for differences in uncertainty over the future.

6. This paper has focused on a clarification of some of the more important theoretical foundations of the applied field of corporation finance. In particular, in order to focus on the more primary issue of whether investors will have basic preferences over *how* given investment budgets are financed and whether "earnings" or "dividend" models provide the appropriate vehicle for further analysis and development, we have assumed capital budgets fixed throughout this paper. The implications of the results of this paper for the functional relation between equity values and size of capital budgets (with optimal finance-mix throughout) and the determination of optimal internal investment and corporate growth are developed elsewhere. We have found that in general theoretical models, non-linearities, complex interactions, and inequalities leading to marked preferences, abound. It remains a question of fact whether models which ignore such important facts of life as issue costs, taxes, and differences in expectations, and which substitute linear for non-linear functions and straight-jacket variable and interacting parts into con-

stant sums, can encompass practical reality to an acceptable approximation—whether differences and distinctions important in more general models really do make a difference that matters in practice. Empirical tests must also be reserved to another occasion.

BIBLIOGRAPHY

1. Bierman, Harold, Jr., Fouraker, Lawrence E., and Jaedicke, Robert K., *Quantitative Analysis for Business Decisions* (Homewood, 1961).
2. Bodenhorn, Diran, "On the Problem of Capital Budgeting," *The Journal of Finance*, XIV (December 1959). Reprinted in this volume.
3. Conard, Joseph W., *An Introduction to the Theory of Interest* (Berkeley, 1959).
4. Dean, Joel, *Capital Budgeting* (New York, 1951).
5. Dorfman, Robert, Samuelson, Paul A., Solow, Robert M., *Linear Programming and Economic Analysis* (New York, 1958).
6. Duesenberry, James S., *Business Cycles and Economic Growth* (New York, 1958).
7. Durand, David, "Costs of Debt and Equity Funds for Business: Trends and Problems of Measurement," *Conference on Research in Business Finance* (New York, 1952).
8. Durand, David, "Growth Stocks and the Petersburg Paradox," *Journal of Finance*, XII (September 1957).
9. Durand, David, "The Cost of Capital, Corporation Finance and the Theory of Investment: Comment," *American Economic Review*, XLIX (September 1959).*
10. Fisher, Irving, *The Theory of Interest* (New York, 1930).
11. Gordon, Myron J., "Dividends, Earnings and Stock Prices," *The Review of Economics and Statistics*, XLI (May 1959).
12. Gordon, Myron J., "The Optimum Dividend Rate," *Management Sciences: Models and Techniques* (London, 1960).
13. Gordon, Myron J., "The Savings, Investment and Valuation of a Corporation," *The Review of Economics and Statistics*, XLIII (February 1962).
14. Gordon, Myron J., and Shapiro, Eli, "Capital Equipment Analysis: The Required Rate of Profit," *Management Science*, III (October, 1956).*
15. Hicks, J. R., *Value and Capital* (Oxford, 1939, 1946).
16. Kuh, Edwin, "Capital Theory and Capital Budgeting," *Metroeconomica*, XII (August–December, 1960).
17. Lintner, John, "Effect of Corporate Taxation on Real Investment," *American Economic Review*, XLIV (May 1954).
18. Lintner, John, "A New Model of the Cost of Capital: Dividends, Earnings, Leverage, Expectations and Stock Prices," mimeo. paper delivered at St. Louis Meeting, Econometrica Society, December 1960.
19. Lintner, John, "The Cost of Capital and Optimal Corporate Growth and Capital Budgeting Under Uncertainty," *Quarterly Journal of Economics*, forthcoming.
20. Lutz, Frederick and Vera, *The Theory of Investment of the Firm* (Princeton, 1951).
21. Markowitz, Harry M., *Portfolio Selection* (New York, 1959).

22. Meyer, John, and Kuh, Edwin, *The Investment Decision* (Cambridge, 1957).
23. Modigliani, Franco and Miller, Merton, "The Cost of Capital, Corporation Finance and the Theory of Investment," *American Economic Review*, XLVIII (June 1958).*
24. Modigliani, Franco and Miller, Merton, "Reply," *American Economic Review*, XLIX (September 1959).
25. Modigliani, Franco and Miller, Merton, "Dividend Policy, Growth and the Valuation of Shares," *Journal of Business*, XXXIV (October 1961).
26. Modigliani, Franco and Zeman, Morton, "The Effect of the Availability of Funds, and the Terms Thereof, On Business Investment," *Conference on Research in Business Finance* (New York, 1952).
27. Preinreich, Gabriel A., *The Nature of Dividends* (New York, 1935).
28. Roberts, Harry V., "Current Problems in the Economics of Capital Budgeting," *Journal of Business*, XXX (January 1957).*
29. Samuelson, Paul A., "Some Aspects of the Pure Theory of Capital," *Quarterly Journal of Economics*, LI (May 1937).
30. Solomon, Ezra, "Measuring a Company's Cost of Capital," *Journal of Business*, XXVIII (October 1955).*
31. Tinbergen, Jan, *Statistical Testing of Business Cycle Theories*, I and II (Geneva, 1939).
32. Tobin, James, "Liquidity Preference as Behavior Toward Risk," *Review of Economic Studies*, XXVI (February 1958).
33. Walter, James, "Dividend Policies and Common Stock Prices," *Journal of Finance*, XI (March 1956).
34. Weston, J. Fred, "The Management of Corporate Capital: A Review Article," *Journal of Business*, XXXIV (April 1961).
35. Williams, J. B., *The Theory of Investment Value* (Cambridge, 1938).

* Reprinted in Solomon, Ezra, Ed., *The Management of Corporate Capital* (Glencoe, 1959).

3. Decapitalization

UNION PACIFIC RAILROAD COMPANY

EARLY IN 1964, the financial officers of the Union Pacific Railroad Company considered that purchasing and eventually retiring some of its outstanding 4% noncumulative, noncallable preferred stock represented an excellent investment for a portion of its available surplus funds, due to the savings that could be realized in the dividends paid out of earnings after federal income taxes. The corporation had followed a policy of utilizing excess liquid funds to purchase its outstanding bonds and thereby accelerate debt retirement. As the company had never before purchased any of its preferred or common stock, the management considered it essential to gain a full understanding of the issues involved before definitely formulating policy.

COMPANY BACKGROUND

Union Pacific Railroad Company was the sixth largest railroad in the United States on the basis of 1963 total operating revenues. Reorganized in 1897, the company had established itself as one of the great and stable railway systems in the country. This success continued through the depression of the 1930's, and in the 1960's the railroad was one of the strongest, operationally and financially, in the United States (see Exhibits 1 and 2 for financial data).

Directly operating 9,701 miles of road, Union Pacific operated in the 13 states of Iowa, Missouri, Nebraska, Kansas, Colorado, Wyoming, Montana, Idaho, Nevada, California, Utah, Oregon, and Washington. The company had achieved an exceedingly favorable operating ratio, in part the result of a long average freight haul, which amounted to 585 miles in 1963, exceeding that of any other U.S. railroad. Also, Union Pacific's location was excellent in respect to connections made with other railroads. The result was that Union Pacific received a higher percentage of traffic from connections not its own than did the average transcontinental carrier.

In recent years, the company had also enjoyed considerable income from nonrailroad properties, including oil and gas wells, mines, pipelines, and lands. Separate divisions of the company were engaged in developing these operations, which had been financed from company funds, as joint ventures, or in relatively small amounts from mortgages on specific properties.

Despite the continuous payment of preferred and common dividends and considerable capital expenditures, Union Pacific possessed a high level of liquid resources in the 1960's. This condition is indicated by the following figures (in thousands):

	1960	1961	1962	1963
Net working capital	$ 87,588	$104,881	$146,377	$207,563
Cash	40,366	36,898	39,385	37,882
Short-term investments	77,510	100,740	137,597	218,220
Gross revenues	494,184	499,325	512,125	519,104

UNION PACIFIC CAPITALIZATION AND POLICY

As of December 31, 1963, the capitalization of Union Pacific was conservative in relation to traffic and earning power, and the carrier enjoyed a high credit standing, which had been reflected in its historical ability to effect refundings with low interest cost. The preferred stock had good investment characteristics, and the common stock was one of the relatively few railroad junior securities that had been maintained on a dividend basis during all the depression years. Exhibit 3 presents a detailed description of Union Pacific securities.

This conservative capital structure was the outgrowth of company debt policy, which had emphasized debt reduction in the 1947–64 period. R. M. Sutton, financial vice president and controller (and chief financial officer) of Union Pacific, described the debt policy as follows.

In the 1945 to 1964 period, Union Pacific had sufficient funds to pay for capital expenditures; hence, we chose to use our own money rather than issue securities. The company has no explicit policy as to an optimal debt–equity mix, but rather a feeling that the less debt a company has, the better its position.

This policy was reflected in statements at various times in the annual reports to stockholders, typified by the two following excerpts.

(1958 *Annual Report*) The reduction in funded debt during the thirteen years since 1945 is shown in the following tabulation:

Outstanding December 31st	Bonds	Equipment Obligations	Total
1945	$333,274,500	$33,040,657	$366,315,157
1958	161,306,000	566,000	161,872,000
Reduction	$171,968,500	$32,474,657	$204,443,157

This reduction represents 56 per cent of total debt outstanding December 31, 1945. During the same thirteen-year period, there was a net *increase* in investment in road and equipment property of $493,346,402, or 48 per cent, over such investment at the beginning of the period.

(1960 *Annual Report*) . . . the two latter bond issues [2½'s and 2⅞'s] aggregating $113,727,000, constituted the total publicly held long-term debt at the close of the year, making the "debt ratio" (percentage of long-term debt to total capitalization) of Union Pacific Railroad Company and Leased Lines only 8.4%, one of the lowest ratios for any major railroad.

The debt retirement had produced a decreasing debt–equity ratio, which averaged about 8.4% in the 1960–63 period, and reached 8.32% as of December 31, 1963.

DEBT RETIREMENT—RATIONALE AND PROCEDURE

Implementation of the Union Pacific debt policy effected an $86.878 million reduction in overall debt in the 1947–63 period. (See Exhibit 4, which gives a detailed breakdown of debt retirement during this period.) The reduction in debt was influenced by three major factors: (1) excess liquid funds; (2) a rising trend in general interest rates during the period; (3) tax considerations incidental to bond retirement; (4) the level of returns available on short-term investments.

As previously stated, the company had maintained continuously profitable operations during this period. In view of the stable volume of revenues and haulage, the concomitant cash flow produced funds considerably in excess of those needed to operate the railroad. This excess liquidity, combined with Union Pacific's historically conservative debt policy, caused the management to investigate reduction of its fixed charges.

The refunding mortgage 2½% bonds, series C (issued March 1, 1946) and the 30-year, 2⅞% debenture bonds (issued February 1, 1946) had been issued during a period of low interest rates. The rise in interest rates during the 1947–63 period caused both bond series to trade at a substantial discount from face value (see Exhibit 5). Given the differential between the trading prices and the call prices, Union Pacific purchased as much as possible of the sinking fund requirements in the open market. The differential between market price and face value of the bonds and the relevant profit treatment of bond repurchase and retirement made the acceleration of debt retirement more difficult.

The profit treatment of a bond repurchase and retirement can be illustrated by an example (this example assumes repurchase at $70).

Face value of bond	$100.00
Repurchase price	70.00
Gain	$ 30.00
Tax at 52%	15.60
Net gain	$ 14.40
Effective purchase price	85.60

Repurchase and retirement of bonds thus resulted in a significant profit realization *in the year of purchase*. The effect on earnings per share, however, was not considered material.

The decision on whether to accelerate bond retirement was based on a comparison of the after-tax yield of a bond repurchase and the after-tax yield available from temporary cash investments in the short-term money market. The yield of a bond repurchase was computed as follows. (Details of this example are given in Exhibit 6, which presents a yield table used in the decisional procedure at Union Pacific.)

1. Given:
   a) An effective purchase price of $85.60.
   b) $2.50 interest payment for life of the bond.
   c) $100 principal value at maturity date.
2. What is the after-tax yield of an investment of $85.60 that will produce $2.50 interest per annum before tax and $100 at final maturity (1991)?
3. Answer (from Exhibit 6): 2.33%.

ROCK ISLAND MERGER AND CONTINGENT CAPITAL STRUCTURE CHANGES

In late 1963, negotiations aimed at merging the Chicago, Rock Island & Pacific Railroad Company into Union Pacific were completed. Managements of both companies reached agreement on an exchange offer, to be submitted to the stockholders of both companies in 1964, in part as follows.

A. In the event that the exchange offer is consummated by merger (two-thirds of Rock Island shares assenting):
   (1) Each share of Union Pacific[1] common stock will continue as authorized and issued.
   (2) Each share of Union Pacific 4% preferred stock, $10 par value, will be converted into $10 principal amount of 30-year, 4¾% new debentures.[2]
   (3) Each share of Rock Island common stock will be converted into one share of new Union Pacific $1.80 dividend convertible preferred stock, convertible into 0.85 share of Union Pacific common stock.
B. In the event that the exchange offer is consummated by control:
   (1) Each share of Union Pacific 4% preferred and common stock will continue as authorized and issued.
   (2) Each assenting share of Rock Island common stock will be exchanged for one share of new Union Pacific $1.80 (dividend) convertible preferred stock, convertible into 0.85 share of Union Pacific common stock.

---

[1] Exhibits 7 and 8 present the relevant Union Pacific common stock information.

[2] It has long been recognized that a noncallable security can be retired only through a successful exchange offer, but this usually leaves a small continuing ownership of the original security. A railroad merger permits extinguishing this minority, although usually at the expense of a cash payment to dissenters.

(3) The ownership of Rock Island shares committed under the offer would be transferred to Union Pacific.

(4) Dissenting Rock Island shareholders would retain their shares of Rock Island common stock.

The managements of both companies strongly favored the merger and its provisions. They felt the two lines were well suited for merger, since the combination of properties would be primarily end to end and thus would unite the two roads in a functional sense. Union Pacific's financial strength would make possible improvements to Rock Island's properties and economies in operation of the company by unification of physical facilities at points served by both lines. Both managements felt confident that the merger would be approved when submitted to the respective stockholder groups. Under Union Pacific's Revised Articles of Incorporation, both the Union Pacific common and preferred stock, each voting separately as a class, would vote on the merger proposal. Approval would require the affirmative vote of at least a majority of the outstanding stock of each class.

EFFECT OF CONVERSION OF THE 4% UNION PACIFIC PREFERRED STOCK TO NEW DEBENTURES

The financial management of Union Pacific favored the retirement of the 4% preferred stock for two major reasons. The 4% preferred stock had been issued in 1897 to raise funds in reorganization of the Union Pacific Railway Company. Because this was an emergency issue, many features attractive to investors at that time had been built into it—for example, a par value of $10, noncallability, and equal voting status with the common stock. Elimination of the 4% preferred would produce a more flexible, less complex capital structure for Union Pacific.

Union Pacific management also foresaw in the conversion a favorable effect on earnings per share. The conversion, although reducing net income, would increase earnings available for common shares and, hence, earnings per share, as follows (using 1963 earnings):

	1963 Actual (in Thousands)		1963 with Conversions (in Thousands)
Net income.................	$68,979	Net income before interest	
Preferred dividends..........	(3,981)	on proposed debentures.....	$68,979
		Interest....................	(4,730)
		Tax shield (52%)...........	2,460
Earnings available for		Earnings available for	
common.................	64,998	common.................	66,709
Earnings per share.........	$ 2.90	Earnings per share.........	$ 2.97

Thus, the conversion would have a favorable effect on earnings per common share; this advantage would increase as the debentures were retired and interest charges decreased. The implications of conversion to the company and to the 4% preferred stockholders were summarized by Union Pacific management in a letter being prepared to present the merger proposal to the stockholders.

The merger would, in addition to the other advantages hereinabove summarized, give to Union Pacific as the surviving company, by reason of the conversion of its 4% Preferred Stock to New Debentures, a more flexible capital structure. The 4¾% interest on the New Debentures will be deductible in the computation of Federal income taxes of the surviving corporation, whereas the dividends on the present Union Pacific 4% Preferred Stock are not so deductible. . . . Holders of the New Debentures will have no voting rights, although holders of the present [Union Pacific] 4% Preferred Stock now have one vote per share on all matters submitted to a vote of the stockholders. The 85% dividends received deduction to corporations and the $100 dividends exclusion to individuals, allowed under the Internal Revenue Code, as presently in effect, will not be applicable to interest on the New Debentures. Holders of 4% Preferred Stock will exchange a non-callable security, which is not a fixed obligation of the company, for an obligation with a definite due date and specific retirement commitments.

CONSIDERATION OF PREFERRED STOCK REPURCHASE

In December, 1963, several corporate holders of the 4% preferred stock approached Union Pacific with offers to sell to the company large blocks of the preferred stock. The exchange of the debentures for the preferred would unfavorably affect the after-tax return realizable by such corporations. This change was the result of the effect of the intercorporate dividend rate, illustrated as follows:

| | After-Tax Yield to Corporations | |
	4% Preferred	4¾% Debentures
Dividend; interest	$4.00	$4.75
85% exclusion	(3.40)	. . .
Taxable income	$0.60	$4.75
Tax at 52%	(0.31)	(2.47)
Net income	$3.69	$2.28

It appeared that over 1.4 million preferred shares were held by corporations.[3] The situation caused the top management of Union Pacific to consider *de novo* the various and complex aspects of preferred stock repurchase. Although areas of extreme uncertainty existed, management perceived two apparent advantages in such action.

1. It would be consistent with a corporate financial objective—eventual elimination of the 4% preferred stock.

---

[3] Union Pacific annually reported to the New York Stock Exchange the top 100 holders of each of its stock issues. The report for April 1, 1963, showed that such holders of the preferred issue had 9,265,610 shares and that corporations held 1,406,000 of these shares.

2. Compared with the alternative use of excess liquid funds—investment in the short-term money market or accelerated debt retirement—repurchase of the preferred appeared attractive.[4]

While the repurchase of the corporate holdings appeared extremely attractive, the possibility of this limited repurchase raised serious questions in the minds of the top financial management of Union Pacific.[5] The superior after tax yield on preferred[6] repurchases in comparison with alternative uses of excess funds indicated that repurchases on a large scale, exceeding those of the corporate offerings, could be a profitable area of funds use. Given the various possibilities of repurchasing, any policy formulation would necessitate decisions on: (1) the method of repurchasing;[7] (2) the desired extent and timing of repurchases; (3) development of procedures in the areas of announcement and purchasing constraints.

As Mr. Sutton prepared his recommendation for submission to the executive committee, he felt it essential to reevaluate the entire policy of retirement of senior securities.

---

[4] Assuming a repurchase price of $9.50, the after-tax return would be 4.21% ($0.40/$9.50). Union Pacific would also realize a profit because the purchase price would be less than the par value, as follows (gains and losses on transactions in stock not being considered as taxable income or loss):

Par value	$10.00
Repurchase price	9.50
Nontaxable gain	$ 0.50

[5] The relevant executive relationships are reproduced in Exhibit 9.

[6] Exhibit 10 presents the volume of Union Pacific preferred stock traded weekly over the New York Stock Exchange during the last half of 1963.

[7] Basically, two methods of repurchase existed:
  a) *Open Market*—the Union Pacific preferred stock was traded on the New York Stock Exchange; private transactions negotiated with individual parties (e.g., corporations) external to the Exchange were possible.
  b) *Tender*—a method of repurchasing securities, in which a prospective buyer announces its intention of making purchases under specified terms, and invites owners to indicate their acceptance, that is, *to tender* their securities.

Exhibit 1

UNION PACIFIC RAILROAD COMPANY

BALANCE SHEETS, AS OF DECEMBER 31, 1960–63
(Dollar Figures in Thousands)

ASSETS	1960	1961	1962	1963
Cash	$ 40,366	$ 36,898	$ 39,385	$ 37,882
Temporary cash investments	77,510	100,740	137,597	218,220
Special deposits	75	121	103	103
Receivables	53,512	56,233	54,452	57,459
Other current assets	29,115	22,240	24,067	24,831
Total Current Assets	$ 200,578	$ 216,232	$ 255,604	$ 338,495
Road and equipment	$1,556,774	$1,582,303	$1,578,660	$1,500,042
Less: Reserve for depreciation	354,441	373,965	391,001	408,060
Road and equipment, net	$1,202,333	$1,208,338	$1,187,659	$1,091,982
Miscellaneous physical property*	$ 47,258	$ 52,583	$ 66,492	$ 53,980
Less: Accrued depreciation	28,436	30,264	42,147	31,776
Net physical property	$ 18,822	$ 22,319	$ 24,345	$ 22,204
Donations and grants	$ (31,096)	$ (42,386)	$ ...	$ ...
General expenditures	52,877	52,367	52,163	32,884
Other elements of investment	...	...	...	141,863
Investment in affiliates	54,952	82,878	86,447	81,517
Other investments	46,799	49,424	48,990	49,422
Reserve for security adjustment	...	(19,132)	(19,132)	(19,131)
Other assets	8,035	9,764	7,363	8,867
Total Assets	$1,553,300	$1,579,804	$1,643,439	$1,748,103
LIABILITIES				
Current and accrued liabilities	$ 112,990	$ 111,350	$ 109,227	$ 130,932
Insurance reserves	32,264	32,729	33,256	33,883
Casualty and other reserves	10,863	12,150	11,600	8,776
Unamortized premium, long-term debt	2,213	2,073	1,934	1,787
Other	8,894	5,016	5,368	2,615
Payable to affiliates	24,821	25,371	9,422	7,915
Funded debt	113,727	112,579	111,992	111,299
Equipment obligations	...	...	19,676	18,154
Preferred stock, 4%	99,587	99,587	99,587	99,585
Common stock	224,302	224,302	224,302	224,302
Capital surplus	8,750	7,323	7,070	7,903
Retained earnings†	914,889	947,324	1,010,005	1,100,952
Total Liabilities	$1,553,300	$1,579,804	$1,643,439	$1,748,103

* Plant and equipment for nonrailroad uses.
† Adjustments in the retained earnings account result from accounting adjustments related to taxes and from liquidation or sale of property.

Exhibit 2

UNION PACIFIC RAILROAD COMPANY

INCOME STATEMENTS FOR YEARS 1960–63
(Dollar Figures in Thousands)

	1960	1961	1962	1963
Railway operating revenues	$494,184	$499,325	$512,125	$519,104
Railway operating expenses*	359,741	360,799	370,157	372,131
Net revenue	$134,443	$138,526	$141,968	$146,973
Railway tax accruals	79,342	85,980	73,469	74,880
Railway operating income	$ 55,101	$ 52,546	$ 68,499	$ 72,093
Rent income	$ 6,418	$ 6,038	$ 6,203	$ 6,157
Rents payable	28,683	26,770	27,926	27,138
Net rents	$(22,265)	$(20,732)	$(21,723)	$(20,981)
Net railway operating income	$ 32,836	$ 31,814	$ 46,776	$ 51,112
Other income, before federal income tax	$ 51,352	$ 56,568	$ 58,467	$ 56,800
Total Income	$ 84,188	$ 88,382	$105,243	$107,912
Miscellaneous deductions	14,810	17,700	19,599	19,909
Income available for fixed charges	$ 69,378	$ 70,682	$ 85,644	$ 88,003
Fixed charges	4,065	3,012	3,154	3,781
Net income	$ 65,313	$ 67,670	$ 82,490	$ 84,222
Net income adjusted†	$ 60,351	$ 66,269	$ 68,630	$ 68,979
Preferred dividends	$ 3,981	$ 3,981	$ 3,981	$ 3,981
Earnings per share	$ 2.62	$ 2.78	$ 2.88	$ 2.90
Common dividends	$ 35,887	$ 35,887	$ 35,887	$ 38,131
Dividend per share	$ 1.60	$ 1.60	$ 1.60	$ 1.70

* Includes annual depreciation as follows: 1960, $35,536,041; 1961, $38,032,536; 1962, $39,103,437; 1963, $41,427,945.

† Net income adjusted reflects the effect of depreciation as computed for federal tax purposes and the 7% investment credit taken as a reduction of tax liability in the year it was granted.

Exhibit 3

UNION PACIFIC RAILROAD COMPANY

DESCRIPTION OF UNION PACIFIC CAPITALIZATION
DECEMBER 31, 1963

LONG-TERM DEBT

Refunding mortgage bonds....................................$	68,606,000
Series C, 2½%..	
Due March 1, 1991.....................................	
Sinking Fund: $430,000 per year........................	
Rating, Aa...	
30-year, 2⅞% debentures...............................	42,693,000
Due February 1, 1976.................................	
Sinking Fund: $235,000 per year.......................	
Rating, Aa...	
Equipment obligations.................................	18,154,000
4.125% to 4.15%.....................................	
Due 1967–70...	
Amounts payable to affiliated companies..................	7,914,818
Total Long-Term Debt..........................$	137,367,818

SHAREHOLDERS' EQUITY

Minority interest in St. Joseph & Grand Island Railway Company..$	52,281*
4% preferred stock...................................	99,585,381
$10 par value..	
Authorized, 20,000,000 shares.........................	
Issued, 9,954,310...................................	
Noncumulative, not callable...........................	
Equal voting rights with common stock.................	
Common stock.......................................	224,250,069*
$10 par value..	
Authorized, 29,617,870 shares.........................	
Issued, 22,429,235 shares............................	
Capital surplus and retained income......................	1,108,855,417
Total Shareholders' Equity.......................	$1,432,743,148

* The common stock account shown in Exhibit 1 consisted of $224,292,350 (Union Pacific par value) plus $10,000 (par value of 100 shares of the St. Joseph and Grand Island Railway Co.). Exhibit 3 shows the minority interest in St. J. & G. I. Ry. Co. separately.

Exhibit 4

UNION PACIFIC RAILROAD COMPANY

DEBT RETIREMENT* FOR YEARS 1947–65
(Dollar Figures in Thousands)

Year	Oregon- Washington 3% Mortgage Bonds†	2½% Mortgage Bonds (Due 1991)	2⅞% Debentures (Due 1976)	Cumulative Accelerated Retirement: 2½'s & 2⅞'s‡	Equipment Obligations	Total Changes
1947	$ (537)	$ (675)	...	$ 10	$ 25,590	$ 24,378
1948	(538)	(713)	...	58	(1,951)	(3,202)
1949	(539)	(1,056)	...	449	(9,922)	(11,517)
1950	(541)	(342)	...	126	(9,712)	(10,595)
1951	(542)	(688)	...	149	(9,712)	(10,942)
1952	(543)	(736)	...	220	(8,471)	(9,750)
1953	(1,085)	(911)	...	466	(7,863)	(9,859)
1954	(5)	(1,255)	...	1,056	9,212	7,952
1955	(1,094)	(3,361)	...	3,752	(9,898)	(14,353)
1956	(2,735)	(760)	...	3,847	(7,864)	(11,359)
1957	(101)	...	...	3,182	(2,432)	(2,533)
1958	...	(247)	...	2,764	(2,432)	(2,679)
1959	...	(233)	$ (742)	3,074	(566)	(1,541)
1960	(45,955)§	(536)	(113)	3,058	...	(46,604)
1961		(1,041)	(107)	3,541	...	(1,148)
1962		(367)	(220)	3,463	19,676	19,089
1963		(75)	(618)	3,491	(1,522)	(2,215)
Total Change	$(54,215)	$(12,996)	$(1,800)		$(17,867)	$(86,878)
Outstanding 12/31/63		$ 68,606	$42,693		$ 18,154	

* All figures represent face value of bonds retired.

† The bonds of the Oregon–Washington Railroad, operated under lease by the Union Pacific Railroad, were guaranteed unconditionally as to principal and interest by the Union Pacific.

‡ Figures indicate excess over combined sinking fund requirement of $665. The indenture provisions of the 2⅞% debenture bonds provided that the sinking fund requirement for the debenture bonds could be satisfied by the retirement of "bonds or obligations of the Company equal or prior in rank to the bonds." (Listing Statement A-12296 of the New York Stock Exchange, March 1, 1946.)

§ Oregon–Washington issue completely retired.

Exhibit 5

UNION PACIFIC RAILROAD COMPANY

PRICE RANGES OF UNION PACIFIC BONDS, 1946–63

Year	2½% Mortgage Bonds*		2⅞% Debenture Bonds†	
	High	*Low*	*High*	*Low*
1946	99⅝	99¾	107½	102
1947	98¾	84⅛	106⅜	96½
1948	94	87½	102½	96½
1949	97¼	91½	104½	100¾
1950	97¼	93¼	104	101
1951	96¾	84	104¾	95
1952	91¼	86	100¼	95⅜
1953	88⅝	79½	96⅝	89
1954	91⅝	86⅝	101	95
1955	90¼	85¾	99¾	95
1956	88¼	74½	96⅝	84
1957	80¾	67	88	79
1958	80½	70	90	81½
1959	73	64⅝	81½	75
1960	72	65	83¼	75
1961	71	66⅞	85	79¾
1962	70½	68	85½	83
1963	72	69½	87⅝	84

* Issuing price for mortgage bonds on March 1, 1946, was 102.19%.
† Issuing price for debenture bonds on February 1, 1946, was 108.50%.

Exhibit 6

UNION PACIFIC RAILROAD COMPANY

YIELDS TO MATURITY ON UNION PACIFIC BONDS TO UNION PACIFIC

Market Price	Yield Before FIT at 48%	Yield After FIT at 48%
2½% Mortgage Bonds, Issue C, 3/1/91		
68½	4.61	2.40
68¾	4.59	2.39
69	4.57	2.38
69¼	4.55	2.37
69½	4.53	2.36
69¾	4.51	2.35
70	4.49	2.33
70¼	4.47	2.32
70½	4.45	2.31
70¾	4.43	2.30
71	4.40	2.29
71¼	4.38	2.28
2⅞% Debenture Bonds, 2/1/76		
83	4.97	2.58
83¼	4.94	2.57
83½	4.90	2.55
83¾	4.87	2.53
84	4.84	2.52
84¼	4.80	2.50
84½	4.77	2.48
84¾	4.74	2.46
85	4.70	2.44
85¼	4.67	2.43
85½	4.64	2.41
85¾	4.60	2.39
86	4.57	2.38

Exhibit 7

UNION PACIFIC RAILROAD COMPANY

COMMON STOCK INDICATORS, 1960–63

	1960	1961	1962	1963
Book value	$51.18	$52.56	$55.35	$59.44
Market price:				
High	$31.00	$37.12	$35.00	$42.00
Low	25.00	27.12	27.50	33.25
Earned per share	$ 2.62	$ 2.78	$ 2.88	$ 2.90
Price–earnings ratio*	10.7	11.6	10.8	12.9
Dividend	$ 1.60	$ 1.60	$ 1.60	$ 1.70
Percentage of earnings paid out	61 %	58 %	56 %	59 %
Yield*	5.71%	4.98%	5.12%	4.53%
Profit/net worth	5.11%	5.29%	5.20%	4.88%

* Using average of high and low market prices for the year.

Exhibit 8

UNION PACIFIC RAILROAD COMPANY

HIGH AND LOW MARKET PRICES OF UNION PACIFIC COMMON
AND PREFERRED STOCK, 1960–63

	Common		Preferred	
	High	Low	High	Low
1960.........................	31	25	8⅝	7¾
1961.........................	37⅛	27⅛	8⅝	8
1962.........................	35	27½	8⅞	8¼
1963.........................				
First quarter................	36¼	33¼	9⅜	8¾
Second quarter..............	42	35⅝	9¼	8⅞
Third quarter................	41¾	37¾	9⅝	9
Fourth quarter...............	41½	38⅜	9¾	9

Exhibit 9

UNION PACIFIC RAILROAD COMPANY

EXECUTIVE RELATIONSHIPS AT UNION PACIFIC

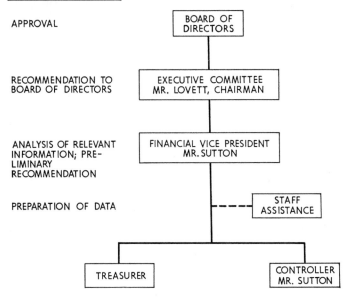

Exhibit 10

UNION PACIFIC RAILROAD COMPANY

NYSE WEEKLY TRADING VOLUMES, JULY–DECEMBER, 1963,
UNION PACIFIC 4% PREFERRED

Week Ending		*No. of Shares*
July	8	11,500
	15	18,100
	22	43,100
	29	18,500
August	5	13,700
	12	36,100
	19	13,900
	26	10,900
September	2	19,000
	9	21,100
	16	10,100
	23	10,300
	30	23,900
October	7	44,200
	14	54,600
	21	35,700
	28	16,700
November	4	14,200
	11	14,400
	18	10,600
	25	21,700
December	2	7,600
	9	18,900
	16	9,400
	23	9,600
	30	3,900
Total		511,700
Weekly average		19,681
Annual rate		1,023,400

MOTEC INDUSTRIES, INC.[1]

At a special meeting on December 27, 1962, stockholders of Motec Industries, Inc. were asked to approve a plan to sell substantially all of the
company's assets. At an earlier date, the Motec directors had unanimously
approved the plan to sell the company's assets to White Motor Company, a
Cleveland producer of heavy-duty trucks and farm implements. White had
offered to buy the assets and to assume the liabilities of Motec for $21 million
in cash. Tax refunds involved would result in another $1 million to Motec.
Since the plan involved basic changes in the company's operation, the approval of holders of two thirds of the outstanding common stock was required
for its adoption.

Motec was the eighth largest manufacturer of farm equipment in the
United States. The company's Minneapolis–Moline Division sold a line of
farm machinery, including tractors, combines, corn pickers, corn shellers,
plows, planters, cultivators, and power mowers, as well as industrial equipment, and repair parts for these units. The Minneapolis–Moline Division
accounted for more than 80% of the company's total sales. Other company
divisions were engaged in the manufacture of lift trucks and diesel engines.

The company's products were sold in the United States and Canada
through approximately 1,800 dealers and 40 distributors. These sales activities were supervised through eight district and eight branch warehouses,
located in the principal farming areas of the United States and Canada. Five
percent of Motec's sales were outside the United States and Canada.

The company's sales had remained relatively constant over the past several
years, but the company had not shown a consistent profit over this period, as
shown in Exhibits 1 through 3. Motec owned and operated 2 manufacturing
plants and employed over 3,000 persons in all phases of its operations. The
company's sources of supply were broadly based throughout the United
States. In addition to raw material, the company purchased such components
as bearings, bolts, wheels, tires, generators, starter motors, radiators, and
brakes.

The common shares of Motec were listed on the New York Stock Exchange,
and were the only security of the company for which a market existed. The

---

[1] Quotations by permission of Dow Jones & Company, Inc., and Abraham L. Pomerantz,
Esq.

high and low sale prices of the common shares and related data for periods during the last four years are listed in Exhibit 4.

On November 29, 1962 a proxy notice, describing the proposed plan of sale and calling a stockholders' meeting for December 27, was mailed to shareholders. A major portion of the notice follows.[2]

Reason for Sale to White

In the judgment of the Board of Directors, the Company is now faced with four conceivable alternatives. These are (1) continuing business on the present basis, (2) merging with or selling the Company's assets to some purchaser other than White, (3) liquidating the Company and selling its assets piecemeal, or (4) proceeding with the presently proposed transaction. Of these four alternatives, your Board of Directors believes that the presently proposed transaction offers the best available opportunity for future growth and earnings in the interests of the stockholders.

With respect to the first alternative, the Board of Directors believes that the Company's prospects for future profitable operation in the farm equipment industry are not good and that continuation of operations on the present basis is not the best available course of action in the interest of the shareholders. The Management believes that the farm equipment market is substantially saturated so that opportunities for increased growth depend upon the ability to overcome competition from competing companies. The Company has not been able, in competition with its much larger competitors, to increase its sales substantially. Its ability to compete has been adversely affected by the fact that the Company is not in a position to offer a full line of farm machinery. The farm machinery business is inherently subject to seasonal fluctuations and the Company lacks the necessary diversification to enable it to maintain a steady level of activity throughout each year. To increase its product line or to diversify successfully would require a substantial capital investment, which the Company has not been in a position to make. The Company's efforts to diversify have not proven profitable as a whole. In addition, the Company's plants are relatively outdated. The nature of the farm machinery business is such as to require large amounts of working capital, primarily for company and dealer inventories. This has necessitated substantial borrowings to enable the Company to operate, with resulting expense for debt service. No material factor of a non-recurring nature is deemed responsible for the unsatisfactory past record. The foregoing factors and the resulting unsatisfactory earnings record of the Company have led your Board of Directors to conclude that the best interests of the stockholders would be served by effecting the presently proposed sale and utilizing the proceeds thereof in efforts to secure income producing properties which, it is hoped, will enable your company to show an improved earnings record in the future.

With respect to the second alternative, in the past, the Management of the Company has held certain discussions or negotiations with other companies in efforts to arrive at suitable mergers or asset sale transactions. The transaction under discussion in each instance was not deemed suitable, either because the Company did not fit in properly with the business of the other companies in question or because the consideration to be received was deemed inadequate. In

[2] "Notice of Special Meeting of Shareholders," November 29, 1962, pp. 4–6, 10.

the judgment of the Board, there is no present prospect of effecting a suitable transaction with anyone other than White.

In the judgment of the Board, the third alternative (liquidating the Company and selling its assets piecemeal) is not an acceptable alternative. It would require the termination of operations in the Company's plants and would cost the jobs of all the Company's employees, an eventuality which the Board believes the Company is morally obligated to prevent if practically possible. The Company's current assets could not, in the judgment of the Board, be sold on a liquidating basis for the amounts at which they are carried on the books of the Company. The Company's inventories, finished products and service parts, and work in process and materials, derive much of their value from the fact that they are among the assets of the Company as a "going concern." The same is true of the Company's properties, plant and equipment. In the judgment of the Board, the net proceeds of liquidating sale of your Company's assets, after payment of its long-term and current liabilities, would probably not be as great as the net proceeds available under the presently proposed transaction. For the above reasons, in the judgment of the Board, the presently proposed transaction (the fourth alternative mentioned above) offers the best available means of enabling the Company to seek more fruitful lines of endeavor.

At August 3, 1962 the Company's net assets were $37,103,158 or $36.46 for each of the outstanding 1,017,551 common shares and the net current assets were $34,502,088 or $33.91 per outstanding common share. The proceeds of the proposed sale (after adjustment for estimated refundable income taxes to be retained by Motec and the payments to be made to the Purchaser with respect to pension costs, but not including an adjustment based on net working capital, described below), will amount to approximately $20.64 per outstanding share.

The Company has been advised by counsel that, under existing laws, a loss of approximately $16,800,000 (adjusted for an estimated anticipated loss on operations between August 3, 1962 and the Take-Over Date and closing adjustments) would be available as a net operating loss carryforward as against subsequent operations for Federal income tax purposes, although a future adverse change in such law is possible. Such net operating loss is available only to the extent that the Company operates at a profit over the five years following the sale and therefore there is no assurance that any benefit can be derived from such loss.

. . . .

. . . The Board of Directors intends to have the Company retain the proceeds of the sale until such time as suitable opportunities for the purchase of new businesses are developed. . . . This does not exclude the possibility that, after the transaction is completed, the market price of the stock or other factors may lead the directors to decide that it will be in the best interests of the Company to acquire some of the Company's shares for its treasury by purchase in the market or by tenders upon reasonable terms and conditions which will be fair to the remaining stockholders. . . .

CONSEQUENCES OF THE PROPOSED SALE
AND MANAGEMENT'S INTENTIONS

The notice to shareholders also explained that the company would cease to be an operating company and its only material assets would be cash if the proposal was approved. Pending the entry of the company into another business or businesses, the board of directors intended to invest such cash temporarily in income-producing securities. The company did not intend to register under the Investment Company Act of 1940, since it did not intend to make investments that would render it an investment company within the meaning of that act. The company had no specific plans for the types of investments it would make, but it would make such investments on an interim or permanent basis as the board of directors from time to time deemed suitable. The company's president, Robert Rittmaster, estimated that in the event the proposed sale was consummated, direct annual remuneration would be as follows:[3]

Name of Individual or Identity of Group	Capacity	Aggregate Remuneration
Robert Rittmaster	President, treasurer, and director	$30,000
Officers and directors as a group	Officers and directors	$95,000

It was also estimated that the company's annual overhead (other than the above-listed salaries) after the sale, but prior to participation in new business activities, would be approximately $89,000.

The staff of the New York Stock Exchange informed the company that, under policies administered by the Exchange for corporations that had ceased to be operating companies, the company's common shares would be delisted if the proposed transaction was consummated. Such delisting would result in the termination of registration of the company's common shares under the Securities Exchange Act of 1934, thus removing the requirements of that act (1) for filing financial statements, and (2) for filing proxy statements with the Securities and Exchange Commission and sending proxy materials to stockholders, giving detailed information regarding officers and candidates for office and other pertinent information. The common shares would cease to be legally acceptable as collateral for loans for the purpose of purchasing or carrying securities by any broker or dealer who was a member of any national securities exchange or did business through such a member. The officers, directors, and principal stockholders of the company would no longer be required to file reports of their trading activities in the company's stock, and any short-term trading profits of officers, directors, and principal stockholders could no longer be recaptured by the company.[4]

The company urged the New York Stock Exchange to allow the shares to remain listed for a reasonable time so that the company could seek suitable acquisitions and return to the status of an operating company. The staff of the New York Stock Exchange, nevertheless, was determined to delist the compa-

[3] "Notice of Special Meeting of Shareholders," p. 10.

[4] The "Notice of Special Meeting of Shareholders" contained this information.

ny's common shares as described above. The board of directors intended to apply for relisting on the New York Stock Exchange or for listing on some other national securities exchange as soon as the board considered such action feasible and desirable. In the meantime, it was the company's intention to distribute to stockholders semiannual and annual reports containing information and financial statements essentially comparable to that contained in the reports previously distributed. Financial statements in the annual reports would be certified.[5]

During the fall of 1962, newspapers quoted Motec's president, Robert Rittmaster, who said the proceeds from the proposed sale of Motec Industries' assets would be used to acquire other companies and would not be distributed in cash to stockholders.[6]

Rittmaster and the other members of the board emphasized that it was particularly inadvisable for Motec to distribute the cash received from the sale of assets to the shareholders, because that would involve the effective dissolution of the company and deprive it of the benefit of the tax loss carry-forward. (Exhibit 5 contains descriptions of Motec board members.) Since the remaining management group after the sale, i.e., the board of directors, had wide experience in business management, including programs of acquisition comparable to that contemplated for Motec, they strongly urged all shareholders to vote against a stockholder's resolution to liquidate the company. This board recommendation as well as the stockholder resolution appeared in the "Notice of Special Meeting of Shareholders." In recommending a vote against the resolution, the board of directors emphasized that the course of action planned for the company afforded the best prospect of using the proceeds of the sale in the best interests of the shareholders.

NAUTEC

In 1955, Mr. Rittmaster and his cousin, Alexander Rittmaster, a New York investment consultant, had joined others in buying control of Motor Products Corporation, a Detroit auto parts and refrigerator firm. After the take-over, new management eliminated manufacturing operations, accumulated cash, and converted the company into a corporate shell with tax credits. On November 2, 1960, the name was changed to Nautec Corporation.

In 1958, having in large measure completed the corporation's program of converting to cash the physical assets of its former operating divisions, Nautec made its first acquisitions—Duncan Parking Meter Corporation and Aero Motor Company, a pump maker. Later acquisitions put Nautec in the pleasure boat construction, lithographing, and warehousing businesses. Robert Rittmaster became chairman of Nautec in November, 1960. Exhibit 6 summarizes Nautec operations during this period.

---

[5] Ibid.

[6] The Wall Street Journal, December 6, 1962, p. 7.

MANAGEMENT CHANGE AT MOTEC
AND SUBSEQUENT DEVELOPMENTS

Rittmaster was also in the group that in December, 1960, gained working control of Motec, which was at that time called Minneapolis–Moline Company. The Rittmaster group first took board positions at the company in 1957, and at that time it was reported they held about 220,000 shares, or about 24% of the 910,000 shares then outstanding.[7] By December, 1960, the group controlled 50% of the shares because of a continuous buildup in their ownership of Minneapolis–Moline common. *The Wall Street Journal* suggested that "the Rittmaster take-over was likely to mean a bolder pace of diversification for Minneapolis–Moline."[8]

Despite management changes and adoption of the name Motec, which "signified the acceleration of a diversification program,"[9] the Rittmaster group was unable to reverse the misfortunes of the farm equipment company. Eventually, they decided to sell the company's assets for the reasons cited above.

In October, 1962, Robert Rittmaster said, "What we did at Nautec, we would do here [at Motec].[10] But we don't expect so much lag here." By this, he meant that Motec expected to make acquisitions quicker and become an operating company sooner than was the case with Nautec.

THE SPECIAL MEETING, DECEMBER 27, 1962

At the special meeting on December 27, shareholder vote on the sale to White was 814,792 (80%) for and 47,000 (5%) against. At the meeting, which lasted nearly four hours, Robert Rittmaster indicated that the New York Stock Exchange had informed Motec that the company's stock would be delisted when the sale to White Motor Company was concluded on January 31, 1963.

At the meeting, David Levin, who identified himself as president of Seaboard Equipment Company, a tractor parts distributor, made an informal offer from the floor to buy Motec stock at about $20 a share, provided at least 51% of the 1.017 million shares outstanding were tendered to his group. On the preceding day, Motec common closed on the New York Stock Exchange at $17.25 per share.

Abraham L. Pomerantz, a Motec stockholder, urged that cash proceeds from the sale of assets be distributed to shareholders. In support of his resolution to distribute the cash to common shareholders, Mr. Pomerantz, a New York lawyer, made the following statement from the floor.[11]

---

[7] *The Wall Street Journal*, December 12, 1960, p. 26.

[8] *Ibid.*

[9] *Motec Annual Report*, 1961, p. 2.

[10] *The Wall Street Journal*, October 22, 1962, p. 10.

[11] The statement was released to the press by Mr. Pomerantz, December 27, 1962.

Mr. Chairman and my fellow stockholders:

I speak for Messrs. R. B. Resnik, A. A. Spiegel and E. D. Mitchell who, together with myself, own 46,800 shares of Motec stock. Our stake in the company is $1,000,000.

We have placed before you and ask your support of the resolution to distribute the cash in the corporate till to all of us stockholders, after we receive the purchase price from White Motors.

The cash value of each share of Motec stock will then be $20.64. But the market price is only about $17 a share—a substantial discount of its cash value.

We demand our cash, and we believe you should too. This is why. We bought into the business of the company, primarily a farm equipment business. We have no quarrel with the sale of our assets—even though it is way below asset value. But now that the business in which we invested has been sold, and we have nothing left but an empty shell, we are, in simple fairness, entitled to get our money back. When the game is over, we are entitled to cash in our chips. After all, we invested in the business of Motec; not in the Rittmasters.

That the business of our company is at an end is attested to by the New York Stock Exchange which has announced its intention to delist our stock. This is bound further to depress the market price of our shares. Moreover, it will deny us the safeguard that listing affords: more complete reporting of corporate transactions, and revelation of all "insider" deals.

Why do the Rittmasters oppose letting us have our money back? They insist on sitting on, and controlling this fund of $21,000,000. They say they will invest this money to our advantage—in some unnamed and unknown business of their choosing. Well, if the past is any guide to the future, we have healthy doubts. We have seen the Rittmasters try this kind of operation before. Not long ago, they and their associates came into control of Nautec Corporation (or its predecessor), sold off its assets, and Nautec became a corporate shell with large tax credits. They then embarked Nautec on an acquisition program. A highly respected national advisory service summed up their record of performance thus:

Stockholders equity during the above period showed only a modest gain. Cash dividends were suspended early in 1962 and Nautec stockholders are currently receiving no return on their investment. The above record, while admittedly short, is in our opinion not very impressive.

Then, turning to the resolution for liquidation now before you, this same advisory service goes on to say:

We recommend that stockholders approve the proposal to liquidate, which is opposed by management. Management's chief argument against liquidation is that such a step would abandon the tax loss carryforward which may have considerable value. However, based on the record of Nautec, which has total assets of $21 million such as the Motec shell would possess, there is considerable doubt that management would earn enough in the Motec shell to use up the $16.8 million loss carryforward before it expires 5 years hence.

The public investors apparently feel the same way because the market price of the shares is selling well below its actual cash value (giving effect to the White Motors deal). This is eloquent testimony to the fact that the stockholders would rather have the cash than the Rittmasters.

But the issue is not whether the Rittmasters are or are not good managers. They have every right to invest *their* money as they wish. We have every right to invest *our* money in a business of *our* choice.

There is a simple solution. Let the Rittmasters give every stockholder an option to redeem his shares for the cash value of $20.64. Then those of us who want out, can have it. And those who want to stay with the Rittmasters may do so. That would be simple justice and corporate democracy.

Failing that, we ask for your vote in favor of liquidation, immediately upon consummation of the sale of our assets to White Motors.

In rebuttal, management contended that dissolution of Motec by liquidating dividends would require "forced sale of the assets" on "disadvantageous terms," and it would deprive the company of the reported benefits of the tax loss carry-forward.

Management had engaged Georgeson & Co., a New York firm, to solicit proxies by the use of mails, telephone, telegram, special letter, and personal visit. Management estimated that the fee and expenses involved in this solicitation had amounted to $5,000, paid by the corporation.

The proposal to distribute the cash to stockholders was defeated by a margin of 558,446 (54.88%) against and 297,041 (29%) for. Where no choice was specified by shareholders on the management proxy, the shares were voted with management.

In mid-January, 1963, Motec disclosed that its management had been authorized to buy shares in the open market.[12] On several days in late January and early February, Motec topped the NYSE in volume of trading, and the stock rose as high as 19¾, although management made no further announcements during the period. Subsequent to the delisting of Motec common stock on the NYSE on February 11, 1963, an article in *The Wall Street Journal* described the Motec annual meeting on February 19, 1963, and company activities during the interim period.[13] This article is reproduced in Exhibit 7.

---

[12] *The Wall Street Journal*, February 7, 1963, p. 31.
[13] *The Wall Street Journal*, February 20, 1963, p. 18.

Exhibit 1

MOTEC INDUSTRIES, INC.

COMPARATIVE EARNINGS DATA
(Dollar Figures in Thousands)

Fiscal Year Ended	Net Sales	Net Earnings (Loss)	Net Earnings (Loss) (Per Share†)
October 31, 1957	$57,479	$(5,031)	$(5.36)
October 31, 1958	53,602	(1,730)	(2.08)
October 30, 1959	53,778	3,238	3.01
October 28, 1960	49,360	2,445	2.44
November 3, 1961	58,314	1,413	1.39
39 weeks ended August 3, 1962*	36,409	(264)	(0.26)

* See Note on Interim Statements, Exhibit 2. Net sales for the period August 4 through November 2, 1962, equaled an estimated $14.94 million (unaudited and subject to final adjustments of reserves for cash discounts and for volume bonuses); earnings figures for this period were not available.
† Based on shares outstanding at end of each period after adjustment for 5% stock dividend issued February 15, 1962.
SOURCE: "Notice of Special Meeting of Shareholders," November 29, 1962, p. 4.

Exhibit 2

MOTEC INDUSTRIES, INC.

STATEMENT OF CONSOLIDATED EARNINGS
(Dollar Figures in Thousands)

	39 Weeks Ended (See Note)		53 Weeks Ended November 3, 1961	October 28, 1960	52 Weeks Ended	
	August 3, 1962 (unaudited)	July 28, 1961 (unaudited)			October 30, 1959	October 31, 1958
Income:						
Net sales	$36,409	$41,672	$58,314	$49,360	$53,778	$53,602
Interest earned	150	232	315	742	198	
Miscellaneous earnings and charges, net	84	280	291	216	533	(174)
	$36,644	$42,183	$58,920	$50,318	$54,508	$53,428
Cost and expenses:						
Cost of products sold	$29,042	$31,905	$44,829	$36,780	$40,223	$42,329
Selling and administrative expenses	7,274	7,779	10,404	9,390	9,581	} 11,101
Provision for uncollectible accounts	179	206	369	522	519	
Interest expense:						
Long-term debt	248	320	420	741	746	} 1,728
Other	397	206	286	382	175	
	$37,141	$40,416	$56,308	$47,814	$51,244	$55,158
Earnings (loss) before taxes on income	$ (497)	$ 1,767	$ 2,611	$ 2,503	$ 3,263	$ (1,730)
Taxes on income (income tax credit)	(233)	810	1,198	58	25	0
Net earnings (loss)	$ (264)	$ 957	$ 1,413	$ 2,445	$ 3,238	$ (1,730)

NOTE ON INTERIM STATEMENTS.—The information for the 39-week periods ended August 3, 1962, and July 28, 1961, is unaudited but includes all adjustments (consisting of normal recurring adjustments) that the management considers necessary to a fair statement of the results of operations for those periods. Amounts previously reported for the 39 weeks ended July 28, 1961, have been retroactively adjusted to allocate major year-end adjustments to the period to which applicable. The results of operations for the 39 weeks ended August 3, 1962, are not necessarily indicative of the results of operations for a full year, because the company's sales are subject to seasonal fluctuations and because, historically, year-end adjustments, particularly those related to inventories, have been substantial in amount and unpredictable in their effect on operations.

SOURCE: "Notice of Special Meeting of Shareholders," November 29, 1962, and Minneapolis-Moline Company, Annual Report, 1959. (Columns may not add because of rounding.)

Exhibit 3

MOTEC INDUSTRIES, INC.

Consolidated Balance Sheet
(Dollar Figures in Thousands)

ASSETS	August 3, 1962 (unaudited)	November 3, 1961	October 28, 1960	October 30, 1959	October 31, 1958
Current assets:					
Cash and short-term securities at cost	$ 2,902	$ 2,506	$ 3,130	$ 8,804	$ 4,805
Receivables, net	26,433	27,726	24,312	25,385	21,317
Inventories, at the lower of cost (first-in) or market					
Finished products and service parts	14,059	10,954	11,238	9,365	14,876
Work in process and materials	10,407	9,921	7,285	5,343	6,521
Prepaid expenses	231	229	124	157	430
Total Current Assets	$54,031	$51,336	$46,088	$49,055	$47,949
Investments in and advances to Argentine subsidiary	$ 150	$ 150	$ 88	$ 43	$ 47
Property, plant, and equipment at cost					
Land	$ 476	$ 510	$ 538	$ 581	$ 662
Buildings	9,435	9,370	9,113	9,582	11,613
Machinery and equipment	11,892	12,920	14,159	14,374	14,829
	$21,804	$22,800	$23,810	$24,536	$27,105
Less: Accumulated depreciation	16,353	16,860	17,068	16,558	16,087
	$ 5,451	$ 5,940	$ 6,742	$ 7,978	$11,018
Total Assets	$59,632	$57,427	$52,918	$57,076	$59,014

LIABILITIES AND SHAREHOLDERS' EQUITY

	August 3, 1962 (unaudited)	November 3, 1961	October 28, 1960	October 30, 1959	October 31, 1958
Current liabilities:					
Notes payable to banks (subsequently paid in full)	$10,000	$ 3,825	$ 8,436	$ 6,701	$ 2,565
Accounts payable and accrued expenses	7,987	8,797			6,162
Dividends payable		242	239		257
Taxes on income	41	1,195			
Current maturities of long-term note	1,500	1,500	1,500	1,500	1,022
Total Current Liabilities	$19,529	$15,559	$10,174	$ 8,201	$10,006
Note payable, 6% due $750,000 semiannually through July 1, 1965, less current maturities	$ 3,000	$ 4,500	$ 6,000	$ 7,500	$ 9,000
Subordinated sinking fund debentures				6,125	6,233
Shareholders' Equity:					
Preferred shares					3,000
Common shares, par value $1: Authorized shares 1,500,000	1,057	1,009	994	986	910
Additional paid-in capital	10,133	9,351	9,190	9,013	7,730
Retained earnings	26,811	27,906	27,458	25,251	22,134
Common shares in treasury, 39,700 shares at cost	(898)	(898)	(898)		
	$37,103	$37,367	$36,743	$35,250	$33,775
Total Liabilities and Shareholders' Equity	$59,632	$57,427	$52,918	$57,076	$59,014

Source: "Notice of Special Meeting of Shareholders," November 29, 1962, and Annual Reports. (Columns may not add because of rounding.)

Exhibit 4

MOTEC INDUSTRIES, INC.

High and Low Quotations for Motec Industries Common Stock on the NYSE and the Number of Shares Outstanding

Period	*High*	*Low*	*No. of shares outstanding*	*No. of shares traded on NYSE*
January 1, 1958 to December 31, 1958 (1 yr.)	20¼	7⅝	910,287	339,800
January 1, 1959 to December 31, 1959 (1 yr.)	29¼	18⅛	985,759	1,097,900
January 1, 1960 to December 31, 1960 (1 yr.)	24¼	17¼	954,097	538,800
January 1, 1961 to March 31, 1961 (3 mo.)	24¼	19	954,097	87,400
April 1, 1961 to June 30, 1961 (3 mo.)	28¼	20⅝	954,097	196,200
July 1, 1961 to September 30, 1961 (3 mo.)	22½	18	969,096	141,400
October 1, 1961 to December 31, 1961 (3 mo.)	25½	17⅝	969,096	184,000
January 1, 1962 to March 31, 1962 (3 mo.)	18¾	17⅛	969,096	112,000
April 1, 1962 to June 30, 1962 (3 mo.)	17¾	11½	969,096	89,000
July 1, 1962 to September 30, 1962 (3 mo.)	17⅞	12½	1,017,551	180,000
October 1, 1962 to October 31, 1962 (1 mo.)	18⅝	14¾	1,017,551	61,000
November 1, 1962 to November 30, 1962 (1 mo.)	17⅞	15⅝	1,017,551	54,000
December 1, 1962 to December 31, 1962 (1 mo.)	18	16⅜	1,017,551	56,000
January 1, 1963 to January 6, 1963 (7 days)	17⅜	17⅛	1,017,551	15,200
January 7, 1963 to January 13, 1963 (7 days)	17½	17⅝	1,017,551	29,900
January 14, 1963 to January 20, 1963 (7 days)	17⅞	18½	1,017,551	91,000
January 21, 1963 to January 28, 1963 (7 days)	18⅛	18¼	1,017,551	15,200
January 29, 1963 to February 3, 1963 (7 days)	18⅛	18⅝	1,017,551	80,300
February 4, 1963 to February 11, 1963 (7 days)	18½	19¾	1,017,551	122,900

Source: *Commercial and Financial Chronicle* and *Bank and Quotation Record.*

Exhibit 5

MOTEC INDUSTRIES, INC.

THE MOTEC INDUSTRIES BOARD OF DIRECTORS, 1962–63*

Name	Position	Principal Occupation
Herbert Adler	Director	Certified public accountant, partner, Clarence Rainess & Co., Certified Public Accountants
Lewis Garlick	Director	Executive vice president, Ivy Hill Lithograph Corporation (subsidiary of Nautec Corp.), printing and lithography
Robert H. Goodkind	Director	President, Goodkind, Neufeld & Co., Inc., members of the New York Stock Exchange
James Heller	Director	President, Heller Bros. Packing Co., citrus growers, shippers and concentrators; Chairman of Finance Committee, Motec Industries, Inc.
Paul H. Hershey	Director	President and treasurer, Hershey Metal Products, Inc., screw machine products
Robert G. Marcus	Director	Vice president, American Biltrite Rubber Co., rubber products and floor coverings
Robert Rittmaster	President, treasurer, and director	President and treasurer of the company (commencing after the sale is consummated) ; vice president, Rittmaster and Co., Inc., business and investment analysis (since 1957) ; chairman of the board, Nautec Corporation, diversified manufacturing and service businesses (since 1960) ; president, Regency Fund, Inc., open-end mutual investment fund (since 1958)
Donald C. Steinhelber	Secretary	Secretary of the company

* All Directors are elected each year at the annual meeting the last Tuesday in February. In 1962, the Articles of Incorporation were amended to preclude cumulative voting for election of directors.
SOURCE: "Notice of Special Meeting of Shareholders," November 29, 1962.

Exhibit 6

MOTEC INDUSTRIES, INC.

SELECTED FINANCIAL DATA FOR NAUTEC CORPORATION
(Dollar Figures in Thousands)

Fiscal Year Ended June 30	Net Sales	Net Earnings (Loss)	No. of Shares Outstanding	EPS on Common
1954	$87,025	$(1,128)	468,300	$(2.41)
1955	83,476	(1,745)	468,300	(3.73)
1956	76,020	(1,195)	467,400	(2.55)
1957	10,088	(336)	198,500	(1.69)
1958	2,883	650	150,000	4.34
1959	8,574	901	300,000*	3.00
1960	13,184	1,739	561,200†	3.10
1961	15,248	967	566,900	1.71

HIGH AND LOW QUOTATIONS FOR NAUTEC COMMON STOCK ON THE NYSE‡

Period	High	Low
1954	23⅞	16¼
1955	32⅛	20
1956	45½	30¾
1957	47	37
1958	75¾	37
1959	27⅛	22½
1960	27½	18
1961	29¼	16¾

* Reflects 100% stock dividend.
† Reflects 2 for 1 stock split.
‡ Not adjusted for changes in the number of shares outstanding.
SOURCE: *Moody's Industrials.*

Exhibit 7

MOTEC INDUSTRIES, INC.

THE WALL STREET JOURNAL
Wednesday February 20, 1963

Motec Bought 350,000 of Its Shares in 1963

It Puts Average Cost at $19 Each; Firm Has $13 Million to Invest, Seeks Manufacturing Concern

By a WALL STREET JOURNAL *Staff Reporter*

NEW YORK—Motec Industries, Inc., purchased more than 350,000 shares of its own stock in the open market since early January, Robert Rittmaster told the annual meeting. Mr. Rittmaster relinquished the chairmanship and was elected president and treasurer by the directors following the annual meeting.

Mr. Rittmaster said the stock purchases cost an average of about $19 a share. The company now has about 640,000 common shares outstanding, he added.

He told a stockholder the purchases were made because the shares were a good investment since they were selling in the open market below their book value. Following the meeting, he said the book value of the stock was slightly over $22 a share.

He also told the stockholder that the purchases gave dissatisfied holders the opportunity to sell their shares. A minority stockholders' attempt to force management to liquidate the company failed at a special stockholders' meeting last December.

Motec sold substantially all its assets to White Motor Co. on Jan. 29 for $20,805,338 in cash. Motec currently is a corporate shell.

Manufacturing Firm Sought

The company now has about $13 million in cash or short-term securities with which to make an investment, Mr. Rittmaster said in reply to a shareholder. The executive added that Motec is seeking to invest these funds in a manufacturing company with a product to sell, but "we haven't confined ourselves to any particular industry."

Mr. Rittmaster said after the meeting that the $13 million "could be increased by institutional borrowing. We could do a $20 million deal."

Mr. Rittmaster will continue as chief executive officer while serving as president and treasurer. His new posts were made vacant when William Foss, former Motec president, and Stacy Angle, former senior vice president and treasurer, resigned to take similar titles with the Motec farm equipment business purchased by White Motor and currently operated as a White Motor subsidiary.

Directors elected James Heller as chairman, to succeed Mr. Rittmaster. Mr. Heller also is president of Heller Bros. Packing Co., of Winter Garden, Fla., a citrus fruit grower, shipper and packer. He is a Motec director.

Daniel B. Lewis, a Motec vice president, was elected to the board, replacing Robert H. Goodkind, who resigned.

Salary to Be $30,000

Mr. Rittmaster, in his new posts, will receive a combined salary of $30,000 a year. He received $30,200 last year as chairman of the board and chairman of the executive committee. In addition, Motec said in its notice of the annual meeting that it paid Rittmaster & Co., a company in which Mr. Rittmaster is a stockholder, $40,000 for financial consulting and statistical services. Motec said it expects to continue retaining Rittmaster & Co.

Mr. Rittmaster was criticized by several stockholders during the sometimes heated annual meeting that lasted nearly an hour. The meeting was attended by about 50 shareholders.

One woman stockholder, who refused to give her name asked, "What is for the common stockholder now?" She stressed, "I have a substantial loss in your company."

"If we invest the money properly, we will make money and pay dividends," Mr. Rittmaster replied.

Motec will reapply for listing on the New York Stock Exchange when it again becomes an operating company, Mr. Rittmaster told the meeting. The Big Board delisted the stock after Motec sold most of its assets. Motec common is currently traded over the counter.

Appendix A

AUTHORS' NOTE.—After classroom use of Motec Industries, Inc., a group of second year MBA students alluded to it in the text of a research report on share repurchase programs. Subsequently, this report was offered for sale, and attorneys for Motec management wrote to one of the report's authors in rebuttal of certain statements. The rest of this appendix consists of excerpts from the attorneys' letter.

The facts are that there was no abuse of stockholders. Stockholders were not misinformed by management; there was fair and meticulous disclosure of all relevant facts. Stockholders were not "persuaded" to sell their shares; purchases were effected only from stockholders desiring to sell.

On December 14, 1962, Motec mailed to its shareholders a letter saying in part:

> *The sale will open the door to possible new business opportunities for Motec.* After the sale, the Company will have about $21,000,000 in cash plus a tax loss carryforward of about $16,800,000. The Management plans to use the cash to acquire businesses which, in the opinion of Management, will produce growth and earnings. The Company's counsel is of the opinion that, under present law, the carryforward would be available against future earnings. Accordingly, to the extent that earnings are realized over the next five years, the tax loss carryforward will reduce taxes and correspondingly increase the earnings available for dividends and growth.
>
> For these reasons your Board of Directors unanimously recommends that you vote *FOR* Proposal 1, the sale. For much the same reasons, we urge you to vote *AGAINST* Proposal 2, the proposal to liquidate the Company which was inserted in the Proxy Statement at the request of three stockholders. Liquidation would prevent the Company from taking advantage of new business opportunities and would sacrifice all tax benefits available through preserving Motec as a going concern. (Emphasis in original.)

On January 10, 1963, Motec made a public announcement of its plans to purchase shares of common stock from time to time in the open market. This announcement received extensive coverage in the press. By January 25, 1963, approximately 105,718 shares had been purchased. On that date, the Company mailed to its stockholders its annual report which included a pro forma balance sheet reflecting the results of the sale and showing approximately $21,000,000 net assets, consisting almost exclusively of cash and referred to the tax loss carryforward of approximately $16,800,000. The annual report reiterated management's confidence in Motec's future:

Your Management is confident that these valuable assets can be profitably utilized through the acquisition of companies with promising growth and earning potential. We are currently examining investment opportunities which appear to have the requisites for successful future operations and which also appear to be in the best interests of your Company.

With your support, the Management looks forward to a successful future.

Between January 25, 1963 and February 14, 1963, approximately 244,500 shares were purchased. On the latter date, Motec mailed to all its shareholders a letter which, among other things, reported the closing of the sale of assets, gave the exact amount of cash received at the closing, mentioned the tax loss short-term interest-bearing securities yielding income at the rate of about 3.15% and stated that potential acquisitions were being analyzed. The letter also reviewed the current status of the stock repurchase program and advised carryforward, advised that the proceeds of the sale had been invested in that "additional purchases may be made if market conditions warrant such action."

Between February 14, 1963 and May 22, 1963 an approximate 133,025 shares were purchased. On the latter date, Motec made a public announcement of the agreement to acquire its present Dolly Madison Foods, Inc. dairy and ice cream business for $10 million in cash plus $1.4 million evidenced by a promissory note. This announcement estimated annual sales of this business at $30 million and pointed out that Motec could expect stable earnings which were particularly desirable in the light of the estimated $16 million tax loss carryforward. The announcement also indicated that the stock repurchase program was continuing.

From May 22, 1963 through June 1963, approximately 34,275 shares were purchased, bringing the total purchase to 517,518.

By means of these stock repurchases, the outstanding common stock of Motec was reduced from 1,017,518 to 500,000 shares. These purchases were made at an average cost of $19.33. Book value per share at the beginning of the repurchase program was about $20.92; as of the conclusion of these purchases, book value per share had risen to about $22.88. Subsequent purchases have reduced the outstanding common stock to 427,000 shares with a book value per share of about $25.00 (reflecting the aggregate effect of purchases below book value, business acquisitions and retained earnings).

During September 1964, Dolly Madison Foods, Inc. (formerly Motec) acquired the business and assets of Huntingburg Furniture Company, Inc., for approximately $6,700,000 plus the asumption of certain indebtedness. Huntingburg's net income before taxes for its 1964 fiscal year was about $1,700,000. Dolly Madison Foods, Inc.'s present earnings prospects are indicated by the fact that, had the Huntingburg business been owned throughout the 1964 fiscal year, its earnings would have been about $4 per share, after applying the tax loss carryforward. Dolly Madison Foods, Inc. currently is paying quarterly cash dividends at the rate of $.80 per annum. Its stock is selling on the over-the-counter market in the range 24⅞ bid, 25⅞ asked. (On

October 8, 1965 the common stock of Dolly Madison Foods, Inc. was quoted at 37¼ bid, and 37¾ asked.)

From the foregoing it is abundantly clear that, far from abusing and misleading stockholders, the Motec management acted in full accord with the ethical standards which you and your co-authors yourselves suggest should govern corporate stock repurchases.

As the report correctly points out, "the heart of the ethical issue" involved in stock repurchases is management's responsibility to make full disclosure of all relevant facts to the stockholders. In most cases it is true, as the report asserts, that corporate management will know more of a company's prospects than the typical shareholder and that some corporate information must be kept confidential. In Motec's instance, however, such was not the case. Literally the only facts concerning Motec's business, assets and prospects in existence at the commencement of the repurchase program were those which had been fully disclosed; namely, Motec's cash position after the sale of assets, the tax loss carryforward, the possibility that some shares might be repurchased and the plan to seek suitable acquisitions of income-producing businesses. There were no specific proposed acquisitions to be disclosed and no predictions or projections of future business and profits could be made. In this unique instance, it can be said that the public stockholders were told literally and precisely every fact about the business and prospects of the company known to the management.

Moreover, as matters progressed, stockholders were kept currently and fully informed. As has been noted, the proxy statement issued on December 3, 1962 clearly revealed the management's plans to acquire income-producing businesses as soon as possible after the sale. This plan was reiterated in the letter to stockholders on December 14, 1962. By February 14, 1963, Motec was able to report, as it did in the letter to shareholders that date, that it was evaluating a number of profit producing asset situations which could enable it to utilize the tax loss carryforward. The Dolly Madison Foods, Inc. acquisition was announced on May 22, 1963, which was the earliest date at which it would have been proper to make any such announcement.

The timing and contents of Motec's public announcements of the stock repurchase program also gave full and fair disclosure. The policy was to purchase shares from time to time as they should become available at prices deemed favorable. There was never a maximum or minimum number of shares which would be purchased and the duration of the program in time was indefinite. The nature of the program thus was fully indicated by the announcements made. As has been noted, the possibility of such a program was clearly stated in the proxy statement issued on December 3, 1962. When the decision to begin purchases was made, there was an immediate announcement, on January 10, 1963. Stockholders were reminded of the program on two occasions while it was going on, namely, by the letter to shareholders of February 14, 1963 and the public announcement of May 22, 1963.

In this context it is ludicrous to assert that the Motec management misled the shareholders and induced them to sell. Indeed, management's position was quite the contrary. Management vigorously urged that the best interests of Motec and the stockholders were for the company to remain intact and not be liquidated. A stockholder heeding management's arguments could only have been induced to hold his shares, not to sell. Management's contention that stockholders should reject the liquidation price of almost $21 per share could hardly be construed as an inducement to sell on the market at $18 or $19.

There can be no claim that the management dealt unfairly with the selling stockholders by purchasing their shares at market prices. As you yourselves correctly point out, valuation is a "subjective" determination and, so long as the management does not through unfair or incomplete disclosure, "manipulate" the determination of value made by the selling stockholders, management quite ethically could repurchase shares at any price acceptable to the selling stockholders. The selling Motec stockholders, after full and fair disclosure, wanted to sell at the market prices, otherwise the shares would not have been available for repurchase. It was certainly fair for Motec to accede to stockholders' wishes and purchase at prices fixed through the operation of the open market.

Certainly it cannot be claimed that the management had any obligation to pay the liquidation value of the shares. As has been noted, a proposal to liquidate had been duly presented and rejected by an 11 to 6 vote of the stockholders. Given these circumstances, the selling shareholders had no right to demand the liquidation price or any other given price, or to assert any claim of right of any sort to the corporate assets which belong as an undivided whole to Motec and to the entire stockholder body. Given the manifest desire of the selling stockholders to sell at market prices, it would have been a waste of the corporate assets to pay a premium over the market prices.

Through hindsight, we see that the Motec enterprise has turned out better for the remaining stockholders than some may have expected at the time of the stock repurchase program. The remaining stockholders took the risk that the outcome would be otherwise. They clearly are entitled to the benefits of the enterprise in which they staked their investment.

The selling stockholders were not willing to take such a risk. They chose to reject the recommendation of their management. Although they certainly have no reason now to feel grateful to the dissidents who urged liquidation, they cannot now be heard to complain of the consequences of their decision. For them, the stock repurchase program afforded a means of selling at prices higher than they otherwise could have gotten.

.   .   .   .

WHY COMPANIES ARE BUYING BACK THEIR OWN STOCK *

By Leo A. Guthart†

THE NUMBER of large, well-known companies listed on the New York Stock Exchange that have been buying back their own common stock has been increasing rapidly in the recent past. At the same time, the number of shares being repurchased by these corporations has been growing rapidly also. In fact, the magnitude of this process, measured as a percentage of total trading on the New York Stock Exchange, has grown from just over 1% in 1954 to approximately 2½% of total NYSE trading volume by 1965. Furthermore, this activity has become so substantial that bills are now pending before Congress to amend the Securities Exchange Act of 1934 to provide for more complete disclosure when corporations purchase their own shares. Because of the rising significance of this activity and its effect upon (1) the financial structure of the corporation buying its own common stock and (2) the character of the market for that company's stock, some knowledge of the magnitude of this activity as well as an understanding of the underlying reasons for its existence are important for the security analyst to understand. In this article, data on share repurchase activity in 1964, 1965, and early 1966 will be presented. Following this, an analysis of the important reasons why companies buy their own common stock will be given.

MAGNITUDE OF THE SHARE REPURCHASE ACTIVITY
1964–1966

In 1964, New York Stock Exchange corporations repurchased 31,120,000 of their own common shares. This amount represented an increase of 17% over the 1963 amount of 26.6 million shares repurchased. By 1965, the amount of shares repurchased on the NYSE grew to 37,170,000. During the period 1954–63, share repurchases grew steadily at an average yearly rate of

---

* Reprinted by permission from the *Financial Analysts Journal*, 23 (March–April 1967), pp. 105–10.

† Executive Vice President, Alarm Device Manufacturing Corporation.

19%. Only slightly more than 5 million shares were repurchased on the NYSE in 1954, less than one-seventh the amount purchased in 1965.

In terms of dollars applied to common stock repurchase, it was estimated that more than $1.7 billion was expended by New York Stock Exchange corporations in 1964 to reacquire their own shares. In 1965, this amount increased to almost $2 billion. These amounts seem startlingly large when compared with money raised from common stock sales during these years. In 1964, U.S. corporations raised $2.6 billion by selling new common stock. In 1965, only $1.5 billion was raised, an amount smaller than that actually applied to common stock repurchases. In 1965, then, total equity capital of U.S. corporations actually declined since repurchases of common shares exceeded sales by almost $500 million.

In both years, the total number of shares repurchased represented approximately 2½% of total trading on the New York Stock Exchange.

During the first six months of 1966, the rate of stock repurchase continued at the same rate as the latter half of 1965. For the six months ending June, 1966, New York Stock Exchange corporations had repurchased 19 million shares.[1]

REASONS WHY COMPANIES BUY BACK THEIR OWN STOCK

In order to gain an understanding of the elements bearing on the decision to repurchase one's own stock, a number of interviews were conducted with the managements of corporations that had been active repurchasers of their own stock during the past decade. Twenty companies, all of whom repurchased 10% or more of their outstanding equity capital during the past decade, were interviewed. In addition to this basic sample, more than 100 other interviews were conducted with (1) executives whose corporations had repurchased their own stock in smaller amounts, (2) executives whose companies had considered purchasing their own stock, (3) brokers, (4) lawyers, (5) educators and, (6) financial writers. The following material represents a summary of the findings of these interviews.

SHRINKING THE EQUITY BASE

The study indicated that by far the most important motivation behind stock repurchase was the desire to reduce the equity capital of the company. Many of the companies that repurchased in large amounts had reached positions where management believed that the company's equity capital was too high in relation to the volume of business to be financed. These companies all had cash or cash generating abilities which far outstripped any needs that

---

[1] For a complete analysis of stock repurchase activity from 1954 to 1963, see Leo A. Guthart, "More Companies Are Buying Back Their Own Stock," *Harvard Business Review*, March–April, 1965.

could be foreseen for either future expansion of plant and equipment or increases in dividend payments.

As a general pattern, most of these companies were in industries that had contracted radically in the recent past, and, as a result of basic changes, no longer required existing equity levels to support their operations. Three typical companies, for example, supplied components to the Big Three automobile producers. When these major manufacturers decided to integrate their operations vertically and to acquire various suppliers, these three typical companies found themselves with their major operations gone and with large amounts of cash. Although other divisions in each were still operating and complete liquidation was not contemplated, all three managements clearly felt that the partial liquidation resulting from the sales to the Big Three auto producers left them with entirely too much cash and too large an equity base in relation to future needs. All three decided to reduce their equity capitalization by repurchasing outstanding common shares.

Another typical company in a similar position but a different industry was a large international owner and operator of hotels. As real estate values of land which its hotels occupied advanced considerably, management decided that certain hotels were not profitable enough to justify occupying such valuable property and therefore should be sold. At the same time, the hotel business in the United States was becoming less profitable as a result of several basic changes in travel habits. As these valuable hotel properties were sold off, management concluded that there were not sufficiently good investment opportunities within the United States to justify reinvesting these funds. It was therefore decided that the company's equity base should be reduced because of the reduced scale of operations foreseen for the future and, in order to accomplish this goal most effectively, a stock repurchase program was instituted.

In addition to companies like these that fit into the general pattern of adopting stock repurchase to accomplish equity reduction after a basic contraction in their industry, there were other companies that adopted stock repurchase after accumulating cash surpluses in a more gradual fashion. These cash surpluses generally resulted from one or a combination of the following three factors:

1) Levelling off of new investment requirements within the industry as a result of technological change or demand shifts.

2) Relating dividend payments to the reported profit level rather than to the total cash flow as funds from accelerated depreciation practices built up substantially.

3) Better management practices which resulted in reducing size of investment required in inventories and accounts receivable.

Companies like these frequently turned to stock repurchase as the logical and best solution to their problems. Many managements interviewed believed that no other method of reducing their equity provided the unique combination of (1) direct effect upon earnings per share as well as (2) minimal risk that stock repurchase offered.

1. *Effect on Earnings Per Share.* When a company utilized redundant cash to buy back its own stock, there was a direct increase in earnings per share as a result of the investment in that share of stock. As each share was repurchased, total earnings were divided among fewer and fewer shares. When compared with the alternative of investing company funds in a different business, the stock repurchase alternative appeared superior to the management because of this fact. If the funds had been invested in a different business, it is likely that only the dividends received on that investment would appear, in the short-term, in the profit statement and reported earnings per share of the investing company. Furthermore, the investment if made in stock of another company would most likely be carried at cost unless a consolidated statement was prepared. Any market appreciation would therefore not be reflected on the financial statements of the investing company until it disposed of its holdings. Stock repurchase provided the advantage of carrying through to earnings per share *directly* the entire earnings yield on the investment without merely being limited to dividends received.

2. *Risk.* From the standpoint of risk, many companies believed that share repurchase presented an attractive opportunity for the company with redundant cash. The research indicated that the officers and directors were likely to feel exceptionally familiar with the company's prospects and problems and very often made forecasts of projected earnings for a five or ten year period before engaging in stock repurchase. Generally, the stock these individuals felt they knew best was their own. For this reason, the risk that management perceived in buying in its own shares was normally very much less than it would be for any other company's common stock that might be considered.

A large oil company, for example, whose basic market was not expanding believed that there was virtually no risk in repurchasing its own common stock with surplus funds. Before determining to engage in stock repurchase, the management made detailed estimates of cash flow per share for ten years into the future and converted these estimates into a net present value for the common stock.[2] So long as market value fell below this indicated present value by an acceptable amount, the company utilized excess cash to repurchase its shares. Management believed that its estimates were informed ones and that there was little chance, over the long term, that the net present value determined from the funds forecasts would not be realized. They adopted stock repurchase, then, on the premise that there was virtually no risk in acquiring their own common shares and that ample funds for all required investments would also be available.

Above and beyond the fact that many corporate managements were familiar with the prospects and problems of their own company, the repurchase of own shares, when looked at from the viewpoint of risk, was attractive to them

---
[2] John G. McLean, "How to Evaluate New Capital Investments," *Harvard Business Review,* November–December, 1958.

for one other reason. The repurchase of "own stock" had the advantage to management of not changing substantially the *risk characteristics* of the corporation. Although it was true that the company became somewhat more highly leveraged as a result of the decrease in equity capitalization, the overall risk of the earnings stream itself, if viewed as a distinct entity from the financial risk of the capitalization of the business, did not change. If, on the other hand, the corporation bought another company's stock, the risk of the total enterprise would be affected by the perhaps unfamiliar risk characteristics of the firm whose stock it purchased.

3. *Income Taxes.* From the standpoint of income taxes, the reduction of excess equity capital, for the shrinking company, by the stock repurchase method provided clear advantages over the alternative of distributing funds by means of increasing ordinary dividend payments. When the company bought back its own common stock, it effectively distributed funds to the stockholder group at tax rates generally at the capital gains level. For the stockholder who held his shares more than six months, the sale of shares to the corporation was treated exactly as any other sale of stock. He subtracted his cost from the selling price and paid a maximum 25% tax on the profits. If his ordinary income tax bracket was below 50%, he paid only half his ordinary tax rate on this profit. On the other hand, if the company chose to distribute its redundant funds to stockholders in the form of increased dividends, the stockholders were obligated to pay taxes on this distribution at full income rates. In addition, the entire amount of the distribution to the stockholder group was taxable at ordinary income rates. Under the stock repurchase method, only the profit portion of the funds returned to the stockholder group was taxable and normally a considerable part of the funds distributed were considered "return of capital." There was no tax at all on the "return of capital" portion of the distribution. At very worst, then, funds distributed by the stock repurchase method were subject to half the tax that dividend distributions were. Furthermore, because of their "return of capital" aspect, they were normally subject to considerably less tax than that.

AVOID INCREASING EQUITY

The second most important reason why many companies repurchased their own stock was to avoid increasing their equity base in the future. The typical company in this position enjoyed considerable cash generation above dividend requirements and did not have large debt or preferred stock servicing requirements *but* foresaw the need to issue shares of common stock from time to time in the future. Because the company's equity position and cash-generating ability appeared to the management to be substantial enough to sustain operations in the future, the management often concluded that it would prefer not to issue additional shares of its common stock. Unfortunately, a number of requirements to issue new common shares were certain to occur and, in spite of the fact that the company did not wish to sell additional equity, it was forced for its own well-being to make certain transactions and to commit itself to issue more common shares. In situations like this, the management often concluded that the company's best alternative was to utilize available cash to repurchase outstanding shares of common stock and then to reissue these common shares when necessary. The net effect of this kind of transaction was that the corporation maintained its current equity level and, in effect, utilized available cash to pay for transactions that ultimately had to be paid for with common shares.

1. Stock Options. The most common use of reacquired shares was to satisfy stock option requirements. A number of large corporations foresaw that when its executives exercised stock options, the company would be required to issue additional shares of common stock. Many managements decided that the company's best interests would be served by maintaining the number of shares outstanding and satisfying stock option requirements by stock repurchase. By utilizing available or surplus cash to repurchase outstanding common shares, the company was able to satisfy the option requirements without increasing the number of shares outstanding. Instead of issuing new shares, they merely transferred shares from one group of stockholders to the executive group that exercised the options. Precisely the same number of shares remained outstanding before and after the stock option transaction and no equity dilution occurred. Many companies reacquired their own shares for this purpose. Among them were General Motors, Jersey Standard, and Chrysler Corporation.

In addition to minimizing the equity dilution problem, some managements believed that stock repurchase provided the opportunity to issue stock options at no cost to the stockholder group. If management was able to repurchase shares at prices equal to or below the prices at which the stock options were exercisable, they reckoned that they accomplished the stock option program without any cost at all, or, perhaps even a profit, to the stockholder group.

2. Acquisitions. The second major reason why companies bought back stock to avoid increasing equity was for the purpose of providing shares for acquisitions. This reason has become an important one in recent years and there were many companies that engaged in stock repurchase for this purpose.

Under today's tax laws, purchases and sales of businesses accomplished with exchanges of common stock generally, with certain specifications, can be consummated without incurring any tax liability for the seller. Generally owners of businesses with large capital gains were very often reluctant to sell their ownership for cash because they would immediately incur a large capital gains tax. Many preferred, if at all possible, to exchange their ownership for stock in a large, prosperous company with a good public market for its stock. If they could make this kind of transaction, they had the advantage of postponing the capital gains tax on their profit for as long as they did not sell the shares they received in payment. When they did decide to sell their shares, they enjoyed the easy liquidity provided by an active, orderly market.

The competition in recent years among large companies to buy prosperous privately owned businesses has become keen. As the economy has witnessed a large upsurge in common stock repurchase programs in the past decade, there has also been a wave of merger and acquisition activity. Because the competition for good businesses was so strong, buyers in many cases were forced not only to pay a full price for the company they buy but also to pay the sellers' tax liability. This additional cost occurred because the purchaser was often forced to absorb the sellers' capital gains tax liability.

The acquisition of a business for stock required that shares be issued. The desire to sell for stock, however, conflicted with the desire of many corporations to utilize their cash and to get more mileage on the existing equity capital.

There was, then, apparently a basic conflict between the desires of many purchasers and sellers. Oftentimes, purchasers appeared to want to buy a business for cash to improve earnings per share. Sellers, on the other hand, wished to take stock to minimize the capital gains tax. Stock repurchase offered a very excellent solution to this dilemma. The purchasing company utilized its cash to repurchase its own common stock. It then traded these repurchased shares for the business that it desired to buy. The net effect on the purchaser's balance sheet was a cash-for-stock transaction since the number of outstanding shares did not change and it merely traded its cash for the new business. For the seller, however, the result was also beneficial since the tax treatment accorded the sale was on the basis of a stock-for-stock exchange and the capital gains tax liability was postponed.

3. *Convertible Debentures and Warrants.*   Finally, corporations that wished to avoid increasing their equity base repurchased shares to avoid dilution resulting from conversion of outstanding convertible debentures and exercising of warrants. In some cases, companies also repurchased shares to avoid the increased number of shares brought about by stock dividend programs. The economic basis behind the repurchase of shares for these purposes was essentially similar to the reasoning behind repurchasing stock to satisfy option or acquisition requirements. Again, the company saw no need to sell additional shares of common stock and did not desire to dilute the existing equity position any further. However, because of other commitments it made or for various business reasons, it was forced to issue additional shares of common stock. To counteract the dilution caused by the issuance of these new shares, the corporation went into the market and bought back already outstanding shares. It then used these outstanding shares to satisfy its obligations and, on the net basis, kept its equity capital the same.

STOCK REPURCHASES AS A GOOD INVESTMENT

The third most important reason why companies bought back their own shares was that stock repurchase appeared a good investment of corporate funds. On the basis of comparative calculations, these companies decided that share repurchase provided for them a more attractive investment opportunity than either investment in new plant or investment in other businesses. They therefore invested funds not needed for the operation of their business in their own stock. In some cases, funds were diverted from investments within the business to the repurchase of outstanding common shares because the investment evaluation appeared so attractive.

The research indicated that the yardsticks used by corporations to determine the profitability of investment in their own common shares were diverse and, in many cases, seemed unenlightened. Many companies used buy-back rules which did not take account of all the factors that were affected by stock repurchase.

In general, the principal yardstick on which most corporations relied was book value. To the extent that the market price of the stock fell below book value, many managements reckoned that repurchase was an attractive investment. Other companies attempted to make some definite evaluation of what their stock was actually worth. Once having arrived at what they considered a fair market price, they repurchased their own stock whenever the market fell below this amount. Finally, some companies attempted to calculate the return on their investment in stock repurchase by selecting either the dividend yield or the earnings yield as the percentage return on their investment. As market price dropped and the yield increased above the rates of return that could be earned on alternative investments of funds, companies diverted cash to stock repurchase in order to take advantage of what they considered a more attractive investment opportunity.

STOCK REPURCHASE TO SUPPORT THE MARKET

The fourth most important motivation among the large stock repurchasers was a desire to support the market for their stock. Obviously, the addition of demand for the company's stock in the market place had an upward effect on the price of the stock. The extent to which the corporation actually supported the market, however, depended a great deal on the extent to which it participated in trading and on the general character of the market for that particular security.

One of the more common forms of stock repurchase for the purpose of market support was to absorb large blocks of stock that were overhanging the market. Typically, in situations of this kind, one stockholder who had a substantial position in the company desired to liquidate his holdings and was not able to do so easily. This brought about a situation where large amounts of stock were overhanging the market and depressing the price. Generally, the management of the corporation desiring to repurchase this block entered into direct negotiation with the seller. In many cases, the holders of large blocks of stock were well known to the management group and it became a simple matter for negotiations to be instituted. In situations of this kind, the corporation very often bought the block of stock at a discount from the market price. This gave the corporation the double advantage of preventing a substantial depression of the market price while acquiring shares for the treasury at prices below the current level. Quite often, in order to be fair, the company also made the same purchase offer to all stockholders via general tender offers.

STOCK REPURCHASE TO ELIMINATE SMALL STOCKHOLDERS

Anachronistic as it may seem in today's world of "people's capitalism," many corporations repurchased their own stock to eliminate small stockholders. The reasoning underlying management's decision to repurchase for this purpose was that the cost of servicing small stockholders was extremely high. Several companies found that a significant proportion of their total cost of shareholder relations was accounted for by a group of stockholders that owned an insignificant percentage of the company. This group was comprised of holders who owned small amounts of stock—usually between 1 and 25 shares.

For most companies, the cost of servicing a small stockholder was virtually the same as for a large stockholder. Dividend checks had to be written regardless of whether the stockholder owned 1 share or 10,000 shares. The cost of processing these dividend checks was essentially the same regardless of the amount of the dividend. Furthermore, all stockholders had to be kept informed of the company's progress. The cost of preparing proxy statements, annual reports, and any other material used for communicating with stockholders was essentially the same for a small stockholder as a large one.

STOCK REPURCHASE TO OBTAIN OR IMPROVE CONTROL

Occasionally, corporations repurchased shares in order to consolidate control of the corporation. While this was not normally regarded as a bona fide reason for repurchasing shares, and companies that did this were likely to find themselves the victims of shareholder suits, there have been a number of instances where managements used corporate funds for this purpose. The mathematics of share repurchase are such that each time the company repurchased one share of its stock, the proportionate ownership of every remaining stockholder in the corporation increased since there was one less share outstanding. A favorite manipulation of several corporate raiders then was to obtain working control of a corporation and then to use corporate funds to buy in stock and increase their control.

It should be remembered that a repurchase program carried out for the benefit of only one portion of the stockholder group is generally considered *ultra vires*. If any stockholder can show that the repurchase program was not carried out for a bona fide corporate purpose but rather for the benefit of a controlling stockholder or only one portion of the shareholder group, a legitimate and strong stockholder-suit can be filed. Although there have not been many cases where stock repurchase has been used for such unethical purposes, there have been in recent years several instances where it appeared that large corporations have repurchased stock principally for this reason. While it certainly would be unfair to conclude that many stock repurchase plans were carried out in order to consolidate the control positions of various groups of stockholders, it cannot be denied that there have been some cases where this has occurred.

SUMMARY

Share repurchase is a rapidly growing and important factor in the stock market. The number of shares repurchased by New York Stock Exchange companies has grown to approximately 2.5% of total Exchange volume.

The underlying reason behind much of this share repurchase activity relates to the large amount of cash being generated by U.S. corporations. Many of these corporations desire to reduce their equity base and select repurchase as the most effective way of accomplishing the reduction. Other companies, however, engage in repurchase to prevent the expansion of their equity as the need to issue additional shares arises. Other major motivations include share repurchase (1) as a good investment, (2) to support the market, (3) to eliminate small stockholders, and (4) to gain or improve control.

A REVIEW* OF LIVINGSTON'S
THE AMERICAN STOCKHOLDER†

By Bayless Manning‡

As MANY READERS will know, Joseph Livingston is the fluent and sharp-penned financial editor of the *Philadelphia Bulletin*. His familiarity with the world of finance and his ability to write lucid English are marks of his skill at his trade; his penchant for asking the embarrassing question and his willingness to turn an irreverent wit upon the totems of society are marks of his personality. In *The American Stockholder*, Livingston has taken as his topic the role of the stockholder in the modern publicly-held corporation. His thesis is that this role is insignificant. He has given the general reader a useful book, an entertaining book, but a book which stops short of its own implications.[1]

Some background facts are needed to put Livingston's book in context. Since the end of World War II, the brokerage profession and particularly the New York Stock Exchange have become persuaded that it is at least good public relations and, hopefully, even good business to broadcast the gospel of "People's Capitalism." The theme is that American enterprise—especially big business—is really "owned" and, by implication, controlled by legions of small stockholders.

The Stock Exchange is in part a business organization and stockbrokers are businessmen. As such, they can be no more criticized than other businessmen for doing their best to puff their product. But securities are not commodities like safety pins, and the Exchange is not just another business corporation. Data on the number of safety pins sold and who buys them disclose relatively little about the American economy or its power structure; data on who owns securities and who controls corporations, however, disclose a great

* 67 Yale Law Journal 1477–96 (1958). Reprinted by permission of the Yale Law Journal Company and Fred B. Rothman and Company. All footnotes except the first have been omitted.

† Joseph A. Livingston, *The American Stockholder* (Philadelphia and New York: J. B. Lippincott Company, 1958).

‡ Dean of the Law School, Stanford University.

[1] In all matters of shareholder relations these days, the watchword is "disclosure"—usually in small print. Let me therefore quickly disclose in this first footnote that Joe Livingston is a personal friend.

deal about our economic system as a whole. When the investment industry
purports to have discovered a People's Capitalism in America, it invites a
rather more critical analysis of its claim and supporting evidence than is
usually accorded advertising copy.

At the request of the New York Stock Exchange, the Brookings Institution
prepared and published in 1952 its well-known report—often called the
Kimmel Report—entitled *Share Ownership in the United States.* This study
found that, as of March 1, 1952, 6,490,000 individuals owned shares in
publicly-held corporations. The results were disappointing, for it had been
hoped that share ownership was more widespread. In 1956, the Exchange's
own Department of Public Relations and Market Development, collaborating
with Alfred Politz Research, Inc., did a bring-down study. This time, the
Exchange was able to announce that "based on new sampling techniques" of
the "vast economic changes that have altered America," none is "more
significant than the emergence of a democratic 'People's Capitalism.' " The
most pointed statistical conclusions of the 1956 Exchange report were that the
number of individuals owning shares in publicly-held corporations had increased to 8,630,000 since the 1952 study and that two thirds of all shareholders earn under $7,500 per year. Since the publication of this report, the
Exchange has done its best to disseminate these statistics and dramatize their
implications.

Concurrently, brokerage firms have developed and been pushing the new
Monthly Installment Plan, calculated to extend still further the base of
stockholdership among the people by making it possible to buy stocks on time
for as little as $40 a month. It was perhaps inevitable that the image of
People's Capitalism should be incarnated in a selected representative stockholder. He was Mr. D. M. Kuehl—age forty-eight, married, two children,
salaried employee earning $7,500 per year, residing near South Bend, Indi-
ana, the geographic metacenter of individual shareowners—a walking statistic
representing the findings of the Exchange's 1956 study. In the summer of
1956, Mr. Kuehl was the well-publicized guest of the Exchange, invited to
spend a couple of days in the canyons of Wall Street to survey the world
which he and his fellow shareholders "own."

Somehow, certainly through no fault of his own, the visiting shareholder
was not convincing in his role as owner of America's business. (Some with an
associative turn of mind thought of another little fellow who, in 1933, had
been set briefly in the lap of Wall Street.) And somehow, certainly through no
fault of the Exchange, energetic repetition of the "two thirds earn less than
$7,500" slogan and wide distribution of advertisements depicting all America
at a stockholders' meeting have not persuaded many to accept the glowing
image of People's Capitalism.

Livingston is among the unpersuaded. Tackling the latter-day dialectic of
People's Capitalism head on, he suggests that one reason converts are few is
that the gospel just isn't so.

He points out that the "two thirds earn less than $7,500" statistic itself is less startling on reflection than it may first appear. In 1952:

More than 65 per cent of all shareowning family units had incomes of $5,000 or more.

The New York Stock Exchange, in its later surveys, found pretty much the same. However, the Exchange is so intent on publicizing the widespread ownership of stocks, or propagandizing the phrase, 'people's capitalism,' that it headlines: 'Two-thirds of Shareowners Earn Under $7,500.' The inference to be drawn is that only one third of America's shareholders are in the upper brackets. But you have to decide where the upper bracket begins—at $5,000 or $7,500. Further, it would be strange, indeed, if a majority of shareholders did not have incomes under $7,500. After all, nearly 90 per cent of the adult population is in the below-$7,500 income group. Only 10.4 per cent is in the above-$7,500 group. Yet, this 10.4 per cent accounts for 36 per cent of the shareholders by the Stock Exchange's own count.

The Exchange's interpretation of its own statistics also seems questionable to Livingston.

On a significant point, Kimmel and Stock Exchange data come close together: For shareholders in the $5,000-and-below income group, Kimmel shows 31.6 per cent, the Stock Exchange 37.7 per cent. The discrepancy—the higher percentage of the Stock Exchange—could well be due to the rise in incomes, the inflation between 1952 and 1956, rather than any important increase in the proportion of shareholders among the lower-income group.

*   *   *   *   *

Families with leftover income—unspent income—are the purchasers of common stocks. These are the better-heeled families. A sample survey by the Ford Motor Company of its shareholders supports this. Only 11 per cent of the Ford holders reported incomes of less than $5,000; only 31 per cent reported incomes of less that $7,500. In other words, 69 per cent had incomes of $7,500 or more. Four out of five purchasers of Ford stock (82 per cent) were already stockowners. Yet here was a security originally tabbed for the man in the denim cap, not the homburg hat.

The conclusion to be drawn is not that, increasingly, farmers and laborers own shares, but rather that as people ascend the income ladder, their savings spill over into the stock market.

And he finds other figures in the 1952 and 1956 studies which accord far more readily with one's *a priori* hunches on who are the country's shareholders. These figures concern the percentages of shareholders in different occupational groups. Though the classifications in the two studies differ somewhat, both show what one would have guessed—that a shareowning laborer is a rare fellow, a shareowning farmer only slightly less so, and a shareowning corporate executive commonplace.

Strangely, Livingston forbears from hammering squarely on the weakest link in the statistical case for People's Capitalism. The 1952 and 1956 reports reveal almost nothing about the concentration of stock ownership. Inescapably, they do show that only a small minority of the population holds any stock at all. But, in studying the 1952 and 1956 reports, one first dimly senses, then sharply awakens to, the fact that the multiplicity of statistics cannot be arranged to reveal anything about share ownership concentration among those who do own shares. The reports deal in terms of "shareholdings," "shareowners" and "issues," not "shares." An owner of one share is a "shareowner" just like an owner of one million shares; a shareowner holding one share of each of five "issues" has five "shareholdings," while an owner of one million shares of a single issue has only one "shareholding." Two thirds of all shareholders earn under $7,500. Probably, too, ninety-nine per cent of all landholders in the Soviet Union are peasants—each with his acre of personal beets—but this statistic doesn't throw much light on the Soviet agricultural system.

In view of the importance of the subject, it may seem surprising that so little information on shareholder concentration is available from any source. Efforts to obtain this data, however, run into serious statistical hurdles— complex problems of properly allocating the holdings of trusts, corporations, and of investment, insurance and retirement funds—and an understandable resistance to disclosure of financial matters felt to be private. A 1949 estimate, which Livingston mentions in passing, was that about 0.5 per cent of the nation's population held slightly over 50 per cent of all marketable securities owned by private investors. Other and later sources report different estimates but imply a similar magnitude of concentration. What indications we have on the subject are unlikely to inspire many to thoughts of "People's Capitalism."

What the available data do show, however, is that there are a large number of shareholders in publicly-held corporations in the United States, perhaps 9,000,000, that the total number is growing, and that the vast majority of these own very few shares. Livingston devotes the major part of his book to an inquiry into the part that this mass of small shareholders plays in the conduct of the modern corporation. He does not attempt to bring down to date the economics of the disparity between "ownership" and "control" documented by Berle and Means; nor does he primarily undertake a showing that management groups do control corporate conduct. Rather, he chooses the other fork of demonstrating that shareholders do not.

As Livingston sees it, an important cause of shareowner impotency is that, despite their numbers, stockholders are a negligible political force. The usual shareholder is an amateur for whom stock investment is a relative sideline. Despite the efforts of Lewis Gilbert and Wilma Soss to create shareholders' organizations, the individual seldom identifies himself with others to form a self-conscious group. Thus, shareholders, however numerous, do not constitute a cohesive, politico-economic bloc.

Ineffective in the halls of the legislature, what can the small shareholder do for his own protection? Livingston sees three choices: the stockholder can sue the corporate management; he can attempt to throw out the management; or he can throw himself out by selling his shares. It is not difficult to show that he usually does the last of these—or nothing.

The law suit against management is an uncertain road, open only in relatively extreme cases of perfidy and subject to heavy toll charges in the form of lawyers' fees. The small, nonprofessional shareholder seldom has a sufficient stake to justify entering upon it. It is hard to disagree with Livingston here. The law today probably protects the shareholder reasonably well against thievery; and the threat of the striker's suit has some salutary consequences. But recourse to the courts hardly offers the shareholder a significant method for overseeing his investment or controlling the corporate enterprise he is said to "own."

What of the shareholders' right to vote and to throw out an offending management? Livingston draws a generally sympathetic profile of intrepid corporate democrat Lewis Gilbert, and retells the saga of Young versus the New York Central. But he sadly concludes that control of management through shareholder election is largely illusory. Managements are virtually never displaced at the polls by their alleged constituency. On the rare occasions when a management is deposed, the insurgents are far more apt to be invaders than rebels—invaders who draw their main strength not from the force of their arguments but from the outright purchase of voting shares for the purpose. The modern proxy fight is usually a battle between heavyweights—in this ring Wolfson v. Avery, in that Young v. White, in the other Silberstein v. Morse. It is no game for the flyweight shareholder. He knows it—or if he should happen not to, his lawyer will tell him. So when he is disgruntled, he either goes along with management anyway, or sells out to another investor who will.

Shareholder impotence would not be much of a problem if one had no reservations about concentrating uninhibited power in the hands of corporate executives. Certainly Livingston has such reservations. He concedes that standards of managerial corporate morality have improved in the last generation with the development of the SEC, the growth of "enlightened" management, and the spread of the concept of the corporation as a Good Citizen. But he is far from convinced that the good citizenship approach provides a sufficient answer for society as a whole and investors in particular.

> The shareholder is the residuary beneficiary of Good Citizen, Inc., and this gives rise to two-toned morality—one set of morals with which executives, corporations, greet the outside world, and another set of morals with which they treat shareholders.

*   *   *   *   *

> Although corporation executives are often criticized—muckraked by union officials and left-wingers—they also have the power of benevolence to dispel said criticism, to symbolize themselves as paragons of thoughtfulness and Good Citizenship. This is the power of the corporate purse. When United States Steel Corporation, General Motors, Procter & Gamble or Ford dispense scholarships, fellowships and wads of cash to universities, the presidents and professors at those

universities are likely to be well disposed toward corporation policies, especially since the fount of largesse is continuous. When corporation executives take to fund-raising for the Red Cross, Cancer, Community Chest and Boy Scout drives, and disburse corporate as well as personal funds in these national and community endeavors, an awareness of the social conscience of the corporation is readily engendered. Benevolence is disarming and self-serving. Criticism is dulled and gratitude whetted by the lively expectation of further favors to come.

And this, the concluding section of *The American Stockholder*, tries to look behind this facade of Good Citizenship and examine the social consequences of the erosion of shareholder power—how the incapacity to correct and restrain corporation executives has become a grant of excess freedom. Executives have become an overprivileged class in a democratic society. Their power to overpay themselves, with legal sanction, could, if unchecked, erode the very structure on which they and their corporations depend for survival. The Good Citizen whom so many young men and women want to emulate, could become the Bad Example.

With the restraining hand of the shareholders atrophied, Livingston sees a tax-sheltered managerial elite inexcusably setting its own extravagant compensation. The most serious consequence is not the diversion of corporate funds to personal use, but the impact which unduly high executive reward has upon the rest of society. This misallocation gives the business corporation an overpowering bargaining advantage in the national competition for talented manpower—an advantage which government, schools, the military and other essential social service institutions cannot hope to match.

Seeing little promise for the toothless shareholder in the world of things as they are, Livingston casts about to find a champion for the shareholders' cause. On the horizon he glimpses a possibility—the mutual investment funds. Manned by professionals, permanently in the market on the equity side, economically powerful, the investment funds may, and in Livingston's view should, develop into a countervailing power to help police management's stewardship of corporate control. The author quickly adds, however, that so far the mutual funds have shown no disposition to assume this role. Indeed, they have adopted the motto, "In Management We Trust." The book concludes with a call to the investment funds and to the tame, uncritical financial press to awaken to their unique responsibility and potentiality as defenders of the helpless small shareholder and of the public.

I have described Livingston's book as useful and entertaining. It is entertaining because it is deftly, professionally and often amusingly written. It is useful because it offers, in a style readily understandable to all, a realistic assessment of the shareholder's position, stripped of slogans and focused on the control of events rather than the symbols of ownership. The book makes its point, and with punch. It deserves wide readership.

But "useful" is a word of measured praise, chosen because the book seems to falter at its most crucial point—the conclusion. The author is a firm and discerning reporter in his description of the shareholder's world as it is. The implications of his findings, however, appear to reach well beyond his stated conclusions.

In 1932, Berle and Means vivisected the modern corporation. They found a virtually omnipotent management and an impotent shareholdership. A quarter century of unparalleled corporate law reform intervenes. In 1958, Livingston surveys the lot of the shareholder in a reformed world—a world of SEC regulation, extensive disclosure requirements, elaborate proxy machinery, Stock Exchange self-discipline, corporate Good Citizenship, People's Capitalism and Corporate Democracy. His finding? A virtually omnipotent management and an impotent shareholdership. The finding itself will not surprise many readers. But a book demonstrating that twenty-five years of reform have not appreciably changed the situation inescapably raises the question whether we have been on the right track for the last two and a half decades. Although Livingston is worried by what he sees, it seems fair to say that he responds primarily with a yearning for re-enfranchisement of the shareholder, with an encouraging though not very optimistic smile for the churnings of Lewis Gilbert, and with a wistful hope that the investment funds will rise to save the day.

Even while suggesting the investment funds for the role of shareholder champion, Livingston spends more time explaining why they have not applied for the part. The case against such a development is probably even stronger than Livingston makes it out. As with other shareholders, the primary interest of the investment fund must be income and profit-taking—not the abstraction of good business management. For the investment fund, too—with only a small part of its fortunes riding on any one company—it is far easier to sell out than to try to reform management policy. In some ways, the funds may find it even harder than small shareholders to assume the policeman's role, since the men who manage investment funds are subject to special social pressures arising from their position as members of the very management class that Livingston expects them to discipline. It is doubtful that the managers of any investment fund would find attractive the expensive and nonconforming posture of Sir Galahad. It is still more unlikely that investors would flock to entrust their savings to a fund which so conceived its function. And at the end of the line is always the question—*quis custodiet?*—for a controlling investment fund is just another holding company. In some circumstances, the funds have the power to make their voices felt; in fewer circumstances will they do so. The far greater probability is that, like other shareholders, they will sell their shares and move on when they dislike the way the wind is blowing. And the problem of managerial responsibility will remain just about where it was before the growth of the mutual funds.

What, then, of improving the situation by redoubling present efforts to re-enfranchise the shareholder?

For the last generation, the prevailing school of thought among corporate reformers, writers and legislators has been that the key to ensuring managerial responsibility lies in the shareholder's power to vote. The common shareholder elects the directors; all he needs is information adequate to form an intelligent judgment and he may be relied upon to vote as his personal

estimate of his economic interests indicates. His interests will thus be protected and management will be checked. Out of the elements of this conception, together with the total failure of the states to include adequate reporting
requirements in their corporation statutes, arose the proxy regulation requirements of the Securities Exchange Act of 1934.

Whatever agitation continues today for corporate reform is in this same
tradition—pressing for more of the same statutory approach. Extreme parti-
sans of this viewpoint have appropriated for themselves a fine, associative
symbol, in character not unlike the Stock Exchange's "People's Capitalism."
They put their faith in what they call Corporate Democracy—a shimmering
conception fusing good old American free enterprise with good old American
Jacksonianism. Apostles of this ideology offer a fully developed program to
cure our corporate ills. The nostrums of Corporate Democracy have a vaguely
familiar quality, for the prescription is largely taken from the municipal
reformers of the turn of the century: more disclosure; greater mass attend-
ance at shareholders' meetings; more policy issues on the ballot for shareholder vote; cumulative voting; more pre-, during, and post-meeting reports,
preferably in color; machinery for submitting shareholder proposals to vote;
and more representation for women. Nearly all of the planks in the platform
of Corporate Democracy find their analogues in the reform agitations of 1900
for the long ballot, initiative and referendum, the direct primary, proportionate representation and women's suffrage.

One would be brave indeed at this date to raise any question about the
nineteenth amendment. But with this exception, the success of these political
reforms over the past fifty years has been at best debatable—and in the case
of the long ballot and proportionate representation, decidedly unfortunate.
More to the point, whatever their desirability in the political life of 1900, the
wholesale importation of these reforms into the area of mid-twentieth-century
business organizations should be preceded by some analysis of their appropriateness to the context. Advocates of Corporate Democracy have been more
ready to invoke the symbols of our political tradition than to undertake such
an analysis, more eager to press for further reforms along the party line than
to assess how well shareholder democracy has worked so far. Every page of
Livingston's book supports the conclusion that Corporate Democracy in its
present form has not accomplished, is not accomplishing and will not accomplish the visitatorial job set for it.

Without doubt, the growth of more rigid disclosure requirements, particularly through the SEC, has had a powerful and healthy effect upon managerial
conduct. No prophylaxis is so effective as sunlight, and to the extent that
Corporate Democracy implies disclosure, it deserves applause. Fact disclosure
by management, however, is not the same as corporate decision-making by a
shareholder "democracy." Once stock is issued, disclosures to shareholders
are made under present rules mainly in conjunction with an election or other
shareholder vote. But tying disclosure to voting is no more than a convenience
and is even incidental. The same or more stringent disclosure requirements

could be set up without being hung on the event of voting. Disclosure is essential; how significant in the publicly-held corporation is the shareholder vote to which it is appended?

Managements are almost never reprimanded or displaced by the shareholder electorate; shareholders remain stubbornly uninterested in exerting control. Management recommendations on mergers, option plans or other corporate matters are virtually never rejected by the shareholders. The SEC machinery for putting shareholder proposals on the ballot is almost never used. When directors and officers deal personally with their corporation, as in compensation arrangements, shareholders are either not asked for their views or else give rubber stamp approval. The once-in-a-lifetime opportunity given the small shareholder to choose sides in a street brawl proxy contest between giants is hardly the democratic process. Livingston is clearly right in his conclusion that, in practice, the mass shareholders' voice is but faintly heard through the creaking of the proxy machinery.

What other dividends has Corporate Democracy paid?

The cost of hiring professional shareholder bloodhounds at meeting time to flush a quorum, and the expense and time required to comply with the legal formalities of a foreordained election, are a nuisance. But they can be borne. Bearable, too, is the increasingly familiar sight of large-company shareholder meetings with a revival-meeting atmosphere—box lunches, flowers for the ladies, wailing infant shareholders, publicity-seekers demanding the floor and—a new benefaction of modern technology—the portable, battery-operated megaphone. Shareholder interjection into the flexible day-to-day operation of the corporation could become a more serious problem, but fortunately shareholder apathy has effectively contained this risk. Experience with cumulative voting in the large corporation has been found to have little practical effect upon corporate conduct, has often introduced an undesirable divisive element into the operation of centralized corporate management and affords a potential nuisance weapon to the minority shareholder motivated to wield it. Again, however, these are results which can be lived with especially since, as in the case of municipal proportionate representation, the spread of the use of cumulative voting in large corporations seems today to have largely been stemmed.

But in the fever of the "democratic" proxy contest, the corporate patient is approaching the period of crisis. The modern proxy contest has become a grotesque travesty of an orderly machinery for corporate decision-making. Largely irrelevant to issues of management policy, fought out between rival cliques competing for personal control of the corporate treasury and the elixir of corporate office, an instrument for attack by wolves from without rather than for surveillance by watchdogs within, increasingly a sideshow performance of hired public relations men, its effectiveness haphazardly dependent on the accidents of stock distribution, available only to those who command the enormous ante the game requires—the modern proxy contest does not significantly touch the mass of small shareholders until the victor, or both victor and vanquished, present their handsome expense accounts to the corporation for reimbursement of costs incurred for the "benefit of the corporation." The modern proxy contest is at best a device for tempering autocracy by invasion. Too infrequent and misdirected to perform the function of policing management responsibility, it is often too frequent for the resources of a corporate treasury when it occurs once.

From the standpoint of the national economy, powerful arguments can be advanced to justify the corporate "raid" as a mechanism for reallocating frozen capital investment. Probably, too, the possibility of a proxy fight in which management will have to look to the good will of its shareholders to retain office has some collateral effect in inducing executives to toe the mark—though the practices adopted by a well-advised management to head off proxy attack will often have little relation to sound management policy from the standpoint of the corporate enterprise. The central point here, however, is that whatever collateral advantages the shareholder proxy fight may have, it cannot be relied upon as an effective device for regularized supervision of management's stewardship.

Perhaps the most serious charge against the myth of shareholder democracy is that its slogans do much to create an impression in the public mind, and in the minds of the potential investors in a People's Capitalism, that a degree of shareholder supervision exists which in fact does not. It is quite arguable that the net effect of the corporate Jacksonians has been to impede their ultimate objective of responsible corporate management. The forms and mechanisms of shareholder democracy divert attention from the real problems of holding business managements to a desirable standard of responsibility. Modern international politics demonstrates that a centralized control group can do much behind a democratic panoply that could not otherwise be done. In actual effect, the paraphernalia of corporate democracy may operate as a first line of defense around management's high ground of control.

Altogether, the tenets of Corporate Democracy have served us little; and it is predictable that they will serve us less and less as public stockownership grows. The reason is not hard to find. In looking to the shareholder franchise for management supervision, we have been trying to design remedies for a make-believe world rather than a real one. We have done this, even though in another compartment of our minds, we have known better.

Thanks to the pioneering work of Berle, Drucker and a few others, we have long known that in our modern industrial system, it is the corporation as an institution which is permanent and the shareholders who are transitory. We have known since 1932 that widespread public holding of shares erodes a chasm between "ownership" and "control" and, particularly since the 1952 and 1956 reports on shareholdings, that the faceless mass of small stockholders is increasing by millions. We have known, too, that today's large corporation may for many purposes be best viewed as an intricate, centralized, economic-administrative structure run by professional managers who hire capital from the investor. In competition with other managements seeking capital, they sell, for what the market will bear, the opportunity to share in the economic results of their managerial efforts. Dramatic illustrations are afforded by the sprawling, all purpose, multidivisional diversified corporate enterprises which have become commonplace since World War II. The purpose clause in the charters of these companies reads simply "to make money." In an interesting and new way these companies offer an opportunity to diversify a portfolio with one purchase—to buy into an operating mutual fund rather than an investing one. Here, the buyer of stock does not know even what business the company may be in tomorrow. He is betting on a management, banking on its expert judgment to steer his small investment through the swift currents of today's commercial stream.

But for a generation, the law's response to these facts has been partially to ignore them, partially to try to exorcise them by mislabeling and partially to decree that the clock of history shall run backwards. Finding the shareholder a passing investor, we have insisted that he is an owner and a member of an electorate. Finding managements to be hirers of capital, we have tried to bury this disquieting fact by calling them hired hands of the shareholder-owners. Finding "control" to have slid away from "ownership," we have sought to put the control back with the ownership where it "belongs." Pressed by the evident economic need for flexible centralized management, we have sought to decentralize decision-making and offer it to the multitude.

The reform efforts of the Corporate Democrats, seen in this light, appear fundamentally misplaced, misdirected and romantic. Their prescriptions have not been effective to date. There is even less to recommend them for tomorrow as the corporate form matures and the number of small shareholders increase.

If our present course of reform toward more Corporate Democracy is misguided, is it possible at this time to project a more satisfactory approach? Probably so. But such an approach would have to proceed from the facts of the modern corporate institution and be accommodated to them, rather than to a bucolic and obsolete image.

An arbitrary model of a corporate structure may prove helpful in attacking the problem. Assume a large modern corporation similar to its typical commercial counterpart in all respects but two. First, the model abandons the *a priori* legal conclusion that the shareholders "own the corporation" and substitutes the more restricted conception that the only thing they "own" is their shares of stock. Second, the shareholder in this model corporation has no voting rights. His position would be quite similar to that of a voting trust certificate-holder with all economic rights in the deposited stock but no power to elect or replace the trustees by vote. Given this corporate model, there can be no talk of "corporate democracy" or rejoining "control" and "ownership." In such a corporate world, how would one go about ensuring the desired degree of management responsibility while permitting corporate officers the necessary discretion to run the business? The problem is difficult but not impossible. Its solution has already been approximated in trust law.

Reflection on the legal implications of this model would doubtless isolate other areas where accommodation in the present law would be called for, but four come readily to mind. First, of course, full and periodic disclosure of the managers' business conduct to the security holders would be necessary; perhaps a responsible judicial or other public agency should be similarly informed. By hypothesis, this information could not help the voteless stock holder to throw the management out by election. But it would offer him data on the basis of which he could decide whether to retain or sell the shares he "owns" and, perhaps, whether to sue for fiduciary breach. An individual investor might not read much of this disclosure material, but the professional investors and the investment funds would; and the market is largely made by them.

Second, in a shareholder world without voting rights it would be necessary to provide—judicially, legislatively, administratively or by new nongovernmental machinery—some supervision of management's behavior in corporate matters affecting their personal interests, such as personal compensation.

Third, since the certificate-holder could not influence the course of the enterprise, he would badly need available avenues for rapidly and inexpensively disposing of his investment interest, and for pulling out, when he objects to the course set by management.

Finally, the entrepreneurial function of this model corporation would demand that management have the broadest latitude for discretion in business matters and that the present business-judgment rule be continued or even extended. In this respect, the law for the model corporation would depart radically from the restrictive operational rules which govern ordinary trusts designed for other economic objectives. A different result would probably follow in nonbusiness matters. The peculiar aspects of this model would invite critical attention to some practices of corporate good citizenship—particularly charitable contributions unrelated to company business. With the elements of stockholder "ownership" and voting control removed by hypothesis, such contributions could no longer be easily described as private donations from shareholders channeled through the corporation. A power of appointment is a special form of compensation. Charitable contributions would be overtly seen in the model as a matter of management's sole discretion and would probably attract some form of external restriction.

This nonowning, nonvoting shareholder corporate model is useful. In the first place, it helps skirt a dangerous semantic pothole. The usual articulation that "the shareholder owns the corporation" is only one step removed from "therefore he should run it." From a premise of shareholder "ownership," one almost inevitably becomes involved in concepts of "shareholder approval," "shareholder contract" and "shareholder estoppel." In large measure, the superstructure of the ideology of Corporate Democracy proceeds from deep emotional associations deriving from the concept that the shareholder "owns" the corporation. It is not at all necessary to say anything about who "owns" the corporation when discussing the problem of the proper distribution of corporate power. The term is best abandoned for this purpose.

More importantly, the model is useful because, in the case of the large, publicly-held modern corporation, it approximates reality. Except in the context of the closely-held corporation, the limited notion of the shareholder as owner of a "share"—a reified legal and economic bundle—is surely more valid than our historical image of the shareholder as "owner of the corporation." To view the shareholder as the owner only of a share of stock—as a bondholder is said to own "the bond"—conforms far more closely to the shareholder's own expectations and describes far more accurately what he in fact handles as his own—buying, selling and giving away. And the model's assumption that the shareholder has no vote is much closer to fact than the Jacksonian metaphor of the voting, independent freeholder.

Our historical absorption with the democratic process, as a process, tempts us always to describe our environment in the verbal categories of democracy. It is not only in Cleveland that any three people at a bus-stop are soon a bus-waiting committee, with three elected officers. It comes hard for us to accept the possibility that any institution not democratically operated can be operated morally. We are not apt at discriminating between organs of the state—which get out of hand if not subjected to internal democratic voting check—and organs of institutions within the state—which, if not democratically controlled internally, may yet be effectively controlled from without. It thus comes easily to us to conceive and treat shareholders as an electorate—though a rather odd electorate which buys and sells its franchise daily on an exchange.

But though the political figure is tempting, it just will not do. As Livingston well documents, the average stockholder does not behave like an active member of an electorate, born into a corporate political environment as a citizen. He is an economic investor. He may choose to put his money in a sock or in pepper-corns for safety. Or if he is a bit more sophisticated and income conscious, he invests in government bonds, or a bank, or a post office savings account, or an investment trust, or in bonds, or debentures, or preferred stocks or common stocks. In none of these but the last does he buy—or is he forced to buy, willy-nilly—any semblance of a "control" over the enterprise in which he invests. The appeal of common stock to the average investor lies in its peculiar economic features—greater return, speculative potential and inflationary hedge. He discriminates among his possible choices of investment largely on economic grounds—or what he conceives to be economic grounds. And as stock ownership becomes more widespread, this disinterest in voting rights may be expected to intensify.

Characterizing the mass of shareholders as an electorate carries the implication that their franchise may be relied upon to police the conduct of the corporation. For the few professionals who buy and sell corporations like used cars, control is of paramount importance. But the usual shareholder's interest in the control factor is reflected in his unlimited boredom with the devices of corporate democracy, in his simple decision to depart when he objects to the way things are going, and in his eagerness to snap up Dodge stock in 1925 and Ford stock in 1956, ignoring the absence of voting control. It may be legitimately speculated that, but for the listing rules of the New York Stock Exchange, enormous blocks of pure nonvoting stock of major corporations would probably be outstanding in the hands of the public. In most situations, the control differences among publicly-held corporations with fully nonvoting stock, the Ford pattern in which the common held by the public is substantially noncontrolling, and the General Motors pattern in which the publicly-held common legally carries voting control, are primarily differences in words.

The model is not to be taken literally of course. Legally votable stock is in fact votable, and the vote can, in some circumstances, make a difference; for some purposes, such as the determination of creditors' rights, shareholders may be conveniently viewed as proprietors; and for the closely-held corporation, the model's assumptions are obviously invalid. But, as a broad generalization for use in thinking about problems of power distribution within the publicly-held corporation, the suggested model offers a much better guide than the unarticulated model we have been following—the homespun Jeffersonian image of the small business owned and operated by sturdy freeholders.

Accepted as a valid working tool, the model points to the likely course of tomorrow's law governing control of the big corporation. The four areas of legal change suggested by it and outlined earlier combine to form a unified general pattern: franker acceptance that centralized managerial control is necessary, a fact and here to stay; less wishful pretense that the shareholders' vote is or can be an effective restraint; emphasis upon disclosure, free exit and transfer as the shareholder's principal protections; and development of new and extrinsic mechanics to supervise management dealings in corporate funds for nonbusiness purposes and for itself.

We are dealing here with trends. De-emphasis of the role of shareholder voting does not imply the scrapping of existing shareholder voting machinery. Although the proxy system of electing directors is largely an engine of, rather than for, management control, someone has to select directors, and there would be no advantage in permitting them overtly to choose their own successors. Further, as already mentioned, improvement of disclosure requirements has been largely linked to shareholder voting. Institutionally, this is the way the law has grown and experience has been amassed; nothing is to be gained by discarding what we have. The need is, rather, to recognize that the important thing is the disclosure, not the electoral process to which it is attached. Similarly, at least until a better solution can be found, the proxy fight will be difficult to dispense with, however much it may have gotten out of focus. We may expect some adjustments in present proxy fight procedures designed approximately to realign them with their asserted purpose, but evolution is to be anticipated, not revolution.

The projection offered here is a broad outline. It is tempting to try to project in more detail. But the essential need is for a major revision in our thinking about the problem. When we shall have made this turn, the concrete forms of change will come with time and trial. One general observation on this process should be made, however. We are not locked into our present corporate control system by our ideological preference for a pluralistic, privately-run society and a less rather than a more regulated economy. The contrary is true. It is this very preference which may be expected to bring about change—in the same way that pluralistic preference has inspired our antitrust laws.

Livingston is vehement on what he considers the undue power position of corporate managers in American society. Without necessarily echoing the same vehemence, one is forced to recognize that the control of corporate managers over employment, over disposition of business property and over their own compensation confers vast community power upon them. The new enthusiasm for the concept of corporate good citizenship is likely to increase this power further. The driving need for funds on the part of educational and charitable institutions and our reluctance to turn to government sources incline us to welcome the prospect of access to the only large accumulations of donatable funds remaining outside of government—the corporate treasuries. Current judicial opinion and tax patterns encourage such contributions, for they are today considered "private" and a healthy example of American capitalist adaptability. In time, however, we may be driven to conclude that though corporate good citizenship is preferable to corporate bad citizenship, unfettered donative power in the board of the large good-citizen corporation may more conflict with than conform to our pluralistic preference. Relatively small, diverse private donations by countless individuals and small businesses are one thing. Quite another is the prospect of vast donations of investors' funds by the directors of publicly-owned corporations. For these must inevitably favor institutions conforming to management's predispositions and add to management's existing community influence the profound power attending the role of a Medici. Past hesitation to permit corporate donations at board discretion arose from concern at giving away shareholders' money. To this will be added tomorrow a broader social concern at the increased community power of management and at the life and death implications of more central-ized donative power upon the charitable and educational institutions them-selves. Avoidance of undue concentration of economic power and supervision of a trustee's personal dealings with the subject of his trust are in the mainstream of conservative legal tradition in America. Corporate manage-ment cannot expect indefinitely to remain outside this current.

It will not be easy to find new ways to police transactions in which management sits on one side of the table and the managers sit on the other, or to deal with management's newly won power to disburse corporate assets to charities of its choice. No responsible source is calling for direct government controls to keep management in line. Neither are we forced to stand still. The genius of the American people has been its history of working out pragmatic solutions to new problems without running to Draco. But this process cannot be brought to bear until the problem is faced—until we stop thinking about the large corporation as though it were a family partnership.

There is one way to head off the legal development projected here—curtail the increase in amateur small stockholders. Something of a case could be made for this course of action. The history over the centuries of stock investment by the unsophisticated has not been particularly happy. If it could be assumed that only pros played the stock market, the necessity for expensive and time-consuming regulatory machinery would disappear. Professionals in smaller numbers could be expected to look after their own interests; if they did not, the social loss would not be great.

Obviously, this theoretical alternative is out of the question. Rising incomes increase the pressure of investable funds. The pull of common stocks as an inflationary hedge and higher income source is powerful, particularly for retirement investment. To exclude the common man from these advantages would be totally repugnant to the American dream. And it is generally agreed that the nation must tap every available source of equity investment if it is to maintain or arrive at an adequate rate of economic growth. Finally, the normal incentives of commercial expansion may be expected to spur the stock exchanges and the brokers to sell their wares where they can. Barring serious depression, public stock ownership will continue to grow.

"People's Capitalism" and "Corporate Democracy" are slogans with an inverse relationship. Each expansion of the first undermines the second. Every sale of common stock to a new small investor adds to the fractionation of share ownership which lies at the root of the impotence of shareholder voting as a check on management. Every extension of common stock ownership to an inexperienced small investor adds to the ranks of those who may be expected to lay claim, both politically and morally, to new legal protection of their interests. Every victory for the cause of the Exchange's People's Capitalism accelerates the development of new legal techniques designed to temper the power of corporate management.

Joseph Livingston's book, though it does not say so, documents the end of one era of corporate reform and foreshadows the beginning of the next.

Chapter 8 Refining the Security Pattern

OREN WEAVING COMPANY, INC.

THE BALANCE SHEET of the Oren Weaving Company, Inc., a family-owned corporation that manufactured synthetic and woolen cloth, as of June 28, 1964 (shown as the first column in Exhibit 1), contained several items reflecting the fact that the corporation had been reorganized under Chapter XI of the Bankruptcy Act, and discharged on that date.

The income statements in Exhibit 2 show that the company's operations after its discharge from bankruptcy were very successful. By December, 1965, it was possible to accurately predict the results for the fiscal year ending January 31, 1966, and to forecast with confidence the result of operations for the ensuing fiscal year, as shown in the last column of Exhibit 2.

The abrupt turnaround in the company's affairs occurred in part because two extremely unsuccessful divisions had been liquidated during the bankruptcy proceeding, but came about also because of the successful introduction, at first on an exclusive basis, of a process of bonding two fabrics of different nature to make a product that was new to the stylists. It was felt that the bonded fabric would continue in large demand indefinitely, but as the process was not patented, competition could be expected to cut gross margins by the 1967 selling season.

The high level of demand for synthetic and woolen products during the recent months had also produced profitable conditions throughout the industry.

The general situation in the industry was seen as follows.

A strong market for synthetic fibers and textiles is being matched by price strength for the leading companies' stocks. Earnings increases will be good in 1966, but most companies will probably be unable to match their tremendous percentages of gain of recent years. . . .

There is a partnership here between the makers of synthetics (or raw materials for them), and the weavers of textiles. Between them, they are achieving changes which are encouraging for the long term, as they point to a lessening of cyclical fluctuations which often were violent in the past. . . .

. . . .

While cyclical variations are unavoidable, all this is reason to remain optimistic about these groups. Projected population patterns also brighten their prospects.[1]

The balance sheet of the company at the beginning of November, 1965, the latest available to the officers in early December, showed not only that many of the debts that had emerged from the bankruptcy had been settled but also that the company had a strong position in liquid funds. Pro forma statements for later dates confirmed this trend. David Oren, Jr., treasurer of the Oren Weaving Company, therefore believed that some rearrangement of the remaining debt contracts was both possible and desirable to allow the company to adopt policies suitable to a profitable, financially strong concern.

The pertinent terms of the various debt arrangements in force at the end of December, 1965, are summarized below. First described are those arrangements that might be classified as in the ordinary course of business; and second are those inherited from the reorganization.

FACTORING

The company maintained a factoring arrangement with the firm that also acted as its exclusive sales agent. This firm, located in New York City, had worked with the Oren Weaving Company for many years. It received commissions on the styling advice it furnished and on the sales it developed, and also was paid .75% of each receivable handled. The receivables charge was considered reasonable by the Oren company officers, since the factor's service relieved the company of all costs usually created by handling customer credits.

The factoring arrangement provided that the Oren company could draw 90% of the amount of any account booked, with an interest charge on these drawings that varied with the general level of interest rates. The remaining 10% was available when the debtor paid the factor. In December, 1965, as for the preceding 2 years, the rate used on the drawings was 5.75%; but at his last interview with the factoring firm David Oren, Jr., had learned that in view of the recent strengthening of rates he could expect an increase to 6.75% in 1966.

On the other hand, the factor had never pressed the Oren company to use its available funds, and there had been times in the past when the financial portion of the factoring arrangement had been unused. This had not been the case, however, since the reorganization.

TRADE ACCOUNTS PAYABLE—TAXES PAYABLE

These were accounts due from current operations, on normal terms, and payments were being made promptly. The company began the 1966 fiscal year with an unused loss carry-forward of about $1,527,500 applicable to offset

---

[1] *Moody's Stock Survey*, December 27, 1965 (Vol. 57), p. 310.

taxable income; so the amounts shown as taxes payable on November 3 and January 31 were exclusively for state and local obligations.

OTHER CURRENT LIABILITIES

These included the usual accrued expenses and, in November and January, about $66,000 for a liability due to the company's pension trust immediately after the end of the fiscal year.

CHAPTER XI DEBT

The November 3 balance of $16,600 was the remainder of the obligation created to settle "all other unsecured debts, as proved or allowed, including those scheduled as undisputed, and including those arising from the rejection of executory contracts." Of the original debts of this class, none above $300 were settled in full, according to the plan. The $16,600 was payable before the end of calendar 1965.

EQUIPMENT PURCHASE OBLIGATIONS

This debt was incurred for machinery purchased on conditional sales contracts. The 1965 balance of about $20,000 had become a current liability. Mr. Oren, Sr., considered the plant well equipped and efficient. He expected that large amounts for new fixed assets would not be needed for at least five years. In fact, production could be substantially increased by more intensive use of shifts, and the plant had excess floor space where new capacity, as needed, could be installed. But in the longer run, it would be necessary to replace much of the equipment as it was made obsolete by changes known to be on the drawing boards.

MORTGAGE PAYABLE

This debt was held by an insurance company. It was secured by a first mortgage on the company's real property in North Carolina. This debt, undisturbed by the reorganization, scheduled monthly payments for principal and interest averaging about $775 in 1965 and 1966. The interest rate was 5.5%. Maturity fell in 1977. Prepayment was not mentioned in the loan agreement.

TERM LOAN

This loan, from a bank in a neighboring city introduced to the Oren company by its New York bank during the reorganization proceedings, was arranged as part of the reorganization plan, although it was not taken down until August, 1964. Originally $350,000, the loan was at 6%, and was payable in quarterly installments of $13,800 (principal and interest) beginning January 1, 1965. Prepayment was not mentioned in the loan agreement, but one prepayment, applied to the most remote payments, had been allowed without comment. The loan was currently scheduled to be paid off during 1971.

The Oren company had not actively used the new banking relationship, but it did try to maintain an average deposit balance of 20% of the loan with the bank, as it had been advised to do by its New York bankers. There had been no talks between officers of this bank and the Oren officers since the prepayment referred to, but the bank had been sent semiannual reports, as required by the loan agreement.

LOAN WITHOUT INTEREST

For many years, the Oren company's only bank connection other than local payroll accounts had been with the Hudson Trust Company, one of the largest commercial banks in New York City. This bank had supported the Oren company with loans for seasonal purposes, and had made a term loan in the early 1960's to assist the purchase of the divisions that later were liquidated during the reorganization. The interest rates charged had usually been "½% over prime" on short-term loans, and the rate on the term loan was 1% over the prime rate at the time the loan was arranged. In December, 1965, the prime rate was 5%, and it was expected to go higher.

At the end of the reorganization, the Oren company owed $1,040,988 to the Hudson Trust Company because of the defaulted term loan, accrued interest on this loan, and a frozen short-term loan with its accrued interest. The bank agreed to the deferred payment of this sum, without any interest, on the following terms. It had been insistent, although only informally through conversations with the Orens, in its expectation of average balances of 20% of the loan. Any drawdown for seasonal or other needs should be offset at other dates.

The schedule of minimum payments on the loan began on July 1, 1965, with $40,000. Quarterly payments of $14,218.80 would be due beginning October 1, 1965. Additionally, the company promised to pay, at times to be chosen by it:

$106.6 thousand by July 1, 1967
42.4 thousand by July 1, 1969
146.5 thousand by July 1, 1971
146.5 thousand by July 1, 1973
47.2 thousand by July 1, 1974

According to this schedule, the loan would be extinguished on July 1, 1974. (Discounted values of this schedule as of January 1, 1966, assuming payments of the above additional sums at the latest possible dates, have been computed by the case writer and appear in Exhibit 3.) However, if 50% of net profits after all taxes from June 30, 1965 to July 1, 1967 should exceed the payments already made, the total payment was to be increased to this sum on July 1, 1967. Similar calculations and payments were to apply to each succeeding two-year period.

No provision had been made to permit more rapid payment of this loan, but in an interview early in December, 1965, Mr. Oren, Jr., learned from the bank vice president who handled the account that the bank would be interested in a proposition to settle the remaining indebtedness for "about $800,000 depending on the exact date."[2] Mr. Oren left the interview feeling that a partial payment would also be welcomed.

COLLATERAL

The first mortgage has already been mentioned. The factoring arrangement was used for the purchase of approved accounts without recourse to the company. The factor also held a security interest in all other accounts receivable of the company, and any interest the company might have in merchandise delivered to customers on account. These were normal arrangements in most factoring contracts. In addition, at the time the Oren company was discharged from bankruptcy the factor had obtained a security interest in all the inventories of the company, to apply until the company had earned $275,000 after taxes in a fiscal year, and total indebtedness (including factor's advances) had fallen below $2.8 million.

The term loan was secured by a second mortgage on the real estate and a chattel mortgage on all machinery and equipment, including after-acquired property of the same kind. This pledge was to be discharged after the final settlement of the interest-free loan, described above, from the Hudson Trust Company.

RESTRICTIVE PROVISIONS OF LOANS

The interest-free loan was unsecured but contained the following restrictive covenants. The term loan also contained the same clauses in wording exactly the same as that of the interest-free loan.

1. Net Operating Loss. A net operating loss (before tax adjustments) in excess of $100,000 in either of the fiscal years commencing in 1965 and 1966 shall be an event of default, except that a net operating profit in the first year can be used as offset in computing the extent of the net loss in the second year.

2. Working Capital. To be maintained at not less than $1 million; or an amount that is $275,000 less than Oren's working capital at June 28, 1964 (Exhibit 1), whichever is less.

3. Accounts Receivable. Oren must not have outstanding at its own risk (i.e., not accepted by the factor) more than $90,000 of accounts receivable at any one

---

[2] If the loan was retired at a discount, the saving would become part of the taxable income of the Oren Weaving Company.

time. (But Oren was not required to draw against the factored accounts before they were collected.)

4. Total Debt.   Must be kept at or below $2.4 million, exclusive of factoring.

5. Real and Personal Property Leasing.   Aggregate rental payment obligations must not exceed $80,000 per fiscal year without prior written consent. (The company had no long-term leases in force at December, 1965.)

6. Dividends.   Except for stock dividends in its own stock, Oren shall not pay dividends or distribute assets to its stockholders, except that when and if net worth exceeds $1,735,393 (150% of the net worth at June 28, 1964) such payments may be made but not to exceed in any 1 year $7,000 or 20% of net earnings after taxes, whichever is less.

7. Capital Investments.   No more than $5,000 per single expenditure; aggregate expenditures, net of cash received from retirements, must not exceed 50% of depreciation accumulated since June 28, 1964.

8. Investments.   Oren shall not invest in securities or obligations of any person, firm, etc., other than short-term U.S. governments or time certificates of deposit issued by banks.

9. Loans to Others.   Oren shall make no loans nor incur contingent liabilities by way of guaranty or otherwise for the obligations of others unless first approved by the directors representing the banks.

10. Salaries.   No changes in salaries of the officers are to be made by Oren or any subsidiary unless approved by the salary committee of the board of directors. (There had been no changes in salary levels since the bankruptcy proceedings were started in 1963.)

11. Voting of Shares.   The family shareholders had agreed to vote their shares so as to elect to the board one representative of each lending bank, as long as the term loan or the interest-free loan remained outstanding. These directors constituted a majority of the salary committee.

As David Oren, Jr., the treasurer of the corporation, discussed the situation with his father in December, 1965, it appeared that the time was fast approaching when a financial policy suitable to a prosperous company should be established. The father was particularly anxious to be rid of "the residue of the bankruptcy," and suggested concentrating all efforts on the reduction of the interest-free loan. He pointed out that this loan, appearing in credit agency reports, probably hurt the company's commercial credit. The son, however, argued that one seldom has the use of $1 million without cost, and thought that the interest-free loan should be regarded as an opportunity instead of a source of shame. He remarked that every supplier was giving the Oren company normal trade terms. There was disagreement also about how much debt should be carried on a long-term basis by a small company in the textile industry. The father was willing to accept the mortgage debt, but preferred to have all other debt financing retired, and to use the factor's services to the full. Finally, both the Orens were aware of pressure from other members of the family (who held the remaining 40% of the shares) for the commencement of dividend payments as soon as warranted. One of the younger shareholders, a law student, had recently suggested that his shares be repurchased, instead.

Exhibit 1

OREN WEAVING COMPANY, INC.

BALANCE SHEETS AS OF JUNE 28, 1964, AND NOVEMBER 3, 1965,
AND ESTIMATED BALANCE SHEET AS OF JANUARY 30, 1966
(Dollar Figures in Thousands)

	June 28, 1964	November 3, 1965	Pro forma January 31, 1966
ASSETS			
Cash on hand and U.S. notes............$	392.6	$ 380.6	$ 905.2
Factored accounts:*			
Cash available......................	280.9	560.9	350.0
Required 10% equity................	198.4	137.8	201.6
Inventories...........................	1,332.1	1,268.6	1,228.3
Prepaid expenses......................	36.2	26.8	24.2
Nonfactored receivables................	82.3	3.2	52.1
Total Current Assets............$	2,322.5	$ 2,377.9	$ 2,761.4
Fixed assets..........................$	3,899.8	$ 3,795.8	$ 3,726.2
Reserve for depreciation..............	(2,561.8)	(2,720.2)	(2,743.5)
Net fixed assets....................$	1,338.0	$ 1,075.6	$ 982.7
Other assets..........................$	7.4	$ 3.5	$ 3.5
Cash value of life insurance†	42.3	46.3	46.3
Total Assets...................$	3,710.2	$ 3,503.3	$ 3,793.9
LIABILITIES AND EQUITY			
Customers' deposits...................$	11.9	$ 5.3	$ 5.8
Trade accounts payable................	71.6	243.1	195.1
Taxes payable........................	81.5	88.5	52.5
Other current liabilities...............	62.3	125.7	93.5
Current portion, debt arrangements......	7.5	121.4	121.4
Chapter XI debt......................	1,054.1	16.6	...
Total Current Liabilities..........$	1,288.9	$ 600.6	$ 468.3
Noncurrent portions of liabilities			
Equipment purchase obligations........$	88.9	$ ...	$ ...
Mortgage payable....................	134.5	121.9	120.5
Term loan...........................	...	208.6	196.6
Loan without interest.................	1,041.0	929.9	915.7
Total Liabilities..................$	2,553.3	$ 1,861.0	$ 1,701.1
Common stock and surplus.............$	1,156.9	$ 1,642.3	$ 2,092.8
Total Liabilities and Equity.......$	3,710.2	$ 3,503.3	$ 3,793.9
Net working capital...................$	1,033.6	$ 1,777.3	$ 2,293.1

* The total of factored accounts can be obtained by multiplying the required equity by 10.
† $150,000 on the life of David Oren, Sr.

Exhibit 2
OREN WEAVING COMPANY, INC.

INCOME STATEMENTS, FISCAL YEAR 1964–65, AND ESTIMATED
INCOME STATEMENTS, FISCAL YEARS 1965–66 AND 1966–67
(Dollar Figures in Thousands)

	Year ended January 31, 1965	*Pro forma Year ended January 31, 1966*	*Pro forma Year ended January 31, 1967*
Sales..................................	$ 6,483.8	$ 8,508.3	$ 9,500
Cost of sales.........................	(5,677.7)	(6,688.3)	(7,300)
Gross profit...........................	$ 806.1	$ 1,820.0	$ 2,200
Marketing expense....................	$ (227.2)	$ (452.6)	$ (450)
Administrative expenses..............	(260.1)	(294.3)	(280)
Provision for profit-sharing...........	. . .	(78.8)	(90)
Total...........................	$ (487.3)	$ (825.7)	$ (820)
Operating profit......................	$ 318.8	$ 994.4	$ 1,380
Interest cost.........................	$ (12.9)	$ (29.1)	$ (25)
Factoring cost.......................	(101.2)	(176.9)	(200)
Purchase discounts...................	*	38.3	40
Gain or (loss) on sale of assets........	14.7	(22.0)	. . .
Other income........................	4.4	1.9	. . .
Total...........................	$ (95.0)	$ (187.8)	$ (185)
Net profit............................	$ 223.8	$ 806.5	$ 1,195
Provision for income tax..............	. . .	. . .	(335)
Profit after tax.......................	$ 223.8†	$ 806.5	$ 860
Depreciation included.................	$ 222.8	$ 185.0	$ 160.0

* Deducted in cost of sales.
† Approximately $115,000 earned after June 28, 1964.

Exhibit 3

OREN WEAVING COMPANY, INC.

DISCOUNTED VALUE OF PAYMENT SCHEDULE,
INTEREST-FREE LOAN, AS OF JANUARY 1, 1966
(Face Amount, $972,550)

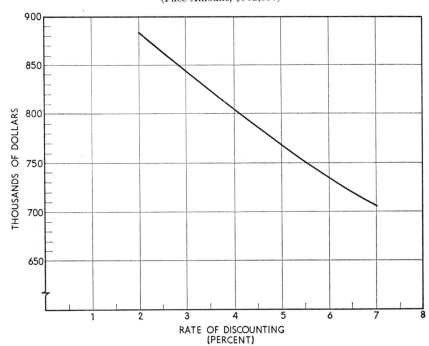

GALESBURG PULP COMPANY

In May, 1962, in view of substantial sales and profits since January, 1960, and the immediate prospect of even larger volume from rising business, the Galesburg Pulp Company was reviewing its financial position. Particular attention was to be given to the special credit arrangements that had been imposed in 1958 by the Fidelity National Bank to obtain security for its loans to the company.

The Galesburg Pulp Company was a closely held family concern, incorporated in Maine in 1880 to produce soda and sulphite pulp for use in paper manufacture. The company operated a large pulp mill. It also owned all the outstanding capital stock of the Galesburg Timber Company (authorized capital, $1.5 million), which it had organized in 1910 for the sole purpose of producing pulpwood for the parent company. The Galesburg Timber Company financed the cost of timberlands by means of advances from the parent company. These advances had ranged between $700,000 and $2 million. In addition, in 1925 the parent company had purchased the controlling interest in Barnes and Conway, Inc., manufacturers of paper.

Since 1947, the Galesburg Pulp Company had been a steady borrower from the Fidelity National Bank under an open line of unsecured credit, at annual rates from 2½% to 5%. The record of its monthly borrowings on open line of credit and balances with the bank from November, 1956, through March, 1959, appears in Exhibit 1. In fiscal 1957 and 1958, the company suffered losses, and it was clear by January, 1959, that losses for the fiscal year ended March 31, 1959, would be especially heavy. The working capital position had weakened to such an extent that substantial current funds would be needed to finance operations for the coming year.

Therefore, in January, 1959, the company requested an increase in its line of credit to $450,000–$550,000, in order to carry operations through fiscal 1960. In requesting the increase, the treasurer explained that pulpwood would come in faster than it could be worked up, and that he had been holding excess cash because he felt that if he paid down the current loan he might have trouble in getting the money back when he needed it.

The immediate business outlook for the company was such that the bank decided to refuse further credit on an unsecured basis. It wanted, if possible, to protect its loan so that in the event of the company's insolvency the bank would not have to share the residual asset values with other creditors, including probable deficiency claims of the existing mortgagees.

The bank recommended that the loan be secured by self-liquidating collateral. For this purpose, it suggested an arrangement that had been used in other situations: the loan would be secured by a lien on the company's woodpile, to be liquidated as the wood was used. A bank officer explained that it would be easy for the company to provide such security by giving to the bank a simple mortgage on the wood then in pile, describing the location and the number of cords. The bank would name an employee of the company as its agent to report weekly on withdrawals and substitutions. Whenever the value of the woodpile got below a proper margin (125% of the face of the mortgage), a supplementary mortgage would be drawn to cover additional wood purchased. Insurance on the woodpile would run directly to the bank.

The Galesburg treasurer thought favorably of the proposed change, because the new arrangement would give the company leeway to increase the loan as pulpwood purchases became larger. The result of these negotiations was that the bank extended a new loan of $195,000 secured by the pulpwood inventory, in addition to the $148,000 loan outstanding on open line of credit.

When counsel for the company studied the details of the plan, however, he was uncertain whether the indenture of the outstanding first mortgage bonds would permit a valid lien on the woodpile to be given to the bank. He suggested that the company pledge the unissued portion ($250,000) of its first mortgage bonds as added collateral for the $195,000 loan. This was done immediately, just before the close of fiscal 1959.

Counsel for the bank, on the other hand, examining the indenture provisions for the outstanding mortgage bonds, concluded that the indenture could not be construed as covering the inventory of pulpwood, which was being continuously used up in operations and replenished through purchases from the subsidiary timber company. This opinion was based on his interpretation of the following provisions of the indenture.

Conveyance clauses:

All and singular the property of said Galesburg Pulp Company now owned or that may be hereafter acquired . . . of whatsoever character[1] . . . including real estate, lands, water powers, water power rights and privileges, dams, mills, lines, machinery and appliances, buildings and structures of all kinds, and each and every of their appurtenances, engines [etc.].

Also, all and singular, the rights, privileges and franchises, legislative or otherwise, of the Corporation now or hereafter owned by it, including all licenses, letters patent [etc.].

Also, all rents, issues, tolls, revenues, profits and income arising or to arise out of the mortgaged property.

---

[1] Counsel advised that in view of *Emerson* v. *European & North American Railway Co.* (67 Maine 387) the mortgage could not be held to cover the pulp or cordwood acquired from time to time. In this case, the court said that general words such as "all and singular of its property" would seem to refer only to kinds of property thereafter enumerated.

Excepting and excluding, however, from the lien of this mortgage, all stocks, bonds, or other corporate securities now owned . . . or that it may hereafter acquire.

Provisions as to default:

Until default the company is permitted to possess, manage, operate and enjoy all the property, estates and franchises hereinbefore described and conveyed . . . and to renew, alter, substitute, and repair the same and to receive, take and use the tolls, revenues, incomes, rents, dividends, interest, issues and profits thereof in the same manner and with the same effect as if this mortgage had not been made, and to retain all the rights, powers, duties, and privileges belonging to or incident to the full ownership thereof, except such . . . as are inconsistent herewith.

Power of trustee in case of default:

Trustee may take possession . . . of all . . . the property hereby conveyed or intended to be conveyed.

Release clause:

Trustee has power to release any of the conveyed property if the Corporation has decided it should not continue to hold it, providing other property equal in value is substituted and made subject to the lien of the indenture, or, the proceeds of sale are paid to the Trustee as a part of the security.

The release clause in the mortgage indenture was emphasized in counsel's argument that the indenture did not create a lien on the pulpwood. It was pointed out that the release clause covered all the property conveyed by the indenture. If the pulp or cordwood was part of the mortgaged property, none could be disposed of unless new inventory was substituted or the proceeds of the sale paid to the trustee. He argued that this meaning to the release clause was certainly unreasonable in any realistic view of company operations.

Finally, counsel said, even though not a word in the indenture would seem to indicate that the mortgage was intended to cover stock in trade, if the mortgage should be construed as covering such merchandise the Maine law was not clear on the question whether the mortgagee would have a lien on the after-acquired merchandise enforceable in equity as against one taking with notice before the mortgagee had obtained possession. The Massachusetts Supreme Court had ruled that a mortgage of such after-acquired property has no validity as against a person who takes the mortgaged property, even though with notice, before the mortgagee takes possession.

Bank's counsel further argued that although some cases in Maine referred with favor to a leading English case, which upheld the validity of such a mortgage, dicta in other Maine cases indicated that the state courts might hold that a mortgage of after-acquired personal property was not good until mortgagee took possession. The counsel concluded that the chances were about even that a Maine court would follow the Massachusetts rule; and much better than even were the chances that the indenture for the outstanding first mortgage bonds would be construed as not including a lien on pulpwood or merchandise.

In view of these differences of opinion as to the validity of the bank's lien on the pulpwood owned by the Galesburg Pulp Company, the bank proposed another arrangement, which was substituted in April, 1959, for the loan secured by the woodpile. The Galesburg Pulp Company set up a new, wholly owned subsidiary, the Pulpwood Purchasing Company, to act as a vehicle for the purchase of pulpwood from the Galesburg Timber Company. The new subsidiary was merely a purchasing corporation. An agreement drawn between the subsidiary and the parent company bound the parent to buy its entire supply of pulpwood from the subsidiary at prices satisfactory to the bank.

As a next step, the parent company paid up its unsecured bank loans of $148,000, retaining only the $195,000 note secured by first mortgage bonds. The bank then made new loans as necessary to the Pulpwood Purchasing Company to cover its purchases from the Galesburg Timber Company. The bank charged interest at 5½%, but agreed to a credit line of $600,000. The Pulpwood Purchasing Company borrowed $300,000 at once, in April, 1959, and had taken the full line of credit by November.

Except for small current operating expenses, the purchasing subsidiary incurred no other debts. The inventory of pulpwood was piled on a plot leased by the Galesburg Pulp Company to its purchasing subsidiary at a nominal rental. Notices were posted on the leased premises as evidence of ownership of the pulpwood by the Pulpwood Purchasing Company. Both the parent company and the purchasing subsidiary agreed to keep account of these transactions, treating them as absolute sales.

The bank required the Galesburg Pulp Company to endorse the notes of the purchasing subsidiary and also to raise additional equity funds of its own. After company counsel had advised that it would be permissible to issue prior preferred stock, despite the existence of outstanding first and second preferred issues, the company found a buyer for $289,000 prior preferred stock. Further restrictions imposed by the bank were that neither company could pay dividends without the bank's consent, and that the Pulpwood Purchasing Company could not issue further stock, incur obligations, or use its assets as security.

Balance sheets and operating statements for the Galesburg Pulp Company for the fiscal years ended March 31, 1957–62, appear in Exhibits 2 and 3, and financial statements for the Pulpwood Purchasing Company for the fiscal years ended March 31, 1960–62, are in Exhibits 4 and 5. Exhibit 6 shows the purchasing subsidiary's borrowings and balances with the bank for the three years ended April, 1962.

As the Galesburg Timber Company continued to show operating losses while the other two companies enjoyed profits, some study was given to possible changes in the relationship of the companies. Balance sheets and operating statements of the timber company for the fiscal years ended March 31, 1961 and 1962, are given in Exhibits 7 and 8. The timber company sold pulpwood at market prices to the Pulpwood Purchasing Company, which in turn sold the pulpwood to the parent company at $1 a cord more.

Because the bank loans of the Pulpwood Purchasing Company had stood at only $139,000 since November, 1961, a question posed in May 1962 was whether the purchasing subsidiary, operating under a loan agreement drawn to meet emergency conditions in early 1959, was needed any longer. The Galesburg management was satisfied that fiscal 1962 represented a return to normal levels of activity and profit, although it was in some doubt about whether fiscal 1963 would be as prosperous as 1962 had been.

Exhibit 1

GALESBURG PULP COMPANY

BORROWINGS AND DEPOSIT BALANCES ON BOOKS OF THE
FIDELITY NATIONAL BANK, NOVEMBER 1956–MARCH 1959
(Dollar Figures in Thousands)

	Own Notes— Open Line*	Average Deposit Balance		Own Notes— Open Line*	Average Deposit Balance
1956:			**1958:**		
November	27	31.5	January	159	38.8
December	27	34.5	February	154	41.9
			March	154	85.0
1957:			April	154	122.6
January	55	29.2	May	154	150.1
February	110	40.3	June	154	135.5
March	165	49.6	July	148	107.3
April	220	48.7	August	148	87.6
May	220	49.7	September	148	83.9
June	247	69.7	October	148	78.9
July	220	58.2	November	148	102.7
August	192	37.9	December	148	94.6
September	192	42.3			
October	192	33.7	**1959:**		
November	192	72.0	January	148	82.2
December	165	39.7	February	148	81.5
			March	148	105.7
			April	paid	

* As of last day of month.

Exhibit 2

GALESBURG PULP COMPANY

BALANCE SHEETS AS OF MARCH 31, 1957–62
(Dollar Figures in Thousands)

	1957	1958	1959	1960	1961	1962
ASSETS						
Cash	$ 21	$ 158	$ 147	$ 79	$ 66	$ 444
Notes and accounts receivable	307	158	123	270	359	361
Merchandise:						
Finished (cost)	39	43	35	11	15	10
Unfinished	5	6	7	6	6	6
Raw materials and supplies	1,477	1,000	664	259	276	347
Total Current Assets	$1,849	$1,365	$ 976	$ 625	$ 722	$1,168
Land, buildings, machinery, equipment	3,437	3,539	3,572	4,460	4,467	4,705
Less: Reserve for depreciation	1,927	2,046	2,152	2,840	2,938	2,999
Land, buildings, machinery, equipment, net	$1,510	$1,493	$1,420	$1,620	$1,529	$1,706
Investments in subsidiaries and others	1,888	1,888	1,914	2,010	2,009	2,009
Deferred charges—prepaid items	58	43	40	45	47	54
U.S. Treasury bonds, partly pledged	23	23	217	208	208	. . .
Advances to subsidiary companies	1,590	1,686	1,399	1,617	1,610	1,941
Improvements	134	68	28	17	23	7
Mortgages, notes receivable	6	4	3	14	14	13
Total Assets	$7,058	$6,570	$5,997	$6,156	$6,162	$6,898
LIABILITIES						
Notes payable for borrowed money	$ 248	$ 193	$ 182	$ . . .	$ . . .	$ . . .
Notes payable, other	45	96	85	100	93	53
Accounts payable	98	50	14	197	165	157
Accruals	. . .	. . .	37	. . .	. . .	. . .
Dividend payable	. . .	. . .	. . .	. . .	. . .	8
Total Current Liabilities	$ 391	$ 339	$ 318	$ 297	$ 258	$ 218
First mortgage 6% bonds	750	750	750	750	750	750
Notes payable secured by first mortgage bonds	. . .	. . .	195	195	195	. . .
Prior preferred stock, $6 cumulative	. . .	. . .	. . .	289	289	289
First preferred stock	329	329	329	329	329	329
Second preferred stock	275	275	275	275	275	275
Reserves, contingent	48	48	48	202	143	221
Common stock (no par value) and surplus	5,265	4,829	4,082	3,819	3,923	4,816
Total Liabilities	$7,058	$6,570	$5,997	$6,156	$6,162	$6,898

Exhibit 3

GALESBURG PULP COMPANY

COMPARATIVE PROFIT AND LOSS ACCOUNT,
YEARS ENDED MARCH 31, 1957–62
(Dollar Figures in Thousands)

	1957	1958	1959	1960	1961	1962
Sales	$2,697	$1,903	$1,442	$3,219	$3,384	$4,600
Less: Cost of goods sold	2,710	2,280	1,964	2,747	2,800	3,135
Gross profit (loss)	$ (13)	$ (377)	$ (522)	$ 472	$ 584	$1,465
Selling and general expenses	246	215	247	411	426	469
Operating profit (loss)	$ (259)	$ (592)	$ (769)	$ 61	$ 158	$ 996
Other income*	281	235	101	46	89	83
Other charges†	65	77	76	116	140	129
Net profit (loss) before federal income tax	$ (43)	$ (434)	$ (744)	$ (9)	$ 107	$ 950
Net profit (loss)	$ (43)	$ (434)	$ (744)	$ (9)	$ 107	$ 950
Dividends on prior preferred stock	...	...	...	13	17	17
Depreciation included in costs above	na	119	106	108	98	100

* Including dividends on common stock of Barnes and Conway, Inc.
† Including interest on mortgage bonds.
Inventories carried at cost. From 1960 includes purchases from Pulpwood Purchasing Company at approximate market prices at date of purchase. No revaluation on a basis of market price was made.

Exhibit 4

PULPWOOD PURCHASING COMPANY

BALANCE SHEETS AS OF MARCH 31, 1960–62
(Dollar Figures in Thousands)

	1960	1961	1962
ASSETS			
Cash	$ 3	$ 4	$ 7
Accounts receivable	...	...	7
Pulpwood and supplies (book value)	798	697	820
Total Current Assets	$801	$701	$834
Deferred charges	4	3	3
Real estate and timberland	137	136	131
Total Assets	$942	$840	$968
LIABILITIES			
Accounts payable, sundry	$ 58	$ 41	$ 20
Accounts payable, Galesburg Pulp Company	236	183	564
Accounts payable, Galesburg Timber Company	...	13	19
Notes payable, bank (endorsed by Galesburg Pulp Company)	484	424	139
Accruals	3	3	17
Total Current Liabilities	$781	$664	$759
Reserve for wood shortage	18	15	21
Capital stock	99	99	99
Surplus	44	62	89
Total Liabilities	$942	$840	$968

Exhibit 5

PULPWOOD PURCHASING COMPANY

PROFIT AND LOSS ACCOUNT, 11 MONTHS ENDED MARCH 31, 1960, AND
YEARS ENDED MARCH 31, 1961 AND 1962
(Dollar Figures in Thousands)

	1960 (11 months)	1961	1962
Sales	$1,209	$1,276	$1,339
Less: Cost of wood sold	1,110	1,188	1,240
Gross profit	$ 99	$ 88	$ 99
General expenses	56	57	61
Net Profit from Operations	$ 43	$ 31	$ 38
Other income	...	10	14
Other charges	37	24	8
Net Profit before Provision for Federal Income Tax	$ 6	$ 17	$ 44
Net Profit	$ 4	$ 12	$ 27

Exhibit 6

PULPWOOD PURCHASING COMPANY

BORROWINGS AND DEPOSIT BALANCES ON THE BOOKS OF THE
FIDELITY NATIONAL BANK, JANUARY, 1959–APRIL, 1962
(Dollar Figures in Thousands)

	Own Notes—Open Line*	Average Deposit Balance		Own Notes—Open Line*	Average Deposit Balance
1959:			**1961:**		
January		12.8	January	457	12.2
February		15.9	February	452	18.3
March		17.2	March	424	12.8
April	300	12.8	April	380	13.5
May	390	13.8	May	259	14.8
June	415	11.7	June	259	18.3
July	475	17.7	July	259	25.0
August	526	11.0	August	314	17.3
September	573	7.1	September	100	63.0
October	585	6.3	October	100	28.4
November	599	4.8	November	139	11.5
December	598	7.2	December	139	14.1
1960:			**1962:**		
January	522	6.6	January	139	22.2
February	522	10.6	February	139	28.8
March	484	6.6	March	139	25.5
April	473	14.7	April	139	21.5
May	445	15.2			
June	423	14.0			
July	478	2.6			
August	467	13.0			
September	506	6.4			
October	478	10.4			
November	467	10.7			
December	457	8.6			

* As of last day of month.

Exhibit 7

GALESBURG TIMBER COMPANY

BALANCE SHEETS AS OF MARCH 31, 1961 AND 1962
(Dollar Figures in Thousands)

	1961	1962
ASSETS		
Cash..................................... $	7	$ 336
Accounts receivable......................	77	39
Lumber and supplies......................	13	13
Total Current Assets................ $	97	$ 388
Advances to subsidiaries..................	22	24
Deferred charges.........................	1	1
Notes receivable.........................	6	8
Investments in affiliates and others (book value)............................	175	145
Timberlands, other real estate, etc...........	3,098	2,681
Total Assets....................... $3,399		$3,247
LIABILITIES		
Accounts payable and accruals.............. $	20	$ 6
Advances from Galesburg Pulp Company.....	1,428	1,376
Mortgages on real estate..................	161	177
Capital stock (authorized 20,000 shares, par $100; issued 14,400 shares)............	1,440	1,440
Surplus..................................	350	248
Total Liabilities................... $3,399		$3,247

Exhibit 8

GALESBURG TIMBER COMPANY

PROFIT AND LOSS ACCOUNT, YEARS ENDED
MARCH 31, 1961 AND 1962
(Dollar Figures in Thousands)

	1961	1962
Sales of pulpwood.................... $ 117		$ 140
Cost of stumpage used.............	45	46
Gross profit..................... $ 72		$ 94
General expenses....................	83	85
Net Profit (Loss) from Operations................. $ (11)		$ 9
Other income.......................	5	3
Other charges......................	12	114*
Net Loss.................... $ (18)		$(102)

* About $100,000 of this sum was loss on sale of interest in timberlands.

QUALITY PLASTICS, INC.

On May 5, 1964, Robert Paxson, president of Quality Plastics, Inc., was attempting to formulate for the company a recapitalization plan that would enable him to obtain control of the corporation from the other two investor groups with whom he shared ownership and voting control at the time. The other stockholders had granted him options to purchase their shares at $150 a share, but Mr. Paxson had not yet been able to command the amount of funds required to exercise the options. He had recently struck on the idea of having the company exercise the options by repurchasing the shares of the other stockholders with borrowed funds, but wondered whether anyone would lend the company the estimated $5 million required on a net worth of only $5.25 million.

Later in the day, Paul Brewer, vice president of the National Commerce Bank, was going to be in Mr. Paxson's office. With the exception of seasonal loans, the company had required only limited bank financing in the past, but Mr. Brewer had mentioned on several occasions the bank's readiness to consider requests for more extensive borrowing on appropriate terms when it was needed. Mr. Paxson's invitation "to discuss the company's future financing requirements" had elicited a prompt response from Mr. Brewer.

BUSINESS

Since its organization in 1955, Quality Plastics, Inc., had been engaged in the production and sale of high-pressure decorative laminated plastic sheets characterized by a hard surface resistant to impact and deterioration. The company offered these plastic sheets in a wide variety of patterns, colors, and surface textures in sizes up to 60 square feet. They were sold for use principally as decorative coverings for sinks and countertops, school desks, and other furniture. In the company's plant, layers of heavy kraft paper impregnated with resins were bonded together by simultaneous application of heat and high pressure in three heavy-duty laminating presses. Resin impregnation of all papers used by the company was performed in the company's own treating department.

The company's primary effort was directed toward the production and sale of its own laminated plastic, but it also sold resin impregnated paper to other companies, which carried on their own laminating processes. Sales of laminated plastic accounted for 95% of the company's revenues for the 6 months ended April 30, 1964; the remainder represented sales of impregnated paper. The company's plastic sheets were sold by its own salesmen, principally to original equipment manufacturers and distributors. Inventories were maintained in six regional warehouses leased in major cities around the country, as well as at the plant. Shipments to these warehouses were made in the company's fleet of eight leased trucks.

COMPETITION

Mr. Paxson did not know the company's position among producers of decorative laminated plastic because no reliable statistics were available. Strong competition on the basis of design, quality, price, and service came from several large manufacturers, including Formica Corporation (a division of American Cyanamid Company), Westinghouse Electric Corporation, Pioneer Plastics Corporation, and General Electric Company. None of Quality Plastics' processes were patented.

FINANCIAL PERFORMANCE

Sales of Quality Plastics had grown to an annual rate of $10 million by the end of the 1963 fiscal year, and annual profits exceeded $1 million (see Exhibit 1). The tremendous financial success of the company was indicated by the fact that each share purchased by the original investors in 1955 for $10 earned $17.50 during fiscal 1963. Mr. Paxson felt that achievement of this success in a highly competitive market was due in large part to the unusual degree of dedication of the company's employees, who were prepared to make considerable personal sacrifices when necessary in order to meet the corporation's commitments.

None of the original investors in Quality Plastics had need of dividends, so most of the company's earnings had been retained to help finance the company's rapid expansion. The modest $1 per share annual dividend paid in recent years was increased in late 1963 to reflect the growing level of corporate profits, but the payout in 1964 remained low (see Exhibit 1).

EXPANSION PLANS

Mr. Paxson hoped to be able to broaden the company's product line at some time in the future to include other laminated plastic covering materials, such as decorative wall coverings. In his judgment, however, a more pressing program was enlargement of the manufacturing facilities and an adjacent warehouse to enable the company to meet its future production and inventory requirements of existing products. The production facilities normally operated with three eight-hour shifts per day on a five-day workweek. On the basis of normal operations, it was estimated that for the past 12 months there had been an annual production capacity of approximately 45 million square feet and that 80.4% of this capacity was utilized during the period. Exhibit 2 presents the company's annual production since its founding in 1955.

Included in the company's expansion plans were an addition to the existing plant, the purchase of a new laminating press, and purchase of other equipment to increase annual capacity for production of plastic sheets by approximately 25 million square feet. Mr. Paxson hoped this expansion program would be completed by late 1966, and he believed the estimated expenditure of $1.5 million could be financed without additional borrowing.

OWNERSHIP AND CONTROL

Since the formation of Quality Plastics in 1955, control of the corporation had been exercised on behalf of the shareholders by nine trustees. Control was vested in these trustees by the Voting Trust and Pooling Agreement drawn up on December 21, 1955, for the purpose of protecting the financial interests of the three shareholder groups who originally formed the corporation. These three previously unacquainted groups—the Paxson interest was one—were brought together by a common desire to invest in a company with growth possibilities. It was finally decided to form a corporation to make decorative laminated plastic, and Mr. Paxson was installed as president because his previous experience in operating a similar business made him uniquely qualified to organize and develop such an undertaking.

The company was originally capitalized at $600,000. Each of the three groups agreed to purchase at par one third of the 60,000 shares of $10 par common stock to be issued by the new corporation, and to become party to the Voting Trust and Pooling Agreement drawn up for the following reasons, as expressed in the trust deed:

It is deemed important to the interests of the subscribers to create a Trust with the shareholding body as beneficiaries thereof, in order that stock of said company shall not be liable to be bought up for speculative control, and to secure safe and prudent management in the interests of the whole number of stockholders. . . .

The termination date of the trust was set at 10 years from its inception, in order to conform with the state law. The important provisions of the document can be summarized as follows.

1. All voting power was vested in the hands of three trustees from each group, elected by the shareholders of that group.
2. Beneficial ownership was represented by voting trust certificates that entitled the holder to all the benefits of the trust agreement, including a proportionate share of all dividends paid, less a proportionate share of the expenses of the trust.
3. The principal powers of the trustees were expressed in the trust deed as follows.

The subscribers hereby constitute and appoint the said Trustees, and their successors in office, their, and each of their, true and lawful attorneys and proxies to appear for, represent and vote for them at all meetings of the stock-holders of said company, with power to vote upon any and all questions which may arise at any such meeting or meetings, including the sale or mortgage of the entire franchise, assets and property of the corporation, or the dissolution of such corporation, as fully and with the same effect as the said subscribers, or any of them, if personally present, could do; and if any difference of opinion should arise among said Trustees or their successors as to the proper vote to be cast, then the voice of three-fourths of said Trustees shall govern; and it shall not be necessary for said Trustees to assemble together to consider any proposition, nor for all of said Trustees to attend all meetings of stockholders, but the wishes of such absent Trustee or Trustees shall be evidenced by a writing signed by such absent Trustee or Trustees, and the said Trustees and their successors are hereby authorized to designate some one of their number to actually cast the vote which all of said Trustees, by reason of their being joint stockholders, shall be entitled to cast.

4. The trustees were empowered to admit to the benefits of the trust, on an equal footing with the original parties, any stockholders who might desire to become a party to the agreement if there was an issue of stock to outsiders.

5. Termination of the trust prior to December 20, 1965, required the consent of the holders of a three-fourths interest in the voting trust certificates.

6. Legal title to all stock transferred under the agreement remained vested in the trustees.

7. If a certificate holder wanted to sell any of his shares and received an offer in good faith from someone not a party to the agreement, he was required to notify the other parties to the trust and allow them the right of first refusal at the same price and terms for at least 30 days. Furthermore, other parties to the trust had a right to participate in the sale to the outside party to the extent of their pro rata share of ownership of the total number of shares held in the voting trust.

THE PAXSON INTEREST

Mr. Paxson's financial interest in Quality Plastics took several forms. As of May 5, 1964, Mr. Paxson held in his own name voting trust certificates representing 12.2% of the outstanding shares of the corporation. Certificates representing another 30.5% were held in the names of other members of his family and a family trust, the Robert Paxson Trust (see Exhibit 3). As president and a director of the corporation, Mr. Paxson received for the year ended October 31, 1963, aggregate direct remuneration of $137,570, of which the major portion was a profit-sharing bonus. Two other members of his family serving as executive officers received for the same period remuneration totaling $126,104. Details are given in Exhibit 4. The board of directors had conferred on Mr. Paxson full and complete authority in the allocation of the profit-sharing bonus. Mr. Paxson was also part owner of the real estate corporation from which the plant facilities were leased, and the owner of properties leased by the company in another city. Lease payments on these two properties totaled $7,350 monthly.

RECENT DEVELOPMENTS

Late in February, 1964, one of the major shareholders of Quality Plastics had received a bona fide offer from an investment firm to purchase his interest at $150 per share. This was not the first time the same firm had attempted to buy into the company, and it was suspected that a bid for control would follow if inroads were successfully made in this manner. When the rest of the shareholders were polled in accordance with the terms of the Voting Trust and Pooling Agreement, it was found that several of them wished to participate in the selling rather than acquire their pro rata share of the stock offered for sale.

Mr. Paxson originally had hoped to deal with the problem of thwarting the outsider's bid for control by channeling the shares offered for sale into friendly hands. By the end of February, the Paxson family had purchased from members of the other two shareholder groups voting trust certificates for 4,398 shares at $150 for a total of $660,000, increasing the family's holdings to 42.7% of outstanding shares. Mr. Paxson also obtained options to purchase all the remaining shares at $150, although he was not sure at the time whether he would be able to find the funds required to exercise them. At the option price, $750,000 would have been required to increase the family's holdings from 42.7% to 51%, and more than $5 million to purchase 100% of the remaining shares. Included in the terms of the options was a provision that the selling shareholders would agree to vote for termination of the Voting Trust and Pooling Agreement if the options were exercised by Robert Paxson or his assigns. Mr. Paxson's attempts during March and April to place a majority of the remaining shares in friendly hands very nearly succeeded, but by late April it was apparent that he would have to find another means of exercising the options.

DEVELOPMENTS FOLLOWING MAY 5, 1964

The May 5 meeting with Mr. Brewer of the National Commerce Bank ended on a cordial note. Mr. Paxson's suggestion that the bank lend Quality Plastics the money required for a stock repurchase had caught Mr. Brewer by surprise. Before the meeting was over, however, he had examined the company's operating statements (see Exhibit 1) and balance sheet as of April 30, 1964 (see Exhibit 5), and had indicated a willingness to pursue the matter further if Mr. Paxson would consider obtaining a large portion of the funds required through a new equity issue. When Mr. Paxson reiterated his concern about losing control of the company, Mr. Brewer pointed out that it might be possible to develop a satisfactory compromise by obtaining a portion of the additional funds required through the issuance of debt subordinated to the bank claims. Subordination of this additional debt to the bank claims would not relieve Mr. Paxson of the responsibility for demonstrating the company's capacity to meet all its contractual obligations, however, since default on any of these could lead to an impairment of the company's ability to meet its commitments to the bank. Mr. Brewer explained that unless the assumption of increasing volume could be made very convincing, the bank would request Mr. Paxson to submit a cash flow forecast based upon the current volume of sales.

As Mr. Paxson reviewed the results of his conversation with Mr. Brewer, he became increasingly aware of the complexity of the network of alternatives facing him. For example, there was the matter of determining to what extent a mixture of equity and subordinated debt might improve his chances of gaining control. Against this potential advantage, he would have to weigh the additional risk the company would incur by taking on more debt. He realized also that it might not be easy to place an issue of subordinated debt. There were the alternatives of attempting a public offering, attempting a private placement, paying some of the other shareholders subordinated debentures for their shares, or attempting to sell a package of subordinated debt and equity in a public or private offering. He also wondered whether or not he should consider offering a conversion privilege on the subordinated debt in order to make it more attractive to potential investors. Mr. Paxson felt he would probably be able to evaluate the alternatives open to him in terms of their effect on his control of the corporation, but he felt less sure of his ability to evaluate the risks involved and very unsure of how he should go about calculating the costs of the various alternatives.

On May 6, Mr. Paxson received a call from Mr. Brewer, suggesting a meeting with Philip Montgomery, a partner in the investment banking firm of Kieth, Whitney & Co.

At the meeting on May 13 with Mr. Brewer and Mr. Montgomery, Mr. Paxson reopened the question of using subordinated debt to raise a portion of the funds required. Neither Mr. Brewer nor Mr. Montgomery seemed interested in pursuing this possibility, however, and the issue was dropped. It seemed the two men had discussed the matter earlier, but the reasons for dismissing subordinated debt as an alternative were never made clear to Mr. Paxson.

Mr. Montgomery pointed out that it would be virtually impossible for the company to precisely synchronize the stock repurchase and sale of new shares. Mr. Brewer then explained that his bank was prepared to consider providing the short-term financing required to bridge the period between the repurchase of shares and the acquisition of new capital. Because of the circumstances of the loan, the rate charged would probably be 5% or more.

Mr. Brewer stated further that the bank was also considering provision of some of the long-term capital required, contingent on a successful stock offering. On the basis of his preliminary studies, he estimated that the National Commerce Bank would be willing to lend the company as much as $2 million for as long as 10 years at a rate of 5–6% if suitable covenants for protecting the bank's position could be included in the loan agreement. The bank probably would not be interested in the assignment of specific assets, but would require the maintenance of working capital in excess of the amount of the loan, and a current ratio of 2 to 1. The company might also have to limit dividend payments and executive compensation so that its ability to meet contractual obligations would not be impaired. The company would be required to regularly submit audited financial statements to the bank, and it might have to agree to some covenants limiting its ability to dispose of assets and take on additional debt.

Mr. Montgomery then stated that his preliminary appraisal of Quality Plastics suggested that a public offering could be successful at roughly 15–16 times 1963 earnings if the price were in the popular $12–$25 range. He added that issues of fewer than 200,000–300,000 shares were often too small to sustain active trading, making such issues more difficult to sell. Mr. Montgomery estimated that the fixed costs of a stock issue of $3–$5 million would be about $75,000. The underwriter's spread would be in the range of 7.5–10%.

Mr. Montgomery suggested that Mr. Paxson give some thought to the type of shareholder he hoped to interest in Quality Plastics and the type of concessions he might have to make in order to stimulate this interest. The areas suggested for consideration were dividend policy, organization of the board of directors, authority concerning the profit-sharing bonus and other forms of executive compensation, and the authority to issue additional shares of common stock in the future.

Mr. Brewer concluded the meeting by suggesting that Mr. Paxson prepare the following as a basis for further discussion:

1. A forecast of funds flow from operations, assuming current sales volume, with a supplementary schedule of current contractual obligations and other major expenses likely to remain fixed in the ordinary course of business (such as maintenance).
2. A plan for recapitalizing the company based on the following assumptions:
   a) The other shareholders could be bought out at a price of $150 per share.
   b) Necessary bridge financing could be obtained from the bank at a cost of 5%.
   c) The bank would lend up to $2 million long-term, as discussed at the meeting.

Mr. Paxson felt that the meeting with Mr. Brewer and Mr. Montgomery was a good start. He was not satisfied with their quick dismissal of the subordinated debt alternative, however. If he could gain control of the corporation with a smaller number of shares, he might be able to sell off some of his own holdings for cash in order to liquidate the debts he was incurring in buying out other shareholders. Although Mr. Paxson wished to retain as many shares as possible, it appeared that he might incur personal debts totaling more than $750,000 before the reorganization was completed. Any profits realized on the sale of shares acquired by Mr. Paxson after March 1 would be taxed as short-term capital gains if the sale was consummated before September 1.

Exhibit 1

QUALITY PLASTICS, INC.

STATEMENT OF INCOME, YEARS ENDED OCTOBER 31, 1956–63, AND 6-MONTH
PERIODS ENDED APRIL 30, 1963 AND 1964
(Dollar Figures in Thousands)

| | Year Ended October 31 | | | | | | | | 6 Months Ended | |
									April 30 1963	April 30 1964
	1956	1957	1958	1959	1960	1961	1962	1963		
Sales: less discounts and allowances	$679	$2,049	$3,698	$6,322	$6,981	$7,737	$8,516	$9,747	$4,360	$5,429
Costs and expenses:										
Cost of sales	523	1,396	2,220	3,737	4,244	4,647	4,915	5,295	2,429	2,926
Selling and warehousing expense	69	245	355	599	770	797	916	1,136	519	706
General administrative expense	73	225	348	518	562	712	819	1,009	460	512
Interest	4	18	15	21	42	43	25	16	10	5
	$668	$1,884	$2,938	$4,875	$5,617	$6,198	$6,674	$7,456	$3,417	$4,149
Income before federal income tax	$11	$165	$760	$1,448	$1,364	$1,539	$1,842	$2,291	$943	$1,281
Provision for federal income tax	3	82	390	747	685	838	993	1,239	513	650
Net Income	$8	$84	$370	$700	$679	$701	$849	$1,052	$430	$630
Dividends paid		$60	$60	$60	$60	$60	$60	$60	$30	$75
Supplementary profit and loss information:										
Maintenance and repairs						$63	$73	$109	…	$67
Depreciation of plant and equipment						253	229	214	…	108
Taxes other than federal income						76	90	118	…	98
Rents:										
Real property*						91	102	110	…	60
Automotive property†						158	186	192	…	110

* Approximately $72,000 charged to cost of sales in each 12-month period, and $36,000 for the 6-month period ended April 30, 1964.
† 100% charged to cost of sales.
Details may not add to totals because of rounding.

Exhibit 2

QUALITY PLASTICS, INC.

PRODUCTION OF LAMINATED PLASTIC SHEET
(Square Feet in Millions)

Fiscal Year Ended	Actual Production
October 31, 1956	2.7
1957	5.9
1958	9.5
1959	16.4
1960	18.4
1961	21.6
1962	25.7
1963	30.5

Exhibit 3

QUALITY PLASTICS, INC.

TRUST CERTIFICATES OWNED BY THE PAXSON FAMILY

	Owned in Name of Robert Paxson	Owned by Paxson Family*
At January 1, 1964:		
No. of shares	2,934	21,222
% of total shares outstanding	4.9%	35.4%
At May 5, 1964:		
No. of shares	7,332	25,620
% of total shares outstanding	12.2%	42.7%

* Includes Robert Paxson.
NOTE.—60,000 shares outstanding.

Exhibit 4

QUALITY PLASTICS, INC.

MANAGEMENT COMPENSATION DURING YEAR ENDED OCTOBER 31, 1963

Name*	Capacity in which Remuneration Was Received	Other Executive Offices Held in the Corporation	Aggregate Direct Remuneration‡	Components of Direct Remuneration	
				Basic Salary Rate	Profit-Sharing Bonus†
Robert Paxson	Director and president	Chairman of the board	$137,570	$24,000	$113,570
Edgar Paxson	Director and vice president	Secretary-treasurer	57,402	10,200	47,202
Norman Paxson	Director and vice president	....	68,702	18,500	50,202
Donald Sullivan	Vice president	Director	65,702	18,000	47,702
All Directors and Officers as a group§			$334,876	$70,700	$262,868

* With the exception of Edgar Paxson, all officers had been active in management since the company's formation. Edgar Paxson had been employed in an executive capacity on a fulltime basis since September, 1960.

† The Profit-Sharing Bonus account was computed as follows: Bonus Account = 13.5% × Annual Income before federal income taxes, management bonuses, and contribution to the profit-sharing retirement plan. The total bonus account for the year ended October 31, 1963 was $374,518; $262,858 was paid to officers and the remainder to other employees.

‡ In addition to direct remuneration, four officers benefited from a profit-sharing retirement program as follows:

	Amounts Set Aside or Accrued under Profit-Sharing Retirement Program	
	Accrued During Year Ended 10/31/63	Total Accrued at 10/31/63
Robert Paxson	$1,812	$ 9,106
Edgar Paxson	866	3,332
Norman Paxson	1,406	7,036
Donald Sullivan	1,370	6,837
All Directors and Officers as a Group	$5,454	$26,311

§ Figures cannot be completely reconciled because of minor omissions.

Exhibit 5

QUALITY PLASTICS, INC.

BALANCE SHEET AS OF APRIL 30, 1964
(Dollar Figures in Thousands)

ASSETS

Current assets:

Cash			$1,370
Receivables:			
Accounts receivable		$2,242	
Notes receivable within one year		384	
		$2,626	
Less allowance for doubtful accounts		200	2,426
Inventories			1,637
Prepaid expenses			94
Total Current Assets			$5,528
Notes receivable due after one year			280
Property, plant, and equipment at cost:			
Land			14
Building and improvements			122
Machinery and equipment			1,825
Leasehold improvements			257
			$2,218
Less: Accumulated depreciation			1,204
			$1,013
Total Assets			$6,821

LIABILITIES AND STOCKHOLDERS' EQUITY

Current liabilities:

Accounts payable	$ 361
Federal income tax	820
Accrued employee bonuses and profit-sharing contribution	270
Other liabilities	116
Total Current Liabilities	$1,568
Commitments (Note A)	
Stockholders' equity:	
Common stock, $10 par value; 60,000 shares authorized and issued	600
Capital in excess of par value	. . .
Retained earnings	4,653
Total stockholders' equity	$5,253
Total Liabilities and Stockholders' Equity	$6,821

NOTE A.—Annual rent commitments under various long-term leases were approximately as follows: Fiscal years through 1971, $120,000; 1972 and 1973, $100,000.

Details may not add to totals because of rounding.

Chapter 9 Acquisitions and Mergers

AMALGAMATED MANUFACTURING CORPORATION

THE AMALGAMATED MANUFACTURING CORPORATION was a large manufacturer of heavy industrial equipment; its main headquarters and production facilities were located in the metropolitan Chicago area. The company had grown over a long period of years with its principal sales volume in a specialized line of industrial equipment. This line accounted for more than half of its 1964 sales volume. In recent years, technological developments had limited sales of new equipment in this major line of the company's production, and it seemed unlikely that original equipment sales would expand beyond their 1965 volume. While the demand for replacement parts would remain high for several years to come, it would eventually be limited by the cessation of growth and possible decline in the sale of new equipment.

The management of Amalgamated was thus confronted with the difficult task of maintaining a satisfactory rate of growth in the overall volume of the company's sales and earnings. Two main strategies were adopted. One was to intensify the company's research and development efforts in product lines that had previously accounted for a relatively small portion of Amalgamated's total volume but seemed to offer more promising opportunities for long-term growth than its main line of industrial equipment. The second was to inaugurate a vigorous search for companies Amalgamated might acquire in industries other than its main product line. The successful implementation of these strategies explains, in part, Amalgamated's growth in recent years (Exhibit 1) and its sound financial position at the end of 1964 (Exhibit 2).

Amalgamated was particularly interested in acquiring small companies with promising products and management personnel but without established growth records. The management of Amalgamated hoped to be able to acquire several such companies each year, preferably before their earning capacity had been sufficiently well established to command a premium price. In this way, Amalgamated hoped over a period of years to build a broad base for expansion and diversification.

The management of Amalgamated was aware that the potential rate of growth of many small companies was limited by inadequate capital resources and distribution systems. Amalgamated's management was convinced that its abundant capital resources and its nationwide distribution system could greatly facilitate the growth of many such companies. Consequently, Amalgamated was hopeful that it would be able to acquire promising small companies on terms that would be mutually attractive because of the complementary character of the contributions Amalgamated and any small companies it might acquire could make to the combined enterprise.

In following the strategy of expanding in part through acquisitions, Amalgamated's management recognized that a variety of problems would be encountered. Such a policy would have to be in accord with the rather strict interpretation by the Supreme Court and the Justice Department of allowable mergers or acquisitions under the antitrust laws. Among other things, this would mean that most of the companies to be acquired by Amalgamated would have to be small in size. Even so, only a few companies could be acquired in any one year. Consequently, if these acquisitions were to have a significant impact on Amalgamated's growth rate it was important that wise decisions be made in selecting the companies to be purchased from the many potentially available for acquisition. The management of Amalgamated anticipated that for each one it should attempt to acquire, many companies might have to be screened.

(There are, of course, many facets to any decision concerning a potential acquisition. Among the most important is the caliber of the management of the company to be acquired, provided that the old management is expected to remain. Likewise, the qualities of the company's product line, research capabilities, and patent position, if any, are a prime consideration. Others are the degree to which the products of the two companies would mesh and the extent to which the value of the acquired company would be enhanced by an association with an established company. The acceptability of the acquisition under the antitrust laws would also have to be evaluated.)

Even after a prospective acquisition had passed the preliminary screening tests established by Amalgamated's management, there still remained the difficult task of determining the maximum offering price that would be placed on the stock or assets of the company to be acquired. Until such an evaluation was made, serious negotiations with the potential sellers could not commence.

In order to apply consistent standards and to minimize the work load, the financial staff of Amalgamated had been requested by its top management to work out a standardized procedure that would be used in evaluating potential acquisitions. The method used in evaluating the Norwood Screw Machinery Company, discussed below, is typical of that ordinarily used by Amalgamated.

The remainder of the case will very briefly describe the Norwood Screw Machinery Company, and then will discuss in more detail the method by which Amalgamated's financial staff arrived at a figure to recommend to management as a possible maximum purchase price. Not all the management members were convinced of the validity of the evaluation method currently being used by Amalgamated. The final section of the case briefly outlines the doubts expressed by these members.

NORWOOD SCREW MACHINERY COMPANY

The Norwood Screw Machinery Company was a relatively small company with a diversified line of screw machinery products. It had a plant with approximately 75,000 square feet, and employed about 75 persons. Its sales organization was rudimentary. In the opinion of both the Norwood and Amalgamated managements, this was one explanation for Norwood's relatively low volume of sales and profits.

Amalgamated had an interest in acquiring Norwood, if a satisfactory price could be agreed on, because Amalgamated was favorably impressed by the quality of Norwood's management and by its promising product lines. Norwood manufactured various standard screw machine products for which competition was severe and growth prospects were limited. It also had several proprietary products on which it earned a much higher rate of profit and from which it expected to achieve substantial growth. In addition, Norwood had several promising products scheduled to be put on the market in the near future. These items—several revolutionary by industry standards—were expected to make a major contribution to Norwood's future growth. The management of Norwood also anticipated production process improvements that would increase its gross margin on sales above the relatively high level already prevailing.

Preliminary negotiations toward an acquisition of Norwood by Amalgamated were begun in mid-1965. The management of Amalgamated had considerable confidence in the quality of Norwood's management and shared its hopes that Norwood would be successful in developing new and improved products. Both managements believed that by the combined organization Norwood's products could be marketed much more successfully than by Norwood acting alone.

Amalgamated's information as to other aspects of Norwood's operations was much more scanty. Norwood had furnished Amalgamated with audited financial statements only for the year ending December 31, 1964 (Exhibits 3 and 4). The financial staff of Amalgamated was informed that the deficit in the retained earnings account (Exhibit 4) and the negligible charge against net income for income tax accruals (Exhibit 3) resulted from operating losses incurred in 1962 and 1963. These losses, however, were attributed to temporary conditions and were not regarded by the management of either company as indicative of Norwood's potential future earning capacity. Preliminary unaudited statements for the first 7 months of 1965 showed sales of approximately $550,000 and profits before taxes of about $100,000.

The management of Amalgamated recognized that a much more thorough examination would be necessary before a firm offer could be made to Norwood for the acquisition of its stock or assets. Among other things, much more detailed financial information would be needed for the years preceding 1964 and for the first part of 1965. Other aspects of Norwood's operations, such as the strength of its patent position, would also have to be subjected to detailed scrutiny by Amalgamated. In the meanwhile, however, preliminary negotiations were instituted. In connection with these negotiations, Amalgamated's financial staff was requested by its top management to prepare, using the limited information then available, an estimate of the maximum price at which Amalgamated might consider acquiring Norwood. Such an estimate might help to determine whether the probability that a deal could be worked out was high enough to justify the detailed examination of Norwood that would have to be undertaken before Amalgamated could make a firm offer.

AMALGAMATED'S METHOD OF EVALUATING ACQUISITIONS

Basic Approach

As previously noted, Amalgamated's financial staff had worked out a fairly standardized method of evaluating potential acquisitions. This value was calculated by discounting at Amalgamated's cost of capital the future cash flow to be derived from the acquisition. The present worth of this future cash flow was the maximum price that Amalgamated would be willing to pay for an acquisition.

The future cash flow of a potential acquisition was obtained by forecasting the future profits, working capital, capital expenditures, depreciation, and other items affecting the cash flow to be derived from the acquisition. The financial staff reviewed these forecasts with other Amalgamated personnel who were familiar with the products and with the industry of the company under consideration.

Forecast of Future Cash Flows

Typically, three forecasts were considered in evaluating a company: an optimistic forecast (quite often the forecast submitted by the company to be purchased); a "most likely" forecast (the one that qualified Amalgamated personnel believed most likely to be realized); and, finally, a minimum forecast (the one that reflected the minimum growth to be reasonably expected from the potential acquisition). The cash flow resulting from each of these forecasts was then discounted at Amalgamated's cost of capital to arrive at a range of values for the company.

Although these three sets of forecasts were normally prepared, the management usually decided on the terms to be offered for a potential acquisition on the basis of the minimum forecast. This procedure was used because management had found that very frequently the *actual* growth rate of its acquisitions had not been so rapid as the minimum forecast.

As an illustration of the divergence often reflected in these forecasts, the president of Norwood estimated that the annual increase in sales would be about $400,000 a year for the next 3 years under *Norwood's* management, but the annual rate of growth could be as large as $2 million if *Amalgamated* were to acquire Norwood. In contrast, the minimum forecast made by Amalgamated's staff for the same three years, on the assumption that Amalgamated acquired Norwood, projected a growth in sales averaging about one third as large as that estimated by Norwood's management. This staff forecast, shown in Exhibit 5, assumes that Amalgamated would acquire Norwood at the beginning of 1966.

Amalgamated's normal procedure was to forecast for a five-year period the cash flows to be used in its evaluation. It then held constant the cash flow predicted for years 6 to 10. The staff preparing the forecasts recognized that this procedure introduced a conservative factor in its evaluation, but this element of conservatism was thought desirable as a means of counterbalancing the tendency, cited above, to overestimate the growth rate for the first five years. Finally, in year 10 a terminal value was placed on the company to be acquired. In effect, then, Amalgamated's procedure valued a potential acquisition as the sum of the present worth of the cash flow to be realized over the next 10 years, plus the present worth of the terminal value at the end of the 10th year.

Assignment of Terminal Value

The decision to use a terminal value at the end of the 10th year was prompted by 2 factors. First, it was recognized that normally Amalgamated would still own a company that cash flows would be derived from and that would, therefore, be of value to Amalgamated at the end of the 10-year period. Second, it seemed impractical to Amalgamated to attempt to forecast cash flows for a period longer than 10 years.

In the past, Amalgamated had used several different approaches to set a terminal value on a potential acquisition at the end of the 10th year. These approaches included: (1) the book value of the acquired company at this date; (2) its liquidating value at this date—that is, an estimate of the value of its assets, but not as a going concern; and (3) a value based on an estimated sale of the acquired company at a specified multiple of earnings at the end of the 10th year.

However, Amalgamated's staff recognized that each of these procedures had serious limitations. Book value and liquidating value often would not reflect the worth of a company based on its present and potential earnings. The sale of a company at a specified multiple of 10th-year earnings was regarded as a more adequate reflection of the company's value in that year. The possible tax adjustments resulting from capital gains or losses arising from the sale, as well as the appropriate price–earnings multiplier for each company, were recognized as presenting additional complications for this method of determining a terminal value. Furthermore, Amalgamated's staff was concerned about a possible internal contradiction in this approach to the problem. It reasoned that to value the company in the 10th year at a specified price–earnings multiplier would be somewhat unrealistic: if the company's performance were satisfactory, Amalgamated probably would not be willing to sell; if its performance were poor, Amalgamated probably would not be able to obtain the value indicated by the price–earnings multiplier.

At the time of the Norwood evaluation, Amalgamated's staff was using a somewhat different approach. The terminal value of the company in year 10 was assumed to be the present worth of 20 years of additional cash flow. The annual rate of cash flow for years 11 through 30 was normally assumed to be equal to that for years 6 to 10, with the possible exception of adjustments for certain noncash expenses such as those shown in Exhibit 5. This procedure was believed to reflect more satisfactorily Amalgamated's intention in making an acquisition, that is, to realize a satisfactory cash flow over the long run.

Obviously, an assignment of a terminal value based on a discounting of the estimated cash flows (or earnings) from years 11 through 30 would not necessarily require Amalgamated to retain the company for 30 years in order for the acquisition to be profitable. For example, if Amalgamated could sell an acquisition at the end of the 10th year for the calculated terminal value, then, disregarding possible capital gains taxes, the investment would be just as profitable as it would be if the assumed 20 years of additional earnings were realized in years 11–30. The Amalgamated procedure ignored years beyond year 30 because their contribution to the present worth of the terminal value with a discount rate as high as 10%, or thereabouts, would be negligible.

Working Capital and Capital Expenditures

In determining the cash flows that would be caused by an acquisition, estimates also had to be made of changes in working capital requirements and of prospective capital outlays. If no better evidence was available, working capital requirements for a proposed acquisition were based on a historical analysis of relevant financial ratios of the company or industry for previous years. Expenditures on fixed assets were estimated at a level designed to maintain physical facilities in good working order and to handle the projected increases in sales volume.

Since sales volume was estimated to increase only for the first five years, as noted above, working capital requirements were generally considered to remain constant after year five. A typical assumption with respect to capital expenditures was that they would be equal to depreciation outlays after year five. The Norwood evaluation was made in this manner (Exhibit 5).

Treatment of Debt

Amalgamated's financial staff eliminated debt from the capital structure of potential acquisitions by assuming in its cash flow estimates that this debt would be paid off in full in year zero. As a corollary, interest charges associated with this debt were also eliminated from the estimates of cash outflows for subsequent years. The rationale for this treatment of debt and associated interest charges was that the future earnings of an acquisition should not be benefited by the use of leverage in the capital structure. This treatment was designed to permit all potential acquisitions to be evaluated on a comparable basis.

Estimate of Cost of Capital

At the time of the Norwood acquisition, Amalgamated's practice was to discount its cash flow estimates for future years at a rate of 10%. This figure was assumed to be an approximation of Amalgamated's cost of equity capital. As Exhibit 2 indicates, Amalgamated's capital structure consisted almost entirely of common equity. Management, however, was not committed to such a capital structure as a matter of company policy; it was, in fact, actively considering the possible benefits that might be derived from having a larger proportion of senior capital in its capital structure.

Application of Above Procedure to Norwood

Exhibit 5 shows in detail how Amalgamated's procedure was applied in the evaluation of Norwood. The cash flow from Norwood was calculated first by estimating after-tax profits in years 1 to 10, and then adding back noncash expenses, such as depreciation and amortization. From this sum, the cash required for additions to working capital and new capital expenditures was subtracted. In addition, all long-term debt was assumed to be retired at the beginning of 1966 and was shown as an initial outlay. The resulting total represents the estimated cash contribution to be derived from Norwood over the 10-year period beginning January 1, 1966. The cash contribution of each year was then discounted at 10% to obtain an estimate of the present worth of contributions from operations over the next 10 years. The estimated terminal value of Norwood at the end of year 10 was then computed as the present worth of 20 additional years of earnings, that is, the earnings of years 11–30 discounted to year 0 at 10%. The sum of the estimated present worth of the contribution from operations for the first 10 years and the present worth of the terminal value assigned to Norwood represents Amalgamated's estimate of the purchase price it would be justified in paying for all the outstanding stock of Norwood. This sum amounted to $4.465 million for Norwood (Exhibit 5).

VIEWS OF OTHER MEMBERS OF AMALGAMATED'S MANAGEMENT

Although the evaluation procedure described in the preceding section was that currently used by Amalgamated, its merits were still under active debate within the company. Some management members, for example, thought that in evaluating a potential acquisition more emphasis should be placed on the effect on Amalgamated's earnings per share. Mr. Simpson, a company director who was especially interested in Amalgamated's acquisition program, shared this view and vigorously contended that the $4.465 million price for Norwood, as calculated in Exhibit 5, was far too high. He prepared the following illustrative data to support his position.

Hypothetical levels of profits after taxes to be derived from Norwood. .$	100,000	$ 200,000	$300,000	$ 400,000
Approximate earnings per share of Amalgamated without acquisition of Norwood.....................	$5	$5	$5	$5
Number of shares of Amalgamated's stock that could be exchanged for all outstanding shares of Norwood without diluting Amalgamated's earnings per share...............	20,000	40,000	60,000	80,000
Approximate market value of Amalgamated's common stock at time of contemplated acquisition..........	$50	$50	$50	$50
Implicit value placed on Norwood by earnings-per-share criterion........	$1,000,000	$2,000,000	$3,000,000	$4,000,000

Mr. Simpson pointed out that even if Norwood's profits after taxes were assumed to expand to $400,000—far in excess of its 1964 or probable 1965 level—the acquisition would result in a dilution of Amalgamated's earnings per share. In no circumstances, he contended, could Norwood's earnings expand sufficiently to overcome this dilution in earnings per share for at least several years. While Mr. Simpson did not deny that Norwood was a promising young company, he argued that no one could foresee the future well enough to predict with confidence that Norwood's profits after taxes would soon reach or exceed a level of $400,000 or $500,000, the minimum range needed to prevent a dilution in Amalgamated's earnings per share.

In this connection, Mr. Simpson urged that his numerical illustration was highly conservative in that it assumed no growth in Amalgamated's future earnings per share. In fact, the $5 figure understated reported earnings in 1964, and even more so the projected earnings for 1965. A reasonable allowance for the growth in Amalgamated's earnings per share over the next several years, he pointed out, would require that Norwood's profits after taxes be substantially larger than the top figure of $400,000 shown in his numerical illustration in order to prevent a dilution in Amalgamated's earnings per share for an indefinite and possibly permanent period.

The proponents of the discounted cash flow method of evaluating acquisitions such as Norwood conceded to Mr. Simpson that it would be preferable for Amalgamated to acquire Norwood for cash rather than by an exchange of stock. But they pointed out to him that since Amalgamated was in a highly liquid position an outright purchase for cash was feasible. Thus, Amalgamated's earnings per share would increase provided that the return on Amalgamated's investment in Norwood exceeded that available from money market securities.

Mr. Simpson responded that he recognized the validity of this argument if the Norwood acquisition was viewed in isolation. As a general principle, however, he stated that Norwood should be considered as one of a series of companies Amalgamated hoped to acquire each year. Mr. Simpson pointed out that while Amalgamated could probably acquire Norwood without resorting to outside financing, such financing would be required if Amalgamated were to vigorously press its planned program of acquisitions. He concluded, therefore, that the Norwood acquisition should be required to pass the same earnings-per-share hurdle he felt would have to be applied to subsequent acquisitions. In summary, then, Mr. Simpson continued to press his original contention, namely, that Norwood should be acquired only if the price was such that no dilution in earnings per share would result if the acquisition was made by an exchange of stock. The most he would concede was that a reasonable time should be allowed so that Norwood's profits would reflect the anticipated benefits from the combined operation before calculating the effect on Amalgamated's earnings per share of acquiring or not acquiring Norwood.

Other influential members of Amalgamated's management were concerned about the impact of the Norwood acquisition on Amalgamated's return on its book investment. They pointed out that Amalgamated was currently earning approximately 8% on the book value of its equity capital. If Norwood were to be acquired for $4.5 million, it would have to earn about $360,000 after taxes to match this rate of return. At best, they contended, several years would pass before earnings of this amount could be reasonably anticipated. Meanwhile, the acquisition of Norwood would dilute Amalgamated's return on its book investment.

With these widely conflicting views regarding the appropriate means of evaluating potential acquisitions, all parties concerned were anxious to arrive at a consensus on the best procedure as soon as possible. Unless such a consensus were achieved, continuing differences of judgment were bound to occur. These differences would inevitably slow down the company's acquisition program. In addition, favorable opportunities might be rejected and poor ones accepted unless a consistent and defensible method of valuing potential acquisitions could be agreed on as company policy.

Exhibit 1

AMALGAMATED MANUFACTURING CORPORATION

SELECTED OPERATING DATA, 1960–64

Year	Net Sales*	Income after Taxes*	Earnings per Common Share	Dividends per Common Share	Market Price of Common Stock
1960	$157.8	$ 9.0	$3.87	$2.20	$33–57
1961	158.4	8.6	3.62	2.00	38–45
1962	167.0	8.2	3.41	2.00	38–54
1963	183.3	10.4	4.50	2.00	45–55
1964	200.6	11.8	5.11	2.00	45–55

* In millions of dollars.

Exhibit 2

AMALGAMATED MANUFACTURING CORPORATION

BALANCE SHEET AS OF DECEMBER 31, 1964
(In Thousands of Dollars)

ASSETS

Current assets:

Cash	$ 5,344
Marketable securities	8,752
Accounts and notes receivable	32,304
Inventories	48,674
Total Current Assets	$ 95,074
Net fixed assets	103,537
Patent rights and other intangibles	3,086
Other assets	2,304
Total Assets	$204,001

LIABILITIES AND STOCKHOLDERS' EQUITY

Current liabilities:

Accounts and notes payable	$ 13,458
Income taxes payable	9,649
Accrued expenses and other liabilities	4,529
Total Current Liabilities	$ 27,636
Other liabilities (provision for pensions, various reserve accounts, and minority interest)	20,258
Mortgage notes and other noncurrent liabilities	2,927
Total Liabilities	$ 50,821

Capital stock:

Preferred stock	8,478
Common stock	47,319
Retained earnings	97,383
Total Stockholders' Equity	$153,180
Total Liabilities and Stockholders' Equity	$204,001

Exhibit 3

AMALGAMATED MANUFACTURING CORPORATION

NORWOOD SCREW MACHINERY COMPANY
INCOME STATEMENT FOR YEAR ENDING DECEMBER 31, 1964
(In Thousands of Dollars)

Net sales	$729.4
Deduct: Cost of goods sold	334.8
Gross profit on sales	$394.6
Deduct: Selling and administrative expenses	252.6
Net operating income	$142.0
Other income less other deductions	14.2
Net profit before income taxes	$156.2
Provision for income taxes	7.8
Net Income	$148.4

Exhibit 4

AMALGAMATED MANUFACTURING CORPORATION

NORWOOD SCREW MACHINERY COMPANY
BALANCE SHEET AS OF DECEMBER 31, 1964
(In Thousands of Dollars)

ASSETS

Current assets:

Cash	$ 109
Accounts receivable	130
Inventories	484
Prepaid expenses	37
Total Current Assets	$ 760
Net plant and equipment	456
Patents and other intangibles	230
Miscellaneous other assets (including large fire loss claim)	218
Total Assets	$1,664

LIABILITIES AND STOCKHOLDERS' EQUITY

Current liabilities:

Accounts payable	$ 88
Advances from officers	84
Notes payable	116
Accrued expenses	19
Accrued taxes	26
Total Current Liabilities	$ 333
Long-term liabilities:	
Debentures payable	273
Total Liabilities	$ 606
Stockholders' equity:	
Common stock	154
Paid-in capital	1,260
Retained earnings (deficit)	(356)
Total Equity	$1,058
Total Liabilities and Equity	$1,664

Exhibit 5

AMALGAMATED MANUFACTURING CORPORATION

Norwood Acquisition Study, Evaluation of Company

(In thousands of dollars)

	Initial Outlay	1966	1967	1968	1969	1970	1971	1972	1973	1974	1975	Total
I. OPERATING STATEMENT												
Net sales		$1,866	$2,500	$3,200	$3,800	$4,400	$4,400	$4,400	$4,400	$4,400	$4,400	$37,766
Cost of sales		840	1,050	1,280	1,444	1,672	1,672	1,672	1,672	1,672	1,672	14,646
Gross profit		$1,026	$1,450	$1,920	$2,356	$2,728	$2,728	$2,728	$2,728	$2,728	$2,728	$23,120
Deduct:												
Selling, general, and administrative		560	750	960	1,140	1,320	1,320	1,320	1,320	1,320	1,320	11,330
Research and development		94	126	160	190	220	220	220	220	220	220	1,890
Net profit before tax		$ 372	$ 574	$ 800	$1,026	$1,188	$1,188	$1,188	$1,188	$1,188	$1,188	$ 9,900
Tax at 50%		186	236	400	514	594	594	594	594	594	594	4,950
Net profit after tax		$ 186	$ 288	$ 400	$ 512	$ 594	$ 594	$ 594	$ 594	$ 594	$ 594	$ 4,950
Cash flow												
Add:												
Depreciation		88	96	96	96	120	...	...	...	...	...	496
Other noncash charges against income		28	28	28	28	28	28	28	28	28	20	272
Deduct												
Increase in working capital		...	...	160	180	180	...	...	...	...	...	520
Capital expenditures		84	...	...	260	...	...	...	...	...	...	344
Long-term debt	$ 218*											218
Mortgages	22*											22
Cash contribution from 10 years operations	$(240)	$ 218	$ 412	$ 364	$ 196	$ 562	$ 622	$ 622	$ 622	$ 622	$ 614	$ 4,614
Present worth contribution at 10%	(240)	198	340	273	134	349	351	319	290	264	237	2,515

II. TOTAL PRESENT WORTH VALUE OF COMPANY AT A 10% DISCOUNT FACTOR

Present worth contribution from operations...$2,515

Terminal value—present worth of 20 add. yrs. of earnings...1,950

Total Present Worth Value of Company...$4,465

* These outlays are assumed to be made on January 1, 1966.

LITTON INDUSTRIES, INC.

In OCTOBER, 1957, C. B. Thornton, chairman and president of Litton, revealed plans to merge Monroe Calculating Machine Company (Orange, N.J.) and Aircraft Radio Corporation (Boonton, N.J.) into Litton Industries, Inc. (Los Angeles). Terms offered to Monroe stockholders were (a) $1\frac{1}{2}$ shares of Litton common for each share of Monroe, or (b) $\frac{1}{2}$ share of Litton cumulative 5% voting preferred ($100 par value) for each share of Monroe. Terms offered to Aircraft Radio shareholders were (a) $\frac{6}{10}$ of 1 share of Litton common for each share of Aircraft Radio, or (b) $\frac{23}{100}$ of 1 share of Litton voting preferred for each share of Aircraft Radio common.

In the preceding month, Litton had reported an agreement to acquire Maryland Electronic Manufacturing Corporation, developers and producers of radar antennas, aircraft blind landing systems, and related electronic equipment. The agreement called for: (1) the immediate exchange of 2 Litton shares for each of the 9,394 outstanding common shares of Maryland Electronic; (2) the pro rata distribution of Litton shares equivalent, at their then market price, to $450,000 in 3 annual installments of $150,000 each, beginning October 1, 1958; and (3) the pro rata payment in common shares (at their then market price) of not more than $200,000 on completion of contract renegotiation for the years 1951 through 1955, provided the refund did not exceed $350,000.

Litton, a Delaware Corporation, was originally incorporated on November 2, 1953, under the name of Electro Dynamics Corporation. In 1954, after purchase of the capital stock of Litton Industries, located at San Carlos, California, its name was changed to Litton Industries, Inc. Litton and its subsidiaries were engaged in the research, development, manufacture, and sale of electronic components, equipments, and systems at 11 locations in 5 states—California, Utah, Indiana, Maryland, and New York.

The company's activities in electronic systems were in the fields of digital computers and controls, inertial guidance, automatic radar data processing, and radar and countermeasures. Equipments developed and manufactured by Litton were classifiable into telemetering and communications, navigation, servomechanisms, instrumentation and test, automatic instrumentation and control, flight simulation, flight control, missile launching and other power supplies, and automatic film magazine equipment for X-ray photography.

Electronic components included magnetrons, klystrons, and related microwave power tubes; color cathode ray display tubes; ferrite load isolators, rotary joints and associated microwave components; transformers, reactors, toroid coils, electronic wave filters, magnetic amplifiers, and related magnetic components; potentiometers; terminals, terminal boards, and other electronic hardware; and printed and etched circuits.

Research was carried on under contract to the Department of Defense and industrial customers, and with Litton's own funds for proprietary purposes. In addition to developmental work, separate laboratory facilities were devoted to fundamental research in the areas of digital computation, space simulation, and electronic color display.

Marketing methods varied among the several classes of Litton products. Sales to the military were handled by personnel of the operating divisions, supplemented by staff members in Washington, D.C., and Dayton, Ohio. Commercial and industrial type products were sold primarily through manufacturers' representatives and distributors.

All Litton's activities were in highly competitive fields. Numerous companies competed in the research, development, and manufacture of military electronic systems. Although a lesser number produced electronic power transmitters, such as magnetrons and klystrons, the competitors in this field included some of the largest electronic firms. There were also several major competitors engaged in the manufacture of other electronic parts and components.

Despite the severity of competition, Litton sales rose from $3.001 million[1] for the first 9 months of operation to $28.13 million for the fiscal year ended July 31, 1957. By the end of calendar 1957, the annual sales rate had reached $34 million. The year-end backlog amounted to $54 million, compared with $35 million in 1956 and $19 million in 1955. The increase in net earnings from $154,000 for the first 9 months before July 31, 1954 to $1.806 million for fiscal 1957 was equally impressive.

Between 1954 and 1957, the total assets of Litton quadrupled. Expansion was achieved through the purchase of other companies, as well as through direct investment. Acquisitions during 1954 included Digital Control Systems, Inc., La Jolla, California, and West Coast Electronics Co., Los Angeles. Acquisitions during 1955 were The Ahrendt Instrument Company, College Park, Maryland; U.S. Engineering Co., Inc., Glendale, California; and The Automatic Seriograph Company, College Park, Maryland. Purchases during 1956 included Triad Transformer Corporation, Los Angeles, and Utrad Corporation, Huntington, Indiana.

Asset growth during the three-year period terminating July 31, 1957, was financed in a variety of ways. Current liabilities rose by $2.872 million; term loans from banks increased by $2.506 million; reinvested earnings grew by

---

[1] There are slight discrepancies between some of the text figures, which come from the Proxy Statement of Litton Industries, Inc., dated November 28, 1957, and those in the exhibits, which were taken from several sources.

$3.161 million; and common shares outstanding more than doubled. During this period, Litton also entered into several lease arrangements. Annual rentals, as of July 31, 1957, were approximately $150,000, plus property taxes and insurance in certain cases.

At the end of fiscal 1957, the capital structure of Litton included subordinated income debentures, convertible subordinated debentures, and convertible preferred stock, as well as notes payable and common equity. In late 1957, the convertible preferred (par value of $100 and conversion rate of $1 per common share) was called for redemption and retired. Under the terms of the subordinated income debentures, due 1959 and callable at par, dividends other than stock dividends were not permitted.

The convertible subordinated debentures featured a conversion price of $13.50 per common share with an antidilution clause.[2] Under the provisions of these debentures, additional funded debt could not be created unless consolidated tangible assets immediately thereafter were $1\frac{2}{3}$ times the consolidated funded debt. The term loan agreement of July, 1957, permitted borrowing up to $3.5 million by December 1, 1957, at interest charges at .75% over the prime rate. The notes were repayable in four semiannual installments starting December 1, 1960; Litton agreed to maintain (1) a current ratio of 2 to 1, (2) a ratio of net fixed assets to unsubordinated debt (excluding bank long-term borrowings of $1.5 million) of at least 2 to 1, and (3) net worth in excess of 80% of Litton's total debt.

Partly because of the restriction noted above, no common dividends had been declared since Litton's incorporation. The number of common stockholders, nonetheless, rose from 1,100 in mid-1955 to 4,500 in mid-1957. Litton shares were admitted to trading on the American and Pacific Coast Stock Exchanges in September, 1956, and were listed on the New York Stock Exchange in July, 1957. The market price of Litton common rose steadily from a low of 10 to a 1957 peak of 56⅝.

Acquisitions proposed by Litton in late 1957 had sales totaling $56.779 million for 1956. Maryland Electronic, with sales of $2.99 million for 1956, was established in the areas of air navigation aids, radar microwave antennas, and telemetering equipment. Its plant facilities consisted of 100,000 square feet of engineering and manufacturing area adjacent to the plant of Litton Industries of Maryland, Inc.

Monroe, with annual sales in excess of $40 million for both 1956 and 1957, had operated successfully in the business equipment field since 1912. It had domestic and foreign manufacturing facilities, and its distribution facilities comprised approximately 325 company-owned branches and subbranches in the United States and 90 dealers abroad. Through these facilities, Monroe produced and marketed a line of calculating, adding, and accounting machines.

---

[2] The antidilution clause did not apply to the issuance of stock in exchange for the shares of other companies.

The Litton directors believed that the business equipment industry would undergo a profound change in the future through the impact of electronics. Litton's activities in electronic digital computers and control, as well as in precision electronic components and other branches of electronics, could be applied to business equipment. With the purchase of Monroe, Litton would benefit from its well-established name, organization, and distribution facilities. The Litton board felt that the transaction would eliminate a substantial amount of time and cost that would otherwise be necessary to effectively establish Litton in the business equipment field. In the opinion of Litton directors, there was a promising long-term potential of profitable operation in the business equipment industry, and the unification of Monroe and Litton would augment the prospect of expansion and profitable operation in that market.

Aircraft Radio, with sales of nearly $9 million for 1956, had operated in the area of airborne communication and navigation equipment for over 29 years. Litton had conducted research in such phases of the airborne communications field as the applications of radar, digital computers and inertial guidance to aircraft navigation and communications. It was the view of the Litton board that (1) the outgrowth of this research offered a promising area of future activity for Litton, and (2) a significant contribution to the company's strength and prospects could be made by combining the research and manufacturing skills and markets of Aircraft Radio and Litton.

Statements of *Business and Properties* of Monroe and Aircraft Radio, obtained from the proxy dated November 28, 1957, to Litton shareholders, are provided in Appendixes A and B. Of the combined sales of Litton, Monroe, and Aircraft Radio for 1957, on a pro forma basis, 45% were made to the armed services. Sales to the armed services generally bore lower profit margins than commercial sales and were subject to renegotiation and termination at any time.

The Litton board of directors believed that the exchange offers for Monroe and Aircraft Radio were fair and equitable to all stockholders. The bases of exchange resulted from arm's-length bargaining conducted over a period of several months. Factors taken into account included relative earning power based on past and anticipated operations and comparative asset and balance sheet positions. Respective market prices of the common shares were also considered over an extended period; and due attention was paid to differences in the nature and volume of the trading in Monroe and Aircraft Radio shares.

A pro forma combined balance sheet, as of July 31, 1957, for Litton and the proposed acquisitions is shown in Exhibit 1. Comparative balance sheets and income statements for Litton, Monroe, and Aircraft Radio, as well as data on stock prices for Litton and Aircraft Radio, are included in Exhibits 2–8. Assetwise, in mid-1957 Litton was roughly half the size of Monroe and twice the size of Aircraft Radio. On an earnings per share basis, Litton was lowest with $1.51 for 1957, followed by Aircraft Radio with $1.97 in 1956, and Monroe with $5.66.

During 1957, the market price of Aircraft Radio common fluctuated around 20, whereas the midrange for Litton common was 43. Aircraft Radio shares were traded over the counter. Monroe common stock had never been listed or traded on any stock exchange. Over 80% of Monroe stock was held by 4 families closely identified with management, and virtually the entire remainder was held by past and present employees. While there were occasional sales of small lots of Monroe stock in 1956 and 1957, the management of Monroe did not believe that the sales constituted a market for the stock.

Unlike Litton, both Monroe and Aircraft Radio consistently paid cash dividends. The 5 year dividend payout ratio was 45.4% for Monroe and 51.1% for Aircraft Radio. It was for this reason that the exchange offers by Litton provided for either preferred or common stock.

The cumulative voting preferred stock offered by Litton in exchange for Monroe and Aircraft Radio shares was convertible into common shares at any time during the first six years after original issuance. The conversion price was $55 per common share; each preferred share was valued at $100 for the purpose of conversion. Provision was made for proportionate changes in the conversion price in the event of: (1) annual stock dividends in excess of 3% (only to the extent of the excess); (2) stock splits; and (3) issuance of stock, or granting of options to purchase stock, at a cash price below $45 per share (to the extent of the difference between the cash price and $45). No provision was made for adjustment by reason of the issuance of common stock in exchange for property or services.

The exchange with Monroe was not to be consummated unless Litton acquired at least 80% of all outstanding Monroe shares. Litton further reserved the right to terminate the agreement provided the holders of more than 50% of Monroe's outstanding stock elected to receive Litton preferred stock. By the middle of October, 1957, holders of some 80% of Monroe's stock had accepted the offer. It was anticipated that the holders of 40% of Monroe shares would elect voting preferred stock.

In similar fashion, Litton was not to be bound by the exchange agreement with Aircraft Radio unless (1) at least 80% of outstanding Aircraft Radio shares were deposited for exchange and (2) holders of less than half of Aircraft Radio shares chose the voting preferred. Of the 304,146 Aircraft Radio shares outstanding on July 31, 1957, it was initially estimated that the holders of 97% would exchange their shares (with 15% allocated to preferred).

During December, 1957, Litton shareholders authorized the increase of common shares from 2 million to 3.5 million and the creation of 160,000 shares of voting preferred stock to be used in the proposed exchanges. Public hearings on the acquisition of Monroe and Aircraft Radio were also held before the California Commissioner of Corporations. In late December, 1957, L. M. Hull, chairman of Aircraft Radio, stated in a letter to stockholders that by a vote of four to two the board of directors had "adopted a resolution recommending acceptance of the proposed exchange offer."

Two directors, Donald Havens and Franz Schneider, declined to recommend acceptance because of potential dilution in the equity of the preferred shareholders scheduled to come into being. Their sole objection was to the provision for future stock dividends up to 3% without corresponding adjustments in the conversion rate on the preferred stock. The opposition directors did not initially specify whether their holdings of over 13,000 Aircraft Radio shares would be deposited under the plan.

Additional opposition to the Litton proposal came from two common stockholders—J. E. Johanson, a former employee of Aircraft Radio, and G. P. McCouch, a Boston engineer. In soliciting the support of other shareholders, Mr. Johanson and his associates contended that the Litton offer would reduce the value and earnings of Aircraft Radio shares. Emphasis was placed on the facts that (1) Litton offered Aircraft Radio holders only one sixth of its total outstanding stock; (2) Aircraft Radio was formed in 1924 and had paid 99 consecutive dividends, while Litton was created in 1953 and had paid no common dividends; and (3) Litton employees on July 31, 1957, held options to purchase 170,317 common shares at $1 per share.

The arguments of the dissident Aircraft Radio stockholders apparently bore fruit. When the Litton offer first expired on February 17, 1958, only 205,699 shares, or about two thirds, had been deposited for exchange. Among these were some 82,000 shares deposited by Laurance Rockefeller. The offer was then extended to February 28.

On February 20, 1958, Mr. Johanson expressed the opinion that insufficient Aircraft Radio shares would be deposited to effect the merger, and he stated that "a vast majority of employee stockholders" had declined to accept the offer. Mr. Schneider also revealed at that time that the 13,000 shares under his control would not be deposited. He announced: "I don't want Litton common because it pays no dividends, and I don't think the preferred is attractive enough."

Exhibit 1

PRO FORMA COMBINED BALANCE SHEET

COMBINING LITTON INDUSTRIES, INC., AND SUBSIDIARY COMPANIES, MONROE CALCULATING MACHINE COMPANY AND SUBSIDIARY COMPANIES, AIRCRAFT RADIO CORPORATION, MARYLAND ELECTRONIC MANUFACTURING CORPORATION, AND DIGITAL CONTROL SYSTEMS, INC.,

JULY 31, 1957

ASSETS	Litton Industries, Inc. and Subsidiary Companies	Monroe Calculating Machine Company and Subsidiary Companies	Aircraft Radio Corporation (August 31, 1957)	Maryland Electronic Manufacturing Corporation	Digital Control Systems, Inc.	Combining Transactions Companies Acquired	Combining Transactions Companies Pooled	Pro Forma Combination
Current assets:								
Cash	$ 982,233	$ 2,857,693	$ 855,530	$ 240,511	$ 105	...	$ 49,550	$ 4,985,622
Accounts receivable, less provision for doubtful accounts	4,145,144	8,027,425	1,024,540	284,367	...	...	...	13,481,476
Inventories, at the lower of cost or market	5,616,126	14,822,931	5,043,252	1,460,083	...	...	...	26,942,392
Prepaid insurance, taxes, and other expense	337,187	510,282	83,721	6,093	...	...	...	937,283
Total Current Assets	$11,080,690	$26,218,331	$7,007,043	$1,991,054	$ 105	...	...	$46,346,773
Investments in and advances to unconsolidated subsidiaries	...	...	75,700	...	...	...	...	75,700
Property, plant, and equipment, less accumulated depreciation	5,338,231	6,688,729	1,072,482	501,474*	...	$ 788,251	...	14,389,167
Intangible and other assets:								
Patents, at cost, less accumulated amortization	238,575	...	1	...	51,262	90,594	...	380,432
Excess of cost over net assets acquired therefor	54,861	...	...	...	...	...	...	54,861
Other	111,026	178,580	...	1,512	291	...	...	291,409
	$16,823,383	$33,085,640	$8,155,226	$2,494,040	$51,658	...	...	$61,538,342

* The true value, as determined by the American Appraisal Company, is approximately $1.3 million.

Exhibit 1 (Continued)

	Litton Industries, Inc. and Subsidiary Companies	Monroe Calculating Machine Company and Subsidiary Companies	Aircraft Radio Corporation (August 31, 1957)	Maryland Electronic Manufacturing Corporation	Digital Control Systems, Inc.	Combining Transactions — Companies Acquired	Combining Transactions — Companies Pooled	Pro Forma Combination
LIABILITIES								
Current liabilities:								
Notes payable to banks	...	$ 1,500,000	$1,400,000	$1,316,764	$10,481	...	...	$ 4,227,245
Accounts payable, payrolls, and payroll taxes	$ 2,951,419	3,523,844	1,025,357	251,583	24,155	...	...	7,776,358
Deferred maintenance contract income	...	4,356,682	...	...	...	...	...	4,356,682
Federal taxes on income and estimated contract refunds	1,311,994	1,638,938	805,399	550,000	...	...	...	4,306,331
Current portion of long-term debt	85,319	425,000	200,000	...	...	...	...	710,319
Total Current Liabilities	$ 4,348,732	$11,444,464	$3,430,756	$2,118,347	$34,636	...	...	$21,376,935
Long-term debt, less amounts due within one year	4,670,136	6,750,000	600,000	...	...	...	...	12,020,136
Minority interest	19,096	...	...	...	...	...	(123,734)	142,830
Stockholders' equity:								
Preferred stock (Litton), par value $100 a share (voting, convertible)	...	...	...	...	...	...	(7,017,800)	7,017,800
Common stock:								
10 cents a share (Litton)	126,994	...	...	...	...	(3,346)	(42,046)	172,386
$10 a share (Monroe)	...	3,000,000	...	...	...	...	3,000,000	...
$1 a share (Aircraft Radio)	...	...	304,146	...	...	...	304,146	...
No par value (Maryland Electronic)	...	...	...	37,576	...	37,576	...	...
$100 a share (Dico)	...	...	...	...	94,400	94,400	...	...
Additional paid-in capital	4,268,187	...	221,892	...	...	(1,268,214)	3,772,316	1,985,977
Earnings retained in the business	3,390,238	11,941,561	3,598,432	338,117	(77,378)	260,739	107,953	18,822,278
Less: Common stock reacquired, at cost	...	(50,385)	...	...	...	...	(50,385)	...
Total Stockholders' Equity	$ 7,785,419	$14,891,176	$4,124,470	$ 375,693	$17,022	...	...	$27,998,441
	$16,823,383	$33,085,640	$8,155,226	$2,494,040	$51,658	...	...	$61,538,342

SOURCE: Proxy Statement of Litton Industries, Inc., dated November 28, 1957, pp. 20–21.

Exhibit 2

LITTON INDUSTRIES, INC., AND SUBSIDIARY COMPANIES

CONSOLIDATED BALANCE SHEETS AS OF JULY 31, 1954–57
(Dollar Figures in Thousands)

	1957	1956	1955	1954
Cash	$ 982	$ 960	$ 648	$ 482
Accounts receivable	4,145	2,300	1,532	192
Tax claim	...	...	40	...
Inventories	5,616	3,064	2,041	995
Prepayments	337	288	148	32
Total Current Assets	$11,081	$ 6,612	$4,409	$1,701
Land, buildings, etc.	7,278	4,648	3,632	2,349
Depreciation and amortization	1,940	1,144	788	316
Net property	$ 5,338	$ 3,504	$2,844	$2,033
Notes receivable	...	240	...	...
Investments	...	65	...	202
Patents	238	253	262	224
Other assets	111	94	34	32
Goodwill	55	58	99	8
Total Assets	$16,823	$10,826	$7,648	$4,200
Notes payable	$ 85	$ 1,181	$1,579	$ 67
Accounts payable	1,667	906	579	169
Accruals	1,284	675	459	180
Federal income tax	1,312	1,195	662	1,061
Total Current Liabilities	$ 4,349	$ 3,957	$3,279	$1,477
5% subordinated debentures, 1965	1,238	1,500	...	...
5% subordinated debentures, 1959	230	230	230	1,430
Notes payable	3,202	591	648	696
Minority interest	19	15	48	...
5% preferred stock	76	91	126	270
Common stock	119	105	97	53
Paid-in surplus	4,200	2,626	2,523	3
Earned surplus	3,390	1,588	655	229
Other surplus	...	123	42	42
Total Liabilities	$16,823	$10,826	$7,648	$4,200

Exhibit 3
LITTON INDUSTRIES, INC., AND SUBSIDIARY COMPANIES
CONSOLIDATED INCOME STATEMENTS, YEARS ENDED JULY 31
(Dollar Figures in Thousands)

	3 months* 1957	1957	1956	1955	9 months 1954
Sales	$8,680	$28,131	$14,920	$8,899	$2,980
Cost of sales	6,462	20,824	10,733	6,928	2,089
General and administrative expense	1,084	3,776	2,042	1,232	522
Net earnings	$1,134	$ 3,531	$ 2,145	$ 739	$ 369
Interest	...	203	149	101	...
Federal income tax	485	1,426	976	243	193
Other income and (charges)	(72)	(95)	...	41	(22)
Net Income	$ 577	$ 1,807	$ 1,020	$ 436	$ 154
Preferred dividends	...	5	5	11	6
No. shares common (000's)	1,202	1,194	1,047	966	525
Earned per share	$0.48	$1.51	$0.97	$0.44	$0.28
Price range common, calendar years		56⅝–29½	32¼–14¾		

* To October 31, 1957.

Exhibit 4
AIRCRAFT RADIO CORPORATION
BALANCE SHEETS AS OF DECEMBER 31, 1953–56
(Dollar Figures in Thousands)

	1956	1955	1954	1953
Cash	$ 358	$ 363	$ 536	$ 868
Accounts receivable	1,561	1,425	1,358	931
Inventories	5,465	3,671	3,075	4,101
Prepayments	80	60	37	45
Total Current Assets	$7,464	$5,519	$5,006	$5,945
Land and buildings	3,187	2,693	2,508	2,445
Depreciation and amortization	2,240	2,111	2,007	1,888
Net property	$ 947	$ 582	$ 501	$ 557
Investments	76	76	...	9
Total Assets	$8,487	$6,177	$5,507	$6,511
Accounts payable	$ 617	$ 521	$ 197	$ 304
Notes payable	2,000	1,000	500	1,500
Accruals	708	577	626	478
Contract price refund	...	...	38	79
Federal income tax	706	774	1,182	1,481
Total Current Liabilities	$4,031	$2,872	$2,543	$3,842
Notes payable	700	...	...	...
Common stock ($1 par)	300	300	300	300
Capital surplus	162	145	15	8
Earned surplus	3,309	2,892	2,720	2,440
Reacquired stock	(15)	(32)	(71)	(79)
Net stock and surplus	$3,756	$3,305	$2,964	$2,669
Total Liabilities	$8,487	$6,177	$5,507	$6,511

Exhibit 5

AIRCRAFT RADIO CORPORATION

INCOME STATEMENTS, YEARS ENDED DECEMBER 31, 1953–56,
AND EIGHT MONTHS ENDED AUGUST 31, 1957
(Dollar Figures in Thousands)

	8 months 1957	1956	1955	1954	1953
Net sales........................	$6,916	$8,685	$7,480	$8,460	$9,425
Cost and expenses................	na	7,292	6,429	6,752	7,682
Depreciation and amortization......	na	129	105	120	109
Net earnings.....................	$1,089	$1,264	$ 946	$1,588	$1,634
Interest..........................	...	82	33	37	43
Other charges....................	...	...	24	...	...
Income taxes....................	619	600	454	975	1,200
Net profit.......................	$ 470	$ 582	$ 435	$ 576	$ 391
Dividends.......................	181	265	262	295	210

SELECTED INCOME DATA

	Net Sales (000's)	Net Profit (000's)	No. Shares (000's)	EPS	Dividend per Share	Price Range
1957, 8 months.......	$6,916	$ 470	304	$ 1.54	$1.25	16½–25
1956...............	8,685	582	296	1.96	0.90	19½–12
1955...............	7,480	435	292	1.49	0.90	21–12¾
1954...............	8,460	576	282	2.04	1.05	17½–7¼
1953...............	9,425	391	280	1.40	0.75	8¼–6¾
1952...............	8,996	390	280	1.39	0.75	8¾–7¾
1951...............	7,444	349	280	1.25	0.70	
1950...............	3,360	296	280	1.06	0.60	
1949...............	2,550	168	280	0.60	0.33	
1948...............	1,822	96	292	0.33	0.20	
1947...............	458	(106)	298	(0.35)	0.22	

na = not available.

Exhibit 6

MONROE CALCULATING MACHINE COMPANY

BALANCE SHEETS AS OF DECEMBER 31, 1953–56
(Dollar Figures in Thousands)

	1956	1955	1954	1953
Cash	$ 2,069	$ 2,426	$ 2,205	$ 1,576
Treasury notes	...	499	599	...
Inventories	11,480	8,924	8,347	9,361
Receivables	6,448	4,825	3,436	4,028
Other	1,098	1,872	1,704	1,452
Total Current Assets	$21,095	$18,546	$16,291	$16,417
Plant and equipment	8,508	7,940	7,723	7,638
Less: Depreciation	2,949	2,469	2,026	1,713
Net property	$ 5,559	$ 5,471	$ 5,697	$ 5,925
Land	325	325	325	332
Investment in subsidiaries	1,113	719	1,019	1,061
Cash value, life insurance	176	173	169	160
Total Assets	$28,268	$25,234	$23,501	$23,895
Accounts payable	$ 1,349	$ 998	$ 760	$ 625
Wages payable	1,924	1,439	1,066	899
Income taxes	1,647	522	222	1,052
Deferred contracts	3,109	2,852	2,636	2,431
Notes payable	325	...	...	...
Total Current Liabilities	$ 8,354	$ 5,811	$ 4,684	$ 5,007
Notes payable	4,675	5,000	5,000	5,000
Loan payable	2,500	...	...	...
7% preferred	...	2,756	2,970	3,370
Common stock	3,000	3,000	3,000	3,000
Earned surplus	9,789	8,701	7,885	7,518
Less: Reacquired stock	(50)	(34)	(38)	...
Total Liabilities	$28,268	$25,234	$23,501	$23,895

Exhibit 7

MONROE CALCULATING MACHINE COMPANY

INCOME STATEMENTS, YEARS ENDED DECEMBER 31, 1953–56
(Dollar Figures in Thousands)

	1956	1955	1954	1953
Sales...............................	$44,909	$36,821	$29,686	$30,862
Costs and expenses....................	40,285	32,991	27,909	28,961
Depreciation.........................	586	555	525	396
Net earnings.........................	$ 4,038	$ 3,275	$ 1,252	$ 1,505
Other income........................	185	197	317	234
Total income......................	$ 4,223	$ 3,472	$ 1,569	$ 1,739
Federal income tax...................	2,025	1,609	593	900
Foreign subsidiary income.............	(416)	(360)	...	...
Net Income..........................	$ 1,782	$ 1,503	$ 976	$ 839
Preferred dividends...................	96	201	231	236
Common dividends....................	521	485	374	525

SELECTED INCOME DATA

	Sales (000's)	Net Income (000's)	No. of Shares (000's)	Earnings per Share	Dividends per Share
1956.......................	$44,909	$1,782	298	$5.66	$1.75
1955.......................	36,821	1,503	298	4.36	1.63
1954.......................	29,686	976	298	2.50	1.25
1953.......................	30,862	839	300	2.01	1.75
1952.......................	30,012	1,256	300	3.37	1.75
1951.......................	30,277	1,844	300	5.31	2.00
1950.......................	24,543	2,035	300*	5.92	2.00
1949.......................	19,983	1,731	150	9.76†	2.50†
1948.......................	20,679	1,608	150	8.91†	2.50†

* Split 2 for 1.
† Not adjusted.

Exhibit 8

MARKET PRICES

LITTON COMMON STOCK

The following table shows the range of the bid and ask prices of the common stock of Litton on the over-the-counter market in New York, New York, during the period beginning on October 1, 1955, and ending on the date the stock was admitted to trading on the American Stock Exchange and the Pacific Coast Stock Exchange.

	Range			
	Bid		Ask	
Period Ended (Quarterly unless Otherwise Indicated)	High	Low	High	Low
December 31, 1955	16¾	10¼	17¼	10¾
March 31, 1956	23⅜	14⅜	23¾	14⅞
June 30, 1956	24⅝	19¾	25¼	20¼
September 26, 1956	29½	24	30¼	24½

The following table sets forth the high and low sale prices of the common stock of Litton on the American Stock Exchange during the period from September 26, 1956, to July 29, 1957, and on the New York Stock Exchange from July 30, 1957, to October 31, 1957.

Period Ended (Quarterly unless Otherwise Indicated)	Range	
	High	Low
Four days ending September 30, 1956	27½	26½
December 31, 1956	32¼	23
March 31, 1957	39⅞	29½
June 30, 1957	48	36⅞
September 30, 1957	56	41⅛
October 1 to November 22, 1957	48	36⅞

ARC COMMON STOCK

The following table shows the range of the bid and ask prices of the common stock of ARC on the over-the-counter market in New York, New York, for each quarterly period within the past two years.

	Range			
	Bid		Ask	
Quarterly Period Ending	High	Low	High	Low
December 31, 1955	15¼	12¾	16	13½
March 31, 1956	19	12	20½	12¾
June 30, 1956	18¾	15¼	19½	16
September 30, 1956	18	15¼	18¾	15¾
December 31, 1956	19¼	16¼	20	17
March 31, 1957	23	16½	24	17½
June 30, 1957	22	16½	22¾	17
September 30, 1957	23¾	19¼	24¾	20¼
October 1 to November 22, 1957	25	19	26	20¼

SOURCE: Proxy Statement of Litton Industries, Inc., dated November 28, 1957, p. 15.

Appendix A: Business and Properties of Monroe

Business

Monroe is a Delaware corporation organized on October 30, 1925 to continue the business of Monroe Calculating Machine Company (N.Y.) incorporated on April 25, 1912. Monroe and its subsidiaries manufacture and market office business machines including calculating, adding, bookkeeping, accounting, punched card and punched tape machines. Substantially all the machines are manufactured and assembled at plants in Orange, New Jersey, Morris Plains, New Jersey, Bristol, Virginia and Amsterdam, Holland. With the exception of one line of adding machines Monroe purchases motors, steel and some components and manufactures and assembles the complete machine. Monroe and its domestic subsidiaries employ some 4,450 people of whom 2,100 are in sales and service. In the United States the Monroe line is marketed through approximately 325 company owned branches and sub-branches. Outside the United States the Monroe line is sold by some 90 exclusive dealers of which five are wholly owned foreign subsidiaries. It has executed union contracts with the International Union of Electrical, Radio and Machine Workers–CIO and the International Association of Machinists–AF of L, the first extending to September, 1960 and the latter to February, 1961. There is no litigation pending or threatened against Monroe. A list of Monroe's subsidiaries is as follows:

Monroe Calculating Machine Company, Inc. (N.Y.)
Calculator Equipment Corporation (N.Y.)
Monrobot Corporation (Del.)—Inactive
Monroe Calculating Machine Company Limited (Eng.)
Monroe Calculating Machine Co. of Canada, Ltd.
Monroe Calculating Machine Company–Holland N.V.
Monroe Venezolana C.A.
Monroe Calculating Machine Company-France S.A.R.L.
Deutsche Monroe Rechenmaschinen G.M.B.H.—Inactive

The products of Monroe are:

1. Calculating Machines	Fully automatic, semiautomatic and hand types. Some 20 different models are currently manufactured with sales prices ranging from $195 to $1,075.
2. Adding-Listing Machines	Adding and subtracting machines with computations recorded on paper tapes. Full keyboard machines are manufactured on approximately 20 different electric and hand models with prices

	ranging from $194 to $861. Ten-key machines are sold at prices ranging from $221 to $535.
3. Accounting Machines	Approximately 14 different base models of the electric type are manufactured. Sales prices range from $750 to over $10,000.
4. Auto Punches	Monroe developed the auto punch machine which may be combined with an adding machine or an accounting machine to create a master record for repetitive use. Models range in price from $1,015 to $1,285 in addition to the basic price of the Monroe adding or accounting machine of which it is an integral part.

Monroe is an aggressive manufacturer and world-wide distributor of a wide line of adding, calculating, accounting and other computing machines. It makes many variations of this equipment, the major characteristic of which is the automatic performance of some or all of the four rules of arithmetic (addition, subtraction, multiplication and division). In some lines amounts are listed and totalled printed on paper tape or specially designed forms. In other cases calculations are performed by the machine and answers are displayed in number dials. The machines are used for a wide variety of figure problems by both large and small businesses, industries, educational institutions, government, etc. They are priced from under $200 to over $10,000.

There are at least twenty different United States companies and many more foreign ones which compete with Monroe in one or more of its lines. The field is so complex and the manufacturers' approach to the customers' problems so diverse that it becomes difficult to precisely define products or end uses of those products. Most of the more mature and well-organized companies, of which Monroe is one, sell machines through determining the customers' figure requirements and recommending equipment which will fulfill these. Various other different products or combinations of products of competitive manufacturers will also be offered.

Competitive companies are both larger and smaller than Monroe. Some well known names which compete directly or indirectly with Monroe in one way or another are IBM, Sperry-Rand, National Cash Register Co., Burroughs, Smith-Corona, Friden Calculating Machine Co., and Marchant Calculators, Inc. There are many more. Foreign competition has historically been active, both in the United States and world markets, but never so intense as in the post war era. Many foreign manufacturers have now established company owned branches and national advertising programs in the United States. The many developments in the research and development field, especially electronics, are altering the character of some of the companies and portend even greater change in the years to come.

Properties

Monroe owns 22 administrative and manufacturing buildings in Orange and West Orange, New Jersey; a manufacturing facility of approximately

100,000 square feet on some 400 acres in the Borough of Morris Plains, Township of Hanover, New Jersey and approximately 160,000 square feet of administrative and plant space on some 30 acres in Bristol, Virginia. Monroe Calculating Machine Company, Inc., the domestic distributing company, rents approximately 325 offices throughout the United States with a gross annual rent of approximately $550,000.00. Monroe Calculating Machine Company N.V. leases approximately 85,000 square feet of administrative, selling and manufacturing space in Amsterdam, Holland, some of which extend to the year 2000.

The main plant and general offices of Monroe are in Orange, New Jersey adjacent to the Highland Avenue Station of the Delaware, Lackawanna and Western Railway. The 22 buildings provide approximately 215,000 square feet of manufacturing space, 50,000 square feet of office space and 50,000 square feet for storage, research, cafeteria and service facilities. Most of the buildings have been purchased—beginning in 1917—but the two newest buildings, comprising some 15,000 and 100,000 square feet, were built by the company in 1936 and 1941 respectively. In the fall of 1952 Monroe completed a modern plant of approximately 100,000 square feet at Morris Plains, New Jersey, some 15 miles northwest of Orange. The building is set on well landscaped grounds with parking area, and houses assembly and light manufacturing departments, the Monrobot Laboratory, a cafeteria, medical department and office suites. In 1947 Monroe constructed a unit containing 90,000 square feet of space in Bristol, Virginia and in 1952 added an additional 90,000 square feet. The buildings include service facilities of the latest type.

SOURCE: Proxy Statement of Litton Industries, Inc., dated November 28, 1957, pp. 6–8.

Appendix B: Business and Properties of ARC

Business

Since 1930 ARC has been a recognized factor in the design, development and manufacture of electronic communication and navigation equipment for military, naval and civil aircraft. Incorporated in New Jersey in 1924, ARC commenced active operations at its present site in 1928, and changed its name to Aircraft Radio Corporation in 1929. Its first products were a radio-range beacon receiver sold principally to commercial airlines, together with special aircraft radio antennas and ignition-shielding systems. Starting in 1930 it developed two-way pilot-operated equipment which was later adopted as standard apparatus for Army aircraft. Other similar equipment designed by ARC was adopted as standard for Navy aircraft and in the case of each service this represented the first equipment of this general type that was so standardized. Outgrowths of these original designs were subsequently adopted as standard apparatus by both services for other phases of two-way, one-way and navigational radio operations, and from 1932 through 1945 ARC's customers were almost entirely confined to various branches of the armed forces.

After World War II ARC commenced a comprehensive program of diversification of both its products and its markets. Its products now include a variety of airborne electronic communication and navigation and radar equipment, and a line of special apparatus for testing and adjusting electronic equipment in customers' laboratories and in the field. Its principal customers are commercial and private aircraft operators, airframe manufacturers, and United States and foreign governments. Throughout its history a basic ARC policy has been the evaluation of operational needs and the development of apparatus to meet those needs, all at its own expense and risk. Sales and field service are accomplished by a staff of company field personnel and by a nationwide network of factory dealers. In 1956 over 40% of ARC's total sales were to civil customers for non-government end use. It operates one twin-engine and two single-engine airplanes for engineering field tests of its products, evaluation of new requirements, and demonstrations to customers.

ARC employs approximately 660 persons on a full-time basis. It enjoys favorable relations with its employees, all of whom are residents of rural communities in the vicinity of the ARC plant. Throughout its history there have been no strikes by company employees or material labor disputes. ARC has no contract with any labor union. There is no litigation pending or threatened against ARC.

ARC is engaged primarily in the design and production of airborne electronic communication, navigation and control equipment. The industry is a highly competitive one.

ARC was a pioneer in this field and, by virtue of its experience and engineering proficiency has been able to meet successfully its competition to date. Its competitors range all the way from very small independent producers up to subdivisions of the largest corporations. It is impossible to authentically estimate the ratio of ARC dollar sales to sales of the entire industry since in the case of large corporations figures are not normally published for subdivision operations, and in the case of many of the small independent producers, no figures are normally published.

ARC is a relatively small factor in the electronic industry. For example, the annual gross sales of one of its principal competitors are more than ten times ARC's gross sales. It is believed, however, that current ARC sales at the annual rate of Ten and One-Half Million Dollars represent a significant part of the sales volume of the independent producers who specialize in similar or equivalent product lines.

Properties

The ARC plant is located in the township of Boonton, New Jersey, about 30 miles from New York City. It consists of a group of masonry and frame buildings built by the company from 1928 to 1957 and a private airport, all situated on a tract of 101 acres owned by ARC. In addition, it leases an adjoining tract of 20 acres which is used principally as an employees' parking lot.

The age of the buildings varies from less than 1 year to 29 years, but the older portions have been remodeled and extensively reconditioned within the past 5 years. About 38% of the present floor space is in the buildings constructed within the past 11 years. Total floor space comprises 148,600 square feet of which 21,540 square feet are devoted to engineering research and development, 89,000 square feet are devoted to manufacturing operations with attendant direct administration and services, 22,000 square feet are devoted to executive, sales, accounting, purchasing and personnel offices, and 10,000 square feet comprise an airplane hangar with office and shop for installation and maintenance of ARC airborne products.

Two grass-covered, drained aircraft runways on ARC property are maintained on a year-around basis as a private airfield for use by aircraft of ARC and its customers.

SOURCE: Proxy Statement of Litton Industries, Inc., dated November 28, 1957, pp. 8–9.

LESTOIL PRODUCTS, INC.

IN EARLY JUNE, 1960, John Bolten, Sr., and Daniel E. Hogan, Jr., members of the executive committee of Lestoil Products, Inc., were studying the details of a proposed offering of the company's capital stock, which was to be traded over the counter. In light of the company's past record, its potential future earnings, and the terms of the issue, they were confident that the proposed stock would be sold with little difficulty. In this final analysis of the offering, they concentrated particularly on the price of the stock to the public. They believed that the offering price would certainly be attractive. They thought, however, that the offering was perhaps underpriced and questioned whether the company should offer fewer units at a higher price to raise the necessary funds.

COMPANY BACKGROUND

Lestoil Products, Inc., was organized in the spring of 1960 for the purpose of purchasing Adell Chemical Company, Inc.; its wholly owned advertising affiliate, Jackson Associates, Inc.; and its wholly owned real estate subsidiary, J.L.B. Realty Trust. Adell Chemical Company had been organized in 1933 by Jacob L. Barowsky to manufacture and sell a synthetic liquid detergent. Until 1954, sales had been made primarily to commercial laundries and the paper and textile industries. In that year, the Adell company brought its detergent to the attention of the household trade through spot television advertising. The company later added several other items, including a concentrated, premeasured dry bleach sealed in individual, water-soluble packets. The two principal products, detergent and bleach, were widely advertised and known under the trade names of Lestoil and Lestare. The company's offices and manufacturing facilities were located in Holyoke, Massachusetts. Financial data for Lestoil Products' predecessor are presented in Exhibits 1 and 2.

ACQUISITION OF ADELL CHEMICAL COMPANY, INC.

In early 1960, Mr. Barowsky, the president and founder of Adell Chemical Company, decided to find a buyer for the company. He turned down several offers. One company, for instance, offered $8 million in its own stock and $4 million in cash, but Mr. Barowsky wanted a cash sale. Another company offered $7 million in cash, but Mr. Barowsky thought that this amount was not enough. Samuel S. Dennis III, a member of the law firm of Hale and Dorr, Boston, Massachusetts, who had been counsel to the Adell company, had been attempting to aid Mr. Barowsky in finding a buyer.

Mr. Dennis was also associated with a family group in Andover, Massachusetts, headed by John Bolten, Sr., and Mr. Hogan, respectively chairman of the board and president of the Standard International Corporation. This corporation was a closely held investment company with substantial interests in a number of corporations. During the time that Mr. Dennis was trying to locate a buyer for Adell Chemical Company, he, Mr. Bolten, and Mr. Hogan concluded that perhaps a group associated with Standard International would find it worthwhile to buy the company. Recognizing a possible conflict of interest, Mr. Dennis immediately notified Mr. Barowsky that he should obtain new legal counsel to represent him in this transaction.

As the result of further negotiations, a contract dated March 25, 1960, was entered into between Adell Chemical Company and its stockholders as sellers and Standard International Corporation and Mr. Hogan, acting for himself and as agent for John Bolten, Sr., John Bolten, Jr., and Mr. Dennis, as purchasers. Lestoil Products, Inc., was formed subsequently by the purchasing group to become the acquiring corporation.

Lestoil Products agreed to pay the sellers a cash price of $8 million and also agreed to assume a conditional liability to pay an additional sum in the maximum amount of $4 million. Payments on the conditional obligation were required annually but only to the extent of one half of annual net profits in excess of $1.5 million after income taxes. The obligation would expire on October 31, 1969, whether or not the maximum amount had been paid in full.

The purchase and sale agreement called for a deposit of $150,000 as option money and gave the purchasing group 90 days to complete the transaction. This sum was to be forfeited as damages in the event that the transaction was not completed within this period. The Standard International Corporation advanced the option money. In addition, employment contracts were made with 3 former officers for 5 years, beginning on June 1, 1960, at the following salaries:

	First Year	Annually, Last 4 Years
Jacob L. Barowsky	$100,000	$ 50,000
Isaac L. Eskenasy	30,000	30,000
Aaron L. Kingsberg	20,000	20,000
	$150,000	$100,000

These officers had received compensation at a higher rate in recent years.

Mr. Hogan had always kept a business diary. The entries in the spring of 1960 included a chronological account of the important dates and events in connection with the acquisition of Adell Chemical Company. A summary of these entries from February 1 to March 25 is given below.

1960

Monday, February 1.   In Palm Beach with Sam Dennis. He called the president of a chemical company in New York and told him about the availability of Adell Chemical and suggested that his company consider the possibility of adding it as one of their divisions.

Friday, March 4.   While in New York on another matter with Mr. Dennis, we decided to visit the president of the chemical company personally and tell him the latest news about Adell Chemical and give him the reasons why his company should buy it, etc. En route to Boston the next day, the thought occurred to us that maybe we could put together a group or a transaction that would be attractive to all concerned, and where Standard International and its stockholders could end up with a fairly good-sized piece of the Adell equity.

Tuesday, March 8.   Visit to Boston and preliminary discussions with William L. Brown, vice president of The First National Bank of Boston, regarding interim financing.

Wednesday, March 9.   Visit to Holyoke and preliminary discussion with Mr. and Mrs. Barowsky.

Thursday, March 10.   Conferences in Boston regarding the amount and terms of the loan the bank was willing to give us to finance the purchase.

[At this early stage of negotiations, the bank indicated a willingness to provide $7–$8 million in turnaround money at an interest rate of $5\frac{1}{2}\%$. The stocks of Lestoil Products and of Standard International were to be pledged as security.]

Friday, March 11.   Conferences in Boston with law firm of Hale and Dorr to go over the preliminary drafts of the proposed employment contract for the owners of Adell Chemical.

Saturday, March 12.   Skiing at Mittersill and met Mr. [X] of a law firm in New York with contacts that might be helpful in a public underwriting.

Monday, March 14.   Conferences at Holyoke with Mr. and Mrs. Barowsky.

Tuesday, March 15.   Conference at The First National Bank of Boston with the senior loan officer.

Wednesday, March 16.   Conference at Andover with Gale Deam and Charles McCarthy, who would be the vice presidents for manufacturing and sales in the new Lestoil organization. Aaron Kingsberg of Adell phoned to emphasize that we would have to show them definitely where the $8 million is coming from fairly soon.

Thursday, March 17.   With McCarthy, Deam, and Sol Sackell, who will be in charge of advertising activities, to Holyoke for more negotiations regarding the purchase and sale contract.

Friday, March 18.   In Andover and Boston, going over the various projections involved in paying off the interim bank loan.

Sunday, March 20.   Conversations with S. Dennis about various financing alternatives.

Monday, March 21.   In New Hampshire, conversations with Mr. [M] regarding the possibility of his firm's joining in an underwriting group re: Lestoil Products, Inc.

Tuesday, March 22.   In Jackson, New Hampshire, more conversations with Mr. [M].

Wednesday, March 23.   In New York City, initial conferences with institutional lenders regarding the possibility of their putting up $3–$4 million of subordinated funds.

Thursday, March 24.   In Andover, conversations with Mr. Bolten, Sr. and Mr. Bolten, Jr., regarding progress of the Lestoil situation.

Friday, March 25.   Signing of purchase and sale agreement of Adell Chemical.

FINANCING THE ACQUISITION

The formal closing of the purchase and sale transaction took place on May 31, 1960, when Lestoil Products paid $8 million in cash to the sellers. It had raised the necessary funds to finance the acquisition of Adell Chemical Company in the following manner:

Sale of Lestoil common stock at 60 cents a share:

Purchasers	Shares	Amount
Standard International Corporation.............	249,406	
John Bolten, Sr..............................	396,599	
John Bolten, Jr..............................	396,598	
Daniel E. Hogan, Jr..........................	396,599	
Samuel S. Dennis III.........................	396,598	
Total...................................	1,835,800	$1,101,480
Loan to Lestoil Products from The First National Bank of Boston on a demand promissory note...		6,900,000
		$8,001,480

The bank loan was a temporary one, granted to serve only as turnaround money while Lestoil Products raised permanent capital to finance the acquisition. The purchasers had spent the past two months working out the details of the permanent financing.

As a part of the financing, on May 27, 1960, the company received letters of commitment from representatives of institutional investors (several pension funds), stating their intention to purchase $3.2 million principal amount of the company's 6¼% notes due in 1970, together with detachable and transferable 10-year warrants, protected against dilution, for the purchase of a total of 339,200 shares of common stock at $7.50 a share.[1] The agreement provided that the obligation of the institutional lenders was conditional on the sale by Lestoil Products to the public of certain of its equity securities as

---

[1] When the financing was completed, 339,200 shares would be approximately 14% of the common stock before conversion of the class A shares, and approximately 11% after conversion.

outlined in management's proposal for a public offering to raise approximately $4 million. Any excess over the $6.9 million needed to repay the bank loan was to be used for general corporate purposes.

Important provisions of the loan agreement relating to the 6¼% notes to be purchased by the institutional lenders were as follows: Annual installments on principal were payable in the amount of $300,000. The notes were redeemable for the first 2 years at a premium of 10%; the premium would be 4% for the 3rd year, and then would diminish annually at the rate of 1% a year until 1966, after which date the notes would be redeemable at par. The company could not create liens or mortgages other than for the purpose of financing a maximum of 70% of plant and equipment purchases. It was required to maintain a minimum net working capital balance of $1.2 million during the period July 1, 1961–June 30, 1962, and $1.5 million after June 30, 1962. It was prohibited from making distributions on account of the common stock until such time and also thereafter if, as a result, consolidated net working capital would be less than $2.5 million. The notes were subordinated to bank loans up to a maximum of $3 million, which in certain circumstances could be increased to a maximum of $5 million.

THE PUBLIC OFFERING OF EQUITY SECURITIES

The major part of the funds needed were to be raised by a public offering of equity securities. Mr. Hogan and a representative of one of the two underwriting firms involved had conceived a plan that they believed would aid in assuring the success of the offering. The securities designed for the public sale were to be split into class A shares and common shares, and would be sold in units consisting of one common share and one class A share. Certificates representing units were to be issued to purchasers. On January 2, 1961, the shares of class A and common stock composing a unit would become separately transferable, and certificates representing units would become exchangeable for separate certificates for shares of class A and common stock.

A complex of factors actually determined the size and price of the offering. The offerers naturally wanted the offering to be successful and hoped, therefore, that no questions would be raised regarding its attractiveness. At the same time, they wanted to hold dilution of their equity within reasonable limits. They knew that Mr. Barowsky had talked earlier with several investment banking houses regarding the possibility of publicly selling the stock of Adell Chemical Company. These discussions had indicated some interest on the part of investment bankers in underwriting such an issue at a price–earnings ratio of 15 to 1. Thus, from the start, the Standard International group had based its thinking on a price–earnings ratio in this range.

In preliminary talks with representatives of underwriting firms, an offering of only one class of common stock had been proposed. After a review of the situation, the underwriters replied that, in their opinion, the company's earnings were not sufficiently stable to justify a 15 to 1 price–earnings ratio on a straight common issue. The package of two classes of stock was then conceived and decided on, one class bearing a fixed and cumulative preferred dividend obligation, to add the appeal of an assured return to the offering for the investing public. As an additional capital gains incentive, the class A stock would be made convertible into common stock at any time prior to redemption and within a limited time after any call for redemption.

On the basis of earnings after taxes in the year ended October 31, 1959, adjusted to allow for $6\frac{1}{4}\%$ interest payments on the notes to be purchased by institutional lenders, it was estimated that earnings after interest and taxes in future years were likely to be at least $1 million. The offerers and underwriters agreed that a fixed dividend commitment on class A stock should be covered a minimum of four times if it and the common stock were to be looked on with favor by investors. A computation revealed that it would be possible to maintain this coverage and still offer as much as a 6% return on the total funds to be raised through the offering ($4 million).

With this information at hand, specific details of the offering were backed into. The conversion ratio of the class A stock was set at two shares of common stock for each share of class A. A price of $14.40 and 60 cents, respectively ($15 a unit), was placed on the class A and common shares on a total offering of 275,000 units, primarily on the following basis: It was determined that a fair offering price for the common shares would be the same as the Standard International group had paid for their shares, namely, 60 cents. The price and conversion ratio of the class A stock were then determined at the amount per share that would give a price–earnings ratio of approximately 15 to 1 on the whole package, allowing for probable future dilution from the warrants issued to institutional investors. This automatically gave an acceptable result in terms of equity dilution on the basis of a $4 million offering. The preferred dividend was then determined at 90 cents, to give a 6% plus return on the class A shares. Other factors involved in setting the conversion privilege at two shares of common for each share of class A were (1) to give additional desirability to the offering and (2) to be substantially consistent with the $7.50 warrant price to institutional investors.

	Shares of Common Stock	Percentage
Owned by promoting group	1,835,800	61.2
Reserved for exercise of warrants	339,200	11.3
Sold to public (275,000 units):		
Common stock	275,000	9.2
Reserved for conversion of class A shares	550,000	18.3
Total	3,000,000	100.0

Earnings for year ended October 31, 1959 (adjusted)	$1,000,000
Total shares of common stock to be outstanding	3,000,000
Earnings per share	$ 0.333
Offering price per unit	$ 15.00
Effective cost to public per share of common stock	$ 5.00
Effective price–earnings ratio (after dilution)	15/1

Both the Standard International group and the underwriters were confident that this combination would make an attractive package for sale to the public.[2]

The red-herring prospectus[3] for the public offering was completed early in June, 1960. Other provisions of the two classes of stock were described as follows: A provision was included for adjustment of the conversion ratio to prevent dilution of the rights of class A shareholders. The class A stock had a liquidation and redemption value of $15 a share. No dividends could be paid on the common stock while any shares of class A stock were outstanding, and the prospectus stated that no dividends on the common stock should be expected in the near future. Management intended to retain all earnings until a substantial amount of working capital had been accumulated. The common shares and the class A shares were entitled to one vote each and would vote together as a single class, except where the separate consent of class A shares was required.

Conferences with underwriters indicated an underwriting commission of 8%. Net proceeds to the company would therefore amount to $3.795 million. The effects of the proposed financing on the company's balance sheet and earnings statements are shown in the pro forma financial statements presented as Exhibits 5 and 6.

Mr. Hogan's business diary noted the development of the plans for the permanent financing.

Saturday, March 26. Conference in New York City with underwriters' representatives re: first studies as to the various methods that could be used in the Lestoil underwriting. We first came up with the possibility of the class A and common stocks package at this conference.

Sunday, March 27. More conferences, New York City—conversations with Sam Dennis regarding the present proposal for the packaged security.

Monday, March 28. Additional conferences in New York City with representatives of the two underwriting firms.

Tuesday, March 29. We are now, in effect, running Lestoil. Held conferences with McCarthy, Deam, and others regarding immediate steps that should be taken to strengthen the business.

---

[2] Exhibit 3 presents selected data on certain other companies, and Exhibit 4 gives data from Moody's Industrial Stock Averages.

[3] Eric L. Kohler, *A Dictionary for Accountants* (2d ed.; Englewood Cliffs, N.J.: Prentice-Hall, Inc., 1957), p. 410, defines *red-herring prospectus* as follows: "An announcement and description of an anticipated issue of securities, given restricted circulation during the 'waiting' period of 20 days or other specified period between the filing of a registration statement with the U.S. Securities and Exchange Commission and the effective date of the statement. It generally takes the form of the final prospectus except that the offering price, commissions to dealers, and other data dependent on price are omitted; also emblazoned across each page is an inscription printed in red, stating that the document is not an offer to sell or the solicitation of an offer to buy and that neither kind of offer may be made until the registration statement has become effective."

Wednesday, March 30.   Conferences with the Barowskys at Holyoke on what is needed in Lestoil.

Friday, April 1.   Finalized the arrangements with underwriters.

Monday, April 4.   Conferences in New York with institutional lenders to discuss the intermediate financing plans and subordinated notes.

Tuesday, April 5.   At Holyoke planning Lestoil strategy.

Wednesday, April 6.   Left Holyoke with Mr. Barowsky, to packaging show in Atlantic City.

Thursday, April 7.   Conference in New York City with a chemical company regarding possibility of bringing out a liquid starch made from their synthetic resins.

Tuesday, April 12.   Picked up representatives of the pension funds in Morristown, New Jersey, and flew them to Lestoil at Holyoke for the day. [One of the corporations controlled by Standard International owned an airplane as its only asset. Mr. Hogan held a pilot's license and often flew the plane on such trips.]

Thursday, April 14.   Conferences in Boston regarding the closing of the Lestoil deal and the details of the underwriting.

Friday, April 15.   In Andover and Boston, discussing details of financing with Messrs. Bolten, senior and junior. Then a luncheon conference with firm of Hale and Dorr to begin giving them the background work for the registration statement.

Monday, April 18.   On the phone most of the day with representatives of pension funds trying to work out the details of their financing versus the underwriting. Pension funds thought the underwriters' deal was too rich, and the underwriters felt that the pension funds were asking for too much. [The institutional lenders thought that the underwriters were making the package more attractive than necessary to raise $4 million. The underwriters thought that the institutional lenders were getting too many warrants for purchase of stock at $7.50 a share.]

Tuesday, April 19.   Writing up the brochure for consideration by the pension funds committees to help push the financing of the subordinated notes.

Thursday, April 21.   Conferences in Boston with the underwriter. Then meeting with president of [XYZ Company]. He was interested in buying Lestoil. We had many feelers from various companies wanting to know if we would like to turn over our deal to them. [Mr. Hogan did not investigate any of these offers in any depth.]

Friday, April 22.   Conferences with underwriter in Boston.

Saturday and Sunday, April 23 and 24.   Revising the brochure for the underwriters and the pension funds.

April 25–May 31.   A lot of activity on the promotions at Lestoil, details of the underwriting, preparing the details for the SEC, etc.

Tuesday, May 31.   We had the closing at The First National Bank of Boston.

FUTURE PROSPECTS

Lestoil Products maintained a research department to study production methods, quality controls, and development of new products by applying to practical uses current discoveries and developments in chemical science. The management intended to place the emphasis almost entirely on development and improvement of discoveries made by others in the field, rather than emphasizing basic research. The policy of the company would be to add to its product line new items for family and household use if and when suitable products were developed and proved. Management's objective was to develop and market companion products to Lestoil and Lestare, and thus offer a family of Lestoil products to the consumer.

In 1959, some of the major soap and detergent companies had introduced new brands of heavy-duty liquid detergents, accompanied by extensive television advertising and other unusually intensive methods of sales promotion. Partly as a result of this competition, sales of Lestoil had declined since September, 1959. Industry sales were also seasonally lower during the winter months. The new owners believed, however, that no permanent or continuing adverse trends in sales volume were necessarily indicated. In fact, they thought that a seasonal increase in industry sales, improvements in sales management, rapidly increasing sales of Lestare, and plans to advertise and market company products in the western and southwestern parts of the United States in the immediate future would push sales volumes to new highs. They felt that company profits before taxes during the calendar year 1960 could reasonably be expected to reach a level of $3 million, and that the before-tax profits for 1961 were likely to show an increase over the 1960 level. In their opinion, existing plant facilities would be adequate for some time. The company's net cash inflow during the next few years would therefore be substantial.

At this time, the Standard International group foresaw no need for additional common stock issues in the future. In fact, they had stated that company policy would be to avoid any such dilution if at all possible. Acquisitions by or additions to Lestoil Products would be made with cash and new debt, with sale of equity only as a last resort.

Exhibit 1

LESTOIL PRODUCTS, INC.

CONSOLIDATED STATEMENT OF FINANCIAL CONDITION OF
ADELL CHEMICAL COMPANY, INC., AND SUBSIDIARIES
ON MARCH 31, 1960
(Dollar Figures in Thousands)

ASSETS

Current assets:

Cash and U.S. Treasury bills	$1,614	
Accounts receivable	1,605	
Inventories (at lower of cost or market)	1,304	
Other	65	
Total Current Assets		$4,588
Fixed assets (net)		3,415
Other assets		184
Total Assets		$8,187

LIABILITIES AND CAPITAL

Current liabilities:

Notes payable (banks)	$1,140	
Other	2,465	
Total Current Liabilities		$3,605
Noncurrent liabilities*		1
Capital stock and retained earnings		4,581
Total Liabilities and Capital		$8,187

* Commitments for noncancelable media advertising for a 3-month period amounted to approximately $1.5 million.

Exhibit 2

LESTOIL PRODUCTS, INC.

CONSOLIDATED STATEMENTS OF INCOME AND EXPENSE OF ADELL CHEMICAL COMPANY, INC., AND SUBSIDIARIES, 1955–60

(Dollar Figures in Thousands)

	Year Ended October 31					Five Months Ended March 31	
	1955	1956	1957	1958	1959	1959	1960
Net sales	$474	$1,641	$7,220	$19,945	$22,467	$9,158	$8,719
Cost of sales*	218	625	2,553	7,319	8,731	3,399	3,959
Gross profit	$256	$1,016	$4,667	$12,626	$13,736	$5,759	$4,760
Advertising expense	$125	$ 497	$2,033	$ 6,008	$ 9,562	$3,648	$3,027
Selling, general, and administrative expenses	100	191	650	1,666	1,974	859	825
	$225	$ 688	$2,683	$ 7,674	$11,536	$4,507	$3,852
Net operating income	$ 31	$ 328	$1,984	$ 4,952	$ 2,200	$1,252	$ 908
Other income (expense):							
Interest income	$ ..	$ ..	$ 6	$ 9	$ 7	$ 6	$ 5
Miscellaneous	(2)	5	14	80	113	41	26
Interest expense	..	(1)	(3)	(14)	(26)	(7)	(24)
	$ (2)	$ 4	$ 17	$ 75	$ 94	$ 40	$ 7
Net income before taxes	$ 29	$ 332	$2,001	$ 5,027	$ 2,294	$1,292	$ 915
Provision for federal and state income taxes	10	178	1,091	2,763	1,226	695	499
Net Income	$ 19	$ 154	$ 910	$ 2,264	$ 1,068	$ 597	$ 416

* Depreciation charges included:
Year ended October 31:
1955 .... na
1956 .... na
1957 .... $ 49
1958 192
1959 318
Five months ended March 31:
1959 .... na
1960 .... $168

Exhibit 3

LESTOIL PRODUCTS, INC.

Selected Data on Certain Companies in the Same and Related Fields of Business

		Price-Earnings Ratios		Cash Dividend Yield on Common Stock, 1959‡	Sales		Date	Capitalization		
	Where Traded	(1)*	(2)†		Year Ended	Amount (Millions)		Long-Term Debt	Preferred Stock	Common Stock and Surplus
Lestoil Products Inc. (pro forma)	O.C.	15§		6.0‖	10/31/59	$22.5	3/31/60	39.5%	45.0%	15.5%
Purex Corporation, Ltd.	O.C.	20	18	2.4%	6/30/59	$71.4	6/30/59	39.1%	...	60.9%

Manufactures and sells bleaches, disinfectants, synthetic detergents, ammonia, and other soaps, cleaners, and toiletries. Products are sold under a variety of trade names. Company was established in 1927.

Procter & Gamble Company	NYSE	20	24	2.7%	6/30/59	$1,368.5	6/30/59	14.7%	0.3%	85.0%

Constitutes the largest factor in the domestic soap industry. Manufactures and sells soap, toothpaste, synthetic detergents, household cleansers, glycerine, cooking fats, peanut butter, cake mixes, and a variety of other products. Its products are marketed under numerous trade names. Company was established in 1905.

Stepan Chemical Company	O.C.	21	18	0.0%	12/31/59	$19.4	12/31/59	36.2%	...	63.8%

Manufactures organic chemicals sold primarily to processors and industrial users. Products include liquid detergents, chemicals for cosmetics, emulsifiers, insecticides, flavoring compounds, liquid fertilizers, and others. Company was established in 1932.

Wyandotte Chemical Corporation	O.C.	20	28	1.9%	12/31/59	$93.9	12/31/59	10.1%	14.8%	75.1%

Produces cleansing products, sanitizing products, soda ash, caustic soda, chlorine, glycols, coke, cement, and other products. Sales are made primarily to industrial users. The existing company was incorporated in 1942.

Witco Chemical Company, Inc.	O.C.	17	11	2.5%	12/31/59	$51.2	12/31/59	...	...	100.0%

Produces chemicals, synthetic detergents, metallic stearates, emulsifiers, plasticizers, asphalts, and other products. Sales are made largely to industrial users. Company was formed in 1920.

* Bid prices (or closing prices) on December 31, 1959, divided by earnings for year ended December 31, 1959.
† Bid prices (or closing prices) on May 31, 1960, divided by earnings for quarter ended March 31, 1960, on an annual basis.
‡ Annual cash dividend rate, divided by average of high and low market prices for the year.
§ Effective price-earnings ratio (after dilution) based on effective offering price per share of common stock ($5.00) divided by earnings for year ended October 31, 1959.
‖ Yield on offering price of unit.

Source of Basic Data: Moody's Industrials

Exhibit 4

LESTOIL PRODUCTS, INC.

SELECTED DATA FROM MOODY'S INDUSTRIAL
STOCK AVERAGES
PRICE–EARNINGS RATIOS OF COMMON STOCKS*

1955..12
1956..14
1957..14
1958..18
1959..19

* Moody's annual composite weighted average prices, divided by composite weighted average earnings for corresponding years (125 industrial common stocks).

MOODY'S PREFERRED STOCK YIELD AVERAGES

	10 Medium-Grade Industrials	*10 Speculative-Grade Industrials*
1959............................	4.99%	5.58%
1960:		
January......................	5.23	5.78
February.....................	5.22	5.72
March.......................	5.21	5.79
April........................	5.25	5.80

Exhibit 5

LESTOIL PRODUCTS, INC.

PRO FORMA BALANCE SHEET GIVING EFFECT TO THE PROPOSED FINANCING
AS IF THE ACQUISITION TRANSACTION HAD BEEN COMPLETED
ON MARCH 31, 1960
(Dollar Figures in Thousands)

ASSETS

Current assets:
Cash and U.S. Treasury bills.........................$1,889
Accounts receivable............................... 1,605
Inventories (at lower of cost or market)*............... 1,374
Other*.. 58

Total Current Assets...........................	$ 4,926
Fixed assets (net)*..................................	4,077
Other assets†...	2,760
Total Assets...................................	$11,763

LIABILITIES AND CAPITAL

Current liabilities:
Notes payable (bank)...............................$1,140
Other‡... 2,525

Total Current Liabilities.......................	$ 3,665
Noncurrent liabilities:	
6¼% notes..	3,200
Other§.......................................	1

Capital Stock:
Class A (convertible, no par value; 275,000 shares)......$3,644
Common stock (50 cents par value; 2,110,800 shares).... 1,055

	4,699
Capital paid in in excess of par value of common stock....	198
Total Liabilities and Capital.....................	$11,763

* Reflects adjustments made on the basis of values as determined by the new management and supported by independent appraisal.
† Reflects excess of cost of total assets over the amount allocated to tangible assets. Payments on the $4 million conditional liability were to be allocated to intangible assets also.
‡ Reflects adjustment for estimated organization and financing charges in connection with acquisition transaction.
§ Commitments for noncancelable media advertising for a 3-month period amounted to approximately $1.5 million.

Exhibit 6
LESTOIL PRODUCTS, INC.

PRO FORMA EARNINGS AS IF THE ACQUISITION TRANSACTION HAD BEEN EFFECTIVE
DURING THE PERIODS COVERED
(Dollar Figures in Thousands)

	Years Ended October 31		Five Months Ended March 31,
	1958	1959	1960
Net income after taxes (as reported)	$2,264	$1,068	$ 416
Pro forma adjustments:			
Interest on 6¼% notes	$ (200)	$ (200)	$ (83)
Amortization of estimated organization and financing expenses	(12)	(12)	(5)
Changes in depreciation charges resulting from revaluation of assets and change in method*	24	54	58
Estimated reduction in income taxes resulting from additional expenses	104	87	16
	$ (84)	$ (71)	$ (14)
Pro forma net income after taxes	$2,180	$ 997	$ 402
Dividends on 275,000 Class A shares	$ 248	$ 248	$ 103
Pro forma net income on common stock	$1,932	$ 749	$ 299
Pro forma net income per share, based on 2,110,800 common shares	$ 0.92	$ 0.35	$0.14

* Lestoil Products, Inc., would not be permitted to use accelerated methods used by the predecessor company.

HIGHTOWER COMPANY

DURING THE SPRING OF 1965, representatives of the boards of directors of the Hightower Company and the Shaw Company were actively discussing a projected merger between them. Both boards believed that some form of combination was desirable and had agreed that this should take the form of a statutory merger, with Hightower as the surviving corporation.

The financial details of the merger, however, were still to be arranged. The boards had made a tentative proposal for an exchange ratio of 0.425 share of Hightower common stock for each share of Shaw common stock. This ratio appeared to them satisfactorily representative of the relationship of the two stocks in the market at the time of the preliminary agreement. However, it was recognized that this ratio was no more than a starting point for the detailed financial discussions, and that it would have to be adjusted after consideration of the problems described below. These included the existence of Shaw preferred stock, outstanding stock options to Hightower executives, pension plans and employment contracts, and the considerable disparity between the capital structures and dividend policies of the two companies. Attempts to solve these problems would require attention to the need for arranging the merger so that it would be classified as tax free by the Internal Revenue authorities.

BACKGROUND OF HIGHTOWER COMPANY

Since its incorporation in 1924, the Hightower Company had been engaged in the production of precision metal parts, primarily for the electrical, automotive, road building machinery, and farm equipment fields. A program of acquisitions in recent years had led to some diversification, including the production of metal die castings as well as both metal and plastic extruded containers. In fiscal 1964, approximately 50% of Hightower's sales were of precision metal parts. Die castings made up a further 11%; 21% of sales were of seat springs for both the automobile and furniture industries; and the remaining 18% was made up of a number of blow-molded plastic products. Approximately one third of total sales were to the automotive industry. All Hightower products sold in highly competitive markets, and in no case did the company have a market share of more than 10%. The company employed 2,400 people in 11 plants.

Exhibit 1 presents income statement data for Hightower for the five fiscal years ended July 31, 1960–64, and the nine-month periods ended April 30, 1964 and 1965. Exhibit 2 presents balance sheet data as of July 31, 1964, and April 30, 1965.

Although sales had increased each year during the time span covered by the exhibits, earnings had shown a downtrend in 1961 and 1962. The drop in earnings in 1961 had resulted from discontinuance of certain product lines. The other-deductions item in 1962, which caused a severe earnings drop, resulted from closing down plants used in the production of these discontinued product lines. The earnings drop in 1962 was also aggravated by losses on the liquidation of obsolete and useless finished inventory and work in process. In early 1965, the president of Hightower believed that the product line had been pruned as much as possible of unprofitable products. A few such products had been continued for marketing and competitive reasons.

The following quotations from the 1964 Annual Report reflect in part the direction of corporate policy.

During the past year, the company served in excess of 2,500 customers in the consumer and capital goods markets. Volume with more than 500 of these accounts totaled from $10,000 to over $1,000,000 each for the year. This select group of customers represents 120 different industrial classifications, a factor that contributes greatly to the stability of the Company and future growth prospects.

Another significant area of improvement [in earnings] was in non-operating income, which increased a net total of $749,421. This net income came about primarily from the reduction of expenses for idle facilities ($412,508), the reduction of interest expense ($138,948), and the increase in gains from the sales and liquidation of divisions ($197,824).

Due to certain legal and contractual obligations the operating loss carry-forward was not available to the company in fiscal 1964. This loss carry-forward, totaling $526,000, will be used by the company to reduce its tax liabilities for fiscal 1965 by approximately $275,000.

The company is currently in the best financial position in its history, completely free of bank debt, with cash and securities in excess of $3,000,000 and with working capital of $9,090,735 at July 31, 1964.

The fact that all bank loans have been paid off should not be construed as a change of company attitude toward further acquisitions and expansion. Companies were investigated during the year for purpose of acquisition but were found to be unsatisfactory from the standpoint of potential return on investment. It was decided, therefore, that prepayment of bank loans during fiscal 1964 was the best way to utilize funds not required for operations.

The company will continue its program to solicit and investigate all interesting acquisition possibilities and to proceed with a balanced program of internal product development. Undoubtedly, these growth programs will again require the favorable financial banking assistance which has proved to be an important factor in company growth in recent years.

BACKGROUND OF THE SHAW COMPANY

The Shaw Company was incorporated on January 30, 1934. In early 1965, Shaw was engaged principally in the manufacture and sale of automotive seat springs and seat spring assemblies for use in trucks, passenger cars, and buses. It also manufactured vinyl plastisol and polyurethane foam pads for automotive and other furniture seating.

Approximately 90% of Shaw's net sales for fiscal 1964 were to the automotive industry. Its nonautomotive products consisted principally of refrigeration condensers, shelves, and evaporators for the refrigeration industry. The major automotive producers accounted for approximately 82% of Shaw's sales of automotive seat springs and assemblies, approximately 96% of its sales of urethane foam pads, and approximately 83% of its plastisol production.

Automotive cushion springs produced were of the zigzag or formed wire type, the modified coil spring type, and the conventional coil spring type, which were the general types of construction used in the automotive industry. Polyurethane foam pads for seating were produced in several forms, including flexible molded and semirigid molded foam. The urethane foam industry generally was highly competitive. All these products were distributed primarily through Shaw's own sales organization to original equipment manufacturers.

Shaw owned and operated 5 plants and had approximately 2,400 employees. Exhibits 3 and 4 present income statement and balance sheet data for the Shaw Company.

MARKET PRICES OF COMMON STOCKS

The Hightower common stock was listed, whereas the Shaw common stock was traded over the counter. Exhibit 5 shows sales prices for Hightower stock and bid prices for Shaw common stock for each quarter during calendar 1963 and 1964 and the first two quarters of 1965.

FUNDS FLOW PROJECTIONS

Exhibit 6 presents pro forma funds flow projections for the merging companies for the fiscal years 1965 through 1968. The statements were developed for the negotiators by combining projections made separately by the Hightower Company and the Shaw Company. Therefore, the statements do not reflect any economies of scale or changes in capital structure, such as might eventually result if and when the proposed merger was consummated.

Planners for both the Hightower and the Shaw companies expected that sales would increase slightly each year over the foreseeable future and that gross margins would also increase slightly from year to year. The actual sales level would depend closely on the national level of automobile production and particularly on the specific performance of those makes that used Hightower and Shaw parts. Both Hightower and Shaw planners believed their companies would be among the last in their industries to be hurt if and when the major automotive companies decided to make rather than buy more semifinished materials.

Additions to facilities were expected to be minimal over the next few years. Both companies had just completed (ending in fiscal 1964) major renovation projects. Depreciation charges were therefore expected to be more than adequate to meet capital expenditure needs.

Annual dividends of 60 cents a share on the 4,800 shares of Shaw Company preferred stock were projected as constant. Common dividends were estimated at a constant annual rate of 60 cents a share, the current rate on Hightower stock. The sinking fund payments in the funds flow statement refer to various loans outstanding to the Shaw Company. Details are discussed in the following section on the capital structures of the two companies.

CAPITAL STRUCTURES AND FINANCIAL POSITIONS

As of April 30, 1965, the Hightower Company had no long-term debt outstanding (see Exhibit 2). Because reporting for tax purposes and reporting for financial accounting purposes were identical, there was no deferred federal income tax account. The common stock of the Hightower Company had a par value of $2.50. As of April 30, 1965, there were 2,753,549 shares outstanding. The company did not hold any shares in the treasury. Its financial position is evidenced by the lack of any long-term debt and the large investment in commercial paper.

The capital structure and financial position of the Shaw Company, however, were quite different. As of April 30, 1965, the company had two classes of stock. One was a preferred stock, with a 60 cent a share cumulative dividend, a par value of $5, and redemption price of $10 a share. In April, the stock sold between $9 and $10 a share. As of April 30, there were 4,800 shares outstanding. During the preceding 6 months, only 25 shares had been transferred on the company's books.

The common share was of $1 par value. At April 30, 1965, there were 763,620 shares outstanding and 14,722 shares in the treasury. During the past 8 months, the Shaw Company had purchased 378 shares at an average price of $9.57.

The long-term debt of the Shaw Company was of two types. The first type consisted of several conditional sales contracts carrying $6\frac{1}{2}\%$ to $7\frac{1}{2}\%$ interest rates. The outstanding principal value as of April 30, 1965, was $98,378. Payment periods on these contracts ranged from 3 to 12 years. The principal value of each could be paid off without any penalty or payment of future interest payments.

The debt issue was a $5\frac{1}{2}\%$ sinking fund subordinated debenture totaling $123,000 in April, 1965, and due in May, 1967. Sinking fund payments were made annually, on May 1, in the amount of $41,000 a year. As of April 30, 1965, there was no penalty for prepayment.

The Shaw Company also owed its major bank $1.75 million on an unsecured basis. The rate was calculated at .5% above the prime rate. The negotiators of the merger were assured that the bank would be pleased to continue this loan to the new company. In fact, they were asked if a larger line would be of use.

THE STOCKHOLDER GROUPS

A large proportion of the shares of the Hightower Company were either owned or controlled by the directors or their families, as witnessed by the following tabulation:

	Number of Shares	Percentage of Total Number of Shares Outstanding
Mr. Simon Iffland	330,687	12.01%
Mr. Iffland's family	33,349	1.21
Iffland Foundation	7,562	0.28
Mr. John Normandie, vice chairman	209,886	7.62
Other directors, total	228,058	8.28
Salaried Employees' profit sharing trust	132,028	4.79
	941,570	34.19%
Total shares outstanding	2,753,549	100.00%

The Hightower executives knew little about the makeup of the rest of the stockholder list, except that there were over 5,400 registered stockholders. The average stockholding, excluding those discussed above, was approximately 280 shares. There were very few stockholdings of less than 100 shares. In the investment community, Hightower shares were looked on as neither a growth stock nor an income stock primarily, but were considered "a stock with better than average potential for price appreciation, which pays a dividend which in turn makes it worthwhile to hold the stock" as an investment adviser stated in a letter.

The major common stockholdings in the Shaw Company were as follows:

	Number of Shares	Percentage of Total Number of Shares Outstanding
Mr. Morris Shaw, chairman	102,495	13.41%
Mrs. Morris Shaw	51,211	6.71
Other directors	7,375	0.97
	161,081	21.09%
Total shares outstanding	763,620	100.00%

The other 602,539 shares were owned by over 1,100 stockholders. About 50% of these shares were owned by relatives of the directors other than Mr. Shaw, or by employees of the company. However, no one of these persons owned more than 10,000 shares.

A rough survey by each company had shown that the largest stockholders of each were in favor of the merger. The surveys covered slightly more than 50% of the outstanding shares of each company. Although only a two-thirds majority was needed under the law to authorize the merger, the negotiators wanted the favorable votes of at least 95% of the shares of each company in order to avoid any chance of cash payments to dissenters.

PROBLEM AREAS

In July, 1965, the negotiators were ready to take up the detailed problems that needed solution before the exact terms for the share exchange could be fixed. It had been agreed, as stated above, that the ratio of .425 share of Hightower Company to 1 share of Shaw Company would serve as the base from which any necessary adjustments could be made. The problem areas appeared to be:

1. Outstanding stock options to executives.
2. The preferred stock of Shaw Company.
3. Redundant assets and debt capacity of the two companies.
4. The disparity in dividend rates of the two companies.

Outstanding Stock Options

As of July 31, 1964, Hightower had 270,218 shares of authorized and unissued common stock subject to options under various restricted stock option incentive plans for key personnel. All had provisions to prevent dilution of the options. In all cases, the option price was at 95% of the fair market value of the common stock at the time the option was granted. All shares had to be paid for in cash.

Options under Hightower's supplemental restricted stock option plan were granted at the end of each fiscal year. The number of shares to be optioned annually depended on the improvement, if any, in the market value of Hightower's common stock from year to year. Options granted under this plan were exercisable at any time during the period of 10 years from the date the option was granted. In the event of the optionee's death, the option was exercisable within nine months from the date of death. In the event of termination of the optionee's employment, his option was exercisable within three months of the date of termination. This plan was to terminate on July 31, 1970.

Options had been awarded to 85 employees. As of April 30, 1965, options were outstanding for 239,125 shares, at prices in the range of $20–$22 per share.

The Shaw Company had no option plans. However, there were pension

plans and employment agreements. The largest employment agreement was
with Mr. Shaw. It provided for $60,000 per annum compensation to him for
active service until retirement, for reduced payments (maximum $30,000
annually) during his lifetime for advisory services after retirement or in the
event of disability, and after his death for payments to his wife until her death
or for 15 years, whichever period was shorter.

Under the Shaw Company's pension plan for salaried employees, eight
officers (including Mr. Shaw) were entitled on retirement at age 65 to
pensions equivalent to $2.25 a month for each year of accredited service. This
plan was trusteed, and it was fully funded.

Shaw Company Preferred Stock

As has been stated earlier, the boards of directors of both companies
wanted the merger to be a tax-free exchange of shares, with the Hightower
Company as the surviving entity. Consequently, they believed there might be
some problems with the Shaw Company's preferred stock. This stock had
originally been sold to common stockholders in March, 1956, in units of 1
$250 debenture and 25 preferred shares ($5 par) for each 100 common shares
held. The price was $418.75 a unit. The preferred, as a class, had preference
for assets and cumulative dividends of 60 cents per share. It was callable as a
whole or in part at any time on at least 30 days' notice at $10 a share and
accrued dividends.

Redundant Assets of Hightower Company

As witnessed by Exhibit 2, Hightower Company had investments in commercial paper and no debt other than current liabilities. Exhibit 6 shows that
operations for the foreseeable future were expected to provide more funds
than the total needed for capital expansion, for improvements, and for capital
service (dividends and sinking fund payments).

During recent months, the financial officers of both companies had been
visited by representatives of the commercial banks with which they did
business, as well as one or two others. It was clear from these visits that both
companies enjoyed high credit ratings and that applications for term or other
loans ("in seven figure amounts") would be welcomed. The bankers, of
course, had not been told officially of the tentative merger agreement, but the
negotiators could not be sure that there had been no leaks.

The possibility of introducing leverage into the merged companies had
been discussed between the negotiators and by each of them with the directors
of the company he represented. There was a general atmosphere favoring the
use of debt in the new capital structure, but the problems of how much to use,
how to get it in place, and how it would affect the basis of exchanging shares
were as yet untouched.

Dividend Payments

Under the provisional agreement, the Hightower shares received by Shaw
stockholders in exchange for their Shaw common shares would rank equally

with existing Hightower common shares for dividend distribution. During the current financial year, the Hightower dividend had been 15 cents per quarter, and the funds flow projection included, as a constant, dividend payments at this rate of 60 cents per share per annum. The provisional ratio of exchange of .425 represented a dividend of 25.5 cents per share per annum on the Shaw common stock. This exceeded Shaw's existing rate of 6 cents per quarter maintained in 1964 and 1965 to date.

The effective increase in the rate of dividend payout on the Shaw common stock was especially disturbing in the context of the possible effects of the merger on earnings per share of Hightower common stock. The earnings per share during 1964, the last full year for which audited figures were available, had been $1.61. The corresponding figure that would have applied if the merger had been in effect during 1964 (produced by adding the net income figures for each organization, assuming no economies of scale, and converting issued and outstanding Shaw common shares into Hightower shares at the .425 to 1 ratio) was only $1.56 a share. The negotiators were convinced that the existing Hightower shareholders would not approve the merger unless they were assured of receiving dividends at least as large as the existing rate. In consequence, the dividend cover would be reduced. Projected pro forma earnings for the joint organization in 1965, however, were considerably higher than those realized in 1964 (see Exhibit 6).

START ON PREPARATION OF FINANCIAL DETAILS

In order to get the needed discussion on its way, the negotiators agreed that the representative of the Hightower Company would prepare a plan to deal with the problems stated above, and would suggest whether and how much the base ratio of exchange would need to be changed in consequence. As he began his work, he realized that it would be worthwhile to consider what each company might do independently, in advance of the merger, to simplify the details of the merger itself. But beyond realization of this dimension of the problem, he had nothing specific in mind.

Since the form of the combination was to be a statutory merger (Type A reorganization), it would be possible to use nonvoting classes of stock in the plan, provided that a substantial amount of voting stock would be received by the holders of Shaw Company voting stock. Debt instruments could not be used except in exchange for like amounts of debt. Counsel advised that to use cash in this type of acquisition was questionable.

Exhibit 1

HIGHTOWER COMPANY

INCOME STATEMENTS FOR THE YEARS ENDED JULY 31, 1960–64, AND THE NINE-MONTH PERIODS ENDED APRIL 30, 1964 AND 1965*

(Dollar Figures in Thousands)

	Years Ended July 31					Nine Months Ended April 30	
	1960	1961	1962	1963	1964	1964 (Unaudited)	1965 (Unaudited)
Net sales and other operating revenues	$28,865	$34,394	$45,601	$56,980	$62,065	$47,244	$51,523
Cost of products and services sold	22,482	26,897	37,549	44,747	47,532	35,406	38,119
	$ 6,383	$ 7,497	$ 8,052	$12,233	$14,533	$11,838	$13,404
Selling and administrative expenses	3,526	4,187	5,479	5,667	6,450	5,477	5,560
	$ 2,857	$ 3,310	$ 2,573	$ 6,566	$ 8,083	$ 6,361	$ 7,844
Interest expense	137	168	315	218	80	69	...
Other deductions (credits), net	(39)	108	1,123†	120	(630)†	(609)†	(232)
Earnings before Income Taxes	$ 2,759	$ 3,034	$ 1,135	$ 6,228	$ 8,633	$ 6,901	$ 8,076
Federal income taxes:							
Provisions for the period	$ 1,405	$ 1,570	$ 625	$ 3,300	$ 4,300	$ 3,500	$ 3,875
Less reduction resulting from carryforward of tax losses of acquired companies	305	...	275	...	...	...	...
	$ 1,100	$ 1,570	$ 350	$ 3,300	$ 4,300	$ 3,500	$ 3,875
Net Earnings	$ 1,659	$ 1,464	$ 785	$ 2,928	$ 4,333	$ 3,401	$ 4,201
Retained earnings at beginning of period	3,962	4,744	5,550	5,563	6,955	6,955	9,729
	$ 5,621	$ 6,208	$ 6,335	$ 8,491	$11,288	$10,356	$13,930
Less:							
Cash dividends	535	658	772	849	1,559	875	1,234
2% stock dividends	342	...	...	687	...	...	...
	$ 877	$ 658	$ 772	$ 1,536	$ 1,559	$ 875	$ 1,234
Retained Earnings at End of Period	$ 4,744	$ 5,550	$ 5,563	$ 6,955	$ 9,729	$ 9,481	$12,696
Per share of common stock‡							
Net earnings	$ 0.75	$ 0.64	$ 0.30	$ 1.10	$ 1.61	$ 1.26	$ 1.53
Cash dividends	0.24	0.29	0.29	0.32	0.58	0.32	0.45

* These statements include the operations of various acquired companies generally from dates of acquisition.

† Other deductions in fiscal 1962 comprise principally costs and expenses incident to disposal and relocation of divisions and idle facilities; other credits in fiscal 1964 and the 9 months ended April 30, 1964, include gains of $627,889 on disposals of divisions and adjustment of properties to income-tax basis.

‡ Amounts per share are based on the average number of shares outstanding during the respective periods, adjusted for subsequent stock splits and dividends.

Exhibit 2

HIGHTOWER COMPANY

CONSOLIDATED BALANCE SHEETS, AS OF JULY 31, 1964, AND APRIL 30, 1965
(Dollar Figures in Thousands)

ASSETS

	July 31, 1964	April 30, 1965
Current assets:		
Cash	$ 1,463	$ 1,786
Commercial paper	...	3,365
Accounts receivable, less allowance of $125,000	4,842	7,293
Inventories, at lower of cost or market	8,005	7,753
Prepaid expenses and other current accounts	511	456
Total Current Assets	$14,821	$20,653
Property, plant, and equipment:		
Land	$ 278	$ 291
Buildings and improvements	6,892	5,513
Machinery and equipment	12,818	15,108
	$19,988	$20,912
Less allowances for depreciation	8,943	9,315
Property, Plant, and Equipment, Net	$11,045	$11,597
Other assets	866	680
Total Assets	$26,732	$32,930

LIABILITIES AND STOCKHOLDERS' EQUITY

	July 31, 1964	April 30, 1965
Current liabilities:		
Accounts payable	$ 1,891	$ 2,008
Accrued liabilities	2,776	4,074
Federal income taxes, less U.S. government securities of $1,695,165 in 1964	1,063	2,844
Total Current Liabilities	$ 5,730	$ 8,926
Stockholders' equity:		
Common stock, $2.50 par value; authorized, 5,000,000 shares; issued and outstanding, 2,735,156 shares in 1964 and 2,753,549 shares in 1965	$ 6,838	$ 6,884
Additional paid-in capital	4,435	4,424
Retained earnings	9,729	12,696
Total Stockholders' Equity	$21,002	$24,004
Total Liabilities and Stockholders' Equity	$26,732	$32,930

Exhibit 3

HIGHTOWER COMPANY

Income Statements of the Shaw Company for the Years Ended August 31, 1960–64, and the Eight-Month Periods Ended April 30, 1964 and 1965
(Dollar Figures in Thousands)

	Years Ended August 31					Eight Months Ended April 30	
	1960	*1961*	*1962*	*1963*	*1964*	*1964* (Not audited)	*1965* (audited)
Net sales	$37,901	$35,673	$33,425	$30,170	$34,839	$24,115	$29,249
Cost of products sold	33,692	33,707	31,397	27,371	31,839	21,664	26,311
Gross profit on sales	$ 4,209	$ 1,966	$ 2,028	$ 2,799	$ 3,000	$ 2,451	$ 2,938
Selling, administrative, research and development expenses	1,938	1,997	1,802	1,765	2,004	1,424	1,502
Operating income (loss)	$ 2,271	$ (31)	$ 226	$ 1,034	$ 996	$ 1,027	$ 1,436
Other charges or (income):							
Interest	$ 81	$ 139	$ 109	$ 25	$ 20	$ 12	$ 68
Miscellaneous, net	(57)	(42)	(21)	3	50	(26)	(18)
	$ 24	$ 97	$ 88	$ 28	$ 70	$ (14)	$ 50
Income (loss) before federal income taxes	$ 2,247	$ (128)	$ 138	$ 1,006	$ 926	$ 1,041	$ 1,386
Federal income taxes (refund)	1,160	(56)	81	481	465	536	700
Net income (loss) before special items	$ 1,087	$ (72)	$ 57	$ 525	$ 461	$ 505	$ 686
Special items, net of federal income taxes:							
Profit (loss) on sale of plants and equipment	266		(144)				
Expenses relating to idle plant	(58)						
	$ 208		$ (144)				
Net income (loss) after special items	$ 1,295	$ (72)	$ (87)	$ 525	$ 461	$ 505	$ 686
Retained earnings at beginning of period	4,202	5,115	4,480	4,389	4,673	4,673	4,947
	$ 5,497	$ 5,043	$ 4,393	$ 4,914	$ 5,134	$ 5,178	$ 5,633
Deduct:							
Cash dividends:							
On preferred stock	4	4	4	3	3	2	2
On common stock	378	384	....	238	184	93	91
Estimated fair value ($11.50 per share) of 15,258 shares of common stock issued as 2% stock dividend		175					
Retained earnings at end of period	$ 5,115	$ 4,480	$ 4,389	$ 4,673	$ 4,947	$ 5,083	$ 5,540
Net income (loss) before special items, per share of common stock*	$ 1.40	$ (0.10)	$ 0.07	$ 0.68	$ 0.60	$ 0.65	$ 0.89
Net income (loss) after special items, per share of common stock*	1.67	(0.10)	(0.12)	0.68	0.60	0.65	0.89
Cash dividends per share, common stock	0.50	0.60	0.60	0.31	0.24	0.12	0.12
Cash dividends per share, preferred stock	0.60	0.60	0.60	0.60	0.60	0.45	0.45

* Based upon net income or loss, after deducting preferred stock cash dividends, and based upon number of shares outstanding at end of each period, adjusted for 2% stock dividend in 1961.

Exhibit 4

HIGHTOWER COMPANY

BALANCE SHEETS OF THE SHAW COMPANY, AS OF
AUGUST 31, 1964, AND APRIL 30, 1965
(Dollar Figures in Thousands)

	August 31, 1964	April 30, 1965 (Not audited)
ASSETS		
Current:		
Cash	$ 1,156	$ 1,155
Accounts and notes receivable, less $25,000 allowance for possible losses	1,971	2,893
Inventories, at lower of cost (first-in, first-out) or market	3,894	3,407
Prepaid expenses	73	53
Total Current Assets	$ 7,094	$ 7,508
Fixed, at cost:		
Land and improvements	121	126
Buildings and improvements	1,885	2,015
Machinery and equipment	6,219	6,916
Leasehold improvements	231	269
Construction in progress (estimated cost to complete, $560,000 at August 31, 1964, and $750,000 at April 30, 1965)	136	767
	$ 8,592	$10,093
Less accumulated allowances for depreciation and amortization	3,298	3,858
Total Fixed Assets	$ 5,294	$ 6,235
Other:		
Deferred tooling and miscellaneous	346	541
Total Assets	$12,734	$14,284
LIABILITIES AND SHAREHOLDERS' EQUITY		
Current:		
Notes payable to bank	$ 1,150	$ 1,750
Accounts payable, including payroll deductions of $200,045 at August 31, 1964, and $122,644 at April 30, 1965	1,598	1,249
Accruals:		
Federal income taxes	303	698
Other taxes	281	463
Salaries and wages	400	693
Pension, profit-sharing, and stock bonus plans	377	228
Miscellaneous	23	41
Current maturities of long-term obligations	57	53
Dividends payable	46	—
Total Current Liabilities	$ 4,235	$ 5,175
Long-term:		
6½–7½% conditional sales contracts on purchased equipment, less current maturities	$ 105	$ 98
5½% sinking fund subordinated debentures, maturing in 1967	123	123
Pensions for retired employees, less current maturities	33	26
Total Long-Term Liabilities	$ 261	$ 247
Deferred federal income taxes	410	444
Total Liabilities	$ 4,906	$ 5,866

Exhibit 4 (Continued)

	August 31, 1964	April 30, 1965 (Not audited)
Capital stock:		
60¢ cumulative preferred, $5 par, at stated value; redeemable at $10 per share; matures April 1, 1968; shares authorized, 100,000; outstanding, 4,825 at August 31, 1964, and 4,800 at April 30, 1965..	40	40
Common, $1 par-shares; authorized, 1,000,000; issued, 778,342; in treasury, 14,344 at August 31, 1964, and 14,722 at April 30, 1965; outstanding, 763,998 at August 31, 1964, and 763,620 at April 30, 1965.............................	764	764
Total Capital Stock.................................	$ 804	$ 804
Additional paid-in capital.................................	2,077	2,074
Retained earnings...	4,947	5,540
Total Shareholders' Equity...........................	$ 7,828	$ 8,418
Total Liabilities and Shareholders' Equity.............	12,734	14,284

Exhibit 5

HIGHTOWER COMPANY

MARKET PRICES OF COMMON STOCK OF HIGHTOWER COMPANY AND SHAW COMPANY, BY QUARTERS, 1963–JUNE, 1965

	Hightower Company Sales Prices (listed)		Shaw Company Bid Prices (over the counter)	
	High	Low	High	Low
1963				
First quarter...............17.000		13.125	9.000	6.375
Second quarter.............16.875		11.875	7.500	5.250
Third quarter..............15.000		12.250	7.000	5.375
Fourth quarter.............15.750		12.250	6.625	5.125
1964				
First quarter...............17.500		14.250	6.750	6.125
Second quarter.............23.875		17.250	6.250	6.000
Third quarter..............24.750		20.500	6.000	5.625
Fourth quarter.............23.375		20.000	7.375	6.375
1965				
First quarter...............25.375		21.000	8.750	7.375
Second quarter.............25.125		23.250	10.250	8.000

Exhibit 6

HIGHTOWER COMPANY

Pro Forma Funds Flow Statements, Years Ended July 31, 1965–68
(Dollar Figures in Thousands)

	1965 Hightower	1965 Shaw	1965 Combined	1966	1967	1968
Sources of funds:						
Sales	$69,000	$41,000	$110,000	$120,000	$130,000	$140,000
Less: Cost of goods sold	50,000	37,000	87,000	96,000	104,000	112,000
	19,000	4,000	23,000	24,000	26,000	28,000
Less: Selling and general expenses	6,700	2,300	9,000	9,500	9,500	9,500
	12,300	1,700	14,000	14,500	16,500	18,500
Less: Interest	10	77	87	65	50	45
	12,290	1,623	13,913	14,435	16,450	18,455
Other credits	260	40	300	...	...	...
Earnings before taxes	12,550	1,663	14,213	14,435	16,450	18,455
Federal taxes	6,087	816	6,903	6,929	7,896	8,858
Earnings after taxes	6,463	847	7,310	7,506	8,554	9,597
Add: Depreciation	2,870	1,551	4,421	4,356	4,212	4,176
Funds provided by operations	9,333	2,398	11,731	11,862	12,766	13,773
Decrease in noncurrent assets*	...	400	400	375	350	325
Total sources	$ 9,333	$ 2,798	$ 12,131	$ 12,237	$ 13,116	$ 14,098
Uses of funds:						
Additions to facilities (net of disposals)	$ 3,981	$ 1,330	$ 5,311	$ 4,200	$ 4,000	$ 4,000
Sinking fund	...	71	71	66	20	15
Preferred dividends paid	...	3	3	3	3	3
Common dividends†	1,652	195	1,847	1,847	1,847	1,847
Total Uses	5,633	1,599	7,232	6,116	5,870	5,865
Additions to Working Capital	$ 3,700	$ 1,199	$ 4,899	$ 6,121	$ 7,246	$ 8,233

* Amortization of certain capitalized and tax deductible past expenditures. Like depreciation, these expenditures were charged off along with costs of goods sold for tax purposes. Therefore, they were to be added back to sources of funds in funds flow analysis.

† Assuming Shaw common stock to have been converted into Hightower common stock at a ratio of exchange of .425 to 1.

Chapter *10* Markets and Intermediaries

S. D. WARREN COMPANY

IN THE FALL OF 1959, Edward B. Gray, treasurer of S. D. Warren Company, was considering whether the company's common stock, currently traded over the counter, should be listed on the New York Stock Exchange. Having given a great deal of attention to the problem, Mr. Gray thought that he would soon be in a position to make a final recommendation to the president and the board of directors.

Founded in 1854 and incorporated in 1918, S. D. Warren Company of Boston, Massachusetts, was a leading manufacturer of high-quality coated and uncoated printing papers for the publishing industry. In 1959, the company owned and operated three completely modernized paper mills—Cumberland Mills and Copsecook Mill in Maine, and Central Mill in Michigan. The company also produced all its own power and a large part of its pulp requirements.

Continuous and active research by the company had developed a product line that was generally considered the standard of quality in the field. Printing papers made up approximately 85% of the total annual product. Nationwide distribution was accomplished, in the words of an investment banker, "through a closely-knit group of leading paper merchants, whose loyalty to the company is considered one of its greatest assets."

FACTORS INFLUENCING THE DECISION ON LISTING

For a number of years, members of management had given much thought to the possibility of listing the common stock. During the 1940's, in fact, the company had registered the stock on the Boston Stock Exchange. The outcome of this decision, in management's opinion, had not been at all satisfactory. The activity in terms of number of shares traded had been very small, which made the market for the company's stock an uncertain one at best. In a typical month on this exchange, for example, transactions in S. D. Warren common stock would be recorded on only 4 or 5 days, and total monthly volume would be less than 500 shares.

Preferring what had been, in Mr. Gray's words, "a reasonably good over-the-counter market," management decided in late 1940 to delist. Acting on this decision proved to be complicated, however, owing to the procedures involved in obtaining permission to delist from the Securities and Exchange Commission.[1] Some time after failing to substantiate its case for permission to delist, the company neglected to make certain changes in proxy material sent to stockholders as required by new and revised statutes; the company's stock was thus "delisted by default."

There was little question in Mr. Gray's mind that general market conditions and the company's situation in particular had changed considerably since the unhappy experience on the Boston Stock Exchange. The number of shares of S. D. Warren common stock outstanding during the period the stock was listed on this exchange, for example, had ranged up to a maximum of about 400,000 shares. Furthermore, a substantial number of these shares was in concentrated or family holdings.

The question of listing had been brought before the management with renewed prominence because of several developments in recent years. Most important of these was the company's growth. If it continued, substantial equity financing—perhaps as much as $25 million—probably would be required within a few years to provide for expansion of production facilities. Management had therefore been considering whether listing would result in a broader distribution of the common stock among noninstitutional investors, and thus improve chances for the success of a large public issue. The existing over-the-counter market for the company's stock was believed to be primarily local and somewhat narrow. The evidence supporting this belief was not conclusive, but rough data obtained from the company's transfer agent indicated that probably over 90% of the activity in S. D. Warren common was taking place in New York and the New England states.

Although management's primary interest in the possibility of listing was a desire to benefit the company and its stockholders, an added incentive for achieving better publicity and better investor acceptance for the company's stock was that several members of the management were executors of an estate and were planning to sell a large number of S. D. Warren common shares to diversify the estate holdings.

Mr. Gray thought that S. D. Warren Company probably would not be troubled with several of the more common questions confronting companies when listing was considered. For example, the company would easily meet all listing requirements of the New York Stock Exchange.[2] In fact, officials of the

---

[1] In accordance with SEC regulations, stockholders must be notified of a proposal to delist, and a hearing must be held by the SEC to determine whether such action is justified.

[2] A brief brochure published by the New York Stock Exchange, *A Listing on the New York Stock Exchange, Its Purposes, Its Advantages, Its Responsibilities*, stated the following with respect to listing requirements:

In reviewing the qualifications of a company for initial listing, the Exchange seeks to deal with each case on its merits. It takes into account not only earnings records,

Exchange had recently approached management and solicited listing of the common stock. Only one suggestion had been made by these officials concerning preparation for listing. They indicated that it probably would be desirable to split the common stock in order to (1) lower the price per share, (2) increase volume in the number of shares traded, and (3) aid in obtaining broader distribution. It was also indicated that the company would have some say in selecting the specialist for the company's stock on the floor of the Exchange.[3] Appendix A presents selected excerpts from the listing agreement that would be required of the company.

Mr. Gray also thought that investor interest and activity (volume of shares traded) sufficient to make listing feasible had existed for several years. Although the exact number of shares actually being purchased and sold could not be determined with accuracy,[4] it seemed probable to him that enough interest in the company's stock existed to assure that sufficient activity would

---

but the degree of national interest in the enterprise, its place and stability within its industry, and the prospects for its industry's growth. Not as an inflexible rule, but as a general guideline, the Exchange looks for these characteristics:

1) A company should have earned over $1 million net annually under competitive conditions.
2) It should have tangible net assets of over $8 million, or at least $8 million in aggregate market value of its stock.
3) It should have at least 400,000 common shares outstanding, exclusive of concentrated or family holdings, and more than 1,500 shareholders, after substantially discounting odd-lots.

It is only when these standards continue to be met that the advantages of listing accrue, and the kind of market can be provided which the company would expect.

Effective April 15, 1965, the New York Stock Exchange revised several of its guidelines for determining the qualifications of a company for initial listing. The following minimum numerical standards were suggested:

1) A company should have earned $1.2 million net annually under competitive conditions.
2) It should have $12 million market value of publicly held shares and (less important) $10 million net tangible assets.
3) It should have at least 700,000 shares publicly held and 1,700 holders of 100 shares or more.

[3] The Exchange assigns a specialist to each listed stock. Specialists are charged with maintaining a fair and orderly market, which implies maintenance of price continuity and minimizing of the effects of temporary disparity between supply and demand. A specialist is often required to take a position in a stock to keep trading and quotations orderly when wide swings occur in the market price. A specialist's activities on the American Stock Exchange have been described in John Brooks, "Profiles," *The New Yorker,* October 1, 1955. The article in book form is *The Seven Fat Years* (New York: Harper & Bros.), 1958.

[4] Unlike the activity of listed stocks, which is recorded and reported daily by the respective stock exchanges, the activity of an unlisted stock is not available from any public source or agency. The main source of information on the activity of an unlisted stock is the company's stock transfer records. At best, however, these records typically provide only a rough approximation of activity. Stock transfer records are maintained to show only date, name, and number of shares for old certificates surrendered and new certificates issued. Therefore, it is often difficult to distinguish between entries that represent actual sale and purchase transactions and those that represent some other kind of action on the part of the holder requiring the issue of new certificates for old.

continue without the benefit of maintenance of a market by a number of dealers. (Exhibit 1 presents an approximation of the activity in S. D. Warren common stock as compared with the activity of listed stocks of two other companies in the industry.) This belief had been reinforced in discussions with a vice president of a large investment banking firm that had banked the street[5] in S. D. Warren common stock for many years. From these discussions Mr. Gray had gained assurances that a fairly hungry market and considerable buying pressure had existed for several years. The vice president of this investment banking firm had said that "over time and through education" his firm had interested many other investment bankers and analysts in the stock, and that in recent years several paper company analysts had been "strongly talking up S. D. Warren Company." In this light, Mr. Gray questioned whether it might not become increasingly difficult for over-the-counter dealers to satisfy the market.

For several years, approximately 10 reputable dealers had been fairly active in maintaining an over-the-counter market for S. D. Warren common stock. On occasion, Mr. Gray had obtained quotations on the stock from one of the dealers, and the spread between the quoted offering and buying prices was often as small as $\frac{1}{2}$ to 1 point. The company's stock was also quoted daily in several newspapers, including *The Wall Street Journal*.[6] Exhibit 2 presents selected common stock quotations for S. D. Warren Company and three other paper companies. Appendix B presents excerpts from a study comparing over-the-counter securities transactions with transactions in listed stocks on stock exchanges.[7]

The nature and source of much of the interest in S. D. Warren common stock in recent years were factors that made Mr. Gray somewhat hesitant about a decision to list. Although some interest in the company as a blue-chip investment on the part of investment bankers, analysts, and professional investors had existed for several years, it had apparently been excited in recent months by glowing reports of analysts and publicity about the company's "long and outstanding record." As one investment banker put it, "Suddenly it seems that everyone is aware that S. D. Warren is truly the 'Tiffany' of the paper companies." In light of this interest, Mr. Gray questioned what

---

[5] Banking the street refers to the activity of an investment banking house that takes a primary position in a company's stock, quotes bid and asked prices, and makes a market at quoted prices for dealers who are maintaining a retail market in the stock.

[6] Newspaper quotations on over-the-counter securities are obtained from the National Association of Securities Dealers, Inc., and a few other selected sources. They do not represent actual transactions, but are intended as a guide to the price range within which the securities could have been sold or purchased at the time of compilation. Newspaper quotations on listed securities, on the other hand, represent the opening, high, low, and closing prices of actual transactions on a stock exchange.

[7] Irwin Friend and others, *The Over-The-Counter Securities Markets* (New York: McGraw-Hill Book Co., Inc., 1958). The excerpts in the appendix were taken from chap. 6, "Pricing and Price Differentials on Over-the-Counter Markets," by Irwin Friend, Morris Hamburg, and Stanley Schor, pp. 312–16, 406–9. Used by permission of McGraw-Hill Book Co.

the actual effect of listing would be with respect to a broader distribution of ownership. Although institutional investors now owned a substantial number of shares, listing would make it possible for many more institutions now legally or otherwise prohibited from owning unlisted common stocks to become holders of S. D. Warren common shares. To date, however, no investment institution had suggested listing to the company's management. Exhibit 3 shows selected ownership data for 1951 and 1959.

The company had been under no pressure from stockholders with respect to listing. Management, however, would make its decision in the considered best interest of stockholders and the company. Mr. Gray had gathered other data, as follows, to guide him in forming a recommendation.

Shares outstanding, October, 1959, 1,060,597.

Approximate number of shareholders, 3,700.

The 10 largest holdings accounted for more than 35% of the shares outstanding.

About 80% of shares outstanding were held by less than 15% of the shareholders.

Over 75% of shares outstanding were held by owners in 3 states—Massachusetts, Maine, and New York.

Exhibits 4 and 5 compare performance of S. D. Warren Company and its common stock with those of several other companies in the industry.

Exhibit 1
S. D. WARREN COMPANY
COMPARISON OF ACTIVITY IN S. D. WARREN COMMON STOCK WITH ACTIVITY IN THE LISTED COMMON STOCKS OF TWO OTHER COMPANIES IN THE INDUSTRY*

APPROXIMATE AVERAGE WEEKLY ACTIVITY

S. D. Warren Company		Oxford Paper Company†	Hammermill Paper Company†
1955	1/1–10/31/59	1/1–10/31/59	1/1–10/31/59
425 shares	3,900 shares	4,000 shares	3,500 shares

APPROXIMATE ACTIVITY FOR MOST RECENT
13-WEEK PERIOD (8/1–10/31/59)

S. D. Warren Company.............................33,000 shares
Oxford Paper Company.............................40,000 shares
Hammermill Paper Company........................35,000 shares

* Activity in S. D. Warren common stock was estimated from entries in the company's stock transfer records. Activity in the common stocks of the other two companies was taken from *The Wall Street Journal.*
† Listed on New York Stock Exchange.

Exhibit 2

S. D. WARREN COMPANY

SELECTED QUOTATIONS FOR COMMON STOCKS OF S. D. WARREN COMPANY AND
THREE OTHER COMPANIES IN THE INDUSTRY

WEEK OF OCTOBER 27, 1958*

Date	S. D. Warren Company† Bid	Asked	P. H. Glatfelter Company† Bid	Asked	Oxford Paper Company‡ Low	High	Hammermill Paper Company‡ Low	High
27th	42¾	45⅞	66	70½	32⅝	32⅞	29½	29¾
28th	42½	45⅝	63	67½	32¼	32½	29	29¼
29th	42½	45⅝	62½	67	32⅜	32½	28½	29⅜
30th	42½	45⅝	62	66½	32⅜	32½	29	29⅜
31st	42½	45⅜	61	65½	32¾	32¾	28⅞	29½

WEEK OF OCTOBER 26, 1959*

Date	Bid	Asked	Bid	Asked	Low	High	Low	High
26th	60¾	64¼	42½	45⅝	29⅛	30¾	34	34
27th	60¾	64¼	42½	45⅝	29½	29⅞	33⅝	34
28th	61¼	64¾	42½	45⅝	29⅝	30	33¾	33¾
29th	62¼	65¾	42½	45⅝	29½	30¼	33¼	33¾
30th	63	66½	42½	45⅝	29¾	29¾	33	33⅛

MARKET QUOTATIONS OF DEALERS ON S. D. WARREN COMMON
STOCK FOR MONTH OF OCTOBER 1959§

Dealer	Location	Date	Wants	Offerings
Ogden Wechsler & Krumholz	New York	10/14/59	100 at 61½	—
First Boston Corp.	Chicago	10/27/59	61½	at 63
Smith Barney & Co.	San Francisco	10/28/59	61½	63
J. B. Maguire & Co. Inc.	Boston	10/30/59	64	65½
Smith Barney & Co.	New York	10/30/59	64½	65½
First Boston Corp.	Boston	10/30/59	64	65½
May & Gannon, Inc.	Boston	10/30/59	64	65½
N.Y. Hanseatic Corp.	Boston	10/30/59	64	65½

* *The Wall Street Journal.*
† Traded over the counter.
‡ Listed on New York Stock Exchange.
§ *The National Stock Summary*, issued by The National Quotation Bureau Incorporated. The Wants and Offerings indicate the prices at which the respective dealers stood ready to buy or sell S. D. Warren common stock on the dates shown.

Exhibit 3

S. D. WARREN COMPANY

SELECTED DATA ON OWNERSHIP OF S. D. WARREN COMMON STOCK

Ownership Group	Approximate Percentage of Shares Held	
	October 1959	June 1951
Professional investors (largely institutions)............................	22.0%	2.5%
Employees and their families................	12.0	
Former employees and their estates..........	22.0	
General public (includes nominees, fiduciaries, stock brokers, and security dealers)†.......................	44.0	97.5*
	100.0%	100.0%

* This breakdown for 1951 was not readily available in company records.
† This ownership group accounted for over 85% of the total number of shareholders.

STOCK DISTRIBUTION SCHEDULE—APPROXIMATION FOR
OCTOBER 1959

Number of Holders	Shares Held	Total Shares
1,900	1–49	72,000
1,300	50–149	150,000
500	150–up	838,000
3,700		1,060,000

Exhibit 4

S. D. WARREN COMPANY

SELECTED DATA ON THE COMPANY AND OTHER COMPANIES IN THE INDUSTRY

Company	Year	Net Sales (Millions)	Net Profits (Millions)	Number of Common Shares Outstanding	Earnings per Share on Common Stock (Unadjusted)	Where Traded	Price Range High	Price Range Low	Capitalization at December 31, 1958 Long-Term Debt	Preferred Stock	Common Stock and Surplus
S. D. Warren Company	1959*	$71.0	$5.0	1,060,597	$4.60	OTC	66½	42	28.3%	4.7%	67.0%
	1958	61.2	3.4	1,060,597	3.15		45	26½			
	1957	58.3	3.0	1,060,597	2.75		50	24¾			
	1956	64.2	4.7	1,060,597	4.31		63	34			
	1955	55.1	2.9	964,759	2.85		35	24⅛			
P. H. Glatfelter Company	1959*	$27.2	$2.4	690,000	$3.30	OTC	49	30	24.9%	9.5%	65.6%
	1958	23.1	2.0	345,000	5.53		68	43½			
	1957	25.3	2.3	345,000	6.18		66	38½			
	1956	21.1	2.3	345,000	6.23		74	53½			
	1955	18.2	2.1	345,000	5.79		57	30			
Oxford Paper Company	1959*	$72.5	$2.3	1,006,434	$1.80	NYSE	38⅝	29⅛	30.0%	12.9%	57.1%
	1958	62.8	2.7	1,006,434	2.13		38¾	25½			
	1957	58.7	3.4	936,470	3.05		43	24			
	1956	61.7	4.6	761,470	5.43		51¾	35			
	1955	56.4	3.7	761,470	4.20		46⅜	34			
Hammermill Paper Company	1959*	$61.4	$3.1	1,232,610	$2.45	NYSE	36¼	28⅛	29.0%	5.6%	65.4%
	1958	46.5	2.3	1,071,655	2.06		33¼	21¾			
	1957	44.5	2.3	1,067,631	2.04		45¼	20½			
	1956	49.2	4.4	1,066,992	4.04		42⅜	33			
	1955	34.5	2.8	850,064	3.10		38¼	21½			

* Net sales, profits, and earnings per share on common stock for year 1959 are projected on the bases of results through September 30. Price ranges of common stocks for 1959 cover the period from January 1 to October 31.

Exhibit 5

S. D. WARREN COMPANY

SELECTED COMPARISONS OF S. D. WARREN COMPANY COMMON STOCK
WITH COMMON STOCKS OF OTHER COMPANIES IN THE INDUSTRY

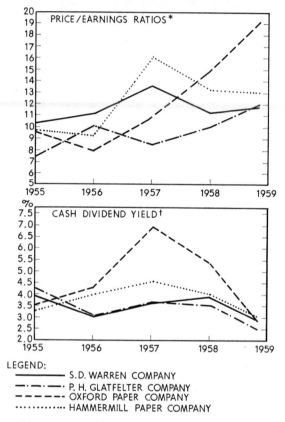

LEGEND:
——————— S.D. WARREN COMPANY
—·—·—· P. H. GLATFELTER COMPANY
— — — — OXFORD PAPER COMPANY
············ HAMMERMILL PAPER COMPANY

* Average of annual high and low market prices divided by earnings per share for the year.
† Cash dividends per share on an annual basis divided by the average of annual high and low market prices.

Appendix A

S. D. WARREN COMPANY (hereinafter called the "Corporation"), in consideration of the listing of the securities covered by this application, hereby agrees with the New York Stock Exchange (hereinafter called the "Exchange"), as follows:

I

. . . .

6. The Corporation will disclose in its annual report to shareholders, for the year covered by the report, (1) the number of shares of its stock issuable under outstanding options at the beginning of the year; separate totals of changes in the number of shares of its stock under option resulting from issuance, exercise, expiration or cancellation of options; and the number of shares issuable under outstanding options at the close of the year, (2) the number of unoptioned shares available at the beginning and at the close of the year for the granting of options under an option plan, and (3) any changes in the exercise price of outstanding options, through cancellation and reissuance or otherwise, except price changes resulting from the normal operation of antidilution provisions of the options.

7. The Corporation will report to the Exchange, within ten days after the close of a fiscal quarter, in the event any previously issued shares of any stock of the Corporation listed on the Exchange have been reacquired or disposed of, directly or indirectly, for the account of the Corporation during such fiscal quarter, such report showing separate totals for acquisitions and dispositions and the number of shares of such stock so held by it at the end of such quarter.

8. The Corporation will promptly notify the Exchange of all facts relating to the purchase, direct or indirect, of any of its securities listed on the Exchange at a price in excess of the market price of such security prevailing on the Exchange at the time of such purchase.

. . . .

13. The Corporation will furnish to the Exchange on demand such information concerning the Corporation as the Exchange may reasonably require.

14. The Corporation will not make any change in the form or nature of any of its securities listed on the Exchange, nor in the rights or privileges of the holders thereof, without having given twenty days' prior notice to the Exchange of the proposed change, and having made application for the listing of the securities as changed if the Exchange shall so require.

15. The Corporation will make available to the Exchange, upon request, the names of member firms of the Exchange which are registered owners of stock of the Corporation listed on the Exchange if at any time the need for such stock for loaning purposes on the Exchange should develop, and in addition, if found necessary, will use its best efforts with any known large holders to make reasonable amounts of such stock available for such purposes in accordance with the rules of the Exchange.

16. The Corporation will promptly notify the Exchange of any diminution in the supply of stock available for the market occasioned by deposit of stock under voting trust agreements or other deposit agreements, if knowledge of any such actual or proposed deposits should come to the official attention of the officers or directors of the Corporation.

. . . .

II

1. The Corporation will publish at least once a year and submit to its stockholders at least fifteen days in advance of the annual meeting of such stockholders and not later than three months after the close of the last preceding fiscal year of the Corporation a balance sheet as of the end of such fiscal year, and a surplus and income statement for such fiscal year of the Corporation as a separate corporate entity and of each corporation in which it holds directly or indirectly a majority of the equity stock; or in lieu thereof, eliminating all intercompany transactions, a consolidated balance sheet of the Corporation and its subsidiaries as of the end of its last previous fiscal year, and a consolidated surplus statement and a consolidated income statement of the Corporation and its subsidiaries for such fiscal year. If any such consolidated statement shall exclude corporations a majority of whose equity stock is owned directly or indirectly by the Corporation: (a) the caption of, or a note to, such statement will show the degree of consolidation; (b) the consolidated income account will reflect, either in a footnote or otherwise, the parent company's proportion of the sum of, or difference between, current earnings or losses and the dividends of such unconsolidated subsidiaries for the period of the report; and (c) the consolidated balance sheet will reflect, either in a footnote or otherwise, the extent to which the equity of the parent company in such subsidiaries has been increased or diminished since the date of acquisition as a result of profits, losses and distributions.

Appropriate reserves, in accordance with good accounting practice, will be made against profits arising out of all transactions with unconsolidated subsidiaries in either parent company statements or consolidated statements.

Such statements will reflect the existence of any default in interest, cumulative dividend requirements, sinking fund or redemption fund requirements of the Corporation and of any controlled corporation, whether consolidated or unconsolidated.

2. All financial statements contained in annual reports of the Corporation to its stockholders will be audited by independent public accountants qualified under the laws of some state or country, and will be accompanied by a copy of the certificate made by them with respect to their audit of such statements showing the scope of such audit and the qualifications, if any, with respect thereto.

The Corporation will promptly notify the Exchange if it changes its independent public accountants regularly auditing the books and accounts of the Corporation.

. . . .

4. The Corporation will publish quarterly statements of earnings on the basis of the same degree of consolidation as in the annual report. Such statements will disclose any substantial items of unusual or nonrecurrent nature and will show either net income before and after federal income taxes or net income and the amount of federal income taxes.

. . . .

6. The Corporation will not make any substantial change, nor will it permit any subsidiary directly or indirectly controlled by it to make any substantial change, in accounting methods, in policies as to depreciation and depletion or in bases of valuation of inventories or other assets, without notifying the Exchange and disclosing the effect of any such change in its next succeeding interim and annual report to its stockholders.

III

. . . .

4. The Corporation will publish immediately to the holders of any of its securities listed on the Exchange any action taken by the Corporation with respect to dividends or to the allotment of rights to subscribe or to any rights or benefits pertaining to the ownership of its securities listed on the Exchange; and will give prompt notice to the Exchange of any such action; and will afford the holders of its securities listed on the Exchange a proper period within which to record their interests and to exercise their rights; and will issue all such rights or benefits in form approved by the Exchange and will make the same transferable, exercisable, payable and deliverable in the Borough of Manhattan in the City of New York.

5. The Corporation will solicit proxies for all meetings of stockholders.

. . . .

Appendix B

EXCERPTS COMPARING OVER-THE-COUNTER SECURITIES TRANSACTIONS WITH TRANSACTIONS IN LISTED STOCKS ON STOCK EXCHANGES[1]

Price Quotations and Differentials

Prices in the over-the-counter markets, while ultimately dependent on the many factors affecting evaluation of securities generally, are immediately determined by the bids and offers of customers and dealers. A customer interested in buying or selling a security in these markets will normally contact a broker-dealer firm to obtain bid and ask quotations before transmitting his order. For many securities, these quotations constitute the only market data available to a customer; for other securities, the financial press publishes daily bid and ask quotations showing composite prices at which representative firms would be willing to buy or sell the security from or to the public. The "spread" between the public bid and ask quotations appearing in the press is usually made sufficiently large so that most firms interested in the security are willing to trade at the prices indicated or even to improve on those prices. There is no published information on actual market prices, as distinguished from quotations.

If the firm carries an inventory in the security, it may buy or sell for its own account, earning a "gross profit," which is simply the difference between the selling price of the security and its cost. Part of this profit (or loss) reflects the movements of security prices between the time of acquisition and the disposition of the issue by the firm, with the relative importance of this portion of the profit likely to vary directly with the duration of positioning. Where the firm acts on an agency basis, the commission it charges constitutes its gross profit.

If the firm does not customarily inventory the security, it may still buy or sell for its own account. However, ordinarily in this, as in the agency case, it is necessary to contact another firm which specializes in the issue. The first firm dealing with the customer has a pretty good idea of the prices at which it can buy or sell the security from or to another dealer on the basis of its

---

[1] Irwin Friend and others, *The Over-The-Counter Securities Markets* (New York: McGraw-Hill Book Co., Inc., 1958), chap. 6, pp. 312–16, 406–9. Used by permission of McGraw-Hill Book Co.

knowledge of the market and of the quotations appearing each morning in the National Quotation Bureau sheets (which give the bid–ask quotation as of the preceding afternoon of each of the dealers making a market in specific issues) ; these quotations are subject to confirmation or bargaining by telephone. The spread between the dealer bid and ask quotations—constituting the so-called "inside market," generally available and disclosed only to dealers—is obviously narrower than the customer spread indicated in the financial press, since the former is essentially a wholesale market and the latter retail.

In both of these types of principal transaction, the gross profit to the firm is the difference between selling price and cost. However, since this difference frequently reflects movements in security prices as well as price and cost differentials attributable to services rendered in effecting the transaction, another measure is commonly used to compare the selling price to a customer (or purchase price from a customer) with the corresponding asking price (or bid) in the "inside market." This measure, which may be called the firm's "markup," indicates the relationship between a price to a customer and dealer quotations and is akin to a retail markup in other markets where speculative profits are not a major factor. The concept of "markup" is not quite so precise as that of profit, depending on the type of dealer bids and offers used as a basis for measurement. Thus, the markup on the "best" dealer bid and offer, i.e., the highest bid and lowest offer, will be higher than the markup on representative bids and offers. Which of these two sets of bids and offers should be used depends on a variety of circumstances, but particularly on the number of shares involved in the transaction and in the quotations.

In either case, it is essential that the dealer quotations used not be nominal bids and offers on which bargaining would improve. The concept of markup may become rather tenuous when the firm which is transacting business with a customer is the only firm quoting a market for the security—unless careful attention is paid to the nature of the "inside market." In spite of these limitations, the concept is useful for segregating speculative profits from charges and return attributable to normal operations of the over-the-counter markets.

One final type of price differential which is of major importance in appraising pricing and costs on over-the-counter markets is what will be called "average customer cost," a term which may be less familiar than those described above. This concept attempts to measure the average cost to a public customer of a simultaneous round-trip transaction in the over-the-counter markets. It can be considered to represent the average difference between the purchase and sale prices of public customers in the same issue at the same time. This measure focuses on cost to the customer, abstracting from movement in security prices rather than profit to the broker-dealer firm. Brokers and dealers are regarded simply as intermediaries between customers, i.e., as instrumentalities for facilitating the exchange of securities between different sectors of the public; and any gross profit (net of losses) involved in transferring securities among broker-dealers in the over-the-counter markets is considered as ultimately paid by public customers. In a sense, the average customer cost may be considered as a measure of the social cost per dollar of customer round-trip transactions in the over-the-counter markets, adding in indirect as well as direct costs arising from one or more firms intervening between public customers.

Comparison with Exchanges

On the organized exchanges, much more of the public trading is on an agency basis, with exchange members acting as brokers. The exchange market is largely an auction market made up of bids and offers of the public, and wide publicity is given to the price and volume of transactions. The over-the-counter dealer generally plays a more active role in pricing than his exchange counterpart, who customarily acts as a broker.

A customer desiring to buy or sell securities on an exchange knows the prices at which previous transactions have been effected and the trading activity in the issue. He gets this information from his daily paper and, on an up-to-the-minute basis, from his broker, who has wire service to the exchange. In a reasonably active issue, he knows within a fraction of a point at what prices he can buy or sell a moderate quantity of securities, and the spread between these two prices is likely to be very small. However, as an issue becomes less active, the spread is much larger, the prices at which transactions can be effected are less certain, and the situation is closer to that found in the over-the-counter markets. In both cases, unless an unusually large volume, requiring special treatment, is involved,[2] the brokerage firm transmits the customer's order, if it is a round-lot or multiple of the unit of trading on the exchange, to a representative on the floor of the exchange or, if it is an odd-lot, to an odd-lot dealer. The floor representative, who has the responsibility of getting the best possible price for the customer, will normally execute transactions with firms representing other customers but will at times be dealing with floor members of the exchange acting for their own accounts. In most of these instances, the floor members will be specialists in the issue involved.

When a floor member trades as a principal, he is behaving in the same capacity as a dealer in the over-the-counter markets, though he is subject to more restrictions as a result of exchange rules and cannot deal directly with a customer. The profits or markups of these specialists and other floor traders are as much a part of customer cost of transactions on exchanges as dealer profits or markups are on over-the-counter markets. Similarly, the additional differential charged by the odd-lot dealer must be added to the regular commission to obtain the total customer cost of these transactions.

---

[2] The special procedures for handling such large transactions are discussed in Chapter 7.

It is only after adjustment for such profits or markups that the cost of effecting transactions on exchanges can be compared with the cost on over-the-counter markets. Moreover, since these costs differ for various kinds of transactions, such comparisons can be meaningful only to the extent that they hold constant the types of securities traded, the size of transactions, and other significant differences of trading activity in the two markets.

However, in appraising the economic or social performance of different institutional arrangements in two markets, it is not sufficient to compare average costs of transactions to customers even if other characteristics of transactions (i.e., characteristics other than cost) are kept reasonably constant. Average costs to customers as a whole could be low and yet market performance adjudged unsatisfactory if, as a result either of generally faulty market evaluation or of erratic fluctuations in prices, one group of customers benefited excessively at the expense of another. For a market to perform satisfactorily, not only should costs of transferring securities among public customers be as low as possible, but prices should represent the consensus of informed buyers and sellers and erratic price movements be minimized. Erratic movements, resulting from significant discontinuities in supply and demand, can be reduced, to some extent, by the intervention of dealers acting as principals in the over-the-counter markets or of specialists acting as principals on an exchange. Faulty market evaluation can be improved by the dissemination of relevant market and security data to public customers and by competent investment advice. It is only by considering all these factors that one market can appropriately be compared with another.

. . . .

Spreads in Dealer and Customer Markets

The average spread on unlisted common stock in the over-the-counter customer markets, i.e., the average difference between bids and offers published in the financial press, was in excess of $1.50 in 1949 and 1952, or somewhat more than 5% of the average price. For issues under $20 in price, the average customer spread in 1949 was 10%; for higher-priced issues, 5%. The differences in the percentage spreads of low- and high-priced issues narrowed somewhat from 1949 to 1952.

These customer spreads, representing the outside public, or retail, market, were, as might be expected, much higher than the dealer spreads, or the difference between bids and offers of dealers in the inside, or wholesale market. The average dealer spread on common stock was somewhat less than 25 cents and slightly under 1% of average price. For issues under $20, the dealer spread was typically about 2%; for higher-priced issues, less than 1%. It is interesting to note that customer bids are much closer to dealer bids than customer offers are to dealer offers.

An analysis of regional variation in customer spreads published in the financial press in different parts of the country indicated that the Boston and

Atlanta areas have somewhat wider spreads than other areas, reflecting in part differences in the types of transactions effected.

Comparison of Quotations with Transaction Prices

This study made available for the first time a comparison of the over-the-counter prices quoted in the financial press and the actual prices at which public customers effected transactions. Typically, on a purchase of unlisted common stock from a dealer in 1949, a customer paid 11 cents less than the published retail offer; on a sale, he received 16 cents more than the published bid. The average prices at which public customers effected transactions were, on the purchase side, $1.07 more than the best (lowest) offer in the dealer, or inside, market, and on the sale side 23 cents less than the best (highest) bid in that market. These figures, of course, are averages and vary widely though the general findings for 1952 were virtually the same as for 1949.

Adjusting for commissions paid, it appeared that over-the-counter customers did not obtain so favorable prices in agency sales and obtained somewhat more favorable prices in agency purchases than in the corresponding principal transactions; but on the whole, the difference was not great.

Gross Profit Margins in Dealer and Customer Markets

The average gross profit margin on principal transactions with public customers in 1949—i.e., the difference between the dealer's sale and purchase prices on transactions with the general public, as a per cent of the value of the transaction—was 3.0% for all common stock combined, 1.7% for preferred, 0.7% for corporate bonds, 0.6% for state and municipal bonds, and less than 0.05% for U.S. Governments. The corresponding margin on inter-dealer transactions in common stock was 2.0%. The average gross profit margin on public transactions in unlisted common stock, which is exclusively traded in the over-the-counter markets, was 3.3% in 1949 and about the same in 1951–1952.

These margins were higher for small common stock issues and small trades, averaging 5% for issues less than $5 million in size and 7.5% for transactions under $100. They were also higher for low-priced shares, for newer issues, for small issues which had been positioned for a considerable length of time, for individuals or noninstitutional customers, for small broker-dealer firms, and, in 1949 but not in 1951–1952, for firms in the south and west central regions.

It may be noted that these estimated profit margins reflect movements in security prices as well as normal markups. However, the influence of price movements is fairly unimportant on the whole, in view of the very small proportion of transactions in which issues had been positioned for any considerable length of time.

Average Customer Costs in Over-the-Counter Markets

Since more than one broker-dealer firm may, and in the over-the-counter markets typically does, intervene between public customers, the study developed a measure of the average cost of transferring securities from one public customer to another. This measure may be considered to represent the average difference between the purchase and sale prices of public customers in the same issue at the same time, expressed as a per cent of the value of the securities transferred.

The average customer cost of transferring unlisted common stock from one public customer to another in the over-the-counter markets was about 5.2% and 5.6% in 1949 and in 1952, respectively. The corresponding cost for transferring through the over-the-counter markets issues listed or traded on the two New York exchanges was estimated at 4.4% in 1952, when only principal transactions were included, and at 3.2% in 1949, when both principal and agency over-the-counter transactions were included. The over-the-counter cost for transferring issues listed or traded on other exchanges was of the same general magnitude as for unlisted issues.

In addition to average customer costs and average profit margins for different types of transactions, the dispersion around these averages is shown. Thus for unlisted common stock, customer costs were 3% or more in 90% of trades, 4% or more in 80% of trades, and 6% or more in 30% of trades.

Comparison with Exchange Markets

The average customer cost of transferring common stock from one public customer to another on the New York Stock Exchange was 2.1% in 1949 and in 1951–1952 (both round-lots and odd-lots). In the relatively small proportion of round-lot Exchange transactions involving a member firm as principal, the customer cost is increased to approximately 3.0%. Obviously, either of these figures is much lower than the average cost in the over-the-counter markets for unlisted issues and somewhat lower than the average cost for listed issues. Apart from these differences in average costs in the two markets, there is, of course, much greater variability in costs incurred in individual transactions in the over-the-counter markets than on the Exchange, where transactions are subject to a fixed schedule of commissions.

When common stock issues on the two markets were classified by size, measured by value outstanding or by number of stockholders, average customer costs in the over-the-counter markets appeared to be about twice those on the New York Stock Exchange for each size class. An over-the-counter issue in a given size class is, of course, likely to be less active than an Exchange issue of the same size. However, it may be noted that average customer costs on the Exchange for issues under $1 million in size, where costs are greatest, were somewhat below the corresponding over-the-counter costs for issues of $100 million and over in size, where costs are smallest. Even when identical listed issues traded in both markets were compared, the over-the-counter costs were higher than those on the Exchange.

While there was significant variation in customer costs by type of transaction, it appears that average customer costs on the New York Stock Exchange are generally lower than on over-the-counter markets for most types of transaction—though not for large "block" transactions. The data suggest that while for common stock transactions up to $100,000 in size average customer costs on the Exchange were lower than in the over-the-counter markets, this was not true for large block transactions.

To the extent that disparities in cost seem to exist for comparable transactions, these may still reflect, at least in part, the different services provided by the two markets. If, for example, a larger number of intermediaries and more selling effort are necessary to effect transfers among public customers of securities traded over the counter, higher costs may be justified.

Moreover, in appraising the performance of the two markets, it should be recognized that not only should average costs to customers as a whole be as low as possible but, to prevent one group of customers from benefiting excessively at the expense of another, prices should represent the consensus of informed buyers and sellers, and erratic price movements should be minimized. There is some evidence that prices at which customers either purchase or sell stock on the over-the-counter markets are slightly more stable in the short run than prices on the New York Stock Exchange.

Finally, it should be pointed out that the above comparison of costs casts only limited light on the quality of prices or desirability of investing in the two markets. It is quite possible that securities might be particularly undervalued, from the point of view of past or prospective return, in the market where customer costs or price differentials are relatively large.

SPEEDATA EQUIPMENT, INC.

THE BOARD OF DIRECTORS of Speedata Equipment, Inc., held a special meeting on August 24, 1961. Ornette Hendricks, financial vice president, treasurer, and director, was about to express his opinion concerning the advisability of listing the company's securities on the American Stock Exchange. Two directors had already indicated that they were in favor of listing, while three others had spoken against it. Michael Pressman, president and director, had not yet given his opinion, but Mr. Hendricks believed he favored listing.

As early as 1959, the management of Speedata had received sporadic letters from stockholders inquiring whether the company planned to list its stock on a national securities exchange. In addition, at the annual stockholders' meeting in 1960 several persons had expressed disappointment in not being able to follow the trading activity and market price of Speedata stock on a day-to-day basis. In fact, since the stock was quoted only on the eastern over-the-counter market, stockholders in other sections of the country seldom, if ever, could find a quotation for the shares in a local newspaper.

On February 28, 1961, Mr. Pressman had received the following letter from Bentley, Wolf & Co., a large New York investment banker, which was reputed to control 90,000 shares, or 14.4%, of Speedata's outstanding stock.

DEAR MICHAEL:

Now that your financing is out of the way and it appears that you have Speedata moving ahead on all fronts, I should like to make a suggestion which would benefit your company and stockholders. I should like to recommend that you list your stock on a recognized exchange at the earliest practicable date. A good time to make the announcement would be when you release your annual report. As you are not eligible for a New York Stock Exchange listing, it should be the American Exchange.

Your stockholders, present and future, are entitled to a better break than they have been or will be getting from the over-the-counter traders. Your stock has been kicked around in the unlisted market like a soccer ball. Unfounded rumors have driven it up and down to unwarranted price levels. The market at times is so thin it is only nominal, all to the detriment of your company and stockholders. Speedata would benefit directly from such a listing, receiving publicity and advertising that couldn't be bought. Your stock at all times would have a fair and orderly market, something it has never had.

For your further information, I am attaching a New York Stock Exchange publication covering the advantages of listing, which I shall not bother to review. There are no disadvantages that I know of to a well-run company.

I hope you feel the same way I do about listing; if not, I should like to discuss it in more detail with you.

With kindest personal regards,

Sincerely,

(signed) CHARLES H. WOLF

COMPANY BACKGROUND

Speedata Equipment, Inc., of Lexington, Massachusetts, was one of several electronics organizations located on the legendary Route 128, labeled by several newspapers as "the hotbed of America's space-age companies." The company specialized in the manufacture of reversible high-speed voltage-to-digital computer linkage equipment, FM and PCM telemetering data transmission and data reduction equipment, digital volt-ohm meters, differential amplifiers, industrial measurement and control systems, and special-purpose computing systems. The company's Neco division produced industrial recording instruments and advanced medical devices such as cardiographs and anaesthographs. These products were marketed to government, institutional, and commercial customers. The company's systems were used extensively in missile and aircraft testing programs; digital and analogue computers; data logging and process control in oil, chemical, and manufacturing plants; automatic control of machine tools; laboratory studies; and telemetering of physical information to remote areas.

Speedata was founded in 1953, when Michael Pressman, an ambitious and imaginative electrical engineer, formed a partnership with Sheldon Russell, a young entrepreneur. Their company, originally named Electronics Maintenance, designed and sold specialized electronic components to large electrical contractors. Sales were modest, totaling $25,000 for 1953. In January, 1954, Messrs. Pressman and Russell dissolved Electronics Maintenance and transferred the company's assets to its successor, Speedata Equipment, Inc., which was incorporated in Massachusetts the following month.

From these humble beginnings, Speedata substantially increased its sales volume every year, reaching $10 million in 1960. (Exhibit 1 presents selected financial data.) Most of the company's growth was attributable to its engineering staff, which was responsible for several major technological innovations in the manufacture and design of data processing equipment. Even so, profits did not keep pace with either sales growth or scientific advances, and the company experienced net losses in five of its first seven years.

In 1957, through A. J. Grant and Company, a large New York underwriter, the company successfully sold 60,000 shares of common stock to the public at $16 a share. The net proceeds to the company of $870,000 were used to repay short-term secured notes payable to banks, to increase working capital, and to provide funds for expansion.

The market price of Speedata shares traded on the eastern over-the-counter market fluctuated between 21 and 8 in the first year of trading. The stock remained volatile, reaching a high of 45 in 1959 and falling as low as 15½ in 1961. (Market price statistics are included in Exhibit 1.)

In 1961, the company employed over 850 people in 4 modern plants, situated in Lexington, Massachusetts (home office); Torrington, Connecticut; Camden, New Jersey; and San Jose, California (West Coast division). Management believed that these facilities were adequate to carry a sales volume in excess of $20 million.

SPIN-OFF

In May, 1961, Messrs. Hillman, Strong, and Young, the top management of Speedata's San Jose division, organized a new company, Altuna Electronics, Inc., for the sole purpose of acquiring the net assets and business of the Speedata West Coast division. The original capitalization of Altuna Electronics was 100,000 shares of common stock, of which 78,000 shares were held by the entrepreneurs. The remainder were sold to other San Jose division employees for 50 cents a share.

Two months later, in exchange for 2 million newly authorized shares of Altuna capital stock, Altuna Electronics acquired the assets of the San Jose division, which had a book value of $526,000 in excess of the liabilities assumed by Altuna. In addition, Altuna Electronics and Speedata commissioned A. J. Grant and Company to underwrite a public financing of 1.65 million shares of Altuna common stock. Of these shares, 1.25 million shares, constituting 62.5% of the Altuna shares held by Speedata, were to be first offered to Speedata stockholders in November, 1961. This offer would be on the basis of two shares of Altuna Electronics for each share of Speedata owned on record, at a subscription price of $2.25. The remaining 400,000 shares were newly authorized stock of Altuna Electronics and would be offered to the public at $2.50 a share. The expected proceeds of the underwriting to Altuna Electronics were $1 million, less commission discounts and expenses. Speedata would receive for its stock $2,812,500, less commission and expenses. Substantial capital gains would result to the parent company.

THE DIRECTORS

As of November 21, 1960, the directors of Speedata, their stockholdings, options, and warrants were as follows:

Michael Pressman, president; shares owned, 46,525.

William Ritter, executive vice president; shares owned, 1,000; options and warrants, 5,124.

Ornette Hendricks, financial vice president; shares owned, 5; options and warrants, 2,000.

Robert Singleton, partner of A. J. Grant and Company; shares owned, 1,000; warrants and options, 500.

Frank Appleton, Jr., vice president of Standard National Bank, New York, which had purchased $2 million, 6% notes from Speedata Equipment, Inc., in 1959. These notes had attached 69,560 transferable warrants, exercisable to December 15, 1965, at $28.75 per common share; and 3,000 nontransferable warrants exercisable at $40 per share to December 15, 1965. Mr. Appleton personally owned 15 shares.

Winslow Roberts, financial vice president and treasurer of Remis Combustion and Generator Company. He was formerly with Granite Air-Dynamics, Inc.; shares owned, 200.

Alan Peterson, partner of Alan Richards & Company; shares owned, 8,000.

In addition, Robert Peterson, father of Alan Peterson, was the holder of record of 57,850 shares.

SPECIAL DIRECTORS MEETING TO CONSIDER LISTING

Following are the opinions expressed by the directors concerning the listing of Speedata on the American Stock Exchange.

Michael Pressman, President of the Company; Owned 46,525 Shares, or 7.5%

All of you know that over the last few years we have received inquiries from stockholders suggesting that Speedata list on a national exchange. Three days before our April board meeting 10 letters expressing an opinion on this subject were brought to my attention. They came from both brokers and stockholders. It is rumored, however, that they were all written by the same person, an eminent investment banker on the Street. [Laughter.] Nevertheless, we have spoken to several officials of the American Stock Exchange in New York about the possibilities of listing our shares. The Division of Securities of the American Stock Exchange is permitted to express an informal opinion as to the eligibility of a particular issue prior to preparation of a complete listing application. Speedata was granted such preliminary approval.

In general, the American Stock Exchange requires a minimum public distribution of 100,000 shares and ownership by a minimum of 500 public stockholders. Our latest audit indicates that 622,607 Speedata Equipment shares are outstanding, and in the hands of 2,168 stockholders.[1]

The cost of joining the exchange is $1,000 plus the printing costs of the application. Since the company already releases interim statements and comprehensive annual reports, and otherwise generally adheres to regulations governing companies listed with the American Stock Exchange, neither the legal nor the accounting requirements need be given much weight in our reaching a decision.

My basic sphere of knowledge is science and not finance. Therefore, at the

---

[1] A sample of the American Stock Exchange listing form for listing distribution of stock is given in Appendix A, with information on Speedata common stock.

moment I am going to throw the discussion open to you without expressing an opinion.

William Ritter, Executive Vice President; Owned 1,000 Shares and 5,124 Warrants

Back in 1954 when I joined Speedata, I envisioned that sometime in the near future the company would grow to the point where listing would become necessary. We are now a national company and a national company should have national posting of its securities. In the course of my travels, I have spoken to numerous stockholders throughout the country who have expressed disappointment over the company's failure to list on a national exchange. At this moment, the only way investors can follow the company's progress is to telephone a stockbroker who, at best, can supply a bid and asked quotation for the shares by calling a New York dealer. No information is available concerning the stock's trading activity.

On the West Coast, several investors mentioned their reluctance to purchase shares of Speedata stock because of poor market communications. Only in New York can market prices for the stock be found in the financial section of a daily newspaper. And even when quotations appear, they may or may not be representative of the true market. It is not uncommon to find spreads of 15% to 20% between quoted bid and asked prices. Investors cannot know what price the shares are physically traded at.

Although we have stockholders in 40 states, over 90% of the company's shares are held on the Eastern Seaboard. [Exhibit 2 presents a geographical breakdown of the stockholders.] Listing on a national exchange should permit wider distribution by stimulating interest for our common stock in other areas of the country.

The customers for our complex scientific systems are interested in knowing that we have stature. They, too, would like to follow our progress. The prestige of listing on a national exchange is irrefutable. In most cases when we submit a contract bid, we are competing with large, well-known electronics organizations, such as Beckman Instruments, Bendix Corporation, Packard Bell, or Texas Instruments. These companies, just by being listed, command respect and carry an aura of soundness and stability which is absent among unlisted companies. In a bidding situation the customer wants to know a good deal about those companies submitting sealed offers. Not only do reporting services, advisory letters, and financial analysts publish more information about companies traded on a national exchange, but listed companies can also expect more comprehensive newspaper coverage, public relations blurbs, and, in a sense, free advertising. And the more you look into Speedata Equipment, the better the company looks. Although it is difficult to pinpoint, I am sure in the past we have lost contracts because the company was not so well known as competitors. I do not think listing will have a decided effect in raising the price of Speedata shares per se, but I do believe it can be used as a lever to increase our business.

Listing on the American Stock Exchange will strengthen our corporate image. Speedata is a major company in specific electronics areas. We could hurt our reputation by staying on the over-the-counter market too long. A grocery chain with $10 million sales is just another grocery chain and is not obligated to list on a national exchange because of its position in the industry, but Speedata is a pace setter, and therefore owes listing to both its customers and its stockholders.

The over-the-counter market is dangerous. The rules and regulations are not as strict as those of the American Stock Exchange. For example, a short sale can be made at any time on the over-the-counter market, while on a national exchange a short sale can only be made on an up tick.[2] SEC laws governing over-the-counter securities are ineffectual. There are so many stocks and so many dealers involved in the over-the-counter market that it is impossible for any law enforcement agency to adequately police the market. There is considerable manipulation by dealers interested in making a fast buck, not in supporting an orderly market. On the American Stock Exchange, Speedata would have the benefit of a specialist, who would be responsible for balancing the supply and demand of those shares offered for trading, even if he is forced, from time to time, to buy or sell for his own account. In addition, every day we receive 30 or 40 telephone calls from over-the-counter dealers desiring information about contract rumors. If we were listed, it would be the specialist's duty to confirm or refute any Wall Street gossip about new business. An accurate source of corporate information would curb some of the severe price fluctuations that have been characteristic of our stock in the past, caused by distorted or completely false news releases.

It is true that several "prestige" Wall Street houses make markets in Speedata shares. However, their participation is known only to financial circles. Besides, with the exception of A. J. Grant and Company, the large Wall Street investment bankers and brokers maintaining a market in our stock do so only because their volume of trading in the securities is sufficient to justify taking a position. As evidenced by the turnover of dealers making a market in our shares, participation is seldom permanent. Trading houses enter and leave the sheets every day. [Exhibit 3 presents lists of over-the-counter dealers maintaining a market in Speedata shares on August 24, 1961, and in August, 1960.]

Winslow Roberts, Outside Director; Owned 200 Shares

For a company of our size, listing on a national exchange is certainly not a necessity. I don't think we have outgrown the over-the-counter market. There are innumerable industrials having far greater asset value, proven earning power, and a long record of dividend payments that are content to remain on the over-the-counter market. Whether or not listing on the American Stock

---

[2] Prentice-Hall, Inc., *Encyclopedic Dictionary of Business Finance* (Englewood Cliffs, N.J.: Prentice-Hall, Inc., 1960) describes an up tick in this way: when a security is sold at one price and the very next sale of the security is at a higher price, the latter sale is called an up tick or a plus tick.

Exchange would benefit our shareholders is the real question facing us today.

Listing should have no effect on the market price of Speedata common shares, which are already depressed; but the American Stock Exchange demands adherence to strict accounting and reporting practices, which is, in my opinion, to the company's disadvantage at the present time because of its poor performance. Since Speedata is relatively well known by the investing public and has shareholders in 40 states and several foreign countries, even wider distribution is of no particular benefit to stockholders or to the company. I would suspect that one reason why stock ownership is high on the Eastern Seaboard is that many stockholders leave their securities in the names of Wall Street houses.

A competitor of Speedata and a company of similar capitalization, Packard Bell Electronics, was traded over-the-counter until July 1959, when it listed on the New York Stock Exchange. Since that time, despite sponsorship from several powerful investment bankers, the shares have declined over 50% in their market value as a result of poor earnings reported in 1960. [Exhibits 4, 6, and 7 include market data for Packard Bell Electronics Corporation.] Listing on a national exchange can be in no way a substitute for earnings or dividends.

In 1959, the shares of Speedata were trading at 40. At that time investment interest in the company was intense. Large profits were believed to be forthcoming as the market for data processing equipment significantly expanded. Failure of these lofty projections to materialize resulted in deterioration of the company's image within the investment community. Until Speedata is able to regain its lost investment status by proving to Wall Street that a scientifically oriented management can earn substantial profits, I think listing on the American Stock Exchange should be abandoned.

Frank Appleton, Jr., Outside Director (Standard National Bank); Owned 15 Shares

Theoretically, I agree with the arguments advanced by Roberts. However, I do believe that broadening the market for the company's shares is desirable. Advisory services and institutions are more inclined to recommend and purchase shares that are listed on a national exchange.

The paramount question is timing. At this stage of the game Speedata cannot afford any major changes affecting its investment status. In less than three months we are going to ask our stockholders to subscribe to the company's rights issue. The Altuna spin-off is a major change, which can create considerable stockholder confusion per se, without complicating the situation by listing on the American Stock Exchange.

Although the support of the over-the-counter dealers has not been particularly effective in preventing a serious decline in the market price of Speedata shares, the company cannot afford to lose their backing in a period of unprofitable operations. Listing on a national exchange, while the company is

in the red, with more bad news still to come, is sheer folly, especially in light
of a rights offering in the near future.

Robert Singleton, Outside Director (A. J. Grant and Company); Owned 1,000 Shares and 500 Warrants

The fact that Speedata is currently an unprofitable operation would be
reflected in the market price of the shares no matter what exchange the
company were traded on. To think that by remaining unlisted we can soften a
poor earnings performance is like an ostrich putting his head in the sand.
Earnings come out, anyway. There are no secrets on Wall Street. I think the
depressed price of our common stock is evidence enough. If the company
switched over to the American Stock Exchange today, I should not be
surprised to see the shares selling at the same price as current over-
the-counter quotations.

In regard to the spin-off of the West Coast division, it would be a decided
advantage to be listed on the American Stock Exchange, and thus to have the
benefit of Wall Street arbitrageurs, who could help insure success of the issue
by promoting an orderly rights market.[3] I cannot overemphasize the importance of arbitrageurs, who purchase and sell rights when a favorable price
differential exists between the rights and their conversion value. Their activities will keep the price of the rights in harmony with conversion value. In
addition, both market prices and trading volume of the rights will appear in
the financial section of every major newspaper. If Speedata remains on the
over-the-counter market, the rights similarly will be traded over-the-counter.
Our stockholders cannot make a rational decision about their rights—exercise
or sell—unless they are kept informed about prices and trading volume.

Over the last four years the over-the-counter dealers have done a very good
job in making a market for Speedata shares. However, in recent months,
despite almost heroic actions, they have been unable to end the decline in the
market price of the stock. It would thus appear that earnings are more
important than sponsorship in determining a stock's price level. Even so, there
is no reason to think that Speedata would lose dealer support by listing, since
the National Association of Securities Dealers permits dealers to sponsor
securities posted on a national exchange.

In the past, investors have inquired whether Speedata had any outstanding
stock, and if so, where it was traded. Listing will increase awareness of the
company among financial institutions and the public alike. It will tend to
broaden and diversify stock ownership. Shareholder interests are safeguarded

---

[3] Prentice-Hall, *Encyclopedic Dictionary of Business Finance, op. cit.*, defines arbitrage
as: buying an item and simultaneously selling another item into which the first is convertible. [This] usually takes place in convertible securities. For example, a bond might
be convertible into a fixed number of shares of common stock. If, for any reason, the bond
price becomes less than the product of the market price of the common stock times the
number of shares into which the bond is convertible, a profit can be made by (1) buying
the bond and selling the stock at the same time, (2) converting the bond into the stock,
and (3) delivering the stock to cover the sale.

because investors know exactly how much the shares are actually traded at. On the over-the-counter market such information is available only to dealers. On the American Stock Exchange orders are executed speedily and conveniently; odd lots are traded at a fixed differential and the market operates in full public view.

The cost of listing is nominal. The strict accounting and financial requirements endorsed by the exchange are a matter of reporting to your stockholders what they have a right to know. If a company cannot meet this requirement, it should close its doors.

In the past Speedata has relied primarily on internal growth to achieve industry leadership. Our plans for the future, however, include an aggressive program of acquiring other companies. Listing on the American Stock Exchange can prove of benefit in three ways: (1) The prestige of national listing will make Speedata generally more attractive to the managements of smaller companies. (2) In negotiations with a potential acquisition where an exchange of stock is contemplated, listing facilitates valuation of our shares. (3) A small company is likely to be more willing to accept stock in exchange for assets if the stock is traded on a national exchange, because of the ready market for the shares.

Although there is no accurate method of determining the volume of trading in Speedata stock, A. J. Grant and Company makes a market in Speedata and is in close contact with over-the-counter houses quoting prices in the shares. Discussions with the back room traders have led us to believe that the volume of trading in Speedata is, on the average, a few thousand shares a day. This is more than ample activity to eliminate any fears that Speedata might wind up a dead issue shortly after listing. [Exhibit 4 presents transfer records of Speedata and trading volume of selected competitors.] On the contrary, moving on to the American Stock Exchange should significantly increase the trading in the stock as the company attracts the curiosity and attention accorded any newly listed issue among brokers, advisory services, and investors.

Alan Peterson, Outside Director (Alan Richards & Company); Owned 8,000 Shares. His Father Owned 57,850 Shares, Totaling 10.6%

One of the most critical factors influencing a company's decision on whether to move to a national exchange is the qualifications of the specialist the exchange designates to keep an orderly market for the shares. True, on the over-the-counter market several dealers maintain such a market, but unlike the specialist they are not responsible to an exchange official for their actions. Needless to say, the activities of an American Stock Exchange specialist bear heavily on the price movements of a stock. Through the efforts of A. J. Grant and Company, if Speedata were to list, Mr. Victor Oppenheimer, a senior member of the exchange and a man of unusual capabilities, could be appointed as specialist. This is certainly a plus factor.

On the other hand, we should question the true value of listing. Will Speedata find a more receptive market for its shares? The answer is of course an unknown quantity. However, experience suggests that the real purpose of listing on a national exchange is the creating of investment interest in the company. In order to successfully alter the investment climate, a company must have a favorable earnings trend. Frankly, gentlemen, what is there to recommend about Speedata Equipment? Since 1957 the company has failed to earn any profits despite growing sales and an increasing market potential for its products. In addition, the near term outlook appears no better. The market price of the shares has, at times, fallen below the initial offering price, and profits may still be as much as a year or two away.

I suspect that quite a few Speedata shareholders purchased their shares at $30 or higher during the "golden age of electronics" two years ago. These people might be more prone to liquidate their holdings if the company was listed, since they could be reasonably certain that a sell order could be executed within a fraction of a point of the previous sale. Such is not the case on the over-the-counter market, where a point or more difference in back-to-back transactions is possible. And remember, a point or more differential in the price of a Speedata share represents almost 8% of the share's value. In a sense, the large spread between bid and asked prices on the over-the-counter exchange, together with the difficulty in finding a market quote in the newspaper, may have a locking-in effect, which is desirable at this time of poor corporate performance. Although the virtues of dealer support are often overestimated, Speedata cannot afford to gamble with the dealers' sponsorship until some public enthusiasm can be created for the stock.

There has been some mention about the prestige of listing on the American Stock Exchange. This may be true, but let us also remember that many of the soundest securities are unlisted. For example, most of the blue chip banks and insurance companies are traded over the counter. G. D. Searle and Weyerhaeuser Timber are just two of many industrials having dynamic and active markets on the over-the-counter market. A good trading climate is dependent upon capitalization, profit performance, dividends, and general investor interest, and is not a matter of listing on a national exchange. Since Speedata has only 622,000 shares outstanding, of which about 250,000 shares are closely held, there is some doubt as to whether an active market could be created for the shares even under a favorable profit picture. [Exhibit 5 presents data on the company's outstanding common shares.]

Also, moving over to the American Stock Exchange is no guarantee of broadening distribution for the shares. This generalization is only applicable to a regional company upon listing. If the A. J. Bayless Markets of Arizona were to join a national exchange, it is likely that many investors residing in other areas, who were unaware of the company's progress prior to listing, might subsequently purchase shares. Speedata, on the other hand, is a national company with customers in all parts of the country. People already know about us. Listing would not even be a frosting on the cake.

Although there is some truth in the argument that financial institutions generally confine their purchasing to listed securities, the desirability of this policy to Speedata is questionable. First, with the exception of International Business Machines (IBM), electronics issues are not well represented in the portfolios of the more substantial financial institutions. Second, when these buyers go into the market, they purchase in large lots, usually in amounts of over $100,000. The small supply of Speedata stock prevents financial institutions from taking a meaningful position in our shares, even if they so desire. This is not, however, necessarily to our disadvantage since ownership of large blocks of Speedata shares by institutions would create an undesirable concentration of stock in a few hands.

And, lastly, the NASD is a good policeman. Manipulation of over-the-counter securities by dealers is, in my mind, nonexistent. To the best of my knowledge there has been no evidence indicating that SEC laws applicable to over-the-counter trading are ineffectual or obsolete.

Exhibit 1

SPEEDATA EQUIPMENT, INC.

SELECTED DATA ON SALES, INCOME, DIVIDENDS, FINANCIAL POSITION, COMMON
STOCK, AND MARKET PRICES, 1954–61
(Dollar Figures in Thousands)

	11 Months Ended December 31, 1954	Years Ended December 31						Six Months Ended June 30, 1961
		1955	1956	1957	1958	1959	1960	
Net sales	$ 96	$ 308	$ 1,496	$ 3,023	$ 3,934	$ 8,703	$ 10,742	$ 5,568
Net income (loss)	(28)	(143)	155	41	(195)	(811)	(228)	(102)
Earnings (loss) per share*	(0.17)	(0.60)	0.64	0.13	(0.52)	(1.62)	(0.45)	(0.16)
Depreciation	2	7	17	90	119	125	156	97
Research and development	na	55	222	420	650	970	1,155	920
Total assets	na	218	1,605	3,126	5,559	8,179	8,621	9,510
Long-term debt	na	200	1,000	995	968	2,076	2,063	2,000
Debt as percentage of capitalization	na	na	84%	48%	58%	53%	58%	39%
Number of common shares outstanding	8,200	11,915	120,400	320,500	373,241	502,057	502,573	622,857
Dividends	...	...	...	...				
High and low market bid prices†	...	...	...	21–8¼	43–15¼	45–28½	30–15	24–17

* Adjusted for ten-for-one split in 1955 and two-for-one split in 1957.
† For Bid and Asked Prices on August 24, 1961, see Exhibit 3.
na = not available.

Exhibit 2. SPEEDATA EQUIPMENT, INC.

NUMBER AND GEOGRAPHICAL DISTRIBUTION OF COMMON SHARES
AND STOCKHOLDERS ON APRIL 28, 1961

State	Number of Shares	%	Number of Stock-holders	%
New England	221,368	36	834	39
Connecticut	9,298	2	103	5
Maine	21,642	4	156	7
Massachusetts	182,906	29	510	24
New Hampshire	4,453	1	17	1
Rhode Island	2,909	*	45	2
Vermont	160	*	3	*
Middle Atlantic	208,952	34	727	34
New Jersey	17,378	3	141	7
New York	181,311	29	490	23
Pennsylvania	10,263	2	96	4
South Atlantic	130,984	21	116	5
Delaware	200	*	1	*
Florida	1,525	*	12	*
Georgia	779	*	6	*
Maryland†	125,869	20	59	3
North Carolina	110	*	2	*
Virginia	2,501	1	36	2
East South Central	1,695	*	10	*
Alabama	830	*	2	*
Tennessee	865	*	8	*
West South Central	2,957	*	17	1
Arkansas	350	*	4	*
Louisiana	205	*	3	*
Texas	2,402	*	10	1
East North Central	27,606	4	154	7
Illinois	18,609	3	62	3
Indiana	273	*	7	*
Ohio	7,512	1	59	3
Michigan	355	*	9	*
Wisconsin	857	*	17	1
West North Central	18,244	3	199	9
Iowa	425	*	9	*
Kansas	263	*	7	*
Minnesota	8,867	2	35	2
Missouri	8,614	1	144	7
Nebraska	45	*	2	*
North Dakota	10	*	1	*
South Dakota	20	*	1	*
Mountain	770	*	11	1
Arizona	350	*	3	*
Colorado	345	*	6	*
Idaho	25	*	1	*
Utah	50	*	1	*
West	5,396	1	71	3
California	3,968	1	55	3
Hawaii	526	*	5	*
Oregon	150	*	3	*
Washington	752	*	8	*
Washington, D.C.	1,650	*	21	1
Canada	2,960	1	7	*
England	25	*	1	*
Total	622,607	100%	2,168	100%

* Less than .5%.
† 120,500 shares owned by Volcano Aircraft and Missile Corporation.

Exhibit 3

SPEEDATA EQUIPMENT, INC.

Over-the-Counter Dealers Offering to Sell and Wanting to Purchase Shares of Speedata Equipment, Inc.

AUGUST 24, 1961

Dealers	Wants	Offerings
	*Prices**	
Troster, Singer & Co., New York	15½	17
May & Gannon, Inc., Boston	16	17½
New York Hanseatic Corp., New York	15½	17
J. B. Maguire & Co., Inc., Boston	16	17½
Singer, Bean & Mackie, Inc., New York	15½	17
A. J. Grant & Co., New York	15½	17
Fahnestock & Co., New York	16	17

AUGUST 1960

Dealers

J. J. FitzGerald Co., New York
Stokes Hoyt & Co., New York
A. M. Lerner & Co., New York
James H. Acker & Co., New York
John J. Laver & Co., Inc., New York
L. Johnson & Co., Syracuse
Theriot & Co., Bronxville
J. F. Reilly & Co., Inc., New York
Newborg & Co., New York
William H. Tegtmeyer & Co., Chicago
Jones Miller & Co., Philadelphia
Troster, Singer & Co., New York
May & Gannon, Inc., Boston
New York Hanseatic Corp., New York
Fahnestock & Co., New York
J. B. Maguire & Co., Inc., Boston
Singer, Bean & Mackie, Inc., New York
Carl M. Loeb, Rhoades & Co., New York
A. J. Grant & Co., New York
Irving Weis & Co., New York
B. W. Pizzini & Co., Inc., New York

* Prices are for inside transactions only—that is, the price for which one dealer will sell to another, or at which one dealer will buy from another. The outside price, which is the one charged to the public, is the inside price plus a commission or a spread that constitutes the dealer's profit.

Sources: The National Quotation Bureau, Inc., *National Daily Quotation Service*, August 24, 1961, and *The National Monthly Stock Summary*, August 1, 1960.

Exhibit 4

SPEEDATA EQUIPMENT, INC.

STOCK TRANSFERS OF SPEEDATA EQUIPMENT, INC., RECORDED WITH THE TRANSFER
AGENT, COMPARED WITH TRADING VOLUME OF PACKARD BELL ELECTRONICS
CORPORATION AND BECKMAN INSTRUMENTS, INC.
Februa⁓y–July 1961

Month	*Speedata**	*Packard Bell*†‡	*Beckman Instruments*†
February...............	102,826 shares	43,900 shares	87,200 shares
March..................	73,133	56,700	89,300
April..................	60,868	53,400	54,700
May....................	41,536	59,800	47,500
June...................	51,573	28,100	46,800
July...................	20,852	49,700	40,800
Total.............	350,788	291,600	366,300

* These stock transfer records are not so accurate as data on actual trading volume because they do not reveal the amount of activity exercised through street certificates—stock certificates so registered that they can be bought and sold without reference to the transfer agent.

† Traded on the New York Stock Exchange.

‡ The high and low market prices of the common stock of Packard Bell Electronics Corporation since its listing on the New York Stock Exchange in July, 1959, were as follows:

Date	*High*	*Low*
1959		
July............................	45¼	39¼
August..........................	41¼	33
September.......................	35	30
October.........................	43	32
November........................	46	37
December........................	45	38
1960............................	39	19
1961, through July..............	26	14

Exhibit 5

SPEEDATA EQUIPMENT, INC.

AUTHORIZED AND OUTSTANDING COMMON SHARES

Year		Shares Outstanding December 31
1954	At incorporation, the authorized capital consisted of 6,000 shares of no-par common stock. The authorized stock was soon increased to 10,000 shares of $1-par Class A common stock and 10,000 shares of $1-par Class B common stock, and each old common share was exchanged for 1 Class A share. Both classes were reclassified into no-par common stock at the end of the year, and the authorized stock was increased to 50,000 shares. During the year, 2,200 shares were sold to officers.	8,200
1955	Private placement of 3,715 shares.	11,915
1956	10-for-1 split and an increase in the authorized stock to 500,000 shares. Exercise of options and warrants for 1,250 shares.	120,400
1957	2-for-1 split; public offering of 60,000 shares. Exercise of conversion rights of subordinated notes, options, and warrants for 19,700 shares.	320,500
1958	Authorized common stock increased to 750,000 shares. Issue of 35,281 shares to purchase Neco Company. Exercise of conversion rights, options, and warrants for 17,460 shares.	373,241
1959	Exercise of conversion rights, options, and warrants for 128,816 shares.	502,057
1960	Exercise of options and warrants for 516 shares.	502,573
		June 30, 1961
1961 (to June 30)	Private placement of 119,454 shares. Exercise of options and warrants for 830 shares. Increase of authorized stock to 1,500,000 shares. Shares reserved for exercise of options and warrants, 151,673.	622,857

Exhibit 6

SPEEDATA EQUIPMENT, INC.

COMPARISON OF INDEXES OF COMMON STOCK PRICES* OF SPEEDATA EQUIPMENT, INC.,
PACKARD BELL ELECTRONICS CORPORATION, AND BECKMAN INSTRUMENTS, INC.,
WITH MOODY'S INDEX OF 125 INDUSTRIAL STOCKS, 1957–61

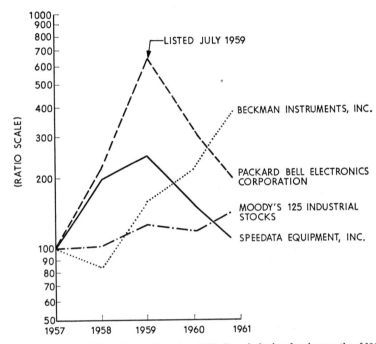

* Averages of annual high and low market prices, 1957–60, and of prices for nine months of 1961.

Exhibit 7

SPEEDATA EQUIPMENT, INC.
COMPARISON OF PRICE–SALES RATIOS* OF SPEEDATA EQUIPMENT, INC.
PACKARD BELL ELECTRONICS CORPORATION,
AND BECKMAN INSTRUMENTS, INC.,
1957–1960

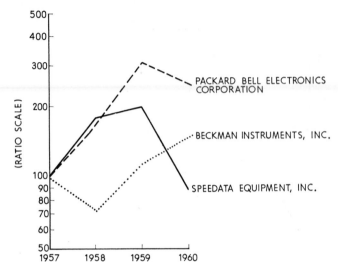

* Comparison of price–sales ratios is believed to be more meaningful than the traditional comparison of price–earnings ratios in the case of electronics companies, which have characteristically experienced deficits in their early stages of development.

Prices are averages of annual high and low market prices.

Appendix A

AMERICAN STOCK EXCHANGE

1M-6-61

LISTING FORM K
(10-30-45)

SAMPLE

DISTRIBUTION OF STOCK

(Separate form to be made out for each class of stock applied for)

Speedata Equipment, Inc.
(Name of Company)

Distribution of .... Common .... Stock
(Class)

on .... April 28 ...., 19 61 ......

I, .. Michael Pressman .... President ......, of ....
(Name)   (Title)

.... Speedata Equipment, Inc. ...., hereby certify that of the .... 622,607 ....
(Company)   (Amount)

outstanding shares of .... Common .... stock of the .... Speedata Equipment, Inc. ....
(Class)   (Company)

there are ...... 556,064 .... shares held by the Public, exclusive of Officers, Directors, and Under-
(See Note A Below)

writers, which publicly held shares are distributed among .... 2,158 .... stockholders, and not
(Number)

pooled, in escrow, non-transferable or restricted as to sale in any manner, whatsoever.

NOTE A—The ten highest holders of the .. 556,064 .... shares certified above as publicly held
(Amount)

are as follows:

	Name		Shares		Name	Shares
1.	Volcano Aircraft & Missile Co.		120,500 shares	6.	Alan Richards, Inc.	9,935 shares
2.	Robert Peterson		57,850 "	7.	Sitwell & Co.	9,130 "
3.	New York Trading		15,036 "	8.	Winston, Boone, Inc.	9,104 "
4.	L. Star & Co.		13,700 "	9.	Sheldon Russell	7,012 "
5.	Evans & Lang, Inc.		13,034 "	10.	Lewis, Clark, Inc.	5,030 "

The .... 66,543 .... share difference (i. e., difference between outstanding amount and

amount certified above as publicly distributed) is held by .... 10 .... stockholders as follows:
(Number)

(Show below holdings of officers, directors, underwriters or others in the "non-public" category. Also include below any outstanding shares which are restricted as to sale, and in center column state that such restriction is the reason for the inclusion of such holdings in this grouping.)

Name	Official Relationship to Company	Holdings
Michael Pressman	President and Director	46,525
A. J. Grant & Co.	Underwriter	9,323
Alan Peterson	Director	8,000
Robert Singleton	Partner, A.J.Grant & Co. & Director	1,000
William Ritter	Executive Vice President & Director	1,000
John Cohen	Clerk	275
A. T. Martin	Vice President	200
Winslow Roberts	Director Certified Correct,	200
Frank Appleton, Jr.	Director	15
Ornette Hendricks	Vice President & Director	5
	By	66,543

891

AMERICAN STOCK EXCHANGE   **LISTING FORM K**
                                                        (10-30-45)

DISTRIBUTION OF STOCK
(Separate form to be made out for each class of stock applied for)

SPEEDATA EQUIPMENT, INC.

Distribution of .... **Common** .... Stock

on ....**August 24**........................, 19..**61**......

					Shares
1,254	Holders of	1 – 99 share lots – – –			**35,676**
482	" "	100 " " – – –			**48,200**
185	" "	101 – 200 " " – – –			**33,397**
67	" "	201 – 300 " " – – –			**19,027**
28	" "	301 – 400 " " – – –			**10,708**
33	" "	401 – 500 " " – – –			**15,892**
53	" "	501 – 1000 " " – – –			**41,190**
66	" "	1001 – up " " – – –			**418,517**

........**2,168**........Stockholders   Total Shares ....**622,607**...........*

* This figure should be the total of all outstanding shares.

Is any of the .... stock pooled, deposited in escrow, non-transferable or held
(Class)
under any syndicate, agreement or control?........................

If so, state the number of shares ...., and attach detailed explanation, including
certified copies of all agreements relating thereto.

Certified Correct,

By...

CUTTER & DUNLOP, INC.

In May, 1961, David Prescott, president of Cutter & Dunlop, Inc., Lynn, Massachusetts, was considering which of four proposals, three from under-writers and one from a small business investment corporation (SBIC), best suited his company's needs. As far back as December, 1959, Mr. Prescott had told his commercial banker, his accountant, and his lawyer that within the next year and a half, if his sales projections proved accurate, the company would have to raise long-term capital. He had therefore asked them to "keep their eyes and ears open" for any capital leads that might arise. In the meantime, he prepared a detailed report on Cutter & Dunlop, covering its history, progress to date, and profit expectations. The president believed that such a study might act as a silent salesman in negotiations with a capital prospect.

COMPANY BACKGROUND

Cutter & Dunlop was incorporated on March 27, 1951, to succeed a partnership formed in 1946 by James Cutter and Foster Dunlop. Both men were graduate engineers, who had had extensive training in the optical lighting industry. The company designed, developed, and manufactured meas-uring instruments as well as miniature assembly lighting and control equip-ment. Virtually all of Cutter & Dunlop's products were proprietary items developed by management.

The company's progress was severely hampered by intense competition from larger and better known firms with superior production and marketing facilities. Up to 1958, Cutter & Dunlop was unable to increase sales substan-tially above the levels reached during the previous decade. Profits were volatile, and sizable losses were recorded in 1955 and 1957. In early 1958, David Prescott, production manager of Inca Camera Corporation, purchased Mr. Cutter's interest and became executive vice president of Cutter & Dunlop. He was elected president the following year.

Under Mr. Prescott's leadership, Cutter & Dunlop completely revised operating policies and procedures. In addition to a cost-cutting program, the president started a research and development program aimed at servicing the needs of the electronics and miniaturization industries. By the end of 1960, despite heavy research expenditures, the company had achieved record-breaking sales and profits. Exhibits 1 and 2 present balance sheets and profit and loss statements for the years 1955–60. Exhibit 3 presents a funds flow statement.

Much of this success was attributable to customer acceptance of the company's new line of optical comparators and projectors. These products were measuring devices that, with the use of light and optics, permitted gauging to very close tolerances. They were also used as quality control instruments, as devices for assembling intricate and minute parts, and as a means of monitoring parts in process. An optical comparator might be described as a microscope in which a magnified image of a part is reflected on a screen marked with a precise measuring scale to test the conformity of the manufactured product with established standards.

As an adjunct to precision measuring and control equipment, Cutter & Dunlop had also developed optically ground and polished lenses coupled with high intensity fluorescent lamps to provide a wide, uniformly illuminated magnified area for examination of precision parts. Like the optical comparators and projectors, these products were designed for industries that required a concentrated source of localized lighting. The company's largest customers, for all products, were major optical manufacturers and missile and electronics firms.

Cutter & Dunlop's sales for the year ended December 31, 1960, were divided among its products as follows:

Comparators and projectors	35.8%
Lighting aids	63.9
Special designing and consulting	0.3
	100.0%

Management believed that most of the company's future growth would come from expansion of its interest in optical instrumentation rather than from lighting aids.

In Mr. Prescott's opinion, the continued success of Cutter & Dunlop depended on the company's ability to strengthen its marketing facilities in order to fully capitalize on several new products: a large-screen machine tool projector, an audio-visual projector, and a projection microscope. The markets for these products were considered by management to be almost insatiable. Mr. Prescott planned to replace manufacturers' representatives with direct salesmen as soon as possible. Robert Tucker, the sales manager, had concluded that the company's existing channels of distribution, which were centered around various forms of wholesalers, were inadequately penetrating the potential market.

Since Cutter & Dunlop expensed rather than capitalized the development costs of its new products, Mr. Prescott believed that the profit statements for 1959 and 1960 were ultraconservative. He said:

In March 1961, we were on the verge of great expansion. The expenses associated with developing a host of new products were well behind us. We then needed funds to merchandise our line to the trade. Our sales objectives of $795,000 for 1961, $1,740,000 for 1962, and $2,845,000 for 1963 are more than realistic. I shouldn't be surprised if we do better. We have declared no dividends in the past, nor can any be expected in the near future.

Estimated profit and loss statements for 1961–63 appear in Exhibit 4.

Cutter & Dunlop employed approximately 50 people, of whom 5 were engineers and 7 were members of general management. For the year ended December 31, 1960, Mr. Prescott received a salary of $15,000, and Mr. Dunlop received $10,000. Otherwise, no employee of the company received remuneration in excess of four figures.

The company had no collective bargaining agreements with any union and had never had a strike. Production facilities, leased for $3,600 a year, consisted of 12,000 square feet of space on the first, third, and part of the fourth floors of a factory building located in Lynn, Massachusetts. Housed in these quarters, Cutter & Dunlop had a well-equipped general machine shop capable of producing all its products. The equipment was owned outright and was in good condition. Management believed, however, that within the next few years a move to a larger, more modern plant was inevitable in light of the proposed expansion program.

PROPOSED FINANCING

At the directors' meeting in March, 1961, Mr. Prescott stated that additional capital of $200,000, plus retained earnings and bank loans, would permit Cutter & Dunlop to achieve its sales goals over the next three years. The company had, at that moment, a $50,000 bank line of credit.

In Mr. Prescott's opinion, the cost of raising $200,000 was substantially the same as the cost of raising $300,000. If a public offering was decided on, underwriting commissions and other related expenses could run as high as $50,000. For this reason, in addition to the desirability of a capital cushion, Mr. Prescott decided to ask for $300,000 when approaching the capital markets. Following is the intended application of proceeds, based upon an estimated $250,000 net to the company.

1. Final research and development of new products................$ 15,000
2. Purchase of jigs, fixtures, and capital equipment for the manufacture of new products..   40,000
3. Sales promotion and marketing program to expand the company's distribution facilities and marketing department................ 120,000
4. Working capital to provide available funds necessary because of expected increases in accounts receivable and to enlarge inventories of materials, demonstration equipment, and finished products....   75,000
                                                                    $250,000

In thinking over what he wanted from either a public or a private offering, Mr. Prescott decided that keeping voting control of the company was the most important criterion. He also wanted to establish a sound basis for mergers and acquisitions, and would expect the underwriter or private capital source to act as a finder and financial adviser when such an opportunity presented itself. Unlike many small businessmen, however, Mr. Prescott was not interested in management consulting services if they were to be offered by the source of capital.

In the event of a public offering, Mr. Prescott wanted wide distribution of the shares. At the same time, he felt that New England stockholders might be more loyal to the company than shareholders in other areas. He described what he termed an ideal stockholder as a sophisticated investor who understood the risks of purchasing shares in a growth situation in its earlier stages of development. He also wanted an orderly aftermarket, which would both instill shareholder confidence in the company and represent a sound situation for a potential merger.

The breakdown of the ownership of Cutter & Dunlop stock on May 1, 1961, was as follows:

David Prescott	380 shares	27.1%
Nancy Prescott	740 shares	52.9
Foster Dunlop	240 shares	17.1
Employees	40 shares	2.9
Total	1,400 shares	100.0%

Mr. Prescott was not opposed to granting warrants as an incentive to an underwriter or to employees. In fact, he believed that by 1963 the company would have to expand its management, and that warrants would be necessary to attract ambitious, capable people into the organization. He said, "When Cutter & Dunlop is better entrenched in the optical industry and in the hands of effective administrators, I won't mind giving up control and relaxing a bit." Nevertheless, although he was not opposed to warrants, he was disturbed by the possibility that an underwriter might exercise the warrants and dump the shares on the market within a short period of time.

Finally, Mr. Prescott believed that Cutter & Dunlop would have to enter the capital market again, perhaps in 1963, to raise substantial funds for expansion. Success in initial financing was important to facilitate a second offering.

OFFER FROM A SMALL BUSINESS INVESTMENT CORPORATION

In January, 1961, Mr. Prescott had approached Oliver Wentworth, an old family friend and a partner of a large Boston brokerage house. Mr. Wentworth told Mr. Prescott that Cutter & Dunlop was too speculative for his company to finance, but that he would put him in touch with George Chesterfield, president of the Wharton Corporation, an established small business investment corporation. Several weeks later, by invitation, Mr. Prescott visited the management of the Wharton Corporation at its office in New York City.

At this meeting, Mr. Chesterfield described the Wharton Corporation. The company was incorporated in New York in 1959 as a small business investment company licensed under the Small Business Investment Act of 1958, with an initial capital of $300,000 raised privately through the sale of 30,000 shares at $10. In June, 1960, through Viceroy Securities, a large investment banker, the Wharton Corporation successfully sold 1 million shares of common stock to the public at $10. The net proceeds to the company were $9 million.

Since that time, the company had invested $1 million in 7 electronics companies, and slightly over $2 million in 10 other small companies actively engaged in the manufacture of chemicals, plastics, and drugs, and in construction. Two of the firms in which Wharton had invested had subsequently raised equity capital by selling stock to the public. Based on current market prices, Wharton's holdings of securities in these two organizations, with a book value of $700,000, had a market value in excess of $3.5 million. The management of Wharton had no intention of liquidating its holdings in either situation, but it felt that the large paper profit had been considered indicative of its ability to spot growth companies and to work closely with them in solving their financial problems. The market price of Wharton stock was about $20 per share, or twice its subscription price. Mr. Chesterfield thought the public appreciated that Wharton was an aggressive SBIC.

Mr. Prescott outlined the progress of Cutter & Dunlop and presented his report. Mr. Chesterfield appeared impressed and subsequently made the following offer: Cutter & Dunlop would be recapitalized by an increase of its authorized common stock to 300,000 shares and conversion of its 1,400 issued and outstanding shares into 161,000 shares of common stock, at a ratio of 115 to 1. The Wharton Corporation would purchase $200,000 of 8% long-term notes due in 1967. The notes would be amortized after the third year in quarterly installments of $15,000. Mr. Prescott would be asked to personally sign the notes, thus giving the Wharton Corporation recourse against his estate in case of default. The Wharton Corporation would receive 5-year warrants to purchase 69,000 unissued shares of common stock, to be protected against dilution, for $150,000. In addition, it wanted the right of first refusal for 50,000 shares at $3 per share in the event Cutter & Dunlop needed additional equity capital within 2 years. The Wharton Corporation would also place on the board of directors a man who would be active in the area of financial planning.

This offer was conditional, depending on the results of a market survey of the optical industry and the company's competitive position. The cost of such a study, to be made by Marlboro Associates, a well-known Boston management consulting firm, was expected to run between $3,000 and $5,000, and would be paid by Cutter & Dunlop.

As the negotiation progressed, Mr. Prescott indicated that he would not commit himself without talking with some investment bankers specializing in underwriting small growth companies. Mr. Chesterfield quickly responded:

Although the new issue market is currently at a historical peak, if Cutter & Dunlop goes public now you will have to give up 45% of the company to get the same amount of funds we are offering. Besides, the small investment bankers you refer to are generally just plain manipulators and thieves. In the long run, such an association will injure the reputation of your company. We, on the other hand, have the best Wall Street connections in New York and will take you public with a prestige underwriter at the proper time. Then, by commanding a higher price/earnings ratio, you could raise a larger sum by selling a smaller proportion of the company to the public.

OFFERS FROM NOVELLI & SPIEL, INC.

The following week, while Mr. Prescott was still weighing the Wharton Corporation's proposal, Frank Novelli of Novelli & Spiel, Inc., a New York investment banker, telephoned. Mr. Novelli explained that Cutter & Dunlop had been brought to his attention by John Collins, chief loan officer at the Lynn Trust Company, which was Cutter & Dunlop's commercial bank. Mr. Novelli indicated that he was impressed by the company's progress and would like to send his engineering group to look over Cutter & Dunlop's physical facilities and product line. Mr. Prescott welcomed such a visit.

A few days later, Mr. Prescott met with Mr. Novelli in New York. Mr. Novelli gave Mr. Prescott several prospectuses of the firm's past underwritings. He pointed out how well the public had received the issues, as witnessed by the market prices appearing in Exhibit 5. Although Mr. Prescott agreed that the price performance had been excellent, he had reservations about the quality of the companies. In fact, several of Novelli & Spiel's underwritings seemed to him like complete speculations.

Mr. Novelli stressed that his firm could guarantee wide distribution if a public offering was undertaken. He further indicated that Novelli & Spiel was known for creating strong markets in its issues. He then made Cutter & Dunlop two offers, one for a private placement and the other for a public offering.

If the private placement was accepted, the company would be recapitalized to 300,000 shares. The existing stockholders would receive 161,000 shares, as in the Wharton Corporation proposal. Novelli & Spiel would purchase $300,000, 7%, 5-year convertible debentures in 3 steps: $100,000 in June, 1961; $100,000 in January, 1962; and $100,000 in June, 1962. The last two purchases would be made only on the company's substantial compliance with sales and earnings projections (see Exhibit 4). Thus, if Cutter & Dunlop failed to meet its sales and profit forecasts, the investment banker could legally withdraw, in January, 1962, or in June, 1962, from purchasing additional debentures. If $300,000 of debentures were purchased, they would be convertible into 86,700 shares of common stock for a period of 5 years and would be protected against dilution. The banker also wanted options for another 30,000 shares if the company went public at a later date. After considerable discussion, this demand was dropped; however, the company did agree that at the first $100,000 purchase of debentures Novelli & Spiel would receive an additional 4,300 shares as a commitment fee.

The public offering involved recapitalizing the company to 153,000 shares, of which 73,000 shares would be held by the present stockholders and 60,000 shares would be sold to the public at $5. This would be a Regulation A[1] issue but a firm underwriting.[2] Novelli & Spiel guaranteed Cutter & Dunlop a minimum of $210,000. The underwriter would also receive 5-year options to purchase 20,000 shares of unissued common stock at $5 per share.

When Mr. Prescott questioned the $90,000 difference between the gross and net proceeds of the issue, Mr. Novelli replied:

There are significant cash outlays associated with an initial public offering. We are required to pay a finder's fee to John Collins and to lay out large sums for advertising, accounting, and legal expenditures. At a later date we will sponsor a financial public relations program. For example, we expect to prepare a research study of Cutter & Dunlop, which will be mailed to salesmen in key brokerage houses as well as to large advisory services. If we interest the financial community in Cutter & Dunlop securities, a strong aftermarket should result. And remember, Novelli & Spiel is known for strong aftermarkets. Not only will we take a position in the shares, but you can also count upon several leading over-the-counter houses like Waldorf & Co. and H. Bick, Inc., who have worked with us in the past, to push your stock. When you are looking for mergers or acquisitions, and an exchange of stock is contemplated, a high market price will permit Cutter & Dunlop to give away only a fraction of the stock you otherwise would.

Mr. Prescott next asked several friends who were active on Wall Street about the reputation of Novelli & Spiel. The reactions to the investment banker were mixed. All agreed that the firm was "a powerhouse which could sell the public anything." One stock broker said, however, that Novelli & Spiel was "exclusively engaged in underwriting garbage," whereas another said that Novelli & Spiel would not handle a company without exceptional promise.

---

[1] Regulation A provided a short form registration, a procedure less expensive and simpler than the full registration prescribed by the Securities Act of 1933. In order to qualify for a Regulation A issue, the aggregate offering price to the public (number of shares offered times retail price per share) could not exceed $300,000. Regulation A also required filing with the Securities and Exchange Commission a notification, which was much simpler than a full registration statement, and the use of an offering circular rather than the much more detailed and expensive prospectus for making security offers.

Under a Regulation A offering, stock purchased by the underwriter through warrants could not be registered for public sale until 13 months after the date of the original offering of stock to the public.

[2] In a firm underwriting, the investment banker purchases the entire issue from the company and offers the shares to the public or other interested parties. The risks associated with selling the issue are exclusively the concern of the underwriter, who has no recourse to the company if the issue cannot be sold successfully.

OFFERS FROM HARRIS & CO.

Mr. Prescott's meeting with a second underwriter occurred when Cutter & Dunlop's accounting firm put him in touch with E. Charles Harris, senior partner of Harris & Co. Before conferring with Mr. Harris, Mr. Prescott made discreet inquiries about the reputation of the firm. Several people in the trade told him that Mr. Harris had boasted of handling a new underwriting almost every week for a period of a year or so. Such a high rate of productivity alarmed Mr. Prescott, since he felt that Mr. Harris could not have been very selective. The underwriter was also known to have dumped the warrants of several companies on the open market as soon as legally permissible. A recent financial article in a New York City newspaper had made generally unfavorable remarks about this investment banker. Even so, Mr. Prescott still wanted to talk with him.

Mr. Prescott later described Mr. Harris as

. . . one of the most personable men I have ever met. Despite his constant use of sailor's language, he possessed a dynamism that I found spellbinding. The moment I walked into the office he sat me down and proudly announced that he was a one-deal firm, that no bargaining or negotiating would even be considered. He admitted that Harris & Co.'s reputation had suffered in the past, but he assured me that era was over. In fact, he said: "Since the beginning of 1960, we have only underwritten two companies, Safti-Lock, Inc., and Southern Paint & Varnish Company. The latter has already moved from the over-the-counter market to the American Stock Exchange. Both companies are quality." He then took a blank check from his top drawer, filled it out for $225,000 payable to Cutter & Dunlop and handed it to me. That check was very tempting.

(Exhibit 5 includes the subscription prices and the May 1, 1961, market prices of Safti-Lock, Inc., and Southern Paint & Varnish Company.)

Mr. Harris' first offer was as follows: Cutter & Dunlop would recapitalize to 200,000 shares, of which 120,000 would be held by the existing stockholders and 60,000 would be sold to the public at $5. The underwriting would be filed as a Regulation A offering, but would be a firm commitment. Harris & Co. would guarantee a minimum of $225,000 to the company after expenses. However, Cutter & Dunlop was required to pay the finder's fee, which was $5,000 plus stock in the amount of 2% of the total number of shares offered to the public. The investment banker also asked for warrants, exercisable until 1966, to purchase 20,000 shares at $1.

Mr. Harris wanted to close an agreement that very afternoon, but Mr. Prescott would not agree to such a request. Mr. Harris wanted the underwriting so much, however, that within the next few days he offered Cutter & Dunlop five different arrangements, each new one better than the last. Finally, he offered either of two propositions.

1. Recapitalize the company to 200,000 shares, of which 120,000 shares would be held by the existing stockholders and 60,000 would be sold to the public at $5.

This, too, would be a Regulation A offering, but a firm commitment. Harris & Co. guaranteed a minimum of $250,000 after expenses to the company, and asked for 5-year warrants to purchase 20,000 shares of unissued stock at the offering price.

2. The second proposition was similar to the first, except that the existing stockholders would receive 140,000 instead of 120,000 shares. However, Mr. Harris asked for 5-year warrants to purchase 25,000 shares from the existing stockholders at $5, in proportion to the original ownership. For example, Mr. Prescott and his wife, who owned 80% of the Cutter & Dunlop stock outstanding before the public sale, would have to sell 20,000 shares to Mr. Harris if he exercised the warrants.

Mr. Prescott did not think it necessary to make inquiries of the managements of any of the companies financed by either Novelli & Spiel or Harris & Co., since, in his opinion, their reactions to the underwriters would be too largely influenced by the market prices of their issues. He thought also that the general Wall Street reputations of the investment bankers would be a better guide to a decision.

OFFER FROM CRANE BROS.

In April, 1961, Mr. Collins suggested that Mr. Prescott talk to a close friend of his, Harvey Jamerson. Mr. Jamerson had recently formed an SBIC, and had numerous contacts with investment bankers and venture capital firms. Several days later, Mr. Prescott met with Mr. Jamerson at the Harvard Club in Boston. Mr. Prescott described his company's need for new capital, and showed Mr. Jamerson the 200-page document giving a detailed history of the company and its plans for the future.

The following week the men met again. This time, having done some research, Mr. Jamerson expressed considerable interest in the company and offered to arrange financing for the firm.

Mr. Jamerson added that although he managed an SBIC, he could also offer Mr. Prescott another source of capital. Several months ago, he had been approached by an old friend, Emil Crane, an eminent financier and professor of economics at a leading university. Mr. Crane and his brother, a successful securities salesman, had recently formed an investment banking firm, Crane Bros. They were interested in an association with a Boston man who would both run the Boston office and act as a finder for underwritings. This was an unusual opportunity, in Mr. Jamerson's opinion, and after careful consideration he had accepted it.

"Therefore," Mr. Jamerson said, "I can offer Cutter & Dunlop a deal with Crane Bros." When Mr. Prescott asked about the companies previously underwritten by Crane Bros., Mr. Jamerson replied:

At the moment we do not have any offerings behind us. We have already contracted with two companies, however, one a medical electronics firm and the other a data processing organization. We are raising $300,000 for each. Both issues will be sold to the public within a month. Our selling group has already been formed and consists of Morris Shiller & Co., A. C. Howard, Inc., and Plato Securities.

These investment bankers were well known to Mr. Prescott as reputable and aggressive firms.

Mr. Jamerson continued:

By signing with us you will be assured of the support of our whole syndicate in both the offering and the aftermarket. Cutter & Dunlop will be one of our first issues, and one which we hope to build a reputation on. Therefore, supporting the issue in the open market will be our primary objective. To most other investment bankers Cutter & Dunlop would be just another underwriting, but to Crane Bros. such an association will be a marriage. Also, unlike other small New York investment bankers, we are opening a Boston office in hopes of interesting New England investors in Crane Bros. securities. Such stockholders are more desirable than New York speculators, who so often purchase new issues just for a quick trade. I am going to continue managing an SBIC as well as running the Boston office of Crane Bros. In the near future I hope to be able to offer financial consulting when needed and to arrange and negotiate mergers and acquisitions for you. In this area my extensive contacts with small business should be of help.

Mr. Jamerson then detailed the terms of the Crane Bros. proposal, which included recapitalizing the company from 1,400 to 300,000 shares and selling 100,000 shares on a Regulation A filing to the public at $3 on a best efforts, all or none[3] basis. The existing stockholders would hold 161,000 shares. The net proceeds to the company would approximate $250,000, from which $15,000 would be deducted for expenses. Any part of the $15,000 not used by the underwriter for expenses was to be deemed additional compensation. Crane Bros. also wanted an option for a term of 5 years to acquire 20,000 shares of unissued Cutter & Dunlop stock at 1 mill per share.

The following day, Mr. Prescott telephoned Ezra Pine, president of a multimillion dollar real estate trust company. Emil Crane had been financial consultant and a director of the organization for several years. When asked about Mr. Crane, Mr. Pine candidly replied, "Emil Crane is a brilliant financier. He has worked out some of our most complex sale-and-leaseback problems. I don't pay a man $500 a day for nothing. He is tops in his field." Mr. Prescott then spoke to several New York security salesmen about Roger Crane. They were all in agreement that he was honest, hard working, and a powerful salesman, with some of the largest and most desirable accounts in the city. It was rumored that Roger Crane had been offered a partnership in a medium-size brokerage house if he wanted to sever his association with Swanson & Co., where he was currently employed.

A summary of all the investment proposals offered to Cutter & Dunlop appears in Exhibit 6.

---

[3] In a best efforts, all or none offer, the investment banker acts simply as agent for the issuer. It does not purchase the issue and makes no commitment. In the event the underwriter does not sell all the shares within 90 days of the date of the offering, all moneys collected from subscribers to the shares will be returned in full.

ADDITIONAL ASSUMPTIONS

Mr. Prescott projected total capital expenditures of $40,000 in 1961, $30,000 in 1962, and $30,000 in 1963. Assuming these capital additions, he estimated depreciation of $7,000 in 1961, $11,000 in 1962, and $13,000 in 1963.

Mr. Prescott had not included in Exhibit 4 the nonrecurring expenses noted on page 895—$15,000 for final research and development, expected to be spent in 1961, and $120,000 for a sales promotion and marketing program, to be spent by the end of 1962.

At present, Cutter & Dunlop had an unsecured line of credit for $50,000 at the Lynn Trust Company. Mr. Collins, the chief loan officer of the bank, had indicated a willingness to increase the line to 90% of accounts receivable and about 40% of inventories on a secured basis, provided total loans bore a reasonable relationship to existing equity.

Exhibit 1
CUTTER & DUNLOP, INC.
BALANCE SHEETS AS OF DECEMBER 31, 1955-60

ASSETS

	1955	1956	1957	1958	1959	1960
Current assets:						
Cash	$ 544	$ 5,968	$ 8,380	$ 6,192	$ 2,191	$ 9,724
Accounts receivable	45,125	49,215	36,633	40,102	59,394	55,375
Inventory	71,026	56,348	46,594	55,453	93,838	110,891
Prepaid expenses and deposits	5,187	3,134	3,168	4,092	1,980	1,932
Due from officers		73	1,131	456	983	9,027
Total Current Assets	$121,882	$114,738	$ 95,906	$106,295	$158,386	$186,949
Machinery and equipment (net)	29,798	21,209	21,300	19,979	19,894	24,556
Total Assets	$151,680	$135,947	$117,206	$126,274	$178,280	$211,505

LIABILITIES AND CAPITAL

	1955	1956	1957	1958	1959	1960
Current liabilities:						
Notes payable	$ 35,000	$ 10,000	$ 20,000	$ 25,000	$ 15,507	$ 25,000
Accounts payable	16,703	10,497	8,424	11,239	57,916	24,009
Advance on contracts				400	3,201	
Accrued salaries, wages, commissions, and payroll taxes	10,804	14,161	10,749	11,206	14,973	19,475
Reserve for federal taxes						12,000
Deposits on projectors	1,649	1,650	1,189	1,100	1,100	1,100
Due to officers	9,000	12,400		746	312	2,245
Total Current Liabilities	$ 73,156	$ 48,708	$ 40,362	$ 49,691	$ 93,009	$ 83,829
Capital:						
Common stock, 1,400 shares (no-par value) outstanding	60,000	60,200	60,200	60,200	60,200	60,200
Surplus	18,524	27,039	16,644	16,383	25,071	67,476
Total Liabilities and Capital	$151,680	$135,947	$117,206	$126,274	$178,280	$211,505
Current ratio	1.67	2.36	2.38	2.14	1.70	2.23
Working capital	$ 48,726	$ 66,030	$ 55,544	$ 56,604	$ 65,377	$103,120

Exhibit 2

CUTTER & DUNLOP, INC.

PROFIT AND LOSS STATEMENTS FOR YEARS ENDED DECEMBER 31, 1955–60

	1955	1956	1957	1958	1959	1960
Net sales	$273,015	$381,989	$323,285	$287,985	$372,785	$629,759
Cost of goods manufactured and sold	188,314	263,899	241,636	194,393	272,760	425,765
Gross profit	$ 84,701	$118,090	$ 81,649	$ 93,592	$100,025	$203,994
Selling and administrative expenses	113,300	107,785	91,231	93,672	90,619	144,065
Operating profit (loss)	$(28,599)	$ 10,305	$ (9,582)	$ (80)	$ 9,406	$ 59,929
Total other income (charges)	1,488	(690)	(313)	(783)	482	(524)
Net income (loss) before taxes	$(27,111)	$ 9,615	$ (9,895)	$ (863)	$ 9,888	$ 59,405
Income taxes	70	1,100	500	500	1,200	17,000
Net income (loss) after taxes	$(27,181)	$ 8,515	$(10,395)	$ (1,363)	$ 8,688	$ 42,405
As % of net sales						
Gross profit	31.0	30.9	25.3	32.5	26.8	32.4
Net income (loss) before tax	(9.9)	2.5	(3.1)	(0.3)	2.7	9.4
Net income (loss) after tax	(10.0)	2.2	(3.2)	(0.5)	2.3	6.7

Exhibit 3

CUTTER & DUNLOP, INC.

STATEMENTS OF SOURCE AND APPLICATION OF FUNDS, 1956–60

	1956	1957	1958	1959	1960
SOURCE OF FUNDS					
Net income (loss).........$	8,515	($10,395)	($ 1,363)	$ 8,688	$42,405
Depreciation...............	1,469	3,511	3,539	3,628	3,175
Increases:					
Notes payable...........	...	10,000	5,000	...	9,493
Accounts payable........	...	...	2,815	46,677	...
Accruals.................	3,357	(3,412)	457	3,767	4,502
Reserve for federal taxes..	...	...	...	...	12,000
Reductions:					
Cash....................	...	...	2,188	4,001	...
Accounts receivable......	...	12,582	...	...	4,019
Inventory...............	14,678	9,754	...	...	...
Machinery and equip-					
ment..................	7,120	...	...	...	...
Other sources.............	2,254	...	489	4,913	...
	$37,393	$22,040	$13,125	$71,674	$75,594
APPLICATION OF FUNDS					
Increases:					
Cash....................$	5,424	$ 2,412	...	...	$ 7,533
Accounts receivable......	4,090	...	$ 3,469	$19,292	...
Inventory...............	...	...	8,859	38,385	17,053
Machinery and equip-					
ment..................	...	3,602	2,218	3,543	7,837
Due from officers.........	73	1,058	(675)	527	8,044
Reductions:					
Notes payable...........	25,000	...	...	9,493	...
Accounts payable........	6,206	2,073	...	...	33,907
Due to officers...........	(3,400)	12,400	(746)	434	(1,933)
Other applications..........	...	495	...	...	3,153
	$37,393	$22,040	$13,125	$71,674	$75,594

Exhibit 4

CUTTER & DUNLOP, INC.

ESTIMATED PROFIT AND LOSS STATEMENTS FOR YEARS ENDING
DECEMBER 31, 1961–63
(Dollar Figures in Thousands)

	1961	1962	1963
Net sales...............................	$795	$1,740	$2,845
Cost of goods manufactured and sold.......	505	1,068	1,720
Gross profit............................	$290	$ 672	$1,125
Total selling and administrative expenses....	190	450	670
Net income before taxes..................	$100	$ 222	$ 455
Provision for state and federal taxes........	35	122	252
Net Income............................	$ 65	$ 100	$ 203

Exhibit 5

CUTTER & DUNLOP, INC.

PRICES OF REPRESENTATIVE ISSUES UNDERWRITTEN BY TWO INVESTMENT BANKERS

OFFERING PRICES AND BID AND ASKED MARKET PRICES ON MAY 3, 1961, FOR UNDERWRITINGS OF NOVELLI & SPIEL, INC., FROM AUGUST 17, 1960, TO MAY 1, 1961*

Company	Date of Issue	Offering Price	Market Prices, May 3, 1961	
			Bid	Asked
Rembo Filter Co.	August 17, 1960	8¾	8	8½
Citti Industries, Inc.	November 13, 1960	5	3⅛	3½
Beta-Tech Labs, Inc.	November 22, 1960	6	11	11¾
Moon Textiles Corp.	February 3, 1961	6	19	21
Finite, Inc.	March 6, 1961	5	8½	9
Hypo Electronics, Inc.	March 18, 1961	5	11⅜	11⅞
Glamor Industries, Inc.	April 4, 1961	6	9	9½

OFFERING PRICES AND BID AND ASKED MARKET PRICES ON MAY 1, 1961 OF UNDERWRITINGS OF HARRIS & CO., FROM DECEMBER 12, 1960, TO MAY 1, 1961

Company	Date of Issue	Offering Price	Market Prices, May 1, 1961	
			Bid	Asked
Southern Paint & Varnish Company	December 13, 1960	12	25	26†
Safti-Lock, Inc.	March 14, 1961	3	10	11*

* Securities traded on the over-the-counter market.
† Traded on the American Stock Exchange.

Exhibit 6

CUTTER & DUNLOP, INC.

DETAILS OF CAPITAL PROPOSALS

	SBIC Wharton Corporation 8% Notes	Novelli & Spiel, Inc.		Harris & Co.		Crane Bros. Public Offering
		Convertible Debentures	Public Offering	Public Offering No. 1	Public Offering No. 2	
Long-term debt	$200,000, 8% notes, due 1967	$300,000, 7%, 5-year debentures, convertible into 86,700 common shares	none	none	none	none
Number of common shares authorized	300,000	300,000	300,000	200,000	200,000	300,000
Retained by existing owners	161,000	161,000 = 97%	73,000 = 55%	120,000 = 67%	140,000 = 70%	161,000 = 62%
Sold	none	4,300*	60,000	60,000	60,000	100,000
Potential from conversion or warrants	69,000	86,700	20,000	20,000	25,000	20,000
Price of offering, per share	...	...	$5	$5	$5	$3
Underwriter's spread	...	...	$ 90,000	$ 50,000	$ 50,000	$ 65,000
Proceeds to company	$200,000	$300,000	$210,000	$250,000	$250,000	$235,000
Earnings per share, 1963 base	$1.21	$1.17	$1.52	$1.13	$1.02	$0.78
Warrants	To purchase 69,000 shares for $150,000; 5-year life. Also, right of first refusal: 50,000 shares at $3	Conversion price, $3.44	To purchase 20,000 shares for $100,000; 5-year life	To purchase 20,000 shares for $100,000; 5-year life	To purchase 25,000 shares for $125,000 from existing stockholders; 5-year life	To purchase 20,000 shares for $20; 5-year life

* Commitment fee.

HOW THE INVESTMENT BANKER

FUNCTIONS*

It was extremely difficult, in the midst of the conflicting statements of counsel and the welter of miscellaneous documents which followed one another into the record without witnesses to describe the attendant circumstances, to get any adequate grasp of just what investment bankers did. Finally, when Harold L. Stuart of Halsey Stuart & Co. was called as a government witness and remained on the witness stand for many months the light began to dawn. I watched him closely for many weeks, asked questions which were designed to test his forthrightness and credibility and checked his testimony with the utmost care against many of the documents already in evidence and much of the testimony taken by deposition, which had already been read into the record. I became convinced that this man, who probably knows as much if not more about the investment banking business than any other living person, was a man of complete integrity upon whose testimony I could rely with confidence.

Thereafter, and with the consent and approval of counsel for all parties, I went with counsel for both sides to the office of Halsey Stuart & Co. and watched one of the large issues "go through the hopper." I examined the bundles of securities, the tickets and slips from which the various book entries were to be made, watched the deliveries and snooped into every nook and cranny of what was going on. This was all done with the understanding that anything that occurred would be placed upon the record if anyone so desired; and, with a similar understanding, the greater part of two weeks was spent in my chambers with Stuart and various assistants and members of his staff going over every aspect and practically every document connected with two typical security issues from beginning to end. One was a negotiated underwritten issue and the other an issue brought out at public sealed bidding.

---

* In a trial opened on November 28, 1950 and continued through May 19, 1953 for 309 courtroom days the U.S. Government brought suit against 17 defendant investment banking firms "to restrain the continuance of certain alleged violations of Sections 1 and 2 of the Sherman Act." In an *Opinion* filed by Harold R. Medina, United States Circuit Judge, October 15, 1953 "The motions to connect, and further to amend the complaint (were) denied; each of the several motions to dismiss the complaint (were) granted, and the complaint (was) dismissed as to each defendant on the merits and with prejudice." The portion reprinted here from the *Opinion* in United States v. Morgan, et al. was Part I, Chapter IV, a remarkably succinct and simple summary of the transactions in which investment bankers engage.

Neither of these issues had any relation whatever to this case and nothing of a controversial character was included. But the result was that for the first time I felt possessed of the necessary background, and could thereafter, with a modicum of assurance, interpret and assess the probative value of the documents which constituted the greater part of plaintiff's proof. As Stuart continued to testify as a witness for many weeks thereafter, the facts relative to the actual operation of the investment banking business were fully developed in the record.

The types of issues, methods of raising money and the general apparatus of finance which I am about to relate are the ABC's of investment banking, known to every investment banker but not to others.

The problem before an issuer is in no real sense that of selling a commodity or a manufactured article. In essence what the issuer wants is money and the problem is how and on what terms he can get it. Basically, it is simply a question of hiring the money.

Thus a knowledgeable issuer, and most of them are definitely such, will scan the possibilities, which are more numerous than one might at first suppose.

The available types of transactions include many which may be consummated by the issuer without using any of the services of an investment banker. In other words, the raising of a particular sum may be engineered and consummated by the executive or financial officers of an issuer according to a plan originated and designed by them; and this may be done after prolonged collaboration with one or more investment bankers, whose hopes of being paid for the rendition of some sort of investment banking services never reach fruition. Thus the necessary funds may be raised by:

1. A direct public offering by the issuer without an investment banker.
2. A direct offering to existing security-holders without an investment banker.
3. A direct private placement without an investment banker.
4. A public sealed bidding transaction without the assistance of an investment banker.
5. Term bank loans, commercial mortgage loans, leasebacks and equipment loans by commercial banks, life insurance companies and other institutions.

Where the services of an investment banker are used, the typical transactions are even more varied. The principal ones are:

1. A negotiated underwritten public offering.
2. An underwritten public offering awarded on the basis of publicly invited sealed bids, an investment banker having been retained on a fee basis to shape up the issue.
3. A negotiated underwritten offering to existing security-holders. Here the investment banker enters into a commitment to "stand by" until the subscription or exchange period has expired, at which time the investment banker must take up the securities not subscribed or exchanged.
4. An underwritten offering to existing security-holders awarded on the basis of publicly invited sealed bids, an investment banker having been retained on a fee basis to render the necessary assistance.

5. A non-underwritten offering to existing security-holders, with an investment banker acting as agent of the seller on a negotiated basis.

6. A private placement with an investment banker acting as agent of the seller on a negotiated basis.

There are many and sundry variations of the types of transactions just described, depending on the designing of the plan, the amount of risk-taking involved and the problems of distribution; and these variations are reflected in the amount of compensation to be paid to the investment banker, which is always subject to negotiation. And it is worthy of note that, where the services of an investment banker are availed of in the preparation of an issue for publicly invited sealed bids, then pursuant to SEC, ICC and FPC rulings, the investment banker who has rendered financial advisory services for a fee cannot bid on the issue.

Moreover, the static data reveal numerous instances where combinations of these types of transactions are used. The avenues of approach to the ultimate goal of hiring the money on the most advantageous terms, and in ways peculiarly suited to the requirements of the particular issuer at a given time and in a certain state of the general securities market, are legion. And issuers, far from acting in isolation, are continually consulting and seeking advice from other qualified financial advisers such as their commercial bankers and others.

Sometimes an issuer knows pretty well in advance which type of transaction it wishes to use. More often this is not determined until every angle has been explored. In either event, the methods to be followed present a complex series of possibilities, many of which involve intricate calculations of the effective cost of the money and a host of other features affecting the capital structure of the issuer, plans for future financing, problems of operation of the business and so on.

Generally the money is needed for a special purpose at a particular time, which may or may not be determined at the will of the issuer. Examples are: for expansion, the building of a new plant, the purchase of existing facilities, the scrapping of one set of elaborate and costly machines and their replacement by others more efficient and up-to-date, or for refunding. Often it is deemed important by the management that there be a wide distribution of the securities or that they be placed with investors in a particular geographical locality or among those who utilize the services of the issuer or purchase its products. When good will is involved or favorable treatment of existing security-holders is desired, the issuer may have sound reasons for not wishing to obtain the highest possible price for the issue.

If a given type of transaction is tentatively selected, the issuer has before it an almost infinite number of possible features, each of which may have a significant bearing on the attainment of the general result. The method to be pursued may be through an issue of bonds or preferred or common stock or some combination of these. If a debt issue is contemplated there are problems of security and collateral, debentures or convertible debentures, serial issues, sinking fund provisions, tax refund protective and other covenants, coupon rates and a host of other miscellanea which may affect the rating (by Poor's or Moody's, Fitch or Standard Statistics), or the flexibility necessary for the operation of the business and the general saleability of the issue in terms of market receptivity. These details must each be given careful consideration in relation to the existing capital structure and plans for the future. If equity securities seem preferable on a preliminary survey, the available alternatives are equally numerous and the problems at times more vexing. What will do for one company is not suitable for another, even in the same industry. At times prior consolidations and reorganizations and an intricate pattern of prior financing make the over-all picture complicated and unusually difficult. But in the end, sometimes after many months of patient effort, just the right combination of alternatives is hit upon.

The actual design of the issue involves preparation of the prospectus and registration statement, with supporting documents and reports, compliance with the numerous rules and regulations of the SEC or ICC or FPC and the various Blue Sky Laws passed by the several States. In view of the staggering potential liabilities under the Securities Act of 1933 this is no child's play, as is known only too well by the management of issuers.

This hasty and far from complete recital of available alternatives will suffice to indicate the milieu in which the investment banker demonstrates his skill, ingenuity and resourcefulness, to the extent and to the extent only that an issuer wishes to avail itself of his services. It is always the hope of the investment banker that the issuer will use the full range of the services of the investment banker, including the design and setting up of the issue, the organization of the group to underwrite the risk and the planning of the distribution. If he cannot wholly succeed, the investment banker will try to get as much of the business as he can. Thus he may wind up as the manager or co-manager, or as a participant in the group of underwriters with or without an additional selling position; or he may earn a fee as agent for a private placement or other transaction without any risk-bearing feature. Or someone else may get the business away from him.

Thus we find that in the beginning there is no "it." The security issue which eventuates is a nebulous thing, still in futuro. Consequently the competition for business by investment bankers must start with an effort to establish or continue a relationship with the issuer. That is why we hear so much in this case about ingenious ways to prevail upon the issuers in particular instances to select this or that investment banking house to work on the general problem of shaping up the issue and handling the financing. This is the initial step; and it is generally taken many months prior to the time when it is expected that the money will be needed. It is clear beyond any reasonable doubt that this procedure is due primarily to the wishes of the issuers; and one of the reasons why issuers like this form of competition is that they are under no legal obligation whatever to the investment banker until some document such as an underwriting agreement or agency contract with the investment banker has actually been signed.

Sometimes an investment banking house will go it alone at this initial stage. At times two or three houses or even more will work together in seeking the business, with various understandings relative to the managership or co-managership and the amount of their underwriting participations. These are called nucleus groups. Occasionally one comes across documents pertaining to such nucleus groups which seem to contemplate the continuance of the group for future business, only to find that in a few weeks or less the whole picture has changed and some realignment of forces has taken place.

The tentative selection of an investment banker to shape up the issue and handle the financing has now been made; and there ensues a more or less prolonged period during which the skilled technicians of the investment banker are working with the executive and financial advisers of the issuer, studying the business from every angle, becoming familiar with the industry in which it functions, its future prospects, the character and efficiency of its operating policies and similar matters. Much of this information will eventually find its way in one form or another into the prospectus and registration statement. Sometimes engineers will be employed to make a survey of the business. The investment banker will submit a plan of the financing, often in writing; and this plan and perhaps others will be the subject of discussions. Gradually the definitive plan will be agreed upon, or perhaps the entire matter will be dropped in favor of a private placement, without the services of an investment banker. Often, and after many months of effort on the part of the investment banker, the issuer will decide to postpone the raising of the money for a year or two.

In the interval between the time when the investment banker is put on the job and the time when the definitive product begins to take form, a variety of other problems of great importance require consideration. The most vital of these, in terms of money and otherwise, is the timing of the issue. It is here, with his feel and judgment of the market, that the top-notch investment banker renders what is perhaps his most important service. The probable state of the general security market at any given future time is a most difficult thing to forecast. Only those with ripe trading experience and the finest kind of general background in financial affairs and practical economics can effectively render service of this character.

At last the issue has been cast in more or less final form, the prospectus and registration statement have been drafted and decisions relative to matters bearing a direct relation to the effective cost of the money, such as the coupon or dividend rate, sinking fund, conversion and redemption provisions and serial dates, if any, are shaped up subject to further consideration at the last moment. The work of organizing the syndicate, determining the participation positions of those selected as underwriters and the making up of a list of dealers for the selling group or, if no selling group is to be used, the formulation of plans for distribution by some other means, have been gradually proceeding, practically always in consultation with the issuer, who has the final say as to who the participating underwriters are to be. The general plans for distribution of the issue require the most careful and expert consideration, as the credit of the issuer may be seriously affected should the issue not be successful. Occasionally an elaborate campaign of education of dealers and investors is conducted.

Thus, if the negotiated underwritten public offering route is to be followed, we come at last to what may be the parting of the ways between the issuer and the investment banker—negotiation relative to the public offering price, the spread and the price to be paid to the issuer for the securities. These three are inextricably interrelated. The starting point is and must be the determination of the price at which the issue is to be offered to the public. This must in the very nature of things be the price at which the issuer and the investment banker jointly think the security can be put on the market with reasonable assurance of success; and at times the issuer, as already indicated in this brief recital of the way the investment banker functions, will for good and sufficient reasons not desire the public offering price to be placed at the highest figure attainable.

Once agreement has been tentatively reached on the public offering price, the negotiation shifts to the amount of the contemplated gross spread. This figure must include the gross compensation of all those who participate in the distribution of the issue: the manager, the underwriting participants and the dealers who are to receive concessions and reallowances. Naturally, the amount of the spread will be governed largely by the nature of the problems of distribution and the amount of work involved. The statistical charts and static data indicate that the amount of the contemplated gross spreads is smallest with the highest class of bonds and largest with common stock issues, where the actual work of selling is at its maximum. While no two security issues are precisely alike and they vary as the leaves on the trees, it is apparent that the executive and financial officers of issuers may sit down on the other side of the bargaining table confidently, and without apprehension of being imposed upon, as data relating to public offering prices, spreads, and net proceeds to issuers from new security issues registered under the Security Act of 1933 are all public information which are publicized among other means by the wide distribution of the prospectuses for each issue.

And so in the end the "pricing" of the issue is arrived at as a single, unitary determination of the public offering price, spread and price to the issuer.

With public sealed bidding issues the whole procedure is radically different. The issue is designed and shaped up by the management of the issuer, with or without the services of an investment banker. As the problems of distribution are not the same, due particularly to the high quality of the securities generally involved, their sale in bulk to institutional investors, and the fact that, as no one knows in advance who the successful bidder will be, there is no time available for preparing the market or setting up any elaborate distribution machinery, the formation of the underwriting group follows a different pattern; and the issuer is not concerned with the public offering price but only with receiving the highest amount bid for the issue. However, when the participating underwriters in a public sealed bidding account confer at their "price meetings" before agreeing upon the amount of the bid to be submitted on their behalf by the manager, they first make up their minds on the subject of the price at which they think the entire issue can be sold to the public.

After the bids are opened, and without reference to the issuer, the underwriters in the winning account promptly decide among themselves the public offering price, the method of sale and the amount of any concessions or allowances. The difference between the bid price and the public offering price thus arrived at is the spread or anticipated gross compensation of the participants and the manager.

This very brief outline has been telescoped into bare essentials by way of general background. As a matter of fact no two security issues present quite the same problems; some are relatively simple and follow somewhat standardized lines, especially in many public sealed bidding transactions. The methods and practices of the various defendant investment banking firms vary greatly. The competitive pattern of the different firms will be found to depend largely on the background, the personnel and matters of policy peculiar to each firm. But one thing stands out. This record has not revealed a single issuer which can fairly be said to be the "captive" of any or all or any combination of these seventeen defendant firms. The reason why private placements of new debt issues, with or without the services of an investment banker, increased from 14.3% of the total of all such issues in 1936 to 72.4% of the total of all such issues in 1948, is because the issuers were free to choose and did choose to use this type of transaction to raise the funds they needed, rather than to go by the negotiated underwritten route or any of the others which were available. And it is equally clear that, although there has never been any rule, regulation or statutory or other law preventing issuers from resorting of their own free choice to public sealed bidding as a means of raising capital, issuers have done so only in rare and exceptional cases, unless compelled to resort to public sealed bidding by the mandate of the SEC or the ICC or some state regulatory body having jurisdiction.

PRICING A CORPORATE BOND ISSUE:
A LOOK BEHIND THE SCENES*

By Ernest Bloch†

MAKING MARKETS for securities means setting prices. This is a demanding job, for it requires a continuous evaluation of the various factors acting and reacting in the markets. Securities dealers must make day-to-day, hour-to-hour, and sometimes minute-to-minute adjustments, and the dealer who falls asleep, even briefly, may find his snooze a costly one.

Underwriters engaged in competitive bidding for new corporate bonds have a special pricing problem in that each flotation involves the distribution of a relatively large supply of securities in the shortest time feasible. While the market for outstanding securities does provide some guidance to the pricing process, it is a rough guide at best. A new bond issue will be similar to, but rarely identical with, any securities being traded in the secondary market. Furthermore, the relatively large amount involved in many new offerings increases the difficulty of gauging the market. Finally, pricing decisions on new securities are not made at the actual time of sale to the ultimate investors but must be made a short time before the bonds are released for trading, while the distribution itself may stretch over a number of days during which market rates may be in motion. The pricing of a new issue even under the best conditions thus takes place at the edge of the unknown.

The specialized job of buying, selling, and pricing new corporate securities is primarily the province of investment bankers.[1] Not all issues are priced through a competitive bidding process, however, and the pricing of some flotations is negotiated directly between borrower and underwriter. But in all successful flotations, investment bankers function as quick intermediaries for

---

* Reprinted by permission from *Essays in Money and Credit* published by the Federal Reserve Bank of New York, 1964, pp. 72–76.

† Federal Reserve Bank of New York.

[1] These firms have traditionally been called "investment bankers" although they are now bankers in name only. As is well-known, the Banking Act of 1933 specifically prohibits commercial banks that accept deposits and make loans from underwriting corporate securities. Under the act, commercial banks are permitted to continue some "investment banking"-type activities, such as underwriting direct obligations of the United States and general obligations of States and political subdivisions. At present, underwriters for corporate issues perform none of the basic functions of commercial banks, but the term "investment bankers" continues in use, and this usage will be followed in this article.

new securities between borrowers and ultimate investors. This involves two distinct, although closely related, objectives. In cases of competitive bidding—formal or informal—the first objective is to "win" the right to offer the security to the public by paying the borrower more for it than any other underwriter. The second is to "reoffer" the security to investors at a price higher than that paid the borrower. If a number of underwriting groups are competing against each other for an issue, each must strike a balance between (1) pressing hard to win the issue by paying a relatively high price to the borrower and (2) increasing the risk that the issue cannot be sold to the public at a price to yield a profit.[2]

This article is concerned with the pricing problem in a competitive underwriting process, the resolution of which boils down to setting the bid price to the borrower. It illustrates how this price is set by following through the process for an actual issue of corporate bonds. Nonessential details that might serve to identify the borrower or the investment banking houses that underwrote the issue have been slightly altered.

Because the offering discussed below was quite sizable, the pricing problem involved an added dimension. The pricing decision was made not by a single underwriter, but by a large underwriting group acting jointly as a syndicate. The pricing decision thus was to be hammered out among the members of the underwriting group, each of which had been tentatively assigned a share of the new issue. And this pricing decision, if successful, had to better that of the strong rival syndicate.

PREPARATION FOR A LARGE ISSUE

When a corporation plans a large financing, it customarily gives fair warning as a means of preparing the capital market. In line with this practice, the firm to be called Large Company, Inc., had announced its intention to borrow $100 million *several months* before the date of actual issue. The early announcement gave potential investors, such as insurance companies, pension funds, and bank trust accounts the opportunity to adjust their financial commitments so as to make room, if they wished, for sizable chunks of the Large Company issue. At the same time, other potential corporate borrowers were made aware that the Large Company underwriting would bring special pressures on the market, making it unwise to schedule other sizable flotations around that period.

A light calendar of flotations makes possible a more eager participation in

---

[2] In a negotiated flotation, the problem of reaching an optimum bid between (1) and (2) would appear to be less than it is under the competitive bidding process. And a negotiated deal clearly offers the short-run advantage to the underwriter that he cannot "lose" the issue to another syndicate. A negotiated underwriting will not necessarily carry a higher borrowing cost, however, for many large borrowers have some degree of choice between competitive and negotiated flotations. If borrowing costs in, say, negotiated deals were to rise out of line with costs on competitively priced flotations, the cheaper method of raising funds would be used to a greater extent.

the underwriting by syndicate members because their over-all market commitments during the flotation period will be less. And the better the demand for bonds among syndicate members, the stronger their bid will be, and the lower the borrowing cost to the borrowing firm. As noted, in the underwriting of the Large Company issue two competing syndicates were formed. One of the groups, managed by X Investment Bank, consisted of more than 100 investment firms, and the competing syndicate, led by Y Investment Bank, was about as sizable.

Managing such large syndicates has become the business of about a half dozen large investment banking houses. Only the largest among them have the capital, the manpower, and the market contacts necessary to propose the proper price for a large offering. If a given house, acting as syndicate manager, wins what the market considers a fair share of the bidding competitions in which it participates, it gains in a number of ways. Not only is its prestige enhanced—which helps in managing future syndicates—but the house that is continuously proving the high quality of its market judgment may be more successful in attracting *negotiated* financings. This concern for the future tends to intensify present competition among managing underwriters.

But while the half dozen syndicate leaders are rivals, they are also potential allies because a grouping of underwriters exists only for a given flotation, and the next offering on the market will involve a different group. Indeed, during the preparation for the Large Company issue, two of the major firms in the rival syndicate led by Y Investment Bank knew that they would be associated with X Investment Bank in a large secondary stock offering within two weeks. As a consequence of the shifting associations and combinations of firms from syndicate to syndicate, the current associate in an underwriting insists on conserving his own independence of action, and this has an important bearing on the pricing process, as we shall see below.

The first informal "price meeting" on the forthcoming issue took place at X Investment Bank two days before the actual bidding date set for the issue. Fifteen senior officers of X Investment Bank actively engaged in trading and underwriting met at this point to discuss pricing recommendations that would win the issue and at the same time find ready acceptance in the market. The terms of the new issue were discussed in the light of current market factors, and each pricing suggestion was, in effect, an answer to a double-barreled question: first, how attractive was the issue in terms of quality, maturity, call provisions, and other features; and, secondly, how receptive was the market at this time? Among the factors discussed as leading to a lower yield was the new bonds' Aaa rating, while factors leading to a higher yield included the lack of call protection and the large size of the issue.

The preliminary discussion of the offering price then shifted to the "feel of the market." Even the proponents of a relatively high yield recognized that the final bid should be close to current market yields on similar securities, owing to the relatively light calendar of forthcoming new corporate flotations.

Another sign pointing to aggressive bidding was a relatively light dealer inventory of corporate securities. The discussion of competitive demands for funds was not confined to the corporate securities market, however, but extended to the markets for municipal and Treasury issues as well. Here the picture was mixed. The light calendar of forthcoming municipal issues was cited by proponents of a lower yield, while those in favor of a higher yield pointed to expectations of a relatively heavy volume of Treasury financing. Finally, the discussion moved on to assess the possibility of changes in significant market rates such as the prime loan rate and Federal Reserve Bank discount rates during the flotation period. It was agreed that the likelihood of such changes during the financing period was small. Each of the officers of X Investment Bank then independently set down his opinion of the proper pricing of the issue (i.e., the combination of coupon rate and price offered the borrower) and the reoffering "spread" (i.e., the difference between the bid price and the reoffering price to the public).

The majority of the fifteen members of the group agreed that the new bonds should carry a rate of $4\frac{1}{4}$ per cent to the borrower with the bonds priced at par, and with a reoffering spread of about $7 per $1,000 bond.[3] One member of the group thought that a lower yield might be needed to win the bid, and two or three others indicated yields higher than $4\frac{1}{4}$ per cent. The aggressiveness of X Investment Bank's price ideas can be judged from the fact that newspaper comment on the likely level for the winning bid on the day of this meeting indicated a yield in the neighborhood of 4.30 per cent.

MARKETING STRATEGY

Simultaneously, assessments of the market for the purpose of establishing a proper bid for the issue were under way in the offices of the allied syndicate members. The comparison of various opinions of the "best" bid of the syndicate members took place a day later, the day before the actual opening of the bids by the borrower. This was the "preliminary price meeting," to which each firm in the syndicate was invited. At the meeting each participant firm named the price it was willing to pay for the number of bonds tentatively assigned in the underwriting.[4] The poll of the 100-odd allied syndicate members revealed far less aggressiveness (i.e., willingness to accept a low yield) by the smaller firms than was shown by the syndicate manager. Relatively few ideas were at $4\frac{1}{4}$ per cent, while one of the "major underwriters" (i.e., a firm tentatively assigned $3 million of bonds or more) put his offering yield at 4.35 per cent, and a small firm went as high as 4.40 per cent.

In this particular underwriting, X Investment Bank seemed quite eager to win the bid, partly because of its optimistic appraisals of the state of the bond

---

[3] It should be noted once again that these rates have been changed from those placed on the actual bond issue.

[4] In this meeting, as in the final price meeting, a number of security measures were taken to prevent a leak of information to the competing syndicate.

market and partly because it is the syndicate manager's responsibility to push for a winning bid and to exercise the proper persuasion to carry his syndicate along. Prestige is peculiarly the concern of the syndicate manager because, rightly or wrongly, the market apparently does not attach nearly so much significance to membership as to leadership in a losing syndicate.

This factor explains the paradox that the followers, rather than the manager, may be more responsible for the failure to win a bid for lack of aggressiveness, even though the market tends to place the blame on the manager. But smaller syndicate members may be reluctant participants at lower yields because their commitment of funds for even a relatively small portion of a large underwriting may represent a larger call (or contingent liability) against the small firm's capital than it does for a bigger firm. Even though the larger firm's capital may be as fully employed as that of the smaller firm in its *total* underwriting business, the commitment of a large portion of capital for a single underwriting may make the smaller firm more hesitant to take that particular marketing risk.

In preparing for the final price meeting, the syndicate manager held the first of a number of behind-the-scenes strategy sessions. At these meetings, some basic decisions were made about ways and means of holding the syndicate together. During the final price meeting, any firm believing that the market risk of the proposed group bid was too great (i.e., that the yield was too low to sell well) had the right to drop out of the syndicate. Conversely, if the syndicate member liked the group bid, he could raise the extent of his participation. Of course, if many syndicate members drop out, particularly major underwriters, too much of a burden is placed on the remaining members, and the result is, in effect, to veto the proposed bid. The aggressive manager thus is placed squarely in the middle of a tug of war: if his bid is too aggressive, and carries a relatively low yield, the syndicate may refuse to take down the bonds; if the bid is too cautious and carries too high a yield, the syndicate may lose the bidding competition to the rival group. This conflict was resolved at the final price meeting.

SYNDICATE TACTICS

On the morning of the day on which the final bids were made to the borrower, the officers of the syndicate manager held their final conference at which decisions were reached regarding their willingness to raise their own share of the underwriting. In effect, a manager who believes in an aggressive bid puts up or shuts up by expressing his willingness to absorb a greater or a lesser share of the total underwriting as firms drop out of the syndicate at lower yields. A strong offer to take more bonds by the manager may induce a number of potential dropouts to stay at a lower yield, partly because their share of the flotation won't be raised by a given number of dropouts since the manager is picking up the pieces. But beyond the arithmetic effect, a strong offer may have a psychological impact, and some reluctant participants may decide that the manager knows more than they do, and that his willingness to raise his share at a given yield is his way of backing the strength of his judgment.

This "psychological" downward push on yields may be small, but some-times even a tiny difference between two competing bids can spell the differ-ence between success and failure. For example, in late 1959, the winning syndicate for a $30 million utility issue bid $\frac{1}{100}$ of a *cent* more per $1,000 bond than the loser; the borrower received exactly $3 more from the winning syndicate for the $30 million issue than was offered by the loser.[5]

Another important factor in holding the syndicate together is the strength of the "book" for the new issue. The "book" is a compilation of investor interest in the new bonds. This interest may have been solicited or unsolicited, and may have gone directly to X Investment Bank from, say, institutional investors or to other members of the syndicate. Thus the book is a sample of market strength. All the interest in the book is tentative since no lender would commit funds for an issue of unknown yield. Nevertheless, it is impossible to exaggerate the importance of a large book to an aggressive syndicate manager in holding his group together at the lowest possible yield. Because reluctant participants in an underwriting are particularly concerned about the selling risk, the larger the book the more reassured they will feel at any given rate. Put another way, the better the book, the more bonds a firm will take at a given rate, thus absorbing more dropouts. Indeed, the size of the book was considered so important that the final price meeting on the Large Company underwriting was interrupted a number of times by the latest indications of interest in the issue.

THE FINAL PRICE MEETING

As a means of preventing information leaks, representatives of the firms attending the final price meeting were locked in a room. The meeting was opened by a vice president of X Investment Bank with a brief review of the good state of the "book"—about half the issue had been spoken for, tenta-tively. He derived further encouragement for an aggressive bid from the healthy state of the bond market. Thus he proposed to make his bid at the $4\frac{1}{4}$ per cent rate agreed upon at the X Investment Bank preliminary meeting two days earlier.

The immediate reaction to this statement was a chorus of moans. Appar-ently, the book was not sufficiently broad to carry the doubters along with the first bid, nor did the manager indicate any other action that would have made his proposal more acceptable. When the group was polled, large and small dropouts cut the $100 million underwriting by about a third. The failure to carry the syndicate at the first go-round was later attributed by some X

---

[5] At times, tie bids are received. On September 12, 1961, two underwriters bid identi-cal amounts, down to the last $\frac{1}{100}$ of a penny per $1,000 bond, for a $3 million issue of municipal bonds. Such tie bids are as rare as a golfer's hole in one, however.

Investment Bank people to the fact that three dropouts occurred among the first set of major underwriters polled (i.e., the eight largest firms, each of which had been tentatively assigned $3 million of bonds). And in the second set ($2 million assigned to each firm) another few had fallen by the wayside.

Thus a new bid proposal had to be presented to the group. Following another behind-the-scenes consultation of the senior officers of the managing underwriter, a 4⅜ per cent coupon was proposed with a bid yield of 4.27 per cent. Amid continued grumbling of the majority of the members of the meeting, this was readily accepted by nearly every firm.

Judging that they might have leaned over too far in the direction of their reluctant followers, the officers of the syndicate manager consulted once again, and decided to present a somewhat more aggressive bid to the syndicate. In the third proposal, the bid price on the 4⅜ coupon was upped by 20 cents per $1,000 bond. The underwriters, still grumbling, were polled again and, following a few minor dropouts, approved the new price. The final allocation of the bonds differed relatively little from the tentative original allocation except that the manager picked up the allotments of the dropouts by adding about $3 million to his own commitment. By this time only a few minutes were left until the formal opening of the competitive bids by Large Company, Inc. The final coupon and price decisions were telephoned to the syndicate's representative at the bidding, who formally submitted the bid to Large Company.

Promptly at 11:30 A.M. the doors of the price committee meeting were thrown open, and within thirty seconds of that time the news was shouted from the trading room that the X Investment Bank bid had lost. The difference in the bid prices between the two syndicates came to little more than $1 per $1,000 bond.

The bonds were released for trading by the Securities and Exchange Commission at around 4 P.M. and were quickly snapped up by market investors. At X Investment Bank the feeling of gloom hung heavy, particularly since the first bid offered to the price meeting would have won the issue.

Would a better X Investment Bank book have carried the defecting major underwriters along on the first bid? Should the manager have been willing to take more bonds to carry the group along in the first recommendation which would have won the issue? And would market acceptance of that bid have been as good as that accorded the actual winning bid of Y syndicate? These post mortems were bound to be inconclusive, and the unremitting pressures of the underwriting business soon cut them short. Within the next several days a number of other securities were scheduled to come to market. Tomorrow was another day, and another price meeting.

THE PRIVATE ROUTE TO NEW CAPITAL*

By Jean Ross-Skinner†

ONE OF LAST YEAR'S most spectacular financial deals was the purchase by the smallish Albemarle Paper Manufacturing Co. of Ethyl Corp., a firm many times its size. To pull off the coup, Albemarle borrowed no less than $200 million in long-term debt on its total book value of $25.8 million.

Admittedly, the transaction was not as unlikely as it sounded. The sellers of Ethyl were two of the country's largest corporations, General Motors and Jersey Standard; and as one investment banker put it, the deal looked like "a clear case of the tail wagging the dog," with Albemarle in effect being engulfed by Ethyl.

Nevertheless, the striking dimensions of the borrowing point up the versatility of an important source of capital. While such a top-heavy sum could scarcely have been raised on the open market, most of the $200 million flowed into Albemarle's coffers smoothly enough by a different route: the private, or direct, placement.

Like a public issue of securities, a private placement is a means of raising long-term capital. There are, however, essential differences between the two. First, title to a public offering passes originally to the underwriters who ultimately resell the securities to the public; a direct placement, though an investment banker often acts as agent, is sold directly to the final buyers.

Secondly, while the public offering is widely distributed to all comers, the private placement is sold to a small group of institutional-type investors— small enough for the issue to avoid registration with the Securities & Exchange Commission. These unregistered securities must be held for investment rather than resold to the public.

While numerous small companies place common stock privately with local investors, employees, customers and suppliers, the overwhelming dollar volume of direct placements takes the form of long-term debt. For the nation's life insurance companies, backed by assets of over $100 billion, provide perhaps 90% of private placement funds; and they are effectively barred from

* Reprinted by permission from Dun's Review and Modern Industry, 81 (January 1963), pp. 35–6, 79–83.

† Formerly Financial Editor of Dun's Review and Modern Industry, and now European Editor of Dun's Review.

substantial equity investments. Pension and welfare funds, foundations, investment companies and savings banks take up most of the balance. The usual range of maturities acceptable to the institutional lenders is from 10 to 25 years.

For more than six months now, interest in private placements has been running unusually high. Although the rate of new corporate issues, both debt and equity, has tumbled by a third since May's market upset, direct placements have boosted their share of total new capital from around 30% in the

---

THE COSTS AND THE CATCH

How do expenses compare for a private placement versus a public issue? For small loans, like the example shown below, the private placement is generally cheaper, despite higher interest rates, because of high minimum outlays on printing and investment banker's fees for the public offering. The catch: for larger loans, of roughly $15 million or more, the economies of size and the lower rate usually make a public issue cheaper.

$4 Million Bond Financing

Out-of-Pocket Expenses	Public	Private
Printing and Engraving Bonds	$16,500	$ 2,000
Counsel Fee (excluding Blue Sky fees)	6,500	5,000
State Blue Sky Fees	2,500	—
Federal Original Issuance Tax	4,400	4,400
Trustee Fee	4,000	1,500
Accounting Fee	3,000	—
SEC Registration Fee	400	—
Miscellaneous (including State Commission fee, if any)	2,700	1,100
Total Out-of-Pocket Expenses	$40,000	$14,000
Underwriter's Compensation or Agent's Fee	$40,000	$20,000
Cost per $1,000 Bond		
Issuer's Out-of-Pocket Expense	$10.00	$3.50
Underwriter's or Agent's Commission	10.00	5.00
Total Cost of Financing	$20.00	$8.50
Net Proceeds to Issuer on Sale at Par (100%)	98.00%	99.15%

---

first quarter of 1962 to well over 45% in the third quarter. By year's end, they were believed to be running at a rate of 50% and had fallen off only slightly from their first-quarter volume.

Much of this upswing, of course, came from the slump in market prices last year. At such times, when interest rates are volatile, the lengthy SEC registration period of three to six weeks can ruin the borrower's chances of getting the rate he calculated on. For the underwriter will not commit himself on the rate until the end of the waiting period. "It's not surprising," remarks Vice President Edward P. Lebens of The First Boston Corp., "that in any uncertain market, there is a tendency for borrowers to use direct placements because of the speed with which a commitment can be obtained."

What kind of speed? "There have been cases," says Lebens, "where we have obtained a verbal commitment on the rate from the lender within 24 hours. This is exceptional, of course, and is only possible where the lender is thoroughly familiar with the credit of the borrowing company."

Speed aside, and in relatively good market times like the present, more and more corporate treasurers are realizing that the private placement offers a goodly number of other valuable advantages. First, although it traditionally carries a higher interest rate than a comparable public issue, it is usually less costly for the small borrower. The reason: the small direct placement avoids substantial printing and engraving costs and incurs lower investment banker's fees. These savings generally offset the higher rate (*see table*). It is only with the really large loans that the economies of size come into play and the rate differential takes its toll.

Consequently the small borrower can use the private placement to bridge the gap that may appear between his graduation from the ranks of small fry, who must rely on bank term loans, finance company loans, real estate loans or perhaps Small Business Administration loans, and the time when he reaches the stature where he can successfully sell bonds to the public. For while direct placements of as little as $100,000 can prove profitable to both borrower and institutional lender, a public offering of less than $2 million is a luxury.

Again, private placements are highly flexible. Unusual provisions which could not be put across in a public sale can be thrashed out with a handful of practiced lenders. Issues can be "tailor-made" to suit the borrower's individual requirements. In a private loan involving a construction project, for instance, the corporation may draw down the funds only as it needs them. A public issue offers no such convenience.

By the same token, if circumstances change and the borrower wants to renegotiate the terms of the borrowing, he can often reach a quick accommodation by talking things over with a handful of creditors around the same table. Because of this flexibility, large corporations will sometimes use direct placements of hundreds of millions of dollars, in spite of the higher cost.

Complicated package deals, too, can be negotiated. Consider, again, Albemarle. Of the full $200 million it raised, as much as $164 million in cash came from private placement. The early maturities consist of $16 million in 5½% bank term loans which will be fully repaid by the end of the second year; of the long maturities, $114 million in 5¾% senior notes, sold to a group of institutional investors, will mature in 1978, and $50 million of 5¾% subordinated notes, also sold to institutional investors, will mature in 1982. As a kicker, each $1,000 of the subordinated notes carries a warrant to purchase eight shares of common stock at $27.50 a share at any time before maturity.

UNDER WRAPS

In addition, the private placement does indeed offer privacy. Some investment bankers, like director of investments William Zuehlke Jr. of fraternal insurance firm Aid Association for Lutherans (despite its somewhat misleading name, the Aid Association is one of the more active smaller private placement lenders), object to the word "private." "We don't like to call them private placements," Zuehlke declares. "It sounds as though it's something that is done in tremendous secrecy. 'Direct placements' is a more accurate term." Certainly, many direct placements are far from private. Either the borrower or the lender or both frequently consider it good public relations to announce a loan in all its details.

On the other hand, the details of a private placement can, like those of a bank term loan, be kept pretty much under wraps. The borrower's financial statement must inform stockholders of the terms of the loan, but the lender's name need not be revealed. The identity of any lending insurance company only appears later on in the relative seclusion of the annual investment schedules that insurance concerns must publish.

The identity need never be published, moreover, if the lender is a pension fund, a foundation, an investment banker (which may use its own capital in a "lock-up") or a private investment company. It was only as a consequence of the difficulties of ex-President Edward Gilbert, for instance, that the shareholders of E. L. Bruce Co. learned that New York investment bankers Lazard Frères had privately bought $2 million worth of E. L. Bruce notes, convertible into 126,800 shares, or 6% of the voting stock.

There are several reasons for a desire for anonymity. Certain insurance companies may avoid publicity simply because they do not want their bigness advertised. "Sometimes," adds one investment bank vice president, "the lender might not like it to be known that it was a buyer of a certain industry or stock. Or it might not be proud of the rate it got for it. When a *borrower* avoids publicity, it may be that he has a new product he doesn't want the world to know about but is prepared to discuss freely with a limited number of people."

One investment banker who never publicizes private placements points out that a flow of publicity for placements gives borrowers useful hints as to going rates and lenders' preferences. "Why should we make this sort of information available free in this way," says he, "when we want borrowers to come and buy it from us?"

Before he takes the private placement route, however, the borrower must weigh certain offsetting drawbacks. For example, the direct placement which seems so much cheaper than a public offering at the outset could turn out to be more costly in the long run. For when it comes to repaying the principal of a privately placed loan, the borrower will find that sinking fund and other prepayments must normally be made at par. "You can't repurchase your bonds held privately at a discount," says Lebens, "in the way that you can buy in your publicly issued bonds at a discount on the open market."

THE PRAGMATIC APPROACH

The financial executive who has weighed the various arguments and decided on a direct placement must first be sure that his firm can qualify for one. And qualifying is not always easy. The institutional investment manager is highly flexible and pragmatic in his assessment of potential borrowers. He tends not to use a set of rigid criteria so much as to judge each case on its own merits, taking into account such intangibles as his impression of the caliber of management. "Before we make a loan," says Vice President Henry Barkhorn of Mutual of New York, "we go out to the company and look at the plant. We hold talks, chiefly with the financial officers, but also with the sales and manufacturing people, to size up the company."

Basically, the successful candidate for a long-term insurance company loan must have reached a certain level of maturity. As a very rough rule of thumb, it should also have had a satisfactory earnings record for the past five years. "We occasionally lend to new companies," Barkhorn adds, "but only if they are contractually supported by having a big customer already lined up, or have other special advantages. In addition we would need good engineering reports and other supporting data."

The would-be borrower can either approach the institutional lender directly, or he can enlist an investment banker as his agent. Such big firms as Blyth & Co., Dean Witter, Eastman Dillon and First Boston Corp. handle scores of private placements each year. The investment banker will make an initial investigation of the client, and if he decides that the financing is "doable," he will undertake to handle the placement.

For a fee ranging from over 2% for some small issues to considerably less than 0.5% for really big loans, he advises the client on such points as what rate he should pay, what equity kickers, if any, must be conceded, suitable sinking fund provisions and what protective provisions will be necessary.

He also draws up a memorandum for potential lenders. "We need to know in detail," explains one insurance company financial vice president, "the full history of the business, supported by at least five years' audited statements, the purpose of the funds, the standing of the company in its industry from the point of view of its percentage of the market, who its competitors and its customers are. And," he adds, "we also need a thorough earnings projection."

Finally, the investment banker lines up a lender or group of lenders. On any sizable loan, he will attempt to bring in one of the "bell-cow" insurance companies. With the exception of The Prudential, which tends to walk alone, the bell-cows are the top half-dozen or so life firms, headed by Metropolitan, Equitable Life and New York Life. With the bell-cow leading, the rest of the lending group will normally fall into line, accepting whatever terms are agreed to by the big company's huge legal and investment departments.

A HELPING HAND?

Should the borrowing company approach lenders directly or work through an investment banker? Bankers not unnaturally point out that no borrowing company can know the market as intimately as they do.

"Many corporations feel that they have acquaintance with the institutions," explains Edward Lebens, "and that they can work out a direct placement on their own without bringing any bankers into it. But we have found this is not the case. A manufacturing firm, for instance, can't possibly know all the companies that are potential buyers or the funds they may have available at a given time and their investment policy. I don't care how sophisticated or efficient the company may be—it can't know all this. We, on the other hand, are talking with buyers every day of the week and are in a much better position to know where the best terms and provisions can be obtained."

Points out another banker: "It's also an advantage having an investment banker as go-between from a trading point of view. It can be awkward for the treasurer to say flatly that he can't agree to something. But it's much easier for us to put it to the lender. Again, if the borrower goes only to one institution, he is pretty much at the mercy of what they tell him."

In addition, both investment bankers and life company investment men warn of common mistakes made by novice borrowers on their own. "Companies in the first phase of their growth cycle, which desperately need funds to expand," says Partner Martin LeBoutillier of Dean Witter & Co., "must turn to risk-capital groups. They are often startlingly naïve about what those funds should cost them in the way of equity kickers. I've seen company after company handicapped because they refused to face up to the cost of capital, and they tend to carry that same naïvete on into the next stage—private placement. But they do get more sophisticated as they go on."

Apart from boggling at the cost of funds, the small borrower tends to be vague about financial data. "Sometimes," says the investment manager of a large New York life company, "they just haven't spent enough time with their cash flow figures. They don't know what they need or when they need it. We like to see them project their expectations. And another good piece of advice to borrowers is that a good audit is vital. The firm should be audited by a good, recognized accounting firm."

Complains an investment banker: "Often the smaller company isn't prepared to release the executive talent to go to work on preparing records and reports, and it's a real tooth-pulling job to get enough information to put a story together that you can sell to the insurance companies. Obviously, if they are going to lend money for fifteen years, the first thing they want is accounts and records they can depend on."

Some institutional lenders, therefore, feel that an investment banker saves them the chore of educating would-be borrowers and extracting orderly information from them. Others are not so sure. "Many investment bankers come in with just a bundle of audits under their arm and an officer of the borrowing company," declares a life company treasurer, "and we have to do considerable further work. We encourage borrowers to come to us directly—we'd rather not plow through other people's work."

INDIVIDUALISTS OF FINANCE

There is no doubt, however, that above all for the newcomer, a good investment banker's fee can be money wisely spent. For a business that funnels over $3.5 billion a year into industry, private placement is surprisingly little standardized.

Investment bankers point to the wide range of styles and preferences among institutional lenders. "We have to be familiar with all their different characteristics," remarks one investment bank partner. "Just as an example, Equitable, Metropolitan and New York Life have pretty set ideas as to rates and would rather stick with a good security than go down the line to get the higher yields. Prudential, on the other hand, is an enigma—you just don't know which way it will react. Again, if you want to sell a preferred, the odds are that Allstate will be interested. Then you have companies like Security Mutual of Worcester—they like to look at out-of-the-way deals, with warrants, options and so forth."

The insurance companies differ enormously, too, in the measures they take to seek out new borrowers. The Prudential, always a loner, has a small-loan division that conducts "cold canvassing" (calling on any potential borrower that comes to its attention). Others describe their role as purely passive. "We don't go out looking for borrowers," declares one life company vice president. "We expect them to come to us."

More typical of the majority, however, is Mutual of New York. "We have no private placement representatives out ringing doorbells," says Henry Barkhorn, "but we do search for loans by approaching investment and commercial banks and by keeping on friendly terms with the larger law firms."

One thing is certain: The way the market is today, any likely borrower can expect an attentive hearing from the institutional investor. "The most outstanding thing about the private placement business recently," declares Dean Witter's LeBoutillier, "has been the tremendous pressure of funds waiting for investment. Hardly a day has passed but that someone in our firm has been approached by an institutional investor asking to be shown private placements. It's been that way for the better part of a year now."

With institutional investors so avid to lend, interest rates on private placements have been falling. While a year ago a well-established company would probably have had to pay well over 5% on a private placement loan, it may get away with as little as $4\frac{1}{2}$% today. At the same time, the differential between public and private placement loans is at its narrowest for many years, a typical spread today being around ten to fifteen basis points.

The drop in rates has been accentuated by much heavier competition that the life insurance companies are meeting from other lenders, chiefly bank-run pension funds. "These pension funds' loans are not reported," notes Henry Barkhorn, "so we can't know exactly what they are doing. We do from time to time run into it in conversation, however, and I'm satisfied that some of them are strongly competitive. Even the commercial loan departments of some of the banks are going out to ten years for good customers."

Not surprisingly, therefore, the borrower is being assiduously courted. The investment banks, spurred by the pressure from big lenders, are out looking for business more intensively than ever before. Says Lebens frankly: "We're searching as aggressively as we know how. This means ranging from reading daily newspapers and annual reports to following up any clue we can get from conversations with commercial banks. We even get ideas walking down the street, seeing a sign up and wondering who that company's banker is."

Appendix

TABLE A

Present Value of $1

Periods until Payment	1%	2%	2½%	3%	4%	5%	6%	8%	10%	12%	14%	15%	16%	18%	20%	22%	24%	25%	26%	30%	40%	50%
1	0.990	0.980	0.976	0.971	0.962	0.952	0.943	0.926	0.909	0.893	0.877	0.870	0.862	0.847	0.833	0.820	0.806	0.800	0.794	0.769	0.714	0.667
2	0.980	0.961	0.952	0.943	0.925	0.907	0.890	0.857	0.826	0.797	0.769	0.756	0.743	0.718	0.694	0.672	0.650	0.640	0.630	0.592	0.510	0.444
3	0.971	0.942	0.929	0.915	0.889	0.864	0.840	0.794	0.751	0.712	0.675	0.658	0.641	0.609	0.579	0.551	0.524	0.512	0.500	0.455	0.364	0.296
4	0.961	0.924	0.906	0.888	0.855	0.823	0.792	0.735	0.683	0.636	0.592	0.572	0.552	0.516	0.482	0.451	0.423	0.410	0.397	0.350	0.260	0.198
5	0.951	0.906	0.884	0.863	0.822	0.784	0.747	0.681	0.621	0.567	0.519	0.497	0.476	0.437	0.402	0.370	0.341	0.328	0.315	0.269	0.186	0.132
6	0.942	0.888	0.862	0.837	0.790	0.746	0.705	0.630	0.564	0.507	0.456	0.432	0.410	0.370	0.335	0.303	0.275	0.262	0.250	0.207	0.133	0.088
7	0.933	0.871	0.841	0.813	0.760	0.711	0.665	0.583	0.513	0.452	0.400	0.376	0.354	0.314	0.279	0.249	0.222	0.210	0.198	0.159	0.095	0.059
8	0.923	0.853	0.821	0.789	0.731	0.677	0.627	0.540	0.467	0.404	0.351	0.327	0.305	0.266	0.233	0.204	0.179	0.168	0.157	0.123	0.068	0.039
9	0.914	0.837	0.801	0.766	0.703	0.645	0.592	0.500	0.424	0.361	0.308	0.284	0.263	0.225	0.194	0.167	0.144	0.134	0.125	0.094	0.048	0.026
10	0.905	0.820	0.781	0.744	0.676	0.614	0.558	0.463	0.385	0.322	0.270	0.247	0.227	0.191	0.162	0.137	0.116	0.107	0.099	0.073	0.035	0.017
11	0.896	0.804	0.762	0.722	0.650	0.585	0.527	0.429	0.350	0.287	0.237	0.215	0.195	0.162	0.135	0.112	0.094	0.086	0.079	0.056	0.025	0.012
12	0.887	0.788	0.744	0.701	0.625	0.557	0.497	0.397	0.319	0.257	0.208	0.187	0.168	0.137	0.112	0.092	0.076	0.069	0.062	0.043	0.018	0.008
13	0.879	0.773	0.725	0.681	0.601	0.530	0.469	0.368	0.290	0.229	0.182	0.163	0.145	0.116	0.093	0.075	0.061	0.055	0.050	0.033	0.013	0.005
14	0.870	0.758	0.708	0.661	0.577	0.505	0.442	0.340	0.263	0.205	0.160	0.141	0.125	0.099	0.078	0.052	0.049	0.044	0.039	0.025	0.009	0.003
15	0.861	0.743	0.690	0.642	0.555	0.481	0.417	0.315	0.239	0.183	0.140	0.123	0.108	0.084	0.065	0.051	0.040	0.035	0.031	0.020	0.006	0.002
16	0.853	0.728	0.674	0.623	0.534	0.458	0.394	0.292	0.218	0.163	0.123	0.107	0.093	0.071	0.054	0.042	0.032	0.028	0.025	0.015	0.005	0.002
17	0.844	0.714	0.657	0.605	0.513	0.436	0.371	0.270	0.198	0.145	0.108	0.093	0.080	0.060	0.045	0.034	0.026	0.023	0.020	0.012	0.003	0.001
18	0.836	0.700	0.641	0.587	0.494	0.416	0.350	0.250	0.180	0.130	0.095	0.081	0.069	0.051	0.038	0.028	0.021	0.018	0.016	0.009	0.002	0.001
19	0.828	0.686	0.626	0.570	0.475	0.396	0.331	0.232	0.164	0.116	0.083	0.070	0.060	0.043	0.031	0.023	0.017	0.014	0.012	0.007	0.002	
20	0.820	0.673	0.610	0.554	0.456	0.377	0.312	0.215	0.149	0.104	0.073	0.061	0.051	0.037	0.026	0.019	0.014	0.012	0.010	0.005	0.001	
21	0.811	0.660	0.595	0.538	0.439	0.359	0.294	0.199	0.135	0.093	0.064	0.053	0.044	0.031	0.022	0.015	0.011	0.009	0.008	0.004	0.001	
22	0.803	0.647	0.581	0.522	0.422	0.342	0.278	0.184	0.123	0.083	0.056	0.046	0.038	0.026	0.018	0.013	0.009	0.007	0.006	0.003	0.001	
23	0.795	0.634	0.567	0.507	0.406	0.326	0.262	0.170	0.112	0.074	0.049	0.040	0.033	0.022	0.015	0.010	0.007	0.006	0.005	0.002		
24	0.788	0.622	0.553	0.492	0.390	0.310	0.247	0.158	0.102	0.066	0.043	0.035	0.028	0.019	0.013	0.008	0.006	0.005	0.004	0.002		
25	0.780	0.610	0.539	0.478	0.375	0.295	0.233	0.145	0.092	0.059	0.038	0.030	0.024	0.016	0.010	0.007	0.005	0.004	0.003	0.001		
26	0.772	0.598	0.526	0.464	0.361	0.281	0.220	0.135	0.084	0.053	0.033	0.026	0.021	0.014	0.009	0.006	0.004	0.003	0.002	0.001		
27	0.764	0.586	0.513	0.450	0.347	0.268	0.207	0.125	0.076	0.047	0.029	0.023	0.018	0.011	0.007	0.005	0.003	0.002	0.002	0.001		
28	0.757	0.574	0.501	0.437	0.333	0.255	0.196	0.116	0.069	0.042	0.026	0.020	0.016	0.010	0.006	0.004	0.002	0.002	0.002	0.001		
29	0.749	0.563	0.489	0.424	0.321	0.243	0.185	0.107	0.063	0.037	0.022	0.017	0.014	0.008	0.005	0.003	0.002	0.002	0.001			
30	0.742	0.552	0.477	0.412	0.308	0.231	0.174	0.099	0.057	0.033	0.020	0.015	0.012	0.007	0.004	0.003	0.002	0.001	0.001			
40	0.672	0.453	0.372	0.307	0.208	0.142	0.097	0.046	0.022	0.011	0.005	0.004	0.003	0.001	0.001							
50	0.608	0.372	0.291	0.228	0.141	0.087	0.054	0.021	0.009	0.003	0.001	0.001	0.001									

SOURCE: Jerome Bracken and Charles J. Christenson, *Tables for Use in Analyzing Business Decisions* (Homewood, Ill.: Richard D. Irwin, Inc., 1965), except for the data on 2½%, the source for which is *Mathematical Tables from Handbook of Chemistry and Physics* (6th ed.; Cleveland: Chemical Rubber Publishing Co. 1938).

AUTHORS NOTE: These values are obtained by compounding at the end of each period. Other tables use different schemes of compounding, without changing the magnitudes greatly.

TABLE B

Present Value of $1 Received Annually

Periods to Be Paid	1%	2%	2½%	3%	4%	5%	6%	8%	10%	12%	14%	15%	16%	18%	20%	22%	24%	25%	26%	30%	40%	50%
1	0.990	0.980	0.976	0.971	0.962	0.952	0.943	0.926	0.909	0.893	0.877	0.870	0.862	0.847	0.833	0.820	0.806	0.800	0.794	0.769	0.714	0.667
2	1.970	1.942	1.927	1.914	1.886	1.859	1.833	1.783	1.736	1.690	1.647	1.626	1.605	1.566	1.528	1.492	1.457	1.440	1.424	1.361	1.224	1.111
3	2.941	2.884	2.856	2.829	2.775	2.723	2.673	2.577	2.487	2.402	2.322	2.283	2.246	2.174	2.106	2.042	1.981	1.952	1.923	1.816	1.589	1.407
4	3.902	3.808	3.762	3.717	3.630	3.546	3.465	3.312	3.170	3.037	2.914	2.855	2.798	2.690	2.589	2.494	2.404	2.362	2.320	2.166	1.849	1.605
5	4.853	4.713	4.646	4.580	4.452	4.330	4.212	3.993	3.791	3.605	3.433	3.352	3.274	3.127	2.991	2.864	2.745	2.689	2.635	2.436	2.035	1.737
6	5.795	5.601	5.508	5.417	5.242	5.076	4.917	4.623	4.355	4.111	3.889	3.784	3.685	3.498	3.326	3.167	3.020	2.951	2.885	2.643	2.168	1.824
7	6.728	6.472	6.349	6.230	6.002	5.786	5.582	5.206	4.868	4.564	4.288	4.160	4.039	3.812	3.605	3.416	3.242	3.161	3.083	2.802	2.263	1.883
8	7.652	7.325	7.170	7.020	6.733	6.463	6.210	5.747	5.335	4.968	4.639	4.487	4.344	4.078	3.837	3.619	3.421	3.329	3.241	2.925	2.331	1.922
9	8.566	8.162	7.971	7.786	7.435	7.108	6.802	6.247	5.759	5.328	4.946	4.772	4.607	4.303	4.031	3.786	3.566	3.463	3.366	3.019	2.379	1.948
10	9.471	8.983	8.752	8.530	8.111	7.722	7.360	6.710	6.145	5.650	5.216	5.019	4.833	4.494	4.192	3.923	3.682	3.571	3.465	3.092	2.414	1.965
11	10.368	9.787	9.514	9.253	8.760	8.306	7.887	7.139	6.495	5.938	5.453	5.234	5.029	4.656	4.327	4.035	3.776	3.656	3.544	3.147	2.438	1.977
12	11.255	10.575	10.258	9.954	9.385	8.863	8.384	7.536	6.814	6.194	5.660	5.421	5.197	4.793	4.439	4.127	3.851	3.725	3.606	3.190	2.456	1.985
13	12.134	11.348	10.983	10.635	9.986	9.394	8.853	7.904	7.103	6.424	5.842	5.583	5.342	4.910	4.533	4.203	3.912	3.780	3.656	3.223	2.468	1.990
14	13.004	12.106	11.691	11.296	10.563	9.899	9.295	8.244	7.367	6.628	6.002	5.724	5.468	5.008	4.611	4.265	3.962	3.824	3.695	3.249	2.478	1.993
15	13.865	12.849	12.381	11.938	11.118	10.380	9.712	8.559	7.606	6.811	6.142	5.847	5.576	5.092	4.676	4.315	4.001	3.859	3.726	3.268	2.484	1.995
16	14.718	13.578	13.055	12.561	11.652	10.838	10.106	8.851	7.824	6.974	6.265	5.954	5.668	5.162	4.730	4.357	4.033	3.887	3.751	3.283	2.488	1.997
17	15.562	14.292	13.712	13.166	12.166	11.274	10.477	9.122	8.022	7.120	6.373	6.047	5.749	5.222	4.775	4.391	4.059	3.910	3.771	3.295	2.492	1.998
18	16.398	14.992	14.353	13.754	12.659	11.690	10.828	9.372	8.201	7.250	6.467	6.128	5.818	5.273	4.812	4.419	4.080	3.928	3.786	3.304	2.494	1.999
19	17.226	15.678	14.979	14.324	13.134	12.085	11.158	9.604	8.365	7.366	6.550	6.198	5.878	5.316	4.844	4.442	4.097	3.942	3.799	3.311	2.496	1.999
20	18.046	16.351	15.589	14.877	13.590	12.462	11.470	9.818	8.514	7.469	6.623	6.259	5.929	5.353	4.870	4.460	4.110	3.954	3.808	3.316	2.497	1.999
21	18.857	17.011	16.185	15.415	14.029	12.821	11.764	10.017	8.649	7.562	6.687	6.312	5.973	5.384	4.891	4.476	4.121	3.963	3.816	3.320	2.498	2.000
22	19.660	17.658	16.765	15.937	14.451	13.163	12.042	10.201	8.772	7.645	6.743	6.359	6.011	5.410	4.909	4.488	4.130	3.970	3.822	3.323	2.498	2.000
23	20.456	18.292	17.332	16.444	14.857	13.489	12.303	10.371	8.883	7.718	6.792	6.399	6.044	5.432	4.924	4.499	4.137	3.976	3.827	3.325	2.499	2.000
24	21.243	18.914	17.885	16.936	15.247	13.799	12.550	10.529	8.985	7.784	6.835	6.434	6.073	5.451	4.937	4.507	4.143	3.981	3.831	3.327	2.499	2.000
25	22.023	19.523	18.424	17.413	15.622	14.094	12.783	10.675	9.077	7.843	6.873	6.464	6.097	5.467	4.948	4.514	4.147	3.985	3.834	3.329	2.499	2.000
26	22.795	20.121	18.951	17.877	15.983	14.375	13.003	10.810	9.161	7.896	6.906	6.491	6.118	5.480	4.956	4.520	4.151	3.988	3.837	3.330	2.500	2.000
27	23.560	20.707	19.464	18.327	16.330	14.643	13.211	10.935	9.237	7.943	6.935	6.514	6.136	5.492	4.964	4.524	4.154	3.990	3.839	3.331	2.500	2.000
28	24.316	21.281	19.965	18.764	16.663	14.898	13.406	11.051	9.307	7.984	6.961	6.534	6.152	5.502	4.970	4.528	4.157	3.992	3.840	3.331	2.500	2.000
29	25.066	21.844	20.454	19.188	16.984	15.141	13.591	11.158	9.370	8.022	6.983	6.551	6.166	5.510	4.975	4.531	4.159	3.994	3.841	3.332	2.500	2.000
30	25.808	22.396	20.930	19.600	17.292	15.372	13.765	11.258	9.427	8.055	7.003	6.566	6.177	5.517	4.979	4.534	4.160	3.995	3.842	3.332	2.500	2.000
40	32.835	27.355	25.103	23.115	19.793	17.159	15.046	11.925	9.779	8.244	7.105	6.642	6.234	5.548	4.997	4.544	4.166	3.999	3.846	3.333	2.500	2.000
50	39.196	31.424	28.362	25.730	21.482	18.256	15.762	12.233	9.915	8.304	7.133	6.660	6.246	5.554	4.999	4.545	4.167	4.000	3.846	3.333	2.500	2.000

SOURCE: Jerome Bracken and Charles J. Christenson, *Tables for Use in Analyzing Business Decisions* (Homewood, Ill.: Richard D. Irwin, Inc., 1965), except for the data on 2½%, the source for which is *Mathematical Tables from Handbook of Chemistry and Physics* (6th ed.; Cleveland: Chemical Rubber Publishing Co., 1938).

AUTHORS' NOTE: These values are obtained by compounding at the end of each period. Other tables use different schemes of compounding, without changing the magnitudes greatly.

TAX TABLE

FEDERAL TAX RATES ON CORPORATE INCOME, AND PAYMENT DATES

(To be used in connection with cases in this book. This is not a complete statement of applicable rates, and it should not be used as a reference for general purposes.)

Income Years	Rate	Income Years	Rate	Income Years	Rate
1940*	24.0%	1949	38.0%	1958	52.0%
1941*	31.0	1950*	47.0	1959	52.0
1942*	40.0	1951*	52.0	1960	52.0
1943*	40.0	1952*	52.0	1961	52.0
1944*	40.0	1953*	52.0	1962	52.0
1945*	40.0	1954	52.0	1963	52.0
1946	38.0	1955	52.0	1964	50.0
1947	38.0	1956	52.0	1965	48.0
1948	38.0	1957	52.0	and later years	

* Excess profits tax also applied for at least part of year.

The 52 percent rate broke down into a normal tax of 30 percent of taxable income and a surtax of 22 percent of taxable income in excess of $25,000. The 50 percent rate broke into a normal tax of 22 percent and a surtax of 28 percent; and the 48 percent rate into a normal tax of 22 percent and a surtax of 26 percent.

Recent revenue acts have moved corporate income tax payments close to current payment. Beginning in 1950, payments were gradually accelerated until in 1954 they were brought entirely within the first half of the year following the tax liability. The Revenue Acts of 1954 and 1964 and the Tax Adjustment Act of 1966, which became law on March 15, 1966, set up even more accelerated schedules. All tax liabilities up to $100,000 are payable in equal amounts on March 15 and June 15 of the year following the tax liability. Tax liabilities over $100,000, for companies on a calendar year, are payable according to the following schedule:

Year	Percentage Paid in Income Year*				Percentage Paid in Following Year†			
	Apr. 15	June 15	Sept. 15	Dec. 15	Mar. 15	June 15	Sept. 15	Dec. 15
1949	—	—	—	—	25%	25%	25%	25%
1950	—	—	—	—	30	30	20	20
1951	—	—	—	—	35	35	15	15
1952	—	—	—	—	40	40	10	10
1953	—	—	—	—	45	45	5	5
1954	—	—	—	—	50	50	—	—
1955	—	—	5%	5%	45	45	—	—
1956	—	—	10	10	40	40	—	—
1957	—	—	15	15	35	35	—	—
1958	—	—	20	20	30	30	—	—
1959	—	—	25	25	25	25	—	—
1960	—	—	25	25	25	25	—	—
1961	—	—	25	25	25	25	—	—
1962	—	—	25	25	25	25	—	—
1963	—	—	25	25	25	25	—	—
1964	1%	1%	25	25	24	24	—	—
1965	4	4	25	25	21	21	—	—
1966	12	12	25	25	13	13	—	—
1967 and subsequent years‡	25	25	25	25	—	—	—	—

* These are percentages of the estimated tax liability on income of the current year.
† These are percentages of the tax liability on income of the previous year.
‡ Until passage of the Tax Adjustment Act of 1966, the payment schedule for 1966–70 was as follows:

Year	Percentage Paid in Income Year				Percentage Paid in Following Year			
	Apr. 15	June 15	Sept. 15	Dec. 15	Mar. 15	June 15	Sept. 15	Dec. 15
1966	9%	9%	25%	25%	16%	16%	—	—
1967	14	14	25	25	11	11	—	—
1968	19	19	25	25	6	6	—	—
1969	22	22	25	25	3	3	—	—
1970	25	25	25	25	—	—	—	—

SOURCES: Derived from *Prentice-Hall Federal Taxes* (Englewood Cliffs, N.J.: Prentice-Hall, Inc., 1965); *Prentice-Hall Federal Taxes*, Vol. XLVII, No. 7 Extra Issue, February 18, 1966; and *Wall Street Journal*, March 16, 1966.